The Complete Encyclopedia of COMMERCIAL VEHICLES

G.N. Georgano, Editor
G.Marshall Naul, U.S. Consulting Editor

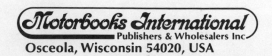

Motorbooks International
Publishers & Wholesalers Inc
Osceola, Wisconsin 54020, USA

First Edition

Distributed by
MOTORBOOKS INTERNATIONAL
PUBLISHERS & WHOLESALERS, INC.
P.O. Box 2
Osceola, Wisconsin 54020 USA

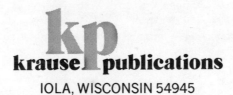

krause publications
IOLA, WISCONSIN 54945

Library of Congress Catalog Card Number 79-88062
International Standard Book Number 0-87341-024-6

Introduction

We have set out in this Encyclopedia to give concise accounts of every commercial vehicle offered for sale throughout the world, from the 19th Century to the Fall of 1978 when the book went to press. However the field of the commercial vehicle is so large that a number of lines of demarcation have had to be drawn. The most important is that we have confined ourselves to vehicles built for use on public roads, thus excluding, among others, works trucks, yard spotters, aircraft tugs and farm tractors. A number of tractors, especially in Germany between the wars, were used with road equipment for highway hauling, and these are included. The same demarcation has been made for steam traction engines where the majority were built for agricultural work, even though they may have been used for short-distance work on the roads. However engines intended for road haulage, which include some of the earliest made, such as Bray, Tennant and Thompson, are covered, as are road locomotives and showmen's engines. Roadmaking equipment such as graders, scrapers and rollers are excluded, but an exception is made for the heavy off-road dumptrucks by such firms as Euclid, Lectra Haul and Wabco. The smaller examples of these are described as on/off road trucks, and often it is only national laws that allow them to run on highways in one country and forbide them in another.

At the other end of the scale is the motorcycle derived three-wheeler. Where these were purpose-built load carriers with the goods compartment ahead of, or behind, the rider they are included, but not the many goods carrying sidecars attached to a motorcycle, for this would lead to the inclusion of a fair proportion of the world's motorcycles.

The Encyclopedia is essentially one of chassis makers, and body builders are only included where they have made a complete vehicle, even if for a limited period. However, the years before and after vehicle manufacture are usually mentioned in order to give a complete picture. Thus firms such as Carpenter and Wayne are listed as 'to date,' although the manufacture of complete buses is no longer undertaken.

Streetcleaning equipment and snowplows are not specifically listed, though they may be mentioned if they were made by firms which built other vehicles as well. The same applies to mobile cranes. Taxi cabs are only mentioned when they were purpose-built for cab work, such as Checker, Yellow Cab, Beardmore, etc.

We have stated that vehicles must have been built for sale to justify inclusion, but an exception has been made when a considerable fleet was made by an operating company for its own use, for example the buses of Pickwick Stages and Pioneer Stages, and the electric delivery vans made by Harrods, the London store. However, vehicles made in ones and twos by haulage and other companies, as often happened in the early days, are not listed.

Carrying capacity. For most vans and trucks the weight given (5-tons etc.) represents the recommended carrying capacity of the vehicle. However this has given way in recent years to the GVW (Gross Vehicle Weight) figure which represents the total weight of chassis, body and payload, and all recent legislation in the United States and Europe relates to GVW. Where these weights are quoted in text or captions they are followed by GVW or GCW (Gross Combination Weight for tractor/trailer units).

The nationality of a vehicle is indicated by the letter(s) used by the International Conventions of 1926 and 1949 (see page 4), and refer to the country where the parent firm was situated. Production under license in other countries is mentioned in the text but not in the heading or addresses. Not all subsidiary plants are listed.

Makes are listed in alphabetical order, but the following points should be noted.

(1) Makes having Christian names as part of their make-up are classified under the Christian name — eg: Georges Irat, not Irat, Georges.

(2) Makes beginning with Mc, as McCurd, are listed between Ma.. and Me.., not at the beginning of 'M.'

(3) Makes beginning with De are classified under 'D.' Thus DeMartini is found under 'D,' not 'M.'

(4) Makes beginning with Le or La are classified under 'L.' Thus Le Moon is found under 'L,' not 'M.'

(5) Makes beginning with St. (Saint) are classified under Saint...

Romanization of Chinese characters. There are three systems of Romanization in common use, Wade-Giles, Pinyin and Yale. For the main reference we have used the Pinyin system as it is more frequently employed by present-day Chinese publications, but where possible we have included the Wade-Giles version as well, followed by the English translation. For example:

TIAO-JIN (p) T'IAO-CHIN (wg) (Leap Forward)

We have tried to give at least one illustration of all the makes of any importance, and to give a selection of photos of the most prominent makes. We are well aware that the quality of some photographs leaves much to be desired, but where nothing better was obtainable, we felt that readers would rather see an indifferent photo than none at all.

Any corrections or additions which readers think may be desirable for future editions will be very welcome. They should be sent to the Editor, Encyclopedia of Commercial Vehicles, c/o Krause Publications, Iola, Wisconsin 54945, USA.

Abbreviations

International Registration Letters

The country of manufacture has been indicated by the International Registration letters, as established by the International Conventions of 1926 and 1949, and as notified to the United Nations. These are as follows:

A	Austria
AUS	Australia
B	Belgium
BG	Bulgaria
BR	Brazil
BS	Bahamas
C	Cuba
CDN	Canada
CH	Switzerland
CHI	China (People's Republic)
CS	Czechoslovakia
CY	Cyprus
D	Germany (Federal Republic)
DDR	Germany (Democratic Republic)
DK	Denmark
E	Spain
ET	Egypt
F	France
GB	Great Britain and Northern Ireland
GR	Greece
H	Hungary
I	Italy
IL	Israel
IND	India
IR	Iran
IRL	Republic of Ireland
J	Japan
KO	Korea
MEX	Mexico
N	Norway
NL	Netherlands
NZ	New Zealand
P	Portugal
PAK	Pakistan
PI	Philippines
PL	Poland
PTM	Malaysia
R	Romania
RA	Argentina
RC	Taiwan
RI	Indonesia
S	Sweden
SF	Finland
SU	Soviet Union
TR	Turkey
US	United States
VN	Vietnam
YU	Yugoslavia
ZA	South Africa

The following abbreviations have been used for frequently repeated terms.

aiv	automatic inlet valve(s)
bbc	bumper to back of cab (measurement)
cc	cubic centimeters
cid	cubic inch displacement
ckd	completely knocked down
fwd	front wheel drive
GCW	Gross Combination Weight
gpm	gallons per minute
GTW	Gross Train Weight
GVW	Gross Vehicle Weight
hp	horsepower
ifs	independent front suspension
irs	independent rear suspension
kg	kilogrammes
lb	pounds
lhd	left hand drive
mm	milimeters
moiv	mechanically-operated inlet valves
mpg	miles per gallon
mph	miles per hour
nhp	nominal horsepower
ohc	overhead camshaft(s)
ohv	overhead valves
psi	pounds per square inch
PSV	Public Service Vehicle
PTE	Passenger Transport Executive
rhd	right hand drive
rpm	revolutions per minute
sv	side valves (L-head)

Drive systems are indicated as 4×2, 4×4, 6×4 etc., where the first figure is the number of wheels, and the second figure the number that are powered.

Contributors

ACT	Alvaro Casal Tatlock, Montevideo, Uraguay
BE	Bill Emery, Sheridan, Wyoming
DJS	Donald J. Summar, Lancaster, Pa.
FH	Ferdinand Hediger, Lenzburg, Switzerland
EEH	Eugene E. Husting, Locust Valley, N.Y.
GA	George Avramidis, Athens, Greece
GMN	G. Marshall Naul, Granville, Ohio
GNG	G.N. Georgano, Milford on Sea, Hants, England
HD	Hugh Durnford, Montreal, Canada
HON	Hans-Otto Neubauer, Hamburg, Germany
JCG	Joaquin Ciuro Gabarro, Lloret de Mar, Spain
JFJK	J.F.J. Kuipers, Amsterdam, Holland
LA	Larry Auten, Gastonia, North Carolina
MBS	Motor Bus Society, Philadelphia, Pa., Albert E. Meier, Eli Bail, John P. Hoschek
MCS	Michael C. Sedgwick, Midhurst, Sussex, England
MJWW	Michael Worthington-Williams, Burgess Hill, Sussex, England

MSH	Marian Suman-Hreblay, Lipt. Mikulas, Czechoslovakia
MW	Martin Wallast, Nieuwerkerk, Holland
OM	Old Motor Magazine, London, England, Nick Baldwin, Ken Blacker, Arthur Ingram, Geoff Lumb, Prince Marshall
RAW	R.A. Whitehead, Tonbridge, Kent, England
RH	Rich Hamilton, Indianapolis, Indiana
RJ	Rolland Jerry, Toronto, Canada
RW	R. Wawrzyniak, Berlin, Wisconsin

Photo Credits

Where several photos are credited to a particular source, the following abbreviations have been used.

AACA	Antique Automobile Club of America (Minnesota Region)
AAR	Avramidis Automobile Register, Athens, Greece
AJHB	A.J.H. Baker Collection, Rossendale, Lancs, England
BE	Bill Emery Collection, Sheridan, Wyoming
BHV	B.H. Vanderveen Collection, 't Harde, Netherlands
BR	British Rail, London, England
CP	Crestline Publications, Sarasota, Florida
CR	Chuck Rhoads Collection, Collinsville, Ill.
DJS	Donald J. Summar Collection, Lancaster, Penna.
DL	Denis Latour Collection, Dorval, Quebec, Canada
EEH	Eugene E. Husting Collection, Locust Valley, Long Island, N.Y.
EK	Elliott Kahn Collection, Clearwater Beach, Florida
ES	Ernest Schmid Collection, Lausanne, Switzerland
FH	Ferdinand Hediger Collection, Lenzburg, Switzerland
FLP	Free Library of Philadelphia
FTS	(the late) Frank T. Snyder Collection, Chandler, Arizona
GB	Glenn Baechler Collection, Waterloo, Ontario, Canada
GMN	G. Marshall Naul Collection, Granville, Ohio
GNG	G.N. Georgano Collection, Milford on Sea, Hants, England
HD	Hugh Durnford Collection, Montreal, Canada
HDB	Homer D. Brown Collection, Canton, Ohio
HFM	Henry Ford Museum, Dearborn, Michigan
HHB	Henry H. Blommel Collection, Connersville, Indiana
HON	Hans-Otto Neubauer Collection, Hamburg, Germany
JCG	Joaquin Ciuro Gabarro Collection, Lloret de Mar, Spain
JFJK	J.F.J. Kuipers Collection, Amsterdam, Netherlands
KCB	K.C. Blacker Collection, London, England
LA	Larry Auten Collection, Gastonia, North Carolina
LIAM	Long Island Automotive Museum, Southampton, Long Island, N.Y.
LTE	London Transport Executive
MAS	Michael Sutcliffe Collection, Chippenham, Wiltshire, England
MBS	Motor Bus Society, Philadelphia, Pennsylvania
MCS	Michael C. Sedgwick Collection, Midhurst, Sussex, England
MHK	Margus-Hans Kuuse Collection, Estonia, USSR
MHS	Minnesota Historical Society
MJWW	Michael Worthington-Williams Collection, Burgess Hill, Sussex, England
MSH	Marian Suman-Hreblay Collection, Lipt. Mikulas, Czechoslovakia
NAHC	National Automotive History Collection, Detroit Public Library
NMM	National Motor Museum, Beaulieu, Hants, England
OMM	Old Motor Magazine, London, England
RAW	R.A. Whitehead Collection, Tonbridge, Kent, England
RJ	Rolland Jerry Collection, Toronto, Ontario, Canada
RLH	R.L. Hamilton Collection, Indianapolis, Indiana
RNE	Railway Negative Exchange, Moraga, California
RW	R. Wawrzyniak Collection, Berlin, Wisconsin
TCV	Thomas C. VandeGrift Collection, Birmingham, Michigan
TT	Truck Tracks Magazine, Lake Grove, Oregon
VP	Vaclav Petrik Collection, Prague, Czechoslovakia
WB	William Boddy Collection, Llandrindod Wells, Wales, Great Britain

In March 1979 the name Old Motor Magazine was sold, but all photographic archives, including those used in this book, have been retained by the owners who are now trading under the name Marshall, Harris and Baldwin Ltd. of London, and are continuing to publish annuals and books on vintage trucks and buses.

1914 International Harvester Co. Autowagon (Henry Austin Clark, Jr.)

1919 White flatbed stake truck (Michael A. Carbone

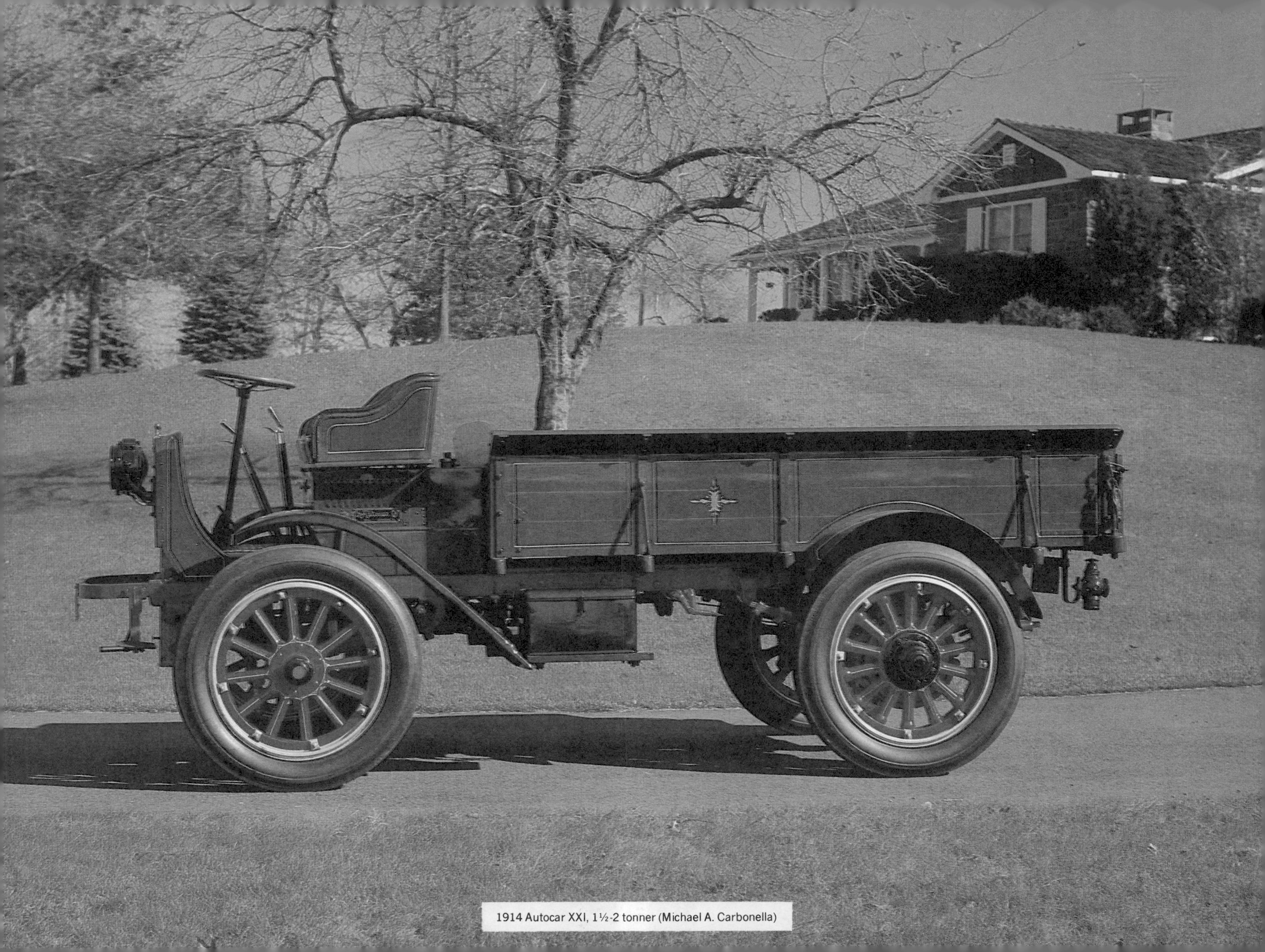

1914 Autocar XXI, 1½-2 tonner (Michael A. Carbonella)

1923 Foden C-type estate tractor (G.N. Georgano)

1927 Mack Bulldog chain drive tractor (Michael A. Carbonell

1928 Dennis fire truck with pump trailer (National Motor Museum)

1929 Ford Model A Pickup (Robert Strand/Robert Lemke)

1933 Scania-Vabis 1½ ton (G.N. Georgano)

1934 Sentinel S4 steam truck (G.N. Georgan

38 Reo fire truck (Robert Lichty)

1939 Leyland fire truck (G.N. Geòrgano)

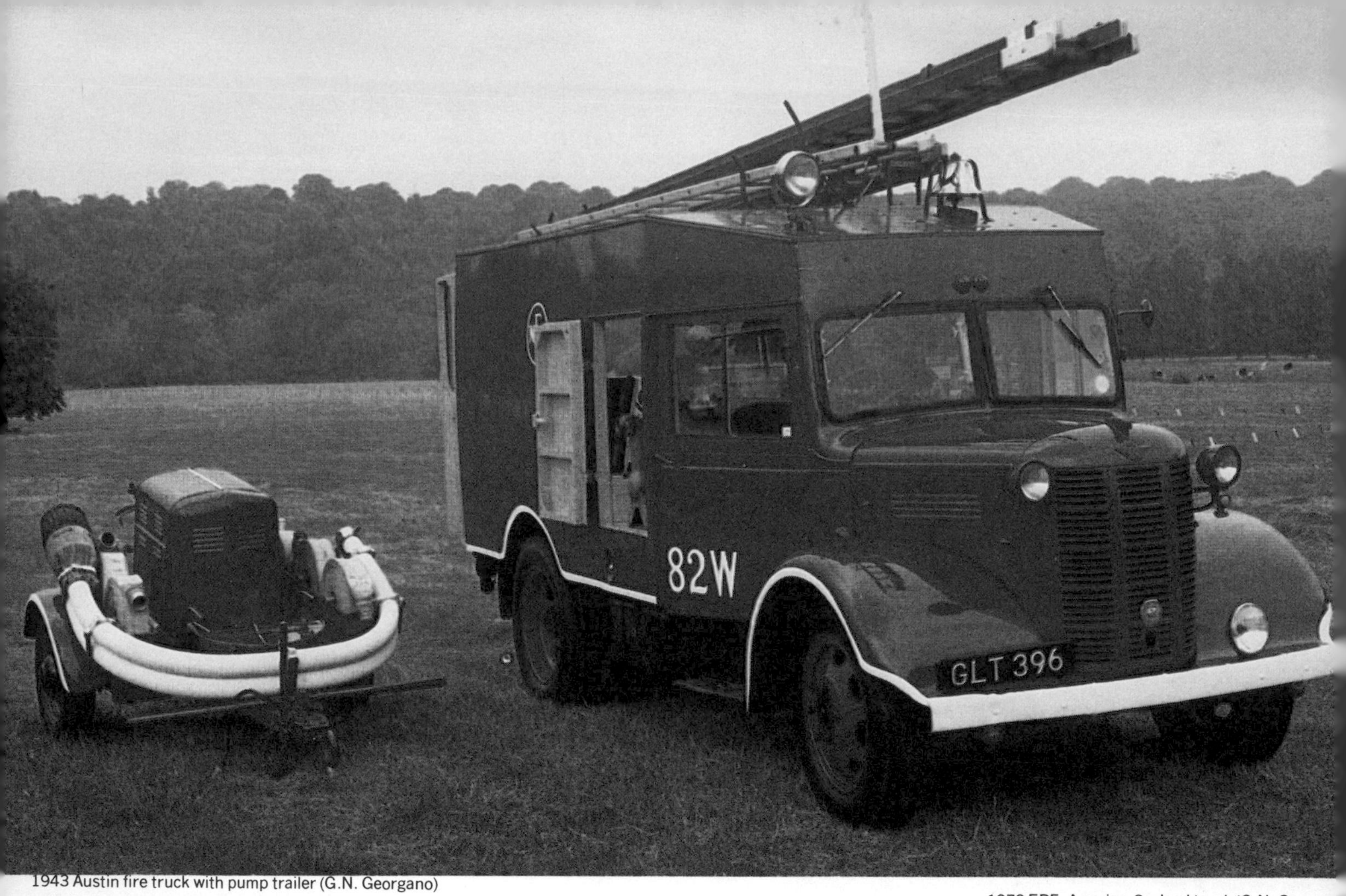

1943 Austin fire truck with pump trailer (G.N. Georgano)

1973 ERF, A series, 8 wheel truck (G.N. Georga

62 Foden tanker (Fodens Ltd.)

1976 Magirus Deutz tanker (F. Hedigar)

Skoda 706 MTS (F. Hedigar)

1975 Caterpillar 777 dump truck (Caterpillar Tractor Co

975 Neoplan 144 passenger Jumbocruiser (Claus Benter)

1978 DAF, Model 4730, articulated low-loader (G.N. Georgano)

1975 Raba (Magyar Vagon es Gepgyar)

1975 Berna 5VF 6x2 articulated truck (F. Hediga

75 Neoplan 144 passenger Jumbocruiser (Claus Benter)

1979 FWD Tractioneer with snow plow (FWD)

1978 APE 600 3 wheel delivery truck (G.N. Georgano)

1974 Chubb Pathfinder (Chubb Fire Security Ltd

shkosh "B" series front discharge cement mixer (Oshkosh Truck Corp.)

1979 International 4300 series Transtar (International Harvester Co.)

1979 GMC General (General Motors Co.)

Oshkosh, largest M-series fire truck (Oshkosh Truck Corp.)

A & B (US) 1914-1922
American & British Mfg. Co., Providence, R.I.

Like Christie and Cross, this company built two-wheeler tractor conversion units for converting horse-drawn steam pumpers to self propulsion. They were gas-electrics, with 4-cylinder engines generating power for electric motors mounted in each front wheel. Commercial trucks were also made, in 3- and 5-ton sizes. *GNG*

A & R (US) 1912-1915
Abendroth & Root Manufacturing Co, Newburgh, NY

Trucks under this tradename were 3-, 4- and 5-tonners and all used 4-cylinder engines with forward control, 3-speed gearboxes and double-chain drive to the rear wheels. The 5-tonner was governed to a maximum speed of only 8½ mph. This make was formerly known as Frontenac, the tradename of passenger cars by this manufacturer. *GMN*

A.A. see All-American

A.A.A. (D) 1919-1922
Aktiengesellschaft fur Akkumulatoren- und Automobilbau, Berlin N 65; Driesen-Vordamm

This firm built electric driven vans and a 2-ton truck, the latter was especially ordered by postal authorities. Later these models were marketed as "Elektric." *HON*

A.B.A.M. (D) 1898-1905
Allgemeine Betriebs-Aktiengesellschaft fur Motorfahrzeuge, Cologne

Electric vehicles — vans, buses and taxicabs — were built by this firm following Krieger principles and using Krieger components to a great extent. *HON*

ABBOTT-DOWNING see Concord

A.B.C. see All-British

A.B.C. (US) 1908-1911
A.B.C. Motor Vehicle Mfg. Co., St. Louis, Mo.
The A.B.C. was a high-wheeler, a typical product of the mid-west during the era. While passenger cars were the major product, some half-ton delivery vans were also built. These were powered by 2-cylinder engines with either water- or air-cooling. The van weighed 1275 pounds, had wheelbase of 192 inches and the price for the 1909 Model F was $650 or $700 depending upon the cooling system. *GMN*

1915 ACASON chassis, LIAM

ABOAG (D) 1913-1917; 1928-1929; 1935-1936
(1) Allgemeine Berliner Omnibus Akt. Ges., Berlin 1913-1917
(2) Berliner Verkehrs-Aktien-Gesellschaft (BVG), Berlin 1928-1929, 1935-1936

This Berlin bus company developed some of their own bus versions. The first one appeared in 1897, an electric driven bus. Actually it was a converted horse bus and remained a single specimen. In 1911 ABOAG started

1915 ABOAG RK-Wagon Berlin bus, HON

production of buses, two years later of chassis. The first own development was the RK-Car of 1913 (RK = Richard Kaufman, director of ABOAG), a double-decker. In 1928/1929 (the company was renamed in the meantime) a front-driven double-decker was developed in co-operation with the Voran company. A 100 bhp Maybach engine was used. But only two of these were built, one of them was sold to General of London. Also during 1935/1936 the company built buses on their own chassis using Bussing engines. *HON*

ABRESCH-KREMERS (US) c. 1910-1912
The Charles Abresch Co., Milwaukee, Wis.

The Abresch-Kremers was an assembled truck, built by a custom automobile body builder in Milwaukee. Little is known about their truck venture. The make is also referred to as the Abresch-Cramer, possibly an error, or a changing of a partner's name to give the marque a better chance in the marketplace. The Charles Abresch Co. survived until 1965, although they were almost certainly out of the truck business by 1913. *TVB*

A.C. (GB) 1914-1954
(1) Autocarriers (1911) Ltd, Thames Ditton, Surrey 1914-1922
(20 A.C. Cars Ltd, Thames Ditton Surrey 1922-1954

The bulk of commercial production by this well-known car maker was under the name Autocarrier, and only a small number of car-based light vans were made, and this over a widely spread period. A 6cwt van was announced in 1914 on the newly introduced 10hp 4-cylinder car chassis, the frame being strengthened to allow for the additional load. The van was not reintroduced after the war, and the next A.C. commercial vehicle was a 10cwt van on the 11.9hp 4-cylinder chassis, of which a few were made in 1924. These were not put on the market, although *Motor Transport* was sure there would be a ready sale for such a high-quality van, but kept for works use. There were no further A.C. vans until 1954 when a 2cwt version of the Petite 3-wheeled car was announced. This had a 346cc Villiers engine, 3-speed gearbox and body by the Buckland Bodyworks company of Buntingford, Herts. It was priced at £308, but very few were sold. *GNG*

ACASON (US) 1915-1925
Acason Motor Truck Co., Detroit, Mich

The Acason began as ½, 2- and 3½-tonners with standard stake bodies and worm drive. In 1917, a 1½-tonner was added and the three types used a 4-speed gearbox. Spotlights were available accessories. By 1918, the

Acason offered a 5-tonner as well as light and heavy duty tractors. For 1921, the line had dropped all but 2½- and 3½-tonners. This was an assembled truck with standard components, all with 4-cylinder Waukesha engines and most models used Timken worm-drive rear axles. *GMN*

1922 ACE moving van, Lawrence A. Brough

ACE (US) 1918-1927

American Motor Truck Co., Newark, Ohio

This company was a reorganization of the Blair Mfg. Co. who made trucks from 1911 to 1918, and their first product was a conventional 2½-tonner with electric starting, powered by a Buda WU 4-cylinder engine. From 1919 to 1924 a range of 1½/2-tonners and 2½/3-tonners was made, both Buda-powered and with the unusual feature of headlights which turned with the steering. The final truck model was the 2½-tonner of 1925/26, but meanwhile the company had turned to bus manufacture. Models A and B were based on truck chassis for 20/22 and 26/28 passengers respectively, while Model C introduced in 1923 had a purpose-built underslung chassis in which the axles passed between the semi-elliptic springs and the frame. The Model C was designed for 30/32-passenger bodies and was powered first by a Midwest engine (1923-24), and then by a Continental 6-cylinder unit for the last two years of production. See also ROYAL. *GNG*

A.C.E.C. (B) 1914-1964

Ateliers de Constructions Electriques de Charleroi SA, Charleroi

1964 ACEC-VAN HOOL Electrobus, JFJK

This major electrical company had several periods of involvement in road vehicles. In 1914 they built a 4x4 gas-electric truck in cooperation with the French company, Balachowsky et Caire. It had a 4-cylinder engine and electric motors in each wheel hub. Then in 1929 they converted a number of Straker-Squire buses belonging to Antwerp transways into trolleybuses (possibly inspired by the British Straker-Clough), and subsequently production of trolleybuses was set up in conjunction with Ragheno and Brossel. In 1935 Brossel and ACEC built a small fleet of 3-axle trolleybuses with central driving axle and steering on front and rear axles, for Liege. They could be driven at the same speed in either direction.

In 1963 ACEC returned to gas-electric drive with the Electrobus, a Van Hool-bodied city bus powered by a 150hp Fiat diesel engine and with drive through motors in the rear wheel hubs. Only a few were produced experimentally. *JFJK*

ACF, ACF-BRILL, BRILL (U.S.) 1926-1953

(1) American Car & Foundry Co., Detroit, Mich. 1926-1932
(2) American Car & Foundry Co., Philadelphia, Pa. 1933-1953

In 1925 the American Car & Foundry Co., a large and established maker of railway passenger and freight cars, acquired the J.G. Brill Co. of Philadelphia and the Fageol Motors Co. of Ohio (see FAGEOL) in a move to diversify into the business of making city transit vehicles. Brill had been the nation's largest streetcar builder since the 1890's and had acquired the C.C. Kuhlman Co. of Cleveland

1930 A.C.F. P-45 coach, MBS

1931 A.C.F. TT175 articulated truck, NAHC

1936 A.C.F. H-15-S 30-passenger bus, MBS

1938 A.C.F. 37-P underfloor-engined coach, MBS

1950 (A.C.F) BRILL C-44 suburban bus, MBS

("Brill of Ohio") and the American Car ("of St. Louis, Missouri"). ACF was content to allow leadership in the declining streetcar business to pass to other hands, though streetcars continued to be built at Philadelphia until 1941.

Production of the Fageol bus was transferred from Kent, Ohio to Detroit in 1926, and the Fageol brothers became vice-presidents of ACF. In 1927 they left the firm when its top management expressed no interest in a radical new design of twin-engined 40-passenger city transit bus; (see TWIN COACH). ACF continued to produce the Fageol bus under that name until 1929, but in 1927 a somewhat heavier and more powerful range of chassis was introduced bearing the ACF name. Many of the bodies for both city transit and parlor car versions were produced in Cleveland by the Lang Body Co.

An underfloor-engine city bus known as the "Metropolitan" was marketed in gas-mechanical and gas-electric versions from 1928 to 1932, but was not particularly successful by comparison with the Twin Coach, upon which it had been modeled. Meanwhile, steady improvements were made in the line of conventional chassis with six-cylinder Hall-Scott engines, resulting in a succession of changes in model designations for basically similar buses. In 1930 a smaller front-engine bus was introduced with a Hercules engine. In 1931 and 1932 approximately 25 ACF trucks were made, using Hall-Scott 160 or 175 engines.

Bus production was transferred from Detroit to Philadelphia, the front-engine models were discontinued, and a new line of underfloor-engine transit buses was introduced, all in the closing months of 1932 and early 1933, when business was at a low ebb. A few operating companies purchased modified versions of these buses for intercity service. In 1937 there was a styling change in the direction of greater streamlining, and the range was broadened to include 26, 31, 36, 41, and 45-passenger versions. Parlor buses in 25, 29, and 37-passenger sizes were brought back into the line and sold fairly well. All these buses used Hall-Scott engines, the largest being the 707 cu in 175 (later 180). As with all other builders, production was suspended late in 1942 so that the plant could be devoted to war work.

A few buses had been equipped with hydraulic transmission in the late 1930's, but ACF never had a diesel engine. After the war, production was begun on models C-36 and C-44 for city transit service and IC-41 for intercity duties. All had underfloor six-cylinder Hall-Scott engines, and beginning in 1947 the city buses were made available with Spicer hydraulic transmission. These buses were marketed under the name of ACF-Brill. In 1948 smaller city buses were offered as models C-27 and C-31, with International gas engines mounted at the rear. These were called Brills to distinguish them from the Hall-Scott group.

While still an independent streetcar builder, Brill had developed a trackless trolley (so-called "railless car") in 1921. The trolley-coach concept did not catch on at that time, but starting in 1930 Brill became a major producer of these vehicles. Many of their body parts were the same as those of the contemporary ACF buses, except that after the war the old design was retained for a time. The gas bus and trolley-bus businesses went into a steep decline together after 1950, and when General Motors introduced air-suspension in 1953, Brill (along with White) dropped out of the competition. *MBS*

ACME (i) (U.S.) 1905-1906

Acme Motor Car Co., Reading, Pa.

The Acme motor car was built from 1904 to 1910. A 1000-pound delivery truck with 16hp 2-cylinder engine was announced after Frank A. Devlin took control of the firm in 1905. The truck had chain drive, a cone clutch, and 3-speed progressive transmission. The truck was listed only until the firm entered a temporary receivership in July 1906. *DJS*

ACME (ii) (US) 1915-1931

(1) Cadillac Auto Truck Co., Cadillac, Mich.
(2) Acme Motor Truck Co., Cadillac, Mich.

The Acme was a thoroughly conventional truck using mostly Continental 4-cylinder engines for the many

1925 ACME (ii) 1½-ton van LIAM

models offered. Beginning with 1-, 2-, and 3½-tonners, Acmes were always in the light to medium-sized class of truck, the largest being a 6 tonner made in 1925 and 1926. Tractors for 7½-ton trailers were made in the late 1920s, when 6-cylinder Continental engines came into use. Bus chassis for 16 to 21 passengers were also made during the 1920s. In 1927 Acme acquired the United Truck Company of Grand Rapids, Michigan. *GNG*

ACME (iii) (U.S.) 1916-1919

Acme Wagon Co., Emigsville, Pa.

This Acme was a typical assembled truck of 1-ton capacity, with 17hp 4-cylinder engine, dry plate clutch, 3-speed transmission, and bevel drive. It was never more than a side-line of the firm, which manufactured farm wagons from 1880 until after 1925. *DJS*

ACOMAL (B) 1972

Acomal S.A., Malines

In 1972 this company showed during the Brussels Motor Show a very interesting fully integral tanker truck, with the tank functioning as a chassis. Unfortunately, no more than a few prototypes were produced. *JFJK*

ACORN (i) (US) 1910-1912

Acorn Motor Car Co., Cincinnati, Ohio

This was a delivery wagon powered by an 18/20hp horizontally-opposed twin engine mounted transversely at the front of the chassis. It had a 3-speed roller friction transmission and double chain drive. Payload was 1,000 lbs. *GNG*

ACORN (ii) (US) 1925-1931

Acorn Motor Truck Co., Chicago, Ill.

This was a conventional assembled truck made in sizes from 1 to 5 tons payload, powered by 4- or 6-cylinder Buda engines. *GNG*

ADAMS (US) 1910-1916

Adams Brothers Co., Findlay, Ohio 1910-1915

Adams Truck, Foundry & Machine Co., Findlay, Ohio 1916

The Adams began with a three-quarter tonner, a light delivery van which used a 2-cylinder engine, a 3-speed gearbox and shaft drive with pneumatic tires. This light commercial used a Renault-type sloping hood with radiator behind the engine, a style continued with all Adams light vans. A one-tonner was added in 1911 on a wheelbase of 10 feet and was powered by a 4-cylinder engine. For 1913 and 1914, 1½- and 2-tonners were added to the line with wheelbases up to 152 inches. A bottom dump was available for 1915. For the last year of manufacture, the Adams line included 1-, 2- and 2½-tonners. *GMN*

ADAMS-HEWITT: (i) ADAMS (GB) 1906-1913

Adams Manufacturing Co. Ltd, Bedford

The original Adams vehicles were based on the American Hewitt, which explains the layout of their original 10hp with its single-cylinder horizontal underfloor engine, 2-speed pedal-controlled planetary transmission, and single chain final drive. This model was available as a ¾-ton van in either forward control or conventional forms, though a bigger 1½-ton truck differed from the 10hp in having its 2.1-litre 2-cylinder engine mounted vertically at the front. Adams commercials never reached the Herculean proportions of the bigger Hewitts, though a big 25hp truck with 4.8-litre 4-cylinder engine, side-chain drive, and 34-inch wheels was delivered to a customer in Kenya in 1907. From 1907 to 1910 Adams offered shaft-driven cabs with 2- and 4-cylinder engines; latterly a 4-speed sliding-type gearbox was optional on these. Conventional gearboxes were also available on the ¾-ton worm-drive truck of 1911, which used a 2.9-litre sv 4-cylinder engine, and could be had with pneumatic tires and the Adams compressed-air starter. This model was offered until 1913, along with a smaller bevel-driven ¾-ton machine on which the traditional 'pedals to push' transmission was not even listed. *MCS*

1928 A.D.C. Series 500 5-ton tanker, OMM

ADC (Associated Daimler) (GB) 1926-1928

(1) The Associated Daimler Co. Ltd., Walthamstow, London E17. 1926.

(2) The Associated Daimler Co. Ltd., Southall, Middlesex. 1927-8.

Daimler and AEC had close ties before World War One when Daimler was responsible for AEC bus sales outside London, and had subsequently supplied engines for some AEC Y-type subsidy chassis. Following a resurgence of interest in commercial vehicles by Daimler's owners, BSA, they formed a joint company with the highly successful Associated Equipment Co. Ltd. in 1926. The intention was that the Associated Daimler Company should control policy and sales while the two separate manufacturing companies should avoid duplication and make components for AEC to assemble at their new purpose-built factory at Southall.

L. H. Pomeroy was chief engineer and for the first year the range was identical to the former AEC's, covering 2- to 6-tonners and numerous passenger models. Then in 1928 two specifically ADC designs appeared, the 423/424 chassis for goods and passengers. These were to an advanced lightweight design and a few were fitted with Daimler sleeve-valve engines. After ADC disbanded these

1908 ADLER 11/18PS van, HON

models became the basis of the AEC 426 and Daimler CF6. An earlier product of the fusion was the LS or London Six, a 3-axle 68-seater with pneumatic tires produced for the LGOC from 1927. It was powered by a 6-cylinder Daimler sleeve-valve 100bhp engine which created considerable internal controversy as to whether Daimler sleeve or AEC poppet valve engines should be used, especially as the Daimler engine was from Daimler's 35hp car. In 1928 the two companies decided to go back to separate sales, service and manufacturing, though vehicles continued to be built under license from ADC for sometime. *OM*

ADE (D) 1932-1933

ADE-Werke AG., Waltershausen

This was a 3-wheeler with front platform and a single driven rear wheel. Ilo 2-stroke engines of 200, 350 and 400cc were used. *HON*

ADLER (D) 1902-1939

1. Adler Fahrradwerke vorm. Heinrich Kleyer AG., Frankfurt 1902-1906

2. Adlerwerke vorm. Heinrich Kleyer AG., Frankfurt 1906-1939

Adler produced vans, small trucks and a small bus based on their designs of private cars, all using a 2-cylinder 1.7 litre engine and cardan drive. From about 1910 a 3-ton truck was available with engines up to 25hp and this chassis was also used for fire engines and buses. In 1921 a 5-ton truck was presented which later also was available as a bus and which was supplemented by a 2-ton express truck with 40bhp engine. The heavier types were dropped at the end of the twenties and only the 1-ton version was continued as van or truck using a 2.9 litre engine. Various Adler private cars, including the fwd types, were the basis for vans and combination cars during the thirties. *HON*

ADMIRAL (US) 1913-1915

Admiral Motor Car Co., St. Louis, Mo.

The Model C was a 1½-tonner with either express or stake body, both priced at $1475. The chassis had wheelbase of 125 inches, a 4-cylinder engine, 3-speed gearbox and double-chain final drive. *GMN*

AEBI (CH) 1964 to date

Aebi & Co. AG., Maschinenfabrik, Burgdorf BE

In 1964 Aebi, one of the leading manufacturers of agricultural equipment and machinery in Switzerland, launched their first multipurpose vehicle. The four-wheel drive Aebi Transporter TP 2000 with an open forward control cockpit, a wooden loading platform and 2 tons payload was offered. The basic model with central-tube chassis was further improved and the present range includes three models: Type TP 1000A for 2 tons with single or twin cylinder gasoline engines of 11 and 16 hp or single cylinder diesel engine of 15 hp. Type TP 20 with an air-cooled Deutz twin-cylinder diesel engine of 28 hp and 2.2 tons payload and the more powerful type TP 50 with a water-cooled Perkins 4 cylinder diesel engine of 43 hp and a payload of 3.3 tons. All models have fully synchronized gearboxes with 6 forward and 2 reverse speeds. Front and rear axle drive can be disengaged and there is a differential locking. Hydraulic brakes are fitted. These versatile vehicles are used mainly in agriculture, forestry and for many general transportation tasks in the alpine region of Switzerland. *FH*

1974 AEBI TP50 3.3-ton multi purpose truck, Aebi

1913 A.E.C. B-type London Bus, Mrs B. Knight

AEC (GB) (Known as ACLO in certain overseas territories) 1912 to date

The Associated Equipment Co. Ltd., Walthamstow, London E17.1912-1926
Southall, Middlesex, 1927-1948
AEC Ltd., Southall, Middlesex, 1949-1967
British Leyland Truck & Bus Division. 1968 to date.

After the London General Omnibus Company merged with the Vanguard Omnibus Company and the London Road Car Company in 1908, they produced buses to their own design at Walthamstow. In 1910 they introduced their highly successful B-type 34-seat double deck model which had a flitched wood/steel frame, worm drive and weighed 3½-tons complete.

In 1912 the Underground Electric Railways Company of London Ltd. bought a majority shareholding in the LGOC and decided to separate the vehicle manufacturing and bus operating sides with the result that the Associated Equipment Co. Ltd. became an independent subsidiary of the Underground Group. Initially, AEC made vehicles solely for the LGOC with some 2500 B-types completed by 1913, a very high production for the time, and in that year they caused considerable anxiety among other bus manufacturers when they announced that their chassis would be available to provincial operators via the Daimler Co. of Coventry, who would act as sales agents. War

1921 A.E.C. S-type single decker bus, LTE

intervened before this could become too serious a threat and immediately several hundreds of the LGOC's B-types were adapted as troop carriers, while the factory at Walthamstow quickly developed a more substantial truck for military use, known soon as the Model 'Y'. This featured an all-steel frame, first tried on a small batch of single-deck B-types in 1915. Virtually unique in Europe was a moving track assembly line which permitted a Y-type to leave the factory every 30 minutes, resulting in a total wartime production of over 10,000, the highest figure of any British manufacturer. Engines for the Y were bought in from Daimler or Tylor.

After the war the Y continued in production as a five tonner, though AEC's immediate preoccupation was with supplying replacements for London's depleted and aging bus fleet. In 1919 they introduced their forward-control 46-seat K-type bus, of which more than 1100 were eventually supplied, mainly to London. This design was followed by a bigger 54-seat S-type in 1921. Both the K and S-types followed pre-war B-type practice in having flitched wood/steel chassis frames. With the re-start of post-war production AEC took the opportunity of beginning an entirely new method of chassis numbering. Whereas before all vehicles produced were in one sequence of numbers, vehicles were now segregated into engine types, i.e., the 28hp as installed in the K-type was the 3-type, followed by the bigger 35hp 4-type and the new AEC 45hp engine replacing the Tylor engine were called 5-types. Trolleybuses were listed as 6-types. Vehicle types fitted with the various designs of engine had chassis No. starting 401, 503, etc., and consequently were known by these first three numbers when marketed. It was not until 1925 that AEC started supplementing the numerical designation by names. The LGOC continued to record all its vehicles, whether K, S, NS, etc., in one chassis sequence starting 20,000.

1923 A.E.C. 4-ton truck with trailer, OMM

November 1923 saw the introduction of a 2-ton range with an L-head 28hp engine, known as the 2-type. At the same time the company announced the 7-type, a 65hp engine fitted into an articulated tractor rather similar to the well-known Scammell. 1923 also saw the introduction of the 405 model, known in London as the NS. This was AEC's first drop-frame chassis and the first to enter production in Britain. It enabled the interior floor line to be dropped to 2 ft. as against earlier models of 2 ft. 11 ins. While the one-step rear platform was a great improvement for passengers, the main attribute of the drop-frame was greater stability, enabling a body to be built with a top cover — a feature that the Metropolitan Police in London would not allow until 1926.

During 1926 AEC made arrangements to move to a new factory on a 63-acre site at Southall, but before they actually moved they joined forces with Daimler, as described under ADC. The arrangement was not satisfactory and the two companies went their respective ways in July 1928. During the ADC period two entirely new models were designed, the 423 and the 801. The 801 was a high capacity six-wheeler with the choice of either the Daimler Mk4 engine — very similar to that fitted in Daimler cars — or the specially adapted engine like that fitted in the NS (same bore and stroke) known as the 8-type. The 801 was not a success and only 20 were ever built. The 423 and its normal control counterpart the 424, announced in 1927, were ultra lightweight designs by Laurence Pomeroy.

When the two companies split, Daimler continued to market the 423 as their CF range, while AEC installed a new detachable-head version of their 35hp 4-type engine and made many modifications to the chassis design, marketing them as 426/427 respectively. About 300 426/427's were sold before being superseded in the spring of 1929 by the 660 Reliance. Basically the same as the 426,

1929 A.E.C. Model 426 28-seater bus, OMM

the Reliance had single servo brakes and the new Rackham-designed 37.2hp 6-cyl. ohv engine which was unique in its design of right angle rockers. The Reliance was an immediate success — nearly 500 being sold in a few months — but before the year was out it was superseded by the 662 Regal. This had the same engine but the chassis design was completely new. Whereas the Reliance followed basic earlier principles, such as gate gearchange,

1930 A.E.C. LT 56-seater bus, LTE

separate engine and gearbox and cone clutch, the Regal had a gearbox forming a unit with the engine via a single dry plate clutch, ball change and Timken semi-floating back axle. The design formed the basis of a slightly shorter wheelbase double-decker 661 Regent chassis and

1930 A.E.C. Mercury tanker, OMM

an entirely new 6-wheeled 663 double-decked Renown and 664 single-decked Renown.

In 1930 the goods range was completely revised along the lines of the new bus chassis with the introduction of the Mercury for 3½ tons and Monarch for 4 tons, sharing the same 31 hp 4-cylinder engine, the 6-cylinder 45 hp 6-ton Majestic, and the 7/8 Mammoth which used the same 6-cylinder unit. A six cylinder diesel engine was also available in the same year, that had been developed during the previous two years and was the first British lightweight, high speed diesel. These models were followed by the Marshal, Matador (a 5-tonner and not a 4 x 4 at this stage), Mandator and 12-ton Mammoth- Major in 1931 and by the four-axle Major 8 in 1934. These replaced the 2½ ton 204, 4-ton 418/1 and 428, the 5-ton 506 and 6-ton 508/1 and 509 of the twenties and greatly extended AEC's heavy vehicle coverage.

Following AEC's acquisition of Hardy Motors, who had used AEC components since 1928, a number of 8 x 8 tractors were produced by AEC for hauling road trains on un-paved tracks in such countries as Australia and the USSR. They could gross 30 tons and typically towed three 8-wheel trailers. Most Hardy/AEC products of the thirties were 4 x 4 and 6 x 6 trucks, which evolved into the Matador and Militant. A new bus development in 1932 was the advanced Q-type with side mounted engine, fluid flywheel and Wilson pre-selective gearbox, available as a double or single decker.

Being so closely involved in the London bus business had advantages and disadvantages for AEC. It kept them busy, but it also restricted their ability to compete with untied manufacturers and from 1926 they had merger talks with Leyland with a view to rationalizing the British heavy vehicle industry. The Chairman of Underground Electric Railways recommended a holding company to acquire the shares of Leyland and AEC and when Leyland turned this down in 1930 it was suggested that the Ford Motor Company should make an offer.

Instead the London Transport Passenger Act of 1933

1934 A.E.C. Mammoth tanker, NMM

instructed the Underground Group to distribute their assets and AEC was converted into an entirely independent public company, which had a ten year contract to supply London with 90% of its buses.

By 1935 most AEC models were available with 4- or 6-cylinder diesel engines and in that year the well-known 6-cylinder 7.7 litre diesel was introduced which was to be the mainstay of the range for over 20 years. The Matador and Militant military vehicles have already been mentioned and these as well as Marshal 6 x 4's, armoured cars and tank engines were AEC's main products during the Second World War. The Matador, of which over 9000 were built during the War, was primarily a medium gun tractor while the 6 x 6 chassis served many roles including aircraft refuelling and mobile crane carrying.

1936 A.E.C. Q-type model 5Q5 side-engined bus, LTE

After the War the Regent Mark III bus developed in 1939 and called the RT for London service, was produced and some 5000 sold to London Transport. AEC's trolleybus interests were merged with those of Leyland in a new company in 1946 entitled B.U.T. Ltd. In 1948 AEC acquired Crossley Motors Ltd. and the Maudslay Motor Co. Ltd. and a new holding company, Associated Commercial Vehicles Ltd. was formed to control all three firms. In 1949 the coachbuilding firm of Park Royal Vehicles Ltd. was acquired along with their subsidiary Chas. H. Roe Ltd. For a time Crossley and Maudslay continued to make distinct models but by the early fifties had become just variations on the AEC theme. Also in 1949 the underfloor-engined Regal IV single deck bus and coach chassis entered production and in 1953 came its successor, the Reliance, whose mechanical components were also available in the integrally constructed Monocoach from Park Royal Vehicles Ltd. This gave AEC experience in chassisless construction which was applied to the prototype Routemaster for London Transport in 1954, and the later Bridgemaster — so named because of the low height (and, incidentally, weight) made possible by not using a chassis.

1949 A.E.C. Mommoth Major 15-ton 8-wheeler, OMM

1957 A.E.C. Reliance 43-seater M.C.W. bodied bus, OMM

In the goods field the new 8-ton Mercury of 1953 lost AEC's traditional radiator in favor of a stylized grille. In 1955 in Mark II form it was modified to accept 9½ tons under the new 14 tons gvw limit with AV410 98 bhp or AV470 112 bhp engine (the number as on the AV 590 and 690 of 1958 indicating the engine capacity in cubic inches).

A new departure for AEC in 1957 was the Dumptruk, an extra heavy duty version of the Mammoth Major with single oversize rear tires and half cab. It was designed to carry a 10 cu. yd. earthmoving body and was joined by a massive 2-axle 18 cu. yd. Dumptruk in 1959 built at the Maudslay Works at Alcester. This had a 340 bhp 6-cyl. diesel able to propel 50 tons gross up a 1 in 3 slope.

During the fifties most of AEC's traditional goods model names remained in being with several available in heavy duty normal control form for export. An additional conventional export model introduced in 1959 was the AEC Mogul, or ACLO Mogul in Spain and Spanish speaking areas of South America, where it and other models achieved considerable popularity following licensed manufacturing agreements with Barreiros in Spain in 1961 and with SIAM DiTella Automotores SA of Buenos Aires soon afterwards. Other overseas manufacturing arrangements at the time included a South African operation where the Kudu bus was produced specially for local requirements and a link with coachbuilder N.V. Autoindustrie Verheul in Holland. In France AEC took an interest in Etablissements Willeme in 1962, which resulted in several Willeme vehicles using AEC engines.

Also in 1962 AEC took over Transport Equipment (Thornycroft) Ltd. and curtailed Thornycroft's ordinary goods vehicles range in favor of special purpose cross-

1960 A.E.C. Mustang twin steer 6-wheeler, OMM

1968 A.E.C. Mandator V8 32 tons GTW articulated truck, AEC

country chassis. In the same year ACV merged with its long-time rivals Leyland Motors Ltd. and over the next decade became increasingly integrated into the British Leyland Truck and Bus division. The first step was the introduction of the Leyland Ergomatic tilt cab in 1964. At the same time a new passenger model, the rear engine Swift, was introduced. This engine layout was also used in the Merlin bus of 1967. In 1968 a 247 bhp V8 diesel engine was introduced and fitted to a number of models including Mandator and Mammoth Major tractive units, the latter being suitable for up to 56 tons combination weight, as well as in the Sabre coach, where it was rear mounted.

AEC's current activities center round the Leyland Marathon which it assembles and for which it produces the TL12 six cylinder 281bhp diesel engine. In normally aspirated form this is also fitted to the Leyland Buffalo L12 introduced in 1977 to replace the AEC Mercury, among others. The uprated 30 ton gvw Mammoth Major gave way to the Leyland Octopus in 1976 and now the only vehicle bearing the AEC name is the horizonal mid-engined Reliance coach. Late in 1978 it was announced that the Southall factory would be closed in June 1979.

AEC trucks and buses have been assembled in South Africa since 1961, and a number of vehicles exclusive to that country have been developed. The best known are the 6 x 4 Super Mammoth tractor with conventional hood, and the Kudu front-engined bus chassis. AEC trucks and tractors are also assembled in Portugal by UTIC using locally-designed cabs of distinctive appearance. *OM*

A.E.G. (D) 1903-1905; 1935-1939
Allgemeine Elektrizitats Akt. Ges., Berlin-Oberschoneweide

This electric concern owned the N.A.G. company (q.v.) but under their own name produced trolley-buses in 1903 following the Stoll patents. But at this early stage they were more experimental, although some lines were operated with these vehicles.

In 1935 a production of electric driven vans and trucks was taken up and a light van and heavier 3-ton and 6-ton versions were offered. *HON*

A.E.M. (F) 1923-1924
Ste. d'Applications Electro-Mecaniques, Gennevilliers, Seine

This was a 10cwt electric van sponsored by the Ste d'Applications Electro-Mecaniques and made in the Chenard-Walcker factory. It had front wheel-drive, a speed of 15/18mph and a range of 50/60 miles per charge. An unusual feature for a vehicle of this kind was i.f.s. by transverse leaf springs. The motor lived under a short, Renault-style hood, and the batteries under the seat. *GNG*

AERFER (I) c.1952-1965
Industrie Meccaniche Aeronautiche Meridionali, Naples

Formerly a well-known aircraft factory, Meridionali was principally concerned with bodies for buses and trolleybuses. In the 1950s and early 1960s, however, they made some light-alloy, integral construction buses using Fiat diesel engines. These included a 150-passenger double-decker of 1960, ordered by Rome as well as Naples. Its 150 bhp horizontal power unit was mounted transversely at the rear, driving the rear wheels via an automatic gearbox. *MCS*

1966 AERMACCHI ND3 1500kg truck, Aermacchi

AERMACCHI (I) 1947-1970
(1) Societa Commerciale Aeronautica Macchi SpA, Varese 1947-1960
(2) Aermacchi Harley-Davidson SpA, Varese 1960-1969
(3) AMF-Harley-Davidson Varese SpA, Varese 1969-1970

After World War II the Macchi aircraft factory, renowned for its fighters and Schneider Trophy seaplanes, branched out into motorcycles and commercial 3-wheelers. The latter, though featuring the two driven rear wheels of the classic Italian *motocarro,* was more sophisticated than most of its rivals. The cab was enclosed, and a 750cc flat-twin engine was underslung in a tubular backbone frame with shaft drive and 3-wheel hydraulic brakes. The gearbox gave eight forward speeds and two reverses, and the payload of 1½ tons could be increased by another ton if a drawbar trailer was used. In 1950 Macchi exhibited a light fwd 4-wheeler with inter-connected, all-round torsion-bar suspension and the same engine, and in 1957 there was a new edition of the 3-wheeler using a 973cc 18 bhp aircooled 2-cylinder diesel unit. In the 1950s Macchi also built some ultra-light open-saddle models with 123cc single-cylinder engines. Financial troubles led to a takeover by Harley-Davidson of Milwaukee in 1960, but the trucks were continued, the diesel being joined by a ¾ ton model on similar lines. This used the ohv 2-cylinder Fiat 500 gasoline engine. After a change of ownership truck production ceased in 1970, but the Aermacchi diesel was continued under the Bremac name by the Brenna brothers. *MCS*

AERO (CS) 1932-1940: 1946-1951
Aero, tovarna letadel, Prague-Vysocany

The 2-stroke Aero light car designed by Novotny was made in commercial form as a delivery van and pick up.

1947 AERO 150 van, Techniart

The Type 662 had a 662cc 2-cylinder engine developing 18bhp, with a capacity of 240kgs, and this was followed in 1935 by the Type 30 with 998cc 28bhp engine and 300kgs load. The latter had front wheel drive. After the end of passenger car production, Aero built the L-150 30cwt truck from 1946 to 1951. This was derived from the Skoda 933 and had a 4-cylinder ohv engine of 2,090cc, developing 52bhp. In 1951 Aero's motor vehicle department was transferred to Praga, and the truck renamed A-150. About 3,700 were made, as trucks, vans and fire engines, and many are still in use today. *MSH*

1940/50 AEROCOACH, MBS

AEROCOACH (U.S.) 1940-1952

(1) General American Aerocoach Co., Chicago, Ill. 1940-1946

(2) General American Aerocoach Co., East Chicago, Ind. 1946-1952

General American Transportation Corp., a builder and lessor of railroad cars, purchased the bus manufacturing business of Gar Wood Industries in 1939 (see GAR WOOD) and set up a new production line in Chicago early in 1940. The principle of the welded tube framework was used in an entirely new and larger type of bus later that year, and these 29 and 33-passenger buses gradually superseded the smaller type on the production line. The Aerocoach name was used for both types, so that the earliest Aerocoaches were indistinguishable (except for their nameplates) from the last Gar Woods.

International engines and five-speed Clark transmissions were standard equipment in the new, larger Aerocoaches, which were to be manufactured into the early1950's without substantial change. When bus production was stopped by material shortages in 1943, the sales record stood at approximately 250 Aerocoaches of the Gar Wood type and 300 of the new type, which was the only design resumed when manufacturing began again in April 1944. From then until the end in 1952, another 2350 buses were made. A Continental engine was offered in addition to the International power plant in 1947, and design changes were made in 1949 and 1951, but Aerocoach by then had been left behind by the changing demands of the U.S. intercity bus industry, and at the end much of its output went to foreign customers.

An effort was made to enter the transit bus business in 1948 with the introduction of handsome 36 and 45-passenger models having fully automatic heating and ventilating systems, but the venture was not successful. An interesting sideline was the rebuilding of prewar Greyhound Yellow Coaches with diesel engines and new interiors in the postwar years, under contract to Greyhound. *MBS*

AETNA (US) 1915-1916

Aetna Motor Truck Co., Detroit, Mich.

The Aetna commercial vehicles used worm-drive rear axles and underslung 3/4-elliptical springs. These trucks were available as 1½- and 2½-tonners. *GMN*

AGA (D) 1921-1928

1. AG fur Automobilbau, Berlin-Lichtenberg 1921-1926

2. Aga Fahrzeugwerke, Berlin-Lichtenberg 1926-1928

Based on the private car of this company, a van was available using the 1.6 litre engine of 6/20 PS. *HON*

AGRICOLA (GR) 1975 to date

Agricola, Salonica

The Agricola is a Unimog-like vehicle based on a ladder-type chassis, powered by a Mercedes-Benz I80D diesel engine and is fitted with allwheel-drive through a Mercedes-Benz gearbox. An all-metal cab seating two, a metal cargo body and a standard P.T.O. complete the specification of the Agricola, which is destined mainly for agricultural uses. *GA*

AHRENS-FOX (US) 1911-1956

(1) Ahrens-Fox Fire Engine Co., Cincinnati, Ohio 1911-1953

(2) C.D. Beck Co., Sidney, Ohio 1953-1956

This company was formed by John P. Ahrens whose family had built horse-drawn steam pumpers since 1868, and Charles H. Fox, assistant chief of Cincinnati Fire Department. Their first motor fire engine to be delivered was completed in 1911 and sold to Rockford, Illinois Fire Department in January 1912. Powered by an 80hp 6-cylinder Herschell-Spillman engine, it had a 2-cylinder pumper with an output of 750gpm. It was followed by eleven similar models in 1912, thirteen in 1913 and eleven in 1914. The last Ahrens-Fox steamer, powered by an electric front-wheel-drive unit, left the factory in 1912. In mid-1914 the Herschell-Spillman engine was replaced by a slightly larger monobloc six built by Ahrens-Fox, and up to 1927 their own make of engine was used in all their fire engines. In 1915 the Model A was replaced by the Model M which employed a new 4-cylinder double acting pump mounted ahead of the engine. This was surmounted by a

1936 AHRENS-FOX Model BT pumper, Techniart

spherical brass air chamber which became the hallmark of Ahrens-Fox pumpers until 1951. The brass sphere was beaten out by hand, and it was said that only one employee knew the secret of its construction. When he died his secret died with him, and a new design of two-piece forged steel ball was worked out.

Although the pumpers were the best-known Ahrens-Fox products, the company also built tractors to pull horse-drawn ladder trucks, articulated aerial ladder trucks with tiller to steer the rear wheels, chemical engines and hose trucks. Most of the specialized equipment was furnished by Peter Pirsch of Kenosha, Wisconsin. Other pioneer features included double banking of ladders, an aerial ladder hoist powered by a small engine-driven compressor, and a hydrant-thawing device consisting of a small boiler attached to the exhaust manifold. In 1917 an Ahrens-Fox was the first pumper to drive water over the then tallest building in the world, the 60 story Woolworth Building in New York City.

6-cylinder pumps were introduced on the 1915/17 Model L and the 1921/30 Model P, the latter having a capacity of 1300gpm. Up to 1920 all Ahrens-Fox machines had chain drive, but shaft drive was optional from that year onwards, and had become universal a few years later. Continental engines were introduced on the 1927 chemical trucks, and by the mid-1930s alternatives to the Ahrens-Fox engines were Hercules or Waukesha units. As well as the famous piston pumps, Ahrens-Fox developed a line of smaller rotary pumpers, and these were mounted on other chassis such as Ford, Dodge, Studebaker and Republic as well as on Ahrens-fox chassis. Because of the Depression, production shrank to very few units during the years 1931 to 1936, when the company merged with another Cincinnati firm, the Le Blond-Schacht Truck Company. This arrangement continued until 1951 when a Cincinnati businessman, Walter Walkenhorst, purchased Ahrens-Fox. Under his management the famous piston pumpers with the steel ball were discontinued as they were becoming obsolete. The last was delivered to Tarrytown, N.Y. in late 1951. A year later Walkenhorst sold Ahrens-Fox to the C.D. Beck Company, manufacturers of buses; production of fire engines was transferred to Beck's Sidney, Ohio plant, while sales and service remained in Cincinnati. The Beck-built Ahrens-Fox followed previous design of conventional centrifugal pumpers, and in 1956 a new line of cab-forwards appeared powered by Continental or Waukesha engines. In 1956 Beck was purchased by Mack who, adopting the Ahrens-Fox forward cab for their own line of fire engines, discontinued the Ahrens-Fox. Total production of Ahrens-Fox chassis over 45 years was not much more than 900 units. Of these, about 200 were still in service early in 1975. Mack fire engines were made at the Sidney plant for a few years before being concentrated at the main factory at Allentown, Pa. In 1961 all assets, machinery, parts and patterns of Ahrens-Fox were acquired by a former employee, Richard C. Nepper, who services and repairs existing fire engines and also builds fire apparatus on commercial chassis. Production of the latter is very slow as Nepper has only one part-time helper, and currently runs at one fire engine every five years. *GNG*

A.I.C. (US) 1912-1914

American Ice Manufacturing Company, New York, N.Y.

A few of the early users of specialized trucks got into the business of manufacturing such trucks because, presumably the unavailability of the desired capacity. This was the route of the builder of the A.I.C., a large capacity (5 tons) and sturdy vehicle. The chassis weighed 7900 pounds and wheelbase was 137 inches. The 4-cylinder engine with 6-3/4 inch stroke was located under the driver's compartment. To accept the high load capacity, the rear wheels used solid tires which were 40 x 5 dual ones. *GMN*

AILSA (GB/S) 1973 to date

Ailsa Bus Ltd., Irvine, Ayrshire

The Volvo-powered Ailsa double decker bus, assembled by the British concessionaires for Volvo vehicles, is unusual in marking a return to the front-engined double-decker bus, the first to be made in Britain since 1969. It is powered by a 6.75-litre 6-cylinder turbocharged diesel engine developing 201bhp, and has a 5-speed automatic gearbox made by Self Changing Gears Ltd. The 70-seater integral construction body is built by Walter Alexander & Co. Ltd. of Falkirk. In the Spring of 1978 more than 400 orders for Ailsa buses had been fulfilled, the majority from South Yorkshire and West Midlands PTEs, and from the Scottish Bus Group. *GNG*

1978 AILSA double decker bus, Ailsa

AIR-O-FLEX (US) 1918-1920

Air-O-Flex Auto Corp., Detroit, Mich.

For 1918-1919, this make was offered as a 2-tonner. For 1920, a 1½-tonner was made which used a 4-cyl. Buda engine with a piston-operated water pump. This model had a 4-speed gearbox and shaft drive. Wheelbase on this last offering was 180 in. *GMN*

AIREDALE (GB) 1908

Leeds Motor Manufacturing Co., Leeds, Yorkshire

The Airedale appeared only briefly during 1908 but incorporated a number of unusual features in its construction. The company concentrated upon a 4-cylinder 20 hp model light van with ohv engine and ohc driven by vertical shaft and skew gear. It was fitted with a McLeod carburetor and boasted Gianoli dual ignition. The radiator hinged forward on trunnion bearings to facilitate engine maintenance, lubrication was by pump (friction driven), the oil tank being located near the exhaust to keep it warmer in winter, and the fan was worm driven through a dog clutch. Three speeds and reverse were provided, driving through a single plate clutch with cardan shaft to a live rear axle. A number of smaller vans were also built, fitted with 2-cyl. engines but the marque does not seem to have survived the end of the year and is not connected with the car of the same name built in Esholt from 1919. *MJWW*

AISA (E) 1952-1957

Actividades Industriales, SA, Barcelona

In addition to a small touring motor tricycle, this company built a light delivery tricycle, powered by a 197cc Hispano-Villiers air-cooled engine driving the rear wheel via a 3-speed gearbox. Suspension was by coil springs. *JCG*

A.J.S. (GB) 1929-1931

A. J. Stevens & Co. (1914) Ltd., Wolverhampton, Staffs.

This well-known manufacturer of motorcycles introduced a line of passenger vehicles in order to reach new markets when their motorcycles were selling badly. Announced in February 1929, the Pilot chassis was available in conventional or forward-control form, and was powered by a 3.3-litre 70bhp 6-cylinder Coventry-Climax engine. It had a four-speed gearbox, worm final drive and vacuum brakes, and was designed to carry 24/26 seat coachwork. In October 1929 it was joined by the larger Commodore, powered by a 5.8-litre 100bhp 6-cylinder Coventry-Climax engine; this was only made in forward-control form. It was intended as a 26-seater coach or 32-seater bus. The buses sold quite well for a while, but in October 1931 the company went into liquidation; the motorcycle interests were sold to Matchless so that the name was perpetuated on two wheelers, manufacturing rights to the light car were sold to Willys-Overland-Crossley who made it for another year, but the commercial vehicles were discontinued. *GNG*

A.K. — ELLAS (GR) 1968 to date

D. Agelopoulos — I. Karkanis & Co., O.E., Nikaia, Piraeus

An ultra-light three-wheeled tricycle powered by a Sachs and later a Kazal 50cc engine, but fitted with a two seat glassfibre cab, full automotive controls and hydraulic brakes. The open rear body was hand-tilted to allow accessibility to the mid-chassis positioned engine. Simplicity of cab design permitted restyling almost every two years. *GA*

AKRON (US) 1913-1914

Akron Motor Car & Truck Co., Akron, Ohio

The Model A was a 3/4-tonner available as either open or closed delivery vans. These ranged in price from $1460 to $1500. Available on special order were bus, hearse, ambulance and police patrol bodies. *GMN*

AKRON MULTI-TRUCK (US) 1920-1921

Thomart Motor Co., Kent, Ohio

Despite its name, this was built only as a 1-tonner with a 133 in. wheelbase. The Model 20 was one of the few truck makes which used a Hinkley Model 400 engine, with four cylinders. This model was provided with pneumatic tires, a 3-speed gearbox and bevel gear drive. One reference claims this make was continued under the name Thomart, but this is unverified. *GMN*

ALBARET (F) 1865-c.1914

Albaret et Cie, Liancourt-Rantigny, Oise.

Though mainly noted for agricultural engines and road rollers, the firm made a range of steam road tractors having locomotive boilers with circular fireboxes, the outer vessel of which was continued upwards above the boiler barrel to form a large steam dome. Other features were an undermounted engine with enclosed all gear drive to the rear axle, geared down steering by horizontal shaft and rack and worm, railway type pannier tanks and an open backed tender. Later Albaret tractors, however, were conventional overtypes closely resembling the corresponding British product and directed mainly at agricultural users. *RAW*

ALBION (GB) 1902-1972

(1) Albion Motor Car Co., Finnieston, Glasgow 1902
(2) Albion Motor Car Co., Scotstoun, Glasgow 1903-1930
(3) Albion Motors Ltd., Scotstoun, Glasgow 1931-1972

After producing a small number of dog-carts, Albion made their first commercial vehicle in 1902, a 10cwt van with horizontal 2-cyl. 8 hp engine and tiller steering. It was followed in 1903 by the 12 hp A3, which remained in production for eleven years and had a more conventional vertical 2-cylinder engine and wheel steering. Various versions could carry up to two tons and the engine was increased to 16 hp. A 1-ton model gained a gold medal in the 1907 RAC trials and the make was often regarded as a Lacre outside Scotland, as that firm was responsible for their English sales.

In 1910 the A10 for 3- and 4-ton loads was introduced with 4-cyl. 32 hp engine and chain drive, while a lighter 25 hp model was popular as a charabanc. After producing over 500 vehicles in 1913 Albion decided to abandon its private car models in favor of commercial vehicles. The A10, or B as it became, was approved by the War Office and approximately 6000 were built during the First World War.

Afterwards Albion continued to produce variations on the B up to 1927, by which time a total of some 9000 had been produced, though they were among the first manufacturers to reorganize themselves after the War with new models.

One of the most important of these was the first Subsidy 30cwt model to enter full production. Introduced in 1923 it remained the basis of Albion's lighter models well into the Thirties.

1913 ALBION 32hp country bus, NMM

In 1913 Albion had produced some attractive torpedo-bodied charabancs and in 1923 they augmented this lead with the Viking, one of the first commercial chassis specifically designed for passenger work. It was low-built, requiring only one step, and had a most attractive streamlined radiator on high-performance touring car lines. 14 and 18 seaters were initially available and could travel at up to 30 mph on giant pneumatic tires. Albion were also one of the first to produce a drop-frame bus chassis in Britain and their new 30/60 hp model did the round trip from Glasgow to London and back in 1925 in under 24 hours.

To give it in excess of 40 mph performance, the Viking could be fitted with the 30/60 hp engine from 1925, and for 1929 it was fitted with Albion's first six cylinder engine producing 90 bhp.

1928 ALBION Viking 24 seater all-weather coach, Chris Taylor Collection

By the end of the Twenties Albion's goods range extended from 30cwt to 5-ton models with few frills and none of the one-off and specialized Colonial models that typified most other important British manufacturers of the period. One exception however, was a six-wheeler based on the 24hp Subsidy chassis. Most models could have forward or normal control and were of simple and rugged design and styling, though an untypical forward control model in

1929 ALBION 4-ton tanker, OMM

1927 with faired-in radiator was rapidly discontinued and Albion's familiar radiator design and archaic cab remained largely unaltered until the Fifties.

For 1931 the goods range was extended up to 6-tons and the first of Albion's highly successful lightweight 3½/4-ton models was introduced which, through the Thirties, were to be the backbone of their range and take maximum advantage of speed and unladen weight regulations culminating in the model 127 of 1935. Also new in 1931 were the Valiant 32 seat 6-cylinder bus and the Victor 20 seater as well as a new 2-tonner. The Valiant and its four cylinder variant the Valkyrie were to be the mainstay of Albion's passenger business in the Thirties. The Victor also remained in production and from the mid-Thirties a six wheel Valkyrie was offered.

1931 ALBION 7/8 ton 6-wheeler, OMM

Announced in time for the Scottish Motor Show of 1932, which Albion always tried to support with a new model, was the Venturer double decker which had a similar engine to the Valiant.

From this time most of the heavier Albion models could be supplied with a choice of Gardner, Dorman or Beardmore diesel engines, though at the end of 1933 Albion introduced their own diesel unit.

In 1935 Albion acquired the premises of Halley at Yoker, to gain more space, and entered the multi-axle field with a 13-ton double-drive six wheeler which was joined by an eight wheeler in 1937 with a choice of Albion 6-cyl. petrol or Gardner 6LW diesel, while later that year most of the heavy models acquired unit-construction engines and gearboxes for the first time.

Before production switched to military vehicles Albion also produced twin-steer six wheel models.

During the Second World War Albion were major producers of 4 x 4 3-ton and 6 x 4 10-ton trucks as well as producing almost 1000 tank transporters. Among the latter was a prototype twin engined 8 x 8 design though

1939 ALBION Venturer CX19G 56-seater bus, MAS

1939 ALBION 15-ton 8-wheel tanker

production models were 140 hp 6 x 4 conventional tractors.

Soon after the War the goods chassis acquired model names like the Chieftain and Clansman (formerly Halley model names) which in 1948, had 75 hp four cylinder diesel engines, and the 12-ton Clydesdale in 1950.

In 1951 Albion Motors was acquired by Leyland Motors and was thus the first step in their vast expansion program. For some time this produced little change at Albion though Leyland engines and other components began to be used.

However it did result in an interesting 39-seat bus project being killed in 1952. This single decker had an underfloor eight cylinder pancake engine. Another unexpected piece of unconventional design in 1954 produced the underfloor engined 4-ton Claymore, but this was not produced in quantity until it had been simplified in 1958. It also became the basis of the Nimbus bus.

1949 ALBION 15-ton 8-wheeler, OMM

An unusual involvement at the time was with the Leyland-engined Albion-Cuthbertson Water Buffalo, a large crawler vehicle for working in swamps.

In 1958 Albion re-entered the eight wheel market with the Caledonian, a design almost identical to the contemporary Leyland Octopus. Other Leyland features of the time were the adoption of the forward control Comet's

1956 ALBION Claymore underfloor-engine truck, OMM

steel cab on the Clydesdale and Chieftain, which differed from the Leyland product in having hub reduction axles. These became an important Albion feature and made them particularly popular for site work, as half shaft breakages were virtually impossible. They were also employed on the 6 x 4 Reiver which, like the 9-ton Clydesdale, was powered by the Leyland 0.400 engine from 1960, although Albion continued to make their own 5.5 litre engine, and also a five speed constant-mesh gearbox which was fitted to most of the range.

Being light in weight and simple, Albions were extremely economical and both the seven and nine tonners regularly achieved over 15 mpg laden, and the 5-ton Claymore 20 mpg in urban driving. They were also cheap and a fleet of Chieftains was even acquired by a United States distribution firm.

In the passenger field Albion continued to offer the Victor and a rear engined Viking for export as well as the Nimbus, and in 1961 introduced the double deck Lowlander, a variation on the Leyland Atlantean.

1963 ALBION Chieftain articulated truck, Scammell

1965 ALBION Reiver 6-wheeler, OMM

1912 ALCO (right) with two MOGULS, RNE

New in 1964 was the Ergomatic cab which differed from the A.E.C. and Leyland versions in having different frontal styling incorporating Albion's rising sun motif and also lighter gauge panelling. Though this was used on normal haulage models the previous cab was retained for more arduous conditions, like on a 4 x 4 Chieftain model produced in conjunction with Scammell in 1966 and on Reiver tipper and mixer chassis. This latter vehicle incidentally soon acquired a more powerful 151 hp engine from A.E.C., as well as the 10-speed gearbox.

From 1969 some Reivers and Clydesdales were fitted with turbocharged Leyland engines, but this was to mark the end of their independent technical development. Albions remained popular in the tipper field and for no-frills road transport, but Leyland decided to phase them out in 1972 because most of their models complemented existing Leyland, A.E.C. and Guy designs.

However, though the Albion name is no longer used on vehicles produced in Glasgow, the model names Reiver, Clydesdale and Chieftain and Viking export bus chassis live on with many of the Leyland vehicles now produced. These still comprise a high proportion of Albion components and now use an updated version of the B.M.C. cab also used on Leyland's other Scottish products from nearby Bathgate. *OM*

ALCO (US) 1909-1913

American Locomotive Co., Providence, R.I.

As one might expect from a locomotive builder, Alco gasoline trucks were all well-built heavyweights, being offered in 2, 3½, 5 and 6½ ton capacities. Some customers even used them to power road trains of four trailers hauling 18 tons of coal.

Alco trucks were all large cab-overs with solid tires, artillery wheels, chain-drive, and semi-elliptic springs. The engines all had four cylinders and were of large sizes: for the 2-ton model, 4½x5½ inches, rated at 32hp, and for the other models, 5x6 inches rated at 40hp. The larger engine displaced 471 cu. in., quite sizeable in its day. The cooling was by water pump, clutch was steel and bronze multiple disc, and transmissions were all 3-speed selective, mounted amidships, a common practice then. The price range was from $2950 to $5500.

In the summer of 1912 an Alco with a three-man crew headed by E.L. Ferguson made the first transcontinental delivery of merchandise (3 tons of soap) by motor truck from Philadelphia, Pa. to Petaluma, Cal., north of San Francisco, a distance of 4145 miles in 94 days. The top speed was 15 mph.

In the transport manufacturing field since 1835, the company in Sept. 1913 decided to suspend all automotive production, including the large Alco car and taxi, and concentrate on their first love, locomotives. Lifetime production of Alco trucks was about 1000, a substantial number for a large truck of that era, some of which were used in Alaska, the Philippines, and elsewhere in the tropics. *RW*

1933 ALFA ROMEO Model 50, Alfa Romeo

ALFA ROMEO (I) 1930 to date

1) SA Alfa Romeo, Milan 1930-1942
2) Alfa Romeo SpA, Milan 1942 to date

This famous producer of high performance cars had an agricultural tractor on the market in 1920, but did not introduce a roadgoing truck until the 1930 Milan Show. This was of light, high speed type, with 3-litre 6-cylinder gasoline engine, but a year later the company had adopted the diesel, offering some Bussing-based 5- and 6-tonners with Deutz-type antechamber engines. The range embraced PSVs as well as a 10-ton 6-wheeler; this latter was also sold in bus form. 1934 saw a 78-seater Macchi-bodied articulated bus, and by 1937 the standard coach chassis was the conventional ALR, with 6.1-litre, 6-cylinder power unit, 4-speed gearbox, and air-hydraulic brakes; its sloping grille was clearly inspired by the contemporary 2.9-litre supercharged sports car. Mechanically, Alfa Romeo's trucks were very similar, and catered for payloads from 3 to 10 tons; the bigger ones, which included a 6-wheeler, were of forward control type with eight forward speeds, and there were special gazogene and

1934 ALFA ROMEO Model 85, Alfa Romeo

1937 ALFA ROMEO Model T500, Alfa Romeo

methane versions. In 1940 there was a full-fronted aerodynamic coach based on the 6½-ton 800, while during the War the smaller conventional 500 models were replaced by an 8-speed 3/4-tonner, the 430, powered by a 5.8-litre 4-cylinder direct injection oil engine. Alfa Romeo built some prototype artillery tractors with 4-wheel drive and steering, but the authorities preferred the rival S.P.A. designs.

Forward control models only were offered after 1945, the 800 evolving into the 8-ton 900 with 130bhp, 9½-litre engine, while the smaller Alfa was given air-hydraulic brakes and coil ifs in 1948. This latter refinement resulted in excessive tire wear, and the 4/5-tonners reverted to beam axles in 1950. The 450 and 900 series were continued until 1957, the latter being in 1951 as an unusual 6 x 2 on which the front and rear pairs of wheels were steerers.

On the PSV side a conventional 450-based coach was joined in 1948 by a new line of advanced vehicles with transversely-mounted rear engines, 900 mechanical ele-

1951 ALFA ROMEO Model 140 city bus, coachwork by Garavini, HDB

ments, and coachwork on Aerocoach and Tubauto lines by Casaro. Developments of this theme included some 157-passenger articulated buses operating in Milan, and a 1954 variant with central driving position. Alfa Romeo also supplied trolleybuses to their home city, while from 1954 onwards they collaborated with Fiat and C.G.E. and in a new model; among the customers was the city of Montevideo.

A light, Jeep-type 4 x 4, the Matta, appeared in 1951. It used the twin ohc 4-cylinder engine, 4-speed synchromesh gearbox, and torsion-bar independent suspension of the 1900 sedan. Some 2,000 only were made; more successful

1962 ALFA ROMEO Mille 8/10 tonner, Alfa Romeo

was the Romeo Autotutto of 1954, a modern 1-ton forward control truck or van. It was all-independently sprung, and could be had with either a 1.2-litre 2-stroke twin-cylinder diesel or a detuned, 35bhp edition of the 1.3-litre twin-cam Giulietta car unit. It was joined in 1957 by a new forward control 8-tonner, the Mille, with 11-litre 6-cylinder diesel engine, air assisted clutch, air-assisted 8-speed gearbox, and air brakes. Coach versions used rear horizontal engines, and the Mille was built under license in Brazil by F.N.M. These basic models were continued with little change for a decade. 1967, however, saw an agreement with Saviem which led to the license-assembly of the French company's Goelette and Galion models, the latter being sold in Italy as the Alfa Romeo A15. Alfa Romeo also developed a new 1-ton fwd model with torsion-bar ifs,

1971 ALFA ROMEO A-15 light truck, Alfa Romeo

the F20; it used 4-cylinder Saviem petrol or diesel engines.

Still being made in 1978 were the A12 and F12, developments of the 1954 Romeo, and retaining that model's fwd, suspension, and 1.3-litre twin-cam gasoline engine, now uprated to 65bhp. Front disc brakes were standard, and the diesel option was the 1.8-litre Perkins 4-108. In addition, there was an all-new range of conventional-drive semi-forward control types for payloads in the 1½/2¼-ton bracket (A30, A32, A35 and A40), powered by 2.4-litre 4-cylinder Sofim diesels produced at Foggia under the joint sponsorship of Alfa Romeo, Fiat and Saviem. 5-speed gearboxes and twin rear wheels featured on bigger variants: in addition to their torsion-bar ifs these latest Alfa Romeo commercials had all-disc brakes. *MCS*

1978 ALFA ROMEO 35 AR8 3½ tonner GVW truck, Alfa Romeo

ALFARO (E) 1953-1957

Construcciones Mecanicas Alfaro, Santa Perpetua de la Moguda, Barcelona

In addition to motorcycles, this firm made a small 3-wheeled van with a load capacity of 400 kgs. *JCG*

1927 ALFI 3-wheeler, HON

ALFI (D) 1922-1928

(1) Aktiengesellschaft fur Akkumulatoren und Automobilbau, Berlin N 65; Driesen-Vordamm 1922-1924
(2) Alfi Automobile GmbH., Berlin N 39 1927-1928

This company started to produce electric vans and trucks (see A.A.A. and Elektric) but also offered a gasoline driven van based on their private car types 4/14 and 5/20 PS. In 1927 a unique design was presented, a 3-wheeled vehicle with a single front wheel, to which a DKW engine was fitted and which could be turned around through 180 degrees for reverse drive. *HON*

ALGE (D) 1927-1937

Motoren- und Fahrzeugfabrik Alfred Geissler, Knauthain nr. Leipzig

This was a tri-van following motorcycle lines with one front wheel and rear box or platform. Villiers two-stroke engines of 6 and 10 bhp were used. *HON*

1920 ALL AMERICAN 1-ton truck, NMM

ALL-AMERICAN (US) 1918-1923

(1) All-American Truck Co., Chicago, Ill. 1918-1922
(2) Fremont Motors Corp, Fremont, Ohio 1922-1923

Sometimes known as the A.A., particularly on the British market, the All-American was a conventional 1-ton truck powered by a 4-cylinder Herschell-Spillman engine. It had a 3-speed gearbox, internal gear drive and a wheelbase of 130 inches. For most of its life the All-American was made in Chicago, in the former Ogren car plant, but in August 1922 production was transferred to Fremont, Ohio. *GNG*

ALL-BRITISH (GB) 1907-1908

All-British Car Co. Ltd., Bridgeton, Glasgow

This grandiosely-named company was formed by George Johnston, formerly of Arrol-Johnston, to build cars and commercial vehicles with 4- and 8-cylinder engines which bore some similarity to Johnston's horizontally-opposed twins used in early Arrol-Johnstons. The engines were made in pairs of cylinders, of which one piston acted directly on the crankshaft, and the other through a rocking lever. In the All-British, these cylinders were paired vertically, making what could be called a U-4 or U-8, rather than the usual V-4 or V-8. Cars and commercial vehicles were listed, and at least one bus was built and ran for a short time in London. It had a 44 hp 4-cylinder engine, 2-speed all-chain gearbox and chain drive. Confusingly, *The Commercial Motor* describes this bus as having a horizontal engine, although the All-British catalogue clearly shows it to be a vertical unit. *GNG*

ALL-POWER (US) 1918-1920

All-Power Truck Co., Detroit, Mich.

The All-Power was made only as a 3½-tonner known as Model SV 4. This used a 4-cylinder Continental engine with a 3-speed gearbox and shaft drive. It was on a 150 in. wheelbase, and was available only as a bare chassis for a price of $4800. The name would imply four-wheel-drive but there is no indication of such a drive system for this make. *GMN*

1905 ALLCHIN compound undertype steam wagon, OMM

ALLCHIN (G.B.) 1905-1931

Wm. Allchin & Co. Ltd., Globe Works, Northampton

The company took over the business of Wm. Allchin, founded in 1847, manufacturers of traction engines, portable engines and a few road rollers.

In 1905 they launched a locomotive boiler compound undertype steam wagon on steel tires with final drive by chain, seven of which were built before 1909 when the overtype engine with single roller chain final drive was adopted. Initially this had a side-fired boiler but firing from behind was substituted in the second and subsequent wagons. A few wagons had the channel chassis cranked down at the front before attachment to the boiler but later wagons had level frames attached to the side of the smokebox by Allchin's own design of expansion socket (c.1912). Allchin wagons were made as 3-, 4-, 5- and 6-tonners while at least three were made (1924) as 10-ton articulated six-wheelers.

Allchin wagons after 1912 followed closely the conventions set by Fodens and generally resembled the Foden 5-tonner. Earlier wagons had chain and bobbin steering and steel wheels but latterly Ackermann steering and solid rubbers were used. Only thirteen wagons were sold after 1924 but one supplied in 1920 ran until 1950 for the Borough of Northampton. The total overtype production was 256.

The wagons made after the design settled down in 1912

1915 ALLCHIN 5-ton overtype steam wagon, RAW

were reliable and good performers, on a par with Fodens, many of whose later refinements, such as roller bearings on crankshaft and countershaft they mirrored, but Allchins never adopted standardization of components to close limits and spares consequently required hand-fitting which told against them in the shrinking market for overtypes in the 1920's.

The firm failed in 1931 because the family initiative and direction upon which it depended ran out. *RAW*

1914 ALLDAYS 2½-ton trucks, NMM

ALLDAYS (GB) 1906-1918

Alldays & Onions Pneumatic Engineering Co. Ltd., Birmingham

The Alldays company had the oldest ancestry of any British motor firm, tracing its history back to an engineering concern of 1650. Quadricycles were made from 1898 and cars from 1903, but the first commercial vehicle was a light van on the 10 hp 2-cylinder chassis of 1906. In 1911 a trivan on similar lines to the Autocarrier, with 7/8hp engine, wheel steering and chain drive, was announced, and this was joined in 1912 by a 5cwt van on the Alldays Midget cyclecar chassis, and a range of larger trucks of up to 5-tons capacity. In 1913 the factory was turning out 30 commercial vehicles per week, of which 20 were Midget vans. The others were the trivan, now christened Expressodel, 12 and 14 hp 4-cylinder chassis for 10 and 15cwt loads, a 20hp 1-tonner, 25/30hp 2-tonner and a 40hp chassis for 3- or 5-ton loads. The 1-tonner and above all had chain drive. Alldays vehicles were used as trucks and ambulances during World War 1, and in 1918 the name was joined to that of the Enfield Autocar Company, which had in fact been owned by Alldays since 1908. *GNG*

ALLEN & SIMMONDS (GB) 1909

Allen & Simmonds Ltd., Reading, Berks.

The Allen & Simmonds was a fully-condensing locomotive-boilered steam tractor designed to run 200 miles on a single charging of water in order to comply with the conditions of the War Department Trials held in 1909. In this

1909 ALLEN & SIMMONDS steam tractor, RAW

it failed. The building of it was sub-contracted to Taskers of Andover and, the condensing apparatus apart, the components were largely those of their own tractors. The firm was later concerned in the development of the Auto Culto agricultural tractor and subsequently became Auto Culto International Limited. *RAW*

1915 ALLIS-CHALMERS B-6 half-track truck, Allis-Chalmers

ALLIS-CHALMERS (US) 1915-1918

Allis-Chalmers Mfg. Co., Milwaukee, Wis.

This commercial vehicle by the prominent manufacturers of electrical apparatus and agricultural tractors, was a five-tonner. Its general layout was a half-track with steel wheels on the front axle. Production of this vehicle was very limited and the general specifications are unavailable. *GMN*

ALLIANCE (US) 1916

Alliance Manufacturing Co., Streator, Ill.

This was a short-lived hearse-make of assembled type, powered by a 40hp 6-cylinder Lycoming engine. *MCS*

ALLREIT (D) 1908-1911

Koln-Lindenthaler Metallwerke AG., Cologne-Lindenthal

Based on the private car design, a van version was offered using a 2-cylinder engine with 1 litre capacity, 5 or 7 bhp and chain or cardan drive. *HON*

A.L.M. (F) c.1964 to date

(1) Ateliers Legueu, Meaux

(2) Ateliers de Construction Mechanique de l'Atlantique, St. Nazaire

This company builds light and medium trucks with particular stress on off-road work. They are made in 4 x 4 and 6 x 6 versions, with British Ford gasoline or Perkins diesel engines, 5-speed transmissions with 2-speed auxiliary, and

1965 A.L.M. TF4-20-SM 2½-ton truck, BHV

reinforced fiberglass cab. A number of the TF4-20-SM 2½-ton pick-ups have been supplied to the armies of France and Chad as light reconnaissance and support vehicles. *GNG*

ALPHA (E) 1927-1936
Fabrica Nacional Espanola de las Motocicletas Alpha, Barcelona

This company was founded by Nilo Maso Miro who built engines and motorcycles under the name Alpha. He also made a delivery tricycle with two front wheels and one rear, which was belt driven. Running expenses of the Alpha tricycle were said to be no more than 5% of a peseta per kilometer. Total production was 600 tricycles. *JCG*

ALPINO (I) c.1952-1960
Alpino SpA, Stradella, Pavia

Alpino's motorcycle range included two light delivery 3-wheelers on classic Italian lines, with 2-stroke single-cylinder engines and 3-speed gearboxes. The 200kg model was chain-driven, with a 49cc unit, but the 300kg Golia was a shaft-driven 125cc machine. *MCS*

1968 ALTA 700 3-wheel truck, AAR

ALTA (GR) 1967 to date
(1) ALTA S.A., Athens 1967-1970
(2) ALTA S.A., Elephsis 1970 to date

The most successful 3 wheeled light truck ever built in Greece, the ALTA 700 was entirely designed and engineered locally by a company associated with plastics. A box section chassis fitted with a rear mounted BMW two-cylinder horizontal engine developing 35 hp driving through an integrated gearbox, a spacious two seater glassfibre cab of nice design and finish and a payload of 800 kgs were part of ALTA specifications. The ALTA truckster was built in large numbers while the same factory later produced also a much modified version of the Fuldamobil cabin scooter. *GA*

ALTER (US) 1914-1916
Cincinnati Motors Mfg. Co., Cincinnati, Ohio

Three models of truck were made under this name, from 1000 to 1800 lbs capacity, all with 4-cylinder engines. When the company moved to Grand Haven, Mich. the name was briefly changed to Hamilton Motors Co. after the original backer, then to Panhard and finally Apex. *GNG*

ALTMANN (D) 1894-1907
1. Ad. Altmann & Comp. GmbH., Berlin 1894-1896
2. Kraftfahrzeugwerke GmbH., Brandenburg 1905-1907

From 1894-1896 Altmann produced various traction engines designed by Keller, but no specific details are known. Later developments by Keller were built under his own management.

In 1905 Altmann took up production of steam trucks and vans of his own design but following Gardner-Serpollet principles. However steam cars were not accepted by the public and production was only on a small scale. *HON*

1962 ALVIS Stalwart 6×6 cross country truck, Alvis

ALVIS (i) (GB) 1923-1924; 1952-1971
Alvis Ltd., Coventry

This well-known car maker had two periods of commercial vehicle manufacture. A few vans were mounted on the 12/40 car chassis in 1923/24, and used for newspaper delivery work, while in 1952 the FV600 range of 6 x 6 vehicles was introduced. Powered by a 6½-litre Rolls-Royce B81 V-8 engine, these were built mainly in military form, as general load carriers (Stalwart), fire engines (Salamander), armored cars (Saladin) and armored personnel carriers (Saracen). All except the last had their engines mounted at the rear. The amphibious Stalwart had a load capacity of 5-tons, and was theoretically suitable for general commercial use. However, despite the appearance of one at the 1962 and 1964 Commercial Vehicle Shows, none was sold to civilian users. Following the marketing agreement between Alvis and Berliet in 1964, there were plans to build the Stalwart in France under the name Auroch, but this was ended by the absorption of Alvis by British Leyland. *GNG*

ALVIS (ii) (E) 1955-1958
Talleres "Alvis" de Construcciones Mecanicas, Barcelona

No connection with the well-known British firm, this Alvis was a delivery tricycle made in 125cc and 175cc forms. *JCG*

A.M. (B) 1951-1952; 1960-1961

Ateliers Metallurgiques, Nivelles; La Brugeoise & Nivelles, St. Michiels-Brugge

In the years 1951-1952 the Ateliers Metallurgiques produced some integral buses using Leyland and Bussing underfloor engines and various other foreign parts. Their success, however, wasn't very impressive so production soon came to an end. A few years later the Ateliers Metallurgiques merged with La Brugeoise, famous constructors of trams, to establish La Brugeoise & Nivelles. This new group again tried to get a foothold in the bus market in 1960, manufacturing very American-like coaches with Detroit Diesel engines, Allison gearboxes and many other American parts. Again it failed and bus production was subsequently transferred to a new company, the Bus & Car Co., founded by the American concern Overseas Inns Co. and granted with a contract to build all the buses for the American bus operator Continental Trailways. (See Silver Eagle.) *JFJK*

1879 AMEDEE BOLLEE steam tractor, "Marie Anne", RAW

AMEDEE BOLLEE (F) 1873-c.1885

Amedee Bollee pere, Le Mans, Sarthe.

Bollee pere designed and built a number of heavy steam tractors using a rear-mounted vertical Field tube boiler with a central uptake in conjunction with a two cylinder vertical engine placed at the front of the vehicle with a level drive to a transverse countershaft from which final drive was by chain. The well-known tractor "Marie Anne" of 1879 had a power-driven tender the wheels of which were powered from a second countershaft coupled to the first.

Most Bollee vehicles, however, though very heavy, were primarily private carriages. His son, also Amedee, built steam cars in the 1880s but turned early to the internal combustion engine. *RAW*

AMERICAN (i) (US) 1906-1912

(1) American Motor Truck Co., Lockport, N.Y. 1906-1911
(2) Findlay Motor Co., Findlay, Ohio 1911-1912
(3) Ewing-American Motor Co., Findlay, Ohio 1912

This company made heavy trucks with 4-cylinder engines from 20 to 60 hp, in conventional and forward-control models, with double chain drive. An unusual feature in the 60 hp was the use of epicyclic transmission, usually found in smaller vehicles. After the move to Findlay the company merged with Ewing, makers of light goods vehicles and taxicabs. *GNG*

1911 AMERICAN (i) 5-ton truck, NAHC

1910 AMERICAN (ii) 5-ton 4-wheel-drive truck, HFM

AMERICAN (ii) (US) 1910-1912

American Motor Truck Co., Detroit, Mich.

This was an unconventional 5-ton truck powered by a centrally-mounted 4-cylinder engine which drove front and rear axles by chains. These axles were duplicates of each other and interchangeable. The truck featured four-wheel-steering as well as drive. *GNG*

AMERICAN (iii) (US) 1913-1918

American Motor Truck Co., Detroit, Mich.

This make began as a 1-tonner using a 4-cylinder Continental engine under a hood with a 3-speed Brown-Lipe gearbox and double-reduction rear drive. Wheelbase was 108 inches. In 1917, this was replaced by a 3½-tonner using a Covert 4-speed gearbox and Sheldon worm-drive rear axle. *GMN*

AMERICAN (iv) (US) 1916-1917

American Motor Truck Co., Hartford, Conn

This was a 2-tonner built for only a short time. It had a stake body, a 4-cylinder engine under the hood, a 3-speed gearbox and worm-drive rear axle. Electric lighting and starting were standard. *GMN*

AMERICAN (v) (US) 1918

American Motor Vehicle Co., LaFayette, Ind

A ½-tonner is listed as being offered by this obscure make. Little is known other than this company also built very light juvenile vehicles. *GMN*

AMERICAN (vi) (US) 1920-1924

American Truck & Tractor Co., Portland, Conn

For 1920 and 1921, this make offered 2½- and 4-tonners. Both were on wheelbases of 159 inches, used 4-cylinder

Wisconsin engines, 4-speed gearboxes and worm drive rear axles. In 1923, the larger model was upgraded to a 5-tonner with no essential mechanical changes, and for the last year of production, only the Model 25 2½-tonner was made. *GMN*

AMERICAN AUSTIN; (ii) BANTAM (US) 1930-1941

(1) American Austin Car Co., Inc., Butler, Pa 1930-1934
(2) American Bantam Car Co., Butler, Pa 1935-1941

The American edition of the Austin 7 differed mainly from its British prototype in its 'mirror-image' engine (to accommodate the necessary lhd) and in the use of fixed disc wheels with demountable rims. The range of bodies included a business coupe and a ¼-ton van, but promises of huge orders were never fulfilled and the 8558 units delivered in 1930 represented the make's best-ever performance. The original company went bankrupt in 1934, but despite a reorganization and a change of name nothing happened until 1937, when the Bantam reappeared with synchromesh gearbox and contemporary American styling to the designs of Alexis de Sakhnoffski. Once again vans and pickups were listed, but a commercial Bantam at $445 was no bargain when $592 would buy a 6-cylinder ½-ton Chevrolet with similar bodywork. 1939 saw a flashy open-drive Boulevard Delivery in the truck range, but neither this nor 1940's new 3-bearing 800cc engine helped much. That year, however, Karl Probst was hired to design a ¼-ton light 4x4 for the Army. This used a 45 hp 4-cylinder sv Continental engine and not the Austin (which had been tried in a 4x2 scout car as early as 1933), but it served as the prototype for the Jeep despite competition from Ford and Willys. Bantam made over 2500 for the Army during 1941, but the small run-down factory could not cope with ever-increasing demands, and thereafter their war effort centered round 2-wheeled trailers, which they had been making as a sideline since 1939. Motor vehicle production was never resumed. *MCS*

AMERICAN CARRIER EQUIPMENT (US) 1971 to date

American Carrier Equipment, Fresno, Calif.

Three 100-passenger open-top double-deck buses with Ford 6-cylinder truck engines (converted to run on propane) and Allison fully automatic transmissions were supplied to Yosemite National Park in California during the summer of 1971 to start American Carrier Equipment in the business of building complete buses. Previously the company constructed truck bodies and trailers, but also offered open-sided sightseeing trailers for parks and zoos under the general name of "Shuttlecraft." Additional double-deckers have been built for Yosemite and other parks. *MBS*

AMERICAN COULTHARD (US) 1905-1906

American Coulthard Company, Boston, Mass.

This very heavy steam truck was based upon the design of the British Coulthard. This used a 30 hp, 2-cylinder, cross-compound engine fed from a vertical boiler located between the seats for the driver and fireman. The wheelbase was 130 inches and the wheels were shod in steel tires. The lack of popularity of steam propulsion at that period precluded any success. Actual manufacture of these vehicles was by Corwin Manufacturing Company of Peabody, Mass. *GMN*

AMERICAN EAGLE (US) 1911-1912

American Eagle Motor Car Co., New York, N.Y.

This was made in a single model, a 11/2-tonner with a 25 hp, 4-cylinder engine. Wheelbase was 108 inches. *GMN*

1974 AM GENERAL city bus, MBS

AM GENERAL (US) 1974 to date

AM General Corp., Wayne, Mich. (plant at Mishawaka, Ind.)

AM General is a new name for the Kaiser Jeep Corp., a manufacturer of military and post office trucks (using former Studebaker plants), which was purchased by American Motors in 1970. Two years later the decision was made to enter the heavy-duty city transit bus business, then divided between GM and Flxible, and arrangements were made with Flyer Industries of Winnipeg for the supply of assembled body shells. Air-conditioning was added, the window arrangement was changed, and Flyer's in line engine placement using a Spicer transmission was given up in favor of transverse engines (Detroit Diesel 6V-71 or 8V-71) with Allison transmissions as on the competing GM and Flxible buses. The initial order was placed by the new metropolitan-area transit system serving Washington and called for 620 buses; approximately 2250 vehicles had been delivered by the end of 1975. AM General buses are offered in 35-and 40-foot lengths, 96-and 102-inch widths with most specifications generally similar to those of GM and Flxible. All sales to date have involved 80 per cent federal funding, under whose terms contracts are made with the lowest bidder and according to which specifications so written as to prevent qualified firms from bidding are illegal. During 1976, AM General was the successful bidder on several interesting contracts for deliveries in 1978-79. A total of 398 articulated buses were to be constructed for 11 different operators; M.A.N. would make the basic shells and engines, which would be shipped to AM General's fabrication plant in Marshall, Texas, for finishing. To be built in both 55-foot and 60-foot lengths and 102 inches wide, tapering at the rear, these are the first true articulated transit buses ever used in the U.S. Also, 219 trolley-coaches are to be built for Seattle (109) and Philadelphia (110), replacing vehicles placed in service between 1940 and 1955. AM General also make 5-ton 6 x 6 trucks for the U.S. and other armed forces, though recent trucks sold under the AM General name have been made for them by the Crane Carrier Corp. The Mishawaka plant closed in June 1978, all production being transferred to Marshall, Texas. *MBS*

1913 AMERICAN LA FRANCE Type 16 front drive ladder truck, LIAM

AMERICAN LA FRANCE (US) 1910 to date

(1) American La France Fire Engine Co., Elmira, N.Y. 1910-1927

(2) American La France Truck Co., Bloomfield, N.J. 1923-1929

(3) American La France & Foamite Corp., Elmira, N.Y. 1927-1966

(4) American La France, Divn A.T.O. Inc., Elmira, N.Y. 1966-to date

America's leading manufacturer of custom fire engines, the American La France company was formed in 1903 from a group of smaller companies the oldest of which dated back to 1832. The name came from the two largest of the companies, American Fire Engine Company of Seneca Falls, N.Y. and the La France Fire Engine Company of Elmira, N.Y. Experimental steam fire engines were made in 1905/06, and in 1910 came the first motor vehicle, a chemical and hose wagon powered by a 4-cylinder Simplex engine. Also in 1910 the company's own designs of 4- and 6-cylinder engines were developed, and soon they were using no bought-out engines. In 1913 came two important developments, the gas-electric Types 16 and 30, and the front-drive conversions for horse-drawn apparatus known as the Type 31. These were made for 16 years, and some completely factory-built front-drive fire engines were also known as Type 31s. The largest conventional chassis was the Type 17 with 105 hp 6-cylinder engine. In 1914 American La France built their last steam pumper, attached to a Type 31 tractor. The larger ladder trucks had rear-wheel steering operated by a steersman with a tiller who sat above the rear axle. Wheelbase of these machines ranged from 239 to 383 in.

Commercial trucks were made by American La France intermittently from 1913 to 1929, in sizes from two to 7½ tons. Like the fire engines they used the company's own engines exclusively. A new factory especially intended for truck manufacture was acquired at Bloomfield, N.J. in 1923 and remained in use until 1929 when the truck side of ALF was merged with Republic to form the La France Republic Corporation.

Conventional and front-drive fire engines continued to be made during the 1920s. Among the smallest was the Type 40 350 gpm rotary gear pumper, and American La France equipment was available on a special Brockway chassis in the mid-1920s. In 1927 the company acquired the Foamite-Childs Corp. which had made fire engines on Kearns-Dughie chassis under the name Childs Thoroughbred. The following year American La France combined with General Motors to make the Buick-powered American La France-GMC Type 199 for medium-sized chemical, hose wagon and pumper work.

The last front-drive tractors were made in 1929, and two years later came one of the most important innovations in the firm's history, their 240 hp 30° V-12 engine. This was used in the larger fire engines and also in Brockway trucks, the Budd Streamliner railroad locomotive and army tanks. It was joined in 1935 by a smaller 170 hp V-12 based on the Auburn passenger car engine. Smaller 500 gpm pumpers used Lycoming straight-8 engines. Four wheel brakes had arrived in 1929, and chain drive was finally phased out on the 1935 400 series.Van-type pumpers came into vogue in 1936.

Probably the most dramatic model of the 1930s was the Metropolitan Duplex Pumper of which four were delivered to Los Angeles in 1937/38. These had two of the large V-12 engines, one to drive the wheels and the cowl-mounted pump, and the other to drive the rear pump. The new 500 Series with streamlined grille and hood came out in 1938,

1953 AMERICAN LA FRANCE Series 700 pumper, OMM

1937 AMERICAN LA FRANCE Metropolitan Duplex pumper, NMM

but of most significance was the cab-forward aerial ladder truck introduced in 1939, which was the precursor of the 700 Series of cab-forwards announced in 1945 and put into production two years later. Unlike their rivals who continued conventionals and cab-forwards side by side, American La France went over exclusively to the new design with the 700 which made until 1956. In 1950 American La France was awarded a big Air Force contract for their 0-10 and 0-11 6x2 airfield crash trucks which had remotely-controlled foam turrets on the roof. A similar design was made by Marmon-Herrington, and a total of 1100 were delivered between 1950 and 1953.

In 1955 American La France departed from tradition by using a proprietary engine, a 6-cylinder Continental, on their lower-priced Ranger, Protector and Crusader

1940 AMERICAN LA FRANCE Series 500 pumper, OMM

pumpers. The 700 was replaced in 1956 by the 800 which was generally similar in appearance and like its predecessor came in open and closed cab models, rigids and articulateds. Engines were the Continental six or American La France's own V-12. Two years later came the 900 Series with completely re-styled cab and a new V-8 engine in addition to the other power units. The V-12 was finally phased out during 1961.

In 1960 three gas-turbine powered fire engines were put into service, but were found to be too noisy and lacking in acceleration, so they were quietly converted to gasoline power. However in 1972 a further gas-turbine experimental fire engine was built. In 1962 a new range of airport crash tenders was introduced — known as the Airport Chief these were based on the 900 Series but had 4-wheel-drive. In 1964 came the Pioneer Series of lower-cost pumpers designed to bridge the gap between commercial chassis and the high priced 900 models. The

1975 AMERICAN LA FRANCE Pioneer pumper, EK

Pioneers had squared off cabs in place of the rounded cabs of the 900s. Diesel engines were introduced in 1965, and were standardised on the 1000 Series of premium pumpers introduced in 1970. Otherwise there were no drastic changes on the 1000 Series which preserved the appearance of the 900s dating back to 1958. In 1971 the Pioneers had 285 hp International gasoline engines as standard, with the option of 216 or 265 hp Detroit Diesels, while a new model in 1972 was the Pacemaker priced between the Pioneer and the 1000. It had a Cincinnati cab and Detroit Diesel engine. A new, wider cab Century Series appeared in 1974 and is still made today representing the top end of the American La France line. It is available in 4x2 and 6x4 forms, and as an articulated tractor-trailer unit. Engines are Detroit Diesels from 216 to 380 hp or Cummins from 225 to 350 hp. *GNG*

AMERICAN MOTOR BUS see Chicago Motor Bus

AMERICAN STEAM (US) 1912-1913
American Steam Truck Company, Lansing, Michigan

A massive vehicle with an unusual engine was the American Steam which used an eight-cylinder, quadruple expansion steam engine. The cylinders had bores of 2.5, 3.25, 5.0 and 7.0 inches respectively, high pressure to low pressure. This engine produced 53 hp from 300 psi steam. The chassis of the Locomotive model weighed 7000 pounds with a wheelbase of 144 inches and was priced at $4500. It is not known whether there was a connection between this company and the later organization of 1918-1922 of the same name but located in Elgin, Illinois. *GMN*

AMIGO see Harimau

A.M.L. (GB) 1920-1923
Associated Motors Ltd., Maida Vale, London W.9

The A.M.L. was a taxicab powered by a 2,297 cc Chapuis-Dornier 4-cylinder engine, with a Rolls-Royce type radiator and a dropped frame. The price was £750 complete, £100 less than the contemporary Beardmore, but few A.M.L.s were sold. *GNG*

1924 AMO F-15 1½-ton truck, MHK

AMO (SU) 1924-1933
Automobilnoe Moskowvoskoe Obshchestvo — Moscow

As part of the plan for the Union of Soviet Socialist Republics, Lenin envisioned the need for an indigenous automotive industry, thus the AMO factory was born out of the vestiges of some small machine shops left from World War One.

The first trucks appeared in November, 1924 and were based on a Fiat 1½-ton design. The AMO F-15 was powered by a 4-cylinder, 35 hp engine providing 50 kmh. Early models had fabric tops, later versions enclosed cabs. All appear to have been right-hand drive and the chassis was modified as a 14-seater bus, open staff car, fire engine, ambulance and mail truck.

During the second Five Year Plan, the factory was rebuilt from 1928 to 1931, however F-15 production was not interrupted.

In 1931 a new truck, the AMO-2, was introduced. This was a 2½-ton vehicle powered by a 93 hp, 6-cylinder Hercules-type engine, the same as used in the Yaroslavl YA—5. This truck had the distinction of being the first Soviet-built vehicle with hydraulic brakes.

The factory is alleged to have also been used as an assembly plant for imported U.S. Ford cars and trucks while the new Gorky (GAZ) plant was being readied.

In 1932 the 2½-ton AMO-3 with strengthened chassis and 60 hp, replaced the AMO-2 and this design continued through the factory name change.

The factory was renamed Zavod Imieni Stalina in honor of Joseph Stalin, in 1933, and for a short time the AMO-3 became the ZIS-3 until production terminated on this model.

Further vehicle development will be found under the ZIS entry. *BE*

AMOSKEAG (US) 1867-1906
(1) Amoskeag Mfg. Co., Manchester, N.H., 1867-1877
(2) Manchester Locomotive Works, Manchester, N.H. 1877-1906

The Amoskeag was one of the best-known makes of 19th Century American steam fire engine, and although most of the steam pumpers were horse-drawn, they made 22 self-propellers. Design changed little in the 39 years that the Amoskeag was made; a vertical seamless copper-tube boiler generated steam for a 2-cylinder horizontal engine with cylinder dimensions of 9½ x 8 inches. Final drive was by single chain at first, then by double chains, to the rear axle. The pump was capable of delivering 1450 gpm. Despite a weight of 17,000 lbs., the Amoskeag could reach 25 mph.

The first self-propeller was delivered to Boston where it was used in the great fire of 1872, while other customers included New York, Detroit and Hartford, Connecticut. *GNG*

ANDERSON (US) 1909-1910
Anderson Carriage Manufacturing Company, Anderson, Indiana

This brand was a high wheeler which was very light, weighing but 1300 pounds. Power came from 2-cylinder engines connected with a planetary transmission then double chain drive. It utilized the then-obsolete reach frame. Its wheelbase was 70 inches and the price was $700. *GMN*

ANDINO see Harimau

ANDOVER (US) 1915-1917
Andover Motor Vehicle Co., Andover, Mass

This was a battery-powered electric with rated capacity of 1½ tons. One source lists the manufacturer for the year 1917 as Joly & Lambert Electric Auto Co, also of Andover, Mass. However, this is unconfirmed and further information has not been found. *GMN*

ANDREAS (D) 1900-1901
Sachsische Accumulatorenwerke A.G., Dresden

This firm built electric driven vans with two motors driving the front wheels. The bogie steering was quite unique by differing the speed of the motors. *HON*

ANDREES (D) 1925

H.W.Andrees, Dusseldorf

A 4-wheeled van was built by this firm in 1925 but no further details are known. *HON*

ANGLO-FRENCH (GB) 1896-1897

Anglo-French Motor Carriage Co., Digbeth, Birmingham.

Anglo-French vehicles were built both in private and commercial guise in about equal numbers. Initially production consisted mainly of modified Benz and Roger-Benz types with driving belts and chains eliminated in favor of a friction disc transmission designed by the Chief Engineer, Lieutenant Day. Bodywork was, however, of all-British construction and was assembled in the Birmingham works. Small charabancs, brewer's drays and delivery vans were produced utilizing horizontal engines of 8 and 10 hp, the former being twin cylindered, but later models employed belt drive from the engine to a geared countershaft and thence, centrally, by chain to the back axle. The company enjoyed a short and chequered career, during which the activities of its French directors were often both questionable and questioned on ethical grounds. This did not prevent firms like Sunlight Soap from buying and operating their vehicles. *MJWW*

ANN ARBOR (US) 1911-1912

Huron River Manufacturing Company, Ann Arbor, Michigan

The lone model of the Ann Arbor was an open delivery van on a light chassis of 100 inch wheelbase. Rated at 1500-pound capacity, it was powered by a 2-cylinder engine, combined with a planetary transmission and double chain drive and pneumatic tires. *GMN*

ANSAIR (AUS) 1958 to date

Ansair Pty Ltd., N. Essendon, Victoria

Ansair is a large multibranch company that builds also buses and coaches. As usual with Australian vehicles, Ansair models are largely inspired by American styling and the first model introduced was the "Transette" series of city and intercity buses, which look like the first post war American buses. Transettes were built on a ladder-type frame and were powered by either a Perkins diesel of 83 hp or an American Ford V8 petrol engine developing 103 hp. Either engine was placed in the rear of the all metal body which was offered in many capacities and seating configurations. A special version introduced in the same period, was the "Bookmobile" mobile library, a window-less bus with purpose-designed interior. Transettes were built for many years and were supplied in many numbers throughout Australia, were replaced, though, in the late 60's by the "Scenicruiser", an air-conditioned rear-engined coach of modern appearance, which resembles the GM coaches of same period. Bus and coach bodies on proprietary chassis, as well as commercial vehicle bodies are also built by Ansair. From 1960-1965 Ansair built the American Flxible Clipper buses under license. *GA*

ANSALDO (I) 1930-1932

Ansaldo Automobili, Turin

Towards the end of their active life as car makers, Ansaldo branched out into trucks, offering 2- and 3-tonners with ohc engines, 4-speed unit gearboxes, and double reduction back axles. The smaller truck used the standard 4-cylinder car engine, but a big 4.9-litre six was fitted to the 3-ton version. From 1932 unsold stocks of cars were remaindered off by the CEVA organization, but this does not seem to have concerned itself with commercial vehicles. The trolley bus activities seem to have been independent. *MCS*

ANSBACH (D) 1906-1930

(1) Fahrzeugfabrik Ansbach GmbH., Ansbach 1906-1918
(2) Fahrzeugfabrik Ansbach A.G., Ansbach 1926-1930

This factory was founded for the production of commercial vehicles. Vans and trucks with payload capacities ranging from 1/2 to 6-ton were produced. In 1918 this firm merged with Nurnberger Feuerloschgerate-, Automobillastwagen- und Fahrzeug-Fabrik Karl Schmidt (see Braun) to form Fahrzeugfabrik Ansbach und Nurnberg (see FAUN).

However in 1926 both firms divided for some reason and Ansbach continued some models of Faun but introduced a new bus using the 70 PS Maybach engine. In 1928 a small car appeared, available as truck or van. It was the "Express" with 2-cylinder Motosacoche engine featuring turbo-cooling.

In 1930 both factories merged again and all subsequent models again appeared as FAUN. *HON*

1950 APE 125cc 3-wheel van, Piaggio

APE (I) 1947 to date

Piaggio/Co., Spa, Genoa

This Italian aircraft manufacturer turned with great success to scooters after World War II, these being marketed under the Vespa (wasp) name. It was thus logical that the commercial edition should be called the Ape (bee). The first Apes were fairly primitive adaptations of the Vespa with a chain-driven differential back axle and torsion-bar rear suspension. There were four forward speeds, and the 125cc 2-stroke engine developed 4bhp. By

1974 APE 400R 170cc 3-wheel truck, Piaggio

the early 1960s, progressive development had led to a more sophisticated 1,000-pound, 169cc model with enclosed cab and electric starter, though handlebar steering was still used, and the hydro-mechanical brakes were uncoupled. 1968 saw the introduction of a simple moped, the 50cc Ciao; a 225-pound Porter version followed, this breaking with Vespa practice in having the driver's saddle at the rear and a single driven wheel, with infinitely variable belt-cum-chain transmission. New for 1973 was the Ape Car, a 30-cwt truck with enclosed 2-seater cab, wheel steering, and rubber swing-arm rear suspension; it was produced under license in Yugoslavia by Tomos. Vespa light commercials have also been made in Britain by (i) Douglas and in France by A.C.M.A. Though the minimal Ciao Porter was no longer quoted in 1978, the Ape Car was still in production alongside other models, which covered payloads from 2 to 12 cwt., and used engines of 50cc, 121cc, 170cc and 187cc. *MCS*

APEX (US) 1918-1921

Hamilton Motors Co., Grand Haven, Mich

For all three production years, this was offered as 1-1½- and 2½-tonners. The two smaller models were on wheelbases of 130 inches, while the largest had 150 inches. All were built with Fuller 3-speed gearboxes and Torbensen internal-gear rear axles. See also ALTER and PANHARD (ii) *GMN*

APOLLO (D) 1914-1922

Apollo Werke AG., Apolda

During WW I Apollo built a truck using a 10/30 PS engine which they carried on until 1922. *HON*

1907 ARBENZ 12/14hp 1½-ton truck, FH

ARBENZ (CH) 1904-1928

(1) Motorwagenfabrik E. Arbenz & Co., Albisrieden-Zurich 1904-1907

(2) Arbenz AG, Albisrieden-Zurich 1907-1923

(3) Oetiker & Co., Arbenz Motorwagenfabrik, Albisrieden-Zurich 1923-1928

Eugen Arbenz' first vehicle was a 1½-ton truck with a 14/16hp 2-cylinder engine under the driver's seat. This was shown at the 1905 London Olympia Show under the name Straker-McConnell, and a taxicab on the same chassis was also offered. Two years later Arbenz listed no fewer than 14 different chassis for trucks and buses, with 2- and 4-cylinder engines from 12 to 40hp. All had chain drive. Arbenz had a keen export policy, and sold vehicles as far afield as Spain, Russia, Java and Sumatra, as well as in Germany and Italy. In 1913 came the first shaft-driven Arbenz, a 3-tonner with 30hp 4-cylinder engine. During World War I production doubled because of orders from the Swiss and German armies, but after the war sales dropped badly, in addition to which Arbenz was not

1917 ARBENZ 30hp 4-ton truck, FH

paid for many of the vehicles and spares he had delivered to Germany. The company collapsed early in 1922 after about 3,000 vehicles had been made, and was taken over by a financial group headed by Edwin Oetiker. They continued to make Arbenz trucks with a greatly reduced workforce of only 35 employees, and for 1924 a 3-ton shaft drive and 5-ton chain drive chassis were offered. In 1927 there were 3, 4 and 5-ton chassis with new 4-cylinder ohv engines. For 1928 they were re-named Oetiker. *FH*

ARDIE (D) 1927-1928

Ardie-Werk A.G., Nuremberg

A tri-van was offered with two front wheels, the driver sitting behind the box. The single rear wheel was driven by a 500cc J.A.P. engine. *HON*

1912 ARGO electric truck, LIAM

ARGO (US) 1911-1915

Argo Electric Vehicle Co., Saginaw, Mich.

As well as electric passenger cars, Argo made electric trucks in ½- and 1-ton sizes. They were conventional machines with 40-cell batteries, shaft drive and a top speed of 16 mph. *GNG*

Argosy Miniature Bus

ARGOSY (US) 1976 to date

Argosy Manufacturing Co.
Versailles, Ohio

Many miniature buses have appeared in the U.S. since provision of service in low-density territories has been in demand by the authorities but uneconomical to provide with standard-size equipment. One is the Argosy, made by an affiliate of the company that builds Airstream aluminum-alloy travel trailers and A-Van truck bodies. The Argosy is offered either 24 or 25 feet long with seats for 25 to 29 passengers (or fewer if a wheelchair lift and securements are specified.) *MBS*

ARGSON (GB) 1935

Stanley Engineering Co Ltd, Egham, Surrey

Well known as makers of gasoline and electric tricycles for invalids, this company made a 3-wheeled parcel carrier with single front wheel, powered by a 1½hp single-cylinder Villiers 2-stroke engine, with an Albion 3-speed gearbox and single chain drive to the nearside rear wheel only. Load capacity was 2cwt and the chassis price £45. *GNG*

ARGUS (D) 1907-1910

Argus Motoren-Gesellschaft Jeannin & Co. KG., Berlin-Reinickendorf

Argus built trucks with their own 6-cylinder engines. The chassis was also used for buses. Production was not on a big scale. *HON*

1970 ARGYLE Christina 16-ton GVW truck, Argyle

ARGYLE (GB) 1970-1973

Argyle Motor Manufacturing Co. Ltd., East Kilbride, Lanarkshire

This company was founded by Argyle Diesel Electronics Ltd. to manufacture trucks in the 16-ton GVW range. Their first model, the Christina, was powered by a Perkins 6.354 6-cylinder diesel engine and used familiar components such as Eaton Yale & Towne 5-speed gearbox, Eaton 2-speed rear axle and Kirkstall front axle. The cab was by Motor Panels. Production ceased by 1973 because of competition from larger firms in that size bracket, and the 24-ton 6-wheeled Karen and 32-ton tractive unit Linsay never left the drawing board. In 1973 Argyle made a special tractor for the British Steel Corporation; named the Trilby. This was powered by a Cummins 220 engine and could pull a load of 120 tons of steel strip. *GNG*

ARGYLL (GB) 1902-1914

(1) Hozier Engineering Co., Ltd., Bridgeton, Glasgow 1902-1905

(2) Argyll Motors Ltd., Bridgeton, Glasgow 1905-1906

(3) Argyll Motors Ltd., Alexandria-by-Glasgow 1906-1914

Argyll started by offering light van editions of their private car chassis, usually with solid tires. First of these was an 8cwt type with 8 hp single-cylinder Simms or M.M.C. engine, 3-speed gearbox, and shaft drive, selling for £240. A 10cwt twin followed in 1903, and 15cwt models with 1.7-litre 2-cylinder or 3.2-litre 4-cylinder moiv engines, both by Aster, in 1904. Front tires were now

1908 ARGYLL 1-ton van, NMM

pneumatic, and by 1906 the commercial vehicle range embraced travellers' vans, brakes, combination cars convertible from tourer to truck, a 26/30hp 4.8-litre 4-cylinder ambulance with dual ignition, and a compact 4-cylinder cab-over-engine taxicab only 10 ft. long. This last was launched with a demonstration drive from Glasgow to London, but it was no more successful than other brougham types, and by 1908 Argyll cabs featured normal control and smaller 12/14hp monobloc engines. 1907 saw a full range of trucks for payloads from 30cwt to 3 tons, with 4-cylinder Aster engines and worm drive: both forward and normal control were available. A 1-tonner with 2.2-liter 2-cylinder engine was added in 1908, while Argyll also made fire engines, most of which went to Scottish or Northern municipalities. The first of the line was sold to Sheffield in 1907, and from 1911 the standard power unit was a huge 13.3-litre six developing 85 hp, with dual ignition and pneumatic starter. 1910 cabs reverted to pair-cast cylinders, the new 2.4-litre engine being of Argyll's own make. *MCS*

1913 ARIES 5-ton truck, OMM

ARIES (F) 1904-1934

SA Aries, Courbevoie, Seine.

Though their private cars had a sporting flavor (an Aries nearly won at Le Mans in 1927) the company's major interest for many years was a range of medium-heavy trucks, mostly with side-chain drive and Aster engines. The original 3-tonner of 1904 wore its 2.4-litre vertical-twin engine under the driver's seat, other features being an armored wood frame, a cone clutch, and a 3-speed gearbox. 4-cylinder engines had made their appearance by 1906, along with PSV variants (single-deckers were later sold to Prague), and in 1909 only fours were used in a range which covered the 3-7-ton bracket. The biggest

Aries ran to 7.4 litres, though the firm also offered a car-type light van with 9hp single-cylinder engine. Their compact V4 engine, advertised as suitable for cab use, seems to have been confined to private cars. The forward control models persisted until World War I, but normal control 3-tonners were available by 1910, and 3000 of this type, with 3.8-litre Aster engines and four forward speeds, were supplied to the French armed forces. Both the 3-ton Aries and a 4.7-litre 5/7-tonner remained in production until 1930, later ones being available with enclosed cabs and pneumatic tires. Between 1923 and 1928 there were also some light vans for 5/15-cwt payloads, based on contemporary car models. The smaller ones had Aries's own ohc 4-cylinder engines of 972 and 1,086cc. The chain-driven trucks were still quoted in buyers' guides as late as 1934. *MCS*

1965 ARKLA ¼-ton truck, OMM

ARKLA (US) 1965

Arkansas-Louisiana Gas Co., Little Rock, Ark.

This company built 100 light trucks for their own use. They were powered by a 45.5 cu. in. (745cc) air-cooled flat-twin engine developing 30 bhp, and had an automatic centrifugal clutch. The cab and hood were of molded fiberglass. Load capacity was 840 lbs. *GNG*

ARMADALE (GB) 1906-1907

Northwood Engineering & Motor Works, Northwood, Middx.

This was a small 3-wheeler with a box van body behind the engine and ahead of the driver, in the scuttle position. It was powered by a 2-cylinder Fafnir engine, and had a friction transmission and chain drive to the single rear wheel. *GNG*

ARMLEDER (US) 1910-1936

(1) The O. Armleder Co., Cincinnati, Ohio 1910-
(2) The Armleder Truck Co., Cincinnati, Ohio -1928
(3) The LeBlond-Schacht Truck Co., Cincinnati, Ohio 1928-1936

The Otto Armleder Company was an old-established wagon-building firm whose history dated back to the 1890s, and whose products were especially popular with Cincinnati brewers. They were an important firm with a 6-story plant that covered more than half a city block. Their trucks were conventional assembled vehicles, at first in the light class with capacities of 1500 to 3000 lbs., but extending up to 3½ tons by 1917. In this year chain drive was replaced by worm, and Armleder's sales network was extended from the previous 100 mile radius of Cincinnati to a more nationwide basis, with dealers in many important cities.

By the mid-1920s Armleder trucks were offered in capacities from 1 to 3½ tons, with Buda, Continental and Hercules engines, Timken worm and bevel axles and Brown-Lipe transmissions. Heavier models employed structural steel I-beam frames at one point. 6-cylinder models were introduced in 1927, though fours were continued as well. Production at this time was running at about 50 to 100 units annually. Like the Cincinnati-built Biederman trucks, Armleders featured variable-rate rear suspension on most models.

In October 1928 Armleder became a division of LeBlond-Schacht, and the lines of the two makes were gradually merged, some Armleders being sold as Schachts while others retained their identity. Continental, Buda and Hercules engines were still used, and a 2½-ton articulated truck was offered, a type which had been originally offered as early as 1920. Armleder's last year was 1936, by which time their owners LeBlond-Schacht had only two years to run. *RJ*

ARMSTRONG (GB) 1914-1915

Armstrong Motors Ltd., London N.W.

The Armstrong was an entirely conventional delivery van built in very limited numbers immediately prior to and just after the commencement of the first World War. Fitted with a 1.2 litre four cylinder watercooled s.v. engine, ostensibly of own manufacture, three speed gearbox and worm final drive, it was designed for carriage of loads of 6/8 cwt, and found favor with firms like Accles and Pollock, the well-known tube manufacturers. *MJWW*

1920 ARMLEDER 6-ton Articulated Truck, FLP

1934 ARMSTRONG-SAURER 10-ton 6-wheeler, NMM

ARMSTRONG-SAURER (GB) 1931-1937

Armstrong-Saurer Commercial Vehicles Ltd., Scotswood, Newcastle-upon-Tyne.

Swiss Saurer diesel engined trucks had been demonstrated in Britain for sometime when Sir W.G. Armstrong-Whitworth & Co. decided to acquire the British manufacturing rights. They produced the first Armstrong-Saurer in time for the 1931 London Commercial Motor Show and all were for the maximum legal weight 4- and 6-wheel goods categories. For a time the make held an important position in heavy diesel transport in Britain. The Defiant four and Dauntless six cylinder four wheel models and the Dominant 6-wheeler were all diesel powered as denoted by their model name commencing with D, while gasoline models commencing with P were also briefly offered.

By 1933 gasoline engines had been discontinued and all models were considerably lightened. The Dynamic replaced the Dominant while a 4-wheel Active 7- to 8-tonner could also be specified as the Effective for trailer work. Dennis were granted sole British rights to use the engines in passenger models. In 1934 a 15-ton 8-wheel Samson was added to the range while in 1935 a new Dual-Turbulence combustion system was introduced, which was used on a small 3.62 litre experimental engine.

Armstrong-Saurer had hopes of using this in a quantity-produced light vehicle range but Government money to help build a suitable factory was not forthcoming and, with re-armament preoccupying the parent company, manufacture was discontinued in 1937. The Saurer engine license subsequently passed to Morris-Commercial Cars Ltd. *OM*

1906 ARMSTRONG-WHITWORTH 4-ton truck, OMM

ARMSTRONG-WHITWORTH (GB) 1906-1914; 1926-1927

Sir W.G. Armstrong, Whitworth & Co. Ltd., Newcastle-upon-Tyne

The first commercial vehicles built by this well-known engineering firm were a series of bus chassis ordered by the Motor Omnibus Construction Co., Ltd. of Walthamstow, London. These were fitted with double-decker bodies in the works later used for assembly of the famous B-type bus, and sold to an operating company, the Motor Bus Co. They had 4-cylinder 32 hp engines, 4-speed gearboxes and chain drive, and those used by the Motor Bus Co. went under the name M.O.C. This company did not take up all the chassis that they had ordered, and those that Armstrong-Whitworth had on their hands were sold off as 4-ton goods vehicles, a few being retained by Armstrongs for their own use. In 1910 a further series of similar chassis were built, some being sold by the Lowcock Commercial Motor Co. of Manchester under the names Lowcock or Locomo. Dual ignition replaced low-tension magneto in 1912. Production was never large, but there were about 90 Armstrong-Whitworth trucks and buses on the road in 1912. The 4-ton chassis was continued up to the outbreak of war in 1914, and was joined by a 1-tonner on Armstrong's car chassis in 1913.

1927 ARMSTRONG-WHITWORTH road locomotive, RAW

After the merger with Siddeley-Deasy in 1919 no more road vehicles were made at Newcastle, but a number of steam rollers were made at the firm's Manchester factory, and in 1926 road locomotives and steam tractors were also listed. The road locomotives were sub-let to Robeys of Lincoln, and so far as can be ascertained no tractors were sold. *GNG/RAW*

1966 ARO M461 4×4 utility truck, AAR

1975 ARO 240 4×4 utility truck, MSH

ARO (R) 1966 to date

(1) Uzina Mecanica Muscel, Cimpulung, Muscel 1966-1970
(2) Intreprinderea Mecanica Muscel, Cimpulung, Muscel 1970 to date

As the continuation of M.I.C.M., ARO built the M461 utility 4x4 vehicle until 1970 when the 240 generation appeared. Much modernized in external appearance, powered by a more powerful gasoline engine developing 80 hp and fitted with an auxiliary gearbox for the first time and coil front suspension, the new 4x4 series include a two and a four door canvas-top utility and a four door station wagon. AROs are sold at comparatively low prices and are exported to many countries, including West Europe, where they are often fitted with Perkins or Indenor diesel engines by local representatives. ARO vehicles are sold in Portugal under the name Portaro. *GA*

ARRAN (GB) 1934-1938

(1) Arran Motors Ltd., Welwyn Garden City, Herts 1934-1937
(2) Wm. Hurlock Jr., Ltd., London, S.W.2 1937-1938

The Arran Dieselet was one of Britain's first medium-capacity diesel trucks designed as such. In its original form it was an American-looking conventional 4-tonner with 48 bhp Perkins Wolf engine, 4-speed gearbox, and hydraulic brakes, but this was soon supplemented by a cab-over 4-ton model with the bigger 4-litre Perkins unit. By 1936 the Arran range had been extended to embrace not only a heavy-duty 7½-ton GD7 with 4-cylinder Gardner engine, but also a 4-ton gasoline-engined model which used the 3½-litre 6-cylinder Austin 20; both these Arrans had overhead worm back axles in place of the spiral bevel type originally used. In 1937 Hurlocks acquired the company's assets, and announced their intention of continuing manufacture at their Brixton works, under the H.A.C. name. In fact only two H.A.Cs were made, one of which served A.C Cars Ltd., another Hurlock company, until the early 1950s. *MCS*

ARROL-JOHNSTON (GB) 1904-1915

(1) Mo-Car Syndicate Ltd., Camlachie, Glasgow 1904-1906
(2) New Arrol-Johnston Car Co. Ltd., Paisley, Renfrewshire 1906-1913
(3) Arrol-Johnston Ltd., Heathhall, Dunfries 1913-1915

Like the closely related Albions, the original Arrol-Johnston high wheelers with the underfloor-mounted, opposed-piston 2-cylinder engines, chain drive, and solid tires were ideally suited for utility work, but the company did not make a purpose-built commercial vehicle until 1904, when a lengthened 12 hp chassis was fitted with 16-

1907 ARROL-JOHNSTON 1-ton van, NMM

seater charabanc body. A full range of commercials for payloads of up to three tons was offered in 1905, the biggest truck having twin rear wheels. Tipper and charabanc versions were listed, and 3-cylinder engines of 16 or 20 hp were used. During the season the range was augmented by a forward control 2-tonner using a detuned version of the horizontal 12/15 hp T.T car engine, but more advanced was a bus chassis powered by 5.1-litre ioe 4-cylinder vertical unit of 24 hp. This one featured lt magneto ignition and detachable heads, the driver sat beside the engine, and 30 saw service subsequently in London. Other interesting departures were some tower wagons for Glasgow Corporation, a few special vehicles with large-diameter disc wheels for use in the Sudanese desert, and a curious one-off with 12/15 hp 4-cylinder vertical air-cooled engine for Shackleton's Antarctic Expedition, made in 1907.

By 1906 the 15 cwt vans were available with shaft drive, and a year later came a 2-cylinder 2-tonner, while the bus chassis could now be had as a normal control ¾-ton truck. 1908 Arrol-Johnston commercials came in a wide range from 1 to 5 tons, the biggest ones with 4-cylinder engines. A 12/15 hp bevel-driven cab appeared the same year, but when T.C. Pullinger became Chief Engineer in 1909 vertical engines were standardized, the heavier 4-cylinder types being dropped. Increasing preoccupation with cars had led to the virtual abandonment of the truck line by 1911, though a 15 cwt van was offered on a modified 15.9 hp worm-driven chassis. This had solid rear tires and a dashboard radiator, but not the car model's fwb. It would remain the staple commercial until 1914, when the company added not only a 10 cwt van based on their 12 hp chassis, but also a 50/60 cwt worm drive truck with 3.7-litre 4-cylinder engine. Both these types marked a reversion to a frontal radiator. In 1913 Arrol-Johnston acquired a manufacturing license for Detroit Electric vehicles, 7½ cwt and 10 cwt battery-electric vans being offered alongside private cars of this type. Few were made, and the only post-1918 commercial products of the group was the Galloway light van. *MCS*

A.S. (i) (PL) 1927-1930

Tow Budowy Samochodow "A.S.", Warszawa

Based on their car designs, A.S. built during its short life a taxi-cab and a light van version called S1 and S2. Conventional in design, both models were powered by proprietary engines of "Chapuis Dornier" or CIME manufacture. *GA*

1936 A.S. (ii) 30-seater bus, JFJK

A.S. (ii) (NL) 1928-1969

Nederlandsche Automobielfabriek Schmidt N.V., Amsterdam.

Schmidt started in business in 1927, importing the American Republic chassis into Holland, but soon found out that it would be cheaper to construct their own vehicles, due to the low wages in Holland, if they would use the American system of assembly. The A.S. trucks and buses emerging from this consideration were using about the same components as the Republic; Lycoming, Continental or Hercules engines, Timken axles, Ross steering units, Spicer transmissions. In 1932 A.S. built its first diesel-engined truck, a forward control vehicle using the Cummins four-in-line diesel engine, thus deserving the honor of introducing the Cummins diesel engine in Holland, and maybe even in Europe. Other diesel engines used were the Hercules units. After World War II Schmidt again started building A.S. trucks and buses, though in much lower quantities now due to the altered situation on the Dutch commercial vehicle market with much import and the quick success of another home-made truck: DAF. After a while A.S. vehicles were only built to order, the last one being constructed for Van Wezel N.V. of Hengelo, part of the world-renowned heavy haulage contractors Mammoet Transport. *JFJK*

ASHOK LEYLAND (IND) 1948 to date

(1) Ashok Motors Ltd., Enore, Madras 1948-1955
(2) Ashok Leyland Ltd., Ennore, Madras 1955 to date

A major Leyland investment outside England, Ashok Leyland builds a variety of truck and bus chassis based on slightly outdated Leyland models. The two axle Comet and Beaver and the 6x4 Hippo series are powered by 100 hp and 185 hp Leyland diesels and are fitted with modified forward control cabs. Military 4x4 chassis and bus chassis complete the range which fullfils the high-tonnage demands of the Indian market. *GA*

ASTOR (US) 1925-

M.P. Moller Motor Car Co., Hagerstown, Md.

The Astor cab was built by Moller, makers of Dagmar passenger cars and Luxor cabs, for Astor Cab Sales Inc. of New York City. It had a 4-cylinder Buda engine, a distinctive V-radiator and disc wheels. Body styles were the usual cab ones of limousine and landaulette. Prices ranged from $2295 to $2607. *GNG*

1975 ASTRA (i) BM196×4 dumper, Astra

ASTRA (i) (I) 1954 to date

Astra Costruzioni Speciali, Piacenza

This firm was founded in 1946 to recondition war-surplus vehicles, the Italian agency for Detroit Diesel engines and Allison transmissions being acquired in 1952. Two years later the production of dumpers was initiated, and by 1978 a wide range of models for payloads in the 12/38-

ton bracket was available, using Fiat and Mercedes-Benz as well as Detroit power units. Roadgoing types included 6x4 and 6x6 types, both half cab mixer chassis and trucks for the Italian Army, with air brakes and a choice of 12-speed splitter boxes or 6-speed Allison automatic transmissions. Astra's production ran at the rate of 60 a month. *MCS*

1958 ASTRA (ii) 5cwt van. GNG

ASTRA (ii) (GB) 1955-1959

(1) Jarc Motors Ltd., Isleworth, Middlesex 1955-1956
(2) Astra Car Co. Ltd., Hampton Hill, Middlesex 1956-1959

Originally marketed under the name of Jarc, the Astra was unusual among minicars of the mid-1950s in that it was conceived as a 3½-cwt van. An air-cooled 2-cylinder 2-stroke engine lived at the rear of an all-independently sprung chassis with hydraulic brakes, the 3-speed Burman gearbox being of motorcycle type. Final drive was by chain. The first Jarcs used the 250 cc Excelsior unit, but after the change of ownership manufacture was undertaken by the British Anzani firm, who installed their own 322 cc engine. Despite a speed of 55 mph, and handling superior to that of some of its private-car rivals, the Astra never caught on. *MCS*

A.T. (GB) 1929-1931

Allan Taylor & Co. Ltd., Wandsworth, London S.W.18

This company made a wide variety of light tractors, rollers and park mowers, mostly Ford-powered although Morris Commercial engines and chassis were also used. Their only specialized road vehicle was a forward-control low-loader cased on the Ford AA, with 20 or 22 in. wheels and solid tires. There were two models, a 30/40-cwt and a 50-cwt, the only difference being extra rear springs on the larger one. Chassis prices were £270 and £285 respectively. *GNG*

ATCO (US) 1919-1921

American Truck & Trailer Corp., Kankakee, Ill.

This brand was originally offered as a 2-tonner only, with a 4-cylinder Buda engine under a hood, 3-speed gearbox and worm-drive. Tires were solid rubber and the wheels were 8-spoke cast steel. For 1920, a 1-tonner with pneumatic tires was also made, as well as was a 2½-ton trailer for a tractor. For 1921, both models were re-rated to 1½- and 2½-tonners respectively, with the latter having a 4-speed Fuller gearbox. *GMN*

ATF (NL) 1974 to date

Asser Transportmiddelen Fabriek, Assen

Based on the remnants of the former Cock company, they are currently manufacturing small vans and motor carriers with electric traction or OLO internal combustion engines. Their range consists of the OL-3, OL/R-4 and OL-4 electric trucks and the IT-15 OLO-engined trucks, while

1975 A.T.F. garbage truck, JFJK

the Little Tyrant is also still in production, though now under the designation Great Tyrant. *JFJK*

ATHOLL (GB) 1907-1908

(1) Angus Murray & Sons
(2) Murray, Workman & Co., Craigton Engineering Works, Glasgow.

Only about a dozen Atholl vehicles of any type were constructed, and most of these were cars. One of two light delivery vans were, however, offered as well, and like the cars they used 4-cylinder 25 hp engines and shaft drive. The most distinguishing feature was a radiator shaped like the Scottish thistle. *MJWW*

ATKEY-GIMSON (GB) 1905-1908

A.R. Atkey & Co. Ltd., Nottingham.

The Atkey-Gimson was designed by A.R. Atkey and built by Gimson & Company of Leicester. The first model was intended for colonial use, and had a 24 hp 3-cylinder vertical engine which could run on gasoline or kerosene, and a 4-speed gearbox. The final drive was unusual, consisting of chain drive to a differential shaft, and thence by two pinions meshing with gearwheels attached to the inside of the road wheels. This system gave the maximum possible ground clearance. The wheels were shod with steel tires. Few, if any, were sold to the colonies, and in 1907 a new home-market model was introduced. This had the same drive system, but was powered by a 30 hp 4-cylinder engine. *GNG*

ATKINSON (GB) 1910, 1925-1975

(1) Atkinson & Co., Preston, Lancs 1910; 1916-1925
(2) Atkinson-Walker Waggons Ltd., Preston, Lance 1925-1930
(3) Atkinson & Co., Ltd., Preston, Lancs 1931-1932
(4) Atkinson Lorries (1933) Ltd., Preston, Lancs 1933-1953
(5) Atkinson Vehicles Ltd., Preston, Lancs 1954-1972
(6) Seddon-Atkinson Vehicles Ltd., Preston, Lancs 1973-1975

After apprenticeship to T. Coulthard & Co., a steam wagon maker in Preston, Edward Atkinson joined a millwright, who, between 1906 and 1908 experimented with Pullcar gasoline engined vehicles. Atkinson left to start his own engineering company, and in 1910 built two White and Poppe engined Victor or Victory vans with three speed epicyclic gearboxes.

Initially most work had been done from the home of a partner in Frenchwood Avenue, Preston, but following a move to Kendal Street in around 1910, Atkinson started to specialize in steam wagon repairs. He took on the agency for the Sentinel Waggon from Glasgow, but following their move to Shrewsbury, he lost the agency and

1925 ATKINSON 6-ton steam tipper, RAW

decided to build his own machines. The first Atkinson 6-ton steam wagon appeared in 1916 to the design of an ex-Sentinel employee. 125 were built at the old works before production was transferred to a new factory at Frenchwood. Here the work force increased to 150 with three wagons being completed each week. These now featured Uniflow engines, an American system claimed to improve fuel consumption and reduce manufacturing costs.

Atkinson wagons were usually 5- to 8-tonners, though one 2½-tonner was produced in 1921 as well as articulated 12-tonners from 1923. In 1925 Walker Bros. of Wigan loaned £3000 to Edward Atkinson and Atkinson-Walker Wagons was formed. The money was intended to provide capital for the development of an overdue replacement for the old design, and to give Walker some work for their machine shop.

The liason was not a success, and after a total of approximately 325 Atkinsons had been built since 1916, production ended in 1929, and Walkers withdrew. Atkinson had taken over the remaining Leyland and Mann steam wagon spares in 1926 and 1929 respectively, and resumed wagon repairs plus trailer building and six-wheel chassis conversions.

A Blackstone oil engined 12-ton 6-wheeler was built in 1931, followed by a Dorman diesel engined 6-ton 4-wheeler in 1932. In 1933 the firm was acquired by two London bus-

1934 ATKINSON FC47 7-ton truck, OMM

inessmen and reorganized to concentrate on diesel vehicles. By the outbreak of war, a total of fifty 4-, 6-, and from 1937, 8-wheelers had been produced, mainly with Gardner engines, David Brown gearboxes and Kirkstall axles. During the war 260 6- and 8-wheelers were produced, 200 with A.E.C. 7.7-litre engines. Following the move to a new factory at Walton-le-Dale in 1947, production increased to 180 chassis the following year.

In 1950 the first Atkinson passenger chassis appeared, the Gardner-engined Alpha coach, followed by a bus in 1952, and in the 14 years of their production, 170 buses and coaches were built, including 4x4 chassis for difficult overseas conditions, 6-wheelers for export, and double

1945 ATKINSON 15-ton 8-wheel tanker, OMM

deckers.

Orders began to be taken for one-off vehicles, an example being the Omega oilfield tractor of 1957. The first of these 100-ton 6x6 tractors had a 275 bhp Rolls Royce diesel and at the time was claimed to be the most powerful truck in the world. Four more were built with Cummins and supercharged Rolls Royce engines up to 335 bhp. Other contemporary special vehicle designs were 4- and 6-wheel Cummins engined half-cab dumptrucks, later given the model name Hy-Lode, and 6x6 snow clearance and gritting vehicles for the new motorway network. Several hundred have been built with Cummins NHE 180 engines and the first load compensated braking system to be fitted as standard.

Conventional haulage models acquired a fibreglass cab with wrap-round windscreen in 1958. They continued to be maximum capacity 4-, 6- and 8-wheelers, joined by a new 14-ton gross 4-wheeler in 1959. Most had Rolls Royce, Cummins, A.E.C. and Gardner engines, though a few of the lighter models had Perkins engines. This maker's V-8 engine was also used in Atkinson's first low-line mobile crane chassis in 1966.

1962 saw 25-ton Scammell-type tractors introduced for Pickfords with Gardner engines, followed by larger 6-wheelers the following year. Also in 1963 cabs without exposed radiators were optionally available on the normal haulage models.

In 1964 Atkinson produced a new Guardsman cab, fitted to articulated tractors with Cummins V-8 engines, though these, and an under floor engined light goods model never seriously entered production.

Heavy haulage tractors of the time included 300 hp Rolls Royce engined 100-tonners built to South African, Australian and New Zealand specifications by Atkinson's subsidiaries in these countries.

A new Viewline cab to the American concept of shallow depth and great height appeared in 1966, but again achieved little success, except on a few heavy haulage

1968 ATKINSON 6×4 articulated tractor with "view line" cab, OMM

tractors. Another unsuccessful experiment was the adoption of Krupp steel cabs in 1969 on some export chassis after the German manufacturer had ceased production.

1967 saw the first of Atkinson's successful 6-wheel tractor units with a second air sprung steering axle close to the back axle.

During 1970 Atkinson haulage models acquired model names like Borderer for the 2-axle tractor, and Defender for the 8-wheeler, and at the same time lost their traditional cast aluminum radiator surround in favor of a fibreglass moulding to allow for larger radiator cores. Also in 1970, Atkinson was acquired by Seddon, after which the joint firms were taken over by International Harvester in 1974. At the Brussels and London Commercial Motor Shows in 1974 a new Motor Panels steel cabbed Atkinson was shown and this entered production at the Atkinson factory in April of the following year as the Seddon-Atkinson 400 four, six or eight wheeler with choice of Gardner, Cummins or Rolls-Royce engines of 184 to 274 bhp.

1968 ATKINSON (Australia) 8-wheel chassis, AAR

1975 ATKINSON Borderer 32-ton GCW articulated truck, Atkinson

Several models of Atkinson are produced in other countries, notably South Africa (1968 to date), Australia (1962 to date) and New Zealand (1968 to date). Cabs in particular are of different appearance from the British models, and a higher proportion of American components such as Detroit Diesel and Cummins engines, and Fuller transmissions are used. *OM*

ATLANTIC (US) 1912-1921

Atlantic Vehicle Co., Newark, NJ

Initial Atlantic electrics were 3½- and 5-tonners with double-chain drive with power supplied by lead-acid batteries. The smaller version carried an express body with top, was claimed to make 15 mph and claimed to travel 40-60 miles per battery charge. The 5-tonner was fitted with a body for carrying brewery kegs and had a wheelbase of 144 inches. This also carried 44 cells of Exide batteries and was priced at $4400. For 1914, this line of electrics was expanded to include ½-, 1- and 2-tonners, all with General Electric motors, and only the smallest having shaft-drive. This group of five models remained essentially unchanged until 1920 when the ½-tonner was discontinued. For 1920-1921, this line was made up of 1-, 2-, 3½-, 5- and 6½-tonners provided with Hycap batteries and still maintaining chain-drive. *GMN*

ATLANTIC (ii) see see Rotinoff

1906 ATLASS (i) 2-ton truck, NAHC

ATLAS (i) (US) 1905-1913

Knox Motor Truck Co., Springfield, Mass.

The first Atlas, Type A, was a 2-tonner with a 2-cylinder, 24 hp engine. This had an 8-foot wheelbase and shaft drive. Type B was a 3-tonner which used the same engine but had wheelbase of 114 inches. For 1907, Model D, a bus, was built as well as the Model C, a 1½-tonner. Later production was limited to 2- and 3-tonners. This company also built the very successful Martin 3-wheeled tractor, sometimes referred to as Knox-Martin. *GMN*

ATLAS (ii) (US) 1908-1912

Atlas Motor Car Co., Springfield, Mass.

Delivery vans with 2-stroke, 20 hp engines and carrying capacity of 1250 lbs. were the first Atlas product. Shortly after, the Model T taxicab was introduced, also with the 2-stroke engine. In 1911, the delivery van was re-rated as a ¾-tonner which had a 3-speed gearbox, shaft drive and pneumatic tires. A 2-tonner express van was made during the last year of production. This was built with a 4-cylinder engine on a wheelbase of 12 feet. There is no known connection between this make and the Atlas made by Knox Motor Truck Co. in the same city. *GMN*

ATLAS (iii) (GB) 1910

Martins Motors Ltd., Tufnell Park, London N.

This company was mainly concerned with selling second-hand vehicles, particularly bus fleets, to home and overseas customers, but they also built small numbers of a 3-ton lorry with 4-cylinder 30 hp engine, 3-speed gearbox and shaft or chain drive. *GNG*

ATLAS (iv) (US) 1916-1923

(1) Martin Carriage Works, York, Pa. 1916-1917
(2) Martin Truck & Body Co., York, Pa. 1917-1919
(3) Martin-Parry Corp., York, Pa. 1919-1920
(4) Atlas Motor Truck Co., York, Pa. 1920-1922
(5) Atlas Div., Industrial Motors Corp., York, Pa. 1922-1923

The Atlas succeeded the Martin truck. The first model was 1500-pound delivery truck with 19.6 hp Lycoming 4-cylinder engine and Hotchkiss drive. Price of the chassis rose from $690 in 1916 to $1,135 in 1919. A 1-ton truck with Buda engine was introduced in 1920 and a 2-ton truck was introduced in 1922, when the 1500-pound truck was dropped. A merger with Selden in 1922 resulted in a takeover of sales outlets and dropping of the Atlas name. Production totaled about 3,500 units. *DJS*

ATLAS (v) (GR) 1968 to date

F. Rigos — G. Rigas O.E., Ag. Ioannis Rentis, Athens

Another of the successful producers of three wheeled light trucks that flourished in Greece in late 60s, Atlas used VW 1.2 litre and 1.3 litre engines combined with Mercedes Benz gearboxes driving through FK (Taunus) rear axles. Both engines and other components used were either new or rebuilt. A spacious fibreglass cab and a payload of 350 kgs, completed the specifications of Atlas 3-wheelers. *GA*

1930 ATTERBURY Model 100 chassis, NAHC

ATTERBURY (US) 1910-1935

The Atterbury Motor Car Co., Buffalo, N.Y.

Formerly the Buffalo, which in its turn was an development of the Auto-Car, the Atterbury was a conventional truck which never gained the sales or fame of its Buffalo rivals, Stewart and Pierce-Arrow. Within a year of the start of production quite a wide range was offered, with trucks of 1-, 2-, 3- and 5-tons capacity, the largest with chain drive. From 1917 worm drive was adopted in place of chains. Continental engines were used, and other familiar components included Brown-Lipe transmissions and Timken axles. The firm's sales were concentrated in the Buffalo area, and their main 'export' market, understandably, was Canada, only 15 miles from the Buffalo plant. Ontario fleet operators bought Atterbury trucks for some years in the 1920s. Sales were never large, though, and in 1929, presumably a good year as it was for most of the industry, they only amounted to 141 units. By this time there were nine models, from 1¼ to 7 tons, with 4- and 6-cylinder engines by Continental, Buda and Lycoming. The last new Atterbury trucks appear to have been the 1931 models, 2- to 5-tonners with 6-cylinder engines which were continued until the firm's demise in 1935. The radiator sheet metal used on these trucks was seemingly identical to that of the earlier and now discontinued Larrabee-Deyo trucks from nearby Binghampton, N.Y. This suggests that Atterbury acquired redundant sheet metal from Larrabee, or perhaps picked up the latter's commitments from supplier firms. *RJ*

ATTILA see Hunslet

AUBURN (US) 1936

Auburn Automobile Co., Auburn, Ind.

Ironically this famous car manufacturer chose a line of ambulances and hearses for a last-ditch stand. This used a lengthened edition of their 852-series private car chassis with 4.6-litre straight-8 Lycoming engine, and hydraulic brakes. The year's sales, were, however, less than 5,000 vehicles, and very few of these were professional cars. *MCS*

AUDENIS (E) 1930-1936

Motor Palace Audenis S.A., Barcelona

Francisco Audenis was a former racing driver, well known particularly at the wheel of Salmson cars, who built delivery tricycles with drive to the single front wheel. The body was similar to that of the contemporary German Goliath. About 100 Audenis tricycles were built. *JCG*

AUDI (D) 1910-1939

Audi Automobilwerke GmbH., Zwickau

Vans and small trucks were available of the first Audi models using the 10/28 PS engine. A heavier express truck appeared in 1913 and was extensively built during WWI for various military purposes. This design was carried on during the twenties using the 14/50 PS engine. Later vans were availxble on private car chassis. *HON*

AUGLAIZE (US) 1911-1916

Auglaize Motor Car Co., New Bremen, Ohio.

The Model B half-tonner was similar in appearance to a high-wheeler although it used wheels of smaller diameter. It was an express van with a water-cooled 2-cylinder engine with planetary transmission and double chain drive. The Model C, rated at 1500 pounds capacity was also an express van but with a 4-cylinder engine and 3-speed gearbox, with double chain drive. Models after 1912 were all ¾-tonners and though the model designations changed to D and H, they were basically the same as the 1912 Model C with shaft drive and solid rubber tires. *GMN*

AULTMAN (US) 1901-1902

Aultman & Co., Canton, Ohio.

This was a highly unconventional steam wagon with friction transmission, surely unique on a steam vehicle and seemingly unnecessary in view of the flexibility of the steam engine. Drive was to all four wheels, by double chains to the rear axle, and by shaft and bevel gears to the front axle, which had a much narrower tread than the rear. Power came from a 16 hp 2-cylinder engine, and the load capacity was 5-tons. *GNG*

AURORA (US) 1908

Aurora Motor Works, Aurora, Illinois

The single model under the tradename Aurora was a light open delivery van of 1500-pound capacity. It used a water-cooled two-stroke engine with two cylinders. Final drive was through a planetary transmission and driveshaft. Its wheelbase was a very short 6 feet, 8 inches. *GMN*

AUSONIA (I) 1903-1906

Camona, Giussani, Turrinelli & C, Sesto San Giovanni, Milan.

This firm continued the manufacture of Gino Turrinelli's S.I.V.E. electric cabs. Private cars were also made. Ausonias were said to have a range of 90 miles and a speed of 18 mph. *MCS*

AUSTIN (GB) 1908 to date

(1) Austin Motor Co. Ltd., Longbridge, Birmingham 1908-1970

(2) British Motor Corporation Ltd., Bathgate, East Lothian 1961-1967

1909 AUSTIN 15hp 15cwt van, NMM

(3) British Leyland Motor Corporation Ltd., (Austin-Morris Division), Longbridge, Birmingham 1970-1977
(4) British Leyland UK Ltd., (Leyland Cars), Longbridge, Birmingham 1977 to date

Herbert Austin had already been responsible for Wolseley's horizontal-engined commercial vehicles before he set up on his own in 1906, but no Austin commercials were offered until 1908. Initially the only such model was a 15 hp driven-over-engine type available as a cab or 15-cwt van. The 4-cylinder power unit was of the usual T-head type, but up to 1910 its cylinders were cast monobloc, there being a reversion to separate cylinders on later versions. By 1909 normal control cabs were offered, and in the same year Austin made one of the world's first mobile homes, to the order of Arthur Du Cros. They also made a specialty of car-based ambulances, a line of business which they pursued for nearly 60 years; later types included the 4- and 6-cylinder 20 hp (1919-38),the 18 hp (1937-39), and the 4-litre Sheerline/Princess family from 1950 onward. After 1959 the big ambulance/hearse chassis was marketed under the Vanden Plas name, production ceasing in 1968. A small number of car-type light vans was also made up to 1914, mainly on the 10 hp and 15 hp chassis.

A novelty of 1913 was the 2-3 ton truck, an unusual design with 25 hp 4-cylinder engine, dashboard radiator, externally mounted steering column, central-change 4-speed gearbox, and an ingenious drive by twin angled propeller shafts. Some 2000 were built to civilian and military account, the last ones in 1919; many went to Russia (which also took 50 hp Austin armoured cars), and some served as double-decker buses in Cambridge.

From 1919 to 1926 the firm built agricultural tractors with 3.6-litre 20 hp car engines; these were made under license in France for many years, while a roadgoing version was briefly offered in 1925. Another use for the 20 hp power unit was found in a 30-cwt solid-tired truck with overhead worm drive; its exposed steering column was inherited from the old 2-3 tonner, but in other respects it was conventional. It had disappeared by 1924, leaving Austin to concentrate for 15 years on car-type light vans. Most significant of these was the 747-cc Seven, introduced at the 1922 Car Show, and available a year later as a 2½-cwt van. Though the Seven was later uprated to 5-cwt, production of commercial models was modest; the 1000 a year mark was not passed until 1931. The model's foreign licensees — Dixi (B.M.W) in Germany, Rosengart in France, and American Austin (Bantam) in the U.S.A. would also produce van variants, and after the Seven was discontinued in 1939 Reliant purchased the design rights of the engine, which they continued to make for many years. Also made in van form were Austin's original 12 hp

1917 AUSTIN 2/3-ton van, OMM

1929 AUSTIN seven van, MJWW

(from 1923), the 1½-litre Light 12/6 (1932-36), and the 10/4 and Light 12/4 (from 1933), the commercials generally retaining styling already outmoded on the cars. Plated ribbon radiator shells, for instance, persisted on some types until mid-1937.

From 1930 Austin began the manufacture of London-type taxicab on the 1.9-litre 12 chassis. Some of the early ones wore bodies transferred from superannuated Citroens, but the marque achieved a 60-70 per cent share of the metropolis's cab traffic, nearly 6000 being delivered between 1930 and 1938. 1934 saw a special low-loading worm-drive taxi model, soon given synchromesh and coil ignition in place of the magneto retained to the end on

1939 AUSTIN 12.8hp London taxicab, GNG

private car models, and in 1938 it received modern front-end styling as well, some of the last models being fitted with 15-cwt truck bodies for the Army. Though cab production was not resumed until 1948, the new FX3 with 2.2-litre ohv 4-cylinder Sixteen engine gave Austin a virtual monopoly of this specialized market, over 7000 being sold in London alone during its ten-year run. 1958 saw the more advanced FX4 with ifs, offered initially with a diesel engine and automatic transmission; gasoline and manual gearbox options came later. It was still in production, with a more powerful 2½-litre diesel, in 1978. Unusual variants offered by the company included a miniature provincial model on the 10 hp car chassis (1938), and an export edition of the FX3 (1949) using the 1.2-litre A40 engine.

A big step forward came in 1939, when Austin challenged the established Morris-Commercial and Bedford with a full light-medium duty range on accepted lines; trucks for payloads of 30cwt to 3-tons and a 26-seater coach chassis. The all-steel 3-man cabs followed the prevailing fashion and chassis design was conventional, but they were the first Austins of any type to be marketed with ohv and hydraulic brakes, features that would not reach the cars until the end of 1947. The 3½-litre 6-cylinder engine served as the prototype of the Sheerline series, and was destined to survive (in 1948 4-litre form) to the end of heavy truck production as the recognized gasoline option. Gearboxes were of 4-speed constant mesh type, and

1944 AUSTIN 3-ton tanker, OMM

Austin built 115,000 vehicles for the Allied war effort between 1939 and 1945, most of them based on these models. The most important types were the 30-cwt K2 (the Army's standard ambulance), the 3-ton 6x4 K3 and K6, and the 3-ton forward-control 4x4 K5 of 1943. Large numbers of 30-cwt tenders were also supplied to the National Fire Service.

The trucks underwent little material change before 1950, though the ohv 16 engine was applied to a new 25-cwt 3-way van introduced in 1946, and ifs reached the commercials with the advent of a 10-cwt van on the 1.2-litre A40 chassis at the end of 1947. Post-war car-based vans would include the 5/6-cwt A30/A35 family (from 1954), the 10-cwt A50/A55 (from 1957), and, from April, 1960, 5-cwt van and pickup editions of Alec Issigonis's all-independently-sprung, transverse-engined fwd 848-cc Mini. From 1946 Austin added battery-electric light vans to their financial interests with the purchase of the Morrison-Electricar firm.

1950 saw revised cabs on a new Loadstar range of normal control trucks, available for the first time with a diesel option, the Perkins P6. In 1952 there was a new Loadstar variant, a 1-ton short wheelbase military type 4x4, and at the same time Austin produced a Jeep replacement, the Champ, which would remain in army service until 1966, A 5-speed gearbox and all-independent springing featured in the specification, Service models using a 2.8-litre ioe 4-cylinder Rolls-Royce engine. A civilian edition with the Austin A90 unit was made in very small numbers.

Meanwhile in 1951 Austin had merged with the Nuffield

1949 AUSTIN 2-ton van, OMM

Group to form the British Motor Corporation. Rationalization, which took some time to penetrate the combined car range, was soon very apparent in the commercial sector. Austin's ohv engines proved more economic propositions than the rival Morris units, but despite the unification of Austin and Morris-Commercial types from 1954, the story remains complex up to 1962, thanks to BMC's practice of assigning different designations to identical models with Austin and Morris badges. What emerged, however, was a range of conventional normal- and forward-control models, the former based on the Austin Loadstars, and the latter Morris-inspired, covering the 30-cwt — 7-ton bracket. Austin's existing 4- and 6-cylinder

1949 AUSTIN 25cwt Three Way van, OMM

ohv gasoline engines sufficed to meet a dwindling demand, but from 1953 a new series of BMC diesels was developed, starting with a 3.4-litre 58 hp four and a 5.1-litre six rated at 90 hp. By 1958 there was a 2.2-litre unit for the under 2-tonners, 1962 saw a 5.7-litre six for the heaviest trucks and tractors. Hydrovac brakes were universal in the higher echelons, and 2-speed axles were also a regular option. Further widening of the range led to the Omnivan of 1956, a unitary-construction forward-control light van with 1½-litre gasoline engine suitable for 12/15-cwt payloads or Minibus use, and the Gipsy of 1958, which revived the Champ theme in simplified civilian guise. The twin hypoid-drive axles and ingenious suspen-

1955 AUSTIN 2-ton van, BR

sion were retained, but power was now provided by the 16 hp engine. Despite lwb and diesel options, and an ultimate reversion to beam axles in 1967, it was never a great success, and was quietly dropped in 1968 when the formation of British Leyland brought the firmly established Landrover under the same management. A better proposition was the FG-series of 1960, forward control trucks with ingenious low-silled, angled-vision cabs, offered with ratings of up to five tons and the usual options.

In 1961 the new truck factory at Bathgate in Scotland

1962 AUSTIN FG K100 5-ton truck, NMM

1971 AUSTIN 250JU 22cwt van, British Leyland

was opened, handling production of the heavier trucks. Also new in 1961 was a smaller 12-cwt forward control van, the J4, notable for its coil spring ifs. It sold over 100,000 units in 10 years, being available with a diesel engine from 1962 and with automatic transmission (also listed on Omnivans) from 1965. On the heavy goods side the FH range of 5/8-ton forward control trucks featured inclined underfloor engines and no gasoline option, while tilt cabs arrived on the FJs of 1965: these also had 5-speed gearboxes, air-hydraulic brakes, air-assisted handbrakes, four-headlamp styling and a power steering option. In 1967 the group introduced a replacement for Morris's old forward control LD parcels van, the 22-cwt 250JU.

From the beginning of 1968 the old Austin and Morris names were dropped in favor of BMC labels on the bigger models, leaving only the lighter types (now augmented, ironically, by a badge-engineered version of the 6-cwt Morris Minor van) as Austins. The British Leyland merger of that year had even more far-reaching results, fusing Austin and Morris into a single division by 1970. The Mini was now a make in its own right, and while the group still made bigger vans, some of these bore the Leyland badge. This applied to the 13/22-cwt Sherpa range new for 1975, though the Austin name was perpetuated the 1978 on commercial editions of the Morris Marina car. *MCS*

AUSTIN (TR) 1968 to date

B.M.C. Sanayi ve Ticaret A.S., Izmir

Produced by a long established tractor factory, still bearing the BMC trademark, Austin trucks are normal control chassis build around the old British WE series of mid 60s. A locally designed sheet metal cab of angular lines, built with ease of manufacture and repair in mind, is fitted, while power comes from BMC diesel engines developing 105 and 120 hp. The feathered Austin "A" is also apparent on all Turkish built chassis. The same company also makes trucks under the Morris name, in three models, 68 to 120 hp. *GA*

1933 AUSTIN UTILITY COACH bus, MBS

AUSTIN UTILITY COACH (US) 1933-1934

Austin System
El Segundo, California

The Pickwick Corp. was a large holding company which defaulted on its obligations and entered receivership in

1932. The general manager of Pickwick's bus manufacturing operation acquired the plant and used it briefly to build his own design of 21-passenger city transit bus. Dwight E. Austin had patented an angle drive that made a transverse rear engine more adaptable than it was with various right-angle arrangements then being tried by larger U.S. manufacturers, and this was the chief feature of Austin's Utility Coach. Austin was hired by Yellow Coach in 1934, and his patent went with him, to be used exclusively by Yellow and GM for the next 30 years. *MBS*

AUSTRAL (F) 1930-1932

Ets. Austral, Puteaux, Seine

Made by a long-established motorcycle manufacturer, the Austral was a 3-wheeled parcel van with single front wheel, powered by a single-cylinder engine mounted under the seat, driving the rear wheels via a 3-speed Sturmey-Archer gearbox and single chain. *GNG*

1912 AUSTRO-DAIMLER M12 4×4 military tractor, BHV

AUSTRO-DAIMLER (A) 1900-1920

(1) Osterreichische Daimler-Motoren-Gesellschaft Bierenz, Fischer & Co., Wiener-Neustadt 1900-1902

(2) Osterreichische Daimler-Motoren-Gesellschaft mbH., Wiener-Neustadt 1902-1910

(3) Osterreichische Daimler-Motoren AG., Wiener-Neustadt 1910-1920

When this firm was founded as a subsidiary of the German Daimler company well-proved engine designs were available. A first truck was presented in 1900 but commercials of a higher standard appeared after Paul Daimler, son of Gottlieb, had taken over the job as chief designer. When he presented two versions of 4x4 vehicles he laid the foundation for one of Austro-Daimler's main activities, the production of specialized vehicles. Emile Jellinek, the initiator of the Mercedes cars, turned to Austro-Daimler after he had ended his activities for the German Daimler company and one of his first new proposals was to employ Ferdinand Porsche as the successor of Paul Daimler, when the latter left in 1906. Jellinek initiated the production of electric and gasoline-electric vehicles which were built to his order and sold by him as "Mercedes Electrique" and "Mercedes Mixte." These were based on Lohner-Porsche designs which were bought by Jellinek. From these they differed by having the electric hub cap engines in the rear wheels while Lohner had placed them in the front wheels. When Jellinek also gave up these activities and withdrew from the field of automobiles in 1908 Austro-Daimler carried on production of electric driven vehicles, especially buses and fire service vehicles. Another specialty was trolley buses, originally known as "Lohner-Stoll" and then as "Mercedes-Electrique-Stoll"; they were built until 1913. Trucks were built to a very great extent for the army.

Various designs of buses were available, for city as well as for overland services. They all used 4-cylinder engines of 14 to 32 hp. The Austro-Daimler tractors became well-known for military purposes. They were either driven by a 6-cylinder 100 hp engine or this engine drove a generator supplying the electric energy for the motors driving the tractor itself and the trailers. After WWI production of commercials was given up.

Austro-Daimler later merged with Puch and Steyr. Some special vehicles, especially 6x4 all terrain vehicles were built from about 1935 to 1942. These were widely known as Austro-Daimler and in fact they retained the type designation AD with a suffix. But they were manufactured in the Steyr plant and marketed as Steyr. *HON*

1941 AUTARQUIA 3-ton electric truck, JCG

AUTARQUIA (E) 1940-1945

Vehiculos Electricos Autarquia .S.A., Barcelona

The Autarquia was a 3-ton battery electric truck built on the Ford Model 51 chassis. Maximum speed was 20

1914 AUSTRO-DAIMLER C-Zug gas-electric road train, BHV

mph and range per charge 45 miles. In addition to trucks and vans, some Autarquías were made with bus bodies for town and suburban work. *JCG*

AUTOAR (RA) 1950-1961

Automotores Argentinos S.A.I.C., Buenos Aires.

Autoar made light front-engined pickup trucks and station wagons and also cab over engine vans and minibuses. The same basic chassis was used for all these models. Pickups and station wagons could be ordered with three different engines: Fiat 1900 4-cylinder, Willys 2,150cc 4-cylinder, or Simca 2,351cc V-8. At first only the Willys engine was offered but later the Simca and Fiat were added. They had a ¾ ton load carrying capacity. Vans and minibuses could be ordered only with the Fiat or Simca engines. They had a 1½-ton load carrying capacity. Four or three forward speeds were available according to the engines. These commercial vehicles were discontinued in 1961. Thereafter Automotores Argentinos continued making only the NSU cars under license until 1966 when the factory closed down. Automotores Argentinios also made several thousand chassis frames for the Rastrojero light truck made by IAME.

Production was low in their later years and in the 1959-1961 period only 204 Autoars were made. *ACT*

AUTOBAMBI (E) 1950-1956

Manufacturas Mecanicas Aleu, SL, Esparraguera, Barcelona

This well-known motorcycle firm made 3-wheeled minicars and light vans and trucks, powered by 125cc M.M. Aleu single-cylinder 2-stroke engines. Capacity was 250 kgs. *JCG*

AUTOBIANCHI see Bianchi

AUTO CAMION (F) 1905-1906

Ste l'Auto Camion, Levallois-Perret, Seine

This company made a 4-ton truck powered by an 18/22 hp 4-cylinder engine mounted under the footboard, with 3-speed gearbox and double chain drive. In 1906 it was joined by a smaller truck powered by a 14 hp 2-cylinder engine. *GNG*

AUTO-CAR (i) (US) 1904-1908

Auto-Car Equipment Co., Buffalo, NY

This make should not be confused with the contemporary and better known Autocar of Ardmore, Pa. The Auto-Car offered a variety of gasoline and battery-powered electric trucks. Initially, there was an electric 2-tonner with a closed delivery body, a 24-passenger bus and a trackless trolley. At the same time, two gasoline delivery vans were made, both with 2-cylinder engines. In 1906 there was a 3-tonner with forward control driven by a 35 hp, 4-cylinder engine. For 1907, there was a 5-tonner available, again with forward control, a 4-cylinder engine, as well as a 20-passenger "brake" or sight-seeing bus. Electrics for that year included a closed 10-passenger Brougham or light bus. The last year under the name Auto-Car there was offered an electric ambulance, an electric 24-passenger bus as well as a 6-tonner with platform body. Gasoline vehicles in that last year included a 20-passenger bus plus 3- and 5-tonners. The name was changed to Buffalo, and later became Atterbury. *GMN*

AUTO-CAR (ii) (I) 1907-1911

Societa Italiana Auto-Cars, Alessandria

Like many an Italian venture of this period, the Societa Auto-Cars advertised every type of motor vehicle. Only buses were, however, actually made, these being assembled from such imported components as Malicet et Blin frames and Aster engines. Auto-Cars were in service in the Brescia and Pesaro areas. *MCS*

AUTOCAR (US) 1908 to date

(1) Autocar Co., Ardmore, Pa. 1908-1954

(2) Autocar Divn, White Motor Co., Exton, Pa. 1954 to date

After nine years of building cars and motorized tricycles, Autocar began to experiment with commercial vehicles in 1907. The following year saw the introduction of the Type XX1 series of forward-control trucks. Powered by a horizontally-opposed 2-cylinder 18 hp engine, these vehicles had 3-speeds and shaft drive. Wheelbase

1921 AUTOCAR Model XXI 2-ton truck, Roger Whitehouse Coll.

was only 8 ft. 1 in., and load capacity 1½ tons. More than 30,000 of these rugged and reliable vehicles were built before production was finally phased out during 1926. Many were bodied as buses, and they were used in World War I by the armies of the United States, Canada and Great Britain. Up to 1919 they were the only Autocar trucks made (passenger car production ceased in 1911), but then a range of 4-cylinder forward-control trucks of 2 to 5-tons capacity was introduced. These came in two engine sizes, 25.6 hp for 2/3 tonners and 28.9 hp for 4/5 tonners. Together with the 2-cylinder Type XX1 and a range of 1, 2, and 3-ton electric trucks, they were made until 1926 when a new series of conventional trucks was introduced, of 1½ to 5 tons capacity, later increased to 7½ tons. These had 4- and 6-cylinder engines.

1924 AUTOCAR bus, FLP

Among developments of the early 1930s was a 4x4 chassis for off-highway work and, in 1933, the re-introduction of forward-control on the U.S. series. This was some-

1926 AUTOCAR Model 26B 3-ton truck, LIAM

1939 AUTOCAR Model U70 tanker, BHV

1946 AUTOCAR 6-wheel truck, NMM

thing of an innovation in the American truck industry, but within two years leading manufacturers such as Mack, G.M.C. and White followed suit. The forward-control models paralleled the normal-control ones, and included 4x2 and 6x2 tractors for articulated units as well as 4x2 and 6x2 rigid chassis. The larger models had 5-speed gearboxes. In 1936 came the UD series with more streamlined cabs, and these were continued with little change until after World War II. From 1938 onwards, forward-control models represented a growing proportion of the range. Most engines were made by Autocar, but the Model DC 4x4 dump truck used a 150 bhp Cummins diesel. In 1938/39 some Autocars, both normal and forward-control, were assembled in Amsterdam using Hercules engines. Known as Autocar-Kromhouts, they were used as fire engines and refuse trucks as well as ordinary load carriers.

From the summer of 1940 Autocar began to supply standard production models to the United States armed forces. Later they were commissioned to build thousands of armoured half-tracks and 4x4 and 6x4 prime movers for the allied forces. Half-track production was phased out early in 1940, and Autocar allowed to build 3,000 trucks for civilian operators. The end of war work in 1945 saw the beginning of a vast expansion of Autocar, with new factories and increased production. A total of 5,320 Autocar trucks were made in 1946, and demand remained strong during the late 1940s, but the curtailment of the heavy truck market in the early 1950s brought trouble, and in 1953 the company was acquired by White. The next year production was transferred to a new factory at Exton, Pa., and henceforth production was more on a custom basis. Engines were White gasoline and Cummins, Caterpillar or Detroit Diesels, and a wide range of gearboxes and axles enabled trucks to be built more or less to customer's specifications. More powerful models were made, for the quarrying, logging, mining and oil industries, the largest being the AP40 powered by a 600 bhp 12-cylinder diesel engine, with a capacity of 40 tons.

In 1958 came a new series of lightweight aluminum chassis called the A series. Chassis weight was reduced by nearly 25%, and an additional legal payload of up to 4,475 lbs. was possible. During the 1960s diesel engines became predominant in Autocar trucks, being supplied by Cummins and Caterpillar. Load carrying trucks and tractors were made in 4x2, 4x4, 6x4 and 6x6 versions, all with normal control, and in addition Autocar has developed a range of special chassis for cement mixers, some with forward control, of 6x4 and 8x4 configuration. Current models range from 46,000 to 120,000 lbs. GCW, with Cummins engines of 230 to 350 bhp and Caterpillar engines of 220 to 375 bhp. Gearboxes give up to 13 forward speeds. A new model for 1975 was the Contractor with offset cab

1962 AUTOCAR Model RP18 heavy articulated low loader, OMM

and short wheelbase, and early in 1978 came the Constructor 2 series which came in three different BBC dimensions, and with axles forward or set back. Engines run from 210 to 430 hp. *LA*

1910 AUTOCARRIER 5/6cwt 3-wheel delivery, BR

AUTOCARRIER (GB) 1907-1920

(1) Autocars & Accessories Ltd., West Norwood, London S.e. 1907
(2) Autocarriers Ltd., West Norwood, London S.E. 1907-1911
(3) Autocarriers (1911) Ltd., Thames Ditton, Surrey 1911-1920

The Autocarrier was an ingenious little 3-wheeled delivery vehicle designed by John Weller who had previously built a 4-cylinder car under his own name, and was later to be responsible for A.C. cars. It was powered by 5/6 hp single-cylinder air-cooled engine of 723 cc with two large flywheels, a multiple disc clutch and 2-speed epicyclic gears. Final drive to the single rear wheel was by chain, and steering by side tiller. Launched on the market in May 1907 at a price of £80, the Autocarrier had gone up to £95 two years later, but became a best seller in its field thanks to its simplicity and robustness, both of which made it suitable for use by young delivery boys. Among leading customers were the Great Western and London & South Western Railways; Associated Newspapers and Carr's biscuit, while export orders took the Autocarriers as far afield as Rumania, Argentina and China as well as France, Italy, Spain and Portugal. For a few years before World War I the Autocarrier was sold by F.B. Goodchild & Co. of London, sometimes under the name Goodchild.

Production was resumed in 1919 but in 1920 the 3-wheeler was withdrawn in favor of a 4-wheeled version known as the Autocarrier Junior. This had a 3½ single-cylinder engine mounted between the narrow-track rear wheels, wheel steering in place of the tiller and disc wheels instead of wire. It was not a success, and Autocarriers, who were now concentrating on A.C. cars, made no further vehicles of this kind. *GNG*

AUTO-ELECTRIC (GB) 1924-1939

Murphy Cars & Trucks Ltd., Cordwallis Works, Maidenhead, Berks.

Early in 1924 the first Auto Electric 3-wheel box body parcel car type of vehicle was introduced as the "errand boy on wheels". Layout was with the driver seated at the rear looking over the 4 ft. x 3 ft. x 3 ft. 8cwt load carrying box and protected by an open fronted curved roof cab if required. The two front wheels on pneumatics beneath the box were steered and the single solid tired rear wheel was

1935 AUTO ELECTRIC (Murphy) 8/10cwt milk float, NMM

chain driven from a Langham 1½ hp 40-volt motor. The 160AH batteries were located amidships beneath the frame.

In 1928 a 10cwt four wheel model made its appearance and in 1930 this was followed by a 15cwt model. An invalid carriage was added to the range in 1933 and the company went into the field of internal works trucks by producing a 1-ton capacity truck. 1935 saw the range extended to cover the MP type 8cwt 3-wheeler, the MT 10/15cwt and MV 20/25cwt, all with direct drive from the Nelco motor to the rear axle. The smallest vehicle had worm drive while the others used double helical spur with single reduction. The largest model was equipped with two motors. The 8cwt 3-wheeler was later given the name of "Servitor" and was unusual because the driver stood on a small platform at the rear of the machine and looked over the body somewhat similar to the original model. Production of all three models ceased late in 1939. *OM*

AUTOHORSE (US) 1917-1922

One Wheel Truck Co., St. Louis, Mo.

The Autohorse was a single-wheel tractor for attachment to 4-wheeled horse-drawn trailers. The 22.5 hp 4-cylinder Continental engine was offset but counterbalanced by the 56-gallon water tank for the radiator. It drove through a Borg & Beck clutch, Warner 3-speed gearbox and internal gear final drive. Unlike other mechanical horses such as Knox and Scammell, the Autohorse had no turntable, but the rear part of the main frame was attached to the front axle of the wagon. In 1918 forty were ordered by the St. Louis Fire Department but they proved unsatisfactory, and only five were delivered. In 1922 it was announced that it would be made in Britain by the steam wagon builders, Taskers of Andover, but this did not materialize although a few US-built Autohorses were used in Britain. *GNG*

AUTO-LUX (I) 1945-1950

Auto-Lux SpA, Milan

Externally the Auto-Lux was a typical Italian commercial 3-wheeler, with two driven rear wheels, handlebar steering, and enclosed cab. Less usual was its battery-electric propulsion. *MCS*

AUTOMACH (E) 1954-1958

Empresa Automach-Movilutil, Barcelona

This company made small passenger cars and trucks powered by a 350cc 2-cylinder 2-stroke engines. The latter had a carrying capacity of 400 kgs. *JCG*

AUTOMATIC (US) 1922

Automatic Transportation Co., Buffalo, N.Y.

Also made in passenger car form, the Automatic was a diminutive electric van for 5cwt loads with a wheelbase of only 5 ft. 5 in. and overall length of 8 ft. 6 in. The 24 volt motor drove the offside rear wheel by chain, and steering was by tiller. *GNG*

AUTO-MOWER (GB) 1925-1947

Auto-Mower Engineering Co. Ltd., Norton St. Philip, Bath, Somerset

This company, established in 1922, was mainly known for its lawn mowers and motor rollers, but they made three types of commercial vehicles:

1) The Auto Truck, a light 3-wheeler powered by a 550cc single-cylinder Blackburn oil-cooled engine driving the single front wheel. The whole power train could turn through 360°, thus avoiding the necessity for a reverse gear. It was intended chiefly for factory and estate work, but could be licensed for use on the road. The design was sold to R.A. Lister & Sons Ltd. of Dursley, Gloucestershire, who have made it in various forms ever since.

2) The Nippy Carrier, a 3-wheeled 10cwt truck whose driver sat at the rear, next to the 500cc J.A.P. Sport single-cylinder engine which drove the rear wheels. Only six of these were made, in 1934.

3) The Auto Tractor, a timber tractor powered by a transversely-mounted 24 hp 4-cylinder Ford engine, with a 4-speed gearbox and chain drive. This was introduced in 1933, and later models had Ford V-8 engines mounted transversely or longitudinally, as well as transverse Meadows or Gardner diesel engines. A total of 48 of these were made up to 1947, after which the company mounted their timber handling equipment on A.E.C. and Leyland chassis. They are still in business today, making motor rollers. *GNG*

1928 AUTOMOTIVE SYNDICATE steam bus, MBS

AUTOMOTIVE SYNDICATE (US) 1928

Automotive Syndicate, Indianapolis, Indiana

The Automotive Syndicate was organized in 1927 by William Parrish, a former vice-president of Wills-Ste. Claire, with backing from a number of men well known in the automotive industry. Its purpose was to develop a steam-powered bus under license from the Electrol Corp., which had patented a flash boiler and control system originally but not successfully tested in the Standard Steam Truck. A six-wheel 40-passenger all-steel prototype was constructed, with an eight-cylinder V-type steam engine beneath the floor and driving both rear axles directly. An auxiliary steam engine powered the water pumps, air compressor, condenser cooling fans, and electric generator — an arrangement similar to that of Clarkson steam buses in England 15 years earlier. The sample bus progressed well into the test stage, but the syndicate's trustees postponed further work after the stock market crash of 1929. *MBS*

1975 AUTOSAN H-9-15 36-passenger bus, MSH

AUTOSAN (PL) 1973 to date

Sanocka Fabryka Autobusow, Sanock

The former Sanok buses and coaches have been marketed since 1973 as Autosan. The same basic integral design was retained, while power comes from a license-built WOLA-Leyland diesel developing 125 hp placed at the rear of the body. A city bus model was also added to the line a year later. *GA*

AUTO TRACTOR see Auto Mower

AUTO-TRACTION (B) 1920-1925

SA Auto-Traction, Antwerp.

The Auto-Traction was a license-built Chenard-Walcker road tractor for 6-ton loads, with such Chenard features as an automatic 5th wheel coupling. The engine was a 3.6-litre 4-cylinder sleeve-valve Minerva, and pneumatics replaced solid tires in 1923. Minerva acquired the company two years later, the Auto-Traction being continued as part of their commercial vehicle range. *MCS*

AUTO-TRUCK (US) 1916

Auto-Truck Co., Bangor, Pa.

The only model offered was a 1-ton stake truck with 20 hp Buda 4-cylinder engine. It cost $1,250. *DJS*

AUTO-UNION (D) 1942

Auto-Union, Zwickau

The Auto-Union combine was formed by the makes of Audi, Horch, D.K.W. and Wanderer, each producing private cars under their own marque. In 1942 several prototypes of a very advanced 4x4 drive 1½-ton truck were presented. A forward control cab was used, the 2.7 litre Wanderer engine was used and placed behind the front axle. However this design was not put into series production as a matter of standardization during the war. *HON*

AVAILABLE (US) 1910-1957

(1) Available Truck Co., Chicago, Ill. 1910-1957

(2) Available Truck Co., Divn. of Crane Carrier Corp., Tulsa, Okla. 1957

The first Available truck was a ¾-tonner with 22 hp flat-twin engine under the driver's seat, 2-speed planetary transmission and double chain drive. It came with, or without, cab, and was in the same class as the famous

1920 AVAILABLE Invincible 7-ton coal truck, FLP

Autocar Type XXI. For 1914 Available offered a larger truck with 32 hp 4-cylinder engine and 1-ton capacity, still with engine under seat, but the next year they went conventional with 1- and 2-ton trucks with 3-speed transmissions and overhead worm drive. By 1917 the range had expanded to four models up to 5 tons with Continental 4-cylinder engines, 4-speeds and Timken or Wisconsin rear axles. In 1920 came the 7-ton Invincible with 50 hp Waukesha engine, but like many manufacturers at this time Available found that such a heavy truck did not sell, and by 1922 the largest model was again a 5-tonner. Pneumatic tires appeared for the first time in 1926 on the 1½-tonner, and 6-cylinder engines arrived in the late 1920s. Hercules was the most used engine at this time, with Waukesha on the larger trucks.

1935 AVAILABLE 6-ton tanker, RJ

A wide range was offered during the 1930s, though actual production was very low, and some models listed may never have been made. Cab-overs were built from 1936, as were 6-wheelers, and at the bottom of the range was a ¾-ton pickup in 1937. Buses, both conventional and forward control were made in the 1930s and 1940s, and were used by the US Armed Forces during World War II, as were Available 6x4 medium wreckers and mobile cranes. These had Waukesha gasoline engines, though diesels by Buda and Cummins were also listed. After the war a custom fire engine chassis was offered, and used by number of fire apparatus makers including Oren-Roanoke and Boyer. Trucks were listed in ten models from 15,000 to 32,000 lbs. GVW with Waukesha gasoline and Cummins diesel engines, Warner, Fuller and Spicer transmissions and Lockheed hydraulic brakes. Available bus chassis of the early 1950s used Ford V-8 engines mounted either below the driver or at the rear of the chassis, while

1947 AVAILABLE 10-ton 6-wheel tanker, OMM

in 1955 came a yardspotter, and 6x4 chassis for concrete mixers or crane carrying. The latter activity led the company to be acquired by Crane Carrier Company, makers of the CCC, and it is possible that a few vehicles were made under the Available name while under CCC ownership.

Sales of Availables were largely confined to the Chicago area, good customers being Blatz Breweries and Borden's Milk, though some crane carriers found their way to the Netherlands. Total production over 47 years was not much above 2,500. *RW*

1966 AVELING-BARFORD SN 30-ton dumper, Aveling Barford

AVELING-BARFORD (GB) 1933 to date

Aveling-Barford Ltd., Grantham, Lincs.

Formed as as amalgamation between Aveling & Porter and Barfords, both well-known makers of road rollers, Aveling-Barford continued in this field and also made site dumpers, originally based on the Fordson tractor. The first shuttle dumper with reversible seat and controls, and a gearbox giving the same number of speeds in reverse as forward, went into production in 1939, and was joined in 1947 by a 6-wheeler version with 12-ton capacity powered by a 128 hp 6-cylinder Dorman diesel engine. In 1957 came the SL series which has been steadily developed up to the present day. A two-axle truck with 6-cylinder Leyland diesel engine and reversible controls, it has grown from the original 10-ton model to the present 17-ton SL340 with 201 hp engine and five forward and three reverse speeds.

In 1958 the SN range was introduced with conventional cab and controls, powered by a 450 hp Rolls-Royce V-8 or 335 hp Cummins 6-cylinder engine, with 6-forward speed gearbox. Capacity was 30 tons, increased to 35 tons in the

1975 AVELING-BARFORD Centaur 50-ton dumper, Aveling-Barford

SN35 which had the Rolls-Royce V-8 or a General Motors V-12 2-stroke engine developing 476 hp. The SNs were replaced in 1970 by the Centaur range with driver-beside-engine layout. These are made in five models from 25 to 50 tons capacity, the largest having a General Motors V-16 2-stroke engine of 18.6 litres developing 635 hp.

Aveling-Barford became part of British Leyland in 1968, and this resulted in the former A.E.C. 690 on/off road dump truck joining the Aveling-Barford range. The only 6-wheeler currently made, it has a 189 hp 6-cylinder Leyland engine. *GNG*

AVELING & PORTER (GB) 1865-1932

Aveling & Porter Ltd., Rochester, Kent

Founded to build agricultural engines, the partnership turned to crane engines (1865), road-rollers (1867) and traction engines for road haulage, notably the "Steam Sappers" supplied to the War Office in 1871 et seq. Until the 1914 war the firm continued to make a limited number of road locomotives mostly of 6 and 8 n.h.p. After the passage of the 1896 Act they commenced to build 3-ton

1900 AVELING-PORTER 8hp compound road locomotive, RAW

steam tractors for road haulage stepping up to 5 tons in 1905.

Between 1909 and 1925 compound overtype steam wagons in 3-, 4- and 5-ton capacities were manufactured, the total output being 292 of which 12 were built under sub-contract by Richard Garrett & Sons Ltd., at Leiston, Suffolk.

All road locomotives were four shaft and tractors three shaft, with all gear drives. Wagons were three shaft with final drive by single roller chain to a differential in the rear axle. The later tractors and locomotives were on rubber tires as were about half the wagons.

1913 AVELING & PORTER *3-4*-ton truck, RAW

In addition to steam wagons the firm manufactured a limited number of gasoline-engined trucks of conventional four wheeled drive layout using a 4-cylinder engine of their own manufacture, the first appearing in 1913 and the last in 1916.

Chain and bobbin steering was used on locomotives, tractors and the earlier wagons but later wagons and all gasoline-engined trucks had Ackermann steering.

The company became part of the A.G.E. combine in 1919 under whose policy steam wagon and truck building

1920 AVELING & PORTER overtype steam wagon, RAW

was allocated to another constituent company, Richard Garrett & Sons Ltd.

Aveling steam tractors were well thought of but all other products were overshadowed by roller building which constituted the bulk of the business. *RAW*

AVERY (US) 1910-1923

The Avery Co., Peoria, Ill.

Built by a company famous for their tractors and farm machinery, Avery trucks had a strong agricultural bias, with extra wide wheels clad in steel tires for good traction on soft ground. They were advertised as either trucks, tractors, combination farm wagons or general farm power machines, having a long front extension on the crankshaft for use as power take-off for sawing wood, pumping water etc. Early models had 4-cylinder engines, open cabs and chain drive, being rated at 1-ton capacity. By 1912 2- and 3-tonners for ordinary road use with solid rubber tires were also offered. A crescent cab was available from 1913, and in 1917 a cab-over-engine truck was introduced with enclosed chain drive.

From 1921 Averys were much more conventional, with rubber tires, electric lights and starter, and square enclosed cab. At this time they introduced a short-lived 6-cylinder model, using their own make of monobloc engine. *RW*

AVIA (i) (E) 1956 to date

(1) Aeronautica Industrial SA, Madrid
(2) Motor Iberica SA, Barcelona

The first road vehicle built by this aircraft firm was a light 3-wheeler powered by a 197cc Hispano-Villiers single-cylinder engine, but they soon turned to a medium-sized truck, the 2500, powered by a 68 hp Perkins diesel engine. Other models in the same range followed including the 1500, 3500, 4000 and 6500, for loads of 3000 to 10,200 kgs, all powered by various sizes of Perkins engines. Buses for 18 to 28 passengers were also made.

In 1970 Motor Iberica, makers of Ebro vehicles, acquired a major shareholding in Aeronautica Industrial, and Avias carried the name Avia Ebro on their grilles; in 1975 Motor Iberica gained complete control and the Madrid company was dissolved. The range of Avia Ebro trucks and buses was continued, however, in addition to Ebro's own range. *JCG*

AVIA (ii) (CS) 1968 to date

Avia n.p., Prague-Letnany

The Avia concern was founded in 1919 for the manufacture of aircraft, and built many well-known sporting and military machines between the wars. From 1946 to 1951 they built Skoda trucks and buses, and from 1961 onwards various models of Praga and Tatra. In 1967 an agreement was signed with the French Renault company

1963 AVIA (i) 3500 3000kgs van, GNG

to make Renault-Saviem light commercial vehicles under license, and production of these commenced at the Prague factory in October 1968. Two types are made, the A15 and A30, both with 3.3-litre 4-cylinder diesel engines. In the A15 this develops 72 hp and in the larger A30, 80 bhp. A total of 20 variants of the A15/A30 series are made.

In 1970 a new 7-ton Avia S7T was built, with a 6-cylinder air-cooled diesel engine of 8.1-litres. Apart from the Prague factory, Avia has branches in three other Czech towns. *MSH*

AVON (GB) 1906

Avon Motor Manufacturing Co. Ltd., Keynsham, Bristol

The Avon Trimobile was a tubular-framed 3-wheeler powered by a 5½ hp single-cylinder engine driving the rear axle by chain. Most were sold as 2-seater cars, but a goods version with 4 cwt capacity was listed in 1906. *GNG*

AVONSIDE (GB) 1913

Avonside Engine Co. Ltd., Fishponds, Bristol.

Due to a misprint in *Motor Traction* when this vehicle was first announced, it is invariably referred to as the Avondale, which is incorrect. Avonside were primarily builders of small locomotives with kerosene and heavy oil engines for colliery, mining and colonial use, and of engines for use by other manufacturers. During 1913, however, they offered a range of gasoline driven trucks, vans and tipping wagons and a large 200 hp road tractor capable of hauling up to 500 tons. The latter utilized a 2-stroke semi-diesel kerosene or heavy oil engine. *MJWW*

A.W.S. (D) 1951

Autowerke Salzgitter, Salzgitter

This was a construction featuring a 4-cylinder 2-stroke radial diesel 2-litre engine. Available were vans and pick-ups but only a few were produced. *HON*

BABCOCK (i) (US) 1911-1913

H.H. Babcock Company, Watertown, New York

The Babcock was a 1500-pound capacity delivery van and essentially remained unchanged during its brief life. It used a two-cylinder engine mounted beneath the driver's seat, a three-speed gearbox and double-chain drive. This Model G was on a wheelbase of 102 inches and was priced at $1650.*GMN*

BABCOCK (ii) (E) 1950-1955

Sociedad Espanola de Construcciones Babcock & Wilcox, SA, Bilbao

This powerful industrial combine entered motor manufacture for only a short period. They made a sturdy 5-ton truck powered by a 4.9-litre 70hp 4-cylinder diesel engine of their own manufacture. Agricultural tractors powered by 4-cylinder diesel engines were also made. *JCG*

1927 BACKUS Speed Truck, FTS

1937 BACKUS bus, FTS

BACKUS (US) 1925-1937

Backus Motor Truck Co., East Rutherford, N.J.

The Backus was a limited-production assembled truck made in various sizes from 1½ to 6 tons capacity. The 1½-tonner used a 27.34hp 6-cylinder engine, but the 2½ to 6-tonners were powered by 4-cylinder units. All engines were Waukeshas, and Brown-Lipe transmissions and Timken rear axles were used. Backus radiators bore some resemblance to those of Packard. In 1927 it was decided to concentrate on bus production, and a very limited series of custom-made bus chassis were built until 1937. Total production of Backus vehicles was about 150. *GNG*

B.A.D.C. (GB) 1905-1907

British Automobile Development Co. Ltd, London S.E.

The B.A.D.C. bus was built by a subsidiary of the Brush company, makers of electrical equipment and bodies for trams. It had a 30hp 4-cylinder engine, 4-speed gearbox with a top speed of 12mph, and shaft drive. It had a 36 passenger double decker body, and was also offered as a 3-ton truck. In 1907 a forward-control version was sold under the name Brush. *GNG*

BAILEY (US) 1912-1914

S R Bailey & Co., Boston, Mass

This was a battery-powered electric van built on a passenger car chassis. There were two commercial models with just 300-pound rating. Batteries were 60-cell Edison alkaline type and motors were by General Electric. The Model E had a sloping hood and very rakish lines for an electric of this period. Wheelbase was 106 inches. The vehicle was furnished with pneumatic tires. Speed was claimed to be as high as 20mph and operating radius 60 miles per charge. The two commercial types were a light van and a "light service car". *GMN*

BAKER (i) (GB) 1907

Joseph Baker & Sons Ltd., Willesden Junction, London N.W.

This company, who were manufacturers of sugar cane mills and soup and jam mixers, built a 3-ton forward-control truck powered by a 16hp flat-four engine of their own design, with 4-speed epicyclic gearbox and shaft drive. After two years of experiments they decided not to put it into production. *GNG*

1914 BAKER (ii) 5-ton electric truck, OMM

BAKER (ii) (US) 1908-1916

(1) Baker Motor Vehicle Co., Cleveland, Ohio

(2) Baker, R & L Co., Cleveland, Ohio

One of America's best-known makers of electric passenger cars, Baker also made a variety of electric trucks. These ranged from 1000 lbs to 5 tons capacity, and all used double chain final drive. *GNG*

BAKER (iii) (US) 1926-1928

Baker Motors, Inc., Cleveland, Ohio

A steam-powered bus chassis was built by Baker Motors in 1926, featuring a five-cylinder rotary reciprocating engine and auxiliaries that were entirely powered by electricity. There is no record that a body was ever put on the chassis or that the vehicle was ever tested. In 1927, however, the Steam Appliance Corp. of America, also in Cleveland, announced a similar chassis called the "Steam Line," in which the rotary engine was identified as a "Rotobaker." This, or a modification of it, was still in existence in 1928, when it was displayed with a parlor car body, but nothing further was ever heard of it. *MBS*

BAKER-BELL (US) 1913-1914

Baker-Bell Motor Company, Philadelphia, Pa.

Small and light delivery vans were made by this manufacturer of passenger automobiles. Capacities of these closed vans are given as 500, 1000 and 1500 pounds. The smallest, with only 90-inch wheelbase and a friction transmission, weighed only 1000 pounds and was priced at $600. *GMN*

1914 BALACHOWSKY et CAIRE gas-electric truck, BHV

BALACHOWSKY et CAIRE (F) 1912-1914

Balachowsky et Caire, Paris

This company made gas-electric lorries and tractors with a 4-cylinder engine generating current, and Belgian ACEC electric motors in each wheel. Two- and four-wheel-drive versions were made, the latter being used by the French Army as a gun tractor in 1914. This had its engine under a hood, but earlier goods carrying versions had engines under the seat. Balachowsky *et* Caire also made a few trolleybuses. *GNG*

BANKS (US) 1923

Banks Motor Corporation, Louisville, Ky

This firm offered a line of carved hearses using their own chassis, and a Ford Model-T engine and transmission. *MCS*

BANTAM see American Austin

1939 BANTAM (American Austin) light pick up, NAHC

BANTAM (GB) 1932-1935

Bantam Carrier Co., Stevenage, Herts.

The Bantam was just one of a spate of small tri-vans which appeared during the Depression period. Built in the Vincent-HRD factory, two single cylinder models were offered initially, of 300cc and 250cc respectively and with a carrying capacity of 2½cwt. During the two final years of production the smaller model was dropped in favor of a 550cc single cylinder model with a pay load of 4cwt. *MJWW*

BARBER (US) 1917-1918

Barber Motors Corporation, Brooklyn, New York

The Barber was a tractor using a four-cylinder Buda engine with forward control. Its main feature was a differential-less worm-drive rear axle. This was practical only because of the very narrow 24-inch track for the hind wheels. Its price was $2500 and it was rated to pull a 12-ton load. *GMN*

BARBER-BUCHANAN (GB) 1905/1906

James Buchanan & Son, Liverpool

The Barber-Buchanan, designed by T.W. Barber, used a three-drum water tube boiler and duplicate compound engines, one to each rear wheel, to which it was connected by roller chain, the valves being push rod operated by a camshaft bevel driven from the crank-shaft. Other unusual features were internal expanding brakes to the rear wheels, sprung wheel centers and a fan-cooled condenser.

Though, in press releases, the makers gave glowing accounts of orders for Australia and South Africa the wagon seems to have defeated itself by combining too many innovations in one vehicle and inquiries suggest that it may not have progressed much beyond the prototype. *RAW*

BARCINO (E) 1960-1966

Talleres Metalurgicos Barcino, Barcelona

This company made delivery tricycles powered by engines of 125cc, 175cc and 197cc. The name is derived from that of Hamilcar Barca, the 3rd Century BC Carthaginian general who founded Barcelona. *JCG*

BARDON (F) 1903-1904

Automobiles Bardon, Puteaux, Seine

Bardons used horizontal opposed piston engines of Gobron-Brillie type with two pistons per cylinder. These drove two crankshafts which meshed with a transverse shaft. This engaged with a differential shaft to provide three speeds, and final drive was by chain. Most Bardons were passenger cars, but a few light vans were built on car chassis, and in 1904 there was a forward-control 3-ton truck powered by an engine of only 8hp. Surprisingly this used single chain drive, unlike the passenger cars which employed double chains. *GNG*

1960 BARKAS V901 pick-up, HON

BARKAS (DDR) 1954 to date

VEB-Barkas-Werke, Hainichen, Saxony

The former IFA Framo F9 light vans were sold under the Barkas name from 1954. A new 1-ton forward-control van, the B1000 came in 1961 and used the 3-cylinder engine employed in the Wartburg passenger cars. It is still made today, and various bodies including pick-up, minibus and ambulance are available. *HON*

BARKER (i) (US) 1912-1917

C.L. Barker Company, Norwalk, Connecticut

The sturdy-appearing Barker trucks had rated capacities ranging from 1000 pounds to 5 tons. In 1914, only a one-tonner was offered which used worm drive rather than the previous chain-drive. In 1915, this was joined by another of two-ton capacity on a wheelbase of 137 inches and a price of $2400. *GMN*

BARKER (ii) (US) 1911-1913

Barker Motors Co., N. Los Angeles, Cal.

Trucks under this name were limited to 3- and 5-tonners. Both used 40hp, four-cylinder engines and a common chassis with wheelbase of 150 inches. Stake, open express and closed van bodies were available in both capacities. There is no known connection with the earlier Barker built in Connecticut. *GMN*

BARON (GB) 1959-1969

Baron Motors Ltd., Boreham Wood, Herts.
Baron Motors Ltd., Far Cotton, Northampton.

The Baron was the culmination of seven years' market research and development by Peter Boulos, the Managing Director of the company. The intention was to produce a cheap, simple and rugged chassis specifically designed for underdeveloped countries, with Africa, Asia and the Middle East generally being the prime target. Two years after the project commenced in 1957, the first prototype was produced and production models followed in 1964. These consisted of 6 and 7-ton chassis designated the Master BN6 and Senior BN7 respectively, and these were also available as 38-44 seat p.s.vs. Powered by the Perkins 6.354 diesel, the Baron was an 'assembled' truck, buying out its frame from Rubery Owen, two speed axle from Eaton Yale and Towne and cab from Airflow Streamlines (as on the contemporary Commer).

It was planned to build only prototypes and c.k.d. kits in Britain for assembly abroad and larger trucks were intended although probably never built. The Baron was technically available abroad until 1969 but never sold in large numbers. *MJWW*

BARRAN (GB) 1865

Joseph Barran, Leeds, Yorks.

Barran designed a locomotive boilered overtype haulage engine with double cylinders and two road speeds. It was unusual for its time in being sprung. The engine had front steerage and the inventor's own arrangement of double rear wheels. Examples were used for a time for haulage in Leeds by Joseph Whitham & Sons and in California for moving copper ores. *RAW*

BARREIROS (E) 1958-1978

(1) Barreiros Diesel SA, Madrid 1958-1963
(2) Chrysler-Barreiros SA, Madrid 1963-1970
(3) Chrysler-Espana SA, Madrid 1970-1978

Eduardo Barreiros Rodriguez set up in business just after the Civil War converting gasoline engines to diesel, in Orense. In 1951 he transferred his works to Madrid and began to manufacture diesel engines, making his first complete vehicle in 1958. This was the Victor 6-tonner, which was followed by other medium-sized trucks under the names Halcyon, Condor, Azor and Super Azor Gran Ruta, the latter a tractor for trailer loads up to 16,000 kgs. Later came the Saeta light forward-control trucks in the 3000 to 4500 kgs range, and several models of military vehicles; these included the Comando 4x4 forward-control and the Panter 6x6 which came in conventional and forward-control form. The conventional Panter III was very similar in appearance to the U.S. Army 5-ton truck made by Kaiser Jeep and others, and these military models are still made today. Early civilian Barreiros trucks had cabs very similar to those of the contemporary Berliet, but new and more individual styles were developed during the 1960s, when the range covered the field from 2500 to 38000 kgs GCW as well as several sizes of bus. Barreiros continued to be a leading manufacturer of diesel engines which are often used as replacement units in older trucks of many makes, and were also supplied to Poland for use in the Star 21 range.

In December 1963 Barreiros became associated with the American Chrysler Corporation, and began to assemble Dodge and Simca passenger cars in addition to continuing their own trucks. The company name later became Chrysler Espana SA, though the trucks were called Barreiros until 1978. Another foreign link was with the British AEC company when a factory financed by Barreiros was built in the suburbs of Madrid to make AEC buses which were sold under the name Barreiros-AEC.

1963 BARREIROS Saeta 35 3000kgs truck, GNG

1964 BARREIROS Super Azor 16000kgs tanker, GNG

1969 BARREIROS Panter 6×6 military truck, OMM

1971 BARREIROS 26/26 17000kgs truck, GNG

Production began in 1961 and lasted until 1974 and included minibuses based on the Barreiros Saeta chassis in 4- and 6-cylinder form. Another bus venture was the Barreiros-Von Hool made in the former Nazar factory in Zaragoza. These had bodies by the Belgian Van Hool company with Barreiros engines and frames.

Current production consists of 22 models from 60 to 275 hp for GVWs from 13000 to 38000 kgs. The large tractor model K.3820P is sold in Britain under the Dodge name and in April 1978 it was announced that the name Barreiros would be dropped completely in favor of Dodge. *JCG*

1936 BARRO 36 seater coach, JCG

BARRO (E) 1930-1942

Barro Fabrica de Chavin, Vivero, Lugo

Jose Barro Gonzalez was a de Dion Bouton agent who built up a large business making spare and accessories, and also bus bodywork. In 1930 he began the construction of complete commercial vehicles with gasoline and later diesel, engines. During the Civil War he made munitions and military vehicles, and then resumed manufacture of commercial vehicles until 1942. *JCG*

BARRON-VIALLE (F) 1912-1937

(1) Automobiles Barron-Vialle, Lyons 1912-1929
(2) Automobiles Barron-Vialle, Arandon, Isere 1920-1937

Antoine Vialle, a coachbuilder from Tulle, transferred his works to Lyons in 1909. Three years later he was joined by A. Barron from Berliet, the partnership making a line of conventional chain-driven 4-ton trucks with 4-cylinder Ballot engines. These Barron-Vialles were offered with a variety of engine capacities from 2.8 up to 5.3 litres. Production continued through World War I, but was dropped in 1920 in favor of railway carriage repairs and (from 1923) the manufacture of private cars. Some guides, however, quoted Barron-Vialle trucks as still available during the 1920s, and with the demise of Gadoux's big luxury cars in 1929 the company concentrated their activities on Arandon, and attempted a commercial vehicle revival. The specialty was now a 30/55-seater bus chassis with all metal coachwork, but there was also a 7½-ton truck. Engines tried were a 65 hp 4-cylinder, a 115 bhp Continental Straight-8, and the Lilloise opposed-piston diesel, but by 1939 the Barron-Vialle's last home was a camp for Spanish Civil War refugees. *MCS*

BARROWS (US) 1927-1928

Barrows Motor Truck Co., Indianapolis, Ind.

The Barrows was a conventional shaft-driven truck powered by 4-cylinder engine with 4-speed gearbox. It was made in 1½, 2½ and 3½-ton sizes. *GNG*

1923 BARTON & RUMBLE 2½-ton truck, GB

BARTON & RUMBLE (CDN) 1917-1923

Barton & Rumble, London, Ont.

These trucks ranged from 1 to 5 tons in capacity, the biggest models featuring an enormous cast-iron radiator. Lycoming, and later, Hinkley engines were used. Production totaled about 50 trucks. *HD*

BASSAC see Citroen (ii)

B.A.T. (GB) 1929-1930

Harris & Hasell (1929) Ltd., Bristol

Harris & Hasell had been concessionaires for various makes of vehicles since 1914. They had been notably successful in marketing Reo passenger and — to a lesser extent — good vehicles, and this led them to design and assemble their own range of similarly-sized vehicles in their Bristol works. There were two models in the B.A.T. (British Associated Transport) range, both of which were assembled mainly from proprietory items. The Cruiser was a six-cylinder Continental-engined model designed to take 20-seat passenger bodies or a gross load not exceeding 2 tons 10 cwt, and the larger Super Pullman as a 32-seat passenger chassis powered by a straight-8 engine. Most of the production consisted of Cruisers which initially sold reasonably well, but the general depression quickly killed the project. *OM*

BATAVUS (NL) 1934-1962

Batavus Rijwiel-en Motorenfabriek, Oudeschoot

Batavus are bicycle and motorcycle manufacturers who introduced a pedal-driven 3-wheeled delivery vehicle called the 'trapcarrier' in 1930 and followed this with a powered version, the 'motorcarrier' in 1934. These were driven by various sizes of JLO engine from 48cc to 250cc as used in Batavus motorcycles. These had two wheels in front but another type of Batavus was the 'triffid' with single front wheel which also drove. Triffids were powered by single-cylinder engines of 60, 120, 145 and 250cc, the smallest having a tiller and the others wheel steering with a vertical colum. The 250 was available with a cab but the others were open, and more suited to works than street use. In 1960 came the 'elec-triffid' powered by a 4½ hp electric motor. Batavus stopped production of all 3-wheelers in 1962, but are still in business as bicycle manufacturers. *GNG*

1975 BATTRONIC electric van, BATTRONIC

BATTRONIC (US) 1964 to date

Battronic Truck Corp., Boyertown, Pa.

This firm, organized to manufacture electric delivery trucks, was backed by Boyertown Auto Body Works, Boyertown, Pa.; Smith Delivery Vehicles, Ltd., Gateshead-on-Tyne, England; and the Exide Division of the Electric Storage Battery Company. Exide supplied the batteries and motors, Smith supplied the chassis, and Boyertown supplied the all-steel forward control bodies and the assembly facilities. Smith withdrew its backing in 1966 and Exide followed in 1969. Battronic has since that time been a subsidiary of the Boyertown Auto Body Works.

Delivery of the first Battronic trucks was made in March 1964. The truck had a 2500-pound capacity, a top speed of 25 mph, and a range of 62 miles per charge. Later models could go more than 75 miles per charge. Since 1966 Battronic has been building its own chassis.

In 1971 Battronic listed four models: panel delivery van, 11 passenger suburban bus, 15 passenger transit bus, and 25 passenger transit bus. Advertising has emphasized the truck's self-contained power cell and rapid battery change-over arrangements. *DJS*

BAUER (US) 1914-1917

Bauer Machine Works Company, Kansas City, Missouri

Bauer trucks succeeded ones under the name of Gleason by the same manufacturer. The only models as Bauers were rated at 1000 and 1500 pounds capacity. Both used a four-cylinder engine, a wet clutch with a three-speed gearbox. All the components were manufactured in house. The prime feature of these light trucks was "double reduction drive." *GMN*

BAUMI (D) 1925

Baugesellschaft Michelsohn, Minden

This firm produced a 16 PS diesel road tractor in limited numbers. *HON*

BAYARD — CLEMENT

BEACH (GB) 1899

James Beach & Co., Taunton, Somerset

The Beach steam van, which weighed about 28½ cwt, had a small liquid fired vertical boiler at the front and a vertical 5 hp single-cylinder engine. Working pressure was 150 lbs. Two speeds, 5 and 10 mph respectively, were provided and gear changes were made by means of friction clutch. *RAW*

BEADLE (GB) 1945-1957

John C. Beadle (Coachbuilders) Ltd., Dartford, Kent

The old-established Beadle coachbuilding firm built an experimental aluminum alloy semi-chassisless (or integral) single-deck bus with Commer running units in 1945, followed in 1946/47 by three further vehicles powered by Leyland, Bedford and Dennis engines respectively. Following evaluation of these early integral vehicles, production commenced in earnest in 1948, most vehicles being supplied to companies in the state-owned Tilling group up to 1950. Service buses were of a most distinctive full-front design with slim pillars; coaches were less distinctive. Both front and underfloor-engined vehicles were produced, those in the former category employing new Bedford or Morris Commercial running units or second hand AEC and Leyland parts removed from pre-war vehicles. Underfloor-engined vehicles were originally built in conjunction with Sentinel; indeed a Beadle/Sen-

1899 BEACH steam van, Autocar

1948 BEADLE semi-chassisless bus, KCB

1955 BEADLE chassisless coach, NMM

tinel of this configuration which appeared at the 1948 Earls Court Show heralded the start of the trend towards the general use of underfloor-engined vehicles in the 1950s. From 1954 onwards extensive use was made of Commer units — including the TS3 two-stroke engine introduced earlier that year — reflecting the purchase of control of Beadle by the Rootes organization. By the time production ceased in 1957 over 500 Beadle integral buses and coaches had been built. *OM*

BEAN (i) (GB) 1924-1932

A. Harper, Sons and Bean Ltd., Tipton, Dudley, Staffs 1924-1925

Bean Cars Ltd., Tipton, Dudley, Staffs 1926-1932

The manufacturers of the Bean were a major motor components firm who adopted the pre-war 11.9 hp Perry car as a mass production project in 1919. A few vans and other light commercial vehicles were built on this chassis, and on the 14 hp car which followed in 1923. However their first serious attempt at commercial vehicles came at the end of 1924 when a 25 cwt chassis was announced which was loosely based on 3 vehicles produced in 1920 by a motor dealer in Glasgow, David Carlaw and Company, who had sold the concession to Harper, Bean. The Bean 25 cwt was intended as a direct rival to the Morris Tonner and equivalent American vehicles, and Harper, Bean

1929 BEAN (i) 2-ton van, MJWW

planned to produce 25,000 per year, a figure they never came anywhere near attaining.

The early commercial chassis used as many 14 hp car components as possible, including engine and in-unit gearbox, and had a spiral bevel back axle with only semi-floating half shafts. It was available with various types of commercial bodywork including 14 seat bus and 16 seat charabanc. A number was sold overseas, especially in Australia, where Bean had established a good reputation for their robust cars.

In 1926 Hadfields Ltd., steelmakers who had been involved in Bean's mass-production plans from the outset, took a controlling interest in the financially ailing Bean company. In an effort to strengthen their export sales, a heavier duty 30 cwt chassis appeared in 1927 which still used the 14 hp car engine, but now had a separate gearbox and fully floating worm back axle. It was considerably stronger than its predecessor and could be distinguished by a new cast-aluminum radiator. Later that year, Bean built a special passenger chassis using a 6-cylinder 3.8 litre engine evolved from the 14 hp engine, and this was also used in the Imperial Six export car. However it is doubtful whether the bus/coach ever entered production.

The 30 cwt or 14-20 passenger vehicle, and a cheaper 25 cwt version, were joined in 1929 by a 50 cwt Empire model using a 22.3 hp version of the 14 hp engine. In the same year Bean abandoned car production in favor of commercials, whose price they substantially reduced in an effort to increase sales. however in the depths of the Depression they were not successful, and despite an extra forward control 4-ton model in 1930 based on the Empire chassis and drastic reductions in price they went out of business in 1931.

The firm was once more reconstituted as a component maker and still exists as part of the Leyland Motor Corporation. *OM*

BEAN (ii) (US) 1973 to date

John Bean Divn., F.M.C. Corp., Lansing, Mich.; Tipton, Ind.

This company developed the 'fog system', a high pressure steam of water broken up into fine particles, during World War II. This equipment was mounted on a wide variety of commercial chassis and John Bean introduced their own cab-forward custom chassis in 1973. *GNG*

BEARDMORE (i) (GB) 1919-1967

(1) Beardmore Motors Ltd., Paisley, Dumbartonshire 1919-1933

(2) Beardmore Motors Ltd., London, N.W.9, 1933-1967

Beardmore was a large engineering concern with a

1923 BEARDMORE taxicab, NMM

1926 BEARDMORE 30cwt van, NMM

1958 BEARDMORE Paramount Mark VII taxicab, NMM

number of factories, making boilers, aero engines and complete aircraft. In 1919 they entered the taxicab market for which they acquired a factory at Paisley formerly occupied by Arrol-Johnston. This was only used for cab manufacture, Beardmore's contemporary passenger cars being made in Glasgow. The cab had a 2.4-litre 4-cylinder engine with detachable cylinder head, and a 4-speed gearbox. As a complete cab it cost $690 with electric lighting and starting, but it could be supplied as a chassis for the customer to choose his own coachwork. The Beardmore soon became one of the most familiar cabs in London and other cities, and apart from slight changes in appearance it was made without change until 1929. During this period goods chassis were also made using the same engine as the cabs, but with longer wheelbases of up to 11' 5". According to wheelbase, they were for 15 or 30 cwt loads. In 1929 a new cab known as the Hyper was announced. This took advantage of new Scotland Yard regulations in having a lower ground clearance and therefore more modern appearance. The engine was a slightly smaller unit of 1,954cc, and for the first time on a London cab, four wheel brakes were fitted. In 1933 the Hyper was replaced by a cheaper cab, the Paramount, and at the same time production was transferred from Paisley to London. Known as the 'Mark IV Paramount' (Marks I to III were the original Beardmores and the Hyper), the new cab had a 1,944cc 4-cylinder Rootes Group engine also used in Commer good vehicles and later in Hillman Fourteen and Humber Hawk cars. Four factory body styles were offered, single landaulet, three-quarter landaulet, four-light saloon and six-light saloon. The Paramount was gradually developed over the next seven years, the Mark V of 1936 having a longer wheelbase and lower appearance, and the Mark VI of 1937 introducing a synchromesh 4-speed gearbox.

Beardmore did not re-introduce a cab immediately after the war, but concerned themselves with selling the Wolseley-built Oxford cab. When production of this came to an end in 1953 they began development of a new design of their own, launched in 1954 as the Beardmore Mark VII. This had a 1,508cc 4-cylinder Ford Consul engine and 4-speed gearbox with steering column change. There was only on body style, a six-light saloon made by Windovers. In 1958 a Perkins Four-99 1,628cc 4-cylinder diesel engine was an alternative to the Ford gasoline unit. The Mark VII remained in production until the summer of 1967. A new design was planned to be known as the Mark VIII, but got no further than a model, and the rights of the design were acquired by Metropolitan Cammell Weymann whose Metrocab of 1970 showed some resemblance to the Mark VIII. Beardmore struggled on for two more years servicing existing Mark VIIs, but went into voluntary liquidation in July 1969. *GNG*

BEARDMORE (ii) (GB) 1936-1937

William Beardmore & Co. Ltd., Dalmuir, Dumbartonshire

In November 1936 another branch of Beardmores announced a new range of heavy trucks to be powered by Beardmore-built oil engines. Four models were listed, a two-axle 8-tonner powered by a 5,579cc 4-cylinder engine, a two-axle 6-cylinder model for a gross load of 13 tons with a full trailer, a 3-axle 13-tonner and a 4-axle 15-tonner, both the latter with 6-cylinder engines. They also announced that they would make single and double decker buses, but apart from a few of the 8-tonners it is not certain that any were made. They had forward control and all-welded steel frames. *GNG*

1930 BEARDMORE MULTIWHEELER python 15-ton tractor, OMM

BEARDMORE MULTIWHEELERS (GB) 1930-1932

Beardmore Multiwheelers Ltd., London SW4

The Chenard *et* Walcker road tractor for towing drawbar trailers had previously been assembled for the British market at the factory of Hall, Lewis and Co. Ltd., Maindy, Cardiff. It was exhibited at the 1929 Commercial Motor Show under its French name, but soon afterward manufacturing rights passed to a subsidiary of the well-known Scottish engineering firm of William Beardmore, who renamed the tractors Beardmore Multiwheelers. They increased the range and by the time of the 1931 Show were offering a version of the original 50 hp ten tonner, now with the model name Cobra, plus the Python for 10 to 15 tons and the 115 hp 6-cylinder Anaconda for 15 tons. The railway companies bought some of the smaller machines but the market for the heavier ones was dominated by articulated tractors of the Scammell type. In 1932 Beardmore disposed of their manufacturing license to Multiwheelers of Harrow, Middlesex who continued to make a few tractors with AEC, and Gardner engines before going over wholly to trailers during the Second World War. *OM*

BEARDSLEY (US) 1914-1915

Beardsley Electric Co., Los Angeles, Calif.

Trucks with this name were battery-powered electrics and were built as half- and one-tonners. These appear to have been sold only in southern California and further data is unavailable. *GMN*

BEAVER (i) (US) 1914-1915

Beaver State Motor Co., Portland, Ore.

The only data on this make of truck indicates it had a wheelbase of 112 inches a 28 hp, four-cylinder engine and the chassis sold for $2650. Other references indicate this manufacturer may also have built electric trucks but his is unverified. *GMN*

1920 BEAVER (ii) 1½-ton truck, GB

BEAVER (ii) (CDN) 1918-1923

(1) Beaver Truck Builders Ltd., Hamilton, Ont.

(2) Beaver Truck Corp. Ltd., Hamilton, Ont.

Produced by a company which claimed to be Canada's biggest truck builder at its peak, the Beaver was introduced as a 2-ton assembled vehicle. Later additions ranged from 1½ to 3 tons. A speed wagon was introduced for 1921, and was called the Beaver Bullet the following year. A specially-adapted model sold well among Niagara Peninsula fruit growers. *HD*

1950 BEAVER (iii) Model B-35PT bus, MBS

BEAVER (iii) (US) 1934-1956

(1) Beaver Transit Equipment Co., Beaver Falls, Ohio 1934-1935

(2) Beaver Metropolitan Coaches, Inc., Beaver Falls, Ohio 1935-1953

(3) National Coach & Manufacturing Co., Beaver Falls, Ohio 1955-1956

G.M. Davis, in charge of the Philadelphia sales office of ACF since 1928, went into the bus building business for himself in 1934, a depression year when an economical lightweight bus was demanded by most operators. Using a standard Ford front-engine commercial chassis, Traver Engineering Co. of Beaver Falls, Pa., built a prototype bus which was shown to city transit companies in the area. Response was good enough that a separate manufacturing company was soon organized. After a short time the original 83-inch-wide design was changed to permit installation of double seats on each side of the aisle, while gradual changes were also made in the exterior styling; the front engine and forward control arrangement were retained. Chevrolet and International power was optional.

The first rear-engine Beaver was announced in 1938, and soon a range of "pushers" was being offered with seating capacities from 20 to 35. An advertised virtue was the ease of replacing all body panels, which were of flat sheet metal except for the four roof corners. Postwar Beavers, basically unchanged, took on a more modern appearance with tilted windshields and optional sliding sash. A flood in 1953 damaged the factory and caused suspension of production, but in 1955 Davis (who had left the company earlier) and some associates acquired the enterprise and attempted to restart it without conspicuous success. Times had changed, and the sort of small-town low-budget bus operator who had formerly constituted Beaver's principal market had turned to second-hand diesel buses or else gone out of business entirely. Incomplete records suggest production and sale of just under 1000 Beaver buses from 1934 to 1956. *MBS*

BECK (i) (US) 1911-1921

(1) Cedar Rapids Auto Works, Cedar Rapids, Iowa 1911-1914

(2) Beck & Sons, Cedar Rapids, Iowa 1914-1916

(3) Beck Motor Truck Works, Cedar Rapids, Iowa 1917-1918

(4) Beck-Hawkeye Motor Truck Works, Cedar Rapids, Iowa 1918-1921

Initial models of this make included a two-tonner on a 10-foot wheelbase and an 18-passenger bus with a 40 hp engine on 130 inch wheelbase. For 1914, two- and three-tonners were added to the line. Late in 1914, a half-tonner was also made. The 1½-tonner for 1915 had wheelbase of 10 feet, 10 inches, solid rubber tires and a three-speed gearbox with double-reduction internal rear wheel drive. This model was continued to the end along with a one- and a 2½-tonner. *GMN*

1940 BECK (ii) Luxury Liner coach, MBS

BECK (ii) (US) 1934-1957

C.D. Beck & Co. Sidney, Ohio

C.D. Beck, a former salesman for the Fremont Metal Body Co., organized a consortium of dealers and operators to buy the Anderson Body Co. in 1932. Anderson had built bodies for the Willys-Knight automobile, which was discontinued during reorganization of Willys, but its first function under its new ownership was the construction of school bus bodies conforming to the unique regulations then in force in New York state. By 1934, a line of low-cost intercity and transit bus bodies with seating capacities from 12 to 33 passengers was being offered for stretched Chevrolet and Ford commercial chassis. A streamline

1957 BECK (ii) 'deck and a half' coach, MBS

"Airstream" body was offered in that year, and the Beck name was first used in connection with the "Fleetway," an 11-passenger sedan stretchout announced at the end of 1934.

Production of composite (wood-steel) bodies for intercity and transit use continued until new regulations dictated all-metal designs for intercity traffic. The "Steeliner," introduced in 1937, was Beck's most popular product and was produced until 1950. Integral Steeliners and Airstreams were introduced in 1938, and both body-on-chassis and integral buses were made until 1940. A rear-engine bus, the "Super Steeliner," and a low-priced version, the "Scout," appeared late in 1938 in imitation of the Yellow "Super Coach" for Greyhound, but fewer than 100 were sold.

These models were superseded in 1940 by the rear-engine 33-passenger "Mainliner" and more costly "Luxury Liner." Both 185 and 220-inch wheelbase versions of these buses were produced, and they competed with the larger FitzJohn and Aerocoach styles rather than with low-priced Flxibles. The usual engine was an International Red Diamond.

The War Production Board stopped Beck production at the end of 1942 after 420 integral buses had been built, but when the small plant was found unsuitable for war work, Beck was allowed to manufacture a modified version of the Mainliner with transit-type seats called the "Commuter Express." A new plant was opened in 1946, and in 1948 the Mainliner and Steeliner were replaced by new models of generally similar external appearance but with welded tubular body and chassis framing, an innovation pioneered earlier by Aerocoach. Production at this time was at the rate of about 150 buses per year.

In the 1950's there was a parade of new models produced in imitation of GM and Flxible designs, with full silversiding, picture windows, air suspension, and diesel power (Cummins) being added in response to demands. But in common with the other small makers of interecity coaches, Beck found that more and more of its output was destined for export, particularly to Cuba and Mexico. Domestic customers were attracted by the financing terms offered by the larger manufacturers, or else had become part of the expanding Greyhound and Trailways systems and were thus committed to certain bus types.

Beck acquired the Ahrens-Fox fire engine line in 1953 and transferred its production from Cincinnati to Sidney, and it was primarily to acquire the fire engine business that Mack Trucks bought Beck in 1956. A single production run of 25 Mack Cruisers was built at Sidney in 1958, and when this failed to attract much attention the plant was sold and fire engine production moved elsewhere. Total Beck bus production was approximately 3150 units.*MBS*

BECKMANN (D) 1905-1926

Otto Beckmann & Co., Erst Schlesische Veloციped-und Automobil-Fabrik, Breslau

The private cars of this make were the basis for some van versions, especially in the 1910-1914 period and during WWI. *HON*

BEDFORD (GB) 1931 to date

Vauxhall Motors Ltd., Luton, Beds 1931 to date: Dunstable, Beds 1954 to date.

The only series production commercial vehicles to bear the Vauxhall name were some ambulances made between 1935 and 1939 on their big 6-cylinder private-car chassis, though in 1905 the company experimented with an extraordinary 3-cylinder motor hansom on which the driver was perched above and behind his passengers.

The Bedford was created as a successor to the 6-cylinder Chevrolet trucks which General Motors had been assembling at their Hendon works since 1929, but though outwardly the original 2-tonner closely resembled a Chevrolet, there were some significant differences. The 3.2-litre 6-cylinder engine had four main bearings and full pressure lubrication, and there were four forward speeds to the Chevrolet's three. In other respects the vehicle typified American light-medium truck practice, with 6-volt coil ignition, 4-wheel mechanical brakes, and spiral bevel drive. Initially only the 2-tonner was listed, but by early 1932 the range was assuming classic shape, with the addition of a 12-cwt van using the smaller Vauxhall Cadet engine, a 30-cwt truck with single rear wheels, and a 14/20-seater PSV chassis which could be had with standardized coachwork by Duple (still closely associated with Bedford in 1978) for less than £600. Like their competitors, Bedford offered a wide range of 'off the peg' specialized bodywork — meat vans, cattle trucks, pantechnicons, a fire engine, and an ambulance on a modified 30-cwt chassis — but such variants as artics, rigid 6-wheelers and forward control trucks were left as yet to the specialist modifiers. 1933 saw the addition of a car-type 8-cwt van on the 1½-litre Vauxhall 12/6 chassis, with synchromesh gearbox. Few major modifications were made to Bedfords up to 1934, apart from the boosting of engine output from 44 to 57 bhp, but the make was immediately successful, sales rising from 12,850 in 1932 to 22,431 in 1935.

Meanwhile Vauxhall Motors had moved up into the 3-ton class with the Stepney Acres-designed WTS/WTL series, which was to serve as the prototype of all Bedford trucks for the next sixteen years. Unladen weight was kept below the British 50-cwt, 30mph class, and the only major mechanical alterations were more power and the provision of vacuum servo assistance for the brakes. The engine was, however, moved forward over the front axle, giving the characteristic short-hood look. The new range was soon extended to include a 26-seater coach chassis, and by 1936 the smaller 30-cwt and 2-ton models had fallen into line: mid-1938 saw not only the first of a catalogued series of Bedford-Scammell artics for payloads of up to 12 tons, but also much-improved 3½-litre, 72bhp engines. Another novelty of that year was a 5/6-cwt van, based on the 1.2-litre Vauxhall 10: the torsion-bar ifs and hydraulic brakes were retained, though the saloon's full unitary construction had given way to a separate X-braced chassis. Within a year the little van had been joined by a 10/12-cwt 4-cylinder model based on the bigger 12hp Vauxhall, and both models were available with specialized Utilecon (station wagon) conversions by Martin Walter. These and their successors were to be the

1934 BEDFORD 2-ton truck, NMM

1933 BEDFORD 8cwt van, NMM

1941 BEDFORD OY articulated tanker, MCS

nearest approaches to private cars offered under the Bedford name, and would lead to even more successful derivatives of the CA (1952) and HA (1964) series. On the eve of war the 1940 Bedfords were announced: appearance was much improved by new streamlined cabs with vee windshields, but more important were the standardization of hydraulic brakes and the addition of a 5-tonner to the range.

Vauxhall's contribution to the British war effort ran to close on 250,000 trucks. Of these, the 15-cwt MW, 30-cwt OX, and 3-ton OY were developments of civilian themes, notable for their angular shovel noses and heavy-duty integral front bumpers, but the Q-type, also a 3-tonner,

1943 BEDFORD QLD 4×4 army truck, NMM

was the Army's most successful wartime 4x4 truck as well as the first factory-built Bedford with full forward control. The company also made the now-universal jerrican, and was responsible for the development, in record time, not only of the Churchill tank, but also of its 21.3-litre 350bhp flat-12 engine. Another wartime experiment was the Traclat, a heavy halftrack troop-carrier on German lines, powered by twin 6-cylinder engines. From 1941 onwards there was also some civilian production of OYs and of the OWB 26-seater bus with austere slatted wooden seats. These latter found favour with schedule operators as well as in the coach business, and by 1951 no fewer than 86

1947 BEDFORD 10/12cwt van, NMM

1948 BEDFORD OB coach, NMM

1951 BEDFORD 30cwt truck, NMM

Bedfords were owned by municipal bus companies alone, though the later tendency towards larger one-man PSVs has tended to reverse this trend since the late 1950s.

The half millionth Bedford was delivered in 1947, but for the first five years of peace production was centered on what amounted to the 1940 lines,from the light vans (with steering-column shift from 1948) to the 5 ton truck and the Bedford-Scammell artics. Nothing new apeared until the 1950 Commercial Vehicle Show, when the 7 ton Big Bedford marked the first upward move for the company. This vehicle featured full forward control, with a new and more powerful 7-bearing 4.9-litre engine developing 110bhp; other improvements were synchromesh gearboxes (the British opposition was still wedded to the crash-type) and hypoid back axles. Brakes, initially hydro-mechanical, soon received full hydraulic actuation, and parallel models were a PSV chassis (Type SB) and a 4x4 truck (Type-R), the latter being commercially available from late 1952, and surviving until 1969.

The next two seasons were to see the replacement of all the pre-War designs. Early in 1952 came a new light van, the 10-cwt semi-forward control CA with sliding doors, which set a fashion and sold well over 350,000 units in a 17-year run. The specification featured ifs and hypoid rear

1952 BEDFORD CA 10/12cwt van, NMM

1954 BEDFORD 7-ton livestock truck, NMM

1956 BEDFORD A3 4-ton truck, NMM

axle, and in Britain at any rate the vehicle became indelibly associated with mobile homes like Martin Walter's Dormobile, which had reached full sleeper status by 1957. The CA was progressively developed, acquiring synchromesh on all forward gears in 1957, a long-wheelbase 15-cwt sister in 1959, and 4-speed and diesel options (the latter, inevitably, by Perkins) in 1961. Finally the normal control line (30-cwt to 5 tons) was updated in 1953, with single unit cabs and modernized front-end styling, plus the synchromesh and (on heavier duty types) hypoid axles of the Big Bedford. At the same time the company, which had hitherto left dieselisation to outside firms (Leyland and Albion units had found their way into 7-tonners during 1952) now offered Perkins engines as factory-fitted options on 4-ton and heavier types. Production passed the 60,000 mark in 1955, by which time the Dunstable plant was in full operation as a manufacturing unit, and the range included a variety of fire engines based on the Big Bedford and SB chassis, with equipment by such firms as Miles, Carmichael and H.C.B.

New for 1957 were 4 to 6-ton variations on the Big Bedford forward control theme, as well as a normal control 6-tonner; at the same time Vauxhall Motors started to make their own diesel engines of direct injection type, first of these being a 4.9-litre 97bhp six, followed a year later by a 3.3-litre four for machines in the 30-cwt-3-ton class; for the time being heavier-duty oil engines were still bought from Perkins and eventually from Leyland. Other new options were 5-speed gearboxes and 2-speed rear axles, while in 1959 the medium-duty range was augmented by low-loader chassis on 16-in wheels. 1960 saw an American style pickup, the JO powered by the 2.7-litre Vauxhall Velox car engine.

The millionth Bedford came off the line in May, 1958; the second million would take barely ten years to achieve, thanks to a steady extension of the range to challenge the efforts of the big bespoke truck makers. Bedford had broken the 100,000 mark for the first time in 1960, and that year's Commercial Vehicle Show saw a new forward control range with wrap round screens, conventionally mounted engines, and lateral access doors to these which were preferred to tilt cabs. These TKs also featured transmission handbrakes and (on the heaviest models) air-hydraulic brakes. Initially the TKs covered only the traditional Bedford spectrum — payloads in the 3½-7-ton bracket — but over the ensuing years the range would be extended both upwards and downwards. First came the bulk-load tippers of 1965, catering for GVWs of up to 12¼ tons and powered by the 6.5-litre 6-cylinder Leyland diesel engine. Then in 1966 there were low-loading urban types for 30-cwt and 2-ton payloads distinguished by front disc brakes, while 1967 saw the KM heavy-duty family, which raised GVWs to the 16-ton mark, and introduced users to Bedford's own big 466 diesel, a 7.6-litre six developing 145bhp. Two years later the company, who had hitherto left rigid 6-wheelers to outside enterprise (Reynolds Boughton already marketed a range of TK conversions), introduced their own 6x2s and 6x4s with 466 engines, 5-speed gearboxes and air brakes. It was not surprising that by 1969 Bedford could claim a 24 per cent share of home market sales in the over 2-ton category, as well as being the world's biggest truck exporters with over 45,000 vehicles sold abroad during the year. Finally in 1970 the old R-type 4x4 (of which 73,135 had been made) gave way to an all-wheel drive TK derivative, the M.

1963 BEDFORD VAL Topaz coach, bodywork by M.C.W.

There were other improvements. The normal control range was updated in 1964 to become the TJ series, and in the same year Vauxhall's return to the small car field with the 1,057cc Viva sedan led to a Bedford derivative, the HA, initially for 6-cwt payloads but available in 10-cwt form by the early 1970s. Bus development continued, the faithful SB being joined by the short-wheelbase (13ft 6in) VAS with a choice of 3½-litre gasoline or 4.9-litre diesel 6-cylinder engines, braking being hydrovac on the former or air-hydraulic on the latter. Even more ambitious was the 6x2 twin-steer VAL of 1963, a 36-footer for 55 passengers, with power steering and 5-speed gearbox, it used the 131bhp 6-cylinder Leyland diesel engine. For 1966 the range was rounded out by a conventional full-fronted 41/45-seater, the VAM.

When the CA disappeared at the end of 1969, the proprietary diesel engines went with it; the new 62bhp 4-cylinder diesel option in the CF series was a Vauxhall product, as were the 1.6-litre and 2-litre gasoline units with their cogged-belt drive ohc. In other respects the CF, though entirely new and heavier (payload range was 14 to 35 cwt) inherited such CA features as ifs, all-synchromesh gearboxes, and hypoid rear axles. Automatic transmission was a regular option by 1973, when the most powerful gasoline engine offered ran to 2.3 litres and 94bhp. With the YRT bus chassis of 1970 Bedford broke new ground again, for their amidships mounted engine was a vertical affair, slung inside the frame. This one was available by 1973 in 10-meter and 11-meter forms with the Bedford 466 engine, 5-speed gearbox, air brakes.

Meanwhile the company was moving slowly up to the maximum load class. Already in 1971 Australian buyers could specify the 195bhp 7-litre 2-stroke V6 Detroit Diesel, with 10-speed Fuller Roadranger gearbox and 2-

1974 BEDFORD KM 16-ton GVW truck, Bedford

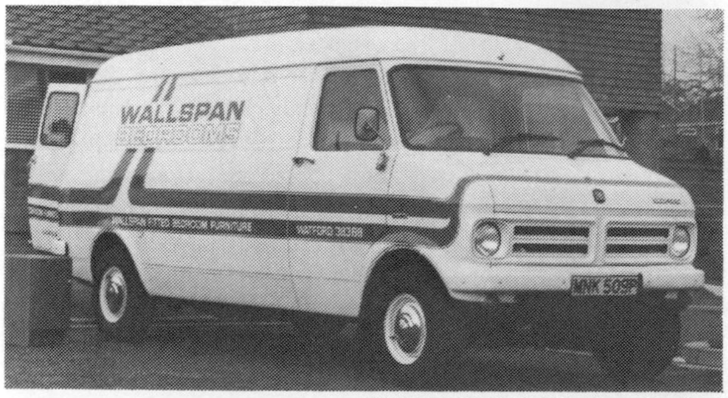

1978 BEDFORD CF 25cwt van, Bedford

speed back axle, in local versions of the KM tractor, and by 1973 such a combination had reached England, complete with dual-circuit air brakes, an air-assisted handbrake, and power steering. The next logical step came at the 1974 Show, when Bedford unveiled their forward control TM range, with short, American-style tilt cabs, Bedford-built Detroit Diesel engines, servo-assisted twin-plate clutches, 9-speed rangechange gearboxes, power steering and air brakes with spring handbrakes. An infinite variety of 4x2s, 6x2s, 6x4s and tractive units covered GVWs of up to 24 tons and GCWs of as much as 32 tons. During 1975 there would be further TM variants using conventional 8.2-litre 4-stroke Bedford 6-cylinder power units and a military 4x4 version featuring the same unit in turbocharged 202bhp form would appear in 1977, by which time the biggest tractors had GCW ratings of over 40 tons, and there was a 44-tonner variant with 380bhp V8 Detroit Diesel and sleeper cab aimed exclusively at the Italian market.

By 1976 the normal control TJ had at long last disappeared, and a year later a demand for a more civilized delivery van was met with the Chevanne, based on the

1978 BEDFORD TM4400 44-tonne GCW articulated truck, Bedford

Vauxhall Chevette sedan. It used the same 53bhp 1.3-litre ohv engine and servo-assisted front disc brakes, though the old HA was continued in derated 42 bhp form. Trials were made with battery-electric conversions of the CF range, while announced in 1977 (though not as yet regularly catalogued) was the JJL, a unitary construction bus evolved in association with Marshalls of Cambridge. The 5.4-litre 6-cylinder diesel engine and its Allison automatic gearbox were mounted at the rear, and brakes were air-hydraulic. In addition to the two light vans and the biggest TMs, the 1978 range embraced petrol and diesel-powered CFs for payloads from 18 to 35 cwt, forward-control Ks in 4x2 and 6x2 forms (the latter included a twin-steer chassis) with GVWs in the 5½-16-ton bracket, and tractor versions with parallel GCW ratings: gasoline engines were confined to the lighter types. In addition there were the four-wheel-drive Ms for 11-ton GVWs, and four bus chassis, of which the YLQ and YMT featured underfloor-mounted engines. Bedfords were being assembled in 20 countries, those produced in Pakistan having been marketed under the Rocket name since 1971. In Argentina, where actual manufacture of TJ range had ceased in 1965, 6-cylinder Bedford diesel engines were still being built for installation in local versions of the Chevrolet truck. Bedford mechanical elements formed the basis of such light commercials as the Malaysian Harimau (discontinued in that country after 1977, but still under development as a Basic Transport Vehicle) and the Uruguayan Grumett. Among former chassis makers who have used Bedfords as the basis for specialist conversions are Merryweather (fire engines) and Lacre and Lewin (municipal vehicles).*MCS*

BEECH CREEK (US) 1915-1917

Beech Creek Truck & Auto Co., Beech Creek, Pa.

The Beech Creek was a 3-ton four-wheel-drive-and-steer truck powered by a 29 hp 4-cylinder P.M.E. engine. Just two trucks were completed, although at least two others were started.The company survived until 1920 as an automobile agency; despite the firm's name no automobiles were built. *DJS*

BEERS (NL) 1933-1950

Adr. Beers N.V., Rijswijk.

Adriaan Beers, for many years the Dutch distributor of the American Diamond T chassis and various other makes (Chenard & Walcker, Berliet, to name a few), also manufactured a few own vehicles. In 1933 the Beers Floating Tractor chassis was shown during the Amsterdam Motor Show, fitted with a Kromhout-Gardner 4LW oil engine. This tractor could also be had with a semi-trailer carrying a bus body, and was in this version sold as Beers Floating Pullman. The Floating Tractor received in 1934 a Dorman-Ricardo 40UR engine. New in this year was the Tramcoach Type A, with a lightweight cross-section frame and a Hercules gasoline engine.

After World War II Beers tried again to establish themselves as commercial vehicle manufacturers with the Handyvan, a walk-through van with front-wheel-drive and either a 4- or 6-cylinder gasoline engine. However, only a few vehicles were manufactured, mainly for the municipality of The Hague. *JFJK*

B.E.F. (D) 1907-1913

Berliner Electromobil-Fabrik GmbH., Berlin

The electric motor of this threewheeled van was

1914 B.E.F. electric 3-wheel van, HON

mounted above the single front wheel, which was driven. The box-van was very popular for city deliveries and the postal authorities ordered a good number of this version. *HON*

BEKAMO (D) 1926-1928

Bekamo Vertriebgesellschaft Donath & Co. oHG., Berlin W 57

In 1926 this firm presented a tri-van following the pattern of the time with two front wheels and front mounted box or platform and one single rear driven wheel and rear driver's seat. But as a variation a version with two rear wheels was also available. *HON*

BELGA (B) 1968

Etn. J. Avonds, Mortsel-Antwerp

The Belga was a battery-electric truck, assembled by Jos Avonds, one of the largest truck importers in Belgium, from foreign parts. Only one prototype was built, but there still are plans for small-scale production at a later date. *JFJK*

1972 BELAZ 540 dump truck, BE

BELAZ (SU) 1959 to date

Byelorussian Motor Works — Zhodino

Some of the Soviet Union's largest trucks emanate from the BeLAZ Works, which first produced model 525 in 1959 as a version of the MAZ-525, 25-ton dumper. This was built under the MAZ name only.

Under the BeLAZ name, the 540 half-cab 4x4, 30-ton dumper for rock quarry use was presented about 1965. The 'A' version currently features a JAMZ-240 V-12 diesel of 360 hp with a 3-speed hydro-mechanical gearbox, 55 km/h. The standard 540 is offered with a tank engine of 375 hp.

A 40-ton 4x4 dumper for open cast workings, the 548, is built with a 560 hp (SAE) V-12, power steering and pneudraulic suspension. The dumper bed can be heated by exhaust gases to facilitate dumping in winter. Many parts of these models are interchangeable.

Modified 'C' versions for northern regions are offered

and models 540B and 548B are built as semi-tractors.

BeLAZ-7525 is a 40-ton coal truck, built since 1972, and BeLAZ-549 is a 75-ton dumper with a 900 hp engine.

BeLAZ-256B, a dumper sold in England, appears to be a KRAZ unit exported under the BeLAZ name. *BE*

1914 BELHAVEN 3-ton truck, OMM

BELHAVEN (G.B.) 1906-1924

(1) Robert Morton & Sons Ltd., Wishaw, Lanarkshire.
(2) Belhaven Engineering & Motors Ltd., Wishaw, Lanarkshire.

The Belhaven 'parent' company, Robert Morton & Sons, dates from 1879, but the Belhaven company was formed to take over the wagon building business of the parent. An experimental steam vehicle was built in 1906, and a Morton steam bus operated on the Glasgow-Eaglesham route. Belhaven steamers employed water tube boilers with compound undertype engines, mostly with rubber tires and based on the Lifu patents and designs. Both wagons and buses were built, the wagons being mainly the lighter type of about 2 tons capacity.

After the company took over the Allanton Foundry in 1907, production of 2-cylinder Aster-engined taxi cabs and light trucks commenced in 1908, and from 1910 these were dropped in favor of heavier, chain driven petrol engined trucks, buses (as used by Perth Corporation) and charabancs. Production of steam vehicles, always limited, was phased out prior to the 1914-18 war, during which some gasoline engined trucks were supplied to the War Department. After the war, production was resumed with a 30/35 hp 4-cylinder 3 ton chassis with chain and spurgear final drive, on some of which passenger vehicles were built, others being supplied to the Scottish Co-operative Wholesale Society as the basis for the latter's Unitas trucks. Some of these were also operated by the United Co-operative Baking Society. Heavy competition forced the closure of the vehicle building plant in 1924, but the company survives to this day as the Morton Machine Company Ltd. *MJWW*

BELL (i) (G.B.) 1905-1918

Bell Bros, Ravensthorpe, Yorks.

Bell vehicles were rarely encountered outside their native Yorkshire and although, initially, a wide range of private cars was offered, production was always limited. Of these, the 2½-litre 16 hp model found favor as a taxicab and a few good vehicles were also built for local operators on the 20 and 30 hp worm-drive chassis. Production of a range of 1 ton, 30cwt and 3 ton trucks was prevented by the 1914-18 war, and in 1919 the Manchester-based Co-operative Wholesale Society Ltd. purchased all the designs and patterns for both cars and commercials. All vehicles subsequently produced by the C.W.S. were known as C.W.S. Bell. *MJWW*

BELL (ii) (US) 1913-1915

Bell & Waring, Yonkers, N.Y. 1913
Bell & Waring Steam Vehicle Co., Yonkers, N.Y. 1914
American Motor Freight Co., Yonkers, NY 1913
Bell Locomotive Co., Yonkers, NY 1913

This was one of the very few American steam trucks built after 1910 and was a massive vehicle with dump body capacities up to six tons. The steam engine which powered these trucks had two double-acting cylinders with bores of 4.5 inches and stroke of 6.5 inches. The manufacturer's name is a matter of confusion, being listed four different ways in a two year period. *GMN*

BELL (iii) (US) 1915-1918

Bell Motor Car Co., York, Pa.

Bell turned out a 1200-pound delivery truck on their touring car chassis. The truck, priced at $775 in 1915, had a 19.6 hp Lycoming 4-cylinder engine and bevel drive. A 1½-ton truck was announced in early 1918 but truck production ceased at the close of that year. Automobiles were built until 1923. *DJS*

BELL (US) (iv) 1919-1923

Iowa Motor Truck Co., Ottumwa, Iowa

The objective of H. L. Bell, president of the company, was to sell the trucks primarily to farmers in Iowa, Nebraska, Colorado, and the Dakotas. The Ottumwa location was chosen because the electric power of the dam in the Des Moines river was economical, labor conditions were better than in the east, and four railroads provided excellent transport facilites.

Bell truck production started April 1, 1919 and reached 15 trucks per month by August. They were quite handsome in their day with good proportions all around. In this era it became fashionable to attach several bright bars (6 for Bell) in front of the radiator enhancing the appearance.

Of conventional layout, the Bell's frame was made by the company of 6-inch channel steel with 5-inch crossmembers. The frame extended well in front of the radiator, serving as a bumper, a somewhat uncommon feature.

The rest of the truck was of assembled units, using a Buda 4-cylinder engine (4¼ x 5½), and final drive was through a Russell internal gear rear axle. Solid tires and artillery wheels were standard.

1920 Bell prices were $2000 for the 1½-ton model for the Iowa short-haul market, and $2650 for the 2½-ton model for the Colorado long-haul market. Regular equipment included crescent cab, driver's seat, cushions, windshield, storm curtains, sidelamps, taillamps, and klaxon horn. Pneumatic tires were optional. Later, a 1-ton model was also offered. *RW*

BELLABEY see Dufour

1912 BELSIZE 14½-litre fire engine, GNG

BELLISS & MORCOM (G.B.) 1907

Belliss & Morcom Ltd., Islington, Birmingham.

Belliss & Morcom were the successors of Richard Bach who made the first Boydell wheeled traction engine in 1854 but their work was chiefly in fixed steam engines and generator sets.

However in 1907 they manufactured a double-decked steam bus, not dissimilar to the Darracq-Serpollet, using a front-mounted semi-flash boiler, undertype compound engine and twin chain final drive. Frank Searle encouraged the L.G.O.C. to licence the bus for experimental running in London between December 1907 and the autumn of 1908, which included, variously, the routes from Hammersmith to Canning Town, Acton to Bow Bridge and Victoria to Cricklewood but the company were not sufficiently impressed by its performance to retain the bus and nothing was heard of it after 1908. *RAW*

BELMONT (US) 1919-1923

Belmont Motors Corp., Lewistown, Pa.

The Belmont was an undistinguished truck made of assembled parts. In 1920 1500-pound and 1½-ton models priced at $1,150 and $1,950 were offered. Both used the 26 hp Continental 4-cylinder engine. The Belmont factory became a sales and service branch for the Kearns truck in early 1924. *DJS*

BELSIZE (GB) 1906-1925

Belsize Motors Ltd., Manchester

The first Belsize car appeared in 1901, and the company was well-established when commercial vehicles joined the range five years later. The first of these was a fire engine with a 4-cylinder 40 hp engine and the unusual feature of double tires on front as well as rear wheels. Like most subsequent Belsize fire appliances its equipment was by John Morris & Sons Ltd., of Salford, and it was delivered to the London fire brigade. In 1907 a 10 cwt van was made on the 20 hp 4-cylinder car chassis, and this was followed by vans and taxicabs with 14/16 hp engines. Taxis remained an important part of Belsize's commercial vehicle output up to the end of production in 1925.

1907 BELLIS & MORCOM steam bus, Bellis & Morcom

In 1911 a shaft-driven 3-ton truck with 28 hp 4-cylinder engine appeared, this being also made with charabanc bodywork. Some very large fire engines with 50/80 hp 14½-litre power units were made between 1911 and 1914, by which dates the goods range had been extended to include 30 cwt and 3-tonners. The smallest was a 5 cwt light van on the popular 10/12 hp Belsize car chassis. The post-war range was considerably reduced, consisting only of vans and taxicabs with 20 hp 4-cylinder engines. *GNG*

BENDIX (US) 1908-1909

The Bendix Company, Chicago, Illinois

The Bendix was a high-wheeler and rather spindly in appearance, despite its rated capacity of up to 2400 pounds. These closed vans were powered by four-cylinder engines and used friction transmissions with chain-drive to each rear wheel. Wheelbases ranged up to 110 inches. *GMN*

1965 BENELLI 3-wheel truck, GNG

BENELLI (I) 1930-c.1970

Fratelli Benelli Spa, Pesaro

This motorcycle factory was early in the field with a light commercial 3-wheeler on class is Italian lines, with motorcycle-type front end and two shaft-driven rear wheels. Pre-War models used 500cc single-cylinder 4-stroke engines, but on the post-War edition a 5bhp 124cc 2-stroke was featured, together with a 4-speed gearbox. By the 1960s enclosed cabs were provided. *MCS*

BENTALL (GB) 1908-1913

E. H. Bentall & Co. Ltd., Heybridge, Maldon, Essex.

Founded in 1792, Bentalls were (and still are) primarily agricultural engineers, and only about 100 Bentalls of any kind were produced. In addition to private cars, however, the company did offer a commercial traveler's brougham and a 10cwt trademens van on the 11hp chassis, examples of each being shown at Olympia in 1908. Both utilized a 2-cylinder vertical engine. A taxi-cab was also made on the same chassis but none of the vehicles achieved currency outside the immediate area of the factory. *MJWW*

BENZ (D) 1894-1926

(1) Benz & Co. Rheinische Gasmotorfabrik, Mannheim 1894-1899

(2) Benz & Cie. Rheinische Gasmotorenfabrik AG., Mannheim 1899-1911 (3) Benz & Cie. Rheinische Automobil-und Motorenfabrik AG, Mannheim 1911-1926

Carl Benz is known as the first man who realized with lasting success the idea of a self-propelled vehicle. A Benz car, a model "Victoria" of 1894 became the first van in the history of the automobile. It was put into service by a coffee-trading firm as a "salesman and delivery car." As a variation of the 5 hp. "Landauer" the first motor omnibus was created in 1895 which ran the world's first motor bus line Siegen — Netphen — Deuz in Western Germany. Although this line lasted for only 9 months it was a remarkable step. One year later the first vans and trucks were built, showing some resemblance to Benz' car models with rear mounted engine, mainly "Victoria" and "Velo". A new design of a truck with front-mounted underfloor engine was realized in 1900 with 6 hp engine and a load capacity of 1.25 tons. This one was supplemented by a 2.5 ton (10 hp) and a 5 ton type with 2-cylinder 14 hp engine. All models were driven by belts and chains to the rear axle. There were no further remarkable developments in the following years.

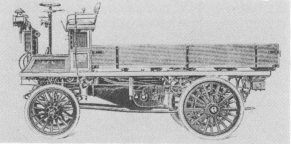

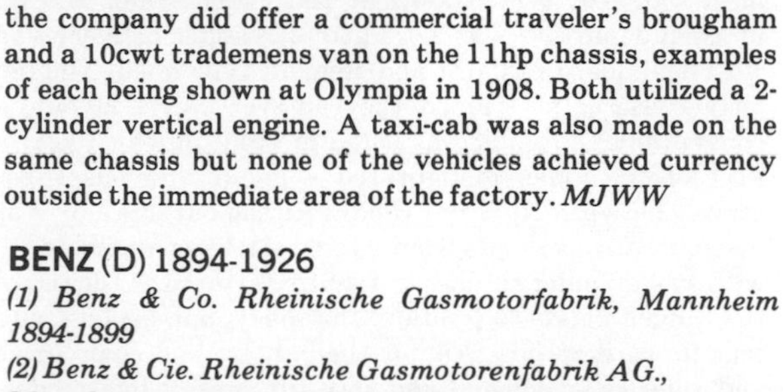

1901 BENZ 6hp truck, NMM

1919 BENZ 1½-ton truck, NMM

In 1910 Benz bought the "Suddeutsche Automobil-Fabrik" of Gaggenau (vide SAF) and from this date the production of commercial vehicles was concentrated here. A wide range of types was offered from ½ ton to 6 ton payload which were available as vans, trucks and buses and for special purposes as municipal vehicles and fire engines.

An epochal development took place after the end of WW I. Benz built their first diesel engines following the pre-combustion-chamber principle developed by Prosper L'Orange. By 1923 the first diesel engines were used for Benz-Sendling agricultural tractors. Consequently they were developed for use in trucks and after a few prototypes of 1923 the world's first diesel engine truck was presented at the Amsterdam Motor Show of 1924. The 4-cylinder engine developed 50 bhp at 1,000 rpm. It was used for a 5 ton chassis with cardan drive.

After the merger of interests between Benz and Daimler the development stagnated as also Daimler had started with diesel experiments and no decision could be reached between the partners which was the right way. Benz built a line of gasoline-engined trucks of 1.5, 2, 3 and 5 ton with engines ranging from 25 to 36 hp. A remarkable development was the "low chassis" version of 1924 with forward control and available as truck, bus and for special purposes, e.g. refuse collectors.

The merger of both companies brought the end of Benz production. For further developments see Mercedes-Benz. *HON*

BERGDOLL (US) 1910-1913

Louis J. Bergdoll Motor Car Company, Philadelphia, PA

Light delivery vans were offered by Bergdoll on their essentially unmodified passenger car chassis. These chassis, priced at $1600, used a four-cylinder engine with inlet-over-exhaust valves. For the same years, one model was termed a taxi but appears to differ not at all from the contemporary Bergdoll town car or landaulet. *GMN*

BERGMANN; BERGMANN-METALLURGIQUE (D) 1907-1939

Bergmann Elektrizitatswerke Akt. Ges., Berlin

At first electric driven vans and trucks were built with chain or cardan drive. They were marketed also under the name "Fulgura". In 1909 license production of Metallurgique cars was taken up and gasoline-driven vans and trucks ranging from 350 kg to 4 tons and buses supplemented the electric vehicles. Also after WW I —

1935 BERGMANN electric van, HON

1939 BERGMANN electric van, OMM

during which the licenses were given up — production of gasoline trucks was carried on and lasted until 1922. But electric vehicles were the backbone of the production. The heaviest type was a two-motored 5-ton truck. A 2 ton van was very widely used by the mail for parcel delivery. Production was carried on until the outbreak of WW II in 1939. *HON*

1906 BERKSHIRE 3-ton truck, GMN

BERKSHIRE (US) 1906-1907

Berkshire Automobile Co., Pittsfield, Mass.

This manufacturer built several open delivery vans using modified passenger car chassis, then offered a three-tonner with forward control, 3-speed gearbox and double chain-drive. Very few of these were built. *GMN*

BERLIET (F) 1902 to date

(1) Automobiles M. Berliet, Lyons 1902-1977
(2) Automobiles M. Berliet, Blainville, Ain 1964-1977

1913 BERLIET CBA 4-ton truck, Berliet

(3) Renault Vehicules Industriels, Lyons and Blainville, Ain 1977 to date

Though his firm was to become France's biggest builders of heavy goods vehicles, Marius Berliet confined his interests to private cars until 1902, when a light chain-drive delivery van was catalogued. An experimental driver-over-engine 2-tonner, also chain driven, with wood wheels and iron tires made its appearance in 1906, and a year later similar models were on sale, with 6.3-litre 4-cylinder T-head engines and 4-speed gearboxes. An early customer was Bristol Tramways, who ordered Berliet buses in 1907. Predictably, a cab was the next arrival: it had a 2.4-litre engine and is of interest as the first shaft-driven vehicle marketed by the company. By 1909 the range embraced trucks from 30cwt to 4 tons, a ventilated meat van had been shown at the Paris Salon, and an unusual departure was a 1.2-litre 2-cylinder delivery van with dashboard radiator and Renault-type hood. Though heavier Berliets retained the cab-over-engine layout, a conventional 2-tonner was listed in 1911, in which year a fleet of the make inaugurated a goods and passenger service between Nice and Evian. At the outbreak of War machines for payloads from 1 to 6 tons were available, all with sv 4-cylinder engines (a 4.4-litre featured at the top of the range), magneto ignition, thermosyphon cooling, and four forward speeds. All but the lightest had chain drive and solid tires; normal and forward control bus models could accommodate up to 30 passengers. Berliet buses were in service in Marseilles and Annecy as well as in Lyons. Between 1905 and 1913 the make had been built under license in the U.S.A. by the American Locomotive Co., trucks and taxicabs being produced as well as private cars. This connection was to be commemorated by the locomotive emblem used on later Berliets.

The company's war effort centered round the CBA, a chain-driven normal control 4/5-tonner with 5.3-litre engine, of which more than 25,000 were made: latterly,

1921 BERLIET ¾-ton pick up, Berliet

1926 BERLIET VMPG producer gas bus, Berliet

Renault tanks were added to the programme. In 1919 Berliet plunged into a two-model range, based on the American-type VB car (and its light truck derivatives), with the faithful CBA representing the heavy goods sector. Unfortunately the VB suffered from teething troubles, while a glut of war-surplus vehicles prevented the firm from selling the 40 CBAs it could make daily. Receivership followed in 1921, but already the VB's more reliable successors had been evolved into 15- and 30-cwt vans with 3.3-litre sv monobloc 4-cylinder engines, spiral bevel final drive, and pneumatic tires, and the range was steadily expanded. By 1926 it covered everything from a 7-cwt van on the little VI car chassis up to chain-driven 7½-tonners. Chain drive continued on a diversity of CBA derivatives, but further down the range worm or double-reduction bevel back axles were finding favor. All 1927 Berliets up to the 4-ton category came with pneumatic tires as standard, but forward control had gone out of fashion, being found only on a few bus chassis, notably the GSB and GSD of 1924/27.

Variety was infinite. All-wheel drive types were produced to military account from 1924 onwards, these including a rear-engined 4x4 command car in 1928, and some front-engined 6x6s. As early as 1921, a worm-driven 25-seater bus chassis with a monobloc edition of the CBA engine had made its appearance, and by 1927 there was a high-speed coach chassis, the VKR, which marked the first use of a 6-cylinder engine in a Berliet commercial. This unit was a 4.1-litre side-valve, but three years later the company's bigger 8-litre type was going into coaches, including some 6-wheeled sleepers. 6-cylinder engines were also fitted to the first 6-wheeler trucks, chain-driven 6x2s for 10/12-ton payloads. Like other French makers, Berliet started to take an interest in gazogenes in 1924, using the Imbert system: these were catalogued items in 1927. In 1924/27 there was also a comprehensive range of electrics, from taxicabs to a 30-seater bus. The small ones were hard to distinguish from i.c-engined delivery vans, and the forward control 5-tonner also sported a dummy radiator. Like its gasoline-engined counterparts it had worm drive, and 2-speed back axles were standard on all Berliet electrics. Ironically the city of Lyons bought its few electrobuses from de Dion-Bouton, though the gas company used Berliet vans for a while. By 1930 the 8-litre 6-cylinder range had been extended to embrace a 4x2 heavy road tractor with solid tires at the rear, not to mention a 6x6 edition with 4-wheel steering and eight

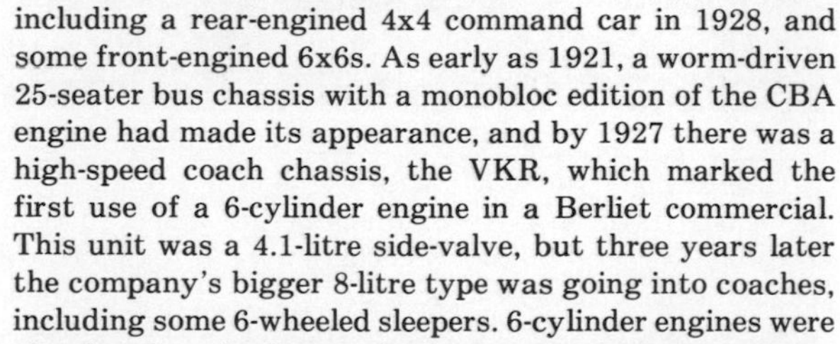

1932 BERLIET GPGF 12-ton van, OMM

1938 BERLIET VDAH6 3-ton producer gas truck, OMM

forward speeds.

Berliets of the 1930s pursued a similar line of development, the CBA surviving into 1933 before its replacement by the GDL with diesel engine and worm drive; other chain-drive types, however, were still listed as late as 1936. The first diesel engines, a 7.2-litre four and a 10.9-litre six, were catalogued in 1932. These were initially confined to models of 5 tons or over, but had reached 3/4-ton types by 1937; air brakes made their appearance on the heaviest Berliets as early as 1933. At the bottom end of the range design reflected private-car influences, with ohv 4-cylinder gasoline engines standardized from 1936 onwards. An unusual departure of 1933 was a 12-ton normal control tank transporter of self-loading type built for the French Army: it used the big diesel six. 1939's offerings covered everything from a 15-cwt van with the 2-litre 11CV engine up to 12/15-tonners: there was also a range of normal control full front and half-cab buses and coaches. Forward control trucks were made, but the bigger Berliets were usually of conventional configuration with the power units projecting well over the axle, a layout which persisted into the 1970s on heavy types. Gasoline engines were standard on lightweights, mediums had a choice of gasoline or diesel power, and in the over 5-ton class (apart from a few gazogenes) the diesel reigned supreme. At the time France fell in 1940, the factory was turning out 40 commercial vehicles a day.

Private car production was not resumed after the War, and with its demise went the lightest Berliets: henceforward 4-tonners would mark the company's bottom limit. Initially, however, a smallish range was offered, consisting of forward-control 4- and 6-cylinder diesel trucks in the 5/10-ton class, all with 4-speed gearboxes, double reduction drive, and air brakes. The PSV element was confined to a 35-seater coach version with 80 bhp, 7.2-litre 4-cylinder engine and single reduction back axle. Conventional models reappeared in 1949, in the shape of a 7-tonner with a 5-cylinder engine giving 120 bhp from 7.9 litres. This typified Berliet's thinking in this category for the next ten years, with its 5-speed overdrive gearbox, air brakes, and double reduction drive, though later ones would be available as 6x4s, and would acquire twin plate clutches and power steering. Engine capacity depended on the GVW, but as well as the 5-cylinder there were a 6.3-litre four, a 9.5-litre six, and an even bigger six of 14.8 litres. Turbocharged editions made their appearance in 1955,

In 1951 Berliet acquired Rochet-Schneider, inheriting from them a 6x6 military tractive unit which they had converted to multifuel operation by 1955. 1953 saw a reversion to gasoline engines on a new 4/5-tonner, the GLA: the latest power unit was a straightforward 5-litre ohv four developing 100 bhp, while a diesel option of like capacity was available. This was to be Berliet's last gasoline-powered load carrier, though a massive 8x8 tractor built for the Army used a 22½-litre V-12 engine with magneto ignition, and gasoline survived in the fire-engine range, later units being of Hotchkiss make after Berliet ceased to develop their own. 1951 also saw the first of a new generation of bus and coach chassis, with full unitary construction and offset horizontal underfloor engines. By 1957 these included big 6x4s for up to 90/100 passengers, a diversity of 5- and 6-cylinder engines of up to 260 bhp could be fitted and Wilson preselective gearboxes were regular equipment, with or without 2-speed back axles. At the other end of the scale, Berliet offered a 26-seater PSV edition of the 5-litre GL, with hydrovac brakes.

1955 BERLIET GLR 8½-ton tanker, GNG

8,144 Berliets were made in 1955, and over 10,000 in 1956, in which year the company started to sell trucks to Communist China. In 1957 the SAVA firm of Valladolid began license-production of Berliets in Spain, producing special variants to suit local conditions, though operations came to an end when the company was taken over by Pegaso in 1971. 1957's principal news was the T100 6x6 tractor intended for service in the Sahara. It was 44 ft. long, cost £55,000, and was powered by a 30-litre 600 bhp Cummins diesel engine. Other features included disc brakes, air conditioning, a radio telephone, a cooker, and even a Dyna-Panhard engine to power the ancillary services. 1958 developments included new and more powerful diesel engines on M.A.N. lines, the 5-cylinder unit now giving 150 bhp, while forward control trucks received new cabs with wrapround screens. In 1960 the front-engined coaches were brought up to date, emerging as the Fugue and Rallye with 5- or 6-speed gearboxes. A new option in lighter trucks was a 6-cylinder Perkins diesel.

1959 BERLIET GBC8 6×6 truck, Berliet

During the 1960s Berliet developed existing themes, with production climbing steadily, to over 15,000 in 1963, and passing the 19,000 mark in 1969. Specialist models now included crane and mixer chassis, while more powerful M-series engines made their appearance: a 12-litre, 240 bhp six in 1965, and a 12.8-litre V8 of 300 bhp at the end of the decade. Perkins units were used in the PAK series of front-engined PSVs as well as in trucks, while 2-stroke Detroit Diesels were fitted to some heavier 6x4s as well as to the biggest off-road dumpers. Synchromesh was in extensive use by 1961, and the biggest bus model was

1963 BERLIET GAK 8-ton van, GNG

the articulated PH180, nearly 18 meters long and capable of carrying 180 passengers. It was of the integral-construction type with horizontal, laterally mounted 6-cylinder engine and a Wilson preselective gearbox. In 1966 the firm also showed a 94-seater double-decker destined for use in Paris. On the military side, an agreement signed in 1964 with Alvis of Coventry added versions of Alvis's 6x6 Stalwart to the range, though plans for an exchange of designs folded when Berliet merged with Citroen during 1967. A little-publicized aspect of this latter alliance was the sale of some light-duty Berliets with Citroen badges.

1966 BERLIET Tekel 5-ton front drive truck, OMM

Interestingly, though, Citroen technical influence had been felt as early as 1965, when Berliet launched their Stradair range of 4-6 tonners. These were of semi-forward control type with lateral radiators, powered by 4-cylinder diesels of 80 and 120 bhp, but outstanding was their use of a combined air-leaf suspension and Citroen-type hydropneumatically actuated brakes. Other features were a hypoid final drive, 5-speed all-synchromesh gearboxes, and sealed-for-life chassis lubrication. Stradairs cruised at an easy 60 mph and were said to handle like sports cars. A year later came the Tekel, a fwd 6x2 for urban delivery work, with Stradair cab and rear suspension: this one also featured air/hydraulic brakes and power steering. Berliet's new suspension system was, however, short-lived, both 1968 Stradairs and their successors, the Dauphin range of 1972, having conventional springing as well as full forward control, and, latterly, tilt cabs.

By 1968 the company controlled 60 per cent of home sales in the over-12 ton GVW category, and it was an open secret that the EEC had authorized the French Government to compensate Berliet should the Community settle on an axle weight loading below the 13 tons eventually agreed. 1970's big Berliets featured forward control, tilt cabs, 300 bhp V8 engines, 8-speed rangechange gearboxes, power steering, air and exhaust brakes, and the added option of triple-reduction back axles. The newest coach model was the Cruisaire, a rear-engined machine with air-leaf suspension, synchromesh gearbox (5- 6-, and 8-speed variants were listed) and either a Berliet or Detroit Diesel engine, both V8s. When Fiat

1975 BERLIET PR100 bus, Berliet

1978 BERLIET GBH260 6×6 tractor and trailer, Berliet

and Citroen (who had entered into an uneasy marriage in 1968) finally settled for a divorce, Renault stepped in at the end of 1974 and acquired the Michelin company's Berliet holdings, thus bringing the latter under the Saviem umbrella. Full integration had been attained by 1977, when Berliet became a division of the newly-found Renault Vehicules Industriels.

Berliet's four plants (assembly was centered on Lyon-Venissieux and Blainville) were capable of making 30,000 vehicles a year, of which some 2,000 were PSVs. The 1978 range of diesel trucks covered GVWs from 6 tonnes upward, with standard engines in the 80-350bhp bracket. Forward control was general practice with the exception of the old-fashioned G range, which came in various forms up to the huge 32-tonne 6x6 GBH tipper/dumper. The medium-range (GVWs from 10 to 20 tonners) KB-types featured tilt cabs and all-synchromesh boxes with 5, 6, or

1978 BERLIET TR280 28 tonner GCW tanker, Berliet

10 forward speeds, while for really heavy loads there were the TR series of tractive units. The 6x4 TRH350 had the latest, 352bhp edition of Berliet's turbocharged V8, a twin-plate air-assisted clutch, and a 13-speed Fuller gearbox: it was rated for GCWs of up to 120 tonnes. Also listed were on-and off-road dumpers, municipal vehicles, fire engines, and PSVs for up to 110 passengers. The smaller ones featured rear-mounted 8.8-litre 6-cylinder engines, synchromesh gearboxes, and air-leaf suspension, but the unitary PR100 service bus combined coil-spring ifs with an air-leaf arrangement at the rear, with automatic gearboxes by Pont-a-Mousson or Voith. An unusual variation was the ER100, a trolleybus with an auxiliary 3-cylinder aircooled Deutz engine which allowed it to move independently of overhead wires. Other Berliet activities included the manufacture of armored cars, stationary and marine engines, and construction equipment. Trucks were being made under license in Algeria by the state-owned Sonacome company, and Pol-Mot of Poland was building buses to Berliet designs. *MCS*

BERNA (CH) 1905 to date

(1) J. Wyss, Schweizerische Automobilfabrik Berna, Olten 1905-1906
(2) Motorwerke Berna AG., Olten 1906-1907
(3) Berna Commercial Motors Ltd., Olten 1908-1912
(4) Motorwagenfabrik Berna AG., Olten (1912-to date)

When J. Wyss founded the Swiss Automobil Factory in Olten, the name Berna was given to it in remembrance of his hometown Berne, where he had built light cars with single cylinder engines since 1900. The first commercial vehicle, the type K, was a 2 ton truck with monobloc 2-cylinder in-line engine (120 x 140mm) mounted under the seats and chain drive. Only a small number of the type K truck was produced. There followed a heavier model with a huge twin-cylinder engine of 150mm bore which was however not successful. Early in 1906 the new model G1 or "Vanguard" as it was called in view of the exports to Great Britain, was launched. It incorporated many up to date ideas and set the pattern for some time to come. It was powered by a 4-cylinder engine of 6.3-litres, developing 35-40 hp. Power was transmitted via a 4-speed gearbox, drive shaft and differential to the small pinion driving the large diameter internal-tooth wheel crown (spur-hub-reduction). This method of power-transmission was to remain the trade-mark of Berna trucks for some 40 years. It was considered by many as being stronger than conventional rear-axle reduction drive at the same time allowing better ground clearance. The "Vanguard" had solid rubber tires and a payload of 5 tons. It was offered as a platform truck and as an omnibus. One of the latter was used for the first scheduled Swiss postal omnibus services. Business however was slack and the newly formed public company was soon in financial troubles. In 1907 about 40 workers were employed. Instead of concentrating on improving the promising "Vanguard" truck a newly hired French engineer began costly development of a new passenger car, which however was not successful. The company had to be liquidated. J. Wyss, its founder had already left.

The British financial group Hudson Consolidated took over the ailing company. Ernst Marti, who had already worked for some time in 1905/6 as a designer technician for Berna, before leaving for England, took over the management. In July 1908 the new owners founded the Berna Commercial Motors Ltd. and soon a wide range of truck based on earlier models was offered. The catalogue of 1909 contains no less than 5 trucks for 1½ to 6 tons, type C, F, G, H and J as well as omnibus chassis for 12 to 36 passengers. Four distinctly different engines were made. The smallest a 2 liter monobloc 4-cylinder in line was built into the 1½ ton truck, the light bus and some touring cars. It had a ball-bearing crankshaft. The other engines were an early attempt at standardization. There were two-, three- and four-cylinder L-head engines with separate cylinders, all with the same dimensions of 120x140mm. Apart from crankcase and crankshaft all parts were interchangeable facilitating manufacturing and spare-part cilitating manufacturing and spare-part stock-keeping. The power rating was 16/20 hp, 26/30 hp and 35/40 hp respectively. All engines had carburetors of Berna design and dual ignition by magneto and coil. Leather cone clutch, 3- or 4-speed gearboxes were used. With the exception of the heaviest chassis, where iron-tired wheels were mounted, all had solid-rubber tires.

One year later the heavy trucks C, F, G and H were still offered but the engine of the smallest model was substituted by a slightly enlarged version of the T-head 4-cylinder (85 x 100mm.). This chassis type L could also be ordered with multi-disc clutch and conventional final drive by a worm-gear. In addition an intermediary model, type V with a new L-head 4-cylinder-monobloc engine of 3.1 liters rated at 20/22 hp was launched. Payload was 2 tons, the wheelbase 10' 6" and top-speed about 18 mph.

Early in 1912 a Swiss group purchased the company and re-named it again into Motorwagenfabrik Berna AG.

1915 BERNA C2 4-ton truck, Berna

Under British ownership and the new management Berna had grown considerably and had expanded its activities especially on various export markets. There were established agencies in Holland, Belgium, Spain, Italy, Rumania and South America. The daughter company in England had to be closed due to the protective custom duties on commercial vehicles but British Bernas were made in that country for several years. With 79 commercial vehicles registered in Switzerland Berna was number 3 after Saurer and Arbenz. On the eve of the outbreak of the first World War there was a hectic search for trucks and increasing numbers of orders were pouring in from abroad. At the Swiss National Exhibition 1914 Berna was awarded the golden medal and the Grand Prix. In the same year Berna took over the Franz Brozincevic factory in Zurich which produced the Franz trucks and later the light Berna E types. Marti having pushed the development of a Berna model especially suitable for military transportation soon could announce the new type C 2 truck, which was to become the most successful Berna. The 30/35 hp engine was a watercooled L-head 4-cylinder in line, cast in two pairs of cylinders of 105 x 160mm. 5.5 liters and developed its maximum power at 1200 rpm. Power was transmitted via leather cone clutch, 4-speed gearbox with direct top and shaft. Fitted with solid rubber tires the Berna C 2 had a payload of 3½ to 4 tons. For the Swiss, British and French armies the driver's compartment and platform usually received a canvas top. This Berna truck was nearly indestructible and became a true working horse in the military services. 30 and more were expected monthly to the Allied transport units. Until production of the Berna C 2 ceased in 1928, several thousand were made.

The new heavier type G was similar in most respects, the engine however had an increased bore of 115 mm. and developed 40 hp, wheelbase was 13' 11" and payload 5 tons. At the lower end Berna offered the type E, a 2-ton truck with a 20 hp 4-cylinder-monobloc engine of 5.3 liters. These two models still had wooden artillery wheels and solid rubber tires. Inspite of continuous efforts by purchasing agents of the central powers Berna did not supply the German and Austrian Armies during the war years. Apart from trucks and various special purpose vehicles, the company developed a heavy short wheelbase tractor to draw the mighty howitzers of the Swiss Army. It was equipped with the 40 hp engine of the Type G vehicles. When the war was finally over in November 1918 demand for army trucks and tractors sharply dropped off. The sturdy Berna C 2 had to be adapted to civilian requirements. A considerable number was sold in Germany, assembly was taken up by Perl in Leising near Vienna and by Jakob & Hegedus in Budapest. Heavy artillery tractors were used for agricultural tasks.

The first peace years were rather difficult and the increasing pressure of cheaper imported commercial vehicles worsened the situation. Berna concentrated on improving their models and especially the heavy G-type chassis which proved to suit the requirements of high payload and performance — it thus became the G 3. Production in the Franz factory had been abandoned in about 1918 and this company was reformed and became a maintenance workshop also selling passenger cars.

From 1922 onward the demand on the home market improved again and later the Swiss Government introduced protective custom duties, at the same time asking all Federal and Cantonal institutions and services including the PTT to order Swiss vehicles whenever

1928 BERNA G5 5-ton tipper, Berna

possible. In 1923 the new G 4 model was introduced. The faithful two-block 4-cylinder engine was modernized and enlarged to 130 x 160 mm. or 8½ litres developing 55 hp. The basic design of the chassis remained with little change but the entire truck was considerably up-dated with a closed and fully weather-protected driver's cab. Payload was 5 to 6 tons. A license agreement was signed with the famous German locomotive factory Krauss in Munich but apparently no production resulted. The excellent quality and workmanship of the Berna vehicles as well as a more aggressive sales policy led to some export contracts but the home market always took the great majority of the production. In 1926 a total of 977 Bernas were registered in Switzerland and the company was runner-up to the market-leader, Saurer. In 1928 Berna took out a license to build Deutz 4- and 6-cylinder diesel engines.

In 1929 the history of Berna took a sharp turn: Saurer, the big competitor on the Swiss market had purchased a controlling portion of the company's shares. The agreement between the two companies for a close co-operation was realized in several steps and it took many years until Berna lost its own design identity. One question however was rapidly settled, namely the choice of an up-to-date diesel engine. Saurer was a pioneer in this field and soon the new BLD 6-cylinder OHV diesel engine of 8 liters developing 105 hp was fitted into Berna chassis bearing then the designation MSRd.

1930 BERNA road tractor, GNG

Market studies had shown an increasing demand for light commercial vehicles. High development costs and a considerable time loss however made it a better proposal to look around for a license agreement instead of beginning from scratch. Such an agreement was signed with the German Adler factory. From 1932 onward Berna offered the new line of type L 1, L 2 & L3 with a payload of 1½ to 3 tons in addition to the heavy range. The two smaller models received a 6 cylinder SV gasoline engine of 2.9 liters developing 50 hp, whereas the L 3 — engine was slightly bigger with 3.1 liters and 60 hp. Some of the major components were purchased from Adler. Later the L 2 d and L 3 d with 4.5 liter 4-cylinder diesel engine were added.

The medium and heavy L4, L5 & L5a chassis, as well as the last of the proper Berna types, the G6a model with the pinion/wheel crown final drive received first the Saurer designed B-line and later the C-line diesel engines with direct injection. A few 3-axle trucks were also built but the new Swiss traffic regulation kept this interesting model from wider spread. The economic climate in the thirties hurt the Swiss automobile industry severely and forced Martini, the last passenger car manufacturer to liquidate. Berna took over the remains and planned to assemble Renault cars, later to establish a large repair workshop but neither of the projects was realized and finally the factory was sold. In Olten some 50 Hispano-Suiza aircraft engines were built.

1936 BERNA L4 5-ton vans, Berna

In 1936 the first model of the new U-range was launched. It corresponded to the C-range of Saurer and was destined to supersede all previous models after some 5 years. At the outbreak of the 2nd World War Berna offered a mixed lot of no less than 9 distinctly different models. At the lower end were the L1 and L2 models with 6 cylinder SV gasoline engines with 7 bearings, Scintilla magneto ignition, 4-speed gearbox, hydraulic brakes, 13' 2" wheelbase and 1 to 2½ tons payload. The medium chassis all had direct injection 4-cylinder OHV diesel engines. Type U2-B with 2.8 liters of 50 hp, type 1U-R with 4.5 liters of 55 hp and the type 2U-R1 with 5.3 liters of 65 hp corresponding to the Saurer "CBD", "CRD", and "CR1D" — engines. All had single plate dry clutches and 5-speed gearboxes with overdrive and the top two speeds synchronized. Brakes were hydraulic, some with vacuum servo assistance and wheelbase varied betweeen 11' 6" and 13' 10". Payload range was 2 to 4 tons. These chassis were also used for buses for private and postal services. The heavy trucks included model 3U-T with the 6-cylinder OHV diesel engine of 6.75 liters developing 105 hp and models 4U-T1, L5a/1D-L and the old-faithful G6a/1D all with the powerful 8 liter engine of 110 hp (Saurer CTD). 5 as well as 8 speed gearboxes with overdrive and 2 or 6 speeds synchronized were offered. Payload was 4 to over 6 tons.

Berna had begun already some years before with the research of the use of substitute fuels and worked closely together with the Imbert company who specialized in wood-gas-generators. It was found that the old gasoline engine Type G5, a monobloc 4-cylinder of 8.3 liters, offered the best combustion chamber and cross-flow properties for this purpose. When the fuel-shortage set in after the outbreak of the war it was therefore this engine which found its way into many Berna trucks. Later the modern diesel engines were also converted.

The Swiss Army required large quantities of trucks and the majority were supplied by Saurer and Berna. Apart from their emblems and designations they were identical. The most common model had 3 tons payload and many remained in service until very recently. During the war years the heavy L5a and G6a were dropped and replaced by the 5U also equipped with the 8-liter 6-cylinder diesel engine. Except on the two lightest models all types now had hydraulic brakes with compressed air servo.

A speciality of Berna since the twenties was the construction of heavy road-tractors using shortened and strengthened chassis of the heaviest truck models. For these vehicles the traditional Berna final drive with a separate driving and a load rear-axle was often chosen. In order to haul railroad wagons on the roads such tractors were used. Requirements set up by the Swiss railroad office asked for a trailing load of 54 tons to be drawn up in a 10% gradient. Other developments during the war included electric vehicles for short-range transportation, tank-engines etc. After 1945 a large number of vehicles with wood-gas-generators had to be re-converted for normal gas and oil use.

The U-range (corresponding to the Saurer C-line) was extended and in addition to the normal chassis, forward control models appeared. The boom in construction and building led to an enormous demand for trucks and soon the time of delivery climbed to one and later up to two years.

1954 BERNA 6U 10-ton truck, Berna

Early in the fifties the 4UM and 5UM four-wheel-drive trucks were launched, which were similar to the Saurer 4CM and 5CM, with the 125 hp 6-cylinder-diesel forward-control, 5x2 speed gearbox, separately engaged front-wheel-drive and the short wheelbase of 11' 2". It had tremendous climbing potential and was often used to haul extra heavy loads on the alpine roads. As the Saurer it was of course also delivered in quantities to the Swiss Army. Urban buses, sometimes with trailers, excursion buses and trolley buses followed closely the pattern set by Saurer.

From 1956 onward the successful U-line was step by step replaced by the newly designed models of the V-range (Saurer's D-models). In 1960 the following Berna vehicles were offered: 2US with either the small R2 (Saurer CR2D) 4-cylinder engine of 5.8 liters and 90 hp or the T4 (Saurer CT4D) 6-cylinder engine of 6.8 liters and 110 hp. It was available with normal and forward-control. The 2x4 speed gearbox had a compressed air actuated overdrive and on request differential-blocking. Springs were semi-elliptic and hydraulic brakes with compressed air servo in addition to the mechanical handbrake and the exhaust-motor-brake were fitted. Wheelbase was 11' 2" to 14' 5" and payload about 4½ tons.

The L4U received the T2 (Saurer CT2D) 6-cylinder-engine of 8.7 liters and 125 hp. It was similar to the lighter model but servo-steering could be had, wheelbase ranged from 13' 5" to 17' 9" and payload from 5½ to 6 tons. The most famous model 5U was offered with the T2 or the T2Lm (Saurer CT2DLm) engine with supercharging and 170 hp or the H2V (Saurer CH2D) 8-cylinder of 160 hp or

1964 BERNA 5VU 8-ton truck, Berna

even the H5-V8-engine with 12.7 liters and 175 hp. Wheelbase was from 9' 2" to 16' 5" and payload about 9 tons. The heaviest Berna chassis, the 6U-H was available only with forward-control and the H2V or H5 8-cylinder engines. Payload was 10 to 11 tons. Of the new line there was the 3 VUR forward-control truck with the under-floor mounted Saurer DCU 6-cylinder-OHV-engine of 10.3 liters and 160 hp or the supercharged DCUL developing 210 hp. The 5VU was similar but had a heavier chassis offering 9 tons payload instead of 6 tons only. Type 2H was a forward-controlled excursion bus with rear-engine R2Lm (Saurer CR2DLm) of 5.8 liters and 115 hp. The two four-wheel-drive models 2VM-4x4 and 5VM-4x4 were similar to Saurer's 2DM and 5DM equipped with the T4 and the DC 6-cylinder-engines of 10.3 liters and 160 hp respectively. Payload U models were 5 and 9 tons.

Five years later in 1965 all the old U-models had disappeared. Berna offered the 2V and 5V models with various Saurer designed engines of 120 to 210 hp. There were normal and forward control as well as under-floor engined types suitable for truck or bus superstructures. The 4x4 types 2VM and 5VM had been improved and engines of 140, 180 and 240 hp were fitted. In addition there were four different trailer-tractors offered on the 2V and 5V bases chassis. This range tailored to the needs of the home market and supplemented with the light OM commercial vehicles was offered with minor modifications for the next seven years.

In 1972 the smaller 2V type was replaced by the modern 4V model (Saurer 4D) with the new CK 6-cylinder engine of 8.8 liters developing 200hp at 2500 rpm. An up-to-date 6x2 speed ZF synchro gearbox and twin-circuit compressed air brakes have replaced the earlier equipment. Wheelbase of the forward-control vehicles are 10' 8" to 15' 5" and payload is about 10.3 tons. Trailer-tractor (4VF) and 4-wheel-drive (4VM) models also received the new engine. THe 5V-line was continued and from 1969 onward a new 6x4 vehicle with the 310 hp D1KT-engine of 11.6 liters and 18 tons payload was added. A range of three different bus chassis is also offered.

By 1974 the heavy 5V models had received the new powerful D2K 6-cylinder-engine of 12.5 liters and 250 hp or the even more powerful turbo-supercharged D2KT engine of 12 liters and 330 hp. This engine is also fitted into the heaviest model ever built in Olten, the 5VF 8x4 with a payload of about 18 tons.

Recently the integration of the marque into the Saurer-line has been taken one step further and all advertising and export efforts are strictly Saurer. In 1976 the designations were changed to comprise the "D" prefix and then the engine output in HP. The current program is identical to the D-series of Saurer. *FH*

BERNARD (F) 1923-1967

(1) SA des Bennes Basculantes E. Bernard, Arcueil, Seine 1923-1928
(2) Camions Bernard, Arcueil, Seine 1929-1964
(3) Camions Bernard, Bagneux, Seine 1964-1967

E. Bernard was a manufacturer of hydraulic tipping gears who exhibited his first complete vehicle at the 1923 Paris Salon. This was a modest affair for 30-cwt/2-ton payloads powered by a proprietary 2.6-litre sv 4-cylinder engine. There were four forward speeds and a double reduction back axle: though pneumatic tires and fwb were standard from the start, electric lighting and starting were not. A 3.3-litre 2½-ton development was available by 1926, when Bernard became the first French maker to offer an American-type high-speed coach with dropped frame. Its 6-cylinder sv engine was initially of American manufacture, Bernard offering their own power units by 1929; these came in 3.6-litre and 5.2-litre sizes and were notable for sparking-plug covers of Citroen type. Coaches were to remain an important part of the Bernard programme, an elegant 1½-decker observation model being shown on their stand at the Salon in 1933. Alongside them, from 1929, the company developed a new range of low-loaders for fast, long-distance goods transport, using a straight-frame version of the coach chassis. 1930 Bernards of this type could be had with oversize 500-litre fuel tanks and sleeper cabs, and were averaging close on 30 mph on the Paris-Marseilles run. New for 1932 was the 6½-ton F8 with 6.8-litre sv straight-8 engine, 5-speed overdrive gearbox, hydraulic servo brakes, and cetralized chassis lubrication. These big Bernards were elegant machines with their long hoods, and liberal use of chromium plate; initially on bumpers and badge, but later extending to the radiator shell itself.

1929 BERNARD Six 3-ton van, FLP

1939 BERNARD DH6 12-ton truck, BHV

After a brief flirtation with the 2-stroke Lilloise diesel in 1931, Bernard acquired a manufacturing license for the British Gardner, which they produced in 70 bhp 4-cylinder and 100 bhp 6-cylinder forms. Diesel models came with air-cooled transmission handbrakes and 5-speed gearboxes as standard, and 1934 saw the introduction of a 3-cylinder derivative of the Gardner for medium duty work. This was made until 1937, and was said to give 25

1962 BERNARD Type 19 DA150 van, NMM

mpg in regular service. After 1935 gasoline engines were dropped altogether, the range being extended upwards to include a 12/15-ton 6-wheeler with 6-cylinder engine and Hispano-type servo brakes fed by twin hydraulic pumps. An electro-magnetic transmission handbrake was an option on 1938 models, and the immediate pre-War range covered the 6/12-ton sector, with coaches for up to 47 seats. Bernards were now averaging as much as 45 mph on the long runs. In 1939 the company produced an experimental armoured tractor with steering by articulation.

Bernard, along with Laffly, Unic and Delahaye, joined the GFA group during World War II, but post-1945 design followed established lines, the coaches being phased out in favor of heavy 4x2 and 6x2 trucks with 8.4-litre 6-cylinder engines, the latter type being much favored for tanker work. Though normal control was retained, engines were mounted over the front axles, other features being 4-speed unit gearboxes in place of the earlier separate type, dry multi-disc clutches, and air-hydraulic servo brakes. The 5-speed gearbox was back in 1948, when a 5.6-litre 4-cylinder engine made its appearance, and over the next few years Bernards were progressively improved, with full air brakes and a 12.1-litre engine option in 1950, disc handbrakes on the transmission in 1953, and aluminum chassis frames in 1954-55, by which time power assisted steering and 2-speed auxiliary gearboxes were also available, and the company were experimenting with turbocharged engines. Two novelties of 1958 were a 200 hp V8 diesel engine and the curious Elephant, a wheeled off-the-road tractor with tracked-vehicle type steering. Standard 4x2 and 6x2 Bernards, however, were now available with full forward control and used 9-litre and 12.1-litre 6-cylinder power units with outputs of up to 150 bhp. Bellows-type air suspension was tried in 1960, when a wide range of trucks, tractors and dumpers were rated at between 19 and 35 tons, and the most powerful six now ran to 12.6 litres and 200 bhp. Unfortunately the vehicles were no longer competitive with Berliet and Unic, this despite changes which included wrap round windows on the normal control cabs, and a new futuristic forward control cab styled by Philippe Charbonneaux. At the same time cylinder capacity was once again increased and 10-speed transmissions standardized, but in 1963 Bernard were taken over by Mack of America. Under the new management, some hybrid types were added to the range. The 35-ton TD211 of 1965, though outwardly a normal Bernard, used a 214bhp 6-cylinder Mack diesel engine, the clutch and 10-speed gearbox being also of Mack origin. Mack's six was also optional in the specialized porte-fers for girder transport, available as 4x2s or 6x4s and distinguished by their centrally-located one-man cabs. The Franco-American partnership was, however, unsuccessful, and the company was wound up in 1966. There was a Bernard stand at the 1967 Paris Salon, but only imported Macks were on display. *MCS*

BERRY (GB) 1902-1903

A.W. Berry, Port Lane Works, Colchester, Essex

A 5-ton vertical firetube boilered undertype using separate compound engines each with three speed gearbox and chain drive to each rear wheel, the Berry also incorporated a condensing arrangement. One example was sold but it was found that the engines used more steam than the boiler could provide and it was not repeated. *RAW*

BERSEY (GB) 1897-1899

(1) Great Horseless Carriage Co. Ltd., Coventry 1897-1898
(2) Gloucester Railway Waggon Co. Ltd., Gloucester 1898-1899

Walter C. Bersey was the general manager of the London Electrical Cab Co Ltd, and gave his name to the electric cabs operated by this company. They had 3½ hp Lundell-type electric motors and a range of 30 miles. The chassis were assembled by the Great Horseless Carriage Company who also made M.M.C. vehicles, and the bodies were by Mulliner. An improved version with larger batteries was made by the Gloucester Railway Waggon Company. Between September 1897 and December 1898 more than 70 Bersey cabs were put on London streets, but breakdowns and the high cost of batteries and tires made the enterprise unprofitable, and in August 1899 the London Electrical Cab Co. closed down. *GNG*

BERTOLINI (I) to date

Bertolini Macchine Agricole SpA, Ferrara

Producers of pumps since 1918 and more general agricultural equipment in recent years, Bertolini now makes small 4x4 tractors and load carriers. 2- or 3-cylinder, air-cooled 36-38 bhp diesels are fitted and seven forward and three reverse gears provided. *OM*

1915 BESSEMER 5-ton truck, Mrs Warren Graeff

BESSEMER (US) 1911-1926

(1) Bessemer Motor Truck Co., Grove City, Pa. 1911-1923
(2) Besser-American Corp., Plainfield, N.J. 1923-1926

Early models were of 1 and 2-ton capacity with Continental 4-cylinder engine, cone clutch, progressive 3-speed transmission, and chain drive. In 1916 Bessemer adopted selective 3-speed transmission and offered a 1-ton model with internal gear drive, a 1½-ton chain drive model, and 2, 3½, and 5-ton models with worm drive. Prices ranged from $975 to $3,400. By 1918 the chain drive model had been dropped and the dry plate clutch adopted for the entire line. A 4-ton model replaced the 3½-ton model in 1919. Prices ranged from $1,825 to $4,285 in 1920.

Bessemer constructed a factory in Philadelphia to expand production but didn't move there when the factory was completed in 1922. The firm merged with American Motors Corporation of Plainfield, New Jersey, in January 1923. A further merger with Northway and Winther was announced in early 1924 but never carried through.

Production of the Bessemer truck was moved to Plainfield in late 1923. Bessemer listed a 1-ton 16-passenger bus from 1923. The only new models thereafter were a 3-ton truck added to the line in 1924 and a 1-ton speed truck with Continental 6-cylinder engine, priced at $1,250 for the chassis, which was announced in 1926, Bessemer's final year of production. *DJS*

BEST (i) (US) 1912-1915

Durant-Dort Carriage Company, Flint, Michigan

The precursors of passenger automobiles, under each of the hyphenated names of the manufacturer, were rather diminutive open and closed delivery vans on a wheelbase of only 76 inches. These were powered by two-cylinder engines. The transmission was a friction type and chains drove each rear wheel. For 1913, the covered delivery van cost $875 and weighed 2000 pounds. *GMN*

BEST (ii) (US) 1913-1914

Best Manufacturing Co., San Leandro, Cal.

The two models by this name were a 1½-tonner and 1-tonner. The smaller was powered by a 2-cylinder engine mounted under the body, with a friction transmission and double chain final drive. The one-tonner used a 4-cylinder engine also beneath the body with a selective gearbox and shaft drive. The latter was on a wheelbase of 106 inches and sold for $1370. The Best company was a well known traction engine manufacturer. *GMN*

BETHLEHEM (U.S.) 1917-1926

Bethlehem Motors Corp., Allentown, Pa.

Bethlehem's first models were of 1¼-ton capacity with 23 hp G.B. & S. engine and of 2¼-ton with 26 hp North American engine, priced at $1,245 and $1,775 for the chassis. Internal gear drive was used. Production exceeded 3,500 trucks in 1919. Bethlehem purchased North American Motors, Pottstown, Pa., to acquire an engine shop. In 1920 four Bethlehem-engined models from 1-ton to 4-ton capacity were offered. In that year the firm introduced a 4-cylinder automobile for export trade, began the production of buses, and enlarged its factories for a proposed annual production of 20,000 vehicles. Receivership occured before the end of the year; new management in 1921 continued the old models in limited numbers. Production dwindled to a mere 42 trucks in 1924. The Bethlehem company disappeared when Hahn purchased their Allentown factory in January 1927. *DJS*

BETZ (US) 1919-1929

Betz Motor Truck Co., Hammond, Ind.

The first Betz was a 2½-tonner with a Buda 4-cylinder engine, a Brown-Lipe 4-speed gearbox and Timken worm-drive rear axle. In 1924, a 1-tonner was added on a wheelbase of 11 feet, 4 inches. For the last four year of production, Buda 4- and 6-cylinder engines were used in trucks of 1 to 1½ tons capacity. *GMN*

BEYER PEACOCK c.1903-1904

Beyer Peacock & Co. Ltd., Gorton, Manchester

How Beyer Peacock, a celebrated firm of railway locomotive builders, came to be interested in steam trucks is not clear, but the influence of Mr. H.A. Hoy, chief mechanical engineer of the Lancashire & Yorkshire Railway at nearby Horwich Works, who had designed his own wagon in 1901, may have been involved as he designed the modified Ackermann steering gear used. The first design, a 5-tonner, had a vertical firetube boiler and a duplex high pressure undertype engine, mounted longitudinally, in conjunction with a countershaft differential and twin chain final drive.

In 1905 Hoy left the railway and became General Manager of Beyer Peacock who had got into rather low water.

As the old boiler was not a sufficiently flexible generator it was superseded in 1906 by a revised boiler conceived by Mr. Hoy in which a large, top fired, circular "bottle" firebox was enclosed in a circular water jacket, very short inclined firetubes enclosed in a short horizontal front extension carrying the flue gases to a smokebox of locomotive type in the front apron. A coil superheater was provided in the smokebox and the top of the main boiler body formed a large steam space. Beyer Peacock and Hoy were interested in the development of a self-contained steam railcar for which a compact but effective boiler was needed and the wagon and its boiler may have served as a test bed. Though the wagon was shown at the Liverpool Motor Show in 1906 and used for works transport it is doubtful if many were made, partly because the company's locomotive building affairs improved so much under Hoy's direction that sidelines were unnecessary. *RAW*

BEYSTER-DETROIT (US) 1910-1911

Beyster-Detroit Motor Car Co. Detroit, Mich.

Beyster-Detroit was announced in Dec. 1909 as a 1200-pound delivery car with a 4-cylinder 25 hp engine. Other features were a cone clutch in oil, selective sliding transmission, double enclosed chain-drive, two sets of brakes on the rear hubs, 105 inch wheelbase, and 34 x 2 inch tires. Although the weight was only 1000 pounds, the company stressed that it was all truck and not a made-over runabout. *RW*

1961 BIAMAX R514 bus, AAR

BIAMAX (GR) 1961 to date

Biamax S.A., Athens

Biamax was established in 1958 as the body building branch of the Daimler Benz representatives in Greece and after a successful career building bus bodies on Mercedes-Benz chassis, introduced in the early 60s the first all Greek designed vehicles. Called the "R" series, they were integrally-built buses in intercity and coach form, powered by a rear mounted Mercedes Benz 6 cylinder diesel engine developing 126 hp. Running gear was of the same origin, while the chassis/body frame was of rectangular tube construction and front suspension was by a patented independent beam system.

1962 saw the introduction of a prototype trolleybus with Italian CGE electric equipment, while Biamax's masterpiece appeared in 1968 in the form of a transit bus chassis. Designated the "F" series and built of steel beams, it is powered by a mid-underfloor Mercedes Benz 6 cylinder diesel engine developing 172 hp and has been supplied in large quantities to both the cities of Athens and Salonica as a city bus, complete with Biamax built bodies. Biamax is a major export to many Middle East and African countries. *GA*

1911 BEYSTER-DETROIT van, NAHC

1950 BIANCHI Civis city bus, HDB

BIANCHI: AUTOBIANCHI (I) 1903-1975

(1) Bianchi-Camions, Brescia 1908-1909
(2) Fabbrica Automobili e Velocipedi Edoardo Bianchi, Milan 1910-1955
(3) Autobianchi SpA, Milan 1955-1968
(4) Fiat SpA (Sezione Autobianchi) 1968-1975

This Milanese cycle maker branched out into cars in 1900, the first trucks, of which little was heard, being produced by an associated concern in Brescia. It was not until 1912 that Bianchi commercial vehicles appeared in any quantity, in the shape of the Model-G, available as a 30-cwt truck or light bus. It had a 2.9-litre 4-cylinder sv monoblock engine, a multi-disc clutch, four forward speeds, shaft drive, and pneumatic tires with twin rear wheels. There were also some 2½/3-tonners with 3.3-litre power units, but demand dropped after the Armistice, and for ever a decade the only Bianchi commercials were light vans and taxis, based on the S4 and S5 ohv private cars with 1.3- and 1.5-litre engines. From 1934 onwards these used the S9 chassis, but alongside them there was a new range of normal control 3-tonners powered by 4.9-litre 60/65 bhp 4-cylinder diesel units of Mercedes-Benz type. Brakes were hydraulic or air-hydraulic, and the inevitable Italian 4x2-speed transmission was used. As well as the standard Mediolanum there were a coach chassis and the Miles variant for the army, all three surviving the abandonment of the private-car line in 1939. In the 1930s and 1940s Bianchi's motorcycle department produced 3-wheel *motocarri* with 600cc engine and two driven rear wheels.

Post-War Bianchi trucks were based on the prototype Cabi-Cattaneo of the mid-1940s, with forward control, tubular frame, and coil ifs. First of the family was the 2-ton Sforzesco with 44 bhp ohv 4-cylinder gasoline engine; a methane-gas model was also listed. Later developments included a light military 4x4, and 2½- and 5-tonners with OM diesel engines and OM's 8-speed transmission. The biggest ones had channel-section frames.

1952 BIANCHI CL51 2-ton truck, BHV

Financial difficulties in 1955 led to a rescue operation by a Fiat-Pirelli consortium from which Pirelli soon withdrew. Under the new management the product was renamed Autobianchi, and private-car production was resumed with the Bianchina, a customized 2-cylinder Fiat 500 introduced in 1957. Also continued was the truck range, consisting of 3- and 4½-tonners, and a 28-seater coach edition of the latter. Engines were 4.4-litre, 88 bhp OMs, and later 4½-tonners featured full air brakes. Sales were, however, modest — only 2,370 units in 1961 and the big Autobianchis had disappeared before the concern was finally integrated into Fiat in 1968. Thenceforward the Bianchina van was the sole commercial vehicle to bear the name: though it outlived its private-car prototypes it was finally withdrawn in 1975. *MCS*

1927 BICKLE fire engine, HD

BICKLE (CDN) 1906-1956

(1) R.S. Bickle Co., Winnepeg, Mann 1906-1915
(2) Bickle Fire Engines Ltd., Woodstock, Ont. 1915-1956

Both motorized and horse-drawn fire apparatus were produced by the R.S. Bickle Company, but after the move to Woodstock and change of name only motor units were made. Piston-pump units were built in the early 1920s under license from Ahrens-Fox, and other apparatus was built on a wide variety of chassis including Bickle's own, Ford, Ruggles, Packard and Gotfredson. In 1926 V. B. King, a nephew of R.S. Bickle, designed a complete new line of Bickles based on the Ahrens-Fox and featuring a classic gabled hood and Rolls-Royce-type radiator, and disc wheels.These were available with pumping capacities from 350 to 840 gpm, and sold very well. Pirsch aerial ladder trucks were later built under license. In 1936 the Seagrave franchise for Canada was obtained, and for the next twenty years the American machines were sold under the name Bickle-Seagrave. In 1938 Bickle offered a line of three trucks for gross loads of 20000, 25000 and 35000 lbs which were, in fact, Gramms to be built under license, but only one unit was ever delivered. In 1956 the company went bankrupt, but King took over and started producing King-Seagrave fire engines. *HD*

BIDDLE-MURRAY (US) 1906-1908

(1) Biddle-Murray Motor Truck Company, Oak Park, Ill., 1906
(2) Biddle-Murray Manufacturing Company, Oak Park, Ill., 1906-1908

Only one model appears to have been made under this tradename. It had a 3-ton capacity with a driven by a four-cylinder engine giving 24 hp at 900 rpm. This had a 4-speed gearbox and chain-drive to the rear wheels. Layout was forward control and the price was $3500. *GMN*

1926 BIEDERMAN 4-ton tanker, NAHC

c.1942 BIEDERMAN C2 6×6 Air Force wrecker, BHV

BIEDERMAN (US) 1920-1955

Biederman Motors Corp., Cincinnati, Ohio

Biederman was a small concern which managed to outlive several larger Cincinnati rivals such as Schacht and Armleder, although production was always very limited except during World War 2. They were early in the field with 6-cylinder engines, the first being introduced in 1921. This was a small-bore Continental unit built to Charles Biederman's design. By 1922 there were two 4-cylinder trucks (1 and 1½ tons) and three sixes (1½ to 3 tons) in the range, and from 1923 onwards only sixes were offered. Variable-rate suspension was a prominent feature on Biederman trucks for years. Continental and Lycoming engines were used in the late 1920s and 1930s, when load capacities were raised to 5/7 tons (1932) and 7½ tons (1936). During the 1930s Biederman built a number of vehicles for the US Army. These included a 3-ton 4x2 tractor and 4- and 5-ton 6x6 trucks. They were not made in large numbers, but their experience of Army vehicles led to large orders during World War 2. By 1938 Biederman listed an enormous range, but it is likely that every order, even for one-offs, entered the catalogs as a production vehicle. Models included trucks from 1 to 7½ tons including a tilt-cab COE, municipal and snow removal trucks, a bus chassis and fire apparatus. Engines were Hercules, Continental and Lycoming gasoline units, Cummins and Detroit Diesels, and Waukesha-Hesselman oil-burning units. Some Biedermans featured Chevrolet cabs at this time.

1947 BIEDERMAN 6×4 concrete mixer, GNG

During World War 2 Biederman built more trucks than at any other time, for their Hercules-engined 6x6 chassis was widely used as a wrecker and crane carrier. It was almost identical to similar models made by Federal and Reo, all being built to Army Air Force specification. Wartime profits enabled Biederman to enter the post-war market in good shape. The new model was called NS (National Standard) and came in 4- and 6-wheeled versions with Hercules gasoline engines, Timken axles and other stock components. For several years Biederman sold as many trucks as the small plant could produce, but the slump in truck sales in the early 1950s hit the company badly, and for the last few years annual production barely reached two figures. One of the last orders was for some COE wrecker trucks for use in New York's Lincoln tunnel. The Biederman plant later became the service department for Cincinnati's largest Chevrolet dealer. *RJ*

BIJOU (GB) 1901-1904

Protector Lamp & Lighting Co. Ltd., Eccles, Manchester

This company made light cars powered by 5 hp single-cylinder horizontal engines, on which van bodies could be fitted. They also made, though apparently not using the name Bijou for it, a fire engine powered by a 7 hp horizontal 2-cylinder engine, with 2 speeds and chain drive. It could carry five men and 300 yards of hose at a maximum of 16 mph. It was delivered in 1901 to Eccles Fire Brigade. *GNG*

BILL see Curtis-Bill

BINDEWALD-ALBRECHT (D) 1905

Motorlastwagen-Fabrik Bindewald, Albrecht, Friedberg

A truck with two driven and steered front axles was produced by this firm in limited numbers only. *HON*

BINGHAM (US) 1914-1915

Bingham Mfg. Co. Cleveland, Ohio

Bingham made a light, conventional, good looking delivery truck of 1250 pounds capacity complete with stake, open express, or panel body and semi-enclosed cab on a 115 inch wheelbase to sell for $800. It had an L-head 4-cylinder Continental engine cast en bloc, and the steering wheel was on the left side. Its friction-drive was claimed to last for 5000 to 10000 miles, and final drive was by imported Coventry chains. *RW*

BIRMINGHAM-TRANSPORT (GB) 1917

Birmingham & Midland Counties Transport Co. Ltd., Birmingham

This company announced a conventional 5-ton truck powered by a 4-cylinder Dorman engine. It was designed by G.E. Ralls, the company's chief engineer, initially for their own use, although they planned to put it on general sale when times were more propitious. So far as is known they did not do so. *GNG*

BISCUTER VOISIN (E) 1951-1958

Autonacional SA, Barcelona

Designed by the distinguished French engineer Gabriel Voisin, the Biscuter was the best-known of the many Spanish minicars made in the 1950s. About 5,000 were built, including a number of small vans for 250 kg loads. They were powered by the well-known 197cc Hispano-Villiers engine. *JCG*

B.J.R. (E) 1953-1960

Contrucciones Mecanicas Bautista Esplugues, Algemesi, Valencia

Don Bautista Esplugues Alvarez was a motorcycle maker who also built a number of vans powered by single-cylinder engines of 125cc, 175cc and 200cc, the former two 2-strokes and the latter a 4-stroke. *JCG*

BLACKBURN (GB) c.1906-1908

A. Blackburn, & Co., Tofts Mills, Cleckheaton, Yorks

This company, which had earlier made passenger cars under the name Norfolk, built a few light goods vehicles and buses, using 10 hp 2-cylinder or 20 hp 4-cylinder engines. The latter included charabancs with seats for 12 passengers. *GNG*

BLACK CROW (US) 1909-1912

(1) Black Manufacturing Co., Chicago, Ill 1909-1912
(2) Crow Motor Car Co., Elkhart, Ind 1912

The first model was a ½-tonner, a high-wheeler which used a 2-cylinder, air-cooled engine with a planetary transmission and double chain-drive. This single Model 30 was a closed delivery van and was priced at $900. By 1912, this make was a somewhat larger vehicle with a 4-cylinder engine, shaft drive with a three-speed gearbox, on wheelbase of 112 inches. Still, a closed van was the only model offered. *GMN*

BLACKER (US) 1910-1912

John H. Blacker & Co., Chillicothe, Ohio

Blackers were made in three sizes: ½-, 1-, and 3-tonners. The smallest, Model N, was driven by a two-cylinder engine of 13 hp and had wheelbase of 78 inches for a price of $670. The largest, designated Model S, had a 40 hp engine and wheelbase of 10 feet. Its price was $3300. *GMN*

BLAIR (US) 1911-1918

(1) Blair Mfg. Co., Newark, Ohio 1911-1914
(2) Blair Motor Truck Co., Newark, Ohio 1914-1918

Founded by Frank M. Blair, this company was an early proponent of the worm-drive rear axle, and also employed a three-point suspended sub-frame on which were mounted the engine, transmission, drive shaft and rear axle, while the front axle, body and controls were on the main frame. Three sizes were made, 1½, 2½, and 3½-tons, all using 4-cylinder Continental engines. Driver's and passenger's seats were placed on either side of the engine, giving forward-control without a high seating position. Only 25 Blair trucks were made during the seven years, and in 1918 the company was re-organized as the American Motor Truck company who subsequently made the Ace truck and bus. *GNG*

BLANC & TREZZA (I) 1923-1924

Blanc & Trezza, Milan

This firm made a few electric taxicabs, with a range of 75/90 miles per charge. *MCS*

BLEICHERT (D) 1928-1939

Bleichert Transport-Anlagen GmbH., Leipzig

Bleichert produced electric driven vehicles only starting in 1928 with a light van. During the 1930's Bleichert had the biggest output of electric vehicles in Germany and they covered the range of one to five tons with one or two motors and with front or rear wheel drive. The largest was a 5-ton 6 wheeler with both rear axles driving. The Bleichert was the origin of the British Q Electric. *HON*

BLITZ (D) 1925-1926

Aufbau Industrie Bremen GmbH., Bremen

When Carl Borgward presented his tri-van "Blitzkarre" he sold a license to this firm which produced this car, while Borgward's own capacities were limited. The vehicle had one front wheel, front mounted platform or box and rear driver's seat. One of the rear wheels was driven by a side-mounted D.K.W. engine. *HON*

1952 BLUEBIRD "Traveler" bus, MBS

BLUE BIRD (US) 1932 to date

Blue Bird Body Co., Fort Valley, Ga.

A.L. Luce was a Ford dealer in Fort Valley and Perry, Georgia. In 1927 he designed and built a bus body with angle iron roof bows in order to improve on the wooden-framed bodies generally available at that time for truck chassis. The first body was sold for school transportation and in spite of being all-metal except for a canvas roof, it had no window sashes. The trend toward consolidation of schools, and the economic depression, which was hard on auto dealers, caused Luce to sell his Ford dealerships and concentrate on bus body production in 1932, when the Blue Bird name was adopted from the color of a demonstrator.

Window sashes and all-steel construction including the roof came in 1937, though wartime buses had wooden cross sills. During a trip in 1948 Luce saw a forward control GMC chassis at the Paris Salon and imported a complete bus from a Belgian body plant because GMC would not sell him a chassis of that type. A forward control Blue Bird named the "All American" was soon offered, and starting in 1952 Blue Bird assembled its own chassis for these buses instead of modifying conventional chassis. Like other builders, Blue Bird supplies various engines and transmissions for both conventional and forward control buses.

A motor home version of the All American called the "Wanderlodge" was introduced in 1962. About 50 tandem-axle bottler's trucks were built in the early 1970's with GMC V-6 gas engines. A pusher chassis was first produced in 1976. Efforts to gain export business began in 1949 with ventures in Latin America, and today Blue Bird has foreign assembly plants in Guatemala and Canada as well as branch assembly plants in Mount Pleasant, Iowa and Buena Vista, Virginia. The three sons of A.L. Luce are owners of the company at the present time. *MBS*

B.M.A. (GB) 1952-1955

B.M.A. & Electrical Equipment Co. Ltd., Hove, Sussex

The B.M.A. was a light electric car of which at least two commercial examples were made. The first was a 4cwt pick-up version of the normal control passenger car, announced at the end of 1952, and the second was a forward-control 5cwt van with central driving position. Both had single chain drive to a rear wheel. This latter type was also announced in 1952, and was theoretically available until 1955, though probably not more than one of each was made. *MJWW*

B.M.C. (GB) 1955-1956: 1968-1970

(1) Austin Motor Co. Ltd., Longbridge, Birmingham 1955-1956

(2) Leyland Motors (Scotland) Ltd., Bathgate, East Lothian 1968-1970

The BMC label was first used briefly for the heaviest model of the 1955-56 Austin-Morris range, a forward control 7-tonner with 5.1-litre 6-cylinder diesel engine, hydrovac brakes, and power steering. Its successors reverted to the old marque names, but twelve years later the name was revived for the products of Bathgate, among them the WF normal control range, and the FG and FJ series covering the 30-cwt - 8-ton sector. It was also applied to the 350EA, a Birmingham-built 2-ton forward control van using gasoline or diesel engines of 2½ litres capacity. 1969 saw several variations on the FJ theme. notably the Laird for GVWs of 9½-13 tons, and the very similar Boxer and Mastiff, both of which broke new ground for BMC by using proprietary 6- and 8-cylinder engines by Perkins. Once again, however, the name had a short life. In July, 1970 the Birmingham-made lightweights became Leylands (even when made by Austin-Morris), while Bathgate's products became Leyland Redlines. *MCS*

B.M.F. (D) 1901-1907

Berliner Motorwagen-Fabrik GmbH., Berlin-Tempelhof

This firm developed out of the Gottschalk company. The program of friction-driven vans and trucks was carried on but soon also belt- and shaft-driven versions were introduced. Also an electric van was offered. In 1902 a 2½ and a 5 ton truck were presented. A type of delivery van which was built for the Berlin department store Wertheim became famous, known as the "Wertheim Type." This was equipped with a horizontally mounted engine and so had no hood. Many cars were delivered to the postal authorities and even the Royal Mail ordered B.M.F. cars. In 1906 B.M.F. presented a truck for beer distribution which seems to have been the first forward control car in Germany. B.M.F. cars were also known as "Tempelhof." After 1907 they were marketed as Eryx. *HON*

B.M.M.O. (GB) 1923-1969

The Birmingham & Midland Motor Omnibus Co. Ltd., Edgbaston, Birmingham

This company, best known as "Midland Red", had been in business as a bus operator for nineteen years before it commenced the design and manufacture of its own vehicles in 1923. This move was inspired by the need for a fast, light pneumatic-tired bus capable of competing with the inexpensive American-built vehicles used by B.M.M.O.'s competitors. No such vehicle was then available on the home market so the company decided to fill the gap by building buses to serve its own needs and also for sale to other companies in the British Automobile Traction group. Group members to whom vehicles were supplied had their names cast prominently into the radiator shell, giving the appearance that they were the manufacturer. The names which could be found thus were NORTHERN, ORTONA, PETERBOROUGH (Electric Traction), POTTERIES, TRENT and TYNEMOUTH. The vehicles became known by the letters "S.O.S." which were carried on the hub-caps and, from 1932 to 1940, also on the radiator. The initials are believed to have stood for "Shire's Own Specification", L.G. Wyndham Shire being Midland Red's chief engineer and a man of outstanding ability.

1925 B.M.M.O. SOS FS bus, Midland Red

The original 1923 design — later known as the S type — was a normal control lightweight 32-seater; in 1925 it was joined by B.M.M.O.'s first forward control model, the FS. these both incorporated spoked wheels combined with pneumatic tires, a most un-British feature for vehicles above the 30 cwt. range, but one which persisted with B.M.M.O. until 1927. Some early vehicles incorporated chassis frames purchased from Tilling Stevens. New and revised models were introduced in most years up to 1933, six-cylinder engines being experimented with from 1927 and being fitted on a large scale from 1929 onwards.

A prototype double-decker was produced in 1931 and production of this type, designated REDD, commenced in 1932. This developed in 1934 into the well-known FEDD design of front entrance double-decker which was constructed up to the war and incorporated, from 1937 onwards, B.M.M.O.'s K-type oil engine. The company had fitted this to its SON-type single-decker chassis from 1935 after trying out proprietary makes of diesel engine from 1934. The SON was the standard single-deck saloon throughout the middle and late 'thirties.

1936 B.M.M.O. SON 39-seater bus, AJHB

B.M.M.O. was renowned for anticipating design trends later adopted by commercial manufacturers. In 1935 an outstanding break from normal practice resulted in the construction of a rear-engined single-decker. Four such vehicles were ultimately built, and they employed B.M.M.O. gasoline engines mounted transversely behind the rear axle. In 1941-44 the four were rebuilt with

1949 B.M.M.O. D5a double decker bus, AJHB

underfloor engines — B.M.M.O. 8-litre diesel units — placed horizontally behind the front wheels in the manner which found general acceptance from the early 'fifties onwards although B.M.M.O. themselves adopted it as standard as early as 1946.

Vehicle manufacture ceased temporarily in 1940 which was the last year in which B.M.M.O. built vehicles for other operators. Post-war production was geared purely to the company's own operating needs. A prototype double-decker of 1944 was the forerunner of the D5 of 1949-50, and it introduced the full-width hood and concealed radiator which later became popularly known as the "new look" front when adopted by other manufacturers. A single-deck prototype was also constructed; this was chassisless and was built in conjunction with M.C.W. Post-war single-deck manufacture began in 1946 with the underfloor-engined S6 which had the conventional separate chassis and body, unlike the chassisless prototype, although the S6 body was itself ahead of its time in employing stressed skin construction with panels pop-riveted on to an all steel frame. Various modified designs of single-decker appeared over the years, culminating in the notable S14 which went into production in 1954 and was a chassisless design employing a steel frame and light alloy panelling, with rubber suspension and disc brakes. The last B.M.M.O. double-decker to be built in quantity, the D9 with set-back front axle and a new 10.5 litre engine, appeared in 1958. This was also a chassisless design incorporating rubber suspension and disc brakes. The first of a pair of

1950 B.M.M.O. C2 26-seater coach, Midland Red

1961 B.M.M.O. D9 double decker bus, Midland Red

underfloor-engined double-deckers of type D10 entered service in January 1961; these were the only double-deckers of this configuration ever to run in regular public service in Great Britain. In 1959 B.M.M.O. brought out the CM5 coach, the first to be purpose-built for motorway use in Britain. With supercharged engine, overdrive gearbox and high ratio hypoid rear axle, the CM5 was capable of running at 85 m.p.h.

Manufacture by B.M.M.O. of double-deck vehicles ceased in 1966. In 1969 the company, now a subsidiary of the National Bus Company, ceased its manufacturing activities entirely. Its last model had been a 51-seat underfloor-engined single-decker designated type S23. *OM*

B.M.W. (D) 1928-1939

Bayerische Motoren-Werke A.G., Eisenach

B.M.W. took over the Dixi (q.v.) works and the production of the Austin Seven based Dixi 3/15 PS. This version also was available as a van. In 1932 a three-wheeled van was presented with front platform and single driven rear wheel. Own 200 cc. and 400 cc. four-stroke engines were used. Production of this type ceased in 1934 while van versions on private car chassis' were available until 1939.*HON*

BOARD (US) 1911-1913

B.F. Board Motor Truck Company, Alexandria, Virginia

Boards were offered as "open panel cars" of various capacities: 1000, 2000, 4000 and 6000 pounds. Only the lightest had shaft drive, but all used 4-cylinder engines and right hand drive, and all had forward control. *GMN*

B.O.E. (US) 1911-1913

Motor Conveyance Company, Milwaukee, Wisconsin

B.O.E. stood for Best On Earth, possibly an over-extended claim. This make was available as a bare chassis or with platform bodies with capacities of 2, 3 or 6 tons. The most interesting of these was the massive 6-tonner whose chassis weighed 8000 pounds, with a structural steel frame and a 4-cylinder engine of 11.3 liter displacement. *GMN*

BOES (D) 1904-1905

Jacob Boes & Co., Berlin-Charlottenburg

This firm produced a three-wheeled van with one front wheel and front driver's seat. Nearly all vehicles produced were brought by the postal authorities and were used for letter collecting. *HON*

BOLLSTROM (US) 1915-1920

(1) Bollstrom Product Sales Co, Battle Creek, Mich 1915-1916

(2) Bollstrom Motors, Inc, Detroit, Mich 1916-1920

The earliest Bollstrom was a 3/4-tonner. The last model on record was the Model A for 1920 which was a five-tonner on a wheelbase of 144 inches. This latter used a 4-cylinder engine of their own manufacture with Bosch ignition and a four-speed gearbox. Some accounts claim this make used 4-wheel-drive but this claim is not substantiated. *GMN*

BOLTON (See Bradshaw)

BOMBARDIER (CDN) 1935 to date

l'Autoneige Bombardier Lt, Valcourt, Quebec

While the Bombardier snowmobile had tracks on the back and skis on the front, and could easily navigate snow covered fields, hill or woods, it was designed primarily for use on roads in the days before they were kept open all winter for ordinary cars and trucks. By 1937 the 7-passenger Ford V-8 powered B-7 model with its Volkswagen-like silhouette and slab sides, was used by priests, salesmen, doctors and taxi drivers. A cargo model, in the style of a panel truck with no rear side windows, appeared in 1940, and a 12-passenger B-12 model, with little porthole windows in the sides, in 1941. Despite its greater size and weight, the B-12 had a better flotation on snow. It was used extensively for mail delivery and as a school bus. Bombardier later diversified into specialized tracked vehicles and Ski-Doos; today they operate a railway locomotive factory, but a modified B-12 is still sold. *HD*

BONACINI (I) 1898

Ciro Bonacini, Modena

One of Italy's first gasoline commercial vehicles, the Bonacini was an omnibus chassis, bodies being the work of Orlandi, a local coachbuilder. Power was provided by a front-mounted 20 hp Bolide engines. *MCS*

BOND (GB) 1951-1970

1) Sharps Commercials Ltd, Preston, Lancs 1951-1964

2) Bond Cars Ltd, Preston, Lancs 1964-1970

1969 BOND 875 6cwt van, GNG

By 1951 the ingenious Bond Minicar with its single chain-driven front wheel had been adapted for commercial use, initially under the name of Sharp's Minitruck. The first type, however, differed from the cars in several respects; the engine was a 250cc 4-stroke Brockhouse, the driver sat centrally, and there was double-coil rear suspension. This one never saw series production, giving way to more conventional goods-carrying car derivatives with 197cc Villiers engines. No vans were offered between 1955 and 1959, the next such vehicle being the more sophisticated Ranger with 250cc reversible Villiers engine, 12-volt electrics, and stressed aluminum structure with glass fibre top. From 1962, a rear door was provided, but the original Minicar line was withdrawn in 1965. Two years later came Bond's last van, a version of the 875 saloon with rear-mounted ohc 4-cylinder Hillman Imp engine, 4-speed all-synchromesh gearbox, and trailing-arm irs. It was a compact little vehicle only 128 in long, but commercial vehicle production ceased when Reliant took over Bond and closed down the Preston factory. *MCS*

BORGWARD (D) 1924-1927; 1938-1962

1. Bremer Kuhlerfabrik Borgward & Co., Bremen 1924-1927

2. Carl F.W. Borgward Automobil-und Motoren-Werke, Bremen 1938-1949

3. Carl F.W. Borgward GmbH., Bremen; Osterholz-Scharmbeck 1949-1962

Borgward's first attempt in car production was a small van, the "Blitzkarren" of 1924. It was a three-wheeler with one front wheel, front mounted box and two rear wheels, of which one was driven by a D.K.W. engine. The driver's seat was at the rear. This vehicle was also

1937 BOMBARDIER B7 van, HD

produced under the name of "Blitz" (q.v.) as Borgward's own capacities were limited. In 1926 Borgward presented a new tri-van design under the name of "Goliath" (q.v.) and gave up the "Blitzkarren" in 1927.

Since 1938 all Hansa-Lloyd (q.v.) cars were marketed under the name of Borgward. The range covered trucks from 1½ to 5 ton payload capacity. Up to 3 tons gasoline as well as diesel engines were available; the heavier versions all had diesel engines. A 3 ton standard truck for the army was also built by Borgward. It was available either as 4x2 or 4x4 version with gasoline or diesel engine. Also the 3 ton half-track truck — developed by Hansa-Lloyd — was carried on. The 8 ton half-track truck was built under Krauss-Maffei license.

1959 BORGWARD 4-ton van, GNG

1961 BORGWARD B2500 van, GNG

After WW II Borgward started in 1945 with a 3 ton truck using a 3.5 litre gasoline engine. It was supplemented in 1947 by a 1¼ ton version with 1.5 litre gasoline engine. In 1952 a 4-tonner appeared whose chassis was also available for buses and as articulated tractor. A light 2-3 ton truck for the army was a new development, a 6-cylinder 2.3 litre 80 PS gasoline engine was installed. One year later a 4x4 private version was presented using a 6-cylinder 5.0 litre engine of 95 PS. Since 1954 the light versions had a new face but still featured normal control. Forward control bodies appeared in 1958 but normal control was further available. 4- and 6-cylinder engines — gasoline as well as diesel — were supplied ranging from 1.8 litre to 5.0 litre and 42 to 110 PS were offered. Production ended in 1962 when financial difficulties forced Borgward to give up. *HON*

BORLAND (US) 1912-1914

Borland-Grannis Co., Chicago, Ill

There were two models of this electric truck, both 3/4-tonners. An open express van designated Model 10 weighed 2500 pounds with a wheelbase of 81 inches. The Model 15 used the same chassis with closed body. Exide batteries weighing 1200 pounds were used and the final drive was by chains to the rear wheels. A top speed of 15 mph was claimed for these trucks with a maximum range of 50 miles per battery charge. This manufacturer was merged into the American Electric Car Co. *GMN*

BOSCHUNG (CH) 1976 to date

Marcel Boschung, Schmitten, FR

Little 4x2 or 4x4 vehicles, called "Pony", are equipped with the 40 VW-engine mounted amidship. The gearbox of six forward and reverse speeds. Payload is two tons and the turning radius 3 m only. Boschung are well known for their snow-clearing machines. *FH*

BOSS (US) 1905-1906

Boss Knitting Machine Works, Reading, Pa

The Boss steamer was a light delivery van rated at 1000-pound capacity with wheelbase of just 72 inches. This was powered by a Mason double-acting steam engine mounted under the driver's seat. Steering was by tiller and price of this Model D was $800. This manufacturer also built steam passenger autos. *GMN*

1940 BOTH electric van, D.J.R. Both

BOTH (AUS) 1940-1943

(1) Both Electrics Ltd, Adelaide
(2) J.A. Lawton & Sons, Adelaide

The Both was a 3-wheel electric delivery van intended mainly for house-to-house bread delivery. It had a 90-volt 3hp motor driving by chain to the single front wheel with a range of 45-50 miles for normal delivery work, and a top speed of 20-25 mph. Bodywork on the early models was by A.P.H. Oke of North Adelaide, and was rather spartan with neither windscreen or doors, but when Lawton took over manufacture they made the bodies as well, with both these amenities. About 100 Both Electrics were made. The designer E.T. Both achieved international fame as the inventor of the iron lung for polio victims, which was sponsored by Lord Nuffield. *GNG*

1978 BOUGHTON RB44 4 × 4 truck, Reynolds Boughton

BOUGHTON (GB) 1978 to date

Reynolds Boughton Ltd., Amersham, Bucks

Reynolds Boughton originally built winches for timber

extraction, followed by off-road conversions for proprietory chassis, and special fire engine chassis for cross country work (see CHUBB). In the summer of 1978 they introduced the Boughton RB 44, a 4 x 4 5 ton CVW chassis for a variety of civilian and military uses. Three wheelbase lengths are available, from 130 to 156 inches, and engine options include three Ford V-6 gasoline units from 100 to 158 hp, and Bedford, Ford or Perkins diesel units from 82 to 100 hp. *GNG*

BOULTI-LARBORDIERE (F) 1903-1904

Boulti-Larbordiere et Cie, Paris.

A 10-ton wagon was shown at the Paris Show of 1903, using a vertical boiler at the front of the chassis with a vertical 2-cylinder engine, reported to drive the rear axle by bevel gear.*RAW*

BOUR-DAVIS (US) 1919

Louisiana Motor Car Co. Shreveport, La.

The makers of the Bour-Davis car also made a 2½-ton truck briefly. Production was slight — perhaps 100 trucks. *RW*

BOURNE (U.S.) 1915-1918

(1) Bourne Magnetic Truck Co., Philadelphia, Pa. 1915-1918

(2) Bourne Magnetic Truck Co., New York, N.Y. 1918

Stephen N. Bourne built several experimental trucks in 1915; they were tested by the Atlantic Refining Company. Production was started in late 1916 with a 2-ton model priced at $3,150 and a 3-ton model priced at $3,850. Sales were conducted jointly with Owen Magnetic in New York. The Bourne factory in Philadelphia was also occupied by the Biddle Motor Car Company.

The most salient feature of the Bourne was the Entz magnetic transmission, a unique feature among trucks. It was used in the Owen-Magnetic and Deering Magnetic cars. The magnetic transmission took the place of the conventional clutch and transmission. The Entz system, manufactured by General Electric, was simple, clean and efficient. The system was, however, rather expensive and this no doubt limited the sales of all magnetic-driven vehicles.

The Bourne was otherwise a conventional truck powered by a Hercules 4-cylinder engine with worm gear final drive. Artillery wheels had solid tires. Steering was left-hand in a semi-enclosed cab. *DJS & RW*

BOVA (NL) 1970 to date

Carrosseriefabriek BOVA B.V., Valkenswaard.

Bova, one of the oldest and most renowned Dutch manufacturers of bus bodies, started in 1970 building integral buses around DAF running units. shaping the body after the good examples set by Van Hool. Three models are currently in production: N 16, N 18 and N 24. *JFJK*

BOVY, BOVY-PIPE (B) 1904-1936

S.A. des Automobiles Industriels Bovy, Brussels-Molenbeek

Soon after they had introduced their first cars in 1904, the construction company owned by Albert Bovy started producing a wide range of commercial vehicles with payloads from some 200 kgs up to about four tons, and engine outputs of 18 to 28 hp. Both cars and trucks were produced up to 1920 under the Bovy-Dheyne trade-mark, in which year the company decided to concentrate on commercial vehicles only. Their strongest point were the lightweight construction, a fact that made Bovy renowned in Belgium and abroad.

1936 BOVY-PIPE 32-seater coach, JFJK

Particularly for colonial use a range of chassis with gasproducer engine were constructed during the 'twenties. Another *specialite de la maison* was a wide track chassis for fire-engines, featured in their catalogues around 1928.

In 1930 Bovy was taken over by Brossel, who would operate the company for several years as their 'Light Vehicles Division' before a final integration. From 1931 onwards Pipe, also acquired by Brossel, was bearing Bovy company as the second member of this division. The vehicles produced were from then on sold under the name Bovy-Pipe. *JFJK*

BOWDEN (GB) 1927

Bowden Brake Company Ltd., Birmingham.

Although best known for the production of cables and brakes, Sir Frank Bowden's company made three attempts to enter the vehicle market: in 1902, with a 2 hp motorcycle; in 1913 with the 2-cylinder Tyseley light car, and in 1927 with a 3-wheeled light van, for local delivery work. This was, unfortunately, attended with no more success than its predecessors. *MJWW*

BOWEN (GB) 1906-1908

Bowen & Co., Mount Pleasant, London W.C.

The Bowen light cars and vans were made by a brass foundry which had been established in 1808. They were unusual in making practically all of the vehicle, including the 9 hp vertical twin engine, in their factory. The van had a capacity of 6 cwt, a 3-speed gearbox and shaft drive. *GNG*

BOYD (US) 1908-1916

James Boyd & Brother, Philadelphia, Pa.

This make seems to have built exclusively as fire engines including hose wagons and chemical wagons. The chassis for these weighed 4600 pounds with a wheelbase of 144 inches. These were powered by 4-cylinder engines, and top speed was claimed to be 50 mph. *GMN*

1857 BOYDELL traction engine (built by Tuxford of Boston), Science Museum, London

BOYDELL (GB) 1855-1862

Boydell & Glaisher, London

James Boydell was the patentee (1846 and 1854) of an early form of track-laying wheel which was equipped with interlocking, iron shod, swamp shoes. Though Boydell & Glaisher exhibited (as at the Royal Show, Chelmsford in 1856) haulage engines which they claimed to have manufactured, the only elements made by them were the patent wheels. The earliest recorded Boydell engine was by Richard Bach (Birmingham) in 1855, the second by Garrett in 1856 and thereafter by Burrell, Clayton & Shuttleworth, Lee and Tuxford. Boydell failed to incorporate an effective device to allow lateral canting of the shoes when in contact with a hard obstacle in their path and because of the wear and tear arising from this and other causes the idea was abandoned on Boydell's death in 1862. *RAW*

BOYER (F) 1906

Boyer et Cie, Puteaux, Seine

This car maker did not offer a commercial vehicle until his last year in business. The Boyer was, however, an ambitious 9.9-litre 4-cylinder affair available as a double-decker bus or 5-ton truck. Other features were a 3-speed gearbox, dual ignition, side-chain drive, and rubber shock absorbers. *MCS*

BRADBURY (GB) 1905-c.1906

Bradbury & Co. Ltd., Oldham, Lancs.

Bradbury was a well-known motorcycle maker who built a few trade carriers powered by their 4½ hp single-cylinder engines, with 2-speed gearbox and chain drive. Load capacity was 2 cwt. *GNG*

BRADFIELD see Kissel

BRADFORD see Jowett

1922 BRADFORD CORPORATION trolleybus, KCB

BRADFORD CORPORATION (GB) 1913-1923

Bradford Corporation Tramways, Bradford, Yorkshire

In the first decade or so of trolleybuses, Bradford Corporation constructed a total of 26 vehicles in its tramway works at Thornbury. At this time there was no established manufacturer of trolleybuses in Great Britain, early design trends being more tram than bus orientated and thus of little interest to established commercial vehicle builders. Most of the Bradford vehicles, which were built entirely for the Corporation's own use, were small single-deckers but there were two interesting exceptions. A vehicle built in 1920 was the first covered-top double-deck trolleybus in the country, and a remarkable four-wheel-steered double-decker completed early in 1922 was the first high capacity trolleybus and seated 59 passengers. It anticipated by several years the wider use of multi-axle passenger vehicles in Great Britain. *OM*

BRADSHAW (GB) 1902-1909

(1) James Bradshaw & Sons, Victory, Bolton 1902-1907
(2) The Bolton Motor Wagon Company, Victory, Bolton, Lancs. 1907-1909

The Bradshaw used an improved de Dion boiler with a small coil superheater, fired with coal or coke. A 4-cylinder single-acting undertype engine was used, at first compound but latterly as high pressure throughout, years ahead of its time. Slip eccentric reversing gear was used. Final drive was by a pair of roller chains.

Bradshaws were quite reasonable performers and much ahead of most early vertical boilered wagons but were outclassed by the Sentinel. Fewer than a dozen were made. *RAW*

BRAMHAM see Stanhope

BRAMWELL (US) 1905

Springfield Auto Company, Springfield, Ohio

The Bramwell was a small delivery van powered by a 2-cylinder, 20 hp engine, with a wheelbase of 76 inches. It used forward control. This vehicle weighed only 1700 pounds and was priced at $1250. *GMN*

BRANTFORD (CDN) 1911-1916

Brantford Motor Truck Co. Ltd., Brantford, Ont.

The Brantford was introduced with a dash-mounted radiator and was available in models from ⅔ to 1½ tons. They introduced the idea of a removable body which could be left at a loading bay while the truck was delivering a full load. In 1917 production was switched to the Brant-Ford, a 1-ton pick-up which was basically an elongated Model T Ford with chain drive. The company is still in business making truck bodies and trailers. *HD*

BRASIE (US) 1913-1917

(1) Brasie Motor Truck Co., Minneapolis, Minn. 1913-1914
(2) Brasie Motor Car Co., Minneapolis, Minn. 1914-1916
(3) Packet Motor Car Mfg. Co., Minneapolis, Minn. 1916-1917

Frank R. Brasie's first product was the Twin City truck, a forward-control, chain-driven 2-tonner, but this was replaced in 1914 by the Packet, a light delivery van powered by a 12 hp 4-cylinder engine, with friction transmission and belt final drive. In 1916 the company name was changed to Packet, and this is sometimes regarded as a make in its own right. *GNG*

BRASIER (F) 1898-1928

(incl. Georges Richard, 1898-1903: Richard-Brasier, 1903-1904)

(1) Societe des Anciens Etablissements Georges Richard, Ivry-Port 1897-1905

(2) Societe des Automobiles Brasier, Ivry-Port 1905-1926

(3) Societe Chaigneau-Brasier, Ivry-Port 1926-1928

This car maker offered a belt-driven delivery van with 6 hp 2-cylinder engine as early as 1898, such light commercials surviving until 1902, by which time Richard's private cars followed the more sophisticated Panhard idiom. A military postal wagon was built in 1900, and a 2-ton truck of 1902 had chain drive. By the end of 1904 M. Richard had departed to build Unics at Puteaux, while Brasier's victories in the 1904 and 1905 Gordon Bennett Races led to an increasing interest in big luxury cars. Their little 10/12 hp vertical twin with 3-speed gearbox was, however, marketed as a cab or light van from 1908 to 1913, some of the cabs finding their way as far afield as Sydney. An interesting departure of 1909 was the production of self-contained avant-train units for the conversion of horse buses and vans to mechanical propulsion. The established twin was used for payloads of up to two tons, but 4-cylinder conversion kits with 18 hp engines were also available. By 1913 the company's 2-litre 12/20 hp private car engine was being used to power a conventional 2-tonner, but there were also heavier Brasiers with driver-over-engine layout, round Solex radiators, 3- or 4-speed gearboxes, and side-chain drive. All had 4-cylinder sv monobloc engines, and the biggest ones wer 4-tonners of 4.7 litres capacity. Brasier also supplied engines to Mass for installation in their trucks.

Specialized vehicles were made for the French Air Service during World War I, but from 1919 onwards Brasier's truck production was rationalized, with normal control, the old 4.7-litre engine, four forward speeds, chain drive (a lockable differential was an option), and twin rear wheels. Payloads ranged from two to five tons, with pneumatics available on all but the largest ones. Production ceased in 1928, two years before the demise of the private cars. *MCS*

BRAUN (D) 1898-1918

(1) Nurnberger Feuerloschgerate — und Maschinenfabrik vorm. Justus Christian Braun, Nuremberg 1898-1911

(2) Justus-Christian Braun Premier-Werke AG.,Nuremberg 1911-1913

(3) Nurnberger Feuerloschgerate —, Automobillast-wagen- und Fahrzeug-Fabrik, Nuremburg 1913-1918

This firm began with the production of fire engines which they supplied with steam, gasoline or gasoline-electric drive. After 1906 trucks were added to the range starting with a 10 ton version with gasoline-electric drive. Later versions had conventional gasoline engines. In 1918 the firm merged with Ansbach to form FAUN. *HON*

BRAVIA (P) 1964 to date

Bravia S.a.r.l., Lisbon

A producer of military vehicles, Bravia builds a variety of 4x4 and 6x6 truck chassis using proprietary mechanical units. Comando, Gazella, Leopardo, and Pantera are the names given to the models that cover a wide range from ¼ to six ton NATO class payloads and are powered by either gasoline or diesel engine.

A range of armored personal carriers were also built since the early 1970s, consisting of the basic Chaimite 4x4 model and its variants. The Chaimite is powered by either a 2IO gasoline or a V6 diesel engine and carries 11 combat equipped men. External appearance is interestingly similar to the American Commando armored behicle, though no connection exists between the two companies. *GA*

BRAY (GB) 1856-1867

Wm. Bray, Folkestone, Kent 1856

Bray's Traction Engine Company, Pall Mall, London 1856-67

Bray, a ship's engineer, constructed his first road locomotive in Folkestone in 1856/57. At first intended for agricultural use, incorporating his patent driving wheels, in which teeth could be made to project from the segment of the rim in contact with the ground by means of an eccentric on the axle, it soon attracted attention for general haulage. It probably achieved the distinction of being the first showman's road locomotive by being used, on hire, by one Jim Myers in 1859 for hauling circus paraphernalia.

On the formation of the company, D.K. Clark, the distinguished locomotive engineer, was appointed consulting engineer and seems to have directed designs. Subsequent manufacture appears to have been by sub-contract or license. F & J. Hughes of New Cross, London, made several in 1860 and engines were made under license by Taylor of Birkenhead, Chaplin of Glasgow and Dubs & Company of Glasgow.

1857 BRAY traction engine. J.P. Mullett Collection

Apart from the patent wheels Bray engines had plate frames, similar to railway practice, twin high pressure outside cylinders driving the first shaft which was geared to the second shaft by gears between the frames. Final drive was by gears on the respective ends of the countershaft engaging with integral ring gears on each rear wheel, one wheel being clutched out of drive on sharp corners. Usually locomotive boilers were used but the Chaplin-built examples used his vertical boiler.

Undermounted haulage engines were developed further on the Continent but interest in them in Britain seems to have waned by the late 1860s, in favor of the conventional traction engine layout, probably because of the onerous legal restrictions, but in their time Bray engines performed notable feats of heavy haulage. *RAW*

BRECHT (US) 1904

Brecht Automobile Co., St. Louis, Mo.

This company made steam and electric passenger cars, and listed a Fancy Steam Delivery Wagon with 12 hp 2-cylinder vertical double-acting reversible engine. Load capacity was 1800 lbs and top speed 15 mph. *GNG*

1943 BREDA Dovunque 6×4 7-ton truck, Breda

BREDA (I) 1920-1945

Societa Italiana Ernesto Breda, Milan.

This huge engineering combine (ordnance, aircraft) also built roadgoing vehicles for the Italian Army. Best known and longest-lived of these was the 32, a 4x4 heavy tractor with 8.1-litre 4-cylinder ohv engine, dual magneto ignition, and 5x2-speed gearbox: diesel-powered developments had appeared by 1940. From 1935 there were also some 6x4 forward control load carriers; wartime editions were 7-tonners with 8.8-litre 6-cylinder diesel engines and air brakes. A small 2-stroke gasoline motor was used for starting purposes. A copy of the German Krauss-Maffei halftrack followed in 1944, and in 1958 Breda (by then owners of the Isotta Fraschini name) attempted to revive the company's trucks. Also produced were trolleybuses, some of which were still in service in Perugia in 1970. *MCS*

BREMAC (i) 1971 to date

Fratelli Brenna, Varese

This company took over production of Aermacchi's 30-cwt 3-wheeler diesel truck, the ND3, fitting a different engine. Features of the design were a 4-speed gearbox, fully enclosed cab, wheel steering, and coupled hydraulic brakes. *MCS*

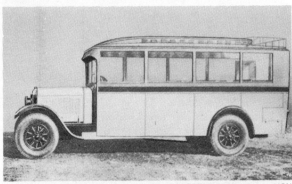

1929 BRENNABOR light bus, HON

BRENNABOR (D) 1905-1932

Gebr. Reichstein Brennabor-Werke, Brandenburg

A motorcycle, based van with two rear wheels started the production of Brennabor commercials. From 1909 also four-wheeled vans were available, based on the private car design. Only in 1924 a 1-ton truck appeared as an independent chassis design but using the 8/24 PS engine of the private car. The newly developed 6-cylinder engine was used for 1½-ton and 2-ton trucks and for a bus with seating capacity of 18 passengers. These models were built until 1932 when production of commercials was given up. *HON*

BRENNAN (US) 1913

Brennan Manufacturing Company, Syracuse, New York

This manufacturer had earlier been a builder of stock engines for motor cars and trucks. Apparently for a single year they offered 2-, 3- and 5-ton stake body and platform body trucks. The larger truck had forward control with a price of $4600 with a stake body. *GMN*

BRETHERTON & BRYAN (GB) 1905-1908

Davey Paxman & Co., Ltd., Colchester, Essex

Frank Bretherton and L.C. Bryan had an engineering and haulage business at Willesden Green, North London for which Bretherton designed a 5-ton wagon using his own design of short locomotive boiler in conjunction with a compound undertype engine, two speed gearing and all gear final drive. Earlier examples had cast steel one piece wheels but later wagons had artillery wheels with steel tires. Some examples were sold to other users, the first made actually going to Finch, the London wine firm and another to Barratt & Co., the Wood Green (London) candy manufacturers.

The boiler was fired through the firebox crown, the chute taking the place of crown stays. Bretherton later designed the boilers of the Ransomes and Robey wagons in which a fully stayless box was used but in the case of his undertype design quickly reached the conclusion the despite its theoretical advantages it was inferior to an overtype in terms of work performed and, so far as is known, all his subsequent design work was on overtypes.

Although sold by Bretherton & Bryan the wagons were actually built by the traction engine maker, Davey Paxman. By 1906 the firm had changed its name to Bryan & Co. *RAW*

BRIDGEPORT (US) 1920-1927

(1) Bridgeport Motor Truck Corp., Bridgeport, Conn.
(2) Morrisey Motor Car Co., Bridgeport, Conn.

Bridgeport trucks were initially made in 4½- and 6-ton models powered by Hercules engines, but after 1923 lighter models from 1½ to 4 tons load were made, using various models of Buda engine. From 1924 to 1925 only a 30-seater bus was offered, known as the Bridgeport 45. *GNG*

BRIGHTMORE see Coulthard and Manchester (i)

BRILL see A.C.F.

BRILLIE (F) 1904-1907

Societe des Automobiles Eugene Brillie, Paris.

Eugene Brillie discontinued his partnership with Gustave Gobron in 1903 and formed his own company in Paris. He concentrated on the design and development of commercial vehicles, particularly buses, which used a Schneider-designed and built gasoline engine. All other parts of the Brillie buses were also manufactured by the Schneider armaments company, in their Le Havre plant, but to the ideas of Eugene Brillie. The most interesting detail of the Brillie buses was the cab-over-engine lay-out. Between the 8th and 24th, December 1905 the Compagnie Generale des Omnibus of Paris started experiments with gasoline buses on a test track between the Bourse and the Cours la Reine. Among the vehicles was a Brillie, the marque which was finally selected as the supplier of their first fleet of motor buses. 150 chassis were ordered in

1906 BRILLE 35/45 hp truck, OMM

1906 BRILLIE 35/45hp van, OMM

1907 BRILLIE 6-wheel Paris bus, OMM

total, in two batches of viz. 90 and 60 units. The model designation was P2, the engine still a Schneider, and the body already mounted by Scemia. On the 11th, June 1906 the first buses were put into service.

The successor of the P2 was the P3, again with a Schneider engine and the characteristic round radiator constructed by the Ets. Goudard & Menesson, currently known as manufacturers of Solex carburetors. The engine had four separate cylinders with a bore and stroke of 125 x 140 mm and an output of 35 hp at 1000 rmp. The weight of a bare/chassis was 3.19 tons, with a body the P3 weighed 5.06 tons.

A very early user of Brillie buses was also the city of Barcelona, which ordered a number 1906. However, Eugene Brillie wasn't in a position to finance his own success and his company went into bankruptcy in 1908. Production of buses was continued by Schneider, under their own name. *JFJK*

BRINTON (US) 1913-1924

(1) Chester County Motor Co., Coatesville, Pa., 1913-1916
(2) Brinton Motor Truck Co., Philadelphia, Pa., 1917-1924

1915 BRINTON Model B 2-ton truck, Mrs. John S. Downing Sr.

Although the 1913 Brinton prototype was a 1500-pound truck with Renault-type hood and radiator and chain drive, the first production model was a 2-ton truck with Rutenber 4-cylinder engine and worm drive. Later models of 1-ton and 2½-ton capacity had Wisconsin or Continental engines. Production for twelve years totaled no more than 287 trucks, of which 76 were built in Coatesville. *DJS*

BRISCOE (US) 1915-1921

Briscoe Motor Corp., Jackson, Mich.

Initially, the Briscoe was a ½-tonner using the passenger car chassis by the same manufacturer. This had a 3-speed gearbox on the rear axle and was available with canopy top or panel body. For 1918, a 1-tonner also was built with double-chain drive, and for 1920, this drive was changed to an internal gear type rear axle. This 1-tonner was the only type made for 1920-1921. *GMN*

1904 BRISTOL (i) steam wagon, RAW

BRISTOL (i) (GB) 1904 — c.1908

Bristol Wagon & Carriage Works Ltd., Bristol.

Though the marque is noted for its body building a few 3- and 5-ton vertical boilered undertype steamers were made up to 1906. The wagons were two speed, the final drive in the larger being by chain and, in the 3-tonner, all gear. In this feature and in general appearance it resembled the Ellis. By 1906, however, the firm had gone over to the short locomotive boiler but sales did not revive and the steam wagons were extinct by 1908. *RAW*

1922 BRISTOL (ii) 4-ton tanker, OMM

BRISTOL (ii) (GB) 1908 to date

(1) Bristol Tramways & Carriage Co. Ltd., Filton, Bristol, 1908-1912

(2) Bristol Tramways & Carriage Co. Ltd., Brislington, Bristol, 1912-1954

(3) Bristol Commercial Vehicles Ltd., Brislington, Bristol, 1955 to date

This old-established concern traces its origins back to the formation of the Bristol Tramways Company of 1874, out of which the Bristol Tramways & Carriage Co. Ltd. was formed in 1887. The company was primarily an operating concern and its rolling stock included electric trams from 1895 and motor buses from 1906. Road vehicle construction did not commence until 1908, in the May of which year the first Bristol passenger vehicle, a 16-seater, was completed. Pre-war production was mainly based on a 4-ton model for passenger and goods use, and after a wartime period of aircraft manufacture, a similar type was again produced up to the mid-'twenties. In 1923 a smaller, forward control model for 2 ton loads or 20-25 passengers was introduced, both this and the four-tonner being available for sale to other operators as well as being used by Bristol Tramways themselves.

1925 BRISTOL (ii) 32 seater bus, Chris Taylor Collection

In 1925 the A-type was announced. This was a heavy, low-loading chassis of which only eighteen were built, mostly double-deckers. A lighter version, the B-type of 1926 (known as the Superbus) was in contrast very successful. In 1930 a 6-cylinder version of the Superbus appeared in the form of the D-type but this found few purchasers as did two other new models of the same year, the C-type double-decker and the three-axle E-type, Bristol's only trolleybus design. The B and D developed into the 27'6" long H and J models and these were joined by the 26'6" long G-type double-decker. Although Bristol had carried out considerable development work on the Redrup axial gasoline engine, Gardner diesel units were installed on request from 1933 and were fitted to nearly all new Bristols from 1935 onwards. The G and J types when fitted with Gardner 5-cylinder engines were known as the GO5G and JO5G respectively and were reliable and economic vehicles. Bristol Tramways came under the control of the Thomas Tilling organization in March 1931, and thereafter Bristol buses were supplied in ever increasing numbers to operators in the Tilling group. No interest was shown in the manufacture of goods vehicles during the nineteen-thirties.

In 1937 the famous K (double-deck) and L (single-deck) models replaced earlier designs and they continued in production, with a wartime break from 1942 to 1944, until well into the post-war era. Added length resulted in the K becoming the KS and the L becoming the LL, while 8 ft. wide versions were developed as the KSW and LWL respectively. The single-decker ceased production in the early 'fifties with the arrival of underfloor-engined ma-

1928 BRISTOL (ii) B-type bus, KCB

chines, but the KS and KSW were available until as late as 1957. Bristol's own diesel engine, which had been under development since 1938, was available in post-war years as an alternative to the Gardner (or the AEC 7.7 which was sometimes specified), but the majority of Bristols continued to be Gardner-powered.

The integral LS underfloor-engined light saloon was introduced at the end of 1950 and later developed into the medium weight MW. But the greatest step forward came with the Lodekka low floor double-decker which permitted a conventional upper-deck seating layout with center gangway to be installed for the first time in a double-decker within an overall unladen height of only 13'4". Two prototypes of 1949/50 had twin propeller shafts, but the final production design of 1953 combined a single propeller shaft with a double-reduction rear axle. There were various models of Lodekka, including a flat floor version from 1959 onwards, and over 5,000 were built before production ceased in 1968. The first VR rear-engined double decker, with longitudinally mounted engine, appeared experimentally in 1966, and from this developed the VRT with transversely mounted rear engine, which went into production in 1968 and is still current. The main single-deck model between 1963 and 1975 was the rear-engined RE. Models designed for use on lightly used services were the SC of 1954, the SU of 1960 and the still-current LH of 1967.

1948 BRISTOL (ii) K-type bus, NMM

Bristol came under state control in 1948 when the Tilling group was nationalized, and thereafter all new orders for Bristol vehicles were confined to state-owned concerns up to August 1965 when Leyland acquired a 25% interest (since increased to 50%) allowing sales to be resumed on the open market. In 1952 goods vehicle production was resumed to use up factory capacity, the whole

1957 BRISTOL (ii) HG 15-ton truck, GNG

1958 BRISTOL (ii) Lodekka bus, GNG

1974 BRISTOL (ii) VRT bus, GNG

output being supplied to subsidiaries of the state-owned Road Haulage Executive. The initial goods model, the HG rigid 8-wheeler, was later followed by the HA articulated tractor. Leyland and Gardner engines were used to power the Bristol goods models which continued in production until 1964. Almost the whole passenger vehicle output between 1949 and 1965 was bodied by Eastern Coach Works Ltd., another concern in the state-owned sector.

In 1943 a new company was formed with the title Bristol Commercial Vehicles Ltd. but it was not activated until 1st January 1955 on which date all manufacturing was divorced from the operating activities of Bristol Tramways and placed under the B.C.V. organization. *OM*

BRISTOL (iii) (US) 1909

Bristol Engineering Co., Bristol, Conn.

This manufacturer of passenger cars built a landaulet taxicab with a 4-cylinder engine, 3-speed gearbox and shaft-drive. This was a 5-seater and used ½-elliptical springs in front with 3/4-ellipticals at the rear. *GMN*

1914 BRITISH BERNA 5-ton truck, BHV

BRITISH BERNA (GB) 1914-1918

British Berna Motor Lorries Ltd., West Kensington, London W.

The British Berna was a close copy of the Swiss version, though with a tubular radiator and large header tank which gave it a different and heavier appearance. It was made by Henry Watson and Sons Ltd of Newcastle-on-Tyne who later made their own truck of similar design under the name Watson. 3½- and 5-tonners were listed, though most seemed to be of the larger size. More than 300 British Bernas were used by the British Army in World War I, in addition to 591 of the Swiss variety. *GNG*

BRITISH QUAD see F.W.D. (ii)

BRITON (GB) 1912-1918

Briton Motor Co. Ltd., Wolverhampton, Staffs

This offshoot of (i) Star was managed by Edward Lisle Jr, and made inexpensive light cars with some affinities to the senior make. A logical development was a 5-cwt van using their 10/12hp chassis with vertical-twin engine, 3-speed gearbox, and detachable wheels. The range was augmented in 1914 by 7-cwt and 15-cwt models using paircast 1.7-litre and 2.4-litre 4-cylinder power units. 1915 saw a 50-cwt shaft-drive truck using a 4-cylinder sv Star engine and a quantity of other Star components. Only about four of these were, however, made, and all commercial-vehicle activity was discontinued after the Armistice. *MCS*

BROC (US) 1909-1914

(1) Broc Carriage & Wagon Co., Cleveland, O 1909-1912
(2) Broc Electric Car Co., Cleveland., O 1912-1914

Two sizes of battery-powered electrics appear to have been built under this tradename. One was a ½-tonner while the other was a 1-tonner. The larger was available with either closed or open bodies and gross weight is stated as 3400 lbs with a wheelbase of 100 inches. Maximum speed was given as 15 mph. The last few years of this company were confused as it was combined in 1914 with Argo and Borland-Grannis to form the American Electric Car Co. In 1916, American Electric Car Co was absorbed by Columbia Motors Co. *GMN*

1912 BROCKWAY 3-cylinder truck, Brockway

BROCKWAY (US) 1912-1977

(1) Brockway Motor Truck Co., Cortland, N.Y. 1912-
(2) Brockway Motor Co. Inc., Cortland, N.Y. -1956
(3) Brockway Motor Trucks, Divn of Mack Trucks Inc., Cortland, N.Y. 1956-1977

Veteran New York carriage builder George A. Brockway built his first motor truck in 1912. It was a high wheel delivery wagon powered by a 3-cylinder 2-stroke air-cooled engine, and had a 2-speed planetary transmission. By 1914 more conventional trucks of up to 3,500 lbs

1920 BROCKWAY gulley emptier, Brockway

capacity were made, with 4-cylinder Continental engines. This firm was to supply the bulk of Brockway's engines up to the 1960s when diesels took over. During 1917 and 1918 the entire Brockway production went to military requirements; in addition to their own designs, Brockway built 587 of the Class B Liberty trucks for the army. Fire engines were also made for the protection of army camps, ports and government explosive plants.

1919 saw a return to civilian production with 1½ and 3½ ton worm drive trucks of conventional layout, joined in 1921 by a 5 tonner. In 1925 Brockway forsook Continental for a while, and used 4- and 6-cylinder Wisconsin engines in their light range of 1½ and 2½ tonners, 6-cylinder engines only being employed from 1928 onwards. By this time Brockway was one of the nation's largest independent truck makers, with an

1928 BROCKWAY Model R tipper truck, Brockway

annual production of 5,500 units. 1928 also saw the purchase of the Indiana Truck Corporation of Marion, Indiana. There was a close parallel between the standards and range of these firms, and the Indiana purchase enabled Brockway to move into the mid-Western and some foreign markets, whereas previously their sales had been largely confined to the Eastern seaboard. However, by 1932 the Depression necessitated the sale of Indiana to White. From 1933 to 1938 Brockway made a range of electric trucks of 1 to 7 tons capacity, and in 1934 came a remarkable machine in the shape of the Model V1200. This monster was powered by an American LaFrance V-12 engine of 240bhp, making it one of the two most powerful trucks in America. (The other was the twin-engined Relay Duo-Drive). It could haul loads of up to 60,000 lbs at 45 mph, and cost $10,500 for the chassis. The V1200 was listed up to 1937, but regulations restricting maximum weights per axle in many states prevented its widespread

1930 BROCKWAY Model 220 tankers, Texaco Archives

1938 BROCKWAY 6-ton truck, Texaco Archives

acceptance. Heavy loads were more likely to be carried by articulated trucks, and Brockway made these too, with capacities of up to 10 tons by 1940. During the late 1930s a range of 16 models was made, from 1½ to 10 tons, all with Continental 6-cylinder engines, some being of semi-forward control layout.

America's entry into World War II saw a return to defense work. The firm was invited by the US Army Corps of Engineers to assist in the development of a 6-ton 6x6 chassis for transporting rubber pontoons and steel treadways used in the building of combat bridges. The chassis was specially equipped with pontoon inflation equipment and a hydraulic loading device. Production got under way in April 1942. Later the same chassis was further adapted for use as a general load carrier, crane carrier and airfield crash tender. As in the previous war, the entire truck production went to defense requirements, smaller 4x2 trucks also being made for the US and British forces.

1949 BROCKWAY 260XW sleeper cab tractor, LA

The early post-war period saw the introduction of the 260 series, powered by the new Continental BD ohv engine. In the 1950s 20 basic models were offered, from 20 to 65,000 lbs capacity, powered by Continental engines, with Fuller transmissions and Timken axles. On October 1st 1956 Brockway became an autonomous division of Mack, and two years later came the Huskie line of all-new trucks. Despite the association, the Huskie was not an example of badge engineering, but remained independent of Mack thinking in truck design. A proud Huskie emblem stood above the radiator of every Brockway from now on. In 1962 the company reached its golden anniversary as a truck maker, and the chrome Huskie emblem gave way to a golden one. Brockway entered the forward-control market in 1963, using a modified Mack F series cab, and forward-control models made up an increasing proportion of Brockway production in the coming years. These, and their normal-control equivalents, were offered with a choice of Continental gasoline, or Cummins or Detroit Diesel engines. Gasoline engines were phased out in 196 , and since then Cummins, Detroit or Caterpillar diesels have been used in all Brockways. In 1968 Huskiedrive was

1970 BROCKWAY 400 Series COE tractor, OMM

1974 BROCKWAY 550 Series 6 × 4 truck, OMM

introduced, consisting of a 5-speed gearbox and 2-speed axle, and this was later increased on some models to an 8-speed gearbox, giving a total of 16 forward speeds. A new model in 1971 was the Huskiteer, with low-profile forward-control tilt cab, originally a 2-axle model, later extended to 3-axles. The 1977 range consisted of normal and forward-control 4x2 and 6x4 tractors for a gtw of up to 73,000 lbs and with engines of up to 500bhp, and rigid 4x2 and 6x4 load carriers of up to 53,000 lbs gvw. In April 1977 the parent Mack company decided to close the Brockway plant, after efforts by the local community had failed to save it. *LA*

BRODESSER (US) 1909-1911

Brodesser Motor Truck Co., Milwaukee, Wis.

Peter H. Brodesser, an immigrant from Cologne, Germany, formed the Brodesser Motor Truck Co. in 1909 as a sideline of his elevator business.

The Brodesser model A had a 2-cylinder horizontally-opposed engine with force-feed lubrication while the model B had a 30 hp 4-cylinder opposed engine.

Both models were large, assembled cab-over trucks of one ton or more, with friction transmission, chain drive and solid tires on artillery wheels. The Brodesser was large enough to carry a 25 passenger bus body.

Brodesser trucks were renamed Juno for 1912, and soon the Juno Motor Truck Co, of Juneau, Wis. was organized and bought out the Brodesser company. *RW*

BRONX (US) 1912-1913

Bronx Electric Vehicle Company, Bronx, New York

The Bronx Electric was available as a very small open van with an 800 pound capacity on a wheelbase of 76

1912 BRONX 4000lbs electric truck, NAHC

inches, or of two ton capacity with 9-foot wheelbase. Ratings of these were 14 mph, 50 miles per charge and 9 mph, 40 miles per charge, respectively. *GMN*

BROOKS (i) (US) 1912-1913

(1) Brooks Manufacturing Company, Saginaw, Mich 1911-1912

(2) Brooks Motor Wagon Company, Saginaw, Mich 1912-1913

This was a light-weight high-wheeler fitted with either open or closed delivery bodies. Power was provided by, 2-cylinder air-cooled engines under the bodies and drive was by friction transmission and double chains. Prices with open or closed bodies were $625 and $675 respectively. This company was bought by Charles Duryea in October 1913 and became Duryea Auto Company with the name Duryea succeeding Brooks. *GMN*

BROOKS (ii) (CDN/US) 1927-1928

(1) Brooks Steam Motors Co., Stratford, Ont.

(2) Brooks Steam Motors Co., Buffalo, N.Y.

An insurance broker named Oland Brooks decided to build steam cars on Stanley lines, making about 180 sedans from c. 1924 to 1926, quite similar to Stanley's last design. An American branch was established in 1927, and a steam-powered bus was displayed by the Canadian company in the fall of that year. Its boiler could build up 750 lbs/sq. in. pressure in 40 seconds and a loaded test chassis achieved 60 mph. The Brooks bus, of which one chassis and one complete bus with aluminum parlor car body, was built, had 4-wheel air brakes. During 1928 the Buffalo factory converted an ACF Metropolitan bus into a steamer, but neither financing nor orders materialized. One of the Canadian buses remained in use until 1937, though latterly with a gasoline engine. *MBS/GNG*

BROOM & WADE (GB) 1907-1913

Broom & Wade Ltd., High Wycombe, Bucks

These were single-cylinder paraffin engined 3- and 4-ton trucks lorries, and colonial type tractors on large diameter wheels. Both types of vehicle were of forward control layout.

The engine was mounted horizontally at the center offside of the chassis and had an extremely large and heavy flywheel. Drive was through a 3-speed gearbox (2-speed in the case of the colonial type), and thence by single roller chain to nearside rear wheel. A speed of 8 mph was claimed for the vehicle operating with full load. The colonial tractor was rated at 6-tons capacity. *GNG*

BROTHERHOOD (GB) 1920-1921

Peter Brotherhood Ltd., Peterborough, Northants.

The Brotherhood 5 ton wagon was designed by G.H. Mann using a double ended return tube locomotive boiler (closely resembling that of the Yorkshire) allied to a compound undertype engine driving the rear axle through a double set of bevel gears and a short longitudinal shaft placed next to each rear wheel.

Only three were made and production was discontinued because Yorkshire had protested about the resemblance of the Brotherhood boiler to their own. *RAW*

BROWN (i) (US) 1912-1914

Brown Commercial Car Company, Peru, Indiana

The Brown was built as a panel delivery van with capacities of 1500 and 2000 pounds. With four-cylinder engines, three-speed gearboxes, shaft drive and pneumatic tires, they were governed to a maximum speed of 16 mph. *GMN*

BROWN (ii) (US) 1916

Brown Carriage Company, Cincinnati, Ohio

This was a light delivery vehicle resembling the better-known Dodge "business car" but without the screens. It was an assembled product with a 4-cylinder L-head Le Roi engine, Walker-Weiss axle, and Allis-Chalmers starting and lighting, and was based on the Brown passenger car, typical of its day. *RW*

BROWN (iii) (US) 1922-1924

(1) Saint Cloud Truck Co., Duluth, Minn.

(2) Brown Truck Co., Duluth, Minn.

The 2½-ton Brown chassis was powered by a 4-cylinder Buda ETU engine, and was available with stake or dump truck bodies. Prices ran from $3,650 to $4,400, with pneumatic tires and electric lighting extra. *RW*

BROWN (iv) (US) 1936-1938

Brown Industries, Spokane, Wash.

Brown Industries introduced the "Sunset Coach" in February 1936. It was one of several streamlined buses of that era to use airplane-type frameless construction in order to reduce weight. The original Brown bus weighed less than three tons, had 24 reclining intercity seats, and was powered by a rear-mounted Ford V-8. Later in 1936 the firm turned from Ford to Hercules engines and announced a 28-passenger version. With minor revisions these two types were the only models Brown built. They continued to appear in tabulations of available bus models published in trade journals until 1938, though there was no advertising after 1936. There is no record of total Brown production, which was probably less than 50 buses. *MBS*

BROWN (v) (US) 1939-1953

Brown Truck & Equipment Co., Charlotte, N.C.

The Brown was unusual in that it was initially built by a haulage operator, Horton Motor Lines, for their own use, and yet over a thousand were built in all. Designed by Horton's chief engineer, J.L. Brown, the first Brown tractors were rugged, handsome, normal-control vehicles. Continental gas engines, Parish frames and Fuller gearboxes were used. In 1942 'Buddy' Horton merged his company with six others to form Associated Transport, and after the war an improved Brown, the Model 513, was offered for sale to the general truck-buying public. The quality was high, but so was the price ($4450 in 1948). Cummins diesel engines were offered as an option in the late 1940s, and in 1952 a new forward-control tractor

1952 (v) BROWN Model R articulated tanker, OMM

appeared. However the end was near, for the management at Associated Transport had decided to switch to cheaper mass-produced trucks. The last batch of tractors was completed in 1953. *LA*

BROWN & MAY (G.B.) 1875-1912

Brown & May, Devizes Wilts 1875-
Brown & May Ltd., Devizes, Wilts 1912

Brown & May were early builders of traction engines but in 1875 launched a 4 ton vertical-boilered, vertical-engined steam wagon with boiler and engine at the rear and the steersman at the front steering by chain and bobbin gear. The vehicle was fitted with a differential on the main axle, an early application. Only one seems to have been built.

Not long before going into liquidation the firm made a few compound three-shaft steam tractors, some of which were used by showmen. They also built at least one 6 n.h.p. showman's compound road locomotive now preserved by John Rundle of New Bolingbroke, Leics. A steam wagon of their manufacture was entered in the War Department Trial of December 1901 but failed to appear. *RAW*

1901 BRULE 20hp 10-seater bus, GNG

BRULE (F) 1900-1901

H. Brule et Cie, Paris

This company manufactured the Brule-Ponsard avant-train unit for converting horse-drawn vehicles to power, and also made at least one complete vehicle, a 10-seater bus. Like the avant-trains, this had an unconventional 3-cylinder engine made by Rozer et Mazurier in which the explosions took place in the outer two cylinders only, from which exhaust gases passed to actuate the center cylinder. This 20 hp unit was mounted at the rear of the bus, driving the rear wheels by chains. There were four speeds.

Subsequently they were licensed to build Thornycroft steam wagons for the French market and were one of the few French makers to show a steam vehicle at the 1905 Paris Show though their interest seems not to have outlasted 1906. *GNG*

1907 BRUNAU 12hp 1¼-ton truck, FH

BRUNAU (CH) 1905-1908

Weidmann & Co., Automobilfabrik, Brunau-Zurich

One of the many small and short-lived Swiss manufacturers showed a small hotel bus for 10 passengers at the 1906 Geneva Exhibition and offered light trucks on the same four-cylinder-chassis. In 1907 two new commercial chassis were launched. The light truck for 1-ton payloads had a 2-cylinder engine of 12 hp and the single-wheeled rear-axle was shaft driven. Pneumatic tires were used. The heavier 3 ton-model had also a twin-cylinder engine 120x140 mm) of 14 hp. *FH*

BRUNNER (US) 1910

Brunner Motor Car Co., Buffalo, NY

This was a particularly obscure commercial vehicle. It was made in ½-, 1- and 2-ton versions with the two larger ones built to order only. The half-tonner used a 2-cylinder engine with twin silencers under the hood. This engine was connected with a planetary transmission and drive shaft. It had full-elliptic springs and used a wheelbase of 90 inches. *GMN*

1907 BRUSH (i) 34-seater bus, NMM

BRUSH (i) (GB) 1904-1910, 1946-1968

(1) Brush Electrical Engineering Co., Loughborough
(2) Brush Coachwork Ltd., Loughborough
(3) Brush Electrical Engineering, Co. Ltd., Bunton-on-the-Wolds, Loughborough

The early entry of Brush into the vehicle manufacturing business was by means of their supplying vehicles using Daimler engined chassis.

1968 BRUSH (i) Pony electric van, OMM

Following this short excursion into vehicle building Brush then settled into two major fields, that of vehicle bodybuilders and as manufacturers of electrical equipment.

Soon after WW II finished Brush began to produce a range of battery electric vehicles with three four wheeled models and one 3-wheeler. This 3-wheeler was the Pony, a front wheel drive tiller steered 75½ inch wheelbase 18-cwt payload truck which was to outlast the four wheeled range by remaining in production until 1963. The 4-wheelers were of 10/14, 18/22, and 25/30-cwt size. Toward the end of the 1940's larger capacity models of the 3-wheel type were produced and by 1951 all models were of this type. About this time industrial works trucks were produced and in the ensuing years more of the production was of vehicles of this type. In 1954 the Cob 4-ton towing tractor was introduced and the range of internal works trucks increased so that by 1963 when pedestrian models were added there were 17 models in the list.

Brush also built bodies for the five experimental Edison battery electric buses supplied to Lancaster in 1916. These were 22 seaters. *OM*

BRUSH (ii) (US) 1908-1913

Brush Motor Car Co., Detroit, Mich.

The Brush runabout was a popular light car powered by a 6 hp single-cylinder engine, with wooden axles and frame, chain drive, four coil spring suspension and solid tires. It was made in light van form with the driver in semi-forward control position, between the hood and wheel. Van production was suspended after 1909, to be revived in 1912 with a more conventional 500 lb machine with pneumatic tires and normal driving position. There was also a light taxi known as the Titan on the same chassis. In 1913 Brush, which was part of the ill-fated U.S. Motor Corporation, ceased production. *GNG*

B.S.A. (GB) 1909-1910: 1931-1933

1) Birmingham Small Arms Co. Ltd., Birmingham 1909-1910

2) B.S.A. Cycles Ltd., Birmingham 1931-1933

B.S.A.'s first commercial vehicle venture was a shortlived taxicab with bevel drive, powered by a 2.5-litre L-head 4-cylinder engine. The light vans of the 1930s were, however, based on F.W. Hulse's ingenious 1929 fwd designs, starting in 1931 with a 5-cwt type on the 1021cc ohv v-twin 3-wheeler chassis. This was followed later in the year by a 4-wheeler development for 6-cwt payloads. Interestingly, this model received a 4-cylinder 1075cc sv 4-cylinder power unit a good six months before it was offered in B.S.A.'s private cars. It was more expensive, at £135, than conventional vans, and few found buyers. B.S.A. dropped their fwd four-wheelers for a year in 1934, and when this line was resumed the Scout range did not include a van. *MCS*

BUCHER (CH) 1976 to date

Bucher-Guyer AG, Niederweningen

This well known company for agricultural machinery offers light all wheel-drive vehicles, especially for municipal work. The forward-control GET 1200 4x4 has a cen-

1911 BRUSH (ii) panel delivery van, NAHC

trally mounted VW 127 4-cylinder flat-four engine of 1.8-litre and 70 HP output. It has an automatic gearbox and a wheelbase of 2 m. The TR 2200K and the TR 2500KK 4x4 have Leyland 1½-litre 4-cylinder diesel engines mounted up front with a 40 HP output and 6 speed gearbox. Payload is 2½ to 3¼ tons. *FH*

BUCK (US) 1925-1927

The Buck Motor Truck Co., Bellevue, Ohio

Buck trucks in their brief history were offered in nine conventional models in a range of 1½ to 7½ tons of which two were 4-cylinder "speed" models, two were 6-cylinder models for even faster service, and five were heavy duty models with transmissions having seven speeds forward and two reverse.

The wheels were steel-spoked and had solid tires, with those on the rear being duals of the block type. Cabs were rectilinear in shape, with doors sliding to the rear. The Rolls-Royce car was the inspiration for the shape of the radiator shell and hood. The trucks were furnished with electric lights, Moto Meter, tow hooks at the front of the frame, and four vertical grille bars in front of the radiator.

For 1926 an additional heavy duty chassis was offered, totalling ten models in all, half with 4-cylinder engines, and the other with 6-cylinder engines. *RW*

BUCKEYE (US) 1910

The Buckeye Wagon & Motor Car Co., Dayton, Ohio

After making light delivery wagons for many years, in 1910 Buckeye made a light, short 100-inch wheelbase cab-over motor wagon with vertical steering column and powered by a 4-cylinder 25 hp vertical motor. Capacity was 1½ tons. It was chain-driven and had four fenders. A special type of selective transmission made it impossible to strip gears, according to the company. They also said that "You can make no comparison until you have looked thoroughly into our product." But you had to hurry — they went bankrupt in only a few months. *RW*

BUCKLEN (US) 1912-1916

H.E. Bucklen, Jr Motor Truck Co., Elkhart, Ind.

The first models designated A, B and C were ¾-, 1½- and 3-tonners, respectively. Bodies available were open express, stake, and delivery van. In 1914, the rating of model C was reduced to 2 1/2 tons but other than this, the models remained unchanged from beginning to end. *GMN*

BUCKMOBILE (US) 1905

Black Diamond Automobile Company, Utica, New York

The lone version of this make was called a "Business Wagon", an open delivery van of one-ton capacity. This was driven by a 15 hp two-cylinder, water-cooled engine through a planetary transmission and double chains of extreme length. Wheelbase was 83 inches and the price was $1100. *GMN*

BUFFALO (i) (US) 1908-1910

Atterbury Manufacturing Co., Buffalo, NY

The Buffalo was a continuation of the Auto-Car. The latter name was changed presumably to avoid confusion with the make of similar name based in Ardmore, Pa. Buffalos were offered in several different models on a single chassis. Two buses were available, one for ten, the other for twenty passengers. Both were quite archaic in appearance. There also was a 1/2-tonner with an engine under a hood and a 2-tonner with either a 4- or a 6-cylinder engine. Both types used solid rubber tires and double-

1910 BUFFALO (i) 1-ton truck, NAHC

chain drive. Supplementing these was a line of battery-powered electrics, a Model F bus as well as a 5-tonner with a stake body. Finally there was the Model O which was a 1-tonner delivery van. In 1910 the name was changed again to Atterbury. *GMN*

BUFFALO (ii) (US) 1912-1916

Buffalo Electric Vehicle Co., Buffalo, NY

The initial model of this battery-powered electric was a one-tonner built with an enclosed express body, the whole weighing 3700 pounds. It used a General Electric motor and drive was by shaft. Solid rubber tires were standard and wheelbase was 102 inches. In 1914, a 3/4-tonner was also built on the same chassis, but this appears to have been the only year this was offered. The 1-tonner was continued essentially unchanged into 1916. This manufacturer also built electric passenger cars. *GMN*

BUFFALO (iii) (US) 1920-1925

(1) Buffalo Truck & Tractor Co., Buffalo, N.Y. 1920-1925
(2) Buffalo Truck Corp., Buffalo, N.Y. 1924-1925

The Buffalo was a conventional assembled truck powered by a Hercules CU-3 4-cylinder engine, with Detroit transmission and Wisconsin or Sheldon rear axles. The first model was a 2-tonner, but for 1921 a 1½-tonner was added, and for 1922 this was uprated to 2 tons and the larger model to 3 tons.

An unusual feature of the 1923 models was a frame holding three copper balls ahead of the radiator. These could be cut into the water circulating system to give extra cooling when the engine was working particularly hard. Despite the slogan "The truck that sells," Buffalo only delivered 45 trucks in 1921 and 25 in 1922. Bankruptcy followed in July 1924, and although the company was reorganized in November it is not certain that any trucks were made in 1925. Lifetime production was probably 125-150 vehicles. *RAW*

1940 BUFFALO (iv) fire engine, RW

BUFFALO (iv) (US) 1927-1948

Buffalo Fire Appliance Corp., Buffalo, N.Y.

Beginning in 1920 this company built fire equipment on commercial chassis including Reo and Larrabee. From

1927 they used their own chassis but commercial chassis such as Ford Model A were also employed. Limousine pumpers were made from 1937, and in 1939 came a new streamlined series; this received a new grille in 1946, but otherwise there was little change until the end of production in 1948. *GNG*

BUFFAUD 1905-c.1910

Buffaud st Robatel, Lyons.

Buffaud et Robatel were a firm of general engineers in Lyons who seems to have built a limited number of road vehicles as a sideline. In addition to building private motor cars they also acted as sub-contractor for the engines and boilers of some of the Scotte buses and tractors of which the chassis were constructed by l'Horme et Buire. About 1905, when Scotte's business was in decline, they began making Johnson steam wagons (presumably by license of the U.S. firm) one for 5/8 ton loads and the other for 8/10 tons — the graduation being presumably in the sprocket sizes and the springing. The wagons were last advertised in 1908 and were probably defunct by 1910. *RAW*

1910 BUICK Model 2 1500 lb truck, CP

BUICK (US) 1910-1918; 1922-1923

Buick Motor Co., Flint, Mich.

Buick's first commercial chassis was the Model 2, powered by the 22 hp flat-twin engine as used in the Model F passenger car. This was mounted under the driver's seat, and drove through a 2-speed planetary transmission and double chain drive. Two wheelbases were available, 92 inches and 110 inches. The most popular body styles were a delivery van and an open stake truck, but there was also a hotel bus. In 1912 the 2-cylinder range was replaced by conventional 4-cylinder trucks of 10 and 15 cwt capacity, known as the Model 3 and Model 4 respectively. Engines were 2.3- and 3.6-litres. Several thousand were made up to 1918, when truck production was discontinued for four years. In 1922 Buick introduced a new cheap car powered by a 2.8-litre 4-cylinder engine, and a truck model of this was made under the name SD4. 2740 were built up to the middle of 1923, when Buick decided to concentrate on passenger cars, a policy they have continued ever since. One experimental van was made in 1928, and extended Buick chassis were used by the Flxible Company for a number of years for their long-distance buses. Buick chassis were also used as a basis for ambulances and hearses by several makers, including Knightstown and Sayers & Scovill. *GNG*

BULKLEY-RIDER (US) 1914-1917

Bulkley-Rider Tractor Co., Los Angeles, Calif.

This was an outsize road tractor powered by a 90 hp engine mounted originally under the hood and from 1916 below the floorboards of the cab, and driving through a 3-speed transmission with double reduction gearing, giving six speeds in all, and double chain final drive. Maximum speed on high gear was 25mph, while the lowest gave a total reduction of 96 to 1, surely a record for a road vehicle. It had a double frame construction the inner sub-frame carrying the power plant on independent springs from those which supported the main frame. Steel tires were fitted, but those on the rear wheels could be replaced by rubber ones for long-distance work on roads. *GNG*

BULL DOG (US) 1924-1925

Bull Dog Motor Truck Co., Galena, Ill.

The Bull Dog was a conventional assembled truck powered by a Continental N 30 hp 4-cylinder engine. A 2-tonner priced at $1800 was the only model listed. *RW*

BULLEY see Mercury (i)

BURFORD (US/GB) 1914-1938

(1) H.G. Burford & Co. Ltd., North Kensington, London W.10 1914-1931

(2) H.G. Burford Co., Fremont, Ohio 1915-1917

(3) H.G. Burford Co. Ltd., Teddington, Middx. 1931-1938

H.G. Burford had a long career in the motor industry, being manager of the vehicle department of G.F. Milnes & Co from 1901, and founding Milnes-Daimler Ltd, of which he became managing director, in 1905. In July 1914 he launched on the British market a new make; sold under his own name it was in fact a Fremont-Mais made in Fremont, Ohio. It had a 4-cylinder 29 hp Buda engine, 3 speeds with central change and internal gear drive. Mounted on solid tires, its load capacity was 2 tons. In 1915 the name Fremont-Mais was changed to Burford, and the trucks were sold under this name in America as well as in Britain. This situation ended in September 1917 when the Taylor Truck Company purchased the assets of the H.G. Burford Company of Fremont, and the trucks made there were renamed Taylor.

1922 BURFORD 1½-ton truck, BR

The Burford name was continued on the trucks sold on the British market, which became increasingly British in content, with the exception of their Buda engines. The 1920 range consisted of 1 and 2 ton trucks with engines of 19.6 hp and 27.3 hp respectively, and the same internal gear drive as the pre-war Burford. The chassis was used for passenger bodies as well, a coach of 1921 having four wheel brakes, though these were not standardized on the good-chassis until 1927. The first forward-control Burford was introduced in 1923, and a year later came an unusual vehicle designed to interest the railway companies. This was a 15-cwt forward-control van powered by a flat-twin British Anzani engine mounted ahead of the driver's seat,

1925 BURFORD 16-seater bus, BR

1895 BURRELL 10nhp crane engine, RAW

between his legs. It had a 3-speed gearbox, single chain drive and solid tires. The price was only £150, but although the Great Western Railway took quite a number of the larger Burfords for goods and passenger carrying, the 2-cylinder model found no customers.

In 1924 Burford entered a new field with the Burford-Kegresse half-track vehicle. H.G. Burford's decision to explore the half-track market may have been inspired by the fact that he imported during World War I the Cletrac crawler tractor, sold in Britain as the Burford-Cleveland. The Burford-Kegresse was powered by a larger engine of 5130cc, but the otherwise based on the forward-control 2-ton chassis. It incorporated a 2-speed auxillary gearbox giving a total of 8 forward and 2 reverse speeds. It was supplied mainly to the War Office, and an armored version was built in 1928.

In 1926 the original Burford company went into liquidation, and the assets were purchased as a going concern by D.C.H. Gray, the former general manager. Production continued on a very limited scale of normal and forward-control 4-cylinder chassis of 30 and 50-cwt capacity. The Kensington works were sold and new premises leased at Teddington in 1931, by which time only normal control models were made, apart from the Kegresse. Three years later Burford was taken over by Lacre, and a small number of trucks turned out of Burford design but with the Lacre name on the radiator. Burfords were listed until 1938, but production in the last two or three years is doubtful. *GNG*

BURRELL (GB) 1856-1932

(1) Charles Burrell & Sons, Thetford, Norfolk 1856-1884
(2) Charles Burrell & Sons Ltd., Thetford, Norfolk 1884-1929
(3) Charles Burrell & Sons Ltd., Leiston, Suffolk 1929-1932

Burrells enjoyed a fame and esteem as builders of steam road vehicles which transcended their importance on a narrowly numerical basis. From first to last the firm produced rather less than 4000 self-propelling vehicles of all classes, including agricultural traction engines and road rollers but, because of its early involvement in the making of road haulage engines on Boydell patent wheels, its association with Thomson in the making of his design of 3-wheeled road locomotives and, finally, its splendid double crank compound sprung road locomotives for heavy haulers and, particularly, for traveling showmen, its products were frequently in the forefront of attention.

Charles Burrell seems to have begun his involvement with Boydell in 1855 and completed his first Boydell locomotive in 1856 devoting his energy and capability to attempted solving of the problems of the system for the next seven years. The system itself is noted under Boydell's own name. Burrell's contribution, apart from his moral encouragement of Boydell, was in the production of soundly engineered and well built overtype locomotive boilered duplex cylindered, road engines, designed to be fitted with Boydell's wheels, and in the efforts he made to solve the metallurgical problem of the Boydell wheels which, quite simply, was that they could not be made strong enough to withstand the battering they received at commercially practicable road speeds. He also made some single cylinder agricultural engines with Boydell wheels. A Boydell road haulage engine moved, on at least one occasion, a test load of 138 tons.

The firm built its first three wheeled road locomotive to the designs of R.W. Thomson in 1871, incorporating Thomson's patent form of India-rubber tire protected by pivoted iron shoes. Burrells built Thomson engines both with his own design of vertical boiler, having the copper "pot" suspended in the firebox, and also with the superior vertical Field boiler. More or less in parallel with the Thomson designs there was in production at Thetford a three wheeled road engine of home design having a locomotive boiler and overtype, duplex cylinders. Designed to run firebox first these engines were fast — up to 20 mph — but found no place on the home market because of legislative restrictions, the examples produced being for export.

The firm went on, however, to build a line of four wheeled road locomotives developed from its agricultural engines. Most were fitted with gear drive but the famous "Oregon" (1883) was the last Thetford chain drive engine. At first these were single cylindered but by the mid-1890s most were compounds. A limited number employed the firm's patent single crank system of compounding in which the high and low pressure cylinders were placed one above the other driving a common crosshead, effectively a variant of the tandem compound. Most compounds, however, were conventional cross compounds, using double cranks. Burrells became celebrated for their road locomotives for traveling showmen built from 1887 to 1930, 207 being made in all, the first three of which had single cylinders. 37 had single crank compound cylinders and the remainder cross compound. Rated capacities were 6, 7, 8 and 10 nhp. The majority were 8's, many having three road speeds. Road locomotives of this final phase were fitted with road springs and were mainly on the makers' three shaft arrangement.

Burrells also designed and built a 5 ton steam tractor echoing most points of design of the road locomotives.

1909 BURRELL compound steam tractor, RAW

1911 BURRELL 5-ton steam wagon, NMM

One of these tractors took a prize in the R.A.C. Trials in 1908 and thenceforth the firm titled the class the "Gold Medal Tractor". The tractors were well-liked but never achieved the popularity of the showmen's road locomotives in which class of machine Burrells were pre-eminent.

After an experimental undertype wagon of about 1900 the firm did not re-enter the wagon market until 1911 when they built their first 5 ton compound overtype wagon, incorporating a differential in the countershaft and final drive by enclosed twin roller chains. A feature unusual in wagons was a differential lock. With interim modifications 13 of these wagons were built by 1922. In 1912 a single chain design appeared with differential in the rear axle but otherwise similar to its predecessor with which it ran in parallel. Chain and bobbin steering was used but was changed to Ackermann in the final design which appeared in 1924. In 1919 Burrells had, like Avelings and Garretts, become part of the A.G.E. combine which allocated the wagon building role to Garretts. It was a surprise, therefore, that the 1924 design appeared at all. A 6-tonner, it had improved driving visibility, lower center of gravity, expanding brakes, and higher boiler pressure (220 psi). Rubber tires were standard and the front wheels were dished to bring the king pins over the point of contact with the road. The wagon was too late on the scene, however, and only fourteen were made. Total wagon production was 114 and the last was delivered in 1928. *RAW*

BUR-WAIN (DK) 1938-1940

Burmeister & Wain A&B, Copenhagen.

The Bur-Wain truck was in fact an American Stewart chassis, assembled in Denmark by Burmeister & Wain, the well-known shipbuilders, and fitted by them with a diesel engine of their own manufacture. The truck division of Burmeister & Wain later became Nordisk Diesel A&B. *JFJK*

BUS & CAR see Silver Eagle

BUSCH (D) 1898-1912

(1) Wagenbauanstalt und Waggonfabrik fur Elektrische Bahnen vorm. W.C.F. Busch, Bautzen 1898-1901

(2) Waggon- und Maschinenfabrik AG., vorm. Busch, Bautzen 1901-1912

This firm specialized in fire engines and supplied versions with steam, gasoline, electric or gas-electric drive. Busch supplied the first self-propelled fire engine for Berlin in 1906. *HON*

1908 BUSSING 5-ton truck, HON

BUSSING (D) 1903-1931; 1950-1971
BUSSING-N.A.G. (D) 1931-1950

(1) H. Bussing, Braunschweig 1903-1920

(2) Bussing Automobilwerke K.G., Braunschweig 1920-1922

(3) Automobilwerke H. Bussing A.G., Braunschweig 1922-1931

(4) Bussing-NAG Vereinigte Nutzkraftwagen A.G., Braunschweig; Leipzig; Elbing 1931-1943

(5) Bussing-NAG Vereinigte Nutzkraftwagen GmbH., Braunschweig 1943-1950

(6) Bussing Nutzkraftwagen GmbH., Braunschweig 1950-1960

(7) Bussing Automobilwerke A.G., Braunschweig; Salzgitter; Osterholz-Scharmbeck 1960-1971

Heinrich Bussing founded a factory especially for the production of commercial vehicles in 1903. His first model was a 3-ton truck with 2-cylinder ohc engine. One year later also a bus, based on the truck chassis, was presented. To prove this design he founded the first German overland bus service which operated in the Harz Mountains. Also in 1904 the first bus chassis' were delivered to London, about 400 being used in the British capital during the next few years. The first Straker-Squires were Bussing based. To further overland transport by trucks Bussing also founded the first transport company of the world operating with automobiles on the road. In 1907 Bussing gave licenses to Fross of Vienna which was followed by licenses to Rathgeber of Munich in 1909 and Ganz of Budapest in 1912. In 1909 Bussing presented the first 6-cylinder engine for trucks which was capable of 90 PS. Best known models of that period were the subsidized 5 tonner and an 11 ton version. In 1914 Bussing presented a 4x4 lorry for the army.

After WW I the Bussing program consisted of a 2-ton express truck, a 2 1/2 ton chassis for buses and 3-and 5-ton trucks. In 1923 the first 3-axle chassis in Germany was introduced which subsequently was used for trucks and buses. Both rear axles were driven and a 6-cylinder 80 PS engine was used. It was claimed that 98% of all 6-wheelers in Germany in the 1920s were made by Bussing. A

1926 BUSSING 6-wheeled bus, NMM

gasoline-electric chassis which appeared in 1924 was not put into production. In 1929 a "twin-bus" was presented, a chassis-less fwc 3-axle bus with body by HAWA. One year later the "Trambus" followed, a 3-axle chassis with forward control body and a 6-cylinder 110 PS engine mounted amidships. When Komnick (q.v.) gave up

1930 BUSSING-NAG Trambus, FLP

production of commercials in 1930 Bussing took over the plant at Elbing. The Komnick tractor was continued by Bussing and from 1932 was equipped with a Bussing diesel engine. At the beginning of 1931 Bussing took over the production of commercials by N.A.G. (q.v.). In the N.A.G. plant at Leipzig (formerly owned by Dux) the production of the light truck type 15 (4-cylinder, 3.1-litre) was carried on. Other types of this period were a 6/7 ton chassis (6-cylinder, 9.35-litre) available for trucks and buses and the 3-axle type with 11.8-litre 110 PS engine. A special version of 1934 was a twin-engined bus using two 6-cylinder engines each with its own gearbox and propeller shafts to one rear axle. Total engine capacity was 27 litres and output 320 hp. Only five of these buses were made, all supplied to the Government of the State of Saxony. Also from 1931 Bussing optionally offered a 6-cylinder diesel engine. Two 6x4 military types appeared in 1931. These were a 1 1/2 ton truck with 4-cylinder 4.0-litre gasoline engine and a 3 ton truck with 6-cylinder 9.3-litre gasoline engine. A new engine for buses was the V-8 cylinder of 7.9-litre and 150 PS of 1933. In the same year also a new 4x4 6 1/2 ton truck equipped with 6-cylinder 6.2-litre diesel engine of 85 PS. Another military version was a five ton

1932 BUSSING-NAG 12-cylinder bus, FLP

half-track intended as truck or prime-mover. It appeared in 1936 with 6-cylinder 3.8-litre Maybach engine. The "Trambus" bus versions of Bussing became very popular and were available with 5-cylinder 6.2-litre or 6-cylinder 7.4-litre engines and as a 3-axle version with 6-cylinder 13.5-litre underfloor engine. Especially for the use of autobahnen was a twin-engined bus with two 145 PS engines placed one in the front and one in the rear. Experimental was a gas-electric double-deck bus of 1935 and another gas-electric bus was tested a few years later. Famous were the 6x4 armored cars for the army, originally based on the 3-axle truck chassis with 4-cylinder 4.0-litre engine. The later version was an 8x8 layout, all wheels driven and steered for forward and backward drive. An own V-8 cylinder gasoline engine of 8-litre was used, later replaced by a 12-cylinder 14.8-litre Tatra engine. In 1939 the program covered a range from 2 1/2 ton (4-cyl., 3.3-litre) to 6 ton plus a 9 ton 3-axle version (both 6-cylinder, 13.5-litre). 4x2 and 4x4 trucks with 4 1/2 ton payload capacity with 6-cylinder 7.4-litre engine and a half-track prime-mover for 8-ton towing capacity with 100

1965 BUSSING Decklaster low-cab truck, OMM

PS Maybach gasoline engine were produced for army use during the war. After WW II production was taken up in 1945 with a five ton chassis for trucks and buses and was later developed into the 7 ton version. In 1949 Bussing presented their first "Trambus" in chassis-less construction with underfloor engine. Trucks and buses with underfloor engines became the construction principle which Bussing consequently carried on in the following years. 1951 saw the debut of a 3-axle chassis with 180 PS diesel engine. A new factory was built in Salzgitter which later took over all production. In 1962 Bussing took over the former Borgward plant at Osterholz-Scharmbeck and

1955 BUSSING D2 Berlin bus, GNG

continued to build Borgward 4x4 3/4 ton trucks for the army until 1968 when this factory was sold to Faun.

In 1965 Bussing presented a "Decklaster" (deck loader) with lowered driver's cabin, air-springing, tandem front axles and 150 PS underfloor engine. By this time the program covered versions for 5- to 18-ton payload capacity. The newly developed standard bus design for city traffic was taken into production by Bussing as the first manufacturer in 1968.

1970 BUSSING BS20 38-ton articulated truck, OMM

In 1969 Bussing started co-operation with M.A.N. (q.v.) which led to the take-over by M.A.N. in 1971. M.A.N. carried on the factory in Salzgitter, especially for the range of underfloor lorries and buses. Subsequently all vehicles were marketed as M.A.N.-Bussing. *HON*

B.U.T. (GB) 1946-1965

British United Traction Ld., London, Wl.

The company was formed in 1946 to bring together the trolleybus manufacturing interests of AEC and Leyland. It later also built multiple unit diesel trains. Though all new trolleybuses from both manufacturers were henceforth sold as B.U.T.s, distinctive designs from each stable were perpetuated. Generally speaking three-axle

1948 B.U.T. Weymann-bodied trolleybus, NMM

single-deckers (model 9641T) and all double-deckers (9611T & 9612T two-axle and 9641T three-axle) were built to AEC design, and two-axle single-deckers (in the ETB range) to Leyland design. Most of the latter were exported, the only examples supplied to the home market comprising 21 RETB1 vehicles for Glasgow Corporation built between 1950 and 1958. The electrical equipment fitted to B.U.T. chassis came from a variety of manufacturers according to the specification of the operator, although Metrovick-built equipment proved the most popular. B.U.T. trolleybuses were assembled in various factories including the Leyland premises in Lancashire and at Ham, the AEC factory at Southall and the Crossley plant at Stockport. The last B.U.T. trolleybuses were a batch of six of type LETB1 built at the Scammell works in 1965 for export to Oporto. From 1947 to 1956 a number of B.U.T. chassis were supplied to Talleres Carde y Escoriaza of Zaragoza, Spain who fitted them with their own bodies and sold them under the name But-Escoriaza. *OM*

BUTLER (U.S.) 1913-1914

Huselton Automobile Co., Butler, Pa.

A 1500-pound truck with 30 hp 4-cylinder engine was the only model offered. It cost $1650.*GMN*

BYRON (US) 1912

Byron Motor Car Co, Denver, Colo.

This brand was built as 1-, 2- and 3-tonners, all gasoline-powered.*GMN*

1906 CADILLAC 9hp van, NAHC

CABI-CATTANEO see Bianchi

CADILLAC (US) 1904 to date
(1) Cadillac Automobile Co., Detroit, Mich. 1904-1905
(2) Cadillac Motor Car Co., Detroit, Mich. 1905 to date

It has been all but forgotten that this prestigious marque once manufactured diminutive single-cylinder delivery vans. During the five model-years the single van offered each year was a closed affair except for the driver's compartment which was even without windscreen. These were mounted on passenger-car chassis; Model-B in 1904, Model-F in 1905, Model-M for 1906-1908. These were the same designations given the passenger car versions. They all had single-cylinder watercooled engines, planetary transmissions and single chain drive to the rear axle. All had pneumatic tires and wheel steering. The usable space in the bodies was but 40 in. by 42 in. and the capacity was given between 600 and 900 lbs. From an initial figure of $900 in 1904, the price rose to $1000 in 1908. These prices were the same as the touring model.

Subsequent 4-and 8-cylinder Cadillacs have been widely used for ambulance and hearse bodywork, Cadillac themselves offering a range of such vehicles on lengthened V-8 chassis in 1926. They then reverted to to practice of cataloguing a commercial chassis for the benefit of the specialist coachbuilders (Eureka, Superior), this being adopted also by firms such as Cunningham, A.J. Miller, and S and S who had hither-to made complete vehicles. Though some 12- and 16-cylinder models served as professional cars (as did Cadillac's companion La Salles up to their demise in 1940), the principal commercial model has always been the 75, top of the V-8 family. Since World War II, deliveries of this type have averaged over 2,000 a year, and in 1975 three major firms (Miller-Meteor, S and S, and Superior) offered regular lines of Cadillac ambulances and hearses. The lengthened 75 chassis (6 inches longer than standard) was powered by an 8.2-litre ohv V-8 engine developing 190 hp, and automatic transmission, front disc brakes, and power steering were standard. 1978's specifications were basically the same, but engine capacity was down to 7-litres. *GMN/MCS*

CAETANO (P) 1973 to date
Salvador Caetano I.M.V.T., S.a.r.l., Vila Nova de Gaia

Following a successful career as a bus and commercial vehicle body manufacturer since 1946, Caetano introduced their integral coaches in the early 1970s. Built of square section tubes in monobloc construction with a high degree of finish and pleasant lines, Caetano coaches are powered by rear mounted GM or DEUTZ diesel engines of 145 and 230 hp and are exported to many European markets. *GA*

1920 CAFFORT ½-ton van, Autocar

1918 CALEDON Model D 4-ton truck, OMM

CAFFORT (F) 1920-1922
Ste des Anciens Establissements Caffort, Paris

The Caffort was an unusual vehicle employing a l-litre flat-twin air-cooled engine mounted over the front wheels which it drove through bevel gears. The front wheels were so close together that the Caffort had the superficial appearance of a 3-wheeler. It was made as a passenger car, taxicab and ½-ton van. *GNG*

CALCOTT (GB) 1914-1915
Calcott Brothers Ltd., Coventry

This well-known maker of light cars offered a 6cwt van on their 10.5 hp car chassis. The price was £185, but sales were limited because of the outbreak of war. *GNG*

1912 CALDWELL VALE 4-wheel-drive truck, Gilltrap's Auto Museum

CALDWELL VALUE (AUS) 1910-1912
Caldwell Vale Truck & Bus Co., Auburn, N.S.W.

The Caldwell Vale was a large truck which could be used either as a load carrier or as a tractor for a road train. It was powered by a 4-cylinder T-head engine with separately cast cylinders and a capacity of over 11 litres. Power was transmitted through a 3-speed gearbox and a transfer box to all four wheels which had steel tires and were 5 ft. in diameter. An unusual feature was power steering by a chain driven shaft from the front of the engine which turned two cone clutches. When the steering wheel was turned it engaged one or other of the clutches which drove a worm connected to the drag link of the steering. About 40 Caldwell Vales were made, being used for the transport of wool and timber by contractors to the Federal Government in the building of Canberra. One was used by a travelling circus in South Australia for many years. At least two survive, in Gilltrap's Auto Museum, Coolangatta. *GNG*

CALEDON (GB) 1915-1927
(1) Scottish Commercial Cars Ltd., Glasgow 1915-1918.
(2) Caledon Motors Ltd., Glasgow 1919-1921.
(3) Scottish Commercial Cars, Glasgow 1922-1926.
(4) Richard Garrett & Co. Ltd., Leiston, Suffolk 1927.

For six years Scottish Commercial Cars had been Scotland's Commer distributors until the Great War intervened and all the Commers were diverted to the War effort. To fill the breach, Harry and Edmund Tainsh, formerly of the Argyll Motor Co. designed a 4-ton chassis for Scottish Commercial Cars to produce under the name Caledon. It featured the well-known Dorman 4JO 40 hp subsidy engine, a four speed constant mesh gearbox made under French Dux patents and chain drive.

Almost 400 were produced during the War with the majority going to civilian hauliers, though the Ministry of Munitions supplied fifty to Russia and forty to the United States Expeditionary Force. A few were also supplied as rail cars for military railways and for Stirling's formerly horse-drawn tram system.

Caledon had their best year in 1919 with around 170 chassis sold and decided to expand their range to cover 30 -cwt to 7-ton machines as well as shaft-drive passenger models. This expansion coincided with the Slump in new vehicle sales, made all the more difficult for Caledon to bear by expensive development work on a sleeve-valve engine made for them by Beardmore Motors Ltd. Between bouts of financial difficulty the company produced under 200 vehicles in its remaining years, including possibly the first British rigid 6-wheeler during August 1924. This used a Buda engine after being found underpowered with the 40 hp Dorman, whilst all the rest of the range had reverted to Dorman, with the exception of a few forward-control passenger chassis with Hercules engines.

The Company's work force had been reduced from 400 to 300 in an effort to remain solvent, but in November 1926 it admitted defeat and sold out to the well-known steam engineers, Richard Garrett, who subsequently produced 2 Garrett-Caledons, but then abandoned the project. *OM*

CALEDONIAN (GB) 1910-1911
Caledonia Motor Construction Co. Ltd., Edinburgh

This company made a small number of taxicabs in the works where Granton trucks and buses had been built in 1906/07. *GNG*

CAMBIER (F) 1897-c.1901

Etablissements Cambier, Lille, Nord

Cambier were specialists in air-compressing equipment who began making rear-engined, Benz-like, cars in 1897, following these with a variety of commercial vehicles, all probably made in single units only. The first of these was a *diligence* for service in Algeria, powered by a 30 hp 3-cylinder horizontal engine. In 1898 they built a fire engine with 30 hp 4-cylinder horizontal engine under the seat, and double chain drive. The pump was capable of delivering 500 gpm, and an unusual feature was a battery operated starter, the batteries also serving to illuminate the scene of the fire. *GNG*

CAMILLO (E) 1940-1947

Jose Maria Camps, Barcelona

During the period of restricted gasoline supplies, Camps built a small number of electric cars and delivery vehicles. Most of his production, however, was devoted to electric trucks for service in railway stations, factories and ports. *JGG*

CAMPBELL (AUS) 1968 to date

R.M. Campbell Vehicle Sales Pty., Ltd., Bankstown, N.S.W.

A bus and coach body builder, Campbell modifies also certain Leyland chassis in order to meet local needs. Due to the more arduous conditions encountered, Campbell modifies mainly truck chassis of many sizes and capacities, modifications including elongation and reinforcement of the chassis, as well as repositioning of the diesel engine in the middle of the chassis, in "underfloor" position, in order that a forward entrance body can be fitted. Campbell chassis are fitted with nice looking metal city and coach bodies. *GA*

CANADIAN (CDN) 1911-1912

The Canadian Commercial Motor Car Co. Ltd., Windsor, Ont.

"Deliver the Goods the Canadian Way" urged the builders of this 22 hp 2-cylinder light delivery truck with a dash-mounted radiator. It had a 2-speed planetary transmission and double chain final drive. The company was the first to build exclusively commercial vehicles in Canada. *HD*

CANADIAN MOTOR SYNDICATE (CDN) c.1897-1899

The Toronto-based Canadian Motor Syndicate turned out Canada's first commercially built truck in 1898 (as well as the country's first commercially-built automobile a year later). The 1898 vehicle was an electric delivery tricycle with a tall compartment for packages behind the driver. It used very efficient lightweight batteries developed by W.J. Still of Toronto. The company apparently also developed a large 4-wheeled delivery wagon, although it is not certain whether this was produced by C.M.S. or by the Still Motor Co Ltd which succeeded C.M.S. after a reorganization in 1899. The large vehicle, adapted from a horse-drawn wagon, used Still's batteries and also his powerful double-acting electric motor in which the armature and field coils revolved in opposite directions, each driving one rear wheel. Another reorganization in 1900 brought the company under British control, and changed its name to The Canadian Motors Ltd. Production of the delivery wagons, as well as passenger vehicles, continued, and the new company also turned out a 15-passenger tally-ho bus, and apparently a fleet of electric taxicabs. *HD*

1960 CANCAR TD51 city bus, DL

CANCAR (CDN) 1945-1962

(1) Canadian Car & Foundry Co. Ltd., Fort William, Ont. 1945-1960

(2) Canadian Car & Foundry Co. Ltd., Montreal, Que. 1960-1962

An established builder of rail vehicles, this company had built bus bodies on A.E.C. and Leyland chassis before World War II. In 1945 it arranged with A.C.F.-Brill of Philadelphia to build the new Brill model IC-41 highway coach, for which it provided the expertise in the use of aluminium. A city transit bus, the C36, was also engineered, both vehicles using Hall-Scott underfloor 6-cylinder engines. A 44-passenger trolleybus was introduced in 1946, and adopted in modified form by A.C.F.-Brill. In 1950 the gasoline engine was dropped in favor of a modified A.E.C. 6-cylinder pancake diesel, and this unit helped CanCar buses establish a remarkable record for reliability. The transit bus was built in larger versions and also in an interurban model. In 1956 air suspension was adopted, and the Brill name dropped as production of Brills in Philadelphia had ceased three years before.

All production up to this point had been in Fort William (now Thunder Bay), Ontario, but in 1960 a new, rather square-looking transit bus in 43- and 51-passenger versions was built in Montreal. It was not successful; only 138 were made, and all bus production ended in 1962, after a total output of some 4,400 buses and 1,100 trolleybuses. The company also made Leyland-Canada trucks from 1957 to 1958. *HD*

CANTONO: F.R.A.M. (I) 1900-1913

(1) E. Cantono, Rome 1900-1905

(2) SA Ligure-Romana Vetture, Rome 1905-1906

(3) SA Ligure-Romana Vetture, Genoa 1906-1913

Cantono offered an avant-train conversion for horse-drawn vehicles. This comprised a battery box housing 44 cells, and two series-wound electric motors driving the front wheels by toothed gearing, a system which offered primitive power assistance for both brakes and steering. Some Cantonos also had brakes on the rear wheels. In 1905 the company built some light rear-drive trolleybuses; these, and 3-ton van derivatives, operated a service between Pescara and Castellamare. After the move to Genoa the vehicles were known as F.R.A.Ms, being produced in both private and commercial guises.

1906 CANTONO front-drive electric truck, NAHC

The Italian Army tested a road train based on the system. Cantonos had already been made under license in America from 1904 to 1906, and though the parent company closed down in 1913, development continued in France, where an agency had been active since 1902. In the last two years of peace a sizable range of F.R.A.Ms was offered from Paris; it was said that de Dion-Bouton were responsible for their manufacture. The biggest model, a 5-tonner, had two 7 hp motors and twin front wheels, while 3-ton F.R.A.Ms with cranked frames were used for refuse collection work by the City of Paris. *MCS*

CAPDEVILA (E) 1960-1965
Talleres Mecanicas Capdevila, Barcelona
In addition to the manufacture of motorcycles and scooters, this company made small delivery tricycles with engines of 175 and 197cc capacity. *JCG*

CAPITOL (i) (US) 1910-1912
Washington Motor Vehicle Co., Washington, D.C.
Capitol electric trucks were made in 1000 and 2500 pound capacities, but for some strange reason these were later reduced to 800 and 1500 pounds. They were of cab-over design with panel bodies. 1910 prices were $1600 and $2300.

Power was furnished by either Edison batteries, or lead batteries weighing 270 pounds more, and they were centrally located below the floor. Mileage capacities were 70 miles for the Edison batteries, 40 for lead. Voltages for the motors were 40 and 80 volts, or about 2 volts for each cell. The 1000-pound car weighed 2400 pounds with Edison battery.

As a chain-drive electric, the Capitol was typical of its type with full elliptic springs in front although the platform springs in the rear were usually found only on expensive quality automobiles. *RW*

CAPITOL (ii) (US) 1914
Capitol Truck Mfg. Co., Denver, Colo.
The Capitol electric light delivery was powered with 30 cells drawing through a General Electric motor of a series-wound type. Four forward speeds and one reverse were provided by a continuous torque drum. Final drive was by shaft to a floating type rear axle. Optional features were tiller or wheel steering and solid or pneumatic tires.

Semi-elliptic springing was provided all around for the conventional chassis with open cargo body. The cab had a folding buggy top and a braced windshield with two headlilights at the bottom. Some of the batteries were under the hood and the others were at the sides. Full length running-boards connected the semi-circular rear fenders with the front ones of unorthodox design. These rose vertically about a foot, then angled sharply at about 50 degrees to the front to a point above the axle, curving then to slightly above horizontal for another foot or so.

The truck weighed 1800 pounds and would use up about half of the battery charge in 40 miles. *RW*

CAPITOL (iii) (US) 1920-1921
Capitol Motors Corp., Fall River, Mass.
This make, with a name of indeterminate origin, was made in three capacities, 1½-, 2½- and 3½-tonners, all powered by 4-cylinder Wisconsin engines. Wheelbases ranged from 12 feet to 14 feet. The 2½-tonner was available with either solid or pneumatic tires with a price differential of $550 for the latter. The other chassis used solid tires and all three models had 4-speed Cotta gearboxes and Wisconsin worm drives. *GMN*

C.A.R (i) (I) 1905-1906
Cantiere Automobistici Riuniti, Palermo
This Sicilian firm advertised ambitiously that it could make cars, buses, trucks, motorboats, and engines from 7 hp to 120 hp. Nothing apparently emerged, however, before the venture was wound up in 1906. *MCS*

C.A.R. (ii) (F) 1907-1908
Ste des Camions et Autobus a Moteur Rotatif, Lyon
The C.A.R. was an unconventional truck designed by Antoine Burlat who had earlier made a car under his own name. Like the car, it had a 4-cylinder rotary engine developing 20 hp. This was designed to run on petrol, heavy oil or naphthalene. The latter was carried in the form of solid blocks which were liquified by the exhaust gases at 60°C, and gasified when they reached 218°C. There was a conventional 3-speed gearbox, and final drive was by chains. Four C.A.R.s were laid down, but it is believed that not more than one was completed. *GNG*

CARAMAGNA (I) 1898-1900
Officine Elettrotechiche Ing. Caramagna & C.,
Caramagnas were chain-driven electric delivery vans with a speed of 8 mph and a range of 30 miles. *MCS*

1926 CARETTE 3-wheeled van, BR

CARDEN-LOYD see Vickers

CARETTE (GB) 1925-1927

Carette Trade Carrier Co. Ltd., London N.W.6

The Carette 3-wheeler was powered by a single-cylinder air-cooled engine, with 2-speed gearbox and chain drive to the single rear wheel. This was smaller than those at the front, and was fitted with a Ducasble semi-pneumatic tire said to be unpuncturable. The front wheels were shod with ordinary Dunlop pneumatics. The price of the Carette was £85 complete. *GNG*

CARHARRT (US) 1911-1912

Carharrt Automobile Corp., Detroit, Mich.

The Carharrt Model T was a 3-ton truck with 38 hp 4-cylinder engine, 3-speed transmission and double chain final drive. the price, including platform body was $3,000. The makers had previously built two models of passenger cars. *GNG*

CARL (US) 1915-1916

Carl Electric Vehicle Co., Toledo, Ohio

Despite several references to this manufacturer and to the electric trucks which they built, details of the commercial vehicles have not been uncovered. *GMN*

CARLSON (US) 1904-1910

Carlson Motor Vehicle Co., Philadelphia, Penna.

Carlsons were cab-over trucks with a gasoline 4-cylinder 4-cycle double-oppsed horizontal motor of 20 hp at 800 rpm. Cooling was by pump. The motor was hung on a cradle directly under the driver's seat (right-hand steering) with cylinders fore and aft and the flywheel on the left. The channel steel frame was made in one piece by-bending the corners instead of riveting or welding. The crossbars, also of channel steel, were hot riveted to the main channels. These early chain-driven models had coil springs, with spring seats being guided in their vertical movement by horn blocks, or jaws riveted to the frame. The first Carlson trucks weighed 1 ton, with a capacity of 1 ton.

By 1910 Carlson had graduated to 3-ton models with the same type of motor and layout but with semi-elliptic springs. Among several unique and distinctive features were: detachability of motor from chassis (for fleet management with one motor in reserve), detachable crank-case cover, Carlson Sliding Case transmission which had been awarded the first basic patents on the sliding case principle, and force-feed lubrication which, the company said, made it possible to operate the motor 3000 miles on 5 gallons of lubricating oil. Shock-proof steering was claimed. Tires were solid, the larger rear ones being of the block type.

With a 108 inch wheelbase, a cargo body having screen sides and full roof, the 3-ton model weighed 4300 pounds. *RW*

CARLTON HILL (US) 1915

Carlton Hill Motor Car Co., East Rutherford, N.J.

This company built a small number of 1½-ton trucks, most of which were supplied to Bobkins & Atkins, a local rose garden. Two or three fire engines were also made, but total vehicle production did not exceed 25. *GNG*

CARMEL (IL) 1970-1973

AUTOCARS Co. Ltd., Tirat Carmel

The well know Israeli factory of Sabra was renamed after the Carmel mountains near Haifa. Products continued being a light van and pick up with an all glassfibre body and British Triumph 1.3 liter or 1.5 liter gasoline engine and running gear. The Dragoon 4x4 utility vehicle was also made under the Carmel trademark, while the factory was renamed, once again, as Sussita and is still active under this name today. *GA*

CARMONT (GB) 1901

H. Carmont, Kingston-upon-Thames, Surrey.

Like a number of others the Carmont was a four wheeled tractor unit designed to convert horse drawn vehicles into articulated six wheelers by taking the place of the original forecarriage. Like many of its kind it steered on the rear wheels. A vertical fire tube boiler was used in conjunction with a 2-cylinder high pressure vertical engine, counter-shaft differential and twin chain drive to the front wheels. In 1903 the designs were taken over by Centre Steer and features of it reappeared in the Lomax in 1906. *RAW*

1901 CARMONT 'motor horse', RAW

1970 CARPENTER bus, EK

CARPENTER (US) 1923 to date

(1) R.H. Carpenter Body Works, Mitchell, Ind., 1923-1941
(2) Carpenter Body Works, Inc., Mitchell, Ind., 1941 to date

Ralph H. Carpenter learned the blacksmith's trade from his father, began making horse-drawn wagons on the side, and set up his own wagon business in Mitchell, Indiana in 1918. The first school bus body built for a truck chassis was produced in 1923, almost entirely of wood, principally oak, with a wood-sheeted roof protected by canvas that was coated with a preservative. Gradually composite bodies replaced the early wood designs, and all-steel construction was standard after 1935.

Carpenter is not an assembly-line producer, and although its conventional school bus bodies are largely standardized, there is a wide range of custom accessories and design variations. Passenger capacities range from 29 to 72 children, overall vehicle lengths from 15' 9" to 32' 8" and headroom can be either 74 or 79 inches. All major truck manufacturers offer chassis suitable for use under Carpenter (and other) school bus bodies, with gas or diesel engines, often these days with automatic transmission.

In the 1970's Carpenter has introduced three new types of buses. The Cadet CV is a small bus seating up to 26 passengers (or 32 children if outfitted for school transportation) that was introduced in 1969 because of increasing demand for small buses of various types; it is designed for the so-called Step-Van type of chassis that is sold by Chevrolet and GMC but made for them by A.O. Smith of Milwaukee. A similar but forward control bus with the typical Carpenter curved windshield is mounted on the Oshkosh V-series chassis, available in wheelbases from 139 to 246 inches and with Ford or International gas engines or diesel engines from Cummins, Caterpillar or Detroit Diesel. The same range of power plants and a similar size variety characterize the Carpenter Corsair series on a pusher chassis designed by the company and built by Hendrickson. *MBS*

C.C. see Commer

CARRIMORE (GB) 1926-1937

Carrimore Six Wheelers Ltd., North Finchley, London N.12.

Primarily producers of trailers, and pioneers with Scammell of the articulated principle, Carrimore did offer a complete vehicle from 1926 to 1928. Designated the Freighter '3000' and of two tons capacity, this employed a 4-cylinder 20 hp engine and a six speed gearbox driving a worm back axle, with solid tires all round. The make of engine is unknown, but a Ford magneto and Holley carburetor were standard on this model, which cost £235 initially and £245 three years later. From 1930, the company appears to have adopted the 6-cylinder 4.9 litre Leyland tractor unit, to be sold, together with their articulated trailer unit, as a Carrimore. Larger trailers with payloads ranging from 220-cwt to 340-cwt accompanied this change, and prices rose accordingly at £1395 for the 1930 SW15 model six wheeler up to £1895 for the EW17 eight wheeler in 1932. From 1937 the company concentrated upon trailers only. *MJWW*

1926 CARRIMORE 2-ton low-loading truck, OMM

CARTER (GB) 1906-c.1909

Carter Brothers Ltd., Rochdale, Lancs.

The Carter used the Ellis-Balmforth patented vertical fire-tube boiler and had a compound vertical engine with piston valves. Three speeds were provided and the gears could be clutched in and out from the driver's seat, an unusual and advanced feature in early vertical-boilered wagons. Reputed to be better than many early vertical boilered wagons it was, nevertheless, unable to hold its own against the Foden and its makers, who are still in business, did not pursue wagon building. *RAW*

CARTERCAR (US) 1906-1912

Cartercar Company, Pontiac, Michigan

The light commercial cars under this name were all fitted with friction transmissions which were the forte of the passenger automobiles by the same company. Delivery van bodies as well as taxis were built on chassis with wheelbases ranging from 96 to 110 inches. All models used double chain drive. *GMN*

CASALINI see David (ii)

CASE (US) 1910-1913

Case Motor Car Co., New Bremen, O

The Model B was a closed delivery van of 1200-pound capacity. This used a two-cylinder, two-stroke engine of 20 hp. This drove through a planetary transmission and double chains. Wheelbase was 100 inches. The only other model, the C, was a 1-tonner with 24 hp, 2-cylinder, 2-stroke engine. This was furnished with an open express body and was on a wheelbase of 96 inches. It has been claimed this make evolved into the Auglaize, but this is not verified. There is no connection with the Wisconsin-built Case. *GMN*

CASS (US) 1910-1915

(1) Cass Motor Truck Co., Port Huron, Mich. 1910-1914
(2) Independent Motors Co., Port Huron, Mich. 1914-1915

The Cass was a conventional truck powered by a 30 hp 4-cylinder engine, with 3-speed transmission and double chain drive. Load capacity was 2 tons. From 1912 there were also models of ¾-ton, 1- and 1½-tons capacity. In 1915 the product name was changed to Independent, following the change of company name the previous year. *GNG*

1910 1-ton van, NAHC

1974 CATERPILLAR 773 50-ton dump truck, OMM

CATERPILLAR (US) 1962 to date

Caterpillar Tractor Co., Decatur, Ill.

The origins of the Caterpillar company go back to the steam tractors of the 1890s built by Daniel Best and Benjamin Holt, and the introduction in 1904 of the latter's crawler tractor. The Caterpillar Tractor Company was formed in 1925 as a combination of Best and Holt interests, and soon became world-famous for crawler tractors. They are now among the fifty largest industrial companies in the world, and as one of their many diversifications they introduced a range of off-highway dump-trucks in 1962. The rigid 4-wheeler rear dump models have capacities of 35, 50 and 85 tons (Models 769B, 773 and 777), and there are also three truck tractors (Models 768B, 772 and 776) and two bottom dump coal haulers with capacities of 100 and 150 tons (Models 772 and 776). Engines are turbocharged Caterpillar diesels, a 415 hp 6-cylinder and 600 and 870 hp V-8s, driving through 9-speed Caterpillar planetary transmissions to full-floating rear axles. Suspension is by independent oil-nitrogen cylinders, one for each wheel, and all models have oil-cooled disc brakes.

Although Caterpillar has a total of eleven factories in the United States, all the trucks are built in the Decatur plant which was opened in 1955. *RW*

CAVAC (US) 1910-1911

Small Motor Co., Plymouth, Mich.

As the company name implies, this vehicle was small. It was a 3-wheel delivery car of light weight and low center of gravity. *RW*

CBM (F) 1975 to date

Car & Bus Le Mans, Le Mans

In 1975 the Autocars Verney plant in Le Mans was acquired by the French Heuliez group, well-known manufacturers already of bus bodies, and reorganized under its new name. Produced currently are the LMB and TDU ranges, both available as 4- or 6-wheeled buses or coaches, and featuring fully independent suspension. The diesel engines used are of DAF or Mercedes-Benz manufacture, the gearbox is a fully automatic Pont a Mousson unit, a further development of the automatic box that was used in the Facel Vega cars years ago. The differential is manufactured by Chenard & Walcker. *JFJK*

1974 C.C.C. Century Series 6×6 chassis, C.C.C.

C.C.C. (US) 1953 to date

(1) Crane Carrier Corp., Tulsa, Oklahoma
(2) Crane Carrier Co., Divn. of C.C.I. Corp., Tulsa Oklahoma

The roots of the Crane Carrier marque to back to 1946 when three ex-servicemen founded Zeligson Truck & Equipment Co. to convert and rebuild surplus military equipment. In 1953 the Crane Carrier Co. was established to build custom-engineered vehicles for the construction industry. A 6-ton carrier chassis was built for the city of Brunswick, Georgia. During the following year a Canadian factory was established near Toronto, and in 1955 a larger plant at Tulsa was acquired from the Hinderlitor Tool Co. In 1957 C.C.C. bought the long-established Available Truck Co. of Chicago, and re-established their manufacturing activities at Tulsa. Two years later another rival, the Maxi Corporation of Los Angeles, was also purchased and moved to Tulsa.

1977 C.C.C. Centaur 6×4 tipper truck, C.C.C.

In the early 1960s the chief products of C.C.C. were carriers for cranes of 9 to 60 tons capacity, on 6x4, 6x6 and 8x4 chassis, but quarry trucks and a small number of integral contruction buses were also made. Engines were Chrysler, International, Waukesha, Cummins and GM Diesels. Many features developed by C.C.C. at this time are now widely used by the specialist vehicle industry. These include all-welded H-beam frames, lightweight carriers and cab design for greater visibility and safety. Crane Carrier of Canada has developed many special vehicles for local use including a line of log carriers of 25 to 75 tons capacity. Current C.C.C. products include 6x4, 6x6 and 8x4 carriers for a wide variety of work but particularly cranes and cement mixers, 6x4 roll-off container carriers, the Centurion low-profile full-cab (most C.C.C.s have half-cabs) range especially designed for the waste disposal industry, but also made as a highway truck, and the conventional 6x4 Centaur range. Engines currently used include Cummins, Detroit Diesel, Caterpillar, and Waukesha; other major components are Fuller transmissions and Hendrickson suspensions.

From 1963 to 1968 C.C.C. had an assembly plant in Sydney, Australia where in addition to regular models, a special Australian dumper with conventional hood and cab was made. *LA*

CECO (US) 1914

Continental Engineering Company, Chicago, Illinois

A delivery van body was substituted for the standard passenger body on this cyclecar. The chassis has wheelbase of 103 inches, and track of just 3 feet. Power was provided by a 2-cylinder engine (with optional air or water cooling), a friction transmission and single chain drive to the rear axle. The weight of this van was 630 pounds and the price was $375. *GMN*

CEGIELSKI (PL) 1920 - c. 1925

H. Cegielski Tow, Akc, Poznan.

The Cegielski works was noted mainly for its railway locomotives and equipment but in the early '20s built also a series of spring mounted compound piston valved steam tractors equipped with Schmidt superheater. The engines had two road speeds and an all gear drive. *RAW*

1930 CEIRANO 50-C coach, HDB

CEIRANO (I) 1925-1931

Societa Ceirano Automobili Torino, Turin

Giovanni Ceirano and his son Ernesto reacquired the S.C.A.T. firm in 1924, introducing a new line of Ceirano cars, the last to bear this name. They also built 3- and 5-ton trucks on orthodox lines, with 4.7-litre 4-cylinder sv engines, magneto ignition, 4-speed gearboxes, fwb, and pneumatic tires, which were widely used by the Italian Army. The smaller CM could be had as a coach on a longer wheelbase. From 1929 marketing of Fiat, S.P.A. and Ceirano commercial vehicles was turned over to a Fiat-controlled consortium, but the economic crisis led the Ceiranos to liquidate their company two years later. The assets were sold to S.P.A., who continued to make Ceirano trucks until shortly before World War II. *MCS*

CENTRE STEER (GB) 1903

Centre Steering Tractive Co. Ltd., Kingston-upon-Thames, Surrey

The Centre Steer was one of the many unsuccessful

avant-train conversion units designed to take the place of the forecarriage of a horse drawn vehicle and was a development of the Carmont. In 1903 a demonstration was arranged for the technical press but was cancelled at the last moment and the project was thereafter lost sight of though elements of it reappeared in the Lomax three years later. *RAW*

CENTURY (GB) 1904-1906

Century Engineering Co. Ltd., Willesden, London N.W.

The Century began life as a tricar made in Altrincham, Cheshire, and 4-wheelers were added to the range after the move to London. These included light delivery vans with 10 hp Aster engines, as well as goods versions of the Century Tandem tricar. In 1906 the company was making 2-ton vans powered by 2-cylinder engines, under the name Princess. *GNG*

C.E.Y.C. (E) 1922-1927

(1) Centro Electrotecnico y de Comunicaciones, Madrid

(2) Compania Euzkalduna de Construccion y Reparacion de Buque, SA, Bilbao

The C.E.Y.C. was designed by Juan Antonio Hernandes Nunez, and originally built by the communications department of the Spanish War Ministry in Madrid. Later, production was taken up by an important company in Bilbao. It was a light vehicle powered by a 792cc 4-cylinder 2-stroke engine, and was made as a 3-seater car for Army communications purposes and also as a light van and armored car. The make disappeared because of lack of official support. *JCG*

1930 C. G. A. 54/60-seater bus, JCG

C.G.A.; C.N.T.-A.I.T. (E) 1929-1942

(1) Compania General de Autobuses de Barcelona, SA, Barcelona 1929-1936; 1940-1942

(2) Colectividad de los Autobuses de Barcelona, Barcelona 1936-1939

After six years' experience operating A.E.C., Laffly and Tilling-Stevens busses, this company decided to build their own buses under the direction of Sebastian Nadal. A total of 68 buses was built up to 1936, using 90 hp gasoline engines and electric transmission doubtless inspired by that of the Tilling-Stevens. There were both single-and double-deckers, the former for 30 to 40 passengers and the latter for 54 to 60 passengers. With the coming of the Civil War the company was nationalized and operated by a workers' committee until January 1939. The name was changed to C.N.T. - A.I.T. (Confederacion Nacional del

1939 C. G. A. 60-seater trolleybuses, JCG

Trabajo — Associacion Internacional del Trabajo) and production of the double-deckers continued. These had disc wheels and pneumatic tires as opposed to the artillery wheels and solid tires of the earlier types. After denationalization the name C.G.A. was resumed, and five more buses made, followed by 33 double-decker trolleybuses. *JCG*

1905 CHABOCHE steam van, RAW

CHABOCHE (F) 1901 - c.1910

E. Chaboche, Paris

Chaboche, a steam car builder, built a steam van in 1900 from which developed a range of steam trademen's vehicles and some steam omnibuses, using a semi-flash boiler and coal fuel. The boiler was mounted in front of the driver and the engine longitudinally beneath the chassis with final drive by cardan shaft.

By 1906 the steam car market was in decline and Chaboche discontinued their manufacture to concentrate upon the steam vans, but the steam commercial never caught on in France and the marque was extinct by about 1910.

Chaboche commercials never exceeded about 2½ tons carrying capacity. *RAW*

CHADWICK (US) 1915-1916

Chadwick Engineering Works, Pottstown, Pa.

The Chadwick firm, makers of the famous Chadwick Six automobile, was virtually closed down by 1915. A 1000-pound delivery truck powered by a 16 hp 4-cylinder LeRoi engine was the firm's final effort before the factory was taken over for war work. The chassis price was $620. Chadwick employed just thirteen assemblers in 1915. *GMN*

CHALLENGE-COOK see Cook (ii)

CHALLENGER see M.C.I.

CHAMBERS (GB) 1904-1925

Chambers Motors Ltd., Belfast

One of the very few motor vehicles produced in Ireland, the Chambers suffered from under-capitalization from the start, and very few — either cars or commercials — were built. The company, which had commenced operations by making a machine for wiring corks on to soda-water bottles, was started by Robert Chambers who joined forces with his brother, J.A. Chambers (previously with Vauxhall) in 1904 to build cars. By 1905, the latter had designed a 10/12 hp delivery van which, for some reason, was not built in the works but was contracted out to Alford and Alder Ltd. of London who were assembling Aster-engined vehicles for a number of firms at the time. A large range of private cars were also offered, and of these the 4 cylinder s.v./2.5 litre 12/16 model introduced in 1908 (latterly with 2.2 and 2.3 litre engine) formed the basis for the firm's commercial chassis and some ambulances. This, with three speed epicyclic gearbox in the back axle, was offered in 15 cwt guise until 1919, when conventional Meadows gearboxes were adopted and the payload was increased to 1 ton. Final drive throughout was by shaft and worm. In landaulette form, the 12/16 also found some favor as a taxicab but all production ceased in 1925 and the make existed 'on paper' only thereafter until the final failure in 1929. *MJWW*

CHAMPION (i) (US) 1904-1905

Champion Wagon Works, Oswego, NY

There was a 1-tonner produced by this manufacturer, a battery-powered electric with forward control and double chain drive. This was built only as an open-sided van with top. There was a Champion brand electric which was marketed in 1906 by McCrea Motor Truck Co., Chicago, Ill. This latter also was a 1-tonner but it is not known whether there was a definite connection between the two makes. *GMN*

CHAMPION (ii) (US) 1917

Champion Motors Co. Inc., Fulton, Ill.

With sales offices in Cleveland, Ohio the Champion compnay made a conventional ½- and ¾-ton delivery chassis powered by a 4-cylinder L-head engine, with 3-speed transmission and shaft drive. *RW*

CHANG-ZHENG (p), CH'ANG-CHENG (wg) (Long March) CHI to date

Hopei Ch'ang-Cheng Motor Vehicle Plant — Hopei Province

(Plant Vehicle Code — XD)

The Long March series of 6x6 trucks includes the 10-ton XD-250 with a V-12 diesel of 170 hp, the 12-ton XD-160 with 180 hp, and the XD-980 tractor vehicle of 5.5 tons.

These units are based on Czech Tatra designs. *(BE)*

CHAPLIN (G.B.) 1859-c.1867

Alexander Chaplin & Co., Glasgow.

Chaplin was noted for his cranes and fixed engines but also built some railway locomotives together with, as a licensee, one or more of Bray's patent traction engines.

He also built a road haulage engine of his own design placing his standard vertical boiler amidships, a transverse vertical engine immediately behind it and geared drive to the rear axle. Chaplin offered engines capable of hauling loads up to 50 tons but no records survive as to the numbers and actual sizes built. *RAW*

CHARRON (F) 1907-1921

Automobiles Charron Ltd., Puteaux, Seine

This make was the successor to the C.G.V. launched in 1901 by three former Panhard racing drivers, Charron, Girardot, and Voigt. There were no C.G.V. commercial vehicles as such, though the firm exhibited a primitive *automitrailleuse* with Hotchkiss machine gun at the 1902 Paris Salon. They followed this up in 1906 with a true armored car with revolving turret on a 30 hp chain drive chassis. A few of these were supplied to the Imperial Russian Army, but Charron's main interest outside private cars was cab manufacture, 2- and 4-cylinder types being offered from 1907. All had sv monobloc engines, magneto ignition, 3-speed gearboxes, and shaft drive. The first fours had underslung frontal radiators, these giving way by late 1908 to the dashboard type with thermosyphon instead of pump circulation. Capacities of these later engines were 1.2 and 2.4 litres respectively, and the cabs had a wide currency, 550 being at work in Paris, Brussels and London alone during 1909. A colonial model with 10-in. ground clearance was catalogued in 1912, and the 4-cylinder chassis could be had with 15-cwt van bodywork. Some of London's Charrons survived into the 1930s, albeit disguised with frontal radiators. In 1908 the firm made a few luxury single-decker omnibuses with pneumatic tires on 30 hp chain drive chassis. A commercial model with 3.4-litre 4-cylinder sv engine was still offered as late as 1921. *MCS*

1912 CHASE Model L 1½-ton wire screen delivery wagon, NAHC

CHASE (US) 1907-c.1917

Chase Motor Truck Co., Syracuse, N.Y.

The Chase was one of the more popular highwheeler vehicles, and was made in both passenger and goods form, although mostly the latter. In 1908 there were two models, a 'business runabout' which could be converted from a four seater car to a 700 lb truck, and a 3-ton forward-control truck. Both had air-cooled 2-stroke engines, the runabout a 10 hp twin and the truck a 30 hp four. Transmission was planetary 2-speed on the runabout and 3-speed sliding on the truck. They were priced at $750 and $3500 respectively. In 1910 a 15 hp 3-cylinder model was introduced, still with air-cooled 2-stroke engine, 2-speed planetary transmission and chain drive. This sold on the British market for £230; it was brought to Britain by Henry Spurrier of Leylands. By 1914 the Chase was a conventional truck powered by 4-cylinder Continental water-cooled engines, with 4-speed sliding transmissions and worm drive. It was made in 1, 2 and 3-ton sizes. The 1917 range ran from 1500 lbs to 3½ tons. *GNG*

CHAUSSON (F) 1947-1963

(1) Ste Anon des Usines Chausson, Gennevilliers, Seine; Meudon, 1947-1960
(2) Saviem, L.R.S., Suresnes, Seine, 1960-1963

Chausson were radiator manufacturers who had supplied more than 80 per cent of all radiators fitted to French vehicles before the war, and who turned to the building of chassisless buses in 1947. The pressings were made at the Meudon factory and brought to the former Chenand & Walcker works at Gennevilliers for assembly, where 8000 workers were turning out 12-14 buses per day in 1948. The standard engine was an 80 hp Panhard diesel, but a 90 hp Hotchkiss gasoline unit was available to special order. The original Chaussons had a rather utilitarian appearance, with similar exterior for all three interurban and long-distance models. However they were advanced mechanically, with 5-speed gearboxes, compressed air braking, servo steering, door operation and tire inflation. By 1950 a wider range of engines was available, with 100 and 140 hp diesels added, and the gas unit uprated to 105 hp. Chausson buses were now in service in Paris, the Hague, Liege, Luxembourg, Copenhagen, Casablanca, Warsaw and Budapest, as well as many provincial French cities.

1957 CHAUSSON bus, NMM

In 1951 a new full-fronted luxury coach appeared, with an underfloor-mounted 6-cylinder 6.98-litre diesel engine made under license by Hispano-Suiza from Hercules. The same coach was available with a front-mounted vertical engine. By 1954 the Hispano/Hercules engine was used in urban buses as well, these having Wilson preselector gearboxes and accommodation for 55 passengers, 32 seated and 23 standing. Chausson were now the major producers of buses on the continent of Europe, and their products had reached Sofia, Istanbul, Cairo, Jerusalem, Djeddah and Madagascar. Their body/chassis unit was used for Vetra trollybuses. Gemmer power-assisted steering was available in 1956, and in 1958 a new urban bus originally designed for Paris appeared. This had its 150 hp Hispano/Hercules engine mounted vertically alongside the driver, a fully-automatic gearbox by Self-Changing Gears Ltd., and accommodation for 80 passengers, of which only 30 were seated. In 1960 Chausson was absorbed by the Saviem group who already owned Somua, Latil, Floirat, Isobloc and the heavy vehicle section of Renault. Production of urban and inter-city buses continued under the Chausson name for three years, latterly with fuel injection Saviem Fulgur 6 engines of 6.84-litres capacity, developing 150 hp. *GNG*

CHAUTAUQUA (US) 1914

Chautauqua Cyclecar Company, Jamestown, New York

This cyclecar was fitted with a van body and used a two-cylinder air-cooled engine of 10 hp, with a friction transmission and belt drive to the rear wheels. Its wheelbase was 102 inches with "standard" track of 4 feet, 8 inches. It sold, probably in very limited numbers, for $415. *GMN*

CHECKER (US) 1920 to date

(1) Commonwealth Motors Co., Joliet, Ill. 1920-1922
(2) Checker Cab Mfg. Co., Joliet, Ill. 1922-1923
(3) Checker Cab Mfg. Co., Kalamazoo, Mich. 1923 to date

America's best-known specialist cab making company, Checker began life as the cab model of the 4-cylinder Commonwealth car, with body by the Markin Auto Body Corp. The name came from the Checker Taxicab Company of Chicago, for whom the vehicles were built. The first few cabs used Lycoming engines, but when Commonwealth turned to Herschell-Spillman in 1921, Checker naturally followed suit. In October 1921 Morris Markin merged his body company with Commonwealth, and seven months later the Checker Cab Manufacturing Company was formed. Production of Commonwealth passenger cars was

1923 CHECKER taxicab, Checker

discontinued and in 1923 Checker moved into a new factory, the former Handley-Knight plant at Kalamazoo. The Herschell-Spillman engine was replaced by a 22.5 hp 4-cylinder Buda which was standardized for the next five years. By 1925 production of cabs had reached 75 per week, making Checker the biggest-selling cab make. Sedan and landaulette bodies were offered, and some of the latter were exported to England. The first 6-cylinder Checker, also Buda-powered, came in 1927, and this was followed by the Series K of 1928 with four-wheel hydraulic brakes. These were as good looking as the higher-priced passenger cars, and several wealthy people chose them for their personal transport.

In 1931 Checker's line was extended to include the Suburban, a station-wagon type vehicle which could do duty as an ambulance or hearse, and a truck. Both of these were available on the K chassis and on its successor, the T, the latter a new model for 1933 powered by a Lycoming straight-8 engine. Truck production was discontinued in 1933 after 500 had been made, but the Suburban was continued in 1934, production totalling about 1,000. In June 1933 E.L. Cord gained control of Checker through purchase of stock from his friend Markin, and the Kalamazoo company began to make a cab for Cord's Auburn Automobile Company, under the name Saf-T-Cab.

1935 CHECKER Series Y taxicab, Checker

This was a Series T with different grille and trim. The Cord era lasted until 1936 when Markin regained control, the company still being in the hands of his family today. In 1935 came the Series Y, a cheaper vehicle than the T, with 6-cylinder Continental engine and the sloping lines typical of cars of that era. A foretaste of the future was lwb version with six doors, ancestor of today's Checker Aerobus. The Y was in turn succeeded by the Series A in 1940; also Continental-powered, this had the streamlined lines of contemporary passenger cars, but retained the landaulette body style.

1940 CHECKER Series A taxicab, RJ

Checker's war production was devoted to trailers of many kinds an experimental four-wheel-drive and steering Jeep. After experimenting with rear-engined and transverse front-engined front-wheel-drive prototypes, they went into production in 1947 with a conventional cab derived from the A, but with updated lines. The landaulette top was no longer made.

A completely new field for Checker was the Series E bus. Checker entered the bus field by building chassis for Transit Buses, Inc. 1948 and 1949. Early in 1950 Checker bought Transit, redesigned the bus slightly, and began selling it under its own name. A Continental engine was used, as in the Transit, and the first customer was the Detroit transit system, which purchased 450 buses. Most of the year 1951 was taken up with their delivery, and then in 1952 and 1953 another 40 or so buses were sold to various small companies, principally in the northeastern states. The basic Checker bus seated 31 passengers,

1950 CHECKER Model O-1 31 passenger bus. MBS

1967 CHECKER Aerobus, GNG

though other seating capacities were avialable in the same body shell. In 1952 a prototype was built of a proposed new line of buses with LeRoi engines mounted straight in at the rear; these were to include both city and suburban designs with seating capacities from 28 to 42. No great amount of interest was aroused, and so the earlier type continued to be built; the last known deliveries were in September 1953.

There was gradual but unspectacular development of the cabs up to 1958 when the A8 with coil ifs, and power-assisted steering and brakes appeared. This was replaced by the four-headlamp A9 of 1959, similar in appearance to the Checker cabs of today. This model saw the introduction of the nine and twelve passenger Aerobuses of wheelbases of 12 ft 10½ in and 15 ft 9 in respectively, with six or eight doors. Throughout this period the faithful side valve Continental six engine was used, but in 1960 an ohv unit was an optional alternative, and in 1965 Chevrolet six or V-8 engines were adopted. Automatic transmission is now standardized, and 1978 Checkers have 4.1-litre 6-cylinder or 5.7-litre V-8 engines. The Aerobus is only available with the larger engine. *GNG/MBS*

CHELSEA (US) 1915

Chelsea Manufacturing Company, Newark, New Jersey

The lone model under this name was a panel van with capacity of 600 pounds using an 18 hp 4-cylinder engine. It was fitted with cantilever springs all around and had a three-speed gearbox on a wheelbase of 102 inches. Standard colors were a dark blue body with black fenders and running gear. *GMN*

1928 CHENARD-WALCKER U5 van, NMM

CHENARD-WALCKER (F) 1905-1951

(1) Chenard, Walcker et Cie, Asnieres, Seine 1906-1907
(2) SA des Anciens Etablissements Chenard-Walcker, Gennevilliers, Seine 1907-1951

This firm did not manufacture commercial vehicles on a regular basis before World War I, though a 12-cwt van was listed on the 16/20 hp chassis in 1906, and a taxicab in 1910. Both had 4-cylinder sv engines, as well as the company's 'double' back axle, on which the drive was taken by two cardan shafts independently of a second, dead axle beam. In 1919, however, Chenard-Walcker introduced a compact road tractor, used in conjunction with semi-trailers of their own or Lagache &Glaszmann manufacture; it was marketed by an associated company, the SA des Trains Chenard-Walcker-F.A.R. Features of the machine were a long stroke sv 3-litre 4-cylinder engine as fitted to contemporary private cars, a cone clutch, a 4-speed gearbox, and double-reduction worm drive. Pneumatic or solid tires were optional. Originally rated for 2/5-ton loads, it could be had in 8-speed, 10-ton form by 1924; among well-known users were the Nicolas wine company in France, and the LMS Railway in Britain. These tractors were made under license in Belgium by Minerva and in Britain (from 1930) by Beardmore. In 1928 the native model was fitted with a 44 hp ohv engine and 5-speed gearbox, heavy-duty versions having vacuum servo brakes as well. A chain-driven 6x4 edition was evolved for timber haulage or other heavy tasks involving GCWs of 25 tons and more, and in 1930 the bigger Chenards came with 4-cylinder sleeve-valve Panhard engines; pneumatic tires were now standard equipment. The ultimate in tractors came in 1931, in the shape of a twin-engined 6x4; the pair of 7½-litre Panhard units were mounted side-by-side, each with its own 5-speed gearbox, and each driving a separate rear axle. Output was in the region of 250 hp, and the model actually went into small-scale production. A diesel option was also catalogued for 1932.

Though Chenard-Walcker controlled the A.E.M. electric-vehicle venture, the tractors were the principal commercial-vehicle offering of the 1920s. It was not until the alliance with Delahaye in 1927 that other types appeared; initially these were light vans based on the 7CV and 9CV 4-cylinder private car chassis. 1932, however, saw a new range covering the 30-cwt/4-ton bracket; these were conventional machines resembling the 6-cylinder Citroens in appearance, but with 4-cylinder sv power units of up to 2.8 litres and vacuum servo brakes. 1933 models included a coach chassis and a 5-tonner with eight forward speeds, while a free wheel was optional on some types. By 1937 there was even a 6-tonner, and the smaller types (like their private car counterparts) used 4-cylinder ohv gasoline or diesel engines of Citroen make. Another 1937 development was license production of the British

1930 CHENARD-WALCKER 20-ton tractor, FLP

Scammell Mechanical Horse, though this, along with the Chenard-Walcker tractor line, was now made under the F.A.R. name by a separate company. In 1941 the parent concern introduced an interesting 20/25-cwt forward control delivery van with fwd and all-independent, torsion-bar suspension, powered by a horizontal-twin 2-stroke 725cc engine; gas and gazogene versions were available. This outlived the Chenard-Walcker car, surviving into 1951, though 1947 and later types used 4-cylinder ohv Peugeot engines, latterly of 1.3-litre 203 type. Peugeot also acquired the Chenard-Walcker assets, and the name disappeared, though the fwd vans continued as Peugeots, the J7 of 1978 being a direct descendant of the Chenard line. *MCS*

CHEVALIER (US) 1974 to date

Monarch Mfg. Corp., Nappanee, Ind. and Chatsworth, Calif.

This former motor home manufacturer markets a medium-duty cab-over truck of high-volume hauling capacity called the Chevalier CC. The chassis is that used for Chevrolet motor homes, and comes with 454 or 350 cid V-8 engine, automatic transmission, power brakes and steering, and dual rear wheels. There are three wheelbase lengths, 125, 137 and 158½ inches, and bodies are aluminum van or stake types. The cabs are made in Indiana and the trucks are assembled by Monarch from supplied parts. Chevaliers are marketed nationally though Chevrolet dealers. *RW*

1922 CHEVROLET Superior van, Chevrolet

CHEVROLET (i) (US) 1918 to date

Chevrolet Motor Co. (Division of General Motors), Detroit, Mich.

Chevrolet entered the 1-ton truck field in the same model year as Ford, but the make's initial impact was much less dramatic. Of the 243,479 vehicles delivered in 1922, less than 2000 were commercials. Their first tonner,-Series T, had a 3.7-litre 4-cylinder splash-lubricated ohv engine with coil ignition, a 3-speed gearbox, full electrics, worm drive, and solid rear tires(pneumatic from 1920). There was also a light van on the 2.8-litre 490 private car chassis; Chevrolet made neither cabs nor bodies, though an express style by Martin-Parry of Indianapolis (whom they would acquire in 1930) was listed. By 1919 Chevrolet engines were also being used in the trucks and farm tractors of Samson, another GM subsidiary, but there were no drastic changes for the first six seasons. Light vans continued to run parallel to the car line, but with the abandonment of the bigger F-series cars in 1923 the tonner received the 2.8-litre power unit and spiral bevel drive. In 1924, H-series form it sold for on £149 as a chassis in Britain, and from 1925 trailing axle 6-wheeler versions began to be listed, a favorite being the Danish Triangel. Enclosed cabs came with the 1926 R-series, and at the same time the light delivery range was extended to embrace a commercial roadster and a roadster pickup. This latter became a favorite style with Chevrolet, who developed a coupe edition in 1928, and continued to offer it as late as 1942. Other styles with which they persevered beyond the normal American limits were the car-type

1927 CHEVROLET LM 1-ton truck, OMM

sedan delivery (retained until 1960), and the traditional canopy express, which survived in the range until 1954. A 4-speed option was first offered on the LM-series tonner of 1927, being standardized (along with fwb) on the LP, last of the 4-cylinder splash-lubricated family.

1929 saw an entirely new 'six for the price of a four', common to both car and truck lines. The legendary 3.2-litre ohv Cast Iron Wonder retained splash lubrication, other features being mechanical pump feed, and disc wheels instead of the wood type hitherto used on Chevrolet commercials. The first International series came as a ½-tonner (Type-AC) on the 3-speed car chassis, and as a 1½-tonner (Type-LQ) with 4-speed gearbox. 1930 saw the advent of the Maple Leaf truck, a Canadian cousin of the Chevrolet 6, while from 1928 Chevrolet commercials had also been built in Britain. These British models were phased out during 1931 to make way for the Chevrolet-inspired Bedford produced by Vauxhall at Luton. Both the older 4s and 6s were widely used for light bus work, 14-seater sunroof coaches on the LQ chassis being especially popular in England. In 1930 Chevrolet sold 118,253 trucks, which still put them behind Ford; they would, however, take the lead in 1933, only to lose it twice again (1935 and 1937) before 1969. Improvements included a twin-rear wheel option and all-expanding brakes on the LS of 1930, and synchromesh on the car-based BA of 1932. Also standardized that year were downdraft carburetters, though styling tended to lag behind the cars, with 1932-type front end sheet metal on 1933 trucks, and 1933's vee

1936 CHEVROLET RB 1½-ton truck, RNE

radiator on 1934-36 types. By mid-1936 a new streamlined low-roof cab and hydraulic brakes had been standardized, and the 1½-tonner came with two wheelbase options, 131 and 159 inches. 1935 had seen the company's first factory-built station wagon, the 8-passenger Suburban; this unlike some of its competitors, was essentially a truck type, and would still be in the range in 1978. Short wheelbase 1½-tonners were selling well as tractive units, Chevrolet promoting this usage by hauling a 5-ton load up Pikes Peak. General Motors' G.M.C. and export-only Oldsmobile commercial lines were now very closely related to Chevrolets, the GM-built Yellow Coach PSVs of the 1937-42 period used Chevrolet mechanical elements, and the General Motors Cab (ex-Yellow) of 1936-38 was merely a long-chassis edition of the Chevrolet Master Six sedan. 3½-litre 4-bearing engines made their appearance in cars and trucks for 1937, when COE (forward control) variants were first seen, with updraft carburation to reduce engine

1930 CHEVROLET LS 1½-ton truck, RNE

1938 CHEVROLET HG 1-ton van, NMM

height. These were export-only items until 1938; the 77 hp Hercules diesel option, another 1937 innovation, was not seen on the home market at all. Vee windshields, new grilles and intermediate ¾- and 1-ton models featured in the 1939 program, along with a new, if short-lived British assembly operation at Southampton. Options included 2-speed back axles and hydrovac brakes, and the cheapest complete truck cost $658. Hypoid rear axles (used on cars and light deliveries since 1937) were standardized in 1940, while a new model was the KP Dubl-Duti, a forward control walk through van for urban delivery work. 1941 saw a new heavy duty engine option of 3.8-litres,

1942 CHEVROLET BK ½-ton pick-up, CP

standardized from 1944 on 1½-tonners, and the 1942 range covered fifteen basic models in the ½/2-ton class, including two school bus chassis. Among the specialist bus builders to use Chevrolet mechanics were Fitz John and Flxible, while the Swiss Lauber unitary construction coach of 1954 would also be Chevrolet-based.

The parent concern's war work included the production of armored cars and half a million trucks, mainly 1½-ton 4x4s with 3.8-litre engines; the 6x6 derivative was the responsibility of G.M.C. Chevrolet cars and trucks of the 1946-47 period were essentially 1942 designs, but the latter received their facelife first, in 1948. The range-structure, however, remained the same, with the sedan delivery, trucks and vans in the ½/2-ton category, a 1½-

1947 CHEVROLET 1½-ton CO truck, Republic Steel Corp

ton forward control variant, and school buses for up to 54 pupils. Engine options were likewise unchanged, the 3½-litre giving 92 hp and the 3.8 105 hp. Step-n-Drive vans with the driver in standing position were added in 1951, and in 1952 GM's Antwerp plant listed a full-fronted bus, the GT30, on a 154 inch wheelbase. Other improvements

1950 CHEVROLET 3100 ½-ton pick-up, GNG

of the early 1950s included a Powerglide automatic option on light models, full-pressure lubrication, and a bigger 135 hp six. During 1952 a 90 hp 4-cylinder 2-stroke Detroit Diesel engine was offered, but seldom seen. Complete restyling, with the fashionable dog's leg windshields, came in 1955, along with 12-volt electrics, 4-speed Hydramatic in place of Powerglide as the automatic option on all but sedan deliveries, and new low-cab-forward, or semi-forward control types replacing the old C.O.Es. Also in 1955 Chevrolet introduced their first short-stroke ohv V8 for trucks, the 4.3-litre, 145 hp Task-master, available only on 2-tonners. Commercial vehicle sales that year were a record 393,315. In 1956 tubeless tires were standard and V8 engines became generally available throughout the range; heaviest types were uprated to 2½ tons and could be had with power steering and 6-speed automatic gearboxes, as well as with a 5-speed manual type; this last was listed in all-synchromesh

1957 CHEVROLET Model 5703 2-ton truck, OMM

form a year later. Other upward moves of 1957 were the provision of an air/hydraulic brake option and more powerful V8s of up to 210 hp in the case of the big 322 unit. Full air brakes arrived in 1958, and a year later Chevrolet had their answer to Ford's Ranchero, the sporty, car-type El Camino pickup with all-coil springing and the usual choice of engine/gearbox combinations. Chevrolet tried torsion-bar ifs on all their trucks in 1960, but gave it up three years later; more lasting, however, was a range of forward-control tilt-cab machines with GVWs in the 37,000-40,000 pound class. 4-cylinder Detroit Diesels reappeared in the options list, and in 1961 the company launched the Corvan, a light forward control delivery van based on their controversial Corvair compact sedan with unitary construction, all-independent suspension, and rear-mounted air-cooled flat-6 engine. 1963 also saw a new 4-cylinder engine, a 2½-litre 5-bearing unit designed for the Chevy II car line, and also offered briefly in light trucks. Also new in 1963 were ladder-type frames in place of the once-universal X-braced type, more diesel options in the heavy-duty bracket and the option of Fuller Roadranger transmissions. At the top of the range were some 6x4s with 195 hp V6 Detroit Diesel engines. In 1964

1962 CHEVROLET Corvan, Chevrolet

1963 CHEVROLET T-series tilt-cab tractor, Chevrolet

1965 CHEVROLET Stepvan, GNG

the conventionally engineered, though still forward control Chevy van with 4- or 6-cylinder inline engine supplanted the Corvan, and there were new V6 gasoline units for the heavy trucks. Other engine developments included city delivery vans using the 3-cylinder Detroit Diesel, and still more powerful V8s, with as much as 252 hp from 6.7-litres. Like Ford, Chevrolet were experimenting with gas turbine-powered tractive units, their Titan III being a complicated affair with automatic transmission, power tilt cab, power windows, retractable headlamps, stereo, and a radio-telephone. Production Chevrolets now catered for GVW ratings of up to 48,000 pounds, and GCWs as high as 65,000, increased by 1970 to 76,800 with the advent of the Titan highway tractor. This was a short-tilt cab model available in 4x2 or 6x4 configurations. Diesel engines available included V6s, V8s and V12s by Detroit, extending up to 14 litres and 390 hp, as well as Cummins units of 255/319 hp. Other features were twin-disc clutches, air brakes, and options such as 10- and 13-speed transmissions, power steering, and air suspension. At the other end of the range were such departures as the Blazer (1969) a light 4x4 in the popular Jeep idiom, and the 7/8-cwt Vega panel (1971), a commercial derivative of the company's new sub-compact car with 2.3-litre 4-cylinder ohc engine. Neither car nor van was successful and the line was discontinued at the end of 1977, leaving the Isuzu-built Luv pickup in the ½/¾-ton class as the smallest commercial to carry the Chevrolet name.

1976 CHEVROLET Titan 90 tandem diesel tractor, Chevrolet

In 1977 the big Titan was joined by a conventional 6x4, the Bison (its G.M.C. counterpart was called the General), with a GVW rating of 50,500 lb. and GCWs in the 80,000 lb. class. Engines, of up to 430 hp, were turbocharged diesels by Detroit or Cummins, and 5-speed automatic transmissions were regular equipment. The 1978 Chevrolet range offered an infinite variety of types. In the lightweight category were the Luv, the El Camino (now using a 3.3-litre V6 engine as standard, but still with all the luxury private-car options), the 4x4 Blazer (with a built-in anti-roll bar since 1976), the Chevyvans, the Suburban, and the latter's pickup relatives, these now available with Oldsmobile's new 5.7-litre diesel V8. Power front disc brakes and coil-spring ifs were regular equipment on such vehicles, though 4x4s retained beam axles all round. Medium conventionals covered GVWs from 13,000 lb upward. A turbocharged 4-cylinder Detroit Diesel joining the familiar gasoline 6s and 8s: brakes were hydrovac with an air option, and there was a choice of 18

1978 CHEVROLET Bruin (left) and 70 series (right) heavy trucks, Chevrolet

transmissions from straight 4-speed synchromesh to a 13-speeder. There were parallel tilt-cab forward control models. Air brakes were in general use on heavy duty Chevrolets, which included the new 90 (Bruin) series, featuring tilt hoods of fiberglass and a choice of Detroit or Cummins diesel power in the 201/335 hp bracket. At the top of the range were the Bison and the forward control Titan, the later now available with a power operated passenger's window and spoiler on the cab roof: Caterpillar power units could also be specified on this one. The Step-Van range continued, while school buses had V8 gasoline engines, and included a new 72-passenger version on a 22 ft 10 in wheelbase. Chevrolet also offered fwd mobile home chassis with gasoline engines, turbodramatic transmission, forward control, front disc brakes and ifs. At peak in 1976 these had been supplied to 18 major specialist producers, but were being phased out two years later owing to the downsizing of the private-car types upon which they were based. *MCS*

1969 CHEVROLET (Brazil) C-1504, 6×6 pick-up, BHV

CHEVROLET (ii) (BR) 1925 to date

General Motors do Brasil S.A., Sao Jose dos Campos, Sao Paulo, S.P.

On 26 January 1925, General Motors Brasiliera S.A. was created by General Motors Corporation with an investment of $245,00re being locally bodied. During the Second World War the firm made equipment for the Brazilian armed forces and also numerous producer-gas plants. In 1948 GM built its first all-metal bus body with Brazilian steel. National production of components was gradually increased and in 1959 the first engine was made, under direct supervision of Brazil's President.

At present, one gas-engined truck is being made, the C-60, with 4.28 litres 6-cylinder engine and 4-speed transmission. These trucks, in different versions have a load-carrying capacity of from 6.5 to 7.6 tons.

Diesel-engined models made at present use the 5.84 litre 6-cylinder engine. The D-6803 is specially made with a bed for sugar-cane transportation. It can carry 13,96 tons of cane and uses a Clark 5-speed transmission. Models D-7403, D-7503, D-7512, D-7803 and D-7812 chassis only differ from one another in wheelbase width which goes from 3.98 metres to 5.00 metres. The D-60 is a heavy-duty model made in four versions: 4x4, 6x6 with conventional suspension, 6x6 with front and rear independent suspension and 6x4. The D-60 versions are made for civilian, military, police and fire-department use. *ACT*

CHICAGO (i) (US) 1910-1911

Chicago Commercial Car Co., Chicago, Ill.

This truck was built in two versions, a ¾-tonner and a 1-tonner. Both used open van bodies. The smaller, called P-16, had a 16hp, 2-cylinder engine with forward control, a planetary transmission, double chain drive and solid rubber tires. The one-tonner, Model S-25, had a 20 hp engine with a selective gearbox and double chain drive. Prices were $1500 and $1700, respectively. *GMN*

CHICAGO (ii) (US) 1919-1932

(1) Chicago Motor Truck Co., Chicago, Ill.
(2) Robert M. Cutting Co., Chicago, Ill.

Chicagos were conventional assembled trucks made in 1 to 5-ton sizes during the 1920s, with a range of 8- and 12-ton worm-drive 6-wheelers being added in 1930. Hercules engines were used up to 1927 when a switch was made to Waukesha, and by 1930 these were all 6-cylinder units. *GNG*

CHICAGO BUSINESS (US) 1912

Chicago Business Car Co., Chicago, Ill.

Very few details are known of this unimportant make as it was made as a single model with wheelbase of 7 feet 3 inches and powered by a two-cylinder, 14 hp engine and had an 800-pound rated capacity. *GMN*

1917 CHICAGO MOTOR BUS front-drive double decker, MBS

CHICAGO MOTOR BUS CO. (US) 1916-1923

Chicago Motor Bus Co., Chicago, Illinois

Beginning in the fall of 1916, the Chicago Motor Bus Co. assembled, for its own use, a fleet of 50 open-top double-deckers. The bodies had been built by the St. Louis Car Co. and the detachable front-wheel-drive power plants were assembled in Chicago using Moline-Knight sleeve-valve engines. Two experimental buses were constructed in 1919, a conventional rear-wheel-drive type which proved too high for the numerous low clearances in Chicago and a front-wheel-drive double-decker with a fully enclosed top, the first such bus in the U.S.

In the process of reorganization during 1920, the operating company split off the bus-building activity under the name of American Motor Bus Co., which built 23 closed-top buses in 1922 and then designed and built a large new rear-wheel-drive open-top bus with 67 seats, later known as "type K." In 1922 and 1923, 71 of these were built.

Acquisition of the parent company by John D. Hertz in 1923 led to the creation of the Yellow Coach Manufacturing Co. (see Yellow Coach) to succeed American Motor Bus. Chicago Motor Coach Co., as the operating company was then called, built only one bus itself after 1923, that being an experimental six-wheel single-decker built in May 1928. *MBS*

CHICAGO MOTOR WAGON (US) 1910-1912

Chicago Motor Wagon Co., Chicago, Ill.

There was only one model under this name, rated at 1500 to 2000 pounds capacity. It was driven by a 2-cylinder, 20 hp engine, connected with a friction transmission to double chains at the rear wheels. The chassis had a wheelbase of 90 inches and the weight of the chassis was 2300 pounds. With open express body, the price was $1000. *GMN*

CHIEF (US) 1910

Michigan Steam Motor Co., Pontiac, Mich.

This was a steam-powered truck produced only for the one year. Further information has not been uncovered. *GMN*

CHILDS see American La France and Kearns

CHINGHAI-HU (Chinghai Lake) QH-10A (CHI) 1970 to date

Chinghai Motor Vehicle Plant, Chinghai Province
(Plant Vehicle Code — QH)

A 4-ton heavy-duty truck that went into production May 1, 1970. 80% of the unit is built within the plant including engine, transmission, axles, frame, body and steering gear.

The engine and chassis is basically the same as the Jay-Fong (Liberation) CA-10B built in Changchun. *BE*

CHIYODA see T.G.E.

CHRISTIE (US) 1911-1918

Front Drive Motor Co., Hoboken, N.J.

John Walter Christie was a pioneer of front wheel drive who had built a number of racing cars using this principle, as well as a prototype taxicab with transverse 4-cylinder engine (1909). In 1911 he began to experiment with two-wheeled tractors which could be attached to horse-drawn steam pumper fire engines. This would give a new lease of life to the expensive steam pumpers which fire departments were naturally reluctant to part with. The first Christie tractor was delivered to New York Fire Department in December 1911; it had a 90 hp 4-cylinder engine mounted longitudinally ahead of the axle. There was a 2-speed gearbox from which power was transmitted by chain to a countershaft at the ends of which were four spur pinions which meshed with gear wheels inside the road wheels. The tractor was attached to the pump by a turntable which was power operated to turn through 60°. This, together with the ordinary steering capability of 30° enabled the tractor to be at right-angles to the trailer and thus turn in its own length. This was of great importance with the ladder truck trailers which were used as well as the pumpers, for these could be up to 80 feet in length.

The first Christie had a longitudinal engine, but all production models, made from 1912 onwards, had transverse engines, either under the driver's seat or under a short hood. Early Christies were hand cranked, but most had Christiansen compressed-air starters. New York Fire Department was the best customer for Christie tractors, purchasing 186 between 1911 and 1918, and other cities which also used them included Boston, Chicago,

1915 CHRISTIE front-drive water tower truck, LIAM

Philadelphia, Pittsburgh and Manila, Philippines. However the conversion tractor business could not last forever as steam pumpers for horse traction were no longer being made (New York bought their last in 1912). Competition from conventional fire engines forced Christie to cease production at the end of 1918, after more than 600 had been sold. His tractors were very long lived, one still being in active service in Toledo in 1945, and theoretically on call until 1959. Other companies who copied Christie's conversion tractors included American LaFrance, Cross, and Seagrave. *GNG*

CHRISTOPH (D) 1906

Maschinenfabrik J.E. Christoph, Niesky

Only a few front-driven tractors with single-cylinder kerosene engine were built by this firm. *HON*

1928 CHRYSLER Series 62 ½-ton van, CP

CHRYSLER (US) 1925-1928

Chrysler Corporation, Detroit, Mich.

The only commercial vehicles offered under the Chrysler name were 10/15-cwt vans for export only. Chassis used were the 3.1-litre 50-series 4-cylinder and (latterly) the small Model-62 six. Hydraulic fwb were fitted, and in 1926 a Paris firm offered a 4-cylinder Chrysler taxicab. The Chrysler name was also used for Plymouth light commercials sold in Britain in 1938. *MCS*

1977 CHUBB Pacesetter fire engine, Chubb

CHUBB (GB) 1970 to date

Chubb Fire Security Ltd., Sunbury-on-Thames, Middx.

Chubb are an old-established manufacturer of safes and locks who entered the vehicle field as a result of acquiring the Pyrene company, makers of fire-fighting equipment. The first complete vehicle to be sold under the Chubb/Pyrene name was the Pathfinder, an advanced airfield crash tender powered by a rear-mounted Detroit Diesel V-16 engine developing 635bhp. Speeds of up to 60mph are possible on good ground, but the Pathfinder is capable of operating on difficult terrain including marsh and inclines of up to 1 in 2.9.The chassis is a 6x6 unit built by Reynolds Boughton of Amersham, Bucks. Chubb were given a Design Council Engineering Award in 1974 for the Pathfinder which has been supplied to, among others, airports at Manchester, Liverpool, Boston, New York, Oakland, Warsaw, Athens, and Belgrade. Other fire engines developed by Chubb and Reynolds Boughton included the Pursuer, a smaller airfield appliance powered by a rear-mounted Chrysler V-8 gasoline engine developing 225 hp, with Allison automatic transmission and a crew of two, and the Pacesetter, a road-going appliance with 230bhp Detroit Diesel V-6 engine giving a top speed of 75mph, and front-mounted multi pressure pump (the engine is at the rear). Chubb also build fire equipment on a variety of chassis including Land Rover, Thornycroft and Unipower as well as foreign vehicles. The Pathfinder is now called the Griffin, and a companion model of similar appearance with a V8 Detroit Diesel is the Aquarius. The Pacesetter has been renamed the Scorpio. *GNG*

1910 CHURCHILL 3-ton truck, OMM

CHURCHILL (GB) 1905-1925

Durham, Churchill & Co., Sheffield, Yorks.

The first Churchill was a conventional chain-driven chassis powered by a 24hp 4-cylinder Aster engine, with gilled-tube radiator and 3-speed gearbox. Load capacity was 3 tons, and it was also used for charabanc work. It was joined in 1906 by a 10cwt van powered by a 2-cylinder Aster engine, and by 1909 the range consisted of five models from 30cwt to 5 tons capacity powered by 4-cylinder engines of 20, 30, 35 and 45 hp. All used chain drive. This range was made up to the outbreak of war in 1914, but when peace returned only one Churchill was listed, a 3-tonner powered by a 40 hp 4-cylinder engine. It had a 4-speed gearbox and chain drive, and was listed without change until 1925. *GNG*

CHUTING STAR (US) 1976 to date

Forward Inc, Huron, S.D.

The first product of this company was a 6x6 front-discharge cement mixer powered by a rear-mounted Cummins VT 555 turbocharged engine, with Sundstrand

DMT 250 transmission. It had a very low cab, and the chassis was planned for other work such as public utility, crane carrying and highway maintenance. *GNG*

CIEM — STELLA (CH) 1904 - 1913

Compagnie de l'Industrie Electrique et Mecanique (CIEM), Secheron-Geneve (1904-1913)

Not satisfied either with the noisy petrol engine nor with the limited range of battery-powered electric cars, CIEM combined the two principles in a number of their passenger cars. The company also built a few commercial vehicles. The earliest models of 1904/5 had a high driver's seat, a vertical steering column and cart-sprung chassis. Two electro-motors drove one of the rear-wheels each. The

1905 C.I.E.M.-STELLA gas-electric truck, ES

batteries were stored in a large compartment amidships. Payload was 1½ to 2 tons and a top speed of 9 mph was claimed. Shortly thereafter an omnibus for 16 passengers was built. Here a 4-cylinder in line engine of 4½ liters drove the rear axle via 4-speed gearbox and shaft. These were offered on the British market by C.S. Rolls & Company under the name Rolls. In 1908/9 there was another omnibus for 8 passengers with a conventional 4-cylinder engine. Total production reached 14 commercial vehicles only. *FH*

CIMARRON (PI) 1975 to date

Chrysler Philippines Inc., Makati, Rizal

In order not to miss the growing market for an easy-to-build utility vehicle, Chrysler introduced a light pick-up with forward control cab of plain, purpose-built design. Called the Cimarron, it was designed by the Japanese affiliate of Chrysler, Mitsubishi Motors and is smarter in appearance than competitive models, in that it features full length doors with sliding windows, twin windscreen wipers, etc. The basic chassis cab can be fitted with all types of bodies. *GA*

CIMATTI (I) 1949-1966

Cimatti Enrico SpA, Bologna

Produced by a motorcycle factory, Cimattis were conventional 3-cwt 3-wheeler vans with 50c 2-stroke engines, three forward speeds, and brakes on all wheels. Early models were of open-saddle type, but the last Mini-Tres had fully enclosed cabs and shaft instead of chain drive. Mopeds are still manufactured by the company. *MCS*

1966 CIMATTI Minitre 50cc van, Cimatti

CINO (US) 1910-1913

Haberer & Co., Cincinnati, Ohio

The first model under this name was a ½-tonner with a 40 hp engine on wheelbase of 113 inches. The second model, built for 1913 was a ¼-tonner whose chassis cost $1300. *GMN*

1929 CITROEN/L.G.C.C4 taxicab, GNG

CITROEN (F) 1919 to date

(1) SA Andre Citroen, Paris 1919-1968
(2) Citroen SA, Paris 1968 to date.

Andre Citroen introduced mass-production methods to Europe with his 1.3-litre sv 4-cylinder Type-A of 1919; this was available in light commercial form as was the 1½-litre Type-B which succeeded it in 1922. Taxicab editions were offered from 1923, and 4-wheel brakes were standardized in 1926, in which year British assembly began at Slough. A 1-ton truck using a reinforced and lengthened edition of the 1.6-litre B14 chassis was first listed in 1927.

From 1921 Citroen offered halftrack vehicles to the designs of M. Kegresse, the former superintendent of Tsar Nicholas II's garages. Intended for military use, the first Citroen-Kegresse was based on the A-type car, with additional cooling surfaces and a 2-speed auxiliary gearbox giving 6 forward speeds. These halftracks remained in the catalogue until World War II, serving in numerous armies as command cars, self-propelled guns, and gun and aircraft tractors. Several firms (Panhard in France, and Burford, Crossley and Vulcan in Britain) produced their own developments of the Kegresse design. Civilian roles included those of hotel bus at winter sports resorts, and barge tug, in which form even a 4-cylinder Citroen-Kegresse could haul up to 1,000 tons. 30 were said to be in such use by 1926. Subsequent editions used the mechanical elements of various 4- and 6-cylinder truck models, with payloads as high as 1½ tons. The last of the

Kegresses, Type 107, was also built for the French Army by Unic, and found its way into German service after 1940. Among the Citroen-Kegresse's most notable exploits were the first automobile crossing of the Sahara (December, 1922-January, 1923); the trans-African Black Cruise of 8 halftracks from Colomb-Bechar to Tananarive (1925/26); and the trans-Asian Yellow Cruise of 1931/32.

The introduction of the 2.4 litre 6-cylinder 4-bearing sv C6 engine in 1929 marked a move towards light high-speed trucks in the modern idiom, though initially only a car-type ambulance was offered. An unusual variant

1930 CITROEN-KEGRESSE C6 half track, Citroen

announced that year was a 4-cylinder taxicab with Citroen mechanical elements built for their own use by the London General Cab Co. In 1930, however, the 4-cylinder 1-tonner (now with 1.8-litre engine) was joined by a 35-cwt 6-cylinder model with 4-speed gearbox and vacuum servo brakes. A year later a wide range of 6-cylinder commercials included a 2-tonner with twin rear wheels, a two-seater coach, a 3-4 ton 6x2, a 5½-ton tractive unit, and the inevitable Kegresse variants. A full-fronted forward-control city bus model did not go into production.

Though the smaller vans followed their car counterparts, there were no other major changes until 1934, when a new range of trucks was introduced with front-end styling similar to that of the contemporary car models. The latest Kegresse (Type 75) and the Type 29 retained sv engines, but the 3½-ton 45 featured an ohv 6-cylinder unit of 4.6 litres' capacity with detachable liners, a twin-plate clutch, and a 4-speed gearbox. It came in three wheelbase lengths, the longest (17 ft 5 in) being reserved for coaches. By 1936 side valves had disappeared, the new lighter Citroens being the 10-cwt 11UA, the 30-cwt 23, and the 2½-ton 32. The first two shared their 1.9-litre 4-cylinder engines with the fwd 11CV cars, but the 32's 3.1-litre unit was reserved for trucks. By 1937 Citroen offered an 80-model range comparable with those of Bedford or Morris-

1939 CITROEN T23 1½-ton truck, OMM

1946 CITROEN T45 3½-ton truck, OMM

Commercial; it included their first diesel, a 1.8-litre four also available in rwd editions of the 11CV private car. The 23 had acquired hydraulic brakes by 1940, while during the War gazogene versions of the 45 were produced. Both these two types were offered again without substantial change in 1946, apart from the standardization of hydrovac brakes on the bigger model. They remained in the catalogue until the end of 1953.

Cars with fwd, unitary construction, and independent suspension had been available as early as 1934, but it was not until 1938 that these principles were applied to a commercial vehicle, the 18-cwt forward control TU van with the 1.6-litre 7CV engine. It used the same 3-speed gearbox and torsion-bar front suspension as the cars, but differed from them in using conventional semi-elliptics at the rear. It gave way in 1947 to the snubnosed H-series with corrugated panels, torsion-bar rear suspension, and a governed, 35bhp edition of the 11CV unit. Early versions had capacities of 17 or 23½-cwt, but latterly the HY could carry over 30-cwt. 1948 saw an even more successful fwd Citroen, the 2CV utility car with 375cc aircooled flat-twin engine developing 9bhp, a 4-speed all-synchromesh gearbox with overdrive top, and interconnected, all-independent springing. The rolltop and detachable trim of the standard sedan rendered this a true dual-purpose vehicle, but 5-cwt trucks and vans were not in fact available before 1951. The 2CV helped to make Citroen France's largest producer of commercial vehicles in 1954, with 50,740 units delivered. A year later the company's new associate, Panhard, was turning out commercial 2CVs in their Ivry factory while these were also being made at Slough, the first trucks to leave there since 1932. The Royal Navy used helicopter-transportable pickups

1954 CITROEN T23 2-ton van, NMM

aboard some of their aircraft carriers, though a subsequent 4x4 twin-engined *tous terrains* model developed in France was made only as a sedan. Capacity went up to 425cc in 1954, and to 602cc with the AK series of 1963, which used the 22bhp Ami engine.

In 1954 the traditional medium-capacity Citroens finally bowed out, though only new front end styling really distinguished their 2-ton and 5-ton replacements, the same engines being used. The 5-speed 55, however, could be fitted with a 76bhp 6-cylinder Citroen diesel engine, and by 1956 capacity of the petrol unit had been increased to 5.2 litres, while tractor and 4x4 versions had been added to the range. An interesting exercise in badge engineering was a further version of the 55 using Panhard's own 4-cylinder diesel engine. The 1960 commercial catalogue featured the 2CV, the faithful H-type, the 55, the 2-ton 23 (now available with semi forward control and also with a British Perkins P4 oil engine), and the first commercial editions of the revolutionary D-series cars with hydropneumatic suspension. These were based on the simplified ID19 and consisted of a *commerciale* (simplified station wagon with detachable seating) and an ambulance, though the ID family soon became popular with the funeral trade as well. 1961 models of the H van could be had with the smaller 1.6-litre Perkins diesel.

As early as the 1961 Citroen had produced a military 4x4 truck with the 6-cylinder gasoline engine and full forward control, and in 1966 this latter feature was applied to their heavy-duty range. Replacements for the 23 and 55 were a new range of 3/6-ton models with 4- or 5-speed all-synchromesh gearboxes and dual-circuit servo brakes similar to those of D-series cars. Gasoline engines were still available, a 2.2-litre short-stroke 4-cylinder DS unit featuring in the smaller 350 as an alternative to 4-cylinder diesels by Perkins or M.A.N. The heavier 600 and 700, however, retained Citroen-built sixes of both types. The H's diesel option was now the 1.8-litre Indenor also used by Hotchkiss and Peugeot.

Citroen's subsequent financial adventures had more effect on their commercial vehicles than on their cars. 1967's purchase of Berliet inevitably made the bigger trucks redundant, and they had disappeared by 1970, albeit Berliet themselves toyed with fwd on their Stradair series. A less felicitous affair was the Citroen-Fiat alliance of 1969, though this had little immediate effect beyond giving Citroen the French distribution rights of Autobianchi's cars and light commercials. There were, however, other developments in the light van sector, notably the Jeep-type 4x2 Mehari of 1969. This combined the mechanical elements of the 602cc 2-cylinder Dyane 6 with glassfibre open bodywork; it was made under license in South Vietnam (and later under Communist control) as the Dalat, being joined in due course by other commercial Dyanes and a local version of the H van. Dyanes and Meharis were also made in Iran from 1971 by Saipac. In 1970 came a 7½-cwt van edition of the 602cc Ami sedan with front disc brakes, following a year later by commercials based on the flat-4 GS with 1,005cc and 1,220cc engines. By this time even commercial Ds had the latest short-stroke units, though the 1934-type 78x100mm 2-litre soldered on in the indestructible H. Though by 1974 2CVs were being built under license in ten countries, Citroen were once again in financial trouble: sales were falling, and this ime they allied themselves with Peugeot. Their new C32/C35 range of fwd vans in the 1½-1¾-ton class were not, however, relatives of the Peugeot J7, but very similar to Fiat's 242, their 2-litre Citroen engines apart. Other features included all independent springing, forward control, and servo assisted 4-wheel disc brakes. In April, 1975, the D-series ended its 19-year run, leaving the 2CV/Dyane family, the Ami, the GS, the new vans and the ageless H to represent the firm in the commercial field. The same line was being offered in 1978, though 2CV commercials were in process of a phase-out in favor of Dyanes. *MCS*

1978 CITROEN J35 1½-ton van, Citoer

C.I.V. (F) 1953

Constructions Industrielles de Versailles, Versailles

This company, mainly known for their refuse collection bodies, built an integral-construction single-decker bus powered by an 80 bhp Hispano/Hercules diesel engine. This was mounted at the rear, and projected into the saloon, with a seat on either side of it. Capacity was 65 passengers, of whom 26 were seated. *GNG*

CLARK (i) (US) 1900-c.1906; 1910-1912

Edward S. Clark Steam Automobiles, Dorchester, Mass.

This manufacturer of steam passenger cars made a few light vans for 1000 lb loads. Later two gasoline models were made of large capacity with ratings of three and of five tons respectively. Both were powered by two stroke, 4-cylinder engines mounted beneath the body. The 5-tonner had a wheelbase of 144 inches, a weight of 7200 pounds and a price of $4400. *GMN*

CLARK (ii) (US) 1910-1912

Clark & Company, Lansing, Michigan 1910
Clark Power Wagon Company, Lansing Michigan 1911-1912

These were delivery or express vans of 1500 and 2000 pounds capacity, driven by two-cylinder, 20 hp engines. Transmissions were planetary but final drive was by shaft. Clark & Company combined with Ferguson Motor Company, also of Lansing, to form the Clark Power Wagon Company. *GMN*

CLARK (iii) (US) 1910-1914

(1) A.C. Clark & Co., Grand Crossing, Chicago, Ill. 1910
(2) Clark Delivery Wagon Co., Chicago, Ill., Detroit, Mich. 1911-1914

The first Clark model was a ¾-tonner delivery van with a 24 hp 4-cylinder engine. This used a 3-speed gearbox, shaft drive and pneumatic tires. For 1912, a 1-tonner with a stake body and forward control was built. In 1914, only the ¾-tonner was made using a 4-cylinder Continental engine with a Brown-Lipe 3-speed gearbox, shaft drive and on a 144-inch wheelbase. *GMN*

1904 CLARKSON steam bus, NMM

CLARKSON (GB) 1899-c.1925

(1) Clarkson & Capel Steam Car Syndicate Ltd., Dalston, London E. 1899-1902
(2) Clarkson Ltd., Chelmsford, Essex 1902-1909
(3) National Steam Car Co. Ltd., Chelmsford, Essex 1909-1911
(4) National Steam Car Co. (1911) Ltd., Chelmsford, Essex 1911-1912
(5) National Steam Car Co. Ltd., Chelmsford, Essex 1912-1920
(6) Clarkson Steam Motors, Chelmsford, Essex 1920-c.1925

Clarkson designed a two-speed chain drive vehicle for the 1899 Liverpool Trials using a modified Merryweather boiler, oil fired and running at 200 p.s.i. A compound vertical engine was placed in the back of the cab and revved at 600 r.p.m., more than double the practice of his rivals. A cab roof condenser was fitted and chain drive was used.

This was followed by a single speed model with duplex cylinders and a spur differential on the countershaft, still with chain drive. Joys gear superseded the Stephenson gear of the first model. Working pressure was 300 p.s.i. raised in Clarkson's own design of paraffin-fired semi-flash boiler.

Later Clarkson used a water tube boiler with horse shoe tubes expanded into a central drum, a coil superheater heating the steam to 700/800° C and an economizer. He also designed a centrally-fired vertical boiler with a wet sided firebox into the upper part of which his patent thimble tubes projected. This boiler, capable of being fired by coke or coal in addition to paraffin was also sold for use in stationary plant.

After using piston valves for some years Clarkson reverted to bronze slide valves on cast iron ports. In about 1903 he adopted progressively improved automatic water and liquid fuel controls and later superseded the chains by shaft drive.

1914 CLARKSON National steam bus, NMM

In 1903 he built his first steam bus for use in Torquay and began to press sales to the London General and other London operators. Clarkson's double decker was shown at Olympia in 1905. Like Serpollet, Clarkson had found that the only effective way in which to secure sales of steam buses was to own or control the operating company. Though he had succeeded in selling 46 vehicles to London fleets by 1907 this was the zenith and by the end of the year they had mainly been discarded in favor of gasoline vehicles. The following year he began, therefore, to build up his own "National" fleet, which at its peak had 173 double deckers at work in London, based on the garages at Nunhead, Poplar and Putney. The shortage of paraffin during the war led to some of these buses being fired on coke. The Nationals outlived the 1914/18 war but the last was withdrawn in 1919. The very last Clarkson bus to run operated from Ryde to Seaview, Isle of Wight, in 1921.

In 1920 Clarkson withdrew from the National group and set about selling an up-dated 3-ton steam truck using his thimble boiler, with emphasis on solid fuels. The engine was a vertical Vee compound with piston valves, totally enclosed, driving, via a single plate clutch, a standard three speed and reverse gearbox. A condenser was mounted like a radiator at the front of the vehicle.

This last design was a better tribute to Clarkson as an engineer than as a business man. Its detail and cost placed it at a disadvantage at a time when war surplus gasoline-engined trucks were swamping the market and few were sold. When well maintained and carefully driven, Clarksons were good and reliable performers with marked fuel economy but did not show up well in the hands of the average haulier. No formal announcement was made of the cessation of manufacture but 1925 marks the effective end. *RAW*

CLAVEAU (F) 1930

Automobiles Claveau, Paris 8

The inventive Emile Claveau built a variety of unconventional cars from 1926 to 1950, and one of these was the basis for a 7cwt van. This had a 750 cc V-twin 2-stroke engine driving the front wheels, coil ifs and integral construction. It was priced at the equivalent of £110, and Claveau announced plans to make it in England, but even in its native France it never got into production. *GNG*

1912 CLAYTON 5-ton overtype steam wagon, RAW

CLAYTON (GB) 1894-1930

(1) Clayton & Shuttleworth Ltd., Lincoln 1894-1926
(2) Clayton Wagons Ltd., Lincoln 1918-1930

Clayton did not set out to be manufacturers of road locomotives for heavy haulage and such engines as they supplied for this purpose may be considered more as sports to the main stem of traction engine production than as a conscious assault upon this field.

Their connection with steam commercial vehicles rests, therefore, upon their single cylinder and compound three shaft 5-ton steam tractors with Belpaire firebox designed to comply with the 1904 regulations and upon their production of steam wagons. Numerically the latter far overshadowed the former which were a neat but unexceptional design that failed to make any pronounced impact upon the limited market in tractors.

After building an experimental and unsuccessful undertype compound wagon in 1902 Claytons did not re-enter the wagon market until 1912 when the first of their 5-ton compound overtypes was sold. Earlier examples came out with, variously, wooden or riveted traction engine type wheels but later examples had cast steel wheels with solid rubbers and a few had Ackermann steering though most

1918 CLAYTON steam tractor, RAW

had chain and bobbin. This design of Clayton overtype was reliable and reasonably economical but outclassed by the contemporary Foden in road speed and hence daily mileage. Sales during the 1914-18 war were undoubtedly helped by the heavy demand for wagons and shortage of Fodens. Despite the introduction of Ackermann steering, internal expanding brakes, rubber tires and an ingenious design of front wheel hub containing the king-pins the

1924 CLAYTON electric truck, OMM

popularity of the 5-tonner decreased progressively after the war and until 1926. In that year an entirely new 6 ton design appeared using a pistol boiler with stayless firebox, ball and roller races on the crankshaft main bearings, marine type big ends, enclosed motion work, improved driver visibility, roller bearing to the road wheels, electric lighting and, optionally, four wheel brakes. The design was, however, too late and only some forty were made though more than 1000 of the earlier 5-tonner had been turned out. A few chain drive steam tractors were made based on the wagon design.

Parallel with the latter overtypes a vertical boilered undertype was designed and launched in 1920. Having a water tube boiler with corrugated firebox and a coil superheater it worked at 230 p.s.i. The duplex-cylindered engine had piston valves below the cylinders with shifting eccentric valve gear driven from a layshaft geared to the crankshaft.

Like the contemporary Sentinel it was a single speed wagon. With 7" x 10" cylinders it was slightly overcylindered compared with the 6¾" x 9" cylinders of the Super Sentinel and was, moreover, rather too heavy in build. Consequently it was a commercial flop, contributing to the downfall of the makers in 1926. After that date steam wagon building was carried on until 1930 by Clayton Wagons Ltd., originally set up to carry on the parent company's railway vehicle building work, which outlived its parent by only four years. *RAW/OM*

CLECO (GB) 1936-1957
Cleco Industries Ltd., Leicester

Introduced in 1936 the Cleco range consisted of an internal works transport stillage truck and a 12 cwt capacity forward control road vehicle. During the next few years many more works trucks than electric vans were produced, although at the outbreak of war two models were being offered, the second being a 5/10 cwt capacity van or dairy truck.

The postwar range continued with the works trucks and a 12 cwt chassis of 7 ft 2 in wheelbase weighing 15 cwt unladen. A 200AH capacity battery was fitted. In 1950 there were two models again — the AV3 of 10/12 cwt capacity and the heavier BV3 offered with capacities of 1 ton, 24 cwt and 28 cwt on a 101 inch wheelbase. About this time the Bijou was announced, being a 10 cwt chassis of only 44 inch wheelbase.

Production of road going vehicles was never very great and in the mid 1950's production was concentrated on internal works trucks. *OM*

CLEMENT: CLEMENT-BAYARD (F) 1903-1914
(1) Clement et Cie, Levallois-Perret, Seine 1903
(2) SA des Etablissements Clement-Bayard, Levallois-Perret, Seine: Mezieres: 1903-1914

Light vans and trucks were being offered by Clement at the beginning of the 1903 season, when Adolphe Clement himself was still associated with Gladiator. These were modern designs with L-head vertical-twin engines of 1.4 litres' capacity, four forward speeds, shaft drive, and pneumatic tires. Clement-Gladiator vans of this type were still available in England as late as 1907, but during 1903 M. Clement had set up on his own, the Clement-Bayard name being selected to commemorate the 16th century Chevalier Bayard. This *chevalier sans peur et reproche* had saved Mezieres (where Adolphe Clement had a factory) in 1521.

Up to 1906 Clement-Bayard commercial vehicles closely resembled the 1903 type, with 2-cylinder engines and shaft drive, though capacity went up to 2.2 litres. A loading height similar to that of railway platforms was publicized, and the range now included a solid-tired 3-tonner. A fleet of Clement-Bayard delivery vans was in attendance on the works team during the 1906 French GP, and by 1907 chars-a-banc with 4.4-litre 4-cylinder engines were in service in Paris. There were also some big forward-control trucks, and 1908 saw the mandatory taxicabs with 2- or 4-cylinder engine and three forward speeds, though the faithful old twin soldiered on in 2-ton trucks as late as 1909. Dashboard radiators had arrived on all but the largest private cars by 1911, and were found on the entire commercial range; this extended from a small delivery van with 921cc 2-cylinder engine at 4,000 fr. up to a chain-driven 2.4-litre 4-cylinder 2-tonner with solids and twin rear wheels. The intermediate 8hp twin and 12hp four were listed with cab bodywork, and the 1913 catalogue covered everything from a 6-cwt van up to a 3½-ton truck. This last, when used in conjunction with a drawbar trailer, was said to be capable of handling 10-ton payloads. Chain drive was standard from 2 tons upwards, and the largest ones were of forward-control type. By this time the twins had gone for good, even the lightest delivery van using a long-stroke (60x120mm) 4-cylinder unit. The same basic range, now headed by a 22hp 5-tonner, was available in 1914. Clement-Bayard did not re-enter the commercial-vehicle field after 1918, and four years later their surviving factory at Levallois-Perret came under Citroen ownership. *MCS*

CLEVELAND (US) 1913-1914
E.C. Clark Motor Co., Jackson, Mich.

This was a ¾-tonner whose tradename was derived from the marketing company, C.D. Paxon, of Cleveland, Ohio. The truck itself was not unusual, having pneumatic tires and shaft drive. Its only unusual feature was its 4-cylinder engine which used overhead valves inclined at 45° to the cylinder head. The valves were driven by an overhead camshaft, possibly the first of this type in a US truck. The name of this vehicle is also given as New Cleveland. *GMN*

CLIMAX (US) 1907
Dunbar Mfg. Co., Sandusky, Ohio

The Climax "convertible" was a light 80-inch car on which roadster, touring, or delivery bodies could be interchanged in a few minutes. As a delivery unit it weighed 1400 pounds with a capacity of 1000 pounds.

The 8 hp one-cylinder horizontal engine was water-cooled, aided by a pump. The transmission of the sliding gear type had two speeds forward, and final drive was by a single chain to the rear axle. Speed was 15 mph. Semi-elliptic springs were provided all around supporting a frame of angle steel. Artillery wheels had optional pneumatic or solid tires. *RW*

CLIMBER (US) 1920-1923
Climber Motor Corp., Little Rock, Ark

This manufacturer of passenger cars also offered a 1½-tonner for the above years. This utilized a 4-cylinder engine built by Herschell-Spillman, a Muncie 3-speed gearbox and a Torbensen rear axle. Wheelbase was 146 inches and the price of the chassis was $2450. *GMN*

1967 CLINE 6×4 truck, OMM

CLINE (US) 1952 to date
(1) Cline Truck Mfg. Co., Kansas City, Mo. 1952-1972
(2) Cline Truck Divin, Isco Mfg. Co., Kansas City, Mo. 1972 to date

Max W. Cline formed his own company after leaving Dart where he had been top salesman for many years. Some other Dart personnel joined Cline in his new small company whose first order was for a truck to be built from an assortment of parts which the customer, a Kansas City construction company, already had on hand. These included a new Waukesha diesel engine. The second order was for nine crane carriers. Cline built eight trucks in 1953 and 24 in 1954. In 1956 the St. Joseph Lead Company ordered two 10-ton underground trucks and later became the first customer to buy $1,000,000 worth of Cline trucks. Max Cline died in 1957 but production of his trucks continued to climb, so that by the end of 1968 it had totalled 169 single-axle tractors, 501 tandem-axle trucks and 91 tandem axle and 4-wheel trailers. The 35-ton 6x4 coal hauler became virtually a standard item in its field; it and drilling rigs accounted for 54 per cent of Cline's sales. Logging trucks accounted for 14 per cent, railroad trucks 13 per cent, trailers 11 per cent and slag haulers 6 per cent. Cline 12 and 20-ton trucks used Detroit Diesel 4- and 6-cylinder engines, the 35-ton 4x2 and 6x4s used Cummins NT-380 engines, while the largest model, introduced in 1970, was the 72-ton 6x6 coal hauler powered by a Cummins 635 hp turbocharged V-12 diesel. Transmissions were five to nine speed Fuller, Allison or Clark, and rear axles were Timken-Cline hypoid with planetary gearset at the outer wheels. Layouts included conventional, offset cab conventional and cab-beside-engine. Cline's own rubber rear suspension is used on many of its trucks.

For 1973 a new model appeared, the IC-A20R front-drive one-man cab articulated 20-ton low-bed dump truck for quarry and road building. It is powered by a Cummins 6-cylinder engine driving through a Clark single-stage torque converter and Rockwell differential, with planetary final drive. Cline has also built some highway trucks which used Hendrickson sheet metal and closely resembled the Chicago trucks. Special vehicles have included railroad wheel-changing vehicles and locomotive and freight car re-railers which have auxiliary railroad conversion wheels.

Since Cline became part of Isco in 1972 many of their trucks have appeared under the Isco name, although the Cline nameplate still appears on some products. *RW*

CLINTON (i) (CND) 1911-1912

Clinton Motor Co. Ltd., Clinton, Ont.

A small number of trucks in sizes from ½ to 3-tons, the larger with chain drive and solid tires, were sold in Ontario. Also produced was the Clinton Combination, a light pick-up to which bench seats could be added for conversion to a passenger car. *HD*

CLINTON (ii) (US) 1920-1934

(1) Clinton Motors Corp., New York, N.Y. 1920-1923

(2) Clinton Motors Corp., Reading, Pa. 1923-1934

This firm assembled trucks in a small way in New York before buying the factory of Schwartz Motors in late 1923. A complete line of worm drive trucks was offered during the mid-1920's. In 1925 Clinton listed eight models from 1¼ to 7-ton capacity. Buda 4-cylinder engines were used. From 1925 to 1928 the firm offered 30 and 35-passenger bus chassis. In 1927, when chassis with 6-cylinder Lycoming engines were first offered, production peaked at 135 trucks. After 1929 trucks were built to special-order only. *DJS*

C.L.M. see Lilloise

CLOUGH-SMITH see Straker-Squire

CLUA (E) 1956-1960

Construcciones Mecanicas Clua, SL, Barcelona

This well-known motorcycle factory made small touring and sports cars, and delivery tricycles of 125 and 175cc. They also made a 4-wheeled light truck powered by a 498cc 2-cylinder engine, with chain drive. Its capacity was 400kg. *JGG*

CLUB (US) 1911-1912

Club Car Co., New York, N.Y.

The Club Car Company was formed as a cooperative to build cars for its members, actual manufacture being the work of Merchant & Evans of Philadelphia. As well as expensive passenger cars there was a 3-ton forward-control truck powered, like the cars, by a 40 hp 4-cylinder American & British engine, with 3-speed gearbox and double chain drive. There was also a taxicab with 16 hp A & B engine. *GNG*

1914 CLYDE(i) 12cwt van. NMM

CLYDE (i) (GB) 1905-1914

G.H. Wait & Co. Ltd., Leicester

George Wait was a cycle and motorcycle maker who built cars and commercial vehicles in small quantities as well. Car production began in 1901, but the first recorded goods vehicle was a 1-ton forward-control van of 1905. In 1912 two vans were offered, both normal-control and based on the company's passenger cars; they were a 6cwt with 8/10 hp 2-cylinder engine and a 12cwt with 10/12 hp 4-cylinder engine. Both had 3-speed gearboxes and shaft drive. The engines were proprietary units, probably Asters. *GNG*

CLYDE (ii) (GB) 1913-1938

Mackay & Jardine Ltd., Wishaw, Lanarkshire.

Both Mackay and Jardine were previously with Belhaven, and initially there was little to distinguish their 3-ton Aster-engined chain driven chassis from the other Wishaw product. The range was, however, augmented by a 1½ tonner with shaft and worm drive in 1914, and this remained their staple offering until the mid-twenties, when a 2-ton and 2½ ton chassis were added and by which time American Buda engines had been adopted. Although an 'assembled' vehicle, the Clyde's gearbox and transmission was built in the works and production ran to about four chassis per month throughout its longish life. Nevertheless, the make was popular in Scotland, particularly with small bus and charabanc operators, with Central SMT Co. Ltd., running several which it had acquired in takeovers until 1932. Production after 1928 is problematical, although the firm remained (and is still) in business and was offering 2, 2½ and 3 ton chassis and 20 and 26 seater buses as late as 1938. *MJWW*

1936 CLYDESDALE 7½-ton 6×6 truck, BHV

CLYDESDALE (US) 1917-1938

(1) Clyde Cars Co., Clyde, Ohio
(2) Clydesdale Motor Truck Co., Clyde, Ohio

The Clydesdale was a typical assembled truck made in capacities from ¾ to 5/6 tons, powered by Continental engines, with Brown-Lipe transmissions and Sheldon axles. The heavier models were distinguished by particularly deep, tapered frame side rails. From 1925 to 1930 4- and 6-cylinder engines were used, but then production lapsed for six years, although there is some suggestion of output for export only. In 1936 a new range appeared, this time powered by Buda and Hercules diesel engines. This was quite early for production diesel trucks in America. Sizes ranged from 1 to 7/10 tons capacity, with 'up to 15 tons' being quoted for tractors. Types covered every possible configuration, conventional, short-conventional, cab-over-engine, and including 4x4 and 6x6 off road models. Some of the latter, powered by 779 cid 6-cylinder Hercules engines, were supplied to the US Army. In 1937 a smaller and lighter range of trucks rounded out what was already an enormous selection of models for a comparatively small firm whose annual production probably never exceeded 200. These last Clydesdales were powered by Waukesha-Hesselman diesel engines. *RJ*

CLYNO (GB) 1927

Clyno Engineering Co. Ltd., Wolverhampton, Staffs.

The well-known Clyno light car was briefly offered in van form with a load capacity of 8 cwt. The standard 1368cc Coventry-Climax engine was used, and the chassis was only modified to the extent of a wider track and stronger rear springs. The price of the van complete was £172 10/-. *GNG*

C.M.V. (E) 1939-1948

SA Industrial de Construcciones Moviles de Valencia, Valencia

This company made trams and trolley-buses and also a light gasoline-engined van and truck during the years 1941/42. Another product of this period was a trailer for camping to be attached to private cars.

In 1946 the company introduced a battery-electric chassis for goods or passengers which was exhibited at that year's Electric Car Exhibition in Madrid. *JCG*

C.N.T.-A.I.T. see C.G.A.

1954 COACHETT, MBS

COACHETTE (US) 1954-1968

The Coachette Co., Dallas, Texas

Coachette was started by Carl Graham, formerly regional sales manager for Marmon-Herrington buses (earlier for Ford). The original design was a 21-passenger city transit bus on a 172-inch wheelbase Ford truck chassis. Most of the bodies were built by Ward Body Co., Austin, Texas, to Coachette's specifications. After 1958 the design was changed to a nearly flat front, and Chevrolet and GM chassis could be specified. Still later seating capacities up to 37 were offered, and options included air conditioning and sliding window sashes. About 330 Coachettes were built. *MBS*

COAST (US) c.1958-1974

Coast Apparatus Inc., Martinez, Calif.

This company built fire apparatus mostly on commercial chassis, but they made some custom chassis, both normal and forward-control, with Hall-Scott engines and International cabs. The company was acquired by Howe in 1974. *GNG*

COBORN (GB) 1908

Coborn Motor Co. Ltd., Bromley, Kent.

Sometimes shown as the Coburn, which is incorrect, this vehicle was interesting in that it employed an unsprung transverse-engined front-wheel-drive unit. Designated the 'SM' motor tractor unit, this consisted of a modified 20 hp 4-cylinder watercooled Alpha engine in-unit with a three speed gearbox, driving the two front wheels by means of short drive shafts and universal joints (as in the modern BMC f.w.d. vehicles). Provision was also made for four-wheel-drive by means of a centrally located propeller shaft driving direct to a live rear axle, or alternatively to a countershaft and thence by twin side chains. The whole unit could be removed en bloc for maintenance or repair and speedily replaced with a spare, thus obviating the neccessity to take the vehicle out of service. *MJWW*

COCK (NL) 1958-1974

Cock N.V., Assen

In 1958 Cock started to produce the Little Tyrant small three-wheeled commercial vehicle, with one front wheel and two at rear. The 2.1 HP single cylinder JLO two-stroke engine drove the front wheel directly without chains or whatsoever, through a 26:1 ratio reduction box. A 1000 kgs and a 600 kgs version were available, top speed viz. 8 and 14 km/h. During the 'sixties an electric version of the Little Tyrant also became available, while Cock started producing four-wheeled vehicles too. One of them was the Colektro IV van with a payload up to 1250 kgs. Mobile shops, based on British Ford components, fol-

1968 COCK Colektro 1V electric van, OMM

1974 COCK Mobile shop, OMM

lowed during the early 'seventies. Imported by Cock were the Italian MV Tevere small three-wheeled trucks which they fitted with their own body. In 1974 Cock went bankrupt. *JFJK*

CODER (F) c.1946-1949

Ets. Industriels Coder, Marseille

This well-known maker of tanker bodies and trailers of all kinds built a small number of light electric trucks for a few years after World War 2. *GNG*

COHENDET (F) 1905-1914

A. Cohendet et Cie, Paris.

Cohendet were component suppliers who advertised in the motoring press as early as 1898; among their customers were Decauville. In addition some rather desultory car manufacture was pursued. Their commercial vehicles were taken more seriously, the firm being regular entrants in the French truck trials of the period. All Cohendets were driver-over-engine types with 4-speed gearboxes, cone clutches, and side-chain drive, for payloads from 3 to 6 tons. A curiosity was the use of T-headed 2-cylinder engines, some of them with comprehensive water jacketing; by 1909 capacity was up to 4.8 litres with square dimensions of 145 x 145 mm. From 1907 there was also a 3-cylinder model. Though by 1912 the heavier Cohendets had a long-stroke (100 x 170 mm) 35hp 4-cylinder unit, the twins and threes survived until the end. *MCS*

1948 COLEMAN (ii) 4 × 4 truck, LA

COLEMAN (i) (US) 1910-1914

F. Coleman Carriage & Harness Co., Ilion, NY 1910-1911
Coleman Motor Truck Co., Ilion, NY 1912-1914

The Coleman commercial vehicles were relatively unsophisticated with the models A-1 and A-2 using 20 hp, 2-cylinder, air-cooled engines mounted beneath the body. The engines were connected to planetary transmissions and then to double chains. These vans had capacities of 1200 pounds and body types were open and closed, respectively. Later models, B and C, were 1- and 2-tonners which used four-cylinder water-cooled engines on chassis of 107 inches and 117 inches wheelbase, respectively. *GMN*

1968 COLEMAN (ii) Space Star twin steer truck, LA

COLEMAN (ii) (US) 1925 to date

(1) Coleman Motors Corp., Littleton, Colo.
(2) American Coleman Co., Littleton, Colo.

G.L. Coleman of Omaha, Nebraska founded his company in 1923, but vehicle production did not start until after the move to Littleton, Colorado in 1925. The first trucks were 4x4 and 6x6 load carriers and tractors powered by 4-cylinder Buda engines. They were particularly used by State Highway Departments, and one was tested by the U.S. Army, leading to military orders for 4x4 and 6x4 trucks. A fire engine was offered to smaller fire services which could pump from a hydrant or streams and throw a jet of water 80 feet in the air.

In 1928 a 7½-ton 6x6 truck was introduced to meet the needs of the logging and oil industries for off-highway work. This had a 6-cylinder Buda GL engine, 4-speed Fuller transmission and 2-speed Coleman auxiliary transmission, giving eight forward speeds in all. One of these chassis was used for aircraft refuelling at a time when this work was in its infancy. By 1936 Coleman had a range of eight models of 2 to 10 tons capacity, all with Buda engines except for the E-57 7 3/4-tonner which used a Sterling engine. In 1938 Cummins or Buda diesels were introduced, but by 1941 the range had shrunk to only one 4x4 6-tonner. During the World War II Coleman crane carriers were supplied to the Corps of Engineers, and after the war production was resumed of 4x4 trucks. A bitter labor dispute kept the factory closed for most of 1949 and 1950, losing the company their dealer network, customers and 350 skilled employees. In 1952, however, Coleman made a comeback when it received a 9½ million dollar contract to build Mule towing tractors for the U.S. Air Force. These had twin cabs, 4-wheel drive and steering and 6-cylinder Buda engines. A similar design was made by Federal.

Since 1954 Coleman's main work has been in producing all-wheel-drive assemblies for the conversion of conventional trucks. In 1961 the firm started to build front steerable drive axles for large O.E.M. accounts. In 1968 Coleman built the Space Star, a forward-control highway tractor with 4-wheel-drive and steering. The semi-trailer was rigidly fixed to the tractor, but a second 4-wheel trailer could be towed as well. Powered by a Detroit Diesel 8V-71N engine developing 318 hp, the Space Star was tested at speeds of up to 80 mph. Other features were roll-bar contruction in the cab and adjustable air suspension giving 8 inches vertical travel to match different loading dock heights. The Space Star remained in the prototype stage. *LA*

COLIBRI (D) 1908-1911

Norddeutsche Automobilwerke GmbH., Hameln

The first Colibri private car was also available as a van using an air-cooled 2-cylinder 860 cc engine which was mounted in the front. In 1910 a 4-cylinder 1320 cc engine was introduced. *HON*

COLLIER (US) 1917-1922

(1) The Collier Co., Cleveland, Ohio
(2) Collier Motor Truck Co., Bellevue, Ohio

The Collier light delivery van was based on standard passenger car design (though so far as is known the company did not make passenger cars) with 4-cylinder engine and a choice of panel or open express bodies. In 1919 the company expanded the range to include 1- and 1½-ton trucks with Continental engines and worm drive. The range was further extended in 1921 and 1922 to include 2- and 2½-tonners, also with Continental engines and worm drive. *RW*

COLLINGS (GB) 1910-1915

J.M.B. Collings, Bacton Hall, Norfolk

John Collings was one of the fortunate (and now defunct) class of men, of comfortable financial position, able to indulge a taste and talent for full scale engineering as a hobby. In his works at Bacton he produced a tandem compound, piston valved, steam tractor, working at 250 p.s.i. and of very much lighter build, as to wheels and gearing, than the contemporary machines of other British manufacturers. A second design, with a superheater, worked at 260 p.s.i. Though the Collings engines worked for many years he seems to have made no serious attempt to market his designs which were a notable attempt to link the best features of British and American practice. *RAW*

COLLINS (US) 1900

Collins Electric Vehicle Co., Scranton, Pa.

Patrick J. Collins designed an electric chassis with both steering and driving done by electric motors. The only vehicle known to have been built was a 1-ton delivery truck completed in November 1900. *DJS*

COLOMBO *(I) 1922*

Officine Mecchaniche Colombo, Milan.

This company exhibited a 3-wheeler delivery van at the 1922 Milan Show. Their principal product was, however, a 4-cylinder light car. *MCS*

COLT see Mitsubishi

1899 COLUMBIA (i) Mark XVII electric cab, CP

COLUMBIA (i) (US) 1899-1907

(1) Columbia Automobile Co., Hartford, Conn. 1899-1900
(2) Columbia & Electric Vehicle Co., Hartford, Conn. 1900
(3) Electric Vehicle Co., Hartford, Conn. 1901-1907

Colonel Albert Pope's Columbia Automobile Company began production of electric cars in 1897, and their first commercial vehicle was a modernized version of the Morris & Salom Electrobat cab, still with the driver in the hansom position, but with equal-sized pneumatic tires, front wheel steering and rear wheel drive. These stubby but practical cabs were made in considerable numbers up to the end of 1902 when they were supplanted by other designs of electric cab, some longer-wheelbase hansoms and others with the driver ahead of the passengers on a box. The Electrobat type was still in use in New York, Boston and other cities as late as 1908.

1904 COLUMBIA (i) Mark LIII 5-ton electric truck, CP

Meanwhile Columbia had begun to make electric vans and heavy trucks of up to 5 tons capacity. The smaller models used single electric motors, but the heavy trucks had two motors connected to the rear driving wheels by double reduction gears and double chains. They had 44-cell Exide batteries giving a range of 25 miles at 6 mph. Larger models had electric power-assisted steering. Columbia was the most popular make of electric truck at a time when these vehicles outnumbered gasoline vehicles for heavy work. Out of 18,000 electric trucks at work in the Eastern States in 1907, 8,000 were Columbias. The company also made the popular observation cars, or 'rubberneck buses' for sightseeing in large cities. At least one of these came to London, but they were largely an American phenomenon. Other smaller Columbia electric

1906 COLUMBIA (i) 6 ton 4 × 4 electric truck, NAHC

vehicles included hotel buses for 6 to 15 passengers, ambulances and police wagons. After 1907 electric vehicles were dropped, and Columbia concentrated on gasoline-engined passenger cars. *GNG*

COLUMBIA (ii) (US) 1916-1925

Columbia Motor Truck & Trailer Co., Pontiac, Mich.

This truck, formerly the Kalamazoo, began as a 2-tonner, and in 1917, a 1-tonner also was made, both powered by 4-cylinder Buda engines, 3-speed Covert gearboxes and fitted with Russell internal-gear rear axles. In 1918, a switch was made to Continental engines, and a 6-tonner tractor also was made. In 1919, the line of trucks was back to 1½-, 2½- and 3-tonners, and this series remained unchanged to the end of production with the exception of a change to Hinkley-built engines. *GMN*

COMET (i) (US) 1914

Comet Cyclecar Co., Indianapolis, Ind.

This was a cyclecar with an attached delivery box. Its price was $450 and it was furnished with a 10 hp, 2-cylinder, air-cooled engine. The drive was through a planetary transmission and belts to the rear wheels. Track was 3 feet and the wheelbase was 100 inches. *GMN*

COMET (ii) (US) 1920-1921

Comet Automobile Co., Decatur, Ill.

This was a conventional assembled truck of 1½ tons capacity, powered by a 4-cylinder Lycoming engine, and employing a Wisconsin worm-drive rear axle. The company also built passenger cars and agricultural tractors. *GNG*

COMMER (i) 1905-1976

Commercial Cars Ltd., Clapham Road, London 1905-1906
Luton, Bedfordshire 1907-1925
Commer Cars Ltd., Luton, Bedfordshire. 1926-1969
Chrysler, U.K. Ltd., 1970-1976

Following experiments with the Linley pre-selective gearbox, a vehicle was built in London embodying this feature. It was intended for 4-ton loads, had chain drive, and was unusual for a British design of the time in having a driver-over-engine layout. The vehicle proved to be successful, and a factory was opened at Luton for the production of a normal control version, variously called a CC, or a Commer Car. In 1907 an RC model Commer won a silver medal in the 3-ton class of the R.A.C. Commercial Vehicle Trials, and this became their staple model for over 20 years. It had a 32 hp engine with its crankshaft running in ball-bearings, chain drive normally enclosed in an oil bath, and a quadrant under the steering wheel for gear selection.

The range extended from 1-to 7-tons capacity by 1911, with additional passenger models and a 90 hp fire engine. All these normally had Commer bodywork, a speciality being rigid charabancs on which doors were only placed on the nearside.

Commer built up a flourishing export trade, and their vehicles were a notable success in the U.S.A. where they were sold between 1911 and 1913 by Wycoff, Chunck and Partridge in New York, who had them assembled by the W.A. Wood Auto Manufacturing Co., Kingston, NY. Such

1909 COMMER 2-ton van, BR

was their potential that Commer set up their own company in Delaware in 1913, though the Great War soon put an end to this project. Other vehicles, some with winches and steel tires, were supplied to several undeveloped countries.

The one-tonner and a new model to the War Office 3-ton subsidy specification were both equipped with shaft drive by 1913, and the latter with a more compact Thomas preselective gearbox. However, when war was declared, Commer were instructed to concentrate on their proven chain-drive RC model, and some 3000 were built for the services by 1918.

1922 COMMER charabancs, NMM

In common with the rest of the industry, Commer was badly hit by the flood of ex-WD vehicles released after the war, and a Receiver was appointed in 1922 in an effort to save them. At the time the range now included 2-, 3-, 4-, 5, 6- and 10-ton goods models and 16-46 seat passenger vehicles. Sales were badly affected by the uncertainty of Commer's financial state and dated designs, many of which still retained chain drive, and indeed, the company did not exhibit at two consecutive London Commercial Motor Shows in 1923 and 1925. However, their vehicles

1928 COMMER 4-ton chassis, OMM

had a good reputation, and early in 1926 Humber came to the rescue and acquired their entire share captial, the company changing its name to Commer Cars Ltd. Early results were new 30-cwt and 4½-ton models, the latter replacing the RC models in 1928.

By 1929 the full effects of the takeover became apparent when the Invader, the Avenger and the G6 appeared. These and the rest of the range were transformed by entirely revised styling. The Invader was a 2-ton or 20-seat chassis with 6-cylinder Humber Snipe engine and silent third gear, while the Avenger was a forward control 32-seat single or 50-seat double decker, sharing a 100 hp 6-cylinder gasoline engine with the 6/7-ton G6. This goods model had a normal control layout with set back front axle for improved weight distribution, an idea used

1931 COMMER Invader 2-ton, OMM

afterwards by Leyland and Thornycroft. In 1931 the goods version of the Invader became the Centaur, while a 30-cwt. Raider model was introduced at only £225. An enlarged Invader became the Corinthian 26-seater.

A number of changes took place in 1933. These included the addition of Commer 6/8 and 15-cwt vans based on the Rootes car range, which by now included Hillman. The 30-cwt and 2-tonners also became the lightest vehicles of the time in Britain to be offered with diesel engines. These engines were made by Perkins and were also available in all the heavy Commers. An entirely new local delivery vehicle with forward control and mid-mounted engine called the Pug for 2-ton loads was also introduced as well as a replacement for the Corinthian, called the Greyhound.

In 1934 Rootes acquired Karrier and transferred production from Huddersfield to the Commer factory. Karrier models thereafter bore a close mechanical similarity to the other Rootes models and used many common components.

1935 COMMER 6/8cwt van, OMM

In 1935 the appearance of Commers was once more radically altered with the N Range, which had pressed metal radiator surrounds and streamlined steel cabs. These replaced all the medium and heavy goods and passenger models, the N5, a 4- to 5- tonner weighing under 2½ tons being particularly successful. They were in turn replaced in 1939 by the Superpoise, or Q range, which had far

1937 COMMER LN5 5-ton truck, NMM

shorter hoods, giving a semi-forward control layout. Full forward control also became available. They were for 1½-to 6-tons and had 6-cylinder gasoline or Perkins diesel engines. In the meantime the car-based models continued with the addition in 1937 of a utility model with all-syncromesh gearbox.

During the Second World War, Commer produced numerous varieties of militarised Superpoise amounting to over 20,000 vehicles, plus a further 10,000 Karriers. After the war, the Superpoise continued, being re-styled in 1948 in line with contemporary Humber cars. It became available in capacities from 1½-tons upwards, and in 1955, two years after the move to a new factory in Dunstable, it was once more restyled with a proprietary cab shared by Dodge, Baron and some export Leylands. It was eventually replaced by forward control models that

1948 COMMER 8cwt van, NMM

had made their first post war appearance in 1948, when a new 8-cwt. Supervan based on the Minx car also appeared. These early forward control models were for 5- to 7-tons and had 6-cylinder gasoline engines canted almost onto their side to permit them to fit under the cab floor. To avoid uneven wear and lubrication problems working in these conditions, the cylinders were given chrome plated liners. The Perkins P6 diesel was also available, and a coach version of the model was once more called the Avenger. Apart from the addition of cab rear quarter windows in 1952, this range changed very little until the arrival of the highly unusual Rootes TS3 diesel engine in 1954. This was produced by Tilling-Stevens, who had joined the group in 1951, and was a 3-cylinder, 2-stroke design with six opposed pistons. It was interchangeable with the under-floor gasoline engine, and had a blower which forced the fuel mixture through ports instead of valves. Each set of three pistons worked rockers at their outer ends, which transmitted power to a crankshaft placed under the central combustion area of the three cylinders. 105b hp was produced from only 3261 ccs.

1955 COMMER TS3 7-ton truck, NMM

Despite the eccentricity of this Kadenacy principle, it worked well and economically, provided it was driven and maintained properly, and in fact remained in production for over fifteen years. However, from 1958 a conventional Perkins substitute was also offered and this eventually replaced the Commer unit. At the same time, a 2.2-litre diesel unit for the smaller Commer models, above 1-ton capacity, was produced for Rootes by the Standard Motor Company.

1956 COMMER Superpoise 1¼-ton van, 1956 COMMER 1½-ton van, NMM

At the time of the adoption of Perkins engines in the larger forward control range, the cab was extensively restyled, though it still retained the inclined engine layout to give a flat floor and three-abreast seating. Most noticeable change was a one-piece windscreen and revised grille.

1964 COMMER Series 1500 ¾-ton van, Chrysler UK

The Cob 7-cwt variation of the Hillman Minx was joined in 1960 by a new forward control 15-cwt van which for a time was the smallest diesel powered van in Britain. Its engine was the Perkins 4:99 I.6-litre diesel. With modifications this vehicle was still in production in 1976.

In 1962 the heavy forward control range acquired larger, more bulbous cabs, though the old style was retained by Karrier. A new model was the Walk-Thru van for 1½- to 3-ton loads with semi-forward control, and easy access to body and driving compartment from doors behind the front wheels, as well as from the rear.

In 1964 a larger capacity version of the 2-stroke diesel, producing 132 hp was fitted to larger 14- and 16-tones gross Maxiload models, and in the same year Chrysler acquired a stake in Rootes and started to integrate their British Dodge commercial range with that of Commer/Karrier. In 1967 Chrysler increased their holding of Rootes shares and in 1973 the company became a wholly owned subsidiary of the Chrysler Corporation. In 1965 a small van based on the Hillman Imp was introduced, and in 1966 certain Dodge models began to be marketed as Commers, thus giving Commer their first tilt cab design. Commer Walk-Thrus were also jointly marketed as Dodges, but neither variation resulted in many sales through the different dealer networks.

1975 COMMER Commando G10 8½-ton GVW van, Chrysler UK

The Commando range replaced several former Dodge (UK) models and was also available with the Karrier name for municipal use. Power for the Commando came from various Perkins or Mercedes-Benz diesels, or the Chrysler V-8 gasoline engine in specialist applications. In 1976 the Commer name was discontinued and replaced by that of Dodge to aid Chrysler's international marketing strategy. *OM*

COMMERCE (i) (US) 1906-1908

American Machine Manufacturing Co., Detroit, Mich.

The initial truck under this name was a 2½-tonner with a 30 hp, four-cylinder engine and forward control. Wheelbase was 109 inches and chassis weight was 3200 pounds. Final drive was by double chains. Later models included 3- and 5-tonners both with chain drive and four-cylinder engines. Model A, the three-tonner had a 35 hp engine and chassis weight of 5800 pounds and wheebase of 111 inches, while Model C, the 5-tonner, weighed 8400 pounds and had wheelbase of 130 inches. *GMN*

COMMERCE (ii) (US) 1911-1932

(1) Commerce Motor Car Co., Detroit, Mich. 1911-c.1922
(2) Commerce Motor Truck Co., Detroit, Ypsilanti, Mich. c.1923-1926
(3) Relay Motors Corp., Lima, Ohio 1927-1932

The first Commerce was a ½-ton panel delivery powered by a 4-cylinder L-head engine of 16.9 hp with right-hand steering and single chain final drive. For 1913 steering was changed to left-hand, and the engine was a 4-cylinder

1911 COMMERCE (ii) ½-ton van, NAHC

Northway in 1914. 800 of these delivery trucks, also made in open express and canopy form, were made with the first three years' production. Capacity went up to 3/4-ton in 1914 and a 1-tonner was added for 1917. This had the same engine as the smaller model, but final drive was by internal gears in place of the 3/4-tonner's bevel drive. By 1922 Continental engines were used, in trucks from 3/4 to 2½ tons, and a 10-passenger charabanc which was an elongated touring car with a fixed top. Claimed to be 'the wonder of motordom' it cost $2350 and could travel at 40 mph easily. Force-feed lubrication and worm drive came on all the 1924 models, and for 1925 four bus chassis from 18 to 28 passengers joined the range, together with a powermatic special lumber truck, dump truck, oil truck and funeral car.

For 1926 Commerce trucks underwent major changes in specifications and styling. 6-cylinder engines, still Continentals, were featured, with 3-speed transmission in place of 4, and semi-floating spiral bevel rear axle. Early in 1927 Relay Motors of Wabash, Indiana bought Commerce and moved truck manufacture into the plant of Service Motors which it had also bought, and later into the plant of another purchase, Garford Truck Co of Lima, Ohio. Under Relay management Commerce trucks were re-engineered again, returning to worm drive. They were now basically the same as the new Relay trucks in eight models from 1 to 4 tons, using 6-cylinder Buda engines, 4-wheel hydraulic brakes and the same sheet metal. Commerce, Garford and Service trucks were now identical except for the nameplates. Of the four makes in the Relay group Commerce fared the worst, with only 65 trucks registered for 1928, and a microscopic 16 for 1929. At the bottom of the Depression Relay was forced into receivership, resulting in the suspension of Commerce and Service production, though they continued Relay and Garford for a little longer. *RW*

COMMERCIAL (i) (US) 1903

Commercial Motor Co., Jersey City, N.J.

After absorbing the Pan-American Co., Commercial started production of several kerosene-burning steam delivery wagons. *RAW*

COMMERCIAL (ii) (US) 1906-1912

Commercial Motor Car Company, New York, N.Y.

The Commercial vehicles were of 1-, 2-, 3-, and 5-ton capacities, although not all were offered each year. All these models used 4-cylinder engines, gear boxes and chain drive with solid tires. The 3- and 4-tonners had forward control, and the engines were rated at 40 hp. *GMN*

COMMERCIAL (iii) (US) 1911-1912

(1) Commercial Truck Co.'s of America, Newark, NJ 1911
(2) Commercial Motor Truck Construction Co., Newark, NJ 1911-1912

The Commercial was built only as a 1½-tonner with forward control and driven by a 4-stroke, 4-cylinder engine. It had a 3-speed gear-box and shaft drive. This was available with either pneumatic or solid rubber tires, and price for the closed delivery van was $2450. *GMN*

COMPOUND (US) 1906

Eisenhuth Horseless Vehicle Company, Middletown, Connecticut

The name for this unusual commercial vehicle was derived from the unique 3-cylinder engine. The engine had a center cylinder much larger in diameter than the two outboard ones, and the center one received the exhaust gases from the more conventional end cylinders. Of course the large central cylinder had no ignition system and merely utilized some of the remaining energy in these exhaust gases. The center cylinder had a diameter of seven inches. The Model Nine delivery van appears to be the only type offered by this manufacturer and had a 3-speed gearbox with double chain-drive. With a wheelbase of 98½ inches, this van was priced at $1400. *GMN*

CONCORD (US) 1916-1933

(1) Abbott & Downing Co., Concord, N.H.
(2) Abbott-Downing Truck & Body Co., Concord, N.H.

Known for one year as the Abbott-Downing, this truck was re-named after the town of its manufacture in November 1917. 1- and 2-ton chassis powered by Buda engines were initially offered, with Timken-David Brown worm rear axles. Later the range was widened to include trucks of up to 3-tons capacity, but engines remained all by Buda throughout the 1920s. *GNG*

CONDOR (US) 1932-1941

Condor Motors Inc., Chicago, Ill.

The Condor was originally simply the Gramm (ii) truck renamed for export markets and sold by a Chicago-based subsidiary. From 1934 onwards Condor specifications diverged somewhat from those of Gramm, with the adoption of a Waukesha-Hesselman engine in place of the Cummins and Hercules units employed in Gramms. The Waukesha-Hesselman was an oil-burning engine with spark plugs and ignition system, thought to be more tolerant of lower grade fuel to be found in many export areas than conventional diesel engines. Gasoline engines were also offered in Condors, but not many were fitted. Condor trucks were sold in more than 30 countries, and with more success than Gramms were on the domestic market. Among Condor's export territories were China where they were sold by Mark L. Moody Inc of Shanghai ('China's largest dealership'), Holland and Belgium where they were fitted with locally-made cabs and bodies, Portugal, Spain, Greece and Turkey. The last Condors were the 1939/40 models which, like Gramms, used the Willys ½-ton pick-up cab which looked odd in conjunction with the long hoods imposed by Buda Lanova diesel engines. Few were made, with the drying up of export markets in wartime and an increasing Gramm interest in truck equipment and trailers. *RJ*

CONESTOGA (US) 1917-1920

Conestoga Motor Truck Co., Lancaster, Pa.

The Conestoga was a typical assembled truck. For 1918 1200-pound and 1½-ton models with the Light 4-cylinder engine were offered. In 1919 1-ton and 2-ton models with Continental engines were listed. All models had worm gear final drive. In 1919 Conestoga also built a 1500-pound truck with a "Victory" nameplate. Production totaled about 700 trucks. *DJS*

CONNORSVILLE (US) 1914-1916

Connorsville Buggy Co., Connorsville, Ind.

This was an electric commercial, battery-powered with a carrying capacity of 1250 lbs. Further information is not available. *GMN*

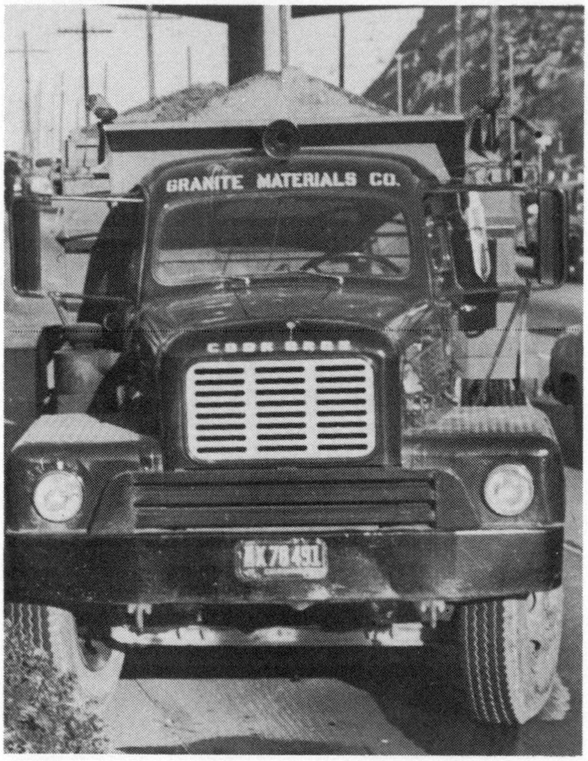

c. 1952 COOK BROS 6-ton truck, GNG

CONTAL (F) 1905-1908

Contal et Cie, Paris 16e

Sometimes known as the Mototri-Contal, this was a typical tricar powered by a 4hp single-cylinder water-cooled engine, with chain drive to the single rear wheel. Load capacity was 3 cwt. The make achieved most of its fame as a result of the ill-starred entry of a tricar in the 1907 Peking-Paris Race, in which it retired and was abandoned in the Gobi Desert. *GNG*

CONTINENTAL (i) (US) 1912-1918

Continental Truck Manufacturing Co., Superior, Wis.

The Model AE, a 1½-tonner was the initial Continental

and had a 4-cylinder engine with forward control, a 3-speed gearbox and double chain drive. In 1914, the engine was moved under a hood and a 1-tonner also was made. In 1915, a 1½- and a 3-tonner were built with optional worm or chain drive. For 1918, this line of vehicles included 1-, 1½-, 2- and 3½-tonners all with worm drive. *GMN*

CONTINENTAL (ii) (US) 1915-1917

Continental Motor Truck Co., Chicago, Ill.

The line of Continental trucks began and ended with the same sizes: 1-, 1½-, 2- and 3½-tonners. All had three-speed gearboxes, 4-cylinder engines and final drives were by worm-gear. *GMN*

1965 CONY AF11 ¼-ton van, GNG

CONY (J) 1946-1966

(1) Aichi Kokuki KK, Nagoya 1946-1949
(2) New Aichi Enterprise Co. Ltd., Nagoya 1949-1952
(3) Aichi Machine Industry Co. Ltd., Nagoya 1952-1966

This former producer of aircraft and aero engines for the Japanese Navy began the manufacture of light commercial 3-wheelers on classic lines after the Second War. By the mid-1950s these had developed into more sophisticated machines with wheel steering and hydraulic brakes on the rear wheels only. Horizontally-opposed engines were used, a 354 cc aircooled twin in the light Cony, and a watercooled 1½-litre four in the 2-ton model, also offered as a tractive unit with 5-speed gearbox. Along with these there was also a 7-cwt 4-wheeler with underfloor-mounted 2-cylinder engine, 3-speed synchromesh gearbox, and hydraulic brakes on all wheels. Coil-spring ifs was standard, but it was found only on the car-type station wagons. Some of these AF7s were exported to the USA. 1961 saw a real pickup in miniature, the Guppy, with a wheelbase of 65¾ inches and a length of only 101 inches. Its 199 cc single-cylinder engine was matched to a single-speed and reverse torque converter transmission, and a top speed of 50 mph was claimed. An association with Nissan in 1965 led a year later to the absorption of the Aichi firm into that group. *MCS*

COOK (i) (US) 1905-1906

Cook Locomotive Works, Paterson, New Jersey

The Cook steamer was rated at 24 boiler hp and was shod with steel tires on wooden spoked wheels. Rear wheel brakes operated directly against the steel tires, a feature of railway trains. The chassis was underslung and had an enclosed cab for the driver. One purchaser of five of these huge steamers found that breakdowns were so frequent and complete that all five were out of use within a year. *GMN*

COOK (ii) (US) 1920-1922

Cook Motors Corp, Kankakee, Ill

In 1920 and 1921, Cook offered 1-tonners only. This model was replaced by a 2-tonner for 1922. The latter used Hercules 4-cylinder engines. *GMN*

1949 COOK BROS T20 8 × 8 army truck, BHV

COOK (iii) (US) 1950-c.1964

(1) Cook Brothers Equipment Co., Los Angeles, Calif. 1950-1958
(2) Challenge-Cook Brothers Inc., Los Angeles, Calif. 1958-c.1964

Cook Brothers built some experimental 8x8 army trucks and tractors at the end of World War II, and followed these up with Ford truck conversions including 6-wheel attachments and chain-drive tandems. They became a make in their own right in 1950 with a line of trucks directed at the construction and building materials industry. These were based on Reo components with modified sheetmetal, though Cummins Diesel and Ford V-8 engines were also used. The units were specially designed for maximum payloads under California weight restrictions which imposed long wheelbases. Cook Bros. allied the special chassis with a variety of bulk-haul bodies for sand, gravel, bricks and similar loads. They also built a small number of articulated bottom-dump earth haulers for on-and off-road work, with offset cabs.

During the 1950s the company began to concentrate on special chassis for crane carriers and cement mixers. These had offset one-man cabs, a choice of gasoline, diesel or propane engines by Reo or Cummins, and single reduction, double reduction or chain drive tandem rear axles. In 1958 they were taken over by Challenge Mfg. Co., makers of cement and ready-mix concrete mixers, who continued to offer Cook chassis with their own mixing equipment, though the bulk of their business became the manufacture of such equipment for mounting on other chassis. Probably to avoid antagonizing truck dealers who might sell the mixer units, they gave up the production of complete trucks in about 1964, though it is possible that a few custom trucks were made after this. Cook were the last truck makers to offer chain drive, which they continued to do into the early 1960s. *RJ/GNG*

1900 COOPER traction engine, RAW

COOKSON (GB) 1905

Cookson & Brothers, Old Trafford, Manchester

This was a 12 hp 2-cylinder light van with chain drive and solid tires, double at the rear. The price was £320. *GNG*

COOPER (GB) 1887-c.1900

(1) T.C. Cooper, Great Ryburgh, Norfolk.

(2) Farmer's Foundry Co. Ltd., Great Ryburgh, Norfolk.

(3) Cooper Steam Digger Co. Ltd., King's Lynn, Norfolk.

Thomas Cooper's 8 n.h.p. compound locomotive boilered overtype engine shown at the Royal Show of 1887 was probably the last design of chain driven traction engine before the introduction of roller chain and was unusual for its time in having a rear axle differential and rack and pinion steering. The chain drive made it very compact in overall width, relatively silent and suitable for haulage work. An example was used for many years by Messrs. Trenowath the King's Lynn furniture removers. *RAW*

COPPOCK (US) 1907-1909

(1) Coppock Motor Car Co., Marion, Ind. 1907

(2) Coppock Motor Car Co., Decatur, Ind. 1908-1909

Described as a one-ton commercial car of "Sterling Quality", the 1907 Coppock model A was a typical cab-over stake truck with 2-cylinder 2-cycle engine operating on the three-port principle. The water jackets were of copper. The transmission was of the 3-speed progressive type, while the clutch had bronze internal-expanding shoes for engagement. These shoes were 10 inches in diameter with a 2½-inch face having cork inserts comprising 8% of the area. Wheelbase was 87 inches and tires were solid. The steering shaft was vertical in the open cab.

In October, 1909 the company was reorganized to continue motor vehicle production under the name of Decatur Motor Car Co., producing the Decatur utility car and a parcel wagon. *RW*

CORBIN (US) 1902-c.1905

Corbin Motor Vehicle Co., New Britain, Conn.

This company, better-known for their passenger cars, made a few light trucks powered by an 8 hp single-cylinder air-cooled horizontal engine mounted under the floorboards. The 1,500 lb vehicle had two speeds, 3 and 10 mph, and single chain drive. *GNG*

CORBITT (US) 1913-1952; 1957-1958

(1) Corbitt Automobile Co., Henderson, N.C. 1913-1916
(2) Corbitt Motor Truck Co., Henderson, N.C.
(3) Corbitt Co., Henderson, N.C. -1952
(4) Corbitt Co., Inc., Henderson, N.C. 1957-1958

Richard Corbitt was a successful North Carolina tobacco merchant during the 1890s, and after being forced out of business by a large trust he set up the Corbitt Buggy Company in 1899. From 1907 to 1913 passenger cars were made, followed by trucks. The first Corbitt was a conventional truck powered by a 4-cylinder Continental engine, with chain drive and a load capacity of 2,500 lbs. During 1915 Corbitt began to supply school and urban transit buses for service all over North Carolina, and during the 1920s the company established a reputation as 'the South's largest truck builder'. In addition they were exported to 23 foreign countries. Corbitts were of conventional design, with 6-cylinder Continental or Hercules engines and up to 1930 made in sizes of 1 to 5 tons. Later models were larger, and included 6-wheeled tractor/trailer units of up to 15 tons capacity. Some of the smaller Corbitts of the mid-1930s used the same grille, fenders and front body panels as the Auburn passenger car.

1922 CORBITT 1½-ton truck, NAHC

From 1933 onwards Corbitt became important suppliers of vehicles to the U.S. Army; these included 2½ton 6x6 cargo carriers powered by Lycoming Straight-8 engines, 8-ton 6x4 and 6x6 artillery prime movers with Hercules 6 engines, and Lycoming-powered armoured scout cars. In 1940 the U.S. Coastal Artillery asked Corbitt to design and build a 6-ton 6x6 prime mover and cargo carrier. Powered by a 855ci 6-cylinder Hercules engine, the Corbitt 50 SD6 became a familiar workhorse for the U.S. Army and its allies. They survived well into the 1950s in the armies of Austria, Denmark, France, Greece, the Netherlands and Sweden. Some of these vehicles are still at work as recovery trucks and heavy haulage prime movers. During the early part of the War Corbitt built 6x4 highway tractors powered by Continental 6-cylinder engines. An 8x8 prime mover and a rear-engined 2½-ton truck were built experimentally.

The early post-war years saw a boom in road tractor sales, and during 1946 Corbitt sold over 600 trucks. These were mostly large 6x2 and 6x4 tractors powered by Continental gasoline or Cummins diesel engines, and they

1934 CORBITT bus, LIAM

1935 CORBITT 2-ton truck (1934 Auburn passenger car sheet metal) HHB

1948 CORBITT Tractor, LA

1958 CORBITT tractor (last one made), LA

were used by some of the biggest fleet operators in the United States. In 1952 "Uncle Dick" Corbitt retired and his loss, combined with falling sales of heavy trucks generally, caused the firm to close. In 1957 an attempt to revive the firm was made, building tractor trucks on a made-to-order basis, but this failed. At this time Corbitt was also rebuilding ex-army Mack 6x6 artillery tractors which were sold to various NATO countries including Great Britain. *LA*

CORNWALL (GB) 1957-1958

Cornwall Motor Transport Ltd., Helston, Cornwall

This company built a prototype 7/8 ton truck powered by a Meadows 4DC 330 diesel engine. It had a 5-speed gearbox, also by Meadows, and the near axle was a choice of Moss spiral bevel or Eaton 2-speed. Other components were a Bowyer plastic cab and Clayton-Dewandre-Girling air-hydraulic brakes. *GNG*

CORONA (D) 1905-1909

Corona Fahrradwerke and Metallindustrie A.G., Brandenburg

The friction-driven Corona private cars were also available as small vans. The friction system followed a Maurer licence and Maurer engines were used, at first a single cylinder 6/8 PS and later a 2-cylinder 9/11 PS. *HON*

CORRE: LA LICORNE (F) 1900-1950

Societe Francaise des Automobiles Corre, Courbevoie, Seine

From the beginning commercial vehicles were offered by this company, which had an entry in the 1900 French delivery van trials. A year later a van was catalogued on their 3 hp voiturette chassis, with de Dion engine and shaft drive. Thereafter little was heard of their trucks and vans until 1912, by which time the La Licorne name was in general use. Commercial Licornes covered the 10/25 cwt bracket, and were entirely conventional, with long-stroke 1.7- and 2.7-litre 4-cylinder sv monobloc engines of Ballot make, 3- or 4-speed gearboxes, shaft drive, and pneumatic tires, though a single-cylinder van, the WXG, was offered in 1912. The bigger models were continued practically without changes until 1929-30, heaviest of the post-War range being a 3½-tonner with 3.8-litre engine and twin rear wheels, but production was on a very modest scale, La Licorne being principally known for the car-type light vans, available on practically every type they offered in the 1920s. All of these used 4-cylinder sv engines, and in 1925 a diversity of 1.4-, 1.6-and 1.7litre-covered payloads from 8 to 25 cwt. The company, indeed, claimed to have pioneered the popular *camionnette Normande* open truck body on their 1920 7CV. 1929 saw a 7 cwt van version of their 905 cc 5CV private car model, this surviving until 1931, when it gave way to a similarly-rated model based on the 1,128 cc LO4.

Lower chassis, 4-wheel brakes and flat radiators characterized the bigger Licornes of the 1930s, which were made on the same small scale until 1939. A 30-seater coach chassis, the D6H, used a 3.2-litre 6-cylinder engine (probably by Delahaye), the only such power unit ever offered commercially by the firm, and between 1933 and 1935 there were even some diesel trucks in the 1/3-ton category, powered by single-or 4-cylinder 2-stroke C.L.M. engines. By 1938, however, the company were back with gasoline units of 4-cylinder type, the biggest model being a 3½-tonner. The 1½-tonner used a development of the short-stroke ohv engine fitted to the latest all-independently-sprung 6CV car, and this, along with a commercial edition of the latter, was revived in 1946. There were, however, very few post-war Licornes of any type. *MCS*

1911 CORTLAND 1500lb delivery wagon, GMN

CORTLAND (US) 1911-1912

(1) Cortland Motor Wagon Co., Cortland, N.Y.
(2) Cortland Motor Wagon Co., Pittsfield, Mass.

The Cortland was a driver-over-engine delivery wagon made in two sizes, ¾-ton and 1½-ton, powered by 2-cylinder engines of 15 and 20 hp respectively. Both had 2-speed planetary transmissions and double chain final drive. Open sided and closed vans were made, and prices were $1,100 and $1,750 respectively. *GNG*

COTTEREAU (F) 1902-1907

Cottereau et Cie, Dijon.

Cottereau cars were first made in 1898, but there is no evidence of any commercial vehicles before 1902, when wagonnette and light omnibus bodywork was available on two chain-driven chassis, a 1.4-litre aiv twin and a 3.2-litre T-head four. 1904 saw a more substantial purpose-built truck, still chain driven, but powered by a 1.8-litre 3-cylinder engine with dual ignition. A year later this had evolved into a 4-speed 4-tonner using a 3.4-litre 4-cylinder unit, but by 1907 Cottereau were past their zenith. Private cars were still offered in 1910, after which the firm was reconstituted under the C.I.D. name. *MCS*

COTTIN DESGOUTTES (F) 1905-1934

Ets. Cottin & Desgouttes, Lyon-Monplaisir

Cottin & Desgouttes, manufacturers of highly renowned, fast and beautifully made cars, also tried to apply these characteristics to their range of trucks. The four-cylinder engines, used in the cars, were also mounted in their range of commercial vehicles, a not so broad as the cars range, but nevertheless offering vehicles from 1½ to 4 tons payload. A very progressive feature in the early days of Cottin Desgouttes trucks was the use of shaft drive. Because of their sturdiness a substantial number of these trucks was ordered by the French army. In fact, the years of World War I were the high point of Cottin Desgouttes commercial vehicle production. Still the range

1924 COTTIN et DESGOUTTES 2-ton van, NMM

included vehicles from 1½ to 4 tons payload, available with three 4-cylinder engines, a small one of 80x160 mm bore and stroke, and two units of 100x160 mm bore & stroke of which one had its cylinders cast in pairs and the others in a monobloc.

After World War I Cottin Desgouttes commercial vehicles retained their conventional lay-out, manufacturing in small numbers trucks and buses, the latter reaching some popularity among the smaller French municipalities with their own transport board. By 1931 Cottin & Desgouttes discontinued the production of automotive parts, though still some cars and commercial vehicles were assembled from stock. The last commercial model was the CR, with a payload of 4 tons and using an engine of 98.4x127 mm bore and stroke, probably of American origin. *JFJK*

1899 COULTHARD 3-ton steam wagon, Autocar

COULTHARD (GB) c. 1895-1907

T. Coulthard & Co., Preston, Lancs.

Coulthards spent five years experimenting before their first "production" model was entered in the 1899 Liverpool Trials. Oil fired, it had a vertical fire-tube boiler providing steam at 200/225 p.s.i. for use in a triple expansion horizontal undertype engine with piston valves. Three speeds and reverse were provided in the gears. Drive from crankshaft to countershaft was by short chain and final drive by twin chains.

Just over a year later this design was replaced by a solid fired wagon with a vertical 2-cylinder compound engine still with piston valves which took a Gold Medal in the 1901 Liverpool Trials. Production continued until 1907 when the firm was taken over by Leyland.

The firm also built at least one example of the Brightmore wagon consisting of a steam powered unit forming the pivotted forecarriage of a more or less conventional four-wheeled dray. It had within it some elements of a good idea but made no commercial progress. *RAW*

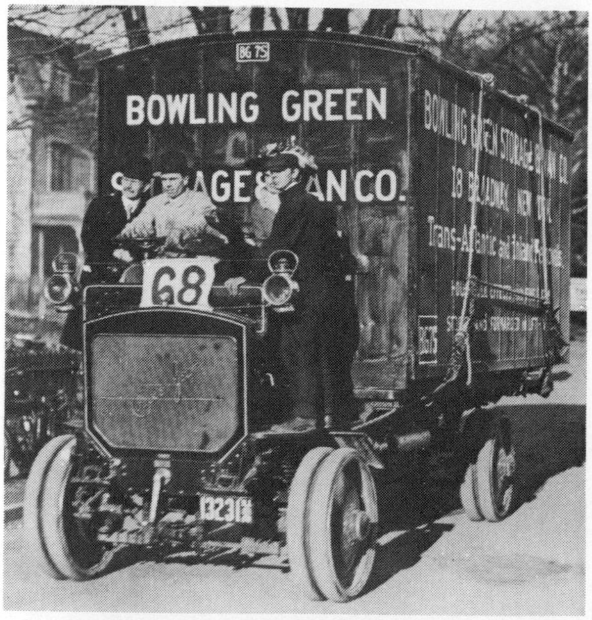

1912 COUPLE GEAR Model HC 5-ton gas-electric truck, NAHC

COUPLE-GEAR (US) 1904-1922

(1) Couple-Gear Freight Wheel Co., Grand Rapids, Mich.
(2) Couple Gear Electric Truck Co., Grand Rapids, Mich.

This company specialized in heavy, slow-moving electric trucks powered by motors in the wheels. The first models were 3 and 5-tonners with 4-wheel-drive and steering, one motor to each wheel. Maxium speed was 6 mph. A gas-electric model was also made, and in 1908 came a lighter truck for 1-to 2-ton loads, on which drive was to the front wheels only. These were disc wheels, with larger carriage-type wheels at the rear. This truck had a speed of 9 mph.

1920 COUPLE GEAR 5-ton gas-electric tanker, RNE

Apart from trucks, Couple-Gear made a large number of fire engines, both electric and gasoline. Their chassis were supplied to such wellknown makers of fire equipment as

Ahrens-Fox, Boyd, Peter Pirsch, Seagrave and Webb. Typical was the Couple-Gear/Seagrave ladder truck supplied to Springfield, Mass FD in 1914. This was 52 feet long, weighed over 10 tons and carried ten different sized ladders. Maximum speed was 20 mph. These fire engines were very long lived, and the city of New Bedford, Mass used several Coupe-Gear ladder trucks for over 30 years.

For 1914 a new range of gasoline trucks and tractors was introduced with all-wheel-drive, tramcar-type controllers and 5 forward and reverse speeds. In case of failure in any one motor, it could be cut out by removing the fuse, and the truck could be run on the other three. After World War I electric trucks and fire engines began to lose popularity, mainly because they could not keep up with the growing speeds of gas-engined vehicles. The last Couple-Gear fire engine was delivered in 1920, and two years later the firm closed its doors. *LA*

COURIER see M.C.I.

1978 COURNIL 4×4 with snowplow, GEVANM

COURNIL (F) 1960 to date

(1) Bernard Cournil, Aurillac 1960-1977

(2) S.A. Gevarm, St. Germain-Laval 1977 to date

The Cournil is a 4x4 cross-country vehicle of the Jeep or Land Rover type, though with a shorter wheelbase (80 in.) than the latter. A variety of gasoline and diesel engines was used up to the take-over by Gevarm, and current models offer a choice of Saviem 2.6-litre gasoline or Peugeot 2-litre or Saviem 3.3-litre diesels. In addition to the 80 inch model a 100 inch wheelbase is also offered. *GNG*

1936 COVENTRY VICTOR 5cwt van, NMM

COVENTRY-VICTOR (GB) 1926-1937

Coventry Victor Motor Co. Ltd., Coventry

These 3-wheelers used their own watercooled sv flat-twin engines in simple chassis with quarter-elliptic springing and chain final drive. A 4/5-cwt van was offered alongside the cars, initially with 688 cc engine and two forward speeds. A reverse was added in 1930; capacity went up to 749 cc in 1932 against to 950 cc in 1934, when 3-speed gearboxes were standardized, and front ends restyled to bring the vans into line with the cars. Sales were always limited. From 1932 Coventry Victor marketed a range of small flat-twin diesel engines for trucks, a version of this being offered in Jowett chassis between 1935 and 1939. *MCS*

COVERT (US) 1906-1907

Covert Motor Vehicle Co., Lockport, NY

The Covert was built only as a ½-tonner with wire-side delivery van body. This had forward control with a 2-cylinder engine, a 2-speed gearbox and shaft drive. Wheelbase was 84 inches and the price was $1000. *GMN*

C.P.T. see Little Giant and Duntley

C & R see Currie

CRAIG-DORWALD (GB) 1904-1906

Putney Motor Co., Putney, London S. W.

This small company made a limited number of commercial vehicles, in addition to a few cars and marine engines, which were their main business. In 1904 they built a 3-wheeled mechanical horse with independent coil suspension for its two front wheels. The track of these was adjustable so that the vehicle could also be used as an agricultural tractor. It had a 2-speed gearbox and final drive by chain to the large single rear wheel. Other Craig-Dorwald designs included a shaft-driven van and a chain-driven truck, and also a double-decker bus which was driven from the upper deck. The driver had a separate ladder to enable him to reach his lofty perch.*GNG*

CRANE & BREED (US) 1909-1912

Crane & Breed Manufacturing Co., Cincinnati, Ohio

Together with Cunningham, this carriage works, founded in 1850, pioneered the American idea of building specialist ambulance and hearse chassis, fitted with their own bodies. All these had 4-cylinder engines, magneto ignition, 3-speed gearboxes, and side-chain drive; the first example of a hearse carried a large reproduction of the tomb of Scipio on its roof. After 1912 they confined their activities to bodies, which they mounted on 6-cylinder Winton chassis, these being offered until 1924.*MCS*

CRAWFORD (US) 1911-1917

Crawford Automobile Co., Hagerstown, Md.

The commercial vehicles by this builder differed from their passenger car chassis. Apparently only one type of commercial car was made with a capacity of 1200 pounds. This had wheelbase of 112 inches and had a 30 hp 4-cylinder engine, a 3-speed gearbox, shaft drive and pneumatic tires. As a closed van, the price was $1350.*GMN*

CRAWSHAY-WILLIAMS (GB) 1904-1906

Crawshay-Williams Ltd., Ashtead, Surrey

This car maker built a limited number of delivery vans powered by a 12 hp 2-cylinder Vautour engine, with 4-speed gearbox and chain drive. Load capacity was 17 cwt. *GNG*

1904 CREMORNE 1-ton steam truck, RAW

CREMORNE (GB) 1903-1906

Cremorne Motor Co. Ltd., Putney, London, S.W.

The Cremorne company made steam cars during 1903/04 but in addition they built a steam omnibus which was listed in *Motor Traction's* "Buyers Guide" as late as 1906. The details given are that it seated 36, had a vertical Field tube boiler fired on kerosene, a 20 hp engine with 4-cylinders and chain drive. If the engine was on similar lines to the cars it was of vertical launch type but details of the Cremorne bus are elusive and it is questionable whether it was ever put into production. Besides the bus a truck of 25/30 cwt. capacity and similar construction was made. *RAW*

1962 CREMSA Toro 500kgs 3-wheeler, JCG

CREMSA (B) 1953-1962

Cremsa Motovehicules, Barcelona

This motorcycle firm made various delivery tricycles including the 125 cc "Rata" and 175 cc "Toro". There was also the "Trailer" model, powered by a 197 cc Hispano-Villeirs engine and designed for pulling an open or closed trailor of 500 bags capacity. Another model was the "Pato 200" with the same engine as the "Trailer" and shaft drive to the two rear wheels. *JCG*

CRESCENT (i) (US) 1912-1913

(1) Crescent Motor Truck Co., Middletown, O 1912-1913
(2) Crescent Motor Truck Co., Hamilton, O 1913

This truck appeared in three sizes: 1-, 2- and 3-tonners. Unfortunately, detailed information is lacking. There was a NY company of the same name in 1917, but a connection is unconfirmed. *GMN*

CRESCENT (ii) (S) 1958-1961

Nymanbolagan AB, Uppsala

This was an ultra-light moped-based 3-wheeler delivery vehicle, powered by 50 or 100 cc Sachs 2-stroke engine, with 3 speeds and chain drive to the single rear wheel. Load capacity was 2 cwt. The 50 cc model had pedals for starting and assistance on hills, while the larger model had a kick starter. *GNG*

CRETORS (US) 1915

C. Cretors & Co., Chicago, Ill.

The Cretors company were well-known manufacturers of popcorn machinery who built nine special popcorn wagons powered by 22.5 hp 4-cylinder Buda engines. They had a complete steam plant with a gas-fired boiler and mill-type steam engine which drove the popcorn popper and peanut roaster. Of the nine made, one survives in Harrah's Automobile Collection at Reno, Nevada. *GNG*

CREUSEN (NL) 1960 to date

Creusen Electro-Mechanische Industrie N.V., Roermond

Creusen is a small manufacturer of electric trucks and delivery vehicles and mobile shops. Their main feature is the drive of the rear wheels with a separate engine for each wheel, transmitting the drive through a worm drive construction. The standard engine produced has a power of 5 hp. Four of these engines are used on the large 6-wheeled mobile shops with payloads up to four tons, two

1970 CREUSEN 1-ton 3-wheeler, A.de Boer

on the medium-weight trucks and delivery vehicles, and one, mounted on the front wheel, on the lightest vehicles. *JFJK*

CRITCHLEY-NORRIS (GB) 1906-1908

Critchley-Norris Motor Co., Bamber Bridge, Preston, Lancs.

This company built both gasoline and steam-engined chassis for goods and passenger work. The former were designed by J.S. Critchley who had previously been with Crossley, and in fact used Crossley-built engines of 25 and 30 hp. They had 4-speed gearboxes, shaft drive and a maximum speed of 12 mph. The steam chassis was equipped with a Lune Valley semi-flash boiler, with central drum having coiled water tubes expanded into its shell, and all being encased in an insulated outer casing. A superheater coil was fitted, designed to deliver steam at 300psi and 500 F. The engine was a vertical in-line 3-cylinder T-head, with poppet valves, cam driven. A short shaft connected the engine to a countershaft differential, and thence power was taken by chains to the rear wheels. Solid tires were standard equipment, and a condenser was provided in the normal radiator position. The exhaust gases were taken to the rear, avoiding the need for a funnel, so the vehicle looked very much like a gasoline-engined one. *RAW/GNG*

1914 CROCHAT 4-ton gas-electric mobile workshop, BHV

CROCHAT (F) 1911-c. 1925

Etablissements Henri Crochat, Dijon

Crochat specialised in gas-electric vehicles, beginning with a 4-ton forward control truck with chain drive which was made before and during World War I when it was used for ambulance work and as a mobile workshop for the French Army and Air Force. In 1919 a remarkable gas-electric road train was built by Crochat, consisting of a tractor and five trailers each of which contained an electric motor and batteries sufficient to enable the trailer to make short journeys to collect or deliver a load and return to the train. Both tractor and trailers had chain drive and solid tires. Also in 1919 a 3-ton gas-electric truck was announced, with 4-cylinder 20 hp Ballot engine, and this was still listed in 1925. Like its predecessors, it had a round Solex radiator giving it a similar appearance to de Dion and Schneider vehicles which used the same radiator. A few Crochat battery electric vehicles were also made in the early 1920s.*GNG*

CROFT (GB) 1932-1936

Croft Commercial Cars Ltd., Bradford, Yorks.

The Croft was a tri-van produced during the Depression years to take advantage of the favorable taxation laws governing three wheelers in Britain. Initially produced in 10 cwt and 5 cwt form with single cylinder engines of 475 cc and 300 cc respectively, a 600 cc single was the only offering from 1934. In that year revision of the taxation laws largely removed the advantages of running three wheelers, and was responsible for the demise of most of the new comers. Prices of the Croft ranged from £66.50 to £79.50.*MJWW*

CROFTON (US) 1959-1961

Crofton Marine Engine Co., San Diego, Calif.

The Crofton Bug was a light utility vehicle of the Jeep type powered by a 722 cc 4-cylinder ohc engine similar to that used in the Crosley. The 1961 Brawny Bug model had a 6-speed gearbox and the option of twin rear wheels. Extras available included a snowplow and an electric winch.*GNG*

CROMPTON-ELECTRICAR see Morrison-Electricar

CROSLEY (US) 1940-1952

(1) Crosley Motors Inc., Richmond, Ind 1940-1945
(2) Crosley Motors Inc., Marion, Ind. 1945-1952

Powell Crosley Jr., a radio manufacturer from Cincinnati, was addicted to miniature cars, which he promoted under the slogan 'Why Build a Battleship to Cross a River?.' His original model appeared in 1939, and was powered by a 655cc flat-twin aircooled Waukesha engine of 13 hp; among its more barbarous features were a graduated dipstick instead of a fuel gauge and a pull-up chain handbrake. Initially only private cars were offered, but a year later came a jazzy Parkway delivery van, followed in 1941 by a full range of commercial bodies. Sales were unimpressive. In 1943 the US Army tested an ultra-light 4x4 based on the 2-cylinder Crosley, but it failed to meet requirements. Post-War Crosleys, though still austere and lacking even in synchromesh, used lightweight copper-brazed 5-bearing 720cc 4-cylinder ohc watercooled engines giving more than double the old twin's output and were good performers even after the company switched to heavier, cast-iron blocks. Along with the usual panels and pickups Crosley offered a Sports

Utility of Jeep type with tailgate. Some 1949 and 1950 models had aircraft-type disc brakes, and an ambitious departure was the Farm-O-Road of 1951, a road-going all-purpose vehicle for the farmer with 6 forward speeds and two reverses. It was said to be able to plough and retailed at a low $800, but nobody was impressed. Though the Crosley fared better than the old, Austin-based Bantam (sales reached over 32,000 units in the peak year of 1948), both private and commercial buyers lost interest once the post-War car shortage was over, and Crosley gave up in 1952. *MCS*

1914 CROSS front drive aerial ladder truck, LA

CROSS (US) 1914-1916

C.J. Cross Front Drive Tractor Co., Newark, N.J. Rochester, N.Y.

This company offered 2-wheeled tractors for motorizing horse-drawn fire appliances, similar in conception to the Christies, although the Cross engine was arranged longitudinally, not transversely. At first it was located ahead of the axle, under a hood, but in 1915 an underseat-engined model was offered. Unlike Christie, Cross also offered front-wheel-drive load-carrying trucks, in 3, 5, 6/7 and 10 ton sizes. Few, if any, of these were actually sold. Cross fire engines were not so well known as Christies, but a number were used by the Fire Departments of New York, Philadelphia and other cities. *GNG*

1915 CROSSLEY 25/30hp RFC-type truck, BHV

CROSSLEY (GB) 1912-1956

(1) Crossley Motors Ltd., Gorton, Manchester 1912-1945
(2) Crossley Motors Ltd., Stockport, Cheshire 1945-1956

Crossley branched out from stationary gas engines into cars in 1904, their 22 hp 4-cylinder engine being supplied to Leyland in 1905 for that company's first gasoline-engined buses. Crossley also supplied engines to Critchley-Norris (J.S. Critchley had designed their first cars), but it was not until 1912 that they made a complete commercial vehicle, this being the legendary tender for the infant Royal Flying Corps. Based on the successful 25/30 hp car, it had a 4½-litre 5-bearing 4-cylinder sv engine; service models differed from civilian types in wearing twin rear tires. Only 58 had been delivered by the outbreak of War, but production continued at the rate of 3000 a year until 1918. The smaller, 2.6-litre 15 was also produced in limited numbers as a light van or ambulance. The basic RFC-type was still available as late as 1926, many being equipped as ambulances, but war-surplus examples were put to many uses, including 14-seater buses or charsabanc. The first vehicles used by Scotland Yard's Flying Squad in 1919 were Crossley tenders, while they were also employed in 1924-26 by the Court-Treatts for their marathon Cape-London run.

In the 1920s Crossley's commercial vehicle department concentrated on military types, a 30-cwt Subsidy model of 1923 using a 5.3-litre 4-cylinder engine in a worm drive chassis with pneumatic tires. There was also a simpler solid-tired model with the RFC-type engine for the Indian Government, as well as a series of machines made between 1926 and 1928 with the 2.4-litre 14 hp car engine. A civilian 1-tonner with fwb came to nothing, but more successful was a 30-cwt rigid 6x4 army version, made also as a one-man tank, and as a half-track under Kegresse

1930 CROSSLEY 3-ton 6×4 army truck, OMM

1935 CROSSLEY Atlas 12-ton truck, OMM

license. A wide range of military types included 2- and 4-tonners with forward or normal control, the 6-wheelers and halftracks featuring 8-speed transmissions, while the bigger types were powered by sv 4-cylinder engines with dry-sump lubrication. The IGL series was progressively developed during the 1930s, and Crossley also made a special 4x4 for the RAF, the Q-type with 90 hp gasoline engine, made both as a 3-ton load carrier and as a tractive unit. Some 11,000 of these were produced during World War II.

In 1928 Crossley entered the bus business, a line which

1929 CROSSLEY Eagle coach, NMM

proved so profitable that it led to the demise of private-car production in 1937. In 1939 23 municipal undertakings, most of them in the North (Maidstone and Portsmouth were notable exceptions) operated a total of 900-odd Crossleys. Logically, Manchester were the top scorers, with 646 buses on the strength. First of the line was the Eagle, a 32-seater half-cab single-decker with the big dry-sump 4-cylinder engine, vacuum servo brakes, and worm drive. New for 1929 were a conventional version, the Hawk, and a double-decker Eagle, which gave way to the similar Condor. A 6.8-litre 6-cylinder engine became available in 1930, in which year Crossley made Britain's first diesel-engined double-decker — initially with a Gardner engine, soon replaced by their own 87 hp 8.4-litre direct injection six. In 1933 the company adopted indirect injection for new 4- and 6-cylinder units, and Crossley buses were progressively developed until 1939, with such transmission options as preselector (first seen in 1933) and the Freeborn 4-speed semi-automatic of 1936. 1939's two basic types were the Alpha single-decker and the Mancunian double-decker, listed only with diesel engines. An interesting 1936 development was a range of trolleybuses, made in four- and six-wheel models with amidships-mounted Metrovick motors, air brakes, and worm drive. Among the trolleybus customers were Belfast, Hull, and, of course, Manchester.

1932 saw the introduction of a line of diesel trucks with 4- and 6-cylinder engines, payloads ranging at various times for three to seven tons. Most of these were of forward-control type, though an exception was the 1933 Delta, which also used a 3.8-litre version of the 4-cylinder gasoline engine, soon replaced by a diesel. Production of these trucks was never on a big scale, and had virtually ceased by 1938, though that year Crossley announced a forward-control 5-tonner with an unladen weight of less than 50 cwt. It featured a gasoline engine and hydrovac brakes, but went the way of another 1939 project, a 12/15-cwt battery-electric light van which never went on sale.

After the War only PSVs were marketed, the trolleybuses sharing axles and other components with the diesel line. This latter had acquired a new 8.6-litre 6-cylinder engine, once again with direct injection, while there were three alternative transmissions — 4 speed constant-mesh, 4-speed all synchromesh, and the Brockhouse Hydraulic Turbo Transmitter, which Crossley had been testing since 1942. A move to Stockport coincided with an order for over 1,000 vehicles from the Netherlands State Railways. This included such interesting types as articulated tractor-trailer outfits for 80 passengers, and high-speed single deckers, some of which were fitted with 5-speed overdrive gearboxes and 140 bhp Marshall-supercharged versions of the standard Crossley diesel engine. In April, 1948, Crossley merged with A.E.C. Crossley designs were still listed as late as

1946 CROSSLEY DD42/3 56-seater bus, AJHB

1951 CROSSLEY DD42 56-seater bus, OMM

1951, but thereafter the marque lost its identity, becoming just a badge-engineered A.E.C, though curiously goods vehicles as well as PSVs went out under the Crossley name. The firm's last appearance at the London Show was in 1956, and two years later the A.C.V Group closed down the Stockport factory. *MCS*

CROW (US) 1912-1913

Crow Motor Co., Elkhart, Ind.

Apparently one model of commercial vehicle, designated C.D., was built by this manufacturer of passenger cars. This was a 3/4-tonner with a four-cylinder engine under the hood. It used a three-speed gearbox and shaft drive. Wheelbase was 114 inches. The enclosed delivery van was capable of 45 mph. *GMN*

CROWDEN (GB) 1901-1902

Charles T. Crowden, Leamington Spa, Warwickshire

Crowden converted several horse-drawn steam fire engines to self-propulsion by installing an undertype double-cylinder engine facing forward immediately in front of the boiler. A countershaft differential and double chain drive were provided to newer and stiffer rear wheels. One of these engines was supplied to the Norwich Union Fire Insurance Company at Worcester. Towards the end of 1902 Crowden built a gas-engined fire engine powered by a 20 hp V-4 engine, with 4 speeds and double chain drive. It had a 30 ft. ladder and accomodation for a crew of six. This was supplied to Leamington Spa fire brigade. *RAW/GNG*

CROWN (i) (US) 1910-1915

Crown Commercial Car Co., Milwaukee, Wis

The initial Crown trucks were ½-tonners with 2-cylinder, water-cooled engines, 3-speed gearboxes and double chain drive. The next Crown offering was a 3/4-ton truck priced at $1200 and powered by a 4-cylinder T-head engine with cylinders cast separately. Clutch was multiple disc with a selective 3-speed transmission mounted amidship, and final drive was by chains.

In 1914 the company presented a broadened line of conventional worm driven trucks in 1- and 3-ton sizes powered by a Wisconsin 4-cylinder T-head engine cast in pairs. Solid tires were standard. The frame deserves special mention. While the channel steel side rails seem to be of more or less adequate size, the cross-members appear to be little more than pipe stems. However, to help keep the alignment of the side rails, a thin X-member of metal strips was added to the frame over the rear axle.

The Crown engineering staff was headed by George Van Rollweiler who came to the USA after having been with the Daimler Motor Gesellschaft and Milnes-Daimler, Ltd., in both Germany and England. This would account for the definite foreign appearance of the truck. *RW*

1965 CROWN (ii) Fire Coach pumper, LA

CROWN (ii) (US) 1933 to date

(1) Crown Body & Coach Corp., Los Angeles, California 1933-1952

(2) Crown Coach Corp., Los Angeles, California 1952 to date

Crown Carriage Co. began building carriages and wagons in 1900 and turned to commercial vehicle bodies of various kinds within the next few years. A major part of the firm's output during the 1920's consisted of school bus bodies built to the specifications of western states, particularly California, and in 1933 Crown first built a complete school bus. It was an all-steel forward-control design with a Waukesha engine and three independent braking systems: four-wheel foot-operated hydraulic, four-wheel hand-controlled vacuum, and an emergency brake acting on the drive line. Underfloor Hall-Scott engines were used beginning in 1937, with Cummins diesel power offered as an option subsequently. Today Crown offers four sizes of school buses, two-axle versions seating 79 or 85 children and three-axle buses with seats for 91 or 97, all with Cummins or Detroit Diesel engines.

Since 1950 Crown has also produced a line of intercity and sightseeing buses based on the school bus design, as well as a wide assortment of special purpose coaches (mobile television transmitters, display coaches, mobile libraries, ambulance conversion coaches, and combination passenger and freight coaches), but these are all built to order and do not constitute a large volume of production.

1967 CROWN (ii) 2 AD 6 × 2 coach, MBS

Fire apparatus has been offered since 1949 under the name of "Crown Firecoach." Each fire engine is custom built to individual specifications, and once again these vehicles have been sold mainly in the western states. In 1961 Crown built the first aerial platform seen on the West Coast, a 65 footer for Downey, Calif. Crown Firecoaches are mostly 4x2s, though some 6x4s are made. Cummins diesel engines are the most popular power units today. *MBS*

CROWTHER-DURYEA (US) 1916

Crowther Motor Co., Rochester, N.Y.

This was another of Charles Duryea's many attempts to commercially produce motor cars and trucks, none of which could really be considered a great success. In this operation he was the mechanical engineer, while Henry Crowther had charge of the motor department as business manager.

The truck itself was light and simple in the tradition of various Duryea vehicles. It had a capacity of 1000 pounds with a 4-cylinder engine, Splitdorf ignition, no clutch, a "Duryea Roller Drive", and had a panel body with no fenders on a short wheelbase. The price was $600.

The roller drive consisted of a small wheel at the ends of a jackshaft which rotated against an annular ring attached to the spokes of the rear wheels. Ring and wheels wee smooth- no gears.

Altogether, the primitive appearance of the truck made it appear as if it had been built ten years earlier. Production was microscopic- about 3 cars and a few trucks. Almost certainly, Crowther-Duryea was the last high-wheeler ever built. *RW*

CROXTON (US) 1911-1913

Croxton Motor Car Company, Washington, Pennsylvania

The Croxton Motor Car Company was one-half of the original Croxton-Keeton organization which was divided in 1910, reversing the normal process of agglomeration. The only non-passenger car types were taxis with landaulet bodies for four paying passengers. Typical of this make was the distinctive sloping hood with the radiator aft of the engine. For 1913, the taxicab chassis was identical with the Model A passenger auto of the same year. *GMN*

CROXTON-KEETON (US) 1909-1910

Croxton-Keeton Motor Co., Massilon, O

The lone commercial version by this manufacturer of passenger cars was a four-cylinder taxicab which used the same chassis as the passenger autos. These were distinctive in appearance with a sloping hood with the radiator aft of the 38 hp, 4-cylinder engine. This was furnished with a three-speed selective gearbox and shaft drive. Wheelbase was 115½ inches and the vehicle weighed 3100 pounds and sold for $3300. *GMN*

CRUSADER see M.C.I.

1956 CSEPEL D420 4½-ton truck, BHV

CSEPEL (H) 1950 to date

(1) Csepel Engineering Works, Csepel near Budapest
(2) Csepel Autogyar, Budapest — Szigethalom

The first post-war Hungarian manufacturer of commercial vehicles was founded in late '40s using the ex-Dunai Repulogepgyar factory of Weiss Manfred and was named after Csepel island, south of Budapest. Csepel products were based at the beginning on contemporary Steyr designs and the first diesel engine was built in 1949, while the first 3.2 ton truck appeared a year later.

As the sole producer of truck chassis in Hungary for many years, Csepel grew rapidly. A variety of chassis with normal and forward control cabs, 4x4, 6x6 and even 8x8 civilian and military trucks, tracked military vehicles and light chassis supplied to Ikarus for bus body mounting are included in Csepel activities. Two to six cylinder, 95 - 145 hp diesel engines of Csepel's own construction powered Csepel vehicles for years and were largely supplied together with gearboxes and other components to Ikarus, Dutra and tractor manufacturers, while 215 hp Raba-Man diesels are currently used on heavier Csepel chassis. A pioneer design of Csepel was the 4x4 chassis fitted with twin propeller shaft transmission to the front driving axle, that permits a very low engine setting.

1965 CSEPEL 706/9 articulated van, OMM

Current models are fitted with Chausson designed forward control cabs as used by Polish Star trucks too, while the Polish Jelcz forward control cab was fitted during the early 70s on certain heavy chassis. A typical Csepel cab, though, was for many years a normal control model derived from the original post war Steyr design.

Csepel has largely exported to Asian and African countries part of its production of 72,000 units of chassis built since 1950. *GA*

CSONKA (H) 1900-1912

Janos Csonka, Budapest

Janos Csonka associated with Donat Banki, pioneered gasoline engine development in Hungary as early as 1880. A passenger car, the first in Hungary, followed in 1896, while two light chassis were also built a year later, all powered by Csonka's own single cylinder gasoline engine. Janos Csonka remained basically the "inventor-engineer" and kept his own repair workshop for years, while light commercial vehicles of his designs were built by contemporary engineering firms on his behalf.

The firm of Ganz es Tarsa built a total of 18 three wheeled vans, the firm of Glattefelder was responsible for one mailvan, while 10 units of postal buses with a capacity of eleven passengers were built by the firm of Rock Istran. *GA*

1911 C.T. 2-ton electric truck, NAHC

C.T. (US) 1908-1928

(1) Commercial Truck Co. of America, Philadelphia, Pa. 1908-1915
(2) Commercial Truck Co., Philadelphia, Pa. 1916-1928

The C.T. trucks were battery-powered electrics and the initial models were ½- 3½-tonners. The smaller was a delivery van for $2200. The larger had General Electric motors geared to each dual-wheeled rear wheel. Wheelbase of this 3½-tonner was 114 inches and it had a gross weight of five tons. By 1912, there were six different models from ¼- to 5-tonners. Beginning in 1913, the 1-tonner used worm-drive. In 1915, a gas-electric tractor, a 5-tonner, was offered and this was continued for two years. By 1921, this series of electrics had expanded to seven different capacities from ½- to 6-tonners. There were some minor changes in rated capacities from year to year and in 1928 there were 12 different types. This company was absorbed by Walker Vehicle Co., another builder of battery-powered electrics. *GMN*

CUB (U.S.) 1950-1951

Cub Industries, Inc., White Pigeon, Michigan

Prime mover in the formation of Cub Industries was Howard Munshaw, formerly with Yellow, Reo, Pony Cruiser and Spartan. The lightweight 19-passenger Cub, based on a 160-inch-wheelbase front-engine Ford truck chassis, was another in a long line of attempts to serve a limited U.S. market for small, economical transit buses. Approximately 40 buses were made in two years. *MBS*

1951 CUB 19-passenger bus

CUDELL (D) 1900-1905

(1) Cudell & Co., Motoren und Motorfahrzeugfabrik, Aachen 1900
(2) AG fur Motor und Fahrzeugbau vorm. Cudell, Aachen 1900-1902
(3) Cudell Motor Compagnie mbH., Aachen 1902-1905

The first Cudell van - following the private car design - had a single cylinder de Dion engine. For the later vans, trucks and small buses 2- and 4-cylinder engines of own make were used. *HON*

CUMBERLAND (GB) 1905-c.1908

Pratchitt Brothers, Carlisle.

Pratchitts used a vertical boiler with cross water tubes, steaming at 200 p.s.i. and providing steam for an under-type compound engine, mounted in a plate sub-frame and driving the rear axle by an all gear drive. Springing was between the sub-frame and main frame and the engine, gearing and rear axle differential were thus all unsprung weight. Though one or two Cumberland wagons were sold the manufacture of them seems not to have been pursued. *RAW*

CUMMINS NORDESTE (BR) to date

Cummins Nordese SA Industrial, Salvador

This Brazilian bus maker uses Van Hool platform chassis in conjunction with rear-mounted Cummins diesel engines and locally-made coachwork by Marcoplo. Two basic models are made, a high floor coach for intercity work and a city bus with perimeter seating for 36 passengers and generous space for standee passengers. *GNG*

CUNNINGHAM (i) (US) 1900-1901

(1) Cunningham Engineering Co., Boston, Mass.
(2) Massachusetts Steam Wagon Co., Boston, Mass.

This was an unconventional 4-wheel-drive steam wagon

1901 CUDELL light postal van, GNG

1901 Cunningham team Wagon, NMM

with chain drive from a centrally-mounted compound engine to both front and rear axles. It had a fire-tube boiler fuelled with either coal or coke. Load capacity was four to five tons. *GNG*

CUNNINGHAM (ii) (US) 1909-1934

James Cunningham, Sons & Co., Rochester, N.Y.

This old established carriage-maker started to assemble cars on a modest scale in 1907, using Buffalo and Continental engines, and other standardized components. Their first ambulances and hearses were announced in 1909, and a year later Cunningham switched to an ohv 4-cylinder engine of their own make. 1916 saw the Lacey-designed sv V8 of 7.2 litres' capacity. A luxury car of the first rank with 3-speed (later 4-speed overdrive) gearbox, multi-disc clutch, and all brakes on the rear wheels. It acquired fwb, with a reversion once more to three forward speeds, in 1926. Surprisingly, however, in the case of a vehicle retailing at around the $6500 mark,

1926 CUNNINGHAM (ii) V-8 funeral coach, LA

a good two-thirds of all the big eights built carried ambulance and hearse coachwork of superb quality, unusual departures being an armored ambulance (1927) and a flower car of pickup type as early as 1931. Also new in the latter year was the ornate Cathedral hearse with the fashionable town car styling, but an indication of hard times was a reversion to proprietary engines, the new W10 series using a Continental straight-8. Only about a dozen of these were made, and though the commercial chassis (and its private-car counterpart) were still nominally available in 1934, most of Cunningham's superb bodies were now being mounted on Cadillacs, Packards and Lincolns. Other activities of the early 1930s included some Cadillac-powered halftracks and armored cars, as well as military halftrack conversions of Ford trucks. All automobile activity ceased after 1936, though Cunningham made garden tractors in the late 1940s, and are still active in the field of specialized electrical switchgear. *MCS*

CURRIE (GB) 1912-1913

R.S. Currie & Co., West Kilburn, London W.

Also known as the C. & R., this was a 5 cwt 3-wheeler, powered by a 9 hp vertical twin air-cooled engine under the seat, with friction transmission and worm drive to the single rear wheel. Tiller steering was used on the first models, but for 1913 a considerably modified version was made, with wheel steering and the driver seated behind the load, as on the Autocarrier. This model had a 7 hp water-cooled engine. *GNG*

CURTIS (US) 1912-1915

Pittsburgh Machine Tool Co., Braddock, Pa.

The Curtis was built entirely in the plant of the Pittsburgh Machine Tool Company, except for wheels and electrical parts. The truck had a 27 hp 4-cylinder engine with force-feed lubrication and thermo-syphon cooling, cone clutch, 3-speed transmission, and chain drive. Although 1½-ton and 2-ton models were listed, they differed only in tire size. The 2-ton model cost $3,000 in 1913. *DJS*

CURTIS-BILL (US) 1933

Bill Motors Co., Oakland, California

Louis H. Bill had been associated with the Fageol plant in Oakland from its early days and went into business for himself in 1933 when Fageol was shut down. Employing the designs of Harry E. Curtis, his company delivered a 20- passenger front-drive bus with an 8-cylinder Lycoming engine and a 144-inch wheelbase. A 10-ton truck was also made. *MBS*

CURTIS-NATIONAL (US) 1934

National Bus Lines was an unregulated interstate operator based in Los Angeles which began in September 1934 with leased vehicles. Later in that year two low-slung streamlined 20-passenger Ford-powered buses were placed in service, known as Curtis-National buses. The company and the buses were sold in 1936 to All American Bus Lines, and only those two Curtis-Nationals were ever built. *MBS*

CUSHMAN (US) 1936 to date

(1) Cushman Motor Works, Lincoln, Neb. 1936-1961
(2) Cushman Motors, Divn. Outboard Marine Corp. (OMC), Lincoln, Neb. 1961-1972
(3) OMC-Lincoln, Divn. Outboard Marine Corp., Lincoln, Neb. 1972 to date

Everitt and Clinton Cushman started their business in 1901 by building 2-stroke engines for pleasure and fishing boats, adding later 4-stroke water-cooled engines for farm use and, from 1922, air-cooled engines. Their first vehicles appeared in 1936, and were lightweight 3-wheelers based on scooter designs. Passenger models included golf course cars which have always been a major part of Cushman production, while goods models were parcel-carriers, either as sidecars or 3-wheelers with two wheels in front.

1975 CUSHMAN police 3-wheeler, GNG

Load capacity was 350 to 414 lbs, and the engines were single-cylinder 4 hp units, with two speeds and chain drive. Many of these were used by the US Army and Air Force in World War II and the Korean war. Although small models are still made, Cushmans have grown up in recent years, with horizontally-opposed twin engines of up to 18 hp, and load capacities of up to 2000 lbs. 3-and 4-wheelers are made, with electric as well as gasoline motors. Road-going Cushmans are generally used for police work, as refuse haulers and for general carrying jobs, while other models have a wide variety of uses inside factories, airport complexes etc. Cabs are open, semi-enclosed or fully-enclosed steel construction. The heavier models have 3-speed transmissions and worm drive, while some lighter models use V-belt drive. About 65% of Cushman production is devoted to golf carts, with industrial and road-going commercial vehicles making up the balance.*RW*

C.W.S. (PL) 1922-1929
Centralne Warsztaty Samochodow, Warszawa

The very first vehicles to be designed in Poland, by engineer Tadinsk Tanski, the C.W.S. TI car chassis was used as the basis for light commercials and ambulance versions. TI model was very simplified in design and construction and was powered by a 4-cylinder, 3 litre gasoline engine developing 61 HP.*GA*

C. W. S. BELL. (GB) 1919-1930
Co-operative Wholesale Society, Ltd., Manchester.

Although variously described as C.W.S. and Bell in contemporary reports, these vehicles were always known as C.W.S. Bell by the C.W.S. themselves and are therefore shown as such. Vehicle production commenced in premises previously owned by the Cotton Industry Motor Transport Ltd., following the takeover of that concern by C.W.S., who had also purchased all the patterns and designs of Bell vehicles from Bell Brothers of Ravensthorpe. Production initially centered upon a 4-cylinder s.v. 2.5 litre engined traveler's brougham and commercial chassis with payloads of 15 cwt, 1 ton and 30 cwt with the same basic specification as the brougham. All these vehicles were bodied in the C.W.S. bodyshops at Broughton and Newcastle and were intended for opera-

1922 C.W.S.-BELL 1½-2-ton van, MJWW

tion by the C.W.S. and retail Co-operative societies only.

In 1922, however, a new 30-40 cwt commercial chassis was introduced. Powered by a 3.9 litre Dorman 4-cylinder engine with 4 speed gearbox and overhead worm drive, this proved suitable for van, truck and charabanc operation and remained in production until 1927. It was then supplemented by a large 30 hp model - the 'P' type - mainly for passenger work with 20 seat bodywork, but production of all types ceased in 1930.*MJWW*

1909 CYKLONETTE 3-wheel van, HON

CYKLONETTE (D) 1902-1922
Cyklon Maschinenfabrik GmbH., Berlin O

The well-known 3-wheeler was also available as a van using the principle of front-drive with the engine mounted above the single front wheel. The single-cylinder 450 cc. model appeared in 1902 and was developed to 2 cylinders and 1.290 cc. It formed a very economical means of transport.*HON*

CZ (CS) 1961-1963
Ceske zavody motocyklove n.p., Strakonice

In 1960 the well-known CZ motorcycle factory tested a prototype of a light 3-wheeler, which was built from September, 1961 to 1963. Known as the CZ 175 Type 505, it employed the front part of the successful Cezeta scooter with single-cylinder 171 cc engine and 4-speed gearbox, and a tubular frame at the rear with independent suspension of the two rear wheels. Load capacity of the van or truck body was 200 kgs, and maximum speed 35 mph.
MSH

1927 DAAG low frame coach, HON

DAAG (D) 1910-1929

Deutsche LastAutomobilfabrik A.G., Ratingen In 1910 this firm started production of subsidised trucks but production was not too significant. During WW I capacity was enlarged and after the war a very well developed construction was available. A remarkable feature was that pneumatic tires were used on all types of the 1½ to 3½ ton range. In 1925 a low-frame bus chassis with 4-wheel brakes and one cardan shaft for each of the rear wheels was introduced. In 1927 DAAG built the first commercial vehicle in Germany with pneumatic springing. By 1928 a new 6-cylinder 90 PS engine was used for all trucks and buses. Production ceased in 1929 and the factory was taken over by Krupp. *HON*

DAB (DK) 1964 to date

Leyland DAB A/S, Silkeborg

Dansk Automobil Byggeri had been truck and bus bodybuilders for over 40 years before they became manufacturers in their own right. Among their more interesting productions was a series of 55 ft. 9 in. long articulated buses using Leyland tractive units, built for Danish State Railways in 1947 and nicknamed 'The Red Worm'. In 1964 they built a large fleet of integral construction buses using Leyland Royal Tiger running units. Over the next three years more than 700 Leyland-powered DAB buses were made, and the company becamse a wholly-owned Leyland subsidiary, though they were not prevented from using other firms' components.

In 1973 DAB began to collaborate with Saurer of Switzerland to build a range of buses using Saurer engines for the Swiss market, Leyland engines for the Danish and other markets, Leyland 5-speed Pneumocyclic gearboxes, and axles from both manufacturers. Leyland-designed four-bellows air suspension was used on each axle. Three two-axle models were offered, joined by a three-axle articulated bus, and this range is still made today. By the use of standard basic running units and flexible modular structure body elements, buses can be tailor-made for all purposes in lengths from 32 ft. 6ins. to 58 ft. 6 ins. *GNG*

D.A.C. (F) 1905-c.1907

d'Espine, Achard et Cie, Paris

The original D.A.C. was a 2-ton truck with a 16/18 hp 2-cylinder engine whose cylinders measured an enormous 165 x 220 mm. It had four forward speeds in all, first being transmitted by belt and the three upper ratios by chains. There were also three speeds in reverse. In 1906 a 20 hp 4-cylinder model with all-chain drive was introduced. *GNG*

DAC (R) 1973 to date

(1) Uzina de Autocamioane Brasov, Brasov

(2) Intreprinderea de Autocamioane Brasov, Brasov

Built along side SR and Roman vehicles in the same factory the DAC range includes two basic models. A medium class normal control chassis, built as truck, tipper and tractor, powered by an MAN license-built 135 hp diesel and featuring a modified SR cab is the main product, while a heavy 3-axled dumper completes the line. With a GVW of 46 tons (latter 42 tons), it is powered by two diesel engines placed side by side. The basic 135 hp unit is used in tandem and mechanics include two clutches and two 5-speed gearboxes. This complexity results in an immense looking hood and a high standing half cab.

Certain Roman forward control chassis were also marketed under the DAC trademark. *GRA*

D.A.F. (NL) 1938 to date

(1) Van Doorne's Aanhangenwagenfabriek NV, Eindhoven 1938-1949

(2) Van Doorne's Automobielfabriek NV, Eindhoven 1950-1972

(3) Van Doorne's Bedrijfswagenfabriek BV, Eindhoven 1972 to date

The brothers Hub and Wim Van Doorne started in a humble way in 1928, manufacturing ladders, metal cabinets, and window frames, whence they branched out into a successful line of semi-trailers. In 1936 they introduced the Trado all-wheel drive truck conversion, applied to Fords and other makes in service with the Dutch Army. Their first complete vehicle (in 1938) was a 6x4 armored car with Ford V8 engine, followed by the MC139, an amphibious prototype 4x4 powered by a transversely-mounted 11CV Citroen unit. During the German occupation Van Doorne's experimented with front- and rear-wheel drive forward control trucks, but there were no further D.A.F. vehicles until 1948, when the company built a 32-seater single-decker unitary construction trolleybus and some bus prototypes with quick detachable front-mounted 6-cylinder gasoline and diesel engines (the former by Waukesha).They were also involved in the construction of Kromhout's contemporary unitary construction bus. Serious vehicle manufacture began in 1950 with a 5-ton forward control truck on conventional lines, with 6-cylinder sv Hercules gasoline engine, and other proprietary mechanical elements. There were four forward speeds, hydrovac brakes were standard, and the regular diesel option was the 4.7-litre Perkins P6. [illegible]00 units found buyers between April and October of that year, the range being extended to cover payloads from 3½ to 7 tons.

Further widening of the range led to light 1-ton vans and pickups using the 2.2-litre 46 hp Hercules four; the A10 van was of forward-control type with hydraulic brakes and hypoid rear axle, normal control being preferred for the truck. Production buses were of conventional full-front configuration with 5.6-litre Perkins R6 diesels and 5-speed ZF constant-mesh gearboxes, while there were also some military vehicles. First of these was a Hercules-powered forward-control 3-ton 6x6 with extra idler wheels and 8-speed transmission, but by 1956 a comprehensive range was offered. Biggest of these was the

1956 DAF 1500DL articulated truck, Daf

YA616, a 6x6 6-tonner featuring double reduction drive, air-hydraulic brakes, power steering, and a Continental 6-cylinder gasoline engine giving 232 hp. Pegaso of Spain took out a manufacturing license for these all-wheel drive types.

Leyland diesels first appeared as a regular option in the 1953 buses; license production of the British company's 0350 engine did not begin at Eindhoven until the summer of 1956. The Hercules and Perkins units continued as standard equipment, though a Leyland-powered 7-ton truck was exhibited at the 1956 London Show, and Leylands were standardized on the 8/9-ton 2000 of 1957. This one came with 6-speed ZF gearbox (air-assisted synchromesh was optional), power steering, and air brakes, and could also be had as a tractor or trailing-axle 6-wheeler. The A10 had been dropped, but the light normal control pickups, now with 4-litre 6-cylinder Hercules engines, were still quoted, and there was a range of heavier normal control types for payloads up to 5/6 tons. The bigger ones had five forward speeds and an air/hydraulic brake option. Buses were little changed, with Perkins diesels as standard equipment, though a few Verheul-bodied 6-wheelers with Leyland engines were produced.

By 1958 D.A.F. had 32 percent of the home market, and had discarded bought-out power in favor of their own versions of the Leyland, outputs ranging from 100 hp up to the 165 hp of the turbocharged 0680s used in the heaviest tractors. Alongside these diesels the company developed a parallel range of 6-cylinder gasoline engines, sharing many components with the D.A.F.-Leyland range. Another novelty of 1958 was D.A.F.'s first private car, a flat-twin 600cc sedan with all-independent springing and their own infinitely variable gear incorporating a belt final drive. This had evolved into a 5/6-cwt van by 1961; a military 4x4 development, the Pony, followed in 1962, and the twin-cylinder engine and transmission were also applied to the Swedish Kalmar vans. D.A.F.'s 1962 production amounted to some 5000 commercial vehicles and 1500 semi-trailers, the former covering payloads from five to 14 tons, with normal control and gasoline variants

1964 DAF A2600DP 8½-9-ton truck, Daf

continued. New that year was the 2600, a modern short-cab forward control machine for GVWs of 19 tons and GCWs approaching the 40-ton mark; its 11.1-litre D.A.F.-Leyland engine developed 220 hp. Features of the model were a 6-speed overdrive gearbox, double reduction drive, dual-circuit air brakes, and power steering. Buses continued to follow orthodox lines, with accommodation for up to 90 passengers, and power steering available on the largest chassis, but underfloor engines made their appearance on the MB200 of 1964, which had a twin-tube frame and all the mechanical refinements of the big trucks. At the same time the company introduced a 6x6 load carrier, the AZ1900, available with 165 hp turbocharged engine. The rear-engined SB200DO bus was the principal novelty of the 1966 season; this one featured the 11.1-litre D.A.F.-Leyland unit and a Voith automatic gearbox. It was adopted by the municipalities of Amsterdam, the Hague,

1967 DAF A16DD 7½-ton truck, Daf

1971 DAF ATE2400DK 6×6 tipper truck, Daf

Rotterdam and Utrecht. The 2600 range was extended, and D.A.F. started to develop their power units. A litre 126 hp s being followed 8.2-litre and 11.6-litre types on similar lines. 1970 saw a complete redesign of the truck range, with square tilt cabs replacing developments of the original 1950 idiom. Bus production centered round variations of the 200 theme with amidships-mounted horizontal engines. With the exception of the light vans, all D.A.F. now featured air-hydraulic or full air brakes, 5-speed gearboxes (synchromesh was optional) being also basic equipment. A curiosity of the 1971 shows was a Jonckheere-bodied coach powered by a Stirling-Philips hot air engine, but D.A.F. themselves were not directly involved with this experiment.

1972 was a year of important business changes. The car

1978 DAF F2800 40-ton GCW cement tanker, Daf

1960 DAIHATSU Trimobile MPA 3-wheel van, FLP

side of the company came under Swedish Volvo control, the 2-cylinder D.A.F.s being phased out as a consequence. International Harvester of America acquired a 33 per-cent stake in the truck business. Gasoline engines would remain available in models of up to seven tons until 1974, and there was more power for the F2600 in the shape of a 304 hp 11.6-litre turbo-charged engine with charge cooling used in conjunction with a 9-speed ZF gearbox. A year later this model was replaced by the 2800 series of 4x2 and 6x4 trucks, tippers and tractors, with engine options of up to 320 hp. Also new was a 26-ton GVW 6x4 tipper with the smaller 168 hp unit, and International's influence manifested itself in a revived, if short-lived range of heavy duty normal control Paystars, essentially I.H.C. designs with D.A.F. engines and running gear.

D.A.F., however, ran into trouble in 1975, when major factory expansion coincided with a sales slump, leaving them with some 3000 unsold vehicles on their hands. They were forced to accept a rescue operation by the Dutch State Mines. Within a year sales had built up again to the 12,000 mark, and in 1978 the company covered most sectors of the medium and heavy duty market, from the modest Club of Four types up to tractors for GCWs in excess of 100 tons. Apart from the 5/7-ton GVW class, which used 3.9-litre 4-cylinder Perkins engines, all models were fitted with diesel sixes of D.A.F.'s own make, capacities ranging from 5.8 to 11.6 litres. Manual steering and air-hydraulic brakes were confined to the bottom of the range. Light D.A.F.s also featured 5-speed all-syncromesh gearboxes whereas 6-speed constant mesh or synchromesh types (with or without splitter) were preferred on heavier models. The heaviest models of all in the 2800 series could be had with 13-speed transmissions incorporating a crawler first. Forward control was general practice, as were tilt cabs, the sole exception to the latter being the ATE2400 DK, a 32-ton GVW 6x4 tipper which retained the old fixed type. D.A.F. 2800s could be had in 8x4 form. PSV types were limited to the unitary 200 with horizontal underfloor engine, and the SB 2000 which wore its 8.2-litre turbocharged unit at the rear of a separate chassis. 6-speed all synchromesh boxes were standard on both models, though the 200 was available with a variety of semi- and full-automatic transmission. *MCS*

DAGSA (E) 1955-1960

Defensas Antigas SA, Segovia

A prototype delivery van powered by a 583 cc 2-cylinder 2-stroke engine was made by this firm who specialized in military equipment. *JCG*

DAIHATSU (J) 1930 to date

(1) Hatsudoki Seizo Kaisha, Osaka 1930-1951
(2) Daihatsu Kogyo Co. Ltd., Osaka 1951-1974
(3) Daihatsu Motor Co. Ltd., Osaka 1974 to date

The Hatsudoki Seizo Co. was founded in 1907 to manufacture internal combustion engines, but complete vehicles were not marketed until 1930. These were motorcycle-type 3-wheelers with single front wheel, sometimes known by the Tsubasa name. In 1937 the company made its first 4-wheelers, a light military 4x4 which competed unsuccessfully against the Kurogane Black Medal, and a conventional pickup which was made only in small numbers. After the War Daihatsu resumed 3-wheeler production; these machines retained handlebar steering, saddles for their drivers, and rudimentary weather protection until 1956. That year's range covered payloads from 15 cwt to over two tons, all engines being of motorcycle type, from a 750 cc single-cylinder air-cooled sv unit developing 17 hp up to 1½-litre water-cooled V-twins. Enclosed cabs, doors, and wheel steering arrived on the miniature Trimobile of 1957, which had a 305 cc engine, and hydraulic brakes on the rear wheels only. At the same time the bigger Daihatsus were also given wheel steering. Some of these were quite sophisticated, with 2-speed back axles on the 13T series, which could be had as dumper, refuse collector, gully emptier, or even fire engine. By 1959 the range had been extended both upward and downward. The ultra-light class was the 249 cc 2-stroke Midget, handlebar-steered and only 100 inches long, while at the other end of the scale was the Vesta, a forward-control 4-wheeled development of the 13T for 2-ton payloads, again with six forward speeds.

The 4-wheeler range was further developed in 1960, when the Vesta was given a conventional 4-cylinder water-cooled engine, and a 23-seater light bus variant became available. There was also a 5/7-cwt van, the Hi-Jet, with 360 cc twin 2-stroke engine, hydraulic brakes on all wheels, and coil ifs, as well as some car-type 1¼/¾-ton pickups with gasoline or diesel power. This range was continued with little alteration until 1965, though more powerful engines (a 1.9-litre 85 hp petrol unit or a 2.3-litre 63 hp diesel) were fitted to the bigger trucks, and the advent of Daihatsu's little 797 cc Compagno private car with torsion-bar ifs led to parallel commercial variants, these including the forward control Newline with beam front axle. The company came under Toyota ownership in 1966, but this had little immediate effect on the trucks. The 3-wheelers were, however, on their way out, the bigger versions disappearing in the late 1960s; the Trimobile, now with 3-wheel brakes, lingered on into 1971. Their place was taken by forward control developments of the

1975 DAIHATSU SV17L 1½-ton truck, Daihatsu

1975 DAIHATSU 360 S-38P light truck, Daihatsu

Hi-Jet family with watercooled 2-stroke engines and 4-speed all-synchromesh gearboxes, and by a 1½-ton Vesta derivative, the SV16T with single rear wheels. Toyota gasoline engines now featured in 4-cylinder trucks, though Daihatsu's own diesel survived. A normal control 6-cwt van based on the 359 cc Fellow minicar was in the 1973 catalogue, but two years later only the forward control lightweights were listed, along with the 1½/2-ton range, available with 80 hp gasoline engine and four speeds, or with a 70 hp diesel and 5-speed gearbox. By 1977 the small Daihatsu commercials had 547 cc ohc engines, while the gap between private cars and trucks was bridged by the Taft, a new Jeep-type 4x4 with a choice of 958 cc or 1.6-litre 4-cylinder gasoline engines. Daihatsu also made diesel-engined road rollers. *MCS*

DAIMLER (i) (D) 1896-1926

Daimler Motoren-Gesellschaft, Stuttgart-Unterturkheim; Berlin-Marienfelde

Gottlieb Daimler's invention of the high-speed internal combustion engine inspired to a great extent the development of motor cars. Ten years after the debut of the first Daimler car the first commercial motor vehicles appeared in 1896. They were based on the "Riemenwagen" and were equipped with rear-mounted 2-cylinder engines of 4, 6, 8 and 10 hp for payloads from 1½ to 5 tons. The further developments saw the engine placed behind the front axle, but the belt drive was retained. In 1898 an improved model was presented with front mounted engine of the same characteristics but with belt and pinion transmission. A motor omnibus was put into operation in 1898 between Kunzelsau and Bad Mergentheim, not too far from Stuttgart. This was a modified "Victoria" model with front-mounted 2-cylinder Phoenix engine of 10 hp, the seating capacity was for 10 passengers. This line how-

1899 DAIMLER (i) bus, NMM

ever was no lasting success; it was only run for about nine months. In 1899 the first bus appeared which was not more or less a modified private car, but was conceived as a bus from the beginning. It had a 2-cylinder 8 hp engine, a 16 passenger capacity and was delivered to England. From 1900 the 2-cylinder engines were replaced by 4-cylinder components.

In 1902 the "Motorfahrzeug-und Motorenfabrik Berlin" at Marienfelde was taken over (see MMB). Henceforth the manufacture of commercial vehicles was concentrated in this plant 2- and 4-cylinder models were produced as vans and trucks up to 70 hp and 5 ton payload. Cardan drive was used for the light models, the heavier ones had chain drive which was succeeded by the unique Daimler Ritzelantrieb (pinion drive). Later also the system of worm drive was featured, especially for buses. As a sideline the production of gasoline driven traction engines from MMB

1905 DAIMLER (i) charabanc, NMM

times was continued for some time. Daimler buses were the first ones to operate in Berlin in 1905 and in the same year a Daimler bus replaced for the first time a mail coach line in the Bavarian Alps. 4x4 vehicles were developed for the army and for use in overseas countries. Some of them were equipped with 6-cylinder 60 hp engines.

In 1907 Daimler built their first fire engines with engine-driven pumps. In co-operation with Austro-Daimler also electric-driven commercials — especially fire fighting vehicles — were built, which were also known as "Mercedes Electrique." They followed the principle of electric wheel hub motors which drove the rear wheels. These first appeared in 1908.

After WW I Daimler produced 3 and 4¼ ton trucks which were available with a wide variety of special purpose bodies and as buses.

Already before the war Daimler had started experiments with diesel engines. These were carried on after the war. Daimler followed the principle of turbocharging. A truck and a bus with diesel engines were presented at the Berlin Motor Show in October 1923. A low-chassis design — especially for bus bodies — was presented in 1924 and a new 5 ton truck appeared featuring pinion drive.

After 1924, when Benz and Daimler started co-operation, there was no further development in diesel engines as no agreement could be reached whether the Benz system or that of Daimler would be better. At the time of the total merger of both companies in 1926 the Daimler program consisted of two truck versions with four and five tons payload capacity. 55 hp and 80 hp engines were available, supplemented by a 60 hp bus and a 3-axle 80 hp bus.

After the merger all commercials were marketed as Mercedes-Benz. *HON*

1899 DAIMLER (ii) light omnibus, NMM

DAIMLER (ii) (GB) 1897 to date

(1) Daimler Motor Syndicate Ltd., Coventry 1897-1904
(2) Daimler Motor Co. (1904) Ltd., Coventry 1904-1910
(3) Daimler Co. Ltd., Coventry 1910-1936
(4) Transport Vehicles (Daimler) Ltd., Coventry 1936-1966
(5) Daimler Transport Vehicles Ltd., Coventry 1967-1972
(6) British Leyland Motor Corporation Ltd., Truck and Bus Division, Leyland, Lancashire 1972-1977
(7) British Leyland UK Ltd. Truck & Bus Division, Leyland, Lancashire 1977 to date

Though the Daimler parcels van driven by J.S. Critchley in the Emancipation Run of November, 1896, was an imported vehicle, the Coventry-Daimler concern had such a model available early in 1897. It had a 4hp vertical-twin engine, tube ignition, 3-speed gearbox with horizontal, dial-type selector, and side chain drive, and by 1899 the company's catalogue depicted such variations as a private omnibus, an Irish-style jaunting car, and a 1-ton van. Two 12 hp cab-over-engine vans were supplied to the Post Office for mail delivery trials in October 1898, but suffered from overheating. Daimler's 1900 range included 2- and 3-tonners with 4-cylinder engines, and the company tested a shaft-driven 2-cylinder charabanc designed by Sidney Straker, but most of the vehicles actually delivered were the classic chain-driven twins; a few of these were still working in London as late as 1912. A spate of financial troubles was followed by the success of a new line of 4-cylinder sv chain-driven private cars (many of which ended their days as truck conversions) in 1904, and hardly any commercials were made in the 1902-1907 period, apart from an 18 hp fire engine supplied to Liverpool in 1903. In 1908, however, Daimler began to manufacture Renard Road Trains under license; in the same year they built a 34-seater normal control double decker bus with worm drive back axle and Auto-Mixte electric transmission. The engine was a 30 hp 4-cylinder, and the hood and radiator were of fluted car type. This came to nothing, any more than did the KPL (Knight-Pieper-Lanchester) unitary construction double decker of 1909. On this one the two 12 hp 4-cylinder Knight sleeve-valve engines were mounted low down, one on each side of the frame, each driving a separate rear wheel via a dynamo. No differential was used. Equally remarkable were wire wheels, front-wheel brakes, and the provision of electric fans in the cooling system.

1900 DAIMLER (ii) 8/10hp van, WB

BSA acquired the Daimler assets in 1910, and a year later came a new and more serious commercial vehicle programme. By 1914 this covered everything from a 10-cwt van to a 5-tonner. All models featured worm drive and Knight engines (also supplied to the London General Omnibus Co. for use in their buses), and even the smallest ones had radiators quite different from those of the cars. A short-lived 1-tonner of 1913 used the 3.3-litre 20 hp car engine and the transaxle also found on some Daimler cars of the period, but more important was the 2/5-ton range. These had 4- and 5.7-litre engines with pump and fan cooling, clutches were of cone type, and frames were flitch-plate. Conventional 3- and 4-speed gearboxes were fitted to trucks, but the buses had the 4-speed chain-drive type also found on contemporary LGOC products. A double-decker cost only £875 complete. In London, the Metropolitan Omnibus Co. ordered 350, and by the outbreak of war Daimler buses were in service in Budapest, Constantinople, Munich, Vienna, and even New York, where the Fifth Avenue Bus Co. placed an order. A longer chassis was available for charabanc bodies. From 1911 Daimler added heavy agricultural tractors to their repertoire, evolving for these a 14.8-litre 6-cylinder sleeve valve engine which was to power the first tanks of World War I. In addition to their regular trucks, Daimler also

1910 DAIMLER (ii) KPL gas-electric bus, NMM

1920 DAIMLER (ii) CV charabanc, NMM

produced a quantity of 20 hp car chassis fitted with truck or ambulance bodies for the Army during the War.

Only the 2/3-tonner (Series CJ and CK) with 4-litre engine reappeared after the War, though by 1920 a built in tire pump was a regular option, and PSV models could be had with electric lighting and pneumatic tires. These models continued without change until 1926, in which year they were joined by the CM, a lightweight omnibus chassis designed with contemporary weight restrictions in view: when equipped with pneumatic tires it was permitted to run at 20 mph. At the same time Daimler and AEC merged their commercial vehicle interests to form the Associated Daimler Co., with all assembly work centered on Southall. Daimler's main contribution to ADC was the supply of 6-cylinder sleeve-valve engines, the 5.8-litre 30/120 hp being fitted to the London Six double decker bus and to the 424 half-cab high-speed coach,

1929 DAIMLER CF6 28-seater coach, NMM

among others. Similar power units were also sold to Guy. The ADC venture was short-lived, the two companies going their separate ways during 1928.

Daimler's renewed independence coincided not only with L.H. Pomeroy's period as Chief Engineer, but also with a boom in long-distance coaching in Britain. They therefore decided to concentrate on buses and coaches, the nearest approach to a truck being occasional horsebox conversions on PSV chassis. First of Pomeroy's commercial Daimlers was the CF half-cab coach (a normal control version was also offered). The engine was the well-tried 35/120 in 90 hp form (later raised to 100hp), with dual coil ignition; final drive was by underslung worm, the four-wheel brakes had vacuum servo assistance, and there was a reversion to the classic Daimler radiator. Initially coach operators were the principal customers, CFs being used on the London-Bradford run, while Daimler Hire Ltd. added

Continental coach tours in Daimler vehicles to their other interests. Single-decker service buses were however ordered by Lanarkshire Traction during 1930, and for 1931 Pomeroy produced the low frame CG6 double decker chassis with offset transmission, this using the famous preselective fluid-flywheel gear just introduced on Daimler's bigger private cars. A year later conventional sliding-type gear boxes had been dropped on cars and buses alike, though the switch to poppet-valve engines was led by the latter, a 6.6-litre ohv 7-bearing 6-cylinder unit being available in 1932. 1934 saw the first catalogued diesel bus, the COG5 with 7-litre 5-cylinder Gardner engine and five forward speeds, and the 1935 range consisted of four double-decker chassis, the new variants using 6-cylinder diesels by AEC and Gardner.

1936 saw the formation of a new company to pursue bus development under the direction of F.G. Couch. Double-decker business was booming; in 1931 Britain's municipal fleets contained only 174 Daimlers, but in 1936 there were 657, and this had grown to 1311 in 1938, when the leading users were Birmingham (622), Edinburgh (150) and

1939 DAIMLER (ii) 37-seater bus, NMM

Coventry (101), this last municipality patriotically proposing an all-Daimler fleet. Leading export customers included Adelaide, Auckland, Bombay, Capetown and Melbourne. In 1936 Daimler, like Crossley, branched out into the trolleybus market, both 6x4 and 4x2 versions being listed. As always, final drive was by worm, other equipment including Metrovick electric motors and Westinghouse air brakes. Trolleybuses remained available until 1955, most of the later ones being exported, though Derby and West Hartlepool were among British undertakings to favor the make.

Daimler brakes were given hydraulic actuation in 1937, but a year later the gasoline models had been discontinued, only Gardner diesel engines being quoted. During the War years Daimler made the very successful 4x4 armoured scout car powered by the 2½-litre 6-cylinder DB18 car engine, this being followed after VJ-Day by the Rolls-Royce-engined Ferret (1951) and the Jaguar-powered Fox (1969). Bus production was resumed in 1942 to help replace air-raid losses, and in 1946 Daimler announced their own direct injection 6-cylinder oil engine of 8.6 litres' capacity, used in conjunction with a 4-speed fluid flywheel transmission. Gardner units were still an option, and a more powerful 10.6-litre Daimler appeared in 1949. With it came the improved CVD650 bus chassis, with servo assistance for handbrake and gear-change mechanism, which could also be applied to steering and to the opening and closing of the rear doors. Some air-braked 6x4 double deckers were supplied to Capetown, while 1949 also saw a brief excursion into specialized ambulance manufacture with the Barker-bodied DC27, basically a 4-litre 6-cylinder 27 hp limousine chassis. Features included ifs and hydro-mechanical brakes, and the London County Council ordered 120 of the 500-odd produced.

The traditional Daimler omnibus was progressively developed, a weight-saving program by both the factory and the MCW coachbuilding firm paring 1¼ tons off a double decker by 1952. A new stylized grille made its appearance, and 1954 examples were available with full air servo brakes. Three years later came the ultimate development of the fluid flywheel, the Daimatic automatic transmission, which eliminated the gearchange pedal. Operators could also specify the basic preselector or a 4-speed David Brown all-synchromesh gearbox with single-plate clutch, as well as having a choice of 6-cylinder Daimler or 5- and 6-cylinder Gardner engines. In addition Daimler were developing a turbocharger which boosted output of their 8.6-litre unit to 137hp.

Since 1951 more modern designs had been explored with a new single decker, the 37/45-seater Freeline with 6-cylinder horizontal underfloor Gardner engine. Transmission was of 5-speed preselective type, and during its run the Freeline acquired all the options, such as Daimatic, air brakes and power steering. The export demand was considerable — Freelines were operated in such countries as Belgium, India, Israel, New Zealand, South Africa and Spain — and by 1956 an extra-long 244 inch wheelbase

1958 DAIMLER (ii) CVG bus, NMM

chassis had become available. 1960 saw double-decker design uprated with the advent of the Fleetline, a 78-seater featuring a quick-detachable transverse rear engine and double-reduction bevel drive in place of the traditional worm. Full air brakes were standard, but suspension was conventional, and steering was normally manual. Power was provided by a Gardner 6LX. At the same time Daimler came under Jaguar control, and as such part of an empire that would embrace Guy commercial vehicles and the engine-building firms of Meadows and Coventry-Climax.

The single-decker SRD prototype of 1962, with transverse horizontal engine and Daimatic transmission, did not go into production, but two years later came a Freeline replacement, the 50-seater Roadliner credited with 77 mph. Jaguar had acquired a manufacturing license for Cummins diesel engines, and thus power was provided by a 9.6-litre V6 of this make, mounted vertically at the rear

1974 DAIMLER (ii) Fleetline bus, British Leyland

on the left. Cooling was assisted by an electric fan, the Daimatic transmission was used in conjunction with a single- or 2-speed back axle, and entirely new was the Dunlop bellows-type air suspension: a rubber system was subsequently offered as an alternative. Daimler's own engines were discontinued in 1963, though municipal demand kept the traditional front-engined buses in production for another five years. By 1967 Cummins units (with the option of Allison automatic transmissions) were being used in Fleetlines as well. The company's share of the municipal market increased steadily despite a tendency towards smaller fleets: 4322 Daimlers were in operation in 1955, 4348 in 1959, 4210 in 1963, and 5577 in 1972, in which year the make was second only to Leyland.

In 1968 the Jaguar-BMC interests had fused with Leyland to form the British Leyland Motor Corporation, but development continued, with 8.4-litre V8 Perkins engines available in the Roadliner, and a choice of A.E.C. or Cummins units in the CR36, notable for its use of a north-south engine in the Roadliner fashion. Though a variety of 6-cylinder Gardners of 120/180bhp were standard, a new option was Leyland's 11.1-litre 0680. By 1971 only the Fleetline still wore the Daimler badge; a year later Leyland-engined machines re-equipped London's Green Line suburban network, and in 1975 turbocharged Leyland units became available. The first LPG-equipped bus on regular service in Britain was a Daimler of Cleveland Transit, fitted unusually with a straight-8 Rolls-Royce engine originally designed to run on gasoline. An impressive backlog of orders kept the Fleetline in production in 1978. *MCS*

DAIN (US) 1912-1917

(1) Joseph Dain, Ottumwa, Iowa 1912
(2) Dain Manufacturing Co., Ottumwa, Iowa 1912-1917

These vehicles were 1-, 2- and 3-tonners all of which used 4-cylinder engines combined with friction transmissions and worm-drive rear axles. In all models, the driver sat to the left of the hood and used a 22-inch diameter steering wheel. During the last two years of production, only the 1-tonner was offered. *GMN*

DAIRY EXPRESS (US) 1926-1930

General Ice Cream Corp, Springfield, Mass.

This company made two lines of truck, a 2-tonner with 4-cylinder Hercules OX engine, and 2½/3-tonner with 6-cylinder Hercules WXB. Chassis prices were $1600 and $2000 respectively. *GNG*

DALAT see Citroen (ii)

DANIELSON (US) 1912-1914

Danielson Engine Works, Chicago, Ill.

The single model by this name, designated Model A,

was a 1-tonner whose chassis weighed 3400 pounds. The engine was of four-cylinders and used a 3-speed gearbox and final drive by chains. The only standard body was a stake type with wheelbase of 115 inches. *GMN*

DANKS (GB) 1914-1918

Fredk, Danks, Oldbury, Worcs.

The Danks overtype wagons were constructed during the wartime period of shortage using a locomotive boiler of Danks' own design and engine and mechanical parts of Foden design. Whether these latter were second-hand or acquired by other means is not clear. It is unlikely that production reached double figures and the make was of little commercial importance. *RAW*

DARBY (US) 1910

Darby Motor Car Company, St. Louis, Missouri

This small delivery van of only 800-pound capacity had a pleasant appearance in contrast with most of its comtemporaries. Its engine was a 2-cylinder, 2-stroke connected with a planetary transmission and double chains to the rear wheels. Its wheelbase was 100 inches and it was priced at $850 for the open body. *GMN*

DARRACQ (F) 1896-1914

(1) Societe A. Darracq, Suresnes, Seine 1896-1905
(2) A. Darracq & Co., (1905) Ltd., Suresnes, Seine 1905-1914

The 1896 Darracq electric coupe with C-spring suspension and underslung, rear-mounted motor was intended for use as a cab, though there is no evidence that it was ever put into service as such. Thereafter preoccupation with light cars prevented any serious exploration of the commercial vehicle market until 1903-04, when the firm built Renard's first Road Trains. There were also some light commercial derivatives of the smaller touring models; 1905 catalogues showed a van on the 1.2-litre single-cylinder 8 hp chassis, and trucks with 12 hp 2-cylinder and 4-cylinder engines. All these featured, 3-speed gearboxes, steering-column change, shaft drive, and steel frames. These were no more than sidelines, but in 1906 the Darracq-Serpollet company was formed to build Serpollet steam trucks and buses; neither this nor an Italian subsidiary was successful. Darracq did better in the taxicab boom which started in 1907, selling 1500 such vehicles that year; the 4000th had been made by 1908 when Darracq cabs were operating in New York as well as Paris and London. The first cab chassis had 2- or 4-cylinder engines and 3-speed transaxles, and were also available with light van bodywork. Interestingly, both the rear-axle gearbox and the column change had been abandoned by 1909 (neither was appreciated by American customers), and some later cabs were made with Renault-style hoods, dashboard radiators and thermosyphon circulation.

By 1910 the fortunes of Darracq-Serpollet were failing, and the cab boom had spent itself. That year Darracq built an experimental 50 hp shaft-driven single-decker bus with round radiator, which was tested in Paris but not adopted. Nothing came, either, of a 3-ton truck with 3.6-litre 4-cylinder engine and worm drive announced in 1912, and thereafter the company's commercial-vehicle efforts were limited to a few delivery vans on the successful 16 hp 4-cylinder touring-car chassis designed by Owen Clegg. Darracq did not return to the field after the War, either, though the British W & G cab of 1922 was based on their 10CV private car with 1½-litre ohv 4-cylinder engine. *MCS*

DARRACQ SERPOLLET (F) 1906-1912

Darracq Serpollet et Cie, Paris

Darracq Serpollet was formed to market the steam omnibuses made under Serpollet's designs, by having associated operating companies. These operated buses in Paris and London (as the Metropolitan Steam Omnibus Co. Ltd.). Manufacture ceased and the company was wound up in 1912.

1907 DARRACQ-SERPOLLET steam charabanc, NMM

G & J Weir, the Glasgow engine and pump manufacturers who, earlier, had provided finance for Darracq also put up a good deal of the money for this venture, Serpollet being beset by a chronic lack of capital, but there is no evidence that they undertook manufacture. The buses were seriously underpowered for hilly routes though passable performers on congenial terrain.

Steam lorries were made on the same (or similar) chassis. *RAW*

1919 DART suburban bus, Techniart

DART; KW-DART (US) 1903-to date

(1) Dart Truck Co., Anderson, Ind. 1903-1907
(2) Dart Mfg. Co., Waterloo, Iowa 1907-1914
(3) Dart Motor Truck Co., Waterloo, Iowa 1914-1918
(4) Dart Truck & Tractor Corp, Waterloo, Iowa 1918-1924
(5) Hawkeye-Dart Truck Co., Waterloo, Iowa 1924-1925
(6) Dart Truck Co., Kansas City, Mo 1925-1961
(7) KW-Dart Truck Co., Kansas City, Mo 1961-1970
(8) Dart Truck Co., Kansas City, Mo 1970-to date

The first Dart trucks were highwheelers of ½ ton capacity with underfloor engines, full-elliptic springs all round and double chain drive. After the move to Waterloo they were completely redesigned, with conventional front-mounted 4-cylinder engines, though still using chain drive. Shaft drive was introduced in 1912 when three models of 100, , 2000 and 3000 lbs were listed. The 2-tonner Model CC was made from 1914 to 1917, 325 of these being used by the US Army. These were conventional worm drive trucks powered by 4-cylinder Buda engines, as were the lighter models of 750 and 1500 lbs. Several models in the under 3-ton range were continued through the 1920s, the company passing in 1924 into the hands of an oil company executive, A.H. Howard, who reorganized it as the Hawkeye-Dart company. After his death in 1925 stock and service parts were bought by Max W. Cline, a Dart salesman, and moved to Kansas City where production continued. During the 1930s a range of 1½ to 5-tonners was made, expanding to 10 ton rigid and articulated 6-wheelers in 1938.

1936 DART 8-ton articulated van, NAHC

1948 DART Model G truck, FLP

A new field was entered in 1937 when Dart built their first heavy-duty trucks for the mining industry, and this field was eventually to replace over-the-highway trucks altogether. In 1939 Dart built a diesel-electric 6x4 tractor which pulled two 40 ton coal trailers and during World War II production was concentrated on 10 ton 6x4 trucks and 40 ton 6x6 tractors for tank transporters. The latter had 6-cylinder 250 hp Waukesha engines. In 1947 Dart was purchased by the George Ohrstrom Co. of New York and in 1950 was acquired by the Carlisle Corp. of Carlisle, Pennsylvania. The most recent change of ownership came in 1958 when it was acquired by Pacific Car & Foundry of Renton, Washington who already owned Kenworth and Peterbilt. They changed the name of the company and products to KW-Dart, but these reverted to Dart in 1970.

1942 DART T13 6×6 tank transporter, BHV

1947 DART Model 50 tractor, FLP

Production of highway trucks was resumed after the war, in the medium to heavy duty tractor category for loads of up to 20 tons, but these were abandoned in the early 1950s in favor of off-highway dump trucks. These have been built in ever increasing sizes, reaching 70 tons by 1958 and 100 tons by 1962. By 1965 the range extended from a small 15 ton rear dump to a huge 120 ton bottom dump tractor/trailer combination. In 1970 there were three lines of Dart trucks; 65, 75 and 110 ton 2-axle mechanical drive, 120 and 150-ton 2-axle electric drive, and 100 and 120-ton mechanical drive articulated 3-axle bottom dumpers. These used Caterpillar, Cummins and Detroit Diesel V-12 and V-16 engines from 635 to 1600 hp.

1965 KW-DART Model D2550 65-ton dump truck, DART

Transmissions on the mechanical drive models were Allison or Twin-Disc manual-electric powershift types with five forward speeds, while the diesel-electrics used two General Electric motorized wheel units flange mounted to the tubular wheel housing, with planetary gear reduction. These were all catalogued models, but Dart were prepared to build even larger trucks to special order. One such vehicle was a 120 ton tractor teamed with three 140 ton trailers, giving a total capacity of 420 tons, a record for any truck in the world. Two of these monsters were built in 1969 for hauling salt from solar evaporation ponds in Baja California to the processing plant. Another order was from Kuwait for a tractor capable of relocating completely assembled and standing oil well derricks from one site to another. Dart developed what has been described as "The world's largest dune buggy" which does the work of 14 conventional 25 ton trucks.

Other Dart products of the 1960s and 1970s included twin-steer 6-wheel aircraft refueling trucks, front-end loaders, log stackers and snowplows. In April 1973 Dart management decided to discontinue production of dump trucks and coal haulers, but later resumed with a range of rear- and bottom-dump trucks with capacities up to 150 tons, powered by Detroit, Caterpillar and Cummins engines up to 1050 hp. *RW*

DASSE (B) 1900-1928

S.A. Gerard Dasse, Verviers

Dasse was a rather popular commercial vehicle make in the Eastern part of Belgium for some 30 years. Gerard Dasse started as an automobile constructor in 1894, building a small threewheeler. Two years later the first four-wheeled car was introduced, being the beginning of a well-accepted range of cars. Based on these were in 1900 the first light commercial vehicles. Till 1920 cars and small commercial vehicles would both be built;, afterwards, however, the car production was dropped in favor of commercial vehicles. One of the last Dasse types produced was an excellent high-speed vehicle, both available as a bus or a truck chassis, and fitted with a Lycoming eight-in-line four litre engine. An interesting feature of the vehicle was a special reduction box, mounted amidships and giving, when selected, an excellent speed for traveling in hilly regions like the Ardennes. In 1928 Dasse was finally wound up. *JFJK*

1928 DAT Model 61 2-ton trucks, BHV

DAT (J) 1924-1932

(1) Kwaishinsha Motor Car Co. Ltd., Tokyo 1924-1925
(2) Dat Motor Car Co. Ltd., Tokyo 1925-1926
(3) Dat Automobile Manufacturing Co. Ltd., Osaka 1926-1932

Kwaishinsha were one of Japan's pioneer automobile manufacturers, building a car as early as 1912. Production of the Dat (named after Den, Aoyama and Takeuchi, the firm's three partners) began in 1915, but there was apparently no serious truck manufacture before 1924, when a Masujiro Hashimoto design was introduced. In 1926 Dat merged with the Jitsuyo Jidosha Seizo of Osaka, as a result of which J.J.S's Lila light car was dropped and production concentrated on Dat trucks, mainly for the Army. These vehicles were on orthodox American lines with normal control and pneumatic tires; among the types offered were 15-cwt and 2-ton machines. Deliveries were on a modest scale — reportedly some 60 units in 1930. 1931 saw the first Datson (later Datsun) light cars, and a year later the Dat concern's activities were split up, with Datsun manufacture transferred to Yokohama. On the truck side, the Ishikawajima and Dat operations were merged under the Isuzu name. *MCS*

1947 DATSUN 600kg pick-up, Datsun

DATSUN (J) 1933 to date.

(1) Jidosha Seizo Co. Ltd., Yokohama 1933-1934
(2) Nissan Motors Ltd., Yokohama 1934 to date

Originally known as the Datson (i.e. Son of Dat), the Datsun light car assumed its present name a year later. It was powered by a 495 cc 4-cylinder sv engine developing 10 hp, there were three forward speeds, and the vehicle, its semi-elliptic rear springs and worm drive apart, bore a marked resemblance to the Austin Seven. 5-cwt vans and pickups were a regular part of the range, and bigger

1954 DATSUN 600kg pick-up, Datsun

1956 DATSUN double cab pick-up, Datsun

1974 DATSUN 620U-1300 pick-up, Datsun

1978 DATSUN C20 ½-ton van, Datsun

commercial vehicles followed with the formation of the Nissan company in 1934, though these latter were always marketed under the Nissan name, leaving the Datsun label for private-car derivatives. 1935 Datsuns had 722 cc, 15 hp engines, and the model continued with little major change until 1952, when capacity and output rose respectively to 860 cc and 20 hp. Other improvements included hydraulic brakes, and the addition of a new deluxe line styled in the fashion of the American Crosley; both the old and the new idioms were found in the commercial line. Crew cab pickups (a model still offered by Datsun in 1978) made their appearance in 1954, and 1955 models had 26 hp engines and 4-speed gearboxes, but a drastic redesign occurred in 1959. The new PG222U pickup featured a 1.2-litre 48 hp ohv engine (a 982 cc unit was available), column shift and ifs, and a variety of models catered for payloads from 5-cwt to 1 ton. Thereafter development of Datsun commercials ran parallel with the private-car line, with 1.3-litre, 67 hp power units and all-synchromesh gearboxes on the 1966 types. The millionth pickup was made in 1969.

The 1978 range embraced 1.2-litre and 1½-litre pushrod types with 4-speed gearboxes and drum brakes, an unusual variant being the double-seater, which resembled a coupe but incorporated a short bed capable of carrying 900 lbs. Delivery van versions of the Cherry and Violet sedans were available in some export markets, and there was also a forward control half-tonner, the 1.2-litre C20, on similar lines to the E20 sold under the Nissan label. *MCS*

DAVEY PAXMAN (GB) 1904-c.1912

Davey Paxman & Co. Ltd., Colchester, Essex

Paxman's essayed a steam tractor to comply with the 5-ton weight restriction introduced in 1904 in both single cylindered and compound types but building engines for road use was a very small part of their total business and few tractors were produced.

In addition to the tractors the firm also produced a compound spring mounted road locomotive designed by William Fletcher but on its joining the A.G.E. combine in 1919 its role was limited to the building of stationary and portable engines and road locomotive work was dropped. Works records are destroyed and no precise total of production survives but it is safe to say it was under a hundred of all types. *RAW*

DAVID (i) (E) 1914-1922; 1942-1945; 1950-1956

(1) Fabrica Nacional de Autocyclos David, Barcelona
(2) David Autos Fabricacion, S.A., Barcelona

The David cyclecar with its transverse spring independent front suspension and belt final drive was the best-known of the Spanish cyclecars, and was also made in taxicab and delivery van form. Engines were British J.A.P. or Blumfield V-twins, French Ballot 4-cylinder and Swiss M.A.G. V-twin.

The second phase of vehicle construction by David came after the Spanish Civil War when battery electric taxicabs and vans were made, using Citroen and Berliet chassis. Few of these were made. The final revival of David came in 1950 with the introduction of a 3-wheeler powered by a 345cc single-cylinder 2-stroke engine driving the single front wheel. Touring and delivery models were made. There was also a 5-wheeled version with the same engine and twin rear axles. *JCG*

DAVID (ii) (I) 1957 to date

Costruzioni Mecchaniche Casalini, Piacenza.

This motorcycle factory also built ultra-light delivery 3-wheelers for 150 kg payloads. These had 3-speed gearboxes and coil rear springing. The 48cc F.B.-Minarelli engine could be mounted either under the cab or at the rear. *MCS*

DAY or, DAY UTILITY (US) 1910-1913

Day Automobile Company, Detroit, Michigan

The 4-cylinder Model D had an open express body with a price of $1500. This vehicle with a capacity of 1500 pounds used a three-speed gearbox and shaft drive with wheelbase of 115 inches. This was convertible to an all-passenger motorcar. *GMN*

1922 DAY-ELDER 1½-ton truck, NMM

DAY-ELDER (US) 1919-1937

(1) National Motors Mfg. Co., Irvington, N.J.
(2) Day-Elder Truck Co., Irvington, N.J.
(3) Day-Elder Motor Truck Co., Irvington, N.J.

As good an example of the assembled truck as one could find, the Day-Elder started out with great expectations. They had national distribution in the early 1920s, and some penetration of the Canadian market too. However sales lagged badly after 1928, and the firm increasingly became a local make until the end in 1937.

Day-Elder's range in the early 1920s consisted of six models from 1 to 5 tons, powered by Continental or Buda 4-cylinder engines, with Corvette, Muncie or Brown-Lipe transmissions and Timken, Sheldon or Columbia axles. From 1925 on Day-Elder standardized on worm drive, so much so that a worm and gear became the firm's insignia. In that year the first 6-cylinder engines were added to the line which was extended to include a 5/6-tonner and a bus chassis. Sales were at their highest at this time. Day-Elder revised its vehicles in 1929 for the new 'Super Service Sixes' in capacities from 1- to 6-tons, all with 6-cylinder Continental engines; internal hydraulic brakes featured on the lighter models. The revised bus chassis was also sold for high-speed van service. Day-Elder used a novel rear suspension for it, a semi-elliptic spring above

1929 DAY-ELDER 2-ton truck, NAHC

the axle and a smaller or auxiliary leaf below it; the main spring carried the heavy loads, the light spring the unladen vehicle, as well as having damping properties. International used the same system on some of its largest trucks in later years. 6-wheelers using the Timken bogie were also featured in the Day-Elder range. In 1930 the trucks were redesigned again, this time in the image of Brockway who provided heavy competition in Day-Elder's by now restricted area of New York City and New Jersey. A range of 1½ to eight tonners plus a bus chassis, now Hercules powered, was made with little change until 1937. *RJ*

DEARBORN (US) 1919-1924

Dearborn Motor Truck Co., Chicago, Ill.

The original line of Dearborn trucks were 1½- and 2-tonners. These used either Continental, Buda or Hercules engines, varying from year to year. In 1923 and 1924, a 1-tonner was made with pneumatic tires and with a wheelbase of 133 inches. *GMN*

DEARNE (GB) 1927-1935

Reynolds Bros (Barnsley) Ltd., Barnsley and Doncaster, Yorks

Reynolds Brothers specialized in forward-control conversions of the Model T Ford, mainly for municipal use. The 1927 model, with solid rear tires, was the first to carry the name Dearne (from a local valley), and in 1928 they introduced a new lowloader with solid tires all round on 22 inch wheels. It was powered by a 4-cylinder 3-litre engine developing 40 hp, and had a 7 cu. yd. tipping refuse body. Load capacity of the normal goods-carrying Dearne was 2½-3 tons. Two wheelbases were available, 96 inch and 126 inch. *GNG*

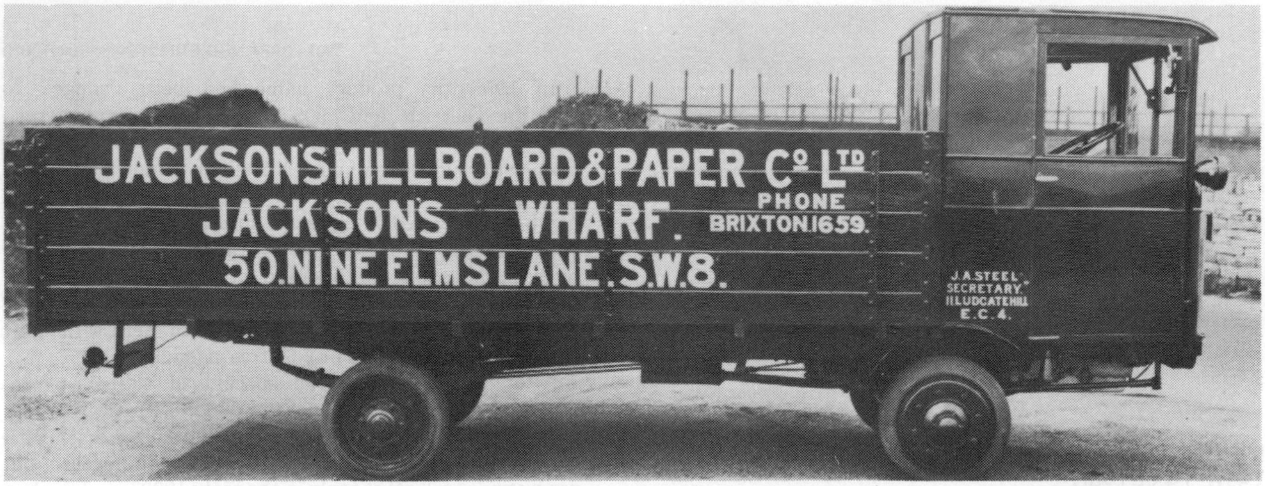

1929 DEARNE 2½-3-ton truck NMM

DECATUR (US) 1909-1915

(1) Decatur Motor Car Co., Decatur, Ind. 1909-1912
(2) Grand Rapids Motor Truck Co., Grand Rapids, Mich. 1912-1913
(3) Parcel Post Equipment Co., Grand Rapids, Mich. 1913-1915

The Decatur Hoosier Limited was a 1½-ton cab-over truck powered by a 30 hp 4-cylinder Rutenber engine, with a 3-speed transmission and dual chain drive. Solid or pneumatic tires were offered, and 25 standard bodies were listed. In 1913 a change of company name marked a complete change of product, for the Decatur Parcel Wagon was an unconventional delivery vehicle in which the driver sat at the rear of the load-carrying area, over the rear axle. It was powered by an air-cooled V-twin or water-cooled 4-cylinder engine, and final drive was by single chain. A central control lever when pulled towards the seat actuated the single external-contracting metal brake band inside the differential housing, and the same lever, when pushed forward and then sharply back, started the engine. Load capacity was 600 lbs and the vehicle was mainly aimed at the Post Office. For 1915 capacity was increased to 800 lbs and a 14 hp 4-cylinder engine standardized. *RW*

DECAUVILLE (F) 1901-1908

Societe Decauville, Corbeil, Seine-et-Oise

The first Decauville commercial vehicles were light vans on the 8 hp and 10 hp 2-cylinder chassis with aiv engines and shaft drive. By 1905 similar body-work was advertised on the 12/16 with 2.7-litre 4-cylinder T-head engine and 3-speed gearbox, this model being available as a cab in 1908. There were also some bigger 4-cylinder chain-driven models in the 1904-1906 period, the trucks being of driver-over engine type and the omnibuses having normal control. 19 of the former type were delivered in 1904.

In addition to the gasoline-engined vehicles the firm built a steam truck which appeared in catalogues as late as 1905. Equipped with an undertype engine with countershaft differential and double chain drive, the truck had a flash type boiler and roof-mounted gilled-tube condenser, but little was heard or seen of it. Some chassis, for omnibus use, were marketed under the Petit-Bourg name. *MCS/RAW*

1902 DE DIETRICH 8-passenger bus, NMM

DE DIETRICH: (i)LORRAINE—DIETRICH: (F) 1897-1916: 1934-1940

(1) De Dietrich et Cie, Luneville, Lorraine 1897-1905
(2) Societe Lorraine des Anciens Etablissements de Dietrich et Cie, Luneville, Lorraine: Argenteuil, Seine-et-Oise 1905-1916
(3) Societe des Moteurs et Automobiles Lorraine, Argenteuil, Seine-et-Oise. 1934-1940

This company's first automobile product was an Amedee Bollee design, featuring a front-mounted horizontal-twin engine with aiv and tube ignition, a huge fire-screen-type radiator, and a complex transmission with three or four forward speeds involving a primary belt and two sets of bevels. It worked surprisingly well in practice and was applied to commercial vehicles as well as cars. A 3-ton truck was entered for the 1897 Heavy Vehicle Trials at Versailles, attaining a top speed of 9½ mph and a fuel consumption of 5½ mpg. Both truck and bus versions were built, and machines were sold to Corsica and the French Sudan, as well as being tried by the army as a load carrier and a heavy field ambulance. A 2-ton cab-over-engine model announced in 1902 featured conventional side-chain drive, but in the meantime de Dietrich had acquired the rights to Turcat — Mery designs, and in 1903 they marketed an orthodox normal control machine with armored wood frame, 4-speed gearbox and side-chain drive, available with 4-cylinder aiv engines of 4.4 or 5.4 litres capacity. In 1905 they progressed to a double-decker bus, remarkable for its pneumatic front tires, and a year later they tried to commercialize the curious 6x2 vehicle already tested by Turcat-Mery in Marseilles. This one featured chain drive to the center pair of wheels, those at front and rear being the steerers. Powered by a 40 hp 4-cylinder engine, it was built as a private car, omnibus and truck, and was still in evidence as late as 1908, alongside a range of normal control trucks and buses with 4-cylinder engines, 4-speed gearboxes, and chain drive.

1907 LORRAINE-DIETRICH 6-wheel truck, BHV

In 1905 the product name had been changed to Lorraine-Dietrich, and 1909 saw a range of commercial models for payloads from 15-cwt to 5 tons, all but the smallest chain-driven fours. A 5½-litre engine was used in the biggest trucks, but the CGP double-decker bus (a fleet of which were used to transport spectators to an from that year's Rheims Aviation Meeting) ran to 8.8 litres. A driver over engine layout was adopted for the 3-ton C3T of 1911, though normal control models were still offered, and in the early War years the company made 1-tonners with shaft drive and engines of 2.1 or 2.6 litres' capacity.

After the Armistice the success of the Barbarou-designed 6-cylinder 15CV car (marketed as plain Lorraine from 1928 onwards) and an increasing preoccupation with aeroengines kept the firm out of truck manufacture, but car business fell off sharply in the early 1930s, and the last 20CV luxury machines were sold in 1934. In their place came a new line of commercial vehicles made under Tatra license and featuring that company's all-independent springing and backbone frames. These included a light 6x4 with 2-litre air-cooled flat-4 engine and the big 8-ton T24/58, powered by a water-cooled inline six of 11.2 litres. In the immediate post-World War II years Lorraine retained their automobile interests as concessionaires for the Nash car, but concentrated their manufacturing efforts on railroad rolling stock. There were, however some road-rail type yard shunters made as late as 1950. *MCS*

DE DIETRICH (ii) (D) 1897-1902

De Dietrich et Cie, Niederbronn, Alsace.

De Dietrich's German branch built cars and commercial vehicles to Amedee Bolle's design. These used 3-litre 2-cylinder engines rated at 10 hp, and were identical to their French counterparts. With the appointment of Ettore Bugatti as designer in 1902, all truck production ceased. *MCS*

1899 DE DION BOUTON steam bus, RAW

DE DION-BOUTON (F) 1884-1950

(1) De Dion, Bouton & Trepardoux, Paris 1884-1894
(2) De Dion, Bouton & Cie, Paris 1894-1897
(3) De Dion, Bouton & Cie, Puteaux, Seine 1897-1931
(4) Societe Nouvelle des Automobiles de Dion-Bouton,uton, Puteaux, Seine 1931-1950

Count Albert de Dion, Georges Bouton, and the latter's brother-in-law Trepardoux went into partnership in 1883 and were testing a small steam truck the following year. Steam vehicles would engage their principal attention during the ensuing decade. A brake was built in 1892, and in 1894 de Dion entered what was almost certainly the world's first articulated motor vehicle in the Paris-Rouen Trials. This consisted of a tractor with a semi-trailer devised by replacing the front axle of a horse carriage with a turntable plate; it put up the fastest performance, but was disqualified because it required a crew of two to drive it. De Dion steamers were vertical boilered undertypes with countershaft differentials and double roller chain drive. The engine was of compound type with slide valves and Stephenson gear, and was widely imitated by other makers. The boiler consisted of an inner firebox, surrounded by a water and steam jacket through which short horizontal fire tubes passed to an outer smoke jacket. De Dion boilers were used by other firms, and were copied in modified form by such builders as Robertson and St. Pancras. In 1897 the company built an articulated bus

1902 DE DION BOUTON 4½hp van, GNG

21 feet long; with its 35 hp tractive unit it weighed 9¾ tons. In the same year de Chasseloup-Laubat's steam brake won the Marseilles-Nice-La Turbie race, and in 1898 de Dions were used on France's first scheduled bus service, from Conde to Vire; this was suspended in 1901 because the iron tires caused too much road damage. Buses were also operated in Australia, Bolivia, Italy, Spain (where 50 were sold), and the U.S.A., later models having pneumatic tires and a speed of 25 mph. The steamers, however, proved an unprofitable venture, and production was phased out during 1903, some of the last ones being water carts supplied to the Paris Municipality in 1904. These paved the way for a long line of municipal vehicles offered by de Dion up to 1939.

Georges Bouton's increasing increasing interest in the internal combustion engine had already aroused the hostility of Trepardoux, who resigned in 1894, and 1895 saw the first of a long series of single-cylinder high-speed gasoline motors capable of 2000rpm. By 1896 these were being fitted to the company's motor tricycles, and a tradesman's trailer was a regular accessory by 1899. New that year was the de Dion voiturette with 2-speed expanding-clutch transmission, rear-mounted engine, and final drive by the de Dion axle invented by Trepardoux. The layout lent itself to commercial work, and the 3½ hp type with 402 cc power unit was available as a 5-cwt van in 1900, a more powerful 4½ hp version appearing in 1901. This latter formed the basis of one of the first publicity vans, with bodywork in the shape of a beer mug, and the brewer's label doubling as a curved windshield. 1903 saw the first postal vans, and though the original rear-engine types persisted for a while in 6 hp and 8 hp forms, they were joined that year by the first of the front-engined variants. Private cars had hoods, but the vans featured underseat engines. Bigger types included 1-, 2- and 3-ton trucks with 2-cylinder engines, three foward speeds, and solid tires, as well as an omnibus on the heaviest 15 hp chassis. 4-cylinder engines were first offered in 1904, and the selection available in 1905 included anything from a 10-cwt van on the 8 hp car chassis to the big 24/30 hp 4-cylinder AT, with separate cylinders, aiv, a 3-speed gearbox and the inevitable de Dion axle. This was intended for omnibus work, double-deckers using the cab-over-engine configuration, with normal control for the smaller single-deckers. Among the many operators to favor the make were LGOC and Vanguard in London and New York's

Fifth Avenue Bus Co; de Dions were also used in Vienna. Honeycomb radiators were first seen in the truck range in 1906, and a year later 4-cylinder de Dions acquired mechanically operated L-head sv, other features being 5-bearing crankshafts and pressure lubrication. At the top of the goods vehicle range was a 5-tonner with 30 hp 4-cylinder engine, while 1908 saw the mandatory taxicab models — a 942cc single and a 1.2-litre twin with conventional gearboxes and vertical gate change. Two unusual machines of the period were an 18 hp fire engine with chain drive and some chain driven motor sleighs for Charcot's Antartic Expedition; these had air-cooled single-cylinder engines and the old expanding-clutch transmission. By 1910 such features as round radiators and hub-reduction drive were to be found on heavier de Dions, which included some single-decker buses with 5.9-litre engines and twin rear wheels for service in Paris. A 7.4-litre 6x2 version was tried in 1911, the drive being taken to the center pair of wheels while those at front and

1914 DE DION BOUTON DA Paris bus

rear steered. Some further machines of this type were built in 1922. Typical of the company's medium truck design in 1913 was the DT, a cab-over-engine 3-tonner with round radiator, 4.4-litre engine, triple-plate clutch, three forward speeds, vertical gate change, and, surprisingly, worm drive; a parallel version with de Dion axle was however listed. Other models catered for payloads from 10-cwt to 2½ tons, though after 1913 the traditional single-cylinder engines of delivery vans gave way to the new long-stroke (56 x 120 mm) EF-type four. The V8 car chassis, new for 1910, was also adapted to commercial use; most of these went to the fighting services as aircraft tenders and searchlight trucks, albeit a special horsebox chassis was offered in 1914.

After the Armistice car-type light vans were once again catalogued, usually with 1.8-litre sv engines; in 1926 there was also a commercial version of the 1.3-litre JP. The bigger 1919 de Dions were the 3½-ton 4.4-litre FR and the 5-ton, 5.8-litre FS with round radiators and solid tires, which found great favor in France and elsewhere as street sweepers and washers. 1921 saw some more modern types with monobloc engines, car-type rounded-vee radiators, double reduction drive, and pneumatic tires, made as 2-

1924 DE DION BOUTON electric bus, NMM

1925 DE DION BOUTON JH 1½-ton van, NMM

1927 DE DION BOUTON JG2 20-seater bus, FLP

ton trucks with 3.6-litre power units, and in 5.7-litre coach form. By 1923 the 3½-tonner had been updated with pneumatics and the new radiator, and new for 1925 was the JE, a low-frame coach chassis with 4-litre, 65 hp ohv engine. 4-speed unit gearbox, and uncoupled fwb. The biggest 6-tonners now featured vacuum servo brakes on all wheels, even if pneumatic tires and electrics were still optional extras. These, the JP light van, the KB 1-tonner the JE and the municipal range formed the 1927 de Dion program; in addition the company was also making autorails and experimenting with gazogenes. de Dion had also shown an intermittent interest in battery-electrics since 1901, these being quoted as late as 1912. In 1926 a 40-seater single-decker bus with 10/12 hp motors of Italian make was operating in Lyons.

After 1919 de Dion never recovered their former commanding position in the industry, and the factory was forced to close down for most of 1927. The private cars had died a lingering death by 1932, but attempts were made to keep the truck business going, with the LC, an improved version of the JE, in 1929, and the standardization of ohv engines on the 1930 line, most of which had coupled servo brakes. Despite a reorganization in 1931, however, production remained modest. The biggest 1930 model had been a 5-tonner, but 1936 saw a 6½-ton truck, the LY, de Dion's first ever six of any type with a capacity of 6.6-litres. Some extremely elegant coaches were built on this chassis, and there was also a companion 4-cylinder 4-tonner with 4.4-litre engine. These and the municipals persisted until the outbreak of the War; though a Deutz-type diesel was briefly announced in 1937, gasoline power units remained standard. The 1939 range included gazogenes, as well as 6-cylinder models with forward control and 8-speed gearboxes.

There was a brief revival in 1947, when the company exhibited a low-slung coach with 40-seater bodywork by Million-Guiet. The Roots-blown 100 hp 6-cylinder opposed-piston engine, of Junkers type, was mounted longitudinally at the rear, the 8-speed gearbox incorporated both synchro-mesh and overdrive, and final drive was by overhead worm. It never saw series production. A portion of the old Puteaux factory remained open as late as 1957, servicing such de Dions as had survived, but by 1973 the once proud factory was Rover's Paris depot. *RAW/MCS*

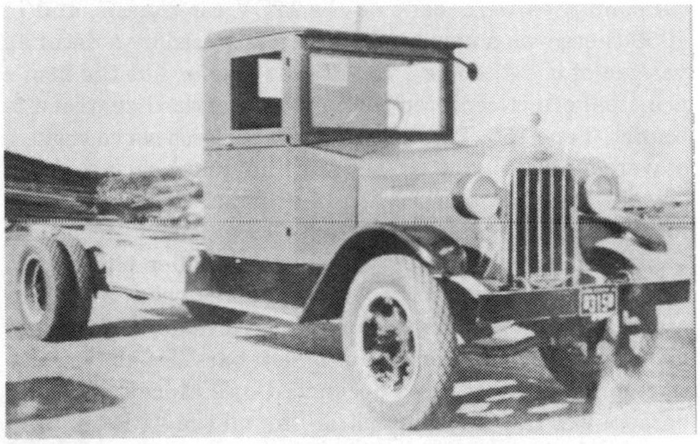

c.1930 DEFIANCE 2½-ton chassis, HD

DEFIANCE (US) 1917-1930

(1) Turnbull Motor Truck & Wagon Co., Defiance, Ohio
(2) Defiance Motor Truck Co., Defiance, Ohio
(3) Century Motor Truck Co., Defiance, Ohio

The Defiance was a conventional medium-sized truck made in one to 3 ton sizes and powered at various times by Continental, Wisconsin and Hercules engines as well as one engine of its own make in the 1927 1½ tonner. There was a short-lived, Continental-powered bus chassis in 1923, but more famous were the fire engine chassis which Howe used for their Defender series. Defiance had a Canadian assembly plant at Digby, Nova Scotia from the mid-1920s to 1930. *GNG*

DE KALB (US) 1914-1918

DeKalb Wagon Works, DeKalb, Illinois

Capacities for the DeKalb trucks ranged from 3000 pounds to 7000 pounds. These were powered by 4-cylinder Continental engines. Prior to 1916, all drives were by chains but worm drive was an option in that year, and in later years only worm-drive was used. It was only in 1917 that the engines were moved forward to reside under the hood. *GMN*

1914 DELAHAYE Type 46 2½-ton truck, BHV

DELAHAYE (F) 1898-1956

(1) Emile Delahaye, Tours 1898
(2) L. Desmarais et Morane, Tours: Paris 1899-1906
(3) Automobiles Delahaye, Paris 1906-1954
(4) Societe Hotchkiss-Delahaye, St. Denis, Seine 1954-1956

The first Delahaye car was made as early as 1894, 19th century offerings being on Benz lines with 2-cylinder horizontal engines at the rear of tubular frames, and belt drive. Commercial bodywork is first mentioned in 1898, in which year Charles Weiffenbach joined Delahaye as Chief Engineer, a post he would occupy for more than half a century. A 9½ hp bus competed in the tourist category of the 1899 Paris-Ostend race, and belt drive persisted on commercials long after it was dropped from the private cars. It was found on a 2-cylinder truck entered for the 1905 French trials. In the meantime, however, power units, while still of horizontal type, had been moved to the front of the frame; 1902 productions included a delivery van on the 1,100 cc single-cylinder OA chassis, and a variety of 2.2-litre twins, among them a tower wagon for Paris's tramways and a postal van for Guadeloupe. The first chain-driven truck was the 2-cylinder Type 15 of 1903, and by 1904 light omnibus coachwork was being mounted on the 24 hp 4-cylinder chassis.

Unlike most of France's bigger car makers of this period, Delahaye took commercial vehicles seriously, with a wide range available by 1906. The bigger ones had 4-cylinder engines, side-chain drive, and the driver over engine layout, these being supplied to the French army. Other important customers included the postal authorities, who had a fleet of 170 Delahayes by 1911, some of them car-type 2-litres and others bigger normal control vans with 3-litre engines, chain drive and solid tires. Inevitably the firm tried their hand at cabs: a modest shaft-driven twin with magneto ignition and 3-speed gearbox found its way to New York, and was succeeded in 1909 by a 9/11 hp monobloc four with double-reduction back axle. A more lasting venture was the manufacture of

1926 DELAHAYE Type 83 2-ton horse box, OMM

fire engines, which began in 1907. Their chain-driven machines had 8-litre 4-cylinder engines developing 72 hp, and Farcot centrifugal pumps; 18 were ordered by the City of Paris, the first of a long line that continued up to World War II. Larger ones used truck chassis, with private-car models serving as the basis of the lighter first-aid types capable of 55-60 mph. A limousine appliance was in service in Paris as early as 1931, and a 6-cylinder half-track engine of Kegresse type was tested in 1935. The 1914 range covered everything from car-type delivery vans up to 5-tonners. Bigger ones were chain-driven, the driver-over-engine configuration being retained for a subsidy-type 3-tonner with 2.8-litre 4-cylinder power unit. Just before the War came the famous 4/5-ton 59, a normal control machine with 5-litre 4-cylinder sv monobloc engine and twin rear wheels; it was made to military as well as civilian account and lasted in 1925, still with solid tires and open cab. A few 59s were even brought out of retirement to serve their country again in 1939.

Weiffenbach's subsequent preoccupation with consortia had little effect on commercial vehicle design. His first 1919 project came to nothing, but in 1927 he teamed up with Chenard-Walcker (Donnet and Unic were also briefly involved). Such rationalization as there was was largely confined to car-type lightweights in the 8/15-cwt class, and even this ceased soon after the divorce of the Delahaye and Chenard interests in 1932. The 1920 commercial range included 15-cwt and 2-ton models with 4-cylinder sv engines, 4-speed gearboxes, full electrics, bevel drive and pneumatic tires, with chains and solids retained on heavier trucks. Though Delahaye had exhibited a double-decker bus as early as 1906, they did not plunge seriously into the PSV market until 1923, and the introduction of the 83-59. This one had fwb, pneumatic tires, a Type 59 engine, and, unusually on a French commercial vehicle, worm drive. In 1926 the 59 itself gave way to the similarly rated and powered 95 with shaft drive, though solid tires were retained. 1928 saw a bid for the trans-African stakes when three modified Type 104 *camionnettes* were successfully driven from Algiers to Chad, and in 1930 came the firm's first 6-cylinder commercial, a first aid fire engine based on the 114 private car.

Delahaye's first diesel was a 7-tonner introduced in 1931. It had six forward speeds and bevel drive, the 10-litre 6-cylinder direct injection engine being made under license from Fiat. A 6-wheeler development had the unusual combination of cable operated front brakes with air actuation for those at the rear. Also in 1931 came a 6-cylinder coach, the Type 111 with 6-litre sv engine, while a year later Delahaye introduced a medium-duty truck in the modern idiom. Under the bonnet of this orthodox 3-4-tonner was a 3.2-litre coil-ignition pushrod six rated at a modest 45 hp, but this unit was to evolve into the famous 135 sports-car type; by 1937 some 160 hp were being extracted from it.

Though 95s were still available in 1934, ohv were standardized on Delahaye's gasoline engines two years later, units fitted to vehicles in the 1-4 ton category being detuned versions of private-car types, a 2.1-litre four and sixes of 3.2 and 3.5 litres' capacity. Coaches with 5-speed gearboxes shared some of the elegance of the contemporary cars; engines were Delahaye's own 6-litre gasoline unit or 4- and 6-cylinder Gardner diesels. The 131 of 1937 had its engine mounted beside the driver, thus permitting the use of aerodynamic full-fronted bodies. 1939's truck models ranged from the 4-cylinder 140 for 1500kg

1950 DELAHAYE Type 163 4/5-ton truck, GNG

payloads up to the the big Gardner-powered 149 with air brakes. Other types included a diesel 103 with 77 hp 6-cylinder engine, and a version of the 6-cylinder 2½/3-ton 140-103 with Gohin-Poulenc gas producer.

During the War Delahaye joined yet another consortium, the GFA group, along with Bernard, Laffly, Simca and Unic, but neither their cars nor their trucks were destined to recover their strong 1939 position. A few camionnettes were made on the 12CV car chassis, and in 1950 there was a new luxury coach powered by a detuned version of the 4½-litre Type 175 car engine, but the firm's principal effort centered round a new forward control 4/5-tonner, Type 163. This was a low loader with servo brakes, powered once again by the faithful four-bearing six; a diesel version had a 5.7-litre 4-cylinder engine and five forward speeds instead of four. 1951 saw a Jeep-type vehicle, the 4 x 4 VLR. Its 2-litre 4-cylinder ohv engine had dry-sump lubrication, other features being a 4-speed main gearbox with synchromesh, hydraulic brakes, and all-independent springing by torsion bars. Delahaye's car sales had, however, been decimated by France's crippling horsepower tax, and the military found the VLR too complex, replacing it by Hotchkiss's license-produced version of the Willys Jeep. In 1954 Delahaye allied themselves with Hotchkiss, both firms abandoning private cars without further ado. Two years later a reorganization spelt the end of the Delahaye truck line. *MCS*

DELAHUNTY (US) 1913-1915

Delahunty Dyeing Machine Co., Pitton, Pa.

The 1915 Delahunty was a 1½-ton truck powered by a 30 hp 4-cylinder Buda engine. It had a cone clutch, 3-speed transmission, and final drive by dual chains. The chassis cost $1800. *DJS*

DELAUGERE (F) 1901-1926

SA des Etablissements Delaugere, Clayette, Freres et Cie, Orleans, Loiret.

Delaugere cars never enjoyed much more than a regional reputation. Their trucks, however, were better known. Initially the commercial vehicle range was limited to omnibus, truck or delivery van bodies on standard chassis, which in 1902 consisted of conventional aiv twins and fours of up to 20 hp with armored wood frames, 3- or 4-speed gearboxes, and side-chain drive, but in the 1905 Industrial Vehicle Trials the company fielded a 3-ton truck in the fashionable driver-over-engine idiom. Its 3.3-litre 4-cylinder engine had overhead inlet valves and coil ignition, and chain drive was retained. Delaugere also offered a 12/16 hp 1-tonner with, surprisingly, pneumatic tires, but though both overtypes and pneumatic-tired light vans were still made as late as 1909, they had settled down to what was to be their staple: a straightforward normal-control model with 4-speed gearbox, solid tires and side-chain drive. Pre-War models covered the 2/5-ton bracket, with 4-cylinder engines of 4.4 or 6.8 litres, and pneumatics still available for PSV chassis. After the War they concentrated on the 4.4-litre 4-tonner, which was tested in gazogene form in 1922 and persisted until the end in 1926. From 1922 there was a car-based 1-tonner on pneumatics, and their 1.7-litre 8/10 hp car of 1923 could be had with *camionnette normande* bodywork. After production of their own designs ceased, Delaugere-Clayette turned to the manufacture of car and commercial bodies for Panhard. *MCS*

1915 DELAUNAY-BELLEVILLE Type C 3½-ton truck, BHV

DELAUNAY-BELLEVILLE (F) 1912-1949

SA des Autos Delaunay-Belleville, St. Denis, Seine.

Though some examples of this famous round-radiatored luxury car were fitted with ambulance bodywork as early as 1908, there was little serious truck manufacture before World War I. In addition to a light truck on the 4-cylinder 12CV private car chassis, some bigger Model-Cs in the 3½/5-ton category were made for the army during the War; they had 4.4-litre 4-cylinder sv engines, 4-speed gearboxes and shaft drive. After the Armistice a more ambitious program was pursued, with additional models in the shape of a 3.8-litre 3-tonner, a big chain-driven 6-tonner, and even a 2-ton battery electric chassis. Delaunay-Belleville explored 4-wheel drive, on a 4-ton truck and on a heavy tractor with twin front wheels, 4 x 2 speeds, and internal-expanding fwb. Its 70 hp 7.9-litre engine was offset to the right, and it could haul 25 tons in addition to carrying another two-and-a-half. Also offered in the early 1920s was the Ara agricultural tractor, but little was heard of Delaunay-Belleville's commercials after 1922, and by 1928 only a car-based 1-tonner was listed. Thereafter their trucks were hardly ever seen, though right up to 1939 a variety of types for payloads from one to four tons were catalogued, as well as coaches for 14/25 passengers. The light DB4U was a direct derivative of their 2.3-litre 4-cylinder sv private car, some heavier types using the 3.6-litre ohv car engine. 4- and 6-cylinder models survived on paper as late as 1949. Interestingly, many of the big luxury Delaunays of the 1907-25 period ended their days as vans and even fire engines. In 1914 the firm's London concessionaires were making a specialty of such conversions, which were listed in 30-cwt and 2-ton forms. *MCS*

1932 DELAUNAY-BELLEVILLE Type CR2 3-ton truck, RJ

DELCAR (US) 1947-1949

American Motors Inc., Troy, N.Y.

This was a light cab-over-engine delivery van with an ultra-short wheelbase of only 60 in. It had a small front-mounted 4-cylinder engine and, unusually, independent suspension all round. The price was $890. *GNG*

DELFIN (E) 1954-1960

Fabrica Espanola de Motocicletas y Tricyclos Delfin, Barcelona

This company made small 3-wheeled goods carriers powered by 197 cc Hispano-Villiers engines. There was a 2-seater enclosed cabin, unlike a number of vehicles of this kind. *JCG*

DELIN (B) 1901

Usines Delin, Louvan

Chiefly known as makers of passenger cars, Delin listed a light van on their 2¾ hp chain driven chassis. It had two forward speeds and a capacity of 5 cwt. *GNG*

DELLING (U.S.) 1930

Supersteam Service Co., Trenton, N.J.

After the Brooks Steam Motors venture folded, Erik Delling, who had been chief engineer of the Canadian Brooks company and who had previously been with Stanley, moved to Trenton as chief engineer at Mercer Auto Co. When that enterprise fell victim to the depression, Delling attracted a few New York investors in the possibilities of steam-powered buses, and they formed Supersteam Service Co. to buy the Mercer plant. As far as is known only a single prototype bus was ever built. *MBS*

DELTA (i) (GR) 1968

Vioplastic S.A., Moschaton, Athens.

Built by the same company responsible for the Attica 3 and 4 wheeled cars, the Delta was an ultra light tricycle fitted with a Sachs 50 cc engine, chain drive to the rear axle and a primitive two seat fibreglass cab with single headlight and no door-windows at all, but with full car-type controls. *GA*

DELTA (ii) (PI) 1975 to date

Delta Motors, Makati, Rizal.

The Delta is a light utility vehicle with a purpose built body and Toyota mechanics, produced by the Toyota distributors in the Philippines. *GA*

DEMM (I) 1954-c.1962

Officine Meccaniche Daldo e Matteucci, Milan.

Made by a motorcycle factory, the Demm was a typical *motocarro* with two shaft-driven rear wheels. It used the company's own 172 cc single-cylinder 2-stroke engine and a 4-speed gearbox. *MCS*

DE MOTTE (U.S.) 1904

De Motte Motor Car Co., Valley Forge, Pa.

In addition to a line of automobiles, De Motte listed a 10 hp 2-cylinder delivery wagon and a 20 hp 4-cylinder truck. The 20 hp truck, built on the touring car chassis, had the driver's seat mounted above the engine in a rather precarious position. *DJS*

DENBY (US) 1914-1930

(1) Denby Motor Truck Co., Detroit, Mich. 1914-1923.

(2) Denby Motor Truck Corp., Detroit, Mich. 1923-1930

The Denby was a thoroughly conventional assembled truck whose best years of production were around 1920. The plant was apparently always too large, and most of it was sold off to a radiator manufacturer in the late 1920s. Most Denbys were in the ¾-ton to 3-ton ranges, though a 7-tonner was listed from 1918 to 1922, and a 30-passenger bus chassis was made from 1926 to 1930. Engines were mostly Continentals, though Hercules were used in 1½ and 2½-ton models from 1924 onwards. Many Denbys had disc wheels. *RJ*

DENMO (US) 1916-1917

Denneen Motor Co., Cleveland, Ohio.

Announced late in 1916, the Denmo was a conventional 1¼-ton truck powered by a 4-cylinder Wisconsin engine, with 3-speed transmission and Torbensen internal gear drive. Tires were pneumatic on the front wheels, and solids at the rear. *RW*

1977 DENNING 6-wheel coach, Denning

DENNING (AUS) 1967 to date

(1) A.B. Denning Pty. Ltd., Brisbane, Queensland 1967 to date.

(2) A.B. Denning Pty. Ltd., Beverley, South Australia 1970-1974

Starting in 1958 as coachbuilders, Denning progressed to actual vehicle manufacture via rebuilds of heavy truck chassis which were re-engined with Cummins, Detroit and Scania diesels and fitted with straight-deck coach bodies. The first Denning Monocoach appeared in 1967. It was of integral type with the stainless-steel panelled body of raised-deck configuration welded to a flat-top frame, at the rear of which was mounted a 2-stroke V6 Detroit Diesel engine. Gearboxes could be either 5-speed Fuller manual or Allison automatic. Dennings have always been

1915 DENBY 1½-ton truck, NAHC

constructed on a bespoke basis, and among variations tried have been horizontal engines and (since they became a Leyland subsidiary in 1968) 6- and 8-cylinder power units of that make. Regular design features are pressurized cooling, power steering and full air brakes: leaf suspension is standard, though air bags are used on the third, non-driving axle of the 6-wheelers. The first of these was made in 1969, but regular production of the variant began when local regulations permitted 40-foot PSVs after 1971. The South Australian branch opened in 1970: initially it built bodies for A.E.C. Swifts and undertook conversion of older buses to conform with out-of State laws, but a few Monocoaches were made at Beverley before the plant closed down in August, 1974, and all production was concentrated on Brisbane. Some 200 Monocoaches had been made by 1974: they are widely used on such long-distance services as those of Greyhound and of the New South Wales Public Transport Authority on their Rail Replacement schemes. 1978's standard types were a 36-foot four-wheeler and the big 6-wheeler. Engines were 6- and 8-cylinder Detroit Diesels, and equipment included air conditioning, refrigeration, galleys, toilets, and reclining, aircraft-type seats. *MCS*

1907 DENNIS 2-ton mail van, NMM

DENNIS (GB) 1904 to date

(1) Dennis Bros. Ltd., Guildford, Surrey 1904-1973
(2) Dennis Motors Ltd., Guildford, Surrey 1973-1976
(3) Hestair-Dennis Ltd., Guildford, Surrey 1977 to date

Dennis Bros. began experiments with motorized tricycles in the late 1890's and moved on to larger cars and then to commercial vehicles in 1904 when a 15-cwt was built for Harrods Ltd. the well-known London store, followed by a motor bus. These were the first commercial vehicles to be fitted with shaft driven worm back axles, standardized by Dennis until the early 1930's and a popular feature with bus operators on account of their silence. Another feature to appeal to bus operators were inswept chassis to give extra steering lock and easy accesibility to the gearbox, which could be dismantled from underneath. Heavier goods vehicles followed and in 1908 the first Dennis turbine pump fire engine appeared. Most early Dennis commercial vehicles had featured engines made by White and Poppe Ltd., of Coventry and from 1909 this make was standardized, leading to Dennis purchasing the company in 1919 and eventually transferring production to Guildford. Dennis employed some 400 men by 1909 and had produced the considerable total of 2000 commercial vehicles by 1912. In 1913 Dennis became a public company and decided to concentrate on commercial vehicles. They built an A-type 3½-ton model to War Office

1914 DENNIS 34-seater bus, NMM

Subsidy specification and during the Great War some 7000 of these were supplied, a small number of which were equipped with gasoline electric drive to the design of W.A. Stevens and called Dennis-Stevens. These were used for searchlight and mobile workshop duties and after the war remained in production for sometime as easy-to-drive bus chassis.

After the War, Dennis continued the Subsidy model in various guises until 1926, but produced a new 2½-tonner in 1919 and a 25cwt vehicle in 1923 which grew into their highly successful and competitively priced 30cwt chassis of 1925 (known as the G in drop frame passenger form).

For 1923 the 2½-tonner had been briefly named Dennis-Portland in honor of a new sales office in London's Portland Street. Dennis chassis were popular with London bus operators, resulting in their supplying the first pneumatic tired bus approved by the Metropolitan Police for operation in London in 1924, the first 4-wheel braked bus, in 1926 and one of the first pneumatic tired double deckers in 1928.

1925 DENNIS E-type bus, NMM

In addition to fire engines, Dennis made a wide selection of other municipal vehicles from the early 1920's including refuse collectors, gully emptiers and street sprinklers. In 1925 Dennis had produced the advanced 33-seat E bus and coach chassis with 4-wheel servo (made under Rolls-Royce license) brakes, a drop frame and 5702cc 4-cylinder L-head engine producing 70 hp. This engine was also used in a new heavy goods range announced in 1926, for 4- and 5/6-ton loads. A smaller version of the same engine was used in a new 2½-tonner and all featured more modern styling with a tapered hood and rounded radiator.

In 1927 the E was joined by a double deck H version which in 1930 was superseded by the Lance. This used Dennis' first 6-cylinder engine, which had been announced in 1929 for the Arrow 32-seat passenger chassis. It was a

6126 cc overhead cam unit of 37.2 hp rating and had a very ingenious rocker assembly which could be rotated round the axis of the camshaft to allow the cylinder head to be removed without upsetting the valve timing. A smaller o.h.v. 60 hp six was used in a small high speed Dart 20 seater, while a third variation was a 7982 cc six based on the side valve 4-cylinder engine used in the E and large goods models. It was used for a time in a 10/12-ton six wheeler and in the largest fire engines. With the elderly but cheap 33-seat E model still in production alongside the far more expensive 6-cylindered Arrow, Dennis decided to replace the E with an even cheaper Lancet model. This was announced in 1931 and was an immediate success with around 1200 built by 1937. It used the 4-cylinder engine from the E but now speeded up

1933 DENNIS 1½-ton van, OMM

with turbulent combustion chamber in which form it produced 85 instead of 70 hp. This engine was also used in a 3½-ton goods version of the Lancet. Though Dennis were working on a diesel engine in 1931 it was not a success, and a revised version did not reach series production until 1936. In the meantime Dorman and Gardner diesels were available in the goods chassis, whilst Dennis obtained the sole rights to use Armstrong-Saurer diesels in their passenger chassis.

In 1933 all the lighter goods and passenger models were replaced by the 40/50 cwt range and Ace respectively. These shared the same 3.77 litre 4-cylinder engine, had spiral bevel back axles for the first time, and were unusual in having set-back front axles for engine accessibility and small turning circle. They could be purchased in normal, or forward control form, when the whole cab was in front of the steering axle. The Ace could seat 20, or 26 as the Mace, while the goods versions soon covered the 2-4-ton payload range and enabled 3½-tons to be carried in a van weighing less than 2½ tons unladen which qualified for 30 miles per hour operation. The chassis was unable to carry four tons under the concession so a new normal control Light 4-tonner was introduced with conventional axle position and this was also available as the Arrow Minor 26-seat passenger chassis from 1936. It was joined in 1937 by a smaller conventional model, the Ajax, for 2- to 3-tons, and later by a passenger variant, the Pike. In 1938 all these light passenger vehicles were replaced by the Falcon which was available with 20 to 32 seats and either used an updated 75 hp version of the old 3.77 litre gasoline engine or a choice of Gardner 4LK or Perkins P6 diesels. With the growing threat of War, fire engine and trailer pump production was drastically stepped up.

A Lancet II had been introduced in 1935 and was, with Maudslay, one of the first single deck chassis to be able to seat 40 passengers within the 27 ft., 6 in. legal length limit, while, the slightly neglected heavy goods vehicle

1936 DENNIS 4-ton truck, OMM

market was joined by the Max in 1937. This was a four wheeler built to take maximum advantage of the 12 tons gross vehicle weight permitted on two axles and used Dennis' by now well-proved 04 diesel engine.

The final peacetime models were the Max Major able to carry 10½ tons, because of the addition of a second steering front axle, and the 5-tonner. This model could carry between 5 and 6 tons and yet still weighed under 2½ tons for 30 mph operation. It used the 3.77 litre engine and reappeared after the 1939-45 War as the aptly named Pax. During the War Dennis made fire appliances, military versions of the Max with simplified cabs, and fighting vehicle components as well as some prototype 6 x 6 and 8 x 8 off-road vehicles.

1937 DENNIS 2/2¼-ton truck, Dennis

1939 DENNIS Lancet bus, Dennis

After the War the Pax was joined in 1946 by a new 6 x 4 6-wheeler called the Jubilant, which used a 7.6 litre 6-cylinder diesel (replaced by an 8 litre unit in 1956) based on the pre-war 4-cylinder unit and producing 100 hp. Also introduced in 1946 was an articulated version of the Pax known as the Horla, for 12 ton gross weight, Brass gave way to chrome on the fire engines with F prefixed model numbers and Rolls-Royce gasoline power, and by 1955 diesel engines became available.

The Lancet became the Mark III in 1948 and Mark IV for overseas use in 1949. A new goods model, the Centaur

1948 DENNIS Pax 5/6-ton truck, OMM

appeared in 1948 to fill the gap between the Max and the Pax. It was powered by a new 5.07 (later 5½ litre) 6-cylinder Dennis oil engine.

1950 saw the arrival of an underfloor version of the Dennis 7.58 litre 6-cylinder diesel, installed in the Dominant passenger chassis, which in 1953 gave way to the underfloor engined Lancet.

Another underfloor engined chassis was the 3.14 litre Perkins-powered Stork goods chassis while the same engine was also used in the AV1 ambulance chassis, with deDion rear axle and Greigoire variable rate suspension introduced in 1954, and also available with 4-cylinder Rolls-Royce gasoline engine. Municipal versions of the Pax were known as Paxits and in addition to the Horla, Pax, Lancet, Stork (now with Perkins P6 engine) and Jubilant the range of 1957 included the Hefty in place of the Max, the Perkins engined Teal 40 seater/ and its goods companion model, the Loline double decker built under license from Bristol Commercial Vehicles Ltd., the Heron, which shared the Perkins engine of the previous/Stork model the Pelican 5.5 litre underfloor engined 40 to 44 seater and the Condor, a seven tonner with the Dennis 5.5 litre engine, which had succeeded the short-lived Centaur. In 1958 two new vans were introduced, one with the Dennis gasoline engine and primarily designed for high speed newspaper deliveries in London, while the other was the Paravan, an easy-access 600 cu. ft. van. This had a Perkins P4 engine mounted behind the driver and access

1956 DENNIS Paxit refuse collector, OMM

through a door initially placed across the front lefthand corner of the vehicle. Another ingenious special purpose vehicle of the period was the Aeroloader with scissor-action hydraulically raised platform for airport use.

Gardner and AEC engines were offered in some of the heavier models, and other outside components began to be used, notably BMC 5.1 litre engines and gearboxes in the Pax. From 1959 fiberglass played an important part in cab construction.

1960 DENNIS Paravan 3-ton van, OMM

Since 1955 fire engines had been available with automatic transmission and in 1962 disc brakes were available as an option. A year earlier the Delta fire chassis with low line cab was announced and this was available with Snorkel hydraulic equipment from 1963. In 1960 an advanced low-loading 30 cwt van known as the Vendor was announced with Standard 2.26 litre diesel or 2.19 litre gasoline engine and front wheel drive. Though this was not a sales success it gave Dennis front wheel drive experience which they applied to a remarkable ambulance in 1968. This had a Jaguar XK engine and Borg Warner automatic transmission, as well as independent suspension and very low rear loading weight. Only three were made. For sometime low-load Pax chassis had been popular with the distributive trade, notably breweries, and in 1964 a small three-axle Pax was introduced to give greater carrying capacity.

In 1964 Dennis acquired the Mercury Truck and Tractor Co. Ltd. (which they later sold to Reliance), makers of airfield and industrial tugs, and in the same year introduced the Maxim 16-32-ton goods vehicle range to take advantage of raised weight limits in the U.K. They

1959 DENNIS Loline 1 56-seater bus, MAS

were powered by Cummins or Perkins V8 diesels developing 178 hp and 170 hp respectively, but proved to be heavy and difficult to sell. After years of profitability the company declared a loss of £90,000 in 1965 and following internal difficulties was acquired by the Hestair Group in 1972, who also own Yorkshire Vehicles Ltd., and who soon sold the Mercury division.

For a time Dennis concentrated on a lightweight DB 15.5 model which permitted more payload than most 16

1966 DENNIS Stork 4-ton van, GNG

1968 DENNIS Pax V 15-ton GVW truck, Dennis

1977 DENNIS Dominator double decker bus, Dennis

tons gvw vehicles but at ½ ton less gross vehicle weight, giving savings in fuel and road tax. This model was also available with a trailing and self steering second front axle or as a 24-ton gross articulated tractor called the Defiant. However all lapsed with increased competition and the decision of Dennis' new owners to concentrate on fire appliances and municipal vehicles. These include conventional D, F and the new R (introduced 1976 for 8.5 and 11 ton gvw) series fire engines, and special escape tenders with Jaguar, Perkins or Rolls-Royce engines, as well as fire crash tenders on 4 x 4 Dennis, 6 x 6 Reynolds Boughton and 6 x 6 Thornycroft chassis. Municipal vehicles include all sorts of street washers, sweepers, cesspool emptiers and refuse compressors. For congested areas an especially narrow Alleycat chassis is produced. Since 1973 vehicles of Dennis design have been made in Cyprus under the name K.M.C.

After a lapse of some twenty years passenger vehicles have been developed since 1975. These include the front-engined Jubilant export chassis and the rear, transverse Gardner, Rolls-Royce Eagle or Perkins VF-640 engined Dominator. Both these models entered production in 1977 and a coach chassis is now in the design stage. A range of 16 ton GVW 2-axle trucks is planned for introduction in 1979. *OM*

1977 DENNISON 6×4 tipper truck, Dennison

DENNISON (IRL) 1977 to date

Dennison Truck Manufacturing Ltd. Rathcoole, Dublin, Eire.

Launched in June 1977, Dennisons are assembled four, six and eight wheelers using such components as Rolls-Royce and Gardner diesels, Eaton axles, Fuller gearboxes and Motor Panels cabs. An output of 250 per year is anticipated by George Dennison, who orginally founded Dennison Trailers and later sold this company to Crane-Fruehauf. *OM*

DENNISTON (US) 1911-1912

E.E. Denniston Company, Buffalo, New York,

A closed delivery van was the only model by this manufacturer. Rated at 1500 pounds capacity, it used a 15 hp, 2-cylinder engine with forward control. Power was transmitted through a 3-speed transmission and shaft drive. It had pneumatic tires and wheelbase of 98 inches and was priced at $2,000. *GMN*

DENONVILLE (B) 1937-1940

Societe Belge des Automobiles Denonille, Brussels-

Denonville manufactured during their existence some 80 tailor-made trucks,of which one is still in service today on a Belgian shipbuilding wharf. Three types were available to choose from: a medium-weight truck with a payload of five tons, a heavy truck of eight tons payload and an articulated tractor for 10 tons payload. The diesel engines mounted in these were viz. a Commins AA600 of 100 hp at 2200 rpm, a Cummins HB600 of 150 hp at 1800 rpm and a Cummins HB400 giving 100 hp at 1800 rpm. Most further components were also of foreign manufacture, only the chassis frame being produced in Belgium by the Fonderies & Laminoirs de Manage. The axles were by Timken, the gear box by Brown-Lipe, the

1938 DENONVILE 5-ton truck, JFFK

clutch by Lipe Rollway, steering by Ross and the vacuum assited hydraulic brakes by Dewandre. Denonville still exists today, though the name has been changed to Cummins Distributor Belgium, and their main occupation is now sales and service of Cummins diesel engines. *JFJK*

DEPENDABLE (US) 1918-1923

Dependable Truck & Tractor Co., Galesburg, Ill

In 1921 this line of trucks included 1-, 1½-, 2½- and 3½-tonners, all with Buda engines, Wisconsin worm-drive rear axles and Fuller 3-speed gearboxes. During the last two years on the market, only the 1½- and 2½-tonners were made. *GMN*

DERBI (E) 1952-1962

Nacional Motor, SA, Barcelona

This concern began as a modest bicycle repair shop in Mollet del Valles, then turned to the manufacture of bicycles, following this with auxiliary-motored cycles and then proper motorcycles. In 1952 a delivery tricycle was introduced, using the rear portion of a motorcycle with a box van ahead of the rider. This had a payload of 300 kgs. Another version of the Derbi had a single front wheel and shaft drive to the rear axle; this had a payload of 500 kgs. *JCG*

DERBY (F) 1922-1927: 1932-1934

Automobiles Derby, Courbevoie, Seine.

The Derby was a typical French cyclecar-voiturette of semi-sporting type with no differential in the rear axle, and 4-cylinder Chapuis-Dornier engine. Initially 900 cc sv units were fitted, growing up progressively to 1100 cc with ohv by 1924; four wheel brakes were available in 1925. The first commercial variant was a traveler's car with box back, but the 1924 range included a *camionnette normande* and a delivery van, these variations surviving until 1927, when the company elected to concentrate on private cars. Production was always modest, no more than 260 Derbys of all types being made up to 1924. In 1932 came the sensational Lepicard-designed forward control fwd 1-tonner, with pull-out engine and transverse-leaf ifs. Prototypes used the 1½-litre ohv 4ED Meadows engine as fitted to some contemporary Derby cars, though it was intended to supplement this with a French-built engine. Very few 1-ton Derbys were, however, made; one of these served its makers as a racing-car transporter at Montlhery. *MCS*

DERLAN (E) 1953-1960

Talleres Basor, Zarauz, Guipuzcoa

The Derlan was a delivery tricycle built in the summer resort of Zarauz. It was a conventional motorcycle-based machine, powered by a 125 cc engine, with a capacity of 300 kgs. *JCG*

DE SCHAUM (US) 1908-1909

De Schaum Motor Syndicates Co., Buffalo, N.Y.

For $650 to $750 you could have one of De Schaum's "Seven Little Buffalos" (the alternate trade name) with a delivery body on an 84-inch wheelbase. They had a 2-cylinder 12-hp motor, air or water-cooled, driving through a friction transmission and double chain final drive. Springs were semi-elliptic front and full elliptic rear. The capacity of this high-wheeler was 800 pounds and the tread was 54 inches. *RW*

DESMARAIS (F) 1906-1907

Desmarais Freres, Paris

This company exhibited a 2-ton forward-control truck with chain drive at the 1906 Paris Salon. *GNG*

DE SOTO (US) 1937-1960

Chrysler Corporation, Detroit, Mich.

Like all (ii) Fargos made since 1933, the De Soto was a simple exercise in badge-engineering intended to give foreign Chrysler Corporation dealers without a Dodge franchise a line of trucks to sell. Initialy catalogued in certain European countries from the 1938 model year, and in Australia after World War II, the vehicles were identical in all respects with the standard Dodge models offered locally: Australian De Soto catalogues, for instance, included some (ii) Dodge types emanating from the Kew factory. Chrysler dropped the De Soto private car line at the end of 1960, and the trucks died with them. There was, however, one curious survival; certain locally-assembled models still carry the name in Turkey. (See Dodge (V). *MCS*

1911 DETROIT ELECTRIC ½-ton van, NAHC

DETROIT ELECTRIC (US) 1909-1927

(1) Anderson Carriage Co., Detroit, Mich 1909-1910

(2) Anderson Electric Car Co., Detroit, Mich. 1911-1918

(3) Detroit Electric Car Co., Detroit, Mich. 1919-1927

Longest-lived of American electric cars, the Detroit first appeared in 1907. Three years later annual sales had passed the 1000 mark, and the range included a 1-ton forward control truck with single Elwell-Parker electric motor and side-chain drive. The latter feature, though not always found on cars, was to be standard equipment on the commercials, which included a wheel-steered ½-tonner as well as a 1½-ton model by 1912. The 1916 2-ton van cost $2000 without batteries, but thereafter little was heard of the trucks, though the cars soldiered on into the late 1930s. In 1922, however the company tested a milk delivery van with four alternative driving positions; at the front, at the rear, and on either running-board. Three years later the Detroit Industrial Vehicle Co. was founded to develop a gasoline engined version, but though other electric manufacturers, notably Ward, persevered with the multi-stop theme, the market was lost to the ubiquitous Divco. *MCS*

DETROIT MOTOR WAGON see Motor Wagon

1936 DEULIWAG light diesel tractor, HON

DEULIWAG (D) 1936-1951

(1) Deutsche Lieferwagen-Gesellschaft mbH., Berlin 1936-1939
(2) Deuliwag Traktoren-und Maschinen GmbH., Hamburg 1949-1951

A mini-tractor was presented by this firm in 1936 using single or 2-cylinder double-piston diesel engines which were mounted in the rear. Another version with front mounted engine was presented one year later using Junkers or Guldner diesel engines. After WW II a new attempt was made with a rear engined mini-tractor using a 3-cylinder MWM diesel engine. *HON*

DEUTZ (D) 1926-1936

(1) Motorenfabrik Deutz A.G., Cologne 1926-1930
(2) Humboldt-Deutz Motoren A.G., Cologne 1930-1936

The Motorenfabrik Deutz have an important place in the history of motoring. They produced the first gas engines invented and designed by Nicolaus August Otto. Deutz engines were used by many manufacturers as proprietary units. Deutz themselves started construction of own vehicles with agricultural machines. The first road tractor appeared in 1926, with a 14 hp single cylinder diesel engine. This was replaced in 1927 by a 2-cylinder engine and this design was produced until 1936 without major changes. Production of agricultural tractors is still undertaken.

In 1938 Deutz acquired Magirus and so developed into a producer of a full range of commercial vehicles. Air-cooled diesel engines by Deutz are still used today by many manufacturers for a wide range of vehicles. *HON*

DE VECCHI (I) 1914-1917

De Vecchi & C, Milan

This car company built a number of trucks and ambulances on their 25/35 hp chassis with 3.6-litre 4-cylinder sv engine and 4-speed gearbox. Final drive was by shaft. *MCS*

DEVON (i) (US) 1912-1914

Devon Engineering Company, Philadelphia, Pennsylvania

Devons were large trucks of 7000, 10,000 and 12,000 pound rated capacities. The most unusual was the Model 6 (for six tons) which was on an articulated chassis with front wheel drive and front wheel brakes. The rear wheels on this model were shod with steel tires. *GMN*

DEVON (ii) (GB) 1937-1938

County Commercial Cars Ltd., Fleet, Hants.

The Devon Distributor was a 15 cwt 3-wheeled van powered by a Ford Ten engine, and was really a load-carrying version of the Ford Tug, described in the Ford (ii) entry. The single front wheel was considerably smaller than the rear ones. County Commercial Cars were responsible for the 6-wheeled Surrey and Sussex conversions to Ford trucks, and also made a small 3-wheeled fire engine to Home Office requirements. Known as the Derby, this had a Ford Eight or Ten engine to drive it, with an Austin Seven engine for the pump. It had a 200 or 350 gallon tank, 30 ft. extensible ladder and accommodation for four firemen. *GNG*

1921 DEWALD KL2 7½-ton tank carrying truck, BHV

DEWALD (F) 1914-1932

Charles Dewald, Boulogne-sur-Seine.

Unlike the cars, which were made in small numbers and hardly at all after 1914, this firm's trucks had quite a long and successful run. First seen in the 1914 Army Trials, they were orthodox normal-control machines with 4-cylinder sv engines, magneto ignition, cone clutches, four forward speeds, and side-chain drive. Capacity on all but the earliest Dewalds was 5.7 litres, and payloads from four to ten tons were quoted at various times, the biggest models being tried as light tank transporters. They were regular competitors in military truck trials, reaching the official French subsidy list. 1925 saw the introduction of special gazogene versions with modified engines and Autogaz generators. By 1930 Dewalds, though still chain-driven, had acquired hydraulic fwb; some of the last ones had 2-stroke Lilloise diesel engines as well. *MCS*

1968 DIAMOND-REO COE articulated truck, GNG

DIAMOND REO (US) 1967 to date

(1) Diamond Reo Trucks Divn, White Motor Corp., Lansing Mich. 1967-1971
(2) Diamond Reo Trucks Inc., Lansing, Mich. 1971-1975
(3) Osterlund Inc., Harrisburg, Pa. 1977 to date

Diamond T and Reo trucks were formally consolidated on a model basis on May 1, 1967, and large black letters reading Diamond Reo were placed on the sides of the hood proclaiming the fact.

Generally, the trucks continued much the same as before. Conventionals came in 4x2, 6x4 and 8x6 (tri-axle rear) configurations, with two models of White cabs, and diesel engines of up to 435 hp. Cab-overs ran from the CF59 compact for urban work which used White cab, through the Trend, now called the CF68, to the CO50 and CO78 long-distance tractors. For 1970 two new LPG engines of 190 and 230 hp were developed, specifically for propane fuel. These were the Cleanaire engines. Diamond Reo now offered the world's largest power train choices with diesels up to 475 bhp, and including a full range of Clark, Fuller and Spicer transmissions and Allison MT automatics. Rear axles were Rockwell standard. Tandems came with a wide range of spring and rubber suspensions, and spread tandems could be ordered.

During the summer of 1971 Francis L. Cappaert of Birmingham, Alabama purchased Diamond Reo from White, thus returning it to independence, a rare event in automotive history. During 1972 and 1973 Diamond Reo re-engineered its range and introduced a completely new highway cab-over called the Royale series, with a wide variety of paint scheme options which were particularly favored by the independent trucker, and made Diamond Reos the most colorful trucks on the highway. Engine options in the Royales were inline 6, V-8, and V-12, all Detroit Diesels. Conventional models were renamed Apollo, and came with a choice of 6- and 8-cylinder Cummins, Detroit Diesel or Caterpillar engines. In the Spring of 1974 came a new conventional, the C119 or Raider. This had a larger grille than any previous Diamond Reo, with a column of seven diamonds in the center, and was available with forward axle for Western use or setback axle for Eastern use. The Raider was mostly made as a 6x4 tractor, although some 6x4 and 8x6 rigids were also made. Engine options were Caterpillar, Cummins and Detroit Diesel. The last new Diamond Reo to be announced was the compact cab-forward Rogue intended for urban delivery or refuse collection work, and powered by a choice of Diamond Reo Gold Comet gasoline or Cummins, Detroit or Caterpillar diesel engines. The Rogue was offered in 4x2 or 6x4 versions.

1971 DIAMOND-REO conventional articulated truck, GNG

Production had been rising rapidly in the early 1970s, reaching a peak of 9136 trucks in 1974. However a variety of problems including an ageing plant, money still owed to White and a serious loss on government contracts led to Diamond Reo's bankruptcy in May 1975. A receiver was appointed, and the last trucks, part of the ill-fated government contract, left the plant in September. The company was then sold to a parts distributor, Consolidated International of Columbus, Ohio, who sold off 163 new trucks included in the deal, and announced that they would continue to supply spare parts for the estimated 200,000 Diamond Reo, Diamond T and Reo trucks still on the road.

c.1925 DIAMOND T articulated tanker, Texaco Archives

After several attempts at revival, production re-started in a small way at the Harrisburg plant of Osterlund Inc. So far, only one model is made, the C-116 Giant 6x4 truck. Early in 1978 production was running at four units per week. *RW*

DIAMOND T (US) 1911-1966

(1) Diamond T Motor Car Co., Chicago, Ill. 1911-1958
(2) Diamond T Motor Truck Co., Chicago, Ill. 1958-1661
(3) Diamond T Division, White Motor Co., Lansing, Mich. 1961-1966

Diamond T's origins go back to 1905 when C.A. Tilt built his first car and continued that line until 1911 when one of his car buyers wanted a truck.

Tilt readily complied, and from that day forward the company specialized in truck building.

The first Diamond T was of conventional design powered by a 4-cylinder engine with a final drive by dual chains. Artillery wheels were fitted with solid tires with duals on the rear. This truck, of about 1½ tons, was in service on the streets of Chicago until the early 1930s.

The famous trademark of a green diamond with a gold border and a "T" inside originated from a trademark used by Mr. Tilt's father who was a shoe manufacturer. The diamond stood for quality and the T for Tilt.

Branching out from a strictly local Chicago market, the company developed an organization of factory branches and dealers by 1915 and was fast gaining recognition as a national manufacturer. Heavy duty trucks assembled from supplied components now came from a new factory built to meet the rising demand and which employed new techniques in a 1000-foot progressive assembly line.

The assembly lines were used to produce some 1500 USA model B 3-5 ton "Liberty" trucks in eighteen months during World War I, quite an accomplishment for the time. Satisfied with this performance, the government gave more orders following the war.

The civilian truck models were made in 2- to 5-ton sizes with an additional 1½-ton farm special complete with crescent cab and body. A Hinkley 4-cylinder engine drove through a 3-speed selective sliding transmission to a semi-floating worm drive rear axle. Pneumatic tires were used on artillery wheels, and a front bumper and radiator guard were included. The steering was left-hand by 1921. The price range was $2220 to $5660.

In 1923 Diamond T pioneered a new enclosed "coupe" cab featuring a 3-point rubber mounting and new designing throughout. Steel spoke wheels appeared on some models.

For 1926 Diamond T's were completely re-styled and re-engineered. They had more powerful 4-cylinder Hinkley or Hercules engines, steel spoke wheels were now standard, and electric light replaced oil.

Even more and larger changes came for 1928. The new 6-cylinder 7-bearing engines drove through a multi-disc clutch and a 4-speed transmission to a spiral-bevel semi-floating rear axle. Brakes were now 4-wheel internal-expanding hydraulic. Disc wheels and double-bar bumpers were standard. Capacities were 1-12-tons, including 6-wheelers.

1930 DIAMOND T 2-ton truck, RNE

1932 DIAMOND T 6×4 1500 gallon tanker, Texaco Archives

1934 DIAMOND T rear-engined 1500 gallon tanker, Texaco Archives

These and other engineering advances were more than matched by the radical, yet tasteful styling which made Diamond T a leader. Chrome-plated metal was used on the radiator shell with its five vertical strips in front, cowl molding, headlights, parking lights, and even the step-plates on the running boards. Diamond T's styling made nearly all other trucks look obsolete. All this solid engineering and advanced styling paid off in a 60% increase in sales over 1927.

In the early 1930's Diamond T engineered a radical forward-control gasoline tanker in conjunction with the Heil Company of Milwaukee, Wis. for the Texaco Oil Company. Among other things, it had glass in both the windshield and the doors curving up into the roof.

More flashy and pioneering styling changes came for 1933. Completely new cabs with a steel roof were given slanting V-type windshields. An attractive V-type grille was flanked by skirted fenders. Fashionable door ventilators graced the sides of the hood. Steel-spoke wheels with chrome hub caps became the standard for many years to come. About this time Diamond T pioneered vari-rate springs.

1935 saw the introduction of the Super Service engine with an electric-furnace alloy block, counterbalanced crankshaft, precision bearings, and Tocco-hardened crankshaft.

For 1936 Diamond T's pioneering styling reached new heights with the cabs being re-designed again, this time with the V-windshield slanted 30 degrees. A new convex V-type stainless steel grille was flanked by one-piece high-crowned full pontoon-styled fenders with tear-drop headlights on the cat-walks. It is recorded that President C.A. Tilt was personally responsible for all Diamond T designs.

Diamond T invaded the low-priced field with pickup and panel trucks, these having chrome wheel covers adding to the flashy styling. Hercules engines, now moved forward over the front axle, furnished the power for the range of 1½- to 6½-tons.

The company furnished the small chassis and basic sheet metal for the Town Taxi of Hagerstown, Maryland.

Two high-speed diesels, Diamond T's own, were introduced in the 2-2½ ton class, and sleeper cabs were available. Body builders also did well with new streamlined designs even to the extent of designing pontoon fenders over the dual wheels and then covering them with detachable fender skirts. With all the solid engineering and sensational styling going for it, Diamond T sales soared to a record peak for 1936 with 8750 registered.

1937 DIAMOND T 900-gallon tanker, Texaco Archives

The cab design was now to last until 1951, being used even on Diamond T's 10-12 ton military truck made during World War II. A few Dart trucks also used this cab.

A face-lift came for 1938 with many more and finer chrome strips in the grille, the top rows virtually encircling the hood from door to door. Another attractive face-lift came for 1940 with fewer but heavier horizontal V-type bars (10) in the grille, which had off-set extensions on the radiator shell somewhat in the manner of the 1938 Cadillac car. This style was to last until 1951 and its influences were seen in various later models even into the mid-1960's. The largest models were now 10-ton, 6-wheel diesels.

Diamond T's first cab-over, a heavy duty model, appeared for 1937. Two other models of cab-overs were added to the range for 1940 using the conventional's cab and grille, only taller. These were really semi-cab-overs, or short conventionals.

Also for 1940, Diamond T startled the whole industry by guaranteeing its trucks for one entire year, or 100,000 miles!

From 1939 to 1941 Diamond T was sales and service agent for the Pak-Age-Car delivery van.

During World War II Diamond T produced 31,245 6x6 4-ton prime movers, 12,424 half-track scout cars, and 6554 diesel-powered 12-ton 6x4 tank tractors. The prime movers and the tank tractors used the civilian cab with major militarized styling changes elsewhere in the sheet metal, but Diamond T still came out the best looking military truck. Some, however, had an open cab with a folding windshield and folding canvas top. One in four of the latter was provided with a track mount for an anti-aircraft machine gun.

The prime movers had Hercules RXC engines of 119 net hp using 70 octane gasoline. Transmission was 5-speed with a single dry disc clutch plate and a 2-speed transfer case. The front axle was double reduction. The truck weighed 18,100 lbs. and payload was 8300 lbs. Several bodies were fitted — dump, wrecker, and cargo, some of which transported pontoon bridge equipment.

1942 DIAMOND T Model 980 former tank transporter, in use in New York in 1970, GNG

The tank hauler was used to pull a 45-ton 12-wheeled full trailer weighing 12½ tons for a loaded gross vehicle weight of 80 tons. Power was a Hercules 6-cylinder DFXE diesel of 178 net hp @ 1600 rpm speed. Transmission was 4-speed, with 3-speed auxilliary. Quite a number of these trucks are still in service in Europe and the United States.

President Tilt, after leading Diamond T for 41 years of car and truck building, retired in 1946 to become board chairman until his death in 1956.

Diamond T resumed production of the 1940-styled civilian range with fourteen models from 8000-36,000 lbs.

1947 DIAMOND T Model 806-C 8-ton truck, Texaco Archives

1960 DIAMOND T Model 430-C tilt-cab truck, GNG

gvw, ten with Hercules engines, three Continental, and one Cummins diesel (HB600). The heaviest, diesel model 910, weighed 14,000 lbs.

Like many other truck manufacturers, Diamond T reached production peaks in 1947 with 10,475 registered and the record of 10,651 in 1948. At this time Diamond T had nine buildings with a floor space of 14 acres.

The next change came for 1951 when the small models were dropped. Other conventionals got the new International cabs with the curved windshield and concave instrument panel. This cab, made by the Chicago Manufacturing Company, was also used by International, Hendrickson, Coleman, Oshkosh, FWD, Cline, and Duplex for varying periods of time; for Diamond T until about 1960.

In 1951 Diamond T won the National Design Award for an industrial product with its new heavy duty tilt-cab COE model, the first time that a motor truck had even been accorded such an honor. This was the cab-over model 723C which had the dip in the bottom of the side-window ventilator wings which was widely copied throughout the world even to the present time. This cab was better known on International trucks with their larger production and was used by both companies until about 1972. Hendrickson also used this cab.

Another heavy duty cab-over of a completely different design appeared, the 923C which was used until 1961. This one was centered over the front axle and had a nearly vertical curved, divided windshield.

The designs remained basically unchanged throughout the 1950's. Production was more or less steady, being in the 5000 to 6000 range yearly.

In 1958 the White Motor Company bought Diamond T and in 1960, having owned Reo Motors for three years, moved the Diamond T operation to the Reo plant at Lansing, Mich. The Diamond T and Reo trucks continued separately with the Diamond T acquiring the use of White's wider conventional "D" cab with the wrap-around split windshield and White's other conventional "R" cab with well-rounded roof and 1-piece curved windshield with the sharper bend in the center. Reo also used both cabs, but mostly the latter.

For 1961 a new tall line-haul tilt cab-over (replacing the 923C for 1962) was shared with Reo, but not with White. This was the 931C model (Reo DCL) with the two grilles slightly trapezoidal in shape, one above the other. The windshield was a flat V-type, but later two wrap-around sections were added at the corners.

One rare style of a flat grille, used with the "R" cab models, which were shared with Reo and White short conventionals, was one that had a diamond at the intersection of a long, thin T. Using the same cab, Diamond T made some conventionals especially for off-highway use, notably concrete mixers. These were the series P which still showed 1940-style grille influences, as well as some other series.

Diamond T's last all-new model was a lighter tilt cab-over of 24,000 lbs. gvw, introduced early in 1966. White started using it that autumn, and Reo, very briefly, in the spring of 1967. Diamond T's HF3000 (White 1200) was

1952 DIAMOND T Model 532 2400-gallon tanker, RNE

1966 DIAMOND T D Series 3000-gallon tanker, GNG

also known as "Trend", but it didn't set any trends because nobody copied it. The cab was made of Royalex plastic. This was Diamond T's only model to use a Chevrolet engine (350). A Cummins V6-140 was optional.

With 56 basic chassis, Diamond T made gasoline-powered models in a complete range from 1½-tons upward, a school bus chassis, conventionals with diesels from 150 to 335 hp, 6-wheelers in all types and sizes, 8x6 drives, plus three tilt-cab models for line-haul and city delivery work with a wide range of components including Spicer, Clark, Fuller, Rockwell, Warner, and New Process. Diamond T made some of its own engines.

Both Diamond T and Reo trucks were turned out from the same location, each with its separate division, but in 1967 White consolidated the two divisions since the ranges were similar, even to much of the sheetmetal, and the next models, introduced May 1, 1967, were known as Diamond Reo. Actual Diamond T production had ceased at the end of the 1966 season.

Production had slumped in the 1960's, hitting a low of only 1800 for 1961 just after the move from Chicago, and the lowest since 1926, but it eventually recovered to 4000 by 1966. Diamond T's 56 year lifetime total, including the World War II group, comes to 250,000 trucks. *RW*

1915 DIATTO 1-ton truck, BHV

DIATTO (I) 1906-1918

(1) Diatto-A. Clement Vetture Marca Torino, Turin 1906-1909

(2) Societa Officine Fonderie Frejus Diatto, Turin 1909-1918

This firm of railway engineers became Adolphe Clement's Italian licensees, producing cars of Clement-Bayard type. In December, 1906, it was announced that trucks, buses and delivery vans would be added to the range, but little was heard of these, though some 12/15 hp Diatto cabs with 2-litre 4-cylinder L-head monobloc engines and 3-speed gearboxes were operating in Sydney, Australia, by 1910. During World War I the company built a range of 1 to 3½-ton trucks for the army, and also for export. All had 4-cylinder engines; the 1-tonner was a 2.8-litre machine with monobloc engine and pneumatic tires. Bigger ones had solids, and the largest commercial Diattos featured side-chain drive as well. *MCS*

DICK (D) 1929-1933

Carl Dick, Frankfurt/Main-Hausen

The tri-van of this manufacturer featured one driven front wheel using an exposed D.K.W. engine and two rear wheels which developed into a version with fully enclosed engine. *HON*

DIEHL (US) 1918-1926

Diehl Motor Truck Works, Philadelphia, Pa.

The Diehl was a small-production truck made in 1- and 1½-ton sizes only. The former was made up to 1923, being powered by a Continental engine, while the 1½-tonner made from 1921 to 1926 was Herschell-Spillman powered. *GNG*

1932 DIFFERENTIAL 2½-ton truck, LA

DIFFERENTIAL (US) 1931-1936; 1960 to date

(1) The Differential Steel Car Co., Findlay, Ohio 1931-1936

(2) Differential Co., Findlay, Ohio 1960-c. 1970

(3) Difco Co., Findlay, Ohio c. 1970 to date

The Differential company began building side dumping equipment for railroad and motor trucks in 1915, and introduced 3-way dump truck bodies in the 1920s. The truck that Differential recommended for this body was the 3-ton Graham Brothers, but in 1931 they decided to build their own chassis for use with their dump bodies. This was a conventional assembled truck powered by a 85 hp 6-cylinder Lycoming engine, with a 4-speed transmission and Timken spiral bevel rear axle. Load capacity was 2½ to 4 tons. It was made until 1936, after which Differential made bodies only.

In about 1960 the company decided to make a complete truck again, this time a large, off-highway 6x4 model. It was designed to carry 30 tons of rock, sand or gravel, plus up to three additional 30-ton short-wheelbase trailers for a total payload of 120 tons and a gross weight of 170 tons. All frames and bodies were of welded construction. The power unit was a Continental AVI 1790-8A air-cooled V-12 of 825 hp driving through an Allison transmission with torque converter and Torqmatic brake; a slightly smaller Continental diesel was an optional alternative. Final drive was via a Timken-Ketroit tandem axle with single reduction differential and final reduction through planetary gears in each wheel. Internal expanding air brakes and power steering were standard. Total length of the Wagon Train was 86 feet. *RW*

1972 DINA 3000 3-ton truck, Dina

DINA (MEX) 1957 to date

(1) Diesel Nacional, Ciudad Sahagun 1957 to date
(2) Diesel Nacional, Monterrey 1975 to date

The name DINA stands for Diesel Nacional, a company owned by the Mexican government. Diesel Nacional not only builds trucks, but automobiles, buses, & tractors as well. The company recently purchased a 60 per cent interest in Motores Perkins, a manufacturer of diesel engines. This move gave DINA a virtual monoply of diesel engine manufacturing in Mexico.

DINA began manufacturing trucks in the late 1950's at a new factory in Ciudad Sahagun. The original DINA trucks used a body based on the American Diamond T truck. In addition to this model, many new models have been introduced in the past few years. Until recently, DINA has concentrated their commercial efforts in the line of heavy duty trucks and buses. In the field of buses, they control 65 per cent of the Mexican market. Their heavy duty trucks account for almost 50 per cent of the Mexican market.

In 1975 DINA entered the fast growing market for smaller pickup trucks. These new pickup trucks were introduced as 1000 and 3000 models, based on International designs. The 1000 model was a 1 ton model, and the 3000 model was capable of carrying 3 tons. These new pickups became extremely popular in a short time. Many luxury options were available to dress up the pickup line. The new DINA 1000 & 3000 series are built in the northern city of Monterrey. they converted the bankrupt Borgward car factory for the exclusive production of the 1000-3000 series. This factory had been vacant since 1971, although it was only three years old at that time. DINA also received the contract to build all of Mexico City's new buses. These buses are totally designed and built by DINA and are ultra modern by current standards. DINA also received a contract to build subway cars for Mexico City's modern "Metro". All in all, DINA has expanded rapidly and continues to take a large share of the commercial vehicle market. Being government owned, they receive favorable treatment from all sectors of business. *RLH*

DINOS (D) 1921-1926

Dinos Automobilwerke A.G., Berlin-Hohenschonhausen

Dinos followed the firm of L.U.C. There were vans based on private cars using 4-cylinder 8/35 PS engines as well as light trucks and light buses. *HON*

DISPATCH (US) 1910-1919

Dispatch Motor Car Co., Minneapolis, Minn.

Dispatch vehicles were made as passenger cars and goods carriers, both with 2- and 4-cylinder 2-cycle air-cooled engines of 16 and 32 hp. They had Renault-type hoods, friction transmission and chain final drive. Load capacities were 600 lbs and 1,100 lbs respectively. From about 1914 a 23 hp 4-cycle Wisconsin engine was used, though chain drive persisted, an unusual feature on light trucks of this size.

DIVCO; DIVCO-TWIN (US) 1926 to date

(1) Detroit Industrial Vehicle Co., Detroit, Mich. 1926-1927
(2) Divco-Detroit Corp., Detroit, Mich 1927-1934
(3) Continental-Divco Co., Detroit, Mich 1934-1935
(4) Divco-Twin Truck Co., Detroit, Mich 1936-1944
(5) Divco Corp., Detroit, Mich 1944-1956
(6) Divco Truck Divn., Divco-Wayne Corp., Detroit, Mich 1957-1967
(7) Divco Truck Co., Transairco Inc., Deleware, Ohio 1968-1972
(8) Divco Truck Co., Correct Mfg. Co., Delaware, Ohio 1972 to date

The original Divco milk truck resulted from an electric prototype built by George Bacon, chief engineer of Detroit Electric Car Co. Built in 1922 it had four driver positions, front, rear, and from the running boards on both sides, and three years later a separate company, Detroit Industrial Vehicle Co., was set up to market a gasoline-engined version. This went onto the market in 1926 as the

1928 DIVCO Model G delivery van, Canada Decalcomania Co

Divco, powered by a 4-cylinder Continental engine with Warner 4-speed transmission. The first 25 Divcos were forward-control vans with a front-hinged door through which the driver could step ahead of the axle. Control from the running boards was also possible. In 1928 came the Model G which had a short hood and was available with van or open-sided bodies. The side control was from the normal position, either sitting or standing. This model was the first Divco to have a drop frame with the walk-through aisle which has been a basic feature ever since.

In 1936 Divco acquired the truck business of the Twin Coach Co. of Kent, Ohio, who were making a similar vehicle, and the company and products were known as Divco-Twin until 1944. In 1937 the Divco was completely redesigned with a welded all-steel van body and a snub-

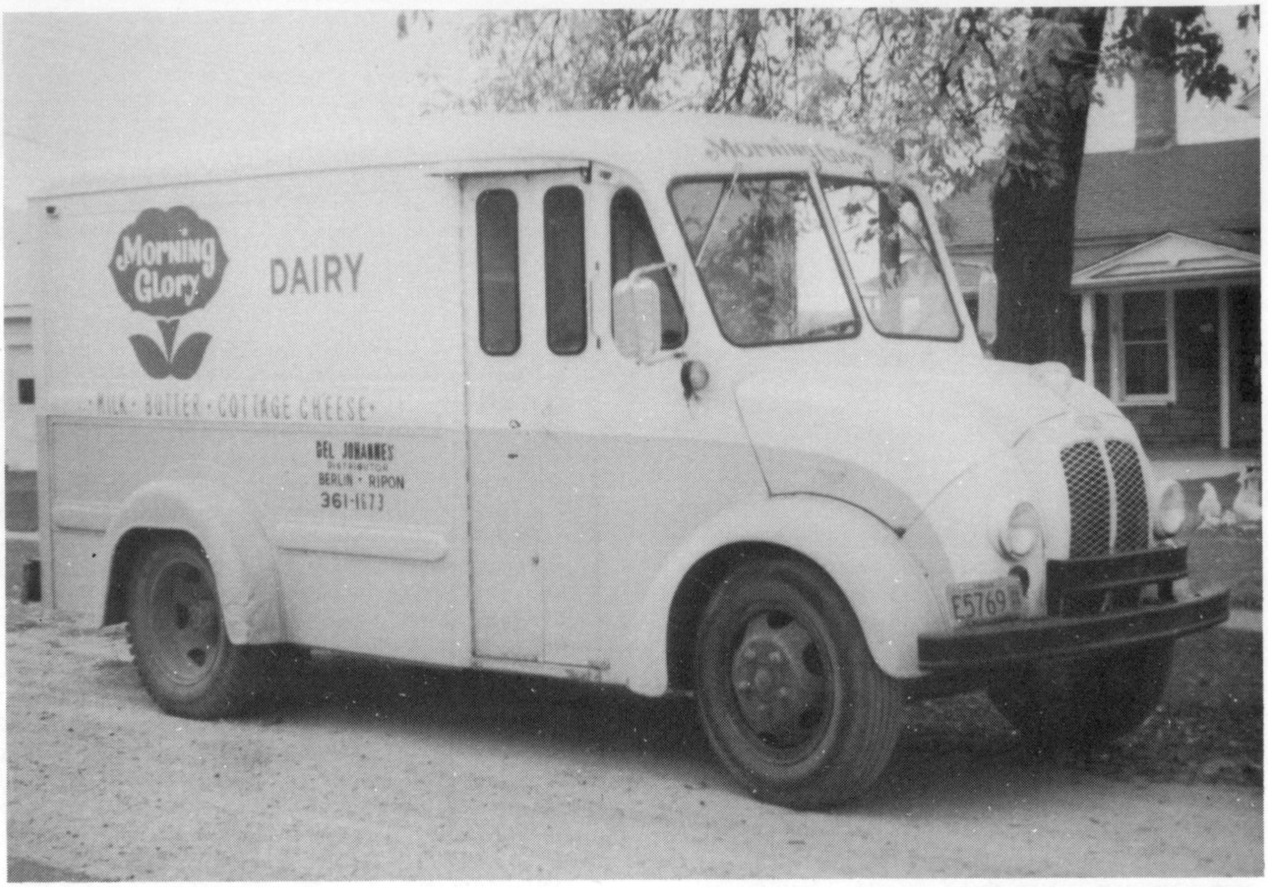

1964 DIVCO 300 Series milk van, RW

nosed hood which has been used with virtually no change up to the present day. The door were of the folding, semi-automatic type, and the power unit was still a 4-cylinder Continental. In 1940 the first insulated and refrigerated unit was built. The 1946 Divcos were basically similar to pre-war, and came in two wheelbases, the 101 inch Model UM and 127 inch Model ULM. GVWs were 9000 and 12,000 lbs. and engines were 4- and 6-cylinder Continentals. In the early postwar years production briefly reached 7000 annually, more than double the best pre-war figure. In 1954 refrigerated vans were offered as a regular production option, and the forward-control Dividend series made its debut in 1956. Continental 4- and 6-cylinder and Hercules 6-cylinder engines were standard in the 1950s, while in the 1960s 6-cylinder ohv Nash engines were used in addition, and there was also the option of a Detroit-Diesel 3-53N 3-cylinder 2-stroke diesel.

Starting in 1963 engine options were Ford F240 and F300 6-cylinder gasoline units, which eventually became standard for the Divco range. The snub-hood models were continued in two sizes and there was also the forward-control Dividend in three sizes, from 5300 to 9200 lbs. payload, made up to 1966. The largest Divco ever made appeared in 1961 — this was a 6½ ton refrigerated wholesale delivery model with Divident chassis and cab, and a separately-attached van body in 14-, 16- or 18-ft. lengths. Current models are the 300 and 200 series with 115 inch and 127½ inch wheelbases, and load capacities from 6000 to 10,000 lbs. The same Ford gasoline engines as in 1963 are available, with an optional 3-speed dual range automatic transmission. Diesels include Detroit, Caterpillar or Deutz. *RW*

1928 DIXON 6-cylinder dump truck, DJS

DIXI (D) 1904-1928

(1) Fahrzeugfabrik Eisenach, Eisenach 1904-1920
(2) Dixi-Werke A.G., Eisenach 1920-1928

Dixi offered vans which were based on the private car designs. Trucks and buses appeared with special chassis' and about 1910 Dixi offered the first heavier truck of the five ton subsidized type which was carried on during WW I. After the war Dixi continued to build trucks and buses for which 4-cylinder 6.2 litre engine was used. Only the 5 ton type had chain drive while the lighter types featured shaft drive. Vans were available based on the 6/24 PS private car and the Austin Seven type 3/15 PS. In 1928 Dixi was taken over by B.M.W. *HON*

DIXON (US) 1921-1931

Dixon Motor Truck Co., Altoona, Pa.

Throughout production, Dixons were noted for their hill-climbing ability. Early Dixon trucks had Continental 4-cylinder engines and worm drive. Later trucks had Hercules 4-cylinder or Lycoming 6-cylinder engines. The 6-cylinder models, introduced in 1927, were fitted with bevel gear drive and pneumatic tires. The Dixon though little known elsewhere, was quite popular in central Pennsylvania. Production totaled 970 trucks, of which at least one survives today. *DJS*

D.J.B. (GB) 1975 to date

D.J.B. Engineering Ltd., Peterlee, County Durham

The D.J.B. is an articulated dump truck made in 25- and 30-ton capacities, using Caterpillar engines and transmissions. It is a 6-wheeler, with articulation behind the front axle and cab. Front and middle axles are driven. *GNG*

D.K. (DK) 1950

Bohnstedt Petersen A/S, Copenhagen

The D.K. was a passenger car or light van powered either by a 600 cc 2-cylinder 2-stroke D.K.W. engine or by a 750 cc 4-cylinder 2-stroke JLO engine. Both drove the front wheels, and speeds were three in the D.K.W.-engined model and four in the larger car. *GNG*

1936 DMX 26-passenger coach, MBS

DMX (US) 1936-1940

Dittmar Manufacturing Co., Harvey, Illinois

Paul O. Dittmar started South Suburban Motor Coach Co. to operate between a Chicago rapid transit terminal and outlying suburbs in 1927, and in 1931 he and others formed SafeWay Lines, Inc. for the purpose of establishing a deluxe nonstop bus service between Chicago and New York. For this venture he teamed with Harry A. Fitz-John to design the so-called Autocoach, a compact 14-passenger sedan-style parlor bus which was built by Reo. SafeWay Lines was soon sold and turned away from the small Autocoaches, but in 1935 Dittmar again designed a bus of his own, this time for the suburban company, now expanded and known as South Suburban SafeWay Lines. The DMX had an aluminum-alloy cab-over-engine body and a Hercules engine, and during the years of its production several different models were offered with seating capacities from 25 to 33. About 150 were built, 33 of them delivered to South Suburban SafeWay itself. *MBS*

DOANE (US) 1916-c.1948

(1) Doane Motor Truck Co., San Francisco, Calif. 1916-1946
(2) Graham-Doane Truck Co., Oakland, Calif. 1946-1948

The Doane was a low-bed truck especially intended for

1916 DOANE 6-ton low-bed truck, John Montville Collection

dockside and warehouse work. The first model of 1916 was powered by a 36 hp 4-cylinder Waukesha engine with double chain drive to a cranked axle dropped for low frame height. It was rated at six tons capacity, but Doanes were overloaded more than most trucks of their era, and loads of up to 20 tons were frequently carried. It was joined in 1918 by a 2½-tonner with 29 hp Waukesha engine, and the range was widened still further in 1920 with a three tonner. In 1924 came a rigid 6-wheeler of 10¾ tons capacity, with Doane's own transmission giving seven forward speeds and three reverse, and a maximum speed of 25 mph. It had chain drive to the leading rear axle only and, like all Doanes up to the mid-1930s, solid tires all round. At least one of the 6-wheelers was used, with a 4-wheeled trailer, by the Mohawk Oil Company of California for delivery of gasoline from refinery to consumer. Total capacity was 4900 gallons. Most Doanes were sold on the West Coast, although sales were also recorded in New York City and Philadelphia in the late 1920s. 6-cylinder engines, still Waukeshas, were introduced in 1928, and in 1933 the company was listing Lo Bed and Hi Bed models as well as 10-ton 6-wheeled dump truck chassis. In the late 1930s three models were listed, 4/6 tons, 6/9 tons and 10/-

1939 DOANE 6/7-ton low-bed track, NAHC

12 tons, all with 6-cylinder Waukesha engines, 4-speed Brown-Lipe transmissions, Timken front axles and Doane's own double reduction rear axles. Chevrolet cabs were used. Floor height varied from 22½ to 24 inches. By this time Doane were also making semi-trailers and offering their low-bed converter frames for use with other makes of truck. Furniture removal, plate glass and horse conveyance were among the more popular uses for Doane trucks.

In 1946 the company name was changed to Graham-Doane, and a forward-control low-bed truck with 6-cylinder Continental engine, Clark 5-speed transmission and Doane rear axle was made in limited numbers. Probably because of the limited mileage covered by many of them,

Doanes were very long-lived, and at least ten trucks of 1916 vintage were reported to be still at work on the West Coast in 1953. *RJ/GNG*

DOBLE (US) 1918-1921

Doble Laboratory, San Francisco, Calif.

Doble is accorded much fame for its steam-driven passenger cars but it is not generally known that this company also built steam trucks. The first model was a 2-tonner with two side-by-side cylinders, both with 5-inch bore and 4-inch stroke. The boiler was paraffin-fired. This model had a wheelbase of 12 feet and was fitted with pneumatic tires and wooden spoke wheels. The standard body was an express van and its price was $3300. For the years 1919-1921, this same model was listed as a 1-tonner. Possibly the original rating was optimistic. *GMN*

1922 DODGE (i) Four screen express truck, GNG

DODGE (i) (US) 1916 to date

(1) Dodge Brothers, Detroit, Mich. 1916-1928

(2) Chrysler Corporation, Dodge Division, Detroit, Mich. 1928-1938

(3) Chrysler Corporation, Dodge Division, Warren, Mich. 1938 to date

The brothers John and Horace Dodge introduced their 4-cylinder touring car in November, 1914; in its first full production year it became America's third best selling make. It was a straight forward 3½-litre sv monobloc affair, notable for its back-to-front gearshift and 12-volt electrics; though chassis were being fitted with light truck bodies as early as 1916, the panel and screen express were not officially listed until the 1918 model year, followed in 1919 by a short-lived taxicab. From 1921 Graham Bros. of Evansville fitted Dodge engines into their trucks, but the subsequent Dodge involvement in this company meant that it became in effect their truck division, thus limiting the Dodge commercial vehicle range to car-based ½-tonners. These had conventional shift pattern, 6-volt electrics and fully enclosed cabs by 1926. Between 1927 and 1929 Graham Bros. trucks (by now fitted with Dodge's new 7-bearing sv 6-cylinder engine) were quietly phased out in favor of a line of Dodge vans and trucks for payloads in the ½/3-ton category. The old 4-cylinder engine was retained in light models, but the bigger ones featured sixes of up to four litres' capacity, 4-speed unit gearboxes, spiral bevel back axles, and the braking arrangements favored by Chrysler, Dodge's new owners; hydraulics on all four wheels with a transmission handbrake. By 1930 Dodge was America's fourth best selling truck, with deliveries of 15,558 units. The four lingered on into 1933, but

1935 DODGE (i) 3-ton truck, Texaco Archives

1931 4-tonners featured a bigger 96 hp six, and from 1933 to 1935 there was even a straight-8 truck, the G80, using the 6.3-litre 9-bearing Chrysler Custom Imperial car engine in unit with a 5-speed gearbox. It was rated for 4/7½-ton payloads, while that year the 2- and 3-ton 6-cylinder models also became available with five forward speeds, and British Dodge production began in the Kew factory. The British Dodge would soon acquire an entirely individual specification.

1937 DODGE (i) MC ½-ton van, OMM

Thenceforward the Dodge commercial range followed the same structure as those of Ford and Chevrolet, covering payloads from half to four tons, with PSV production confined to normal control school bus chassis. At the bottom of the pre-War range were car-type light vans, though front end sheet metal did not always follow that of the cars. 1936 truck grilles closely resembled those of the contemporary D2 sedans, but thereafter there were no major styling changes on the commercial vehicles until they fell into line once more in 1939. A new 5-speed 3-tonner with 5.1-litre 6-cylinder engine appeared in 1935, in which year Dodge evolved a special type of Airflow-styled tanker for Texaco. 265 of these, the last in 1940, were built on various heavy-duty chassis. By 1936 the largest Dodges had hydrovac brakes, and 2-speed rear axles were a regular catalogue option in 1937, in which year sales approached the 65,000 mark. Also new in 1937 was the first forward control Dodge, a 1½-tonner. The conversion was, however, undertaken to factory order by Montpelier; factory-built COE models did not appear until 1939. By 1938, when truck activities were centered on a new plant in the Detroit suburb of Warren, buyers had a choice of four 6-cylinder engines. The selection was even wider in 1941 — six engines, 17 axle ratios, 23 frames, four clutches, six types of brakes, and eight rear axles. Other Chrysler Corporation commercial vehicles included a line of Plymouth commercial cars (some of them closely related to the parallel Dodges), and the badge-engineered DeSoto and Fargo ranges, intended to give greater dealer coverage, mainly in Canada and overseas. Further exten-

1941 DODGE (i) VC ½-ton pick-up, GNG

sions to the Dodge line include the company's first diesel; introduced in 1939, it was a 7-bearing, 95 hp six, available on 2- and 3-tonners. New for 1942 was a ½-ton Route Van with 6-cylinder gasoline engine for urban delivery work, though since 1939 Dodge had been developing a range of light all-wheel drive vehicles for the U.S. Army, initially with civilian-type cabs and front end sheet metal, but from 1941 in full military guise. The wartime range embraced ½- and ¾-ton 4x4s and a 1½-ton 6x6, made as trucks, weapons carriers, command cars and ambulances, and all powered by 3½-litre, 92 hp engines. In 1944 a limited selection of 1942-type ½-ton civilian models went back into production to fulfill esential home-market needs.

The first postWar Dodge commercials were basically modified 1942s, the biggest being the 3-ton WK with 5.4-litre, 128 hp engine, 5-speed gearbox, double-reduction drive, and hydrovac brakes. Curiously, the diesels did not reappear, though the forward control types did. Nor did

1948 DODGE (i) BLD multi-stop delivery van, LA

Dodge reintroduce a car-type sedan delivery to compete with the popular Chevrolet; their ½-ton panels and pick-ups were truck right through, with 3-speed synchromesh gearboxes, hypoid rear axles, and semi-elliptic springing, only the 6-cylinder sv engines being shared with the car line. Also in the catalogue was a civilian edition of the ¾-ton 4x4 Power Wagon; it was still available with the old flathead engine as late as 1963. By 1949 Dodge offered some 6x4 trucks (with optional full air brakes) based on their ¾-tonner, as well as an updated Route Van with electric parking brake and the Fluidrive semi-automatic transmission used on contemporary Chrysler Corporation cars. All engines were sv sixes, with outputs from 95 hp upwards. 1950 saw the introduction of a 5-speed synchromesh gearbox on the heavy duty line, and in 1951 came the T, V, and Y series for 4/5-ton payloads available with

1951 DODGE (i) 4×4 Power Wagon, LA

air brakes, and powered by twin-carburetor engines of 145/151 hp. One piece curved windshields were featured on restyled 1954 models, and power steering became an option for the first time. Dodge applied V8 engines to their trucks, these being of short-stroke ohv type with hemi-heads during the same year. Models in the 1½/2½ ton class used a 4-litre (241 cid) unit rated at 133 hp, but heavies had the bigger 5.4-litre 331 cid type giving 153 hp. 1955 improvements included 12-volt electrics and tubeless tires, while both smaller V8s and fully automatic transmission were available on light duty Dodges. There was a further restyling in 1957, and the 4-headlamp configuration was adopted in 1958. In 1957 a new range of tandems (6x4) had been launched, all with V8 engines, from 201 hp 5.1 litre up to a twin-carburetor 354 developing 232 hp.

New for 1960 were the short cab conventionals, normal control models with swing-out front fenders facilitating engine access. These replaced the traditional forward control types. Smallest of the Cs was the 5-ton C600, available with sixes of 125 or 130 hp, and a wide range of V8s of up to 202 hp, other options being 5-speed manual and 6-

1969 DODGE (i) 700 Series articulated truck, OMM

speed automatic gearboxes. The series, however, also covered 6x4s and tractors with GCW ratings as high as 53,000 lbs., and full air brakes on the heaviest types. There was also a return to diesel power for the first time since 1942, Dodge offering a variety of normally aspirated and turbocharged Cummins units from 175 to 228 hp, matched with twin-plate clutches and 8- or 10-speed transmissions. At the other end of the scale, simplified Dodge sedans were becoming popular as taxis, these being a regular line in the 1960s and 1970s.

Plymouth's Valiant compact sedan of 1960 soon had its Dodge counterpart, while the Valiant's new 2.8-litre and 3.7-litre ohv Slant 6 engines with their alternators found their way into ½-ton and 1-ton Dodge commercials. Also fitted with the slant engine was the P300 Multi Stop van, descendant of the Route Van line, though the old sv units

1973 DODGE (i) Kary Van, Dodge

were still fitted to the Power Wagon, some medium duty models, and the less elaborate school bus chassis. 1962 saw a derivative of the school bus family, the first Dodge specifically designed for recreational vehicle use; by 1975 mobile-home chassis had become a regular business, and Dodge could supply such units with V8 gasoline engines and automatic transmission as standard. Perkins diesel engines became a medium-duty option in 1963, and a year later came the company's answer to Ford's Econoline, the side- and rear-loading forward control Handyvan. Wheelbase was a compact 90 inches. The vehicle could handle payloads of up to one ton, and options included automatic transmission. The engine was the slant 6, though V8s were available from 1965. At the other end of the scale was a bid for the heavy haulage market with the L-line of short tilt cab (49 inch bcb) forward control models with GVW ratings in the 50,000 lb. class. Engines were V6 and V8 Cummins diesels, and at least one 8x4 trailing axle tractor for an 80-ton GCW was built, along with some formidable C-line truck mixer chassis. These included a gasoline-powered 10x6 with 15 forward speeds. By 1970 the big Dodges used such powerful engines as the 335 hp turbocharged Cummins and the 318 hp V8 Detroit Diesel. Other features included air-assisted clutches and parking brakes, and 10-, 12-, and 16-speed transmissions. Ifs reached both the Tradesman (the handyvan's successor) and the light D100/300 pickup family in 1972, these latter having long been available with four wheel drive, while at the top of the normal control range was the 9-ton 6x4 short-cab Bighorn.

During 1975 Dodge discontinued their entire heavy truck line, with profitable consequences: production built up from 319,694 units that year to a record 469,197 in 1977. These deletions apart, the 1978 program typified an American mass-producer's thinking, with the Tradesman and the light pickups at the bottom: all these now featured servo front disc brakes. A new engine option was a 4-litre 6-cylinder diesel, while there were also fancy color and trim packages (Warlock, Macho) to appeal to the new generation of custom truck enthusiasts. The normal-control mediums had GVW ratings in the 15,000-30,000 lb. bracket, and came with gasoline V8s of 5.2 or 5.9 litres (a 6-cylinder Perkins diesel was also offered), 4- or 5-speed synchromesh gearboxes, and hydrovac brakes: options included automatic transmission. Since 1974 Dodge has also offered a light 4x4, the Ramcharger, intended to compete against Chevrolet's Blazer and the Ford Bronco. Power front disc brakes were standard, and engines ranged from the Slant Six up to a 7.2-litre V8. *MCS*

DODGE (ii)(GB) 1933 to date

(1) Dodge Bros. (Britain) Ltd., Kew, Surrey 1933-1967
(2) Rootes Motors Ltd. (Dodge Division), Dunstable, Beds 1967-1970
(3) Chrysler United Kingdom Ltd., Dunstable, Beds 1970 to date

1937 DODGE (ii) Major 4-ton tanker, OMM

1975 DODGE (i) LN-1000 tanker truck, Dodge

Though Dodge trucks had been assembled in England since 1927, these were standard American types, as were the car-type light vans offered by Kew until 1939; this range, interestingly, included a woody station wagon from 1935 onwards. 1933 and later heavy duty models were, however, largely British, only engines and gearboxes being imported; they were sold in some export markets as Kew-Dodges or Kew-Fargos to avoid confusion with the American models. Initially only 30-cwt and 2-ton trucks and a 20-seater passenger chassis were listed, all with 3.3-litre sv 6-cylinder engines, coil ignition, four forward speeds, hydraulic brakes, and spiral bevel drive. Capacity was soon increased to 3.6 litres, and forward control models added, these including a 4-tonner which was popular for gravel haulage. New for 1937 was a streamlined cab with vee windshield, and thereafter the styling of British Dodges changed little for twelve years. At the top of that year's range was the 4-ton Major with 4-litre engine, 5-speed gearbox, and a handbrake working on all four wheels; it had the short hood found on most medium-duty forward control British trucks of the period. A diesel engine (the ubiquitous Perkins P6) was a regular option on some Dodges as early as 1938, and some 1940 models had hypoid back axles.

A simplified range of 2-3 ton, 5-ton and 6-ton trucks reappeared after the War, with a choice of Dodge or Perkins engines, but the line was completely restyled in 1949, emerging with cabs not unlike those of contemporary Leyland Comets, while hydrovac brakes were standard on the heavier types. There was no further serious change until 1957, though the adoption of the bigger Perkins R6 engine allowed for payloads of up to seven tons, and variations included PSV chassis (for export only), 4x4 and 6x6 conversions by Unipower, and a full forward control 6/7-ton pantechnicon chassis. Interestingly, these 1949-type Dodges were still being made by Premier in India as late as 1972, with a choice of Dodge gasoline or Meadows diesel engines.

From 1957 onwards Dodge moved up a class, with nothing smaller than a 3-tonner listed. Though the old sv gasoline engine, now a 4.1-litre developing 116 hp, soldiered on

1959 DODGE (ii) 15 ton 8×4 truck, OMM

until 1960, there was a tendency towards assembly, with a variety of 4- and 6-cylinder diesel units from Perkins, Leyland, and A.E.C. Some Dodges used B.M.C-built constant-mesh gearboxes, while the new cabs introduced in 1957-58 were hardly original, the normal control type being that of Commer's Superpoise, while forward control models had a Motor Panels cab also fitted to certain Leyland Group products. By 1961 normal control Dodges spanned the 3-7 ton bracket; the forward control range (which also included tractive units) ran from a 5-tonner to a 9-tonner, this last with 6.2-litre 100 hp diesel engine, 5-speed gearbox, 2-speed spiral bevel axle, and air-hydraulic brakes. PSVs were now available on the home market as well, these being full-fronted models with 39-45 seats, and a further upward extension of the range had led by 1963 to heavy 6x2 and 6x4 trucks with A.E.C units. The normal control trucks were withdrawn in 1963 (the front-end sheet metal was inherited by the short-lived Baron), but they were replaced by new 5- to 7-tonners of similar type using imported American cab assemblies, Perkins engines, and 4 and 5-speed gearboxes.

The Chrysler-Rootes fusion of 1964 gave Dodge a new status as the heavy duty truck of the combined range, the buses being restricted once more to the export market and disappearing altogether by 1968. Though certain lighter duty Commer models were briefly offered from 1968 to 1970 with Dodge badges, the basic line from 1966 onwards was the K family of forward control machines with low built tilt cabs, 5-speed gearboxes, full air brakes on all but the smallest, and such accepted options as 2-speed back axles and power steering: automatic transmission had become available by 1968. The range embraced 4x2, 6x2 and 6x4 types as well as tractive units, with gross weights

1969 DODGE (ii) KP 1000 28-ton GCW truck, Chrysler UK

1974 DODGE (ii) K3820P 32-ton GCW truck, Chrysler UK

from 10 to 24 tons. 6-cylinder Perkins engines were retained at the bottom end, with Chrysler-Cummins V6 or V8 diesels for the bigger trucks. These latter engines, however, had a short life, and from 1968 there was a switch to Perkins's big 8.4-litre V8-510, which engine was still in use in 1975, by which time the Ks had synchromesh gearboxes. New that year was a heavy tractor, the K382OP, made for Dodge by another Chrysler subsidiary, Barreiros, of Spain. In 1976 the Commer name was discontinued, Commers being produced henceforward as Dodges. The 1978 Dodge line embraced the 18-cwt and 25-cwt Spacevans, inherited from Commer along with the Walk-thrus for payloads from 25-cwt to 3 tons, and the Commando trucks for GVWs in the 7/12-ton class. The gasoline option in the Walkthru was, incredibly, still the aged 2267cc ohv four inherited from the Humber Hawk car and with roots going back to 1933! Dodge's own K range was now restricted to three-axle rigids and two-axle tractors for GVWs and GCWs of between 22 and 29 tons: all had 8.8-litre Perkins V8-540 engines, air brakes, and power steering. Still being imported were the Spanish Barreiros tractors with GCW ratings of 36/37 tons, air and exhaust brakes, and 11.9-litre turbocharged diesel sixes giving 266 hp. During 1977 the Dodge company launched an experimental fleet of 35-cwt Silent Karriers, KC60-series Walkthrus converted to battery-electric propulsion. *MCS*

DODGE (iii) (AUS) 1939 to date

Chrysler Australia Ltd., Adelaide, S.A.

The Dodge name is another of the big American names established in Australia for a long time, as an assembler of U.S. models modified accordingly, in order to fulfil local needs. The basic model for the first years was the coupe utility pickup based on American Dodge car models, but featuring larger wheels, reinforced suspension and other modifications and powered by a 6-cylinder 90 hp gasoline engine. The first Australian designed model, appeared, though, in 1958, when series 1 to 10 were introduced sporting a twin headlight American-style normal-control cab, 6-cylinder 114 hp or V8 180 hp gasoline engines and no less than eight basic models and many variants, including panel vans, coupe utilities, etc. The British Kew-Dodge forward control model was introduced the same year, with a slightly modified cab, powered again by the V8 gasoline engine and fulfilled the heaviest class with its 25,000 lbs. GVW. A major restyling took place in 1966 when an all-Australian line was introduced, fitted with a nice-looking modern normal control cab with twin headlights, sloping hood and panoramic windscreen. Modelled series 1 to 7, the range covered the 6000 to 27,000 lbs. GVW, while three-axled tandem-drive models in the 37,000 lbs. GVW were introduced a few years later. Power for the range came for either 6-cylinder 133 hp or from V8 gasoline engines developing 212 hp, while the heaviest models feature also diesel engines, either a Perkins 6-cylinder 131 hp or a Cummins V8, 185 hp. The Valiant light pickup is also marketed under the Dodge trademark and covers the lightest class with its 750 kilos payload and 6-cylinder 145 hp gasoline engine, while a heavy duty forward control model was introduced in 1971 in the 27,000 lbs. GVW. Powered by either a Chrysler V8 gasoline of 202 hp or a Cummins V8 diesel of 185 hp it was fitted with the British Commer metal cab, slightly modified and equiped with twin headlights. Dodge trucks cover a large portion of Australian needs for commercial vehicles. *GA*

DODGE (iv)(IND) 1946-1972

(1) Premier Automobiles Ltd., Bombay

(2) The Premier Automobiles Ltd., Kurla, Bombay

Established in 1944 by one of the leading and progressive Indian industrialists, P.A.L. as the company is generally known, grew immensely through the years, and today is considered as India's national auto-manufacturer, operating three individual factories. The early cooperation with Chrysler Corp. of U.S.A., led to the building of a variety of truck chassis of 1 to 8 tons payload and to all capacity buses. Locally-built almost 100%, Dodge vehicles use the old British Kew semi-forward cab as well as American Dodge cabs together with Indian-designed ones. Power comes from PAL-built gasoline engines developing 110 hp or Perkins 83 hp and 120 hp diesels. Large station wagons, vans and ambulances, 4x4 chassis for military and civilian uses and buses complete the range of products that include also stationary and marine engines. As a companion to Dodge, PAL markets the whole range of products under the Fargo trademark too, but vehicles are similar to each other. In 1972 the trade name was changed to Premier. *GA*

DODGE (v) (TR) 1964 to date

(1) Chrysler Sanayi A.S., Kadikoy, Istanbul 1964-1970

(2) Chrysler Sanayi A.S., Cayirova Gebze, Kocaeli 1970 to date

The Chrysler factory in Turkey started building of the "D" series American trucks fitted with a locally designed cab on angular lines, easy to build and repair. Lighter models are offered as pickup, 4x4 chassis, van and large station wagon versions, while heavier models are always chassis/cabs. Chrysler's own 140 hp gasoline engines power the bottom of the line, while top models use the Perkins 6.354 diesel developing 130 hp as standard equipment. The whole range is simultaneously marketed under the DeSoto and Fargo trademarks. *GA*

D-OLT (US) 1920-1923

D-Olt Motor Truck Co. Inc., Woodhaven, L.I. N.Y.

The D-Olt came in two sizes, a 1-1½-tonner powered by a Herschell-Spillman engine, and a 2½-tonner made in 1923 only and powered by a Midwest 402 engine. *GNG*

1915 DOMINION articulated truck, HD

DOMINION (US) 1915-1917

Dominion Motor Truck Company, Detroit, Michigan

This was a short wheelbase (90 inches) truck tractor with a T-head 4-cylinder engine between the two single seats. It had a 3-speed gearbox and worm drive with torque taken up through the springs. The manufacturer moved from Canada in 1915, hence the name. *GMN*

DOMINO (AUS) 1976 to date

Domino Coaches, Brisbane, Queensland

This company offered two coach models, both with 6-cylinder Detroit diesel engines, a choice of 6-speed Spicer manual or Allison automatic gearboxes, ZF power steering, air and Jacobs brakes, and Rockwell axles. Ground clearances as high as 20 inches were available to suit local conditions. The S was of conventional straight-chassis configuration with vertical engine located either centrally or at the rear, but the integral DC was built up round an ingenious twin-tier frame. The power unit was mounted underfloor between the two levels. *MCS*

DONAR (D) 1921-1926

Frankfurter Maschinenbau AG. vorm. Pokorny & Wittekind, Frankfurt/Main

Only one basic type was produced by this firm, a 5-ton chassis with their own 4-cylinder 9-litre engine. This was used for trucks and buses. *HON*

DONAU (YU) 1964-1968

Industria Motornih Vozil, Novo Mesto

Donau was a sideline of IMV light commercial vehicles as marketed only in Germany and Austria. Powered by imported DKW 3-cylinder 2-stroke gasoline engines developing 44 hp, driving the front wheels, they were built as vans, microbuses and ambulances. The appearance of the BMC-engined series in 1968 led to the discontinuation of the Donau name, but IMV vehicles are still built, slightly redesigned and in a larger model range. *GA*

DONG-FENG (P), **TUNG-FENG** (WG) (East Wind) BM-021 (CHI) to date

A 3-wheel truck in general use in mainland China, the East Wind is powered by an aircooled 2-stroke, single cylinder engine of 248.5 cc developing 12 hp at 4,750 rpm.

Chain drive is used and maximum speed is 65 km/h. The producing factory is unknown. Chinese sources report this firm also produces heavy-duty trucks (c.1971 to date), built for provincial use. *BE*

DONISELLI (I) c.1953-1957

Fratelli Doniselli SA, Milan

Doniselli offered a range of light 3-wheeled delivery trucks. More powerful models had two shaft-driven rear wheels, differential back axles, backbone frames, and 2-stroke engines of 125 cc or 175 cc, but the 100 kg Metropoli was little more than a powered delivery tricycle. The single rear wheel was chain-driven and there were two forward speeds. *MCS*

1934 DONNET 7/9 CV van, NMM

DONNET: DONNET-ZEDEL (F) 1925-1934

SA des Automobiles Donnet, Nanterre, Seine

Jerome Donnet's venture was built up from the remains of Vinot-Deguingand and Zedel, hence the name Donnet-Zedel sometimes applied to the product. The firm's main interest was inexpensive family cars, a field in which they never challenged Mathis, let alone Citroen, and only two commercial types were seriously marketed. Of these the smaller was a 10-cwt van on the 7CV light-car chassis, while the C16 was a straight-forward 20/25-cwt machine with 2.1-litre 4-cylinder sv engine, magneto ignition, 4-speed unit gearbox, uncoupled fwb, and bevel drive. The 7CV was briefly offered as a taxicab in 1927, and both themes were progressively developed until 1934, later versions having coil ignition and updated editions of Donnet's car engines. There was also a *commerciale* based on the Violet-designed 4CV of 1931, a typical minicar with 740 cc water-cooled vertical-twin 2-stroke engine, transverse front suspension, and a differentialless back axle. After Donnet went bankrupt, the factory was acquired by Simca. *MCS*

1914 DORRIS fire engine, LA

DORRIS (US) 1912-1925

Dorris Motor Car Co., St. Louis, Mo.

This manufacturer began the manufacture of passenger automobiles in 1906, but the first commercial vehicle was not launched until six years later. This original model was a ¾-tonner with pneumatic tires, later joined by a 2-ton stake truck and a 3-tonner chassis. These all used Dorris-built 4-cylinder ohv engines. From 1916 to 1925, there were only seven basic models, with the K-4 dating from 1918 and the K-7 from 1919. These were 2½- and 3½-tonners respectively. During the last three years of commercial production, Dorris also offered two models of buses, models M-4 and L-6 with 4- and 6-cylinder engines, respectively. There was also a gasoline-electric bus made in 1925 which had a General Electric generator and motor. During 13 years of commercial production, there were 3951 Dorris trucks built. *GMN*

1921 DORT 1-ton van, OMM

DORT (US) 1921-c.1924

Dort Motor Car Co., Flint Mich.

Product of a well-known horse-carriage maker, the Dort passenger car went into production in 1915 and was built in considerable numbers. A ¾-ton van version appeared in late 1921, using like the cars, a 19-ghp 4-cylinder Lycoming engine and 3-speed gearbox. *GNG*

DOT (GB) 1947-1956

Dot Cycle and Motor Manufacturing Co. Ltd., Manchester

The Dot was a light delivery vehicle of motorcycle type with front-mounted box for 300 lb. payloads. Power was provided by a 197 cc 2-stroke Villiers engine, and speed was 30 mph. Variations included an ice cream tricycle and a rickshaw for export to the Far East. *MCS*

DOUBLE DRIVE (US) 1919-1930

(1) Double Drive Truck Co., Chicago, Ill. 1919-1922
(2) Double Drive Truck Co., Benton Harbour, Mich. 1922-1930

Double Drive and Front Drive trucks were made by the same company, the former being listed in sizes up to 3½ tons, while the Front Drive was only made as a 1½-tonner powered by a 4-cylinder Buda engine. The Double Drive used a Rutenber engine from 1919 through 1922, then changed to Buda power for most models, though a Hercules Model K was used in the top-of-the-range 3½-tonner. The company made their own front and rear axles, and worm drive was employed on the later models. *GNG*

DOUGILL see Frick

DOUGLAS (i) (US) 1917-1935

Douglas Truck Mfg. Co., Omaha, Neb.

A successful but low-volume assembled truck, the Douglas was designed to meet the needs of operators in the American middlewest and southwest. The onset of regional truck weight restrictions triggered an early interest in rigid 6-wheelers, and these became a Douglas speciality before such vehicles were available from the better-known makers. Douglas launched its operation with a conventional range of 1,1½, 2 and 3-ton models powered by 4-cylinder Buda and Weidely engines, with Timken axles and Brown-Lipe transmissions.

In 1928 came the F66 6-wheeler, conservatively rated at only six tons. It had a Douglas-built bogie suspension consisting of two worm-type Wisconsin axles, and was intended for long-distance moving and livestock transportation. Wheelbase was approximately 200 inches and body length 24 feet. Animals were carried on two levels in the Douglas-built rack body. *RJ*

1946 DOUGLAS (ii) 10/15cwt electric van, Jeff Clew Collection

DOUGLAS (ii) (GB) 1946-1952

Douglas (Kingswood) Ltd., Bristol

This well-known motorcycle manufacturer announced a range of battery electric vehicles after World War II, known as the Douglas-ACM. They had been developed during the war by Leicester electric vehicle specialists A.C. and A.E. Morrison, and their most distinctive feature was the rear axle which contained two aluminum yoke motors. Two models were made, the 10/15 and 20/25 cwt, both with plywood panelled bodies. Range was 30-50 miles depending on the capacity of the batteries. Larger models of 30- and 40-cwt were announced in 1946 but were

1948 DOUGLAS (ii) Handyvan milk float, Jeff Clew Collection

not made, and in 1952 all production of battery electrics ceased. Douglas had made industrial trucks since 1928, and in 1948 they brought out a modified version for road use, known as the Handyvan. It was a 3-wheeler with 596 cc flat-twin engine driving the front wheel, and governed to a maximum road speed of eight mph. Intended for general delivery work especially of milk, the Handyvan was much too noisy for this work, and in addition an insuperable problem was that of oil fumes filling the cab. Of the 100 laid down, only eight were sold. *GNG*

1958 DOUGLAS (iii) 7-ton dump truck, GNG

DOUGLAS (iii) (GB) 1947-1966

Douglas Equipment Ltd., Cheltenham, Glos.

Douglas specialized in cross-country machinery with all-wheel drive, a complex range embracing forestry tractors, oilfield trucks with sand tires, fire engines and snow ploughs. Gasoline and disel engines used included AEC, Commer, Leyland, Meadows, Perkins, and Roll-Royce. Often cabs and front end sheet metal were of proprietary origin, as on the original AEC-engined forestry tractor of 1947, which had a Matador type cab. Smallest of the regular types was the all-independently sprung Pathfinder pickup with 6-cylinder Commer gasoline or

Perkins diesel engines; at the other end of the scale was the 30-ton DH 30/64, a hooded 12-speeder with 220 bhp Leyland diesel and air brakes, available in 6x4 or 6x6 configurations. Two unusual 1959 productions were a 6x6 motorway gritter with 8-cylinder Rolls-Royce gas engine and automatic transmission, and a conventional 4x2 single-decker bus chassis for South Africa using a 4-

1965 DOUGLAS (iii) Cargo master NS.2 6-ton truck, OMM

cylinder Meadows diesel. On- and off-road dump trucks were also produced with Commer, Cummins, or Rolls-Royce oil engines. 1952, however, had seen the introduction of the Tugmaster, first of a line of aircraft servicing and stevedoring units, and though a Commer-based normal control 5-ton 4x4 truck was still listed in 1966, Douglas's subsequent activities have centered round derivitives of the Tugmaster family. *MCS*

DOVER (US) 1929-1930
Hudson Motor Car Co., Detroit Mich.
The Dover was a ½-ton light commercial version of the Essex Super 6, using the same splash-lubricated 2.6-litre sv engine. Hudson subsequently made vans and pickups under the Essex and Terraplane names, as well as under their own. *MCS*

DOWAGIAC (US) 1909-1912
Dowagiac Motor Car Company, Dowagiac, Michigan
The Dowagiac was a very light van with a two-cylinder, 24 hp engine on a chassis with 102-inch wheelbase. The open version was priced at $1400. In 1912 this company was moved to Tulsa, Oklahoma and became part of Tulsa Auto Manufacturing Company, which built the later Tulsa truck. *GMN*

DOWNING (US) 1914
Downing Cyclecar Company, Detroit, Michigan
A delivery van was available on this cyclecar chassis. The chassis had a track of 56 inches and wheelbase of 105 inches and used a three-speed gearbox and shaft drive. Weight of the vehicle was 600 pounds and its price was $450. *GMN*

D.P. (GB) 1907-1910
Dawfield, Phillips, Ltd., West Ealing, Middx.
The D.P. was a taxicab powered by a 12/15 hp flat-twin engine mounted halfway between front and rear axles, and driving the latter via a 2-speed epicyclic transmission and single chain. It had a very small turning circle of only 20 ft. *GNG*

D.P. Taxicab

D-RAD; D-WAGEN (D) 1927-1931
Deutsche Kraftfahrzeugwerke AG., Berlin-Spandau
The pattern of two front wheels and one rear driven wheel was followed by this firm. They used their own 4-stroke motorcycle engine of 500 cc developing 10 hp. *HON*

DRAKE (US) 1921-1922
Drake Motor & Tire Mfg. Corp. Knoxville., Tenn.
Nearly all trucks used 4-cylinder engines at this time but the Drake used a 6-cylinder Herschell-Spillman #11000 engine. The wheelbase was 140 inches, weight was 3500 pounds for the 2-ton chassis with pneumatic tires and the price was $2595 but reduced $100 in its second year. *RW*

DRAULETTE (F) 1899
Capt. E. Draulette, Puteaux, Seine
Capitaine Draulette designed and built an electric hansom cab with seats for four passengers arranged in semi-circular position. The rear-mounted motor drove the rear axle, there being four speeds with a maximum of 12 mph. It was announced that several hundred Draulette cabs would ply in Paris, but very few in fact were made. *GNG*

DRAUZ (D) 1951-1962
Karosseriewerk Drauz KG, Heilbronn
This well-known coachbuilding firm developed a light-metal chassis-less fwc bus with rear-mounted Ford Hercules diesel engine developing 120 PS. At first it was marketed by Ford but in 1956 Drauz sold it under their own organization. Production lasted until 1962. *HON*

DREDNOT (CDN) 1913-1915
Drednot Motor Trucks Ltd., Montreal, Que.
A wide range of trucks from one to three tons, with 2- or 4-cylinder engines, was offered by this company. An armored car prototype was built in 1914 but probably did not get into production. *HD*

DUCOMMUN (D) 1903-1905
Werkstatte fur Maschinenbau vorm. Ducommun, Mulhausen
A small production of commercials in the range from 2½ to 6 tons was carried out by this firm. All of them featured shaft drive. A small number of Ducommun buses ran in London in 1906. *HON*

DU CROS see W & G

DUCROISET (F) 1897-1900
Ducroiset et Fils, Grenoble.

Ducroisets were rather ponderous machines with front-mounted watercooled horizontal 2-cylinder engines, three forward speeds, and belt drive; later examples were wheel-steered. Brake-type bodies were often fitted, and a 15-cwt delivery van was also available. The make was sold in Britain under the Hercules name. *MCS*

DUCSON (E) 1958-1960
Industria Ciclista S.A., Barcelona

Founded by Don V. Sola, this company was mainly a maker of bicycles and motor scooters, but briefly made a 125 cc delivery tricycle. *JCG*

DUDLY (US) 1914-1915
Dudly Tool Company, Menominee, Michigan

This vehicle was also known as the Dudly Bug and qualified as a cyclecar with tread of 40 inches and wheelbase of 90 inches. A light closed delivery body was offered on this chassis for $375, with an air-cooled 2-cylinder engine. *GMN*

DUER (US) 1910
Chicago Coach & Carriage Company, Chicago, Illinois

The Model C light delivery van was a high-wheeler with tiller steering. It had an air-cooled, two-cylinder engine with double chain-drive and solid tires. With wheelbase of 7 feet, 1 inch, it weighed 1,400 pounds and its capacity was given as 1000 pounds. *GMN*

DUFOUR-BALLABEY (CH) 1897-1914
(1) Dufour & Tissot, Nyon, VD (1897-1905)
(2) Societe des Camions Dufour, Nyon, VD (1905-1913)
(3) Etienne Ballabey & Cie, Nyon, VD (1913-1914)

Dufour & Tissot produced stationary single-cylinder engines. In 1897 a flour-mill owner asked them to mount one of these engines on a platform vehicle and thus one of the very first rudimentary motor-trucks in Switzerland took the road. By 1903 a new model with many improvements was offered. A flat-twin-engine of 16 hp mounted in the longitudinal axis of the truck just aft of the front axle drove the large wooden and iron-tired rear-wheels via leather belt, 3-speed gearbox and final chains. Maximum speed was 9 mph.

In 1908 Dufour brought out an interesting new model with a tranversally mounted 3-cylinder engine, which was again placed behind the front axle and under the driver's seat. The old-fashioned transmission to the gearbox by a large belt was retained as was the final drive by chains and the iron-tired, large diameter wooden wheels. One of these trucks is said to have been exported to Argentina and the firm had many customers in France. The 3-cylinder design was used with improvements till 1914. The last Dufour-Ballabey trucks, with 2½- to 3-ton payload, had twin rear wheels and solid-rubber tires. Speed increased slightly to 15 mph. The engine dimensions were 100 x 140 mm, for a capacity of three litres and the indicated performance 18/24 hp. With the outbreak of the first World War the company had to close down. Production was limited over the years and less than 10 Dufour lorries were counted in 1912 in Switzerland. The company was re-established in the mid-twenties but production of commercial vehicles was not resumed. *FH*

1904 DUFOUR-BELLABEY 16hp truck, ES

DUNJO (E) 1954-1960

Talleres Mecanicos de A. Dunjo, Barcelona

Mainly a workshop for the construction of motorcycle and scooter chassis frames, this company also made a small number of delivery tricycles. *JCG*

DUNLAP (US) 1914-1915

Dunlap Electric Co., Columbus, Ohio

There was a ½-tonner built by this company, powered by batteries. The price was $1000. *GMN*

DUNTLEY (US) 1910-1912

Chicago Pneumatic Tool Co., Chicago, Ill

Built by a well-known manufacturer of air compressors, pneumatic and electric tools, this was a delivery truck powered by a 20 hp horizontal-opposed twin engine with 2-speed planetary transmission and shaft drive. Payload was 1500 lbs. It was sometimes known as the C.P.T., and this name survived on the models sold in England up to 1914, although in America the name Little Giant was generally adopted after 1912. *GNG*

DUPLEX (i) (GB) 1907

Duplex Motor Engine Co., London

This company listed two commercial vehicle chassis, in addition to passenger cars. They were a 20 hp 2-cylinder 20 cwt chassis with shaft drive, and a 30 hp 3-cylinder 30-cwt chassis with chain drive. *GNG*

1909 DUPLEX 4×4 truck, LA

DUPLEX (ii) (US) 1908 to date

(1) Duplex Power Car Co., Charlotte, Mich. 1908-1916

(2) Duplex Truck Co., Lansing, Mich. 1916-1955

(3) Duplex Divn., Warner & Swasey Co., Lansing, Mich 1955-1975

(4) Badger & Crane Divn., Warner & Swasey Co., Winona, Minn. 1975 to date

The Duplex Power Car Company was formed from the reorganization of the J.L. Dolson company which made passenger cars from 1904 to 1907. The new product was a ¾-ton 4-wheel-drive delivery wagon powered by a 20 hp 2-cylinder water-cooled engine under the seat, with internal gear final drive on all four wheels. Within a few years a larger 4-wheel-drive model of 3½ tons capacity was added, joined by a 1½ ton rear drive truck. These had conventional layouts with engines ahead of the driver. By 1917 the range was restricted to 4-wheel-drive models, in 2, 3, and 3½-ton sizes, but in the 1920s both 2-and 4-wheel drive trucks were made. Hinkley engines were used in the

1918 DUPLEX 4×4 truck, Warner & Swasey Co.

1923 DUPLEX Model A 1½-ton truck, Warner & Swasey Co.

smaller, rear drive models, and Budas in the 3½-ton 4-wheel-drives. These still used internal gear drive, with solid tires, vertical steering columns and exposed wheels without any fenders. The larger Duplexes sometimes hauled road trains of four or five trailers before state legislatures put an end to these operations. They were also used in the logging industry and as fire engines. By 1929 there was only one 4-wheel-drive model in the range, the 3½-ton Model EF, but other trucks ran from 1½ to 5/7 tons in size, with 4- and 6-cylinder engines. The 3-ton SAC had a 7-speed gearbox. During the 1930s the range from 2/3 to 6/7 tonners, with a 9/10 tonner added from 1938 to 1940. Engines were Buda and Hercules.

During World War 2 Duplex supplied 6x4 trucks for searchlight carrying, and after the war resumed production of conventional trucks powered by 6-cylinder Hercules engines of up to 140 hp, driving through 5-speed Fuller transmissions and full-floating Timken rear axles with bevel gear or double reduction. Styling was conservative, though in the 1950s the models T-H and L acquired the well-known Chicago cab which was also used by International, Diamond T, Oshkosh, F.W.D., Coleman, Cline and Hendrickson.

Duplex continued to make 4-wheel-drives, including the model LC600-4 powered by a Cummins 6-cylinder diesel engine. From the 1950s onwards crane carriers became an increasingly important part of Duplex's output, these being mostly one-man-cab models of 6x4 layout with Continental engines, joined in the late 1960s by an 8x4 25-ton model with GVW of 77,000 lbs. powered either by International gasoline or Detroit Diesel engines. Many of these carried the name Gradall on the front, for use with Gradall earth-moving machinery and the Hoptoe back-hoe, both products of Warner & Swasey who had acquired Duplex in 1955. Other specialised products include a 4-wheeled road/rail maintenance unit, tunnel maintenance trucks and a 4x4 rear-wheel-steering airport snowplow. Fire engine chassis are also made, with three cab-forward

1963 DUPLEX 4×4 dump truck, Warner & Swasey Co.

1975 DUPLEX fire engine chassis, Warner & Swasey Co.

models currently listed in 4x2 and 6x4 drive systems. Detroit Diesel engines are used. Current conventional trucks are 4x4s using a forward-slanting windshield cab shared with Oshkosh, and Caterpillar or Detroit Diesel engines from 225 to 318 hp. Transmissions are by Fuller or Allison, and Rockwell-Standard axles are used front and rear. Power steering is standard.

Duplex was never a high volume producer, annual production during most of its life not exceeding 50 trucks per year, though current production is running at about 300 per year. At the end of 1975 Duplex moved its truck business to a new plant at Winona, Minnesota. *RW*

1912 DURABLE DAYTON Model K 3-ton truck, NAHC

DURABLE DAYTON (US) 1912-1917

(1) The Dayton Auto Truck Co., Dayton, Ohio 1912-1913
(2) The Durable Dayton Truck Co., Dayton, Ohio 1914-1917

This open cab-over truck came in three models, H, K, and M, in order, of 2-, 3-, and 5-ton capacities with a choice of stake or express bodies at prices of $2500, $3500, and $4500. Power was furnished by 35, 45, and 60 hp 4-cylinder T-head engines cast in pairs with water pump cooling. Transmission was 3-speed selective, and final drive was by chains. Steering was left-hand with a vertical shaft. Curiously, each size truck had had a different service brake location-in order, on the transmission, external contracting on the rear wheels, and jackshaft. Emergency brakes were all internal expanding on the rear wheels.

The specifications changed little during the production run, except that later the Durable Dayton was offered in models U,A, and E, in size order, of 2-,3½-, and 7½-tons with a price range from $2650 to $4950. *RW*

DURANT see Star (ii)

DUREY-SOHY (F) 1899-1903

Automobiles Durey-Sohy, Paris

This company made an electric hansom cab in addition to their gasoline-engined passenger cars, and late in 1920 they acquired the Hanzer company, selling, the Hanzer cars and commercial vehicles under their own name. At the 1902 Paris Salon the Hanzer catalogues were overprinted with the name Automobiles Durey-Sohy. *GNG*

1905 DURKOPP 20hp charabanc, BR

DURKOPP (D) 1901-1929

(1) Bielefelder Maschinenfabrik vorm. Durkopp & Co. A.G., Bielefeld 1901-1913
(2) Durkopp-Werke A.G., Bielefeld 1913-1929

The first vehicles which were available as trucks and vans had a 2-cylinder 8 hp engine and appeared in 1901. The first bus appeared one year later with an increased engine output of 15 hp. During the following years Durkopp offered a wide range from 3/4 ton van to a 5 ton truck plus various buses. All were equipped with 4-cylinder engines and had cardan drive. The chassis were also used for fire engines and with special equipment for municipal purposes. In 1908 Durkopp took over the Oryx works in Berlin and so commercials were also built in this plant. Vans were offered as Eryx while heavier types and buses continued to be sold as Durkopp. During the war a 4 ton truck was built for the army. After the war a 3/4 ton van and a 3 ton truck were continued, supplemented by a 2-tonner. Also some low-frame buses were offered. Since 1927 only one type was on the program, the L2, using a 4-cylinder 4.1-litre engine with 2½ ton payload capacity.

1927 DURKOPP 1½-ton truck, HON

This type was available as a bus too. In 1929 Durkopp presented a 2-axle chassis whose low-frame layout made it especially suitable for bus bodies. A 6-cylinder engine developing 100 hp was installed. But only a few of this type were produced as Durkopp gave up production of the cars in the same year. *HON*

DUROCAR or DURO (US) 1914-1916

Amalgamated Motors Company, Alhambra, California

Under this name was produced a 1000-pound capacity chassis, and little more is known of this make. This seems to have had no connection with the earlier California-built passenger auto of the same name. *GMN*

DURYEA (US) 1899-1917

(1) Duryea Power Co., Reading, Pa 1899-1909
(2) Charles E. Duryea, Reading, Pa 1909-1911
(3) Duryea Automobile Co., Reading, Pa 1911-1913
(4) Duryea Laboratories, Philadelphia, Pa 1915-1917

The complex history of this pioneer American make began with a car constructed by the brothers J. Frank and Charles E. Duryea in 1892-93, but the four firms listed were the only ones to have offered commercial vehicles and even then production was not on a regular basis. The first recorded light van was shown in 1899. It was based on the Duryea 3-wheeler with single front wheel. The 8 hp ohv 3-cylinder engine was mounted transversely at the rear, driving the rear wheels by chain, and ingenious features included a 2-speed and reverse epicyclic gearbox with single-lever control, the steering tiller also operating throttle, gears and brakes. Pneumatic tires were regular equipment; one of these three-wheelers was tested as a machine-gun carrier by Major R.P. Davidson, the father of the American armored fighting vehicle. From 1902 Duryea concentrated increasingly on a 4-wheeled derivative of their basic design; in 1905 form it was rated at 12/15 hp and could be had as a 750-pound delivery van or light stage. This type was still available in 1908, but in the meantime Charles Duryea had made a bid in the high-wheeler market with his Buggyaut, powered by a rear-mounted air-cooled opposed-twin 2-stroke engine. Single-lever control was again used, and the central location of the tiller allowed for rhd or lhd at will. Drive was by twin grooved rollers on the crankshaft engaging with the rear wheel rims, and the price was $750. Both private and commercial editions were marketed, and the Buggyaut outlived most of its competitors, surviving into 1913. 1914 saw a 3-wheeled Duryea parcelcar with single driven rear wheel, but little was heard of this. The Philadelphia company, however, produced a 10-cwt high-wheeled van with wheel steering, priced at $600 in chassis form. *MCS*

DUTRA (H) 1950-1973

Dutra Works, Budapest

The combined interests of steam traction engine producers Clayton, Shuttleworth & Co. of Lincoln, England and Hoffherr & Schranz of Vienna, resulted in the formation of Hoffherr es Schranz Mezogazdasage Gepgyar at Budapest which built its first traction engine in 1908 and introduced the first diesel-engined tractors in 1926. Following the reorganization of the Hungarian automotive industry in the post WW II years, the same company launched a 6-ton dumper with half cab and twin controls under the Dutra trademark. Powered by a diesel engine of 60 hp and running gear of Csepel origin, the range was soon enlarged with heavy all-wheel-drive tractors for agricultural and industrial uses. The same dumper design continued unchanged for 23 years, while a self loading variant was later added to the range. A new 4x4 10-ton dumper appeared in 1968 based on an older Raba design and was powered by a 125 hp diesel engine of Csepel manufacture. Both models were built until late 1973, when the factory transferred its activities to Voros Csillag Traktorgyar at Godollo and was amalgamated with Raba producing only axle components since then. *GA*

DUTY (US) 1920-1922

Duty Motor Co., Greenville, Ill.

The Duty truck was made in only one size, a 2-tonner powered by a 35 hp 4-cylinder Gray-Bell engine, with a Covert 3-speed transmission and Russel, internal gear drive. The 6 inch channel steel frame had its flanges turned outward, a very rare feature. Solid or pneumatic tires could be fitted, and a cab was a $85 extra. Total production of Duty trucks was between 300 and 400. *RW*

DUX (D) 1909-1926

(1) Polyphon-Werke A.G., Wahren nr. Leipzig 1909-1916
(2) Dux Automobilwerke A.G., Wahren nr. Leipzig 1916-1926

Dux vans were available on the private car chassis of this make. During WW I 3- and 4- ton trucks were produced. After the war light trucks, vans and special vehicles (e.g. ambulances) were available. Very successful was the version with 4-cylinder 3.1 litre engine. In 1926 Dux was acquired by Presto. *HON*

DYNAMIC (US) 1911-1912

Cleveland Motor Truck Manufacturing Company, Cleveland, Ohio.

This truck was available with either electric or gasoline power and was of considerable complexity for the age. In versions, the chassis had both four-wheel-drive as well as steering on all four wheels. The gasoline engines were horizontal 4- and 6-cylinder types which were spring-mounted. Power to each axle was through a transmission which featured herringbone gears, and drive-shafts to front and rear axles. Air or mechanical brakes were available for all four wheels. *GMN*

EADON (GB) 1927
South Lincolnshire Engineering Co. Ltd., Spalding, Lincs.

The Eadon was a conventional normal-control 2½-ton truck powered by a 6-cylinder 3.8-litre engine. The price complete was £650. *GNG*

EAGLE (i) (GB) c.1903-1904
Eagle Engineering & Motor Co. Ltd., Altrincham, Cheshire

The Eagle was a typical tandem tricar which was also made in commercial form, carrying a 2-cwt load ahead of the driver. It was powered by a 4½ hp single-cylinder engine, and had wheel steering. At least one was used by the General Post Office in 1904 for mail collection work. The Willesden-built Century Tandem was an almost identical design to the Eagle, both being the work of Ralph Jackson. *GNG*

EAGLE (ii) (US) 1920-1928
Eagle Motor Truck Corp., St. Louis, Mo.

The Eagle was made in quite a wide variety of sizes, from ½-ton to 5-tons in capacity, all of them using various models of Buda engine. *GNG*

1928 EASYLOADER refuse truck, OMM

EASYLOADER (GB) 1928-1933
(1) Easyloader Motors Ltd., London N.W.9 1928-1931
(2) New Easyloader Motors Ltd., Islington, London N.7 1932-1933

One of several low-loading vehicles introduced to cash in on the success of the S.D. Freighter, the Easyloader was powered by a 4-cylinder 2,176 cc E.T. White engine as used in the S.D. This unit was mounted ahead of the front axle, and drove via a 3-speed gearbox to the rear axle. The original Easyloader had small wheels with solid tires, although later versions had pneumatics. It was designed to carry at least three times its unladen weight (22-cwt), at speeds up to 30 mph. In January 1932 the business was taken over by a new company headed by Mr. White, formerly with Duple coachworks and Mr. Tapper, a former Brockway concessionaire. They launched a new model, the 3½-tonner T-type with a more powerful engine and 4-speed gearbox. A 2-tonner on a shorter wheelbase was also made. Most of these New Easyloaders had pneumatic tires. They were used largely as municipal vehicles, although intended for general load-carrying as well. *GNG*

1956 EBRO 2000kgs truck, OMM

1961 EBRO C-152, 1500kgs truck, GNG

1977 EBRO E-70 7000kgs GVW truck, Motor Iberica

EBRO (E) 1956 to date
Motor Iberica SA, Barcelona

Ford commercial vehicles had been made in Spain from 1920 to the outbreak of the Civil War in 1936, and was resumed in 1956 with license production of the British Ford Thames normal control trucks, supplemented by a semi-forward control model of Spanish design. These were named Ebro after the Spanish river, just as the Thames was named from an English river. (When Ebros came to be sold in Syria, they were called Frat after the river Euphrates). Later models were for loads of between 1500 and 5000 kgs, and in 1968 the D Series with tilt cab was introduced for loads of 1½ to seven tons. These were based on the British D Series but with some styling differences; the range grew steadily to cover models from three to 27 tons, with two or three axles, and also articulated models. Engines were Perkins Hispania. The current range is the E Series with distinctive Spanish cab, made in six models from 3,500 to 11200 kg GVW, all Perkins Hispania powered. There is also the larger P Series from 13000 to 27000 kg GVW.

In 1967 Motor Iberica began to distribute Alfa Romeo light vans and in 1972 they launched a new model under the name Romeo-Ebro which was made until 1975. In modernized form, with Perkins 4-108 engine, it is still made today. They also made smaller Ebro-Siata vans and minibuses from 1971 to 1975. *JCG*

E.B.S. (D) 1925-1927

Ernst Bauermeister & Sohne, Berlin-Baumschulenweg

The front part of this tri-van was built very closely to motorcylce lines having two rear wheels and a rear mounted box. Engines of E.B.S. design were used. *HON*

ECHASA (E) 1956-1958

Echasa, Arizmendi y Cia S.A., Eibar, Guipuzcoa

This was an important Basque metallurgical company which made motorcycles, scooters and delivery tricycles powered by engines of 125 cc and 175 cc. *JCG*

ECKLAND (US) 1931

Eckland Brothers Co., Minneapolis, Minn.

Eckland were builders of truck and bus bodies whose work was seen on a number of locally-built chassis including Twin City and Will. When the Greyhound company who owned Will sold the firm to Yellow Coach and turned to buying Yellows, Eckland were short of work, so they tried their hand at bus chassis construction. Their only product was an unusual vehicle, patterned on the Twin Coach but employing four wheel drive. The two 6-cylinder Waukesha engines were located half way down the chassis, one on each side of the frame, each with its own 3-speed gearbox and propeller shaft. The nearside engine drove forward to the front axle, the offside to the rear. There were two separate radiators at the front of the bus, one for each engine. It is thought that only one prototype was made, although Eckland remained in business as body-builders until 1935. *GNG*

ECLIPSE (US) 1911-1913

Eclipse Motor Truck Co., Franklin, Pa.

The Eclipse was offered in four models from 1-ton to 4-ton capacity. All models featured a 4-cylinder engine fitted with a compressed air self-starter. Double chain drive was used. The Eclipse enjoyed a brief popularity in Pennsylvania's oil fields. *DJS*

1952 ECONOM twin-steer chassis, HON

ECONOM (D) 1950-1953

Econom-Werk Hellmuth Butenuth, Berlin-Haselhorst

Butenuth equipped some Ford trucks with steam engines during WW II, but built up his own production of commercials later. His first truck was presented in 1950. It was a 5-tonner with two-stroke 2-cylinder 2.3 litre diesel engine by MWM. This also was available as an articulated tractor. A 3-wheeled street-sweeper with single cylinder diesel engine followed and later versions ranged up to a six ton truck and a nine ton articulated tractor, using 3- or 4-cylinder diesel engines. Econom vehicles were mainly used in Berlin because of the unique political situation of this city, which made exports to other parts of West Germany difficult. *HON*

ECONOMY (US) 1909-1912

Economy Motor Car Company, Joliet, Illinois

These commercial vehicles began as a relatively crude high-wheeler with a 2-cylinder engine. In the final two years of production there were produced 1000- and 2000-pound light vans, still with two-cylinder engines but had graduated to pneumatic tires while retaining planetary transmissions and double chain drive. *GMN*

E.C.W. (GB) 1950-1957

Eastern Coach Works Ltd., Lowestoft, Suffolk.

E.C.W. had been building bus and coach bodies from July 1937 onwards although its predecessors had been manufacturing bus bodies at Lowestoft since 1921. As the state-owned manufacturer of bus and coach bodies for the nationalized passenger transport undertakings, E.C.W. produced a batch of 16 chassisless 32-seat buses for the Eastern Counties Omnibus Co. Ltd. in 1950. Based on an aluminum alloy frame, these were odd-looking half-cab vehicles with ugly dummy radiators and rear entrances. Their Gardner 4LK engines and certain other components were reconditioned units taken from pre-war Dennis Aces. An experimental chassisless double-decker with Leyland running units was built for London Transport in 1957 and was a double-deck coach based on the "Routemaster" design. *OM*

c.1927 E.F.A.G. electric gulley emptier, OMM

E.F.A.G. (CH) 1919-1937

Elektrische Fahrzeuge AG., Zurich-Oerlikon

In 1919 the old-Tribelhorn company was reformed and became E.F.A.G. Whereas the production of heavy electric-trucks was given up in the 1920's there was a great variety of electric vehicles used as delivery vans, light trucks and for internal works transportation in factories. Electric tankers for aircraft refueling and electro-tractors for hauling heavy loads on road and rail were built as well. The Swiss postal services were regular customers. In 1937 the company was once again reformed and renamed N.E.F.A.G. *FH*

EHRHARDT (D) 1906-1922
Heinrich Ehrhardt A.G., Dusseldorf; Zella-St. Blasii

Ehrhardt built special vehicles for military purposes but also normal trucks up to 6 ton payload capacity. Vans were available on the passenger car chassis. *HON*

EIBACH (D) 1921-1925
Eichler & Bachmann GmbH., Berlin NW7

A tri-van following motorcycle lines was produced by this firm. There was one driven rear wheel and a forward box. A 200 cc D.K.W. engine was used. *HON*

EICHER (D) 1963-1967
Gebr. Eicher, Forstern

A 3-ton truck and a prime-mover were introduced in 1963. They used a 4-cylinder 4-litre diesel engine by Deutz developing 60 hp in the tractor and 70 hp in the truck. After 1967 the truck version was included in the Magirus program but was still produced by Eicher. *HON*

EISENACH (D) 1900-1903
Fahrzeugfabrik Eisenach, Eisenach

Under this name electric vans were offered, while gasoline driven cars were marketed as Wartburg (q.v.) *HON*

EISENHAUER (US) 1945-1946
Eisenhauer Mfg. Co., Truck Division, Van Wert, Ohio

The Eisenhauer was a most unusual truck powered by two separate Chevrolet 6-cylinder engines mounted in line, one under the hood and the other under the cab. It had two steerable front axles, and three axles at the rear, each with double wheels, giving a total of 16 wheels. The truck was 35 ft. long and the payload was 20 tons, a record for a rigid chassis at the time. *GNG*

ELBIL (N) 1971-1972
Elbil A/S, Oslo

This was an electric van powered by two 13Kw motors, one driving each rear wheel. It was 7 ft. wide and had a floor height of only 15½ins. The body was of aluminum and the payload 3300 lbs. or 18 passengers in bus form. It was developed under a Norwegian government-sponsored contract by Elbil, a company in which 13 of the country's leading engineering companies had a stake. The first prototype was tested by Oslo Electricity Board, and others went to the Post Office and Norwegian State Railways. *GNG*

1927 EL DORADO coach, MBS

EL DORADO (US) 1925-1930
Motor Transit Co., Los Angeles, Calif.

In common with other large California stage operators, Motor Transit Co. was drawn into equipment manufacturing by its dissatisfaction with commercially available buses. From modifications through reconstruction efforts to full-scale assembly, Motor Transit progressed from a buyer (mostly of Whites) to a builder of buses. The most significant step was taken in 1925, when Buda six-cylinder engines began to be used in place of White fours (White did not have a six until 1926). Use of an emblem and slogan indentifying the company as the "El Dorado System" led to the use of the name El Dorado for the buses.

Approximately 70 buses were built for Motor Transit's own use, plus possibly a few for other southern California carriers, during the five years of production. They ranged from small stages and bus-truck combination vehicles (generally referred to as "combos") with compound transmission to large 33-passenger buses for heavy suburban work. Production ceased when Motor Transit came under the control of the Pacific Electric Railway. *MBS*

ELDRIDGE (US) 1913-1914
Eldridge Manufacturing Company, Boston, Mass.

The Eldridge was a four-wheel gasoline-electric tractor for the hauling of unpowered wagons. This unit was a modified Couple Gear power plant with front-wheel drive. Two very small diameter wheels were used at the rear merely for balance. *GMN*

ELECTRACTION (GB) 1976 to date
Electraction Ltd., Maldon, Essex

This firm announced a range of light battery-electric private cars and trucks in 1976, using 7.5 hp Lansing Bagnall motors and Vauxhall running gear. The truck version had a GVW of 2700 lb.: it was of forward control type with tubular steel frame, fiberglass cab, all-coil springing and hydraulic drum brakes. Overall length was a compact 11 feet, and range was 50/60 miles at 20 mph. In February 1978 the company merged with AC Cars Ltd. *MCS*

1930 ELECTRICAR 2-ton refuse truck, OMM

ELECTRICAR (GB) 1920-1939
Electricars Ltd., Birmingham

Late in 1920 Edison Accumulators Ltd. announced that the vehicle production part of their business had been sold to Electricars Ltd. and that a range of 1-ton, 2-ton and 5-ton vehicles would be offered.

The 1-ton W type was made by Walker Vehicles and used their design of having the motor and differential enclosed within the rear axle and driving the rear wheels by means of epicyclic gearing. The 2-tonner was of two-motor layout, these being slung beneath the chassis frame about midway between the axles. Drive was by means of short enclosed chains to short propellor shafts outside of the chassis frame and thence by bevel gears mounted on the

1937 SCAMMELL-ELECTRICAR refuse truck, OMM

inside of the rear wheels. The largest of the trio, the 5-tonner used the more conventional single motor although it was somewhat unconventional for the period, being mounted behind the rear axle and driving through a short shaft to a countershaft mounted in front of the rear axle and thence by outside chains to the rear wheels.

1939 ELECTRICAR 4-ton refuse truck, NMM

During the next few years the range consisted of four models — 1-, 2½-, 4- and 5-ton, with the Walker system of drive being used for the 1-ton and 5-ton vehicles while the other two sizes utilized the two motor shaft and bevel arrangement. 1928 saw a change in design with the Walker system being dropped in favor of worm drive for a 30-cwt chassis and bevel drive for 2½-, 3½- and 5-tonners. The smallest model had single motor drive while the others retained the old Edison style of two motor drive. From 1929 onwards the range underwent a change with the old Edison style being ousted in favor of the lighter single motor and worm driven axle layout. There was a great expansion of models and internal works trucks were produced in quantity. Road going vehicles ranged from 8-cwt van chassis to a 14-ton drawbar tractor and included bakery and dairy vans, lorries for municipalities, tower wagons, seven ton rigid six wheel models, articulated refuse vehicles in collaboration with Scammell and a promenade toastrack 'bus.

In 1934 an assembly plant was established in Ireland.

After joining Associated Electric Vehicle Manufacturers in 1936 the smaller payload vehicles in the range were dropped in favor of those produced by A.E. Morrison. The name Electricar survived in the name of the vehicles produced by the new firm — Morrison-Electricar, although not long after the Electricar designs were phased out and the vehicles became Morrison Electric. *OM*

1907 ELECTROBUS (i) London bus, NMM

ELECTROBUS (i) (GB/F) 1907-1909

The Electric Vehicle Company, West Norwood, London

The London Electrobus Co. Ltd. was formed in April 1906 to operate a fleet of battery-powered double-deck buses in the metropolis, and they imported a chassis from France for test purposes. Operation commenced in July 1907 with Electrobuses supplied by an associated company, the Motor Car Emporium, and assembled for them by the Electric Vehicle Company of West Norwood. In all, twelve vehicles were purchased and, though assembled locally, they contained components imported from France, including a French Thomson Houston electric motor with a nominal 14 hp. 40 miles were expected from one charge of the batteries, which contained 44 cells and weighed 1½ tons. Slow-moving though quiet, they were financially unrewarding and were sold in 1910 to the Brighton Hove & Preston United Omnibus Co. Ltd. who had themselves purchased three new Electrobus vehicles in 1909. All were withdrawn from service by 1911. *OM*

1975 ELECTROBUS (ii) Model 20 MBS

ELECTROBUS (ii) (US) 1974-1975

(1) Electrobus, Inc., Van Nuys, Calif. 1974
(2) Electrobus Division, Otis Elevator Co., Stockton, Calif. 1974-1975

Electrobus was organized in 1973 to produce and market a 20-passenger low-platform battery-driven bus for shuttle services, and delivered three such vehicles to Long Beach, Calif., in August 1974. A single 72-volt battery mounted in the rear and arranged for quick exchange by means of a fork-lift was connected to a DC traction motor rated at 50 hp (continuous), and also furnished power for the air conditioner, ventilating equipment and air compressor. Brakes were air-assisted hydraulic, and the complete bus weighed 15,000 lb. Although a few others were built, and there were plans to add battery-powered vans to the line, Otis Elevator Co. discontinued the division's business in September 1975 because of low volume. (See also Westcoaster)*MBS*

1920 ELECTROMOBILE 4-ton electric truck, OMM

ELECTROCICLO (E) 1945-1956

Electrociclos S.A., Eibar, Guipuzcoa

This company made very small electric vehicles, of which the commercial versions had a capacity of up to 300 kgs. Running costs were estimated at no more than 1/10th of a peseta per kilometer. *JCG*

ELECTROMOBILE (i) (US) 1906

American Electromobile Co., Detroit, Mich.

This 3-tonner was a battery-powered electric van and was offered for just one year. Additional information is unavailable. *GMN*

ELECTROMOBILE (ii)(GB) 1914-1933

Electromobile Ltd., Otley, Yorks

The early range of Electromobile consisted of imported American chassis of Buda manufacture-works trucks and tractors and CT road vehicles proper. The CT range included five models of between 10- and 100-cwt capacities, all being powered by 42 cell Ironclad batteries which gave an operating range between 25 and 40 miles according to load carried. The 10-cwt was of 96 inch wheelbase, the 20-cwt of 104 inches and the 40-cwt 116 inches, all being on wooden wheeled chassis. The 70-cwt and 5-ton models were carried on cast steel wheels and were of 134 inch and 145 inch wheelbase respectively. The three smaller models were of the 2-motor type these being geared to the rear wheels one each side by means of double reduction epicyclic gearing. The motors were fitted between a pair of I-beams forming the rear "axle." The heavier models were powered by no less than four motors — one to each wheel. As with the rear wheels the front motors were bolted direct to the epicycle gear cases on the back plates of the wheels and the whole assembly turned when being steered, with pivots above and below the motor casing.

Toward the end of the 1920's two new models were added to the range at payloads of 15-cwt and 30-cwt, these being of the single motor type, and in 1930 a further 40/50-cwt model was offered. The 2-ton, 3½-ton and 5-ton CT models continued up to the end when the company was absorbed by Electricars in 1933. *OM*

ELECTROVIA (E) 1905-1909

SA Azarola, Madrid

This company built trolley-buses under license from the pioneer German makers of road vehicles, Schliemann of Wurzen, Saxony. A small number of battery electric buses and trucks were also made. *JCG*

1959 ELECTRUK Rider 25cwt milk float, GNG

ELECTRUK (GB) 1937-1961

(1) T.H. Lewis Ltd., London, N.W.1
(2) T.H. Lewis Ltd., Cricklewood, London, N.W.2
(3) T.H. Lewis Ltd., Watford, Herts

Established in 1854 as bodybuilders the company specialized in hand and horse carts for the dairy trade and later became the bodybuilding subsidiary of Express Dairy Co. Ltd. In 1937 the first electric pram milk float (pedestrian controlled) was produced, being a 3-wheeler powered by a 12-volt battery with ¾ hp motor connected directly to the differential in the rear axle. Capacity was 6/7 cwt with a working radius of about 10 miles.

The improved EA model followed after the 1939-45 war and was similar in layout, but was powered by a 24 volt battery and rated at 12 cwt capacity. In 1949 the uprated model EB was put on the market, this being a 1-ton 4 wheeler with a more powerful motor, spiral bevel axle, a reverse gear and capable of surmounting a 1 in 4 hill.

The Rider model EC with driven on the vehicle came in 1954 and featured a 25-cwt payload, 32 volt battery of 161 AH capacity, 16 mile range, batteries carried pannier style and a 56 inch wheelbase. The EB and EC remained available until 1961. *OM*

ELEKTRIC (D) 1922-1924

Aktiengesellschaft fur Akkumulatoren — und Automobilbau, Berlin N 65; Driesen-Vordamm

This firm started to offer their electric driven vans under the A.A.A. name Small vans and a 2 ton version were offered, the latter was extensively used by the postal authorities. Also an electric driven bus was offered. *HON*

ELIESON (GB) 1898

Elieson Lamina Accumulator Syndicate Ltd., Camden Town, London N.

This company made an electric vehicle with narrow front track and chain drive which was fitted with passenger car, taxicab and delivery van bodywork. Though sold by Elieson who made the batteries, the vehicles were in fact made by John Warrick & Co. Ltd. of Reading, who later made the Warrick Carrier 3-wheeled parcel vans. *GNG*

ELITE (i) (D) 1920-1930

(1) Elite Motorenwerke A.G., Brand-Erbisdorf 1920-1922
(2) Elite-Werke A.G., Brand-Erbisdorf 1922-1927
(3) Elite-Diamant-Werke A.G., Brand-Erbisdorf 1927-1928
(4) Carl Richard & Co. GmbH., Ronneburg 1928-1930

Based on the private car design, van versions were available, especially with the 4-cylinder 3.1 litre 12/40 PS engine. The later 6-cylinder engines were used for vans and trucks 1-, 2 and 3-ton payload capacity. *HON*

ELITE (ii) (E) 1955-1958

Elementos de Transporte, Barcelona

A small number of delivery tricycles powered by 197 cc Hispano-Villiers engines were made under this name. *JCG*

ELITEWAGEN (D) 1921-1928

Elitewagen Akt. Ges., Berlin; Ronneburg

This make succeeded the make of Geha (q.v.). The Geha three-wheeler was continued for a short time under the old name. In addition also electric driven vans and trucks from 1- to 5-ton payload capacity were produced as well as gasoline engined trucks. *HON*

ELIZALDE (E) 1914-1928

(1) Biada, Elizalde & Cia, Barcelona
(2) Fabrica Espanola de Automoviles A. Elizalde, Barcelona

Well-known as passenger car makers, Elizalde built chassis for 500-600 kg loads and light hotel buses, using the 4-cylinder car engines, and later a 2-ton chassis which could carry bus bodies for up to 24 passengers. This was also used as an army truck and saw service during the Moroccan War. In 1922 they introduced the 30C, for 5 ton loads or 45 passengers. This had a 55 hp engine and dual ratio rear axle giving a total of eight forward speeds. It could be used with a drawbar trailer. All the larger Elizalde commercial chassis had fully floating rear axles. Aircraft engines were made from 1917, and in 1928 the company gave up road vehicles to concentrate entirely on these. *JCG*

ELK (US) 1912-1914

Elk Motor Truck Company, Charleston, West Virginia

Elk trucks were in three capacities: 2-, 3- and 5-tons. All had four-cylinder engines with forward control. The smallest model was on a wheelbase of 120 inches and had a maximum speed of 15 mph. *GMN*

ELKHART see Huffman

1903 ELLIS 4-ton undertype steam wagon, RAW

1906 ELLIS 5-ton overtype steam wagon, RAW

ELLIS (GB) 1897-1907

Jesse Ellis & Co. Ltd., Maidstone, Kent

In 1897 Ellis patented his Colonial buck-wagon in which a vertical Field tubed boiler with a superheater mounted at the rear of the vehicle powered a 3-cylinder radial engine, of which type a second, and similar, wagon was made in 1899. A 2-ton vertical boilered undertype wagon with chain drive was shown in 1898 at Maidstone and the following year a four tonner using a de Dion boiler, compound undertype engine, and chain drive was supplied to Fremlins, the Maidstone brewers.

Thereafter Ellis abandoned chains and concentrated upon an all-gear drive, in each case with the compound undertype engine and two road speeds. Spring movement was catered for either by mounting the engine, gears and axles on a rigid sub-frame or by the use of the Stevens spring bar and flexible couplings. Boiler design vacillated between water tube and fire tube types and finally settled in his last few wagons as a short locomotive type with top firing. His last fling in wagon design, in 1907, was a two tonner with a Fairfax 3-speed epicyclic gear box. Ellis made only one essay into gasoline vehicles, a 15/20 cwt van fitted with a 14/16 hp engine and the Fouillaron expanding and contracting pulley speed change but the firm closed before it was put on the market. Total production was of the order of 40 wagons, mostly four or five tonners. *RAW*

ELLSWORTH (US) 1916-1920

Mills-Ellsworth Company, Keokuk, Iowa

The Ellsworth was a light delivery van of 1000-pound capacity, available with either open express body or a panel delivery in steel. Power was by a Lycoming Model K four-cylinder engine. These models had pneumatic tires, shaft drive and the chassis price was $635. *GMN*

ELMIRA (US) 1916-1921

(1) Elmira Commercial Motor Car Co., Elmira, NY 1916-1920

(2) Elmira Commercial Motor Car Co., Oswego, NY 1920-1921

The lone model under this trade name was a ½-tonner. Further details are lacking. *GMN*

ELWELL-PARKER (US) 1906-1908

Elwell-Parker Electric Co., Cleveland, O.

These were large electric vans operated from storage batteries. Models were from 5-tonners to 7½-tonners. All used double chain drive and all were furnished with flat platform bodies. Output for the 7½-tonner was claimed to be as great as 30 hp for short periods. This company later built battery-powered industrial lift trucks. *GMN*

ELYSEE (US) 1929-c.1932

M. P. Moller Motor Car Co., Hagerstown, Md.

The only goods vehicle made by the Moller company, whose other products included Dagmar and Standish passenger cars and a variety of taxicabs including Luxor, Paramount and Astor, was the Elysee panel delivery. This used the same radiator grille and Continental Red Seal 6-cylinder engine as the Standish car, and was made in four models, the Band Box. Fifth Avenue, Courier and Mercury, the first two having a 15 cwt capacity and the latter two 30-cwt. They were stylish vehicles and were intended for the delivery of high-class goods to wealthy homes. *GNG*

E.M.A. (CS) 1971 to date

Vyzkumny ustav elektrickych stroju tocivych, Brno

E.M.A. 1 was an electric passenger car built in 1970, and E.M.A. 2 is an electric van using the chassis and body of the East German Barkas B 1000 1-tonner. The batteries are located between the axles under the floor, and drive from the electric motor is via a 2-speed clutchless gearbox to the front wheels. The E.M.A. has a range of 35 miles and a speed of 28 mph. Two vans are in daily use, and others are being prepared. *MSH*

EMPOLINI (I) c.1930 to date

Empolini Milano di Silvestri Aldo, Milan

Unusual among Italian makers of ultra-light delivery 3-wheelers, Empolini have always specialized in this type of vehicle. The 1978 edition followed the classic formula, with shaft-driven rear wheels, 48 cc single-cylinder F.B. Minarelli engine, 3-speed gearbox, handlebar steering, and uncoupled hydro-mechanical brakes. Payload was 300 kg, and bodies available included a miniature tipper and a refuse collector. *MCS*

EMRESS (B) 1906-1907

This obscure Belgian manufacturer made a 4-cylinder bus chassis with chain drive and normal control. *GNG*

E.M.W. (i) (D) 1927-1930

Motor-Transportwagenwerk H. Schivelbusch, Leipzig

This firm produced a tri-van on motorcycle lines with two front wheels, forward box and one driven rear wheel. A choice of 200 cc. D.K.W. and 340 cc Villiers engines was offered. *HON*

E.M.W. (ii) (DDR) 1951-1955

Eisenacher Motoren-Werke, Eisenach

Based on the E.M.W. 340 private car, a van version was available under the type-designation 340-3 using the 6-cylinder 2-litre engine. *HON*

ENFIELD (GB) 1907-1915

(1) Enfield Autocar Co. Ltd., Redditch, Worcs. 1907-1908

(2) Enfield Autocar Co. Ltd., Sparkbrook, Birmingham 1908-1915

The first commercial vehicle made by this company, originally an offshoot of the famous Royal Enfield cycle and armaments firm, was a 3-ton forward control truck with 25 hp T-head 4-cylinder engine and single chain drive. Few were made, and there was little commercial vehicle activity after the change of address which coincided with the acquisition of Enfield by the Alldays & Onions company. In 1914, however, Enfield announced a 5 cwt light van on their 1100cc 4-cylinder Nimble Nine car chassis. This was known as the Parcelette. *GNG*

ENFIELD-ALLDAY (GB) 1920-1923

Enfield-Allday Motors Ltd., Sparkbrook, Birmingham

This company was the result of the merger between the Enfield Autocar Company and Alldays & Onions Ltd. Though both companies had made commercial vehicles before the war, Enfield-Allday was best-known for passenger cars, and only one commercial model was listed. This was a 2-ton chassis powered by a 4-cylinder 25 hp engine of 4.4-litres capacity. It had a 3-speed gearbox and enclosed chain drive. Not many were made, and after 1923 the company decided to concentrate on light cars. *GNG*

ENGESA (BR) 1969 to date

Engenheiros Especializados S.A., Sao Paulo, S.P.

The firm of Engesa started life building gears, winches, P.T.O. units, transfer cases and similar equipment, as well as front driving axles and bogies, for fitment on various Brazilian made truck chassis. Following this practice and the conversion of normal chassis to 4x4, 6x4 and 6x6, Engesa extended their activities introducing a military 4x4 cargo truck of 1.5 ton payload, cross-country. The first model was much like the U.S. Dodge M37 military truck, except for being a little bigger in general appearance, but an improved version was soon offered fitted with a more militarized angular-line, soft-top cab with built-in headlights. Power for both models was by either a Perkins 6 cylinder diesel engine developing 140 hp or a gasoline Chevrolet of 149 hp, both of Brazilian manufacture, while a forward control fiberglass cab was later offered as an option. In contrast to the winch which was a standard equipment on both models.

Engesa builds also 6x6 armoured personnel carriers and reconnaissance vehicles, powered by either gasoline Ford and Chrysler or diesel Perkins and Mercedes-Benz engines. These are used by the Brazilian army and have been exported as far as the Arabian gulf countries. They pioneered the construction of a twin-engined 8x8 amphibious truck of 20 ton/10 ton payload, but the main activity of Engesa remains the conversion of Brazilian-built Chevrolet, Dodge, Ford, FNM, Mercedes-Benz and Scania 4x2 chassis in all-wheel-drive militarized units, that find their way to the Brazilian and other South American armies. *GA*

1903 ENGLISH steam wagon, NMM

ENGLISH (GB) 1903-1907

English Steam Wagon Co., Hebden Bridge, Yorks.

Built under the patents of A. Herschmann of New York the English steam wagon had a vertical fire tube boiler placed behind the driver, compound undertype engine and all gear drive, the final drive being to internal rings of gear fitted to the rims of the rear wheels.

Wagons of 2/3 ton and 5-ton capacity were made. Well known users included Pickfords. *RAW*

ENGLISH ELECTRIC (GB) 1926-1939

The English Electric Co. Ltd., Preston, Lancs.

Already a supplier of trolleybus traction equipment to other manufacturers, and a builder of trams, English Electric began producing complete trolleybuses on a small scale in the old Dick Kerr tramcar works at Preston in 1926. Most of the company's output was in the years 1929-1931 when over 70 trolleybuses were produced to two designs; 2-axle single-deckers and 3-axle machines of both single and double-deck type. Construction ceased in 1931 when an arrangement was made with AEC to co-operate in the introduction of a new range of AEC/EEC trolleybuses using chassis and mechanical units supplied by AEC powered by equipment supplied by English Electric. Thereafter only one more complete trolleybus was built by Preston; this was a lone chassis-less double-decker incorporating AEC running units which was built experimentally for London Transport in 1939. *OM*

1921 ENSIGN 4-ton truck, OMM

ENSIGN (GB) 1914-1923

British Ensign Motors Ltd., Willesden, London N.W. 10

Announced in December 1914, the Ensign was a conventional 3-ton truck powered by a 35 hp 4-cylinder Tylor engine, with a 4-speed gearbox, bevel or worm drive and solid tires. The same model was re-introduced in July 1919 and made with little change until the end of production four years later. Two wheelbase lengths were available on the post-war models, 162 inches and 177 inches. Trucks were also known as British Ensign, the name normally used for the firm's passenger cars. *GNG*

1902 ENTWISLE & GASS steam wagon, RAW

ENTWISLE & GASS (GB) c.1902

Entwisle & Gass Ltd., Bolton, Lancs.

The Entwisle & Gass was a vertical boilered undertype wagon incorporating a double frame and all gear drive. It was unusual in having an entirely open fronted cab but the makers have records of only one example used commercially. *RAW*

EPPERSON see Neustadt

ERAZ (EPA3) (SU) 1966 to date

Erevan Automovile Factory, Erevan.

The ERAZ-762A delivery van is very similar to the RAF-977 microbus series built in Latvia.

An Elektro van was shown in 1976 with a maximum speed of 65 kmh. *BE*

EREWASH (GB) 1936-1940

Erewash Electric Traction Co., Heanor, Notts

Of particularly short duration was the Erewash with two models being introduced in 1936, a 15-cwt and a 20/25-cwt.

The 15-cwt was of accepted battery vehicle layout having a single motor driving to a worm gear rear axle. The chassis was of 78 inch wheelbase carrying a 194AH battery and weighing 13-cwt unladen. Three forward speeds were provided.

The larger 20/25-cwt model was of similar layout having a 78 inch wheelbase and three forward speeds. A larger, 294AH battery was fitted and the chassis carried on 23 in. x 5 in. tires.

In general appearance the Erewash was in the 1930's streamlined style with the composite body having a long sloping cab front and nicely curved rear end. It shared with Newton Derby (qv) the distinction of having a door in the front of the vehicle, although in case of the Erewash this was of the sliding type in the left front panel of the cab. *OM*

1962 E.R.F. Model 88R tanker, OMM

1935 E.R.F. articulated low-loader, E.R.F.

1939 E.R.F. twin-steer 12-ton van, OMM

1960 E.R.F. Model 56GSF 18½-ton truck, GNG

1974 E.R.F. Model LAG320 16-ton GVW truck, GNG

E.R.F. (GB) 1933 to date

E.R. Foden Ltd., Sandbach, Cheshire

E.R. Foden had retired from the family truck firm Fodens Ltd., following disagreements over steam vehicle policy. In 1933 he designed a Gardner 4LW diesel engined six tonner in a conservatory in Sandbach and with his son and two helpers produced the first E.R.F., initially bearing the name E.R. Foden, in time for the London Commercial Motor Show that year. This could carry 7½ tons and was the first British diesel vehicle to do so that weighed less than 4 tons unladen. His 50 year connection with the heavy vehicle industry and good contacts with hauliers, contributed to the success of the vehicle and fourteen were built by the end of the year.

In 1934 10 and 12 ton 6-wheelers joined the 4-wheelers. The first vehicles were built in a workshop rented from bodybuilders J.H. Jennings and Son, who are now owned by E.R.F., and there was room for only three chassis to be assembled at a time, so a new works was acquired in Sandbach.

In 1935 E.R.F. added 15 ton 8-wheelers to their range as well as a 5LW Gardner-engined articulated tractor.

They were also the first to use the Gardner 4LK which replaced a 3-cylinder LW Gardner engine in their smallest 4-ton model. This and its 7½-ton stablemate acquired a new streamlined cab, which had a grille in place of a separate radiator shell for the first time.

In 1937 E.R.F. introduced the first twin steer 6-wheeler in Britain, a 9 tonner with 5LW engine.

The 4-wheel C14 model was supplied as a military 6

tonner during the Second World War and six and eight wheelers were built for civilian transport.

After the War the company expanded into the heavy haulage market with 25 ton tractive units and heavy duty chassis built to export order as well as continuing their maximum capacity four, six and eight wheelers with a high proportion of bought-in proprietary parts.

From 1954 traditional coachbuilt wood and steel cabs were changed to streamlined styling with two piece wrap-round windscreens, though cabs with flat panels continued to be available, especially for export.

New additions in 1958 were semi-forward control chassis which were popular with breweries and as the basis for heavy haulage tractors. The 54G seven cubic yard dump-truck was also produced which featured the first application of front wheel disc brakes to a production commercial vehicle. For the first time engines other than Gardner became optional with Rolls-Royce engined 50-ton tractors and eight wheelers.

In 1960 the familiar cab was modified and received twin headlamps; two years later its eventual replacement, the fiberglass LV cab with access step in front of the wheel arch was first introduced. Also in 1962 ERF offered the first ordinary haulage model, a Gardner engined eight wheeler, with automatic transmission. It also had disc brakes on its front axles and the first use of a Hendrickson air suspended rear bogie in Britain. An additional new model was a 6x6 desert tractor for fifty tons gross operation with Cummins 212 hp diesel.

Cummins engines became available in most of the heavier road-going models two years later, by which time annual E.R.F. production had reached 729 chassis, with a significant proportion going to Australia and South Africa.

1977 E.R.F. B Series 32-ton GTW truck, E.R.F.

A new market in 1966 for E.R.F. was fire fighting chassis, the first being a 235 hp Rolls-Royce gasoline engined chassis with crew cab and Simon hydraulic boom. Various versions were produced with Rolls-Royce and Perkins V8 engines until 1977, when one of the last was a 6x4 Snorkel for export. ERF now build fire appliance bodywork on other makes of chassis. Also in 1966 E.R.F. introduced fail-safe spring activated emergency/parking brakes for the first time in Britain on the 64CU180 30/32 ton articulated tractor. This had a Cummins 180 hp diesel, but Rolls-Royce Eagle diesels were now also available.

1968 saw an unsuccessful lightweight goods model using the lowline fire engine cab plus a new Rolls-Royce engined 50-ton tractor with Motor Panels Steel cab, of which 50 were supplied to Jordan.

In 1970 the normal goods range was simplified as the A Series to improve parts interchangeability, and these could be recognized by a revised frontal styling with horizontal louvres.

In 1973 E.R.F. started work on a steel cabbed 42,000 kg range to meet all foreseeable European legislation and this in turn led to the current B Series with new steel safety framed fiberglass cab in 1974. Total E.R.F production to date is around 30,000 with more than 2000 chassis currently produced per year. Four, six and eight wheelers continue to be produced and E.R.F. is one of the largest independent heavy truck makers in Britain. A new M range of 16 ton four wheel and 26 ton six wheel trucks with lowered B cabs for was introduced in 1978.

Since 1966 E.R.F.s have been made in South Africa with locally-designed and built cabs and Cummins engines. A purely South African model is a conventional 6x4 tractor for use in heavy road train outfits. *OM*

ERIE (US) 1914-1922

Erie Motor Truck Manufacturing Co., Erie, Pa.

This make was produced as 1½-, 2-, 2½-, and 3½-tonners, all driven by 4-cylinder Continental engines and equipped with 4-speed gearboxes. Wheelbases of the several chassis ranged from 144 inches to 168 inches. As early as 1919, these had Timken worm-drive rear axles. For 1921, the line of models was reduced to a single model, the 2½-tonner. *GMN*

ERSKINE (US) 1928-1929

Studebaker Corporation, South Bend, Ind.

Studebaker's first compact car, the Erskine, was announced for 1927, and a 10-cwt van edition was listed for two years. It used a 2.6-litre 40 hp 6-cylinder sv Continental engine. *MCS*

ERYX (D) 1907-1914

(1) Berliner Motorwagenfabrik GmbH., Berlin-Tempelhof 1907-1909

(2) Oryx Motorenwerke, Zweigniederlassung der Durkopp-werke A.G., Berlin-Reinickendorf 1909-1914

Eryx succeeded B.M.F. and carried on their successful van versions with shaft drive. Friction drive was abandoned. As Eryx was a part of Durkopp later van models virtually were based on Durkopp private cars. *HON*

1933 ESCO 2-ton van, Esco

ESCO (US) 1933-1937; 1945-1946

Esco Motor Co., Pittsburgh, Pa.

Esco was a subsidiary of Exhibitors Service Company, a trucking concern, and their vehicles were based on Sterling designs. Esco offered 2-ton and 3-ton models powered by Continental 6-cylinder engines. In 1934 the 2-ton model cost $2500 for the chassis. All Esco trucks featured a 5-speed transmission with direct drive in fifth gear. Production totaled just 50 trucks, including a dozen built during a brief post-war revival of production. *DJS*

ESPANA (E) 1917-1927

Fabrica Nacional de Automoviles F. Batllo S en C, Barcelona

Espana cars and commercial vehicles were made by Felipe Batllo Godo, a textile engineer. The small commercial models were based on passenger cars, being powered by 8-10 hp Altos or M.A.G. engines. Larger trucks were also made, for capacities up to 4 tons, with 40 hp 4-cylinder engines. *JCG*

ESSEX see Hudson (i)

1955 ESSLINGEN electric postal van, HON

ESSLINGEN (D) 1927-1956

Maschinenfabrik Esslingen, Esslingen

Only electric commercials were produced by this firm starting with improved electric platform trucks with steering wheel and 2-seater cabins. Payload capacity was ¾ to 2½ ton. It was succeeded by various models of trucks and vans showing a conventional body design with hood. Production lasted until 1939 and was resumed in 1948 with a 3 ton model. Later the versions covered a range from 1½ to 5 tons and electric tractors with a maximum towing capacity of 30 tons. *HON*

E.T. (A) 1913-1918

Post-Betriebszentrale, Vienna-Stadlau

The Austrian Postal Authority had a big demand for motor buses for their extensive network of long-distance passenger services. So there was the idea that all Austrian factories should participate. Josef Altmann designed the "Einheits-Type" (E.T. = standard type), which was assembled in the own postal workshops in Vienna. The following firms were engaged: Austro-Daimler (4-cyl. 40 hp engine), Laurin & Klement (chassis, radiator), Saurer Austria (complete front axle), Graf & Stift (complete rear axle), Austro-Fiat (clutch, gearbox), Fross-Bussing and Puch (all accessories). Bodies were built by Petera of Hohenelbe and Rohrbacher of Vienna. During WW I assembling was continued on a small scale but now platform bodies were fixed for military purposes. After the war the "Einheits-Type" was not continued. *HON*

EUCLID (US) 1934 to date

(1) Euclid Crane Hoist Co., Cleveland, Ohio 1934-1936
(2) Euclid Road Machinery Co., Cleveland, Ohio 1936-1953
(3) Euclid Divn. of General Motors Corp., Cleveland, Ohio 1953-1968
(4) Euclid Divn. of White Motor Corp., Cleveland, Ohio 1968-1977
(5) Euclid Divn. of Daimler Benz AG, Cleveland, Ohio 1977 to date

1934 EUCLID Trac-Truck 10/11-ton dump truck, Euclid

1958 EUCLID 120-ton twin-engined dump truck, Euclid

1977 EUCLID R-35 70000lb dump truck, Euclid

The Euclid Crane Hoist Company was acquired by the Arlington family's construction machinery business in 1931, and given the title Euclid Road Machinery Company in 1936. The first Euclid Trac-Truk, was a 10/11-ton dump truck with gasoline engine, steel cab, tractor-pattern double rear tires and scow end steel tipping body, built for the construction and quarrying industries. It was followed by the 15-ton 1FB in 1936. Scrapers, loaders, crawler tractors and dump trucks became the firm's staple products, the latter going up to the 3-axle 45-ton 1LLD in 1951. This had twin 300 hp Cummins diesel engines. A later contender for the title of the world's largest truck was the 3-axle tractor with 2-axle dump trailer supplied to Western Mining in 1958, and capable of carrying 120 tons. It was powered by two Cummins engines totalling 750 hp, and cost $170,000.

In 1953 Euclid was acquired by General Motors, but they were forced to sell the division in 1968 under the Anti Trust (Monopolies Commission) law. White bought GM's American-based Euclid interests, but a Scottish factory which had been established in 1950 continued under GM ownership making dump trucks etc. under the name Terex. In 1972 GM began to make dump trucks under the Terex name in America as well. Meanwhile Euclids continued to be made under White ownership, and plants were set up in Belgium, Canada and Australia. All these interests were bought by Mercedes-Benz in 1977.

Current Euclid production includes the R Series 2-axle rear dump trucks, for 22 to 170 tons, B Series articulated bottom dumps up to 110 tons, and CH Series articulated coal haulers for loads of up to 150 tons. They have Cummins or Detroit Diesel engines of 228 to 1600 hp, the largest R-170 having diesel-electric drive. An experimental R-210 with AVCO-Lycoming 1884 hp gas turbine powered generator and 4 x 4 with twin tires all round was developed in 1974, but was soon discontinued because of rising fuel costs. *OM*

EUCORT (E) 1946-1953

Automoviles Eucort SA, Barcelona

Eucort passenger cars used 2-stroke engines similar to the pre-war D.K.W., of 2 cylinders and 750cc or 3 cylinder and 1250cc. Commercial versions included vans, pick-ups and taxis on the 2-cyl. chassis, and a 'fast van' on the 3-cylinder chassis. Eucorts were exported to Morocco and the Argentine in particular. *JCG*

EUGOL (US) 1922-1923

Eugol Motor Truck Co., Kenosha, Wis.

The model 752 was a 1-tonner with a 4-cylinder Buda engine, pneumatic tires, a 3-speed gearbox, Timken rear axle and Ross-built steering gear. This lone type was the only product of this obscure manufacturer. *GMN*

EVANS LIMITED (US) 1912-1913

Automobile Manufacturing & Engineering Company, Detroit, Michigan

The Evans appears to have been limited to a single model, and this for just one year. The Model 1 had a claimed capacity of 1500 pounds and was driven by a 4-cylinder, water-cooled engine. It used a three-speed transmission, shaft-drive and pneumatic tires. Its wheelbase was 112 inches and price was $1200. *GMN*

1976 EVO Model 1650 front drive refuse truck, Lodal Inc

EVO (US) 1968 to date

Lodal Inc., Kingsford, Mich.

Ray Brisson, now Lodal president, began building a rear-end bucket loader for trucks in the Brisson Brothers Machine Shop at Norway, Mich. in 1948. To expand the trucks' use the booms were faced forward for low loading, and an improved front-end loader called Lodal led to the formation of a new company, Lodal Inc. in 1953. Loaders were built on regular truck chassis, but in 1968 the EVO truck was developed to meet special needs of refuse collection in residential areas, taking its name from the EVOlutionary loading developments.

The EVO system separates collection from hauling, in a similar manner to the Pagefield system of the 1930s, and uses two types of vehicle; a compact house-to-house collection truck called the EVO 1650, and a huge 34 cu. yard transfer truck called the LAM (Load-A-Matic) which is mounted on regular truck chassis. The low cab-forward EVO 1650 has both left and right hand steering, with loading hopper amidships. Only one or two crewmen are needed, who both load and drive the EVO. When the body is full the EVO goes to a transfer yard where the 8 cu. yard load is lifted by a loader on the LAM into its body to be taken to the dump site. A city would normally use several EVOs for each LAM. A 12 cu. yard self-dumping EVO is also made. Standard components are used in the EVO, including Chrysler V-8 gasoline engines, Allison automatic transmissions and Rockwell-Standard front-driving axles. *RW*

EVYCSA (E) 1952-1963

Favrica de Motocicletas Evycsa, Barcelona

This company made motorcycles and small delivery tricycles powered by engines of 125 cc and 200 cc. *JCG*

EXPRESS (D) 1901-1905

Express-Werke A.G., Neumarkt

Based on the private car design of this make, light vans were available with 10 hp engines. *HON*

EXSHAW see Purrey

FABCO (US) 1938-1939; c.1955 to date

(1) F.A.B. Mfg. Co., Oakland, Calif.
(2) Fabco Division, Kelsey-Hayes Co., Oakland, Calif.

Fabco is a specialty manufacturer which produces several series of one-man-cab forward control trucks with the cab beside the engine, and also a cab-over utility vehicle, though they entered vehicle manufacture with a small series of fire engines built for California Fire Departments before the war.

Smallest of the one-man-cab vehicles is a yard trailer-spotter, the Fab 151, and there are several models of flat deck trucks with loading area for the entire length of the truck, interrupted only by the one-man cab at the front behind which is a Remy 10,000 lb. hydraulic crane. On these FT models the engine, a Ford gasoline 534-V8, is below the deck and drives through an automatic transmission. This series is made in 4x2 and 6x4 layouts, and is used for handling pipes and power poles up to 45 feet in length. The WT series is a flat top with the engine above the deck and beside the cab, intended for harvesting of agricultural produce with the minimum of plant damage. A 6x6 truck with single tires and 80 in. wide track, the WT is powered by Ford gasoline or Detroit Diesel engines. A combination of 5-speed Clark main and 3-speed Spicer auxiliary transmissions together with 2-speed Fabco transfer case gives a total of 30 forward speeds and 6 in reverse. Lowest speed is one mph, invaluable for harvesting purposes.

The Fabco UV cab-over series was introduced in 1972, and uses a conventional full-width cab and a choice of Ford gasoline or Caterpillar or Detroit Diesels. GVWs range from 27,000 to 56,000 lbs, and the trucks are available in 4x2, 4x4, 6x4 and 6x6 drives. In addition to these complete trucks, Fabco offer 4-wheel-drive conversions on Ford, GMC and other makes which are particularly used in power line erection. *RW*

FACCIOLI (I) 1905

Societa Ing. Aristide Faccioli, Turin

After resigning from the post of chief engineer of F.I.A.T. Aristide Faccioli tried his hand at manufacture, but without any success. One of his efforts was a 24/30 hp chain-driven single-decker bus exhibited at the 1905 Italian Motor Show. *MCS*

FACTO (US) 1922

Facto Motor Trucks, Inc., Springfield, Mass.

The sole model of Facto truck was a 2½-tonner powered by a Buda 4-cylinder engine. *GNG*

FADA (E) 1955-1958

F.A.D.A., Vallodolid

This little-known vehicle was a 3-wheeler powered by a single-cylinder 673 cc 20 hp engine. It had a 5-speed gearbox and shaft drive to the rear axle. The frame was of tubular steel, and the carrying capacity 1,500 kgs. *JCG*

FAFNIR (D) 1908-1926

Aachener Stahlwarenfabrik, Fafnir-Werke A.G., Aachen

The vans and light trucks of this manufacturer were based on the private car models. 4-cylinder engines of own construction were used. In 1922 two versions appeared with 1- and 1-½-ton payload capacity using a 2.5 litre engine. *HON*

FAGEOL (i) (US) 1916-1939

(1) Fageol Motors Co., Oakland, Cal. 1916-1932
(2) Fageol Motors Co., Kent, Ohio 1925-1926 (buses only)
(3) Fageol Truck & Coach Co., Oakland, Cal. 1932-1939

This company was formed by Frank R. Fageol, William B. Fageol, Louis H. Bill (president) and others to make luxury cars and orchard tractors. Car production was killed by America's entry into the war, and the tractors were over-priced, but as the Fageol brothers had built a few trucks before the formation of the company it was decided that these should be the main product. Fageols were conventional assembled trucks in the 2½ to 6-ton range, with 4-cylinder Waukesha engines, some paircast, some monobloc, Fageol's own transmission and a Timken worm rear axle. They had solid tires on artillery wheels, with the option of duals at the rear. A distinctive styling feature, used on nearly all subsequent Fageol vehicles, was the row of finned ventilators along the hood top. In the early 1920s the range was shifted to 1½- to 5-tonners, and prices ran from $3000 to $5700, substantially higher than the average American truck, but typical of California-built vehicles which had to be capable of climbing long, steep grades.

Concurrently the Fageol brothers developed a bus business which eventually involved several other companies. By 1920 the passenger stage business had achieved sizeable proportions in California, but neither extended touring cars nor light truck chassis were suitable, and to fill this need Fageol launched their Safety bus, shortly re-named Safety Coach, in 1921. This achieved a phenomenal success, and not only in California. It featured a 4-cylinder Hall-Scott engine and a fully-enclosed 22-passenger body carried between wide track wheels, the vehicle being lower than anything that had

1922 FAGEOL (i) Safety Coach 22-passenger coach, RNE

1921 FAGEOL (i) 6-ton truck, RNE

been seen before. Soon there was a 6-cylinder bus for 29 passengers, which had a luggage boot at the rear. An eastern sales agency was opened in Cleveland in 1924 by Frank Fageol, and the former plant of the Thomart Motor Co. in nearby Kent, Ohio was acquired for assembly of Safety Coaches. 260 were sold in 1923 and 503 in 1924.

In 1925 the American Car & Foundry Co. of Detroit, desiring to enter the transit vehicle manufacturing business, acquired the J.G. Brill Co. of Philadelphia, a major maker of streetcars and trolley coaches, and offered to buy the Fageol plants too. The Fageol brothers and most of the Ohio stockholders agreed to sell, the brothers becoming A.C.F. vice-presidents, but the Oakland plant remained independent. It also remained quite small, producing about 100 buses and a rather larger number of trucks per year in the late 1920s. Their buses included some double deckers. A.C.F. transferred Fageol production from Kent to Detroit in 1926, and continued to use the Fageol name on a type of bus that strongly resembled the Safety Coach, but other models introduced after 1927 used the name A.C.F. The Fageol brothers left A.C.F. in 1927 to form the Twin Coach Co. at Kent.

The Oakland plant kept pace with developments in the truck industry, with pneumatic tires, electric lighting and starting, full pressure lubrication and, in 1929, 4-wheel hydraulic brakes. The range expanded to include a 10-ton 6-wheeler with a 6-cylinder Hall-Scott engine as an option. A merger with Moreland was proposed in 1930 but fell through because of Fageol's operating losses, which led to receivership and a reorganization with bank leadership as Fageol Truck & Coach Co.

1932 FAGEOL (i) 10-ton truck and trailer, RNE

Diesel engines, by Cummins and Waukesha, were available from 1932, as were aluminum frames. In the mid 1930s a new streamlined cab with V-windscreen was adopted, and a cab-over joined the range in 1937. At this time the range ran from 2- to 10-tonners, with prices from $1340 to $10,800. A 1938 tandem tractor with a two-

1938 FAGEOL (i) articulated truck, RNE

section Fruehauf lowbed trailer measured 74 feet overall length, and hauled a transporter weighing 104 tons. As a result of continuing financial difficulties Fageol's assets were sold in November 1938 to Sterling of Milwaukee, and on January 1st 1939 Fageol truck production was suspended. Sterling retained the sales outlets and sold the rest to T.A. Peterman who renamed the truck Peterbilt and continued production. *RW/MBS*

1954 FAGEOL (ii) FV24 van, GNG

FAGEOL (ii) (US) 1950-1954

Twin Coach Co., Kent, Ohio

In 1950 Twin Coach revived the Fageol name for a line of furniture moving vans using many International components, with Twin's own integral construction. Fruehauf stampings were used for the bodies, which resembled Fruehauf trailers in their lines. They came in eight wheelbase lengths, from 108 to 222 inches. Though made by Twin Coach and sold through International dealers, the vans were known as Fageol Super Freighters. There was also a short-lived multi-stop delivery van of 1954 known as the Fageol Pony Express. *GNG*

FAIRBANKS-MORSE (US) 1908-

Fairbanks-Morse Co., Chicago, Ill.

This company was better-known for its agricultural tractors, which were made until about 1921, than for trucks, but for a short time they made a line of delivery wagons of 1000, 1200, and 3500 lbs capacity and also a 3-ton forward-control truck powered by a 25 hp 4-cylinder Sheffield engine. This had a constant-mesh 4-speed gearbox, double chain drive and a governed top speed of 10 mph. *GNG*

FAKA (D) 1951-1957

Fahrzeugwerk Kannehberg KG., Salzgitter-Bad

This firm produced a 3-wheeled van following motor-scooter lines. A 118 cc Jlo two-stroke engine was mounted above the single front wheel which it drove. A van box was mounted on the rear.

In 1956 a forward control bus was presented using a 120 hp Henschel diesel engine mounted at the rear. *HON*

FALCON (US) 1915-1916

Falcon Motor Truck Co., Detroit, Mich.

This was light ½-tonner which had pneumatic tires. Driving position was optional: either right-hand or left-hand. *GMN*

FALKE (D) 1900-1908

1) Fahrrad-und Automobilwerke Albert Falke & Co., Monchengladbach 1900-1907
2) Falke Motorfahrzeuge Albert Falke & Co., Monchengladbach 1907-1908

Falke vans and small trucks were based on the private car designs of this firm. They featured 2- and 4- cylinder engines by Fafnir and Breuer from 700 cc to 1600 cc. *HON*

F.A.M. (I) 1948-1950

Sarl F.A.M., Pesaro

This firm built light motorcycle-type 3-wheeler trucks on conventional lines. *MCS*

FAMO (D) 1937-1945

Fahrzeug-und Motoren-Werke GmbH., Breslau

Famo built the heavy type of half-track prime movers for military purposes using at first 9.8 litre, later 10.8 litre Maybach engines developing 250 hp. Also a tractor with 4-cylinder 45 hp Famo-LHB diesel engine and a heavy tractor using the 125 hp 2-stroke Junkers diesel engines were made. The latter was available also as articulated tractor. *HON*

FAMOUS (US) 1917-1919

Famous Trucks, Incorporated, St. Joseph, Michigan

This company orginated in Chicago, Illinois, but moved to St. Joseph before production began. Its Model B 10 was a one-tonner using a Continental 4-cylinder engine with a 3-speed gearbox and shaft drive. Apparently it was available only as a chassis on a 10-foot wheelbase at a price of $1690. *GMN*

F.A.P. (YU) 1951 to date

Fabrika Automobila Priboj, Priboj na Limu

FAP started life building medium-class truck chassis under Saurer license. First models bore a strong resemblance to post-war Austrian Saurers, while diesel engines used were of Yugoslavian origin. FAP dominated the medium to high tonnage class and lack of competition

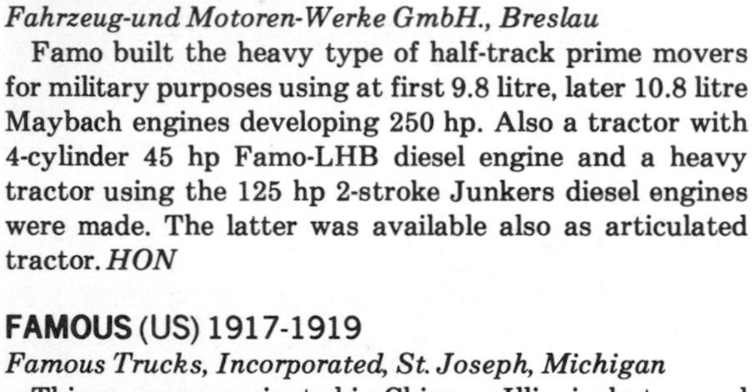

1962 F.A.P. 46EL/K 6-ton truck, AAR

1965 F.A.P. Model 18B 18-ton GVW truck, OMM

led to an intensive growth of the factory that soon was building trucks, tippers, 4x4 chassis and buses. Main supplier of diesel engines developing 90-180 hp was the Famos factory, that belongs to the ITV concern along with FAP, while gearboxes, axles and other components were also produced by ITV concern member factories. Proprietary bought engines, at certain stages, included Leyland 240 hp and IMR (Perkins) 110 hp diesels. Forward control cabs were, at a time, based on old-style OM Cabs, while the typical normal control cab was retained since the Saurer days and for many years remained unchanged, the introduction of twin headlights in the latter years. Buses and coaches, very conventional in design, were always based on front-engined chassis and were bodied by some of the ITV members, like Autokaroserija, Ikarus, II Oktomvri, etc. A trolley bus series was marketed in mid 60s with Elektrosrbija equipment, while Karoserija II Oktomvri pioneered the integrally-built coach at the same time. Integral construction coaches were soon marketed under the FAP Sanos trademark and were powered by rear placed Famos diesels developing 145 to 190 hp. Sometimes referred simply as Sanos, these coaches have a high degree of construction and finish. An articulated city bus was added in 1968 using an underfloor horizontal engine of 160 hp, while a later addition was a 12m Sanos city bus of integral construction, powered again by an underfloor Famos diesel developing 210 hp. The range included 6.5 to 13.5 ton payload normal and forward control trucks, 4x4 chassis and 44 to 160 passenger buses and coaches. Following an agreement with Daimler Benz in 1972, certain Mercedes Benz coaches, mainly 0302 models, are built in Priboj and the use of Mercedes Benz diesels and cabs is envisaged for the near future. *GA*

F.A.R. (F) 1937 to date

Tracteurs F.A.R., Gennevilliers, Seine

The name F.A.R. dates back to 1919 when a 4-wheeled road tractor of this name was put into production by Chenard Walcker. This was made throughout the 1920s and early 1930s, but in 1937 a new and separate company was set up to manufacture the British Scammell 3-wheeled mechanical horse under license. This was the first independent F.A.R. and was made up to the outbreak of the war, powered either by Chenard Walcker or Citroen engines, gasoline and diesel. They were widely used by French Railways and also by the wine merchants, Nicolas et Cie. The French Air Ministry placed a contract for over 300 for use as aircraft tugs.

After the war the 'Cheval Mecanique' was supplemented by the smaller 'Pony Mecanique', also a 3-wheeled tractor but powered by the air-cooled flat-twin Dyna-Panhard engine, for hauling loads in the 2 to 2¾ ton

1965 F.A.R. 6-ton articulated truck, HON

1970 F.A.R. 8-ton articulated truck, OMM

range. A new cab of different appearance from the Scammell was introduced. The Pony Mecanique was used as the basis for a street sweeper/sprinkler made by the Material de Voirie company, from 1952 onwards. These 3-wheelers, powered by Renault gasoline or Perkins diesel engines, were made up to about 1970, and were joined by various models of 4-wheeled tractor. Some of these were based on other makes of truck such as Renault and Saviem, but there was also the S model of individual F.A.R. design powered by a 6.8-litre 4-cylinder Panhard diesel engine for loads of 10/12 tons. Made in the mid-1960s this conventional tractor was short-lived, but was replaced by the cab-over design using a Berliet cab which is still made today. Powered by a 60 hp 4-cylinder Perkins diesel engine, it is for trailer loads of up to six tons. *GNG*

FARGO (i) (US) 1913-1921

Fargo Motor Car Company, Chicago, Illinois

The original Model E was a 1500-pound capacity panel van with a 2-cylinder engine and friction transmission on a wheelbase of 98 inches. It had forward control. Later models were limited to two-tonners on 144-inch wheelbase using Continental 4-cylinder engines. Chassis price for the last models was $2200. *GMN*

FARGO (ii) (US) 1928 to date

(1) Fargo Motor Corporation, Detroit, Mich. 1928-1932
(2) Chrysler Corporation, Dodge Division, Detroit, Mich. 1932-1938
(3) Chrysler Corporation, Dodge Division, Warren, Mich. 1938 to date

Fargo was essentially a name rather than a make. The Fargo Motor Corporation acted as Chrysler's fleet sales division, which explains the presence of Fargo badges on Plymouth sedans sold to the US Army in the 1930s. From 1935 onward the Fargo name was applied to some vehicles sold in the Canadian and other export markets, either to give Corporation dealers without a Dodge franchise a line of trucks to sell, or to assure an extra import quota. Such Fargos were identical in all respects to parallel (i) Dodges, while in some countries the British-built (ii) Dodge was sold as a Fargo. So were Australian Dodges produced at Keswick, Adelaide, and after the Chrysler acquisition of Rootes Motors the Commer sometimes masqueraded behind a Fargo badge. The Canadian Fargo line ceased in 1972, but the name was still widely used in 1978 — mainly in Scandinavia, the Middle East, and Africa.

Until 1932 there were, however, some genuine Fargos with no exact Dodge equivalent. Of these, the Packet was a light delivery van using the mechanical elements of the 4-cylinder Plymouth private car, the Clipper bore the same relation to the K- and CK-series DeSoto Sixes, and the Freighter was a 1-ton truck on Dodge lines. In 1931 and 1932 the Fargo name was also used on Dodge buses, of which about 75 were sold; engines were sixes and straight-8s. Thereafter the Fargo PSV line was limited to chassis, primarily for school bus work. *MCS*

1930 FARGO Packet Six delivery van, Chrysler

1964 FARMOBIL ½-ton light truck, OMM

FARMOBIL (GR) 1962-1967

(1) Kodogouris Bros., Neo Kordelio, Thessaloniki, 1962
(2) Earco S.A., Neo Kordelio, Thessaloniki, 1963-1964
(3) Chrysler Hellas S.A., Neo Kordelio, Thessaloniki, 1965-1967

Designed by the West German factory of agricultural machinery Fahr A.G. and intended as a utility-agricultural vehicle, the Farmobil was series-produced in Northern Greece at first by a Greek owned company. Powered by a rear mounted BMW horizontally opposed twin cylinder engine of 38 hp, it featured an open top rear body and a canvas top cab for two. After a few units were delivered, the company reorganized and soon became a subsidiary of Chrysler International. Farmobil was largely exported through the Chrysler network and was even tested by the British army. Nevertheless the whole project collapsed in 1967. *GA*

FARRIMOND (GB) 1931

Diesel Motor Co. Ltd., Thornton Heath, Surrey

Designed by Thomas Farrimond who had formerly built trailers, this was a road tractor powered by a large single-cylinder oil engine with a bore and stroke of 8 7/8 x 10¼ inches, running at maximum speed of 540 rpm. This horizontal 2-stroke unit was said to be able to run on pure gasoline, pure oil or a 50-50 mixture of the two. It had three speeds, shaft drive, pneumatic tires and a fully-enclosed cab. When hauling its gross load of 15 tons it had a top speed of 12 mph. Starting was effected by detaching the steering wheel and applying it to the hub of the fly-wheel; this was at the side as the engine was mounted transversely. *GNG*

FAUBER BI-CAR (US) 1914

W.H. Fauber, New York, N. Y.

The Fauber was just one of the many abortive cyclecars of the year 1914 and was offered with a delivery van body. This was priced at $285 and was powered by a two-cylinder, air-cooled engine. Gross weight of this vehicle was 500 pounds. *GMN*

FAUN (D) 1918 to date

(1) Fahrzeugfabriken Ansbach und Nurnberg, Nuremberg 1918-1920

(2) Faun-Werke, A.G., Nuremberg 1920-1926

(3) Faun-Werke GmbH., Nuremberg; Neunkirchen; Butzbach;

Osterholz-Scharmbeck 1926 to date

The firm of Faun (Fahrzeugfabriken Ansbach und Nurnberg) came into existence by the merger of Fahrzeugfabrik Ansbach (see Ansbach) and Nurnberger Feuerloschgerate-, Automobillastwagen- und Fahrzeugfabrik Karl Schmidt (see Braun). Both were special factories for the production of commercials. Faun presented a line of vehicles with gasoline, gas-electric and electric drive. There were 3½- and 5-ton trucks with 45 hp gasoline engine, a 2-ton electric-driven truck with hub cap motors and a gas-electric bus with the same 45 hp engine.

In 1926 the firms divided for various reasons, Ansbach manufacturing vehicles under their own marque but these were Faun designs. Faun itself carried on a line of gasoline-electric trucks and buses now using a 70 hp Maybach engine. In 1927 a forward control bus with gas-electric drive was presented.

1932 FAUN refuse truck, OMM

In 1930 both firms were again united. The program consisted of a gasoline-electric refuse collector, a very unique gasoline-electric three-wheeled street sweeper, a universal vehicle for municipal services with interchangeable bodies and a 55 hp 6-cylinder Rasmussen engine, and other municipal vehicles with a 100 hp 6-cylinder Maybach engine. Further there was a bus with 90 hp Maybach engine and also some prototypes of trolleybuses with hub cap motors. Moreover Faun presented the first diesel-electric vehicle as a refuse collector. During the thirties the Faun line consisted of a 2-tonner with 4-cylinder gasoline engine, several versions in the 3½ to 6-tons category with 6-cylinder diesel engines and a 9-tonner with 8-cylinder diesel engine. Faun did not have their own engine production but used Deutz engines. In 1934 the first 3-axle truck appeared, in 1938 Faun presented the first German 4-axle truck with steerable tandem front wheels. It was a forward control version, the engine was placed behind the driver's cab. Very advanced was a road tractor for 20-ton towing capacity.

After WW II Faun started production in a new factory at Neunkirchen near Nuremberg. The type M 6 was the

1938 FAUN 15-ton 8-wheel truck, HON

1950 FAUN 8-ton truck, GNG

1952 FAUN bus with trailer, Techniart

c.1960 FAUN F68 articulated tanker, OMM

first one, mainly used for refuse collectors and equipped with 6-cylinder gasoline engine by Maybach. Compared with other makes Faun very early introduced forward control truck. This was the L 7 of 1949, a 7-tonner with a 6-cylinder 150 hp Deutz diesel engine. This also was available as bus under the type designation 0 7 V. A wide variety of normal control trucks, articulated tractors, dump trucks was developed during the next years, all equipped with Deutz diesel engines. In 1956 a light truck was presented with a payload-capacity from 2- to 2-¾ tons. This was available with gasoline engine or water or air-cooled diesel engines and a wide variety of bodies. Faun continued to build trucks until about 1969. The last type was a 3-axled F 6103 VL for 12 ton payload and equipped with a 10-cylinder 250 hp Deutz diesel engine.

1962 FAUN F24 2-ton van, HON

An articulated tractor with the same engine and a 3-axle chassis for concrete mixers remained in the program. But in about 1970 Faun started to concentrate on special vehicles.

The range today comprises crane carriers up to a 16 x 8 version with 530 hp MTU engine, airport fire fighting vehicles up to an 8 x 8 vehicle with 2 x 500 hp engine, special front-driven transporters for iron and steel mills with payload capacities up to 90 ton and prime movers with 4 x 2 to 8 x 8 drive which also are available as articulated tractors with an engine output up to 730 hp. All these versions are manufactured in the main plant at Neunkirchen. The plant at Butzbach is specialized on dump trucks with payload capacities from 15 to 80 tons and engines ranging from 157 to 811 hp. The former Borgward plant at Osterholz-Scharmbeck produces municipal vehicles, a small self-collecting street-sweeper and the well-proved three wheeled street-sweeper. Moreover susperstructures of street sweepers, refuse collectors and other purposes are built here and fixed to various chassis to the customers order. Also at Osterholz-Scharmbeck various military vehicles are built with 4 x 4, 6 x 6 and 8 x 8 drive. For all vehicles mainly Deutz diesel engines are used, but also for some versions MTU, General Motors and Cummins engines are available. Faun today is a manufacturer for special vehicles and to a great extent builds to order, so it is possible to realize special demands of customers. *HON*

1977 FAUN HZ32.25/40 heavy tractor, Faun

FAVEL (F) 1941-1944

Fabrique de Vehicules Automobiles Electriques Legers, Marseilles

This company made a 400 kg forward-control electric delivery van on the same chassis as its passenger cars. *GNG*

1965 FAUN K30 35-ton dump truck, OMM

FAWCETT-FOWLER (GB) 1907

Fawcett Preston & Co. Ltd., Liverpool

The Fawcett-Fowler was a light goods or passenger chassis with a 4-cylinder single acting horizontally opposed engine, of which the cylinders were 3 inch bore and 3½ inch stroke with camshaft driven poppet valves. The boiler was of liquid fired flash type mounted at the rear. The engine was at front. Shaft drive was employed to the differential on the countershaft and, from thence, twin chains to the rear wheels. The power rating was 20/25 hp. The makers are still in business and their records show that only two vehicles were made. *RAW*

FAWICK (US) 1913-1916

Fawick Motor Car Co., Sioux Falls, SD

This was an obscure make and apparently sold locally only. For the three production years, ½-, ¾- and 1-tonners were offered. *GMN*

FBW (CH) 1910 to date

(1) Franz Brozincevic & Co., Zurich, 1910-1914
(2) F~anz AG., Zurich, 1914-1918
(3) FBW Franz Brozincevic & Co., Wetzikon, ZH, 1918-1930
(4) FBW AG Franz Brozincevic & Co., Wetzikon, ŹH, 1930 to date

Franz Brozincevic the founder of the company was born in 1874 in Kroatia, (present-day Yugoslavia). He came to Switzerland in 1893 and built his first truck, largely by hand, in 1910. It had a 15/20 hp 4-cylinder engine.

In 1911 Brozincevic moved into a small factory still in Zurich. Total staff was about 80 persons only 4 of which served for the management and administration. At this time it was not planned to start manufacturing commercial vehicles but rather to build postal delivery trucks only. A small series of closed postal vehicles with shaft-drive and fully weather protected driver's cab with windshield and side windows was completed and put in service. These light trucks were much admired for their modern appearance, quiet running and high reliability. In view of this favorable reception and also in order to recuperate some of the considerable development costs Franz Brozincevic then decided to offer Franz vehicles also to the public. The company rapidly expanded and still in 1911 claimed having launched the first shaft-driven 5-ton truck. This however is highly doubtful as Berna had offered already one year before a full range of trucks with shaft-drive. Anyway, this heavy model received a 30/35 hp 4-cylinder engine of 5.4-litres. Power was transmitted via multiple disc clutch and 4-speed gearbox to the twin-wheel rear-axle. One year later Franz offered the first mechanically actuated tipping device for their trucks. Business was flourishing and about a dozen trucks of 2½, 3½ and 5-tons were made per year. Franz was still a rather small company but a foreign group was interested to purchase the firm which would then have become a real threat to the larger Swiss manufacturers. This induced Berna, Olten to make a very good offer and early in 1914 the agreement was signed according to which Franz became part of Berna with Franz Brozincevic remaining general manager and owner of a minority of shares of the newly formed company.

A few months later the first World War broke out and this brought unparalleled prosperity to all manufacturers of commercial vehicles. In order to follow a policy of neutrality the Berna management decided to export its own products to the Allies only and to offer the Franz trucks to Germany and Austria. The pre-war types were continuously improved. In 1916 a 4-ton model for military transportation in mountainous country was presented to the press. Due to differences with the Berna management,

1916 FRANZ (F.B.W.) 3-ton truck, F.B.W.

Franz Brozincevic left the company he had founded and established a new firm FBW in the old premises of the Schweizer Motorwagenfabrik in Wetzikon where he started manufacturing tractors and tool machines. His contract did not allow him to produce commercial vehicles for the next 2 years.

Franz continued to supply their trucks in three sizes to the military forces. In 1917 a total of 74 trucks were registered in Switzerland but several times as many had been exported. One year later the armistice was signed, the demand for commercial vehicles dropped off and the Franz company was reformed into a repair and maintenance workshop with agencies for passenger cars and the commercial vehicles of Fiat, Renault and Presto. It was never involved again with the production of commercial vehicles thereafter.

On the other hand FBW Wetzikon took up manufacturing of trucks in 1918 relying mainly on improved earlier designs and also on previous customers. During the difficult years after the war FBW employed between 60 and 100 persons and the yearly output was an average of some 60 to 80 vehicles. In 1922 FBW launched a new model with a very up-to-date monobloc pressure lubricated 4-cylinder OHV engine of 5.3-litres and 35 hp. The conventional chassis with semi-elliptic springs all around had shaft-drive and a wheelbase of 13'. Payload was 3 tons. For the heavy 5-ton models FBW introduced a double-ratio rear-axle. FBW soon began to offer pneumatic tires as an optional and then as standard equipment. In 1924 a licensing agreement allowed the famous German locomotive factory, Henschel & Sohn in Kassel, to build and sell commercial vehicles of FBW design for 10 years. One year later a total of 288 FBWs were registered in Switzerland.

The FBW trucks of the twenties were sober looking vehicles with fully enclosed driver's cab, often with one door only on the left-hand side as the spare rim and tire was mounted on the driver's side. The radiator shell of pleasing form was nickel plated. As on all Swiss trucks the turning radius was of prime importance due to the narrow alpine roads with tight hair-pin curves. 4-cylinder engines of 20 to 60 hp were fitted. Four-wheel brakes and steel-spoke wheels with pneumatic tires became standard. One of the better customers of FBW was the Swiss Army which purchased not only medium and heavy trucks but also a number of light chassis for their ambulances. The 1½-ton chassis had a 4-litre 4-cylinder engine of 35 hp.

From about 1926 onward FBW pioneered a new form of

the heavy truck and large capacity buses in Switzerland, namely the three-axle vehicle. As is well known Renault had proved to the world in 1923 that such vehicles had excellent cross-country properties. FBW however had other goals in mind. One was to offer a considerably increased payload and longer loading platform. The other to provide better traction on snow covered alpine roads. Already in the winter 1927/8 the Swiss postal bus administration was putting one of the new FBW 6x4 buses on scheduled service in the St. Moritz area with good results. The chassis of the early version was straight, subsequently it was lowered and bent over the two rear axles. Semi-elliptic springs were fitted, one pair of extra long and strong springs taking care of the two rear axles which had single wheels only. 40x8" tires and

1928 F.B.W. 6-wheel postal bus, F.B.W.

mechanical 6-wheel brakes were fitted. Whereas the first models received the 4-cylinder engine, later types after 1927 were equipped with the new 90 hp monobloc 6-cylinder OHV engine of 7.9-litres. From the outside this could be detected by the additional "6 Zyl" after the trade-name on the radiator. This powerful and very clean looking engine was of course also mounted into the heavy 2-axle models. There was also a smaller 6-cylinder OHV engine of 6.3-litres and 72 hp. Both had detachable cylinder-heads. The engine-block, sump and valve-cover were made of aluminum. The crankshaft had 4 bearings and double ignition (coil and magneto) was fitted. All the heavy FBW engines had a patented exhaust-brake.

In 1930 FBW was reformed and became a public company with a capital of 1 million Swiss Francs which of course remained in the family. The three sons of the founder were all engaged in the company and when he died three years later, the oldest son Franz took over the general management assisted by Kirchensteiner who had helped his father to build the very first Franz vehicle in 1910.

FBW by that time had established itself firmly on the Swiss market in third position behind Saurer and Berna and a total of 574 of their vehicles were running in Switzerland. The depression forced FBW to reduce staff and production. Furthermore the new Swiss law regarding motor-traffic and transportation further reduced the sales possibilities of heavy vehicles. Maximum gross weight of trucks was severely restricted in order to favor rail transportation.

In 1934 FBW launched their first diesel engine model D34, a 6-cylinder OHV engine of 8.5-litres and 100 hp.

Over the years FBW chassis were steadily developed and in 1939 the following models were offered: Type F 2½-ton truck with 4-litre sv 6-cylinder gasoline engine of 55 hp. Type A 4½-ton truck with 5.7-litre 4-cylinder OHV diesel engine of 66 hp. The 3-side tipper type FA with a 13' 2" wheelbase instead of 14' 9" and the lower omnibus chassis had the same engine. The heavy models L 40 6-ton truck and L 50 6-ton tipper truck as well as the LN 40 bus received the D34 6-cylinder OHV diesel engine of 100 hp.

1941 F.B.W. L40 6-ton truck, F.B.W.

This was also fitted into the 6x4 truck type 60 with 7-tons payload. The type 51 two-axle and three-axle omnibus low-floor chassis however had a 90 hp gasoline OHV engine of 6-cylinders and 8.3-litres displacement. All FBW chassis had multiple disc clutches, mechanical fuel pump and four-wheel servo-hydraulic brakes. Whereas the trucks received 4-speed gearboxes with or without overdrive the bus-chassis had 5-speed gearboxes with overdrive and two synchronized ratios.

During the war years FBW apart from changing many of their vehicles to the use of substitute fuels (wood-generators) and supplying medium and heavy trucks, built and furnished a number of special purpose vehicles to the Army. Furthermore studies were conducted regarding trolley buses. In this field FBW was a pioneer. More and more town administrations in Switzerland became faithful customers. Zurich for instance had a fleet of some 30 refuse trucks on the durable FBW 5-ton chassis and buses of various sizes and passenger capacities were in service in many towns.

The boom in construction and building of houses, roads, bridges etc. which set in soon after the 2nd World War, led to full order books and the time of delivery climbed to up to two years. In view of the limitation of 4½-tons payload for all imported utility vehicles there was an especially great demand for the heavy trucks and tipper trucks.

In the late forties FBW offered trucks for up to 7½-tons payload. The 4.7-ton truck type RD-A35 had a 6-cylinder OHV diesel engine of 5.7-litres and 72 hp. It was equipped with a FBW 5-speed gearbox with the two top speeds synchronized. Wheelbase was 44 cm and steering could be had left or right hand. The type DD-L 40 and DD-L 50 had the improved 6-cylinder OHV diesel engine of 8.5-litres with direct injection developing now 112 hp at 1800 rpm. The 4-speed gearbox had an overdrive ratio. Payload was 6.3 and 7.5-tons respectively. The same engine was also fitted to the various bus chassis. The 7-ton truck could also be ordered with a forward control cab.

In 1949 FBW claimed another first in Switzerland by presenting the type EDU horizontal underfloor mounted 6-cylinder OHV diesel of 11-litres and 145 hp. It was soon fitted into long distance trucks as well as in a lowered chassis version for buses. This powerful engine had wet cylinder liners and was also made in a normal vertical version called ED for heavy normal and forward control commercial vehicles. One year later an excursion bus with underfloor engine and semi-automatic planetary gearbox was on display at the Geneva Motor Show. The Swiss postal administration as well as a number of urban transportation services were quick to appreciate the advantages of this construction and FBW for a time had difficulties to keep up with the orders.

1950 F.B.W. AS50V 7½-ton truck, F.B.W.

Also in 1950 the 4x4 forward control truck type 5 T 4x4 was introduced serving for civilian and military duties. It was equipped with the improved version of the trusted 8.5-litre diesel engine developing 115 hp. The 4-speed gearbox was supplemented by a mechanical reduction and distribution gearbox offering two ratios. Rigid axles, semi-elliptic springs, hydraulic brakes with compressed air servo assistance, exhaust engine brake, a wheelbase of 11' 2" and 5-tons payload were further specifications. The Trilex wheels were equipped with 10.00x20 tires and on request Westinghouse servo assistance for the steering was available.

The following years brought a consolidation with steady improvements of the well-proven engines and chassis-designs. By 1960 the following types were manufactured: the L 40 and L 50 normal control and the L 40 V and L 50 V forward control trucks with the DD-6-cylinder diesel of 8.5 litres and 115 hp. Wheelbase ranged from 13' 5" to 16' 5" and payload was 5- to 8-tons. The L 50 and L 50 V could also be equipped with the 150 hp 6-cylinder OHV diesel engine of 11-litres. All these types had Scintilla or Bosch injection pumps, multiple disc clutches, mechanical 4-speed gearboxes with additional compressed air actuated overdrive gearboxes, compressed air brakes, mechanical hand brakes with Westinghouse servo, exhaust engine brake, servo-steering and 10.00x20 tires on Trilex wheels. For the buses the following chassis were offered: Type L 70 U, CA 40 U and B 51 U all with the underfloor mounted horizontal EDU 6-cylinder OHV engine of 11-litres developing now 155 hp. Unlike the truck chassis these had hydraulic clutches combined with a mechanical 4-speed planetary gearbox operated by compressed air pre-selection and an additional electro-pneumatically operated planetary overdrive gearbox. Semi-elliptic springs all around and brakes similar to those on the truck chassis were fitted. In addition there was the 4x4 truck 5 ASX already described.

From 1962 onward a modernized program was introduced. The small 8½-litre engine which had served in a number of versions as the successful power-plant for many years and the types L 40, L 40 V and 5 ASX were dropped. The new line included the L 50 V/ED forward control truck, the new heavy normal control 3-side tipper truck L 70 3 SK/ED and the forward control 4x4 X 50/70 all with the ED-engine now developing 170 hp. The underfloor engined bus chassis L 50 U and B 51 U were both equipped with the horizontal EDU engine of similar size and power. This range was offered unchanged for six years.

It was felt however that with the heavy models alone it was not possible to fill all the requirements of the clientele and in 1968 a considerably expanded range was presented. At the lower end there was the new L 35 U, a forward control truck with modern cab fitted with the new underfloor horizontal 6-cylinder OHV diesel engine of 7-litres developing 130 hp at 2400 rpm. A hydraulic single plate dry clutch and a 5-speed synchro-gearbox or a 4-speed unit with electro-pneumatically controlled overdrive ration were fitted. Two circuit compressed air brakes, handbrake on the rear wheels with servo-assistance and exhaust engine brake were chosen. Payload 5.6-tons. The slightly bigger L 40 UA received the same powerplant but with turbo-supercharging it was called type CUA and developed 160 hp. Payload 7.1-tons. The next in line was the L 45 UA with heavier chassis and 8.5-tons payload. Still available remained the L 50 V/ED and the L 50 U types. Another new model was the L 70 U3 with the improved underfloor mounted engine EU 3 with increased bore, 11.5-litres displacement and 210 hp. The 6-speed gearbox with an additional intermediary gearbox which was electro-pneumatically controlled by a small switch. Wheelbase was 16' 5" and payload 8 to 10 tons. Other types remaining in the program were the L 70 3SK/E3 normal control tipper truck now with the more powerful E 3 engine of 11.5-litres and 210 hp, the B 51 U chassis and the 4x4 truck X 50/70.

1974 F.B.W. articulated trolleybus. F.B.W.

1974 F.B.W. 50V 15-ton articulated truck, F.B.W.

In the following years this line was further expanded. The turbo supercharged underfloor engine EUA of 11-litres and 230 hp was fitted into the L 50 U chassis. The road tractor with normal control received the vertical supercharged EA engine of similar size and power output. As on the bus chassis a semi-automatic transmission with torque-converter and electro-pneumatically operated pre-selection planetary gearbox with 2x4 speeds was fitted. Payload of this heavy vehicle was 14 tons. Then followed the articulated bus type 91 UA 52/64 L with three axles and a wheelbase of 17' and 21'. This received the improved supercharged underfloor engine EU2A of 260 hp and a full automatic transmission with pre-selection. Total length was 16.5 m and air-cushion suspension was fitted. In 1970 a total of 2190 FBW commercial vehicles and buses was registered in Switzerland and in the following year 82 new vehicles took the road.

During the past few years the FBW range has expanded, especially since 3-axle trucks with a total weight of 26 tons have been allowed on Swiss roads. The current range consists of the Model 40 U in the 10-14 ton GVW range, and 50 U and 50 V in the 16-19 ton GVW range, the U models having horizontal underfloor engines and the V models vertical engines, all 6-cylinder units developing between 230 and 280 hp. In addition there are the Model 70 N conventional tippers with 4x2 drive, 70 X

1978 F.B.W. 8X4 tanker, F.B.W.

4x4 and 80 X 6x6 conventional tippers, the latter with 320 hp engines. The largest trucks are the 75 U 6x2 and 85 V 8x4 with GVWs of 26 and 30 tons respectively. The 50 V is made as a tractor for trailer weights of 30 tons GCW. Among FBW passenger vehicles are the Model 55 U and 91 U city buses and Model 91 GL 3-axle articulated city bus.

In order to enter the market for smaller vehicles, FBW distribute the Japanese Mitsubishi Canter 2-tonner and Fuso 6½-tonner under the name MMC-FBW. *FH*

F. C. S. (US) 1909-1910

Schmidt Brothers Co., South Chicago, Ill.

There was a 1-tonner made under this trademark and this had a closed delivery body. This was powered by a 2-cylinder engine mounted beneath the body. This air-cooled engine was connected to a planetary transmission and then by double chains to the rear wheels. Solid rubber tires were used, and it was claimed this truck could attain 20 mph. It is possible the tradename was later changed to Schmidt. *GMN*

FEDERAL (US) 1910-1959

(1) Bailey Motor Truck Co., Detroit, Mich. 1910
(2) Federal Motor Truck Co., Detroit, Mich. 1910-1952
(3) Federal Motor Truck Div. Federal Fawick Corp., Detroit, Mich. 1952-1954
(4) Federal Motor Truck Co., Div. Napco Industries Inc., Minneapolis, Minn. 1955-1959

Martin L. Pulcher organized the Bailey Motor Truck Co. in Feb. 1910 with a capitalization of $50,000 and was the president and general manager. But by the time the first truck appeared its name was Federal.

Federal was an assembled truck throughout its long history. In design, whatever Federal did was in line with general industry practices, with only rare exceptions. "Never an experiment" they said. All Federals were conventionals until cab-overs were added to the range for 1937.

The first models used a Continental 4-cylinder engine with 3-speed selective transmission, and a final drive by double chains. A 1-ton chassis was offered at $1800 and it weighed 3200 pounds. Bodies available were panel with cab roof, stake, and open express. Already, by May 1913, Federal had produced its 1000th truck with 25 in the US

1911 FEDERAL Model D 1-ton truck, NAHC

Postal Service in New York City and shipments to 20 foreign countries.

1916 FEDERAL Model W 2-ton truck, RNE

Timken worm drive replaced the chain-drive for 1916, and the range was now 1½ to 3 tons. For 1917 a 5-ton model was added, and a 7-ton for 1918. Tractors for semi-trailers were also made, using Continental 4-cylinder engines. Crescent-styled cabs were the rule. Artillery wheels were standard, but large models had steel spoke wheels, all with solid tires.

U.S. Cord tires and disc wheels came on the 1921 1½-ton models; others had steel spoked wheels and retained solid tires. Road speeds were 25 mph for the 1½-ton model, 15 for the 2-ton, and 12 for the 3½- and 5-ton models, generally somewhat below the average for contemporary trucks. Chassis price range was $1800 to $4500 in this era.

By 1923 Federal truck production totalled 27,017 units. Bus chassis for 18 and 25 passengers with 6-cylinder engines and all-steel bodies were offered now. In June 1924, Federal introduced the Willys-Knight engine to the motor truck industry and engineered a light chassis for it with a new low price of $1095. This model was continued into 1928, at which time Willys-Knight started putting these engines in their own trucks.

More powerful 6-cylinder engines of higher rpm were a development of the mid-1920's, and in late 1927 Federal was offering a choice of Waukesha 4- or Continental 6-cylinder engines and bevel or worm drives in 1- to 7½-tons capacity. These 6-cylinder engines had 7-bearing crankshafts.

1928 and 1929 were years of more industry advances, most visibly obvious in the widespread adoption of pneumatic tires for the heavy trucks, and much refinement in styling. Federal kept pace, and also had one of the first sleeper cabs on the large tractors. Brakes on the front wheels became nearly universal now, and Federal's were 4-wheel vacuum-operated hydraulic, expanding, with the hand brake contracting on the drive shaft.

Federals in the early 1930's were generally much like other trucks in styling, especially GMC. Four and six cylinder engines had, in order, 50 and 72 hp for a range of

1932 FEDERAL Model U6 articulated tanker, NAHC

1 to 8 tons, including 6-wheelers, with the rear axle trailing.

In October 1931, Federal announced a new bevel gear tandem axle drive for 4- and 6-cylinder 3-ton models. Developed by Federal's chief engineer George B. Ingersoll, assisted by the Clark Equipment Co., the second bevel ring gear was driven by a short pinion shaft from the bevel ring gear on the first axle (most other truck tandems had worm or double reduction drives.)

1931 FEDERAL Model E6 1½-ton truck, George Ingram Collection

The following month a 4-ton, 6-cylinder, 6-wheeler of 18,000 pounds gvw was added, with the rear axle driving and using swivel type central spring seats. Styling changes for 1934 included a slightly slanted one-piece visorless windshield, a V-type radiator grille. Continental, Hercules, or Waukesha 4- or 6-cylinder engines were offered in the 50 to 114 hp range, the 4-cylinder size being restricted to the ¾- to 1½-ton truck, whose chassis price was $645; 2-ton $845, both with full-floating rear axle.

The era of streamlining had come, and the new 1935 Federals had the latest styling with a deluxe cab featuring a V-type windshield. Fenders got skirts, and the hood got horizontal louvres. The 1½- to 4-ton models had bevel gear drives, and the 4- to 6-ton models had double reduction drives, with worm drive optional on the 6-ton size. Some models up to 2½ tons had drop-frames. By this time Federal also had a Canadian factory at Windsor, Ontario.

A big revival of the cab-over-engine type (also known as the "camel back") occurred in the mid-1930's after being generally out of fashion sine 1920, and Federal's first cab-over made its appearance for 1937 in four sizes from 1½- to 3-tons. The split grille on the cab-overs, large conventionals, and forward-control delivery vans resembled the one used on the 1938 International D-300 cab-over.

1934 FEDERAL Model 50 5-ton truck, NAHC

Federal styling reached a peak in the conventionals with a new, more slanted grille and high crowned fenders with larger skirts and full coverage in front down to the hub level. The engine and the dash panel were moved a bit forward for better load distribution. Mr. Pulcher, still president, announced ¾-ton panel and pickup trucks, each with a 4-cylinder 50 hp engine, to fill an existing gap in the general truck market. Federal now had four lines of trucks. Altogether, 18 models with 99 different wheelbases were offered at prices from $645 to $5345. The largest Federal (6-ton) weighed 10,000 pounds for the first time.

1938 FEDERAL Model 11 1½-ton truck, NAHC

New styling came on the smaller conventionals for 1938 with Henry Dreyfuss doing the work. The deluxe cab was redesigned and the massive new rounded grille was nearly all a sheet of chromium plate with only 9 large slots from top to bottom. Liberal use of chromium was obvious elsewhere, too. This basic style was to continue through 1950.

A rare milestone for a truck manufacturer was passed early in 1939 when lifetime Federal truck production passed 100,000, with a yearly average then of about 4,000 trucks. R. W. Ruddon was now president.

The heavy duty line got new sheet metal, but using the previous cabs. On the heavyweights, too, chromium was

1939 FEDERAL Model 8 metro-van, NAHC

liberally used on the massive vertical V-type shutter-like grille and on the bumper. Some had sleeper cabs. 115 hp Waukesha and 138 hp Continental engines were used, with Hercules engines powering the smaller models, all having 6-cylinders and 7-bearing crankshafts. Heavy duty transmissions were 5-speed Clark. Air brakes were featured.

Several new conventional and forward-control delivery vans stretched that range to 2 tons. From this point on, the civilian line was continued basically unchanged through 1950, with all but the largest Federal getting Her-

1950 FEDERAL Style Liner Artic. Van, RJ

cules engines by 1942. After Stewart truck production came to an end in 1941, Federal adopted the Stewart slogan "Federals have won by costing less to run." Federal also got Stewart's president, Thomas R. Lippard. During World War II Federal made large 6x6 7½-ton wreckers to a common design with Reo, but looking more like Federal's civilian heavyweights. 180 hp Hercules 6-cylinder HXD engines were used with 5-speed transmissions having 2 ranges. Cleveland Pneumatic air springs were used in front, a rare item by this time. Federal also made a 20-ton 6x4 heavy transporter tractor using a 130 hp Cummins 6-cylinder 2-stroke diesel. This was the heaviest Federal yet, weighing 20,000 pounds.

After World War II the civilian Federals continued much as before and the next big change came for 1951 with the completely new Styleliner 1800 conventionals.

An entirely new 6-cylinder ohv Power Chief engine was engineered by Federal, developing 145 hp @ 3000 rpm. Hypoid gear axles and radius-rod drive were standard and single-speed and double reduction axles were offered. Weights for chassis and cab started at 7200 pounds. The gross vehicle weight was 25,000 pounds, and the gross combination weight (with semi-trailer) was 45,000 pounds.

Ten other Styleliner models of smaller capacities were also offered, as well as the full line of conventional heavy duty and 6-wheeler gasoline and diesel units.

Federal US registrations reached the peak of 6020 units in 1947. But, in spite of a good product and new models production thereafter slid to only 874 by 1954.

Some specialties were produced about this time. One was a tall, unusual tractor having the cab set high over the wheels and with the engine and hood in front. The cab for a crew of several was fabricated by removing the rear walls of 2 GMC cabs and welding them back-to-back. The US Air Force used these for towing planes, and an identical design was made by Coleman.

Another highly unusual specialty, of 1954, was a cab-over truck called "The Octo-Quad" built as a show unit for the Timken-Detroit Axle Co. The Octo-Quad used tandem Timken axles, front and rear. The cab was fabricated from the front of a large bus.

Shortly after, Napco Industries bought Federal and moved manufacturing operations to Minneapolis, Minn.

The Air Force ordered about 100 large conventional civilian-styled 4x4 Federals with RXC Hercules and Continental 6-cylinder engines driving through Allison Torqmatic transmissions, and fitted with 5-yard Galion dump bodies. 1956 Ford cabs with the new wrap-around windshield were used. For snowplowing these Federals were fitted with Gledhill 3-way V-blades.

Another heavy duty Federal, the Golden Eagle series, of 30,000 to 70,000 pounds gvw, was fitted with a modern cab closely resembling that used on the Hendrickson and International Fleetstar of the early 1970's.

The 1958-1959 Federal Golden Eagle's biggest change was the cab which had vertical straight door pillars, again with a wrap-around windshield, the total effect being substantially the same as with the Ford cabs. Not many of these were made, as yearly production had dwindled to a few dozen now.

About this time Napco was awarded a $10,000,000 contract from Curtiss-Wright for axle assemblies for the 2½-ton M-series US military truck, and, after making the final shipment of bus chassis to Pennsylvania in March 1959, Federal production came to an end.

However, there was an after-glow, of a sort. For some years afterwards Napco shipped bus kits of mechanical components under the trade name "Mexican Bus" to Argentina where the complete buses were constructed.

Also, the Masa Motor Coach with unitized body was built overseas with components supplied by the Federal Division.

Lifetime Federal truck production is estimated at 160,000, with many being sold in world-wide markets for decades. *RW*

F.E.G. (D) 1904-1908

Friedrich Erdmann, Gera

Erdmann was, together with Maurer, the main representative of friction drive in Germany. His design was unusual as it was only used for moving off and for steep gradients. For normal drive the power was transmitted directly to the shaft-driven axle. Van and trucks were on the program. The small hotel buses were quite popular. 2-cylinder engines by Korting and Fafnir and 4-cylinder engines by Fafnir and Horch were used. *HON*

FEJES (H) 1925-1928

Jeno Fejes Lemezmotor es Gepgyar P.T., Budapest

A roughly built vehicle with angular lines, using welded parts and no castings at all, especially designed to be built by unskilled personel. Even the 4-cylinder 1.2 gasoline engine was built of sheet metal and was reported to be 20-25% lighter than cast engines. Built primarily as a car, the same chassis was also used as the basis for light commercials and mainly postal vans. The Fejes construction technique was ultimately sold to the British Ascot firm. *GA*

FEROLDI (I) 1914

Enrico Feroldi, Saluzzo

Enrico Feroldi was better known for his carburetors and private cars, but after his move to Saluzzo in 1914 he made a small number of trucks. They used the same 3.3-litre 4-cylinder sv engine as the cars. *MCS*

FERRANDO (I) 1954

Ferrando Autocostruzioni, San Benigno Canavese, Turin

This maker of agricultural equipment showed a 10-cwt forward control van in 1954. It had a front-mounted single-cylinder 4-stroke 250cc N.S.U. engine, a 4-speed gearbox, and swing-axle rear suspension. *MCS*

FERRARI (I) to date

Officine Meccaniche Ferrari, Reggio Emilia

Not connected with the famous car firm of the same name, Ferrari makes small 2- and 3-cylinder tractors and agricultural and general purpose load carriers of up to 45 hp. *OM*

1960 F.H. 325cc light truck, GNG

F.H. (E) 1958-1964

This small company whose address is unknown made light vans and pick-ups powered by 325 cc Hispano-Villers 2-cylinder engines. Load capacity was 400 kgs. A total of 390 were made. *JCG*

F.I.A.T. (I) 1902-1906
FIAT (I) 1907 to date

(1) Fabbrica Italiana Automobili Torini, Turin 1902-1918
(2) Fiat SpA, Turin 1918 to date

Giovanni Agnelli's Fiat empire enjoys a virtual monopoly of the Italian commercial vehicle industry, having absorbed directly or indirectly S.P.A. (1925), Ceirano (1931), O.M. (1933), Bianchi (1955) and Lancia (1968). Even in 1927 the company had a good 80 per cent of the market.

Though car manufacture began in 1899, their first commercial vehicle was not seen until 1902. This was a small delivery van on the front-engined 8 hp chassis with 1.9-litre aiv vertical-twin engine, 3-speed gearbox, and side-chain drive. More ambitious was a 4 ton truck of 1903, with iron tires; the driver sat over the 6.3-litre T-head 4-cylinder engine, which itself was mounted ahead of the front axle. It attained 7½ mph, and had evolved by 1907 into a 5 tonner with 7.4 litres and 40 hp. The same engine was used in F.I.A.T.'s first buses, which had twin watercooled transmission brakes, and could carry 36-seater double-decker bodies; by 1907 such models were operating in Bristol and the Isle of Wight as well as in Italy. Fiat (the periods vanished from the name at the end of 1906) also collaborated with Diatto in the design of a gasoline-engined tram, but the demand for heavy vehicles was still very limited, and only 338 commercials had been delivered by the end of 1910. The Austro-Fiat concern began the assembly of Fiat trucks under license in 1907, but design ideas soon diverged, and post-Armistice Austro-Fiats would owe little or nothing to Turin. Though the Italian Army was testing F.I.A.T.s in 1905, the factory's principal early success was with cabs. The 15/20 hp 3.1-litre Brevetti of 1906, first of the shaft-driven models, was available with taxi or hotel bus coachwork, but far more significant was the 2-litre Tipo 1 of 1908, designed as a cab and exported in this form to Britain, the U.S.A. and Brazil among other countries. Its L-head monobloc engine, unit 3-speed gearbox and bevel drive set the fashion for Fiat private car design in the 1910-14 period, and four forward speeds were standard by 1910. It was still available with detachable wheels and full electrics as the 1T taxi as late as 1923. Thereafter no purpose-built cabs were laid down from scratch, but Fiat worked in close co-operation with Italian operators, and subsequent car types to see such service were the 1½-litre 502 (1923), a small-bore edition of the 6-cylinder sv 520 (1928), the 1.4-litre 515 (1931), and the excellent 508L with 1089 cc ohv

1906 FIAT 24/40hp 36-seater bus, NMM

engine (1938-52). As late as 1963 there was a bid for taxi business with a long-chassis edition of the Pininfarina-styled 1500 sedan.

In 1912 Fiat became a bus operator with the foundation of the SITA line in Tuscany, this venture being followed after World War I with SADEM in Turin and Autostradale in the Milan area. There was also a new generation of trucks with L-head monobloc 4-cylinder engines, the 2.8-litre 15/20-cwt Tipo 2 using a car engine and pneumatic tires, the bigger 4.4-litre Tipo 15 family on similar lines, and the 3 ton Tipo 18 with side-chain drive, solids, and cylinder dimensions of 100x180 mm. These were made in immense numbers for the Allies in World War I, production reaching 1900 units a month in the summer of 1917. Other wartime products included the 5/7-ton forward control Type 30, armored cars, Italy's first tank, and a 70 hp artillery tractor with lockable differential (tried by the company as early as 1911) capable of hauling 100 tons on level ground. Versions of the smaller Fiat trucks were produced in Japan by (i) Mitsubishi, and on a far larger scale in the USSR by Amo.

1915 FIAT 18BL 3½-ton truck, NMM

1920 FIAT Tipo 2 charabanc, NMM

The flood of war surplus vehicles had its effect on Fiat, whose truck production fell from 10,618 in 1919 to 1328 in 1921, and the only new departure of the immediate post-Armistice period was the introduction of their first agricultural tractor in 1919. There was also a light van based on the 1½-litre sv 4-cylinder 501 private car, first of a long series of car-based commercials which would be offered until 1955. Others of this family were the worm-driven 15 cwt 502, the 20/25 cwt 2.3-litre 505F which was a best-seller in Australia, and the 5 cwt 509F of 1925 with 990cc ohc engine and fwb. Other models to receive this treatment were the 1.4-litre 514 (1929), the 995cc sv 508 Balilla (1932), and the tiny 569cc 500 of 1936, the first Fiat commercial vehicle with ifs. The 508s were made under license in Germany (N.S.U), France (Simca) and Poland (Polski-Fiat), though only the Polish factory turned out bigger commercials, the 618 and 621 of the early 1930s.

Though a curious full-fronted 2-tonner with worm drive and 4-litre 4-cylinder ohv engine (1923) was stillborn, 1925 saw a new generation of pneumatic-tired Fiat trucks in the 2/2½-ton class, powered by 4-and 6-cylinder sv car engines; fwb arrived on the 605 model, and these new types had the PSV equivalents, including a 50-seater on a wheelcase of 216 inches. The acquisition of S.P.A.in 1925 had two effects; the establishment of a sales consortium to market Fiat, S.P.A, and Ceirano trucks and buses, and the concentration of Fiat's own efforts on lighter types, existing S.P.A models covering the 3/5 ton sector until 1931, when the factory was turned over to specialist machinery. New for 1929 was a high-speed 30/35-cwt model in the American idiom; this 621, also available as a 17-seater coach, used the 2½-litre 7-bearing sv 521 car engine coil ignition, and fwb. A 3½-ton 6-wheeler development appeared in 1930, and a version with 4.6-litre 4-cylinder diesel engine (subsequently standardized) was available from 1934.

1929 FIAT Tipo 621 coach, HDB

1929 FIAT Tipo 605 6-wheel touring coach, HDB

The first of a new generation of heavies appeared in 1930 in the shape of the 640, a 6x4 worm drive double decker bus chassis powered by a 7-litre 6-cylinder sv engine. This was easily detachable for servicing, other features being dual ignition, and Westinghouse servo brakes on all wheels. At the other end of the scale some battery-electric municipal vehicles were produced, but more important were the first Fiat diesel trucks, introduced in 1931. These were the 4-ton 632 and 6 ton 634N, both normal control machines with engines mounted over the front axle in the fashion of later S.P.A.s, 4-wheel servo brakes, transmission handbrakes (as fitted to Fiat cars from the 1930s), and double-reduction worm

1934 FIAT Tipo 618 1½-ton truck, GNG

drive. Engines were a 5½-litre four and an 8.4-litre six, these types being paralleled on the PSV side by the 40-seater 635 family, available with gasoline or diesel power to choice. Trolleybuses were also produced, and from 1934 some Fiat commercial models (the 621 was the first) could be had in gazogene form. Gasoline engines were quietly phased out, their use being confined to military versions of medium trucks and to models in the under 2-ton class like the 1-ton 614 and the 30/35 cwt 618. Larger buses now had 10-litre 6-cylinder oil engines rated at 115 hp, came in 6x4 as well as 4x2 guise, and could carry up to 70

1939 FIAT Tipo 665 S-ton truck, OMM

passengers. Forward control and streamlined cabs came with a new range of trucks for pay loads from 3½ to 6½ tons introduced in 1939; engines were diesel sixes of 70 and 105 hp respectively, 5-speed gearboxes were standard, and brakes were air-hydraulic. The smaller 626 was available as a 26-seater coach chassis, and the range was rounded out during the war years by the A1000, a 9/10-ton 6x4 with ten forward speeds, a 10-litre engine, and full air brakes.

1948 FIAT Tipo 680ORN coach, Fiat

These heavies, the 500 and 1100 vans, and a line of trolleybuses for 100 passengers with amidships-mounted 100 hp motors represented Fiat's contribution in the immediate post-World War II period. Forward control was now standard practice in the over 3 ton classs, and improved types for 4/8 ton payloads came in 1949, all with 6-cylinder

1949 FIAT 64ON 4½-ton truck, Fiat

diesels (the most powerful ones ran to 10.2 litres and 123 hp), as well as eight forward speeds. Their bus counterparts carried 80 passengers, and were widely used with 4-wheeled trailers. Brakes were air/hydraulic or full air, according to payload rating. In 1951 Fiat launched their light jeep-type vehicle, the Campagnola, powered by a 1.9-litre 4-cylinder ohv gasoline engine. It had coil spring ifs, could be had with a diesel engine for 1955, and was still available in 1978, albeit with all four wheels independently sprung and an 80 hp ohc power unit. Fiat, like Bianchi, also used ifs on a new 30/35 cwt normal control, short-hooded model, the 615. Its 4-speed synchromesh gearbox, column change, coil rear springs and 1.4-litre ohv gasoline engine were derived from the 1400, the company's first all-new post-War private car, but in its original guise it was underpowered. It soon acquired a 1.9-litre diesel, the first of a series of upratings which carried the series into 1975 as the sole surviving normal control Fiat truck.

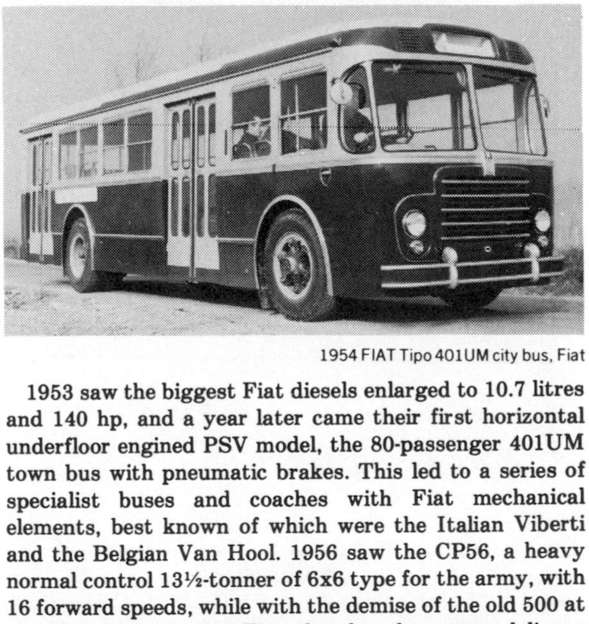

1954 FIAT Tipo 401UM city bus, Fiat

1953 saw the biggest Fiat diesels enlarged to 10.7 litres and 140 hp, and a year later came their first horizontal underfloor engined PSV model, the 80-passenger 401UM town bus with pneumatic brakes. This led to a series of specialist buses and coaches with Fiat mechanical elements, best known of which were the Italian Viberti and the Belgian Van Hool. 1956 saw the CP56, a heavy normal control 13½-tonner of 6x6 type for the army, with 16 forward speeds, while with the demise of the old 500 at the beginning of 1955 Fiat abandoned car-type delivery vans and pickups for the modern forward-control idiom, typified by the 1100T of 1957, using the mechanics of the 1100-103 sedan as well as its ifs. More advanced was the compact rear-engined Multipla announced in 1956, effectively a unitary-contruction 6-seater minicoach. Its running gears and 633cc ohv 4-cylinder engine were those of the rear-engined 600 sedan. Only 132 inches long, it proved very successful as a taxicab: O.M. also marketed a side-loading van edition. In 1958 turbocharged diesel engines became available in some heavy trucks, and there was also a short-lived range of 4/5 ton normal control

1956 FIAT Tipo 615N 1½-ton truck, Fiat

1958 FIAT Tipo C50N 4-ton truck, Fiat

models (C40, C50), with 4.7-litre 6-cylinder oil engines, 5-speed synchromesh gearboxes, hydrovac brakes, and surprisingly, two-tone finish; the front end sheet metal subsequently found its way into the French Unic range. All but the smallest Fiat PSVs now featured horizontal underfloor engines, with integral-construction and separate chassis types catering for up to 88 passengers, and such features as clutchless electro-pneumatic gearboxes, power steeering, and air suspension. There were also companion trolleybus models with similar

1960 FIAT Tipo 690N 10½-ton truck, GNG

running gear. 1960 production was 27,323 trucks and 1,622 buses, well ahead of O.M. in second place. The heavy goods range was continued with relatively little change, though the heaviest members of the 690 6x4 family now had 12.9-litre 6-cylinder engines rated at 210 hp. A diesel engined edition of the 1100T van was listed in 1964, and a year later van and minicoach editions of the 850 sedan appeared, replacing the original 600 derivatives; these, like their predecessors, had full forward control. A new forward control 3 tonner, the 625N with 2.7-litre diesel engine bridged the gap between the 615s and the heavies; this had a 5-speed synchromesh gearbox. The 1966 truck line covered the 30 cwt/12 ton bracket, with synchromesh gearboxes standardized; at the top of the range double-reduction drive, air brakes, and multi-range boxes with up to 16 forward speeds were the order of the day.

The principal news of 1967 embraced some new light vans with ifs and car-type 4-cylinder engines. The smaller 238 was the more sophisticated of the two, with east-west mounted power unit driving the front wheels and ifs as well. Unic of France had come under Fiat control in 1965, and in 1968 both O.M and Autobianchi were finally integrated into the parent company. This led to a steady process of interchangability between Fiat, O.M, and Unic (Autobianchi's medium duty truck and buses had already

1970 FIAT Tipo 238 1-ton truck, GNG

1974 FIAT Tipo 619TI 38-tons GCW truck, Fiat

been discontinued). By 1974, light vans were the responsibility of Fiat's car division, vehicles of three to ten tons GVW (i.e. from the 616 upwards) were made by O.M, Unic handled the 10/16-ton GVW bracket, and the Fiat truck plant at Stura (formerly S.P.A) produced the real heavies. Tilt cabs made their appearance: typical of Fiat heavy truck practice in the early 1970s was the 619 with 13.8-litre 240 hp 6-cylinder power unit, servo-assisted, twin-plate clutch, 8-speed all-synchromesh gearbox, double-reduction drive, power steering (available on the biggest models since 1958), and air brakes: Tractor versions were also listed. The bus range covered models for up to 117 passengers, the big 12-metre 421A featuring a front horizontal engine of 250 hp, an automatic gearbox, and pneumatic suspension. In 1973 collaboration between Fiat and Citroen produced a new 35 cwt van, the forward control 242 with all-disc brakes and all-independent suspension. Fiat's version used a 2-litre twin ohc 4-cylinder gasoline engine derived from the 132 car.

In accordance with their dislike of monopolies, Fiat formed a new consortium (Iveco) in 1975 to handle truck production and marketing. Associated with this were not only their own truck-producing plants but Magirus—Deutz of Germany, though there was no indication that this firm would abandon its aircooled diesels. The Fiat group's own range of trucks now extended from 35/40 cwt model up to 12-tonners, all with diesel engines. New types announced for 1976 consisted of the 170/190 series for 17-ton, and 65-75-90 series of cross-country 4x4s. The 170s introduced the first V-formation oil engine to bear the Fiat name, a 17.2-litre V8 rated at 330 hp in normally-aspirated form. Other characteristics were air brakes, power steering and the choice of 8-speed ZF all-synchromesh or 13-speed Fuller gearboxes. The new 4x4s, built in the old Lancia works at Bolzano, had 3½-litre 4-cylinder or 5.2-litre 6-cylinder engines, tilt cabs, power steering, and air-hydraulic brakes.

During 1977 rationalization within the Iveco group took root, with such hybrids as the big 38 ton 320 M19 tractor using Magirus-Deutz's 320 hp aircooled V10 diesel, and a range of normal-control 4x4, 6x4, and 6x6 dumpers, Fiat's only heavies of this configuration for many years. Design was pure Magirus though power was provided by 14.8-litre watercooled Fiat sixes. A novelty at the bottom of the range was the Fiorino, a car-type delivery van based on the fwd 127 sedan, and 1978 saw a long overdue 616 replacement, the Daily for 3/4 ton (with OM badges it was known as the Grinta), featuring the 2.4-litre 4-cylinder Sofim diesel common to the latest Alfa Romeos, torsion-

1978 FIAT Daily ¾-ton truck, Fiat

bar ifs, 4-speed all-synchromesh gearbox, and disc/drum brakes. Light-medium Fiats covered from four to ten tons, and the heavies embraced of GVWs 19 tons and of over 40 tons, with the big diesel V8s at the top of the range. A wide selection of buses and coaches began with the 20-seater 50A1, a full-front design using the 50 truck chassis, and extended up to unitary coaches with horizontal underfloor engines, air brakes and suspension, and accommodation for as many as 52 passengers. The standard city bus, the 421, though also air-sprung, wore its 13.8-litre engine horizontally under the floor forward of the front axle, with a dropped rear axle to lower platform height. This one had an automatic gearbox, and could carry up to 120 passengers. While most of Fiat's numerous licensees and associates abroad have concentrated on passenger cars, trucks are produced in Argentina by Concord and in Yugoslavia by Zastava. *MCS*

FIDES (I) 1908-1911

Fides Fabbrica Automobili Brevetti Enrico, Turin

Fides started life making Brasier cars under license, but their later products were designed by Giovanni Enrico, formerly of Fiat. A normal control 4-cylinder omnibus was entered for the 1908 Italian Commercial Vehicle Trials, and a year later Fides cabs (presumably based on the factory's 12 hp sv four) were in service. After the company's demise, the factory was used by Lancia. *MCS*

FIEDLER (D) 1899-1900 *Berliner Electromobil- und Accumulatoren-Gesellschaft, Berlin*

Electric driven vans were built by this company. *HON*

1924 FIFTH AVENUE COACH Model 2L bus, MBS

FIFTH AVENUE COACH (US) 1916-1925 *(New York Transportation Co., owner)*

Fifth Avenue Coach Co. New York, NY

The Fifth Avenue Coach Co. started as a horse bus operation in 1885, became part of the New York Electric Vehicle Transportation Co. syndicate in 1899, and began running gasoline buses in 1906 after efforts to produce a workable battery-powered design had failed. (The holding company later became New York Transportation Co.). After 1912 a standardized design for double-deckers combined DeDion-Bouton chassis, Daimler sleeve-valve engines, and J.G. Brill open-top bodies. Engines were later puchased from the American licensee, Root & Vandervoort Engineering Co.

In 1916 the French army commandeered 25 DeDion chassis for which Fifth Avenue already had bodies on order. When no manufacturer could be found to take on the task, the company purchased the necessary chassis components and built the buses in its own shops. As buses became more efficient and the city grew larger, the fleet expanded; eventually some 275 "Type A" double-deckers were constructed, and a few were also sold to other operators. The basic European design was modified over the years with storage batteries instead of acetylene for lighting, exhaust-pipe heating, illuminated destination signs, copper-tube radiators, and enclosed driver's cabs.

When the operating company's former general manager endeavored to establish a similar type of boulevard bus operation in Detroit in 1919, he found that the standard Fifth Avenue "Type A" bus was too high for that city's clearances. Starting in 1921 Fifth Avenue produced the "Type L" "Low", for a 55-passenger double-decker distinguished by an underslung drive shaft. Production of this model and the larger "Type 2L" with 64 seats reached over 300. A single-deck bus designated "Type J" was also built starting in 1923 and about 200 had been constructed (mostly for sale to other operators, especially Detroit) by the time Fifth Avenue sold its bus building business to

Yellow Coach in 1925. As early as 1923, the best features of the Type L had been combined with those of Chicago's Type K to provide Yellow Coach with the initial specifications for its own Type Z. Yellow, Fifth Avenue, and Chicago Motor Coach were commonly owned at that time.

Fifth Avenue Coach Co. continued to build and rebuild bus bodies for its own use until 1930 and extensively rebuilt its buses in its sizable shops into the modern era. *MBS*

FIRESTONE-COLUMBUS (US) 1912

Columbus Buggy Company, Columbus, Ohio

The Model 71-C was convertible from a light delivery van to a passenger car for four to five passengers. It had a 4-cylinder engine, a 3-speed gearbox and shaft drive with a wheelbase of 106 inches. This manufacturer was better known for its passenger cars. *GMN*

FISCHER (i) (US) 1901-1905

Fischer Motor Vehicle Co., Hoboken, N.Y.

The Fischer was a gasoline-electric vehicle with a 20 hp 4-cylinder engine coupled to a 16 Kw 5-pole dynamo. Two 10 hp electric motors drove the rear wheels independently. Both passenger and goods bodies were fitted, the latter being popular with breweries while passenger vehicles included city buses and sight-seeing charabancs. One double-decker bus was tried by the London General Omnibus Company in 1903, but its consumption of gasoline and tires was so heavy that it was returned to the makers after a few months. *GNG*

FISCHER(ii) (D) 1912-1913

Westautohaus Alex Fischer & Co., Berlin

Light electric driven vans were manufactured by this firm. Alex Fischer was later connected with the production of A.A.A. and Alfi. *HON*

FISKEN (GB) 1878

Fisken Bros., Hunslet, Leeds

The Fiskens built Willsher's patent undermounted road engine in which the cylinder was placed beneath the boiler with the crankshaft just in front of the firebox. Two road speeds were provided and the flywheel was concentric with the near-side road wheel. *RAW*

FISHER, FISHER-STANDARD see Standard (iv)

FITZJOHN (US) 1938-1958

(1) FitzJohn Body Co., Muskegon, Michigan 1938-1939
(2) FitzJohn Coach Co., Muskegon, Michigan 1939-1958

FitzJohn had its origin in 1919, when the FitzJohn-

1902 FISCHER (i) gas-electric bus, NMM

Erwin Manufacturing Co. was started in Muskegon by Harry A. FitzJohn to build truck and bus bodies. In 1924 a new plant was purchased, five times the size of the old one, and it was announced that its principal line of work would be the manufacture of a line of standard bus bodies for Reo chassis. The enterprise survived several changes of name and reorganization, and when demand turned away from body-on-chassis designs in the mid 1930's, FitzJohn was prepared. Model 300 was modified from a body to a complete bus for city transit service, generally with 27 seats and a Chevrolet truck engine, and models 500 ("Duraliner") and 600 ("Falcon") were introduced for intercity duty, with seating capacities from 24 to 36 and generally with Hercules engines. All were front-engine designs.

1948 FITZJOHN Model 310 Cityliner, MBS

1954 FITZJOHN Roadrunner coach, MBS

After a brief hiatus during 1943, bus production picked up with similar models being offered, except that the city bus was redesigned with its front entrance door ahead of the front axle. In 1946, model 500 was replaced by a slightly larger 510. A Canadian factory at Brantford, Ont. was opened in 1949 and delivered about 200 "Cityliners" during its existence. By 1950, postwar trends in the transit industry were clear, and rear-engine buses were demanded as well as diesel power. Production of intercity buses fell off except for export sales (to Cuba and Mexico), as that side of the U.S. industry became more concentrated and less able to support small producers. Silversiding, picture windows and air conditioning marked the intercity Roadrunner of 1954, most often supplied with Cummins diesel engine mounted longitudinally at the rear. FitzJohn produced over 2600 complete buses in its history. *MBS*

FLADER (D) 1904-1910

E.C. Flader, Johstadt

This firm's specialty was fire fighting equipment but they also built fire engines themselves. Until 1906 electric drive was featured; later, gasoline engines were used. Production was not on a great scale. *HON*

F.L.A.G. (I) 1905-1908

Fabbrica Ligure Automobili Genova, Genoa.

F.L.A.G. was Thornycroft's Italian licensee, but their private cars showed little affinity with contemporary Thornycrofts. By contrast, F.L.A.G. trucks seem to have existed solely on paper, though both trucks and buses were advertised in 1906. The company went into liquidation two years later. *MCS*

FLEET (GB) 1932-1936

Fleet Motors Ltd., Selly Oak, Birmingham

The Fleet was one of a number of light commercial 3-wheelers using motorcycle components to appear in the early thirties. It was produced by Ariel and had a single cylinder 557 c.c. side valve engine with turbo-fan cooling and three speed gearbox: Its single driving wheel was at the rear with a 10-cwt capacity load compartment and steering front axle ahead of the driver. Approximately 900 were produced. *OM*

FLEXI-TRUC see Ibex

FLINT (US) 1912-1915

Durant-Dort Carriage Company, Flint, Michigan

The Flint was a companion marque to the Best and a slightly larger version with a capacity of 1600 pounds for the lone model. It was a more advanced vehicle than the Best, with a 3-speed gearbox and shaft-drive. Its power was provided by a 4-cylinder engine. The chassis was priced at $1285 to $1375. *GMN*

1948 FLOIRAT coach, Techniart

FLOIRAT (F) 1948-1956

SA Sylvain Floirat, St. Denis, Seine

This company was founded to manufacture integral-construction buses using mechanical components by Latil. Besides complete buses, chassis were supplied, some of which were bodied in Belgium by Van Hool between 1948 and 1950. In 1956 Floirat was acquired by the newly-formed Saviem group which integrated the various bus models into its own program. A fleet of Floirat buses was still operating in Mulhouse in 1975. *JFJK*

FLORENTIA (I) 1901-c.1906

1) Fabbrica Toscana di Automobili, Florence 1901-1903
2) Fabbrica di Automobili Florentia, Florence 1903-1906

The first Florentia vehicle shown to the public was a light charabanc with 6 hp Buchet engine which appeared at the 1901 Milan Show. Though their cars became well-known, there is only one further mention of commercial vehicles, in 1906, and no indication that they were produced seriously. *MCS*

FLXIBLE (US) 1924 to date

1) The Flxible Co., Loudonville, Ohio 1924-1974
2) The Flxible Co., Delaware, Ohio 1974 to date
3) Flxible-Southern, Evergreen, Alabama 1963 to date

The Flxible Side Car Co. was founded by Hugo H. Young and Carl F. Dudte in 1913 to build a patented type of motorcycle sidecar invented by Young. Its name was spelled without the "e" for use as a trade mark; the sidecar was so designed as to allow its wheel to stay on the ground in high-speed cornering. Availability of low-priced automobiles ended the demand for motorcycle sidecars, and Flxible turned first to hearses and ambulances on passenger car chassis, then in 1924 to small parlor car style buses made by rebuilding Studebaker or Buick chassis and mounting new bodies on them.

1932 FLXIBLE 12-passenger coach (Buick sedan rebuilt), MBS

Chevrolet truck chassis began to be used instead of automobile chassis in 1936, with a streamlined type of body known as the "Airway." A Chevrolet or Buick engine mounted longitudinally at the rear marked the Clipper of 1939, those with Chevrolet engines generally having 25 seats and the Buicks 29. Production of ambulances and funeral cars slowed to a complete stop as Flxible buses gained popularity. The "Clipper" was largely a standardized product capable of being built in quantity, and it therefore earned a better profit and supported a more extensive marketing effort than the small cars, often custom-built.

In 1941 Flxible devised a styling feature since seen on countless buses: slanted or parallelogram-shaped windows. Lengthening of these into "picture windows" produced the Visicoach in 1950. With comfortable chairs arranged two-and-one, the basic bus (dating to 1939) became the Airporter in 1946, and these dominated airport bus services in the U.S. for many years.

1951 FLXIBLE Visicoach, MBS

With the turn to diesels by parlor bus operators after 1950, Flxible lost ground. Flxible cooperated with Twin Coach in producing hundreds of U.S. Army "convertible" buses, also usable as trucks or ambulances, and a small group of intercity buses exported to Brazil. In 1953 Twin turned over its line of underfloor-engine city transit buses to Flxible and continued with other types of business. For several years Flxible's city bus output consisted in the main of propane-powered buses for Chicago, the only large city to stay with propane after its brief popularity in the early 1950's. In 1961 Flxible introduced its version of the so-called "new look" transit bus (pioneered by GM), at first with GM (Detroit Diesel) engines mounted longitudinally and driving through Spicer torque converters. One group of new-look buses was supplied to Chicago with propane engines.

In settlement of a government lawsuit, GM agreed to permit other bus builders to use its patents, most notably angle drive. Since 1966 Flxible buses have been fully comparable to GM's. Most transit buses in the U.S. today are purchased with an 80-per cent federal subsidy, and contract awards are customarily to the lowest bidder. Flxible has tripled its annual sales of buses since 1966 and has recently moved from its original plant to new facilities. Since 1970 Flxible has been a subsidiary of the Rohr Corp., an aerospace company which also builds rapid transit cars. Production of intercity buses ended in 1969.

1973 FLXIBLE 40 foot transit bus, MBS

In about 1963 Flxible purchased Southern Coach Co. *(see Southern)* of Evergreen, Alabama, sold its new motor home plant to Clark Equipment Co., and undertook to build truck bodies and small front-engine buses under the Flxible Southern name. The buses generally had seats for about 19 passengers, were equipped with Ford V-8 truck engines, and were known as Flxettes. They are still in production at Evergreen. The main plant at Delaware produces city transit buses of a single basic type in 33-, 35- and 40-foot lengths, 96 and 102 inch widths (33-footers in the 96-inch width only) and equipped with Detroit Diesel 6V-71 or 8V-71 engines (33-footers with 6V-71 only) and Allison fully automatic transmissions.

Rohr Industries announced an agreement to sell Flxible to the Grumman Corp., primarily a maker of military aircraft but also owner of a truck body concern that also makes small buses, during September 1977. Flxible is continuing to build new-look transit buses while planning to start production of a new design late in the summer of 1978. Flxible builds about 1400 buses per year.

Clipper coaches were made in Australia under the name Ansair-Flxible from 1960 to 1965. *MBS*

FLYER (CDN) 1930 to date

(1) Western Flyer Coach Co., Winnipeg, Man.
(2) Flyer Industries Ltd., Winnipeg, Man.

This firm first produced bus bodies, then Western Flyer highway coaches including the Standard and Canuck models. An unusual model was the Bruck, a bus with the last few rows of seats replaced by a closed cargo space accessible through a large rear door, making the vehicle part bus and part truck. In 1968 production of the diesel Model 700 transit bus began, and a few years later the vehicle name became simply Flyer. A trolleybus version of the Model 700 was also made. Today Flyer provides bus shells for AM General which builds Flyer diesel coaches under license in the United States. Flyer, now owned by the Manitoba government, is one of Canada's biggest bus producers. Its vehicles, coming from one of the coldest cities in the country, have always been noted for their warmth in winter. Total production to date is over 1150 units. *HD*

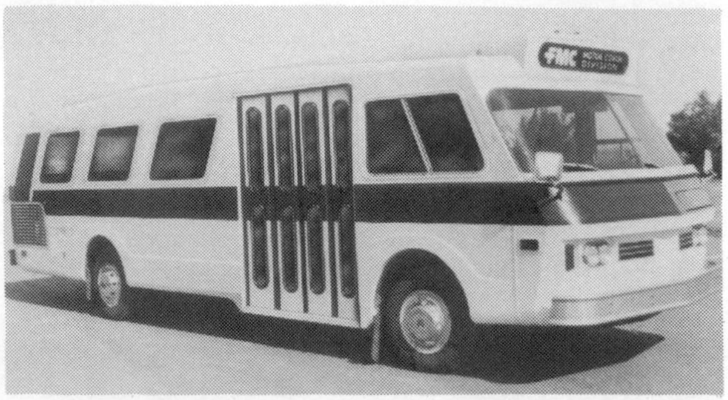

1975 FMC transit coach, MBS

FMC (US) 1974 to date

Motor Coach Division, FMC Corp., Santa Clara, Calif.

The parent company is a diversified corporation; this division used to be the Recreational Vehicle Division, and the "transit coach" is a modified motor home. The first ones built were delivered in November 1974 to Denver, and after extensive trials and reworking were placed in service early in 1975. These are equipped with hydraulic wheelchair lifts and internal locking devices to secure several wheelchairs in position. Similar features may be had on other recently-introduced makes of small buses, in response to a demand from handicapped persons and politicians for accessibility to public transit. *MBS*

F.N (B) 1920-1965

Fabrique Nationale d'Armes de Guerre, Liege

This celebrated small-arms firm produced a car in 1899, and their first motorcycle two years later. No commercial vehicles, however, were offered until after World War I, and even then F.N confined themselves to light truck versions of such private car models as the sv 4-cylinder 2200 and 3800, and the very successful series of ohv fours launched in 1923 and produced up to 1933. There was also a 1-tonner based on their last private car, the 2¼-litre sv Prince Albert of 1934, this surviving until 1939 in 35-cwt form.

1932 F.N. 8-cylinder 3-ton truck, F.N.

1937 F.N. 63C 3-5-ton truck, F.N

A more serious entry, however, came in 1932 with the introduction of a conventional 2½-tonner with 4-speed gearbox, using the company's new 3.3-litre sv straight-8 engine. It could also be had in coach form, but had given way by 1937 to a forward control 5-tonner, the 63C, using either the 8-cylinder unit or a new 3.9-litre, 75bhp six of F.N's own design. Once again PSV variants were offered, as well as a military 4x4 with 8-speed transmission and three lockable differentials. Other F.N commercials of the 1930s included a series of trolleybuses for Liege (1933), and some Kegresse-type military halftracks using 6-cylinder Minerva or F.N engines. From 1932, the motorcycle department offered a line of delivery 3-wheelers, which in 1937 form featured flat-twin engines, enclosed cabs, and shaft drive. F.N engines were also used in another Belgian 3-wheeled truck, the Spiegel, and the Belgian Army used an open-bodied variant. The type was revived after the War, with a 1-litre engine and five forward speeds.

1950 F.N. 62C fire engine, F.N.

1953 F.N. TB V1 trolleybus, F.N.

Truck production was resumed in 1946, though most of F.N's output was reserved for the army; such civilian models as there were went to such Government departments as the fire service and the Belgian State Railways. The new F.Ns were 5- and 6½-ton developments of Type-63 with 4.3 litre engines and 5-speed synchromesh and overdrive gearboxes. Their 4x4 derivatives were made in association with Brossel and Miesse, and included the Ardennes artillery tractor (also available as a 30-cwt

1963 F.N. 4RM Ardennes 4×4 personnel carrier, F.N.

truck) with 4.7-litre ohv power unit, eight forward speeds, and air brakes. Unusual for a Continental firm, F.N never listed a diesel powered type, though they showed an oil-engined coach at the 1948 Brussels Salon., following this up in 1960 with the AB11 prototype city bus. This one had twin Perkins P6 units mounted horizontally over the rear axle, a semi-automatic gearbox, and air suspension. The only PSVs to be made in series were, however, a batch of 25 100-passenger trolleybuses, once again for Liege, delivered between 1953 and 1955. 1960 saw the ingenious AS24, an air-transportable 3x2 device weighing only 3½ cwt, and powered by a 243cc single-cylinder 2-stroke engine. This and the Ardennes were commercially available by 1963, but two years later F.N abandoned regular vehicle production. *MCS*

1965 F.N.M. 6×4 10-ton truck, F.N.M.

FNM (BR) 1949 to date

Fabrica Nacional de Motores S.A., Rio de Janeiro.

The Fabrica Nacional de Motores was founded on 13 June, 1942 with the stated objective of building airplane engines with machinery imported from the USA. This objective was never accomplished. At first FNM made refrigerators and afterwards the American tools and equipment were used for producing trucks. The first model was designated FNM-R-80. It was introduced late in 1949 and these vehicles were made under an agreement with Isotta Fraschini. The first fifty R-80s paraded in Rio de Janeiro. In December, 1950 FNM signed a new contract, this time with Alfa Romeo-inspired badge but with their own lettering and by 1952 they had a 31% Brazilian content. This was the first true Brazilian commercial vehicle. In 1953 production of the D-9 500 truck started and by 1955 FNM had made 2,426 trucks, later examples being equipped with 54% Brazilian parts. In 1957 FNM introduced their heavy Diesel-engined truck, designated FNM D-1 100. By 1959 the D-1 100 had 85% nationally made components. In 1960 FNM entered the automobile producing area with a copy of the Alfa Romeo 1900, was designated the JK as a homage to President Juscelino Kubitschek, and made their 15,000th truck. In 1965 FNM made an experimental armored military reconnaissance vehicle, designed in 1958 by the Instituto Militar de Engenharia, but this did not go beyond the prototype stage. FNM's association with Alfa Romeo continues at present only in the automobile field. Commercial vehicles introduced late in 1975 are FIAT designs, as a consequence of a new association with this make.

The latest models use FIAT Diesel engines. There are three variations. The FNM-70 has a 4-cylinder 5-litre engine, 5-speed gearbox and a 4.3 tons load carrying capacity; the FNM-130 has a 6-cylinder, 7.4-litre engine, 5-speed gearbox and a 9 ton load carrying capacity; and the FNM 210/S uses a 6-cylinder, 13.8-litre engine, 12 forward speeds and has a 12.6 tons load carrying capacity. *ACT*

F.O.D. (I) 1925-1927

Fonderie Officine de Benedetti, Turin

The F.O.D. was an advanced little car with unitary construction and a largely aluminum 4-cylinder ohc engine of only 565cc. A 3-cwt van version was offered, but production of the make was very limited. *MCS*

FODEN (GB) 1887 to date

(1) E. Foden Sons & Co. Ltd., Sandbach, Cheshire 1887-1902

(2) Fodens, Ltd., Sandbach, Cheshire 1902 to date

At the Royal Show of 1887 Fodens captured attention by exhibiting an 8 hp compound engine working at the unusually high pressure of 300 psi. The excellent workmanship of the engine, its sound design and the high performance it put up under test led to Foden engines of 6, 7 and 8 hp sizes being taken up by road hauliers. These engines were fitted with Fodens' patent spring gear, permitting much softer riding than many of their competitors possessed. Fodens supplied 12 engines new to showmen, the first in 1898, and others were converted.

The principal product of the firm was, however, the compound overtype, locomotive boilered steam wagon. After an early dalliance with an undertype wagon Foden built his first overtype in 1900 using a launch type boiler, soon discarded in favor of the conventional locomotive type which was used for the wagon entered in the War Office Trials of 1901. In this wagon the rear wheels were mounted inside the frame and the final drive from the gear shaft to the rear axle differential was by tandem roller chains, no single roller chain strong enough to transmit the engine load being then available. It proved, in practice, impossible to keep the tension on these tandem chains exactly equal so that one chain tended to take more load than its twin, leading to breakages. At an early date, therefore, a single, larger, chain was submitted.

The wagon was redesigned after the promulgation of the Heavy Motor Car Order 1904 with smaller rear wheels repositioned outside the frame but the engine and gearing remained unchanged. This 5-ton design became the mainstay of Foden production until about 1925, despite limited excursions in the production of tractors based upon it and of a rather curious 2-tonner (1905). There was also a Colonial version on larger wheels giving enhanced ground clearance. This design did more than any other to estab-

1911 Foden 4-ton steam wagon, Foden

lish the steam wagon as a practical working tool and made the name of Fodens and overtypes practically synonymous. By the twenties, however, it was severely dated, though it had been updated to some extent by the use of solid rubbers as standard. Poor visibility from the driving position, the chain and bobbin steering and insufficient brake capacity for the speeds in vogue by the twenties led to it being superseded by the 'C' type 6-tonner about 1925.

In this new design the driving position was raised up, with the cab floor at chassis height and powerful camoperated brakes were provided together with Ackermann steering and the use of roller bearings. Alterations to the engine and boiler were more matters of detail but three road speeds were made standard and an improved cab was

1927 FODEN 12-ton steam wagon, Foden

fitted. This design of wagon formed the basis of the tractor of an articulated 6-wheeler built until 1928 but defeated like many early articulated vehicles by the difficulty of effectively braking the semi-trailer. It was superseded by a rigid 6-wheeler for 10/12 ton loads, virtually an extended 6-tonner with the Foden patent rear bogie and with the steam pressure raised from 220 to 230 psi.

By this time the sales of steam wagons as a class had been heavily eroded by i/c vehicles and Sentinels were taking an increasing share of the depleted market. To compete with the Sentinel, Foden produced an undertype design, the first of which was sold in 1926. In this a vertical water tube boiler, pressed to 250 psi, was paired with a two cylinder double acting engine placed longitudinally in the chassis with cardan shaft and worm drive to the rear axle. Produced as four and six wheelers and as tractors the new class, known as the E's, had too high a tare to gross weight ratio and only 51 were made. After some experiments with a modified 'E' type and other variants the makers launched the 'O' type wagon in four and six wheeled versions in 1930, initially with a vertical boiler, then with a horizontal boiler with wet-bottomed firebox

1930 FODEN O-type Speed Six 6-ton steam wagon, Foden

and finally with a reversed horizontal "pistol" boiler with cross water tubes in the barrel and a circular stayless firebox fired through a top chute. This boiler, of all welded construction, was lightened in every possible way and by the use of pressed steel chassis weight was reduced. The outer case of the two speed gear box was of aluminum and great efforts were made throughout the engine and drive assembly to reduce weight. The double cylinder, double acting engine and cardan shaft drive were retained and pneumatics were fitted. This final Foden design was a phenomenal performer, capable of road speeds in excess of 50 mph and, moreover, a prodigious producer of steam. The welded boiler was, however, regarded with suspicion by insurers and in 1932 faced with the changed vehicle taxation conditions the firm decided to move out of steam wagon building into diesels. Nevertheless 135 "O" class wagons were made.

Traction engine building ceased in 1914 but the building of steam tractors based upon wagon designs continued until 1934. Foden timber hauling tractors with larger rear wheels and power winches were produced in the twenties and were used, in many instances, until about 1950 when superseded by ex W.D. Matadors and similar tractors. No Foden steamers are currently in commercial use, the last having been a tar sprayer used by the Mechanical Tar Spraying & Grouting Co. of Reading until the early 1970's.

1933 FODEN 7-ton trucks, Foden

With the drop in orders for steam wagons, Fodens were only working a three day week when their first R-type diesel engined truck was sold in July 1931. It had a Gardner 6L2 engine and four speed gearbox, and was rated for six tons. At the same time a small number of timber tractors were produced to use up various steam wagon parts. These were powered by Gardner diesels mounted transversely behind their cabs. As diesels gradually replaced steam at Foden an attempt was made to introduce lighter vehicles to occupy the works more fully, and in 1934 trucks of two to seven tons capacity were available. The smallest machines had Meadows gasoline engines while medium weight machines could have Dorman or Perkins diesels or Austin 20 hp 6-cylinder gasoline engines. However with the exception of about 100 Dorman engined vehicles and 30 with 3-cylinder Gardner engines, none of these was a sales success. Nor were the 32 seat single and 56 seat double decker buses offered at the end of 1933.

Thereafter Foden concentrated on maximum capacity Gardner engined machines, producing about 150 in 1935, some of which were 10 and 12 ton six wheelers. At the end of 1935 the range was altered and now featured very streamlined forward control cabs with their windshields raked and divided both vertically and horizontally. A Gardner 4LK engined 4-tonner appeared, weighing only 2½ tons unladen, but once more was not as successful as the heavier models as it was not possible to combine the Foden qualities of ruggedness and long life with the low price offered by mass-produced vehicles in this weight range. At the same time a 15½ ton 8-wheeler appeared, followed in 1937 by a twin-steer 10-ton 6-wheeler. To improve fuel economy a five speed gearbox became optional that year and styling reverted to a less revolutionary

1937 FODEN 15-ton 8-wheel truck, Foden

appearance with a more vertical scuttle and windscreen to improve driving visibility. Thereafter the DG range changed little. During the war, in addition to tanks and armaments, some 1750 6- and 10-ton 4- and 6-wheel DGs were produced. Another wartime production, continued from the thirties, was timber tractors with unusual rigidly-mounted front axles able to pivot on uneven ground. In other respects however, they were unlike the original Foden timber design, and were closely related to the DG. After the war the updated FG range appeared as well as two major developments which were considerably to affect Foden's future. The first was the dump truck of 1947. This was the first vehicle of its type to be produced in Britain and was initially based on the 12-ton 6-wheeler chassis suitably reinforced for extra heavy duty off-road service at the Steel Company of Wales. Special half-cab dump trucks soon became an important part of Foden's production and were joined in 1954 by a six cubic yard 4-wheel version and in 1958 by the massive FR6/45 normal control Rolls-Royce diesel engined 300 hp vehicle which had torque converter transmission. The other important development was Foden's own diesel engine introduced in 1948. This was a two-stroke supercharged unit producing 126 hp from only 4.09 litres. It was exceptionally light in weight and economical, and gave Foden an unusual distinction among the smaller vehicle manufacturers of making virtually all their own components. It remained in production for replacement and marine purposes until February 1977. In 1949 the FG (or FE with two-stroke engine) acquired an all-steel cab with faired-in radiator, and a half-cab version of this was also used on the contemporary passenger models.

1949 FODEN PVSC5/6 bus, Foden

Single and double-decker bus chassis were introduced in 1945, with Gardner 5LW and 6LW engines; from 1948 the Foden 2-stroke was an optional alternative. In 1950 came a rear-engined coach chassis, usually with the 2-stroke engine though the Gardner 6LW could be fitted. The engine was mounted transversely. This and the front-engined chassis were made until 1956.

Further ingenuity was shown in 1952 when a 2.72 litre 4-cylinder 84 hp version of the two-stroke diesel was installed in a new 4/8 chassis which weighed 3½ tons unladen and could carry 8 tons. In order to keep the engine working close to its optimum revs, a new Foden gearbox was employed which was a three speed unit plus an epicyclic train of three further gears. This gave a combination of nine forward speeds, while another version fitted to the dump trucks had four main gears giving no less than 12 forward ratios. This gearbox remained a common feature on two-stroke Fodens and on dump trucks until the latter began to acquire semi-automatic transmissions in the early seventies. Also made were heavy road tractors for up to 80 tons gross train weight, and these and medium and heavier models became a Foden specialty.

At the 1956 London Commercial Motor Show a Foden with air brakes and power steering was displayed and in 1958 disc brakes and air suspension were shown. A very wide range of different cabs were offered by Foden from 1958 including ones made from steel for export and alloy or fiberglass for British use.

Special vehicles produced at the time were mobile crane carrying chassis with divided cabs to permit the jib to lie between the driving and passenger compartments when traveling. This in turn led, in the early sixties, to lowline crane chassis on which the cab was mounted in front of the front axle with the engine behind.

1952 FODEN PVRFG coach, Foden

1954 FODEN, 4/8 8-ton truck, Foden

During the fifties the output of the Foden two stroke diesel engine was steadily increased and in 1960 in turbocharged form it gave 210 hp from 4.09 litres, though by 1962, as the Dynamic, it had increased to 4.8 litres, when it gave 175 hp, or 225 when turbocharged. In the same year Fodens were offered with tilt cabs for the first time. An interesting development in 1964, which did not catch on among operators, was a rigid 8-wheeler load carrier to which was attached an articulated trailer. The 42 foot 7 inch outfit could gross 32 tons in Britain.

By 1966 the 45 tons gross dump truck had been discontinued, though smaller forward control 4- and 6-wheel models were an important part of Foden's production, and a new 15 ton capacity 4-wheeler was announced followed by a larger 39 tons gross 6-wheeler in 1967. Most models of both road-going and special purpose vehicles had Cummins, Gardner or Foden engines though following a financial stake taken in the company by Leyland Motors a number of Leyland engines were fitted. Leyland later decided to concentrate capital on its own production and sold its minority interest in Foden.

Developments in 1968 included the fitting of ceramic-lined clutches and the availability of half cabs with forward angled windshields on all models. These cabs were seldom popular for ordinary road use though they achieved later success on heavy duty on/off site 6x4 and 8x4 tippers and mixer chassis. A full-width version of this cab in fiberglass or steel was available from 1970 and was initially fitted to a twin-steer articulated tractor, though the earlier rounded designs of cab remained more popular,

1972 FODEN (Australia) Deltacab 8×4 truck, AAR

except in South Africa and Australia, where Foden by now had assembly plants. Steel cabs by Motor Panels continued to be supplied both at home and overseas, though in 1974 a new S90 steel cab was developed for the Universal range, which used a wide choice of proprietary parts for the first time, to improve overseas spares availability. The Universal started as a Continental type tractor but from 1976 was usually sold as a Cummins 290 or 355 hp engined export six or eight wheeler for 26 and 42 tons GVW or up to 100 tons as a tractor.

In 1973 Fodens were awarded a £10 million NATO contract to build high-mobility military trucks, and in addition to these they produced 4- and 6-wheeled dump trucks for up to 35 ton loads with various engines

1974 FODEN 8×4 tanker, Foden

including Cummins and Leyland, and various 4, 6- and 8-wheeled road vehicles, Fodens being the largest British producers of the latter category. The majority of these now use Gardner, Cummins and Rolls-Royce engines.

In 1974 a new factory with flow-line production methods for a capacity of up to 150 vehicles per week was opened. In the same year a reciprocal trading agreement with

1978 FODEN Fleetmaster 38-tonne GCW truck, Foden

Faun of Germany was signed, but this ended two years later because of currency disparity. In 1976 a lightweight six wheeler for mixer tipper work readopted the S39 cab and Foden re-entered the bus market with the Foden-NC (Northern Counties, the bodybuilders) transverse rear Gardner 6LXB engined double deck bus, which featured Allsion automatic transmission and a Ferodo friction retarder. In 1977 Foden avoided a takeover bid by Rolls Royce and introduced two new models in November, the Haulmaster and Fleetmaster tractive units. The former is for 32 tons operation in Britain and uses Cummins Rolls Royce or Gardner engine of 184 to 265 hp and mainly Foden components, while the latter is for 38 ton export use and has Cummins or Rolls Royce 290 hp diesels and a majority of proprietary components. *RAW/OM*

FOIDART (B) c.1914

Camions a Vapeur Foidart, Brussels

M. Foidart, who had already a number of patents for details of road vehicles, announced in 1914 his intention to market an undertype steam road vehicle.

Superheated steam was generated in a kerosene fired modified flash boiler. The power unit seems to have been a pair of horizontal two cylinder compound engines with piston valves to the high pressure side and slide valves to the low pressure with chain final drive. Cast steel wheels, without rubber tires, were used, a retrograde step for the time. The upheaval of the German invasion killed off the project. *RAW*

FORD (i) (US) 1905 to date

1) Ford Motor Co., Detroit, Mich. 1905 to date
2) Ford Motor Co., Louisville, Ky. 1970 to date

1911 FORD (i) Model T delivery van, NAHC

Before the advent of the Model T, Ford showed little interest in commercial vehicles. Their first such effort was Model E, a delivery van on the underfloor-engined, opposed-twin C private car chassis with dummy hood, 2-speed planetary transmission, and central chain drive. A taxicab edition of the Model B, the company's first shaft-driven vertical-four, was sold in London in 1905, while the 15 hp Model N, a successful $500 4-cylinder runabout of 1906, was briefly catalogued with cab bodywork.

The Model T appeared in October, 1908. It had a 2.9-litre 4-cylinder L-head monobloc engine with detachable head, and its foolproof 2-speed-and-reverse planetary transmission made it ideal for light delivery work. A commercial roadster at $590 and a van at $700 were available by the 1911 season, but these official models made up only a fraction of the T's used for commercial work, and the nominal payload of 7½-cwt was often grossly exceeded. Conversions included a lengthened chassis and side chain drive, which made a cheap 1-ton truck out a private car; there were also light artics with or without chain drive, and agricultural tractor conversion with detachable straked driving wheels. A popular adaptation in the United States was the jitney bus, a 'pirate' vehicle which competed successfully with streetcar lines until the early 1920s, when the practice was outlawed in most communities. T's also saw extensive taxicab service, the town cars of the 1913-16 period lending themselves especially to this role. 1917 saw the introduction of the first Fordson farm tractor, of which 7,000 were supplied to the British government alone during the last two years of World War I.

1922 FORD (i) Model TT 1-ton van, RNE

Along with the T's switch from brass to black radiator in 1917 came the first purpose-built 1-ton Ford truck, Model TT, of which over a million were delivered in ten years. A lengthened chassis, lowered gearing and worm-drive back axle were the principal changes, though on early ones solid rear tires were standard and cabs were of open-sided type. The retention of the 2-speed pedal-controlled transmission meant brisk business for the accessory makers, who marketed 2-speed overdrives (and underdrives like the Supaphord for hilly districts). Initial list price of the chassis was $600, reduced to $325 without starter by 1926, and all manner of bodies were fitted to the TT, including fire engines, ambulances, and 14-seater buses and coaches. Ford tonners even served on light railways as railcars. The vehicle's popularity is reflected not only in Ford's 41 per cent share of all British motor-vehicle registrations by 1919, but in their 51 per cent of the U.S. truck market in 1926. (By contrast Chevrolet, with an established 1-tonner, commanded only 1¾ per cent). Pneumatic rear tires were generally used on the TT by 1923, and a year later came enclosed cabs and a balloon-tire option at the back. The car-type lightweights evolved alongside the cars, TT's being available with roadster pickup or panel van bodywork; some 1926 and 1927 models had the cars' nickel radiators. An unusual prototype of 1926 was the 3-ton Fordson (the only regular American use of this name except on tractors) a modern looking forward control truck with twin rear wheels. It never saw production.

1928 FORD (i) Model AA hauling Model A cars, NMM

The last of fifteen million-odd T's was produced in May, 1927, its replacement being the A, with a 3.3-litre 4-cylinder, coil ignition engine, conventional 3-speed sliding-type gearbox, tw6, and bevel drive, though Ford's traditional transverse suspension was retained. Early AA trucks, rated as 1/1½-tonners, followed similar lines with worm drive, but by 1929 had acquired spiral bevel back axles, 4-speed gearboxes, steel wheels instead of wire, and a twin-rear-wheel option. A stake truck was priced at a low $540. The car-type A came as a delivery van, roadster pickup, or taxicab. Still regarded as a commercial vehicle was the station wagon, a novelty of 1929, which sold for a little over $600; it would acquire private-car status in the ensuing decade. 1930 AA's featured longitudinal cantilever rear suspension, a long (13 ft) wheelbase option, and new cabs with a distinctive front end treatment. A short lived model was a town car delivery on the A chassis, and PSV editions of the AA were supplied through Ford's dealer network, in city transit, intercity, or school bus forms. The school bus version was redesigned in 1932 with Union City Body Co. coachwork constructed entirely of steel apart from the roof; this accommodated 32 pupils. 1930 saw Ford truck sales approach the 200,000 mark, the company being the nation's best-seller both in that year and in 1931. Also in 1931 the Russian Gorki automobile plant (GAZ) began production of A and AA derivatives which were produced without major change until 1946. Russia's first Jeep-type light 4x4, the GAZ of 1943, was also Ford-based.

Cars and trucks were redesigned as the B and BB in 1932, while by the end of the year the new 3.6-litre 65bhp V-8 engine had been adapted for commercial use. Initially the old 4-cylinder engine was retained in production as an insurance against teething troubles with the V-8 (it was preferred for its economy by the school bus operators), but during 1933 it was phased out of American truck production, though retained by such foreign branches as the British plant at Dagenham. Raked radiator grilles distinguished the 1933-34 models, but in 1935 the ½-ton and 1½-ton Fords were restyled to bring them in line with the latest private cars, and Ford regained the first place they had lost to Chevrolet in 1933. That year Marmon-Herrington introduced their first 4x4 Ford conversions. On the bus side the long wheelbase V-8 attracted

1936 FORD (i) 3-ton articulated truck, FLP

attention from city transit lines looking for an economical vehicle, and various body manufacturers were commissioned to fit different styles of transit bodywork. Those sold through Ford dealers carried the same designation (Model-48) as contemporary 1½-ton trucks (Model-51). After a successful test of 35 Fords starting in 1934, Detroit's municipal transit system acquired around 300 additional Model-51 buses, and then in 1936 announced a plan to buy 1,000 chassis, to be equipped with bodies constructed in their own shops. Detroit at the time had the policy of running small buses on extremely close headway (less than one minute on some lines). In the end the plan was changed, and 500 complete vehicles with Union City coachwork were acquired. Ford then decided to market their own Transit bus (Model-70), deliveries of which began to Detroit in October, 1936. Features were seats for 25 and air brakes. Considerable interest was aroused, and in 1937 a second version, 2 feet longer, was introduced as Model-70B, the original model being redesignated the 70A. These two models were continued with annual modifications until 1939, and it is possible that as many as 11,000 were delivered in this period.

1939 FORD (i) 1½-ton COE truck, NMM

The 3 millionth Ford truck was produced during 1936, the range consisting of a car-type sedan delivery (also offered briefly in 1937 as a coupe pickup), and the ½- and 1½-tonners. 1938 saw two additional types, a 1-tonner and a forward-control 1½-tonner, and in 1939 Ford trucks (along with the cars) were given hydraulic brakes. Both trucks and buses were now available with the 3.9-litre 95 hp Mercury V-8 unit and some Fords for export were fitted with Hercules diesels, though these were not a regular catalog option. In co-operation with Detroit the factory also developed a new Union City-bodied 27-seater bus with transverse, rear-mounted 95 hp engine. Coachwork was all steel, the canvas roof apart, wheelbase was 12 ft 4½ in., and the overall length was 25 ft 9 in. Detroit bought 500, and the front-engined buses were discontinued. In 1941 Ford formed a new PSV sales organization, Transit Buses Inc.: it was closely affiliated with Ford Motor Co., but not apparently owned by them. Sales of Transits through Ford dealers continued in large quantities during the war years, some 11,000 finding customers between 1939 and 1947.

The truck line was again restyled in 1940, with a steering column change on the lightweights, and a hydrovac brake option on heavier types. Some models in the 8-cwt/1-ton class were assembled from American parts for the British Army by the Ford factory at Dagenham, which had by now developed an independent range. 1941 saw Ford's first inline six since 1908, a 3.7-litre affair which became a regular option throughout the commercial vehicle range. There was also a short-lived small four of tractor origin, available only in the under-l-ton category. Ford's war effort included 12,000-odd armored cars and nearly 14,000 Universal Carriers, as well as conventional trucks. In 1941 they had built their own light 4x4 design using the 45 bhp 4-cylinder tractor engine, and they subsequently collaborated with Willys on Jeep manufacture, as well as being responsible for the entire series production of the amphibious (GPA) variant of the family.

For the first two postwar seasons Ford — now under the control of the founder's grandson Henry II — was content to revive the 1942 range. One of the consequences of this conservatism was that Transit Buses, anxious to update their wares, went their own way. The big Detroit operation remained faithful to Transit, Ford's PSV sales fell to around 500 in 1948 and 1949. To replace the Transits the company commissioned a line of Wayne-

1939 FORD (i) Transit bus, MBS

bodied 27- and 31-seaters, distributed by yet another associate concern, Metropolitan Motor Coaches Inc. This organization was liquidated in January, 1950, and Ford bus production ceased apart of course from the almost mandatory school bus chassis. Within a few months, however, the old Wayne designs were back on the market under the Marmon-Herrington name.

The trucks were completely restyled in 1948, and with this redesign came the first step in a process of range-widening which has characterized all the USA's volume producers. First step was the introduction of a heavy-duty line of 2/3-tonners, the F6, F7 and F8; 5-speed gearboxes and hydrovac brakes were found on the heaviest ones, and most powerful V-8 was uprated from 100 to 135 hp. The F8 could be had as a 6x4 and in 1949 came a 6-cylinder forward control parcels delivery chassis. A bigger, 110

1949 FORD (i) Series F5 truck, OMM

bhp six was featured in 1950, and some 2-tonners were now available with synchromesh gearboxes.

Ohv power units — a 3.6-litre six and two V-8's of 145 and 155 hp — made their appearance in 1952, the flatheads disappearing for good in 1954. Automatic transmissions were available on 1953 lightweights, while there

1955 FORD (i) C-500 truck, GNG

1955 FORD (i) P Series van, OMM

was now a hydrovac option on 1½-tonners. The 6x4 and forward control ranges were extended in 1954, in which year power steering was first listed as an option on trucks. Tubeless tires and 12-volt electric systems were standardized on the 1956 line, which offered six and V-8 power up to 200 hp. 1957's novelties came at either end of the line-up; the car-type Ranchero pickup available with 6- or 8-cylinder engines and all the regular private-car options, and the C-range of forward control tilt cab types in the 5/9-ton class, which replaced the more traditional COEs. These had 4- or 5-speed synchromesh gearboxes with a new Transmatic automatic-box option, hypoid back axles, and an infinite variety of braking systems (hydraulic, hydrovac, air/hydraulic, or full air, according to payload rating). Engines were gasoline V-8's from 4½ litres and 178 hp up to 5½ litres and 190 hp. A year later the normal control range was augmented with extra-heavy duty types, and the most powerful V-8 disposed of 534ci (8.7-litres) with an output of 277 hp. Diesels also made a tentative reappearance, but these were British 6-cylinder Perkins units and confined to the medium-duty range. Ford tested a gas turbine engine in 1960; three years later they had a 600 hp unit of this type installed in a 6x4 tractor for artics with air suspension and 5-speed automatic gearbox.

New in the ½-ton light van class in 1961 was the forward control unit-construction Econoline, powered by a front-mounted 2.3-litre 6-cylinder engine also used in the Falcon compact car. At the top end of the range were the H-series of forward control, tilt-cab tractors, ancestors of the Intercontinentals launched by Ford of Europe in 1973, as well as of the even bigger American Ws of 1971. As originally announced they covered GCWs in the over 30-ton class, with 6x4 variants, and a choice of either gasoline

1960 FORD (i) C Series Luverne-bodied fire engine, Luverne

V-8's or Cummins diesels of up to 220bhp. Twin-plate clutches and air brakes were features, as were a variety of transmissions with up to 12 forward speeds.

Cummins V-6 engines made their appearance shortly afterwards in the short-hooded, conventional NS. Independent front suspension had spread from the car-based types (which had had it since 1949) to light trucks by 1965, and there were 1,000 different models of Ford commercial listed in 1966. That year's principal novelty was a Jeep-type 4x4, the Bronco. This came initially with the 105hp 6-cylinder engine and 3x2-speed synchromesh gearbox, but the usual V-8 and automatic options soon followed. More and more bought-out components were to be seen, with 6-cylinder Caterpillar diesels available in the heavier trucks. In 1968 power front disc brakes became an option on light and medium types; they would be standard on such models as the Econoline by 1975.

New for 1970 was the L family of heavy conventional trucks built in Ford's just opened Louisville plant. A wide variety of 4x2 and 6x4 types was available for GVW ratings as high as 64,000 lb., air brakes were regular equipment (though 'light' Ls made do with hydrovac), and multi-speed transmissions were offered. The fiberglass hood/fender assembly tilted forward to give access to the engine, and GM-built V-6 and V-8 Detroit Diesels were added to the list of options. A set-back axle version (Series-LN) followed, while 1971 saw the W-series of extra heavy forward control tractors with tilt cabs and Hendrickson suspension on 6x4 members of the family. Though Ford failed to hold their 1974 position as Americas' best-selling truck (892,736 units sold) they still lay third in the over 11-ton class, behind I.H.C. and Mack.

1975 FORD (i) W Series (left) and L Series (right), Ford

A huge range was offered for 1978. Among the lightweights were the Ranchero, an updated Bronco with 5.8-litre V-8 engine, and a formidable selection of Econolines, now offered with 4-speed overdrive gearboxes and a choice of engines from a 4.9-litre inline 6 to a 7½-litre V-8. The 4-cylinder Courier pickup was made for Ford by Mazda of Japan, but native light and medium duty types included 4x4s as well as the F (normal control) and C (forward control, tilt cab) families with GVWs in the 24,000-56,000 lb. bracket. Variants included 6x4s, numerous different transmissions could be specified, and there was a choice of six 6- and 8-cylinder gasoline engines as well as Caterpillar diesels of 175 hp and 210 hp. Louisville Fords now catered for GVWs of as much as 80,000 lbs., with 10-, 13- and 16-speed transmissions on the heaviest types: both gasoline and diesel power was available. An all-new replacement for the W-series was the CL-9000, its light-alloy cab having a bbc measurement in basic form of only 54 in. Caterpillar, Cummins and Detroit engines of up to 600 hp could be specified, and though the standard GCW rated stayed at 80,000 lb., special versions were available to cope with 138,000 lb. Other specialized Ford commercial types included the B series of normal-control school buses and the P family of forward-control parcel vans with 4-speed gearboxes and 4.9-litre 6-cylinder engines. *MCS*

FORD (ii) (GB) 1911 to date

(1) Ford Motor Co. Ltd., Trafford Park, Manchester 1911-1931

(2) Ford Motor Co. Ltd., Dagenham, Essex 1931 to date: Langley, Bucks 1960 to date: Swaythling, Southampton 1971 to date

Commercial vehicles were always part of Ford's British program, starting with the Model-T light van and progressing to the 1-ton TT. In 1929 production of Fordson agricultural tractors was transferred from the Irish factory at Cork; during the 1930s Dagenham was to be the staple producer of these vehicles. There were no major differences between American and British Ford trucks until 1932, in which year a 3-speed 1-tonner with the 3.3-litre 4-cylinder sv engine was introduced, this being made alongside a 10-cwt van on the car chassis, and the stand-

1978 FORD (i) CL9000 Line hauler tractor, Ford

ard 30-cwt truck with 4-speed gearbox and longitudinal rear springs. Later in the year came a 5-cwt van with 3-speed synchromesh box, based on the new 933 cc Model-Y saloon. The Fordson name, previously found on tractors only, was first applied to a truck with the advent of a new 2-tonner in 1933; it was in general use for commercial vehicles by 1935. The 1934 Dagenham Fords covered payloads from 5 cwt to 2 tons; there were also 6×2 (Surrey) and 6×4 (Sussex) derivatives of the 2-tonner for heavier work, but only the smallest van and the 1-ton truck were entirely British in concept; the others were distinguishable for their American counterparts chiefly by the retention of 1933 styling. Interestingly, the 3.6-litre V8 engine was only available in a 20-seat coach; it was not offered in trucks before 1935, in which year a purely British type made its appearance in the shape of a forward-control 2-tonner notable for semi-elliptic suspension all round and a sliding roof as standard equipment on the cab. V8 engines were standardized for all 1936 models from 15-cwt upward, the normal-control range continuing on American lines until the outbreak of World War II. An unusual variation on the Model-Y theme was the Fordson Tug, a 3-wheeler tractive unit only 10 ft long, with 4-speed gearbox and coil-sprung single front wheel, while a new 25cwt truck introduced for 1937 combined the American-type normal control cab with forward control and the small 60

1939 FORD (ii) 3-ton van, OMM

hp 2.2-litre V8 engine. The old 4-cylinder engine was reinstated as an option during the year, and the all-British forward-control range was extended, with 3-tonners and 6-wheelers in 1938, and 4-5-tonners by 1939. The 5-cwt van was restyled along with its sedan counterparts, and a new model was the E83, a compact 10cwt van on a 7 ft 6 in wheelbase using the mechanic elements of the 1,172 cc Ten. Early in 1939 medium and heavy duty Fordson

1944 FORD (ii) Thames 7 V 3-ton truck, OMM

trucks were given the Thames designation, which came to be regarded as a make-name after World War II and was not finally dropped until 1965.

1944 FORD (ii) Thames 3-ton truck, OMM

Vehicles produced for the Allied war effort in the 1939-45 period included 15- and 30-cwt 4×2s, 30-cwt and 3-ton forward control 4×4s, and 3-ton 6×4s, to which should be added large numbers of tracked Universal Carriers using the V8 engine, 2-ton forward control fire tenders with Jensen bodywork for the NFS, and 262,000 V8 engines for sundry purposes. The RAF also used normal-control Fordson-Sussex 6-wheelers as balloon barrage tenders. All these trucks were powered by the 3.6-litre V8 engines.

1950 FORD (ii) Thames ETg 4-ton truck, Ford

Initial postwar offerings consisted of the 5- and 10cwt vans and a range of forward control V8 trucks in the 2/5-ton class. These latter were replaced in 1949 by new normal-control Thames models 4×2s, 6×4s, artics, and a PSV chassis. Payloads ran from 2 to 8 tons, and new features were semi-elliptic front suspension, and hydraulic brakes, with vacuum servo assistance on heavy duty versions. The Perkins P6 diesel engine was a factory option, but those who preferred gasoline had to stay with the old V8 until 1953, when Ford introduced a 5 bearing 3.6- litre ohv 4-cylinder engine developing 70 hp, this serving as a basis for their first diesel design announced in 1954. 4-tonners and over, however, retained the V8 until 1957. Commercial vehicle production passed the 50,000 mark for the first time in 1955, by which time the old 5-cwt van had been replaced by new 5-cwt and 7cwt models with ifs and hydraulic brakes (but still with sv engines and three forward speeds) based on the latest 100 E Anglia and Prefect sedans. Thence forward the car-type light vans would keep pace with their opposite numbers, switching to 997 cc short-stroke ohv engines and 4-speed gearboxes after the final demise of the 100E line in 1962, and emerging in 1968 as members of the Escort family, with 1,100 cc and 1.3 litre engines and a front disc brake option.

There had been no forward control models since 1949, with the exception of a 3-ton 4×4 military truck in 1952, using a Commer cab and a Canadian-built V8 engine, but this configuration returned in 1957 on the Thames Traders with synchromesh gearboxes and hypoid back axles. All engines were Ford-built, the existing 4-cylinder types being joined by gasoline (4.9-litre, 115 hp) and diesel (5.4-litre, 108 hp) sixes. Initially only 1½- to 7-ton trucks and the usual artics were offered, but the range was later extended to include low frame models, all-wheel drive conversions by Vickers, 6×2 and 6×4 adaptations by County Commercial Cars, and a 41-seater PSV chassis: one of these last was fitted with unusual double-decker bodywork for transporting cyclists and their machines through the Dartford-Purfleet Tunnel. 5-speed gearboxes and 2-speed back axles were regular options by 1962, in which year there were normal control Traders as well, distinguished by their curved windshields and alligator hoods.

1963 FORD (ii) Thames Trader 75 7½ ton truck, Ford

Also during 1957 the faithful old 10-cwt E83 disappeared in favor of a new generation of 10/15-cwt Thames vans with full forward control, unit construction, side loading facilities, 3-speed gearboxes with column change, ifs, hypoid final drive, and the 1.7-litre 4-cylinder Consul car engine already used in Beardmore's taxicabs. This one kept pace with its rivals; a 1.6-litre Perkins diesel unit was available from 1962, and an extra forward ratio from 1964.

In 1960 the final assembly of commercial vehicles was transferred to Langley, and two years later Special Vehicle Operations (svo) came into being to tailor vehicles for special customers: it handled around 7,000 orders in 1963. Over 85,000 commercials were made in 1965, in which year Ford launched the beginning of an all out effort in the heavy duty sector, as well as with buses. The whole existing range was scrapped, with the exception of the lightest vans and the normal control trucks, known henceforward as the K-series.

The 10/15-cwt Thames models gave way to the semi-forward control Transit, also built in Ford's German factory. A wider payload range (12-35-cwt) called for a reversion to semi-elliptics at the front as well as for twin rear wheels on some models, and gasoline options were Ford's new V4s of 1.7 and 2 litres' capacity. Until 1971 Perkins remained responsible for diesel engines, but that year saw Ford's own 2.4-litre 4-cylinder inline 61 hp type with cogged belt drive for the camshaft. Other improvements to the Transit range (made at Southampton from 1971 onwards) were an automatic option (1967), 2½-litre V6 gasoline option (1972), and such variations as light artics and high-capacity parcels vans. In 1972 a Transit Diesel set new international class records for 2/3-litre oil-engined cars at Monza, including 10,000 miles at 73.6 mph.

More important still was the D range of forward control trucks with tilt cabs and inclined engines, initially covering the 2- to 9-ton sector, as well as the usual tractors and tippers. Air-hydraulic brakes were standard on heavy-duty types, all the usual options being supplemented by a very popular custom cab which from a 4-litre 83hp four up to a new 6-litre 128hp six. The 6-cylinder gasoline engines of 129 and 149hp were imported from the U.S.A: these were discontinued in 1968.

Parallel with the D were the R192 and R226 buses (the designations indicated wheelbases in inches) for up to 53 passengers. Gasoline or diesel engines were initially available, and 5-speed gearboxes were standard on the more powerful type. In 1966 Ford delivered 113,623 commercial vehicles to become Britain's number one producer.

1978 FORD (ii) A Series crew-cab refuse collector, Ford

Though the K's survived into 1972, the D was now Ford's principal offering outside the lightweight class. By 1969 the heaviest load carrier was a 6x4 of 24 tons' GVW, available with 8.3-litre Cummins or 8.4-litre Ford V8 diesel engines of up to 185hp. Another new departure was a 150hp turbocharged edition of the 6-litre 6-cylinder Ford unit. 1971 saw a new range of heavy-duty all-synchromesh

1977 FORD (ii) Transcontinental 32-tonner GCW truck, Ford

gearboxes (4-speed, 6-speed, and 8-speed rangechange), while svo evolved such variants as low loaders on 17-inch wheels and miniature urban artics for 11¼-ton GCWs. The heaviest 1972 D's could be supplied with 6-speed Allison automatic transmissions and air suspension at the rear. PSV sales boomed, Midland Red ordering 100 R-type buses in 1970, with subsequent repeats; by the end of 1972 220 Fords were in service on State-owned, non-municipal lines. In 1973 the gap between the Transits and the D-series was filled by the A-line, close relatives of the former for GVWs in the 3½/ 5½-ton bracket. Dual-circuit servo brakes were standard, buyers had the choice of four or five forward speeds, and a wide selection of engines included a 3-litre gasoline V6 and a new 3½-litre 4-cylinder diesel developing 89 hp.

In 1977 the company scored an unprecedented success: the Ford was Britain's best-selling truck and farm tractor

1978 FORD (ii) D 1614 16-ton GVW truck, Ford

1978 FORD (ii) Transit truck, Ford

as well as private car. The 1978 commercial range embraced the R buses (now with 144 hp 6-litre turbocharged diesels as standard), with the Escort, Transit and A-series covering the light-medium sector. The latest Mk.II Transits had servo front disc brakes as standard, and 4-cylinder gasoline engines were now of inline type exclusively. There was also a wide selection of Ds, including 4-wheeled trucks for GVWs from 5¾ to 16 tons. Engines were 4-, 6- and 8-cylinder diesels of Ford make, or Cummins V8 diesels, with full air brakes on the heaviest types. Exhaust brakes were an option with 6- and 8-cylinder power units.

During 1975 the process of market coverage had been completed with an answer to Bedford's TM, the huge Transcontinental made in Ford's Dutch plant at Amsterdam. A wide range of 4×2 and 6×4 trucks and tractors was offered, for GVWs and GCWs from 32 to 44 tons. Features included forward control with 3-man tilt cabs, twin-plate clutches, 9- or 13-speed Fuller constant-mesh gearboxes, single-reduction hypoid rear axles, power steering, and air brakes. Engines were 14-litre 6-cylinder inline Cummins diesels, the most powerful 1978 versions with turbocharger and aftercooling disposing of 355 hp. Certain British Ford models are also made in Spain under the Ebro name. *MCS*

FORD (iii) (AUS) 1934 to date

(1) Ford Motor Co. of Australia Pty., Ltd., Geelong, Victoria 1934-1965
(2) Ford Motor Co. of Australia Ltd., Campelfield, Victoria 1966 to date

Ford was assembling T models in Australia since the mid 20's, but introduced the first original Australian commercial vehicle in 1934 in the form of a car-based coupe utility pick-up. The basic model for every year since, was the current American V8 car and these pick-ups were the only original Australian Ford built until hostilities started. War needs led Ford to the assembly of Canadian Military Pattern all-wheel-drive vehicles, to 6x6 conversions of normal chassis and to the introduction of two Australian-designed armored vehicles. The lighter model called the Dingo, after the name of a native wild dog, was based on a short wheelbase chassis with Marmon-Herrington 4x4 conversion and was fitted with a V8 gasoline engine developing 85 hp, while the heavier model was based on the 6x6 chassis as converted by Ford in Australia. Coupe utilities based on contemporary American car models were built throughout the war, while the Mainline pick-up utility appeared in 1955 and was based on a largely modified American car model, sporting the same V8 ohv gasoline engine. Since then coupe utilities were always built alongside car models and since 1960 they are based on the Falcon cars. Both pick-up and vans are produced and are often redesigned following the Falcon car development. Engines are gasoline units of 6 and V8 configuration ranging from 85 hp in 1962 up to 170 hp sixes and 240 hp V8s in 1972. Falcon vans are high-top models offering a large volume capacity, and both models are heavy-duty built meeting local demands. A Falcon 4x4 pick-up was built in 1972 powered by a 155 hp 6 cylinder engine, but it was never produced in quantities. Along with Australian models, the whole US and UK medium ranges of commercial vehicles are also built, but these models remain identical to their overseas counterparts. Ford of Australia was also one of the two companies, along with International, to meet Australian army demand for a light 4x4 1 ton vehicle to replace imported models. A few pilot models were delivered in 1975 and are currently under evaluation. UK bus and coach models are also built in Australia and are marketed with locally built bodies. *GA*

FORD (iv) (D) 1935 to date

Ford-Werke A.G., Cologne

The German Ford plant presented its first truck in 1935. It was the model BB with 4-cylinder 3.2-litre engine. In 1936 a 3-tonner appeared with 3.6-litre V-8 engine developing 95 hp. This was available as van, truck or bus. Vans were based on the private cars, they were the Koln (933 cc), Eifel (1,157 cc), Taunus (1,172 cc) and V-8. The 3-ton truck was built also during the war for the army. Also based on this model was a half-track version with the 3.9-litre V-8 engine.

1950 FORD (iv) Taunus ½-ton van, OMM

After the war the 3-ton type was carried on and was available also as a bus. In 1948 a 4-cylinder 3-tonner was presented as the Ruhr and the V-8 version got the name Rhein in 1949. In the same year the first forward control bus with V-8 engine was presented. In 1951 the type designations FK 3000 (4-cylinder, 3,285 cc, 3 ton) and FK 3500 (V-8, 3,924 cc, 3½ ton) were introduced and henceforth all commercials bore the prefix FK which stood for "Ford — Koln". The FK 3500 D followed with 4,080 cc 94 hp diesel engine and this version also was available with 4x4 drive. A one ton forward control transporter with 1,172 cc engine came in 1953 under the type designation FK 1000. Later it also was available with 1.5-litre engine. The program was enlarged and cars appeared with new styling in 1956. The FK 2500 was available with 8-cylinder 3.9-litre 100 hp gasoline engine or a new V-4 2.8-litre 80 hp Ford-List two-stroke diesel engine. Also the FK 3500 and FK 4500 were equipped with new two-stroke 6-cylinder diesel engines of 4.2-litre and output of 120 hp. Production of trucks ended in 1961 and Ford of Germany concentrated on transporters.

1970 FORD (iv) Taunus 12M ½-ton van, GNG

The FK 1000 got the name Transit in 1961 and was available with 1.2, 1.5 or 1.7-litre engines. In 1965 the forward control Transit was succeeded by an Anglo-German short hood version which got the type designation FT 600 to FT 1750 according to the payload capacities ranging from 600 kg to 1750 kg. Since 1971 a 4-cylinder diesel engine of 2,358 cc is available for the Transit range. Trucks which are distributed by Ford of Germany are of British or Dutch manufacture. *HON*

1954 FORD (v) Cargo 5-ton truck, OMM

FORD (v) (F) 1947-1954

Ford SAF, Poissy, Seine-et-Oise.

Ford SAF were the successors of the Matford concern, and initially they continued that firm's all-French forward control 5-tonner. In postwar guise the French Ford used a more powerful 3.9-litre sv V8 gasoline engine. A new modern all-steel cab made its appearance in 1949, and a 4.1-litre 6-cylinder Hercules diesel option in 1952. Soft-cab editions were supplied to the army, and later models featured 4-speed synchromesh gearboxes, a 2-speed back axle option, and hydrovac brakes. From 1950 the company also offered the Abeille, a typically French 5-door conversion of the 13CV Vedette sedan with 2.2-litre V8 engine. Simca acquired the French Ford interests in November, 1954, continuing the trucks, though not the Abeille, under their own name. *MCS*

FORD (vi) (ZA) 1972 to date

Ford Motor Co. of South Africa (Pty) Ltd., Port Elizabeth, Cape Province

Assembling various models since the mid-20s, the Port Elizabeth based factory introduced in November 1971 a pick-up version of the British Cortina, a model never produced by the mother company in England. The vehicle is intended to provide a locally built light commercial to compete with the Japanese, most of which run their assembly facilities in South Africa. Keeping Cortina's front-end and side doors, the rear-end was designed as a very attractive looking pick-up. Engines used were the Cortina 1.6 litre and 2 litre gasoline units, while later a Ford 2.5 litre unit was also added. 1975 saw the introduction of the heavier Ranchero pick up based on American designs, but with a redesigned front end. *GA*

1973 FORD (vii) Fiera basic transportation vehicle, AAR

FORD (vii) (PI) 1972 to date

Ford Philippine Inc., Makati Rizal

Like GM's Harimau, the Philippine Ford Fiera was an ultra-simple light truck for Asian markets. Powered by 4-cylinder (ii) Ford Escort engines of 1,100 cc or 1.3 litres, it had a 4-speed all-synchromesh gearbox, a straightforward chassis with beam axles all round, and an open cab. Improved 1978 models featured beam-and-coil front suspension of American Ford Bronco type. A heavy duty 1¾-tonner was now available with a choice of 1.6-litre gasoline or 2.4-litre diesel engines. MCS

FORDSON see Ford (ii)

FORREST (GB) 1908-1914

J.A. Wads & Co. Ltd., Liverpool

The Forrest appeared as a two-seater passenger car, powered by an 8 hp V-twin engine, with friction transmission and shaft drive. A light van was offered on this chassis from 1908, and there was also a taxicab with a front pening hansom-style body, though the driver sat in a conventional position. The later Forrests were sold in London under the name Realm-Forrest. *GNG*

FORSCHLER (US) 1914-1922

(1) Phillip Forschler Wagon Co., New Orleans, La 1914-1918

(2) Forschler Motor Truck Manufacturing Co., Inc., New Orleans, La 1919-1922

Initial Forschlers were 1½- and 3-tonners using water-cooled, four-cylinder engines, on frames with 10-foot, 4-inch wheelbases. These also used three-speed gearboxes and double chain drives. Engines and gearboxes were mounted on a separate frame, spring-mounted. By 1917, the drive had been converted to a worm gear at the differential. Capacities were varied from year to year and included ¾-tonners as well as 1-, and 2-tonners. These trucks were sold locally only. *GMN*

FORT GARRY see M.C.I.

FORT WAYNE (US) 1911-1913

Fort Wayne Auto Manufacturing Co., Fort Wayne, Ind.

The Model A was a 1-tonner with a gross weight of 3500 pounds. This was driven by a water-cooled four-cylinder engine with a three-speed gearbox and double chain drive. This was available only with a stake body. Speed was governed to a maximum 18 mph. Model B was a 3-tonner also with four-cylinder engine, with a maximum of 15 mph and a chassis price of $3000. *GMN*

FOSTER (GB) 1904-1934

William Foster & Company Ltd., Lincoln.

The Foster marque is best know for its 6, 7 and 8 hp compound four-shaft showmen's road locomotives. A total of 68 of these were built between 1904 and 1934 and were popular in the Midlands and North of England. Being four-shaft, they did not have the gears overhung as in a Burrell and were preferred by some for collar work for this reason, the Burrell being generally considered, however, the speedier of the two.

In common with many other makers Foster launched a design of a 3-ton (3 hp) tractor within the limits imposed by the 1896 rules, available with either a single cylinder or duplex cylinders. These never achieved great popularity. Better success, however, attended their 5-ton compound three shaft tractor built to the less onerous limits of the 1904 rules. The most notable feature of the tractors was the employment of Foster's own systems of rear springs. Earlier examples had a transverse spring with pivoted compensating levers, placed beneath the rear axle. Later, however, the firm substituted a pair of longitudinal springs above the axle more akin to motor practice which, in association with an all gear drive led to more troubles than it solved.

1904 FOSTER 5-ton steam tractor, RAW

After the building of an experimental overtype wagon in 1905 wagon making was allowed to lapse until in 1919 the company sold the first 60 overtype compound wagons of 5-tons carrying capacity. The boiler, like the Aveling and Clayton overtypes, used a flat topped Belpaire firebox.

1916 FOSTER road engine, converted to showman's type by the makers in 1922, RAW

The 2-speed version was generally not unlike the 5-ton Foden i.e. by the time it appeared it was obsolescent. From the driver's point of view the geared feed pump was excessively noisy and the internal expanding brakes sometimes gave a dangerous kick-back on the pedal when used in reverse. The arrangement of the optional third speed was very noisy. Nevertheless the wagons were soundly built and durable and No. 14630, sold in 1934, was probably the last overtype wagon to be delivered new. The market in overtype wagons was beginning to shrink when the Foster wagon was first sold and in an atmosphere of contracting demand the sales were depressed by the emergence of the improved postwar Fodens.

Fosters did not set out to be builders of internal combustion engined vehicles but they were responsible for the production of the military tank, first used in 1917. *RAW*

FOUILLARON (F) 1901-c.1907

G. Fouillaron, Levallois-Perret, Seine.

Common to all Fouillaron cars right up to the end in 1914 was an infinitely variable gear consisting of belts running over expansive pulleys to a countershaft and side chains. Engines were of proprietary make, and the 1902 catalogue showed light vans on the de Dion-powered 6 and 8 hp chassis. There was, however, little serious truck manufacture: in December 1906 a 32-seater omnibus was said to be under construction, but this did not materialize.

In 1907 Jesse Ellis, the Maidstone steam wagon maker, announced a 15/20-cwt van with 2.8-litre 4-cylinder gasoline engine and Fouillaron transmission, and it is possible that the French firm were responsible for the entire vehicle. There is no further trace of anything except private cars. *MCS*

FOURMI (F) 1919

The Fourmi light van was powered by a M.A.G. V-twin engine in unit with a 3-speed gearbox mounted over the front wheels which were driven by chain. The track of the front wheels was much smaller than those at the rear, giving the Fourmi the superficial appearance of a 3-wheeler. *GNG*

FOUR WHEEL DRIVE (US) 1904-1907

Four Wheel Drive Wagon Co., Milwaukee, Wis.

As its name implies, this truck was driven by all four wheels, and also had four wheel steering. Power came originally from a 30 hp 4-cylinder Rutenber engine, with separate chain drive from the gearbox to each of the wheels. The 1906 models had a 40 hp engine and shaft drive to differentials on front and rear axles. Early models of this truck had wooden tires. There was no connection with the later, and much better known, Four Wheel Drive Auto company, makers of the F.W.D. truck. *GNG*

FOWELL (GB) 1877-1896

(1) G.J. Fowell, St. Ives, Hunts.1876-78
(2) Joseph Fowell, Sons & Co., St. Ives, Hunts. 1878-82
(3) Fowells & Hunt, St. Ives, Hunts. 882-86
(4) Fowell & Son, St. Ives, Hunts. 1886-96

The bulk of the 109 steam engines made by the firm were for agricultural use but in addition they made five of William Box's patent "narrow gauge" road locomotives in which the final drive was by side rods to the rear wheels from a jack-shaft beneath the boiler, permitting the rear axle to be properly sprung and rendering the overall width less than with gear drive. The first had its single cylinder over the firebox, as in a portable engine, but later examples used the conventional traction engine layout. Box patent engines (also built by Robeys) were used to found the famous Manchester heavy haulage business of Edward Box. *RAW*

FOWLER (GB) c.1880-1935

(1) John Fowler & Co., Leeds C.1880-1886
(2) John Folwer & Co. (Leeds) Ltd., Leeds. 1886-1935

John Fowler & Co. achieved their world fame as manufacturers of steam ploughing engines and machinery, followed by traction engines and from about 1880 onwards marketed their B class engines specifically for heavy haulage. Fowlers began to supply engines to showmen in the mid-eighties. A few single-cylinder engines were sold for heavy haulage but the majority were compounds. Fowler engines never achieved with showmen the popularity of the Burrell but, nevertheless, 82 Fowlers were supplied new to showmen and many others converted from road hauliers' engines. The most celebrated Fowler heavy road locomotives were the Little Lion, Big Lion and Super Lion classes of 7, 8 and 10 hp respectively, the penultimate showman's engine supplied in the world being the celebrated Super Lion "Supreme" supplied in 1934 to Deakins of Brynmawr. For the very heaviest classes of haulage Fowlers were pre-eminent. Road engines were also supplied fitted with cranes.

In addition to heavy road locomotives Fowlers also supplied steam tractors complying with the 1904 Regulations. The majority of these were double crank compounds on the three shaft principle (as opposed to four shafts in the heavy engines) but a few of the 'E' class had tandem compound cylinders. The tractors were good machines but not outstanding to the same degree as the heavy locomotives.

Both tractors and heavy locomotives were supplied to

1880 FOWELL 7hp road locomotive (Box's Patent), RAW

the War Department for military use and Fowler locomotives predominated amongst the military engines used in the Boer War (1899-1902), a few being equipped with armored protection which proved an embarrassment. The supply of a special class of artillery locomotives to Russia in 1917 was frustrated by the Revolution and most of the class were ultimately sold in this country.

1893 FOWLER 8nhp Class B3 showman's road locomotive, RAW

1908 FOWLER 8nhp Class R2 road locomotive, RAW

Fowlers, like Burrells and Fodens, paid particular attention to rear axle springing using a great freedom of spring movement which was taken up in their patent universal joint in the third shaft gearing, of which two versions existed, the later being a type of modified Oldham coupling.

The company also persisted in experiments with roadless vehicles. Early examples included traction engines with 12'0" and 9'0" diameter rear wheels. Shortly before the 1914-18 war they carried out experiments with the "Botrail" system of shoed wheels, a twentieth century variant of the Boydell system. In 1909 Fowlers supplied the engine and boiler parts for the Hornsby fully tracked steam tractor for the Yukon. Further experiments took place in 1923 when their "Snaketrac" fully tracked steam locomotive was constructed, only to fail on grounds of weight. Tracked tractor manufacture for agricultural and construction industry use was resumed using the oil engine after the building of other vehicles had ceased in the late thirties, and continues to date.

In 1924, faced with falling sales in other fields, Fowlers produced a steam wagon of advanced design using a vertical vee-twin compound engine, vertical fire-tube boiler, 3-speed gear-box and shaft drive with final drive by worm. All working parts had a high ground clearance but the wagons were let down by the inherent flexibility of the fire-tube boiler. They enjoyed, however, reasonable success as street gully emptiers and a fleet thus equipped was supplied to Warsaw Municipality (Poland).

1924 FOWLER steam gulley emptier, OMM

The company's venture into diesel vehicle building was no more successful. In 1931 they offered their Marathon 6-tonner equipped with their own 6-cylinder direct-injection diesel, developing 90 hp at 1400 rpm using separate 120 x 180mm cylinders, multiplate clutch, 4-speed main box, 2-speed auxiliary box and worm drive. With this were teamed the Crusader short wheelbase tipper and the Warrior heavy haulage tractor. They were all beautifully engineered but the engines were over large and heavy for road work and consequently, the selling prices being corresponding high, they failed to find buyers. Surplus tractor chassis were bought by Union Cartage in London and completed using Gardner engines in which form they ran for many years. By 1934 the 6/7 tonner was offered with a Gardner engine but even so the chassis at works cost £1368 compared with £1150 for the Leyland Beaver oiler.

In 1935 Fowler announced a diesel-engined tractor intended to replace steam showman's engines in fairgrounds. Powered by an 80 hp Fowler-Sanders 6-cylinder engine, it had two gearboxes giving a total of 6 forward and 2 reverse speeds. The rear wheels had a diameter of 6 ft. 9 in. and carried solid tires 18 in. wide, while the front wheels were a normal 3 ft. 6 in. diameter, and had pneumatic tires. Very few were made. *RAW*

F.R.A.M. see Cantono

FRAM (CS) 1927-1939

Vozovka a.s., Kolin

This factory assembled the modified Austrian Perl buses fitted with their own built bodies at first, but only a few units were built. These "Fram" city buses served in the town of Kolin up to 1936. In the years 1929-1939 the factory produced 71 bus bodies on several makes of chassis, and were used by the Prague and Brno travel companies as well as by the State bus travel companies.

The make "Fram" went bankrupt in 1939. *MSH*

FRAMO (D) 1927-1940

(1) Metallwerke Frankenberg GmbH., Frankenberg 1927-1933

(2) Framo Werke GmbH., Hainichen 1933-1940

In 1927 production of the light D.K.W. vans was transferred from D.K.W. to the Framo plant, both owned by J.S. Rasmussen, the founder of D.K.W. The tri-van TV 300 with engine mounted above the single front wheel was produced until 1930 when it was succeeded by the LT 200 with single-cylinder 200 cc engine following more modern lines with enclosed engine, closed cabin and steering wheel. The first fourwheeler appeared in 1932 with D.K.W. engine and front-drive. The van version had a conventional chassis while the pick-up featured a self-supporting body. The threewheeler became available with a 2-cylinder engine and the modernized 4-wheel 1-tonner got the 600 cc. D.K.W. engine, which in 1937 was supplemented by a 1.1 litre Ford engine. In 1939 a new 1-tonner, the model V 501 appeared, but was produced in small numbers only due to the war. This design was taken up again after the war (see IFA). *HON*

FRANCISCO (PI) 1948 to date
Francisco Motors Inc., Manila

Francisco is a big producer of the typical Jeepneys, so much in favor in Philippines. A WW II surplus or a newer model of Jeep is the basis of a much customized elongated body accomodating up to 12 passengers. Powered by the original Jeep engine or an alternative unit of same capacity, gasoline or diesel, Jeepneys are extremely popular as taxis or minibuses, throughout the Philippines. In 1975 Francisco introduced also the "Pinoi", a Mazda engined utility vehicle of many uses. *GA*

1910 FRANKLIN 1-ton van, NAHC

FRANKLIN (US) 1905-1912
H.H. Franklin Manufacturing Co., Syracuse, N.Y.

Franklin's cars featured air cooling, wooden frames, and full-elliptic suspension. As early as 1905 the works were utilizing a normal control truck on the longitudinal-engined 4-cylinder chassis with barrel-shaped hood, and a year later a forward-control 1-tonner was marketed. Its ohv engines had a capacity of 1.8-litres, other features being a 2-speed gearbox, solid tires, and shaft drive. By 1908 there were also a 2-ton model and a ½-tonner with normal control; a police patrol wagon was sold to the make's home town of Syracuse. The biggest Franklin truck had disappeared by 1912, the firm's last commercials having three forward speeds and pneumatic tires. The ½-tonner had a Renault-type hood and was also listed as a taxi, while the bigger forward control model had semi-elliptic springs at the rear. A prototype 1-tonner with 4-cylinder engine and full electrics was made in 1920, and as late as 1931 the US Quartermaster Corps was experimenting with 6-cylinder aircooled Franklin power units in army trucks. *MCS*

FRANZ see F.B.W.

FRASER (GB) c.1920
W. & D. Fraser & Sons Ltd., Arbroath

The Fraser 5-tonner was equipped with a liquid fired monotube boiler, vertical 3 cylinder, single acting, poppet valved engine, countershaft differential and chain drive. Later coke firing was used. Working pressure was 750 psi. Though a channel chassis was used the body and cab were all steel on tubular framing. The wagon was too revolutionary for the market and few were made, possibly one only. *RAW*

FRAT see Ebro

FRAYER-MILLER (US) 1906-1910
(1) Oscar Lear Auto Co., Columbus, O 1906-1910
(2) Kelly Motor Truck Co., Columbus, O 1910

The Frayer-Miller was a 1½-tonner driven by an air-cooled, 4-cylinder engine and equipped with a 4-speed gearbox. Final drive was by double chains. With a stake platform body, the price was $3000. In 1907, a cab was offered under the tradename of Nichols Frayer-Miller. This had tiller steering from the rear top. Frayer-Miller was better known for air-cooled passenger cars. It eventually became part of the later Kelly-Springfield Truck Company. *GMN*

FREEMAN (US) 1928-1934
(1) Freeman Motor Co., Detroit, Mich.
(2) Freeman Quadrive Corp., Detroit, Mich.

The Freeman was a 4-wheel-drive truck powered by 6-cylinder Buda engines of three sizes, 65, 75 and 110 hp. The largest model, when towing two 4-wheeled trailers, had a total load capacity of 20 tons which it could haul at a speed of 25 mph. Drive to the rear wheels was by internal gears, and to the front via a live axle above the fixed axle; this axle drove the wheels by a system of bevel gears at each end which did away with the need for a differential. The Freeman had eight forward speeds and two reverse. *GNG*

FREESTONE (GB) 1911
G. Freestone. Saffron Walden, Essex.

Produced by the inventor of the British Square Turn agricultural tractor, the Freestone was an unconventional little vehicle. A three-wheeler, of the light delivery/parcel carrying variety, it employed front-wheel-drive, an air-cooled 7/9 hp vee-twin engine mounted transversely above the single front wheel, which it drove by vertical roller chain. Variable gearing by means of a friction disc and twin rollers was provided, this apparently also being adaptable for four wheeled versions with rear wheel drive, and wheel steering was achieved by bevel gearing to a vertical shaft on which the front wheel was mounted. A later version boasted a box van body with enclosed driver's cab. *MJWW*

FREIBAHN (D) 1905-1913
Freibahn GmbH., Seegefeld

Steam tractors were a speciality of this manufacturer which developed into steam road trains with up to four trailers and a total payload capacity of 20 tons. *HON*

FREIGHTLINER/WHITE FREIGHTLINER (US) 1940-1942; 1947 to date
(1) Freightways Mfg. Corp. Salt Lake City, Utah Subsidiary of Consolidated Freightways, Inc. Spokane. Wash. 1940-1942

(2) Freightliner Corp. Portland, Oregon Subsidiary of Consolidated Freightways, Inc. Spokane, Wash. 1947 to date
(3) White Motor Co. Cleveland, Ohio (Sales and Service) 1951 to date

Freightliner's origin is unusual. Leland James, president of Consolidated Freightways, Inc. was dissatisfied with the trucks on the market in the late 1930's. He wanted something better — a lightweight truck for heavy duty line-haul work which would give the maximum legal payload capacity. But when he told truck builders what he wanted, none of them would build it. The only solution left was to do it himself.

So, Mr. James and a hand-picked group of mechanics began experimental work in Salt Lake City, Utah in 1939 under the name Freightways Mfg. Corp., and the new diesel-powered lightweight model CF-100 cab-over-engine truck they developed went into production in 1940 using standard components. The parent company, Consolidated Freightways, Inc. took all of the production, but war time metals priorities forced a shut-down in March, 1942.

After World War II a few trucks were turned out by the CF maintenance shop in Portland, Oregon, and Freightliner production was resumed there in 1947 by a new subsidiary, Freightliner Corp., under the leadership of L.E. Kassenbaum, president, and Thomas Taylor, general manager. Metallurgical advances during the war, especially in aluminum and magnesium, were applied to truck manufacturing so that the new Freightliners were one ton lighter than comparable units then on the road. The performance of the new diesel trucks was admirable.

CF and its subsidiary grew, and in 1948 the first Freightliner (model 800) was sold to an outside customer (Graziano). As in all subsequent production, this truck was custom-built to the customer's requirements from supplied components.

1949 FREIGHTLINER Model WF800 tractor, Freightliner

In 1949 a Freightliner appeared with a custom-built sleeper cab for Transcontinental hauling.

In 1951 the White Motor Co. of Cleveland, Ohio became the sales and service organization for Freightliner trucks so that Freightliner Corp. could concentrate on production, and the trucks were now available nationally and in Canada. At this time the truck nameplate was changed to White Freightliner.

During the 1950's Freightliner unveiled some new developments, including three industry firsts: a new 48-inch cab in March, 1953 with a grille about one half of the

1951 WHITE FREIGHTLINER 6×4 tanker, LA

1952 WHITE FREIGHTLINER Model WF-8164 6×4 chassis, Freightliner

former size; the first roof-mounted sleeper; and the first four-wheel-drive tractor designed exclusively for highway transport.

A new cab evolved from basic sketches drawn by Kenneth Self, later president, and introduced in Nov. 1953. These new cabs had the first basic changes since 1940, together with new styling and moving the cab forward over the axle. With a new grille in 1958, this is the basic style still made today.

In May, 1954 Freightliner introduced a sleeper model with a bumper to back-of-cab dimension of only 75 inches.

July, 1958 saw the introduction of a full-tilt cab which opened to 90 degrees in 38 seconds. The cabs are of all-aluminum re-inforced monocoque construction with 12 panels riveted together, so that the cab sheet metal is the basic load-carrying member. The riveted system allows a great many choices for sleeper cab lengths. Cab backs are usually straight vertical, but sometimes slightly slanted forward. All Freightliner glass is flat all around with the V-type windshield slanted backward in line with the upper front of the cab. Cab height is 114 inches. Dual headlights are optional.

A new half-cab series with forward-slanting windshield and grille, the latter offset to the right, was introduced in

1969 WHITE FREIGHTLINER Model WF-8164 6×4 truck, Freightliner

1964 for use in the construction industry. This, too, was a cab-over, and available in a choice of 6 x 4, 6 x 6, or 8 x 6 drives.

For 1974 Freightliner introduced an all-new lightweight conventional model in which 80% of the parts are interchangeable with the full-width cab-over, even to some of the aluminum sheet panels which are of riveted construction. For both models, the basic drive trains are Cummins Diesel NTC290 with Fuller clutch and Roadranger 10-speed transmission, and Rockwell rear axles in 4 x 2 or 6 x 4 drives. Tires are 11 x 22½ 12-ply tubeless nylon with duals on the rear. Freightliner makes its own suspensions, semi-elliptic front and rear, while the tandems are of the 4-spring multi-leaf type. The weight of the conventional 4 x 2 tractor chassis and cab is 10315 pounds, the 6 x 4 weighs 12465 pounds. These are lightweights in their class and only 100 to 200 pounds more than the cab-overs.

1975 WHITE FREIGHTLINER Model WFT-8164 conventional tractor, Freightliner

A new Powerliner cab-over series is also available with a much larger grille and radiator (2000 sq. in., contrasted with the standard 1070 sq. in.) to accommodate the coming generation of 400 to 650 hp diesels. Current engine for the Powerliner is Cummins NTC400.

Other Cummins Diesels are offered throughout the Freightliner range as well as Detroit, Caterpillar, and Allis Chalmers diesels and a wide choice of components, accessories, trim and paint schemes.

Historically, the large majority of Freightliner production has been road tractors, although straight trucks can be ordered. Freightliner has been known to build specials. Among standard or sleeper cab-overs, the rear wall is about over the axle. Ameron of Monetery, Calif. even had one built with the cab entirely ahead of the axle, which was informally known as "Andy Gump", after a well-known comic-strip character.

Over the years Freightliner Corp. has grown considerably, but not just in one place. Beside the main plant in Portland, Oregon, manufacturing locations now include Fremont and Chino, Cal., Indianapolis, Ind. (half-cab models) and Vancouver, British Columbia. Production has risen from only 56 in 1949 to around 18,000 per year, accounting for about 25% of all US cab-over trucks and making Freightliner a major truck manufacturer. *RW*

FREMONT-MAIS (US) 1914-1915

Lauth-Juergens Motor Car Company, Fremont, Ohio

This truck was built in a single model with a rating of 3000 pounds. Powered by a four-cylinder Buda engine, it used a Warner gearbox and had shaftdrive, with either 11-foot or 12-foot wheelbase. This make was succeeded by the Burford. *GMN*

FRERA (I) 1930-c.1939

Srl. Leonardo Frera, Tradate

This motorcycle factory marketed a delivery 3-wheeler with two driven rear wheels and 500cc single-cylinder engine during the 1930s. *MCS*

FRICK (GB) 1904-1908

(1) A. Dougill & Co. Ltd., Leeds, York 1904-1907
(2) Clift's Engineering Co. Ltd., Brighton, Sussex 1908

Dougill's commercial vehicles were sold under the name of Frick; they featured a friction-and-chain transmission made under Maurer licence. A 30-cwt forward control model of 1905 had a 9 hp single-cylinder underfloor engine, but front vertical units were usually found on a range which covered payloads from 7-cwt to 3 tons, the heaviest truck using a 4.6-litre twin motor. Even more ambitious was a 22-seater bus of 1906 with 7.2-litre 3-cylinder engine, at least one of which (with special large diameter wheels) was sold for operation between Cairo and Port Said. The company went into receivership late in 1907, but Clift exhibited a 1-ton truck at the London Commercial Vehicle Show the following April. It had a 12/16 hp Alpha engine, and may well have been simply a case of stock clearance. *MCS*

FRISBEE (US) 1922-1923

Frisbee Truck Co., Webberville, Mich.

The sole model of Frisbee truck was a 2½-tonner powered by a Continental C4 engine. *GNG*

FRITCHLE (US) 1911-1916

Fritchle Auto & Battery Company, Denver, Colorado

Advertised as the "100-mile Fritchle" as a passenger auto, the claim for the commercial versions was reduced to 80 miles per charge on an average. The light truck had a capacity of 1000 pounds, could attain 15 mph and used shaft drive to the rear axle. Its wheelbase was 7 feet, 6 inches and with panel body it was priced at $2000. *GMN*

FRONTENAC (US) 1906-1912

Abendroth & Root Manufacturing Co., Newburgh, NY

The first model under this name was a 5-tonner with double chain-drive. In 1910, this was joined by a 3-tonner with a 4-cylinder, 50 hp engine. During the last two years of production, a 3-tonner was built with forward control as well as a 2-tonner and the original 5-tonner with flare-board body was governed to a maximum of 12 mph and was priced at $3800. *GMN*

FRONTMOBILE (US) 1918-1919

Camden Motors Corporation, Camden, New Jersey

This was a chassis rated at 1500-pound capacity with front-wheel-drive similar to the passenger auto of the same name. It was powered by a four-cylinder engine made by Golden, Belnap & Swartz, used half-elliptical springs all around with a wheelbase of 11 feet, 7 inches. It was offered only as a chassis. *GMN*

FROSS-BUSSING (A, CS) 1909-1945

(1) Maschinenfabrik A. Fross-Bussing, Vienna, 1909-1945
(2) Tavarna na stroje A. Fross-Bussinga Liberta, Prague, 1920-1931

The Fross-Bussing started out as a license-built Bussing made in Austria, and the company supplied a large

1922 FROSS BUSSING 5-ton truck, OMM

number of 3-ton subsidy trucks to the Austrian Army during World War 1. Some of these were converted for use on railroads. In 1920 a branch factory was set up in the newly formed state of Czechoslovakia, and the Prague-built vehicles often went under the name Liberta. During the 1920s both factories produced a wide variety of goods and passenger vehicles, with capacities from 2 to 5 tons, and from 20 to 55 passengers. The Austrian factory supplied a considerable fleet of single-decker buses for Vienna, some of which were still in service in 1960. Engines were mostly Bussing 4- or 6-cylinder units but from 1930 onwards Maybach engines were used in the new VL truck and FB bus range. These were 75 or 100 hp 6-cylinder engines, and in the largest 55-passenger buses the 150 hp DSO 8-litre V-12 engine was employed, similar to that used in the Maybach Zeppelin luxury car.

The Prague factory closed in 1931, but the Vienna works continued to operate up to the end of World War 2. *MSH/GNG*

FROST-SMITH see P.F.S.

F-S (US) 1912

F-S Motors Co., Milwaukee, Wis.

This company offered three models, a ¾- and 3½-tonner along with one rated at 800 lbs. capacity. The smallest was a closed van with a single-cylinder engine and shaft-drive on a wheelbase of 7 feet, 6 inches. The larger trucks used 4-cylinder engines and the 3½-tonner had forward control and a 10-foot wheelbase. *GMN*

F.T.F. (NL) 1966 to date

Floor's Handel & Industrie N.V., Wychen

Floor's was a hauling firm who turned to making trailers, followed by the importation and assembly of Mack trucks. When Mack set up their own European assembly plant in 1964, Floor's decided to make their own vehicles, and the first F.T.F. appeared two years later. This used many Mack components including the engine, and had Floor's own cab, but later F.T.F.s have employed Detroit Diesel engines, Allison or Fuller gearboxes, Timken-Rockwell on Kirkstall axles, Spicer driveshafts, Gemmer steering and a British Motor Panels cab. F.T.F.s are all either articulated vehicles or 6 x 4 tractors for drawbar trailers, the largest having a drawbar capacity of

1976 F.T.F. MS4050 6×4 tractor, BHV

over 100 tons. In 1973 a military version was developed for the Dutch Army for tank transport, and the latest of these uses a Detroit Diesel V-12 engine of 475 hp. GCW is up to 200 tons. In the summer of 1975 production was running at about 100 units annually, but this was expected to increase considerably with the opening of a new factory at Nijkerk. *JFJK*

F.T.H. (AUS) 1915-c.1918

Fred T. Hack Ltd., Adelaide

The first F.T.H. truck used a 20 hp M.A.B. 4-cylinder engine in a chassis and body made by the Hack company, and had a load capacity of 30-cwt. Others followed with varying sizes of M.A.B. engines from 14.4 to 22.5 hp. About 17 were made in all. *GNG*

FUCHS (D) 1926-1932

(1) H. Fuchs Wagenbaufabrik A.G., Heidelberg 1926-1929
(2) Fuchs Lastzug- und Schlepper-Bau GmbH., Munchen 1930-1932

An articulated truck was the speciality of this firm. The first model was available with an own 6.7 litre gasoline engine or a Deutz diesel engine. Later a 100 PS Maybach engine was used. The trailer was available with one or two axles, in the latter case both axles being steerable. *HON*

FUKIEN #130 CHI 1970 to date

Fukien Motor Vehicle Plant — Foochow, Fukien

The Fukien #130 is a 2.5 ton truck of conventional design, built in limited quantities for use mainly in the province. *BE*

FULGURA see Bergmann

1920 FULTON 2-ton truck, OMM

FULTON (US) 1917-1925

(1) Clyde Motor Truck Co., Farmingdale, Long Island, N.Y. 1917
(2) Fulton Motor Truck Co., Farmingdale, Long Island, N.Y., 1915-1925

(This manufacturer had no connection to any other company using the name "Clyde")

William F. Melhuish, president of Clyde, was the driving force behind the design and production of the Fulton Truck. He set out to produce a conventional medium-sized truck of solid quality embodying the latest engineering practice at a low price. 1000 units were planned in the first year.

Initially the 1-1½ ton chassis sold for $1090 which included a 4-cylinder 30 hp L-head engine cast en bloc, 34 x 3½ tires in front, 34 x 2½ duals in the rear, all solid; and Russel internal gear axle.

The radiator was notable in more than one respect. It was circular and the hood was cylindrical to match, and its capacity was not surpassed by any truck then made — it was an enormous seven gallons!

The radiator shell, somewhat larger than the hood, had a prominent flange at the horizontal joint near the top. These visual features gave the Fulton an unmistakable identity.

By 1919 the prices went up considerably, which included larger tires and capacities: 1½ ton, $1850; 2 ton, $2350. By 1924 the corresponding prices were reduced to $1495 and $2135, while the weights were 3450 and 4950 pounds. These made the Fulton something of a heavyweight in its class. *RW*

FUSI (I) 1949-1957

A. Fusi & C SpA, Milan

This motor cycle factory specialized in 250cc solo machines after World War II. They also offered conventional motorcycle-based light trucks with two driven rear wheels. *MCS*

FUSO see Mitsubishi (i)

FWD (i) (US) 1912 to date

(1) Four Wheel Drive Auto Co., Clintonville, Wis. 1912-1960.
(2) FWD Corporation, Clintonville, Wis. 1960 to date.

The FWD truck was the outgrowth of a crucial invention by Otto Zachow who, with his brother-in-law William Besserdich, ran a machine shop in Clintonville, Wis. This invention was a double-Y universal joint encased in a ball-and-socket joint which allowed power to be applied to the front driving wheels of a car and still be steered. An automobile manufacturing company was formed with Besserdich and Zachow being given stock shares in exchange for the patent rights to the invention. A 2-ton truck was included in the early production run of 7 cars.

One of the FWD cars was sold to the US Army, converted to a scout car with a truck body, and sent with several other makes of trucks on a 1500 mile cross country test journey from Washington to Atlanta to Indianapolis over very difficult terrain.

As a result of this and other tests, and catalyzed by the outbreak of World War I in Europe, orders for 3- and 5-ton FWD trucks mushroomed to the point where three other manufacturers; Kissel, Mitchell and Premier were licensed to produce FWD trucks in addition to those in a greatly expanded factory at Clintonville. Ultimately, 15,000 3-ton Model B FWD's were produced for the US Armed Forces. The company had easily become the largest producer of four-wheel-drive trucks in the world.

This famous model B cab-over was powered by a

1920 F.W.D. (i) 4X4 3-ton truck, NAHC

Wisconsin 4-cylinder engine, with a 3-speed Cotta constant-mesh transmission and FWD's own front and rear driving axles. Propulsion was taken by the torque arms. High gear ratio was 8.90-1, and the road speed was 16 mph, slightly better than par for a 3-ton truck. Service brakes were external-contracting on all four wheels. The steering was righthand, and the cabs were generally open.

With the end of the war, the US Military found itself with some 30,000 trucks on hand. The sale of the huge surplus glutted the motor truck market in Europe and America. The majority here went to state highway departments for much-needed road-building.

Since about half of the surplus trucks were FWDs, the company kept operating by providing the needed parts and services. Eventually, as new trucks were needed, the pay-off came with orders for them. Allied to this program was the opening of a factory at Kitchener, Ontario, in 1919, and the purchase of the Menominee Motor Truck Company of Menominee, Michigan in 1921.

The model B, which weighed 6,400 pounds sold for $4,000, and remained in production until the early 1930's, with many refinements, the most visible being the adoption of pneumatic tires. Meanwhile, a conventional FWD was developed in the late 1920's, the civilian ones having a fully enclosed cab and some of the military having a crescent cab.

FWD's were used in many specialized fields — snowplowing, road construction and maintenance, public utilities, fire-fighting, logging, military, and oil fields, notably the Halliburton Oil Well Cementing Company of Duncan, Okla. As these markets developed, FWD engineers worked with these companies to meet their specialized needs. One of these was in transmissions. Early model B's had a low gear ratio of 48-1. After buying the manufacturing rights to the Cotta transmission, FWD re-engineered it and, together with new advances in metallurgy, gave later trucks a low gear of 140-1. Five-speed transmissions were adopted and later FWDs had optional transmissions of 10- and 12- speeds with auxilliaries providing a low of 600-1 for tremendous pulling power. The 4-wheel-brakes were also improved, and by the late 1930's double reduction axles were added and later, multiple speed axles.

1931 F.W.D. (i) 4×4 3-ton truck, NAHC

A range of lighter trucks of about 2-ton capacity was added in the mid 1930's having more modern cabs with a 1-piece slanted windshield and V-type radiator grilles. For 1937 FWD offered a new streamlined cab-over model with a V-type windshield. At this time, too, FWD brought out a 4-door crew-cab on the cab-over models for transporting a full crew to public utility sites. Very likely this was a world's "first" in the commercial truck field. Cummins diesels were available by 1938.

1936 F.W.D. (i) 6×4 tanker, NAHC

1939 F.W.D. (i) T-40 articulated truck, RW

FWDs were never well known for the popular pontoon fender styling, but there was one heavyweight conventional series that did have them in the late 1930's, the T-40, T-60 and possibly others.

A re-styled cab-over model T-32 was announced in mid-1940 with a 40,000 pound gvw and powered by a 98 hp 6-cylinder gas engine driving through a 5-speed transmission or an optional overdrive transmission to full floating front and rear axles. These were of the single-reduction, spiral-bevel type with manually locking differentials for use on slippery road conditions. A conventional TT32 was also offered, with a rounded grille and a V-windshield.

Other conventionals including SU, SUA, CUA, and MJ5 in the 4- to 6-ton range were offered.

Generally, 6-cylinder FWD and Waukesha engines of 33.75 — 79.4 SAE hp powered the over-all FWD range of 1½-15 tons, with 4 models having diesels, and the price range was $2440 to $12,225.

During World War II FWD supplied the Armed Forces with heavy duty civilian-styled trucks, notably the cab-overs, plus a special SU-based cab-over which had an open cab with two individual windshields, one for the driver, and one for his mate. This was a Marine Corps truck.

After World War II FWD added a series of 4x4 conventionals for light duty work, medium duty high-frame models for road scraping, and a heavy duty long-nosed U

1940 F.W.D. (i) SU 4×4 dump truck, Missouri State Highway Dept.

1943 F.W.D. (i) SU-COE 4×4 army truck, BHV

series of 44,000 pounds gvw.

In the 1950's FWD adopted new cabs; for the conventionals the principal one being the "Chicago" cab also used by International and several others.

Cab-overs were generally of two types. The first used a conventional Chicago cab stretched in width while the second was the 1958 Ford C-line cab-forward modified with a wire mesh grille and different fenders.

Several other new models appeared about this time. A very short wheelbase model was specially designed to go anywhere off-highway to do earth-boring for utility poles. The cab was of the forward-slanting type. This was model BXU, better known as "The Blue Ox."

The Tractioneer line first appeared in 1958 and is still current. The flat-nosed cab-over version was soon joined by conventionals, some of which had the front axle set back under the cab. As usual, all of these came with full-time power to all four wheels. The cab at this time was that used by Dodge with the relatively shallow wrap-around windshield, and the fenders came in a variety of angular shapes. Additional varieties included 6x6, 10x8 with tandem front axle on some, and the ultimate, a 12x10, also with a tandem front axle. The Tractioneers are used mostly as concrete mixers and in the construction industry.

The most sensational vehicle ever developed by the company was the FWD Teracruzer 8x8 off highway carrier. These were built for commercial service such as needed by the Pak-Stanvac Pakistan project in East Pakistan to haul full loads of oil well drilling equipment and supplies in monsoon climate areas inaccessible to conventional vehicles. The chassis weight was a hefty 22,000 pounds, but because of the enormous watermelon-

1955 F.W.D. (i) H Series 4×4 truck, GNG

shaped tires the ground pressure was very low. The Teracruzer's capacity was 8 tons, and it was powered by a NHHT-6B Cummins horizontal turbocharged diesel of 250 hp driving through a 10-speed Fuller R96 transmission and FWD transfer case.

Another FWD development of the later 1960's was the 8x8 CFR truck (Crash and Fire Rescue) for airport standby emergencies. These P-2 models are enormous heavyweights at 65,000 pounds and are powered by two 340 hp engines driving through an FWD-designed collector-box to dual transmissions, and either engine may be used to power the truck or its pumps, or both may be used to power the truck giving it an acceleration of 0 to 55 mph in 55 seconds or less. Single tires are used all around on the double tandems. The P-2 carries 2300 gallons of water and 200 gallons of liquid foam concentrate.

In 1963 the FWD Corp bought the fire apparatus division of the Seagrave Corp. of Columbus, Ohio, to further expand its efforts in that field.

In the mid 1960's the Forward Mover series with a non-powered front axle and 6x4 drive was introduced for highway service. Conventionals (B5-2178) looked much like the Tractioneers with the Dodge cab and had smoother fenders although some had an optional cab with a forward-slanting windshield.

Crane carriers have been a regular part of FWD's line-up for many years, the big majority being one-man cab-overs with drives up to 10x8. Even as early as 1939, FWD removed the right half of a conventional cab and used the space for the shovel boom when in transit.

1972 F.W.D. (i) sleeper cab tractor, RW

In a typical year, 1970, 93 models were listed in five different drives in conventional, set-back conventional (axle under the cab) and cab-over models using International, Detroit, and Cummins engines of 4, 6, and 8 cylinders in a range of 145 to 238 hp, mostly Fuller 5-speed transmissions, FWD single reduction rear axles and variety combinations of vacuum, air and hydraulic brakes. Production for the year was 1097 trucks, a bit below the average in a yearly range of 829 to 1645 in the 1956 to 1970 era.

For 1978 there were three series, the RB conventional 4x4, the CB conventional 6x6, 8x6, 8x8 and 10x8, and the DF 4x4 cab-over. Engines, all diesels, ran from 195 to 350 hp.

FWD can build you special types, such as a front-drive low-bed truck, or a four-wheel-steer. An almost endless variety of component combinations, cabs, and sheet metal over the years show that FWD does a great amount of custom truck building. *RW*

F.W.D. (ii) (GB) 1918-1931

(1) British Four Wheel Drive Tractor-Lorry Co., Brixton, London, SW9, 1918-1920

(2) Four Wheel Drive Tractor-Lorry Engineering Co. Ltd., West Ealing Middx. 1920-1927

(3) Four Wheel Drive Motors Ltd., Slough, Bucks, 1927-1931

Large numbers of F.W.D. 4x4 trucks came to Britain during World War 1, and many saw civilian service after the war. In addition, the British Government acquired a license to produce them under the name British Quad. These were generally similar to the American models, but had Dorman engines. Later, peculiarly British variants appeared, including an articulated 6-wheeler called the Harford Haulier in 1922, and an extraordinary fwd 3-wheeler in which the driver sat behind the load, with the engine behind him. Steering was by the single rear wheel which was much smaller than the front driving wheels. Another British model was a front wheel drive low-loading 6-tonner with pneumatic tires on the front wheels and small solids at the rear.

In 1927 F.W.D. Motors introduced a 6-ton 6x6 truck powered by a 6.6-litre Dorman 6-cylinder engine, which was later built for the War Office as a tractor under the name R6T. In October 1929 F.W.D. entered into an agreement with A.E.C. as a result of which the Dorman engine was replaced by a slightly smaller A.E.C. unit of 6.1 litres. The A.E.C.-engined truck was made in military and civilian form, the latter rated for a capacity of 8 tons. A half-track version was tested by the War Office though not adopted, but a few of these were used for many years by the Royal National Lifeboat Institution for launching lifeboats. In 1931 it was announced that, in order to avoid confusion with the American F.W.D. the British products would be sold under the name Hardy. This came from Hardy Rail Motors, an associated company which made railcars and shunting locomotives using F.W.D. components. *GNG*

1908 GAETH 1-ton van, NAHC

GABRIEL (US) 1913-1920

(1) Gabriel Motor Truck Co., Cleveland, O. 1913-1919
(2) Gabriel Auto Co., Cleveland, O. 1919-1920

This line of trucks began as a 1-tonner and this was joined in 1914 by a 2-tonner. Later models included 1½-, 3½- and 4-tonners. The 1917 1½-tonner used worm-drive, a 4-speed gearbox and a 4-cylinder engine. *GMN*

GAETH (US) 1906-1910

Gaeth Automobile Works, Cleveland, Ohio

The first commercial vehicle venture by this passenger car maker was a light truck called the Type K, powered by a 10/12 hp single-cylinder horizontal engine under the floorboards, driving through a 2-speed gearbox and double chain drive. Load capacity was 1500 lbs. Later some vans with 4-cylinder engines under a hood were made, based on the company's passenger cars. *GNG*

GAGGENAU (D) 1905-1910

Suddeutsche Automobilfabrik GmbH., Gaggenau

Based on the private cars also van versions were available, especially the types 6/16 PS and 10/20 PS.

Earlier models were marketed as Liliput; trucks and buses were available under the brand-name S.A.F. *HON*

GALBUSERA (I) 1950-c.1955

Moto Galbusera & C, Brescia

This company produced some light 3-wheelers for 300 kg payloads. Like their contemporary motorcycles, they were powered by 125 cc Sachs engines. *MCS*

GALE (US) 1905-1906

Western Tool Works, Galesburg, Ill.

The diminutive Gale was an enclosed van with wheelbase of 73 inches and a track of 4 feet, 6½ inches. This had a watercooled 1-cylinder engine of 8-10 hp. The engine was mounted beneath the body and was connected with a planetary transmission and single drive chain to the rear axle. Pneumatic tires were standard. The body was hinged at the rear so that the entire structure could be elevated for access to the drive system. The Model H was fitted with a false hood, had a capacity of only 200 pounds and was priced at $750. This manufacturer also built passenger autos under the same tradename. *GMN*

GALLAND (F) 1927-c.1934

Ets. Galland, Paris 15e

This company began by making a 3-wheeled parcel van with motorcycle-type rear portion, powered by a 500 cc J.A.P. engine driving through a Burman 3-speed gearbox. It had handlebar steering. By 1930 the range had been extended with 350 and 600 cc J.A.P. engines, and there was a completely new model, much more car-like in appearance, with single front wheel. This was powered by a choice of 500 cc Train or 600 cc J.A.P. engines, driving either front or rear wheels according to the model. *GNG*

GALLINARI (I) 1906-1908

Cantieri Gallinari, Livorno

Gallinari were unusual among the ephemeral Italian makers of this period in that they concentrated on trucks. These were substantial 5-tonners with 3-speed gearboxes, pressed steel frames, and shaft drive. The 10.6-litre 4-cylinder engine gave 40 hp at 600 rpm and boasted not only a 5-bearing crankshaft but ohc as well. *MCS*

GALLOWAY (GB) 1924-1927

Galloway Motors Ltd., Heathhall, Dumfries.

Arrol-Johnston's light car was offered for a few seasons with light van bodywork, appearing first in 8-cwt guise with 1460 cc sv engine, and subsequently as a 10-cwt model powered by a 1669 cc ohv unit. *MCS*

GANZ (H) 1913-1920

Ganz Waggon es Gepgyar, Budapest

Ganz was a large engineering firm, at the premises of which engineer Gyorgy Jendrasik built the first Hungarian diesel engine in 1912, pioneered the construction of diesel locomotives and made a brief venture in the automotive field with the production of a series of middleweight trucks powered by Ganz's own diesel engines. After 1920 Ganz returned to its original activity, dropping truck production, and is still today one of the largest producers of railway stock in Hungary. *GA*

GARDNER-SERPOLLET see Serpollet

GARDNER (US) 1927-1932

Gardner Motor Co. Inc., St. Louis, Mo.

Like Kissel and Auburn, Gardner sought to recoup the falling sales of their private cars with a line of ambulances and hearses, produced in association with the St. Louis Coffin Co. These were based on their Lycoming-engined straight-8s with all expanding hydraulic brakes; some had 4-speed gearboxes. Gardner's fortunes, however, continued to decline and by 1930 their cheaper professional cars were largely Chevrolet-based. In spite of this, the hearses outlived the cars by a year, though 1932 models were little more than modified V8 Pontiacs. *MCS*

1916 GARFORD 5-ton truck, NAHC

GARFORD (US) 1909-1933

(1) Garford Co., Elyria, Ohio 1909-1915
(2) Garford Motor Truck Co., Lima, Ohio 1915-1927
(3) Relay Motors Co., Lima, Ohio 1927-1932
(4) Consolidated Motors Corp., Lima, Ohio 1933

Early Garfords were 5-ton cab-overs with 4-cylinder L-head engines, 4-speed transmissions amid ships and dual chain final drive. The cabs were distinctive, with 'Roman Chariot' type cowl and a curved filler pipe prominent over the radiator. This model was joined by a 3½-tonner with worm-drive, also a cab-over, in 1916, and there were also smaller conventional models of 1-, 1½- and 2-tons capacity. The larger Garfords were intended to be used with 2- or 4-wheeled trailers, and were fitted with drawbars as standard. For 1917 three models of short-wheelbase tractor were offered which, with semi-trailers, had capacities of 4½-, 7- and 10-tons. Garford trucks were widely used in World War I, including some conventionals with Holt-Caterpillar tracks in place of rear wheels. In

1920 GARFORD 20-seater bus, NMM

1925 GARFORD 1-ton van, NMM

addition, Garford made about 1,000 of the Liberty trucks.

By 1920 the cab-overs had been dropped, and the range consisted of four conventionals from 1¼ to 5 tons, with Buda 4-cylinder engines, 4-speed transmissions and either Timken worm drives or Garford's own chain drive. These models were continued into the mid-1920s, the 5-tonner still having optional chain drive. 7- and 8-speed transmissions were used on some models, with 2- and 4-speed reverse gears. A special 25-29-passenger bus chassis was offered at $4350, with a low frame and kick-up over the rear axle. For 1925 and 1926 parlor car and passenger coach chassis for 17 passengers were offered with 6-cylinder engines.

In August 1927 Garford was bought by Relay Motors of Wabash, Indiana, which promptly moved its headquarters to Lima, Ohio and became a four-truck combine, with Commerce, Garford, Service and Relay. The new Garfords were greatly changed from their predecessors, having 6-cylinder Buda engines and closely resembling Relay trucks in the one to four ton range of eight closely-spaced models, except for retaining worm drive and using steel disc wheels instead of the Relay's artillery-type. Garford production declined dramatically during the late 1920s, from about 700 in 1926 to little over 100 in 1929, and still fewer after the Depression had set in. Still, it was the second best seller of the Relay group, so after Relay went into receivership in December 1932 a new owner, Consolidated Motors, attempted to make Garford (and Relay) production profitable, but failed to do so. *RW*

GARNER (GB) 1915-1941

(1) Henry Garner Ltd., Moseley Motor Works, Birmingham 1915-1926
(2) Garner Motors Ltd., Tyseley, Birmingham 1927-1933
(3) Sentinel Wagon Works, Shrewsbury, Salop 1934-1936
(4) Garner Motors Ltd., London NW 10 1936-1941

Henry Garner Ltd. was a successful car sales organization in Birmingham which began to import trucks made by Gramm-Bernstein from America in 1915 to help reduce the shortage of vehicles for civilian transport needs. They were typical assembled products for 2- to 6-ton loads with Continental engines and Fuller gearboxes. Several hundred were imported and were joined at the end of the war by a 30-cwt model and by an agricultural tractor made by Wm. Galloway & Co. of Waterloo, Iowa, which, like the trucks, had its identity hidden by Garner nameplates.

In 1921 Garner introduced the Busvan for carrying goods, passengers or both, on otherwise uneconomic country routes. This was followed by dropframe four-wheel-braked chassis specifically for passenger work in 1925, the same year in which Garner began to build their own vehicles in Britain. The English Garner was initially a 2-tonner made from proprietary parts with a 24.8 hp Dorman engine. Production was transferred to a new factory in Tyseley, Birmingham in 1926, and forward control models began to be built with ingenious hinge-out wings and cab floor for engine access.

1931 GARNER JO6 6-ton truck, OMM

In 1929 a military specification 6-wheel 2½-tonner was introduced followed by a wide range of goods models and, from 1933, Progressor and Precursor passenger chassis with Austin 20 engines. Other engines used at the time were Meadows and Coventry Climax. In 1934, production was moved to the Sentinel Wagon Works at Shrewsbury and in 1935 a new range of Sentinel-Garners appeared. However, Sentinel were in financial difficulties and unwilling to transfer their backing from steam to gasoline and diesel (Garner was fitting Perkins engines by now) so in 1936 they sold Garner to a group of London businessmen, many of whom had worked for Chrysler-Dodge at Kew. 10 to 12 chassis were soon being completed each week at Garner's new home, and a very modern 2- to 5-ton range appeared in 1937 with Austin, Perkins and Meadows engines plus a few from Waukesha and Buda.

In 1938 Garner collaborated with Nicholas Straussler, consulting engineer to Alvis, and maker of cross-country vehicles, to design some light 4x4 military trucks. Several prototypes were produced, though the only one to go into production was a twin Ford V-8 engined 3-tonner originally conceived by Manfred Weiss in Budapest. Around 50 were built in the early stages of the war before Garner ceased vehicle production in favor of other military supplies, though some experiments took place with light delivery vehicles and the Q electric van. After the war, Garner concentrated on bodywork, and in 1947 introduced a small single cylinder 6 hp J.A.P.-powered agricultural and horticultural tractor which remained in production into the early Fifties, by which time several hundred had been made. The body-building side merged with Hawes of Sunbury, and still trades as Hawson-Garner Ltd. *OM*

1903 GARRETT 8nhp road locomotive, RAW

GARRETT (GB) 1856-1960

(1) Richard Garrett & Sons, Leiston, Suffolk 1856-1897
(2) Richard Garrett & Sons Ltd., Leiston, Suffolk 1897-1932
(3) Richard Garrett Engineering Works, Ltd., Leiston, Suffolk 1932-1960

Although the firm sent a Boydell wheeled traction engine to the Royal Agricultural Show at Chelmsford in 1856 the main-stay of its production until this century was the threshing machine and its attendant portable engine. A 3-ton steam tract or with a single cylinder was made in 1903 under the provisions of the 1896 Act but achieved no worthwhile sales. In 1903/04 6 hp compound four-shaft road locomotives were made, one of which was belatedly sold as a showman's engine in 1907. A small number of 6 and 7 nhp road locomotives were made, some of which were fitted up as showmen's engines.

The most noted Leiston production was probably their No. 4 compound steam tractor, a 3-shaft design which first appeared in 1907 and continued to be supplied until 1930. Those built after 1920 were of a somewhat heavier design and were dubbed the "big G" by users, partly from their increased size and partly from the large brass "G" on the smokebox. Some tractors were supplied with a simple steam drying coil in an enlarged chimney whilst others had a superheater of bank coils in an enlarged flat topped smokebox. The greatest number, however, had neither dryer nor superheater. The tractors were not as fast on the road as Avelings but were very sturdy and reliable and excellent working engines, popular with the lesser showmen.

In 1904 an experimental compound undertype wagon with vertical firetube boiler was a failure but two of a modified design were sold for export. Wagon building in earnest began in 1909 when a 5-tonner, closely modeled on the Foden, was introduced followed by a 3-tonner, on rubber tires, in 1911. A few early wagons had the drying coil like the earlier tractors but after 1912 a full superheater in conjunction with piston valves to the cylinders was adopted as standard though non-superheated wagons with slide valves would be supplied to order. A few 4-tonners were also supplied. In 1917 a solitary reversed boiler overtype wagon was made with the driving position at the extreme front. In 1926 an entirely redesigned overtype 6-tonner was brought out, with Ackermann steering, improved driving position and better brakes but it was too late and only eight were made.

Undertype wagon building was resumed in 1922 using double cylinders with piston valves and Joy's valve gear

1920 GARRETT 1½-ton electric van, RAW

1925 GARRETT 6-ton overtype steam wagon, RAW

taking steam from a vertical cross water tube boiler so close in design to the Sentinel boiler as to cause Sentinels to threaten action over copyright. All subsequent wagons were fitted with a modified boiler of entirely Leiston design using a cast-steel superheater body with looped tubes. In 1927 a poppet-valved engine with cam-operated valves was introduced with an improved cab and modified, fully forward, driving position. A rigid 6-wheeled version followed in 1928 launched straight off the drawing board with the result that users sustained the teething troubles, and various modifications, notably stiffening of the chassis had to be introduced. Total wagon production of all types numbered 948.

In 1916 a battery electric truck of 3½ tons capacity was supplied to the Great Railway but the marketing of a full range of chain drive electric vehicles of 1½-, 2½- and 3½-tons capacity was not started until after the Armistice. In 1924 a 1-ton trademan's chassis and a similar but heavier 1½/2 ton version were added as well as a 5/6-tonner for municipal duties, mainly dust collection, all with shaft drive. The last design of electric was the revolutionary GTZ low line refuse vehicle for Glasgow & Paisley Corporations which continued to be built until 1939, latterly on pneumatics. One example was built with a Blackstone diesel engine.

In 1926 the company bought the goodwill and stocks of the Caledon Motor Company but only one Caledon was sold though another was assembled for works use and a third was assembled for Avelings to use as a test bed for their "Invicta" diesel engine. Two oil engined trucks were made and sold in 1928 using McLaren diesel engines and the chassis and body components of steam wagons, the

1928 GARRETT 12-ton undertype steam wagon, RAW

1929 GARRETT Suffolk Punch 6×4 steam tractor, RAW

first all-British oil engined truck, but work on two prototype trucks of more advanced design, using respectively a Meadows gasoline engine and a Blackstone diesel had not reached the production stage when the old company was wound up in 1932 and the project was not revived by its successors.

The company's solitary venture into the passenger transport field was a run of 99 electric trolley buses built between 1925 and 1930. Ten were six wheeled double deckers and the rest single deck four-wheelers of which 16 were on solids and the remainder on pneumatics. Home users included Bradford, Doncaster, Hartlepool, Ipswich, Swinton & Mexborough Traction, St. Helens and Southend. Abroad they were used in Copenhagen and Lima (Peru).

In addition the company made between 1919 and 1960 various diesel tractors, using at first the Blackstone diesel but after 1932 the Gardner. The latter diesel tractors were high specialized machines for the peat fuel industry. *RAW*

1939 GARRETT GTZ electric refuse truck, RAW

1936 GAR WOOD Model C coach, MBS

GAR WOOD (U.S.) 1936-1938

Gar Wood Industries, Detroit, Michigan

William B. Stout was an aircraft designer (the Ford Tri-Motor) who worked on a streamlined streetcar design for Pullman in 1934 and then undertook to plan a lightweight bus. The result was a framework of welded tubes covered by a thin aluminum-alloy skin, with a Ford V-8 engine mounted at the rear and driving forward to the rear axle. A prototype was built by Gar Wood Industries, a truck body and boat builder, and when no one could be found to take over full-scale manufacture, Gar Wood entered the bus business with a slightly modified version of Stout's idea. Ford running gear was standard, but Chevrolet or Dodge engines could be had, and about 175 buses were built in just over two years. The operation was sold in August 1939 to the General American Transportation Co. of Chicago (see *Aerocoach*). *MBS*

GARY (US) 1916-1927

(1) Gary Motor Truck Co., Gary, Ind. 1916-1922
(2) Gary Motor Corp., Gary, Inc. 1922-1927

The first models of Gary were Continental-powered trucks in four sizes from ¾-ton to 2-tons, and a 1-tonner was continued until 1922. The change of company name coincided with a change in engine supplier, Budas being used from 1922 onwards. A wider range was made, from 1- to 5-ton capacity. *GNG*

GAUBSCHAT (D) 1951-1955

Gaubschat Elektrowagen GmbH., Berlin

This firm built electric driven vans of 1- and 2-ton payload capacity. They were mainly used by the postal authorities for parcel delivery. *HON*

GAUTIER-WEHRLE (F) 1896-1900

(1) Rossel, Gautier et Wehrle, Paris 1896-1897
(2) Societe Continentale, Paris 1897-1900

The first Gautier-Wehrle steamers were made in 1894, with gasoline-engined models available from 1896, the first year in which commercial bodywork is mentioned. Ingenious features of the gasoline models were the 3-speed gearbox and shaft drive to an articulated rear axle. Initially the 2-cylinder horizontal engines were mounted amidships. but in 1897 they were moved to the front of the chassis. Light omnibus bodywork was listed on these later Gautier-Wehrles. *MCS*

GAVONI see Motom

GAY (US) 1913-1915

S.G. Gay Co., Ottawa, Ill.

Under this name were built ¾- and 1-tonners. Both used 4-cylinder engines under hoods with 3-speed gearboxes and double-chain final drive, and both used solid rubber tires. Semi-elliptical springs were used all around. *GMN*

GAYLORD (US) 1910-1913

Gaylord Motor Car Co., Gaylord, Mich.

The Gaylord offered a utility model based on their regular line of assembled open passenger cars which were priced from $1000-$1500. It had various 4-cylinder engines in the 20 to 40 hp range, usually with a right-hand drive, and a hood with unusually long sloping shoulders. This car was generally typical of its day, except for the utility feature: two slots were provided in the rear of the body for insertion of two rails, and a short truck box could be mounted on them.

Besides the standard semi-elliptic springs, rear platform springs were used on some models. This was an uncommon type usually found only on high-priced cars of the day, and used two semi-elliptic springs attached, as usual, at the front ends to the frame while the rear ends were connected to the ends of an inverted transverse spring attached at its center to the middle of the rear frame cross member. This arrangement provided better riding qualities and greater vertical travel of the rear wheels over bumps and depressions.

Gaylord's lifetime production was about 350 cars of all models. *RW*

GAZ (SU) 1932 to date

Zavod Imieni Molotova, Gorky

The Molotov factory at Gorky was, at one time, the largest automotive complex in Europe and was constructed with the aid of American firms including the Ford Motor Company.

1932 GAZ Model AA 1½-ton truck, MHK

The first cargo trucks, the ½-ton 4x4 GAZ-AA and the 6x4 GAZ-AAA were based on Ford designs of c.1929. The AA was powered by a 4-cylinder, 40 hp side-valve engine providing 70 km/h. The twin bogie AAA was generally powered by a 50 hp M-1 engine and could carry up to 2500 kg of goods. Both had four speeds forward. The AA was later modified, in 1938, as the GAZ-MM primarily for military use, with squared fenders and increased horsepower. It was built until 1950.

The Ford-based GAZ chassis was used for numerous special purposes including bus (03-30), ambulance (GAZ-55), dumper (410), half-track (GAZ-60) and armored cars. A gas-generator truck was built as the GAZ-42.

Prior to and concurrent with the opening of the Gorky plant, Model-A Ford cars and trucks were assembled in Moscow from American parts. These units are reported to have varied slightly from both their U.S. and GAZ counterparts.

Light pickup trucks were built in the '30s and '40s on the GAZ car chassis. Some 4x4 passenger cars were also constructed on the M-1 chassis and later on the postwar Pobieda.

Field cars using the Ford-influenced GAZ M-1 car chassis were tested about 1941 and led to the construction of the 4x4, 50 hp GAZ-64. This vehicle evolved as the

GAZ-67 in 1942. A GAZ-67A was developed with a wider tread and still later a 67B was introduced with modified grill and extra fuel tank under the seat. Power was from a 54 hp, 4-cylinder engine. This vehicle saw extensive service in World War Two and the Korean War as well as in the Warsaw Pact countries.

c.1955 GAZ-63 1½-ton truck, FH

The GAZ-67B remained in production until 1953 when the larger, more modern GAZ-69 replaced it. This 4x4 was built as a five seater, 4-door and an eight seater, 2-door. A 4-cylinder engine of 55 hp, later 65, was used. Top speed was 95 km/h. Springing was semi-elliptic and the gearbox was three speed with transfer case.

The 69 stayed in production through the change over to the new UAZ plant at Ulyanovsk, but was eventually replaced there by the UAZ-469. A version continues to be built in Romania as the M-461.

After the war, as Ford-type trucks were phased out, new models were added including the 2½, 5-ton GAZ-51 cargo, the 1½-ton 4x4 GAZ-63 and the GAZ-93 dumper.

The GAZ-51 also appeared as an ambulance, bus (PAZ), and ATA-9-AZ 2-ton truck holding 123 bread trays.

The engine was a 6-cylinder 70 hp @ 2800 rpm with four speeds forward. These trucks were built under license in Poland as the Lublin-51 and are currently constructed in North Korea as the Sungri-58.

A GAZ-53 was introduced about 1964 and is now built as a 4-ton cargo, dumper, tanker and for specialized needs. Power is from a V-8 of 130 hp @ 3,200 rpm with four speeds forward.

A cab-over-engine 4x4 GAZ-66, of 2.4-tons, is also in current production and features power-steering, centralized tire pressure control and can tow a 2-ton trailer.

1967 GAZ-53F 3½-ton truck, OMM

GAZ-built Volga (M-24) passenger cars are offered in ambulance form and the ZIM limousine (M-12), built from 1950 to 1957, was modified for hospital use.

The Ulyanovsk UAZ factory has taken over some GAZ manufacture to ease pressure on the now aging plant. *BE*

GEHA (D) 1910-1023

(1) Electromobilwerke Gebhardt & Harborn, Berlin-Schoneberg 1910-1917

(2) Elitewerke AG., Zweigniederlassung, Berlin-Schoneberg 1917-1923

This was an electric 3-wheeler with the engine mounted above the single front wheel. A van-box was mounted at the rear. *HON*

GEIST (D) 1907-1908

Ernst Heinrich Geist Electrizitats A.G., Cologne.

This firm built some lorries with gasoline-electric drive. Argus gas engines were installed. *HON*

GEM (US) 1917-1919

Gem Motor Car Corporation, Grand Rapids, Michigan.

The Gem was a light delivery van rated at 1000 lbs. It used 4-cylinder Golden, Belknap & Swartz engine, a 3-speed gearbox and shaft drive with wheelbase of 108 inches. *GMN*

GENERAL (i) (GB) 1903-1905

(1) General Motor Car Co. Ltd., Norbury, London S.W. 1903

(2) General Motor Car Co. Ltd., Mitcham, Surrey 1903-1905

This company made passenger and goods vehicles, the first of the latter being a light van for 200 lb. payloads powered by a 4½ hp single-cylinder engine, with single chain drive. In 1905 two models were offered, a 7 cwt van with 6 hp single-cylinder Aster engine, and a 15 cwt van with 12 hp 2-cylinder Buchet engine. Both had single chain drive. Several Generals of various sizes were supplied to the Post Office, but they were not adopted in large numbers. *GNG*

GENERAL (ii) (US) 1903

General Automobile & Manufacturing Co., Cleveland, Ohio.

Formerly known as the Hansen Automobile Company, this firm made a light runabout with an 8 hp 2-cylinder engine which was also offered as a delivery van for loads of up to 1000 lbs. *GNG*

GENERAL CAB (US) 1930-1938

Yellow Truck & Coach Mfg. Co., Pontiac, Mich.

The General Cab (sometimes called General Motors Cab) was the former Yellow Cab re-named in 1930. It had a 6-cylinder Buick engine which was replaced from 1931 to

1932 GENERAL CAB Model O-12 taxicab, TCV

1934 by a GMC-built 6-cylinder engine. The 1933/34 cabs had a Pontiac-like appearance. There was no production in 1935, and the following year a new model, the 0-16, was introduced which was simply a long-wheelbase Chevrolet in appearance, using a rear axle from Chevrolet trucks. Wheelbase was 124½ inches compared with 113 inches for the passenger cars in 1936, and 127 inches compared with 112 inches in 1937 and 1938, when the cabs bore the designations 0-17 and 0-18. General Cabs were fitted with jump seats as standard, but a single front seat and divider between front and rear compartments were optional. *GNG*

GENERAL-DETROIT (US) 1937-1955

(1) General Fire Truck Corp., Detroit, Mich. 1937-1955
(2) General Pacific Corp., Los Angeles, Calif. 1948-1955

In 1937 General Detroit made a 600 gpm pumper using their own chassis, a Packard Eight engine and Ford cab, and the following year several pumpers using complete Packard V-12 chassis, also equipment on other chassis including Ford, G.M.C. and Federal. In 1939 they offered a complete range of apparatus including ladder trucks and quadruple combinations. In 1948 a subsidiary in Los Angeles started making custom chassis pumpers of their own design under the name General-Pacific, while the Detroit company built on Available, Duplex and other chassis. One of the last fire engines made by General-Detroit was a quad combination on 1955 Federal chassis. *GNG*

GENERAL-MONARCH (US) 1932-1935

General Fire Truck Corp., St. Louis, Mo.

This company made assembled fire engines powered by 200 hp engines, and distinguished by a large spotlight between the headlights. 1934 models had styling worthy of a classic car, with V-grille and windshield, and fully faired fenders. *GNG*

GENEVA (US) 1912-1919

Geneva Wagon Co., Geneva, NY

Geneva trucks were light vans with open or enclosed bodies. These were ½- and ¾-tonners. Little improvement is evident in either of these models as in 1919, the ¾-tonner was still using a 2-cylinder Beaver engine with a planetary transmission and double chain-drive. This was on a wheelbase of 96 inches. *GMN*

GEORGES IRAT (F) 1941-1949

(1) Automobiles Georges Irat S.A., Levallois-Perret, Seine 1941-1943
(2) Irat et Cie, Begles-Tartifumes, Gironde 1949

Georges Irat was a well-known builder of sports cars who turned during World War II to small battery electrics, which were made in passenger and goods form. The latter was a 3 cwt van powered by a 3 hp rear-mounted motor whose armature shaft was parallel to the rear axle. The batteries were carried under the hood. The van had a speed of 20 mph and a range of 60 miles.

In 1948, with a new company and a new factory, Irat began the manufacture of diesel engines under the name D.O.G. These were 2-, 4- and 6-cylinders and were intended for road vehicles, agricultural tractors and industrial use. Among vehicle customers was the bus maker, Isobloc. In 1949 Irat exhibited a tanker truck at the Paris Salon in which the tank was the main stress-bearing member, on the same principle as the Scammell frameless tanker, only the Irat was a complete vehicle instead of a trailer. The 4-cylinder 4.3-litre D.O.G. engine drove the front wheels via a Cotal gearbox, and there was independent coil springing at the rear. *GNG*

1942 GEORGES IRAT 150kg electric van, BHV

1906 G.E.R. 32-seater bus, NMM

G.E.R. (GB) 1906

The Great Eastern Railway Company, Stratford Works, London E.

In 1906 the railway built twelve motor buses at its Stratford locomotive works for use on pioneer bus services in East Anglia. They employed 30 hp. Panhard engines and were very heavy vehicles and initially prone to breakdowns, though replacement of the original very rigid springs improved matters. All were built as double-deckers, but charabanc bodies were sometimes carried in summer months and some finished their lives as goods vehicles. *OM*

1904 GERMAIN 16/20hp 32-seater bus, NMM

GERMAIN (B) 1902-c.1907; 1937-1939

S.A. des Ateliers Germain, Monceau-sur-Sambre

The Germain company was founded in 1873 for the manufacture of railway equipment which always remained an important part of its activities. Car production began in 1897, with vehicles of German Daimler type, and in 1902 the first commercial models appeared. These ranged from a 500 kg delivery van powered by a 7½ hp single-cylinder engine to a 5-ton truck. The larger Germains had a rather crude type of forward control, with a conventional hood on top of which was mounted the driver's seat, and ahead of which was a small dashboard and an almost vertical steering column. Passenger versions of these were made, including a charabanc for South Africa and a 32-seater double-decker bus for London which operated the Hammersmith-Oxford Circus route in 1904. In 1907 a more modern normal-control bus chassis was announced with 28 hp 4-cylinder engine. Like its predecessors it had chain drive, but most of Germain's activities were now directed towards their Chainless passenger cars, and the new bus had a short life.

Germain ceased car production in 1914 but continued to make railway wagons, and in the 1930s they took out a license for the C.L.M. 2-stroke diesel engine. In 1937 they announced a 5-ton truck powered by a C.L.M. 3-cylinder opposed-piston engine, and a similarly-powered agricultural tractor. *GNG*

GEROSA (I) c.1953 to date

Moto Gerosa, Brescia

Gerosa's lightweight motorcycle range included a delivery model with baskets front and rear. They also built 3-wheeler vans with two driven rear wheels, which had become their principal product by 1964. In 1975 form, the van had a 48 cc 2-stroke F.B.-Minarelli engine, a 3-speed gearbox, tubular frame, and enclosed cab. Payload was 3 cwt. *MCS*

1922 GERSIX 3½-ton truck, Kenworth

GERSIX 1916-1922

(1) Gerlinger Motor Car Co., Portland, Oregon 1916-1917; Tacoma, Washington 1917

(2) Gersix Manufacturing Co., Seattle, Washington 1917-1922

Although construction of the first Gersix truck began in the fall of 1916 it was not finished until early in 1917. The trade name derives from the last names of Louis and Edgar Gerlinger and the 6-cylinder Continental engine used in the truck, one of the first such power plants to be factory-installed.

Wisconsin 6-cylinder engines were the principal make subsequently used. The steel frame and castings were made at the Gerlinger plant, with other parts bought from suppliers. Later, Gerlingers also made their own axles when World War I dried up the supplies. With a small number of employees it took nearly a month at first to build a truck, even when truck production became a full-time operation. These trucks were all worm-driven conventionals.

Although Gersix trucks were well made, the total production was only about 100 units, some of which were used in the logging industry.

In 1922 E.K. Worthington, a major stockholder, acquired enough additional stock to re-organize the company. H.W. Kent was the other major stockholder. It was decided to use a Buda 4-cylinder engine, therefore a new trade name was necessary. The directors meeting late in 1922 decided on a combination of the names of the two principal stockholders, and so the Kenworth Motor Truck Co. came into being, production continuing under that name. *RW*

GFV (D) 1900-1901

Gesellschaft fur Verkehrsunternehmungen, Berlin

This company produced a tram like battery-electric bus which was in service in Berlin for some time. Characteristic were four small contact bows on the roof which were used for battery recharging at the two end stations of the line. *HON*

GIANT (US) 1918-1922

(1) Chicago Pneumatic Tool Co., Chicago, Ill. 1918
(2) Giant Truck Corp., Chicago, Ill. 1918-1922

Trucks under this name were 1-, 1½, 2- and 3-tonners. For 1918, these all used 4-cylinder Continental engines and bevel-gear drive with solid rubber tires. For 1919, a Buda 4-cylinder engine was used in the 1½-tonner and all four models had been changed to worm-drive. The Giant line for 1922 eliminated the 1-tonner. *GMN*

GIFFORD-PETTIT (US) 1907-1908

Gifford-Pettit Manufacturing Company, Chicago, Ill.

A lone Model A is the only recorded commercial vehicle from this manufacturer. Its capacity was three tons with a chassis weight of 5000 pounds. It used a 35 hp, four-cylinder engine with forward control. It also had a three-speed gearbox and double chain-drive. Its wheelbase was 120 inches, and chassis price was $3500. *GMN*

GIHO (NL) 1976 to date

GIHO B.V., de Klomp

After a less successful attempt to produce the GTS truck in 1973, GIHO tried again to get a foothold in the heavy tipper market. Two prototypes of a truck using a Diamond-Reo chassis, Timken axles, Fuller automatic gearbox and a DAF DH engine were produced in 1975 under the name Hobri. The cab used is by DAF, and the tires were Michelin super singles. For 1976 small scale production under the name Giho was planned. *JFJK*

GILBERT (GB) 1899

Ralph Gilbert & Son, Birmingham

The Gilbert was a 12-passenger charabanc powered by 10 hp horizontal-twin engine with bore and stroke of 5 x 8 inches. It had a separate coil and battery for each cylinder, 2-speed belt-and-pulley transmission and chain drive. The whole front axle swiveled in steering. The company planned to make smaller passenger cars with single-cylinder engines, but it is likely that the charabanc was the only vehicle they made. *GNG*

1939 GILERA Urano 250cc 3-wheel truck, Piaggio

GILERA (I) 1939-1960

Moto Gilera SpA, Arcore, Milan

Like many Italian motorcycle factories, Gilera also offered motorcycle-based *motocarri* with single-cylinder aircooled engines and two driven rear wheels. The first models had foot change, all-chain drive and disc wheels; the smallest type featured a 250 cc sv power unit and three forward speeds, while bigger 30 cwt trucks came with 500 cc and 600 cc ohv engines and 4-speed gearboxes, with the option of a semi-closed cab on the 600VT. The 30-cwt Gilera reappeared on the market in 1945, later versions having spiral bevel back axles. They were joined in 1956 by a 6-cwt lightweight using a 150 cc ohv engine, a 4-speed unit box, and uncoupled hydraulic brakes. After 1960 Gilera elected to concentrate on motorcycles, which they still manufacture as a subsidiary of the Piaggio (Ape) company. *MCS*

GILFORD (GB) 1925-1935

(1) E.B. Horne and Company, London N.7. 1925
(2) Gilford Motor Company Ltd., London N.7. 1926
(3) Gilford Motor Co. Ltd., High Wycombe, Bucks, 1927-33
(4) Gilford Motor Co. Ltd., Park Royal, London N.W. 10. 1934-35

E.B. Horne and Co. were ex-War Department Garford specialists who imported some new chassis from the United States, but realized that the future lay with import duty-free vehicles assembled in Britain. In 1925 they built 30-, 40- and 50- cwt vehicles respectively called C, D and F, with 4-cylinder Buda engines bearing a very close resemblance to the Garford, and with a name deliberately intended to sound like their former speciality.

In 1926 they introduced a passenger version of the F called the Swift, and a low-frame Safety Coach chassis with optional four wheel brakes and a 6-cylinder Buda engine. It combined a modest price, simplicity, and lightness, with more power and agility than available in most other British vehicles of the time, and did much to expand coaching in Britain. Gilford moved to a new factory at High Wycombe at the end of 1927 to give increased production facilities, and where up to six chassis a week were made. They also established their own body building company, Wycombe Motor Bodies Ltd. 1928 saw the introduction of their first forward control designs, the 150T and 1660T, of which the larger had 6-cylinder Lycoming engines. The 1660T was also used as a large capacity van chassis and was joined in 1929 by another goods or passenger model, the 2½-ton CP6.

1927 GILFORD LL15 Pullman coach, NMM

A more important introduction in 1929 however, was the 1680T which, for the first time, bore a familiar Gilford feature, Westinghouse Gruss air springs on the front dumb irons. A normal control version and an unsuccessful double deck chassis were also offered.

In 1930 the entirely and very successful normal control 20-seat AS6 and its 50-cwt derivative the DF6, appeared, while in 1931 they were joined by the 1680T with a British engine (by Meadows) for the first time. Lycoming engines were concurrently being made for Gilford by Coventry Climax. An unsuccessful Australian assembly venture followed by the development cost of front-wheel-drive single and double deck buses adversely affected the company's economic position. This was further weakened by Gilford's failure to sell to the big municipal fleets and

1930 GILFORD AS6 20-seater coach, OMM

1930 GILFORD 1680T Weymann coach, OMM

their reliance on uncertain hire-purchase repayments from the small coach operators who were their largest customers.

The two revolutionary buses were of integral construction and were intended to have Junkers opposed-piston, 2-stroke diesels, though these were never completed, and following trials with a Meadows engine, and the double decker's conversion into a trolleybus, both were scrapped.

1932 saw a less unconventional, but equally unsuccessful, Zeus double decker with Vulcan 6-cylinder engine, followed in 1933 by a single deck version, the Hera, which, with Vulcan and Leyland gasoline engines and Tangye diesel engines did a lot to revive the company at a new smaller works in north London. Production was down to one per week in 1934 when Perkins and Dorman diesels were offered in certain goods and passenger models for the first time, followed by Gardners and a new Coventry Climax gasoline engine in 1935, when the firm finally went into liquidation.

The name had a brief new lease of life when High Speed Gas (Great Britain, Ltd.) took over the works to produce HSG-Gilford producer gas vehicles. A few were made, including a bus in 1937, before the firm moved to the Sentinel Waggon Works in 1938 and disappeared. *OM*

1936 GILFORD-H.S.G. 4/5-ton producer-gas truck, OMM

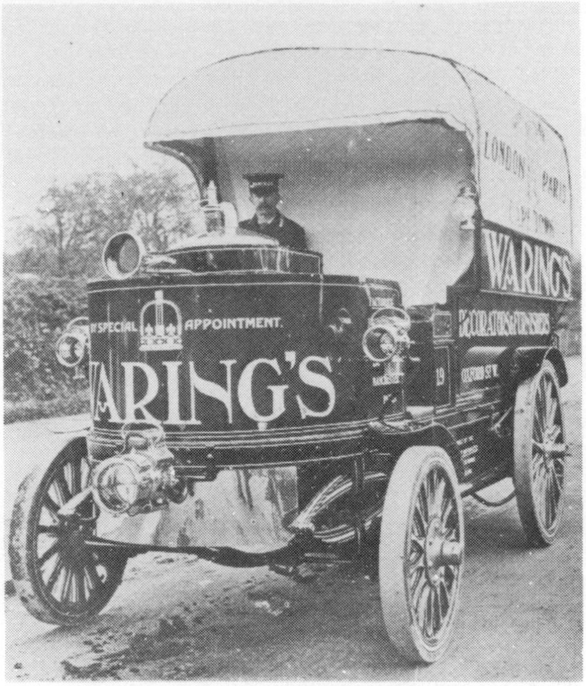

1903 GILLETT steam van, NMM

GILLETT (GB) 1898-1903

The Gillett Motor Co., Hounslow, Middlesex

The first mention of Gillett is the supply of a double deck bus to Lawson's Motor Omnibus Syndicate Ltd. of London in 1898 which seems never to have run in public service, after which nothing is recorded until the appearance of a steam wagon designed by E.H. Gillett, using a compound piston-valved engine, equipped with Joy's valve gear and combined in a single oil tight casting with the rear axle. The wagon was single speed but a simpling valve was provided. The boiler was vertical of the water-tube type fired by paraffin, and the wagon had rubber tires to all wheels.

The only documented example was supplied to Waring & Gillow, the London furnishers in the autumn of 1903. This ran until 1909 when the owners rebuilt it extensively but it was dispensed with the following year. *RAW*

GILLET-FOREST (F) 1902-1907

Ste Gillet-Forest, St. Cloud, Seine

Gillet Forest cars and commercial vehicles were

1902 GILLET-FOREST ½-ton van, Autocar

characterized by their large, curved gilled-tube radiators which acted as condensers for the steam given off by the water-jacket around the engine. The condensed water was returned to the cylinder head, while any surplus went to a tank at the rear. In 1902 there were six goods models of Gillet-Forest, ranging from 300 to 3000 kg capacity, and having engines of 6/7, 9/10 and 12 hp. Final drive was by chains. By 1905 shaft-drive had been adopted, and there were two models, a 12 hp single-cylinder with dimensions of 145 x 170mm, and a 24 hp 4-cylinder with more modest dimensions of 108 x 140mm. The large single-cylinder model was still offered in 1906, when it propelled a 2-ton truck. *GNG*

GILLIG (US) 1932 to date

(1) Gilig Brothers, San Francisco, Calif. 1932-1938
(2) Gillig Brothers, Hayward, Calif. 1938 to date

Jacob Gillig, a New York carriage builder and upholsterer, opened a carriage and wagon shop in San Francisco in 1890. Leo Gillig joined his father's business in 1896, and after the original shop burned in 1906, he reopened as the Leo Gillig Automobile Works and made automobile bodies, hearses, truck bodies, and bus bodies. Chester Gillig joined his brother in 1914, when a three-story plant was built, and in 1920 he patented a "California top," a lightweight affair with a hard roof and sliding windows that was used by the hundreds to convert open touring cars to closed models. In 1932 the first school bus body was built, and within five years this line of work occupied the entire capacity of the plant.

A transit bus was produced in 1937 and sold in small numbers. Production was transferred to a new factory in Hayward, south of Oakland, in 1938, and in 1941 an underfloor-engine design was introduced with Hall-Scott power and chassis by Fabco. Rear-engine buses were produced starting in 1945, and by 1950 production was about 75 complete buses and 100 bus bodies per year, mostly school bus types.

Diesel engines have been used exclusively for many years, and currently Gillig offers Cummins, Caterpillar and Detroit Diesels, designating its school buses by the engine displacement (in cubic inches) and the number of rows of seats. In the early 1970s Gillig designed a front-

1966 GILLIG Model 534-13 49-passenger coach, MBS

1968 GILLIG Model 855-15 6-wheel school bus, MBS

1977 GILLIG-NEOPLAN Model PT-477-35 bus, MBS

engined bus known as the Microcoach and built about 75 of them before selling the rights and tools to Sportscoach in 1974. Returning to the transit bus market, Gillig began building German Neoplan buses under license during 1977, with the addition of American components such as air conditioning and an optional wheelchair arrangement built into the front stepwell. The first batch of these interesting buses was for Santa Clara County, Calif. and were equipped with propane-gas burning Ford truck engines. *MBS*

1976 GINAF Model KFS 16 8×8 truck, BHV

GINAF (NL) 1967 to date

Ginaf Automobielbdrijvan B.V., Ederveen.

Ginaf was one of the many Dutch truck dealers starting during the 50's to recondition U.S. Army surplus material. In 1967 their own share had become sufficiently important that they started to sell the vehicles under their own name. Initially fitting U.S. Army Diamond T and Reo vehicles with new engines, mostly DAF, and a new cab, they gradually grew into real manufacturers, assembling parts from various manufacturers — partly still bought from U.S. Army stock — like ZF, DAF, Timken, to very rugged highway and off-road vehicles, both forward-control and normal-control versions. JFJK

GIRLING (GB) 1911-1914

(1) Girling Motors Ltd., Woolwich, London S.E.1
(2) Girling Motor Manufacturing Co., Bedford
(3) New Girling Commercial Cars Ltd., London W.C.

Yet another 3-wheeled light delivery vehicle, the Girling was built in considerable numbers during the period shown, and quite a number were exported to Ceylon, Chile and New Zealand mainly for postal delivery work. Two transverse front springs replaced the normal front axle, and power was provided by either 4-or 6-hp aircooled engines for 5 cwt and 7 cwt payloads. Final drive was via a variable speed friction disc (providing seven forward speeds) and shaft to bevel gearing on the single rear wheel, although the larger model employed a simple epicyclic gear to hold exceptional power for very hilly districts. By 1913 the standard offering was a 6 hp watercooled model and in this guise even found favor as a small fire engine. Prices ranged from £98. *MJWW*

GIRON single-decker bus

GIRON (C) c.1974 to date

The only Cuban-built vehicle, the Giron (pronounced hiron) is made mainly as a single-decker bus with front-mounted Hino diesel engine, Hino chassis and local bodywork. Some have transmission by the British Self-Changing Gears company, which probably come from the Leyland buses which have been in use in Cuba since the 1950s. A few Giron trucks have also been made. *GNG*

G. & J. see Gotfredson

G.J.G. (US) 1912-1913

G.J.G. Motor Car Company, White Plains, New York

The initials stood for George J. Grossman, a financier who backed this enterprise which also built passenger autos. The lone commercial model was based upon the passenger car chassis and was offered as either a closed van or with stake body, both rated at 1000 pounds capacity. The closed van had a rakish appearance enhanced by windshield attached to the front of the frame. *GMN*

1904 GLADIATOR 1-ton van, OMM

GLADIATOR (F) 1902-c.1906

Societe Gladiator, Pre-St. Gervais, Seine

The Gladiator company was better known for its passenger cars than commercials, and their first vans were closely based on cars, with 12hp vertical-twin engines and chain drive. These were made from 1902 at least until 1905, but in 1904 they were joined by a purpose-built truck with forward control and a 2-ton payload. The engine was the same 12hp twin, which cannot have given it a very sparkling performance, but it was stated that it 'had a more robust character than the motor fitted to the pleasure car.' The truck had a 3-speed gearbox, chain drive and the option of solid tires all round, or pneumatics on the front wheels and solids at the rear. *GNG*

GLASGOW see Halley

GLIDE (US) 1911-1912

Bartholomew Co., Peoria, Ill.

This was a ¾-tonner with either open or closed bodies. It used a 4-cylinder water-cooled engine with a 3-speed gearbox and shaft drive. Wheelbase was 120 inches and this chassis was identical to the passenger car of the same name for both years it was built. *GMN*

GLOBE (i) (GB) 1913-1914

Tuke & Bell Ltd., Tottenham, London N.

The Globe cyclecar was powered by an 8 hp single-cylinder Aster engine which drove via belt to a 2-speed epicyclic gear, thence by single chain to the rear axle. The 10 cwt delivery van version cost £150. *GNG*

GLOBE (ii) (US) 1916-1919

Globe Furniture Company, Northville, Mich., 1916
Globe Motor Truck Company, Northville, Mich., 1917-1919

The Globe was one of the earliest commercial vehicles using a side-valve 6-cylinder engine, although this was dropped in favor of 4-cylinder types by Continental in 1918. Rated capacities ranged from 1500 pounds to two tons. The largest version used wheelbase of 154 inches. *GMN*

1933 GLOSTER-GARDNER-seater coach, OMM

GLOSTER-GARDNER (GB) 1933-1934

The Gloucester Railway Carriage & Wagon Co. Ltd., Gloucester

The company embarked upon a program of vehicle manufacture to occupy its works at a time when railway work was slack. The Gloster-Gardner coach chassis was a fast, robust machine employing a Gardner 6LW oil engine and overdrive gearbox. It is doubtful if more than ten vehicles were produced, the majority (six in all) going to Red & White of Chepstow who operated the first Gloster-Gardner from Aberdare to London on 17th July 1933. A solitary trolleybus was constructed experimentally in 1934; an unusual double-decker with center doorway and with front axle set back to give a short wheelbase. It was bought by Southend-on-Sea Corporation while on exhibition at the Olympia Show of 1935. *OM*

GLOVER (i) (GB) 1904-c. 1907

Glover & Co, Bury St. Edmunds, Suffolk

The Glover was the product of a firm well-known for the manufacture of horse-drawn vans. The first motor vehicle was powered by a 12/14 hp 2-cylinder Aster engine under the seat, had a 3-speed gearbox and chain drive. Payload was 50 cwt. On the 1905 models the whole body could be slid back to facilitate maintenance of the engine and transmission, and in this year models varying from 10 cwt to three tons were listed. Most Glovers were of the driver-over-engine layout, but in 1906 conventional models were also offered. *GNG*

GLOVER (ii) (US) 1911-1912

George T S Glover, Chicago, Ill

The 5-tonner bearing this tradename was provided with a stake body and a 6-cylinder engine of 590 ci displacement. This engine was mounted in the center of the chassis, level with the bed. It used a 3-speed gearbox with drive by double chains which straddled the single rear wheel. A companion to this peculiar truck was a ¾-tonner with a 4-cylinder engine, but also with a single drive wheel in the center of the rear axle. *GMN*

GMC (US) 1911 to date

(1) General Motors Truck Co., Pontiac, Michigan 1911-1925
(2) General Motors Truck and Coach Division, Pontiac, Michigan 1925 to date

GMC came into being in 1911 by the merger of the Rapid and Reliance truck firms already under General Motors' control: the individual names were retained for at least a year, while some early GMCs were made in the former Rapid plant at Owosso, Michigan. The 1-2 ton Rapids were normal control 4-cylinder machines with side-chain drive, 4-speed gearboxes, and solid tires: even in 1911 they featured lhd. By contrast Reliances, though also chain-driven, were high-built forward control trucks for 3½- and 5-ton payloads: their 6.4-litre engines were easily demountable, and three forward speeds sufficed. In addition a range of chain-driven battery-electrics (some with short Renault-style hoods) in the ½- 6-ton bracket was offered until 1915, but in that year gasoline-engined GMCs switched to shaft drive, with straight bevels on the ¾-ton series and worm-type axles on heavier models. Engines were sv monobloc fours with magneto ignition, and 3-speed gearboxes were found only on smaller GMCs. In 1916 William Warwick, accompanied by his wife, drove from Seattle to New York in two months on a 1½-tonner: the return trip took appreciably longer, but was successfully accomplished. GMCs contribution to the US war effort embraced 16,000 2-tonners, and 5000 light ambul-

1925 GMC Model K-16 1-Ton Truck, Goodyear

ances on the Model-15 chassis as well as participation in the manufacture of standardised Light Aviation trucks.

Post-War production centered round the K range on similar lines. 1-tonners featured 3.6-litre engines, 3-speed unit gearboxes, bevel drive and pneumatic tires, but types like the 5-ton K101 and its tractor version for 15 tons retained solids and worm drive. Starters were not standard on heavies even in 1925, and their 6.2-litre power units developed a modest 37 hp, but interesting was the 7-speed dual range gearbox, and from 1925 the division offered the formidable Big Brute (K102), noted for an outsize front bumper, a 6.8-litre power unit and a GVW rating of 22,000 lb. From 1922 GMCs were also built in Canada, while bus chassis made their appearance, early ones based on the 1½-ton K16 and 2/3-ton K41, the latter with dual-range transmission. GM's mainstream bus operation was of course Yellow Coach, which merged with GMC in 1925. Yellow production was transferred to the Pontiac plant two years later. Subsequent purpose-built PSVs would be marketed under the Yellow or General Coach label, though truck-based buses remained GMCs: there would be several variations on the T theme in 1930, and school buses were still listed in 1978. Some of GM's standardised export-pattern bus bodies evolved for local assembly in 1946-7 found their way onto GMCs as well as Chevrolets. An odd departure of the 1936-8 period would be the Gen-

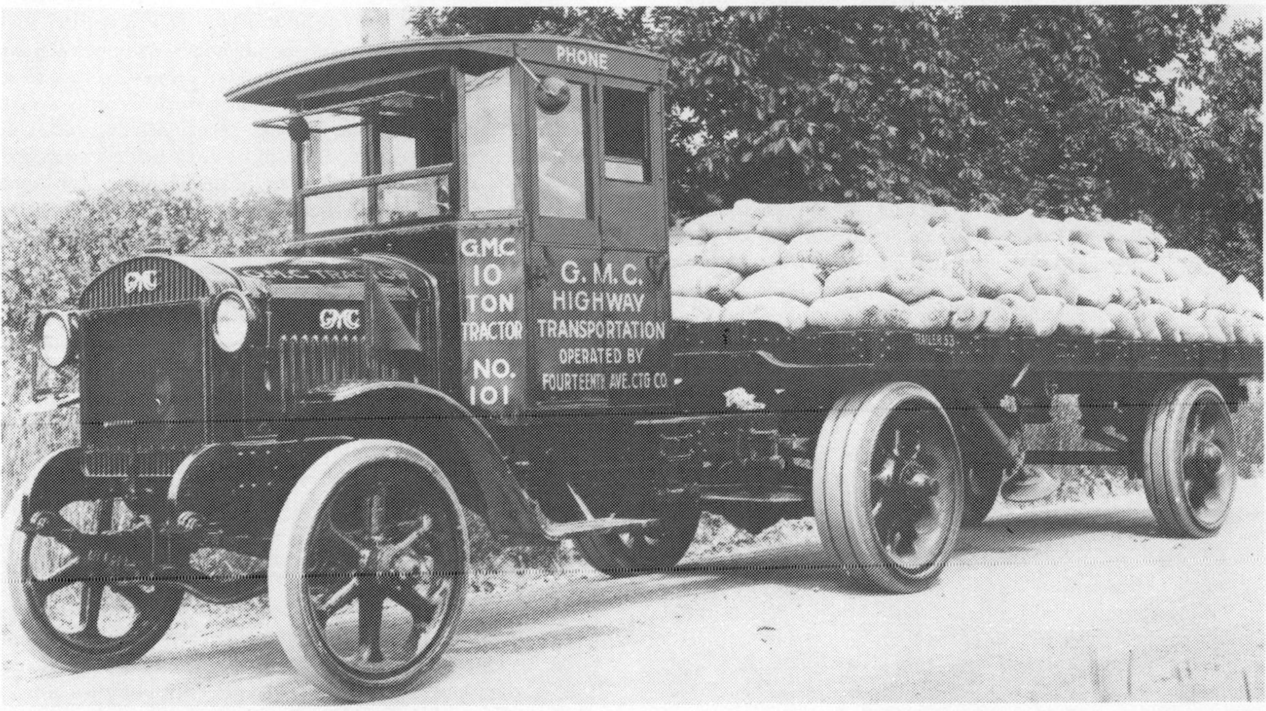

1923 GMC Model K-41T 10-ton articulated truck, GMC

eral Motors Cab, an elongated Chevrolet of passenger-car type.

Though the Big Brute survived into 1929, the remaining GMCs were supplanted during 1927 by the T-line, which set the pattern for subsequent development. The range covered everything from a ½-ton panel delivery to 5/6-tonners: common to all were pneumatic tires, full electrics and 6-cylinder engines. Worm drive was confined to the top of the range, and though the smallest 1927 Ts had rear wheel brakes only, fwb were standard by 1928. 4-speed gearboxes featured on all but the car-type delivery vans, which were close relatives of the contemporary Pontiac 6, and 58 hp sv Pontiac engines were used in these and the 1-tonners. Bigger GMCs shared their 4-bearing ohv units with the Buick range, outputs running as high as 89 hp from 5.1 litres in 1929, and nearly 100 hp in 1930, when capacity was 5.4 litres. Buick switched to straight-8s on their 1931 line, but GMC took over the development of the 6-cylinder line, adding some huge 7-bearing units of their own design with hydraulic valve lifters, intended in the first instance to replace the unloved sleeve-valve type fitted to Yellow Coaches (they even bolted up to existing Yellow gearboxes) but later applied to heavy

1932 GMC Model T-95C 10-ton truck, GMC

trucks as well. By 1931 the GMC lineup covered payloads of up to 15 tons, 6-wheelers were available, and there was even a range of trailers which continued for ten years. The year's sales were some 10,000 units, and heavy duty trucks made extensive use of proprietary components: falling demand led to the introduction of the T18, a cheap 1½/2-tonner at under $600, using the current 3.3-litre sv Pontiac engine and sharing its bodies with similarly rated Chevrolets, though there was no other interchange between General Motors' two makes. 1933's main innovations were a sleeper-cab option on heavies, downraft carburetors, and a new 3.6-litre ohv engine to supplant the flatheads in the 2-ton bracket, while an 8/15-ton range was launched with the new 7-bearing engines in 10-litre and 11.7-litre forms (the latter gave 173 hp), twin-plate clutches, 5-speed overdrive or underdrive gearboxes, and Westinghouse air brakes: worm drive was retained on tandems. The largest engine in wide use by 1934 was how-

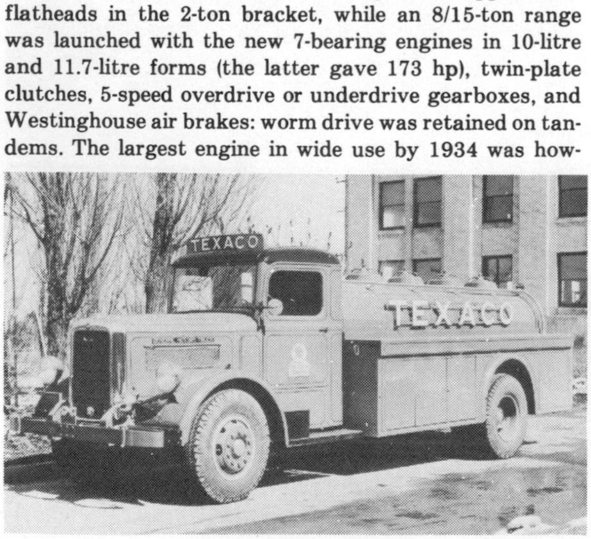

1934 GMC Model T-61 5/6½-ton tanker, Texaco Archives

1934 GMC Model T-74HC 12-ton truck with sleeper cab, GMC

ever, a 7.3-litre 120 hp affair, a 70 hp side valve was still fitted to 1½-tonners, and ohv medium-duty units covered the 69-110 hp bracket. 5-speed gearboxes were regular equipment at the top of the range, and medium-duty models received vacuum servo brakes. New that year was a forward-control range with slide-out engines, covering payloads from three to nine tons: a low loader municipal version was used in New York.

1935 GMC Model T-16 3-ton truck and trailer, FLP

1936 GMC Model T-18 10-ton articulated truck, RNE

From 1935 GMCs, like Chevrolets, received regular stylistic facelifts, the new streamline cab arriving a year earlier than on the cheaper line. Also offered for the first time in 1935 were hydraulic brakes, with hydrovac systems on heavier trucks, full air operation being retained at the top of the range. Some light duty models switched from Pontiac to Oldsmobile engines, still sv 6s, and these were offered in certain export markets (notably Britain and the Low Countries) with Oldsmobile badges. Sales passed the 50,000 mark in 1937, and 7-bearing engines spread down the range, 1938's smallest being the 4½-litre 278 fitted to 2-ton GMCs. Synchromesh came in 1939, while a more important departure, not to be found for many years on Chevrolets, was a supplementary range of diesel-powered models with nominal ratings from two to six tons. Engines were 3- and 4-cylinder 2-stroke Detroits made by General Motors. During World War II the Division became America's largest producer of military vehicles, contributing over 560,000 editions of their famous normal control 2½-ton 6x6, with 104 hp engine, 5-speed main gearbox, and hydrovac brakes. Also built were over 20,000 units of its amphibious development, the DUKW. Development of both themes continued after VJ-Day: GMC had a new 6x6 with Hydramatic transmission in service by 1951, and the DUKW's successor, tested in 1956, was the Drake, an 8½-tonner of 8x8 configuration.

Post-War GMC's returned to 1941 themes - the sv eng-

1940 GMC Model AY-720 1270-gallon tanker, GMC

1940 GMC Model AFWX-354 3-ton searchlight truck, NMM

ines had already gone in 1939 — and the standard light duty unit was a 4-bearing ohv 6 of 3.7 litres capacity. Alongside the conventional small panel deliveries was a forward-control urban type introduced in 1940, while the latest heavies covered GVWs to 55,000 lbs and GCWs to 90,000 lbs. Worm drive, 5-speed gearboxes, air-operated 2-speed back axles and diesel engines characterised the top of the range, the latest Detroit units being a 133 hp four and the latest 6-71 six giving 200 hp from 6.9 litres. Variations included some West Coast Specials with no front wheel brakes and liberal use of aluminium to save weight, as well as a 6x4 normal control tractor of 1950 with 275 hp engine. The regular 7-bearing gasoline sixes were now giving up to 200 hp. The Hydramatic transmission already tried on military GMCs had reached the civilian range by 1953: initially offered only on light vans and pickups it had reached the medium-duty class a year

1942 GMC Model CCW-353 2½-ton 6X4 army truck, BHV

1948 GMC Model ADCR-902 articulated tanker, OMM

1954 GMC Model 101-24 1-ton pick-up, OMM

later. The smaller models now closely resembled Chevrolets, with one-piece curved windshields in 1954 and the dog leg type (together with an Oldsmobile-like/grille) in 1955, when the new short-stroke ohv gasoline V8s became available: outputs ran up to 232 hp. GMC production broke the 100,000 mark for the first time in 1960, the Division, like Chevrolet, trying its luck with ifs on medium trucks and air springing on some heavies. Parallel to Chevrolet's development were the latest forward control tilt-cab types for GVWs of 19,500 lbs upwards, while GMC instituted a new program of high-performance V6 gasoline engines: these came in capacities of 5, 5.6, 6.6, and 7.7 litres, with outputs in the 165-235 hp class, though at the top of the range was the vast 702 V12 (11.2 litres, 275 hp), this package calling for a twin-plate clutch, ten

1962 GMC Model 6500 8X6 dump truck, OMM

forward speeds, and air brakes. It was not quoted after 1964, thanks to the evolution of a new line of 4-stroke diesels to supplement the traditional 2-stroke Detroits, still offered: most powerful of these was the 637, a V8 rated at 220 hp. A wide choice of cabs was listed in the heavy range: as well as the conventionals and the 1960 tilt type there were a 'short' version of the former and a new forward model of only 48in bbc. 8-, 10- and 16 speed transmissions were listed.

GMC set a new production record of 150,180 units in 1969, their last season as an individual make: henceforward only badges and names would distinguish the

1964 GMC Model D sleeper cab articulated truck, GMC

1976 GMC Astro 95 articulated truck, GMC

1978 GMC Brigadier 6×4 dump truck, GMC

breed from Chevrolets, though most heavy-truck customers tended to prefer GMC if only on grounds of sentiment. Heaviest of the 1978 range were the forward control Astro (Chevrolet Titan) and normal control General (Chevrolet Bison), rated for GCWs in the 80,000 lb. bracket and available with the usual engine options - Cummins and Caterpillar sixes, and 6-, 8- and 12-cylinder Detroit Diesels of up to 412 hp. Lower down the range, Chevrolet's car-type El Camino pickup was sold as the Sprint, the Chevyvan became the Vandura, and the light 4x4 Blazer the Jimmy. *MCS*

G.N. (GB) 1920-1928

G.N. Ltd., Wandsworth, London, S.W. 18

Like their competitors Sabella and Bedelia, G.N. offered a light van suitable for local delivery work or the carriage of commercial traveler's samples, on their standard cyclecar chassis. Built in the erstwhile British Gregoire factory at Wandsworth, these employed the large V-twin G.N. engine and chain drive also used by the sporting versions, but relatively few left the works. In 1928, by which time production of cyclecars and conventional shaft driven models with D.F.P., Chapuis Dornier and Anzani engines had ceased, an unsuccessful attempt was made to market a single cylinder 3-wheeled light van at £85, but this was probably the last vehicle to be built by the works although GNs were technically available until 1929. The firm survives as a Vauxhall agency in Balham. *MJWW*

G.N.R. (EIR) 1937-1952

Great Northern Railway Company (Ireland), Dundalk, Co. Louth

The company commenced construction of bus chassis in its railway works at Dundalk in 1937, the vehicles so produced being intended entirely for use on its own network of services, most of which ran within the Irish Republic. Only single-deckers were produced, and these incorporated many parts made in the company's own works, including chassis frames, radiators and springs. Major units bought from outside sources were axles, gearboxes and steering. The power unit was the Gardner 5LW which was mounted on a very efficient flexible suspension of GNR design. 40 vehicles were built in 1937/8, 13 in 1941/2, and 42 in 1947-52, making a total of 95. The bodies, which seated between 27 and 35 according to luggage space, were also built in the Dundalk works, the post-war ones utilizing frames purchased from Harkness and Park Royal. Following bankruptcy of the railway company, those GNR vehicles which still remained in service on 1st January 1959 passed to the ownership of Coras Iompair Eireann, the Irish state transport company. *OM*

GOBRON-BRILLIE (F) 1899-1909

Societe Gobron-Brillie, Boulogne-sur-Seine.

Gobron-Brillie speciality was the opposed-piston engine with pair-cast cylinders and four pistons per pair. In its early form this was a vertical-twin, mounted either amidships or at the rear of a tubular frame, and driving the rear wheels by central chain. Thanks to the use of a metering device in place of a conventional carburetor, the Gobron unit was said to run happily on alcohol, or even on spirits. In spite of these characteristics, the make was seldom seen in commercial-vehicle form, though the Societe Nanceiene made trucks under Gobron-Brillie license, and 8 hp 2-cylinder Gobrons were quoted up to 1903 with wagonnette, brake, or delivery van bodywork. Later ones had front-mounted engines and side-chain drive. In that year Eugene Brillie resigned from the firm and went to work for the Ateliers Schneider of Havre, on conventionally-powered trucks and buses. After his departure Gobron-Brillie, while retaining the opposed-piston principle, concentrated on high-performance private cars. This did not, however, prevent them from offering 2- and 4-cylinder cabs in 1909. Their power units apart, they were orthodox, with ht magneto ignition, 3-speed gearboxes, and shaft drive. *MCS*

GODOLLO (H) 1974 to date

Voros Csillag Traktorgyar, Godollo

Following Dutra's amalgamation with Raba in late 1973, the 4 x 4 10 ton dumper design was transferred to the Voros Csillag Tractor factory and was renamed after the city where the factory is situated. Same technical specifications, including Csepel 125 hp diesel engine and planetary axles, were retained. *GA*

1958 GOGGOMOBIL TL400 ¼-ton van. OMM

GOGGOMOBIL (D) 1956-1966

Hans Glas GmbH., Isaria Maschinenfabrik, Dingolfing

The Goggomobil was available as a pick-up and van based on the firm's private cars . Engines of 250 cc, 300 cc and 400 cc were available. The latter powered a 5 cwt forward control van known as the TL400 and widely used for postal work. From 1962 to 1966 Goggomobil cars and commercial vehicles were made in Spain by Munguia Industrial S A of Bilboa. *HON*

GOLDEN EAGLE see Silver Eagle

GOLDEN WEST (US) 1913-1914

Golden West Motors Company, Sacramento, California

This 2-tonner had 4-wheel drive with worm drive and 4-wheel steering. It had a four-cylinder Continental engine and underslung springs to obtain minimum bed height. Wheelbase was 132 inches. In 1915 the tradename was changed to Robinson. *GMN*

GOLDONI (I) 1960 to date

Goldoni SpA, Modena

Primarily makers of agricultural equipment since 1926, Goldoni added small tractors to their range in 1956, from which were developed 4 x 4 load carriers in the following decade. The latest 3500 RTS has a 3-cylinder, air-cooled, 38 hp Slanzi diesel and can carry 1760 kg up an 80 percent slope. *OM*

1906 GOLDSCHMIDT steam truck, RAW

GOLDSCHMIDT (B) c.1906-c.1913

Ste de Construction Mecaniques et d'Automobiles, Brussels

The Goldschmidt was a light steam truck of 20/30 cwt. capacity using a flash steam boiler (patented in 1904), undertype engine with countershaft differential and final drive by twin roller chain. Alternative wheels available were artillery type with steel tires or steel discs with armored pneumatics.

The only known examples were made for the government of the Belgian Congo using wood fuel but the dates of manufacture are conjectural. The actual manufacture is thought to have been at Liege. *RAW*

GOLIATH (D) 1926-1959

(1) Goliath-Werk Borgward & Co., Bremen 1926-1931
(2) Hansa-Lloyd und Goliath-Werke Borgward & Tecklenburg, Bremen 1932-1937
(3) Hansa-Lloyd-Goliath-Werke Carl F.W. Borgward, Bremen 1937-1938
(4) Carl F.W. Borgward Automobil- und Motorenwerke, Bremen 1938-1949
(5) Goliath-Werk GmbH., Bremen 1949-1959

The first Goliath was presented in 1926, a tri-van following a layout which was very popular at that time. It had

1939 GOLIATH F200 200cc 3-wheel truck, Halwart Schrader Collection

two front wheels and front mounted platform or box. The driver was placed above the single rear wheel which was chain-driven by a 200 cc Ilo engine. After some time this version replaced the "Blitzkarren" (see Borgward). Payload capacities were increased and engine capacities also. A forward-control 4-wheel van "Express" was presented in 1928, the 500 cc Ilo engine was placed under the seat, and entry was by a front door. The tri-vans were replaced by another layout: one front wheel and two-seater cabin and rear platform or box plus shaft drive of the rear wheels. These were made through 1939.

A new start was made in 1949, again with tri-vans using the layout of one front — two rear wheels of which the latest type was the "Goli" of 1955 with 2-cylinder 500 cc air-cooled engine. The 4-wheel transporter came in 1950, a forward control version with 2-cylinder 465 cc engine placed under the seat. A later version had a 586 cc engine. The type designation "Express" was revived for these 4-

1954 GOLIATH 460cc 3-wheel truck, GNG

wheel transporters. In 1953 this was the first transporter using fuel injection for the 2-cylinder 700 cc engine. Two-stroke engines were used until the appearance of the "Express 1100" in 1957 which had a 4-cylinder 4-stroke engine of 1,093 cc. It was available as pick-up, van and micro-bus. *HON*

GOODCHILD (GB) 1912-1914

F.B. Goodchild & Co., Westminster, S.W.

Goodchilds were primarily a sales organization, and prior to 1912 they held the agency for the A.C. Autocarrier, Oryx delivery vans, Le Zebre taxis and Belhaven trucks. They also maintained extensive bodybuilding workshops, however, and from 1912 until the outbreak of war they offered a multiplicity of vehicles under their own name, some of which at least were actually built. Those for which concrete evidence does exist include a 10 hp commercial traveler's car, with 'box' for 5 cwt of samples, a 6 hp single cylinder two-seater 'surveyor's' car with shaft drive, and a massively built 4-ton truck fitted with 4-cylinder 35 hp Drayson engine and worm drive. The latter was built for them by W.S. Laycock Ltd., of Sheffield and was marketed as the Laycock-Goodchild. In addition, however, chassis of similar layout were said to be available in 30, 40 60, and 100 cwt capacity or as charabancs, and smaller vehicles included a 4-cylinder 12 cwt van with chain drive and solid tires in 1912, a 6 cwt vertical twin engined van with primary and secondary chain drive, and 10 and 15 cwt bevel driven vans in 1913. *MJWW*

GOODWIN see Guilder

GOODYEAR (US) 1920-1926

Goodyear Tire & Rubber Co., Akron, Ohio

Goodyear was not interested in producing trucks and buses per se, but did build a small number of them to prove a point. Pioneering in the late 'teens with pneumatic tires for trucks in the 5-ton range, the tires, all singles, got so large that this caused considerable mis-matching between the trucks' cargo floors and the loading docks.

Goodyear wanted some 6-wheel tandem trucks built so tire sizes could be reduced under a spread load, but since no truck manufacturer was interested, Goodyear designed and built their own 5- and 6-ton trucks with the help of Ellis W. Templin, an automotive engineer.

Templin's first bogie was chain-driven from a central Timken worm axle and longitudinally oscillating beams, one on each side having one wheel at each end. Later he developed a dual drive using two Timken worm axles at the ends of inverted semi-elliptic springs in conjunction with torque arms which were slightly telescoping.

Except for the tandem drives, Goodyear trucks were of conventional layout. They were well made, used bought-out components, and were fitted with van bodies. Enhancing their appearance was a smooth radiator shell of polished aluminum at the front of a well-shaped hood, flanked by fenders of unusually good style. Artillery wheels were used with, naturally, Goodyear pneumatics, singles all around. The trucks weighed about 8500 pounds.

Several Goodyear buses were also built, the first type using the 6-wheel truck chassis. The second type used a trolley car body with forward control and rear tandem, and the third, also with a trolley car body, used tandems in front as well as rear, with single pneumatics all around. The Goodyear Heights bus line in Akron, Ohio operated them as the first tandems in commercial service in the early 1920's.

One of the Goodyear trucks was driven 3500 miles from New York to Los Angeles in 6½ days, setting a new transcontinental record. Maximum speed was 45 mph, much more than contemporary 5-ton trucks could attain.

The 6 x 4 Goodyear trucks were part of the Goodyear Wingfoot Express fleet hauling cargo between the Akron, Ohio and Boston, Mass. plants, together with some 4 x 2 White and Packard cargo trucks and tractor semi-trailer combinations.

1921 GOODYEAR 5-ton 6-wheel truck, Goodyear

Promotions such as this eventually proved Goodyear's point to heavy truck operators as truck pneumatic tire production surpassed that of solids by 1926, and Goodyear trucks were ultimately withdrawn from service. *RW*

GOOSENS-LOCHNER (D) 1924-1928

J.P. Goossens, Lochner & Co., Brand, / Aachen

This company produced one type only, a 4-5 ton truck following conventional chassis design but using a Soden preselector gearbox and an 8.1-litre B.M.W. engine. *HON*

GOPHER see Robinson

GORDON (i) (GB) 1914

East Riding Engineering Works, Beverley, Yorks

The Gordon cyclecar, powered by a rear-mounted 9 hp V-twin J.A.P. engine, was made in light van form with an open driver's compartment. Final drive was by chain, and load capacity was 5-10 cwt. *GNG*

GORDON (ii) (GB) 1931-1933

Metropolitan-Vickers Ltd., Trafford Park, Manchester

This was a light 3-wheeled electric vehicle with very small wheels and solid tires, intended for retail delivery work. It had tiller steering which could be operated by a man walking alongside the vehicle. Drive was to the single front wheel, and top speed was 12 mph. *GNG*

1926 GOTFREDSON 2-ton chassis, OMM

GOTFREDSON (CDN/US) 1920-1948

(1) Gotfredson & Joyce Corp. Ltd., Walkerville, Ont. 1920-1922
(2) Gotfredson Truck Corp. Ltd., Walkerville, Ont. 1923-1932
(3) Gotfredson Corp., Detroit, Mich. 1923-1929
(4) Robert Gotfredson Truck Co., Detroit, Mich. 1929-1948

This company was American-owned, but it began in Canada and Canadian operations were on a much larger scale than the American, although the latter survived for longer. Originally known as the G & J, the Gotfredson was an assembled vehicle using such well-known conponents as Buda engines, Timken axles, Brown-Lipe and Fuller transmissions and Ross steering. Production included trucks from ¾ to 7 tons, 4- and 6-wheeled buses and coaches, fire engines and taxicabs, as well as car bodies. Annual production reached 2000 at its peak in the late 1920s, and the vehicles were sold all over Canada and also in England where the 12/14 passenger coach was popular. Gotfredsons featured an attractive cast alum-

1926 GOTFREDSON 6-wheel bus, FLP

1931 GOTFREDSON 2-ton truck, RJ

inium radiator. The American company failed in 1929 and was reorganized on a more modest scale, and after the Canadian plant discontinued manufacture in 1932 it was acquired by Ford. Production continued in Detroit on a very small, largely custom-built, scale using Buda gasoline and Cummins diesel engines, and GMC cabs and fenders. The employment of Cummins engines led Gotfredson into a new field, and they became Cummins sales and service for the whole of Michigan. In the 1940s Cummins engines were used exclusively, mostly big 150 hp units for trucks of up to 100,000 lbs GCW. Production was reduced to one corner of the large Detroit plant, but on this very limited scale it continued at least into 1948, and possibly the early 1950s. *HD/RJ*

GOTTSCHALK (D) 1900-1901

Berliner Motorwagen-Fabrik Gottschalk & Co., Berlin W

A delivery van based on the private car using a 3 hp engine was available together with a 3-wheeled van on motorcycle lines. For trucks and buses (up to 10 passengers) engines by de Dion, Aster, Daimler and Hille were used. Transmission was by friction drive and shaft. For later models see B.M.F. *HON*

GOVA (NL) 1955 to date

GOVA Trucks B.V., Wormerveer

Gova started as a manufacturer of small 3-wheeled delivery vehicles, powered by single-cylinder 2-stroke engines. These original GOVA's had a single-powered front wheel and two wheels at rear. For the last five years GOVA has specialized in large mobile shops, using VW engines to power them. *JFJK*

GRAAFF (D) 1952-1954

Niedersachsische Waggonfabrik Joseph Graaff Gmbh., Elze.

This coachbuilding firm presented a forward-control chassis-less bus in light metal construction in 1952. The Henschel diesel engine was rear-mounted. *HON*

GRABOWSKY (US) 1908-1913

Grabowsky Power Wagon Co., Detroit, Mich.

Max Grabowsky was the designer of the Rapid truck made from 1902 to 1911 which became part of General Motors in 1909. The previous year Grabowsky left Rapid to make trucks on his own. These had 22 hp horizontal-opposed twin engines which could be slid out of the frame for maintenance, planetary transmissions and double chaindrive. Chassis came in 1- and 1½-ton sizes for all kinds of goods bodies and also sightseeing buses. In 1910 larger 4-cylinder models were added to the line. *GNG*

GRAF & STIFT (A) 1909 to date

(1) Wiener Automobilfabrik vorm. Graf & Stift, Vienna
(2) Graf & Stift Automobilfabrik AG, Vienna
(3) Oesterreichische Automobilfabrik OAF Graf & Stift AG, Vienna

This well-known maker of high-grade passenger cars took up production of commercial vehicles in 1909 with a 45PS 2½-ton truck which was made until 1912. Then new 3- and 5-ton models were introduced, many of which were supplied to the Austrian Army, being very similar to other subsidy trucks made by Austro-Fiat, Fross-Bussing and Saurer. In 1916 a mobile workshop truck and trailer, with solid rubber front and iron rear tires was made. After the war these 3- and 5-tonners were continued, being replaced in 1926 with a 2½-ton 'express truck' with

1930 GRAF & STIFT 2-ton truck, GNG

1938 GRAF & STIFT 4½-ton truck, OMM

pneumatic tires and a top speed of 30 mph with full load. Larger models of 3- and 3½-ton payloads, and also buses, were made during the 1930s, when diesel engines were added to the range.

After World War 2 production concentrated on one model, the Typ 120 6-tonner powered by a 125 hp 6-cylinder diesel engine. This was made in many different versions including fire engines and buses. In 1953 two completely new buses were introduced, a front-engined 37-seater powered by a 125 hp 2-cycle V-4 diesel engine mounted well ahead of the front axle, and a chassisless rear-engined coach powered by the 125 hp V-4 or a 180 hp V-6 engine. These were made alongside the Typ 120 which was continued into the 1960s with only styling changes and a slight increase in size and power, when it was known as the LVT8. Meanwhile a new range of cab-overs was introduced in 1957, including a twin-steer 6-wheeler of 10 tons capacity powered by a 200 hp V-6 engine, with 6-speed gearbox. The rest of the cab-over range covered trucks and tractors with load capacities of up to 22 tons, and 4x4 and 6x6 dump trucks. These were powered by 145 hp 6-cylinder engines made by Graf & Stift under

1962 GRAF & STIFT SF-145 articulated truck, HON

Mercedes-Benz license. Sleeper cabs were added during the 1960s, and many of the all-wheel drive models were supplied to the army. Buses made during this period included an enormous 103-passenger 6-wheeled double-decker powered by a Bussing engine, and single deck buses and coaches which were Henschel or Deutz powered.

1968 GRAF & STIFT ZA 200/1 8-ton 6×6 truck, BHV

In 1970 Graf & Stift merged with OAF (formerly Austro-Fiat), and truck production was taken over by this company. Buses continued to be made by G & S, and still are today. Engines are by M.A.N., and the largest in the current range is a 141-passenger (31 seats, 103 standing) articulated bus with 230 hp 6-cylinder engine and Voith-Diwa automatic transmission. *HON/GNG*

GRAHAM BROS (US) 1919-1928

(1) Graham Brothers, Evansville, Ind. 1919-1927
Detroit, Mich. 1922-1927
(2) Graham Brothers Divn of Dodge Brothers, Detroit, Mich. 1928

The three Graham brothers, Joseph, Robert and Ray, began by offering the Truck-Builder which consisted of frame, cab, body and Torbensen internal gear drive by which a passenger car could be converted into a truck. Fifth wheel turntables were available for making light articulated trucks. Capacities were 1, 1½ and 2 tons for the trucks, and 3 and 5 tons for the artics.

It wasn't long, however, before the Graham brothers were assembling their own complete truck.

The Dodge brothers, John and Horace, both passed away in 1920 and were succeeded by Frederick J. Haynes who then arranged with Graham Brothers (and bought a majority interest in them) to manufacture trucks in Detroit under the Graham name but with Dodge 4-cylinder engines and transmissions, and with marketing through Dodge Brothers dealers everywhere. It logically followed that Graham Brothers trucks came to resemble the Dodge Brothers cars and light trucks.

Graham Brothers trucks were typical medium-sized vehicles of their day. Pneumatic tires became standard on, progressively, disc, artillery, and cast steel spoke wheels. Spiral bevel rear axles came by 1924, and by 1928 the range was expanded to include ½, ¼, and 2½-ton sizes with 6-cylinder engines now in some models. The price

1924 GRAHAM BROS 1½-ton truck, NMM

1925 GRAHAM BROS YB bus, MBS

range was $670 to $1665. More than 60,000 units were going into service yearly at this time, making Graham Brothers a major producer.

In many ways the truck was pretty much Dodge Brothers' anyway, so in 1927 they made it complete by purchasing the entire operation.

Part of the agreement was that the Graham brothers would not build trucks in the future. However, the three brothers wanted to continue in the automotive business, so they bought the Paige-Detroit Motor Car Co. and continued that car as Graham-Paige (1928) and later Graham (1931).

Meanwhile, the truck was renamed Dodge Brothers for 1929, and later Dodge (1936) which continues as a major producer today. *RW*

GRAHAM-DOANE see Doane

GRAISELEY (GB) 1937-1939

Diamond Motors Ltd., Wolverhampton, Staffs.

This company launched a conventional battery electric delivery van powered by a 3½ hp motor by the Electric Power Engineering Company. Maximum speed of the 8/10 cwt van was 16-18 mph, and the range 35 miles per charge. This was listed for only two years, after which Diamond Motors concentrated on pedestrian-controlled 3-wheeled vehicles and industrial machinery such as fork-lift trucks. *GNG*

GRAM (F) 1953

Ste Gramme, Pantin, Seine

This was an 18 cwt battery electric van with batteries under a hood, and the unusual feature of a 2-speed epicyclic gearbox made in unit with the motor. Drive was to the front wheels, and the Gram had a speed of 23 mph and a range of 77 miles per charge. One was brought to England in an attempt to find a concessionnaire, but none was sold there. *GNG*

c.1912 GRAMM (i) 3-ton truck, Canadian Pacific

GRAMM (i) (US) 1910-1913

(1) Gramm Motor Car Co., Lima, Ohio
(2) Gramm Motor Truck Co., Lima, Ohio

This company was a continuation of the Gramm-Logan, the name change taking place after the move from Bowling Green to Lima. The former Gramm-Logan Model X 3-ton COE truck was uprated to five tons, and other models for 1911 included smaller trucks of 1-, 2-and 3-tons capacity. Conventionals supplemented the cab-over in 1911. These were continued until 1913 when the plant was acquired by John N. Willys. Gramm had meanwhile formed the Gramm-Bernstein Company. *GNG*

GRAMM (ii) (US) 1926-1942

(1) Gramm Motors Inc., Delphos, Ohio
(2) Gramm Motor Truck Corp., Delphos, Ohio
(3) Gramm Truck and Trailer Corp., Delphos, Ohio

Successor to the generally similar Gramm-Kincaid, the second Gramm company was formed by Benjamin A. Gramm and his son Willard J. Gramm, the former being in charge of finance and marketing and the latter of engineering. A wide range of trucks and buses was offered, with 4- and 6-cylinder Continental, Hercules or Lycoming engines, in sizes from one to five tons. From 1929 only 6-cylinder engines were used. In the late 1920s there were strong links between Gramm and Willys; 1, 1½, 2 and 2½ tonners and a bus chassis using the Willys-Knight passenger car engine were built by Gramm for Willys-Overland's export subsidiary from 1927 to 1930, and were also sold in the US and Canada from 1928 to 1930.

1931 GRAMM (ii) 8-ton articulated truck, NAHC

The Gramm family always had a keen eye to the export market, and in 1932 introduced the Condor as an export vehicle, in fact marketed by a new Chicago-based subsidiary, Condor Motors Inc. Condors were originally identical to Gramms, but from 1934 variations appeared, particularly with regard to the make and type of engines used. Gramm trucks were used by African explorer Martin Johnson, and by the US Government who bought them for use in penal institutions. A new range appeared in 1934 with sharply vee'd radiators and new fenders and cabs similar to those of the Stewart. Ratings were still 1 to 5 tons, but in 1936, the introduction of diesel engines by Hercules and Cummins extended the capacity of the largest Gramms to 7½ tons. With optional twin trumpet horns the 1936 Gramms were the best-looking the company had made. Apart from the Condor export trucks, Gramms were to be assembled in Canada by Bickle, the Woodstock, Ontario fire engine makers, but only one was made. On these, British-built Perkins diesel engines were optional alternatives to Hercules and Cummins. While Bickle was attempting to sell the Gramm in Eastern Canada, a truck dealer in British Columbia was distributing essentially the same vehicle, not as a Gramm or a Bickle, but as a Condor!

A new series of Gramms was introduced in 1939 using the cab from the Willys ½-ton pick-up. These were somewhat confined for a heavy truck but saved the outlay on tooling for a new cab. From 1942 Gramm dropped truck building, to concentrate on trailers and specialist bodywork. The plant is today owned by Fruehauf Trailers. *RJ*

GRAMM-BERNSTEIN (US) 1912-1930

(1) Gramm-Bernstein Co., Lima, Ohio 1912-1916
(2) Gramm-Bernstein Motor Truck Co., Lima, Ohio 1916-1923
(3) Gramm-Bernstein Motor Truck Corp., Lima, Ohio 1923-1930

B.A. Gramm was a truck pioneer who had made Gramm-Logan and Gramm trucks before starting a new company in conjunction with Max Bernstein.

Early Gramm-Bernsteins came in 2- and 3½-ton sizes, but by 1915 there was a 6-tonner, a large capacity for that time. The company achieved fame during World War I in being one of the two pioneer manufacturers of the US Army Class B Liberty truck (the other was Selden), of which they built about 1000. Civilian Gramm-Bernsteins were made in seven models from 1½ to six tons in 1917, and all had worm drive. Continental engines were mainly used, though Gramm-Bernsteins of the 1920s made use of Lycoming engines as well, and one model was Hinkley-powered. The first British Garner trucks were made by Gramm-Bernstein. During the 1920s a wide range of trucks was made, from 1½ to six tons capacity, with 6-cylinder engines entering the range in 1926. In 1925 B.A. Gramm formed a new company with his son W.J. Gramm, Gramm and Kincaid, and after a few years the Gramm-Bernstein was discontinued. *GNG*

GRAMM-KINCAID (US) 1925-1926

(1) Gramm & Kincaid Motors Inc., Lima, Ohio 1925
(2) Gramm & Kincaid Motors Inc., Delphos, Ohio 1925-1926

This company was formed by B.A. Gramm, after he had left Gramm-Bernstein, in partnership with R.M. Kincaid, formerly vice-president of Garford, another Lima truck company. Their trucks were handsome assembled machines in the one to four ton range, with 4- or 6-cylinder Continental, Lycoming or Hercules engines. In 1926 came a bus chassis with unusually low double drop cruciform-stiffened frame and four wheel brakes. It was made in two forms, a 20-passenger inter-city coach and 21-passenger city bus. After Kincaid left, the company name was changed to Gramm Motors Inc., though possibly some vehicles were still sold with the Gramm-Kincaid name for a while afterwards. *RJ*

GRAMM-LOGAN (US) 1908-1910

Gramm-Logan Motor Car Co, Bowling Green, Ohio

Three models of Gramm-Logan trucks were made, the Model Y 20/24 hp delivery van, the Model V 25 hp 1½-ton truck and the Model X 45 hp 3-ton truck with chain drive. They were designed by B.A. Gramm, and in the latter part of 1910 the company moved to Lima, Ohio and was renamed Gramm. *GNG*

1909 GRAMM-LOGAN 3-ton truck, NAHC

GRANT (US) 1918-1923

Grant Motor Car Corp., Cleveland, Ohio

Grant trucks all used 4-cylinder Continental engines with Grant-Lees 3-speed gearboxes and Torbensen rear axles. In 1918, this line included ¾-, 1½- and 2-tonners on frames with wheelbases up to 160 inches. For 1920, the ¾-tonners were discontinued. *GMN*

GRANT-FERRIS (US) 1901

Grant-Ferris Co., Troy, N.Y.

This was a light van with horizontally-opposed 2-cylinder engine and fast-and-loose pulley transmission. It had a load capacity of 500 lbs. and a speed of 12 mph. *GNG*

GRANTON (GB) 1905-1907

Scottish Motor Engineering Co., Granton Harbour, Edinburgh

This company made a bus chassis powered by a 40 hp 4-cylinder engine with dual ignition, and double chain drive. They also made a truck powered by a 2-cylinder engine. *GNG*

1930 GRASS-PREMIER straight-8 6×4 truck, RJ

GRASS-PREMIER (US) 1923-1937

Grass-Premier Truck Co., Sauk City, Wis.

Made in a small community near Madison, Wisconsin, the Grass-Premier was a low-production assembled truck which managed to stay in production for 14 years. They began with three models, two 1½-tonners and a 3-4-tonner, powered by Continental or Lycoming engines with Clark or Timken axles. The first year's production was fewer than 10 vehicles. By 1926 the series had been broadened to include 2, 2½ and 3½-tonners with 4- and 6-cylinder engines by the same makers as before, while in 1930 they added several heavy-duty models powered by Lycoming straight-8 engines. The range now reached up to 5-, 7-, 10- and 15-tonners included 6-wheelers. Waukesha engines and Wisconsin axles now figured in the specifications, with the need for heavier components. 1932

1936 GRASS-PREMIER Ford V8-engined truck, RJ

saw the widest range yet, from one tonners to 12 ton tractors. A short-lived novelty promising at the time was Grass-Premier's Ford V-8-powered cab-over-engine truck of 1935. The object was to make a heavy-duty chassis (3½-5 tons) using the easily maintained Ford engine and other components for heavy-duty service such as Timken axles, Warner and Fuller transmissions, assembled into a rugged chassis. The cab on this model had similar lines to that of the contemporary Available COE. Four of these trucks were supplied to a Chicago operator but the Ford-powered COE never figured in Grass-Premier's published specifications. *RJ*

GRAY (US) 1923-1925
Gray Motor Corp., Detroit, Mich.
Two commercial versions were made of the Gray car, both using the 4-cylinder 2.7-litre sv engine that powered the firm's passenger cars. The ½-ton van was built on the car chassis with an 104 inch wheelbase, while the 1-ton version used an extended wheelbase of 120 inches. *GNG*

GRAY'S (US) 1911
Gray's Motor Co., Newark, NJ
This was a 1-tonner with a 24 hp, 2-cylinder engine and a planetary transmission. Pneumatic tires were standard and the wheelbase was 103 inches. *GMN*

GREAT EAGLE (US) 1911-1914
United States Carriage Co., Columbus, Ohio
Great Eagle was the name of a line of passenger cars and on the same chassis, was also built a variety of special service vehicles which included funeral coaches, ambulances and patrol wagons. These used the standard passenger car chassis, either that for Model 4-50 or the Model 6-60. The latter, with 6-cylinder, 60 hp Rutenber engine and ambulance body and on chassis of 138 inch wheelbase, sold for $4250. Very elaborate coachwork was used for the funeral cars. *GMN*

GREAT SOUTHERN (US)1915-1917
Great Southern Automobile Company, Birmingham, Alabama
This commercial vehicle was proceeded by several years of publicity before building its first product, a 25-passenger bus. The 2- and 4-tonners used underslung worm-drive to give minimum frame height. This resulted in minimum clearance of only seven inches. The Great Southern was one of the few commercial vehicles built in the deep south. *GMN*

GREAT WESTERN (US) 1911-1912
Great Western Transportation Co., Chicago, Ill
The sparse information on this gasoline-electric truck indicates it was a 10-tonner with a wheelbase of 172 inches. Its solid rubber tires were 48x12 for all four wheels. *GMN*

GREBESTEIN (D) 1929-1931
Mitteldeutsche Schlepperwerke Johann Grebestein, Eschwege
A diesel engined tractor using 2- or 4- stroke engines of 30 hp was produced by this firm. *HON*

GREEN (GB) 1906-1911
Thomas Green & Sons Ltd., Smithfield Ironworks, Leeds
Although noted mainly for road rollers Green built six steam tractors between 1906 and 1911, of which two were

c.1908 GREEN 5-ton compound tractor, RAW

single cylindered and the remainder compounds, all (except one 6-ton for export) being built to the 5-ton weight limit. *RAW*

GREENWOOD (GB) 1907
J.W. Greenwood Ltd., Halifax, Yorks.
This company built a 5 cwt light van powered by a 6 hp single-cylinder de Dion Bouton engine, with 3-speed gearbox and chain drive. *GNG*

GREENWOOD & BATLEY (GB) 1907-1908
Greenwood & Batley Ltd., Leeds, Yorks.
This old-established electrical engineering firm built an experimental gas-electric bus powered by a 35 hp 4-cylinder Mutel engine generating current for two electric motors. They also made chassis for Electromobile taxicabs. *GNG*

1902 GRETHER fire engine, GNG

GRETHER (D) 1902
Grether & Co., Freiburg, Baden
The Grether was a fire engine powered by a 15 hp 2-cylinder Deutz engine, with two speeds and chain drive. It had two clutches, one connecting the engine with the drive system, the other with a triple-acting pump mounted in the center of the vehicle. It could be driven from either the left-hand front seat or a platform at the rear, and there were seats for four firemen. The pump could throw a jet of water 160 feet, and deliver at the rate of 165 gpm. *GNG*

GREYHOUND (US) 1914-1915
Greyhound Cyclecar Co., Toledo, Ohio
This was a typical cyclecar fitted with a van body, using an unmodified passenger car chassis. It was driven by a 4-cylinder, 10 hp water-cooled engine. Shaft drive was used, after a planetary transmission. Track was only 2 feet, 6 inches with wheelbase of 104 inches. Weight of this vehicle was 650 pounds and its price $385. *GMN*

GROUT (US) 1901-1905

(1) Grout Brothers, Orange, Mass. 1901-1903
(2) Grout Brothers Automobile Co., Orange, Mass. 1904-1905

Grout steam trucks came in several capacities and were of the cab-over design with the narrow one-man semi-enclosed "pilot house" centered on the platform and ahead of the front axle, with the center steering wheel horizontal. The pilot house was tall, about twice the height of the long steering column, with an overhanging roof in front and tall rectangular window in the three sides.

For their 2½-ton model, the engine was a 12 hp slide-valve type midway in the truck, with a 15 hp fire-tube boiler, 24 inches in diameter by 16 inches high, under the driver's seat. 26 gallons of kerosene and enough water for 20 miles running were carried to operate it at a speed of six to eight mph and on grades up to 15 degrees.

The drive was by chain to countershaft and then by chain to each rear wheel. *RW*

G.R.P. (F) 1923-1928

G. et R. Paul, Paris 15e

Built by Georges and Rene Paul, the G.R.P. taxicab was the first in Paris to be provided with front wheel brakes as standard. It was powered by a 1690cc 4-cylinder ohv S.C.A.P. engine with 4-speed gearbox in unit, and was normally supplied in landaulette form. *GNG*

GRUBE see I.F.A.

1970 GRUMMAN Model B-100 19-seater bus, MBS

GRUMMAN (US) 1963 to date

Grumman Allied Industries Inc., Garden City, N.Y.

The Grumman aerospace company bought the J.B. Olson Corp, makers of aluminum alloy truck bodies, and launched a line of aluminum-bodied vans under the name Grumman Kurbmaster. These were in addition to Olson aluminum bodies supplied on regular chassis/cab units by well-known manufacturers. While Kurbmasters use chassis by such manufacturers as Ford, Chevrolet and G.M.C. they are of distinctive design and are sold only by Grumman dealers. In 1970 a 19-passenger bus was added to the Kurbmaster range, and in 1978 the vans came in a wide range of wheelbases from 102 to 178 inches. *GNG*

GTS (NL) 1973

GIHO B.V., De Klomp.

A not so successful specimen of that typical Dutch breed of U.S. Army truck reconditioners was the GTS, built by Giho, still well-known U.S. truck parts merchants. They came in 1973 with a 6x6 vehicle using the German Karmann cab mounted on the normal control Hanomag-Henschel trucks, but only a few prototypes were eventually built. *JFJK*

GUAZZONI (I) 1949-c.1964

Officine Meccaniche Guazzoni, Milan

In addition to their motorcycles, Guazzoni offered a simple light delivery 3-wheeler with single front wheel, chain drive, four forward speeds, and a 163 cc 2-stroke engine. *MCS*

GUILDER (US) 1924-1936

Guilder Engineering Co., Poughkeepsie, N.Y.

The Guilder was a development of the Goodwin truck built by the Goodwin Car Mfg Co. of Poughkeepsie. This company specialized in railway rolling stock, switching in 1922 to a line of heavy-duty trucks, quite striking vehicles with big cast-aluminum radiators. Guilder was an engineer in the firm, and his name first appeared on a vehicle with the announcement in December 1922 of a bus chassis called the Goodwin-Guilder. This was an advanced design with a drop-frame whose side rails were complex one-piece pressings, costly to produce. By contrast the better-known Fageol Safety Coach, announced a few months later, had fabricated side rail arches initially. Power for the Goodwin-Guilder was a Buda engine.

The Guilder emerged as a make in its own right in 1924, with truck and bus chassis powered by Hercules, Buda and Continental engines, Timken and Shuler axles. By 1927 load capacities ranged from 1¼-to 7-tons, and by the 1930's 8-10 and 12-16-ton 6-wheelers were being offered, together with 21-, 25- and 30-passenger bus chassis. At this time Guilder began to make a complex trailing third axle adaptable to all makes of truck but particularly fitted to Fords, Internationals and Autocars. Because of their concentration on these axles, truck production, never high, declined steeply during the years 1930 to 1936. *RJ*

GUILLIERME (F) 1906-1908

Automobiles Guillierme, Paris

This company made passenger cars and commercial vehicles, the latter being delivery vans with engine under seat and chain drive. Two models were offered, a 10/12 hp for 500 kg loads, and a 15/17 hp for 1200 kg loads. *GNG*

GULDNER (D) 1969-1971

Guldner Motorenwerke, Zweigniederl der Gesellschaft fur Linde's Eismaschinen, Aschaffenburg

The hydraulic transmission of this vehicle — which was also known as "Hydrocar" — was the main feature of this construction. Payload capacities available were 2½, 3 and 4 tons. *HON*

GURGEL (BR) 1976 to date

Gurgel Veiculos, Sao Paulo

This company began as a maker of Volkswagen-powered beach buggies, but has now added a range of light commercial vehicles, usually with VW engines, square-tube space frame chassis and VW suspension using coil springs instead of torsion bars. A wide variety of bodies are offered, including pick-ups, vans and special adaptations such as fire engines. At the 1978 Sao Paulo Motor Show a mini-articulated van was shown, intended for commercial travellers who could leave their samples in the trailer while they used the tractor part for personal transportation. *GNG*

GURNEY (GB) 1828-1832

Sir Goldsworthy Gurney, London

After some initial experiments Gurney built a steam carriage using his own design of coke fire double drum water tube boiler in conjunction with an undertype double cylinder engine, one rear wheel being keyed to the crankshaft and the other running free though provided with a device to cause it to drive when required. Subsequently he made a separate steam tractor quite distinct from the coach and it was with vehicles of this type that Sir Charles Dance ran a service for four months in 1831 between Gloucester and Cheltenham until prevented by the turnpike authorities. Gurney's works were in Albany Street, near Regents Park. *RAW*

1952 GUTBROD Atlas 600kg truck, GNG

GUTBROD (D) 1946-1954; 1976 to date

(1) Gutbrod Motorenbau GmbH., Plochingen; Calw 1946-1954

(2) Gutbrod-Werke GmbH., Bubingen 1976 to date

Before WW II Gutbrod produced vans under the name of Standard. In 1946 a new version with a 4-cylinder opposed engine of 500 cc was presented, the engine was placed behind the rear axle. In 1949 capacity was enlarged to 577 cc, but a 2-cylinder engine was used. Type designations were "Heck 504" and "Heck 604." A version with forward control cabin, the "Atlas 800" was the successor, the engine again being the 2-cylinder 577 cc and again placed behind the rear axle. The "Atlas 1000" followed with increased payload capacity and a 662 cc engine. In 1953 the type 1000/3 appeared. This had a 3-cylinder 990 cc engine and pick up, van and micro-bus versions were available.

In 1954 production of automobiles was given up and only machines for cleaning and agricultural purposes were built. In 1976 a new small all-purpose vehicle, the "Kommutrac 34" was presented. It can be used as a small tractor and with various applications for a wide range of municipal duties. *HON*

GUY (GB) 1914 to date

(1) Guy Motors Ltd., Fallings Park, Wolverhampton, Staffs 1914-1960

(2) Guy Motors (Europe) Ltd., 1961-1964

(3) Guy Motors Ltd., 1965-1968

(4) Division of British Leyland 1968 to date

Sydney Guy had been works manager of the Sunbeam Motor Car Co. when he started the company bearing his own name in 1914. Initial production was of advanced 30 cwt and 2-ton chassis for goods and passenger work. They had White and Poppe engines on highly articulated three point mounted subframes (a Guy feature for many years), road speed, as opposed to engine speed, governors worked off the propellor shaft, overdrive fourth gear, and bevel and spur double reduction back axles to reduce floor height. These models were made with few changes until 1922, apart from two years during the war, when only armaments were produced. In 1920 a 2½-tonner was introduced, and this with lighter models were to be Guy's staple goods production through the twenties, though all sorts of one-offs and colonial vehicles were also made. These included a cross-country farmers truck with retractable wheel strakes in 1920, battery electric trucks between 1922 and 1925, twin engined tractors for working on road or rail in 1923, producer gas-driven trucks from 1927, and all manner of military types. These included half-track trucks from 1924, 6-wheeled armored car chassis in 1928, and 6x6 and 8x8 designs in 1931, as well as Guy's successful subsidy pattern 3-ton 6x4 produced in large quantities from 1926.

Early passenger chassis were identical to those for goods, though from 1921 the road speed governor was omitted. However, from 1922 Guy began to develop separate passenger models, the first being a small-wheeled, low-loading charabanc for holiday resorts. This was followed in 1924 by one of the first drop-frame passenger chassis to be produced in Britain, and in 1926 by a drop-frame 6-wheeler, of which several hundred were built during the next five years. Though Guy normally built their own engines, or bought them from the neighboring Meadows factory, many of these 6-wheel buses, as well as some 4-wheelers in 1925, had Knight sleeve-valve engines produced by Daimler. Guy's own engines had an unusual inclined side valve layout, and often had a cylinder head canted to one side to allow for this feature. In 1926, Guy introduced the world's first pneumatic tired 6-wheeled trolleybus, and these remained in production until after the acquisition of Sunbeam Trolleybuses by Guy in 1948.

1927 GUY Model FBB 30 seater bus, BR

In 1927 Guy produced a 4-wheel double deck bus, which in common with many of the passenger models, was given offset transmission to reduce gangway height in 1929, when many of its mechanical components were also used in Guy's heaviest goods transport model, a 6-tonner. Thereafter Guy moved into the still heavier goods market with an 11-ton 6-wheeler, again based on the bus, whilst by 1930 over 200 major British fleets included Guy buses.

In 1927 Guy had taken over their car and commercial vehicle neighbors, Star, though due to expensive production methods, and the slump, Guy stopped Star production in 1932.

The light goods and passenger models had been replaced by the 20-seat, 30 cwt. and 2-ton ON range in

1927 GUY 20-seater speed model coach, OMM

1928 GUY 2½-tonner animal ambulance, OMM

1929, and in 1933 they were in turn replaced by the Wolf. This had a 4-cylinder Meadows engine and carried two tons, whilst a heavier contemporary model was a 6-tonner which could have Guy 4- or 6-cylinder gasoline or Gardner diesel engines.

Although the rigid 6-wheel buses were a Guy speciality until 1930, they also built some more conventional 32-seat forward control 4-wheelers from 1926, followed by the Invincible double-decker, and in 1933 completely revised their 4-wheel heavy bus program with the Arab for single or double deck bodywork. These used the Gardner 5LW or 6LW diesel as standard, a make of engine that had first been offered in the 1931 Goliath 11 tonner.

1930 GUY Model FCAX 7-ton 6-wheel van with trailer, OMM

1934 GUY 4-ton Luton van, OMM

For a manufacturer producing quality vehicles in hundreds rather than thousands per year, Guys were always remarkably cheap, and the Wolf was highly successful in the 3-ton market at only £239. It was joined by the Vixen 3/4-tonner in 1934 which could be powered by the Dorman 4-cylinder diesel. In 1935 came the Otter 4½-tonner with an enlarged version of the Wolf's engine, and its trailing axle 6-wheel sister, the 5-ton Fox, as well as an enlarged 4-wheeler at the top of the range for 7½ tons.

On the passenger vehicle side Guy adopted the Cotal electro-magnetic 4-speed epicyclic gearbox, which was produced under license by Beans Industries. It incorporated a pre-selective system evolved by Guy which simply involved switching to the gear required and then pressing the clutch pedal.

Guy were not very successful with their heavy goods vehicles in the Thirties, and these were suspended in 1936 in favor of a military design which employed a high proportion of components, and the Meadows engine, from the Wolf/Vixen range. The Ant, as it was called,was a 4x2 truck for 15-cwt. loads with minimal styling, but cheap and rugged. From 1938, it replaced all Guy's other models with the exception of the Arab bus, and some 6x4 military trucks. It was produced in 4x4 form after 1937 as the Quad-Ant, mainly as a gun tractor. With rear engine, it was the basis of 4x4 armoured cars, which were the first to have welded armour plate, a process evolved by Guy.

1941 GUY Vix-Ant 8-ton articulated truck, OMM

Quantity production of these was, however, undertaken by Humber. Wartime production also included a few heavier 4x4 Lizard vehicles with Gardner engines, and versions of the Ant for essential civilian transport from 1941 called the Vix-Ant. Total production for the wartime services, made possible by a moving track assembly line installed in 1939, was almost 13,500 vehicles, and on top of this over 2000 Arab doubledeck buses were produced for essential fleet replacements. These were simplified and strengthened for extra long service life, and because of a shortage of lightweight metals, weighed 20 percent more in chassis form than their pre-war namesakes.

1948 GUY Vixen 4-ton truck, OMM

1949 GUY Wolf 3-ton van, OMM

At the end of the war the Wolf and Vixen were revived, followed by a new Otter 6-tonner in 1950. This had a Gardner 4LK diesel with the option of the Perkins P6.

Because of Gardner engine shortages, Guy and Meadows jointly evolved a 10.35-litre diesel for the Arab in 1948, and in 1950 an underfloor Gardner engined version of the Arab became available. Meanwhile in Mark IV form in 1949 the Arab acquired streamlined frontal styling with the traditional Guy radiator fared in and a stylized version of the traditional Indian's head radiator mascot fitted. Other Guy passenger vehicle products were conventional Vixens for London Transport in 1953, bearing a close resemblance to the contemporary Ford Thames, whilst in the same year the Arab could again be specified with traditional styling. From 1948 Wilson pre-select gearboxes were offered in the passenger models and

1950 GUY Arab Mark 111 33-seater coach, AJHB

from 1952 a lightweight underfloor engined Arab LUF chassis was produced, which after 1956 was gradually replaced by the new Warrior LUF. In 1957 Guy had the distinction of building ten of the largest doubledeck buses of the time for Johannesburg. They seated 105 passengers on 6-wheel chassis with Rolls-Royce 12.17-litre diesel engines. Guy had a thriving export bus trade and produced numerous other special types including the lightweight Perkins engined Seal as well as the heavier Victory single decker and versions of Meadows and Guy engined Arabs.

However, their traditional home market bus business was severely damaged by the revolutionary Wolfrunian of 1958, which was intended to replace the Arab, but which failed to live up to its reliability, and was expensive to develop. It was the first British commercial vehicle to feature disc brakes and air suspension, and was initially powered by a mid-mounted Leyland 150-bhp horizontal diesel engine, though Gardner engines were used in most production versions.

Meanwhile the medium weight goods models continued, acquiring steel cabs in 1952, and after a 20 year gap were once more joined by a heavy range in 1954. These used a high proportion of AEC parts, including chassis and axles, plus Gardner and later Meadows engines. They were available as 4-,6-or 8-wheelers and were given the pre-war model name Goliath, though after objections from the German manufacturer using the same name, this was changed to Invincible in 1955. To fill the gap between the 6-ton Otter and the smallest Goliath, a 10-tonner, the Meadows engined Big Otter appeared, though by the time production started in 1955 it had become the Warrior.

1957 GUY Invincible 15-ton 8-wheel truck, OMM

In 1957 a new heavy articulated tractor briefly appeared, the Meadows 8-litre engined Formidable with Boalloy cab, while in 1958 all the Otter, Warrior and Invincible goods models were revised with glass-fibre cabs. The lighter models did not sell well, although a lightweight AEC-engined 4-axle version of the Warrior was a success, whilst the Invincible range was extended to include normal control export and heavy haulage tractors with Rolls Royce and Cummins engines.

Sydney Guy had died in 1957, and following the unsuccessful Wulfrunian and the expense of developing the new goods range, Guy got into financial difficulties and was bought by Jaguar Cars Ltd. in 1961, following their purchase of Daimler a year earlier. Soon afterwards the Meadows engine and transmission firm also joined the Group.

1965 GUY Invincible 15-ton 8-wheel truck, OMM

The Otter, Warrior and Invincible range continued until 1967, though few of the lighter models, by now powered by BMC diesel engines, or the Leyland engined 4- and 6-wheel Warriors were built.

Jaguar's first step was to simplify the Wulfrunian and to introduce a Mark V version of the Arab, some of which were later to use Daimler Daimatic semi-automatic gearboxes. Then in 1964 a brand new Big J heavy goods range appeared. These had steel tilt cabs and Cummins engines, which Jaguar initially intended to produce under license from the manufacturer. A fixed cab Gardner engined version was also available.

Following the Jaguar Group's merger with British Motor Holdings, Guy were intended as the new Group's heavy goods vehicle division, but the subsequent Leyland takeover in 1968 changed this plan. However, as the other members of the Truck and Bus Division made

1974 GUY Big J8 30-ton GVW 8-wheel truck, British Leyland

increasingly sophisticated vehicles, the Guy Big J changed very little over the years and came to earn a reputation for rugged and rather spartan simplicity. Engines came from AEC, Rolls Royce, Perkins, Leyland, Gardner and Cummins, and a number of extra heavy duty export variations were produced, including a 350 hp 8-wheeler for up to 56 tons gross train weight in 1970.

In 1975 British Leyland announced that when demand for the Big J range dwindled, it would not be replaced, and the last were made a year later. However Guy continues to make components for other members of the group and ckd chassis for overseas assembly, like the single and double deck Victory under the Leyland name. *OM*

GUYMAR (GB) 1935

The Guymar was a light 3-wheeler delivery van with single front wheel, powered by a single-cylinder 598 cc Phelon & Moore engine which, with the Burman 3-speed gearbox, was mounted at the extreme rear of the van. Final drive was by spur gear to the rear axle. The Guymar had a tubular frame, and the carrying capacity was 8-10 cwt. *GNG*

GUZZI see Moto Guzzi

1914 G.V. (i) 1000 lb. electric van, NAHC

G. V. (i) (US) 1906-1920

General Vehicle Co., Long Island City, L.I., NY

The G.V. battery-powered electrics were produced in a bewildering array of models. For 1907, nine different types were offered, from flatbed trucks to a "Chatsworth bus". G.V. electrics ran the gamut of sizes from vans with rated capacity of 750 lbs. to 5-tonners for brewery service. G.V. apparently manufactured their own wet-cell batteries but used General Electirc motors which were mounted amidships and drove the rear wheels by roller chains. For at least one year (1916), G.V. built gasoline-electric tractors for the New York Sanitation Dept. General Vehicle Co. succeeded the previous Vehicle Equipment Co. also of Long Island City. *GMN*

G.V. (ii) (GB) 1916-1935

General Vehicle Co., Hay Mills, Birmingham; Tyseley, Birmingham.

First produced in America in 1906 GV electrics were introduced into Britain in 1916 and were based on a design that had been current for almost 10 years. Five models of 10-cwt, 1-ton, 2-ton, 3½-ton and 5-ton capacity were offered with either Ironclad or Edison batteries ranging in capacity from 133 to 450AH over the range. The vehicles were of forward driver position with batteries slung beneath the frame amidships. The single motor was positioned just ahead of the rear axle and drive was by means of chain to a countershaft and thence by side chains to the rear wheels, except in the case of the 10 cwt which was worm driven.

From 1921 the 10 cwt and one ton models were dropped from the range presumably through lack of sales,

1925 G.V. (ii) 10-ton articulated electric Truck, OMM

although the larger models became very popular with brewers, municipalities and railway companies. Something of a stir in the field of electrics was caused by the introduction of the "Giant" articulated six wheeler in 1924. This 10 ton payload vehicle consisted of a 90 inch wheelbase tractor unit coupled to a drop frame semi-trailer, the whole outfit being 38 ft. overall. As with the medium capacity models the vehicle was driven by a single motor with outside chain final drive. The 500AH rated battery was located in a large box at the rear of the driver's cab above the frame.

Another "first" followed in 1930 with the introduction of a rigid six wheel chassis for carrying a large tipping refuse body for Birmingham Corporation. In this model the single motor drive was retained but final drive was by means of a propellor shaft to the two overhead worm axles, a practice that had been introduced in 1926.

A revision in the range in 1934 provided models of 5/7-cwt, 10/15-cwt, 15/20-cwt and 25/30-cwt with worm or spiral bevel back axles. The smallest was of the type with driver standing at the rear of the small box body. With things being at a very low ebb in the industry. G.V. soon faded from the scene. *OM*

G. V. MERCEDES (US) 1913-1918

General Vehicle Co., Long Island City, NY

Initially known as American Daimler, this gasoline-engined truck was mader under license from the German company. The lone model, a 6-tonner appears to have been a direct copy of the European truck, including Teutonic-type cast steel wheels. It used a 4-cylinder, water-cooled engine of 5.4 litre capacity. Wheelbase was 169 inches with a tread of 5 feet, 1 inch. A 4-speed gearbox was used with shaft drive. Even in its final year of production, kerosene lamps and hand-cranking were maintained, a surprising lack of progress for this company which specialized in electric commercial vehicles. Fitting for the years of production, the standard color was termed Lead. *GMN*

G.W.K. (GB) 1914-1924

(1) G.W.K. Ltd., Datchet, Bucks 1914
(2) G.W.K. Ltd., Maidenhead, Berks 1914-1924

The friction-driven G.W.K. was an early example of a rear-engined light van. Powered by an 1100cc watercooled vertical-twin Coventry-Simplex engine, it offered a 5-cwt payload and a 46 cu. ft. loading space. By 1918 the company, while retaining their infinitely variable gear, had switched to a front vertical 1.4-litre 4-cylinder engine of the same make, and a light van was soon added to the range. A trial order for 50 was placed by the GPO, but these proved troublesome and drivers accustomed to horses had acclimatisation difficulties. The model was still quoted in 1924. In 1930 G.W.K tried their hand at a 3-wheeler industrial truck, also friction-driven, but this came to nothing. *MCS*

G.W.W. (US) 1920-1925

Wilson Truck Mfg Co., Henderson, Iowa

This was a small-scale truck assembler using a Weidley engine in the 1½-ton chassis and Wisconsin SU in the 1½-2-ton model made from 1924 to 1925. The smaller model was also listed as a bus chassis. *GNG*

GWYNNE (GB) 1922-1928

Gwynne's Engineering Co. Ltd., Chiswick, London W.4

Gwynne's principal business was pumps, which they supplied to Dennis for use on the company's early fire-engines. Cars were added to their line in 1922, but the only complete commercial vehicle offered was a miniature fire tender on their 950 cc ohv light-car chassis. The Gwynne pump was driven by its own clutch and separate propeller shaft. *MCS*

1903 HAGEN (ii) 2/3-ton tanker, NMM

H.A.C. see Arran

HAGEN (i) (GB) 1898-1900

A. Dougill & Co. Ltd., Leeds

Between the dates mentioned above Dougills offered an undertype vertical boilered steam wagon under the name of Hagen, though whether as manufacturers or sales agents is not clear and no further details are known to survive. *RAW*

HAGEN (ii) (D) 1902-1903

Rudolf Hagen & Cie. GmbH., Koln-Mungersdorf

This firm produced trucks and buses. Unique was the lever transmission. A single cylinder engine was used. The design was sold to Helios (q.v.) *HON*

HAGEN (iii) (D) 1903-1908

Kolner Accumulatorenwerke Gottfried Hagen, Cologne-Kalk

Electric vehicles were a speciality of this firm which already before built electric batteries. There were vans and trucks with one and three ton payload capacities. Fire engines, street cleaners and hotel buses were also available. Vehicles were also marketed under the names of K.A.W. and Urbanus. *HON*

HAHN (US) 1907 to date

(1) W.G. Hahn & Bro., Hamburg, Pa., 1907-1913
(2) Hahn Motor Truck & Wagon Co., Hamburg, Pa., 1913-1920
(3) Hahn Motor Truck Co., Hamburg, Pa., 1920-1926
(4) Hahn Motor Truck Corp., Allentown, Pa., 1927-1930
(5) Selden Hahn Motor Truck Corp., Allentown, Pa., 1930-1931
(6) Hahn Motors, Inc., Hamburg, Pa., 1931 to date

After building one truck and one automobile in his wagon works in 1907, W.G. Hahn decided to build trucks as well as wagons. Truck production was minimal prior to 1913. Hahn built conventional chain drive trucks powered by the Continental 4-cylinder engine. The 1½-ton chassis cost $2,400 in 1914.

Five models from 1500-pound to 3½-ton capacity were built from 1915, when Hahn also began building fire apparatus. A 5-ton model filled out the line in 1918. Hahn

c.1915 HAHN chemical fire truck, Hahn

used worm drive from 1916, although the first 5-ton trucks had chain drive. Postwar inflation resulted in a chassis price of $10,000 for the 5-ton truck in 1920.

1919 HAHN 2½-ton truck, Hahn

In 1922 Hahn offered eight models from 1-ton to 6-ton with prices from $1,750 to $4,650. Production in the 1920's averaged 600 trucks per year until 1927 and increased thereafter. Hercules engines were used from 1923. When the first 6-cylinder models were introduced in 1926,

Continental and Hercules engines were used in both the 4-cylinder and 6-cylinder lines. Hahn offered 27 and 35-passenger bus chassis with the 6-cylinder Continental engine and a 20-passenger bus chassis with the 4-cylinder Hercules engine.

Hahn took over the former Bethlehem plant in Allentown in 1927 and moved their offices there, although the Hamburg plant was continued. A line of trucks with the 6-cylinder Continental engine was announced in August, 1929. Seven models priced from $1,098 for the ¾-ton to $4,950 for the 5-ton were offered. All models featured 4-wheel hydraulic brakes and a distinctive cast aluminum radiator shell. A merger with Selden lasted 16 months, during which time some Hahn models were offered under both name plates.

Hahn returned to Hamburg in 1931 and retrenched in their own factory. Some trucks built in the early 1930's were powered by the 4½-litre Franklin 6-cylinder engine. Hahn concentrated on fire apparatus from 1933, although a complete line of trucks powered by the Waukesha 6-cylinder engine was offered on special order until 1941.

During World War II, Hahn manufactured mobile machine shops and special recovery trucks for the U.S. Engineer Corps. Hahn's only post-war truck production consisted of a large order of delivery trucks built on Ford chassis for United Parcel Service. Since 1948 the firm has limited manufacture to a line of custom fire apparatus.

1968 HAHN ladder truck, GNG

Since the 1950's the forward control cab has been used to increase chassis space for the many new pieces of fire fighting equipment. Chassis and body are of Hahn manufacture; engines used are either Detroit Diesel or Waukesha gasoline. Production in the early 1970's has averaged 100 custom fire engines a year. *DJS*

HAL-FUR (US) 1919-1931

(1) Hal-Fur Motor Truck Co., Cleveland, Ohio
(2) Hal-Fur Motor Truck Co., Canton, Ohio

For most of its life this company produced typical light and medium-duty trucks with Hinkley 4-cylinder engines, Brown-Lipe transmissions and Timken worm or bevel axles. Sizes were 1 to 3½ tons, and there was also a tractor for 3-ton semi-trailer work. In 1928 they introduced their Model 6YB 6-wheeler with 6-cylinder Hinkley engine, Hal-Fur's own bogie suspension, air brakes and balloon tires all round. The tires were singles even on the bogie. Claimed to be the world's largest moving van, the 6YB was rated at 6 tons. Later Hal-Furs were handsome vehicles with four-piece, bolted cast-aluminum radiators of Rolls-Royce pattern. Production was little more than 50 units annually, falling off to a handful by the end. *RJ*

HALL (US) 1915-1922

Lewis-Hall Iron Works, Detroit, Mich.

This brand of trucks was mainly of large capacity, from 2-tonners to 7-tonners. However, for the first two years, only 3½- and 5-tonners were offered, the 3½-tonner with either worm-drive or double chain-drive. By 1918, only the 7-tonner still used chain-drive while the smaller versions all had worm-drive. All models used 4-cylinder Continental engines and 3-speed gearboxes. Very few changes were made in the models from the beginning to the end. *GMN*

HALLEY (GB) 1901-1935

(1) Glasgow Motor Lorry Co. Ltd., Glasgow 1901-1906
(2) Halley's Industrial Motors Ltd., Yoker, Glasgow 1906-1927
(3) Halley Motors Ltd., Yoker, Glasgow 1928-1935

The most interesting feature of Halley steam trucks (made between about 1901 and 1907) was the patent vertical boiler of 1904 in which a water jacket round the firebox was linked to an upper water space, containing vertical fire-tubes, by means of vertical water tubes spaced around the upper firebox. Apart from the boiler the wagons which were undertypes of 3 and 5-ton capacity had Ackermann steering, compound engines, twin roller chain final drive and a steam brake. Some early steamers were known as "Glasgow" wagons. A few gasoline driven vehicles were produced by Halley during their early years at Finnieston, Glasgow where they adjoined the original Albion factory. However, following their decision to abandon steamers the company was reconstituted in 1906 and moved to Yoker, Glasgow. In 1907 their foresight was rewarded by Gold and Silver medals in the 2-ton and 30-cwt classes of the RAC Trials, one being given a special prize for "simplicity and freedom from liability to derangement".

They produced a wide range of commercial vehicles before the Great War including chassis for 1-6 tons and 10-40 passengers and even a pioneer mobile home in 1911.

The lightest vehicles had shaft-drive and 2-cylinder Crossley engines. Tylor engines were used in the larger chain-drive models, gradually giving way to Halley engines from 1911. These were produced at Linwood and had dual magneto and battery and coil ignition. Halley were very early users of 6-cylinder engines in commercial chassis and a 60/70 hp version was employed in a charabanc model of 1911. They were also used in fire engines, which became an important part of Halley's business from 1910. Halley were able to produce around ten vehicles per week by 1912, and though primarily successful in

1914 HALLEY 2½-ton truck, OMM

Scotland, their vehicles also had limited sales in England and the Colonies.

During the First World War their three ton trucks became better known south of the border as a result of some 400 being supplied to the War Department and many more impressed from civilian operators.

After the War Halley decided on an unwise one-model policy based on a 3½-ton or 25-35 seat worm-drive chassis introduced in 1920. This was unique among standard British commercial chassis in having a 6-cylinder engine.

In the slump in new vehicle sales which followed the War this refined but expensive eccentricity plus the death of the founder, George Halley, in 1921 caused a rapid reversal from former models. From 1922 many of these were available in forward control form. Municipal vehicles,

1923 HALLEY sprinkler/gulley emptier, OMM

some with forward control half-cabs, plus fire engines helped Halley out of their difficulties. The 6-cylinder engine found a new lease of life when special high-speed coach chassis became popular in 1925, and to cater for this market Halley introduced the Kenilworth 31 seater and the Ivanhoe charabanc chassis, while the Talisman was a contemporary 4-cylinder 20 seater. In 1925 Halley also produced a chassis to comply with the War Office 30-cwt Subsidy.

In 1926 the company once more ran into financial difficulties but was reformed. Five years later it was saved again by the North British Locomotive Company.

In 1928, a new and exceptionally efficient and economical 4-cylinder 85 hp engine embodying Ricardo combustion chamber patents was introduced and this was adopted in many of the goods chassis and in a new bus called the Conqueror which replaced the former Marmion 32-seater. In the same year rigid 6-wheel buses were offered which, by 1929, had acquired the model name Challenger and could be fitted with double or single deck bodywork. The Conqueror had a chromed radiator of the vee-shape that had been a Halley feature since 1925. In 1931 these all gave way to a radiator design with a wider top than bottom with a very narrow chrome surround and a Scottish lion on the badge. Among the first vehicles with this revised styling were the Neptune double deck and Clansman single deck 115 hp 6-cylinder passenger vehicles. Neither was successful in the face of competition from the new diesel buses on the market, though the 4- and 6-cylinder goods models continued to sell moderately well and from 1929 included a rigid 6-wheel 8-tonner, the BS3. Fire engines and municipal vehicles also continued to be produced.

For 1934 the range covered 4 to 13-ton goods and 26 to 51 seat passenger models including new 6½ and 4½ ton

1934 HALLEY B60 4-ton tanker, OMM

models. At the Scottish Show that year Halley exhibited a 4-ton chassis employing the Perkins Leopard diesel engine, but this innovation came too late to save the firm and in September 1935 they went into liquidation. The company was then bought by Albion Motors Ltd., who retained the factory for their own expansion, but sold Halley's goodwill and spares and produced no further Halley vehicles. The last was a fire engine for Clydebank Brigade. *RAW/OM*

HALLFORD (GB) 1907-1925

J. & E. Hall Ltd. Dartford, Kent

The Dartford Ironworks of J. & E. Hall was founded in 1785. Among other activities in the 19th Century they made marine steam engines and, from 1888, refrigeration units. In 1907 they entered the commercial vehicle market with a conventional 3-ton chain-driven truck which was largely a Saurer, though with a number of modifications including Hallford's own design of cast aluminum radiator shell. Some early chassis were fitted with double deck bus bodies while an important development of 1909 was the association between Hall and W.A. Stevens Ltd. of Maidstone, England, makers of electrical equipment. The Hallford-Stevens was a gasoline-electric chassis in which the gearbox and final drive were replaced by dynamo and electric motors mounted on each side of the frame, driving the rear wheels by worm gear. These vehicles were made in small numbers up to 1911 when the Stevens works were

1910 HALLFORD 4-ton truck, OMM

acquired by Thomas Tilling for the manufacture of complete vehicles under the name Tilling-Stevens.

By 1911 Halls were making engines of their own design in three sizes, the 25 hp CC, 32 hp EA and 40 hp EE, all 4-cylinder pair-cast units. These powered a range of trucks extending from 35 cwt to 5 tons. All had 4-speed gearboxes and chain drive. These were made with little change up to the outbreak of World War I, when Hallford production was devoted entirely to their 3-ton trucks.

1920 HALLFORD 4-ton truck, NMM

Because of the need for maximum production, Hallford only made the chassis, the engines coming from Dorman and White & Poppe. With the end of the war Hallford revived their pre-war range, using the CC engine in a 2½-tonner and the EA and EE in the 4 and 5-tonners. These were made in dwindling numbers up to 1925, still with chain drive, and in the last two years a 10-ton 6-wheeler was listed, although it is not certain if any were made. It was not worth Halls' while to develop a more modern design, and after 1925 they reverted to other activities. These were joined later by the manufacture of elevators and escalators, in which field the nearly 200 year old firm is still active today. *GNG*

HALSEY (US) 1901-1907

(1) Halsey Motor Co., Philadelphia, PA 1901-1902
(2) James T. Halsey, New York, NY 1904
(3) Halsey Motor Vehicle Co., Philadelphia, PA 1905-1907

James T. Halsey designed a heavy steam truck which featured front-wheel-drive and steering. Two single-acting 4-cylinder steam engines drove through spur gears to the front wheels. The vertical water-tube boiler consumed 125 gallons of water every 12 miles. A 12 hp truck built in 1901 proved successful. A second truck was lost in a fire in 1902. Trucks with dual 30 hp 8-cylinder steam engines were built in limited numbers from 1904. A top speed of 6 mph when loaded was claimed for the 8-ton model. Steel-rim wagon wheels were used. *DJS*

HAMPTON (GB) 1914

Hampton Engineering Co. Ltd., King's Norton, Birmingham

Mainly known as passenger car makers, Hampton offered a 10 cwt van on their 12/16 hp 4-cylinder chassis, but as it was announced in September 1914, a month after the outbreak of war, it is unlikely that many were made. *GNG*

HANDY WAGON (US) 1911-1916

Auburn Motor Chassis Company, Auburn, Indiana

The commercial vehicles under this name were both typical high-wheelers and more conventional 1000-pound trucks. The high-wheelers used a two-cylinder, air-cooled engine mounted beneath the body with chain-drive and carrying capacity of 500 to 600 pounds for the Junior and Senior models, respectively. For only two years there was offered a 1000-pound version which used a four-cylinder engine under a hood. *GMN*

HANGER (US) 1915-1916

C.F. Hanger Company, Cleveland, Ohio

The light, 1000-pound capacity Hanger had a worm-drive rear axle. Electric lights and electric starting was available as options. The company was originally the C.F. Hanger Carriage Company and had built auto bodies as early as 1905. *GMN*

HANLEY (US) 1940-1941

Hanley Engineering Service, Prospect, Ohio

Keenan Hanley, former chief engineer for the Prospect Fire Engine Company, formed his own company in 1934 and built a number of small pumpers on commercial chassis. In 1940 he built a quadruple pumper combination powered by a V-16 engine of Marmon design, though built by Hanley. This used GMC sheet metal, but two more V-16s built in 1941, a triple combination and a ladder truck, had custom-built cabs somewhat resembling the postwar Ahrens-Fox. These were the only 16-cylinder fire engines ever made. *GNG*

HANNIBAL (US) 1916

Hannibal Motor Car Co., Hannibal, MO

This truck, from Mark Twain's home town, is listed as a 1-tonner but further data has not been found. *GMN*

HANNO (D) 1936-1950

Hannoversche Fahrzeugfabrik Hoffmann & Co., Hannover-Laatzen

Hanno produced mini-tractors with Junkers and Deutz diesel engines from 1936. After an interruption by the war a new type, again with a Deutz diesel engine, was introduced in 1949, but production did not last for long. *HON*

HANOMAG (D) 1905-1908; 1925-1968
HANOMAG-HENSCHEL (D) 1968-1973

(1) Hannoversche Maschinenbau AG., vorm. Georg Egestorff, Linden nr. Hanover, 1905-1908; 1925-1932
(2) Hanomag Automobil- und Schlepperbau GmbH., Hannover-Linden, 1932-1935
(3) Hannoversche Maschinenbau AG., Hannover-Linden, 1935-1952
(4) Rheinstahl-Hanomag A.G., Hannover-Linden, 1952-1969
(5) Hanomag-Henschel Fahrzeugwerke GmbH., Hanover-Linden; Kassel; Hamburg-Harburg; Bremen, 1969-1973

In 1905 Hanomag took up a license for production of steam vehicles by Peter Stoltz. Other licensees were Gaggenau (q.v.) and Krupp (q.v.), but Hanomag became the one which built quite a considerable number of these vehicles. Mostly trucks were built, but also some buses and one line in Berlin was operated with these buses. Also the first street sprinkler in Germany was mounted on a Hanomag steam chassis.

After this there was a long gap in production of cars which lasted until 1925. A small 2/10 two-seater private car was also available as a small delivery van with a rear mounted box. With the same engine a forward-control truck was introduced in 1925 with a 3/4 ton payload. From the Hanomag agricultural tractors a road version was developed which also appeared in 1925. From 1928 diesel engines of their own manufacture were used in the tractors. In 1933 Hanomag presented a new truck with a COE and an underfloor engine which was placed amidships. This engine was a 4-cylinder diesel engine of 5.2 litres developing 60 hp. Payload capacity was 3__ to 4 tons. Also a bus was available following this layout. The same engine was used for an express road tractor and for a

1934 HANOMAG 4-ton underfloor-engine van, HON

15 t articulated tractor. In 1935 a 20 ton road tractor was developed with a 5-cylinder 8.5 litre diesel engine developing 100 hp. This was very successful and was built until 1950. Various vans were available on private car chassis during the thirties. Also a light road tractor, the

c.1938 HANOMAG SS100 road tractor, BHV

SS 20, was based on a private car, it had a 2 litre diesel engine. In 1950 Hanomag presented their first new model after the war, a 1½tonner with a 4-cylinder diesel engine

1950 HANOMAG 1½-ton truck, Hanomag

of 45hp. This was supplemented by versions of 2, 2½ and 3 tons payload capacity. All had the same engine but output varied from 50 to 70 hp by installing a Roots blower. The 1½ton version also was available as 4x4 truck, the 2½ tonner was the basis for a very handsome bus version.

A new forward control type appeared in 1958 with a payload capacity from 1¾ to 2½ ton. These models carried the names Kurier, Garant and Markant (the two first ones revived from pre-war private cars). In 1963 Hanomag took over Tempo (q.v.) but until 1966 the well-proved front-driven transporter models Matador and Wiking were sold under their old name. A new Hanomag range with various versions was presented in 1967. These were the types F 45, F 55, F 65, and F 75 with 4-cylinder diesel engines of 2,835 cc/65 hp and 3,142 cc/80 hp. They were supplemented by a 6-cylinder version with 4253 cc/100 hp, the types F 55, F 76 and F 85. Payload capacities ranged from 1 3/4 to 5½ tons. The new face was also to be found on the former Tempo transporters which now were designated F 20, F 25, F 30, F 35, all available with 4-cylinder 1622 54 hp gasoline engine or 50 hp diesel

1968 HANOMAG F45 1¾-ton van, GNG

engine. A merger of Hanomag and Henschel took place in 1968, but vehicles were still offered under their original names.

One year later Daimler-Benz took a 51% interest in Hanomag-Henschel and after the foundation of the new firm Hanomag-Henschel Fahrzeugwerke (HHF) all types were offered under this combined name. The models ranged from the ex-Tempo 1-tonner through the Hanomag range from 2 to 5½ tons to the Henschel range from 10 to 22 tons. The Henschel versions were available with normal

1969 HANOMAG F35 2-ton truck, GNG

or forward control cabs, 4x4 drive and 6-wheeled articulated tractors.

In 1970 Daimler-Benz took over Hanomag-Henschel altogether. Mercedes engines were now installed in various types, e.g. the transporter got a 2 litre Mercedes diesel engine but curiously enough also the Austin gasoline engine from Tempo times was still available. Until 1973 production under the name of Hanomag-Henschel was carried on when both names died. But some types were carried on under the Mercedes-Benz brand name, notably the ex-Tempo transporters which were made until 1977. *HON*

● *From 1938 Hanomag built the army standard half-track lorry under license which originally was developed by Hansa-Lloyd.*

HANSA (D) 1906-1914

(1) Hansa Automobil GmbH., Varel, 1906-1913
(2) Hansa Automobil A.G., Varel, 1913-1914

1919 HANSA-LLOYD 1½-ton electric trucks, OMM

Hansa private cars were also available with van bodies, especially between 1910 and 1914. A speciality was a light truck with changeable platforms.In 1914 Hansa merged with Lloyd to form Hansa—Lloyd. *HON*

HANSA-LLOYD (D) 1914-1938

(1) Hansa-Lloyd-Werke A.G., Bremen; Varel, 1914-1931
(2) Hansa-Lloyd and Goliath-Werke Borgward & Tecklenburg, Bremen, 1931-1937
(3) Hansa-Lloyd-Goliath-Werke Carl. F.W. Borgward, Bremen 1937-1938

1937 HANSA-LLOYD Bremen 2-ton truck, FLP

Hansa-Lloyd began with the merger of Hansa and Lloyd (q.v.). During WWI a large quantity of trucks were built based on the former Lloyd designs. Also electric vehicles were continued, which had been a speciality of Lloyd.

In 1921 a new 2 ton express truck appeared which also was available as a 16-seater bus. Characteristic was the worm-gear drive which was kept also for the later models of 1 and 3½ tons. A standard chassis for electric cars was developed which was characterized by bogie (fifth wheel) steering and front drive. This principle was used for some years for trucks and buses when it was replaced by conventional rear wheel drive. A 4x2 or 4x4 electric tractor for 10 ton towing capacity was widely used for urban traffic.

A speciality was an express bus which appeared in 1925. It had a low-frame chassis and the body had doors for each line of seats. A new 3-axle chassis was presented in 1929 which was destined for trucks and buses with gasoline or gas-electric drive.

At the beginning of the thirties trucks ranging from 1½ to 5 tons were available and designated as types "Columbus" (1½ ton), "Bremen" (2 ton), "Europa" (3½ ton), "Merkur" (4 ton, 2 cyl. Junkers diesel engine), and "Roland" (5 ton, 6 cyl., 100 PS).

Hansa-Lloyd started to build the 6x6 standard truck for the army in 1935, at first as a 2½ ton version. Later it appeared as 4x2 or 4x4 version for a 3 ton payload. Also a 3 ton half-track version with 3.5 litre gasoline engine was built under Krauss-Maffei license.

In 1938 the name Hansa-Lloyd was dropped in favor of Borgward (q.v.). *HON*

HANZER (F) 1902-1903

Hanzer Freres, Petit Ivry, Seine

This small French company built light cars and also listed two commercial models, a 6½ hp single-cylinder 400 kg van, and a 9 hp 2-cylinder 800 hg truck. Both had 3-speed gearboxes. Late in 1902 they were taken over by Automobiles Durey-Sohy who marketed the Hanzer range under their own name in 1903. *GNG*

HARABAS see Harimau

HARBILT (GB) 1947 to date

Harborough Construction Co. Ltd., Market Harborough, Leics.

One of the postwar additions to the battery electric market, the Harbilt range started with the 551 model which was a pedestrian controlled four wheel truck of 4 ft. wheelbase with 128AH battery and rated at 1-ton capacity. Various body styles were offered including

1965 HARBILT Model 760 electric truck, GNG

tipping models and during the 1950's a rider type vehicle of the same capacity was introduced (model 750). Later a 25-cwt model was added to the range and improvements introduced as customers demanded something different.

During the 1960's other models of internal works types were added to the range including 3- and 4-wheeled works trucks, low-loading trucks, towing tractors and platform trucks. In addition the range of pedestrian trucks for municipal use has increased and rider types with capacities up to 30-cwt were made. More recently the company has gone in for producing internal works transport vehicles almost exclusively and the Harbilt-Melex 3-and 4-wheeled battery personnel carriers are the latest trend in this expanding market. *OM*

HARDER (US) 1910-1913

(1) Harder Fire Proof Storage & Van Company, Chicago, Illinois, 1910-1912
(2) Harder's Auto Truck Company, Chicago, Illinois, 1913

1911 HARDER Model C 1½-ton truck, NAHC

The medium to large capacity trucks by these companies began as vehicles for moving operations. The later and larger trucks had capacities up to five tons. They all used three-speed gearboxes, four-cylinder engines and final drive by roller chains. Like most trucks of the period, they were governed to a maximum speed, and typically, to 10 mph for the largest models. A number of fire engines were made in 1911-1912. *GMN*

HARDY (GB) 1931-1937

(1) Hardy Rail Motors Ltd., Slough, Bucks, 1930
(2) Hardy Motors Ltd., Slough and Southall, Middx, 1931-1937

Hardy were associated with British FWD and during the Twenties built rail-going conversion of FWD vehicles. Following the link between AEC and British FWD and Hardy in 1929 the latter developed off-road vehicles using AEC components. During 1930 and '31 these 4x4 and 6x6 3½ to eight tonners were listed alongside the traditional and similar FWD products, but from 1932, to avoid confusion with American FWD, the name Hardy was adopted for all the off-road trucks. These now not only used AEC components but looked like them with the addition of two speed auxiliary gearboxes and all-wheel-drive.

1931 HARDY 4-ton 4×4 truck, OMM

Hardy continued to make railcars, though these mostly went under the name AEC, as did an increasing proportion of their trucks, including special 8x8 colonial models in the mid-Thirties. The make was not exhibited at London Commercial Motor Shows after 1933, but was still listed as a separate entity in 1935, though by now based at AEC's Southall works.

Hardy 4/4 and R68 were the direct forerunners of AEC's famous wartime Matador and 6x6 models. *OM*

HARIMAU (PTM) 1972-1977

General Motors Malaysia Sdh Bhd, Johore Bahru.

This was a very simple normal control light truck intended for sale in Asia. Mechanical elements were essentially those of the Bedford HA light van, with 1.3-litre 4-cylinder ohv engine, 4-speed all synchromesh

1973 HARIMAU 1 basic transportation vehicle, Bedford

gearbox, and hypoid final drive. The Series II Harimau of 1975 had transverse ifs in place of the beam front axle of earlier models.

The Harimau design was also made in a number of other countries where it was known under different names. These include Portugal (Amigo), Ecuador (Andino), the Phillipines (Harabas), and Suriname (Moetete). Malaysian production ceased in December, 1977. *MCS*

HARMENING (D) 1954-1957

Hermann Harmening, Buckeburg

This coachbuilding firm presented their own chassisless bus-the so-called "Club-Bus". An 85 hp Henschel diesel engine was installed in the rear. *HON*

HARMER KNOWLES (CDN) 1923

Harmer Knowles Motor Truck Co. Ltd., Toronto, Ont.

A truck of apparently-normal configuration built in quite limited numbers. *HD*

HARPER (GB) 1898-1900, 1908

Harper Motor Co., Holburn Junction, Aberdeen.

The first vehicles to bear the Harper name appeared in the period 1898-1900 and were built by John Harper and his sons and Thomas Mowat. These were crude tractor-types with Benz or Cannstatt-Daimler engines. Gasoline engined cars based on the single cylinder Cadillac occupied the firm from 1905 until 1906, and in 1908 a few steam trucks were built. These achieved no currency outside the immediate area of the works, however, and little is known of them. *MJWW*

HARPER RUNABOUT (GB) 1922-1923

A. V. Roe & Co. Ltd, Stretford, Manchester

The Harper Runabout was the smallest 3-wheeler made in the early 1920s, having tandem seating and a single-cylinder Villiers 2-stroke engine of only 269 cc. Mostly seen as a passenger car, it was briefly offered with a parcel box in place of the rear seat. Load capacity was 120 lbs. *GNG*

HARRINGTON (GB) 1951-1956

Thomas Harrington, Ltd., Hove, Sussex.

Following upon its wartime experience with aircraft manufacture, the old-established Harrington coachbuilding concern introduced a light alloy underfloor-engined chassisless coach known as the Contender in 1951. Designed in collaboration with the British Aluminum Co. Ltd., the coach embodied running units from the Commer Avenger range. These included the Commer six-cylinder gasoline engine, although an early version of the Contender for the British Overseas Airways Corporation was fitted with the eight-cylinder Rolls Royce gas engine and automatic transmission. A diesel-powered version emerged in 1954 incorporating the compact 3.26 litre TS3 two-stroke engine, and the majority of Contenders were supplied in this form. A number of Contenders, notably a batch of eleven supplied to Maidstone & District Motor Services Ltd. in 1955, were built as service buses rather than coaches. The Contender never achieved great popularity and remained only a minor part of Harrington's coach body construction program (which ceased entirely in 1965). Another chassisless Harrington design was a crew car accommodating twelve passengers plus luggage and employing Ford running units including the Cost Cutter four-cylinder gasoline engine. Specially designed in 1954 for BOAC, its design was suitable for adaptation as a nineteen-seater bus, ambulance, or general purpose vehicle, but it failed to find a market as such. *OM*

HARRIS see Mendip

HARRISON (US) 1911-1917

Robert Harrison Co., South Boston, Mass.

The original models built by this company included 3½-, 5- and 12-tonners, all with forward control. The 12-tonner, probably the largest US truck of the period, weighed 13000 pounds as a chassis. Only the 3½-tonner survived to 1917, still using a four-cylinder engine, 3-speed gearbox and double chain-drive, with a wheelbase of 11 feet, 10 inches. *GMN*

HARRODS (GB) 1937-1939

Harrods Ltd., Knightsbridge, London S.W.1

During the 1930s the well-known London store Harrods decided to build a number of 1-ton battery electric vans to their own designs. For many years they had operated Walkers, and a number of Walker features found their way into the new designs. The Harrods vans used electrical equipment supplied by Bruce Peebles & Co. Ltd., while the chassis and bodywork were carried out by Harrods themselves in the Engineering and Coachbuilding Works at Barnes in south west London. A total of 60 vans were built, and many were in use until the late 1960s. *OM*

1939 HARRODS 1-ton electric van, NMM

HART-KRAFT (US) 1907-1913

Hart-Kraft Motor Co., York, Pa.

Prior to 1911 all models were high-wheelers with a 2-cylinder unit power plant under the seat. All parts were made in the company's factory. Early models of 500-pound capacity cost $800; from 1909 models of 1000-pound capacity cost from $1,350 up. The introduction of a complete line of 4-cylinder trucks with Hart-Kraft's own water-cooled engine led to receivership in early 1911. All featured cone clutch, double chain drive, and armored wood frame. The receiver continued production for two years with Continental engines. *DJS*

HARVEY (US) 1911-1932

Harvey Motor Truck Works, Harvey, Il.

The first Harvey trucks were in the 1½- to 3-ton class, joined by a 5-tonner in 1916. In the 1920s models ran from

1½ to 5-tons, all Buda-powered. One of the more interesting Harveys was the 1927 Road Builders' Special, a dump truck with seven speeds forward and two reverse, aimed at the road construction market in the same way that Hug and Super Trucks were. 6-cylinder engines were used from 1929, when 6- and 10-ton tractor trailer units were offered as well as the smaller trucks. *GNG*

HATFIELD (i) (US) 1907-1908

Hatfield Motor Vehicle Company, Miamisburg, Ohio

This high-wheeler was made only as a light open delivery van with a two-cylinder engine mounted beneath the body. Typical of high-wheelers, it used friction transmission and double chain-drive. Its carrying capacity was given as 800 pounds with a vehicle weight of 1100 pounds. *GMN*

HATFIELD (ii) (US) 1910-1914

(1) Hatfield Motor Vehicle Co., Cortland, NY 1910
(2) Hatfield Motor Vehicle Co., Cornwass-on-Hudson, NY 1911
(3) Hatfield Automobile Truck Co., Elmira, NY 1911-1914

The Hatfields were small ½- and 1-tonners of quite primitive design, with 3-cylinder, air-cooled engines, friction transmissions and double chain-drive. Some models had forward control and all were available with a variety of open and closed bodies including a 10-passenger bus. *GMN*

HAULAMATIC (GB) 1961 to date

Haulamatic Ltd., Heanor, Derbyshire

1974 HAULAMATIC 6-15 32000lb dump truck, Haulamatic

Haulamatic entered the field of dump truck manufacture in 1961 with a modified Commer. This had a strengthened chassis, heavier duty suspension and Allison 6-speed automatic transmission. The subsequent GP8 and QM8 models had Commer chassis with Haulamatic's own design of cab, and in 1969 the company introduced a range of 2- and 3-axle dump trucks substantially similar to those being made today. These are the 4-10 and 6-15, the former a 2-axle 10-tonner with 146 hp General Motors engine, and the latter a 3-axle 15-tonner with 215 hp Perkins V-8 engine. Both have fully automatic Allison gearboxes, the former with 4 speeds in conjunction with a 2-speed rear axle, and the latter with 5 speeds. Haulamatics are suitable for on- or off-road operation. *GNG*

HAULPAK see Wabco

HAWA (D) 1923-1925

Hannoversche Waggonfabrik A.G., Hannover

Based on the electric private car, a single-seater van was available. The body consisted of a wooden frame construction planked with plywood. *HON*

HAWKEYE (US) 1917-1933

Hawkeye Truck Co., Sioux City, Iowa

The Hawkeye began as a 1½-tonner assembled from standard parts and was joined in 1919 by a 2-tonner and in 1921 by a 3½-tonner. All used 4-cylinder Buda engines, with Fuller gearboxes with 4-speeds in the two larger models. 6-cylinder engines came in 1927, and from 1931 Hercules and Wisconsin units were used in addition to the Budas. *GMN*

HAY (GB) 1905-1906

Hay Motor Co. Ltd., Liverpool

This wagon had a vertical cross tube boiler, a single cylinder (10" bore x 12" stroke) and a ratchet and pawl final drive at 80 strokes a minute — a reversion to Cugnot's tractor of 1769. Understandably buyers, even in 1905, treated the wagon as belonging to the lunatic fringe and ignored it, though at £425 it was offered at a price about £125 cheaper than most of its contemporaries.

At the Cordingley Show of 1906 a compound wagon was entered but the marque disappeared soon afterwards. *RAW*

HAYES (i) (CDN) 1925-1928

Hayes Wheel Co. of Canada Ltd., Toronto, Ont.

1936 HAYES (ii) low-bed truck, RJ

The Hayes was an assembled taxicab chassis powered by a 2.4-litre 4-cylinder Continental engine, with a 3-speed gearbox and artillery wheels. A number were sold in Britain with bodies built by various London firms. British price was £425 complete, which was considerably less than the Beardmore or Unic. *GNG*

HAYES (ii) (CDN) 1928-1975

(1) Hayes Manufacturing Co. Ltd., Vancouver, B.C. 1928-1969
(2) Hayes Trucks Ltd., Vancouver, B.C. 1969-1975

Originally known as the Hayes-Anderson, this was the best-known Canadian West Coast make of truck, and earned its reputation in the logging industry. Hercules, Continental and Leyland engines were used, and production of logging trucks ran at about 100 per year during the 1930s. The company developed a special hitch which permitted trailers to track closely behind their tractors. Models ranged from 1½ to 15 tons, but actual loads often reached 50 tons or more. Another Hayes speciality in the 1930s was that of dockside and warehouse trucks with dropped frames giving a low platform for easy loading, similar in conception to the American Doane trucks. Like the Doanes, the Hayes low-loaders were very long-lived, many surviving in Vancouver's dockland into the 1960s. Other Hayes products of the 1930s were buses and coaches, some of which were supplied to Greyhound Lines, and tandem-axle conversion sets to make a 5-6 ton 6-wheeler from a Ford Model AA or Chevrolet truck.

In the late 1930s Hayes became British Columbia distributors for Leyland vehicles, rounding out their own range with the British product. They also used an increasing proportion of Leyland components such as engines, axles and transmissions in the trucks, and as

1939 HAYES (ii) 15-ton 6×4 truck, LA

1949 HAYES (ii) Model 28-22 logging truck, LA

these carried a lower tariff than United States-built components, Hayes vehicles were exceptionally good value. After World War II a line of highway tractors was added, and these were steadily developed during the 1950s and 1960s, along with the logging trucks. Engines used included Rolls-Royce, Cummins, Detroit Diesel and Caterpillar, the largest logging truck, the HDX 1000 using a 430 bhp Detroit Diesel V-12 in conjunction with an Allison 5-speed transmission and Clark rear axle. Buses were no longer made after 1947.

In 1969 Mack acquired a two-thirds interest in Hayes, and continued the range with the addition, in 1970, of the Clipper 100 cab-over-engine highway truck similar to the F series West Coast Macks. These were made in rigid and

1971 HAYES (ii) Model HDX logging truck, HD

articulated models, together with the conventional Clipper 200s, the HS series of rigid off-highway trucks including dump trucks, andd the HDX logging tractors. These used Detroit Diesel and Caterpillar power. In 1974 Hayes was sold to a subsidiary of Pacific Car & Foundry of Seattle, Washington, and a year later the new owner shut down the operation. *HD*

HEATHFIELD (GB) 1966 to date

Heathfield Engineering Ltd., Newton Abbot, Devon

Heathfield is a division of Centrax Ltd., manufacturers of axles, gearboxes and gas turbine compressor blades. In 1966 they launched a 7 cubic yard 2-axle dump truck powered by a Perkins 6-354 engine, with a David Brown 5-speed gearbox and Centrax rear axle. This was followed by the generally similar DF20 with an E.N.V. gearbox and

1971 HEATHFIELD DF20 8cu yd dump truck, Heathfield

a longer wheelbase, and the DF24E and 25E, designed specifically for earthmoving work. In 1972 the DF series was renamed the H11, and in 1974 was replaced by the H19 and H28. These were larger dump trucks of 19 and 28 ton payloads, powered respectively by an 11.1-litre 200 hp Leyland UE680, and 310 hp 14-litre Cummins NT310 turbocharged engine. The H19 transmission was offered with a 5-speed Fuller manual gearbox, while the H28 was offered with a choice of 9-speed Fuller manual or an Allison automatic box. In recognition of increasing export trade, the H19 and H28 were offered in left-hand drive form only, unlike their predecessors. 1978 models are generally similar, but are called the H20 and H30. Engines

1978 HEATHFIELD H20 12cu yd dump truck, Heathfield

are the Leyland UE680 or Rolls-Royce CE220 in the H20, and Cummins NT310 or NTA855C in the H30. Payloads are 40,000 and 60,000 lbs respectively. A feature of all Heathfields is their independent front suspension with rubber spring units.

Leading British customers for Heathfield dumptrucks are the British Steel Corporation and the National Coal Board, while export markets include Yugoslavia, Iran, Malaysia, South Africa and Ghana. *GNG*

HEBE (E) 1918-1922

Fabrica Espanola de Automoviles Hebe, Barcelona

This company made motorcycles and also a light chassis with 6/8 hp 4-cylinder engine which was fitted with passenger car bodies and as a light delivery van with capacity of 250 kgs. This was known as the 'Camioncino'. *JCG*

HEILUNGKIANG (CHI) c.1970 to date

Tsitsihar Vehicles Plant, Tsitsihar, Heilungkiange

The Heilungkiang # 1 is reported to be a large truck for use in the province, and Model #04 is an auto-load version. *BE*

HEI-YAN (p), HAI-YEN (wg) (Sea Martin) CHI c.1958 to date

Shanghai Small Passenger Car Plant, Shangai (Plant Vehicle Code — SW)

The little Sea Martin appears in several forms including model SW-710 4-seated sedan, sometimes used as a taxi.

The plant produces the SWH-600 which is a ½ ton micro truck using an aircooled 2 cylinder engine of 20 hp. *BE*

HELECS (GB) 1950-1957

Hindle, Smart & Co. Ltd., Merefield Works, Ardwick, Manchester.

As bodybuilders and suppliers of Wilson Electric vehicles, Hindle Smart at first offered the Wilson Major 25 cwt and Wilson Junior 18 cwt vehicles as well as their own 10 cwt Helecs 10.

The Helecs vehicles were of straight forward design. They were called the Tough 10 with 8 ft. 10 in. wheelbase and a larger H25 model was rated at 25 cwt with 9 ft. 7 in. wheelbase.

In 1953 the smaller model became the 10/15 cwt Avenger and the H25 was called the Intruder as well as being given a more streamlined body. A 30 cwt model, the Endeavour was also available. 1954 saw the introduction of the Help-Mate, a 5 ft. 6 in. wheelbase model with very narrow (4 ft. 1½ in.) body for work in congested areas. This model was aimed at getting operators away from the pedestrian controlled aspect of vehicle operation and these early models became known as rider prams because the operator rode on the vehicle standing at the front.

Helecs are perhaps best known for their link with Jensen Motors when for a period in the early 1950's they supplied the electrical equipment for two models of a battery electric version of the Jen-Tug automatic coupling articulated tractor unit. The Jen-Helecs as it was called was of 4 ton capacity, had a 5 ft. 10 in. wheelbase and was fitted with either a 192- or 240AH capacity battery. *OM*

HELIKAK see Italindo

HELIOS (D) 1903-1906; 1924-1926

(1) Helios Elektricitats A.G., Cologne-Ehrenfeld 1903-1906
(2) Helios Automobil-Bau A.G., Cologne-Ehrenfeld 1924-1926

Helios continued to build trucks and buses formerly manufactured by Hagen. The principle of lever transmission was used in the beginning. Later vans, trucks and buses featured normal chain-drive.

In 1924 this firm again entered the field of car production with a small private car which also was available as a van. It had a horizontally opposed 2-cylinder 972 cc engine. *HON*

HENDRICKSON (US) 1913 to date

(1) Hendrickson Motor Truck Co., Chicago, Ill.
(2) Hendrickson Motor Truck Co., Lyons, Ill.
(3) Hendrickson Manufacturing Co., Lyons, Ill.

Magnus Hendrickson built his first truck in 1900, and later was chief engineer for Lauth-Juergens. Leaving this company in 1913, Mr. Hendrickson returned to Chicago and formed his own company with sons George and Carl, and also David Nyman and Al Ostby. Son Robert joined later, after leaving Lauth-Juergens, and some years later, Edward, the fourth son, joined the company when he became of age.

The first truck from the Hendrickson factory was a cab-over and chain-driven, with artillery wheels and solid tires. The front windows of the cab were built like a 3-section bay window of a house, like the last ones Hendrickson designed for Lauth-Juergens. Right from the start, Hendrickson trucks were specialties, with Magnus Hendrickson's inventive genius providing the solution to a variety of customers' requirements, such as a patented hoist for stone-hauling trucks and special dump bodies for refuse hauling.

In 1920 the regular Hendrickson line-up included three models of 2½-to 5-tons priced from $3200-$5250, with worm drives, and solid tires all around.

The 1922 line-up included a 1½-ton model $2200 with worm drive and pneumatic tires. Other sizes had solids, duals on the rear, with pneumatics optional except the 5-ton model. All had multiple disc clutches, most had 4-speed transmissions and all had Timken worm drives. By 1924 a 6-ton model replaced the 5-ton. Special chassis sizes were also made to order.

In 1926 Magnus, with sons Robert and George, designed a tandem suspension unit using the now-famous equalizing beam with center pivot to distribute the load evenly to the rear axles and also reduce the effects of uneven terrain by 50%.

An assembly plant was built in 1927, and by 1930 there were some 30 employees.

1928 HENDRICKSON 10-ton 6×4 garbage truck, LIAM

1934 HENDRICKSON 10-ton 6×4 van and trailer, LIAM

A major lift for the company came in 1933 when the International Harvester Company of Chicago signed an exclusive contract for use of the tandem suspension. The results were mutually beneficial; to Hendrickson for the necessary business at the bottom of the Great Depression; and to International for the large percentage of the heavy duty market it captured with those early 6-wheeled units. This relationship continued until 1948 when International agreed to let Hendrickson, at its own request, make the suspensions available to all truck manufacturers. These suspensions are a major production item today.

Hendrickson also built fire engines on International chassis and installed diesel engines in International's large trucks.

The regular Hendrickson truck range by 1936-1939 included some cab-overs again, and had expanded from 2½- to 12-tons at $1760 to $9000, with 6-cylinder Waukesha engines being the standard, since 1932, and having SAE hp from 33.8 to 60. Cummins diesels were also offered by 1938. The 1940-1941 range was 2-to 10-tons with more SAE hp; 35.8 to 79.4. Many of Hendrickson's sales were in the Chicago area.

During the 1930's Mr. Hendrickson invented a power divider which enabled both tandem axles to be powered, and in World War II the company was kept busy supplying Hendrickson suspensions to International at the rate of 600 per week. Other varieties of suspensions were developed through the years, including the use of air.

The conventional Hendrickson trucks used the standard K (or KB) series International cab and had a set-back front axle and a long hood. These same ideas were carried over then the B series came in 1950, also using International's cab, this one with the curved windshield. Model B came in several variations; long nose, standard length, and a short sloped nose with a somewhat higher cab. The latter had a simple screen mesh grille, very flat. The successor H series for 1970 was a larger, but sometimes lighter truck, again using International's Fleetstar cab, and this model is still current. The hood, one of the longest on conventional highway trucks today, is made of steel re-enforced fiberglass.

Diamond T won a National Design Award in 1951 for a new tilt-cab-over, and this was also used by Hendrickson and International until the early 1970's, each with its own grille. Hendrickson also had its own tilt cab-over in the early 1950's, this one tilting to the rear, including the

c.1958 HENDRICKSON 8×4 COE tilt cab truck, LA

1940 HENDRICKSON 6-ton coal truck, LIAM

upper part of the bull-nose hood. A taller line-haul cab-over was added about 1950, using International's cab once more (this one CO-405). Some cab-over and cab-forward designs other than International's were also used in small numbers.

Hendrickson's truck production was small in numbers with 60 to 100 units or so per year in the early 1950's,, and they became more and more custom-built with the customers' wide choice of components and equipment to choose from. They included diesel, gasoline, or propane engines, and aluminum, fiberglass or steel construction.

As time progressed, more and more specialties came from the active engineering department. Some long-nosed conventionals in the B series came with the cab over the front axle, or even over tandem steering axles.

The company expanded into the crane carrier field with a wide variety of cab-over and cab-forward types, including low profile cabs, tandem axles front and rear, and even tri-axles front and rear, in an over-all range from 15 to 200 tons.

Hendrickson's airport ground support equipment includes fuel tankers, plane towers, snowplows, and special cargo and passenger vehicles, the bodies of which reach plane-loading heights by scissors elevators.

Other truck manufacturers come to Hendrickson for truck sub-assemblies, or even the entire vehicle with the customer's own label. The new Ryder truck is one of these. The Manitooc crane carrier is another. The Cline Truck Company of Kansas City, Missouri, bought some of Hendrickson's sheet metal for its trucks. Hendrickson also built chassis for International fire engines.

Several companies operate fleets of Hendricksons, mostly around Chicago, in heavy duty local or interstate hauling. Mid-America Truck Lines, which has possibly the largest fleet, operates about 140 line-haul tractors in the general 7-state area betwen Chicago and Kansas.

1972 HENDRICKSON 6×4 tractor and trailer, Hendrickson

Yearly production is 300-command for the early 1970's, all custom-engineered and hand-built. Lifetime production of Hendrickson (trademarked) trucks is estimated at 5500 units.*RW*

HENNEGIN (US) 1908

Commercial Automobile Company, Chicago, Illinois

This was one of many light delivery vans on high-wheeler chassis built during the period prior to 1910. This Model A had a typical 2-cylinder engine mounted beneath the body, a friction transmission and double chain-drive to the rear wheels. Wheelbase was 7 feet, 3 inches and its price was $650. *GMN*

HENNEY (US) 1916-1932

John W. Henney Co., Freeport, Ill.

The Henney was a typical assembled professional car, available from the start as ambulance or hearse, and powered by various types of 6-cylinder Continental engine. By 1924 a 70 hp unit was standard, and Henneys were distinctive vehicles, both the radiator and the cycle-type front fenders resembling those of contemporary Kissels. When Kissel themselves entered the funeral business, Henney switched to Lincoln-like lines, while 1927 saw the introduction of the Eureka 3-way loading system on hearses. Lycoming straight-8 engines replaced the Continental sixes in 1929, but after 1932 Henney elected to concentrate on bodywork only. This was mounted exclusively on Packard chassis from 1938 until the end in 1954. Other Henney ventures included an ambulance aircraft (in association with the Great Lakes company) in 1929, some sports cars in the early 1920s, and the manufacture of semi-custom private car coachwork for Packard in 1953/4. *MCS*

HENRIOD (CH) 1896-1898

Henriod Freres, Bienne

c.1899 HENRIOD light bus, ES

After early steam-vehicle experiments (1886) and rear engined cars, Henriod pioneered the air-cooled flat twin engines with opposed cylinders. Shortly before the turn of the century a handsome small omnibus for 6 to 8 passengers with a front-mounted flat twin engine and chain-drive was built. *FH*

HENSCHEL (i) (D) 1899-1906

Berliner Maschinenfabrik Henschel & Co., Berlin-Charlottenburg

The first Berlin electric taxi-cab was supplied by this firm. In the following years also electric driven vans and lorries were available. *HON*

HENSCHEL (ii) (D) 1925-1969

(1) Henschel & Sohn GmbH., Kassel 1925-1928; 1937-1957
(2) Henschel & Sohn A.G., Kassel 1928-1937
(3) Henschel-Werke GmbH., Kassel 1957-1962
(4) Henschel-Werke A.G., Kassel 1962-1965
(5) Rheinstahl-Henschel A.G., Kassel 1965-1969

The old established locomotive building firm of Henschel started manufacturing commercial vehicles in 1925 under a Swiss F.B.W. license. This was a 5-ton truck with a 4-cylinder 50 PS engine and chain-drive. One year later a change to 60 PS and shaft drive was made. Also a low-frame chassis for bus bodies became available. In 1928 Henschel began to build diesel engines following the air-chamber system of Lanova. In 1930 a 3-axle truck with a 12-cylinder 250 PS gasoline engine was presented, which was the most powerful on the market at that time. A new diesel engine was a 6-cylinder developing 100 PS.

The Henschel program in 1930 consisted of trucks with payload capacities from 2½ to 10 tons, articulated vehicles of 6 and 16 tons and in addition various buses,

1934 HENSCHEL 12-ton steam truck, HON

special and municipal versions were available. In 1932 Henschel started experimenting with steam engines following Doble principles. This led to the production of steam-driven trucks and buses, of which 18 were made from 1933 to 1936. Most of them went to the German State Railways. Henschel was also a well-known manufacturer of trolley-buses.

In 1933 Henschel took up production of a 6x4 all-terrain 3 ton truck with a 10.8 litre 6-cylinder gasoline engine developing 100 PS. This was supplemented in 1937 by a 100 PS diesel version, which was laid out as a standard truck for the army. Another military version was the 6x6 standard truck which Henschel launched in 1937. It was a 2½ tonner with a 6-cylinder 6.2 litre diesel engine.

1938 HENSCHEL 6-ton truck, FLP

In 1936 Henschel presented a chassis with an opposed 12-cylinder diesel engine of 300 PS. Also the first buses of integral construction were shown.

1939 HENSCHEL streamlined bus, Halwart Schrader Collection

1955 HENSCHEL HS100 5-ton truck, OMM

1956 HENSCHEL HS90 4.3-ton truck, GNG

After WW II Henschel recommenced production of trucks. An interesting bus version was the forward control "Bimot-Bus", equipped with two 6-cylinder diesel engines transversely mounted in the front. This layout was also used for a 3-axle articulated tractor. A range of normal control trucks of 4½, 6½ and 8 tons was in the program. Buses and trolley-buses completed the line. In 1952 a 4x4 truck with 4½ ton payload capacity and 100 PS engine appeared and one year later Henschel adopted the underfloor engine for their model HS 200 UN using a 6-cylinder 200 PS engine. It was sold as forward control truck and bus alike. Normal control and forward control trucks were now available covering the range from 4 to 14 tons payload capacity. A new front for both versions was

1963 HENSCHEL HS16 8-ton truck, GNG

introduced in 1961. In the same year Henschel entered into an agreement with Saviem for mutual development and distribution. Although this lasted only until 1963 Saviem used Henschel engines for their heavy trucks. Later Saviem was replaced as a partner by Commer.

In 1964 the Rheinstahl concern took over Henschel and as they also owned Hanomag the connection with Commer was given up as the Hanomag and Commer lines conflicted. With Henschel, Hanomag and Tempo — which

1966 HENSCHEL HS 14TS 20-ton articulated truck, GNG

was owned by Hanomag — the Rheinstahl concern offered the widest range of trucks on the German market from 1 to 20 ton. Buses were no longer offered. After 1969 vehicles were sold as Hanomag-Henschel as a result of the formation of a new company in which Daimler-Benz had a 51% interest. In 1973 the remaining interests were taken over by Daimler-Benz and together with Hanomag the old-established name of Henschel died. *HON*

HERCULES (i) (CH) 1900-1913

(1) Carl Weber-Landolt, Menziken, AG, 1900-1906
(2) Hercules AG, Menziken, AG, 1906-1913

1906 HERCULES (i) 3½-ton truck, FH

Carl Weber, who had obtained his engineering degree in Paris, decided in 1900 to build his first cart-like truck, which he promptly sold. Two years later the small company offered a full range of commercial vehicles with payloads of 1 to 7½ tons. Front-mounted twin-cylinder engines of 6, 10, 14 and 30 hp, iron-tired wheels and chain-drive were used. It is highly doubtful whether all the models listed in their catalogue actually were built. There was also a more modern small omnibus for 8 passengers with either a 6 hp twin-cylinder or a 12 hp 4-cylinder engine and solid-rubber tires. In 1907 a new large 4-cylinder engine cast in pairs was built for the heavy chassis. The nearly square cylinder dimensions, 140 x 150 mm, gave a 9.8 litre capacity and output was claimed to be 50 hp at 1000 rpm. As on the earlier models a 4-speed gearbox and final drive by chains were used. The foot-brake worked on the transmission-shaft. The hand-brake was still of the old-fashioned cart-type pressing a wooden block directly on the iron-tired rim of the rear-wheels.

Hercules successfully took part in the Swiss Commercial Vehicles contest in 1907 but it could not cope with the increasing competition of technically more advanced products. *FH*

HERCULES (ii) (GB) 1903-c.1909

Hercules Motor Wagon Company, Levenshulme, Manchester

The early Hercules wagons were built around the Perkins & Rowcliffe vertical fire tube boiler in which a dished top tube plate which formed a primary smokebox, kept all tubes fully submerged, the outer wrapper plate being belled out to suit, so that an annulus, the upper part of which acted in some measure as a steam dome, surrounded the dished tube-plate. Outside the wrapper plate was a further annular structure forming a secondary smokebox, linked to the primary (or inner box) by a circle of short inclined tubes. Firing was by central chute. Like most vertical boilers, for wagons, based on fire tubes the Hercules boiler did not generate fast enough or flexibly enough for the designed purpose. A short, conventional, locomotive boiler was substituted about 1907 and seems to have been offered as an alternative to a transverse double ended locomotive boiler superficially resembling the Yorkshire but without the return banks of tubes and hence needing a chimney at each end.

All these boilers were paired with a compound undertype engine, using a countershaft differential and chain drive — an unremarkable layout, but the front suspension, based upon the parallel ruler principle, was interesting.

In 1906/07 a small number of Hercules gasoline-engined chassis were made, with 36hp 4-cylinder engines and double chain drive.

1906 HERCULES (ii) 5-ton steam wagon, NMM

The Hercules seems to have gone out of production about 1909 though the actual date is not known. *RAW*

HERCULES (iii) (D) 1909-1926

Nurnberger Hercules-Werke A.G., Nuremberg

1921 HERCULES (iii) 4-ton truck, HON

The trucks of this manufacturer appeared from the beginning with cardan drive. Their own engines were used and payload capacities ranged from ¾ ton to 4 ton. *HON*

HERCULES (iv) (US) 1913-1915

Hercules Motor Truck Co., South Boston, Mass.

This less well known Hercules was represented by a 1-tonner with either express or stake bodies, priced at $1775. Further data has not been located. *GMN*

HERRESHOFF (US) 1911-1912

Herreshoff Motor Company, Detroit, Michigan

The Model 25 Herreshoff light delivery van used the same chassis as the passenger auto by this manufacturer. With the closed body it was priced at $950. For this, the purchaser got a van rated at 750 pounds carrying capacity, using a 4-cylinder engine under a front hood, a 3-speed gearbox and shaft drive and fitted with pneumatic tires on a wheelbase of 8 feet, 2 inches. *GMN*

HERSCHMANN (US) 1902-1903

(1) American Ordnance Co., Bridgeport, Conn. 1902
(2) Columbia Engineering Works, Brooklyn, N.Y. 1903

The Herschmann was a 3-ton steam truck with vertical fire-tube boiler placed behind the driver, compound undertype engine and all-gear drive, the final drive by internal gear rings on the rims of the rear wheels. Few were made, but Herschmann patents were used in the English steam wagon built from 1903 to 1907. *GNG*

HEWITT (US) 1905-1914

(1) Hewitt Motor Co., New York, N.Y. 1905-1909
(2) Metzger Motor Car Co., New York, N.Y. 1909-1911
(3) Hewitt Motor Co., New York, N.Y. 1911-1912
(4) International Motor Co., New York, N.Y. 1912-1914

Edward Ringwood Hewitt's first commercial vehicles were light vans on the single-cylinder passenger car chassis, whose engines and planetary transmissions were manufactured by the Adams Manufacturing Co. Ltd. of Bedford, England. In 1906 a 4-ton truck with 4-cylinder engine was announced, but the one which went into production was a 5-tonner. This had a 36 hp 4-cylinder engine mounted between the seats, 2-speed planetary transmission and chain drive. A line of similar 2- and 3-ton trucks with flat-twin engines followed in 1907, and two years later came the Hewitt 10-tonner, the largest capacity American truck of its day. This had the same engine as the 5-tonner, but with larger springs and wheels. Maximum speed was 6-8 mph. These trucks were chiefly used for coal delivery, but a number were ordered by breweries. They were made in the factory of the Machine Sales Co at Peabody, Mass. in 1909, and by Philip H. Gill & Sons of Brooklyn in 1910 and 1911. The smaller Hewitt models were made in the New York City plant.

A merger with the Metzger Motor Car Co, makers of the Everitt car, led to a new 1-ton light van to replace the single-cylinder machine. This had a 17 hp 4-cylinder Everitt engine and a conventional 3-speed transmission. The latter spread to the larger Hewitt trucks in 1910 and 1911. In 1912 Hewitt became part of the International Motor Company, a consortium which also included Mack and the American Saurer Company. The smaller Hewitts were dropped, but the 5- and 10-tonners were continued, as no trucks so large were included in the Mack or Saurer ranges. However the old-fashioned and slow Hewitts were phased out altogether by the end of 1914. *GNG*

1910 HEWITT 10-ton truck, Mack

HEWITT-LINDSTROM (US) 1900-1901

Hewitt-Lindstrom Electric Co., Chicago, Ill.

No connection with the New York-built Hewitt truck, this company was formed by financier John Hewitt and engineer Charles A. Lindstrom to make electric vehicles of all types. These included town cars, runabouts, trucks and buses. A 14 seater example of the latter operated a service on Fifth Avenue, New York for a short time. *GNG*

H. H.; HUTTIS & HARDEBECK (D) 1906-1907

Huttis & Hardebeck Motorwagenfabrik, Aachen

Based on the private cars of this firm, vans and light trucks were available with 24 or 28 hp engines. *HON*

HIGHWAY (i) (US) 1918-1919

Highway Tractor Co., Indianapolis, Ind.

This was listed as a 3-wheeled 3-tonner with steering by a single front wheel. The powerplant and the driver's compartment turned with the front wheel. It was fitted with a Martin fifth wheel for connection with a trailer. It had a Weidely engine and other standard components. There is no known connection with the contemporary Highway Knight. *GMN*

HIGHWAY (ii) (US) 1960-1975

Highway Products, Inc., Kent, Ohio

After the Twin Coach Co. ended production of buses in 1953, manufacture of Fageol-Twin Coach gasoline engines and marketing of Fageol-Leyland diesels was continued. By 1959, however, both types of engines had fallen from favor among truck and bus manufacturers, and Twin Coach entered the truck body business to utilize excess plant capacity. Starting in 1960 the company was able to bid successfully on special vehicles for the Post Office, thanks to the efforts of a local businessman and company director named J.T. Myers. He formed Highway Products, Inc. to bid on these contracts and at first arranged to have the vehicles built in leased space within the Twin Coach plant, but in 1962 Highway Products acquired part of the former Twin factory. In addition to 40 ft. long 6-wheel Highway Post Offices with underfloor Cummins or

1962 HIGHWAY 6×4 mobile post office, MBS

1968 HIGHWAY 5-ton Compac-Van, LA

Fageol-Leyland engines and postal delivery vans, the company made the Compac-Van for general commercial use. This was a forward-control van for 18,000 to 26,000 lbs. GVW, powered by a choice of Chrysler, Ford, Cummins or Perkins engines. Some had one-man cabs and loading at front as well as rear. Prior to 1965 Highway had produced the Compac-Van for White, but subsequently it was marketed by Highway.

In 1968 Highway Products introduced a 25-passenger bus with a rear-mounted Chrysler V-8 engine and automatic transmission, in an effort to capitalize on a renewed interest in mass transit for small cities generated by the availability of federal grant funds. The Twin Coach name was used for the new bus, which was joined by a 29-passenger version in 1969. A single batch was completed with Perkins diesel engines, but the Detroit Diesel 4-53 powerplant has been the most popular since it was first offered in 1970. Brakes were originally hydraulic, changed to air in 1970, and full air suspension was introduced in 1971.

Highway Products operated at a loss during 1974 while fulfilling substantial contracts at guaranteed prices during a time of rapid upward pressure on costs of labor and materials. Production stopped temporarily in February 1975, when creditors refused further financing, and resumed briefly from June to October while existing commitments were honored but no further selling efforts were undertaken. The last Highway Products "Twin Coach" buses were delivered in October 1975. Approximately 900 buses were built in eight years, with a variety of engines, the later ones being equipped for the most part with Detroit Diesel 4-53's. *MBS*

HIGHWAY-KNIGHT (US) 1919-1921

Highway Motors Co., Chicago, Ill.

1920 HIGHWAY KNIGHT 4-ton truck, RNE

The hyphenated Knight in this tradename came from the 4-cylinder sleeve-valve engines by Root & Vandervoort Engine Co., under Knight license. The trucks were 4- and 5-tonners on a common chassis with wheelbase of 13 feet, 3 inches. Both models used Brown-Lipe 4-speed gearboxes and final drive by worm gear. *GMN*

HIGRADE (US) 1917-1921

(1) Higrade Motors Co., Grand Rapids, Mich. 1917-1918
(2) Highgrade Motors Co., Harbor Springs, Mich. 1918-1921

Higrade began as a ¾-tonner with a Wisconsin-built 4-cylinder engine and Cotta 3-speed gearbox on wheelbase of 9 feet, 7 inches. Late in 1917, a 1-tonner was introduced with similar specifications. Both models were carried into 1920. For 1921, the ¾-tonner was discarded and only the 1- and 1½-tonners were offered. *GMN*

HIJIRI (J) 1935-1943

Hijiri Motor Vehicle Manufacturing Co. Ltd.

This company organized by the Japan Automobile Parts Manufacturers' Association, originally supplied components to the Japanese Ford works. It subsequently built 30-cwt/2-ton trucks mainly for the army. Early ones bore a close resemblance to the 1933 Model-BB Ford; later Hijiris had front-end sheet metal in the style of Ford's 1935/6 trucks. *MCS*

HILLE (D) 1924-1926

Hille-Werke AG., Dresden

Two types of trucks were offered by this firm. The 3 ton version used a 45 hp ohc engine while the 5 ton had an 50 hp engine. The smaller version had shaft drive while the heavier one had chain drive. *HON*

HILLMAN (GB) 1908-1914: 1931-1932

(1) Hillman-Coatalen Motor Car Co. Ltd., Coventry 1908-1909
(2) Hillman Motor Car Co. Ltd., Coventry 1909-1932

Hillman announced a shaft-driven truck with a 25 hp 4-cylinder engine in 1908, but it is unlikely that any were built. They did, however, market a taxicab version of their 12/15 hp car with a 2.4-litre 4-cylinder sv engine in 1909 and 1910, before offering an interesting light van in 1913. This had no production car equivalent, and was powered by a 1.8-litre watercooled V-twin engine with dual magneto ignition mounted under a very short hood. Other features were a 2-speed gearbox (3 speeds were optional), bevel drive, and pneumatic tires, but after a year this gave way to a conventional 10-cwt model based on their 9.5 hp 4-cylinder light car chassis. Hillman did not return to van manufacture until the 1931 Show, at which they exhibited a 6-cwt van on the 1,185cc 4-cylinder Hillman Minx chassis, and a 15-cwt type based on the 2.8-litre 6-cylinder Wizard, with a detuned 48 hp engine and silent 3rd gearbox. During 1932 these models were transferred to the Commer range, and subsequent Commer light vans have borne close affinities to Hillman cars. Light utility versions of the 8-cwt Commer supplied to the Armed Forces during World War II in fact wore Hillman badges. *MCS*

HINDE & DAUCH (US) 1907-1908

Hinde & Dauch, Sandusky, O.

The single model by this name was a ½-tonner delivery van with a single-cylinder engine, a 2-speed gearbox and single chain-drive. It had forward control, a wheelbase of 7 feet, 6 inches and was priced at $800. *GMN*

HINDLEY (GB) 1904-1908

E.S. Hindley & Sons, Bourton, Dorset

Hindley's first wagon, a 2-tonner, seems merely to have been intended for works use, to tranship coal from the railway station to the works. Using a vertical firetube boiler and undertype compound engine it was notable only for possessing spring spoked wheels and for the method of final drive which consisted of a roller chain from crankshaft to the countershaft, which incorporated the differential, and thence spur gear drive to the rear axle. A second design of undertype was sold in small numbers commercially but Hindley was too practical an engineer to continue to use the vertical fire-tube boiler and compound undertype engine in melancholy combination, and by 1906 had adopted a short locomotive type boiler with a circular firebox, the flat topped outer of which extended well above the top of the horizontal barrel so that the latter was completely water filled. This was allied to a vertically inclined totally enclosed, compound engine, of the type for which Hindley was noted for stationary work, placed transversely, immediately behind the firebox. Offered in 3 and 5-ton sizes this design appeared to have a reasonable hope of success but failed to prosper against the competition of Foden and similar overtypes in the very restricted market of the time and production ceased in 1908. *RAW*

HINDUSTHAN (IND) 1968 to date

Hindusthan Motors Ltd., Calcutta

The automotive branch of the huge Hindusthan engineering complex was established as early as 1942 and built since then a variety of vehicles, including Studebaker, Chevrolet and Bedford truck chassis along with Hindusthan cars based on Morris designs. The first commercial models to bear the Hindusthan trademark, though, appeared in late 60s and were normal and forward control truck and bus chassis based on Bedford designs. The normal control cab used is the same as Bedford's J4/J6 series of the early 60s, while forward control models are fitted with locally designed cabs. Power comes from a Bedford diesel developing 112 hp, built locally, as are almost all other chassis components. The same engine powers also the bus and coach chassis which are conventional in design. Hindusthan produces a light commercial variant of its car model too. Built as chassis/front-end unit with cab doors, it forms the basis for a ½ ton van, pick up, station wagon and ambulance. External appearance is the same as Morris Oxford MkII of the late 50s, while its gasoline engine develops 50 hp. Cranes and earthmoving equipment complete the range of Hindusthan products. *GA*

HINO (J) 1942 to date

(1) Hino Heavy Industries Ltd., Tokyo 1942-1946
(2) Hino Industry Co. Ltd., Tokyo 1946-1948
(3) Hino Diesel Industry Co. Ltd., Tokyo 1948-1959
(4) Hino Motors Ltd., Tokyo 1959 to date

Hino was originally an offshoot of the Tokyo Gasu Denki KK (see T.G.E.) specializing in heavy diesel trucks. The first model offered commercially was a normal control 7-tonner with 4-speed gearbox, spiral bevel back axle, and

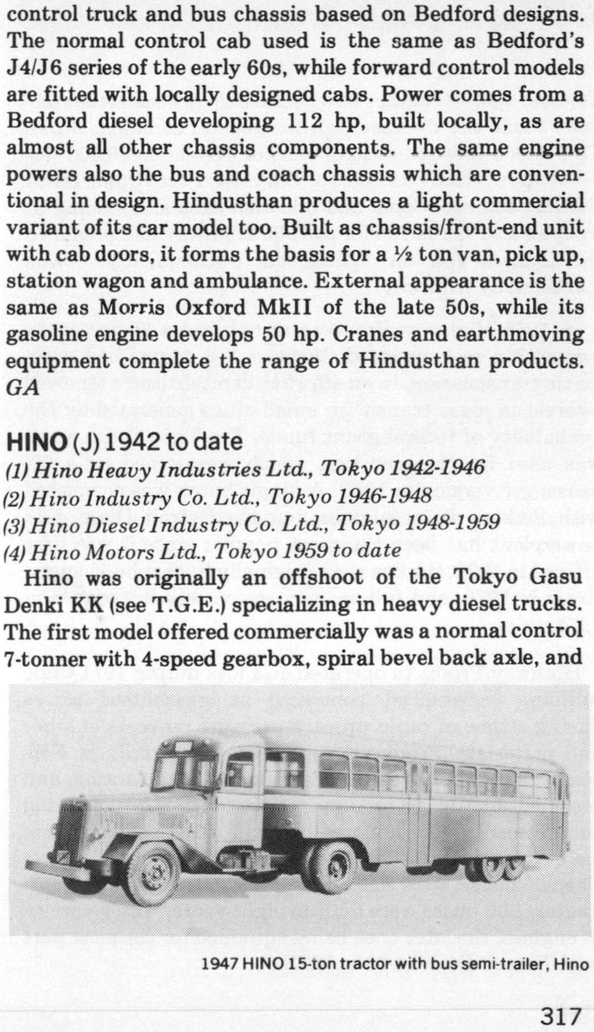

1947 HINO 15-ton tractor with bus semi-trailer, Hino

air brakes, powered by the company's own 110 hp, 7-litre 6-cylinder engine. In tractor form it was the basis for Japan's first heavy-duty artic, a 15-ton outfit, and a 150-seater articulated bus version made its appearance in 1947. The range was progressively widened, with trolleybuses added to the program in 1949, and an all-wheel-drive machine, the 6 x 6 ZC with 5-speed overdrive gearbox, in 1951, this being supplied to the local US armed forces as well as Japan's own army. A later 4 x 4 edition carried the ZH designation. The first of a long series of ZG heavy-duty half-cab dumpers with 6-speed gearbox made its appearance in 1953, and by 1956 Hino trucks catered for payloads from 5 to 8 tons, heavier ones having 150 hp 7.7-litre engines and 5-speed gearboxes.

Initially postwar bus production centered around normal control machines on lengthened truck chassis, but 1952 saw another Japanese first in the shape of a high-speed coach with amidships-mounted horizontal underfloor engine, 5-speed constant-mesh gearbox, and air brakes. Production rose steadily from 1,416 units (nearly half of these buses) in 1953 to 8,000 in 1960, 2-speed back

1953 HINO Blue Ribbon bus, Hino

1960 HINO TA 6-ton truck, Hino

axles being optional on trucks from 1956, and automatic transmissions on some coaches. Air suspension was first tried on PSVs in 1958, when the firm also built its first forward-control heavy truck, a twin-steer 6 x 2 which reached the market in 1961 as the TC series with tilt cab, 195 hp 6-cylinder engine of 10.2 litres capacity, and such options as power steering and a sleeper cab. At the other end of the scale Hino's license agreement with Renault (they had been building the latter's 4CV light car since 1953 led) to an interest in light gas-engined models. First of these was a 10-cwt fwd light van with all-independent suspension, closely modelled on Renault's Estafette, but by 1961 Hino were also marketing Humbee 3-wheelers under their own name, and were making the conventional 15-cwt Briska pickup with 893cc 4-cylinder engine, 4-speed gearbox, and coil-spring ifs.

The big normal control TE&TH series continued, but alongside these Hino made the parallel forward-control tilt cab KC series, as well as exploring the medium capacity market in 1964 with the 4-ton KM on similar lines. This featured a 4.3-litre 6-cylinder diesel engine, a 4-speed synchromesh gearbox, and hydrovac brakes. The 1966 catalogue embraced everything from a more powerful 1-ton Briska with 1¼-litre engine up to normal and forward control models in the 10/15-ton class, all powered by 6-cylinder diesel units. All the regular coach and bus models were of underfloor-engine type, with 5-speed gearboxes as standard. Top of the PSV range was the unit construction RA100 intended for high-speed motorway work. Power was provided by a 16-litre flat-12 diesel rated at 320 hp, air suspension was used, and top speed was quoted as 87 mph.

Hino joined forces with Toyota during 1966, a step which led to the elimination of private cars and light gas-engined models, leaving the KM at the bottom of the range with outsize Hinos represented by the normal control 6 x 4 ZM logging truck with a 10.2-litre engine, 5 x 4 speed transmission, and an auxiliary exhaust brake. The KM range itself was extended with the introduction of a 4 x 4 version, the WB; a 29-seater fullfront bus derivative, the BM: and a heavier truck edition, the KL with 5-litre 6-cylinder engine. A vast diversity of heavies came in 4 x 2, 4 x 4, 6 x 2, 6 x 4, and 6 x 6 forms with forward or normal control. Engines developed from 170 up to 230 hp, 5-, 6- and 10-speed transmissions were available, and power steering was a regular option. Rear engines and unitary construction featured on the latest RE and RC buses, and in 1972 Hino made a bid in the 40-tonne GCW class with the HE series of tractive units with forward control and high, short cabs in the American idiom. Alongside their established sixes the company introduced a new, square-dimensioned 270 hp V-8 of 13.8 litres' capacity, used in conjunction with a 10-speed splitter gearbox.

1975 HINO KM 5-ton truck, Hino

1975 HINO ZM 14-ton truck, Hino

In 1975 the Hino factories were capable of turning out 300 commercial vehicles a day, as well as handling some private car production for Toyota. Forward control and tilt cabs predominated in a range catering for GVWs of up to 30 tons, but there were still conventional models in the KB, KE and TE series. All but the lighter models had air brakes as standard, biggest of these being the KR with a 5.9-litre 6-cylinder engine and 5-speed synchromesh gearbox. On the PSV side, the BM retained the front-engine layout, the 76-seater BT was powered by a central underfloor engine of 8 litres' capacity, the RF was a separate-chassis type with 9.8-litre unit at the rear, and the RC and RE were on similar lines, but of monocoque construction, regular options on these series being power steering, air suspension, and a 5-speed electro-pneumatic epicyclic gearbox. For fast motorway work the rear-engined RV with V-8 unit, 5-speed overdrive box, air, exhaust and maxi brakes, and air suspension offered over 80 mph. This one was not quoted after 1976, though 1978 editions of the RE had 10.2 litres and 200 hp. The specialist range covered crane and mixer chassis, as well as a modernized ZG dumper with 10-speed overdrive gearbox and a 210 hp turbocharged 6-cylinder engine. The 1978 truck range showed little changes, apart from an increasing emphasis on the heavier-duty types. By this time Hinos were being assembled in Australia, New Zealand, eleven countries of the New World, nine in Asia, nine in Africa and six in Europe. The Irish plant alone had put together some 10,000 vehicles between 1967 and March, 1978. *MCS*

HIRANO (J) 1936-c.1940

Hirano Seizakusho Ltd., Nagoya

This firm of loom makers was well known for its scooters in the 1952-61 period. Before the War, however, it had marketed a delivery 3-wheeler of motorcycle type. *MCS*

HISPANO (E) 1952-1960

Hispano, S.A., Barcelona

No connection with the well-known Hispano-Suiza, this firm was the motor division of a machine tool works who made small delivery vans powered by a 200cc single-cylinder Hispano-Villiers engines. Later a slightly larger van powered by a 326cc 2-cylinder Hispano-Villiers engine driving the front wheels was built. *JCG*

HISPANO-ARGENTINA (RA) 1929-1942

Ballester Molina, Buenos Aires.

Carlos Ballester Molina was the Hispano-Suiza agent in Argentina. In 1929 he erected a large workshop which occupied a whole block, facing Tampico Street in Buenos Aires. There he started to manufacture cars and heavy trucks under Hispano-Suiza licenses and using some imported components. The vehicles were named Hispano-Argentina. Several examples were made and sold but finally in 1942 the Ballester Molina factory closed motor manufacturing activities and opted to make exclusively firearms which still is their main activity. *ACT*

HISPANO-SUIZA (E) 1908-1946

La Hispano-Suiza, Fabrica de Automoviles SA, Barcelona

Designed by the Swiss engineer Marc Birkigt, the Hispano-Suiza was Spain's best-known passenger car, and the company was also a prominent maker of commercial vehicles. The first commercial chassis appeared in 1908, the 12/15 hp for 1,000 kgs or a 10 seater bus, and the 24/30 hp for 2,000 kgs or 18 seats, the latter being made until 1916. In 1911 a larger chassis appeared, with a 4-cylinder long-stroke engine (100 x 180mm, the same dimensions as the famous Alfonso passenger car), and many of these were supplied to the Army. These had chain drive. A most unusual feature of early Hispano-Suiza commercial chassis was an auxiliary brake which was operated by a wheel at the driver's right side, in the manner of 19th Century horse-drawn carriages.

1925 HISPANO-SUIZA 40/50 bus, JCG

From 1912 to 1925 the 15/20 hp 4-cylinder chassis was made, initially with three speeds and then with four, and also in 1912 was announced the famous 30/40 hp chassis for 3 tons or 22 passengers. Many hundreds of these were made and together with the larger 40/50 was normally sold with solid tires, though pneumatics were available for passenger work, but the 30/40 came with pneumatics as standard. The 40/50 became the standard 5-ton truck of the Spanish Army, and was also exported in large numbers to the Argentine.

In 1930 a new range of five chassis from 17 to 70 hp with 4- and 6-cylinder engines was introduced, for loads of 2500

1939 HISPANO-SUIZA 26-seater bus, GNG

to 7000 kgs or 18 to 50 seats. Hispano always made their own engines, with the exception of an experimental 6 tonner of 1934 which used a Ganz-Jendrassik diesel. From the mid-30s onwards they made their own diesel engines. During the Civil War special vehicles including fire engines and trolley-buses were made, and in 1944 the new '66' 7-ton diesel engined chassis for goods and passenger work was introduced. The last new model was the 110/120 hp gasoline-engined coach chassis for 55 pasengers introduced in 1945. The following year Hispano-Suiza merged their vehicle building activities with the aero engine and armaments divisions to form the new group, Empresa Nacional de Autocamiones SA (E.N.A.S.A.) which began to produce trucks under the name Pegaso. *JCG*

HITACHI (J) 1935-1937

Hitachi Ltd., Tokyo

This was a short-lived normal control truck of American appearance powered by a 5.8-litre 4-cylinder diesel engine. *MCS*

HMW (B) 1937-1940

H.M. Willems N.V., Antwerp

This was a truck make started by a member of the Willems family that owned the Willems truck manufacturing company. The HMW again was mainly assembled truck using generally foreign parts, except for the engine which was a Belgian made Gardner-Miesse diesel. *JFJK*

HOADLEY (US) 1916

Hoadley Bros., Gosport, Ind

This make is listed as available as a 2-tonner only, without further details. *GMN*

HOBART (GB) 1905-c.1907

Hobard Bird & Co., Coventry

This was a typical tricar-based trade carrier powered by the 4½ hp water-cooled White & Poppe engine, with chain drive to the single rear wheel. The company made motorcycles until 1923. *GNG*

HOBRI see Giho

HOEK (NL) 1907-1913

Machinefabriek W.A. Hoek, Schiedam, Rotterdam

Hoek used a coke-fired vertical cross water tube boiler, with coil superheater to steam his 4-ton wagon of which other features were a compound totally enclosed undertype engine, countershaft differential and double chain drive. Five were made in 1907/08. In 1913 the firm produced two self-propelled steam fire engines designed for oil fuel.

Hoek's object in designing his trucks was to produce a vehicle more suitable for use on the uneven roadways of Rotterdam than the British made wagons of the period which were considered too heavy and too stiffly sprung. He succeeded in reducing the unladen weight to about 2½ tons and solved his springing problem by using very long laminated springs but at the expense of durability, and maintenance costs are believed to have defeated him. *RAW*

HOFFMAN (US) 1913-1914

Hoffman Motor Truck Co., Minneapolis, Minn.

The Hoffman was a conventional 3-ton truck powered by a 4-cylinder Waukesha engine, running on solid tires. Final drive was by single chain, which was unusual for so large a vehicle, and probably contributed to the Hoffman's reputation for troublesome transmissions. *GNG*

HOLDEN (AUS) 1951 to date

General Motons Holden's Pty Ltd., Melbourne, Victoria

The firm of Holden was established in 1856 as a leather business and entered the automotive field by producing car uphostery, as early as WWI years. Holden expanded their activities in 1923 by building complete car bodies, mainly on imported GM chassis and was finally associated with GM in 1931. Following post WWII reconstruction plans, the need for a national automotive industry was faced and GMH was soon the first to introduce their "all Australian" car in 1948. The first model powered by a 6-cylinder gasoline engine was soon followed by a van derivative and since then Holden utilities are always part of every year's range and follow

1966 HOLDEN HR coupe utility, General Motors Holden's

the sedan's styling and mechanical improvements. The original 6 cylinder gasoline engine steadily gained power starting from a 70 HP and reaching 145 HP by 1969, while a V8 option of 210 HP was introduced a year earlier, but was also augmented through the years. 1972 saw the introduction of a 1 ton utility delivered in chassis/cab form, while the 500 kilo payload models were always the favorite taxi-cabs, also, and are widely used throughout the Pacific area. Holden vehicles are exported worldwide and a series of assembly plants operate in many countries. *GA*

HOLLMANN & JERABEK (A) 1907-1913

Hollmann & Jerabek, Plzen

This company was established in 1861 to build fire equipment, which was always their main business, initially of course horse-drawn and later on motor chassis. In 1907 they introduced a 3-ton truck with a 2-cylinder

1907 HOLLMANN & JERABEK 3-ton truck, MSH

engine and chain drive, designed by Frantisek Kec, later famous for his work with Praga. By 1913 trucks of up to 10 tons capacity were being made, but after that date only fire equipment on other chassis was produced. Hollmann & Jerabek continued in this line until 1942. *MSH*

HOLSMAN (US) 1908-1910

Holsman Automobile Company, Chicago, Illinois

Holsman was one of the best-known manufacturers of high-wheelers and offered light delivery van versions of their passenger cars. Two commercial models were produced, one with an air-cooled two-cylinder engine, the other with water-cooled four cylinder type. Both had friction transmissions and double chain-drive. Wheelbases were 6 feet, 3 inches and 7 feet, 8 inches, reespectively. *GMN*

HONDA (J) 1962 to date

Honda Motor Co. Ltd., Hamamatsu

The world's largest producer of motorcycles, Honda added light cars and vans to their model range in 1962. The tiny 350cc dohc 4-cylinder 4-carbureter engine, 4-speed synchromesh gearbox, coil ifs, and hydraulic brakes were common to both types, but the underfloor mounting of the van's detuned unit allowed of a semi-forward control layout. Later models had a bigger 531 cc engine developing 38 hp but in 1955 Honda introduced a new 350 cc minicar with a transversely-mounted 2-cylinder ohc engine driving the front wheels, and a van model followed shortly afterwards. Forward control returned on the TN350, similarly powered but now with central engine and rear wheel drive; this was still catalogued in 1978 by which time light commercial production was centered on the company's Sayama plant. Honda also manufacture light agricultural tractors. *MCS*

HONG-HE (p), HUNG-HO (wg) (Red River) (CHI) c.1970 to date

Kochiu Truck Works, Kochiu, Yunnan

This is reported by the Chinese to be a 2.5-ton truck built primarily for use in the province. *BE*

HONG-WEI (p), HUNG-WEI (wg) (Red Guard) GZ-140 (CHI) 1968 to date

Kuangehou Motor Vehicle Plant, Kuangehau (Canton), Kwangtung (Plant Vehicle Code-GZ)

First assembled as a prototype in 1966, the Red Guard GZ-140 3.5-ton truck has been produced in some quantity since 1968.

A cab-over-engine design, the vehicle is powered by a model 6940 engine of 120 hp @ 3,400 rpm driving 4 speeds forward.

Chinese sources report a 2.5 ton Red Guard truck has been in production in Shansi Province since 1970. *BE*

HONG-YAN (p), HUNG-YAN (wg) (Red Rock) (CHI) 1965 to date

Chichiang Gear Plant, Chungking, Szechuan (Plant Vehicle Code - CJ)

Among the various trucks turned out by this plant, the Red Rock, or Red Crag, is a 25-ton dumper somewhat similar in appearance to the Russian MAZ.

The truck can travel at 30 km/h fully loaded and can empty its load in 25 seconds. *BE*

1966 HONGYAN 25-ton dump truck, BE

HOGRA (NL) 1955-1960

Van Hoek's Automobiel fabriek N.V., Ravenstein.

Under the marque Hogra Van Hoek manufactured a range of normal control trucks mainly using Austrian-built Steyr parts and a Dutch cab. Vehicles in various lengths were available, both with or without driven front axle, but the marque never became a success and slowly faded away. *JFJK*

HOOVER (U.S.) 1911; 1917-1920

Hoover Wagon Co., York, Pa.

Hoover's first truck production was a batch of 1500-pound electric trucks built on special order in 1911. The firm made truck and auto bodies. A 1-ton gasoline truck was introduced in 1917. It had a 20 hp Continental 4-cylinder engine and bevel drive. In 1919 the chassis cost $1,435. Many Hoover trucks were fitted with mail van bodies for the government. *DJS*

HOPE STAR (J) 1952-1962

Hope Jidosha Co. Ltd., Tokyo

Hope Stars were conventional 7-cwt 3-wheeled trucks remarkable only for their 350 cc twin-piston 2-stroke engines. In 1960 the company introduced a 5cwt 4-wheeler, the Unicar, with a 17 hp 2-cylinder power unit, 3-speed synchromesh gearbox, and coil ifs. They also made some ultra-light 4x4s along similar lines. *MCS*

HORA (GB) 1905

E. & H. Hora Ltd., Peckham, London S.E.

Hora's were principally known as bodybuilders but around 1905 they sold, under their own name, a few undertype steam wagons having vertical water-tube boilers and compound undertype engines with chain drive. They also sold gas engine trucks and buses with 24 hp 4-cylinder engines below the driver's seat. These were of French origin, probably Brillie. *RAW*

HORBICK (GB) 1907-1909

Horsfall & Bickham Ltd., Pendleton, Manchester

This textile machinery company built cars in various sizes from 1902 to 1909, and offered their 12/16 hp 4-cylinder chassis with either 8 cwt delivery van or taxicab bodywork. *GNG*

HORCH (D) 1912-1945

(1) A. Horch & Co. Motorwagenwerke A.G., Zwickau 1912-1932

(2) Auto Union A.G., Werk Horch, Zwickau 1932-1945

From 1912 Horch vans were available based on the private car designs. In 1913 trucks and buses followed which in the following years were built especially for military use.

After WW I Horch continued to build commercial vehicles. These were a 1½ tonner with 4-cylinder 10/20 PS engine and a 3½ tonner with 4-cylinder 25/42 PS engine. In about 1925 production of trucks was discontinued. A 6-wheeled all-terrain vehicle was presented in 1926 using an 8-cylinder 3.5 litre engine. Vans were further available on various private car chassis'. These were also used for small fire engines, ambulances, hearses etc. A 4x4 vehicle with V-8 engine of 3.8 litre capacity was developed to military specifications. For postwar production see IFA. *HON*

HORLEY (GB) 1905-1909

Horley Motor & Engineering Co. Ltd., Horley, Surrey

Horley's principal interest was in cheap light runabouts, and from 1905 these chassis were also offered with light van bodywork for payloads from 5 to 15 cwt. Specification was conventional, with sv engines of various makes. The smallest 9 hp had a 1.3-litre single said to be of their own make, the 10-cwt used a 905 cc White & Poppe twin, and the 15-cwt of 1908-09 cost £245 and used a 1.7-litre vertical-twin Aster. *MCS*

HORNER (US) 1913-1918

Detroit-Wyandotte Motor Co., Wyandotte, Mich

This make began as a single model, a 5 tonner, but in 1914, this was joined by 1-, 1½-, 2- and 3-tonners. All but the largest were on a single chassis with wheelbase of 12 feet, 1 inch while the 5-tonner used 13 feet. All models used 4-cylinder engines by Continental mounted beneath a sloping French-type hood. The entire line of models used 3-speed gearboxes and double chain-drive. *GMN*

HORN LITTLEWOOD (GB) 1905-1907

Horn, Littlewood & Co. Ltd., Gainsborough, Lincs.

This company made a 30 cwt van powered by a 15 hp 2-cylinder engine under the driver's seat, with chain drive. The price was £385. They also advertised 3 to 5-ton trucks, buses and cabs, but it is unlikely that these were made. By August 1906 the name had been changed to Hornwood. *GNG*

HOTCHKISS (F) 1936-1970

(1) Automobiles Hotchkiss, St Denis, Seine 1936-1954

(2) Societe Hotchkiss-Delahaye, St. Denis, Seine 1954-1956

(3) Societe Hotchkiss-Brandt, St Denis, Seine 1956-1968

(4) Compagnie Francaise Thomson-Houston-Hotchkiss-Brandt, St. Denis, Seine 1968-1970

It was not until 1936 that the famous French car and ordnance works took up serious truck production, though before 1914 their heavier chassis had been much favored for fire engine work, and between the Wars their engines went into commercial and military vehicles made by Laffly, La Licorne and Morris-Bollee. Their first truck was a straightforward normal control 2-tonner with 4-speed gearbox and double reduction drive powered by the 2.3-litre 4-cylinder ohv unit also fitted to their 13CV car. Like the cars, Hotchkiss trucks came with rhd as standard. The postwar PL20 was much the same, though payload was up to 2½ tons, the traditional horseshoe radiator gave

1956 HOTCHKISS PL25 2½-ton van, GNG

way to an American-style grille, and brakes were hydraulic, latterly with servo assistance. This model continued with little further change until 1954, the range being augmented by a forward-control 22-seater coach chassis (1954), and a diesel option (the ubiquitous Perkins P4) in 1958. An interesting military experimment of 1952 was a 6-cylinder light 4x4 intended to replace the ¾-ton Dodge, but this was not adopted, and a year later Hotchkiss took out a Jeep license, continuing to manufacture these vehicles until the end in 1970. Later ones could be had with Indenor diesel engines. The Hotchkiss-Delahaye merger of 1954 killed off both makes of private car, and in the early 1960s the company sought to widen the appeal of their trucks (never big sellers) by an

1965 HOTCHKISS 3-4-ton truck, OMM

agreement under which they sold Leyland products - and also Leyland-engined Belgian Brossel buses - in France. This did not last long. By 1962 Hotchkiss had introduced a diesel-engined unitary construction coach, produced in association with the Currus coachbuilding firm, and two years later the aged 13CV gasoline engine disappeared, though the PL range of trucks was still available as late as 1967. The last new Hotchkiss model, introduced in 1964, was a 3/4-ton forward control machine with tilt cab and 4- or 5-speed all-synchromesh gearbox, available with 3½-litre short-stroke 4-cylinder gas or diesel engines of their own make. Sundry variations on this theme were offered, including a coach chassis, civilian and military 4x4s, and

1967 HOTCHKISS PL90 3-ton 4×4 army truck, OMM

even a full-track truck for the army; more powerful 6-cylinder engines - the gasoline version gave 215 bhp - came in 1968. After 1970, however, the company devoted itself entirely to the manufacture of ordnance. *MCS*

HOUGHTON (US) 1915-1917

Houghton Motor Co., Marion, Ohio

This was an assembled 1-tonner with a 22 hp 4-cylinder engine and pneumatic tires. It was usually seen with the company's hearse bodywork. *MCS*

HOWARD (i) (US) 1903

Howard Automobile Co, Yonkers, N.Y.

Designed by W.S. Howard who had previously been with the Grant-Ferris company, the Howard was made in passenger and goods versions, the latter with a 3-cylinder engine and a load capacity of 1,000 lbs. There was also a 4-ton gas-electric truck with a 25/30 hp 4-cylinder engine mounted vertically under the floor driving a dynamo which fed two General Electric motors, one for each rear wheel. Its speed was 5 mph loaded and 9 mph empty. It had two coil radiators, at front and rear. *GNG*

HOWARD (ii) (GB) 1903-1904

J. & F. Howard Ltd., Bedford

Howards were noted makers of agricultural machinery and had built steam plowing and traction engines in the nineteenth century. Their wagon was shown at the Smithfield Show in 1903. It employed a vertical boiler incorporating coiled steel water tubes but the actual

1904 HOWARD (ii) steam wagon, Autocar

design is obscure. The undertype enclosed engine was compound, had Stephenson's link motion and was provided with a simpling valve. Experience of wagon building quickly persuaded Howards, however, that other fields were more profitable. *RAW*

HOWARD (iii) (US) 1915-1916

Robert G. Howard Motor Truck Co., Boston, Mass

This was a light open delivery wagon of 1500 lbs payload powered by a 4-cylinder Continental engine, with Covert 3-speed transmission. This was unusual in that it was mounted in unit with the Salisbury rear axle. *GNG*

HOWE (US) 1932 to date

Howe Fire Apparatus Co., Anderson, Ind.

The Howe company was founded in 1872, and built their first pumper on a motor chassis in 1907. They were building on Ford Model T chassis in 1917, and in the 1920s built the Howe Defender on Defiance chassis. When Defiance production ceased in 1930 they began to make their own chassis, also called Defender, as well as using commercial chassis such as Ford, Chevrolet and International. The New Defender on a Waukesha-engined Duplex chassis came in 1953, with 750, 1000 and 1250 gpm pumpers, open or closed cabs. Pumpers on commercial chassis were still made in the 1950s and 1960s. In 1967 came a new custom cab-forward chassis with Detroit Diesel engine and open or closed Cincinnati cab, still called the Defender. In 1974 Howe acquired the Oren-Roanoke and Coast companies. *GNG*

HUAINAN (CHI) 1970 to date

Huainan Motor Vehicle Plant, Huainan, Anhwei

Production of trucks at this plant commenced July 1, 1970 with the appearance of Huainan and Miner brand vehicles. No details are available as to construction. *BE*

HUANG-HE (p), HUANG-HO (wg) (Yellow River) (CHI) 1964 to date

Tsinan General Motor Vehicle Plant, Tsinan, Shantung (Plant Vehicle Code - JN)

From a prototype in 1959 to production in 1964, the cab-over-engine Yellow River JN-150 8-ton diesel truck has evolved as an important part of the growing number of Chinese - built commercial vehicles.

Power is by an in-line 4-stroke, 6-cylinder diesel engine of 160 hp @ 1,800 rpm driving five speeds forward.

Maximum speed is 71 km/h with a fuel consumption of 24 liters/100 km.

A JN-151 of slightly less capacity is also produced as well as dump trucks and buses. *BE*

HUANG-HE (p), HUANG-HO (wg) (Yellow River) OD-351 (CHI) to date

Tsingtao Motor Vehicle Manufacturing and Parts Plant, Shantung (Plant Vehicle Code - OD)

This is a 7-ton dump truck that uses a Shangai-built diesel engine identical to that used in the Yellow River JN-150.

The all-metal cab seats one, there are five speeds forward with power assist and top speed is 63 km/h. *BE*

HUBBARD (GB) 1905-c.1906

Hubbard Motor & Engineering Co. Ltd., Coventry

This was tricar-based trade carrier powered by the firm's own make of 3½ hp single-cylinder engine and using belt drive to the single rear wheel. The 3 cwt load was carried in a wicker basket between the front wheels. *GNG*

HUBER (US) 1903

Huber Automobile Co., Detroit, Mich.

A two-ton delivery wagon was built to move at 25 mph and they were designing a 30 to 40 passenger bus. Production appears to have been extremely limited. *RW*

1947 HUDSON (i) ¾-Ton Pickup, EK

HUDSON (i) (US) 1933-1947

Hudson Motor Car Co., Detroit, Mich.

Though light truck and ambulance versions of the Super 6 car were made for the US Army in 1917, and some Essex pickups produced for factory use in 1922, the first Hudson-built commercial vehicle offered to the public was the Dover of 1929. Thereafter there was a lull until 1933, when a range of ½-ton models was offered on the new inexpensive Terraplane 6 chassis. Hudson commercials were marketed as Essex Terraplanes in 1933, as Terraplanes from 1934 to 1937, and as Hudsons thereafter: all were closely based on the cars, and all used splash-lubricated sv 6-cylinder engines. From 1934 onwards capacity was 3½ litres, with the short-stroke 112 unit used in the ½-tonners of 1938 and 1939 only. A forward-control ½-ton short-stop delivery van made a brief appearance in 1941, in which year the company's regular ¾-ton pickup had the longest wheelbase (10ft 8in) of any vehicle in its class. Production ceased with the advent of the advanced Stepdown series of cars at the end of 1947, though a prototype Stepdown pickup was tested. *MCS*

HUDSON (ii) (GB) 1963

Robert Hudson (Raletrux) Ltd.

This was an unusual example of a vehicle built purely as a cement mixer. Called the Frontomatic Transit Mixer, it was powered by a 125 hp Leyland diesel engine and had a 5-speed gearbox. The 4½ cu yd mixer discharged from the front over the one-man cab. *GNG*

HUFFMAN (US) 1919-1927

(1) Huffman Bros Motor Co., Elkhart, Ind. 1919-1927
(2) Valley Motor Truck Co., Elkhart, Ind. 1927-1929
(3) Elkhart Motor Truck Co., Elkhart, Ind. 1929-1931

Huffman trucks were orginally offered in 1½-tonner form, with either worm or bevel gear rear axle. Both had Fuller 3-speed gearboxes and Continental engines were normally used. From 1923 a Buda engine was used in the bevel drive model, and in 1925 the range was extended to include larger trucks of up to 3½-tons capacity. In 1927 Buda, Continental, Hercules and Wisconsin engines were all offered in a range of 1½ to 4-ton trucks, but in the same year the name of company and product was changed to Valley or Valley Dispatch. Hercules engines were chiefly used in the 2½-4-ton Valley trucks, up to 1929 when the name was changed again to Elkhart. Few of these were made, and all production ended in 1931. *GMN*

HUG (US) 1922-1942

The Hug Co., Highland, Ill.

C.J. Hug was a roadbuilder who found that none of the trucks on the market satisfied his requirements as they were too low geared and lacked suitable bodies, so in 1921 he built a prototype of his own design, and went into production with it early in 1922. Powered by a 34 hp 4-cylinder Buda MU engine, the Model T had a Warner 3-speed gearbox and Clark spiral bevel rear axle, giving a top speed of 45 mph, a high figure for even a 1-tonner in 1922, let alone a 2-tonner which the Hug was. It had pneumatic tires, and open cab and the choice of a rectangular body for dry loads or an inverted trapezoidal body for wet mixed concrete. For 1925 the T was joined by

1925 HUG Model 60 Roadbuilder, CR

the 3½-ton Model CH, followed in 1927 by the 4-6-ton Model 88 powered by a 43 hp Buda KUBI engine with Brown-Lipe 7-speed transmission and Wisconsin rear axle. By the early 1930s Hug Roadbuilder trucks were getting larger and larger; the 1937 range included 6½, 18

1934 HUG Model 99 6×4 dump truck, CR

1936 HUG Model 15AS 2½-ton milk tanker, CR

and 20-ton Roadbuilders with 6-cylinder Buda gasoline or 4-cylinder Caterpillar diesel engines. These were 4x2 or 6x4 trucks with shaft drive, but for quarry work there were 6x2 and 6x4 chain-driven models, the chain-drive units being made by the Six Wheel Co. of Los Angeles who made even larger trucks themselves under the name Maxi. A long overhanging shelf, serving as a roof, was built into the front of the dump body as a shelter for the driver. Chassis prices for the quarry trucks ran as high as $18,320 for the 120,000 lb GVW Model C99MA, the largest Hug ever made. A special option for the 6-wheelers was a J. Walter Christie detachable half-track to loop the tandems for work on soft ground. For 1939 a general change from Buda to Waukesha gasoline engines was made, though diesels were still Caterpillar. Hugs were widely used in roadmaking, housing estate construction and dam building; one of the most important customers was the Tennessee Valley Authority who bought 29 of the large 6-wheelers which were made from 1929 to 1940.

Although Roadbuilders and quarry trucks formed the major part of Hug's production, and earned the company fame as they were the first purpose-built trucks of this kind, there were also a number of highway trucks called "Xpress" in 2,3, and 3½-ton sizes, powered by 6-cylinder Buda engines. Some of the tractors had sleeper cabs when these were far from usual, and there were some cab-over tractors powered by Buda gasoline or Cummins diesel engines. The 1938 Model 16 10-ton cab-over tractor used a 468cu in Caterpillar diesel engine.

In about 1938 the Hug Company began building rear-engined bus chassis, and also undertook the conversion of standard truck chassis. For a brief period Hug offered

1941 HUG rear-engine bus, MBS

completely assembled buses, with a body design of sectional construction which was the basis for the later "Mate" series of bodies built by the Wayne works–not surprising since C.J. Hug's office was in the Wayne factory at Richmond, Indiana.

After war broke out in Europe Hug built eight of the Model 50-6 cargo trucks, 6x6 7½-tonners powered by Hercules engines and generally resembling the Marmon-Herringtons of the period. These went overseas under Lend-Lease. After 1939 the number of giant truck models was reduced, and Hug built a series of highway trucks looking identical to the 1941 round-nosed Reos since they bought sheet metal from Reo. Most of these were sold to the Pet Milk Co which, over many years, had bought a total of 177 trucks from Hug. The last Hug truck left the factory on June 10th 1942, ending a 20-year production run of 4,014 units, including about 50 trailers. Hugs were widely distributed, being sold in 41 states and 7 foreign countries including Mexico and South America. *RW*

HUMBEE (J) c.1947-1961

Mitsui Precision Machinery Co. Ltd., Okegawa

Humbees were handlebar-steered 3-wheeled light trucks and vans using 285cc 2-stroke single-cylinder engines. Later ones had fiberglass bodies, and the range included a Surrey with detachable top for three passengers or goods. The company undertook sub-contract work for Hino, and 1961 Humbees were marketed under the Hino name. *MCS*

HUMBER (GB) 1904-1915: 1939-1945: 1951-1954

(1) Humber Ltd., Beeston, Notts 1904-1908
(2) Humber Ltd., Coventry 1904-1945
(3) Humber Ltd., Ryton-on-Dunsmore, Warwickshire 1951-1954

Humber's first light van was based on the 6½ hp single-cylinder Royal Humberette. It had a 2-speed gearbox and shaft drive, and carried 8 cwt on Post Office service, with a fuel consumption of 20 mpg. The quest for more power led to a van version of the miniature 2-litre 8/10 hp four, with pneumatics at the front and solids at the rear, selling for 250 guineas, and light vans were available on Humber's smaller 4-cylinder chassis until 1909. 1907 saw the beginning of Britain's big taxicab boom, and Humber made several types.. Initially these were Coventry-built, with a compact 7 ft wheelbase achieved by the use of a cab-over-engine layout, 15 hp 4-cylinder engines, coil ignition, 3-speed gearboxes, and auxiliary transverse springs at the rear. In 1908 the cab range embraced coe and normal control versions of the smaller 10/12 hp, plus a 2½-litre Beeston-Humber cab with magneto instead of coil ignition. By 1910 only the normal control 10/12 was still offered, though Humber Ltd ran a fleet of 40 such cabs in London. Thereafter commercial vehicle manufacture lapsed until 1914, when a 2½-cwt van version of the 998cc V-twin watercooled Humberette cyclecar was marketed, followed soon after by 10- and 12-cwt delivery vans on car chassis, with 4-cylinder sv monobloc engines, 4-speed gearboxes, and detachable wheels. These were to be the last Humber commercials to go on sale, though during World War II the Allied Armies used a vast diversity of light trucks, ambulances, utilities and armoured cars based on the 4.1-litre 6-cylinder Super Snipe car. Both 4x2 and 4x4 types were produced, and their success led to the retention of the Humber name on the 1-ton 4x4 FV1600 designs built for the Army between 1951 and 1954. These

1952 HUMBER FV1604(A) 1-ton 4×4 truck, BHV

were powered by a 4-litre 6-cylinder Rolls-Royce B60 engine, other features being 5-speed gearboxes, hydraulic brakes, and all-independent suspension. About 3,500 were made, the mechanical elements being produced in the old Tilling-Stevens factory at Maidstone, and assembled at Ryton. *MCS*

HUNSLET (GB) 1905
Hunslet Engine Co. Ltd.. Leeds. Yorks.

1905 HUNSLET 4-ton truck, OMM

Also known as the Attila, this was a short-lived 4-ton truck powered by a 20 hp 3-cylinder engine. Final drive was by shaft. *GNG*

HUPMOBILE (US) 1912-1914
Hupp Motor Car Co., Detroit, Mich.

The Model H-32 was a closed delivery van with rated capacity of 800 lbs. This used a 4-cylinder water-cooled engine under the hood, a 3-speed gearbox and shaft-drive. This chassis was the same as used for the Hupmobile Model H-32 passenger automobile, of the year 1913. Springs on this model were semi-elliptic in front and transverse at the rear, and wheelbase was 8 feet, 10 inches with a price of $950. In 1918, Hupp announced it would produce a ½-tonner but there is no evidence this proposal was ever brought to reality. *GMN*

HUPP-YEATS (US) 1911-1912
R.C.H. Corp., Detroit, Mich.

This battery-powered electric truck was a ½-tonner with several closed and open types of bodies. Gross weight of the vehicle was 2700 pounds of which the 27-cells of acid batteries weighed 920 lbs. This was furnished with cushion-type solid rubber tires and was priced at $1600 for a screen-sided express van. The name Hupp-Yeats was also applied to a line of passenger cars. *GMN*

HURACAN (E) 1955-1960
Huracan Motors S.A., Barcelona

This company made a series of light vehicles including 3-wheelers with 125 cc and 197 cc single-cylinder Hispano-Villiers engines, and a 4-wheeler known as the Autocarro, powered by a 325 cc 2-cylinder engine, with 3-speed gearbox and shaft drive. *JCG*

HURLBURT (US) 1912-1927
(1) Hurlburt Motor Truck Co., New York City, N.Y. 1912-1915
(2) Hurlburt Motor Truck Co., Bronx, N.Y. 1915-1919
(3) Harrisburg Mfg. & Boiler Co., Harrisburg, Pa. 1919-1927

This make began with a line of 1, 2, and 3½ tonners which by 1918 had been expanded to include 5 and 7 tonners, the two largest with 6-cylinder engines. These were Buda units, while other components included Brown-Lipe gearboxes and worm-drive rear axles. For the first five years, all Hurlburt production was taken up by firms in the metropolitan New York area, including John Wanamakers, Tiffany Studios and Schulz bread; after 1917 sales were extended to other areas on the East Coast. In 1918 a V-radiator was introduced. The 6-cylinder 7-tonner was discontinued in 1920 but reintroduced four years later, and by the end of production in 1927 the Hurlburt range consisted of five models from 3 to 10 tons capacity, the latter an articulated 6-wheeler. Buda engines were used throughout. *GMN*

HURLIMANN (CH) 1957 to date
Theodor Hurlimann, Transporte, Wetzikon, ZH

1975 HURLIMANN 8×4×4 (4-wheel steering) tipper truck, FH

Hurlimann was a truck operator who built a 4x4 tipper to suit his own requirements. It was an unconventional machine, articulated just behind the front axle so dispensed with conventional steering arrangements. Twin wheels were used at front and rear, and the power unit was a 90 hp 6-cylinder Mercedes-Benz engine. Only one was made, but in 1964 he produced a new truck on similar lines, of which five were made by Jules Egli of Wetzikon. These had payloads of 7 tons. In 1974 Hurlimann built another one-off, this time an 8x4 tipper powered by a V-10 Mercedes-Benz 320 hp engine on which axles 1 and 3 were steered, while 2 and 4 transmitted power. It again has an articulated chassis, and a turning circle of only 37 feet which must be the smallest of any 8-wheeled vehicle made. *FH*

HURLINCAR (GB) 1914-1915

Hurlin & Co. Ltd., Hackney, London E.

The Hurlincar was a conventional light car powered by a 4-cylinder 10 hp Ballot engine, which was also made in 5 cwt van form. *GNG*

HURMID (GB) 1909-1910

Hurst & Middleton Ltd., Holloway, London N.7.

George Hurst was initially a model maker with premises at 293, High Holborn. From 1897 until 1900, he built cars with Lewis A Lloyd under the name Hurst & Lloyd and after the latter's departure other models were marketed under the Hurst name. R.B. Middleton joined Hurst in 1906 and from 1907 the cars were known as Hurmids. In common with many other firms, the new company offered a taxicab during the period shown with 10 hp twin cylinder engine, and a 15/18 hp 4-cylinder engine first shown at the Stanley Show in 1905 was also offered to other manufacturers. *MJWW*

HUSTLER (BS) 1976 to date

Arawak Motors Ltd., Antigua

The Hustler is a small general-purpose vehicle on the lines of the Mini-Moke, but using Hillman Imp components. Passenger and goods-carrying models are made. Production was running at about five per week in the Spring of 1978, but with the end of Imp production, the company was looking for alternative component supply. Most Hustlers are exported to neighboring Caribbean islands such as St. Kitts. *GNG*

HYUNDAI (KO) 1974 to date

Hyundai Motor Co. Seoul

Korea's first independent automobile factory was set up under the direction of former British Leyland executive George Turnbull. The Pony sedan was launched at the 1974 Turin Show, and this conventional design, with 1.2-litre ohc 4-cylinder Mitsubishi engine, 4-speed gearbox, coil-spring ifs, and disc/drum brakes, was also available as a light pickup. In 1978 a program of heavier commercial vehicles was put in train. Built to the designs of Trevor Lacey from Bedford, these were to be fitted with locally assembled Perkins Diesel units. The small 4-108 featured in 1-tonners, but the heaviest 7-tonners employed turbocharged editions of the 6-354. *MCS*

1972 IBEX 6×4 tractor with low bed trailer, Jelco Inc

IBEX (US) 1964 to date

(1) Hafer-Ibex Corp., Salt Lake City, Utah
(2) Ibex Motor Truck Corp., Salt Lake City, Utah
(3) Ibex Division, Jelco Inc., Salt Lake City, Utah

Named from an Asiatic mountain goat, the first Ibex trucks were custom-built conventionals made in 4x4, 6x4 and 6x6 models, both rigid trucks and tractors. Engines were 195 hp Detroit Diesel 6-cylinder, 270 hp Caterpillar 6-cylinder or 340 hp Caterpillar V-8, and other components included Spicer and Dana transmissions, Rockwell and American Coleman transfer cases, Rockwell and Eaton axles and Hendrickson suspensions. Although suitable for highway travel, the Ibex was engineered for tough off-highway work as well, such as construction, exploration and oil drilling.

In 1970 Ibex introduced a completely different type of vehicle, a short-wheelbase trailer spotter named the Flexi-Truc. These were marketed by Flexi-Truc Inc. of Secaucus, New Jersey. There are two models, with low and high cabs. Another Ibex product is the 900 series 6x4 construction truck in low cab-forward and high cab-over models. Engines of Flexi-Truc and 900 series are Ford gasoline, or Cummins, Caterpillar or Detroit Diesels. *RW*

IDEAL (i) (US) 1910-1915

Ideal Auto Co., Fort Wayne, Ind.

The Ideal began as a ¼-tonner and a 1-tonner, with the two smaller powered by 2-cylinder, water-cooled engines while the largest had a 4-cylinder version. All had planetary transmissions, double chain drive and solid rubber tires. For 1912, all types had 4-cylinder engines and forward control. Stake and express types were available on all the chassis. During the last year of manufacture, 1-, 1½- and 2½-tonners were offered with selective gearboxes but maintained the drive chains. *GMN*

IDEAL (ii) (E) 1915-1922

Fabrica Espanola de Automoviles y Aeroplanos Talleres Hereter S.A., Barcelona

This company made agricultural and marine engines, aircraft engines and complete airplanes as well as cars and commercial vehicles. The latter were made in two sizes, an 8 hp van with a capacity of 500 kgs, known as the Ideal, and a 15 hp truck or bus chassis (1000 to 1500 kgs capacity) generally known as the T.H. Few of these were made as the company concentrated on touring cars and aircraft. *JCG*

IDEN (GB) 1905-1907

Iden Motor Car Co. Ltd., Coventry

Formerly works manager of M.M.C., George Iden set up his own firm in 1904 and made a small number of cars and commercial vehicles. The latter included a 25 hp 4-cylinder chassis intended for a 2 ton load or 25 passengers, and a front-wheel-drive taxicab with 12 hp V-twin engine under the front seat. The former was shown at Olympia in November 1905, and the latter introduced at the end of 1907, but few were made of either vehicle. *GNG*

1949 IFA-LOWA SD65 steam tractor, HON

c.1958 IFA-Sachsenring S4000 articulated tanker, OMM

c.1970 IFA W50LA 4½-ton 4×4 tractor, OMM

IFA (DDR) 1948 to date

IFA Vereinigung Volkseigener Fahrzeugwerke

This combine of nationalized factories in Eastern Germany was formed in 1948 as a head organization for various manufacturing plants.

(1) VEB Kraftfahrzeugwerke Horch, Zwickau 1946-1957
(2) VEB Sachsenring Kraftfahrzeug- und Motorenwerk, Zwickau 1957-1958
(3) VEB Sachsenring Automobilwerke, Zwickau 1958-1960

In 1946 the production of a 3 ton H3 truck was taken up in the former Horch factory. A 6-cylinder 4.2 litre Maybach engine of 100 hp was used which was available in larger quantities from wartime production. From 1950 a 6.1 litre diesel engine was used. Some changes appeared in the models Sachsenring S 4000 in 1958 (6.1 litre, 80 hp) and S 4000-1 in 1959 (90 hp), the latter staying in production until 1967.

(4) VEB Lokomotiv- und Waggonbau, Werdau 1949-1952
(5) VEB IFA Kraftfahrzeugwerk Ernst Grube, Werdau 1952-1967

This factory started production of commercials in 1949 with a steam tractor Lowa SD 65, using a 3-cylinder 65 hp engine. Also production of trolley buses was taken up using the brand name Lowa. A unique development were articulated double-deck trolley buses. In 1951 a few buses were built using 120 hp Maybach engines (type W 500), followed by a forward control bus version of the Horch H3. A 6 ton truck H6 was taken into production in 1953 and was also available as a bus version. In 1960 production of the S 4000-1 truck was transferred from Zwickau to Werdau and was produced until 1967.

(6) VEB IFA Automobilwerke, Ludwigsfelde 1965 to date

As a successor to the S 4000-1 a new type W 50 (5 ton) was designed. A 4-cylinder 6.5 litre diesel engine of 100 hp is used. A 125 hp version is available since 1967 and is installed in the 16 ton prime-mover, 10 ton articulated tractor and the 5 ton tipper, the latter being also available with 4x4 drive.

(7) VEB IFA Kraftfahrzeugwerk Framo, Hainichen 1949-1957

(8) VEB Barkas-Werke, Hainichen 1957-1961

In 1949 production of cars was taken up again with the type V 501 with a 500 cc two-stroke engine. In 1952 a modernized version with 3-cylinder 2-stroke engine of IFA-F-9 origin appeared. Since 1954 the name "Framo" was replaced by "Barkas". For further models see under this heading.

(9) VEB IFA-Werke Phanomen, Zittau 1949-1957

(10) VEB Robur-Werke, Zittau 1957-1960

Production in the Phanomen works was resumed in 1949 with a 1.5 ton model "Granit 27" using a 4-cylinder 2.7 litre engine with compressed air cooling, well known from pre-war Phanomen cars. Engine capacity was increased in the following years. In 1956 the name "Phanomen" was dropped in favor of "Robur". For further models see under this heading. *HON*

I.H.C. see International

1956 IKARUS (i) 30 bus, Techniart

1974 IKARUS (i) 255 coach, MSH

IKARUS (i) (H) 1948 to date

Ikarus Karosszeria es Jarmugyar, Budapest, Matyasfold

The best known Hungarian post war factory was a result of the automotive industry reorganization that took place in the mid '40s. Ikarus was established as a continuation of the firm Uhry Imre es Flai engineering works, body builders since the turn of the century. First Ikarus buses were constructed on Csepel chassis and were powered by 85 hp Csepel diesel engines, but integrally-built buses and coaches were soon added to the range. Ikarus buses are well equipped and built to high quality standards, two factors that permitted exports to rise, early. By 1970 80% of all units built were exported, while production was 17 times larger than in 1948. Ikarus buses and coaches according to customer's demands were powered by Csepel, Perkins and Henschel diesels developing 95 - 172 hp, while underfloor units fitted to the 180 family of buses and coaches that was introduced in 1960, were also Leyland, Saurer and of course Raba M.A.N. developing 170 - 200 hp. An articulated city bus was soon added to the range and a general facelift was evident with the 200 series introduced in 1967. This series was awarded the silver cup at the 19th Motor Bus Week in Nice in 1969. In the field of cooperation, Ikarus built integral bodies on Scania underframes and bodies on Volvo and Austrian Saurer chassis, while specialized bodyworks include also fire-fighting vehicles and refrigerated vans of integral construction. In 1978, Ikarus articulated buses were offered on the U.S. market by Crown Coach Corp. *GA*

IKARUS (ii) (YU) 1970 to date

Karoserija Ikarus, Zemun

A long established aircraft factory, with body building facilities, that must not be confused with the Hungarian bus factory bearing the same name, Ikarus entered the automotive field introducing an integrally built city bus of 100 passenger capacity. The bodywork is of Ikarus construction also and has a pleasant external appearance, while a Hungarian built 192 hp Raba M.A.N. underfloor diesel engine and Raba axles provide motive power for the bus. *GA*

IKEGAI (J) 1934-1940

Ikegai Automobile Manufacturing Co., Ltd., Kawasaki

This firm built a diesel engine in 1932, progressing to complete trucks two years later. 2- and 3-ton diesel models were produced, the former with a 4-cylinder engine and the latter with a 6.6-litre six developing 70 hp. Production (which included buses) ran at 30 units a month until 1940, when the company concentrated on marine engines. *MCS*

IMP (US) 1913-1915

W.H. McIntyre Co., Auburn, Ind.

The Imp was a light ¼-tonner based on a cyclecar chassis. It used a 2-cylinder, 4-stroke air-cooled engine with V-belt drive, transverse springs and had a gross weight of 600 lbs. The single-seater parcel van was priced at $395. *GMN*

IMPERIA (D) 1927

Imperia-Werk A.G., Bad Godesberg

The tri-van of this firm followed motorcycle lines, having two front wheels and one driven rear wheel. Own engines were used. *HON*

I.M.V. (YU) 1960 to date

Industrija Motornih Vozil, Novo Mesto

The firm of Motomontaji at Novo Mesto had assembled DKW light commercials since 1955 and consequently introduced their own designed series of light commercials based on DKW experience and still using the same engine, front wheel drive principle and mechanical units. Built as a van, truck, minibus and ambulance the IMV 1000 was powered by the DKW 3-cylinder, two stroke gasoline engine developing 44 hp until 1958, when an agreement with the British Leyland concern calling for the local assembly of Austin cars led to the introduction of the well proven BMC 1.6 litre gasoline developing 62 hp. IMV vehicles were always very like the light Hanomag (ex Tempo) range and resembled them even more, when the 1.5 ton series was introduced featuring three axles, the front driven and the rear 2 trailing. At the time when British Leyland was exchanged with a new partner, Renault of France, engines were once again changed for French units, while at the 1975 Belgrade Motor Show IMV exhibited a slightly redesigned 1.5 ton range powered by a Mercedes-Benz diesel engine as an alternative to the gasoline units. *GA*

INBUS (I) 1975 to date

Industrie Autobus, Milan

These integral-construction buses were the products of a consortium — Breda of Pistoia, de Simon of Udine, Sofer of Naples, and Sicca of Treviso, the last-mentioned firm being responsible for the ladder-type frames and air suspension units. Other features were Fiat diesel engines with electric fan-assisted cooling, power steering, and Allison automatic gearboxes. The smallest 8.5-metre 150 series was made in urban (U) and suburban (S) forms: it had air-hydraulic brakes and side-mounted power unit, whereas on bigger models brakes were of full air type, and engines were at the rear. At the top of the range was a 12-metre Grand Touring coach with V8 engine and a hydraulic retarder incorporated in the transmission. *MCS*

1969 IMV 1000 pick-up, AAR

INDEPENDENT (i) (US) 1917-1921

Independent Motor Truck Co., Davenport, Iowa

Two sizes were built under this name, a 1-tonner and a 2-tonner. These were standardized types assembled with Continental engines, Fuller 3-speed gearboxes and Russel bevel-gear rear axles. Wheelbase for the smaller was 135 inches, while the 2-tonner had 146 inches. *GMN*

INDEPENDENT (ii) (US) 1918-1923

Independent Motor Co., Youngstown, Ohio

During the first two years of manufacture, 1-tonners and 2-tonners were made but beginning in 1919, this line of trucks included 1-, 1½, 2- and 3½-tonners. This was another assembled truck using 4-cylinder engines by Continental, 3-speed gearboxes by Fuller and worm-drive rear axles. *GMN*

INDIANA (US) 1911-1939

(1) Harwood-Barley Manufacturing Co., Marion, Ind. 1911-1919

(2) Indiana Truck Corporation, Marion, Ind. 1920-1932

(3) Indiana Motors Corporation, Marion, Ind. 1932-1933

(4) Indiana Motors Corporation, Cleveland, Ohio 1933-1939

For an assembled truck, the Indiana had a long run. The first models used 3.3-litre 4-cylinder Rutenber engines, 4-

1930 INDIANA Six 2-ton van, Techniart

1933 INDIANA 3-ton 4×4 truck, OMM

1934 INDIANA Model 16 bus, MBS

speed gearboxes, and side-chain drive. Rated as 1½ tonners, they were available with pneumatic tires, though solids were standard. By 1920 the factory was said to be capable of making 4000 vehicles a year (their contribution to the American war effort had been 600 units), and a comprehensive range for payloads from 1½ to five tons was offered. Engines were all fours, by Rutenber or Waukesha: capacities extended from 3.8 to 7.7 litres, with worm drive, and 4-speed gearboxes on all but the lightest. A Waukesha-powered 7-tonner followed soon afterward, and from 1924 the 4-cylinder Hercules was standardized in the up- to 3-ton class. An interesting departure of 1925 was a 4/5 tonner with 7-speed transmission and aggressively-styled, detachable sloping radiator grille; the 6½-litre Waukesha engine and back axle were made quick-detachable for servicing. A similar Hercules-engined 3 tonner, the 126, followed in 1926. From 1927 to 1932 the company was under Brockway control, and with the new management came further makes of engine, Continentals as well as the ohv Wisconsin 6, first encountered in a modern 3 ton Speed truck. This one had spiral bevel drive, pneumatics, and full electrics, though brakes were still on the rear wheels only. Spiral bevel back axles soon became standard on light-duty Indianas, but worm drive persisted on the big ones, notably a 4/5-tonner introduced later in 1927. Its Wisconsin unit gave 78 hp, and there were seven forward speeds, but pneumatic tires remained a high-cost option, as they would until 1930 in the 3 ton class and over. A smaller 3.7-litre Wisconsin 6 and fwb made their appearance on the bevel driven 1 ton Ranger of 1928. Standard power units in 1929 were 6-cylinder Wisconsins of up to 6.2 litres. Some of the largest Indianas featured 5-speed gearboxes, and the 1930 catalog included a heavy tractor and a 5½ ton 6-wheeler, both with (10-litre) 6-cylinder Continental units. The fours, however, still came from Hercules.

Control of the company passed from Brockway to White in 1932, and shortly afterwards production was transferred to Cleveland. The new owners, however, preferred to buy 6-cylinder engines from Hercules, other features of White's Indianas being 4- or 5-speed gearboxes, hydraulic brakes, and (except on tandems) spiral bevel drive. The heavier models featured double-reduction back axles, and the medium-duty, 90 hp 95 range included 6x2 and 6x4 versions with all wheels braked. An Indiana had been used by Clessie Cummins, the American diesel pioneer, for long-distance demonstrations of his new design and in the summer of 1932 the company announced the U.S.A.'s first series-production diesel truck. This was a conventional 5 tonner with 125 hp Cummins 6-cylinder unit, but subsequently the Indiana range was curtailed, with nothing bigger than a 2½ tonner listed in 1936. Larger Indianas were, however, still produced, for in accordance with their practice of patronizing smaller firms, the US Army commissioned some 6x6 trucks for payloads of up to 7½ tons. The heaviest ones featured 161 hp Hercules sixes, by contrast with the 73 hp of the 4-6-litre units fitted to civilian models. Interestingly, the White M3A1 military scout car introduced in 1939 was regarded as an Indiana, hence its retention of the Hercules engine (its close relative, the M3 halftrack, had White's own six). 1706 Indianas were sold in 1936, but thereafter the line was quietly run down. In 1937 and 1938 there was still a wide selection of 1- to 5-ton normal control trucks, all with Hercules engines. The 5 tonner had a 5-speed gearbox, hydrovac brakes, and the option of a 6-cylinder Hercules diesel instead of the regular 7-litre gasoline unit. A 50 hp four was optional in the 1 tonner. A plan to make Indianas for the British market at Wolverhampton was announced in 1937, but came to nothing, and by 1939 only the lighter trucks were offered. Some listings, however, suggest that the make was continued into 1940. *MCS*

INLAND (US) 1919-1920

Inland Motor Co., Evansville, Ind.

The sparse information on this tradename indicates there were both 1-tonners and 2-tonners available for just two years, with no details of their construction. *GMN*

INTER-STATE (US) 1916-1917

Inter-State Motor Co., Muncie, Ind.

While this make claims to have built its first commercial vehicle in late 1916, there is a possibility this may have been pre-dated by some activity earlier than 1912. However, the 1917 model was a light commercial vehicle rated at 850-pound capacity. This had a 4-cylinder engine under a hood with pneumatic tires and was priced at $850. The name Inter-State was well-known as a passenger car. *GMN*

INTERBORO (US) 1913-1914

Interboro Motor Truck Co., Philadelphia, Pa.

A 1 ton truck with 23 hp 4-cylinder engine was the only model listed. It cost $1850. *DJS*

1912 INTERNATIONAL Model MW 1-ton truck, TT

INTERNATIONAL (i) (US) 1907 to date

International Harvester Co., Chicago, Ill. (Office) 1907 to date

Factories:

Chicago, Ill. 1907-1961
Akron, Ohio 1907-1925
Springfield, Ohio 1921 to date
Fort Wayne, Ind. 1923 to date

(Engines Only):

Indianapolis, Ind. 1939 to date
Emeryville, Cal. 1946-1963
San Leandro, Cal. 1963 to date

Although the International Harvester Co., per se, dates from 1902, its predecessor companies have roots which go far back in the nation's history-back to 1840 when Cyrus H. McCormick sold two grain reapers. IHC and its predecessors' main program was a continuing mechanization of agriculture, and as an extension of that program, IHC started to manufacture motor vehicles in a fashion that the company thought would be acceptable to the farmers.

After more than two years of prototype development by Edward A. Johnston the first production run of 100 IHC "Auto Buggies" was made in 1907. These were high-wheelers, with some of the wheels reaching 44 inches across. The power plant was a 20 hp 2-cylinder 4-cycle air-cooled gasoline engine with the horizontal cylinders fore and aft under the driver's seat driving through a 2-speed planetary transmission operated by one lever. The transverse propeller shaft had a single chain transferring power to a final double chain drive. The frame was steel, and full-elliptic springs were attached. Tread was the

1916 INTERNATIONAL Model K 1½-ton screenside delivery, Goodyear

standard 56 inch, but a model B had a 60 inch tread for southern and western roads. Steering was right-hand, by wheel.

In 1909 the "Autowagon" model was added, having a wagon body on the rear. This was joined in 1912 by model M along somewhat more conventional lines with a 2-cylinder water-cooled engine under the short hood which had a front radiator. In 1914 the name "International" first appeared on the trucks replacing the "IHC" logo.

For 1915 International's mechanical and styling changes were revolutionary with 4-cylinder L-head engines, 3-speed selective transmissions, and shaft drives to internal gear rear axles. Springs were now semi-elliptic. The radiator was behind the engine which was covered by a front-opening Renault-styled hood. The capacities ranged from ¾- to 2-tons at prices from $1850 to $2800. The 2 ton model, however, was a tall flat-nosed cab-over truck. The high-wheelers were phased out, being almost the last of that type made by any company. Internationals were good sellers, capturing 4% of the truck market in the 'teens. Pneumatic tires were optional on some models for the first time.

For 1921 International joined numerous manufacturers in introducing a ¾ ton speed model which had a 115-inch wheelbase. A thoroughly orthodox design was used for the first time with the radiator in front of the 4-cylinder Lycoming engine, the latter an unusual item, since the company made most of its own components. The clutch was multiple disc followed by a 3-speed selective-sliding transmission and final drive by internal gear. "Speed" trucks of all makes generally went 25 to 30 mph in their time. International produced 7000 trucks in 1921 in a range of 1- to 5-tons, and the speed model from the newly-opened Springfield, Ohio, plant. McCormick-Deering used a fleet of red "speed" Internationals as service trucks. With a pick-up body, this model was known as the "Red Baby."

For 1924 another revolutionary styling change took place on the 1- to 5-ton models. Gone was the French hood; the radiator was now in front and the engine was covered by a butterfly hood. Solid tires had steel spoke wheels. Final drive was plain bevel, double reduction, but a few chain drives were known to have been specially made to order. Models included S, SD, SL, 33(½-ton), 43(2), 63(3), 94(4½), and 105(5), sold by 1500 dealers which were served by 102 branches.

Occasional truck chassis had been used for buses, but

1928 INTERNATIONAL Model S Lang-bodied bus, MBS

now a special bus chassis joined the range in about 1925. Capacity was 25 to 33 passengers, and it had a 6-cylinder engine cast in pairs, spiral-bevel herring-bone drive, full-floating rear axle, and 4-wheel brakes.

In 1926 enclosed cabs started to make their appearance in numbers, and the following year solid tires were phased out. 6-cylinder engines made their appearance in the truck range alongside the four. 1927 production totalled 25000.

The 1 ton International became known as the "6-speed special" (with 2 reverse) with the addition of a 2-speed axle (1928). It also had 4-wheel brakes. 1½- and 2½- ton speed models were added, and a special milk delivery stand-and-drive chassis joined the range. Of the heavyweights, the 3 ton model 63 was the most popular. By 1929 International had expanded to 170 branches, and production reached a record 50,000 trucks that year.

For the 1930 season a whole new line of trucks was announced. The A-series with 2- and 3-ton speed trucks, plus the larger A-series models and the special W-series, covered the overhead-valve type with removable

1929 INTERNATIONAL logging truck, TT

1933 INTERNATIONAL Model A 3-ton tanker, Texaco Archives

1934 INTERNATIONAL C Line articulated truck, TT

cylinders, a "first." 5-speed transmissions were the rule (with 2 reverse), with spiral-bevel drives on the A -series and double reduction herringbone drives for the W-series. Production dropped to 29,000 due to the economic slump.

Demands for greater power were answered by the start of International's producing its own diesel engines in 1933. The smaller A-series became the B-series with scarcely any visible changes, and the following year the company started making its own axles.

For 1934 the new C-series debuted with a V-type aluminum grille and a slightly slanted windshield without the traditional visor. The range broadened with 18 models from ½- to 7-tons, and extended in 1935 to a 10 ton 6-wheeler, using a Hendrickson tandem axle. International now had 217 branches.

A radical new cab-over C-300 joined the range for 1936, the first of its type in some 20 years for International.

The C-series was replaced by the D-series for 1937 which had some really good styling with modern cabs having V-windshields, pontoon fenders, and dashing lines. A newly-designed cab-over was offered, and other models in the range of ½- to 6-tons, and additional tandem capacities. The flat-faced larger models of the A-series were somewhat modernized and continued to 1942, with many A-7's and A-8's being used in New York's subway construction.A new diesel DCO-25 sold well, and with all this going for it, International's production went over 100,000 for the first time.

A sleeper cab appeared in 1938. Metro delivery vans joined the range, with the body made by the Metropolitan Body Co. Bridgeport, Conn. Later this company became an IHC subsidiary.

From 1934 to 1939 International also made station wagons, a couple of which went along on Attilio Gatti's 10th African expedition in which he used 2 special International tractors and semi-traliers. The talented Alexis De Sakhnoffsky designed these.

1940 saw the handsome K-series launched replacing the D-series and having a range of ½- to 8-tons. In that year some 86,000 trucks were built which helped push the lifetime total past the 1,000,000 mark during 1941. International had become the third-ranking truck producer in the United States and said that it sold more trucks of two tons and over than any three other

1937 INTERNATIONAL D Line panel delivery, TT

1941 INTERNATIONAL K Line 3-ton tanker, Texaco Archives

1942 INTERNATIONAL KR8 10-ton articulated truck, NMM

manufacturers combined.

During WWII International made a series of civilian and military 2½- and 5-ton trucks in 4x2, 4x4, and 6x6 drives and a large number of half-trucks, scout cars, and full-tracked personnel carriers. Total combat vehicle production was about 100,000. Marmon-Herrington and Kenworth also built International's H-542-11 military open cab-over truck with the slanted hood and bull-nose.

International's current logo, the red I over black H, first appeared in 1945.

For 1946 the K-series, now KB, was resumed with a face-lift on the smaller models, by extending the grille over the lower fender aprons.

Also, for 1947, International's new Emeryville, Cal. plant started production of a large western-type model with gross vehicle weights up to 90,000 pounds including off-highway use. It was made for west coast trucking, but was soon found elsewhere. The new W-series had a wider cab, flatter V-type windshield, flat radiator and fenders without skirts. The same cab appears to have been used on a western cab-over model with a bull-nose. Two gasoline and three diesel engines were offered with a large variety of transmissions and wheelbases.

The 4 ton Jay-Fong truck made in communist China and the Russian ZIS-150 were very nearly carbon copies of the KB-series International. For 1950 the L-range of 87 basic light- and medium-duty models replaced the KB-range. International designed a new conventional cab with curved windshield and concave instrument panel, and headlights were now in the fenders throughout the range.

1956 INTERNATIONAL 200 COE van, OMM

This cab, made by the Chicago Mfg. Co., was shared, starting in 1953, with the heavier R series conventionals which had three heavy horizontal bars low in the grille, and also shared with Diamond T and several others.

The L-range became, in succession, the S-, A-, and B-ranges, reaching to 1962, each with its own styling changes. In 1963 the Loadstar range succeeded the B-range and continues to date. But the cab-over Loadstar became the current Cargostar, still using the same sheet metal 10 years later, then face-lifted. Meanwhile, the current Fleetstar series was introduced in March, 1963, eventually succeeding the R series after 1967 as the heavy-duty haulers for shorter runs. Currently, the Fleetstar conventionals use two different cabs and two different hoods - steel butterfly or fiberglass tilt.

The first cab-overs of the early 1950's were tall and narrow (LCFD - 405 and others), with a short, rounded hood and styling akin to the R series conventionals. One of the longest production runs was of the new tilt cab-over designed by Diamond T and which was last offered in 1972. This was the cab-forward CO model with the taller side window ventilator than the roll-down section, and also rear quarter side windows. As the VCO, it had a V8; and a DCO, a diesel. Taller line-haul cab-overs had their own ranges, including the CO-405 and Transtars with the trapezoidal grille. Conventional DC-400 Transtars first appeared in 1963, also as line haulers. These were the ones with the tall vent window, resulting in a tall windshield and low hood. They were replaced by the new Transtars 4200 and 4300 in 1971. The Transtars are all diesels.

For 1962 the conventional M-series and F-230 heavyweights of up to 78000 pounds gvw were offered for the construction industry. These had angular tread-plate fenders. Some of these 6x6 concrete block carriers of 15 tons were the legal limit of 35 feet long for a straight truck. The Paystar 5000 series of 1973 was the successor.

About 1964 International started making giant 4x2 and 4x4 quarry dump trucks of up to 154000 pounds gvw (payload is about 5/8 of gvw). By the 1970's IH had 7 models from 80950 to 168445 pounds gvw, powered by 12- and 16-cylinder diesels of 280 to 560 hp with 9-12 speed Allison or Twin Disc transmissions and IH axles. Tires are 16.00 to 18.00x25. These are the largest four-wheel-drive trucks in the world.

1966 INTERNATIONAL R185 6-ton truck, GNG

Currently, the International range of highway trucks includes 12 series: Scout (since 1961) 4x2 and 4x4; Travel All station wagon (since 1960); light-duty series, all 4x2's; Loadstar conventionals some diesels, 4x2, 4x4, 6x4; Fleetstar conventionals some diesels, 4x2, x4; Cargostar cab-overs 4x2, 6x4, some diesels; Transtar conventionals 4x2, 6x4, diesels; Transtar cab-overs, 4x2, 6x4, diesels; Paystar construction trucks, 4x4, 6x4, 6x6, diesels; and school buses. All cab-overs tilt. A CO-8190 cab-forward no-tilt fire engine chassis is also made.

Some 75 Internationnal models are offered with gvw's from 5200 to 180,000 pounds. The range of engines is IH 6-cylinder, 193-215 hp gasoline; IH 200 hp V8 diesel; and diesels by Cummins, Detroit and Caterpillar up to 450 hp; also LP (liquid petroleum) gas (since 1953). Transmissions are New Process, IH, Fuller, or Warner; and rear axles are IH or Spicer.

1966 INTERNATIONAL Fleetstar 2110 articulated truck, GNG

1965 INTERNATIONAL VCO series articulated truck, OMM

1973 INTERNATIONAL Loadstar 1800 6×4 tipper truck, International

International is currently the 5th-ranking US truck manufacturer, after Ford, Chevrolet, Dodge, and GMC; and its lifetime production is one of the largest ever attained in the world. Foreign operations make the total even larger, as International trucks are built in many plants located around the world. Some have their own locally developed models, as in Dandenong, Australia, while others, as in Saltillo, Mexico, built current American versions such as the Loadstar series. There was a British plant at Doncaster, Yorks, from 1965 to 1969. Two other International truck assembly plants are located in Manila, Philippine Islands, and Durban, South Africa.

International's operations are world-wide, with 19 subsidiary companies manufacturing motor trucks, farm machinery, power units, and heavy construction equipment for sale through several thousand dealers in 166 countries around the globe. International has truly lived up to its name. *RAW*

1974 INTERNATIONAL Transtar 4200 6×4 tractor with three-axle trailer, International

1974 INTERNATIONAL Paymaster 5000 10×6 24-ton truck, RW

1975 INTERNATIONAL Cargostar tanker, GNG

INTERNATIONAL (ii) (US) 1908

International Motor Co., Philadelphia, Pa.

This company built 3- and 5-tonners apparently for a single year. Both used four-cylinder water-cooled engines, friction transmissions with front-wheel drive. Roller chains were connected to each front wheel and the power unit was mounted on the front axle which pivoted for steering. Wheelbase for this vehicle was 146 inches and chassis weight was 9500 pounds. *GMN*

INTERNATIONAL (iii) (AUS) 1950 to date

- International Harvester of Australia Pty., Ltd., S. Melbourne, Victoria 1950-1974

- International Harvester Australia Ltd., S. Melbourne, Victoria 1974 to date

International was established in Australia at the turn of the century, but production facilities were built only in the late '30s, too late, though, as the outbreak of WW II didn't permit the building of trucks until well in 1950. Largely expanded in the first postwar years, on contemporary US models, but modified according to local needs. Following local practice, one of the very first models to be built was a large coupe-utility pick-up, a model produced for many years and based on the lighter IH ½ ton commercial. 1959 saw the introduction of the very first Australian designed truck, which was a 2½ ton 4x4 chassis contracted by the Australian Army. Featuring an angular forward control cab, this miltary truck was powered by a 6 cylinder 148 hp gasoline engine of local manufacture, and it soon gave birth to the ACCO series of civilian trucks which was introduced in 1961. Using the same forward control cab and powered by either the 6 cylinder or a V8 gasoline engine developing 177hp and even by a Perkins 6.354 diesel of 120hp ACCO trucks were produced in cargo, tractor and tandem-rear axle versions. The 2.5 ton military truck was followed in 1966 by a 6x6 version, while the civilian range was still modernized in the form of ACCO-A series of 1972. ACCO-A were offered in up to 31,000 kilos GCW rigs and were powered by a variety of IH V8 gasoline or Cummins V8 diesels developing up to 225 hp. The forward control cab was much modernized again. In the meantime the original normal control US based range was developed into series C of medium capacity trucks offered in 4x2 and 4x4 versions and fitted with an all Australian designed cab similar to the cab fitted to Australian Dodge range. Series C was soon developed to series D, while Metro vans and light bus chassis were also built since the mid '60s. To commemorate its 25th year, IH introduced the series ACCO 510A/410A trucks, a modern class of "intermediate" chassis offered in 4x2 and 4x4 versions, featuring a forward control cab and powered by an IH V8 gasoline engine developing 177 hp. IH was also the only Australian company, besides Ford, that met Australian Army demand for a 1 ton 4x4 military truck and submitted a series of prototypes in 1975, that are currently under evaluation. Agricultural machinery is also part of IH production range which is split to three individual factories employing a work force of some 4000 employees in 1975. *GA*

INTERNATIONAL (iv) (TR) 1970 to date

Turk Otomotive Endustrileri A.S., Yenisehir, Ankara

An assembly factory for trucks and tractors, TOE introduced in early '70s the 1200 series of light vehicles fitted with a locally designed and built cab of simplified construction. The range includes a pick-up, a double cab pick-up, a large capacity station wagon and a forward control 17 seater minibus, all based on the International chassis and powered by imported 6 and V8 cylinder gasoline engines developing 145 hp. *GA*

INTRAMOTOR-GLORIA (I) 1972 to date

Intramotor-Gloria SpA, Arcole, Verona

These were ultra-light delivery 3-wheelers with 49 cc F.B.-Minarelli engines, uncoupled 3-wheel brakes and leaf spring rear suspension, made by a cycle and motorcycle factory. The range included a miniature refrigerated van. Early machines were designed for 150 and 200 kg payloads, but the 1978 Titano could carry 250 kg. *MCS*

IRANATIONAL see Paykan

1956 IRESA 200 200kgs 3-wheeler, GNG

IRESA (E) 1956-1959

Industrias Reunidas Espanolas S.A., Madrid

This motorcycle manufacturer also made 3-wheeled vans and trucks powered by 200 cc engines. Final drive was by shaft to the rear axle. *JCG*

IRGENS (N) 1899

Jacob Irgens, Bergen.

Irgens steam bus, so far as is known the only one made in Scandinavia, used a Toward patent boiler, 3-cylinder single acting engine and all-gear drive onto the front (steering) axle. The vehicle was an eighteen seater and provision was made for steam heating the interior in winter. *RAW*

IRIS (GB) 1905-1910

(1) Legros & Knowles Ltd., Cumberland Park, Willesden Junction. London. N.W.

(2) Iris Cars Ltd., Willesden Junction. London. N.W.

(3) Iris Cars Ltd., Aylesbury, Bucks.

The first commercial vehicles offered by Legros & Knowles under the Iris name appeared in June 1905 and utilized the rather crudely engineered 4-cylinder 20 hp double chain driven chassis which had first appeared as the Legros & Knowles car, in February. On this chassis, the firm offered buses, trucks, road tractors and express delivery vans, but with the introduction of an improved range of 4-cylinder engines in November 1905 for the private cars, a 4.2 litre 25/30 hp unit was adopted for the commercials, including a 36-seater omnibus. By 1906, the commercials were utilizing the characteristic diamond-shaped radiator of the private cars, and a shooting brake was added to the range. The company even supplied a tower wagon to Halifax Corporation in May 1906, but no serious production of commercials was ever undertaken. After 1910, and following the takeover by American George Mower's Bifurcated & Metal Rivet Company of Aylesbury, no commercials were made at all, with the exception of a crane truck constructed from pre-war parts in 1919 for Cogger & Hawkins. *MJWW*

IROQUOIS (US) 1906

Iroquois Iron Works, Buffalo, N.Y.

Named after the American Indian tribe which inhabited western New York State, this company made two sizes of trucks as well as steam and gasoline-driven rollers. The smaller truck had a 25 hp 4-cylinder engine and a ½ ton capacity, while the larger had a 60 hp engine under the driver's seat and capacity of four tons. Final drive was by shaft in the smaller, chains in the larger model. *GNG*

ISCO (US) 1972 to date

Isco Mfg. Co., Inc., Kansas City, Mo.

Interstate Securities Company, active in finance, insurance and communications fields, merged four separate companies to form a wholly-owned subsidiary, Isco Manufacturing, in 1972. These were the Cline Truck Manufacturing Co., Hardwick Manufacturing Co. (Eject-All rock-hauler), W.T. Cox's Ryd-A-Rail products, and Shuttle Wagon Corp. All companies were relocated in one plant. A wide range of products was offered under the name, Isco, including off-highway trucks for mining (both above and below ground), quarrying and construction work, and road/rail vehicles of many kinds. The trucks include seven conventional 2-axle trucks, from 13 to 50 tons, one 15 ton cab-over, one 22 ton articulated front-wheel-drive rock hauler, three Eject-All horizontally-unloading rock hauler semi-trailers to fit any prime mover, a 60/75 ton steel and copper mill articulated single-axle slag hauler, 70- and 90-ton coal haulers and a logging tractor. There are also underground personnel carriers and truck-tractors, the Shuttle Wagon rail car mover and trailer spotter, locomotive re-railers and Ryd-A Rail conversions for up to 80,000lbs GVW. Most of the truck range was inherited from Cline, and often bore the Cline name as well as Isco, although this practice is disappearing. Standard Isco power plants are Cummins 6-cylinder diesels from 250 to 420 hp, or turbocharged Detroit Diesels in 4-, straight-6, V-6, V-8 and V-12 cylinder forms, from 140 to 434 hp. The Shuttle Wagon uses a Ford V-8 gasoline engine as an alternative to the 140 hp Detroit Diesel, while Ryd-A-Rail conversion units can be fitted to a wide variety of passenger cars as well as trucks. Allison transmissions, mostly 6-speed, are used in two powershift and one automatic version.

Some models in the Isco range have resulted from an individual customer's order which has then been evaluated for general production. Such a case was the underground truck-tractor with 22 ton side dump low-bed semi-trailer for hauling gypsum. *RAW*

ISHIKAWAJIMA (J) 1918-1936

(1) Ishikawajima Shipbuilding & Engineering Co. Ltd., Tokyo 1918-1929

1925 ISHIKAWAJIMA (SUMIDA) CG bus Isuzu

1932 ISHIKAWAJIMA (SUMIDA) sprinkler, Isuzu

(2) Ishikawajima Jidosha Works Ltd., Tokyo 1919-1933
(3) Jidosha Kogyo Co. Ltd., Tokyo 1933-1936

This company acquired a manufacturing license for Wolseley cars and trucks, building a pneumatic-tired version of the British company's 1914 30 cwt CP model with 3-litre 4-cylinder sv engine. Wolseley variants were still being quoted as late as 1929, but production was modest, running at a little over 100 units a year. From 1923 vehicles were built under the name of Sumida, most of these going to the army; 1929 and later Sumidas were normal-control trucks and buses in the American idiom with 6-cylinder engines, The Jidosha Kogyo Co. was formed in 1933 in association with Dat and T.G.E. and eventually fused with the Kyoda Kokusan Jidosha KK, which had been making Isuzu trucks for the armed forces. *MCS*

1957 ISETTACARRO 500 500kgs van, GNG

ISO (I) 1950-c.1960

Iso SpA, Bresso, Milan

This scooter maker produced the almost mandatory commercial 3-wheeler for 300 kg payloads, with 125 cc engine and differential back axle. In 1953 there was a commercial edition of the Isetta 4-wheeled bubble-car, using the same underseat-mounted 236 cc 2-stroke twin unit, 4-speed gearbox, and forward opening cab door, with jointed steering column. Biggest of the Isos was a 15 cwt van of 1958 featuring transverse ifs and front-mounted

1958 ISO 400 500kgs light truck, GNG

1963 ISOCARRO 400kgs 3-wheeler, GNG

aircooled 4-stroke flat-twin engine, but after the collapse of the bubble-car and scooter markets the company turned to the manufacture of granturismo cars.

Both the 3-wheeler and the Isetta-based van were made under license in Spain, the former by Borgward Iso Espanola SA under the name Isocarro, and the latter by Iso Motor Italia SA under the name Isettacarro. Production of the Borgward-built Isocarro outlasted the Italian model, continuing until 1966 with an improved model for 400 kg loads which had a 4-speed and reverse gearbox. *MCS*

ISOBLOC (F) 1937-1956

(1) Carrosseries Besset S.A., Annonay.
(2) Societe d'Automobiles et Carrosseries d'Annonay

Besset, well-known manufacturers of bus bodies in the France of the pre-1940 years, acquired in 1937 the rights to produce the American GarWood integral coach under license, and sold it under the name Isobloc. The engine used was a V-8 Matford gasoline unit, or a George Irat diesel engine, both mounted in the rear part of the vehicle. The George Irat engine, however, soon disappeared from the list of options.

After World War II production of the Isobloc was continued, by the Societe d' Automobiles et Carrosseries d'Annonay, as Besset was now named. Power was supplied by a Panhard diesel engine. The body was reshaped and updated in the early 'fifties.

Isobloc had meanwhile become associated with Floirat, and both companies merged in 1956 with Saviem, after which each of the makes disappeared though the former Isobloc plant still is the main bus plant of the Saviem company. *JFJK*

1949 ISOTTA FRASCHINI diesel coach, HDB

ISOTTA FRASCHINI (I) 1906-1918: 1934-1949: 1958-1959

(1) Fabbrica Automobile Isotta Fraschini, Milan 1909-1949
(2) Fabbrica Automobili Isotta Fraschini e Motori Breda, Milan 1958-1959

Though cars were made as early as 1900, Isotta Fraschini did not venture into commercials until 1906. The first ones were car-based and usually carried hotel bus bodywork. Variations on this theme with 3.2-litre and 4.4-litre 4-cylinder engines were still being made in 1914, but since 1911 there had also been a range of purpose-built trucks, all with side-chain drive, 4-speed gearboxes, and solid tires. Payloads ran from 1½ to six tons, the biggest ones having 7.2-litre 4-cylinder power units. Production ceased after World War I: there was then a lapse until 1934, by which time sales of the expensive 8B private car were down to a trickle. The new Isotta trucks were normal-control 4- and 7 tonners based on German MAN designs, with 6-cylinder diesel engines. These gave way in 1937 to a new range of which the heaviest, the 8 ton D120, had a 9.5-litre oil engine giving 120 hp. Early ones had 4-speed gearboxes and mechanical brakes, later examples coming with five or eight forward speeds and hydraulics, with air actuation on the heavy duty models. The 6/7 ton D80 was also supplied in bus form. During World War II the company built a 3½ ton forward control truck on modern lines, with cab by Zagato, 8-speed transmission, and air-hydraulic brakes. The army version used a 5.8-litre 4-cylinder gasoline engine and magneto ignition: it evolved in 1946 into a diesel-powered 4½ tonner not unlike Fiat's 626 in appearance. Some bus models were exported to India. Unfortunately, Isotta Fraschini's attempts to re-enter the private car market were costly and unsuccessful, and the Italian Government ordered the closure of the factory in 1949. The name (and such profitable activities as remained) became the property of Breda, who attempted a revival in 1958. Their D160 was an advanced heavy truck with 10.2-litre 155 hp 6-cylinder diesel engine, 8-speed all-synchromesh gearbox, pneumatically-assisted clutch, air brakes, and double reduction drive. Also offered was a coach version featuring an amidships-mounted turbocharged underfloor engine, automatic gearbox, and power steering, but nothing came of this venture. Trolleybuses had also been made by the old company, some of these surviving into 1970. *MCS*

1914 ISOTTA FRASCHINI 4-ton truck, OMM

1958 ISOTTA FRASCHINI D160 chassis, Breda

1938 ISUZU TU10 6×4 truck, Isuzu

ISUZU 1933 to date

(1) Kyodo Kokusan Jidosha KK, Kawasaki 1933-1937
(2) Tokyo Motor Industry Ltd., Kawasaki 1937-1949
(3) Isuzu Motors Ltd., Kawasaki: Fujisawa 1949 to date

Kyodo Kokusan Jidosha KK was set up in 1933 to integrate the military vehicle interests of DAT and Ishikawajima, and to produce standardized trucks for the Japanese Army: T.G.E.'s truck interests were absorbed in 1937. Bearing the name of one of Japan's sacred rivers, the Type-94 (=1934) Isuzu was a conventional 30 cwt/2 ton machine in the American idiom, with 4.4-litre 6-cylinder sv engine and 4-speed gearbox. It was also made as a 6x4 with bevel or worm drive, and as a halftrack. Heavier versions used diesel engines, though not of the aircooled type tried by Isuzu as early as 1936. Some new oil-engined normal control 4x2 and 4x4 models were under development in 1942, and at the top of the conventional range was a 7 tonner with 8.6-litre 6-cylinder diesel unit and 5-speed gearbox. This formed the basis for the postwar 5 ton TX series; these had four forward speeds, hydrovac brakes, and a choice of gasoline or diesel engines including, by 1955, a supercharged version of the latter type giving 120 hp from 5.7 litres. The TX was subsequently uprated to 6 tons, in which form it had a 5-speed overdrive gearbox; there was also a military 6x6 edition, the TW, and some normal control bus derivatives. The bus range was extended by 1963 to include conventional full-front types, as well as a rear-engined model, the BX91. Two years later came the monocoque BC20,with transversely-mounted 9.3-litre diesel engine at the rear; it was said to be capable of 90 mph.

In 1953 Isuzu added private cars to the repertoire when they began license production of the Hillman Minx. This led in 1959 to the company's first light commercial, the 1-ton forward control Elf. Its 1½-litre 4-cylinder ohv engine and 4-speed synchromesh gearbox were Hillman-inspired, but a 52 hp diesel was optional, and a year later it had been joined by the 35 cwt normal-control Elfin on similar lines, but with ifs. Isuzu also extended their heavy truck range to include 7- and 8-tonners with 10.2-litre diesel engines and air-servo brakes, while their newest rear-engined buses had 5-speed synchromesh boxes, and such option as turbocharged engines, air suspension, power steering, and exhaust brakes. This range was progressively developed over the ensuing decade, though Isuzu replaced their Hillman with a car of their own design in 1961, the Elfin giving way to a lighter car-type pickup, the 1.3-litre Wasp with torsion-bar ifs. The Elf was uprated to 2 tons, and newcomers to the heavy TX/TD range were some forward-control 8 tonners with tilt cabs. Big Isuzus could now be had in 4x2, 4x4, 6x2, 6x4, and 6x6 configurations, as well as dumpers and tractive units. An equal variety of PSV types was available, from the minibus edition of the Elf through medium-sized normal control and full front machines to the transverse-rear-engined BU, now with over 200 hp in standard form. By 1968 postwar production of heavy trucks alone had passed the 400,000 mark, and 155,203 commercial vehicles of all types were delivered in 1969. Isuzu was the best selling make over 7 tons on the home market, as well as enjoying 61 per cent of all home sales of 6 tonners. In 1971 General Motors acquired a 35 per cent interest in Isuzu, and the company moved into the booming American light pickup market with the KB20, a 1.6-litre, 84 hp development of the Wasp; it was to be marketed in the U.S.A. as the Chevrolet Luv (Light Utility Vehicle). The Elf series covered the 1/2_ ton sector with a choice of 1½- or 2-litre 5-bearing gasoline engine and diesels of up to 3.3 litres, while a vast diversity of heavy duty models catered for GVWs of up to 20 tons and GCWs to 30 tons. Most of these had full air brakes and 5-speed gearboxes, and 6-cylinder direct injection diesels from 5-12 litres were used, though the heaviest roadgoing model, the TV402 6x4 tractive unit, had a 16½-litre V8 engine with 330 hp. On the bus side, air suspension had been abandoned along with the normal control types, but a gap had been bridged with a 260 seater based on the medium-weight Elf chassis. New for 1973 was an answer to Hino's KM and the traditional Nissans and Toyotas, the Forward for 8½ ton GVWs. This had forward control, a tilt cab, a 5.4-litre 6-cylinder oil engine, hydrovac brakes, and a 5-speed all-synchromesh gearbox. At the same time Isuzu introduced the SP (and VP tractor), 6-wheelers for GVWs of over 20 tons. These could be had as twin-steer 6x2s as well as in the classic 6x4 configuration, power steering and 5-speed synchromesh gearboxes were standard, and the engine was a 12-litre 240 hp six, also fitted to the largest rear-engined monocoque bus models. Other types available were the KC20, a wider Elf range headed by a heavy-duty type powered by a 3.6-litre 100 hp 4-cylinder diesel, and a vast diversity of TX and TD models in the 12-16-ton GVW category, with forward or normal control. There were now 4x2, 4x4, 6x2, 6x4 and 6x6 variants powered by diesel engines from 6.1 litres and 125 hp up to 10.2 litres and 195 hp.

1975 ISUZU Elf 1-ton pick-up, Isuzu

1978 ISUZU SBR 9-tonne GVW truck, Isuzu

This range structure was continued into 1978, with the addition of a new low loader version of the Elf on an 8ft 1½in wheelbase, with small-diameter rear wheels and a diesel engine. The smaller Isuzu diesels were also being adapted to power canal boats in Thailand, while certain Isuzu truck models assembled in Australia by GMH were being sold under the Bedford name. *MCS*

1915 ITALA Tipo 17 1½-ton truck, BHV

ITALA (I) 1908-1926

Fabbrica Automobili Itala SA, Turin

Itala's first commercial vehicles, introduced in 1908, were 30 cwt trucks and light buses using reinforced 4-cylinder private car chassis with shaft drive; a cab based on the 1.9-litre 12 hp four followed in 1910, in which year a 16/20 hp street sweeper was also built. This, unusually, had side chain drive, whereas all Itala's private cars, even the biggest, favored bevels. By 1913 a full range of trucks was available, from 12 cwt up to six tons. All had 4-cylinder engines, four forward speeds, and magneto ignition; all but the lightest, however, favored the T-head configuration and solid tires. The big ones had watercooled transmission brakes, and the 5.4-litre 6 tonner had side chains once again. PSVs and fire engines were listed, unusual catalogued options being paraffin carburetors and internally sprung wheels. 1914 saw the T17, a 30 cwt military truck with cranked frame, intended for mountain work. Itala's finances suffered severely from the War, and truck production was not resumed after 1918, though up to 1926 the firm offered taxicab editions of their smaller 4-cylinder car models. The last of these was the 2-litre Tipo 56, a straightforward sv machine with 4-speed gearbox. *MCS*

ITALINDO (RI) 1970 to date

P.T. Italindo, Jakarta

The company of Italindo assembled Lambretta 3-wheelers and built a taxi cab on the same chassis, powered by a 148 cc, single cylinder, two stroke engine. Called the "Helicak.", it had a capacity of three passengers plus the driver and was tiller steered. In 1973, though, Italindo introduced a large 3-wheeled taxi cab of angular lines powered again by a single cylinder, 125 cc, two stroke engine, under the name "Super Helicak." The body is generously dimensioned and is especially high, permitting easy access to the interior. There are two doors each side and the taxi cab is delivered in standard and de lux versions. "Super Helicak" has full automotive controls and is built in large quantities to fulfil the vast transportation needs of Indonesia and neighboring Asian countries. Current production uses British Reliant chassis and a slightly redesigned body; the company introduced "Helitruck" and "Helipickup" versions in 1976. *GA*

1975 ITALINDO Super Helicak taxicab, AAR

ITAR (CS) 1928-1929

Itar tovarna motocyklu, Prague-Radlice

Established in 1920, this motorcycle maker built a few delivery tricycles powered by 350 cc engines, with a load capacity of 100 kgs. Some of these were exported to Yugoslavia. *MSH*

IVY (GB) 1926-1930

S.A. Newman Ltd., Birmingham

The original Ivy was a ¾ cwt trade carrier powered by a single-cylinder J.A.P. engine, with Moss 3-speed gearbox and chain drive. It had car-type steering and brakes on all three wheels. In 1929 a new model known as the Karryall was introduced; this had a 348cc single-cylinder 2-stroke engine and Sturmey-Archer 3-speed gearbox. The motorcycle engine and front frame were mated with a car-type channel steel chassis, and the Karryall had much better weather protection than most vehicles of its kind. With a 3 cwt capacity, it was priced originally at £70, later raised to £85. *GNG*

IWASAKI (J) 1932-c.1942

Asahi Nainenki K.K.

A motorcycle-type delivery 3-wheeler with two driven rear wheels, it was among the machines used by the Japanese Army in World War II. *MCS*

IZH see Moskvitch

1908 JACKSON (i) ½-ton van, NAHC

JA, JAAZ, see YAAZ

J & J (US) 1920-1921
Lorain Motor Truck Co., Lorain, O.
This is an obscure brand of commercial vehicle and little is known other than its years of manufacture and that the lone model was a 2-tonner. *GMN*

JACKSON (i) (US) c.1907-1923
Jackson Motor Co., Jackson, Mich.
This company had made passenger cars since 1903, and built a number of delivery vans and light trucks on the car chassis from about 1907. The first purpose-built trucks, however, did not appear until 1920, when the company launched a 4-wheel-drive 3½-tonner powered by a 4-cylinder Continental engine. A 4-speed transmission and self-starter were featured. The company slogan was "No Hill Too Steep — No Sand Too Deep". *GNG*

JACKSON (ii) (GB) 1912-1913
Reynold Jackson & Co. Ltd., Notting Hill Gate, London W.
Makers of a variety of passenger cars, Jackson built a parcelcar on his 3-wheeled cyclecar chassis. It was powered by a 12 hp J.A.P. V-twin engine, with chain drive to the single rear wheel. It had a substantial channel steel frame, so was more car-like than many of its contemporaries. *GNG*

JACKSON-HOLROYD (GB) 1919
James Whitely Ltd., Halifax, York.
This was a conventional shaft-driven 30cwt truck powered by a 25.6 hp 4-cylinder engine. *GNG*

JAMES (GB) 1929-1939
James Cycle Co. Ltd., Birmingham
This famous factory's first commercial 3-wheeler, the Handyman, was a simple affair with a motorcycle front end and a chain-driven rear axle. Power was provided by a 247 cc 2-stroke Villiers engine, and payload was 5-cwt. More sophisticated were the 1931 models, which had 500 cc sv v-twin engines of James's own manufacture and some driver-protection, but car ideas emerged for good on the 1933 1096cc Samson, which boasted a welded steel frame, wheel steering, 3-speed unit box, and spiral bevel final drive. There were still no doors, however, and the body was panelled in plywood. Doors and steel panelling became standard wear in 1934, and 1935 Samsons were made in 8-cwt and 12-cwt forms, with room for a passenger seat; an interesting factory option was a 2-wheeled trailer with van bodywork. The last James vans were simpler affairs with more angular styling and doorless cabs. In 1938 the company marketed an open-bodied 15-cwt industrial truck equipped for road use. *MCS*

JAMES & BROWNE (GB) 1904-c.1909
James & Browne Ltd., Hammersmith, London W.
The first commercial vehicle by this car-making firm was a light van with a 9 hp 2-cylinder horizontal engine mounted amidships, and final drive by single chain. This was a passenger car chassis, but in 1905 the company announced a 5-tonner powered by a 20 hp 4-cylinder horizontal engine with transverse crankshaft, mounted

mid-way between front and rear axles beneath the floor, and double chain final drive. This truck had a much larger loading area than most of its day, but was not successful, probably because it was underpowered. A 25/30 hp engine was also listed. A smaller van with a 14/16 hp 4-cylinder engine was sold in modest numbers. In 1907 James & Browne commercials followed the lead of the passenger cars in adopting vertical engines; there was a forward-control 3-tonner powered by a 2-cylinder oversquare engine, the entire output of which was bought by Lacre and sold under the name J & B Lacre. The last of these Vertex models was a 5-tonner of 1909, powered by a 45 hp 4-cylinder engine. James and Browne made the chassis of the experimental Railless trolleybus built for Metropolitan Electric Tramways in 1909. *GNG*

JAMIESON (US) 1901-1902
Jamieson Automobile Works, Warren, Pa.
Mark W. Jamieson designed a small delivery truck. Several were built on a light chassis with a 7 hp 2-cylinder engine under the seat. Final drive was by a single chain. Tiller steering was used. *DJS*

JANNEY STEINMETZ (US) 1901
Janney, Steinmetz & Co., Philadelphia, Pa.
This company advertised coal-burning steam wagons, vans and buses, of 1 to 10 tons capacity and engines of 20 to 120 hp. They claimed that there were 'no odors, no stoking, no visible exhaust, no ashes, no vibration', which would have made them paragons among steam vehicles, then or at any other time. It is not known what types, if any, were actually made. *GNG*

JANSON (NL) 1934-1940
W.A., Janssens & Zoon, Rotterdam
Janssens started in 1934 manufacturing three-wheeled vans of which some were modelled on British examples like the Raleigh, etc. (notably the heavier models) and some were only motorcarriers, like the German Tempo, having two front wheels and one at rear, and the loading space in front of the driver, who was seated above the rear wheel. In 1935 three models were in production: 2K, with a payload of 500 kgs powered by a 6½ hp two-stroke single-cylinder JLO engine; 2G, with 650 kgs payload, powered by a 10 hp JLO engine; and the 5G, giving a payload of 1000 kgs and receiving its power from a two-cylinder two-stroke JLO engine.

In 1938 the heaviest model was the 52, having a payload of 1250 kgs and a 400 cc 12 hp JLO two-stroke two-cylinder engine.

Some models also had four-stroke Norton engines. With the outbreak of World War II, production of Jansons came to an end. *JFJK*

JANVIER (F) 1905-1907
V. Janvier, Paris
Victor Janvier built a 6-wheeled car in 1903, and two years later he applied this principle, more logically, to a truck.. With a claimed load capacity of 7 tons, the Janvier was powered by a 30 hp 4-cylinder engine, and was of 6x2 layout, with double chain drive to the rear wheels, and steering to both front axles. The rear wheels were braked by wooden blocks acting on the axle shaft which projected outside the wheels, as well as by shoe brakes on the solid tires. *GNG*

1906 JANVIER 7-ton 6×2 truck, OMM

JARRETT (US) 1921-1934
J.C. Jarrett Motor & Finance Co., Colorado Springs, Col.
The Jarrett Truck came about through the dissatisfaction of James C. Jarrett Jr. with the poor hill climbing abilities of another make he was selling, and Jarretts were specifically built for the mountainous Colorado country. They used Waukesha 6-cylinder engines with 7-speed transmissions and double reduction rear axles. 2½ and 5-ton models were made, and they were widely used by highway and street departments in Colorado and Texas. About 300 were made. *GNG*

JARVIS-HUNTINGTON (US) 1911-1914
Jarvis Machinery & Supply Company, Huntington, West Virginia
Capacities of these trucks ranged from 1½ tons to 5 tons. All had four-cylinder engines and forward control. The larger models had four-speed gearboxes while the smaller ones had but three speeds. Double chain-drive was used on all models. The five-tonner had a wheelbase of 12 feet, with speed limited to 10 mph and was priced at $4250. *GMN*

JAWA (CS) 1950-1952
Zbrojovka Brno n.p., Prague-Nusle
This well known motorcycle maker built a small number of delivery tricycles derived from the Jawa 250 Type 11 motorcycle. This had a single-cylinder 250cc 2-stroke engine driving the rear wheels by chain. The front forks, engine, fuel tank and saddle were stock motorcycle. Load capacity was 200 kgs. *MSH*

JAY-FONG (Anglicized for export), JIE-FANG (p), CHIEH-FANG (wg) (Liberation) (CHI) 1956 to date
No. 1 Automobile Plant, Changchun, Kirin (Manchuria) (Plant Vehicle Code — CA)
Built with the help of Soviet technicians, the No. 1 Automobile Plant commenced production of the Liberation CA-10 truck on Oct. 15, 1956.

1956 JAY-FONG CA1OZ 4-ton truck, BHV

This 4-tonner is based on the Russian ZIS-150 which in turn was strongly influenced by old American International K-series designs.

The engine is a 6-cylinder, side valve model of 95 hp at 2,800 rpm. There are five speeds forward.

Appearing in a number of variations, the CA-10 is produced as the CA-10BE high rail truck, the CA-10BD chassis for bus and trolleybus use, and the CA-10M6 6-wheel model.

The Szuping Municipal Machinery Plant in Kirin Province builds the DD-340 dump truck and the DD-400Y oil tank truck on the CA-10BB short frame chassis. Crane trucks and fire engines are also built on this chassis. A CA-10 logging truck has recently been pictured in Chinese publications.

The Jay-Fong CA-30A is a 6x6 2.5-ton all-terrain truck capable of driving on sand, deep snow and mud.

It is powered by a 6-cylinder, 110 hp engine. Tire pressure can be regulated from the driver's cab and a winch is optional.

There are reported to be other truck models built at this plant including 3, 5, and 7 ton units. Some Liberations are exported.

Also in very limited production is the Red Flag luxury limousine.

A Liberation 8.5-ton diesel truck is alleged to have been built at the Tsinan Motor Vehicle Plant since 1964. *BE*

JEANTAUD (F) 1895-1906

C. Jeantaud, Paris

One of the most famous battery-electric pioneers, Charles Jeantaud made his first prototype in 1881, and started to build vehicles for commercial sale twelve years later. By 1896 he was experimenting with electric cabs of wheel-steered type, with motors mounted under the driver's seat, chain drive, and an unusual form of double transverse front suspension. Though the cabs themselves were no more successful than any of their contemporaries, Jeantaud won the two-seater class of the 1898 Paris Cab Trials: more important, his constant rivalry with Camille Jenatzy led to the first onslaughts on what is now the World's Land Speed Record, and to the 65.79 mph achieved by Jenatzy's *La Jamais Contente* in 1899. In the same year Jeantaud tried a curious hansom-type cab with batteries mounted under a short frontal hood; this necessitated the removal of the motors to the rear. Chars-a-banc were available in 1900, by which time Jeantauds had five forward speeds and a range of 38 miles. A vast variety of private and commercial types offered in 1903 included a gasoline-engined light van, as well as all manner of electrics: a postal model had the driver's seat over the rear axle, in the manner of the later de Dion-engined Rovals. There was even a trolleybus, though it is unlikely that any were sold. 1905 Jeantauds had front-wheel drive, but the designer's suicide in 1906 brought the venture to an end. *MCS*

JEEP (i) (IND) 1949 to date

Mahindra and Mahindra Ltd., Bombay

A branch of the large engineering firm of Mahindra & Mahindra builds the old style forward control FC150/160 Jeep in pick-up, minibus, van and ambulance versions, which were never built in the U.S.A. Powered by the Hurricaine 75 hp gasoline engine and available in 4x2 and 4x4 models, Jeeps are the main transportation means in the remote Indian areas. The old style Universal Jeep and station wagon are also built along with trailers and other automotive products. *GA*

JEEP (ii) (US) 1963 to date

(1) Kaiser Jeep Corporation, Toledo, Ohio 1963-1970
(2) Jeep Corporation, Toledo, Ohio 1970 to date

After Willys Overland changed their name in 1963, their product assumed the name of its most famous product. The commercial range of Jeeps was inherited complete, and consisted of the Universal Jeep family, and the Panel Delivery and Gladiator truck using Willys's recently introduced 3.8-litre 6-cylinder ohc engine. The 4x2 sv Dispatcher and the forward control types, though still listed in early Kaiser Jeep catalogues, soon disappeared. The Gladiator family was also produced for the Army, along with some big 2½- and 5-ton 6x6s with Continental gas or Cummins diesel engines, later replaced with Continental multi-fuel units. None of these heavies were commercially available, and in 1971 American Motors formed a new company, AM General, to take over the development and manufacture of the military models and also of specialized vans for the U.S. Post Office, and buses.

In 1965 the Gladiators were fitted with AMC-built 3.8-litre 6-cylinder and 5.7-litre V-8 engines, which replaced the ohc six. The basic Jeep, however, retained the ioe 4-cylinder unit, with the same Perkins diesel option, a 3.7-litre Buick-designed V-6 being catalogued as a further option from 1966. Growing interest in recreational vehicles led to a new short wheelbase semi-commercial model, the Jeep Commando, in 1969, as well as an abbreviated type intended as an artic for camper work. American Motors acquired Kaiser Jeep in 1970, and within two years the old four had gone; in its place AMC-built inline sixes and V-8s of up to 5.9 litres and 175 hp were standardized. An innovation on the 1973 trucks (successors to the Gladiators) was the Quadratrac full-time four wheel drive. New for 1974 were a Commando replacement, the Cherokee Sports Utility, while power front disc brakes became an option on the truck range: they were standardized in 1977. In that year, too, a 2.7-litre Perkins diesel became an option in certain European export markets. With Jeep sales approaching 110,000 a year (more than three times Willys's 1950 output) emphasis in 1978 was on fancy trim packages for recreational-vehicle enthusiasts. The truck models came in two wheelbase lengths, with 6- and 8-cylinder engines of up to 6.6-litres and 205 hp, automatic transmission being mandatory with the most powerful V-8. In 1977 Jeep products were being manufactured or assembled in 21 foreign countries. *MCS*

1976 JEEP J-10 pick-up, American Motors

JEEP (iii) (TR) 1968 to date

Turk Willys Overland Fabrikalari A.S., Tuzla

Established in 1959 as an assembly line for the Universal Jeep, the Turkish Willys factory introduced the Gladiator range in 1968 fitted with a much modified front end and rear body, simplified in appearance and construction. Following the reorganization of the company in 1974, production was suspended for a while, but was restarted in early 1976. *GA*

JEEP (iv) (IR) 1969-1973

Sherkate Sahami Jeep, Tehran

Assembling various Jeep models since 1956, the Tehran based company introduced a locally designed pick-up called the "Simorgh 500" in the form of a long wheelbase Universal Jeep with an all-enclosed metal cab and full length cab doors, powered by the Hurricane 75 hp petrol engine. The introduction of the Gladiator series pickup, though replaced the necessity for this old style model, production of which was dropped early in 1973. *GA*

JEEP-VIASA see Willys-Viasa

JEEPNEY (PI) 1948 to date

(1) U.S. Auto Co., Manila
(2) Sarad Motors Inc., Manila

A typical product of the Philippines the Jeepney started life as a civilian version of the WW II Jeep. Based on surplus military Jeeps with extensively customized appearance and an elongated rear body accomodating as many as 12 passengers, Jeepneys are used as taxi-cabs or minibuses. According to current availability the original Jeep engine or an alternative Mercedes Benz gasoline or diesel units are fitted. Jeepneys are built by a handful of artisan workshops, the best known of which are Sarad Motors and U.S. Auto Co. *GA*

JEFFERY (US) 1914-1917

Thomas B. Jeffery Co., Kenosha, Wis.

1913 JEFFERY Quad 2-ton 4X4 truck, BHV

Formerly making passenger cars under the name Rambler, the Jeffery company launched a delivery truck with 1500 lb payload in 1914, followed by others of ¾-ton, 1- and 1½-ton ratings. These were soon overshadowed by the famous Jeffery Quad 4x4 army truck for 1½-2-ton loads, which was developed as a result of a visit by the US Army Quartermaster Corps to the Jeffery factory. It was powered by a 36 hp Buda 4-cylinder engine which drove through 4-speed transmission and central differential to both front and rear axles. Unlike its larger rival the FWD, the Jeffery Quad had 4-wheel steering which gave it a turning circle of only 45 feet. Although available to commercial users, most Quads were supplied to the Army, and with the coming of World War 1 demand was so great that production was farmed out to three other factories (Hudson, National and Paige) as well as taking up the whole of the Jeffery plant's capacity. In July 1916 the company was bought by Charles W. Nash, and from 1917 onwards the trucks were sold under the name Nash Quad. *GNG*

JELCZ (PL) 1968 to date

Jelczanskie Zaklady Samochodow, Jelcz k/Olawy

c.1970 JELCZ 8-ton truck, OMM

Originally building Zubr trucks, the JZS factory modified their old-fashioned cab, changed over to a Wola-Leyland license-built diesel of 200 hp and started life under the new name with an 8 ton truck chassis. The range was completely restyled in 1972 when a modern western style cab was introduced and a 3 axled chassis, as well as tractor versions were announced. Powered by the same 200 hp diesel engine and uprated Wola-Leyland diesels developing up to 240 hp, Jelcz trucks are currently the heaviest vehicles built in Poland having up to 32 ton capacity for the tractor version. Latest additions to the range include 6x4 tippers powered by the same license-built Leyland diesels, while 6x4 tractors are fitted with Steyr engines developing 320 hp. Special bodies, including fire-fighting vehicles were always Jelcz's specialty, as were buses, built along with trucks from as early as 1968. An old style Star chassis fitted with Jelcz built fire-fighting body and 6x6 Star chassis fitted with a workshop body are also marketed under the Jelcz trademark. Basic bus model for many years was the Skoda 706 RTO series built in many versions, as city, intercity, coach and even articulated bus under license from the Czech factory. Power for these buses came from original Skoda 160 hp engines that were imported. This old-fashioned series is being phased out, though by a newly signed contract between JZS and Berliet of France, for the production of the ultra modern 100 passenger PR100 city bus at Jelcz, Power in this case comes from an underfloor diesel of Berliet manufacture, developing 170 hp, or by a locally built 185 hp Leyland diesel engine. *GA*

JENKINS (US) 1901-1902

Jenkins Automobile Co., Washington, D.C.

Claimed to be the largest self-propelled bus in America in 1901, the Jenkins Observation Automobile was a 22 passenger steam bus powered by a 20/30 hp horizontal 4-cylinder compound engine, with marine-type water-tube boiler. Power was transmitted via a differential shaft to ring gears on the insides of each rear wheel. Intended for sightseeing in the capital, the Jenkins bus had revolving seats for its passengers. *GNG*

JENNINGS (CDN) 1911-1914

Jennings & Co., Montreal, Que.

Arthur Jennings was a blacksmith-turned-wagon-builder who built bodies on Gramm chassis, but in 1914 he offered a conventional light truck. The firm also built

1914 JENNINGS 1½-ton truck, GB

three fire engines, and in the 1920s had a Reo agency and did conversions on Reo cars and trucks. *HD*

JENSEN (GB) 1938-1960

Jensen Motors Ltd., West Brommich, Staffs.

The Jensen brothers made their name first as builders of sporting bodywork for private cars and then (from 1937) as makers of specialist cars, but their commercial vehicle interests go back to 1931, when they purchased the business of W.J. Smith and Sons, whose main concern had been truck bodies. In 1938 Jensen collaborated with the Reynolds Tube Co. on the design of a lightweight truck for long loads which would still have an unladen weight of less than 2½ tons and so be eligible for the British 30 mph class. This objective they achieved by the use of a unitary-construction space frame of hiduminium tubes, and between 1939 and 1944 several prototypes were made with wheelbases of 15 ft and lengths of over 27 ft. These included a 6x4 model with wrap-round windscreen. All mechanical elements were of (ii) Ford origin, both 4- and 8-cylinder engines being tried. Other wartime activities included the construction of fire tender bodies on Ford chassis.

The definitive version of their unitary 6-tonner went into production in 1945. It was an assembled COE machine with 4730 cc Perkins P6 diesel engine, 5-speed Moss gearbox, 2LS hydraulic brakes, and worm drive. The power unit was easily detachable for servicing, the front grille spelt out the JNSN symbol by which the truck line was known, and later improvements included servo brakes, 4-speed boxes, and the use of moulded plastic for grilles and cab roofs. In 1948 Jensen introduced a 38/40-seater full-fronted coach 'chassis' for which Sparshatt built the bodies, and by 1955 they were offering a 30-footer truck with a platform space of 25 ft. 6 in. JNSNs were especially popular with furniture movers, many being seen with pantechnicon coachwork.

In 1947 they introduced the Jen-Tug, a small

1947 JENSEN Jen-Tug articulated truck, NMM

mechanical horse for 2-ton payloads designed by George Reikie. This had a quick-detachable power pack mounted below and behind the cab, hydraulic brakes, and a very narrow rear track which dispensed with the need for a differential, though in fact one was standardized after 1951. Various models were produced; the first Tugs had 1172cc (ii) Ford engines and 3-speed gearboxes, replaced in 1952 by a 1200 cc Austin A40 with four speeds, which gave the Jen-Tug a 3-ton rating. Subsequent models were still more powerful, with a choice of 1500 cc Austin gasoline or 2200 cc BMC diesel units. There was even a shortlived Jen-Helecs electric model in 1949, on which the batteries were slung in panniers alongside the frame side-members.

1948 JENSEN JNSN 6-ton truck, NMM

After 1958 the 6-tonner was no longer quoted, but by now Jensen's commercial vehicle interests included the building of bodies for Austin's light 4x4 Gipsy, and a license agreement whereby they were to build the German Tempo 15cwt fwd truck, already fitted as standard with an Austin A50 engine. A full range of Jensen-Tempos, including a minibus and a tower wagon, was listed, but sales were disappointing, while the poor reception accorded to the Gipsy rendered their Austin contract none too profitable. After 1960 Jensen decided to concentrate on their cars. *MCS*

JIANG-HUAI (p), CHIANG-HUAI (wg) (River Huai) HF-140 (CHI) 1969 to date

Chinese Peoples Liberation Army Nanking Military Region Anhwei Production and Construction Corps - Chianghuai Motor Vehicle Plant, Anhwei Province (Plant Vehicle Code- HF), Hofei, Anhwei

The HF-140 is a 3-ton cab-over engine truck featuring a Chianghuai 6-cylinder engine of 120 hp driving four forward speeds. Maximum vehicle speed is 85 km/h. *BE*

JIAN-SHE (p), CHIEN-SHE (wg) (Construction) (CHI) 1958 to date
Antung Automobile Plant, Antung, Liaoning
Little is known of the Antung-built Construction other than it is a 2-ton truck powered by a 50 hp engine. *BE*

JINGGANGSHAN (p), CHINGKANGSHAN (wg) #27 (CHI) 1968 to date
Chingkan Mountains Motor Vehicle Plant, Kiansi Province
The Jinggangshan 2.5-ton truck was trial produced in April 1968 but design flaws delayed full production until March 1969.

The engine and chassis construction are similar to the Nanking-built Tiao-Jim NJ-120. Power is by a 6-cylinder 79 hp engine with 4 speeds forward giving a maximum speed of 82 km/h. *BE*

JIPTARA (P) 1975 to date
Marques, Pereira e Teles Lda, Cascais
A beach-buggy like vehicle based on a VW platform-chassis and powered by either a 1.2, 1.3 or 1.5 litre VW gasoline engine placed in the rear, the Jiptara is an all purpose utility vehicle. The body is made of fiberglass, has angular lines and provides seat for two and a generous rear load space, while a canvas hood is supplied for the driver's compartment. The Jiptara is marketed either completely built-up or as a kit. *GA*

JOHNSON (US) 1901-1912
Johnson Service Co., Milwaukee, Wis.
Johnson made both internal-combustion and steam vehicles, beginning with a 1-ton cab-over steamer in 1901 with underfloor boiler and single chain drive. Steamers were made until 1907, a fleet of at least four vans being used for mail collection and delivery in Milwaukee. These were the first motorized fleet used by the US Mail Service. Gasoline-engined Johnsons used Renault power units made under license in the Johnson factory. Three sizes were used, 30, 40 and 50 hp, for a wide variety of vehicles including fire engines, police patrols, ambulances and hearses (all conventionals) as well as conventional and cab-over trucks and buses in 1 to 4-ton sizes. Final drive was by shaft on the passenger cars and smaller trucks, and double chains on the larger trucks.

With the death of Professor Johnson in 1912 vehicle production was suspended, and the Johnson company turned to the temperature control industry, at that time in its infancy. They are today the largest supplier of Total Building Automation Systems in the country. *RW*

JOLIET (US) 1912
Joliet Auto Truck Company, Joliet, Illinois
Electric trucks by this tradename were of low capacity (to 500 pounds), light-weight delivery vans. Of the models offered in the single year of production, the smallest had tiller steering, wheelbase of 5 feet, 10 inches, weight of 1400 pounds, maximum speed of 10 mph and a claimed 30 miles per battery charge. *GMN*

JONZ (US) 1912-1913
American Automobile Manufacturing Company, New Albany, Indiana
The Jonz was available in models capable of carrying 1000 pounds, one-ton and three tons. A light delivery van with shaft drive, selective gearbox and pneumatic tires used a three-cylinder engine. This name was better-known for passenger autos. *GMN*

JOWETT (GB) 1924-1954
Jowett Cars Ltd., Bradford, Yorks.
Jowett entered the commercial vehicle market in 1924 with a traveler's car based on their 7 hp 2-seater with 907 cc sv flat-twin engine, 3-speed gearbox, and bevel drive. This was soon joined by a 7-cwt van on the long (8ft.6in) wheelbase; from the earliest days Jowett, unlike many of their British competitors, offered a truck version as well, not to mention a commercial tourer in the French idiom. The War Office ordered some Jowett tenders in 1928, when a free wheel was optional on cars and vans alike, but there were few changes before the end of 1929, when the commercial range was brought up to date with 4-wheel brakes and detachable cylinder heads. At the same time the commercial tourer was replaced by a 5-door commercial traveler's saloon on the car chassis.

Thereafter Jowett vans and trucks remained virtually unchanged until 1934, when wire wheels were standardized, and the 1930 front end sheet metal gave way to styling similar to that of the 1933 cars. An interesting variant, offered by a Hull firm, was a lwb 1-tonner with chain final drive, similar to early Model-T Ford conversions. Styling was then left alone for a couple of years, and even then there were differences between the private and commercial types, the latter retaining 3-speed gearboxes to the end. 1936 saw a large capacity 10-cwt variant, as well as a special model powered by a 1005 cc flat-twin Coventry-Victor diesel unit, marketed by Auto Diesels Ltd.; this was available until the outbreak of World War II. Both cars and vans received bigger 946 cc engines in 1937, while 1938 Jowett vans had new styling, steel-spoke wheels, and rod-operated brakes. Entirely new was a 10-cwt type using the 1166 cc sv flat-four engine and an angular grille never seen on any Jowett car.

1934 JOWETT ¼-ton pick-up, NMM

During World War II the flat-twin engine was adapted for use in agricultural tractors. In 1946 the company came out with a new 10-cwt 2-cylinder van, the Bradford. Though this was also offered with station wagon

1953 JOWETT Bradford 8-cwt. van, OMM

bodywork, it was strictly a commercial type with a new, robust chassis frame, 1005 cc 25 hp engine, and synchromesh gearbox: wheelbase was 7 ft 6 in. Some 30,000 were made before production difficulties on the car side forced Jowett to suspend production at the end of 1953. They had, however, already tested a Bradford replacement, the CD-type with F-head engine, for which a whole range of private and commercial bodies had been planned. *MCS*

JUMBO (i) (US) 1918-1924

Nelson Motor Truck Co., Saginaw, Mich.

The Jumbo was named for an elephant and used such a figure as its trademark. It began as a 2½-tonner and this remained the sole model for two years. By 1921, this line had expanded to include 1½-, 2-, 3-, 3½- and 4-tonners, all driven by 4-cylinder Buda engines. Also common to all models was a 4-speed Fuller gearbox and Clark-built bevel-gear rear axles. The six models were kept into 1924. *GMN*

JUMBO (ii) (NL) c.1926-1930

Jumbo Motor Co., Helmond

This company started in 1923 as an offshoot of the Eindhoven Ford agents, for the production of trailers, and they became one of the largest trailer manufacturers in the Netherlands. During the late 1920s they assembled a number of trucks for existing Ford customers who wanted a larger payload than could be supplied by the current Ford range. They used Ford components as far as possible, including engines and radiators, but axles and chassis frames came from outside. The trucks had the appearance of a 'beefed-up' Ford Model TT, with setback front axle, and carried the Jumbo name on the Ford radiator. *GNG*

JUNGBLUTH (D) 1950-1951

Karosserie- und Fahrzeugbau Jungbluth & Co. KG., Bad Lauterberg

The forward-control chassis-less bus was built in small numbers only. A 95 hp Henschel diesel engine was mounted in the rear. *HON*

JUNIOR (E) 1954-1961

Junior, S.L., Barcelona

This company made a delivery tricycle powered by a 197 cc Hispano-Villiers engine which drove the single rear wheel. It had a tubular frame, and wooden or metal box bodies were mounted ahead of the driver. A tipper model was also made, but did not achieve much popularity. *JCG*

JUNO (US) 1912-1914

(1) Brodesser Motor Truck Co., Milwaukee, Wis. 1912
(2) Juno Motor Truck Co. Juneau, Wis. 1912-1914

The Juno truck was at first the Brodesser truck renamed, but soon the Juno Motor Truck Co. was organized and bought the Brodesser Motor Truck Co. of Milwaukee, Wis. moving the operation north to Juneau, Wis.

It was, like its predecessor, an assembled cab-over having a chain drive and solid tires in 36x3 and 36x4 sizes. Wisconsin 4-cylinder T-head engines cast in pairs in either 30 or 40 hp powered Juno trucks of 2- and 3-tons. Clutch was multiple disc and transmission was 3-speed selective mounted amidships. Service brakes were external; emergency, internal. Spring were semi-elliptic front; platform rear; and the Juno truck chassis sold for $2650 and $3250, about average for its time. *RW*

KADIX (US) 1912-1913

Kadix-Newark Motor Truck Company, East Grange, N.J.

All Kadix vehicles were fitted with 4-cylinder engines, three-speed gearboxes and jackshafts with double chain-drive. The line of models consisted of 3-, 4-, 5-, 6-, and 7-tonners. Engines were underhood. Chassis lengths were not standardized and customers could choose from a range of 144 inches to 186 inches. The 7-tonner used 40 x 7 dual rear wheels. *GMN*

KAELBLE (D) 1926 to date

Carl Kaelble GmbH. Backmang

In 1926 Kaelble presented their first road tractor under the name of "Suevia" which was equipped with their own 2-cylinder diesel engine. An improved version which was available with 2- or 3-cylinder engine was of chassis-less construction and had a rear swing-axle. In 1933 Kaelble built the first heavy prime-mover for the German Railway

1933 KAELBLE s GR/1 heavy road tractor, JFJK

to transport railway carriages on special low-loader trailers. Since this time Kaelble has delivered many of these special vehicles to the railway. In 1938 the heaviest tractor of the world was presented, a 6 x 6 version with two steerable axles and a 200 hp diesel engine placed amidships. Also one truck was on the program, having a forward control body. In 1949 Kaelble, making a new start after WW II, presented a 7-ton truck with 6-cylinder 130 hp engine. The prime mover was again put into production and also an articulated tractor was available. The tractors were improved and became available in various versions.

In 1951 a new engine was presented, a V-8 developing 200 hp. this was used for a new truck and when Kaelble started production of dump trucks in 1952 they had available an adequate engine. In 1953 new forward control trucks appeared of 6½-, 8- and 11-ton payload capacity

c.1955 KAELBLE 7-ton cement truck, HON

using 6-cylinder engines of 120 and 150 hp respectively. The 13-tonner was equipped with the V-8 engine. In the early '60s Kaelble concentrated on one fwc 9-ton truck, three-axled road tractors with 240 and 300 hp V-8 engines and a line of dump trucks. A few years later the last truck model was dropped. However Kaelble took up a new line of vehicles in 1973: special carriers for cranes, fire escape ladders and other special purposes. These are offered as 6x4, 8x4, 10x6, 12x8 and 14x8 versions and use engines

c.1950 KAELBLE heavy road tractor, HON

from 192 to 1100 hp. Dump trucks are equipped with 6- or 10-cylinder engines ranging from 265 to 475 hp and payload capacities from 20 to 35 tons. Several models of prime movers are in the line with output up to 880 hp and towing capacities of 100 to 300 tons. Most Kaelbles are powered by Mercedes-Benz engines. *HON*

KAISER (U.S.) 1946

Permanente Metals Corp. plant of Kaiser Industries, Permanente, Calif.

1946 KAISER INDUSTRIES articulated bus, MBS

A pilot model of a 60-foot articulated over-the-road coach was constructed as a speculation and operated between Los Angeles and San Francisco by Santa Fe Trail Transportation Co., a member of the National Trailways association. The body was constructed of a magnesium-aluminum alloy. A 6-cylinder Cummins diesel engine was mounted beneath the floor of the forward section, with a separate air-conditioning unit under the floor in the rear. There was space for 378 cubic feet of baggage in underfloor compartments. Suspension was the so-called "Torsilastic" system of rubber bonded between the walls of concentric tubes, a design pioneered by Twin Coach and later used by Flxible and Bus & Car (on the Silver Eagle). The pilot was never duplicated; it operated in regular service until 1951. *MBS*

KALAMAZOO (i) (US) 1913-1920

(1) Kalamazoo Motor Vehicle Co., Kalamazoo, Mich. 1913-1919
(2) Kalamazoo Motors Corp., Kalamazoo, Mich. 1920

A 1½-tonner was the only size truck built under this name through 1915. This was available with either a stake or express body for $1590. It used a side-valve 4-cylinder Buda engine under the hood with a three-speed gearbox and double chain drive. In the last four production years, 2½- and 3½ tonners were also made. In 1915 the Kalamazoo was sold on the British market under the name Shakespeare. *GMN*

KALAMAZOO (ii) (US) 1920-1924

Kalamazoo Motors Corp., Kalamazoo, Mich.

Initial models of the Kalamazoo were 1½-, 2½-, and 3½-tonners. These all had 4-speed gearboxes and worm-drive with Wisconsin engines for the two larger models. The 1½-tonner used a Continental engine and had a wheelbase of 144 inches. The last two model years saw a large line of seven different sizes from 1- to 5-tonners, all but the smallest with 4-speed gearboxes and worm-drive. The last models used a mix of Continental, Hercules and Wisconsin 4-cylinder engines. *GMN*

KALAMAZOO CRUISER see Pony Cruiser

KALMAR (S) 1965-1974

Kalmar Verkstads AB, Kalmar

To the order of the Swedish postal authorities in 1965 the Kalmar Verkstads AB designed a new fibreglass-bodied delivery vehicle called "Tjorven", and based on the Dutch DAF 750 car, whose engine and Variomatic transmission were used. A civil version of the Kalmar appeared in 1968.

Two years later Kalmar introduced a heavier vehicle, a rather revolutionary tractor for terminal use, which was

1968 KALMAR terminal tractor with postal van, OMM

entered through the front of the cab. It was powered by a Cummins V8-210 diesel engine and had an Allison automatic gearbox.

Unfortunately, however, Kalmar was sold by its owner, the Swedish Government, in the year 1974, thus ending production. *JFJK*

KAMAZ (SU) 1976 to date

Kama Automobile Factory — Naberezhnie Chelni

As part of the ninth Five Year Plan the largest truck plant in the world, covering 40 square miles, has been built on the Kama River 550 miles east of Moscow with the assistance of a number of European and American firms.

Current models include cab-over-engine 8-ton trucks, 6x4 chassis, dump truck and semi-tractors, totalling 150,000 units per year.

Three sizes of direct-injection diesel engines are also built, some of which are supplied to other truck plants as well as Kamaz. *BE*

KAN (CS) 1912

Kralovohradecka tovarna automobilu Alojs Nejedly, Kukleny

In addition to single- and 4-cylinder cars, this company made a small number of 10 hp delivery vans with a load capacity of 300 kgs. *MSH*

KANAWHA (US) 1911-1912

Kanawha Auto Truck Company, Charleston, West Virginia

The sole model under this name was a two-tonner weighing 5000 pounds and powered by a 4-cylinder engine. This had a three-speed gearbox, jackshaft and double chains to the rear wheels. The wheelbase was 10 feet, 10 inches and price was $2850. One reference lists this make to 1916 but without detailed references. It is also possible this company built fire-fighting equipment. *GMN*

KANSAS CITY (US) 1905-1917
Kansas City Motor Car Company, Kansas City, Missouri

This make was also referred to as Kansas City Car. The line of commercial vehicles included light delivery vans, buses and heavy trucks to two tons capacity. For 1906 only, two-cylinder engines were used with ratings to 35 hp. One two-tonner had track of 5 feet, 9 inches with wheelbase of only 91 inches. All models used double chain-drive. *GMN*

KAPI (E) 1950-1957
Gefisa, Barcelona

Federico Saldana Ramos, an infantry captain, built small 3-wheeled cars under the name Kapi, and also a 4-wheeled van powered by a 325cc Hispano-Villiers engine. This Jeep-like vehicle was sometimes called the Jip or Jip-Kapi. *JCG*

KARAVAN (US) 1920-1921
Caravan Motor Corp., Portland, Ore.

Available informations shows that Karavan trucks were 1½-tonners only. *GMN*

KARBACK (US) 1906-1908
Karback Automobile & Vehicle Company, Omaha, Nebraska

There was a model under this name with a 1½-ton capacity. This used a two-cylinder engine of 20 hp, a three-speed gearbox and double chain-drive. Also available was an 18-passenger bus on the same chassis. *GMN*

KARIVAN (i) (GB) 1930-1936
Stepney Carrier Co. Ltd., London W.C.1

The original Karivan was a 4 cwt trade carrier powered by a 2½ hp 2-stroke Villiers engine, with an Albion 3-speed gearbox and motorcycle type rear portion. Steering was by tiller. In 1932 a new model appeared with the same general layout but having an enclosed cab and wheel steering. The engine was now a 350cc unit and a Burman gearbox was used. Carrying capacity was 10 cwt. *GNG*

KARIVAN (ii) (US) 1955
Tri-Car Inc., Wheatland, Pa.

Using the same chassis as the Tri-Car passenger car, the Karivan was a forward-control 3-wheeler van powered by a 30 hp Lycoming vertical-twin engine, with Westinghouse-Schneider torque converter and drive to the single rear wheel. The Karivan had Goodrich torsilastic rubber suspension on all three wheels. Load capacity was 700 lbs. and the price $1045. *GNG*

KAROSA (CS) 1965 to date
Karosa, n.p., Vysoke Myto

This company grew out of the famous pre-war coachbuilding concern, Joseph Sodomka. From 1948 to 1965 they built bus bodies on the Skoda-LIAZ 706 chassis, as well as a number of other special vehicles including fire engines. The first complete Karosa vehicles were the integral construction SM, SD and SL buses introduced in 1965, and continued to the present day. They had 180 hp (now 210 hp) 6-cylinder horizontal diesel engines, and come in three versions, the SM and SMK city buses the SL sightseeing and SD long-distance touring coaches. The latter can be had with sleeper trailer.

Karosa buses and trailers are made under license in Poland by Jelcz, and the old 706 RTO buses are still made for export, mainly to Albania and Bulgaria. *MSH*

KARPETAN (E) 1963-1968
Lerma Autobastidores Industriales SA, Zaragoza

1964 KARPETAN 6000kgs truck, GNG

Also known by the abbreviation L.A.I., this company made medium and heavy trucks powered by Spanish-manufactured Perkins diesel engines or imported M.A.N. diesel engines. Capacities ranged from seven to 12 ton, and rear axles were either Timken or Eaton. The company also made a bus and coach chassis under the name Layetan. *JCG*

KARRIER (GB) 1908 to date
(1) Clayton & Co.(Huddersfield) Ltd., Huddersfield, Yorks 1908-1920
(2) Karrier Motors Ltd., Huddersfield, Yorks 1920-1934
(3) Karrier Motors Ltd., Luton, Beds 1934-1968
(4) Rootes Motors Ltd., Dunstable, Beds 1968-1970
(5) Chrysler UK Ltd., Dunstable, Beds 1970 to date

In 1908 Clayton & Co. began producing Tylor-engined commercial vehicles under the slogan "For commerce

1911 KARRIER B/50 2-ton truck, Chrysler UK

In 1908 Clayton & Co. began producing Tylor-engined commercial vehicles under the slogan "For commerce 'Karrier Cars' ". These early 'Karriers', all 'A' types, were designed specially for hilly districts. To the ordinary user, 'Karrier' cars did not look pretty: the design was unconventional, the object being to combine a short wheelbase with as large a platform as possible. The short wheelbase enabled awkward entrances and docks to be entered and left easily. The driver was positioned over the engine which left maximum space for the load. This type became known later as the overtype, and many manufacturers copied the layout.

In 1911, the first normal control type Karriers, the 'B' type appeared and in 1913, a 3- to 4 ton truck was designed to comply with the War Dept. subsidy specification. This vehicle was granted a subsidy certificate after the October 1913 trials arranged by the War Office. This type was ordered by the War Office, and by a fortunate coincidence were ready for delivery when WWI started in August 1914.

Approx 900 type A and B chassis were produced in the period 1908 to 1921, used for both goods and passenger carrying vehicles, with a load range of 1 ton to 5 tons. About 2200 type WDS chassis were produced in the period 1914 to 1921, and considerable numbers of these were rehabilitated by Karrier Motors after the war, rapidly finding new owners in haulage and passenger carrying businesses, some even being fitted with open-top double-deck bodies. The war was to mark the turning point for Clayton & Co., and in Feb. 1920 a new company 'Karrier Motors' Ltd. was formed to take over the business of Clayton & Co. A new works had been built on a ten acre site during the last few years of the war, and these works were extended to cater for the expansion.

In late 1920 the first new design since the war appeared, being normal control 3-, 4- & 5-ton 'K' type, which were developments of the W.D.S. model, and were powered by the Karrier 50 hp engine which was a development of the Tylor engine.

During 1922, forward control versions of the 'K' type became available, and in 1923 the first of the 'C' type appeared being a 30 cwt chassis; the other new model was the 'H' type, a 2 ton chassis. The 'C' type was fitted with Dorman 4JU engines and the 'H' type with Tylor FC4 engines.

By 1924 the 'CY' type was available as a 2 ton chassis, the 'H' type being reclassified as a 2½ ton chassis with a further variant, the 'JH' being a 3 ton chassis. In 1924 the 25 cwt 'Z' type chassis appeared, being the first to be equipped with pneumatic tires. At this time the various models were fitted with either goods or passenger bodies to suit the operator; however, in 1926, the first purpose-built chassis for passenger vehicles appeared being the 'CL', 'KL' and the rigid frame six-wheelers 'WL6' and 'CY6' models. All these were low loading type chassis, except the KL being fitted with Dorman engines. 1926 was also the year in which the ZX model appeared. This was a Dorman engined 30 cwt chassis and was used for both goods and passenger vehicles. The first specially designed Road Sweeper Cleaner, the RSC model appeared, earlier machines being adapted K type chassis.

In 1927, the WO6 appeared being developed from the CY6. The WO6 6-wheel chassis was very popular with the War Office and was ideal for traversing rough terrain, a couple of vehicles being the first ones to travel around Australia with the MacRobertson expedition. The WL6 became available in 26 ft. and 30 ft. lengths for buses and in late 1927, the sleeve-valve engined DD6 appeared, being a 72-seat 6-wheeled double decker. By 1928, the goods chassis available were the 2 ton CY2, 3 ton CWY, 4 ton GH4, 5 ton K5, 7 ton K7 and the 12 ton K6 tractor unit and the WO6 which was a 2/3 ton vehicle. The passenger chassis were the 4-wheeled 20-seat ZX, the 26-seat CL4 and the 32-seat JKL, the 6-wheeled chassis were the light weight 32-seat CL6, the 37-seat WL6, the 40-seat WL6/1 single deck models. The double decker was available as a 66-seat DD6 or a 72-seat DD6/1, the earlier WL6/2 being discontinued. The E6 trolley bus was introduced to fill the demand for high capacity vehicles.

1927 KARRIER WL6/2 66-seater bus, GNG

1929 KARRIER CYR 2½-ton truck, OMM

In 1929, a new 30 cwt ZA chassis appeared being an improved Z type. The 2½ ton CYR was also new and was used extensively for municipal work. The heavy duty KW6, a 6-wheeler, also made its appearance for 7 ton and 8 ton loads. By 1930 the K5 was uprated to carry six tons, the WO6 being revitalized as the FM6 and the RM6 capable of carrying five tons. The KW6 reappeared as an 8 ton KWR6 or a 9 ton KWF6 chassis. The only new additions to the range in 1931 were the 4-wheeled double deck chassis, the Monitor and the 2 ton, three-wheeled Cob and Colt which were designed in conjunction with the L.M.S. railway and were powered by 7-hp Jowett flat twin engines. These were the original mechanical horses.

By 1932, Cob and Colts were available with larger engines by Coventry Climax and were called Cob Major and Colt Major, carrying four tons and two tons respectively. A 12 ton rigid 6-wheel truck became available called the Colossus. The passenger chassis available were the 28-seat Coaster, the 35-seat Chaser 6, the 50-seat Monitor and the 68-seat Consort, but these did not find many buyers.

The Bantam was the smallest four wheeler, being of 50 cwt payload on an 8 ft. wheelbase chassis using a 4-cylinder gasoline engine and 4 speed gearbox. It is significant that the Bantam remained in production after the Rootes takeover and in fact probably spelled the end of the Commer Pug which started life as the T.S.M. GG model in 1932. Karriers were finding difficulty in

1933 KARRIER Bantam 2-ton refuse truck, OMM

1933 KARRIER Cob 3-wheel tractor with drawbar trailor, OMM

remaining viable and various mergers were considered. Oil engines were offered as a alternative power unit but the Gardner engines were too late for Karriers to continue in business. A receiver was appointed on behalf of the debenture holders in June 1934. A new company Karrier Motors Successors Ltd., was formed in August 1934, to take over the assets and goodwill of Karrier Motors Ltd., Huddersfield. This new company was owned by Rootes Securities Ltd. By the summer of 1935, the production of new vehicles had been transferred to Luton.

With the transfer of such a line of commercial vehicles to a position alongside an already complete line of middleweight vehicles such as the Commer range it was obvious that some rationalization would result. It was announced that the revised — and smaller — range of Karrier vehicles from the new works would embody some standard parts in common with the existing Commer range. Another outcome of the change of ownership was that Karrier trolleybus production did not move to Luton but continued at Huddersfield until the later acquisition of Sunbeam by Rootes when it was possible to combine the trolleybus ranges of both concerns.

Returning to Luton we find that the "Colt", "Cob Junior", "Cob Senior" and "Bantam" models remained in the Karrier list, and for the municipal market — which was to be the Karrier forte in the future — the CK3 and CK6 models were introduced. The CK range was for 3 ton payloads with the CK6 being a rigid six wheeler. Both 6-cylinder gasoline and 4-cylinder oil engines were offered in this series.

In the years leading up to the war the range stayed as outlined above except that a tractor version of the "Bantam" was offered in 1939. Naturally work was underway with orders for the military, and wartime production included rigid six wheelers of the 3 ton CK6 series, model K6 4x4 3 tonners, "Bantams" for the RAF and some KT4 4x4 gun tractors.

The postwar range reintroduced the "Bantam" 2 tonner and tractor models, the CK3 3-4 tonner and the municipal types such as gulley emptier and refuse bodies on the CK3 chassis. Gulley emptiers were built in collaboration with Yorkshire and an unusual road sweeper was produced by the same concern using a modified Commer "Superpoise" chassis of 110 inch wheelbase. This RSC model used the 6-cylinder Commer gasoline engine and employed a special half cab and left hand control.

1946 KARRIER W trolleybus chassis with 1956 63-seater body by East Lancashire Coachbuilders, AJHB

1948 KARRIER CK 3-4 ton truck, OMM

In 1948 a new all steel cab was introduced for the Bantam. In 1950 the CK3 became the Gamecock with a new style cab incorporating a new 6-cylinder underfloor engine. 1951 saw the introduction of a 4-cylinder chassis for ambulance work and in 1954 the revolutionary Commer TS3, 3-cylinder, six piston two stroke oil engine was offered as an alternative in the Gamecock. The oil engine alternative for the Bantam was the Perkins P4.

In 1958 there were improvements to the Gamecock range with a new style cab incorporating a one piece screen and a variation of the Perkins 6.305 6-cylinder diesel engine. The Bantam models were up dated also about this time with a new design of cab, and a battery-electric version of the Bantam tractor was produced in 1959 in collaboration with Smiths-NCB.

1961 KARRIER Bantam 2-3-ton truck, NMM

In 1962 a new version of the ambulance chassis was offered, it being based on the popular Commer Walk-Thru van and being designed in collaboration with Dennis Brothers. 1963 saw the Bantam again updated and offered with a choice of a gasoline or diesel engines of two sizes. Because of larger refuse collection bodies being sought by local authorities there was a need for a heavier chassis to accomodate them and so the larger Commer CC8 and VB7 chassis appeared in 1965 with the Karrier emblem, and in 1968 the still larger 16 ton gross CE16 was offered with a body of 22 cu. yd. capacity. In 1966 control of the company had passed to the American Chrysler concern with the parent company being known as Rootes Motors Ltd. In 1970 this style was changed to Chrysler United Kingdom but with the marque still entitled Karrier.

Recent changes to the range of vehicles offered by Commer/Karrier has been a completely new Commando series of models with a distinctive new design of cab — the

1978 KARRIER Commando G15 refuse truck, Chrysler OK

Hi-Line, and in this model range are chassis ranging from 7.38- to 16.0-tons GVW all with diesel engines by Perkins except for the largest type which has the Mercedes-Benz OM352. Although the Commer name was dropped in 1976, municipal vehicles are still called Karrier.*OM*

KASSBOHRER see Setra

KATO (US) 1909-1913

Four Traction Auto Co., Mankato, Minn.

1909 KATO 1½-ton 4×4 truck, MHS

Designed by a candy maker, Ernest Rosenberger, the Kato was a 4-wheel-drive truck of 1½-tons capacity, powered by a 4-cylinder engine under the driver's seat. Power was transmitted by propeller shaft to a transfer box mid-way between axles, and thence forward to front axle and back to rear axle by additional shafts. A 3 ton model was offered in 1913. Total production of Kato trucks was about 30. *GNG*

K.A.W. see Hagen (iii)

KAZ (KA3) SU c.1951 to date

Kutaisi Automobile Factory — Kutaisi

Prior to 1961, KAZ manufacture consisted of units nearly identical to ZIS/ZIL designs and utilizing their chassis.

In 1961 a cab-over-engine tractor-truck of indigenous design, using a ZIL-164A chassis, was introduced. This was built from 1961 to 1966 as the KAZ-606A "Kolhida." Power was from a ZIL 6-cylinder engine that slid out of the front for major maintenance.

In 1967 a cab-over-engine KAZ-608 "Kolhida" went into production. It contained a ZIL V-8 (130-YA-5) engine of 150 hp at 3,200 rpm. The cab tilted forward for engine repair.

This "Kolhida" was refined in 1973 and is now built as model 608B.

"Kolhida" refers to a stretch of land on the Black Sea (Kolhis) shore known from ancient legends. *BE*

KEARNS (US) 1909-1928

(1) Kearns Motor Car Co., Beavertown, Pa. 1909-1912
(2) Kearns Motor Truck Co., Beavertown, Pa. 1912-1920
(3) Kearns-Dughie Corp., Danville, Pa. 1920-1928

The Kearns automobile was a high-wheeler introduced in 1907. The first truck, a brewery wagon, was built in 1909. The high-wheelers, built until 1913, were powered by a 3-cylinder 2-stroke air-cooled Speedwell engine and had a friction transmission, dual chain drive, and wheel steering. In 1912, when water-cooling was optional, the 1500-pound truck cost $900 for the chassis.

In 1914 a standard truck with 20 hp 4-cylinder water-cooled engine, cone clutch, 3-speed transmission, and Hotchkiss drive was introduced. It cost $1175 for the chassis. A few touring cars were built on the truck chassis in 1915. The firm also built the LuLu cyclecar in 1914.

Post war models included a ½ ton model with Lycoming engine and 1½ ton model with Herschell-Spillman (later Continental) engine. The trucks, priced at $850 and $1800, had dry plate clutches and internal gear drive.

After the move to Danville the firm specialized in the manufacture of fire engine chassis which carried bodies and equipment by the Foamite-Childs Corp of Utica, N.Y. and were sold under the name of Childs Thoroughbred. In addition a complete line of worm-drive trucks from one to five tons was offered until the factory was closed down in 1928. *DJS*

KELDON (US) 1919

House Cold Tire Setter Co., St. Louis, Mo.

This tradename was applied to a 2 tonner in the one year given. The manufacturer's name is peculiar, and its origins unknown. *GMN*

KELLAND (US) 1922-1925

Kelland Motor Car Co., Newark, N.J.

The Model A was a ½-tonner, Model B a ¾ tonner and Model C a 1 tonner. All were battery-powered electrics on a common chassis with wheelbase of 102 inches. Solid rubber tires were standard and motors were made by General Electric. The smallest model was priced at $2200. *GMN*

KELLER (D) 1902-1903

Keller, Hoerschel nr. Laggenbeck (Westphalia)

Keller designed some types of tractors which originally were built to his orders by MMB at Marienfelde. In 1902 Keller established his own production. Very unusual was his system of a track-ring-drive for his tractors. These were able to tow 13 trailers with a total payload of over 40 tons. *HON*

KELLY (US) 1910-1912
KELLY-SPRINGFIELD (US) 1912-1929

(1) Kelly Motor Truck Co., Springfield, Ohio 1910-1912
(2) Kelly-Springfield Motor Truck Co., Springfield, Ohio 1912-1926
(3) American Bus & Truck Co., Springfield Ohio 1926
(4) Kelly-Springfield Truck & Bus Corp., Springfield, Ohio 1926-1929

The Kelly succeeded the Frayer-Miller, and through 1912 continued to use air-cooled engines with which its predecessor had long been connected. Water-cooled engines, 4-cylinder pair-cast units of Kelly's own manufacture, were adopted in 1912, and the trucks featured a Renault-type hood with radiator behind the engine. Transmission was via a 3-speed gearbox and double chain drive. Through 1912 1-, 2-, and 3-tonners were made, principally a stripped chassis, though the 2- and 3-tonners could be had with open express bodies. The range of models extended during the next few years, and by 1918 there were eight, from 1½ to 6 tons capacity. Worm drive appeared on the 1918 1½-tonner, though chains were still seen on the 6-tonner as late as 1926, and other models of the early 1920s used internal gear drive.

1920 KELLY-SPRINGFIELD 5-ton truck, Goodyear

During this period steel disc wheels began to replace artillery spoked wheels, and eventually became standard. The Renault-type hood was continued on the larger models until the end of production, but smaller Kelly-Springfields adopted conventionally-placed radiators after 1924. These also used proprietary engines for the first time, the 1½-tonner having a Continental K4, and the 2½- and 3½-tonners Hercules engines. While some lists carried Kelly-Springfield to 1929, it is likely that production actually came to an end two years before. *GMN*

KEMNA (D) 1912-1914; 1926

1 Kemna, Breslau

Kemna was one of the very few manufacturers of steam traction engines in Germany and production was limited to the 1912-1914 period. In 1926 a diesel engined tractor was introduced but production did not start on a great scale. *HON*

KENWORTH (US) 1923 to date

(1) Kenworth Motor Truck Corp., Seattle, Wash. 1923-1973
(2) Kenworth Truck Co., Seattle, Wash. 1973 to date

The Kenworth company took its name from H.W. Kent and E.K. Worthington who had been directors of its predecessor company, the Gersix Manufacturing Co. Their early days were helped by the failure of the only other truck makers in Seattle, H.R.L. and Vulcan, from

1923 KENWORTH 3-ton trucks, Kenworth

whom Kenworth bought parts. Early Kenworths came in three sizes, 1½-, 2½- and 4-tons, all powered by 4-cylinder Buda engines. The first year's production was 78 trucks of which only two were the 4-tonners. By 1925 there were five models, from one to five tons, and in 1926 annual production reached 99 trucks. At this time and for many years afterwards Kenworth production was sufficiently small for a wide variety of customer's requests to be incorporated, so it is misleading to speak of a standard range; almost any type of vehicle would be built if asked for. In 1927 a new 78 hp 6-cylinder engine was used, and Kenworth began to cater more noticeably for the West Coast market, with 7-speed transmissions, stronger axles and sometimes supplementary springs at the front. In 1929 Kenworth set up a branch factory at Vancouver, B.C.

1929 KENWORTH 25-seater bus, Kenworth

In 1932 Kenworth became the first American truck maker to offer a diesel engine as a factory option; this was a 4-cylinder 100 hp Cummins HA4. Other developments of the early 1930s included torsion-bar suspension and

1930 KENWORTH 10-ton articulated van, Kenworth

vacuum boosters for the hydraulic brakes. New types of vehicle included 6-wheelers, either with trailing 3rd axle or tandem drive, and fire engines. Buses had been made from the late 1920s, and were a small but interesting part of Kenworth's business until the late 1950s. They were mostly intercity coaches, some with 'one and a half deck' bodies, and either conventional or forward control. Some

1933 KENWORTH 6×4 tanker with 3-axle trailer, Kenworth

in the late 1930s had underfloor pancake engines, while an interesting hybrid built in 1951 for Northern Pacific Railroad was the 'Bruck', a combination bus and truck for 17 passengers at the front and a taller cargo van, 18 ft long over the tandem axle at the rear. It was powered by a 136 hp Hall-Scott engine.

In 1935 Kenworth began to build their own cabs and sheet metal, a result of which was an attractive chrome grille which is still recognizable in the appearance of today's Kenworths. Although special requests could still be made, such as chain-drive trucks in order to get an axle capacity for a larger load, there was a standard range of Kenworths in the late 1930s from 2- to 10-ton trucks in the price range $1245 to $11646. Basic power plants were

1936 KENWORTH one-and-a half-decker coach; Tricoach body, MBS

Hercules, Buda and Herschell-Spillman gasoline, and Cummins diesels, all 6-cylinder engines. The first four-wheel-drive truck was made in 1937, and cab-overs appeared in the same year. Other special models were low-

1937 KENWORTH 15-ton articulated van, Kenworth

bed trucks, milk delivery trucks and sleeper boxes in the rear of the cabs. In 1941 Cummins built the world's first aluminum diesel for installation in a Kenworth at the request of the company.

During World War II Kenworth made some 1900 M1A1 wrecker trucks similar to those of Ward LaFrance, and also pilot models of an 8-ton 6x6 truck. Using the experience gained in war-time metallurgy, Kenworth engineers developed in 1944 an extruded aluminum truck frame, and extended the use of aluminum to cabs, hoods and transmission housings. In 1945 Kenworth was bought by Pacific Car & Foundry who relocated it in the former Fisher body plant in Seattle where it has operated ever since. Later a Kenworth plant was established in Kansas City which specialized in extra-heavy duty models.

1946 KENWORTH Model 523 12-ton 6×4 with 3-axle trailer, Kenworth

Production of civilian trucks never entirely ceased during the war, though it was down to only 87 units in 1943. In the late 1940s it climbed to some 600 per year, and passed the 1000 mark in 1952. Conventionals and cab-overs were made, together with fire engines and a dwindling number of buses. The radiator on the conventionals had become vertical in 1940 in place of the sloping grille used since 1935, and this vertical design has been steadily developed up to the present without any radical change. In 1947 Kenworth developed desert trucks for oilfield work in the Middle East, culminating in the Model 953 of 1958 which had a Cummins NTC350 engine, tire sizes of up to 29.50, and cost over $100,000. These trucks are so large that a low sports car can be driven under them, and they have been used for transporting full-sized locomotives across the desert. In 1950 a Boeing turbine was installed in a Kenworth and although it did not go into production it was the first gas turbine in scheduled freight service. Another special project was the T-10 Heavy Equipment Transporter for the US Army, a double-ended unit with tractors in front and rear of a 250mm gun, with a total weight of 85 tons.

1953 KENWORTH 18-ton articulated van, LA

In 1953 Kenworth introduced an original cab-beside-engine design for line-haul work in the mountains where the drivers wanted maximum visibility. Some were 6x4s with the sleeper box behind the engine and entrance to the

1954 KENWORTH CBE (cab beside engine) tractor, Kenworth

cab. This was really a single seater, though a small canvas seat behind the driver could carry a passenger. The cbe style was too unconventional to last for long. Another Kenworth original developed in conjunction with Pacific Intermountain Express, in 1956 was a 4-axle 'Dromedary' with twin steering axles and a short cargo van between the cab and the 5th wheel coupling for the semi-trailer. Peterbilt also built 'Dromedaries' for P.I.E.

From the late 1940s onwards, tractor-trailor units began to gain increasing importance in Kenworth production compared with straight trucks, and today make up the bulk of trucks built. The familiar flat-faced full-width cab-overs (K Series) have been made since 1950 with little change, this cab being shared today with Peterbilt. For the past 20 years or so all Kenworths have used diesel engines, the basic units being Cummins, with Caterpillar or Detroit Diesels as regular options. In 1971 came the PD series, later renamed the Hustler; this was a straight cab-forward design mainly intended for the urban delivery trade, and used the same cab as Peterbilt's 200 series. In 1973 a new model was the Brute, a 6×4 conventional intended for the construction industry. Current models include the Brute and Hustler, W-series conventional line-haul tractors and K-series cab-over line-haul tractors. GVWs range from 50,000 to 89,000 lbs. for the construc-

1975 KENWORTH K-124, 6×4 sleeper tractor with 8-axle dump trailers. Kenworth

1977 KENWORTH C-500 6×4 concrete mixer, Kenworth

tion models, and GTWs with semi-trailers for the W and K series from 76,800 to 130,000 lbs. Production has grown dramatically in the past 15 years, from under 2000 in the early 1960s to 10,000 to 11,000 in the mid-1970s. In addition to the Kansas City plant, Kenworth has factories at Mexicali, Baja California and Bayswater, Victoria in Australia where some special models for the local market are made including ones with tandem front steering axles. Kenworth has gained an unusual record in being the fastest recorded truck in the world, with speeds of 132-154 mph for a tractor, and 92.083 mph for a tractor and semi-trailer. Both records were set in 1975. *RW*

KERR STUART (GB) 1929-1930

Kerr, Stuart & Co. Ltd., Stoke-on-Trent, Staffs.

The product of a well-known firm of locomotive builders, the Kerr Stuart was the first British diesel-engined lorry to be built as a complete entity rather than a converted steam wagon, as the first Garrett diesels were. The prototype had a 6-cylinder Helios engine, but production models used a 11-litre 4-cylinder McLaren-Benz of 60 hp. A single-cylinder 4 hp J.A.P. engine in the cab was used to start the diesel, which was governed to a maximum of 800 rpm, giving a road speed of 20 mph. Drive was through a 4-speed gearbox and double chain drive, the latter distinctly archaic for a new design in 1929. Only five production models were sold before the bankruptcy of Kerr Stuart put an end to the project. *GNG*

KERRY (I/GB) 1965-1968

Kerry's Ltd., London, E.15

Like the company's mopeds, the Kerry Carrier was made specially for them in Italy. It followed classic ultralight 3x2 lines with 50 cc 2-stroke F.B-Minarelli engine, 3-speed gearbox, and uncoupled 3-wheel brakes. Few were sold. *MCS*

KEYSTONE (US) 1919-1923

(1) Commercial Car Unit Co., Philadelphia, Pa. 1919
(2) Keystone Motor Truck Corp., Oaks, Pa. 1920-1923

The Keystone 2-ton truck was powered by a 26 hp 4-cylinder engine of the firm's own manufacture. The truck was first built by the firm which made Truxton conversion units for Fords. A 1-ton model was offered from 1921 on. H.W. Sofield, who was responsible for the Keystone truck, left the firm in 1921 to found Penn Motors Corporation, which bought out Keystone in 1923. Buda engines were used from 1921. *DJS*

KIDDER (US) 1900-1901

Kidder Motor Vehicle Co., New Haven, Conn.

This company made steam-driven passenger and goods vehicles powered by two separate cylinders of 3 hp each, mounted horizontally on each side of the boiler. The passenger model had direct drive to the rear axle but the delivery van used a train of gears to give a lower ratio. *GNG*

KIMBALL(US) 1917-1926

Kimball Motor Truck Co., Los Angeles, Cal.

The initial line of Kimball trucks consisted of 1½-, 2-,, 2½-, 4- and 5-tonners. All had 4-cylinder Wisconsin engines and used worm-drive rear axles. By 1922, the models had been reduced to 2-, 3½- and 5-tonners. Later, in 1924, 1½- and 4-tonners were added with wheelbases as large as 14 feet. During 1925-1926, only a 2½-tonner was built, still with a Wisconsin engine and worm-drive. *GMN*

KING (US) 1912-1918

A.R. King Manufacturing Company, Kingston, New York

The only King model was designated "3½" for its capacity in tons. It had a 4-cylinder engine with a three-speed gearbox and double chain-drive. It had forward control, wheelbase was 120 inches and the early price for the 6000-pound chassis was $3350. *GMN*

KING-SEAGRAVE (CDN) 1956 to date

King-Seagrave Ltd., Woodstock, Ont.

After designing new Bickle fire engines in 1926, V.B. King went on to operate a prosperous truck and trailer company. In 1956 he took over the remains of the bankrupt Bickle company including the Seagrave franchise, and started producing King-Seagrave fire engines. Most King-Seagraves are on conventional truck chassis. *HD*

KING-ZEITLER (US) 1919-c.1929

King-Zeitler Co., Chicago, Ill.

Successor to the Zeitler & Lamson, the King-Zeitler was made in a wide variety of model from ¾-ton to 5-ton, the latter being known as the King-Zeitler 90. All used various sizes of Continental engine. A bus chassis was listed in 1923 only. *GNG*

KISSEL (US) 1908-1931

Kissel Motor Car Co., Hartford, Wis.

The first Kissel truck was mounted on a regular 4-cylinder shaft-drive passenger car chassis, but by 1910 the company was offering large trucks up to five tons capacity with chain drive on the bigger models. These used Wisconsin or Waukesha engines and carried names such as Heavy Duty, Dreadnought and Goliath. A patented differential lock to aid traction on soft surfaces was featured, as was a removable winter cab with all-enclosed plate glass windows. The 1912 range consisted of five models from 1500 lbs. to 5-tons.

During World War I Kissel engineers made important contributions to the design of the Class A and B trucks (see Liberty), and in 1918 the factory was turned over entirely to the manufacture of F.W.D. 4-wheel drive trucks. During the 1920s conventional trucks in the 1- to 5-ton range were made, using their own, Buda or Waukesha engines. In 1923 they introduced the 18-passenger "Coach Limited," a bus styled like the passenger car line, with double drop frame and 20-inch disc wheels. Wheelbase of this "stretched sedan" was 202 inches. This design led, in 1925, to the "Heavy Duty Safety Speed Truck" with the same low chassis and Kissel 6-cylinder engine of the bus. Ambulances and hearses became a major part of Kissel's production from 1926 onwards, on lengthened stock car chassis with Kissel 6-55 engines to 1928, and Lycoming WS after that. They were distributed by the National Casket Company, hence their name National-Kissel. Further attempts to bolster falling sales resulted in a deal with Bradfield Motors Inc. of Chicago to distribute taxicabs, trucks and buses. The former Yellow Cab officials who formed Bradfield collaborated with Kissel in creating a handsome taxicab body. These Bradfield or New Yorker cabs with Continental engines were offered even after Kissel's failure, assembled by Bradfield in space rented from the receiver well into 1931. *EEH*

1924 KISSEL 18-seater Coach Limited, EEH

KLATTE (D) 1952-1954

Metallwarenfabrik Theodor Klatte GmbH., Bremen

This firm had not been active in the field of car manufacturing before when they presented a new concept in bus design in 1952. It was a forward control chassis-less light metal construction with independently sprung wheels. Later versions had hydrostatic all-wheel drive. An air-cooled Deutz diesel engine was placed at the rear end. *HON*

KLEIBER (US) 1914-1937

(1) Kleiber & Co., San Francisco, Cal.
(2) Kleiber Motor Truck Co., San Francisco, Cal.
(3) Kleiber Motor Co., San Francisco, Cal.

Kleiber was a small West Coast operation which began manufacture with a thoroughly conventional range of assembled trucks in the 1½ to 5 ton capacity areas. Engines were by Continental, supplemented by some Buda units from the mid-1920s, when 6-cylinder models were offered. By the end of the 1920s the range had been extended at both ends, the smallest being a ½-ton pickup and the largest a 10-tonner. In 1930 the first Kleiber 6-wheeler appeared, and the firm subsequently built up quite a reputation for this type of work. They had Timken bogies and big air springs at the front. Kleiber was very early in the diesel field, producing trucks in ones and twos from 1932 onwards, according to customer demand. West Coast users appreciated the diesel engine's torque characteristics, and gradually Cummins-powered diesel trucks became a more important part of Kleiber's limited production. This never exceeded a few hundred units annually, and was smaller than Kleiber's two California rivals, Fageol and Moreland.

1930 KLEIBER 2-ton chassis, NAHC

In the early '30s Kleiber acquired the Studebaker franchise for San Francisco, a very profitable business, and from then until 1937 truck "production" was more a matter of fitting in the occasional unit between Studebaker sales and servicing. Statistically at least the firm could supply seven chassis in ratings from 1½ to six tons, plus three 6-wheelers from five to nine tons with Hercules, Continental or Cummins engines. Typical of the occasional order filled by Kleiber was a KD-4 Cummins-diesel powered tandem tractor with 100 gallon fuel tank which gave a range of 1000 miles. *RJ*

KLIEMT (D) 1899-1901

C. Kliemt Wagenfabrik, Berlin

Electric vans were produced by this firm. Their electric driven taxicabs were used in Berlin. *HON*

KLINE (US) 1909-1914

(1) B.C.K. Motor Car Co., York, Pa. 1909-1911
(2) Kline Motor Car Corp., York, Pa. 1911-1912
(3) Kline Motor Car Corp., Richmond, Va. 1913-1914

The prototype Kline truck was built in early 1909 by the York Carriage Works prior to the organization of the B.C.K. firm in mid-1909 to manufacture the Kline-Kar. The truck had a 12 hp 2-cylinder engine and chain drive and looked much like the Hart-Kraft. It was manufactured until 1913. After the move to Richmond some delivery trucks were built on the Kline-Kar 4-cylinder touring car chassis. Truck production ceased 1914; automobile production was prolonged until 1922. *DJS*

K.M.C. (CY) 1973 to date

K.M.C. Ltd., Nicosia

A branch of the Kaisis industrial enterprise undertook local production of Dennis truck and tractor chassis after production at Guildford, England was dropped in favor of fire engines and municipal vehicles. A whole range of truck and bus chassis are built, the former fitted with the familiar Dennis fibreglass cab, but all models are sold under the KMC trademark. Power comes from 6.354 Perkins diesels. Lighter KMC vehicles were introduced a year later and are based on the Commer "Walk Thru" range, but have a redesigned grille and powered by Chrysler gasoline engines, having diesels as an option. *GA*

KNICKERBOCKER (US) 1911-1916

Knickerbocker Motor Truck Company, New York, N.Y.

These electric vehicles were first offered in capacities of 3½, 4- and 5-tons with various body types including a coal dump truck. By 1915, this line had expanded to include a 2-tonner, all with double chain-drives and 4-cylinder gasoline engines as well as forward control. In the last year of manufacture only 2- and 3½-tonners were built which used worm drives and engines under hoods. *GMN*

KNOX; KNOX-MARTIN (US) 1901-1924

(1) Knox Automobile Co., Springfield, Mass.
(2) Knox Motors Co., Springfield, Mass.
(3) Martin Tractor Co., Springfield, Mass. 1913-1916
(4) Martin Rocking Fifth Wheel Co., Chicopee Falls, Mass. 1916-1918
(5) Martin Rocking Fifth Wheel Co., Longmeadow, Mass. 1918-1924

The first commercial vehicle produced by this company was a delivery van version of their light 3-wheeler car. It had a 4 hp single-cylinder engine, air-cooled like all Knoxes up to 1908, two forward speeds by epicyclic gears, no reverse, and tiller steering to the single front wheel. The first 4-wheeler came in 1902; this had a larger single-cylinder engine pointing forward instead of rearward as on the first model, two forward speeds and one reverse. Early in 1904 a 2-cylinder model was introduced. All these were simply goods-carrying versions of Knox passenger cars, but late in 1904 came the first purpose-built commercial chassis with forward control, 96 inch wheelbase and carrying capacity of 1¼ tons or 14 passengers. A 3-ton truck with double chain drive came in 1905, supplemented by a 1½-ton model in 1906. These chassis carried a wide variety of bodies, including sightseeing buses and combination passenger and goods vehicles for rural routes in the West. Knox's first fire engine, a normal control 4-cylinder Model G, was delivered in September 1906 to Springfield Fire Department, and this became an important part of Knox business in succeeding years.

From 1908 water-cooled engines gradually replaced the air-cooled units, familiarly known as "Old Porcupines" because of the 2 inch pins screwed into the cylinder jackets in place of the more conventional cooling fins. The last air-cooled model was a light delivery wagon with single-cylinder engine and double chain drive, announced in August 1908. By 1911 the company was making a range of forward-control trucks of 2-, 3-, 4- and 5- ton capacity and also a normal control fire engine using the same 40 hp engine as the 5-ton truck.

1910 KNOX-MARTIN 3-wheel tractor and trailer, Wallace S. Phinney

In 1909 a former Knox employee, Charles Hay Martin, returned to the company, and his work soon gave a new direction to the firm's products. He patented a system for attaching two-wheeled trailers to tractive units, known as the Martin Rocking Fifth Wheel. In this the turntable was carried by semi-elliptic springs attached directly to the rear axle of the tractor, so that the weight of the semi-trailer was carried by the tractor's rear wheels, while the much lower weight of the tractor itself was carried by separate lighter springs. The first Knox-Martin tractors were 3-wheelers powered by 40 hp 4-cylinder ohv engines, and were employed for pulling horse-drawn fire pumpers and also general haulage work. Because of shortage of space Martin set up a new factory 200 yards from the old one, in March 1913, and formed a new company, the Martin Tractor Company. Two models of the 3-wheel tractor were made, for pulling five and ten ton loads. The same engine was used, and the main difference was a longer wheelbase on the ten tonner. The normal top speed was 10 mph, but by altering the drive sprockets this could be increased to 33 mph for fire apparatus. The steering column extended right over the hood to a steering box immediately over the single front wheel. This had a lock of almost 90 degrees, enabling the tractor to turn in little more than its own length. In 1915 the 3-wheel tractor was

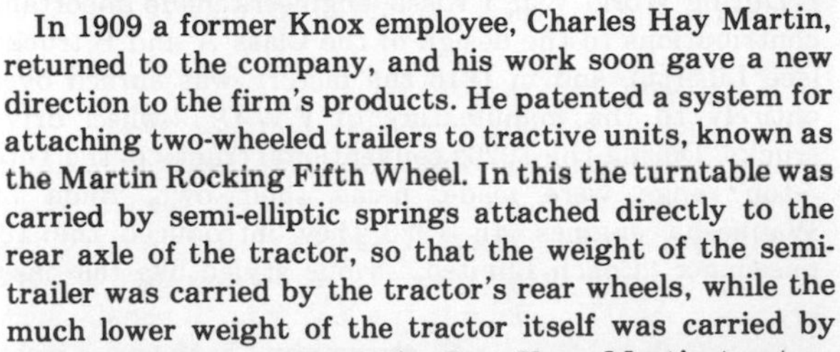

c.1916 KNOX-MARTIN 4-wheel tractor and logging trailer, BHV

replaced by a 4-wheeler, largely because it was found more suitable for rough ground to have two tracks instead of three. The same size of engine was used, but cylinders were separated instead of pair cast. As on the 3-wheeler, final drive was by double chain. Many of the 4-wheelers were used during World War I, and in France they pulled tank-carrying trailers, being probably the world's first tank transporters. Ex-army Knox tractors were in use in Britain and France until well into the 1930s. Production continued for several years after the war, but although pioneers in the fifth wheel system Knox gradually lost out to better-established truck builders. *GNG*

KNUCKEY (US) 1943-c.1955

Knuckey Truck Co., San Francisco, Calif.

The Knuckey was a dump truck made in 2- and 3-axle versions for loads of up to 125,000 lbs. Engines were Cummins diesels, with Fuller transmissions and Timken axles. Most Knuckeys used chain drive, with the firm's patent center pivot double chain system on the 6 x 4 trucks. This had been used on Pacific tank transporters during World War II. As they were largely custom made, Knuckeys could be supplied with gasoline, diesel or butane power units, and with worm or double reduction drive in place of the chains. They were widely used in mining and dam construction in the Western United States. *GNG*

KOBE (J) 1935-c.1939

Kobe Steel Works Ltd., Kobe

Kobe diesel trucks used 3.6-litre 4-cylinder and 5.3-litre 6-cylinder engines, the latter unit developing 70 hp. *MCS*

KOCKUMS (S) 1961 to date

Aktiebolaget Kockums-Landsverk, Landskrona

One of Sweden's two specialist manufacturers of dump trucks, Kockums began with two models, the 36,302 kg KL-420 and the 54,000 kg KL-440, the latter powered by a 385 hp 6-cylinder diesel engine. The current range consists of three conventional dump trucks and an unusual vehicle with articulated chassis which can pivot both horizontally and vertically. Known as the 412, it is powered by a 7.8-litre Scania 08 diesel engine and has a payload of 18 tons.

1975 KOCKUMS Model 412 center-articulated 18-ton dump truck, Kockums

1975 KOCKUMS Model 422 32-ton dump truck, Kockums

Unlike other Kockums models, the 412 has 4-wheel drive. The conventional dump trucks are the 25-ton 425 powered by a 11-litre 285 hp Scania DS11 engine, the 35-ton 442 powered by a 14.2-litre 365 hp Scania DS14A V-8 engine, and the 45-ton 445 with 510 hp Detroit diesel V-12 engine. All have 6-speed Allison Powershift gearboxes. *GNG*

KOEHLER (US) 1913-1923

(1) H.J. Koehler Sporting Goods Co., Newark, N.J. 1913-1915
(2) H.J. Koehler Motor Corp., Newark, N.J.
(3) H.J. Koehler Motor Corp., Bloomfield, N.J.

This company made conventional 1-ton trucks with 4-cylinder ohv engines of their own manufacture, supplemented by a 1¼-tonner in 1918. After that they turned to proprietary engines by Hercules and Herschell-Spillman for a range of 1½ to 5-ton trucks made up to 1923. *GNG*

KOMAREK (A) 1901-c.1912

F.X. Komarek, Vienna 10

Komarek, who were an old established firm of boiler makers and engineers, began design work on their wagon in 1899 but the first example to be put to commercial use was employed in transporting machinery to the new municipal power station in Vienna in 1901.

1901 KOMAREK steam wagon, Vienna Technical Museum

The Komarek wagon had a vertical boiler, placed at the front of the chassis, undertype compound engine with countershaft differential and double chain final drive. Steering, unlike many of its undertype contemporaries elsewhere, was by a patent chain and bobbin system of the maker's own design. Initially wooden wheels with steel tires were used but subsequently steel wheels were used. In 1903 the firm supplied steam buses for use on a route from Mank to Kirchlberg and Saint-Poelten in Austria. *RAW*

KOMATSU (J) 1953 to date

Komatsu LTd., Tokyo

Originally manutacturers of mining machinery, Komatsu progressed in 1932 to crawler tractors, and to dump trucks, mostly of off-road type, in 1953. Since 1961 they have had a license agreement with Cummins, whose diesel engines have been used in almost all their dumpers. The 1978 range covered off-road types for payloads from 20 to 68 tons. The largest Komatsu was a half-cab machine with the company's own 6-speed torque converter transmission, air-hydraulic brakes, and power

1975 KOMATSU KD 320 dump truck, Komatsu

steering. It used a 28-litre V12 Cummins engine developing 775 hp. *MCS*

KOMNICK (D) 1907-1930

1. F. Komnick Autofabrik, Elbing 1907-1922
2. Automobilfabrik Komnick A.G., Elbing 1922-1930

The private cars of this firm were the basis for various van versions and light trucks. In 1913 the first heavier truck was presented, a 5-tonner. After WW I trucks with three and five tons payload capacity were available as well as buses. In 1926 a road tractor was added which was very popular. This and the 5-ton truck had a newly developed 6-cylinder 75 hp engine. The geographical situation of Komnick in East Prussia resulted in their wide-spread use in Eastern Germany and exportation to Eastern Europe.

1929 KOMNICK 3-ton diesel truck, FLP

The road tractor was carried on by Bussing when they had taken over Komnick in 1930. *HON*

KOPP (US) 1911-1916

Kopp Motor Truck Company, Buffalo, New York

The Kopp trucks ranged in capacity from 1 to 5 tons, with in between models of 1½, 2 and 3 tons. The largest, Model 5, had forward control with a four-cylinder engine of 605 cid displacement. The chassis weighed 6900 pounds with wheelbase of 126 inches and was priced at $4500. *GMN*

KOPPEL (B) 1901-c.1903

Compagnie Belge de Velocipedes, Liege

This company made a light van on their car chassis. It was powered by a rear-mounted vertical single-cylinder engine geared to the rear axle. It could be started by a lever from the seat. *GNG*

KOSMATH (US) 1914-1916

Kosmath Co., Detroit, Mich.

The Kosmath was a ½-tonner which in 1914 was priced at $850. The end of this make was in sight when the 1916 ½-tonner was launched with a smaller gasoline engine, shorter wheelbase and a price of $675. This make was a continuation of a truck built by Miller Car Co. in 1914, as Miller. *GMN*

KRAKA (D) 1963 to date

(1) Zweirad Union, Nuremberg
(2) Faun-Werke GmbH., Neunkirchen

Kraka stands for "Kraftkarren" (Power Cart) and means a unique small cross-country cart. It was developed by Faun and built by Zweirad Union (then owned by Faun) and used a 400 cc two-stroke Goggo engine. It is universally used for farm and forestry purposes, can be equipped for various municipal purposes and is used also by military forces. Gradients of 55% can be mastered. A special feature is that this vehicle can be folded to 2/3 of its original size when not being driven.

The current model is the type 640 with an air-cooled opposed twin B.M.W. engine of 697 cc developing 26 hp and giving a maximum speed of 55 kph. *HON*

KRAMER (D) 1956-1974

Kramer-Werke GmbH., Uberlingen

This firm built a 4x4 and 6x6 chassis which was used as a prime mover and for various purposes. Moreover a front-drive component including cab was available which was could be coupled to a large variety of equipment. A 6-cylinder air-cooled diesel engine by Deutz developing 100 hp was used.

Since 1974 only a 4x4 special purpose tractor is built. *HON*

KRAUSS-MAFFEI (D) 1931-1965

Krauss-Maffei A.G., Munich

The Maffei road tractor was carried on by this firm. It was available with a 4-cylinder 60 hp Deutz engine of 4.7-litre; a diesel was available too. It was supplemented by a heavier type in 1933, using a 6-cylinder 7-litre Maybach engine of 95 hp. Both types were produced until 1939.

After WW II Krauss-Maffei started with buses. The first one was the KMO 130 of 1946 with forward control body and a rear-mounted 6-cylinder 6.2-litre Maybach engine. Based on this chassis also a truck was offered

1951 KRAUSS-MAFFEI bus, Techniart

which was the first one with its engine mounted behind the rear axle. Some other fwc buses followed. In 1954 the first one in chassis-less construction appeared. In 1959 Kraus-Maffei entered into co-operation with M.A.N. using engine and other components for their buses. Sales were also organized by M.A.N. In 1963 this co-operation was given up. Later Krauss-Maffei built some bus versions to order for Bussing, but the "K M" sign also appeared. This lasted until 1965 when production of buses ended. *HON*

KRAZ (KPA3) SU 1959 to date

Kremenchug Automobile Plant, Kremenchug

In 1959 YAAZ truck production was transferred to the new KRAZ plant and with it the YAAZ-214, 219, 221 and 222 became KRAZ models and continued until about 1966. Revised designs were then introduced and most have remained in production with some modification.

c.1966 KRAZ-222 6×4 dump truck, FH

KRAZ-257 is a 14-ton 6x4 general purpose truck, 255B is an 8-ton 6x6, 255L is a timber truck, 256B is a 6x4 quarry truck (sold in Western Europe under the BELAZ name) and 258 is a 6x4 semi-tractor.

Power has been increased and these vehicles now contain V-8 diesels of 265 hp at 2100 rpm. Gearboxes are 5-speed and power steering is provided.

Engines used in these units are YAMZ, built in the former YAAZ plant now converted to diesel manufacture. *BE*

KREBS (i) (US) 1912-1916

Krebs Commercial Car Company, Clyde, Ohio

Krebs trucks were early exponents of styling in commercial vehicles having French-type sloping hoods with radiators behind the engines which were 2-cylinder, 2-stroke types. Vehicle capacities ranged from 1500 lbs. to three tons and as late as 1916 were not yet equipped with electric starting. This company occupied the plant of the Elmore Manufacturing Company after the latter was absorbed by GMC and moved to Michigan. *GMN*

KREBS (ii) (US) 1922-1925

Krebs Motor Truck Co., Bellevue, Ohio

The Krebs was made in various sizes from ¾ ton to 6 tons, all using Continental engines. In 1925 the name was changed to Buck, made until 1927. *GNG*

KRIEGER (F) 1897-1909

(1) Compagnie Parisienne des Voitures Electriques (Systeme Krieger), Paris 1897-1907

(2) Compagnie Parisienne des Voitures Electriques, Colombes, Seine 1907-1909

The first Kriegers were converted horse cabs using a forecarriage. A Postel-Vinay electric motor was attached to each front wheel, giving a form of power steering; immunity from sideslip was also claimed, and range was quoted as 40 miles at a speed of 7 mph. By 1898 the company had progressed to complete vehicles, still with fwd;

1905 KRIEGER searchlight truck, BHV

wheel steering was standard, and lighter Kriegers wore pneumatic tires on their driving wheels. Their cab won first prize in the 4-seater category of that year's Electrocab trials, in which they also entered quite a large truck with driver's seat perched high above the ground. Though a fleet of cabs was supposed to be in service in Paris by the autumn of 1898, only one was actually working by November, and Krieger turned to delivery vans and small omnibuses. Gasoline electric vehicles joined the range in 1903, when the regular electric vans were available in forward control or 'loaded' forms. By 1905 the gas-electric assumed more serious proportions, and included a cab-over-engine 4 tonner using a 4.1-litre 4-cylinder power unit. This had final drive by side chains, though a bus version had direct drive to electric motors on the rear wheels. 1906 Krieger electrics still featured forward control, with lowered frames, but nothing came of a gas-turbine electric design patented in 1908, and in the last two years the firm concentrated on two basic types of gasoline-electric. Of these, the cabs had 4-cylinder Brasier engines and fwd, whereas the trucks were rear-drive normal-control 2/3 tonners with the fashionable round radiators. Kriegers were produced under license in Britain by the British Electromobile Co., in Germany by NAMAG (Lloyd), and in Italy by S.T.A.E., though most of these were private cars. The German Gaggenau firm also made at least one fwd charabanc of Krieger type.

An experimental Krieger van with all-independent suspension and centrally-mounted electric motor driving the rear wheels appeared in 1923, but this was developed under Peugeot sponsorship and never went into production. *MCS*

K-R-I-T (US) 1911-1914

Krit Motor Car Company, Detroit, Michigan

The Model KD closed delivery van was on the same chassis as the Model K passenger car by this manufacturer. This used a 4-cylinder engine, a two-speed gearbox and shaft drive. It was on wheelbase of 106 inches and cost $900. *GMN*

K.R.C. (GB) 1925-1926

White, Holmes & Co. Ltd., Hammersmith, London W.6

Named after its designers, Kingston, Richardson and Crutchley, the K.R.C. was a light car which was also made briefly in taxicab form. Powered by a 4-cylinder 9.8 hp Coventry-Climax engine, the K.R.C. cab had a landaulette body for two passengers, and was intended to be one of the 'jixis' or two-seater cabs that were expected to run in London. These never caught on, and only one K.R.C. was licensed by Scotland Yard, although a small fleet ran in Harrogate, Yorkshire. *GNG*

KROMHOUT (NL) 1935-1961

Kromhout Motoren Fabriek D. Goedkoop Jr. NV, Amsterdam

The Kromhout marine engine firm acquired a manufacturing license for the British Gardner diesel in 1935, installing 4-, 5- and 6-cylinder units of this make in a range of conventional medium and heavy trucks. Bus and coach variants were also available: a forward-control Kromhout coach took part in the 1936 Monte Carlo Rally, completing the course. Listed in 1939 were trucks and tractive units for payloads from three to 30 tons, and PSVs for up to 60 passengers.

After the War the Kromhout-Gardner truck range reappeared. Chassis were usually of normal control type with power units mounted well over the front axle, other features including a 6-speed gearbox and full air brakes, with an engine brake option. The basic 4x2 carried a 7½/8-ton payload, but by 1953 there was also a forward-control 10-tonner with its supercharged 8.4-litre 6-cylinder engine mounted vertically under the floor. Two years later the catalogue included a 6x4 with forward or normal control

c.1955 KROMHOUT Type TC articulated van, OMM

and dual Kirkstall worm-drive rear axles. A 6x6 development for oilfield work had a GVW rating of 28 tons, while by 1957 Kromhout's version of the Gardner six was giving 140 hp, and 6x4 models could be had with Rolls-Royce engines. In 1949 Kromhout undertook the assembly of Leylands for the Dutch market.

Post-War Kromhout buses began with a straightforward forward control single-decker using the Gardner six, but in 1948 they developed a unitary-construction 48-seater in association with Verheul; this had the supercharged 6-cylinder engine, a 5-speed overdrive gearbox, power steering, and pneumatically operated doors. Verheul's Holland bus of 1950 featured a Kromhout frame. By 1953, however, Kromhout themselves had abandoned unitary construction, concentrating instead on new horizontal-engined designs, still power-steered and with Gardner-based diesels. A one-man-operated 97-seater of 1955 introduced both the Leyland engine and a pneumocyclic gearbox, other PSVs featured the old Gardner six, a ZF 2-pedal transmission,

1955 KROMHOUT V6D 6 × 4 tanker, M. Wallast Collection

and auxiliary rubber suspension. Kromhout and Verheul merged in 1959, some examples of the latter make being fitted with Kromhout engines, though Rolls-Royces were also used in trucks. The Kromhout name disappeared after 1961: Verheul were to survive another ten years. *MCS*

KRUPP (D) 1905-1908; 1919 to date

(1) Fried. Krupp Akt. Ges., Germania-Werft, Kiel 1905-1908
(2) Fried. Krupp, Motoren- und Kraftwagenfabriken GmbH., Essen 1919-1944
(3) Sudwerke GmbH., Kulmbach; Essen 1944-1954
(4) Fried. Krupp Motoren- und Kraftwagenfabriken GmbH., Essen 1954-1968
(5) Fried. Krupp GmbH Kranbau, Wilhelmshaven, 1969 to date

1924 KRUPP articulated logging truck, JFJK

A first attempt in automobile production was made by Krupp in manufacturing steam wagons under Stoltz license. This was at the shipbuilding yard in Kiel.

A tractor for military purposes appeared in 1914, another step towards car production. But a start on a larger scale was only made just after WW I in 1919 with a 5 ton truck using a 4-cylinder 28/45 hp engine and chain drive. This vehicle was also used for various municipal purposes. In 1921 it was supplemented by a 10 ton articulated tractor. And in the same year a 3-wheeled street-sweeping machine was presented which in its basic design stayed in the line for many years. In 1924 two lighter models of 1½- and 2-ton were added using a 50 hp engine and featuring shaft drive, to which in 1925 also the old 5 tonner changed. It also got a new 6-cylinder engine of 75/90 hp output. This design was developed into a 6 tonner and a 3-axle 8 tonner which appeared in 1928. A low-frame chassis was especially used for buses. A 90 hp engine was used for a new 3-axle cross-country truck which also was presented in 1928.

A forward control version came in 1930, either in 2-axle or 3-axle layout now using 100 and 110 hp engines which later were also available with 150 hp. Another new development was a 6x4 cross-country vehicle using an air-cooled 4-cylinder 55 hp engine, which later was uprated gradually to 110 hp. This vehicle was used for military purposes to a great extent.

1931 KRUPP-FLETTNER 6-wheel-steering articulated truck, HON

A very interesting development was the Krupp-Flettner chassis, an articulated type version with five axles. The tractor had one axle only which was steered, the first two axles of the trailer were steered automatically and the two rear axles were driven. Payload capacity of this version was 13½ tons and it was also used as bus. Not many were built.

The first trolley-bus line in Germany after the early attempts at the beginning of the century was opened in 1931 between Mettmann and Gruiten in Western Germany. Krupp components were used, while the vehicle was built by Uerdingen (q.v.). After experiments with their own diesel engine Krupp took up production of Junkers diesel engines under license in 1932. These were of the double-piston two-stroke type and were available as 2-, 3- or 4-cylinder units with an output of up to 125 hp. Krupp did quite a lot of improving these engines.

In the mid-thirties the line consisted of a wide range of trucks and buses up to the 3-axle 10 ton fwc version. In

1937 KRUPP 49-passenger coach; coachwork by Emmelmann, FLP

1944 production was transferred to Kulmbach and vehicles were also known as Sudwerke. Here also the first post-war models were produced, starting with a 4½ ton truck with 110 hp engine. In 1951 production was again taken up in Essen. A 6 tonner and a new 8 tonner Titan with 6-cylinder 210 hp engine followed, still using the two-stroke diesel engines. Other models were the 6½- 7-ton 4-cylinder 145 hp Mustang and the 5- 5½-ton 3-cylinder 110 hp Buffel. A variety of the Mustang was a special fwc chassis for a 1½-decker bus design by Ludewig. The

1953 KRUPP Mustang 1½-decker bus; coachwork by Ludewig, Techniart

Cyklop of 1952 using the 210 hp engine was one of the early German dump trucks. In 1953 the Drache was presented as a 6-8 tonner 4x4 version with 4-cylinder 145 hp engine. A fwc range of trucks was started in 1956 which was improved in 1959. They were available with 3-, 4- or 5-cylinder two-stroke engines ranging from 3.2-litre 120 hp to 7.2-litre 200 hp. Normal control as well as forward control versions and 2- or 3-axle chassis' were

c.1955 KRUPP 16-ton articulated van, OMM

available. One bus was in the range, the type O 124 with 4-cylinder 3.2-litre 120 hp engine, but this was dropped in about 1961. Since 1963 the two-stroke engines were supplemented and later replaced by Cummins 4-stroke

c.1963 KRUPP LF 901 15½-tons GVW truck, OMM

diesel engines which Krupp built under license and at first a dump truck with 30 ton payload capacity was equipped with a 15.5-litre 430 hp Cummins engine. Also a range of trucks appeared with 4-cylinder Cummins engines of 200 hp output. By 1965 two-stroke engines were only used for a few lighter dump-trucks. A 4x4 tractor with V-8-cylinder 265 hp engine was the novelty of 1967. In 1968 production of ordinary trucks ceased at the Krupp factory in Essen as a result of a diminishing demand. Apart from trucks and dump trucks Krupp established production of truck cranes in their Wilhelmshaven plant in 1959. They build their own chassis but use Deutz diesel engines. The present range of hydraulic cranes covers models from a 6x4 chassis with 232 hp engine to a 12x6 chassis with 450 hp engine. *HON*

KRUSE (D) 1898-1902
Gebr. Kruse, Hamburg

Electric driven vans were produced by this firm. Production was on a small scale only. *HON*

KUANGCHOU (CHI) 1966 to date
Kuangchou Motor Vehicle Plant, Kuangchou (Canton), Kwangtung

The city of Canton, now referred to as Kuangchou since the Cultural Revolution, lends its name to this rear-engined bus.

Engineering details are unavailable. *BE*

KUANG KUNG CHI 1970 to date
Chaohu Truck Parts Plant- Hofei, Anhwei

The Kuang Kung is reported to be a cab over engine 4.5 ton truck. 8-ton dumpers are also in production at this plant. *BE*

KUHLSTEIN (D) 1898-1902
Kuhlstein Wagenbau, Berlin-Charlottenburg

Kuhlstein started production of electric cars which were available also as vans. In 1899 gasoline driven cars were added. A speciality were "avant trains" for the conversion of horse-drawn vehicles into motor cars. Vans, truck and buses were further manufactured. Extraordinary was a large "mailcoach" of 1900. In 1902 Kuhlstein produced the first gasoline tanker in Germany with internal combustion engine, and in the same year the firm was taken over by N.A.G. *HON*

KUMMER & STOLL (D) 1899-1900
A.G. Elektrizitatswerke vorm. O.L. Kummer & Co., Niedersedlitz und Wagenfabrik C. Stoll, Dresden

This firm produced some electric driven buses. Stoll was later connected with Lohner of Austria in building trolley buses. *HON*

KUNKEL (US) 1915-1916
Kunkel Carriage Works, Galion, Ohio

Kunkel were specialists in hearse bodywork whose coaches appeared on numerous makes of chassis, from Ford to Cadillac, and were still being offered in the mid-1920s. They also produced a few hearses on their own assembled chassis. *MCS*

KUNMING CHI 1970 to date
Kunming Motor Vehicle Plant, Kunming, Yannan

The Kunming is a 4.5 ton truck built especially for mountainous areas. Many small factories near Kunming supply parts to the main plant to produce this vehicle. *(BE)*

KUROGANE (J) 1937-1945: 1949-1962
(1) Nippon Jidosha Co., Ltd., Tokyo 1937-1945
(2) Japan Internal Combustion Engine Manufacturing Co. Ltd., Tokyo 1949-1957
(3) Nippon Motor Industries Co., Ltd., Tokyo 1957-1959
(4) Tokyu Kurogane Co., Ltd., Tokyo 1959-1962

Like the New Era (iii) which preceded it, the Kurogane was a light motorcycle-type 3-wheeler with shaft drive and 3-speed and reverse gearbox. Vee twin engines were used, a bigger unit of this type with ohv powering the company's best-known military model, the light 4x4 Black Medal scout car widely used in World War II. Production lapsed for a while after the end of hostilities, but was resumed in 1949, when 10 cwt 3-wheelers were again offered. Soft top cabs were regular equipment by 1952, and the 1956 catalog listed a diversity of types from 15 cwt to two tons,, with 4-speed gearboxes and cylinder capacities from 875 cc up to 1.4 litres. The biggest Kuroganes had ohv and water cooling. In 1957 the Ohta concern was acquired, and heavier duty models were given wheel steering and ohv 4-cylinder inline engines. 1-litre and 1½ litre 4-cylinder engines and enclosed cabs were standardized on the 1959 3-wheeler line, while there were new normal and forward control 4-wheelers for 1-ton payloads, all with 4-speed synchromesh gearboxes. As a replacement for the lighter 3-wheeler types the firm introduced the Baby, a 7 cwt forward control truck or van on a 69 inch wheelbase; the 356 cc ohv vertical-twin engine was watercooled and rear-mounted. These types were continued until 1962, when Tokyu Kurogane went bankrupt. *MCS*

KYOHO (J) 1937-1941

Kyoho Automobile Co. Ltd., (factory location unknown)

2050 Kyoho trucks were made. They were conventional 3-wheelers with two driven rear wheels. *MCS*

KYOSAN (J) 1931-c.1935

Kyosan Electric Manufacturing Co. Ltd., Tokyo

Kyosans were light, car-type pickups with 2-cylinder 2-stroke aircooled engines of 500 cc or 750 cc. *MCS*

1967 LABOURIER Model HUD 4×4 tractor-truck, NMM

LABOURIER (F) c. 1947-c. 1970

Labourier et Cie, Mouchard, Jura

Labourier were mainly makers of agricultural and forestry tractors, but in the late 1940s they also offered a low-loading truck for 5 to 7-ton loads, powered by a Unic diesel engine. The 1947 model had offset drive from gearbox to rear axle, and a year later a front-drive model was introduced which was listed until 1954. The forestry tractors had 4-wheel drive and steering, and were similar to the contemporary Latils. They were powered mainly by Perkins 6-cylinder diesels, though the CLM opposed-piston 2-stroke diesel was also used in the 1950s. The largest model was a 10-ton 4 × 4 tractor intended for oilfield work, powered by air-cooled Deutz or water-cooled Berliet engines. In 1960 there was a brief return of road-going trucks with a lightweight forward-control model of 5½ tons GVW. This had a fiberglass cab and 1.8-litre 50 hp Peugeot diesel engine. One of the last Labouriers was the HUD of 1967, a 4 × 4 tractor-truck with optional 4-wheel steering, powered by a Perkins 6.354 5.8-litre 120 hp diesel engine. *GNG*

LA BUIRE (F) 1906-1929

(1) Societe des Automobiles de la Buire, Lyons 1907-1909

(2) Societe Nouvelle de la Buire-Automobiles, Lyons 1910-1929

La Buire's first commercial vehicles were of driver-over-engine type with 15 hp 4-cylinder power units. They were most frequently encountered with 10/15-seater bus bodywork, in which guise they were favored by French railway companies for feeder work. By 1908 there was a more comprehensive range; postal vans with front pneumatic tires, shaft- and chain-driven trucks and buses for payloads of up to 3 tons (or 25 seats), and the almost mandatory light taxicab, a 1.9-litre four rated at 8/10CV. Trucks of the 1910-14 period were noted for their long-stroke 4-cylinder engines of 80 × 160 mm and 90 × 160 mm (also used in contemporary La Buire cars), other features being magneto ignition, pump cooling, pressure lubrication, 4-speed gearboxes, worm drive and solid tires. Models of up to 4 tons were offered, the 2- and 3-tonners being Subsidy types, and the bigger ones being sold also to the Russian Government. The 3-ton B-type with 4.1-litre engine was available as late as 1925, but latterly the only commercial vehicle listed was a car-based 1½-tonner, still with long-stroke 4-cylinder unit. *MCS*

LACOSTE ET BATTMANN (F) 1906-1908

Lacoste et Battmann Ltd., Paris

This company was best known as a supplier of components (and complete cars) to other firms. Thus their products were more frequently encountered under sundry aliases. In 1906, however, they launched a comprehensive range of commercial vehicles under their own name, from a parcelcar with 4½ hp de Dion or 6 hp Buchet engine up to 4-tonners with 3-speed gearboxes, side-chain drive, and a choice of 4-cylinder engines of 3.6 or 3.9-litres by Gnome, Mutel and Aster. 34-seater Lacoste et Battmann buses were used in London. *MCS*

1906 LACOSTE et BATTMANN doubledecker bus, NMM

LACRE (GB) 1904-1952

(1) Lacre Motor Car Co. Ltd., London W. 1904-1910
(2) Lacre Motor Car Co. Ltd., Letchworth, Herts. 1910-1928
(3) Lacre Lorries Ltd., Kings Cross, London N. 1928-1936
(4) Lacre Lorries Ltd., Welwyn Garden City, Herts. 1936-1952

This company derived its name from an earlier firm, Long Acre Motor Car Company, named after the London district where it was first established. By 1904, when truck production started, the factory was in Poland Street, Soho. The first vehicle to bear the Lacre name was in fact a 25 hp 2-cylinder Albion chassis with Lacre body. Early customers included Shoolbreds and Harrods, the London stores, and T. Wall & Sons. In 1907 Lacre was selling a 4-cylinder forward-control 2-tonner made for them by James & Browne of Hammersmith, under the name J. & B Lacre, in addition to the smaller models. Two years later a new range was introduced, made entirely by Lacre. Five engine sizes were used, 15 and 18 hp twins and 20, 30 and 38 hp fours, for vehicles of 10 cwt to 5 tons capacity. There was also a 15 hp 2-cylinder taxicab chassis. The two larger 4-cylinder engines, of 4,820cc and 7,117cc respectively, were used in the O-type which became the best-known Lacre truck, and was made until 1928. The chain-drive chassis was used as a basis for tippers, tower wagons, charabancs, fire engines and ambulances, as well as for ordinary freight carrying. An articulated version was used for lumber transport during World War I. Among the armies which used Lacres during the conflict were those of Great Britain, Canada, Belgium, India and Siam.

1918 LACRE Model O 30hp 2-ton articulated truck, BHV

During 1910 the company moved to larger premises in the newly-established Letchworth Garden City. Their chief engineer in the years 1911 to 1922 was J.S. Drewry who later founded another Letchworth firm, Shelvoke & Drewry. In 1917 an important step was taken when Lacre launched their first road sweeper, a 2-cylinder 4-wheeler. Two years later came the L-type 3-wheeler which soon became the staple product of the company and kept them going when ordinary trucks were difficult to sell. The L-type had a 12 hp 4-cylinder engine, and later a 6-cylinder was offered as an option. Ordinary goods chassis continued to be made, the O-type getting shaft drive in 1922, and an interesting new model was the E-type of 1926. This was a 2½-ton forward control chassis whose engine, radiator and gas tank were mounted on a sub frame so that they could be slid out for easy maintenance. In 1928

1926 LACRE Model E 2½-ton van, showing detachable engine, FLP

the Letchworth works were sold, and production transferred to the former service depot at Kings Cross. Manufacture of the L-type continued to 1943, but very few load-carrying trucks were made after 1928. In the early 1930s Lacres acted as selling agents for municipal models of the Low Loader, and they also took over Burford in 1934. After World War II only sweepers were made, the 1946-49 M-type with 4-cylinder Meadows engine, and the 1949-52 T-type which was based on the 3-wheeled Opperman Motocart. The last of these was made in 1952, after which Lacre concentrated on sweeping and cleansing equipment on Bedford chassis. *GNG*

LA CUADRA (E) 1899

Cia General Espanola de Coches Automoviles E. de la Cuadra S en C, Barcelona

As well as touring cars, Emilio de la Cuadra Albio built a battery-electric 15-passenger bus in collaboration with Marc Birkigt and Domingo Tamaro. The single-decker bus with solid rubber tires was designed to reach a speed of 15 mph and to climb gradients of up to 12%, but owing to its considerable weight of 6 tons unladen, and the poor road surfaces of the day it failed to achieve these figures. After numerous tests in Barcelona and Vich it was returned to the factory to be broken up. Birkigt went on to become chief designer for the Castro and later, Hispano-Suiza companies. *JCG*

LADOG (D) 1971 to date

(1) Ladog Fahrzeugbau, Nordrach 1971-1975
(2) Albrecht Bertsche, Braunlingen 1975 to date

This is a small all-purpose vehicle which was developed for municipalities and is available with a variety of equipment. Two versions are equipped with VW engines. They are also available with 4-wheel drive and 4-wheel steering. A new type was presented in 1975 using an air-cooled flat four engine by Citroen. *HON*

LAFFLY (F) 1922-1953

Ets. Laffly, Asnieres

After a successful life as a manufacturer of fire engines and municipal vehicles, mainly constructed on Schneider and Somua chassis, Laffly grew in 1922 into a real truck manufacturer. The first vehicles, built up to 1925, still carried the Laffly-Schneider name, because they were powered by Somua/Schneider engines. These first vehicles were a 3-tonner, available in two chassis lengths and powered by a 22.5 hp engine, and a 7-tonner with a 30 hp engine.

From 1925 onwards all vehicles were sold exclusively under the Laffly name, and the engines were partly bought from CGA, until Laffly could produce enough for its own needs. The first true Laffly range consisted of 15 hp 15 cwt chassis, an equally powered 25 cwt chassis, a 2-tonner with a 30 hp engine, a 3-, 4-tonner and a 5-tonner both powered by a 40 hp engine, and finally an 8-tonner with a 60 hp engine. With the adding of some special bus chassis this range was in production up to about 1930.

Laffly still used its own chassis in large quantities for the mounting of municipal and fire fighting bodies. Particularly the Laffly fire engines were very renowned vehicles, in use with many French municipalities.

In the year 1930 the oil engine entered the Laffly range of vehicles. It was the Junkers opposed piston unit as manufactured under German license by the Compagnie Lilloise des Moteurs in Lille, France. They powered the Laffly vehicles for some ten years. One of these CLM-Junkers powered Lafflys made a test run between London and Glasgow in 1930, to demonstrate its low fuel consumption. The distance was completed in 18 hours, for a fuel cost of 35p.

1933 LAFFLY AR35 4-ton truck, BHV

Laffly produced a very broad range of vehicles in these years, featuring ten gasoline-engined types and four oil-engined vehicles besides the various municipal derivatives. In 1934 Laffly added to this range a very important novelty, a 6 × 6 vehicle with fully independent rear bogie. According to their traditions, this type of vehicle was also available in many varieties; one specially for high-speed cross-country work, another for towing heavy trailers, etc. The engines mounted in these vehicles were generally produced by Hotchkiss, who for some years also produced these Laffly 6 × 6 vehicles under license. The heaviest vehicles in this range were the S35 and the S45, powered by a 100 hp engine of Laffly's own manufacture. Some of these chassis were fitted with armor plating and converted to anti-tank gun carriers and reconaissance carriers.

Very impressive vehicles were the huge Laffly ladder trucks, the latest among the Laffly fire engines.

A novelty in the civilian Laffly range was the ADRHS, introduced in 1936 and being a heavy 6 × 4 truck, fitted with a 100 hp CLM oil engine. By 1938 the Laffly range of vehicles had still grown further and now offered sixteen gasoline models, from 2.7 to 10 tons payload and with three various engines, and six diesel types from 4 to about 7 tons payload.

By 1940, however, the CLM diesel engines had gradually disappeared from the Laffly range: it had been replaced by a conventional four-in-line oil engine, powering two truck models each with a payload of 10 tons.

After World War II production was taken up again, though not for long. It started in 1945 with two 3.2 ton payload vehicles, available with two different gasoline engines, each having four cylinders. Two years later two 6-cylinder engines were also available, so that the range had broadened to four models. One year later payloads were

c.1947 LAFFLY fire engine, GNG

also increased by adding further models, starting now at 2.5 tons and ending at 6.5 tons payload. The diesel engines made their come-back in the Laffly range in 1952. One year later, however, all Laffly truck production was discontinued and the company concentrated again on the manufacture of fire fighting and municipal bodies, maintaining it up to the present day. *JFJK*

LA FRANCE-REPUBLIC (US) 1929-1942

(1) La France-Republic Corp., Alma, Mich. 1929-1932
(2) La France-Republic Corp., divn. Sterling Motors Corp., Alma, Mich. 1932-1942

This corporation was the outcome of a merger between two ailing companies, the commercial truck side of American-LaFrance, the fire-engine makers, and Republic Motor Truck Company. The latter had been America's largest truck manufacturer in 1918, but the firm slipped badly through the 1920s. However they had a substantial dealer organization while LaFrance had some limited acceptance in the heavy-duty field. Republic had just introduced a new range, and these made up the bulk of the program of 1 to 6½ tonners, the top of the line representing the American LaFrance content. The first year, 1929, saw a peak of 815 units sold, which fell to 598 in 1930, 461 in 1931 and even fewer thereafter. Efforts were made to develop the Canadian market, one of

Republic's old stamping grounds, but with little success. In 1931 LaFrance-Republic introduced a 'super truck', the Mogul 6-wheeler powered by a 240 hp American-LaFrance V-12 engine, intended for speeds of up to 60 mph with a gross weight of 20 tons. The bogie was a Timken unit, and the firm claimed that oversize tires eliminated the need for rear springs. As with another 'super truck', the Relay Duo-Drive, nothing came of the Mogul.

In 1932 LaFrance-Republic was acquired by the Sterling Motor Truck Co. of Milwaukee; the Alma plant was closed, though offices, parts and service were continued there, and production transferred to Milwaukee. In their purchase of LaFrance-Republic, Sterling had the same motive as White had in purchasing Indiana, a lighter popularly-priced vehicle for Depression budgets. However, they simply attached LaFrance-Republic nameplates to some Sterling models, and this example of badge-engineering lasted until World War II. *RJ*

LAGONDA (GB) 1905-1906; 1914-1915

Lagonda Motor Co. Ltd., Staines, Middx

Before they made their well-known cars, Lagonda produced motorcycles and tricars, and some of the latter, like so many of their kind, were supplied with load-carrying compartments between the front wheels. Capacity was 4 cwt, and they had V-twin engines. About 12 were supplied to the Post Office in 1906. The only other commercial vehicle venture by Lagonda came in 1914 when a 5/7 cwt light van was offered on the 11hp car chassis. This employed unit construction of chassis and lower part of the body, to which the van top was added. *GNG*

LA LICORNE see Corre

LA HISPANO (E) 1917-1932

La Hispano, Fabrica Nacional de Automoviles Aeroplanes y Material de Guerra, Guadalajara

Popularly known as La Hispano-Guadalajara, this company built aeroplanes, touring cars and trucks, mostly for military use. The smallest commercial vehicles were 500 kg light trucks on the 8/10 hp car chassis, but the company also made larger models of 15/20, 30/40, 40/50 and 50 hp for loads of 1,500 to 6,000 kgs. For some years Hispano-Guadalajara built Post Office vans and also a large number of fuel tankers for the C.A.M.P.S.A. oil company. In 1932 they were taken over by Fiat of Italy, and the factory was used for the production of the Fiat 514 passenger car under the name Fiat-Hispania. *JCG*

LA MARNE (F) 1930-

The Paris-built La Marne was a motorcycle-based 3-wheeled parcel van powered by a 2-stroke engine, with Staub gearbox. *GNG*

LAMBOURN (GB) 1937-1939

Lambourn Garages, Lambourn, Berks.

Built in a well-known British racehorse training district, the Lambourn was a horsebox developed by Lambourn Garages and Universal Power Drives, makers of Unipower tractors. The first examples were built to the order of the trainer Sir Hugh Nugent. They had rear-mounted Ford V-8 engines driving forward to the rear axle. This enabled the horses to face forward and all to be carried within the wheelbase. The 1937 models carried a dummy Ford radiator at the front, but in 1938 a more attractive smooth rounded front was adopted. The chassis was offered for bus work, but it is unlikely that any were actually sold for this purpose. In 1939 a new horsebox appeared, with a front-mounted Ford V-8 engine and front wheel drive. This had independent rear suspension and accomodation for three horses, compared with two in the earlier designs. Lambourns continued to be used for a number of years after the war, but production was not resumed. *GNG*

LAMBRETTA; LAMBRO (I) 1948-1972

Innocenti SpA, Milan

Ferdinando Innocenti's Milanese steel-tube firm, founded in 1931, turned to scooters after World War II, becoming one of the world's most successful producers of this type of vehicle. Unusually, the first commercial variants featured a frontal box and single driven rear wheel, though in 1950 there was also a 3 × 2 rickshaw variant for the Far East, and from earliest days Lambretta marketed their own box sidecars. By 1955, however, the Lambretta had adopted the conventional configuration, a 150 cc single-cylinder 2-stroke engine was standard, and the 3-speed gearbox lacked a reverse. Other characteristics were shaft drive, quarter-elliptic rear springing, and hydraulic brakes on the rear wheels only. A year later enclosed cabs made their appearance, and in its final form the commercial Lambretta (now sold under the Lambro name) was a sophisticated little machine for payloads of up to 11 cwt. The 197 cc 2-stroke engine was mounted under the floor, there was a 2-seater cab, and wheel steering had replaced handlebars. *MCS*

1961 LAMBRETTA 175cc light articulated truck, OMM

1972 LAMBRO 197cc Model 600V truck, GNG

LAMSON (US) 1911-c.1919

Lamson Truck & Tractor Company, Chicago, Ill.

There were five sizes of Lamson trucks ranging from one ton to five tons, on wheelbases of 12 feet to 15 feet. All used 4-cylinder engines under hoods with three-speed gearboxes with final worm-drive. Possibly this make was taken over by United Four Wheel Drive Company and the Lamson continued to 1920, but conclusive evidence is lacking. *GMN*

LANCASHIRE see Leyland (i)

LANCASTER (GB) 1946-1952

Lancaster Electrical Co. Ltd., New Barnet, Herts

This company made a small number of electric cars and vans during World War II, under the name Lecar, and in 1946 launched a conventional 15 cwt electric van under their own name. This had a range of 30 or 60 miles per charge, according to the load and capacity of the batteries, and a speed of 15 or 20 mph. Production continued for six years, and in 1952 it was joined by Lusty, a 12 cwt model with small wheels (18 × 4 ½in tires). This was for strictly local deliveries, having a range of only 15 miles and a speed 11 mph. *GNG*

LANCIA (I) 1911-1970

Fabbrica Automobili Lancia & C., Turin

Vincenzo Lancia's factory had been existence five years when it began the manufacture of trucks in the former Fides plant. A batch of 100 30-cwt IZ lorries was made for the Italian Army in 1911. These had 4.9-litre sv 4-cylinder monobloc engines developing over 50 bhp, 4-speed gearboxes, shaft drive, and pneumatic tires: electric lighting was available by 1914. The IZ evolved into the very similar Iota and Diota series, widely used by the Allied armed forces; some armoured car versions survived on the active list in Northern Ireland as late as the 1950s.

1915 LANCIA Model 1Z army truck, BHV

After the war development continued with the Triota and Tetraiota series, rated as 2½-tonners, though they were usually operated as 20-seater buses, coaches and chars-a-banc. Fwb arrived on the Pentaiota of 1925, and the low-loading Esaiota of 1926 was even tried as a double-decker, though the engine was found to develop insufficient power for this role. Though descendants of the Iota family were still available as late as 1935, a modern bus chassis was announced for 1928. This Omicron was a low-loading type powered by a 7.1-litre 8-cylinder 7-bearing hemi-head ohc engine; the rod operated fwb were soon given vacuum servo assistance, and the 4-speed gearbox was of unit type. 550 were made up to 1935,

1928 LANCIA Pentiota sun roof coach, MJWW

1929 LANCIA Omicron city bus; coachwork by Garavini, HDB

Omicrons being used by the city of Rome, as well as on sleeper-coach services in the Italian Sahara. In 1931 Lancia acquired a manufacturing license for the Junkers opposed-piston 2-stroke diesel engine, a 3.2-litre 2-cylinder version being fitted to the first of a new series of normal control trucks, the 6½-ton Ro. Later editions used either a 4.8-litre 3-cylinder sv gasoline unit. Subsequent developments included servo braking and eight forward speeds and in 1938 the firm switched to 4-strokes on the 3RO, which used a 6.9-litre 5-cylinder engine; it was also

1934 LANCIA 3-RO N 6½-ton truck, BHV

made for the Army with a gasoline unit of similar capacity and configuaration. Longer engines called for a mounting well over the front axle, a layout retained on the post-war 8½-ton Esatau. This, however, used an 8.4-litre, 150bhp 6-cylinder diesel, double reduction drive, and air brakes; the eight speeds favored by Italian makers were retained. Alongside their range of heavies, Lancia also offered light-duty car-based commercials, all with ohc V4 engines and the classic coil ifs. The 1.9-litre Artena of 1932 was popular as an ambulance; it was followed by vans based on the 1.4-litre Aprilla (1937) and 903cc Ardea (1939). The latter model survived the war, being supplanted in 1954 by an 1,100cc Appia delivery van. Lancia also built trolleybus chassis, mainly for export. Among the cities which favored the make were Athens, Cairo, Istanbul and Oporto, the last-mentioned municipality's fleet including double-deckers.

Forward control arrived in 1950 on a 2½-tonner, the

1949 LANCIA 6-RO M 6½-ton truck, BHV

Beta. It was powered by a 46bhp 4-cylinder gasoline engine, there were five forward speeds, and transverse leaf it was used in place of the coils found on car-based types A Roots-blown 2-litre 2-stroke twin-cylinder diesel was offered as an option in 1953, and subsequently standardized. Also new in 1950 was a bus version of the Esatau with 18ft wheelbase; the engine was mounted horizontally at the front, beside the driver. Forward

1951 LANCIA Esatau P city bus; coachwork by Garavini, HDB

control was applied to 1955 Esatau trucks, and the engine was moved to an amidships position on the PSV' two years later: both goods and passenger versions now featured 8.9-litre engines and a pneumatically-assisted gearchange, while truck variants included models with Vibeti sleeper cabs and a 10½-ton 6 × 2. 1958 saw a medium duty model, the 5/7-ton forward control Esadelta on classic lines with 8.2-litre diesel power, and the company fell into line with prevailing trends when it replaced the Appia van with the Jolly, a forward control 1-tonner utilizing Appia mechanical elements. Production, however, remained modest, only 1,195 trucks and 379 PSV chassis leaving the works in 1960; Fiat's figures were 27,-323 and 1,622 respectively.

Lancia's offering in the 1960s consisted of forward control light vans, trucks in the 7/12-ton class, and PSV derivatives of the latter. The Esagamma of 1962 was designed for GVWs of 19 tons; power steering and air brakes were standard, and the 10½-litre 6-cylinder engine, which gave 187bhp in its original form, was developing 210 bhp with the aid of a turbocharger by 1964. Also available were 6 × 2 and 6 × 4 variants, the latter having its undriven axle ahead of the driven one. The horizontal-engined buses could be had with turbochargers, SRM automatic gearboxes, and air/leaf suspension as a regular option. By 1964 the Jolly had give way to the more sophisticated 30-cwt Superjolly, developed from the 1½-litre Flavia saloon, and featuring that car's 58bhp flat-

1966 LANCIA Superjolly 1½-ton van, OMM

1970 LANCIA Esadelta C van with 3-axle drawbar trailer, OMM

4 engine, front wheel drive, semi-elliptic rear springing, all disc brakes, and 4-speed all synchromesh gearbox. There were also a number of specialist military models. First of these had been the CL51, a light gasoline-engine 4 × 4 with 5 × 2 speed gearbox introduced in 1951. This was

1970 LANCIA Esagamma E 6×4 truck, Lancia

followed by the heavier 506 of 1958, with 195bhp 6-cylinder gasoline unit inclined under the floor. In 1965 Lancia fromed a consortium with Hotchkiss of France and Bussing of West Germany to develop all-wheel drive types for the NATO Powers.

The Lancia family relinquished control of the company in 1956, and thereafter Lancia fought a losing battle against the big battalions. A revival in the mid-1960s was not sustained, and by the end of 1969 formidable debts resulted in a Fiat takeover. A year later the commercial vehicle range was dropped. Thereafter the only trucks produced by Lancia were specialist military vehicles to Fiat design, bearing the Fiat name. *MCS*

LANDA (E) 1916-1930

(1) Tallerres Landaluce, Madrid 1916-1922
(2) Sociedad de Automoviles Landa, Madrid 1922-1930

Juan A. de Landaluce was mainly known as a maker of small passenger cars, some of which were fitted with light truck bodies. In 1922 a new company brought out chassis powered by larger 4- and 6-cylinder American engines, and these were used as the basis for hearses, being the only Spanish hearse make similar to the American Henney. Some of these were still in use by Pompas Funebras of Madrid in the mid-1960s. *JCG*

LANDMASTER (GB) 1978 to date

S. Metherell Ltd., St. Dennis, Cornwall

Aimed at the Land Rover market, the Landmaster is a 4×4 pick-up powered by a British Ford V-6 engine, with Borg-Warner automatic transmission and permanently engaged 4-wheel drive through Dana axles. Later models will have German Ford engines and Chrysler Loadflite automatic transmission. *GNG*

LAND ROVER see Rover

LANDSHAFT (US) 1911-1920

William Landshaft & Son, Chicago, Illinois

Original trucks under the name were ½- and 1-tonners using two-cylinder engines with forward control, planetary transmissions and chain drive. An intermediate model for 1913 was a 1½-tonner. For the last four model-years only one- and two-tonners were offered which used three-speed gearboxes with shaft-drive. *GMN*

LANE (US) 1916-1920

Lane Motor Truck Co., Kalamazoo, Mich.

The initial model of the Lane was a 3/4-tonner with a 4-cylinder engine and worm-drive rear axle. This was continued into 1917. For 1918, there were three models: 1½-, 2½- and 3½-tonners. All three had engines by Continental, the two larger ones having 6-cylinders. These were continued into 1920 with wood spoke wheels, solid rubber tires and Timken worm-drive rear axles. *GMN*

LANGBRIDGE (GB) c.1914

Langbridge Engineering Co., Accrington, Lancs.

Researches disclosed that a solitary wagon, resembling the contemporary Foden, may have been made by this firm. *RAW*

LANGDON-DAVIES see Soames

c.1920 LANGE 2-ton truck, Goodyear

LANGE (US) 1911-1931

(1) H. Lange Wagon Works, Pittsburgh, Pa. 1911-1912
(2) Lange Motor Truck Co., Pittsburgh, Pa. 1912-1931

The Lange was a conventional assembled truck made originally in 1- and 2-ton form, later increasing to a top model of 3 tons from 1923 onwards. Continental engines were used. *GNG*

LANGHAM (GB) 1924

Auto Electric Co., Slough, Bucks.

This was a 3-wheeler electric van made by a company already well-known for its electric motors, dynamos and equipment. The 1½ hp Langham motor drove the single rear wheel, and the driver sat behind the load in the manner of a motorcycle-based parcel van. Carrying capacity was 8cwt, and the price complete was £220. *GNG*

LANPHER (US) 1910

Lanpher Motor Buggy Company, Carthage, Missouri

The Lanpher was a high-wheeler delivery van which was typical both of the period and the manufacturer's location. Also typically, it used a 2-cylinder, 14 hp engine mounted beneath the body, along with a planetary transmission, jackshaft and chains to the rear wheels. Springing was of the transverse type both front and rear, and wheelbase was 6 feet, 4 inches. *GMN*

LANSDEN (US) 1905-1928

(1) The Lansden Co., Newark, N.J. 1905-1912
(2) The Lansden Co., Allentown, Pa. 1912-1913
(3) The Lansden Co., Brooklyn, N.Y. 1914-1920
(4) The Lansden Co. Inc., Danbury, Conn. 1921-1928

This was a long-lived make of battery-powered electrics and initially built passenger cars as well as commercial types. The first commercial was an open delivery van called Type 36, Style A with a DC motor rated at 3/4 hp, with double chain drive and a wooden frame on a wheelbase of 7 feet, 3 inches. For 1906, there were three types offered and for 1907, there was a ½-tonner and a 1½-tonner. For 1910, five types were made, all with double chain drive. In 1912, a 5 tonner was added, with a claimed 50 miles per battery charge, and a wheelbase of 11 feet, 4 inches. During succeeding years, chassis rating varied with capacities as small as ½-tonners and as great as 6 tonners.

The geographical change from Newark,, NJ to Allentown, Pa. was during an interval when the company

1910 LANSDEN 8-ton electric truck chassis, NAHC

was controlled by Maccarr. It is claimed that Thomas A. Edison had a hand in the original backing of the Lansden. This seems likely, as all Lansden trucks used the Edison alkaline storage batteries exclusively. *GMN*

LANSING (US) 1917-1920

Lansing Company, Lansing, Michigan

Battery-powered electric trucks were made under this tradename with capacities of 2½ and six tons and these were offered in each of the above years. No further details are available. *GMN*

LANZ (D) 1928-1953

Heinrich Lanz A.G., Mannheim

Lanz built his first agricultural tractors with gasoline engine and his name became connected with the construction of his first oil-engined tractor in 1921. This agricultural version developed into the first road tractor which appeared in 1928. It followed the well-proved principle of the oil hot-bulb two-stroke engine with a single cylinder of 10.3 litres capacity and an output of 35 hp. Various versions were developed during the thirties with 20, 25, 35, 45 and 55 hp output, but all retained the single cylinder hot bulb engine. They received the name of the old agricultural tractors "Bulldog" in the combination of "Verkehrs-Bulldog" (traffic bulldog) and "Eil-Bulldog" (express bulldog). They were a most familiar sight in the streets during the thirties. After WW II production was carried on until 1953. Since 1955 Lanz has been owned by John Deere & Co. *HON*

LAPEER (US) 1916-c.1920

Lapeer Tractor Truck Co., Lapeer, Mich.

This was a 5-ton articulated truck powered by a 4-cylinder Wisconsin engine, with 3-speed transmission and Torbensen internal gear drive. It had a completely enclosed cab, quite rare at this time. Production of the tractor truck did not last long, but the company continued with the manufacture of trailers for many years. *GNG*

LAPORTE (F) 1922-c.1925

S.A. des Automobiles Electriques Laporte, Toulouse

The Laporte was a heavy electric truck with a capacity of 5 tons. It was powered by two 7½hp motors mounted directly behind the rear axle which they drove by internal gearing. The range per charge was 60 miles and the maximum gradient which could be climbed when the truck was fully loaded was 1 in 5. Laporte also made producer-gas conversions for gasoline trucks. *GNG*

LARRABEE (US) 1916-1932

Larrabee-Deyo Motor Truck Co., Binghamton, N.Y.

The Larrabee company was named for H. Chester Larrabee and R.H. Deyo, president, and was one of many companies producing standard assembled trucks with the general range of 1 to 5 tons. Major components were generally Continental 4-cylinder monobloc engines, Brown-Lipe transmissions, and Sheldon worm rear axles. Solid tires were the rule in the early days.

In 1922 a 1-ton speed truck was offered with a 6-cylinder Continental monobloc engine (an early one for trucks), a Salisbury spiral-bevel axle, and pneumatic tires.

Following general industry practice, Larrabee in the later 1920s adopted 6-cylinder engines in the range as the

1927 LARRABEE 1½-ton stake truck, NAHC

standard power plants, along with 4-speed transmissions, spiral-bevel rear axles, steel spoke wheels, 4-wheel hydraulic brakes with hand brake expanding on the rear wheels, electric lights, starter, instruments on the dash, and 2-bar front bumper. The gravity fuel system was retained. Single pneumatic tires were used all around.

Almost the only unusual things on the Larrabee were the inclusion of 4 fenders, with the front ones having wide-pointed front edges, full-length running boards even on the larger models, and a side-mounted spare at the cowl.

Prices were competitive, generally ranging in 1919 from $1950 for the 1-ton model to $4750 for the 5-ton model, and 10 years later, $1350 (1-ton) to $3755 (3-ton). A bus chassis was also offered for $3900.

During the late 1920s Larrabee assembled several hundred 4-cylinder taxicabs by the trade name of "Majestic" for use in New York City.

Larrabee truck production was 300-400 per year during 1928 and 1929.

1930 LARRABEE 6-cylinder 3-ton truck, Techniart

In business since 1881, including the predecessor Sturtevant-Larrabee Co. which built wagons, carriages, and sleighs, the company ceased production in the Great Depression of the 1930s. *RW*

LA SALLE-NIAGARA (US) 1906

LaSalle-Niagara Auto Company, Niagara Falls, New York

The sole model under this euphonious name was a flat-bed delivery van of one-ton capacity with a chassis of 7 feet, 6-inch wheelbase. This was powered by a horizontal two-cylinder engine mounted under the seat. Drive was by double chains and price was $1500. *GMN*

LATIL (F) 1898-1956

Automobiles Industriels Latil, Suresnes

Mr. George Latil, an engineer from Marseilles, developed in 1898 the world's first gasoline-engined front-wheel-driven vehicle. Using a De Dion Bouton tricycle's rear axle, he fitted it with hollow axle stubs and cardan joints, thus creating the first driven front axle. Based on this system were soon a complete range of tractors and trucks which, because Mr. Latil didn't have any own premises, were built to his order by other manufacturers: the trucks by Ets. Charles Blum at Levallois-Perret and the tractors by Ets. Tourand.

1904 LATIL front-drive truck, Autocar

In 1914 Mr. Latil had acquired his own plant in Suresnes, at 8, Quai Gallieni, where currently still the headquarters of Saviem is situated, the truck group among other formed by Latil. Here he started the production of a revolutionary new vehicle, the Latil LL, a tractor with all-wheel-drive and all-wheel-steering, that came just in time to be used by the French army, in the first world war. The LL remained in production up to 1920, when a new and improved version was announced. Apart from tractors Latil also manufactured more conventional commercial vehicles. When in the year 1906 trucks trials were organized in France, Latil entered three vehicles: a three-tonner, a 2½-tonner and a 1¾-tonner. They all had front-wheel drive and the coal-scuttle engine hood that was so characteristic of Latil for a long time. Particularly popular for mountain work in the French Alps were the front-wheel-driven Latil buses.

1924 LATIL Type TP 8-ton articulated truck, NMM

The heaviest of the contemporary Latil vehicles was the TAR tractor, of which several thousands were built for the French Army during World War I. It had four-wheel-drive and four-wheel-steering and was powered by a 50 hp four-in-line engine. The towing capacity was 12 tons, enough to manage the heaviest artillery. It still retained the coal-scuttle front, but received a more conventional engine cover in the postwar versions, with the radiator mounted

1924 LATIL Type B 14-seater coach, NMM

in front of the engine. The last model of this TAR range was the TARS, produced up to about 1935, with the engine now developing 61 hp. After the turn of the decade the TARH was announced as an accompanying type, with a heavier engine, six-speed gearbox and pneumatic tires, soon succeeded by the even more improved TARH2.

More'civilized' Latil tractors were found in the TL and KTL range, which were very popular: Latil had their own plant in Brussels to produce these vehicles for Belgium and Holland, and in Britain there was a license production by Shelvoke & Drewry, who used Meadows engines to power them and marketed them as Trauliers.

Trucks also were produced in a wide variety: in 1925 the catalog offered a range of vehicles from 1½ to 10 tons payload. One of the features mentioned with great pride

1929 LATIL Type 13 5/6-ton truck, OMM

was the low loading height: just 146 cm above road level, due to the front-wheel-drive most trucks still retained. The smallest one of the most popular Latils was the B-type, manufactured in various versions up to the early 'thirties: its four-in-line engines was also used by Peugeot in their 1543 Speedvan. Afterwards it was known as Latil M1B1, and M2B1 from 1938 onwards.

1932 LATIL Traulier 4X4 tractor, OMM

During the early 'thirties Latil entered two new fields: that of the diesel engine by starting to produce under license the British Gardner engine, and that of the tandem-axle vehicle. The first tandem-axle chassis was

1938 LATIL M2B1 1½-ton trucks, BHV

the H2Y10, fitted with a six-cylinder oil engine. A few years later 6x6 road tractors were also introduced, like the model V3Y10, for trailer or semi-trailer use and with gross train weights of up to 45 tons. As a power plant both a gasoline or an oil engine was available.

A very interesting Latil vehicle built in these years was a special 6x6 tractor for off-road transport, powered by a V-8 gasoline engine of 100 hp. The same engine had been used before in a 6x4 truck chassis, constructed about 1933.

Like most French manufacturers Latil was also experimenting with substitute fuels such as coal, gas, etc. One of the most interesting examples was a bus chassis with a special kind of gas-producer equipment called Gazomalle. It didn't use a huge round boiler like the conventional gas-producer equipment, but a neat, small unit that could be stored in the rear luggage compartment of a bus. The conventional gas-producer outfits were reserved for the Latil trucks and tractors.

In 1938 one Latil tractor was converted for road/rail service, fitting it at front and rear with railway bogies. On the road it was capable to haul loads up to 10 tons, on the tracks, however, it would pull up to 250 tons.

After World War II Latil went on producing its well-known range of trucks, buses and tractors, now offering them mainly with diesel engines though a 90 hp gasoline engine could still be mounted in the lightest vehicles.

It was again a wide range, featuring normal control and forward control vehicles, the smallest vehicle being the

1955 LATIL Type H14 378 GVW truck, OMM

H14A1B3, and the heaviest a huge 6x6 truck, used among others as chassis for some airport fire engines for LeBourget. The oil engines were available in two sizes:

1963 SAVIEM-LATIL refuse truck, OMM

with four or six cylinder, three outputs: 85, 112 and 150 hp. Up to 1955 Latil was still independent, but in that year it decided to join forces with Renault and Somua to establish Saviem. *JFJK*

LAURIN & KLEMENT (A;CS) 1907-1925

Laurin & Klement AS, Mlada Boleslav

Vaclav Laurin and Vaclav Klement built their first passenger car in 1905, and added a light truck version two

1907 LAURIN & KLEMENT Type B 8/9 hp van, VP

years later. It had a 9 hp V-twin engine and load capacity of 300 kgs. Later came a 4-cylinder engine and chain drive on which was built a 22 seater bus for Prague, and on which 4 ton trucks were made up to 1913. There was also the Type F 1½ ton lorry with 14/16 hp 4-cylinder engine and chain drive, made also as a hotel bus for 10 pasengers. A few years later L & K were making 2,3,4, and 6-ton trucks and 8 to 21 passenger buses with 18,22 and 35 hp engines. These included special short-wheelbase trucks and postal vans for the Kingdom of Montenegro, which had their 22 hp engines under the driver's seat. A wide range of vehicles was built in the years up to 1914, from taxicabs and light vans on car chassis up to 5/6 ton trucks including special ones for the transport of beer, and military trucks supplied to the Armies of Austria, Russia and Japan.

During the war years the M series was developed, with 5.9-litre 22/40 hp 4-cylinder engine and a load capacity of 2-4 tons or 18-24 passengers. After the war the M range was continued, the smallest being an 8 passenger hotel bus. Other models made in the 1920s included the 0.9-ton

1924 LAURIN & KLEMENT Type 540 articulated bus, FLP

with 2.4-litre engine, 1.2-ton 300N with 4.7-litre engine, and 4-ton 540 with 5.9-litre engine. All had solid or pneumatic tires. An interesting version of the 540 was an articulated 6-wheeled bus for 24 to 30 passengers, made in 1924. The last type made under the Laurin & Klement name was the Type 115 1.2 tonner introduced in 1925. In that year the company was acquired by the Skoda syndicate, and all vehicles made after August 20th 1925 were called Skoda. *MSH*

LAUTH; LAUTH-JUERGENS (US) 1907-1914

(1) J. Lauth & Co., Chicago, Ill. 1908-1910
(2) Lauth-Juergens Motor Co., Fremont, Ohio 1910-1915

Magnus Hendrickson built the first trucks for Jacob Lauth & Co., a tanning plant. These were light, conventional, chain-driven, gasoline-powered vehicles with a closed delivery body and cab roof.

Theodore Juergens joined Lauth in 1908, and they built light cars and trucks on a limited scale. As their employee, Mr. Hendrickson, a talented inventor, designed the first hollow-spoke steel wheel (1906), a 3-speed transmission (1909), a quiet 2-speed bevel-gear transmission for chain-driven vehicles, a jaw-clutch transmission, and the first worm-drive axle. For a decade or so, worm drives became popular on trucks although only rarely on cars (Stutz was one).

In 1910 Lauth-Juergens moved their operations to Fremont, Ohio. to build trucks exclusively, at which time Lauth-Juergens became a stock company. Magnus Hendrickson was appointed chief engineer and designer, and his sons, George and Carl, also followed to the Fremont location.

Lauth-Juergens trucks and buses were assembled vehicles in one of the common fashions of the day, the cab-over type with chain-drive, artillery wheels, solid tires, and right-hand drive. These vehicles had full cabs, the truck having a flat vertical windshield area, while the bus had a windshield built like a 3-piece bay-window. This latter feature carried over into the design of Mr. Hendrickson's own trucks in 1913. Lauth-Juergens' 1913 models were offered in capacities of 1,2,3, and 5 tons, while the motor was guaranteed for life.

1912 LAUTH-JUERGENS Model 1 3-ton truck, NMM

Robert Hendrickson, another son who had joined Lauth-Juergens, took charge of the plant for one year after Mr. Hendrickson and his other two sons left Fremont to form their own truck manufacturing company in Chicago.

In 1914 the name of the truck was changed to Fremont-Mais; this lasted until 1915 when it was purchased by the H.G. Burford Co. *RW*

LAVIGNE (US) 1914-1915

Lavigne Cyclecar Company, Detroit, Michigan

This was yet another cyclecar which was offered in delivery van version on an 8-foot wheelbase and 4-foot, 2-inch track. It had a four-cylinder, air-cooled engine with planetary transmission and shaft-drive. Gross weight was 650 pounds and price was $600. *GMN*

L.A.W. (US) 1912-1913
L.A.W. Motor Truck Company, Findlay, Ohio

Under this tradename were offered 1- 1½- and 2-tonners. The smallest of these used a four-cylinder engine with a French-type sloping hood. It had shaft drive and double-reduction gears in the drive axle. With early left-hand drive it was priced at a reasonable $2200. *GMN*

LAWIL (I) 1973 to date
Lawil Construzioni Meccaniche e Automobilistiche SpA, Varzi (Pavia)

This Italian minicar with front-mounted 246cc 2-cylinder 2-stroke engine, 4-speed gearbox and conventional shaft drive was also offered as a 350 kg van. *MCS*

LAWSON (US) 1917-1918
Lawson Manufacturing Company, Pittsburgh, Pennsylvania

This make lasted but one year and offered only one type, the ½-ton Model 35. This used a four-cylinder engine by Golden, Belknap & Schwartz. It used a three-speed gearbox, shaft-drive and was on a wheelbase of 8 feet, 6 inches. *GMN*

LAYCOCK (GB) 1913-1915
Laycock Engineering Co. Ltd., Sheffield, Yorks.

This well-known engineering firm who made Charron-Laycock cars during the 1920s built a small number of trucks powered by a 4-cylinder 35 hp engine made by the Commercial & Marine Engine Company of Hanwell, Middlesex. The first Laycock to be announced was a 3-tonner, but other models of 1, 2, 4, 5 and 6 tons capacity were planned. In 1915 a War Office subsidy type 3-tonner was made, powered by a 4-cylinder Dorman engine. Laycocks were sold by F.B. Goodchild & Company, and were sometimes known as Laycock-Goodchild. *GNG*

LAYETAN see Karpetan

LAYZELL (GB) 1900
E. Layzell, Southend-on-Sea, Essex

Layzell, the proprietor of a small engineering works at Southend, built a single steam wagon in 1900 used, or experimented with, by Essex County Council. Though he remained in business until the 1950s he is not known to have made any other vehicles. *RAW*

LAZ (SU) c.1957 to date
L'vov Motorbus Works L'vov

One of the largest bus works in the Soviet Union, the L'vov plant has built many award-winning units.

1962 LAZ-697M 33-seater coach, GNG

The LAZ-695 Lvov is offered as a city or suburban model carrying from 32 to 65 passengers with a rear-mounted V-8 engine of 170 hp @ 3200 rpm. Wheelbase is 13 ft. 9 in. and the gearbox is mechanical with synchromesh on 2-5.

The LAZ-697 Tourist is an intercity bus on the same chassis with provision for luggage, special night lights, and a sliding roof.

A newer, larger bus, the LAZ-699 Karpatia has recently been introduced. *BE*

L.D.V. (GB) 1949-1952
Light Delivery Vehicles Ltd., Wolverhampton, Staffs.

A subsidiary of Turner Manufacturing Company, L.D.V. made two models, the ByVan and TriVan. The former was a motorcycle with a 148cc single-cylinder 2-stroke engine driving the front wheel. It had a 5¾cu. ft. locker for a 1½cwt load under the saddle. The Tri-Van used the same engine and front wheel drive, but had two wheels at the rear and a much larger load area of 23 cu. ft. for a 3cwt load. When first announced, the ByVan cost £120 and the TriVan £150, but these were later reduced to £110 and £130 respectively. In 1951 a 2-passenger taxi called the Rixi was announced on the TriVan chassis, and engine capacity increased to 168cc. *GNG*

LEACH (US) 1899-1900
Leach Motor Vehicle Co., Everitt, Mass.

This company made a typical light steam passenger car with 2-cylinder reversible slide valve engine of 6 hp, with single chain drive, and offered a 750 lb. delivery wagon on the same chassis. *GNG*

LEADER (AUS) c.1972 to date
Leader Trucks Australia Pty. Ltd., Sydney, NSW

Built by a company with 40 years experience in road transport, the Leader is an assembled truck using mainly

1977 LEADER A8 Midranger 8×4 concrete mixer, Leader

American proprietary components such as Caterpillar 6 and V-8 engines, Fuller or Allison gearboxes, Hendrickson suspension and Rockwell rear axles. They are made in 4-, 6- and 8-wheeled form and also as articulated trucks. *GNG*

LE BLANT (F) 1892-c.1907
Societe des Trains Routiers Le Blant, Paris

Maurice Le Blant's earliest steam vehicles were light steam wagonettes for private use. Using a rear mounted Serpollet type flash boiler he coupled it to a 3-cylinder single acting high pressure engine driving a countershaft behind the rear axle, each rear wheel being chain driven. From these wagonettes he developed a steam tradesman's van, an example of which took part in the 1894 Paris-Rouen trial. At the same time, or a little before, he had made a steam tractor on similar principles. The entry in the 1900 Paris trial consisted of a tractor and road train, the boiler unit being a horizontal double drum water tube type by Niclausse of Paris, the famous builders of industrial and marine boilers. The vehicle was desperately short of adhesion.

Le Blant had disappeared from lists by 1908 but actual manufacture may have ended earlier. *RAW*

LE BLOND-SCHACHT see Schacht

LECAR (GB) 1941

Lancaster Electrical Co., New Barnet, Herts.

Made by an electrical equipment firm originally, for sales and service of their own products, the Lecar was a 5/7 cwt battery electric van with the unusual feature of a 3-speed gearbox. With this it was claimed that a smaller motor and battery could be used. The power unit was a 4 hp White motor, and a range of 25 miles per charge was obtainable. Because of wartime shortages the chassis of the Lecar were reconditioned gasoline vehicles. The company also made a few electric cars, and after the war built electric vans under the name Lancaster. *GNG*

LECTRA HAUL (US) 1963 to date

Unit Rig & Equipment Co., Tulsa, Oklahoma

This company was founded in 1935 and soon became one of the major US manufacturers of oilfield equipment. The company also developed and manufactured various off-highway military vehicles for the US and foreign governments in addition to its trailer-mounted oilfield machinery, truck-mounted ditching machines and other specialized equipment.

In 1963 Unit Rig introduced the giant Lectra Haul 4 x 2 dump trucks, and has produced these in various sizes from the M-85 85 tonner to the M-200 200-tonner, the largest 2-axle truck in the world. All models have much in common including lift-out engines and electric final drive. A wide variety of engines is available, by Cummins, Caterpillar, Detroit and, on the M-200, EMD (the Electro-Motive Division of General Motors). Output runs from a 700 hp Cummins VTA-1710 in the M-85, M-100 and M-120-15, to a 2,475 hp EMD V-12 in the M-200., The engines drive through General Electric generators to General

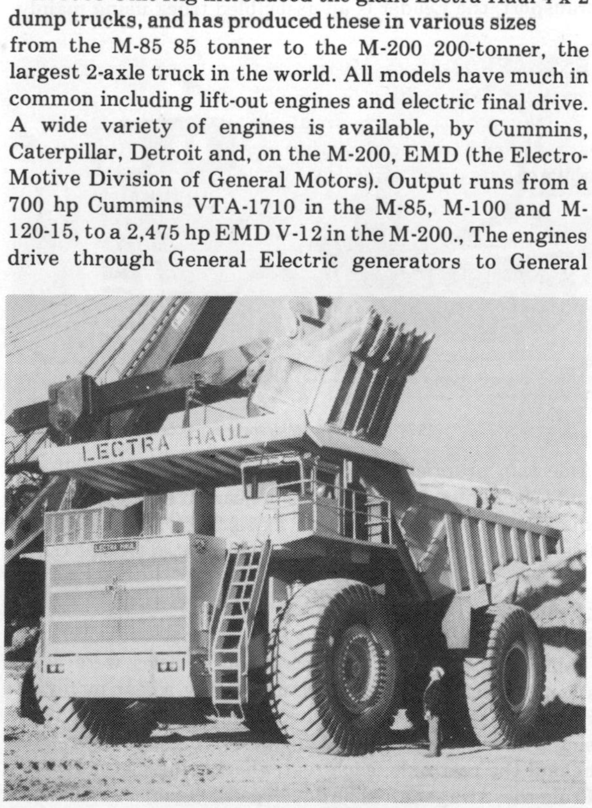

1975 LECTRA HAUL M-200 200-ton dump truck, Unit Rig

Electric wheel motors with planetary gears. Suspension is rubber-cushioned Dynaflow column type on all wheels.

In 1973 an articulated bottom-dump coal hauler, the BD-180, was introduced. Powered by a Detroit Diesel V-12 engine of 1,100 hp, it has a capacity of 180 tons making it the largest coal hauler in the world. Unit Rig also make very large airport tow tractors and fork lift trucks. Total production of dump trucks and coal haulers to the end of 1975 was over 2,000. *RW*

LEHIGH (US) 1925-1927

Lehigh Co., Allentown, Pa.

Three models of 2-tonner Lehigh were made, two using Hercules engines and one a Buda HS-6. In 1927 the company merged with the better-known Bethlehem Motors Corp. *GNG*

LEILA (D) 1925-1928

(1) Heinrich Kaiser & Co., Frankfurt am Main 1925
(2) Dr. ing. Gieren & Co., Frankfurt am Main; Offenbach 1926-1928

LEILA stood for "LEIchtpLAstwagen" (light truck) and was a truck with cycle type wheels and a rear mounted flat-twin engine by Breuer of 500 cc or 750 cc. A

1926 LEILA ¼-ton truck, HON

later version was a bit sturdier and had a V-twin engine of 1,100 cc., again rear mounted and driving the rear axle. *HON*

LEMOON; NELSON-LEMOON (US) 1910-1939

(1) Nelson & LeMoon, Chicago, Ill. 1910-1927
(2) Nelson-LeMoon Truck Co., Chicago, Ill. 1927-1939

Although LeMoon claimed to have built their first truck in 1906, there are no records until 1910 when a conventional 1-ton truck with 4-cylinder engine and double chain drive was made. In 1911 A.R. LeMoon won his class in the Chicago-Detroit-Chicago commercial vehicle trial with one of these trucks, which was joined by a similar 1½-tonner for 1912. Righthand steering was used, and persisted until 1920, very late for this feature. For 1913 2- and 3-tonners were added, and in 1915 the chain drive was replaced by Timken worm drive except on the 3-tonner. Continental engines were used at this time, and indeed on most models until 1930. From 1913 to 1927 the name Nelson-LeMoon was used rather than plain LeMoon, though this latter was resumed thereafter. In 1918 a Buda-engined 5-tonner joined the range, which otherwise consisted of Continental-powered 1 to 3½-tonners, and these were made with little change during the 1920s.

In 1928 6-cylinder Continental engines were adopted for the smaller trucks of what was now an 8-model range, from 1 to 5-tons, and in 1930 no fewer than eleven models were listed in a price range from $1500 to $7300. Waukesha 6-cylinder engines were used in the larger models. By 1931 LeMoon had a 12-ton 6-wheeler with double worm drive which featured cycle-type fenders and dragon-finned ventilators on the hood top, a la Fageol. Lycoming straight-8 engines were offered briefly in the early 1930s, and a Cummins diesel joined the range in 1932. By 1936 capacities were 2 to 12 tons, including cab-over models in truck and tractor form. These resembled

1936 LE MOON 6×4 dump truck, OMM

the Mack CH range, but in 1938 a new more streamlined cab appeared which was similar to that used by Available. Caterpillar diesel engines were offered in addition to Cummins, and Continental or Waukesha gasoline units.

1938 LE MOON 6×4 tractor with low-loading trailer, Caterpillar

LeMoon diversified in its late years by building taxicabs and a motor home designed and marketed by Brooks Stevens which was sold also as a portable office or showroom. All production ceased in April 1939, when LeMoon bought the Chicago branch of Federal and became Federal-LeMoon Truck Co., dealers rather than manufacturers. Some Nelson-LeMoon employees went to the nearby Available Truck Company.

The great majority of LeMoon's sales were in the Chicago area, a prominent user being Bowman's Dairy. Production averaged 100 per year, up to 200 in a good year but only 35-50 in poor ones. This points to an estimated lifetime production of 3000 trucks. *RW*

LEON BOLLEE: MORRIS-LEON BOLLEE (F) 1896-1933

(1) Automobiles Leon Bollee, Le Mans 1896-1924
(2) Morris Motors Ltd (Usines Leon Bollee), LeMans 1925-1931
(3) Societe Nouvelle Leon Bollee, Le Mans 1931-1933

Leon Bollee's rapid if temperamental 650 cc single-cylinder belt-driven tricar could be had with a box-carrier in place of the front-mounted passenger seat, and examples of this version actually went into service in Paris and Bordeaux. With the switch to 4-wheelers at the turn of the century, however, Bollee lost interest in commercial vehicles, the only traces of such types being the 2.4-litre 4-cylinder sv car chassis with 10-cwt van bodies used by *The Star* for newspaper delivery in London from 1912. In 1923 these were replaced by new vehicles based on the 10CV ohv M-type. W.R. Morris purchased the company from Bollee's widow in 1924, and five years later serious truck manufacture began with the 30-cwt T-type, a relative of the 12CV car, with which it shared its Hotchkiss-built 2.4-litre ohv 4-cylinder engine. The 4-speed gearbox and worm drive paralleled contemporary Morris-Commercial thinking, though the servo fwb were not to be found on any light truck as yet offered by the latter factory. Morris jettisoned his unprofitable French subsidiary in 1931, production being continued (under the Leon Bollee name once more) by A. Dunlop Mackenzie and Harry Smith. Though a smaller ohv unit replaced the Hotchkiss in private cars, the lattter was retained in the 1932 trucks, the T-type being joined by a lighter duty model, the ELB with bevel drive. Two heavier 3/4-ton vehicles were added to the range, both with coil ignition, engines being a 3.7-litre four and a 4.1-litre six. In 1933, the last year of production, there were three truck models only (the bigger four was dropped), as well as a low-frame 22-seater coach chassis using the Hotchkiss power unit. *MCS*

LESSHAFT (D) 1925-1926

Lesshaft & Co., Berlin N 65

A tri-van with single front wheel, which was tiller-steered, was announced by this firm. A 131 cc Rinne two-stroke engine was used. *HON*

LESSNER (SU) 1905-1910

G. Lessner Works-St. Petersburg

1905 LESSNER postal vans, MHK

During its short span, the Lessner Works produced a very limited quantity of buses, fire engines, ambulances, a 2.5 ton truck and a van of 3300 lb. loading capacity. *BE*

LEWIS (US) 1912-1914

Lewis Motor Truck Co., San Francisco, Cal.

This make was built as 2½-, 3- and 5-tonners, all powered by 4-cylinder, side-valve engines. Engine location on the largest was under the seat and optional location is given for the other types. All used three-speed gearboxes and jackshafts with double chain drive. A single chassis served all three capacities with a 12-foot wheelbase, semi-elliptic springs in front and platform springs at the rear. Body types included flat-bed, end and sided pump as well as special bodies for brewery use. *GMN*

LEY; LORELEY (D) 1906-1931

Rudolf Ley Maschinenfabrik A.G., Arnstadt

Under the name of Loreley van versions were available, based on the private car. In 1925 an express truck of 2 ton payload capacity was presented, using a 3.1-litre engine. This was carried on until 1931 when a change to a 6-cylinder 3.6-litre engine was made. Also a new bus was presented, but these models were not put into production. *HON*

LEYLAND (i) (GB) 1896 to date

(1) Lancashire Steam Motor Co., Leyland, Lancs. 1896-1903

(2) Lancashire Steam Motor Co. Ltd., Leyland, Lancs. 1903-1907

(3) Leyland Motors Ltd., Leyland Lancs. 1907-1962

(4) Leyland Motor Corporation, Leyland, Lancs. 1963-1967

(5) British Leyland Motor Corporation, Truck & Bus Division, Leyland, Lancs. 1968-1978

(6) Leyland Vehicles Ltd., Leyland, Lancs. 1978 to date

James Sumner built an experimental and unsuccessful steam wagon between 1880 and 1882, subsequently turning his commercial attention to steam lawn mowers. Real success in steam vehicle building began when the Spurrier family bought an interest in the firm in 1896 and built a 2-ton steam van, generally resembling the French Le Blant, using a paraffin-fired vertical firetube boiler, vertical compound engine, three road speeds (controlled by friction clutches) and chain drive. This van appeared in *The Engineer* trial at Crewe (1897) taking a Silver Medal Developed into a 4-ton platform truck this design took first prize in the 1899 Liverpool Trials. In the 1901 2-speed wagon a new coal (or coke) fired vertical firetube boiler was substituted for the first design, together with a horizontal compound undertype engine, with Stephenson's link motion, changed to Joy's gear in the 5-tonner introduced in 1905, the year after the firm's first gasoline engined vehicle appeared.

The firm purchased Coulthards of Preston in 1907, when the title was changed, and marked the event by introducing the new 2-speed 'H' class 5-tonner, with "improved constant lead valve gear and Flat-Stone's Metal Valves" but still with the Spurrier boiler. The engine and gears were totally enclosed and chain drive was retained from a countershaft differential. For the first time bushed bearings superseded most of the split, adjustable, bearings in the engine. Production of steamers averaged about 30 a year in 1905, 1906 and 1907. An enlarged version (1909) was known as Class T.

The year 1909 saw also the first of a range of shaft driven wagons using the standard gasoline engine chassis and axles, with the 3-cylinder poppet-valved single-acting forward-mounted engine and the standard design of vertical boiler but pressed to 250 psi. A condenser was mounted in place of the radiator. The original 3-ton gear driven wagon (KX class) was joined in 1910 by a 5-tonner (class K) and a 6-tonner (class KW).

c.1898 LEYLAND (i) steam wagon, NMM

Steam vehicle production ceased from 1914 to 1920. Postwar models were 5 and 6-tonners using a vertical cross water tube boiler, with a 2-cylinder high pressure engine using cam operated mushroom valves, 2-speed gearbox, countershaft differential and twin chain drive. Examples of this excellent design remained in use in Liverpool until about 1950 but the last was made in 1926. Total production of Leyland steamers was less than a thousand but they were well made machines and the only ones to use a compound undertype engine in conjunction with a vertical firetube boiler in a commercially viable vehicle, though even so the firm changed to a duplex high pressure engine and cross water tube boiler in their 1920 models.

In 1904 Leyland produced their first internal combustion engined vehicle, which had a two cylinder 12 hp engine and could carry 30 cwt. It was followed by goods and passenger models, most with Crossley engines, for up to five tons, and production reached over 60 by the time the company was reorganized and obtained its present name in 1907. In that year the makers of the Coulthard steam wagon were taken over, Coulthard having supplied half of the original Lancashire Steam Motor Company's capital.

New L-head engines replaced the T-head models in 1910, and in the same year Leyland produced a 6-cylinder 85 hp unit for fire engines. At this time Leyland were also taking on haulage contracts, though this was discontinued in 1914 after complaints from customers who were running Leylands in competition. Leyland also offered guaranteed maintenance contracts and insurance facilities.

In 1912 a 3-ton Leyland was approved under the War Office subsidy scheme and by the outbreak of War a total of just over 2,000 gasoline driven Leylands had been built, putting Leyland on a par with the other major British manufacturers, Dennis, Thornycroft, Albion and A.E.C. Steam wagon production of about two per week was relegated to a new fire engine factory at Chorley in 1913

1913 LEYLAND (i) 4-ton municipal tip wagon, NMM

and thereafter was not actively promoted, though examples continued to be built until their spares were sold to Atkinson in 1926.

The Subsidy-model, or RAF-type Leyland as it came to be known, initially had a 32 hp engine and worm driven back axle, though it was modified to 36 hp and double-reduction spur and bevel axle, in which form it was probably the most successful and satisfactory British wartime truck. Approximately 6,000 were built between 1914 and 1919.

Afterwards Leyland re-purchased 3,000 of them and they were extensively reconditioned at Kingston-on-Thames. They were then sold to operators with a two year guarantee for less than the cost of a new vehicle.

However, not even this exercise saved Leyland from great financial difficulties during the slump in new vehicle sales which followed the War. In an attempt to diversify they acquired the manufacturing rights of the Trojan utility vehicle and this was produced at Kingston until 1928, when the division was sold.

Immediate post-war models covered the 2 to 6-ton range

1920 LEYLAND (i) Q-type 4-ton truck, NMM

with corresponding passenger versions. Bus production increased by 100% per year between 1922 and 1924 as fleets were modernized and increased, and in 1925 Leyland

1923 LEYLAND (i) GH bus, OMM

introduced their L-range, which was to establish them on a par with AEC in the bus world. The L-range included the forward control drop-frame 52 seat double deck Leviathan, the normal control Lioness coach and charabanc, most significant of all, the drop frame Lion forward control single decker. This was one of the first of its type to enter quantity production and by the end of 1928 over

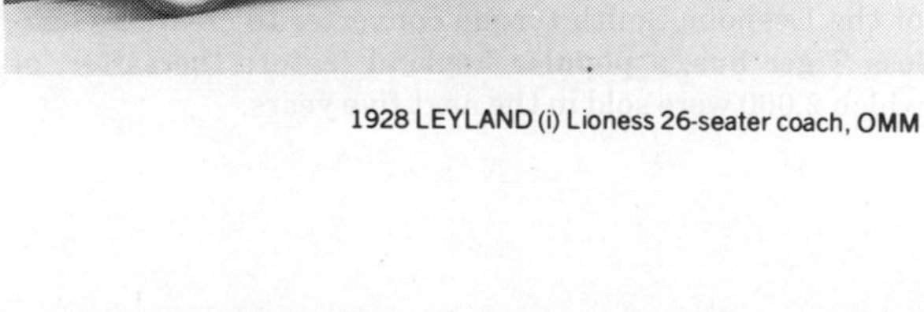

1928 LEYLAND (i) Lioness 26-seater coach, OMM

2,500 of the range had been sold. On the goods side Leyland had little success with a 30 cwt overhead camshaft model introduced in 1923, but the successors to the RAF model, the QH2 with 40 hp engine, also used by the Leviathan, was doing well as a 6-tonner.

Other well-known models of the period were the SWQ2 forward control 10-ton 6-wheeler introduced in 1927 and the 6-cylinder Titan bus announced at the same time, which had a low upstairs gangway to create the enormously successful 'low-bridge' layout, a feature that allowed double deckers to work routes formerly restricted to single deckers. Leyland built most of their own bus bodies until production ended in 1954, and in 1934 replaced traditional construction methods with an all-metal, steel-framed design. They also built up an important trolleybus sideline, initially with converted passenger chassis, but in the thirties, with specially designed machines.

Although Leyland made no particular effort to produce vehicles for the 30 cwt War Department Subsidy scheme they did introduce an important model in 1928 for the 6 x 4 3-ton class, the Terrier.

In 1929 Leyland revised their heavy goods models with the introduction of a range using a high proportion of interchangeable parts, both between themselves and between the bus models. They included 2½-ton to 12-ton models bearing the familiar names Beaver, Bison, Buffalo, Bull and Hippo.

The combination of these and the successful passenger models transformed Leyland's fortunes and there were even plans made at the time for AEC and Leyland to merge to strengthen the British commercial vehicle industry.

1933 LEYLAND (i) Bull 7¼-ton vans, NMM

The end of Trojan production at Kingston led Leyland to plan another light model to be produced there. This materialized in 1931 as the 6-cylinder Cub 2-tonner or 20 seater. Also in 1931 Leyland demonstrated their new diesel engine in a Rhino normal control 6-wheeler. This was followed by diesel units interchangeable with gasoline ones in all models and by the end of 1934 almost half the diesel buses in service in Britain had Leyland engines, while two thirds of all bus operating municipalities had Leyland buses in their fleets.

In 1932 came the bus-based Llama 6½-tonner, the Titanic 6-wheeled double deck bus, and a 4-cylindered Cub, primarily for municipal work. 1933 saw the adoption of the Lysholm-Smith torque converter to create a Gearless Tiger bus, a popular Leyland feature thereafter, of which 2,000 were sold in the next five years.

1933 LEYLAND (i) Tiger coach, NMM

1934 LEYLAND (i) Cub 2-ton truck, OMM

1936 LEYLAND (i) Titan 56-seater bus, Leyland

In 1934 the Octopus 8-wheeler was introduced while in 1935 a Leyland Metz 150 foot turntable escape was the biggest fire appliance of its type produced. A new model in

1935 LEYLAND (i) Octopus 15-ton truck, NMM

1935 was the Cheetah lightweight 6-cylinder bus which shared some similarities with the Cub range, which had been steadily growing in carrying capacity and now included 4-ton rigids and 5 to 6-ton artics. The Cub was gradually replaced by Kingston from 1937 by the semi-forward control Lynx, which managed to carry up to 6 tons on a vehicle weighing under 2½ tons complete.

1935 LEYLAND (i) 60-seater trolleybus, LTE

Also in 1937 Leyland experimented with a twin steering Beaver which resulted later that year in the Gnu bus and Steer 10½ ton goods models.

Leyland were important producers of tanks during the War, but also produced some 1,500 Lynx and 7,500 other models, notably 6 x 4 Retrievers in the early days and over 1,000 6 x 4 Hippo Mk IIs after 1943.

Though one of the largest British commercial vehicle makers by the end of the Thirties it was in the next thirty years that their enormous growth took place. To begin with it closely mirrored that of their arch-rivals A.E.C. The two companies pooled their trolleybus resources in B.U.T. Ltd., in 1946 and thereafter for every independent vehicle manufacturer that A.E.C. bought, Leyland would buy another as if to keep in step. Thus Albion Motors became Leyland owned in 1951 followed by Scammell Lorries Ltd., in 1955.

Though Leyland had long been successful exporters, it was the Government-backed export drive that followed the Second World War that established them as the largest exporter of heavy commercial vehicles in the World. The first step was the 5/7 ton Comet in 1947 named after Leyland's famous wartime tank. It was a normal control design also available as a 35 seat export bus from 1948.

The Octopus was revived in 1948 with a new steel cab also used by the Beaver, while a Leyland speciality of the time, still available in modified form twenty years later, was extra heavy duty normal control export trucks with traditional radiators, like the Super Beaver and Super Hippo.

Following development with Metropolitan-Cammell-Weymann Motor Bodies Ltd., the Olympic integral export bus appeared in 1950 along with the Royal Tiger chassis for separate bodybuilding. Both had underfloor engines. 1952 saw the introduction of the lightweight Tiger Cub with horizontal mid-mounted Comet engine, followed in 1954 by the 150 hp Royal Tiger Worldmaster, many

1950 LEYLAND (i) Comet 5/7-ton tanker, NMM

thousands of which became the basis of overseas bus fleets. Another important development in 1954 was the semi-automatic Pneumo-Cyclic transmission for Leyland passenger models. During this period Leyland established a number of overseas manufacturing plants and also supplied engines to numerous other British and foreign manufacturers.

Amid the boom in Leyland buses the goods range remained largely unchanged, but for the addition of a primarily military 6 x 6 design, the Martian, until 1958. Then the forward control Super Comet 9-tonner appeared and many of its components including cab spread to Albion and to other Leyland models. Also in 1958 the revolutionary Atlantean double deck bus appeared after development going back to 1952 and a showing at the 1956 London Commercial Motor Show. It had a vertical, transverse, rear-mounted 125 hp engine driving the rear axle, via a fully or semi-automatic gearbox and diagonal propeller shaft. From 1960 it was also available as a single decker for export called the Lion, and the Atlantean eventually ousted the more conventional Titans, which had been extensively redesigned in 1956 as the PD3.

In 1961 Leyland acquired Standard-Triumph in a seemingly David and Goliath feat, and the first outcome of this merger was the Leyland 2-tonner built at the Triumph factory from 1962 and using a Standard 2.26-litre diesel engine. Also in 1962 Leyland acquired their age-old rival A.E.C. along with their vehicle making subsidiaries Thornycroft and what was left of Maudslay.

1963 LEYLAND (i) Super Comet 15-ton articulated truck, Leyland

Following the introduction of the Power-Plus range of engines in 1960 the medium and heavy goods models were completely redesigned in 1964 as the Freightline range, with Ergomatic tilt-cab for the first time. Earlier that year the rear, underfloor-engined Panther followed by Panther Cub passenger chassis had made their appearance to join the Leopard introduced in 1959, while an order for several thousand Comets for Iran resulted in an untypical normal control model using an Airflow Streamlines proprietary cab, also shared by Dodge, Commer, Baron and others.

In 1965 Leyland began negotiations with the State-owned Transport Holding Company, which resulted in their acquiring Bristol Commercial Vehicles and their coachbuilding subsidiary, Eastern Coachworks, and in 1966 Rover, who also controlled Alvis, joined the group, followed by Aveling-Barford in 1967.

Following overseas use of Leyland goods vehicles with semi-automatic transmission this feature was made available for Britain in 1966 on the Steer and Beaver models.

At the same time Leyland started their own electrical components subsidiary, Butec Ltd., to be independent of outside suppliers for dynamos and starter motors.

After twenty years of gas turbine development by Rover, Leyland started prototype trials of a gas turbine 38 ton tractive unit which was shown in public for the first time at the 1968 Commercial Motor Show. A number of pre-production versions were built and some started operator trials in 1971, though to date the high cost of manufacture and need for specialized maintenance, as well as no clean-cut fuel cost advantage, has held back the project.

Concurrent with gas turbine development Leyland introduced their new 500 series diesel engines in 1968, which returned to the vintage system of non-detachable cylinder heads to obviate gasket problems, especially with turbochargers. The first of these standardized engines was fitted in the Lynx and Bison models, which were given a restyled version of the Ergomatic cab.

In a merger of enormous consequences in 1968 British Motor Holdings joined forces with Leyland to create the British Leyland Motor Corporation. In addition to the many makes of car involved, Leyland now had several new commercial vehicle ranges including B.M.C., Austin, Morris, Guy and Daimler. By 1970 these had been rationalized to some extent with Guy and Daimler keeping their identities, the light vans produced by B.M.C. becoming Austin-Morris, Nuffield agricultural tractors becoming Leylands and the B.M.C. trucks produced in Scotland becoming Leyland Redlines. This helped to differentiate them from the non-mass-produced Blue line range of traditional Leylands.

Another far-reaching change in 1970 was the Leyland National Bus. This was developed jointly by the operating

1973 LEYLAND (i) Atlantean 75-seater bus, Leyland

1975 LEYLAND (i) National 44-seater bus, GNG

body, the National Bus Company, and British Leyland. It first entered series production at a new factory in Lillyhall, Cumbria, in 1972 with an initial target of 2,000 complete vehicles per year. It was of fully integral construction with air suspension and a horizontal turbocharged version of the fixed head engine available in 150, 180 and 200 hp forms. To avoid complicated drive-line angles this was mounted at right angles to the rear axle, but behind it, and its propeller shaft drove forwards through the axle casing and was then brought back via reduction gearing into the front of a conventional differential.

The initial Redline models in 1970 were the Terrier, Laird, Boxer and Mastiff for 6.5 to 28 tons gross, and they

1974 LEYLAND (i) Terrier 6½-tons GVW truck, Leyland

were joined in 1972 by other models produced in the former Albion factory, which now had the same cab as the Redline models. This was an extensively modified version of the cab originally inherited from B.M.C.

An important new model developed by A.E.C. and Leyland in 1973 was the Marathon, which was intended for the higher gross weights above Britain's 32 tons permitted on the Continent and anticipated on the home market. This has a 280 hp 6-cylinder diesel and is at the top end of an extensive range which also includes the Buffalo for 32 ton articulated operation in Britain with a 212 hp turbocharged version of the 500 engine or from late 1976 a normally aspirated L12 version of the Marathon's TL12 (from 1976 Cummins and Rolls-Royce engines were also available in the Marathon to extend its usage to old proprietary-engined Guy customers.) Leyland are particularly successful in the maximum capacity 4 and 6-wheel market with the Comet and Perkins engined Mastiff, and Bison and Beaver, as well as the medium weight Terrier and Boxer, and lightweight Sherpa van, (introduced in 1974). Overall they have 30% of the British

1975 LEYLAND (i) Marathon 32-tons GCW truck, Leyland

Commercial vehicle market as well as extensive worldwide sales.

In 1975, following cash liquidity problems largely brought on by the Austin-Morris car division and the oil crisis, the Group obtained State backing and was nationalized.

Also in 1975 Leyland unveiled its new generation double decker, the B15 (later renamed Titan) which entered production in 1978. It features integral aluminum construction, air suspension (independent at front), fully automatic transmission and choice of transverse rear mounted engines (normally Leyland or Gardner) of 170 to 250 bhp. It was joined in 1977 by a single deck export bus or coach version of the National called the B21 with chassis to enable local bodywork to be fitted.

For 1976 Leyland re-entered the rigid 8-wheel market with a new Octopus, the cheapest and lightest in Britain.*OM*

LEYLAND (ii) (CDN) 1920-1958

(1) Leyland Motors Ltd., Toronto, Montreal, Vancouver 1920-1948

(2) Leyland Motors (Canada) Ltd., Longeuil, Montreal 1948-1956

(3) The Canadian Car & Foundry Co., Ltd., Longeuil, Montreal 1956-1958

Leylands were launched on the Canadian market with the RAF 4 tonner which accounted for the bulk of Canadian sales until 1926-27. A few trucks were assembled in the company's branches in Montreal, Toronto, Winnipeg and Vancouver, and nearly all had Canadian-built cabs and bodywork, giving them a distinctive appearance from their British counterparts. They made no impression on the bus and coach market until the appearance in 1925 of the Lioness (later called Canadian Lioness). This found many customers with the rapid growth of long-distance passenger travel in Canada, and numerous Lionesses were still in service in the 1950s. The Canadian Lioness differed in wheelbase, tire sizes and other modifications.

Other Leyland models popular in Canada included the rigid-6 Terrier, of which a few were sold to the Army, the Cub in 4- and 6-wheeler versions, the Lynx and Beaver. Practically all Canadian Leylands were normal control; in the later 1930s rounded and more shapely cabs were fitted which seemed at odds with the flat vertical Leyland radiator. Conventional versions of the Cub, Badger, Hippo, Lynx and Terrier were quite unlike their British counterparts.

In 1932 Leyland introduced their diesel engine to the Canadian market, and by 1936 could claim that four fifths of the diesel vehicles sold in Canada (perhaps 150) were Leyland-powered. Also in 1936 the Hayes Mfg. Co. Ltd. of Vancouver were appointed West Coast distributors, and this move resulted in the Hayes-Leyland, a Canadian make incorporating Leyland engines and chassis components.

Leyland Canada had nothing to sell from 1939 to 1948 when an attempt was made to launch the Comet. With only 75 hp this was under powered, and although there were plans to assemble Comets near Toronto, the model was a complete failure on the Canadian market. In 1951 a new series of Canadian-built trucks were assembled in an ex-aircraft plant at Montreal. These were the Beaver, Bison and Bull Moose in GVWs from 24,000 to 36,000 lbs.

1954 LEYLAND (ii) tractor, RJ

All had Leyland 600 diesel engines, and cabs which were substantially reworked versions of the Comet. In 1952 a new series was introduced with improved appearance and 155 hp engine, but sales were still disappointing compared with prewar days. In 1956 Leyland Motors became associated with the Canadian Car & Foundry Co. Ltd., well-known bus makers, and an all-new range of trucks made which still used Leyland engines but had Spicer or Brown-Lipe transmissions, Eaton or Timken axles and styling sheetmetal which included an International cab. Made in rigid and articulated versions (24,000 lbs. GVW to 100,000 lbs. GCW), they were known first as Leyland-Canada, and then simply as Canada. The last model was the 680WT, a heavy-duty highway tractor. Total postwar production of Canadian Leylands probably did not exceed 200, and since 1958, apart from the occasional test vehicle or demonstrator, Leylands have been absent from the Canadian Market. *RJ*

LEYLAND (iii) (IL) 1960-1973

Leyland Ashdod Motor Corp., Ltd., Ashdod

In order to meet the need for conventional truck chassis, so much in favor in the Middle-East markets, Leyland established an Israeli factory where two basic models were built in truck, tractor and tipper versions. The 2 ton GVW "Super Chieftain" used a conventional fiberglass cab called "Ashdod Vue" and was powered by a 6-cylinder diesel developing 106 bhp, while the heavier 20-ton GVW "Super Beaver" used a 200 hp 6 cylinder diesel and was fitted with an angular heavy-looking conventional front end. This model featured also the option of a 2 pedal pneumo-cyclic gearbox. Bus and coach chassis were also built along with trucks, in this case identical to British models. The same factory was later engaged in the assembly of Mack trucks under a new company name. *GA*

LEYLAND (iv) (IR) 1970 to date

Haml Va Naghle Dakheli Iran Co., Tehran

The large demand for normal control chassis in the Middle East markets led Leyland of England to introduce the so called "Bonneted Comet" which was built for a short period at Leyland factory in England. Early in 1970, though, the design was transferred to the Tehran factory and later on the cab was locally redesigned and much simplified. The Tehran factory assembles various other Leyland truck chassis and builds also the Israeli "Carmel Dragoon" 4x4 utility vehicle, which is marketed as the Leyland "Pirouz". *GA*

L.G.O.C. (GB) 1908-1913; 1924; 1926; 1930-1931

(1) The London General Omnibus Co. Ltd., Walthamstow, London 1908-1913

(2) The London General Omnibus Co. Ltd., Chiswick, London 1924-1931

The L.G.O.C. was London's largest bus operator when it merged in 1908 with the Vanguard Omnibus Company and the London Road Car Company. The combined talents of the new company developed the 34-passenger X-type double-decker bus, of which 661 were produced in the old Vanguard works at Walthamstow, followed by the B-type in 1910 made for their own special operating requirement. This had a wood/steel flitched chassis and worm drive. It weighed 3½ tons complete with 34-passenger body, and was an immediate success. In 1912 the manufacturing facilities at Walthamstow were hived off and became the Associated Equipment Co. (A.E.C.) who thereafter supplied the vast majority of the L.G.O.C. fleet.

The L.G.O.C. then concentrated on running and maintaining their bus fleet, though from time to time they produced experimental vehicles or ones for their particular needs at their large and well-equipped repair and coachbuilding works at Chiswick. Vehicles produced included 50 1½- and 2-ton truck chassis with Dorman engines made in 1924 which were used by the company for general work for many years, and with all-weather touring coaches with Daimler sleeve-valve engines and early examples of all steel bodywork, made in 1926. Then in 1930-31 they built three 4-wheeled single deckers and four 6-wheeled double deckers. These were fitted with Meadows engines, later replaced by A.E.C. units. *OMM*

1930 L.G.O.C. CC-type 66-seater bus, LTE

LIAONING No. 2 (CHI) c.1971 to date

Shenyang Automobile Factory, Shenyang, Liaoning

This is reported to be a light heavy-duty truck built for provincial use. *BE*

LIAZ (i) (CS) 1951 to date

Liberecke automobilove zavody n.., Jablonec na Nisou

The Liaz concern was founded in 1951 and put into production the former Skoda 706 7-ton truck which had been made by Avia since 1946. A wide variety of models was made, including tipper and bus versions, all with a 6-cylinder 11.78-litre diesel engine. In 1957 the modernized 706RT was introduced with forward control and diesel engine developing 170 bhp. Bus versions were built by Karosa on the 706RTO chassis.

The 706 range was improved in 1968 with the MT series

1972 LIAZ-SKODA 706MT fire engine, MSH

which had 11.94-litre 200 hp engines and longer wheelbases. This range, which is still in production today covers 10 to 12 ton 4x2 trucks, 4x4 and 6x4 tippers and articulated units up to 32 tons GCW. At the end of 1974 these were joined by a new range, the 100 series. These were made in two basic models, the 100.05 4x2 and the 100.45 articulated unit of 38 tons GCW, with 270 or 304

1977 LIAZ (i) 100.45 38-ton GCW truck, Liaz

hp turbo-charged 6-cylinder diesel engines and two-range 5-speed gearboxes. There is also a 6x4 tipper, the 090.22. A special model, made in a branch factory at Zvolen is the Ferona 22.22.21 D for carrying long metal bars; this 3-axle truck has a horizontal engine as used in Karosa buses mounted midway along the frame. *MSH*

LIAZ (RNA3) (ii) SU c.1959 to date
Likino Bus Plant - Likino

Early production included a model-158 which was a 32-60 passenger bus similar to the ZIL-158.

Power was by a Liaz 6-cylinder engine of 109 hp, the wheelbase was 15 ft. 11 ¼ in., and overall length 30 ft.

1966 LIAZ (ii) 677 bus, JFJK

Current models include the Liaz 677, a city and suburban bus with pneumatic suspension, floor level regulator and a 200 hp V-8 engine. Seating permits 25-41 passengers to be carried with a maximum speed of 70 km/h. This design won a gold medal at the Leipzig Fair. *BE*

LIBERTY (i) (US) 1917-1918

The Liberty or USA was not a make in the accepted sense, but was a standarized design built in large numbers by fifteen different truck makers. In March 1917 the US Army issued specifications for two types of truck, a 1½-tonner and a 3-tonner (Class A and Class B respectively). Only the latter was built in quantity, and came to be known as the Liberty, or sometimes as the USA from the

1917 LIBERTY Class B 3/5-ton army truck, BHV

letters carried on the radiator header tank. The engine was a 424ci 4-cylinder unit of which Continental made the cylinder block, Waukesha the cylinder heads and crankcase, and Hercules the pistons. The 4-speed transmission and fully floating worm drive rear axle were likewise joint efforts by the leading firms in their fields.

Design began in August 1917, and by October the first two trucks were ready. These were assembled by Selden and Gramm-Bernstein who were to be among the leading builders of Liberty trucks, delivering about 1000 each. Other important firms who contributed to the total output of 9452 Libertys were Garford, Pierce-Arrow and Republic (about 1000 each), Bethlehem (675), Diamond T (638), Brockway (587) and Sterling (479).

Production ceased with the end of the war, but the Liberty was the basis of many US Army designs of the 1920s including 6x4 trucks, half-tracks and fire engines. Unlike the wartime Libertys, these were built at various U.S. Army depots. The Liberty was widely used on civilian work in Europe well into the 1930s, and was the basis of the French Willeme trucks. *GNG*

LIBERTY (ii) (B) 1920-1940
Societe Franco-Belge des Camions Liberty, Brussels

During the years up to about 1920 Liberty was initially reconditioning Army surplus stock trucks of the Liberty type, and later manufacturing these vehicles by means of assembly from American parts. During the 'thirties Liberty manufactured a range of lighter and more modern vehicles using mainly six-in-line gasoline engines. Since about 1936 diesel engines were generally mounted, bought from Deutz or Hercules. Though there is no proof, the name of the company suggests that there has been some link between the Belgian Liberty company, at least during the first years of its existence, and Willeme, the French truck manufacturer who also produced the Liberty for some years. *JFJK*

LIFANTE (E) 1952-1960
Juan Lifante, Barcelona

This firm made motorcycles and accessories, and also a delivery tricycle called the 'Mot-Auto Lifante'. This had a single-cylinder Hispano-Villiers 200 cc 2-stroke engine and shaft drive to the rear axle. It had a tubular frame. Payload was 400/500kgs, and top speed of 30 mph. The Lifante company is still in business making small invalid cars. *JCG*

c.1952 LIFANTE Motor Auto 400 kg 3-wheel truck, JCG

LIFU (GB) 1897-1905

Liquid Fuel Engineering Co. Ltd., East Cowes, Isle of Wight

Before taking an interest in road vehicles the makers had supplied boilers and burners of their design for use afloat but a 1 ton steam van was shewn at *The Engineer* Automotor Exhibition of 1897, resembling externally the Le Blant vans made somewhat earlier in Paris. The two-drum patent water-tube boiler was placed amidships and twin tandem compound engines drove each rear wheel through a countershaft and an internal gear on the wheel. The rate of combustion of the paraffin fuel was regulated by a needle valve actuated automatically by boiler pressure.

The following year a 2-ton dray was entered in the Liverpool trials. In this boiler was removed to the front and a horizontal compound engine with piston valves and a totally-enclosed all-gear drive to the rear axle was used. The wagon took second prize. That year a steam van with passenger trailer was supplied for service between Fairford and Cirencester.

1899 LIFU steam van, NMM

The Lifu enjoyed only a limited success. Based on the concept of a light fast vehicle it was ahead of the thinking and road surfaces of its time, was expensive in first cost per ton of payload (the boiler was in copper throughout) and required the services of a skilled driver/mechanic to run it.

The parent company ceased to list the wagon after 1905 but licensees (notably Belhaven) continued rather longer. After 1900 production was probably sub-contracted as in that year the works in Cowes was closed and sold.

The designer behind the Lifu patents was H.A. House who was also responsible for the Lifu steam car.

Some Lifu vehicles were made under license in Belgium by Malevez Freres of St. Servan-lez-Namur. *RAW*

LIGHT (US) 1913-1914

(1) Light Commercial Car., Marietta, Pa. 1913

(2) Wayne Light Commercial Car Co., New York, N.Y. 1914

The Light was a 3-wheel parcel van of 750-pound capacity. Early units had a 6 hp 1-cylinder air-cooled engine, soon replaced with 14 hp 2-cylinder engine. Drive was by chain to the single rear wheel. The 2-cylinder machine cost $475 in 1914. *DJS*

LIGIER (F) 1978 to date

Automobiles Ligier, Vichy

This well-known maker of sports and racing cars launched a small forward-control truck for 1½-ton loads, powered by a Fiat engine. *GNG*

LILA (J) 1923-1926

Jitsuyo Jidosha Seizo Ltd., Osaka

J.J.S. had previously built the Gorham 3-wheeler with tiller steering and drive taken to the righthand rear wheel. This, though not itself a commercial vehicle, was the true ancestor of the Japanese commercial 3-wheeler. The Lila, by contrast, was a more conventional 4-wheeler powered by a 10 hp aircooled engine; it was available as private car or light van. In 1926 J.J.S. merged with Dat of Tokyo, and production of the Lila was discontinued. *MCS*

LILIPUT (D) 1904-1907

(1) Bergmann's Industriewerke, Gaggenau 1904-1905

(2) Suddeutsche Automobilfabrik GmbH., Gaggenau 1905-1907

The small friction-driven Liliput cars were available also as vans. They used a single-cylinder 4 hp engine and later also a 2-cylinder 9 hp engine. These vehicles were also marketed as Bergmann. *HON*

LILLOISE (F) 1929

Compagnie Lilloise de Moteurs, Lille.

This Peugeot subsidiary (also known as C.L.M.) did not normally build complete vehicles: its main product was the Junkers opposed-piston 2-stroke engine for which it held the French license, and which was widely used by French truck makers in the early 1930s. A miniature diesel 1-tonner was however displayed at the 1929 Paris Salon. Of forward control type, it bore a close external resemblance to an electric truck, and was powered by the smallest single-cylinder Lilloise engine. Unusual features on so small a vehicle were the solid tires, twin rear wheels, and transaxle. *MCS*

LIMA (US) 1915-1916

Lima Light Car Manufacturing Co., Lima, O

The only model by this name was a ½-tonner, but further information unfortunately is not available. *GMN*

LINCE (E) 1954-1962

Industrias Cerza, Barcelona

The Lince (Lynx) was one of many Spanish makes of delivery tricycle, powered by a single-cylinder Hispano-

1959 LINCE 400kgs 3-wheel truck, JCG

Villiers 2-stroke engine. It had a payload of 450 kgs, shaft drive to the rear axle, and hydraulic brakes on all three wheels. *JCG*

LINCOLN (i) 1910-1914
Lincoln Motor Car Works, Chicago, Ill.
This company was the successor to Sears and made light vans and trucks of 500 to 800 lbs. capacity, powered by a 14 hp 2-cylinder air-cooled engine driving through a friction transmission and single chain final drive. Solid or pneumatic tires were available, and prices varied from $585 to $685. *GNG*

LINCOLN (ii) (US) 1916-1917
Lincoln Motor Truck Company, Detroit, Michigan
The only model offered by this manufacturer was a 1500-pounder with a four-cylinder ohv engine connected with a three-speed gearbox. This was on a wheelbase of 10 feet, 2 inches. This company absorbed the O.K. Motor Truck Company in 1916. *GMN*

LINDSAY (GB) 1906-1908
Lindsay Motor Car Co., Woodbridge, Suffolk
This car maker also built light vans powered by 8/10 hp 2-cylinder Stevens or 14 hp 4-cylinder Fafnir engines, the former to carry 7cwt and the latter, 10cwt. Both had 3-speed gearboxes and identical chassis. *GNG*

LINDSLEY (US) 1908-1909
J.V. Lindsley & Co. Seymour, Ind.
For $600 this high-wheeler came with a 1500-pound capacity delivery body on a wheelbase of 96 inches. It had a 2-cylinder air-cooled engine with force-feed lubrication. Drive was through a multiple disc clutch, 2-speed planetary transmission and double chain to the axle.

A larger model with a 2500-pound capacity was also available. *RW*

LINN (US) 1916-1950
Linn Mfg. Corp., Morris, N.Y. 1916-1950
The Linn was a half-track intended either as a load carrier or tractor, and was particularly used for snowplowing, logging, mining and construction work. The tracks were mounted between the main framerails and the outside auxiliary extensions, and the rear axle was gear driven. Apart from the tracks, the Linn was conventional, with 4-cylinder Continental engines at first, followed by 4- and 6-cylinder Waukeshas, and 6-cylinder Cummins and Hercules diesels. A special military version of 1933, the 8-ton T3, used an American LaFrance V-12 engine of 246 hp. In the later 1930s the clutch was a special heavy 2-plate type in unit with a high-speed reversing transmission. These transmissions were optional 4 or 8-speed, each with a high speed reverse enabling the Linn to have the same

1934 LINN T3 8-ton half-track truck, BHV

1928 LINN 15-ton half track side dumper, RW

speed in either direction. Bottom gear was as low as 116.1. Cabs were open at first, but soon a variety of wooden cabs were used, some fully enclosed, and just before World War 2 a steel cab with visor adopted. Fenders were never standard equipment, but they could be ordered. Prices were as high as $15,000 in the later years.

In 1927 H.H. Linn left the company, and formed the indicated Linn Trailer Corp. at nearly Oneonta, which later became Lyncoach. In 1940 Linn built a 5-ton truck with front wheel drive and a pair of wheels behind the tracks. These could be lowered for use on hard surfaces, while for rough ground the tracks were lowered, in which case drive was by tracks and front wheels. This truck had a 105 hp 6-cylinder Hercules engine, and a forward-control cab similar to that of the F.W.D. SU-COE model. At this time Linn also made a conventional front-wheel-drive truck with twin wheels at the front and an overall length of about 37 feet. *RW*

LION (US) 1920-1921
Lion Motor Truck Corp., New York, NY
This make is listed as producing a single model, a 3/4-tonner. Further data is not available. *GMN*

LIPPARD-STEWART (US) 1911-1919
Lippard—Stewart Motor Car Company, Buffalo, New York
Early models of this make were of 1500-pound capacity and were vans with French-type sloping hoods with radiators aft of the four-cylinder engines. Later versions ranged in capacity from ½-ton to 2-tons, each with a

1911 LIPPARD-STEWART 1500lb truck, NAHC

different wheelbase. These used four-cylinder Continental engines, three-speed gearboxes and worm-drive. *GMN*

LITTLE GIANT (US) 1912-1918
Chicago Pneumatic Tool Company, Chicago, Illinois
Through 1915, this make used two-cylinder engines, planetary transmissions and double chain-drive on their ¾- and 1-tonners. All had forward control. Later models

1912 LITTLE GIANT Model D 1-ton trucks, NAHC

had capacities up to 3½ tons and used four-cylinder Continental engines with three-speed gearboxes and worm-drive. This manufacturer, still in existence though not in the truck-manufacturing business, also built trucks under the names of C.P.T. and Chicago. *GMN*

LIUCHIANG LZ-130 (Liu River) CHI 1969 to date
Liuchou Farm Machinery Plant & Liuchou Machinery Plant-Liuchou, Kwangsi (Plant Vehicle Code - LZ)
Introduced April 2, 1969 through the combined efforts of two machinery building plants, the Liuchiang LZ-130 is a heavy duty truck for provincial use. *BE*

LIWABA (D) 1930-1931
Lieferwagenbau GmbH., Hamburg-Stellingen
Following the layout of two front wheels and one driven rear wheel this was one of the typical tri-van designs of that time. A 200 cc Jlo engine was used. *HON*

LLOYD (i) (D) 1906-1914; 1948-1962
(1) Norddeutsche Automobil- und Motoren A.G., Bremen 1906-1914
(2) Lloyd Motoren-Werke GmbH., Bremen 1948-1962
The name Lloyd was chosen for Krieger electric cars built under license. Since 1908 also gasoline-engined cars were in the program, the first being a 5-ton truck with 40 PS engine and chain drive, representing the state-subsidized type. A few years later there were vans and trucks of 1½, 3 and 5 tons payload capacity and a bus. Also electric vehicles were now of Lloyd's own design. Various versions were built for the use by the postal authorities and as fire engines. A speciality were trolley buses designed by Kohler. The first one appeared in 1910. One electric motor was used, transmission being by cardan shaft and differential. The Brush Electrical Engineering Co. built these vehicles under license and they were put into service in Stockport. In 1914 Lloyd merged with Hansa and further products were marketed as Hansa-Lloyd (qv.).

1914 LLOYD (i) front-drive electric tractor, NMM

The name Lloyd was revived in 1948 by Borgward for a small car with 293cc 2-cylinder engines. This was made in van form, and later a 596cc engine was used. This car-based van was called the LS500, joined in 1954 by the LT 500 (later LT 600) with semi-forward control. This appeared as ½ tonner van or pick-up using a 2-cylinder two-stroke engine of 386cc (later 596cc) placed in the front and driving the front wheels. Also electric vans and trucks

1955 LLOYD (i) LT600 ½-ton van, GNG

were built from 1948 to about 1958. The BE 3000 was a 3 ton normal control truck; a forward control van was used by the postal authorities for parcel delivery. With the breakdown of the Borgward concern production of Lloyd cars ceased in 1962. *HON*

LLOYD (ii) (GB) 1939-1950

Lloyd Cars Ltd., Grimsby, Lincs.

Encouraged by an order from the Gas Light and Coke Co. Ltd. for a batch of their standard 2-seater minicars, Lloyd introduced a 5-cwt van edition at only £95. It was mechanically similar to the cars, with rear-mounted 350cc watercooled single-cylinder 2-stroke Villiers engine, backbone frame, and all-independent springing. Few were sold; their van edition of the post-war 650cc fwd 2-stroke roadster, however, never progressed beyond the prototype stage. *MCS*

1939 LLOYD (ii) ¼-ton van, NMM

LLOYD & PLAISTER (GB) 1905-1911

Lloyd & Plaister Ltd., Wood Green, London N.

This company was formed by Lewis A Lloyd (late of Hurst & Lloyd) and W.E. Plaister, a maker of confectionery machinery. Lloyd was something of an experimenter, who loved tackling difficult engineering jobs, and the firm specialized in making experimental or prototype machines of all types.

In addition to making the original V-8 two stroke engines fitted to the Dolphin car, and a range of 4-cylinder L & P cars of 10, 16, 20 and 40 hp, the company also offered a 2-cylinder horizontally engined taxicab in 1905 and built various commercial vehicles to special order thereafter, including delivery vans and fire engines, one of which, with the 16 hp engine, solid tires and chain drive, was delivered to the Municipality of Alexandria in 1908. Between 1912 and 1914 the company produced about 50 Vox cyclecars fitted with 2-cylinder two-stroke engines of Dolphin type. *MJWW*

L.M.C. (US) 1919-1920

Louisiana Motor Car Company, Shreveport, Louisiana

The lone truck by this company was called Model 2-20 and was rated at 2½ tons. It used a four-cylinder Continental engine, had a four-speed gearbox and bevel gear drive. Its wheelbase was 13 feet, 8 inches and the price for the chassis was $2950. *GMN*

LOCOMOBILE (US) 1912-1916

Locomobile Company of America, Bridgeport, Connecticut

The initial model of truck under this prestigious name was a five-tonner on a chassis of 11-foot, 8-inch wheelbase. Its four-cylinder engine had a displacement of 431 ci. This drove through a four-speed gearbox and jackshaft with roller chains to the rear wheels. For 1915, this line was expanded to include 3-, 4- and 6-tonners. In 1916, only 3- and 4-tonners were offered. In 1917, the name of this truck was changed to Riker. *GMN*

1912 LOCOMBILE 5-ton truck, NAHC

LOCOMO see Armstrong-Whitworth

LOCOMOTORS (GB) 1949

Locomotors Ltd., Birkenhead, Cheshire

Developed by a body-building company, the Locomotors was a 25cwt delivery van based on a chassis built by the Mercury Truck & Tractor Co. It was powered by a Ford Ten engine and had a forward-control cab with sliding doors. A few were supplied to S. Reece & Sons, a Liverpool dairy. *GNG*

LOHNER (A) 1898-1908

Jacob Lohner & Co., Vienna

When Lohner in 1898, two years after starting car production, engaged Ferdinand Porsche as a young engineer, he also adopted a design principle of Porsche's for his cars. This was the "Radnabenmotor" (hub cap motor), where an electric motor was fitted to each of the front wheels. Subsequently these cars were known as "Lohner-Porsche". This principle was used for various commercial vehicles, but mostly it was used for fire engines which were very famous at that time. The principle of hub motors was also used for trolley buses. The collector was designed by Stoll and the system became known as "Lohner-Stoll". When the design of electric cars was taken over by the Mercedes Electrique company vehicles were marketed under this name. *HON*

LOKKERI (SF) 1967 to date

Rauma Repola Oy,. Lokomo Works, Tampere

A branch of the famous Rauma Repola engineering concern producing cranes, road rollers, etc., builds forest tractors with all-wheel-drive and automatic transmission, powered by Perkins 130 hp diesel engines. An articulated 4×4 model is the basic design, while a 6×6 log transporter is also built on the same principle. *GA*

LOMAX (GB) 1906

John Goode, London E.C.

The Lomax was an *avant train* tractor with front mounted vertical boiler fired through a central chute, twin high pressure cylinders 6½" bore x 7" stroke, geared to a countershaft differential from which twin chains drove the front wheels. A single speed only was provided. The steering was by the rear wheels. Though the original vehicle was sold to Groves & Witnall Ltd., the Salford (Lancs.) brewers, it is believed to have been a failure. *RAW*

LOMBARD (US)1901-1919

Lombard Auto Tractor-Truck Corp., Waterville, Maine

Alvin O. Lombard built his first half-track vehicle in 1901; this resembled a steam railroad locomotive with tracks at the rear and skids at the front. In 1916 he began

1907 LOMBARD 100hp steam log hauler, Hartford Steam Boiler Inspection & Insurance CO

the commercial manufacture of half-track tractor-trucks powered by 75 hp 4-cylinder Model engines, of which 104 were ordered by the Russian army. These were for hauling artillery and supply trains, but the main civilian work of Lombards was in the logging industry where they hauled trailers of up to 60 tons. An unusual feature was that the tracks were mounted inside the chassis frame. *GNG/GMN*

LOMOUNT see Rotinoff

LONDON (GB) 1900-1906

John Stewart & Son Ltd., Poplar, London E.

Wagon building was an incident in the career of the firm, who were noted providers of engines for ships built in the Thames, which trade was in serious decline by 1900. The Stewart 5 and 6 ton wagons had a vertical firetube boiler, undertype compound engine with Stephenson link motion, two road speeds, countershaft differential and chain final drive. With these characteristics they are unlikely to have been brilliant performers, and had ceased to be listed in the Motor Traction buyers' guide by 1906.

The wagon was also known as the Stewart. *RAW*

LONDONDERRY (GB) 1903-c.1908

Marquis of Londonderry, Seaham Harbor Engine Works, Co., Durham

Initially produced for use only on the maker's collieries the Londonderry was subsequently made in limited numbers for other users. The 1903 Londonderry had a vertical water-tube boiler and double high pressure cylinders with steam vents controlled by a rotary valve driven from the crankshaft. Subsequently a vertical firetube boiler and a totally enclosed compound undertype

1904 LONDONDERRY 5-ton steam wagon, RAW

engine with overhead valves and the company's own design of valve gear were used. Slide valves were used for both cylinders. The wagons were two speeders with an all-gear final drive to a rear axle differential. One-piece cast-steel wheels were standard. The usual capacity was 5 tons. The workmanship in Londonderry wagons is reputed to have been first class but like all of their type they were rather shy steamers. The gear drive was open and, it seems, very noisy. The most famous fleet of Londonderry wagons was that owned by the North Eastern Railway.*RAW*

LONE STAR (US) 1920-1921

Lone Star Truck & Tractor Association, San Antonio, Texas

The Lone Star appears to have been a 1½ tonner. *GMN*

LONGEST (US) 1910-1916

Longest Brothers Co., Louisville, Ky.

This truck was made in two sizes, a 3-4 tonner and a 5-6 tonner, both using a 40 hp 4-cylinder engine mounted under a hood, with four speeds and double chain drive. They had solid tires all round and cost $4,250 and $4,750 respectively. *GNG*

LONGSTAFF & PULLAN (GB) 1860

Longstaff & Pullan, London SE

In many respects this engine was ahead of its time having a chassis in which the locomotive boiler was carried in trunnions enabling it to be leveled for work on hills. The double cylinders were side mounted and inclined, each cylinder driving one rear wheel by annular gearing. Pullan's design of superheater was fitted. *RAW*

LOOMIS (US) 1901

Loomis Automobile Co., Westfield, Mass.

Gilbert Loomis was a pioneer experimenter with steam cars, but his production vehicles used 5 hp single-cylinder Crest gasoline engines. These included light vans as well as passenger cars. *GNG*

LORD BALTIMORE (US) 1911-1916

Lord Baltimore Motor Car Company, Baltimore, Maryland

Model A was a three-tonner with a stake body and having a four-cylinder engine, a three-speed gearbox and roller-chain drive. For 1913, five models were offered from one- to 5 tons capacity. Each of these models used a different chassis. In the final two years of manufacture, only one- and two-tonners were built. *GMN*

LORRAINE (US) 1919-1924

Pilot Motor Car Co., Richmond, Ind.

Lorraine hearses were a sideline of the Pilot company, a minor assembler of 6-cylinder private cars. Specification was conventional, only the house colors of silver and dark grey distinguishing Lorraines from other contenders in this class. Sv power units by Herschell-Spillman or Teetor-Harley were fitted. *MCS*

LORRAINE-DIETRICH see De Dietrich

LOTHIAN (GB) 1913-1924

Scottish Motor Traction Co., Ltd., Edinburgh

The Lothian was designed initially as a bus chassis by W.J. Thompson, the manager of S.M.T., assisted by A. Bracken and E. West.

An 'assembled' vehicle, the Lothian utilized a pressed steel frame with tubular cross members fitted with a 38 hp Minerva Silent Knight sleeve-valve engine, four speed and reverse chain driven gearbox (chains from Coventry Chain Co.) and steel worm and phosphor bronze wheel back axle from David Brown of Huddersfield. The radiator and bodywork were built in the company's own workshops, and initially vehicles were built solely for SMT's own fleet. In 1914, however, the Tylor 35 hp engine was adopted, and the Lothian chassis, designated the 3 ton, was marketed for both bus and truck use by outside firms. Buses were supplied to both Autobus Car Company, Dunfermline and Perth Corporation, and at least eight trucks were built for firms in England and Scotland, although several of the latter were subsequently bought back for rebodying as buses in the SMT fleet. Although most vehicles were of the driver-beside-engine type, one with a charabanc body was supplied to McKirdy and Macmillan. During the fuel shortages in 1917/18 all the SMT fleet were run on town gas.

The last Lothian was delivered to SMT's own fleet in September 1924, and most of the 97 built (including two chassis numbered 69 and 70 with six cylinder Minerva engines) remained in use until 1929/30, some being kept as salvage vehicles until 1935. SMT assembled a number of American Bethlehem trucks in the immediate post-war period. *MJWW*

LOTIS (GB) 1908-1912

Sturmey Motors Ltd., Coventry, Warwickshire

After making British Duryea cars and Parsons light vans, Sturmey launched a range of larger vehicles under the name Lotis. They had 18 hp V-twin Riley engines under the seat, with 2-speed epicyclic gearboxes. These were made as vans, hotel buses and taxicabs, the latter finding their way to a number of foreign cities such as Warsaw, where they were said to be the first motor cabs to ply in a Russian city, and Rio de Janeiro which took 50 in 1910.

1908 LOTIS 1-ton van, NMM

In 1911 most Lotises had 2- or 4-cylinder engines under a hood, the range consisting of a 15cwt van with 2-cylinder engine, a 25cwt van or taxicab with 20-24 hp 4-cylinder engine, and a 3 ton truck with 30 hp engine. Forward control was still available, and colonial models were made which could run on kerosene. *GNG*

LOTZ (F) 1865-

Lotz Fils, Nantes.

In 1865 Lotz built a vertical boiler steam tractor with front steering and engine mounted amidships, the arrangement of the gears and final drive not being stated, said to have been constructed under license from Thomson. If this was the case the design must have been very loosely applied, for the resemblance is mainly superficial. This tractor was paired with, *inter alia,* a passenger bus. He seems to have continued for some years but the date when building ceased is not known. *RAW*

LOUET et BADIN (F) 1906

E. Louet et Badin, Auxerre, Yonne

This car-making firm built a few 2-ton forward-control trucks powered by 15 hp 4-cylinder engines. Final drive was by chain. *GNG*

LOUGHEAD (CDN) 1919-1923

Seagrave-Loughead Co. Ltd., Sarnia, Ont.

The first Lougheads were conventional heavy trucks of up to 7 tons, built by the amalgamation of a Sarnia munitions maker and the remains of the W.E. Seagrave branch plant in Walkerville (now Windsor) Ont. Lighter pnuematic tired trucks, including a speed wagon, were added later. *HD*

LOUTZKY (D) 1899-1900

Gesellschaft fur Automobilwagenbau, Berlin

Apart from a light private car Loutzky built a light 4-wheeled van with a front-mounted box and rear driver's seat. The 2-cylinder 5-hp engine was mounted under the seat, driving the rear wheels. *HON*

LOWCA (GB) 1909

New Lowca Engineering Co. Ltd., Whitehaven, Cumberland

The Lowca tractor, designed by Mr. H. Bently, for the 1909 War Department trials used a V-eight engine, with four pairs of tandem compound cylinders (i.e. 4 high pressure and 4 low pressure) steamed at 700 psi by a paraffin fired flash boiler. Ball bearings were used throughout the engine. High pressure steam admission was by cam operated valves and exhaust by the uniflow system. Despite much thought put into it the tractor was too complicated and expensive to appeal to commercial users. *RAW*

LOWDECK (GB) 1926-1927

Corber & Heath Ltd., Dartford, Kent.

Like the S.D. which it resembled, the Lowdeck was powered by a 2,176cc 4-cylinder E.T. White engine mounted transversely under the driver's seat. It had a 4-speed constant-mesh gearbox and shaft drive to the rear axle. The 22 inch wheels were shod with solid tires, and the load capacity was 2½ tons. Few were made. *GNG*

1926 LOW-DECK 2½-ton truck, OMM

LOW LOADER (GB) 1929-1934

Low Loaders Ltd., London W.12

The Low Loader originated as the Roberts Mobile Truck, a platform or works truck powered by a 596cc air-cooled flat-twin engine driving the front wheels. One of these was tested by the G.W.R. at Temple Meads Station, Bristol in 1928. The larger Low Loader was a road-going version of this, powered by a 4-cylinder Coventry-Climax engine mounted transversely on the near side next to the driver. Bevel gearing took the drive to a 2-speed epicyclic gearbox, and thence a vertical shaft drove the front axle. There was no reverse gear, but the narrow-track front axle could be turned through 360° to give reverse movement. Three wheelbases were offered, 8 ft, 9 ft and 10ft, and prices ranged from £415 to £475. The municipal version of the Low Loader was sold by Lacre. *GNG*

LOYAL (US) 1918-1920

Loyal Motor Truck Company, Lancaster, Ohio

The Loyal was available in 1000 and 1500-pound capacities for 1918 and 1919. Both used 4-cylinder Herschell-Spillman engines. For 1920, a one-tonner was added to the line and a LeRoi four was used in the 1000 pound chassis. Significant increases in prices between 1918 and 1919 foreshadowed the end of this brand name. *GMN*

LOZIER (US) 1910-1912

Lozier Motor Co., Detroit, Mich.

This commercial vehicle was one of the last efforts of this one-respected manufacturer of high-grade passsenger cars. The Model 25 was a 5-tonner with forward control and used a four-cylinder, water-cooled engine. This was fitted with a four-speed gearbox with a jackshaft and double roller chains to the rear wheels. The truck was governed to a maximum speed of 13 mph. With a wheelbase of 11 feet, 2 inches, the chassis was priced at $4500. *GMN*

L.S.D. (GB) 1920-1924

(1) Sykes & Sugden Ltd., Huddersfield, Yorks 1920-1923
(2) L.S.D. Motor Co. Ltd., Mirfield, Yorks 1923-1924

The L.S.D. was mainly seen as a two-seater passenger car, but it was also made in 5cwt van form. A 3-wheeler

1922 L.S.D. ¼-ton 3-wheel truck, OMM

powered by an air-cooled V-twin J.A.P. engine, it had a 3-speed gearbox and chain drive. An unusual feature for the time was independent front suspension by coil springs. *GNG*

LUAZ (RYA3) SU 1966 to date
Lutsk Automobile Factory Lutsk

Factory production in the 1950's and early 60's consisted of spares for GAZ trucks and special bodies for autoshops and refrigerator trucks.

In 1966 a two-wheel drive version of the ZAZ-designed #969 field car was produced and in 1970 a four-wheel drive model was added.

The name was changed to the LUAZ-969 and the latest version, the 969M, is powered by a 40 hp engine and features headlight wipers among various accessories. *BE*

LUBLIN (PL) 1951-1959
Fabryka Samochodow Ciezarowych, Lublin

Named after the city where the factory was situated, Lublin trucks were built under Soviet GAZ license. Based on GAZ 51 low-tonnage chassis with normal control cab, Lublins were built in large quantities, attaining the target of 25000 units per year in 1958. The introduction of Polish designed chassis and the reorganization of the automotive industry, eliminated the outdated Lublin designs after 8 years of production. *GA*

L.U.C. (D) 1910-1920
(1) Loeb & Co., GmbH., Berlin
(2) Loeb-Werke A.G., Berlin-Charlottenburg

Luc vans were available on the private car chassis featuring Knight engines. Production of trucks was started in 1913 and was carried on during the war. After 1920 Luc cars were offered as Dinos. *HON*

LUC COURT (F) 1900-1950
S.A. des Anciens Ets. Luc Court & Cie, Lyon

Luc Court was one of the many small French commercial vehicle manufacturers, which were very often known only locally. Luc Court experienced its heydays during the Edwardian years, producing since 1909 as one of the first manufacturers a four-in-line engine with overhead valves. It had a bore and stroke of 70x140 mm and a capacity of 2150 cc and was installed in both car and commercial vehicle chassis. With some modernization — replacing the oil-bath chain-drive by cardan drive — the complete range of vehicles was in production up to 1936. In that year the cars were dropped, but the commercial vehicles were continued up to 1950, when the company finally closed its doors. Trucks and buses with gasoline and diesel engines were made. *JFJK*

LUCK UTILITY (US) 1913-1914
Cleburne Motor Car Manufacturing Co., Cleburne, Tex.

A ½-tonner was the only size built under this name. It used a four-cylinder engine under a hood mounted between the two single seats. This was furnished with a three-speed gearbox and shaft drive. Semi-elliptic springs were used in front with ⅔-elliptic at the rear. Bodies were delivery van type with "special bodies to order". *GMN*

LUDERS (D) 1930
Luders-Werk, Bremen

This manufacturer presented a 1½ ton truck with the type designation Express, but no more details are known. *HON*

LUDEWIG (D) 1968 to date
Gebr. Ludewig CmbH., Essen-Altenessen

This was a coachbuilding firm which formerly bodied private cars as well as coaches, but for many years has concentrated on various versions of buses and coaches. In the 1930's they built some striking aerodynamic coaches on Opel and other chassis. In 1968 the firm produced a first series of trolley-buses which was designed in connection with the municipal traffic board of the city of Solingen. This design was not based on any bus components but was of a chassis-less construction with two rear axles which were both driven. Although this was the first and only new development on the trolley-bus scene in many years, it did not succeed on a wider basis and is only built for the city of Solingen. *HON*

LUEDINGHAUS (US) 1920-1933
Luedinghaus-Espenschied Wagon Co., St. Louis, Mo.

Like Armleder, Luedinghaus was an old-established wagon builder who turned to trucks when the demand for horse-drawn vehicles dwindled. They offered a range from 1 to 2½ tons, using Waukesha engines, Shuler and Wisconsin axles and other proprietary components, extending the range to 5 tons by 1925. In 1928 they built an outsized 6-wheeler for a local operator, with set-back front axle, enormous balloon tires and a Hendrickson tandem axle. Possibly only one of these was made. Production lingered on until 1933, by which time only 1½ to 2½-ton trucks were being made. *RJ*

LUMB (US) 1918
Lumb Motor Truck & Tractor Company, Aurora, Illinois

The only model with this name had an odd rating of 4500 pounds capacity. It used a four-cylinder Buda engine with a three-speed gearbox. Wheelbase was 12 feet, 4 inches and chassis price was $1900. *GMN*

LURQUIN-COUDERT (F) 1906-1907
Lurquin et Coudert, Paris

This was a typical load-carrying tricar powered by a 4½hp vertical single-cylinder engine, with 2-speed gearbox and chain drive. Load capacity was 3cwt. *GNG*

LUTHER & HEYER (D) 1933-1937
Fahrzeugbau Luther & Heyer GmbH., Berlin

This firm built in very limited numbers a tri-van using a 200 cc D.K.W. engine. *HON*

LUTZMANN (D) 1893-1898
F. Lutzmann, Dessau

This pioneer firm produced cars only on a small scale. A van and a bus version are known but these were built to order and were based on the private cars. The engine design showed Benz influence. *HON*

LUVERNE (US) 1912-1923
Luverne Motor Truck Co., Luverne, Minn.

The Leicher brothers began to make passenger cars in 1903 and were particularly known for the 'Big Brown Luverne' of the 1914-1917 era. In 1912 they produced their first hearse and fire engine, both using 6-cylinder Rutenber engines, and truck production began shortly afterwards. Passenger cars were dropped in 1917 because

1923 LUVERNE 3-ton van, NAHC

trucks were more in demand, but by 1923 they found that there was too much competition from bigger manufacturers in this field too, and they concentrated on making fire engines on other people's chassis, in which business they are still active today. The last truck was a 3-tonner powered by a Continental 7N 4-cylinder engine. *GNG*

LUX (D) 1898-1902
Lux'sche Industriewerke, Ludwigshafen

Based on the private car design a 2-3 ton truck was available with an opposed twin 6 hp engine. A later model used a 2-cylinder 10/12 hp engine and also an electric van was offered. *HON*

LUXOR (US) 1924-1927
(1) Luxor Cab Mfg. Co., Framingham, Mass.
(2) M.P. Moller Motor Co., Hagerstown, Md.

The Luxor was a taxicab made by the M.P. Moller company in the former Bay State automobile factory at Framingham. It had a 4-cylinder Buda engine, and was available in limousine and landaulette versions. Later Luxors were made in the Moller factory at Hagerstown which was also making other cabs such as the Astor as well as Dagmar passenger cars. *GNG*

L.V.L. (GB) 1923-1926
Light Vehicles Ltd., Wolverhampton, Staffs.

The L.V.L. was a conventional chassis for 25/30cwt loads, powered by a 20hp 4-cylinder Dorman engine, with 4-speed gearbox and overhead worm drive. The chassis was also used for 14/16 seater coach bodies. *GNG*

1923 L.W.D. 3-ton truck, HON

L.W.D. (D) 1923-1925
Lippische Werke A.G., Detmold

The characteristic feature of this remarkable design by Fritz Mayer was a hydraulic transmission. The engine was a 2.5 litre developing 30 bhp driving the front axle. Also very advanced was the forward control cabin. *HON*

LYNCOACH (US) 1938-c.1970
(1) Lyncoach & Truck Mfg. Co., Oneonta, N.Y. 1938-c.1970
(2) Lyncoach & Truck Mfg. Co., Troy, Ala. 1960-c.1970

Lyncoach was founded in 1929 to build truck and bus bodies, later making specialized vehicles such as traveling salerooms, classrooms and libraries. In 1938 they assembled their first complete vehicle, a Waukesha-powered radio operations truck for Station WOR in New York City. General Electric ordered a number of traveling showrooms, and during World War 2 Lyncoach made complete ambulances with Ford V-8 and Dodge 6-cylinder engines as well as bodies on other chassis and trailers. From 1945 to 1952 a series of Waukesha-powered front-drive vans was made, but body building was always the main activity of the company.

A new plant at Troy, Alabama was opened in 1960 to make aluminum truck bodies and trailers, and this plant made the Lyn Airvan using Ford and other chassis in varying sizes from ½-ton to 3-tons. The name was later changed to Lyn Arrow, but by the 1970s productions was back to bodies and trailers only, and the Oneonta plant was closed. *GNG*

MABECO (D) 1925-1926

Mabeco GmbH., Berlin NO 65

The tri-van presented by this firm was a three-wheeled motor-cycle with a rear-mounted van box. *HON*

MACCAR (US) 1912-1935

(1) Mac-Carr Company, Allentown, Pa. 1912-1913
(2) Maccar Truck Company, Scranton, Pa. 1914-1929
(3) Maccar-Selden-Hahn Corp., Allentown, Pa. 1929-1935

The Mac-Carr Company was formed by Jack Mack, one of the brothers who formed Mack Truck Company, and Roland Carr, their first products being conventional 1500 to 3000lb delivery trucks called Maccarr. For a brief period their Allentown plant also housed the Webb Motor Fire Apparatus Company and the Lansden electric truck, but this combine collapsed and Maccarr was reorganized without the participation of the founders, as the Maccar Truck Company in nearby Scranton. The new company made 1500lb to 2 ton trucks with Wisconsin engines, extending the range to 3½ and 5½-tonners by 1917. During the 1920s sales were quite substantial, and a tight network of factory branches backed by many dealers assured good coverage in Pennsylvania, New York and the New England states, although trucks were sold elsewhere in some numbers too. The range in the early 1920s consisted of 1-to 6-tonners with 4-cylinder Continental engines, Brown-Lipe transmissions and Timken axles.

In 1926 6-cylinder engines were added to the range, these being of Buda and Wisconsin manufacture, with Shuler front axles and heat-treated frames in heavier models. Maccars of this period were quite distinctive, with attractive cast-iron radiators and particularly robust sheetmetal details. Some of the heavier units featured a forward-located engine and radiator set off by a sharply raked front bumper. Maccar entered the 1930s with a comprehensive range including a 6-wheeler, some of which used the Hendrickson tandem axle. In 1931 came two new heavy-duty high-speed 4 and 5 ton models with four-piece lightweight cast-aluminium radiators, big 6-cylinder engines and air brakes. There was also an experimental 6-wheeler for loads of 10-15 tons powered by a 6-cylinder Sterling Petrel engine; this had Maccar's own tandem bogie which was a springless walking beam type, both axles driving. Possibly no more than one of these was built. 6-cylinder engines were used exclusively from 1930.

In 1929 Maccar joined Selden and Hahn in a little combine at Allentown, but the depression defeated them, and both Maccar and Selden were out of production by 1935. *RJ*

MACCHI see Aermacchi

MacDONALD (US) 1920-c.1952

(1) MacDonald Truck & Tractor Co., San Francisco, Calif.
(2) Union Construction Co., San Francisco, Calif.
(3) MacDonald Truck & Mfg. Co., San Francisco, Calif.
(4) MacDonald Truck & Mfg. Co., Divn Peterbilt Motors Co., Oakland, Calif.

Like the Doane, the MacDonald was a low-bed truck particularly intended for dockside and warehouse work, although highway models were also offered. It was made in two models, the 5 ton Model O with front-wheel-drive and the 7½ ton Model AB. Both used 4-cylinder Buda engines, and internal gear drive. A very advanced feature for the era, though essential with the heavy front axle load, was hydraulic power steering which was featured on both models. The frame was structural steel, deeply lapped behind the cab to negotiate the drop to the 16½ in. floor height to the load carrying-area. Solid tires were used all round, singles at the rear on a wide-track, cranked axle to facilitate the low platform. The Model O's rear axle had neither springs nor brakes, and a ground clearance of 5 in. compared with 11 in. at the front. The Model O was particularly used for the carrying of plate glass, flour,

1931 MACCAR Model S6 3-ton truck, NAHC

1923 MACDONALD low-bed truck RNE

cement and newspapers, while the higher and faster Model AB was used in furniture removal and with tipper bodies.

Although listed intermittently until the early 1950s, MacDonald production was not continuous, and there are many gaps in published specifications. Post-war MacDonalds were made by Peterbilt, and were all rear-drive trucks, still low-loaders. Production at the end was very limited; four trucks in 1948, two in 1949, and no figures given thereafter. *RJ/GNG*

MACK (i) (US) 1902 to date

(1) Mack Brothers Co., Brooklyn, N.Y. 1902-1905
(2) Mack Brothers Motor Car Co., Allentown, Pa. 1905-1911
(3) International Motor Co., Allentown, Pa. 1911-1916
(4) International Motor Truck Corp., Allentown, Pa. 1916-1922
(5) Mack Trucks Inc., Allentown, Pa. 1922 to date
(6) Mack Trucks Inc., Hayward, Calif. 1966 to date

The Mack brothers, Willie, Jack and Gus, had a successful wagon-building business in Brooklyn where they built their first motor vehicle. This was an 18-20 passenger sightseeing bus powered originally by a 24 hp horizontally-opposed 4-cylinder engine, soon replaced by a 36 hp vertical unit. Final drive was by double chains and a top speed of 20 mph was possible, though 12 mph was a more normal cruising speed. The prototype was completed and sold in 1902, and a second bus ordered in 1903, but it was not until 1904 that the Mack sightseeing vehicles, now powered with their own make of 4-cylinder engine, were produced on a quantity basis. Carrying the name Manhattan, last used for Mack trucks in 1910, they were sold not only in the New York area, but as far afield as New Orleans, Boston and Havana, Cuba.

Only 15 vehicles were made at Brooklyn, and early in 1905 the Mack brothers acquired a plant at Allentown, Pa. This move brought another brother into the business, for Joseph S. Mack, the youngest of the family, had a silk mill in Allentown, and became treasurer of the new company. At first production was concentrated on the Manhattan bus, joined by hotel buses and combination goods and passenger vehicles. Trucks were tested during the summer and autumn of 1905, and put on the market before the end of the year. These were a normal control 1½/2 tonner and forward control models of 3, 4 and 5 tons capacity. The original Brooklyn-built engines had been of the F-head layout, but at Allentown new T-head designs were introduced. The most widely used was a 50/60hp four, although there was also a 90hp six used in boats and railcars but not in trucks. The basic engine was made with little change until 1915. Another long-lived feature was the constant-mesh selective gearbox designed by Gus Mack in 1905. At first the heavier trucks, 3 tons and up, were all forward control, but in 1908 a parallel line of normal control models up to 5 tons was available. In 1909, in order to enter the important market for lighter trucks, a new line of 1, 1½ and 2 tonners was introduced with 32hp engines and pressed steel frames in place of the rolled channel steel of the larger models. Later these became known as the Junior line, and the 3 to 7½ tonners as the Senior line.

1910 MACK (i) 4-ton truck, Texaco Archives

Up to 1911 production was modest, fewer than 100 per year, but then the figure rose to about 600. This expansion involved the Mack brothers in a search for increased capital, and in October 1911 the International Motor Company was formed. This was a holding company, backed by the Wall Street banking house of J.P. Morgan and Company, for both Mack and the newly-formed American Saurer company. Manufacturing continued separately, but sales of both makes of truck were combined. In March 1912 Hewitt joined the group and for a few years all three makes were often carried in the same advertisement. At this time the Mack range covered trucks from 1 to 7½ tons, as well as buses and fire engines which had been introduced in 1911. The merging of the company into I.M.C. led to the departure of the Mack brothers themselves, though not all at once. Gus and Joe left the vehicle business altogether while Jack formed the Mac-Carr (later Maccar) company which made trucks under that name until 1935. Willie remained with I.M.C. until he retired during the 1920s, but in 1916 he formed a company of his own, Metropolitan Motors Inc., which made a few light trucks under the name Mackbilt.

In 1913 the smallest Mack yet made was introduced, the ⅔-ton Model S with 4-cylinder monobloc engine, though still with chain drive, an unusual feature for so small a truck of this date. The S was supposed to be part of a whole new range of trucks from ⅔ to 6 tons, but apart from 98 of the S and one prototype Model T, this series was stillborn. However the years 1914 to 1916 saw the introduction of two new models which were to bring greater fame to Mack than anything that had appeared before. These were the AB and AC models, both designed by Edward R. Hewitt who had become chief engineer in 1914. The AB was a replacement for the Mack Junior line, although production of the latter continued up to 1916, and was listed in 1, 1½ and 2 ton forms. It was powered by a 30 hp 4-cylinder engine with pair-cast cylinders, and had a worm-drive rear axle, a new departure for Mack. The first series relied on a number of bought-out components such as Timken axles, Gemmer steering and Brown-Lipe transmissions, but from 1915 onwards these units were all made by Mack. Chain drive was offered as an alternative to worm from 1915. The AB remained in production until 1936, by which time a total of 51,613 had been made. Major changes of course took place during this period, including the substitution of double reduction for worm drive in 1920, chains remaining optional, while styling kept pace with the general changes in the truck industry. The AB was used as a basis for medium-sized fire engines, but more important was the AB bus chassis introduced in 1921, and improved in 1924 with drop frame and pneumatic tires. More than 3,800 AB buses, some with gasoline-electric drive, were made up to 1934. The bus chassis was also used by some truck operators for high speed work, these vehicles being known as Bus Commercials.

1921 MACK (i) AC 7½-ton tar spreader, Virginia Dept. of Highways

In 1916 came an even more famous Mack than the AB, the heavy-duty AC (3½, 5½, 7½-tons) soon christened Bulldog by British Army engineers. Like the AB, the AC had a 4-cylinder pair-cast engine with inspection ports in the crankcase and governor built into the camshaft timing gear. The engine was slightly smaller than that of the old Senior Macks (5 x 6 inches compared with 5½ x 6 inches) but developed 75 hp against the 50/60 hp of its predecessor. Like the lighter Macks from 1909 onwards the AC had a pressed-steel frame. Its best-known characteristic were the hood and dashboard-mounted radiator, though these were not unique to the AC. Chain drive was standardized and remained so until the model's disappearance in 1938. However a shaft-driven model of similar frontal appearance called the AK was made from 1927 to 1936. Other variants using the same hood and radiator were the AC 6-wheelers and the 6-cylinder AP made in 4- and 6-wheel versions. The latter had a capacity of 7½ tons as a 4-wheeler, 10 tons as a rigid 6 and 15 tons as an articulated 6-wheeler. From 1936 Buda and Cummins diesel engines were available in the AC and AP. The AC and its relatives were among the strongest trucks ever made, and solid-tired examples from the 1920s were still familiar sights in New York and other cities 30 and even 40 years after they were built. Among their most important contributions to the American economy were their widespread use in construction and road-building and in the Hoover Dam project. Both AC and AP chassis were used for fire engines, pumpers and rigid and articulated ladder trucks. Total production of the AC from 1915 to 1938 was 40,299, together with 2819 AKs and 285 APs.

1925 MACK (i) AB parlour coach, MBS

1929 MACK (i) AB 3/5-ton truck, OMM

The first Mack to use a 6-cylinder engine was a bus, the AL, which was introduced in 1926 and made until 1929. It had vacuum brakes (on the rear wheels only) and a 4-speed transmission. It was superceded by the BK which had an altogether new and more powerful engine as well as air brakes. Other front-engined models followed in response to specific needs; in all Mack built and sold about 6,000 buses of this type between 1921 and 1938. So-called streetcar-type bodies were supplied for front-engined chassis to meet the competition starting in 1931, but were not especially successful, and in 1934 they were replaced by a new line of streamlined rear-engined buses. The first of these was the 30-passenger CT. Mack installed its rear-mounted engines transversely, and during the pre-war years the engines used were small enough for right-angle

1930 MACK (i) AK 10-ton truck, Texaco Archives

drive to be possible. The rear-engined Macks of the 1930s were widely sold to the number of over 7,000 in less than 10 years, the largest fleets being in Buffalo, Philadelphia, Portland and St. Louis. Two sizes of trolleybuses were also built, from 1935 to 1943. Diesel buses were offered starting in 1938, the engine being built by Mack on the Lanova precombustion chamber principle. Standardized school bus chassis based on the E-series truck were also listed, beginning in 1938.

Meanwhile truck production was being diversified into fields both smaller and larger than had hitherto been made. The smaller line was represented by the Mack Juniors (1936-1938) which were in fact Reos sold with Mack badges and minor trim changes. This resulted from an agreement to sell Reos through Mack agencies. Mack Juniors came in ½, 1½, 2 and 3-ton models as well as a bus chassis. The larger Macks were the F series, introduced in 1937. These were chain-drive 4x2 and 6x4 trucks of up to 100,000lbs GVW, the largest intended for off-road use in quarrying and mining. Gasoline and diesel engines were featured, the latter being at first of Buda or Cummins manufacture, though Mack's own diesel was launched in 1938 and soon supplanted the proprietary makes.

In addition to the heavy-duty models Mack made a comprehensive range of trucks in the medium category. the BJ was a 3-4 tonner with 126 hp 6-cylinder engine and front wheel brakes. Introduced in 1927, it was uprated to 5/8 tons in 1931 and was often used in tractor/trailer form with a 10 ton capacity. Other models in the B series ranged from the 1-ton BL with Lockheed hydraulic brakes to the 8 ton 6-wheeled BQ. An important step was the

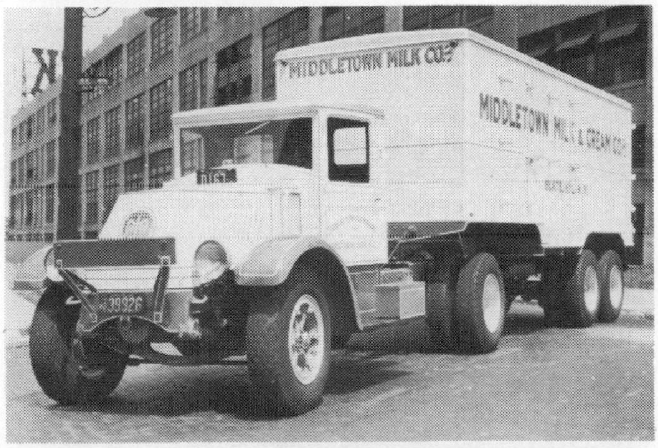

1932 MACK (i) AP 15-ton articulated truck, NAHC

1933 MACK (i) BX 4-ton van, Mack

reintroduction in 1933 of a cab-over-engine range which Mack had not made since 1916. These were the 3/5 ton CH 4-wheelers and 3½/6 ton CJ 6-wheelers, both of which became popular for work in crowded and narrow city streets, though the CH was also made as a tractor for long-distance hauling. Some of the first sleeper cabs on

1934 MACK (i) BC 7-ton 6×4 tanker, Texaco Archives

1933 MACK (i) BJ 5-ton truck, Mack

American trucks were seen on the CH tractor. In 1936 came the EC and EB small coe trucks in the 1½ to 4 ton range, and the following year the Cs were restyled to eliminate the snub-nosed hood of the earlier models. Others in the E range were the ⅔ ton ED, 2½ ton EE, 4 ton EH, 6 ton EM (shaft drive) and ER (chain drive) and 10/12 ton EQ tractor. These, together with the MR (Mack Retailer) 1 ton multi stop delivery van, the heavy duty F and L series, and the buses previously mentioned took Mack up to the eve of World War 2. Truck production was running at over 10,000 per annum, making Mack America's largest makers of heavy trucks.

1936 MACK (i) Junior 20MB 2-ton truck, Mack

Mack production of military trucks had begun two years before Pearl Harbor, several hundred 6x4 EXBU and NR4 trucks being supplied to the French and British forces in 1939 and 1940. The US Army also had 700 cab-over-engine 4x4 Model NJU 5/6 tonners in 1941. The most important specifically military Mack was the NO, a 7½-ton 6x6 which could be used as a load carrier or tractor for the 155mm Long Tom field gun. A total of 2,053 NOs were built between 1940 and 1945.Other aspects of war work included the production of 2,600 power trains for tanks in Mack's gear plant at Brunswick, N. J., and Vultee naval torpedo bombers at the bus plant at Allentown. Fire apparatus was built on Brockway and Kenworth chassis. Some experimental vehicles including a double-ended twin-engined tank transporter were also made.

1939 MACK 2/3-ton truck, LA

After the war the E, F, and L series of medium and heavy trucks were reintroduced but the lighter models of up to 3 tons were not. In addition the first truck built specifically for West Coast needs was announced, although there was to be no actual West Coast plant until 1966. These LTSW models had longer wheelbases and more powerful engines of up to 306 hp, and 10 speed Mack Duplex transmissions. Another aspect of post-war production was the increasing importance of off-road dump trucks. Mack had got into this market with the AC and AP trucks built for the Hoover Dam construction in 1931, followed by the larger F series and the LMSW-M 6x6 model of 1944. This was used in mining, logging and oilfield work, and featured power steering and an offset cab, the latter to find its way to on-highway Macks in the 1960s. From 1940 to 1960 Mack catered for the off-highway market with a variety of 2- and 3-axle trucks in the L series. Largest of these was the LRVSW of 1952, a 3-axle 34 ton dump truck powered by a 400 hp Cummins V-12 engine. In 1960 the L series was replaced by the even larger M series, 2- and 3-axle trucks of 30 and 45 tons respectively. These were developed into the 1962 M70SX, a 60 ton 2-axle dumper, the 1965 M70X, a 70-ton 3-axle truck, and in 1970 the 75 ton M75SX, powered by 700 hp Cummins or Detroit Diesel engines. These were the top end of a wide range of off-highway trucks, catering for the same market as Caterpillar, Terex and Wabco.

1941 MACK (i) LD bus, MBS

When bus production was resumed in 1945 only a single 41-passenger bus, the C41, was marketed. This was an integral bus with welded subframes assembled in jigs. It was supplied with a larger engine than had previously been used, requiring an angle driveshaft between the transmission and the rear axle. In 1947 a Spicer torque converter became standard equipment in place of the 3-speed gearbox and air-operated clutch, and all buses delivered with the older equipment were converted in the field.

A 45-passenger bus, the C-45, joined the line in 1947, and later in that year an adaptation of the 672 cu in gasoline engine with precombustion chambers produced a diesel engine just in time to catch the growing trend to diesel power among the large transit systems which constituted Mack's most likely market. A few hundred small 33-and 37-passenger buses were produced between 1948 and 1951, and a 50-passenger diesel requested by the City of New York was put into production in 1950. Initially this bus, the C-50, was all-hydraulic, but later ones had air brakes. One of these was built with left hand doors and exported to Sweden where it became the basis for a long series of Scania-Vabis buses used in Stockholm and elsewhere. By comparison with GM which was by far the largest selling postwar US bus, Mack had the reputation of building heavy, durable buses that cost too much to run. An effort to lighten the superstructure led to the introduction of new models in 1954, which had the same basic appearance as the old ones but incorporated a direct-injection diesel engine derived from a Scania-Vabis design. Sales picked up slightly, but a significant share of Mack's bus business from 1955 to 1959 was made up of a 450-unit lease to the San Francisco Municipal Railway. In September 1956 Mack acquired the C.D. Beck Company of Sidney, Ohio which built intercity buses and fire engines, and in 1958 a single production run of 25 Mack parlor buses was constructed at Sidney. In spite of a new-look front end paid for by a customer and subsequently offered as an extra-cost option, Mack bus sales slumped to 200 in 1959. The decision was made to utilize the large plant for other, more profitable work, and bus production ended with a group of 75 for San Juan, Puerto Rico in January 1960.

1941 MACK (i) EH articulated truck, Mack

1944 MACK (i) NO2 7½-ton 6X6 army truck, BHV

A curiosity among the on-highway Macks of the post-war period were the FT and FW models which retained chain drive as late as 1950. With GVWs of 35,000 and 50,000lbs respectively, they had a rugged old-fashioned appearance and did not even offer side windows in their cabs. In 1950 came the A series which replaced a number of earlier lines and catered for a wide range of trucks from 17,000 to 40,000lbs GVW. In addition tractor/trailer units were made. They were replaced in 1953 by the B series

1956 MACK (i) B42 articulated truck, GNG

which was made in a very wide range up to the mid-1960s. These were the staples of Mack's conventional trucks and tractors and were supplemented by the cab-over-engine rigid 6 W71 for the West Coast market and the H series COE tractors, nicknamed 'cherry pickers' because of their very high cabs. These were powered by the new Mack END673 Thermodyne diesel engine, gasoline engines being also available in many models. A return to the short-wheelbase COE city truck came with the D series of 1955, with vertical-lifting cabs, followed in 1958 by the N series with Budd tilt cabs, and the MB series with Mack-built tilt cabs in 1962.

Fire engines had been a small but important aspect of Mack production since the earliest days. In the 1930s Mack had pioneered the limousine fire engine in which all the firemen were enclosed instead of being perched precariously on the vehicle's sides. However most of the Macks of the 1940s and 1950s were of the older, open pattern, probably to keep costs down. Ladder trucks and pumpers were made, including a 2,000 gpm pumper for Minneapolis which was the largest single-pump engine of its time. Mack's acquisition of Beck in 1956 led to a new line of forward-cab fire engines similar to the last Becks. Known as the C series they came in pump sizes of 500 to 1,250 gpm, and as ladder trucks, both rigid and articulated, of 65 to 100 feet. Cabs were either open or closed, and automatic transmission was optional. These were made alongside the conventional R series and the forward-cab CF series. These had lower cabs and many other new features including power steering. An exceptional Mack fire engine was the articulated Super Pumper built in 1965 for New York Fire Department. This was pulled by a 6x4 F series tractor, the trailer containing an 18-cylinder 2-stroke Napier Deltic turbocharged diesel engine of 2,400 hp, connected to an 8,800 gpm DeLaval centrifugal pump. In addition there was another articulated unit called the Super Tender whose trailer carried 2,000 ft. of hose and a 10,000 gpm water cannon.

In 1959 came a new series of COE highway tractors which were direct ancestors of the 1978 models. The first was the G series designed for West Coast operators, followed by the F series in 1962. Both of these had very short cabs with BBC (bumper to back-of-cab) measurements of as little as 50 in., or 80 in. with deluxe sleeper cab. Engines were Mack or Cummins diesels, normally aspirated or turbocharged, with a maximum output of 335 hp. Alongside these were the conventional C series of tractors, replaced in 1965 by the U series with offset cabs, and the B series conventional rigid trucks which were replaced by the R series in 1966 and a new line of heavy duty trucks especially intended for the construction industry, known as the DM series. 1966 saw the opening of the West Coast plant at Hayward, California, which built the RL conventional and FL cab-over series for Western operators.

1959 MACK (i) G73 tractor, Mack

1963 MACK (i) B53 6×4 concrete mixer, GNG

1965 MACK (i) MB400 truck, GNG

1965 MACK (i) R Series 6×4 tractor, Mack

The opening of the Hayward plant was only part of Mack's expansion during the 1960s. In 1963 assembly plants were set up in Australia, Venezuela and Pakistan, followed by a Canadian plant at Oakville, Ontario in 1964. These have mostly built trucks of the US Mack type, although there have been local variants such as the rigid 8-and 10-wheelers built in Australia for transport of cattle and sheep. Mack also acquired a number of other truck builders including Brockway in 1956, Bernard in 1963 and Hayes in 1969. For several years Macks were sold in France by Bernard alongside that company's own trucks.

In 1973 came a new type of bottom dump off-highway truck called the Mack-Pack. This had a 475 hp Detroit Diesel V-12 or Cummins engine mounted at the rear, driving forward to both rear and front axles. The Mack-Pack is articulated just behind the front axle, ahead of which is a one-man cab. Load capacity is 35 tons. 1975 saw

1974 MACK (i) DM Series 8×4 asphalt mixer, Pennsylvania Dept. of Transportation

1975 MACK (i) W Series Western Cruiseliner tractor, Mack

the introduction of a new COE highway tractor, the W series Cruiseliner; more roomy, luxurious and powerful than the F series which it supplements. Cabs are only slightly longer, with BBC measurements of 54 to 90 in. There are 31 engine options in the Cruiseliner, from a 235 hp Mack six to a 430 hp Detroit Diesel V-8. Other models in the 1978 range include the conventional R series full-cab and U series offset cab models with Mack, Mack-Scania, Cummins or Detroit engines, Western conventional RL and RS models with Mack, Cummins, Caterpillar and Detroit engines, and the DM rigid 3- and 4-axle trucks. There is also the HMM 8x6 front-discharge cement mixer with Mack Maxidyne Six engine, and a range of off-highway dump trucks, the M series. These run from 15 to 75 tons capacity in rigid 2-axle trucks, with the top of the line being a 120 ton articulated 3-axle bottom dumper. They use engines varying from the 180 hp Mack END673E to the Detroit 16V71TI 800 hp V-16. *GNG/MBS*

MACK (ii) (GB) 1954-1964

Mack Trucks (Great Britain) Ltd., Barking, Essex

This company was formed after World War 2 to provide service and spare parts for the large number of ex-military Mack trucks which were running in Britain. A few new trucks were imported from the United States for display purposes at Motor Shows, but currency restrictions prevented this becoming a commercial enterprise. In 1954 a British Mack was built, with Perkins R6 diesel engine and 5-speed David Brown gearbox. The prototype 7 tonner had an American Mack hood and cab, but the 'production' models exhibited at the 1954 Commercial Motor Show had British-built hoods and cabs generally similar in appearance to the contemporary American product. They were shown in long and short-wheelbase forms, and were joined in 1955 by a forward-control 7 tonner with 6-cylinder Leyland engine, Albion 5-speed gearbox and Bonallack all-metal cab. A year after production had been announced, only these three trucks had been built. In 1956 came the H9T, a normal control 9 tonner with Leyland engine, Albion gearbox and cab a modified form of that used in the larger Bedfords. One of these was sent to the Mack agent in Turkey in 1959, and the model was still catalogued in 1961. An unusual feature was a disc handbrake acting on the transmission. Another 1961 model was the PA8-125, a 4-wheel-drive forward control 8-tonner with Commer TS3 engine and cab. In 1963 a 6-wheeled chassis for crane carrier work, powered by a Leyland 0680 engine was built, and in 1964 an A.E.C.-engined truck for seismographic work in oilfields. These last two vehicles were special orders, and all British Mack production was very limited. It is probable that not more than 20 trucks left the small factory in 11 years. *GNG*

MACKBILT (US) 1917

Metropolitan Motors, Inc., New York, N.Y.

This company was founded by William C. Mack, formerly with Mack Brothers, and announced a ¾-tonner early in 1917. The single chassis had wheelbase of 9 feet, 7 inches, was fitted with pneumatic tires and had a water-cooled, 4-cylinder Buda engine. Only prototypes of the Mackbilt were ever produced, in a small factory in the Bronx. *GMN*

MADSEN (US) 1948-1973

(1) Jay Madsen Equipment Co., Inc., Bath, N.Y. 1948-1971
(2) Jay Madsen Division, Air Springs Inc., Allentown, N.Y. 1971-1973

1968 MADSEN with school bus body by Carpenter, EK

Madsen offered a wide range of custom-built chassis, mainly buses, though fire engine and refuse disposal chassis were also made. They were built to order, so a considerable choice of engine and other components was available. Bus chassis were mostly 2-axle models with front or rear-located engines, though several 3-axle chassis with mid- or rear-mounted engines were available. Engines were Ford, Hall-Scott, International or White gasoline, and Cummins, Detroit or Waukesha diesels. One of the last Madsen designs was a refuse truck with two cabs on either side of the Ford V-8 engine, the front of the cabs being over 7 feet ahead of the front axle. *GNG*

MAFFEI (D) 1928-1931

J.A.Maffei A.G., Munich

This firm developed a road tractor following the designs of Chenard-Walcker. A 4-cylinder 60 PS Deutz engine of 4.7 litre was installed. In 1931 the design was taken over by a new firm Krauss-Maffei and continued to be marketed under this name. *HON*

MAGIRUS; MAGIRUS-DEUTZ (D) 1903 to date

(1) C.D. Magirus, Ulm 1903-1911
(2) C.D. Magirus A.G., Ulm 1911-1938
(3) Klockner-Humboldt-Deutz A.G., Ulm; Mainz 1938-1974
(4) Magirus-Deutz A.G., Ulm; Mainz 1974 to date

Magirus was a specialist firm producing fire fighting equipment. In 1903 they introduced steam drive for the fire engines, later experimented with gas-electric drive before they turned to gasoline in about 1906. In 1914, the first time in Germany, Magirus built a fire escape ladder with the ladder operated by the driving engine. In addition to all kinds of fire fighting vehicles, Magirus took up production of trucks in 1916, the first model being a 3-tonner with 40 hp engine. Buses followed in 1919 using the same engine and featuring shaft drive. Since 1925 pneumatic tires have been used. The basic type was a 2-3 ton chassis which had a 4-cylinder 4.7 litre engine. A low frame bus came in 1927 and for this a 6-cylinder 7-litre Maybach engine was used which was succeeded in 1930 by a V-12 Maybach engine developing 100 hp. Fire fighting vehicles had own engines of 10.3 litres capacity. In the early thirties the range consisted of 2, 2½, and 4 ton trucks with 60 to 70 hp 6-cylinder engines and various bus versions in addition to a complete range of fire fighting vehicles. In 1931 the highest fire escape ladder in the world of that time with a height of about 147 ft. was presented. A 1-ton forward control truck appeared in 1933 using an air-cooled 2-cylinder two-stroke Jlo engine of 670 cc.

In 1933 Magirus introduced the first diesel engines for their vehicles. They were of their own design and had 7.5 litre capacity. Later also a 6 × 6 diesel truck and a 3-ton 4 × 2 or 4 × 4 truck with diesel engine were built for the

1936 MAGIRUS-DEUTZ streamlined diesel bus, FLP

army. In 1936 the first forward control truck and bus were presented; an opposed 12-cylinder diesel engine of 150 hp was placed under the driver's seat. In the same year Deutz took an interest in Magirus vehicles. Two years later this led to a total takeover.

The first air-cooled diesel engines were built in 1943 and these were used for all subsequent models. In 1946 a 3 ton truck appeared which was also the basis for a bus. A new front with a typical rounded hood was introduced in 1951 and was applied to trucks, buses, municipal and fire fighting vehicles. Only the 4 × 4 versions retained the square hood. Air-cooled diesel engines of 4 or 6 cylinders in line or V-6 or V-8 engines were available. A specialty was a three-wheeled street sweeper. A new forward-control bus was added to the program also in 1951, the type 0 3500 H. The engine was mounted in the rear and was a 6-cylinder with a 8 litre capacity developing 130 hp. In 1956 production of buses was passed to the Mainz works. One year later the first fully air-sprung bus was presented, the "Saturn II". Since 1956 normal control was well as forward control was available for nearly all trucks. The type designations were taken from astronomy, being Sirius, Mercur, Saturn, Jupiter and Pluto. These were

c.1956 MAGIRUS-DEUTZ Sirius 4-ton truck, GNG

1956 MAGIRUS-DEUTZ tractor with drawbar trailer, GNG

abandoned in 1964 in favor of numerical designations. Payload capacities ranged from 4 to 11 tons and engines from 4-cylinder in line 5.3 litre to V-8 12.6 litre.

The Eicher truck was taken into the Magirus program in 1967 as the lightest version with a 3½ ton payload capacity; production was carried on by Eicher. Other types at this time were 6-, 8- and 10-cylinder types with 5.1 litre to 14.6 litre capacity and developing 100 to 250 hp. Normal control as well as forward control was still available and 4 × 2, 4 × 2, 6 × 4 and 6 × 6 drive was featured. A standard city bus following the VOV standards (VOV = Association of Public Transport Enterprises) also were presented. The 150 hp engine was mounted in the rear or amidships. Experiments with gas turbines capable of 250 — 450 hp were started in 1968.

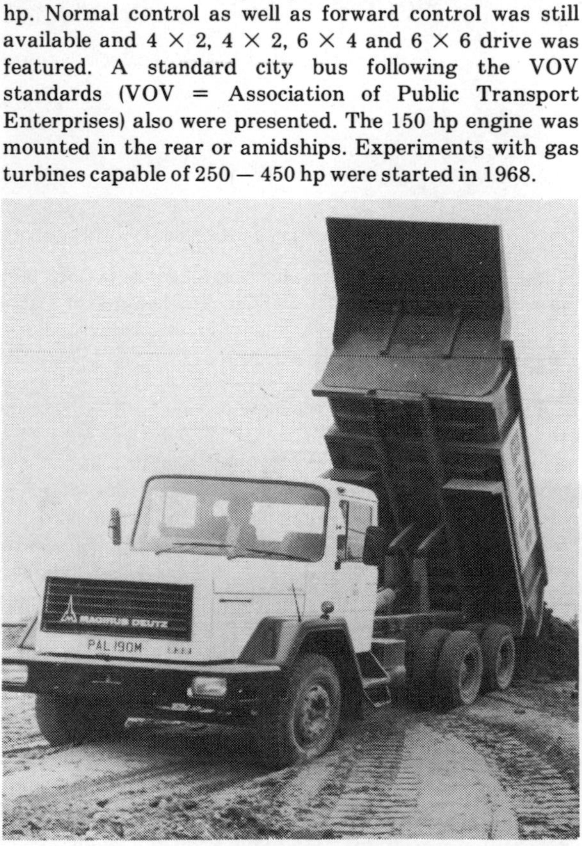

1974 MAGIRUS-DEUTZ 23D 6×4 tipper, Magirus-Deutz

1974 MAGIRUS-DEUTZ 232D 30FK 8×4 tipper, Magirus Deutz

In 1971 Magirus entered into co-operation with Volvo, Saviem and D.A.F. forming the E.T.D. (European Truck Design), the so-called "Club of Four". This co-operation developed new standardized versions in the 3½ to 8½ tons range which are independently built by each partner, Magirus versions being the only ones to use the air-cooled Deutz engines. Available in 87, 130 and 160 hp sizes. These versions appeared in 1975. The further Magirus program consists of forward and normal control versions up to 22 tons payload capacity. The engines range from 4-cylinder 4.1 litre 92 hp to 10-cylinder 14.7 litre 340 hp. In 1975 Magirus pooled their interests with Fiat's commercial range (Fiat, OM, Lancia, Unic) forming the IVECO (Industrial Vehicles Corporation). The first practical result for Magirus was the incorporation of the Fiat NC trucks in their program covering the payload capacities 2¼ to 4½ tons. These vehicles are equipped with the 4-cylinder air-cooled Magirus-Deutz 4.1 litre diesel engines developing 92 hp. Moreover Magirus has its extensive program of municipal vehicles. With their fire-fighting vehicles they have 38% market share in Europe, being the largest manufacturer. Buses are available following the standard principle for city and inter-city traffic and for normal line and tourist service, seven different versions at all. *HON*

MAGIRUS DEUTZ (ii) (GR) 1973

VELO S.A., Athens

In order to meet a specific requirement for a front-engined city bus-chassis demanded by Thessaloniki Bus Undertaking, the Greek representatives of Magirus Deutz modified a rear engined Magirus Deutz chassis fitting the air cooled V8 engine in the front of the chassis. An attractive looking 12m city bus body with a capacity of 100 passengers was built by the Velo body building company on a batch of chassis that have been in regular use in Thessaloniki since 1973. *GA*

MAGISTRAL (B) 1938-1940

Magistral was one of the numerous less important Belgian makes manufactured during the 'thirties. They used Hercules gasoline and oil engines in a range of truck and bus chassis from 3.5 to 5.5 tons payload. Most important feature of these chassis was their light construction, though this went obviously at the cost of quality: Magistral vehicles never were very renowned for their ruggedness. *JFJK*

MAIS (US) 1911-1916

(1) Mais Motor Truck Co., Peru, Ind.
(2) Mais Motor Truck Co., Indianapolis, Ind.

The Mais truck was first made as a single model for

3000 to 4000 lb. loads, powered by a 24 hp 4-cylinder engine mounted under a short hood, with 3-speed transmission and internal gear drive. It was said to be the first US truck to employ this principle. By 1912 the range had been extended to include trucks of 1½-, 2½- and 5-tons capacity, and further models from 1000 lbs. to 3 tons capacity were made up to 1916 when the company was acquired by the Premier Motor Manufacturing Company, also of Indianapolis. *GNG*

MAJA (D) 1923-1924
Maja-Werk fur Motor-Vierrad-Bau AG., Munich

This was a small van with opposed-twin-cylinder 500cc B.M.W. engine. *HON*

MAJESTIC CAB see Larrabee-Deyo

MAKO (D) 1926
Norddeutsche Waggonfabrik A.G., Bremen

A 1-ton truck with 4-cylinder engine and shaft drive was manufactured by this carriage builder. Production was on a small scale only. *HON*

MALEVEZ see Lifu

MALTBY (GB) 1905-1922
Maltby's Motor Works, Sandgate, Kent

John Maltby's company was originally a coachbuilders, but early in the twentieth century they acquired the agency for a number of cars including M.M.C. Walter Iden was chief engineer of the latter company at the time and this connection was cemented when, in 1904/5, Maltby's commenced building charabancs under their own name. These utilized Coronet engines and gearboxes from Iden's own factory at Foleshill, Coventry, and a number were built for local operators in the Hythe, Sandgate and Sandwich area. Production was always sporadic and catered for a local market only, but by 1911 'toast rack' charabancs with worm drive and solid tires and fitted with 40 hp White and Poppe engines had replaced the earlier types. A number of these were absorbed into the East Kent Road Car Company's fleet as a result of post-war takeovers of smaller operators, but litte change in specification had taken place in the meantime. The company concentrated increasingly upon specialized coachwork for private cars and it is doubtful whether an order for 200 White and Poppe-engined trucks for the Indian Government was ever completed. The company was eventually absorbed by Caffyns Ltd. *MJWW*

MAMMUT (D) 1928-1929
Mammut-Werke A.G., Nuremberg

The tri-van of this manufacturer followed motorcycle lines with a single front wheel. Own engines of 200cc, 250cc and 300cc were used. *HON*

1912 MALTBY charabanc, MJWW

M.A.N. (D) 1915 to date

(1) KG Lastwagen-Werke MAN-Saurer, Lindau 1915-1916
(2) Kraftwagenwerke MAN-Saurer GmbH., Lindau; Nurnberg 1916-1918
(3) Maschinenfabrik Augsburg-Nurnberg AG., Nurnberg; Munchen; Penzberg; Salzgitter-Watenstedt 1920 to date

M.A.N. (Maschinenfabrik Augsburg-Nurnberg) has its place in the history of engineering and of the motor car in building the first diesel engine in co-operation with its inventor Rudolf Diesel. This was in 1897 and naturally this was a stationary engine. Only in 1915 M.A.N. took up production of commercial motor cars, but used conventional gasoline engines. These were produced under a Saurer license in the former branch factory of Saurer at Lindau on Lake Constance. This factory was taken over by M.A.N.

1916 M.A.N. log hauling truck, MAN

The first truck was a 4-tonner with 36 hp engine and chain drive. In 1920 a new program was presented. Three engines of 30, 37 and 45 bhp were available and all types were obtainable with cardan or chain drive. These types were used as trucks, municipal and fire fighting vehicles and buses. In 1924 M.A.N. presented their first diesel engined truck at the Berlin Show. The engine was a 4-cylinder of the injection type developing 45 hp. A 3-axle chassis with two driven rear axles was presented in 1926. This had a 6-cylinder 150 bhp gas engine but one year later M.A.N. also had available a 6-cylinder diesel engine developing 100 bhp. Along with this a 5-ton low-frame chassis with 6-cylinder 80 bhp diesel engine for buses appeared and a 4-cylinder 53 bhp diesel engine especially intended for municipal vehicles. In 1931 the program consisted of a 5-ton truck available with 80, 100 or 120 bhp gasoline engines or the 120 bhp diesel. A 3-axle chassis had the 120 bhp gasoline engine and was used for trucks and buses and also for trolley buses which had their debut that year. As the most powerful diesel engine for road vehicles a 16.6 litre unit developing 140 bhp was

1932 M.A.N. S1H6 150hp diesel truck, MAN

presented in 1932 and was installed in the 3-axle chassis. Later the 3 tonner truck only had the 4-cylinder engine, while the 3½ 4, 5, 6 and 8-tonners had 6-cylinder diesel engines with capacities ranging from 6.7 to 13.3 litres. The 3-ton type was delivered to the army as lorry or bus in large numbers as well as the 4½ tonner with 4x2 or 4x4

1938 M.A.N. 32-seater bus, FLP

drive and the 2½-ton standard truck with 6x6. In 1938 M.A.N. took over Austro-Fiat and re-named it "Oesterreichische Automobil-Fabrik (OeAF)".

After WW II M.A.N. re-started production in 1945 with a 5-tonner with 110 bhp diesel engine under the type designation MK. This developed into the 120 bhp MK 25 — also a 5-tonner — which under the type designation MKN was also available as a bus. The MK 26 was a 6½ tonner, also built as an articulated tractor. 1951 saw the unitary bus with forward control body and rear mounted engine. It was the MKH 2. And in the same year the first turbocharged diesel engine was built. This was used for some of the heavier types of trucks. The world's first V-8 diesel engine was built by M.A.N. also in 1951 and was used for the type F 8 truck. Another first for Germany was an all-fuel engine of 1955; this was subsequently used for various types, such as the 4-ton 4x4 630 with 6-cylinder 130 bhp engine.

The production of commmercials was transferred from Nuremberg to Munich in 1957 where M.A.N. had acquired ground from B.M.W. and built a new factory. Also in this year the first bus with underfloor engine was presented.

1960 M.A.N. Model 415 8-ton truck, GNG

By 1960 M.A.N. offered a wide range of trucks with normal and forward control covering payload capacities from 5 to 10 tons and with 4x2 or 4x4 drive. Buses were built in co-operation with Krauss-Maffei and both badges appeared on these versions. In 1961 also two three-axle models became available and payload capacity was uprated to 17 tons. A new presentation of 1963 was the HM combustion system using a faster air swirl and giving more power at slightly reduced peak pressures.

In 1967 co-operation began with Saviem to cover the lighter range also, and 1¾ and 3½ ton Saviem versions became part of the M.A.N. program appearing under their

1974 M.A.N. Model 32-232 DHK 6×6 dump truck, MAN

marque. In the same year another new factory took up production, this was at Penzberg and here the production of buses was concentrated. Touring and line service buses had rear-mounted 160 bhp engines, while the articulated buses were equipped with 192 bhp underfloor engines. A new-long-distance truck was equipped with a new V-8-cylinder engine of 15 litres and 275 or 300 bhp. Development of a gas turbine capable of 350 bhp was started in 1969. This year also the first standard city bus was presented which was supplemented one year later by a standard articulated bus. Co-operation with Bussing was started also in 1969 which led to some standardization and a total takeover of Bussing by M.A.N. in 1971. Since then the Bussing lion marque appears together with the letters M.A.N. on all vehicles. The Bussing plant at Salzgitter is retained and produces mainly buses.

M.A.N. is also active in experimenting with new means of propulsion. An electric bus with batteries stored in a single-axle trailer is on test in some German cities. Experiments are being made with liquid natural gas.

1976 M.A.N. Model 19.330FT 32-ton GCW tanker, MAN

1977 M.A.N. 8×8 10-ton army truck, MAN

The present program of M.A.N. covers trucks with payload capacities ranging from 1 to 24½ tons. In most categories normal as well as forward control versions are available as trucks, tippers, articulated tractors and dump trucks. Engine outputs range from 70 to 320 bhp. Moreover there are refuse collectors and other municipal vehicles as well as fire fighting vehicles. Three versions of touring coaches form the bus program together with a standard city bus and a standard articulated bus with underfloor engine placed amidships and — as the only producer in Germany — a standard double-deck bus. M.A.N. has collaborated with several German manufacturers in building a range of 4x4, 6x6 and 8x8 army trucks. Several models of M.A.N. trucks are made in Rumania under the name Roman. *HON*

1902 MANCHESTER (i) steam wagon, NMM

MANCHESTER (i) (GB) 1905

Turner, Atherton & Co. Ltd., Denton, Manchester

The Manchester was the name selected for the attempted marketing of the strange steam wagon designed by Dr. Brightmore in which a boiler and engine were mounted upon a two wheeled forecarriage intended to replace the forecarriage of a common four-wheeled dray, thus converting it to steam propulsion. A Manchester was shown at the 1905 show at the Agricultural Hall, Islington, London but it is doubtful if it was used commercially. *RAW*

MANCHESTER (ii) see Overland (ii)

1975 MANCHESTER GNU 3-wheel truck, Nigel Engineering

MANCHESTER GNU (GB) 1973-1975

Nigel Engineering Co. Ltd., Swinton, Manchester

The Manchester Gnu was a 3-wheeled truck with a load capacity of 1 ton, which could be increased by the attachment of a 2-wheeled trailer. The engine was either a Ford Escort 1300 or Cortina 1600, while gearbox, prop shaft and rear axle were also of Ford manufacture. Truck, van or 3-way tipper bodies could be fitted, while the use of wide-section tires enabled grassland to be crossed without damage to the turf. *GNG*

MANDERBACH (D) 1929-1954

Louis Manderbach & Co., Wissenbach

The first van version of this manufacturer was very loosely related to motorcycle lines, although this firm did not produce motorcycles themselves. There were two front wheels and one driven rear wheel. One year later there was one front wheel, cabin and rear platform or box. Both versions used D.K.W. engines. The later version was built in improved form until about 1937. After WW II a 4-wheeled van was built for and later 1-ton payload capacity. For these the 1.2 litre 34 PS Ford engine was used. *HON*

MANHATTAN see Mack (i)

MANLY (US) 1917-1920

(1) Manly Motor Corporation, Waukegan, Ill. 1917
(2) O'Connell Manly Motor Corporation, Waukegan, Ill. 1918
(3) O'Connell Motor Truck Corporation, Waukegan, Ill. 1919-1920

Three models, designated 30, 40 and 50 respectively were offered in all of the years. These had ratings of 1½, 2 and 2½ tons, respectively. These all had four-cylinder Waukesha engines under frontal hoods. The 2½-tonner used a four-speed gearbox and all had worm-drive rear axles. *GMN*

MANN (i) (GB) 1897-1928

(1) Mann & Charlesworth, Hunslet, Leeds, Yorks 1897-1900
(2) Mann's Patent Steam Cart & Wagon Co. Ltd., Hunslet, Leeds, Yorks 1900-1928

Mann & Charlesworth began building agricultural traction engines in the early nineties and in 1897 launched their steam cart, based upon the patent of P.J. Parmiter in which a small overtype compound steam tractor with a side fired locomotive boiler carried a large transport box pivotted directly onto the rear axle which was gear driven. Early examples, intended for agricultural use had a single broad rear wheel — in effect a driven roller — but this was soon supplanted by a pair of wheels. Carts of this basic design continued to be made until after the 1914/18 war.

1902 MANN (i) Patent Steam Cart, GNG

In 1898 an amended version with longer wheelbase was launched for industrial use in which, by extending the hornplates well to the rear and the introduction of cross members a much longer wheelbase was obtained, the engine being mounted under the body so as to retain the gear drive. The body, similar to a "Lancashire flat", was demountable and had its own wheels on stubs, which straddled the main rear axle so that the wheels of the body and the basic machine could be locked together, when necessary, by locking pins passing through both.

From this design a series of plate-framed undertype wagons of load capacities varying from 4 tons to 6/7 tons in the Colonial wagon, was developed and remained, nominally, in production until about 1911. After the amended Heavy Motor Car regulations of 1904 came into force a second class of undertype wagon was developed in which a steel-channel main frame was employed, with the engine and gear assembly in a plate sub-frame, pivotted at one end on the rear axle and at the front end on a central hanger suspended from a chassis cross member. In practice the new design superseded the earlier plate frame wagons and the range was extended to include 2 and 3 tonners, some of the 2 tonners being fitted up with a self feed firing system from an overhead hopper.

1912 MANN 5-ton overtype steam wagon, RAW

In 1909 Manns began to build a 5 ton overtype wagon, retaining the side-fired locomotive boiler and compound engine but with Stephenson's link motion instead of the firm's patent single eccentric valve gear used in the carts. Gears giving initially 2, and subsequently 3, speeds were placed between hornplates and behind the boiler, final drive being by roller chain to a rear axle differential. Earlier examples had steel tires, but solid rubbers on wooden artillery centers or cast steel wheels increased in popularity after a few years. In 1910 a 3 tonner, basically similar to but different in detail from the 5 tonner, was launched and from this a 4 tonner was developed (c.1915). By the end of the 1914/18 war the 5 tonner was very dated but the revised overtype design, a 6 tonner, first sold in 1921 did little to remedy the situation and sales began to fall off.

1924 MANN 6-ton overtype tar spreader, RAW

In a last attempt to retain a useful share of the market the firm launched their "Express" vertical boilered undertype in 1924, embodying a cross water tube boiler with superheater, undertype double cylinder, double acting engine, 2-speed enclosed gearbox and cardan shaft drive. For the first time Ackermann steering was used in place of the rack and pinion used on the overtypes but the new wagon, a very sturdy and reliable machine, was too late to retrieve the fortunes of the firm. In 1926 a receiver was appointed and in 1928 it went into liquidation. All the

Mann registers are destroyed and it is difficult to estimate the number made but perhaps a thousand would be a fair indication. Many Aitken type tar sprayers were built on Mann chassis and examples of that type worked in Scotland until the early nineteen fifties. *RAW*

MANN (ii) (GB) 1907-1908

G.H. Mann, Holbeck, Leeds, Yorks

In 1907/8 G. H. Mann made, at his own small works, a vertical-boilered undertype steam wagonette with a fire tube boiler, in which all tubes were fully submerged, designed to burn creosote. The arrangement of engine, gear and final drive was that which he used some twelve years later in his design of the Brotherhood wagon and is described under that marque. It is thought that only one wagon of this design was built. *RAW*

MANTON see Rutland

1914 MANNESMANN-MULAG 3-ton truck, NMM

MANNESMANN-MULAG (D) 1913-1928

Mannesmann-Mulag Motoren- und Lastwagen A.G., Aachen

This firm continued the production of Mulag trucks. The monthly output before WW I was about 80-100 vehicles. They specialized in the heavier type of trucks ranging from 3½ to 5 tons payload capacity. Also buses were available. From 1921 cardan drive was featured. In 1928 a 6x4 all-terrain vehicle was presented which had 2-ton payload capacity. But in the same year production was given up. The factory was taken over by Bussing. *HON*

MANULECTRIC (GB) 1948-c.1969

(1) Sidney Hole's Electric Vehicles, Brighton, Sussex.
(2) The Stanley Engineering Co. Ltd., Egham, Surrey.
(3) The Stanley Engineering Co. Ltd., Exeter, Devon.

The first models were the No. 1 pram, a 10 cwt capacity pedestrian controlled truck, the No. 2 pram of 17 cwt size and the No. 3 pram rated at 21 cwt. These were all 3-wheeled.

In 1953 model No. 4 was introduced, being a 4-wheeled pram of 1 ton capacity and 4 ft. wheelbase. The first rider type was introduced in 1954 being a 1 ton vehicle called the "Standon." It had a wheelbase of 6 ft., single motor drive, 126AH battery and was a rather narrow chassis in order to take a body only 4 ft wide. This was for operation in narrow streets by drivers normally used to pedestrian controlled models. Toward the end of the 1950's the "Mobile" was added to the range, being a 25 cwt chassis of 5 ft. 9 in. wheelbase with bevel final drive. In 1961 the larger capacity Model 7 was introduced with 30-cwt

1964 MANULECTRIC 1-ton milk float, GNG

payload on a 6 ft. 6 in. wheelbase chassis, and in the following year the only pram was the Model 4, the other trucks all being of rider type.

Toward the end of production there were 5 rider models listed, all being in the 1 ton to 30 cwt bracket and this state of affairs lasted until the end of the 1960's. *OM*

MAPLELEAF (i) (CDN) 1919-1922

Mapleleaf Mfg. Co. Ltd., Montreal, Que.

An assembled vehicle for loads from 1½ to 5 tons with a heavy ribbed radiator, the Mapleleaf was basically the Menard transplanted to Montreal. It had special rims for use in snow. *HD*

MAPLE LEAF (ii) (CDN) 1930-c.1948

General Motors of Canada Ltd., Oshawa, Ont.

The Maple Leaf was basically a heavy-duty Chevrolet truck similar in appearance to the Chevrolet and using its engine, except in larger, late model units which used a G.M.C. engine. *HD*

MARATHON (i) (US) 1912-1913

Marathon Motor Works, Nashville, Tennessee

Marathon commercial chassis were ¼-, 1½-, 3- and 5-tonners. The three larger trucks had four-cylinder engines with forward control and worm-drive rear axles. The ¼-tonner, a delivery van had the same four-cylinder engine as was used in the Model M passenger auto by the same tradename. *GMN*

MARATHON (ii) (GB) 1920-1925

James Walmsley & Co. Ltd., Preston, Lancs.

This was a conventional 30 cwt chassis powered by a 4-cylinder Dorman MR engine, with 4-speed gearbox and David Brown worm rear axle. The chassis price was £500, and apart from an increase in wheelbase in 1921 the Marathon was made without change throughout its six years' life. *GNG*

MARATON (E) 1936-1939

General Motors Peninsular, Empresa Collectivizada, Barcelona.

General Motors set up their first Spanish branch at Malaga in 1925, moving to Madrid in 1927 and to Barcelona in 1932. Here they assembled Chevrolet, Bedford and Opel trucks, and during the Civil War the factory was taken over by a workers' collective who built vehicles of General Motors type under the name Maraton. They had 86 hp 6cylinder engines and were for loads of up to 4 tons, or as buses. Almost all went for troop carrying or for government work for the anti-Franco General Council of Aragon. Production ceased at the end of the war. *JCG*

MARMON (i) (US) 1912-1915

Nordyke & Marmon Manufacturing Co., Indianapolis, Ind.

This well-known passenger car make also appeared as a ¼-tonner delivery van. Wheelbase was 10 feet although loading area was only 2 feet, 10 inches by 4 feet, 4 inches. This was powered by a four-cylinder, T-head engine connected with a three-speed gearbox and shaft drive. Maximum speed was 20 mph. Price of this delivery van was $2500. *GMN*

MARMON (ii) (US) 1963 to date

Marmon Motor Co. Denton, Texas 1963
Marmon Motor Co. Garland and Dallas, Texas 1964 to date.

Certain assets of the Marmon-Herrington Co. were sold to Mr. Adrian Roop who then changed the name to Marmon Motor Company and acquired the Marmon name for domestic use on trucks produced for sale only in North America.

1975 MARMON HDT-BC-86 6×4 tractor, Marmon

Marmon produces custom-built light-weight heavy duty road tractors in both conventional and cab-over versions in which the standard model specifications are identical in components. The frame is of completely bolted construction with 10-inch heat treated alloy steel channels with steel crossmembers and gussets.

Basic drive train consists of a Cummins NTC 350 or Caterpillar diesel engines, Spicer 14-inch 2-plate clutch, 13-speed Fuller Roadranger transmission with overdrive, and Rockwell-Standard single reduction tandem axle with a 38000-pound capacity.

Front suspension is 12000-pound Marmon spring, and rear is Reyco 101 4-spring, 36000-pound capacity. Tires are 10.00 x 20 12-ply nylon. Two 75-gallon aluminum fuel tanks are provided. The radiator's area is 1200 sq. in., big enough to accommodate the larger engines yet to come.

To make Marmons lightweight, liberal use is made of aluminum and fiberglass, notably in the cab, which is aluminum with fiberglass inserts, and the hood on the conventional which is a single full width tilt of fiberglass. The cab-over series features a 90 degree full-tilt cab for servicing the engine. A wide variety of major components and other options are available on order.

Sleeping compartments are available — behind the conventional cab, or within the cab-over with a longer cab. Both are lined with padded naugahyde as well as the driver's compartment.

Production averaged almost 100 trucks per year until the Interstate Corporation of Chattanooga, Tenn. purchased the company from The Space Corporation in April , 1973. The new management made some styling changes for 1974 and accelerated yearly production to 700 units for nationwide distribution to owner-operators. *RW*

MARMON-BOCQUET (F) 1964 to date

S.A. Marmon-Bocquet, Villiers-le-Bel

This company is the continuation of the French Marmon-Herrington concern and developed a version of the Marmon-Herrington MH600 known as the MH600BS. This is a 1½-ton 4 × 4 truck mainly intended for military use and manufactured by the Unic division of Simca In-

1964 MARMON-BOCQUET HH600BS 4×4 army truck, BHV

dustries. More specialized military vehicles such as armored cars are also made, based on the MH600BS. Alternative names for Marmon-Bocquets are S.U.M.B. (Simca-Unic-Marmon-Bocquet) or more simply Simca-Marmon. *GNG*

MARMON-HERRINGTON (i) (US) 1931-1963; 1973

(1) Marmon-Herrington Inc., Indianapolis, Ind. 1931-1963
(2) Marmon Trasmotive, division Marmon Group, Knoxville, Tenn. 1973

This company was formed by Walter C. Marmon and Arthur W. Herrington to develop all-wheel-drive trucks, initially for military purposes. Production began in March 1931 when the company received an order for 33 T-1 4 x 4 aircraft refuelling trucks powered by 6-cylinder Hercules engines. These were followed by a variety of 4 x 4 and 6 x 6 vehicles for the US and Persian armies used as general load carriers, mobile machine shops, wreckers and balloon winch trucks. Reconaissance, scout and armored cars were also made, some with 4-wheel-steering as well as 4-wheel-drive.

1932 MARMON-HERRINGTON DSD-800-6 6×6 tractor with desert bus trailer, Marmon

In 1932 Marmon-Herrington built the first all-wheel-drive truck and trailer combination for oil pipe construction in Iraq. Also in 1932 there was a very special project, a 40-passenger articulated coach ordered by the Nairn Brothers for the Damascus to Baghdad desert run. The 6 x 6 tractor was powered by a 90 hp 6-cylinder diesel engine and fitted with a sleeper cab. This was coupled to a luxurious tandem-axle coach 66 feet long, the combination weight being 30 tons. Air springs were added to the tractor's front semi-elliptic springs. This freighter-bus was still in service during World War II, now operated by the Royal Air Force.

More important than the complete trucks that Marmon-Herrington buit was their work on the conversion of light vehicles to 4-wheel-drive. They began with a 1936 Ford V-8 ½-ton open cab pick-up which was supplied in some numbers to the US and Belgian armies, and followed this with a variety of Ford conversions, 6 x 6 as well as 4 x 4, for use as military squad cars, fire trucks, mortar carriers, machine gun trucks, earth boring machines, ambulances, bomb carriers and others. Cabs were either full-enclosed originals or completely open without doors or even a windshield. Civilian conversions were also made on Ford V-8 cars and trucks, and sold with the Marmon-Herrington nameplate. In 1937 a ½-ton Ford was completely reworked with semi-forward control and a canvas-top cab for use as a US Army ambulance. Another important development was the conversion of a Ford 1½-tonner into a half-track with powered front axle, the first time this layout had been seen. Most of Marmon-Herrington's conversions were on Fords, but some Dodge, Chevrolet, GMC and International trucks received the treatment, all carrying M-H nameplates. Civilian production was always less important than military, but a range of Ford- and Hercules-powered trucks were offered during the 1930s, in sizes from 1½- to 20 tons. A number of these were used in road-building projects. During World War II Marmon-Herrington built 4 x 4 cab-overs to Autocar design, and 4 x 2 short slope-nosed tractors to International design, as well as 8-wheeled armored cars, half-tracks and snowplows.

1937 MARMON-HERRINGTON ½-ton 4×4 ambulance chassis, BHV

In 1945 Marmon-Herrington branched out into two completely new fields, those of multi-stop delivery vans, and passenger vehicles. The vans had forward control and front-wheel-drive, and were known as Delivr-Alls. They were made in two wheelbase lengths, and the engine was removable as a unit together with the front frame section, drive train and steering wheel. The Delivr-All was in production from late 1945 to 1952. Trolleybus production began when Charles O Guernsey, midwest sales manager of ACF-Brill, persuaded Marmon-Herrington that there was a substantial market for lightweight trolleybuses which Brill were no longer producing. About 1,500 trolleybuses were built by M-H between 1946 and 1955, and virtually every US transit system that operated such vehicles bought some of them. The largest fleet was operated in Chicago, whose transit system purchased 349 in a single order in 1950. In April 1950 M-H got into the lightweight motor bus business by taking over production and sale of the 27- and 31-passenger transit buses formerly offered by Ford. Both these and the trolleybuses became unprofitable by the mid 1950s, and the company

1941 MARMON-HERRINGTON 7½-ton 6×6 army truck, Marmon

1946 MARMON-HERRINGTON TC-44 trolleybus, MBS

turned to the manufacture of mining machinery, although they continued to make some all-wheel-drive conversions, and in 1959 made a final batch of trolleybuses for Brazil. For 1961 they listed three school bus chassis, powered by Ford V-8 engines, and in the same year they won a contract to re-engine almost 1,000 Greyhound Scenicruisers with Detroit Diesel 8V-71 engines. This was their last major piece of automotive work, and in 1963 Colonel Herrington's 25% of stock was acquired by the Fritzker family of Chicago who later acquired most of the rest, and converted the company into a private holding company for a diverse group of enterprises. These included the all-wheel-drive conversions on a variety of chassis, but the highway tractor which M-H were working on was sold to their Southwest distributor who put it into production under the name Marmon. In 1973 Marmon-Herrington's Knoxville, Tennessee plant built a single one-man cab Ford-powered 4 x 4 construction truck. *RW/MBS*

MARMON-HERRINGTON (ii) (F) 1957-1963

Marmon-Herrington S.A.F., Villiers-le-Bel

The French Marmon-Herrington company followed the pattern of their American parent in making 4-wheel-drive conversions of Ford trucks, but they also made a number of vehicles of more individual design, especially for the French army, although they were sold on the civilian market as well. They were the MS600B and MG600BP 1½-ton forward-control 4 x 4 trucks powered by Simca V-8 or 4-cylinder 2-litre Panhard engines respectively, and the FF6 normal-control 6 x 6 powered by Simca V-8 or Perkins P6 diesel engines. After the demise of the American Marmon-Herrington company the name was changed to Marmon-Bocquet after the president of the French company. *GNG*

MARPLES (GB) 1907

This was a taxicab designed by Stephen A. Marples for the London Improved Taxicab Company who at the time owned 500 horse cabs. It had a 12 hp vertical-twin engine mounted partly under a hood and partly under the floorboards. The body was a coventional four-seater landaulette. *GNG*

MARQUETTE (US) 1910-1912

Marquette Motor Vehicle Company, Chicago, Illinois

Under this name were built seven different body types on a single chassis model. This chassis had a wheelbase of 8 feet and used an opposed two-cylinder engine, planetary transmission and double chain-drive, with solid tires. Body types ranged from an open stake body to a twelve-seater bus. *GMN*

MARS (D) 1906-1908

Mars-Werke A.G., Nuremberg

The private cars with single-cylinder 6/7 hp and 2-cylinder 8/10 hp engines were available also as vans. Both models featured friction drive on Maurer principles. *HON*

1907 MARSHALL road locomotive, RAW

MARSHALL (GB) 1895-1925

Marshall Sons & Co. Ltd., Gainsborough, Lincs.

Agricultural traction engines and steam rollers far outweighed other Marshall self-propelled steam engines in importance to their makers but, nevertheless, from 1895 onwards Marshalls offered a more developed range of compound and single-cylinder traction engines, with springs, belly tanks, motion covers, plated flywheels and more generous journal areas designed with road haulage in mind. They were not, however, despite catalogue descriptions, road locomotives in the same sense as a Burrell, Foden, Fowler or (later) Foster. Early springing on Marshall driving axles was by a pair of heavy helical springs but this was subsequently amended to use a single transverse laminated spring.

In common with most traction engine builders Marshalls designed a compound spring mounted road tractor to comply with the 1904 Heavy Motor Car Regulations. Though neat and well made machines these tractors never achieved great popularity. During the early 1920's the makers made a determined effort to sell these tractors as convertibles (i.e. with conversion parts to turn them into road rollers when required) but this in common with all other attempts to market "conventional" steam tractors expired by about 1925, which date has been taken as the effective end of Marshall participation in commercial vehicle manufacture within the definitions of this book.

The firm never marketed a steam wagon though designs for one were rumored to have been made during the period of the 1914-18 war. *RAW*

1913 MARTA 3-ton truck, Haris Auto Muzeum

MARTA (H) 1909-1918

Magyar Automobil R.T., Arad

Marta built light trucks and buses under license agreement with the French firm of Westinghouse and their vehicles were conventional in design, but high quality in construction and were powered by 4-cylinder gas engines and chain drive. In 1913 Marta entered into an agreement with Austro-Daimler and started producing T16 model taxicabs, the very first to be used in Budapest. A total production of 187 taxis, 100 trucks and 60 buses was recorded until 1918, when the city of Arad was transferred to Romania. Marta's facilities were used in post WWII years by the S.R. factory, when the city of Arad was renamed Brasov. *GA*

MARTIN & CAMPBELL (GB) 1926

Martin & Campbell Ltd., Perivale, London W.13

This was a 4 cwt 3-wheeled van on solid tires driven through the single front wheel. It was exhibited without an engine at the 1926 Motor Cycle Show, and it is not certain if it ever went into production. *GNG*

MARTIN (i) (US) 1909-1915

Martin Carriage Works, York, Pa.

The Martin was initially a high-wheeler of 1000-pound capacity with a 16 hp 2-cylinder engine, planetary transmission, and chain drive. The chassis, with magneto ignition, cost $1,500. The truck was designed by Edward C. Kraft, formerly of Hart-Kraft. A line of 4-cylinder trucks of c.o.e. design was announced in 1911; four models from 1½ to 6-ton capacity were built. These models had 29 hp or 36 hp Wisconsin engines, disc clutch, and 3-speed transmission. In 1913 the 2½-ton model cost $2,750 and the 3½-ton model cost $3,500. The 2-cylinder models were last built in 1913 and the 4-cylinder Martin truck was discontinued at the end of the 1915 season and replaced with the Atlas. *DJS*

MARTIN (ii) (GB) 1925-1926

Martin Cultivator Co. Ltd., Stamford, Lincs.

This company made agricultural tractors and trailer fire pumps for a number of years, and also a short-lived complete fire engine, powered by a 4-cylinder Dorman engine. It had a 4-speed Martin gearbox and 250/300 gpm pump. *GNG*

MARTINI (CH) 1901-1933

(1) F. Martini & Co., Frauenfeld, TG 1901-1903
(2) F. Martini & Cie, St. Blaise, NE 1903-1906
(3) Martini Automobiles Co. Ltd., St. Blaise, NE 1906-1908
4) Ste. Nouvelle des Automobiles Martini, St. Blaise, NE 1908-1933

Martini had built passenger cars from 1897, and in 1901 they were one of the first Swiss manufacturers to make a true commercial vehicle. This was a 4-tonner with a 10 hp 4-cylinder engine and chain drive. In 1904 Martini 14-passenger buses operated one of Switzerland's first regular services between Yverdon and Moudon. They were equipped with heating using exhaust gases from the engine. In 1905 Martini was offering a wide range of trucks from 3 to 10 tons payload with engines from 12 to 60 hp, but it is doubtful if all were built. The company was British-owned from 1906 to 1908, hence the English-sounding title.

In the years up to World War I a shaft-drive 2½-3 tonner was the main commercial product, and these were sold to the Dutch Army as well as the Swiss. During the war a

1917 MARTINI JL 1½-ton truck, BHV

1929 MARTINI 2½-ton truck, FH

number of passenger cars were converted into vans and trucks, and the company prospered. However the post-war slump brought problems to Martini as to many other firms and production dropped. There was a new 1½-ton chassis in 1920 which used the 3.8-litre 4-cylinder engine from Martini's passenger cars; many different bodies were built on this including alpine touring coaches, hotel buses and fire engines.

Towards the end of the 1920s there was another change of capital and Martini came under the control of the German car maker Walter Steiger, who offered new 6-cylinder passenger cars. From 1928 the same 4.4-litre engine was used in new 1½-2-ton truck chassis, later raised to 2½ tons, and in 1930 the smaller 3-litre engine was also available in this chassis. In 1931 Lockheed vacuum servo brakes were offered on some models, and this range lasted until the end of production in 1933. *FH*

MARTYN (GB) 1898

David Martyn & Co. Ltd., Hebburn-on-Tyne, Northumberland

All the boiler and mechanism of the Martyn steam bus was carried beneath the passenger platform. The boiler was described as a horizontal diagonal multitubular type designed to run on coke. The engine had twin cylinders with link motion reversing gear and a good deal of aluminum was used in its manufacture. Final drive was by chain and the bus was single speed. The commercial impact was negligible. *RAW*

MARYLAND (US) 1900-1901

Maryland Automobile Mfg. Co., Luke, Md.

This company made passenger and goods vehicles powered by 12 hp 2-cylinder vertical double slide valve steam engines. The delivery model had a 1,000 lb. payload, and a top speed of 30 mph. *GNG*

MASERATI (I) 1940-1952

Officine Alfieri Maserati, Modena.

A little-known departure by the famous sports and racing car manufacturers was a range of electric trucks announced in 1940. The ½-ton EC10 was a 3-wheeler with single front wheel rated at 4/5 hp, but the forward control 1-tonner, which could be had with hearse or tanker bodywork, as well as a truck, had a 6½ hp motor, a single-plate clutch, and a 4-speed gearbox. Both machines had hydrau-

1940 MASERATI E10 Tipo 2 3-wheel electric truck, MCS

lic brakes, and were available until 1944. In 1948 came the Muletto, a lightweight forward control diesel 1-tonner on a wheelbase of only 7 ft. 10½ in. Front wheels were independently sprung, the 547cc watercooled 2-stroke 2-cylinder engine developed 15.5 hp, and a top speed of 47 mph was claimed. *MCS*

MASON; MAYTAG (US) 1908-1911

(1) Mason Motor Co., Des Moines; Waterloo, Iowa 1908-1909

(2) Maytag-Mason Motor Co., Waterloo, Iowa 1910-1911

Mason and Maytag vehicles followed a continuous line of development with no change of design to accompany the change of name and address. Three models were made, all using the same 14 hp flat-twin air-cooled engine and 2-speed planetary transmission with double chain final drive. Model 10 was a delivery van, Model 11 a delivery wagon and Model 12 a combination car with touring car or light delivery body. These versions cost $1,150 and $1,175 respectively, and with both bodies the price was $1,250. The bodies were said to be interchangeable in only 20 minutes.

In 1910 the Mason company was reorganized with fresh capital provided by F.L. Maytag, founder of a million dollar agricultural machinery company, and the name of the products changed to Maytag. After vehicle production ended in 1911 Maytag concentrated on washing machines which are still made today. From 1908 to 1912 the Duesenberg brothers worked for Mason and Maytag, before building racing cars under their own name. *RW*

MASON ROAD KING (US) 1922-1925

Mason Motor Truck Co., Flint, Mich.

The Mason Road King was William C. Durant's entry into the 1-1½-ton truck market, to supplement his smaller trucks which were sold under the name Star. Originally a 1-tonner, its capacity was uprated to 1½ tons in 1923, though the same engine was used, a 25.6 hp 4-cylinder Herschell-Spillman Model O. A 3-speed transmission was used with double reduction final drive. There were two wheelbases, 130 and 150 inches. *GNG*

MASS (F) 1907-1914

Automobiles Mass (L. Pierron) Courbevoie, Seine

Originally made for export to Britain (the name derived from its English sponsor, a Mr. Masser-Horniman), the Mass was an assembled car of no great distinction. Early commercial vehicles appeared infrequently, and were based on the cars, a light van on the 8 hp 2-cylinder shaft driven chassis being exhibited in 1907. In 1912, however, the firm introduced an interesting forward-control fwd truck, features including a round radiator, cone clutch, 4-speed gearbox, and chain final drive. The power units, Brasier-built fours of 2.8 or 3.6-litres, were mounted in sub-frames well forward of the driving axle, and models for payloads from 3 to 6 tons were offered. *MCS*

MASTER (US) 1917-1929

(1) Master Trucks Inc., Chicago, Ill.

(2) Master Motor Corp., Chicago, Ill.

(3) Master Motor Truck Co., Chicago, Ill.

Master trucks were made in a variety of models from 1¼ to 6-tons capacity, mostly using Buda engines, although from 1925 onwards some models were Jackson-powered. From 1921 to 1924 two models of bus chassis, for 21 and 29 passengers, were offered. *GNG*

1975 MASTER Truck garbage truck chassis, Master Truck Co

MASTER TRUCK (US) 1972 to date

(1) Engineered Fibreglass Co., Fountain Valley, Calif.

(2) Master Truck, Division of Hallamore Inc., Fountain Valley, Calif.

The Master Truck is a low, cab-forward truck intended principally for the refuse-collection market. A choice of diesel engines is offered, Detroit 6V-52N, Cummins V-210, Caterpillar 1150 or Perkins 180, and drive layouts are 4x2, 6x2 or 6x4. Because of the necessity of working close to residential buildings, Master's engineers have studied carefully the question of sound damping, and by the use of fibreglass insulation material around the engine and exhaust system they have kept noise emission down to 78 decibels. On the current 6000 model the one-piece fibreglass cab tilts for engine access. *RW*

MATFORD (F) 1935-1946

SA Francaise Matford, Poissy, Seine-et-Oise

Ford's acquisition of the Mathis factories in 1934 led to the abandonment of Mathis cars in favor of local editions of the (i) Ford V8 in both private and commercial forms.

1939 MATFORD F917WS 5-ton truck, BHV

By 1938 the car range included a 5-door *commerciale* with the small 2.2-litre engine, but while these differed considerably from the native American product, the trucks followed American lines closely, typical of the 1936 range being the 15-cwt van and 3-ton truck. Like Dagenham, however, Poissy evolved their own forward control models for 5-ton payloads, these subsequently being produced to German account during World War II. After 1947 these were made by the reorganized French Ford company. *MCS*

MATHESON (U.S.) 1906

Matheson Motor Car Co., Wilkes-Barre, Pa.

Matheson built a massive 5-ton truck with a 40 hp 4-cylinder engine mounted between the seats. Production of this truck was very limited. *DJS*

MATHIAN (F) 1903-1904

This company exhibited a truck powered by a large 2-cylinder engine, with double chain drive and steel tires. *GNG*

MATHIS (F) 1919-1936

SA Mathis, Strasbourg

Delivery vans were offered by Mathis when they assumed French nationality after World War I. All had 4-cylinder sv engines and 4-speed gearboxes, and the smallest ones, like the 760cc 2-cwt P-type of 1924, had differential-less back axles as well. By 1926 the standard commercial Mathis was a 12-cwt edition of the 1.6-litre GM, but latterly some heavier models were offered, with 4-cylinder engines in the 30-cwt/2½-ton bracket, and sv sixes of 3-litres or more in the biggest trucks, which included a 3-ton 6x4 with 4-speed silent 3rd gearbox by 1930, and a 4-tonner by 1933. These models, however, never achieved the popularity of the delivery vans and were seldom seen. 1935 saw Ford's acquisition of the Mathis factories, and the replacement of both cars and trucks by the new V8 Matford range; a delivery van edition of the 1½-litre 4-cylinder Mathis Emyquatre was, however, still listed in 1936. *MCS*

MATTES (D) 1932

A. Mattes & Co., Ulm

This three-wheeled small truck followed the "avant-train" principle, the engine driving the single front wheel. No further details are known. *HON*

MAUDSLAY (GB) 1903-1960

(1) Maudslay Motor Co. Ltd., Parkside, Coventry 1903-42
(2) Maudslay Motor Co. Ltd., Castle Maudslay, Alcester, Warwickshire 1943-1960

Henry Maudslay was co-founder of the engineering firm bearing his name in 1798. Known as 'the master of metals', he was responsible for the Maudslay screw-cutting lathe, the slide rest, which made repetition machining practicable for the first time, and the micrometer. His firm also made 80% of the steam engines for Britain's navy and in 1833 with Field he produced a steam carriage at his Lambeth, London works for the enterprising pioneer steam bus operator Sir Charles Dance. It regularly towed a 15-seat omnibus trailer from London to Greenwich and on trial covered the 60 miles from London to Brighton in 5½ hours.

Though it remained in use for many years, stiff turnpike charges and restrictive legislation brought the British steam bus boom to an end by 1840. Maudslay's company moved to Coventry and was involved in component and

1905 MAUDSLAY 14hp 14-seater bus, BR

tool production for the infant motor industry from a former bicycle works in Parkside. In 1903 Reginald Maudslay, a relative of Henry Maudslay started the Standard Motor Co. Ltd. a year after Maudslays themselves began to produce cars and the same year in which they built their first commercial vehicle.

A feature of all was their overhead valve layout, a Maudslay speciality over the years which incorporated numerous ingenious ideas to speed valve grinding or replacement. In fact on the earliest engines the overhead camshaft, which incidentally drove the dashboard mounted magneto from its rear end, could be hinged away from the valves by undoing only 2 nuts, and a valve could be removed in 2 minutes. During the twenties this was still further refined with the valves and springs housed in separate detachable caps which stuck out from the cylinder head, giving it a porcupine-like appearance. Pistons could be removed within 15 minutes with the aid of large trap doors in the crankcase. Initially commercial vehicles, particularly buses, were based on Maudslay 3-cylinder 20 hp car chassis, but from 1905 most became 4-cylindered. As befitting Henry Maudslay's pioneer interest in precision, all parts were guaranteed interchangeable. Unusually, on the heavy vehicles produced as early as 1905, shaft drive was available from the outset.

1906 MAUDSLAY 30/40hp bus, LTE

Early customers included the Great Western Railway who obtained the first of a large fleet of 40 hp Maudslays with railroad-type brakes worked by a handwheel pressing on the steel rear tire rims. In 1907, a chain-drive 3-ton millers dray won a medal in the RAC Trials and was awarded an Army Council Diploma for ease of engine accessibility. However private cars had been selling better than commercial vehicles so production of the latter was virtually abandoned until 1912, when new 30 cwt and 3-ton models appeared. The smaller continued the distinctive semi-circular radiator of the earlier commercial models and used the 17 hp 4-cylinder engine from the car range. It had worm instead of the bevel drive of its predecessors. The 3-tonner had a 32 hp engine and was joined by a 40 hp version to War Office Subsidy specification in 1913. This was produced in considerable quantities both by Maudslay and the Rover Co. Ltd. under license during the Great War, and, at the end, some 1550 were in service. Variations on the 32 and 40 hp models continued for several years and were joined in 1923 by one of the earliest British 7-tonners, a forward control 50 hp chassis, and by 2 new light models with 25 hp engines for 30 cwt and 2-tons, the smaller having pneumatic tires.

In 1924 Maudslay were amongst the first to produce low-frame passenger chassis. All had 4 wheel servo brakes and could seat 22 to 35 or 54 as double deckers. The 7-tonner became an 8-tonner in 1925 and in 1927 an overhead valve 6-cylinder engine of 120 bhp became available in passenger models. The lighter goods models were gradually phased out as they became less competitive in price, but the upper end of the range was increased with a 4-cylinder 40 hp 10-ton 6-wheeler in 1929. Three axles were also applied to a double deck bus model at the same time. This was not a sales success though Maudslay continued to do well with high speed touring coaches and single deck buses.

1924 MAUDSLAY 5/6-ton truck, OMM

1928 MAUDSLAY ML3 37-seater bus, BR

1929 MAUDSLAY L10 10/12-ton 6×2 truck, OMM

1929 MAUDSLAY ML7 50-seater bus, OMM

In 1933 Maudslay introduced a new six-four 6-ton goods model with their 4-cylinder overhead valve gas engine, whilst a significant option was the Gardner 4LW diesel.

In November 1934 Maudslay announced a very modern design of passenger chassis (SF40) with long front overhang to permit the exit to be forward of the front axle. This made maximum use of the floor space and was one of the earliest designs to accomodate 40 seats within the 27'6" maximum permitted length. Another development that year was an infinately variable gearbox to Hobbs design, which however never reached quantity production.

A feature of the passenger models since 1932 had been the adoption of model names in addition to numbers, such as Masta, Montrose, Majestic and Meteor and this was extended to the Mogul goods model of 1937 for 7½-ton payloads, and Mikado 8-wheelers of 1939.

During the Second World War the Mogul remained in production for various essential civilian haulage duties and was joined by a military version, the Militant.

1948 MAUDSLAY Mustang 10-ton twin-steer truck, OMM

1948 MAUDSLAY Marathon coach, OMM

During the War a Shadow Factory was established in the countryside near Alcester and following extensive blitzing Maudslay gradually transferred production to it. Peacetime models included the Marathon coach, Mogul and Militant 4-wheelers, Maharanee articulated tractors, Mustang twin steer 6-wheelers and Meritor 8-wheelers. In 1948 the firm was acquired along with Crossley by AEC, with the parent company becoming known as Associated Commercial Vehicles.

The Maudslay range gradually blended into the AEC range, and from 1954 was identical, though the name continued to be listed until 1960. However some of the old model names are still current on AEC vehicles. For a time Maudslay built the largest of the AEC dump trucks but eventually became solely a supplier of axles and other components. Production was never large; about 1500 vehicles of all kinds were made in the 1920's, and 600 in the 1930's. After the War this was increased to 500 to 1000 per year for a while. *OM*

MAURER UNION (D) 1902-1908

Nurnberger Motor Fahrzeug-Fabrik Union GmbH., Nuremberg

A specialty of this firm were their friction driven cars. The 2-cylinder model of 1902 also was presented as a van and light truck. Also a later 4-cylinder model with twin-disc-drive was available as a truck and bus. It is reported that in 1904 a Maurer Union bus was the first one used for passenger and mail transport on an overland route in Bavaria. *HON*

1932 MAVAG 4-ton tanker, RJ

MAVAG (H) 1924-1940

Magyar Allami Vas-Acel es Gepgyar, Budapest

A railway locomotive producer since 1905 and builder of agricultural machines since 1910, Mavag introduced its first truck chassis in 1924, while the first bus followed three years later. In 1928 Mavag following an agreement with Daimler Benz, started producing gasoline engined 2.5 and 3.5 ton trucks, while the range was further extended with 4.5 ton gasoline and 6 ton diesel trucks in 1934, built again under Daimler Benz license. The war stopped Mavags automotive activities after 2800 truck and 200 bus chassis had been built. Mavag was revived after WW II amalgamated with Ganz and have specialized since then in the construction of railroad locomotives, and similar equipment. *GA*

MAXFER (US) 1917-1919

Maxfer Truck & Tractor Co., Chicago, Ill.

Maxfer made rear-end units to transfer Ford Model T cars into 1-ton trucks, and also made a complete conventional 1-ton truck of assembled units including a 31 hp 4-cylinder engine and a David Brown-type semi-floating worm drive with a Bailey non-stalling differential. Electric lights and starter were standard, items still uncommon on trucks in 1917. Tires were pneumatic at the front and solid at the rear. *RW*

MAXI (US) 1940-1942

Six Wheels Inc., Los Angles, Calif.

Intended for extra heavy-duty off-highway work, the Maxi was a 6 × 4 tractor which foreshadowed the heavy dumpers of post-war years, and was possibly the largest truck of its time. Powered by a 225 hp Waukesha-Hesselman engine, it had a Fuller clutch and transmission, and the maker's own rear axle and drive which was through a walking beam that housed a set of reduction gears. From there chains transferred power to the tandem wheels. Drawbar pull was 32,000 lbs, and the maximum load capacity was 220,000 lbs. The cab was open and the tires, all singles, reached above the shoulders of the average man. As well as building Maxi trucks, the Six Wheels Company completed some of the larger Hug trucks, fitting their own tandem axles. *RW*

MAXIM (i) (US) 1911-1914

(1) Maxim Tricar Manufacturing Co., Thompsonville, Conn. 1912-1913

(2) Maxim Tri-Car Co., Port Jefferson, LI, NY 1913-1914

Based on the German Phanomobil, this was a 3-wheeler rated as a ¾-tonner with a driven and steered single front wheel. The engine had two cylinders, was air-cooled and drove the front wheel by a single chain. Wheelbase was 7 feet, 6 inches and the price was $395. The name Maxim was from Hiram Maxim, the founder of this company and an early experimenter with Pope Manufacturing Co. of Hartford, Conn. *GMN*

MAXIM (ii) (US) 1914 to date

Maxim Motor Co., Middleboro, Mass.

This well-known producer of fire apparatus entered vehicle production with a light assembled truck, but after a few had been sold they concentrated on fire engines. The first of these had been built on a Thomas chassis in 1914, and in 1916 came the first on Maxim's own chassis with 6-cylinder triple ignition engine and wormdrive. By 1918 there was a complete range of motor pumpers, combination, and hook-and-ladder trucks, which was continued through the 1920s and 1930s. There were also some specials such as the 6 × 4 pumper-tanker for unmade roads supplied to Falmouth, Mass. in 1938. Also in 1938 Maxim planned to re-enter the commercial truck market with a highly re-worked 2-ton Ford chassis (stronger frame, heavy-duty Timken axles, oversize tires) to carry 3 to 5 ton loads. It was the same kind of vehicle as the earlier Ford-powered Grass-Premier. At least one was built but production never went ahead.

1927 MAXIM Model BA1 fire engine, Maxim

1937 MAXIM Model M-3 fire engine, Maxim

In 1946 came a line of pumpers (750 to 1500 gpm), ladder trucks and quad combinations with open and closed cabs, and a new V-grille which lasted until 1961. In 1952 Maxim acquired the license for the German Magirus rear-mounted aerial ladder which they built on their own chassis. They sold aerial ladders to competitors such as Ward La France and Mack, in rigid and articulated form. The Seagrave Corp acquired Maxim in 1956, but the Massachusetts firm continued to operate independently, building all their own apparatus and major components including bodies and aerial ladders. Maxim's first cab-forward models, the F Series, came in 1959, though conventionals have continued to be made up to the present day, and are now the only American fire engines to use this layout. In 1960 came new short wheelbase conventionals known as the S Series with a hood design which has also lasted up to the present. These two basic series are still made today, in a wide variety of pumpers and ladder trucks, rigids and articulateds, with open and closed cabs. Engines are Waukesha gasoline or Cummins or Detroit diesels, and transmissions Spicer synchromesh or Allison automatics. *GNG*

1956 MAXIM custom pumper, GNG

1976 MAXIM Model S custom pumper, Maxim

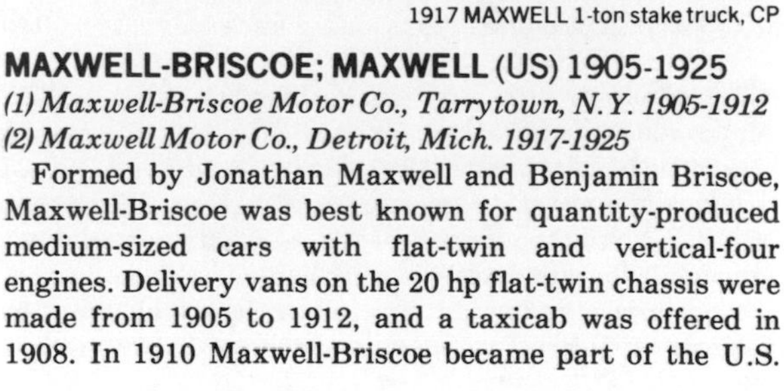

1917 MAXWELL 1-ton stake truck, CP

MAXWELL-BRISCOE; MAXWELL (US) 1905-1925

(1) Maxwell-Briscoe Motor Co., Tarrytown, N.Y. 1905-1912

(2) Maxwell Motor Co., Detroit, Mich. 1917-1925

Formed by Jonathan Maxwell and Benjamin Briscoe, Maxwell-Briscoe was best known for quantity-produced medium-sized cars with flat-twin and vertical-four engines. Delivery vans on the 20 hp flat-twin chassis were made from 1905 to 1912, and a taxicab was offered in 1908. In 1910 Maxwell-Briscoe became part of the U.S.

Motor Corporation, one of whose architects was Benjamin Briscoe, but this would-be rival to General Motors collapsed in 1912. Jonathan Maxwell transferred production to Detroit. Passenger cars only were made until 1917 when a conventional 1-ton truck was introduced, powered by the 21 hp 4-cylinder engine used in Maxwell cars. This was a 10 ft. 4 in. wheelbase, but in 1918 there was also a delivery van on the 9 ft. line car chassis. Capacity was uprated to 1½ tons in 1920, but the truck remained the same in engine and wheelbase until 1923 while the car-based vans lasted until 1925. Fire engines and bus bodies were mounted on the Maxwell chassis as well as ordinary load-carrying trucks. *GNG*

MAXWERKE (D) 1900-1901

"Maxwerke" Elektrizitats-und Automobil-Gesellschaft Harff & Schwarz A.G., Cologne

Electric vans with two motors driving the rear wheels were produced by this company. They were available as vans and buses. *HON*

1962 MAYOR 2-cylinder milk truck, GNG

MAYOR (CH) 1960-1966

Arnold Mayor, Constructions Mecaniques, Bramois VS

The earliest Mayor agricultural multi-purpose "Monotrac" was equipped with a MAG twin-cylinder of 12 hp and rear wheel drive. The heavier "Chassis-Trac" had 4-wheel drive, a 34 hp VW 4-cylinder engine or optionally a Mercedes diesel engine. The forward control vehicle with a front from the Ford Transit delivery van had 6 cross-country speeds and 3 road speeds and hydraulic brakes. The platform could be tipped to 3 sides and payload was 1½ tons. Some vehicles built by Mayor had the BMW flat twin engine of 30 hp.

The last model "Chassis-Trac M.B.2" was generally similar but had a new driver's cab and was the only 4 × 4 multipurpose vehicle with all 4 wheels steered. It could in fact turn on the spot and had an automatic differential lock on both axles. A total of about 200 Mayor vehicles was built before production ceased. *FH*

MAYTAG see Mason

MAZ (MA3) SU 1947 to date

Minsk Motor Works — Minsk

A major manufacturer of Soviet trucks, the MAZ Works commenced in 1947 with model 200, a 7-ton cargo unit of 110 hp @ 2,000 rpm. A semi-tractor version and a model 205 6-ton dumper were also built.

Since 1965, production has centered around the cab-over-engine 500A. This is a 9-ton truck with a 200 hp V-6

1955 MAZ-500 7-ton truck, BHV

diesel, five speeds forward and power steering. A sleeping berth is provided behind the seat.

MAZ-503A is a 9-ton dumper for quarry work and MAZ-504A is a semi-tractor truck, both powered by the 200 hp V-6 diesel. MAZ-504B is a more powerful version using a 265 hp 8-cylinder engine, capable of towing a semi-trailer of 25.7 tons.

A 4 x 4 timber carrier is built as MAZ-509 and the 500 chassis is used for a multitude of other purposes including cement truck, milk tanker and fuel tanker.

1968 MAZ-516 10-ton truck, Motor Jahr

1975 MAZ-500 8-ton chassis, BE

MAZ trucks of larger capacity have been built through the years including model 525 dumper of 25 tons, 40-ton dumper model 530, the 537 10-ton 8 x 8 cargo prime-mover, and the 15-ton 8 x 8 military and civilian 543 using a V-12 diesel tank engine of 525 hp. *BE*

MAZDA (J) 1931 to date

Toyo Kogyo Co. Ltd., Hiroshima

Founded in 1920 as the Toyo Cork Kogyo Co. Ltd. to manufacture cork products, this firm (which assumed its present style in 1927) branched briefly into motorcycles in 1930 before marketing its first light truck a year later. Early Mazdas used 486cc single-cylinder sv engines, with chain primary drive to a 3-speed gearbox, and shaft-driven back axle. Development of this theme was resumed after

World War II, and by the late 1950s a wide range of models was available, with enclosed cabs, electric starting and hydraulic brakes on the rear wheels. Engines were ohv vee-twins of 356cc, 577cc, 1,005cc and 1.4 litres, with 1,130cc and 1½-litre fours also listed. While most Japanese 3-wheeler specialists confined their efforts to 15-cwt and smaller trucks, Mazda made some quite hefty machinery, including a 2-tonner in 1961 with wheelbase options of up to 12 ft. 6 in. The ultimate in 3-wheelers was the T2000 of 1965 powered by an 81 hp 4-cylinder diesel engine, and capable of 65 mph. A year later, however, this configuration was on its way out, only the 10-cwt T600 with 577cc engine surviving into 1972 as Japan's last representative of a once-popular theme.

Mazda had experimented with a conventional light car in 1940, but it was not until 1958 that the D range of semi forward control 4-wheeler trucks reached the public. These shared their ohv 4-cylinder engines with the larger 3-wheelers, but were otherwise entirely orthodox machines in the ½-ton category with 4-speed synchromesh gearboxes and steering column shift. 1960 saw not only the company's first minicar, but also a parallel light commercial in the shape of a diminutive front-engined pickup with the same hemi-head 356cc aircooled vee-twin power unit and hydraulic brakes; the car's torque-converter transmission was not available. Later developments of this family had mid-mounted inline twin or underfloor, front-mounted 782cc 4-cylinder engines, but most of the light duty Mazdas followed car lines, with 4-cylinder power units, 4-speed synchromesh gearboxes, torsion-bar ifs, and hypoid final drive. The B1600 introduced in 1971 had a 1.6-litre ohc engine. By 1960 the D series was available in microbus form, and an agreement signed with Perkins of England in 1965 paved the way for heavier-duty full forward-control 2/3-ton Mazdas with twin rear wheels a year later. Also offered as aerodynamic coaches with wrap round windscreens, these had

1974 MAZDA D1500 pick-up, Mazda

1974 MAZDA B1600 pick-up, Mazda

hydraulic or hydrovac brakes according to payload capacity, and came with either 2-litre 86 hp gasoline or 2½-litre 4-cylinder diesel engine, the latter in unit with a 5-speed gearbox. 1969 saw the 4-ton E3800 with 6-cylinder diesel engine, this evolving by 1974 into the 4.1-litre E4100. 1978's range was headed by gasoline and diesel Es for 2/3½-ton payloads: a 26-seater bus version was known as the Parkway. Smaller Mazdas were the traditional D

1978 MAZDA Titan 2-3-ton truck, Mazda

series with 1½-litre gasoline engines, the car-type pickups, the rear-engined 982cc F1000 8-seater minibus with all-independent suspension, and some even smaller 350kg forward control machines using 359cc 2-stroke twin units from the Chantez minicar. Since 1970 certain light 3- and 4-wheeler commercials have been made under license in Greece by Mazda Hellas SA. *MCS*

M.B.B. (D) 1970 to date

Messerschmitt-Bolkow-Blohm GmbH., Ottobrunn

MBB at first developed an experimental electric car. But subsequently they produced a greater number — mainly as micro-buses — of which some were used during the Munich Olympic Games in 1972 as escort vehicles etc. Also they were supplied to various institutions, but full scale series production did not start. Main characteristic features are a self-supporting plastic chassis of sandwich construction. Payload capacity is 1 ton and the operation range with one battery charge is about 60-100 km.

Following the same design principles for the chassis an amphibious cross-country vehicle was developed, but this used a gasoline engine. This development is still in the experimental stage. *HON*

McBRIGHT (US) 1953-1955

McBright Inc., Lehighton, Pa.

The McBright was an unconventional truck powered by a White engine which, with transmission and radiator, was mounted at the rear, below the floor and behind the rear axle. Two, three and four axle models were made. *GNG*

1914 McCURD 2-ton tipper, NMM

McCURD (GB) 1912-1927

(1) McCurd Lorry Manufacturing Co. Ltd., Hayes, Middx.
(2) McCurd Motors Ltd., Slough, Bucks.

W.A. McCurd was a retailer of passenger cars who announced a conventional 3½-ton chassis in November 1912. It was powered by a 42 hp 4-cylinder engine, had a 4-speed gearbox and worm drive. The same model was revived after the war, but from 1921 there was a lapse in production for several years. In 1925 a new lighter chassis for 2/2½ ton loads was introduced, powered by a 25 hp 4-cylinder monobloc engine, with 4-speed gearbox and overhead worm drive. This was intended for goods and passenger bodies, but in 1927 a special passenger version with lower chassis was offered, for 26/30 seater bodies. These models were carried on some lists to 1931, but production probably did not survive beyond 1927. *GNG*

MCI (CDN/US) 1937 to date

(1) Fort Garry Motor Body Co. Winnipeg Man. 1937-1942
(2) Motor Coach Industries, Winnipeg, Man. 1942 to date
(3) Motor Coach Industries, Pembina, N.D. 1963 to date

An established maker of truck and bus bodies in Winnipeg, the Fort Garry Motor Body Co. made its first few complete buses to meet the special needs of operators in western Canada, where gravel roads and severe weather combined to place unusual demands on buses. They mostly had front-mounted International engines. Yellow Coach (U.S.) styling was copied for five buses built in 1938. Then in 1940 the Greyhound Corp. expanded across the border and acquired two large operating companies: 22 more Fort Garry buses were soon purchased for their major lines.

After World War II bus traffic grew rapidly, and the company, by then renamed Motor Coach Industries, was kept busy turning out buses as fast as it could, generally about one every other week, most of them for the Greyhound lines in Canada. The rear-engined Courier was introduced in 1946. In 1950 Greyhound bought MCI and began to expand its plant capacity to take care of increasing requirements. In 1957 Greyhound Lines of Canada was formed to own MCI and the franchises within Canada.

1950 MCI Courier 85 coach, Denis Latour

A new system of bus model numbers was started in 1959 with the MC-1 Challenger, the first MCI type to have a distinctive pattern of slanted and straight window dividers. In 1963, after approximately 750 buses had been built since the start of Fort Garry production, an assembly plant was opened in Pembina, North Dakota, and Greyhound began filling a large share of its substantial annual bus requirements for U.S. routes with MCI's. (Biggest intercity operator in the nation, Greyhound had purchased bus manufacturing operations in 1930). The then current model was the MC-5, a 39-passenger 35-foot single-level bus with a Detroit Diesel 8V-71 engine and Spicer mechanical transmission. Greyhound had found that belt driven accessories were more reliable than gear drive arrangements and specified belts for all MCI production, the only real distinguishing mechanical feature compared to other U.S. intercity buses.

Approximately 2300 MC-5's and modified versions have been produced, and the type is still in production, but major route and charter carriers today prefer greater seating capacity. Model MC-7 was a 47-passenger design with

1972 MCI Courier Challenger MC-7 coach, GNG

a tandem rear axle introduced in 1968 with the same drive train as the smaller bus; 2550 were built in five years, half of them for Greyhound. The MC-8 was again mechanically similar but looked somewhat different and was produced between 1973 and 1978 to the total of 3000 vehicles. In 1975, because of sporadic labor trouble at the Winnipeg plant, Greyhound set up Transportation Manufacturing Corp. in Rosewell, New Mexico. Here Greyhound's own buses are built from stampings produced at Winnipeg. By contrast the Pembina plant completes shells that are fabricated in Canada and supplies independent U.S. and overseas customers. Canadian orders are filled entirely at the original Winnipeg plant.

Model MC-6, of which only 100 were made, was a Greyhound experiment with a 12-cylinder Detroit Diesel engine in a bus that measured 102 inches in overall width. The U.S. standard for intercity buses is 96 inches, thou some local transit buses are 102 inches wide. A campaign to alter state laws so as to permit operation of the wider buses everywhere was not successful, and the MC-6 fleet is now concentrated in California. Some have 8V-71 engines now.

Current MCI production comprises chiefly the new MC-9, generally similar to the earlier 47-passenger types but with a new window treatment. MCI has been the largest U.S. builder of intercity buses for the past decade and makes about 40 per cent of all such buses produced in the U.S. and Canada. *MBS*

McINTYRE (US) 1909-1915

W.H. McIntyre Co., Auburn, Ind.

The first trucks made by McIntyre (formerly Kiblinger) were little more than elongated motorized high-wheeler chain-driven buggies with a light cargo body.

The 1910 McIntyre commercial power wagon was of conventional design with the axle set back under the dashboard. It was powered by a 24 hp water cooled gas engine and driven through a transmission of 2 speeds forward and 1 reverse. Its appearance was generally primitive, with solid tires, chain drive, and open cab. Weight was 2200 pounds, price $1350, and speed was 4 to 12 miles per hour, typical of its day.

In 1913 the line was greatly modernized in appearance including front fenders, crescent cab, and the axle was now under the engine. The line was also greatly expanded to include ¾, 1½, 3, and 5 ton models, some with pneumatic tires, at prices from $1500 to $4200. All were still chain-driven.

In vehicle building since 1880, McIntyre faded rapidly from the scene with successive failures of their Imp cyclecar (1914), their truck (1915) and their car (1916). *RW*

McLAREN (GB) 1880-1940

J. & H. McLaren Ltd., Leeds, Yorks.

McLarens began building road locomotives in 1880, the first being their works No. 52, an 8nhp single. Engines of 6nhp began to be built the same year and in 1884 they built a 12nhp compound which survived until 1952. In 1885 a fast road locomotive and passenger bus was supplied to India and in 1886 three road engines for maintaining a parcel service between Lyons and Grenoble (France). A number of 6 and 8nhp single cylinder engines were supplied to showmen between 1880 and 1887 and subsequently four 8nhp compounds and one 7nhp were made for showmen though others were converted from road engines. McLarens built the last steam heavy haulage locomotive made anywhere in the world (No. 1870 of January 1938) a compound with 50 ton crane and electric light supplied to South Africa and preserved in Johannesburg.

1899 McLAREN 10nhp road locomotive, RAW

They also made gear-driven steam tractors for road haulage from 1909 to 1936, somewhat heavier in build than most and unusual, for tractors, in having the 4 shaft layout. Again it fell to McLarens to build the last steam tractor made in this country.

McLarens specialized in building, with the finest materials and workmanship, uncomplicated engines of very robust design much esteemed for colonial use though, on the whole, too expensive to attract more than a limited clientele in Britain. They are also remembered for their willingness to experiment with spring wheels both of their own design and also by outside patentees and for their use of Boulton patent wheels with wood block tread inserts.

1936 McLAREN steam tractor, B.J. Finch

They were one of the few major steam manufacturers who did not essay a wagon. The main part of their trade was in very heavy fixed steam engines.

From 1925 to 1940 they built oil engines, at first of Benz design and later, Ricardo. These were employed in agricultural tractors, in the Kerr-Stuart truck, and also in one McLaren-built road tractor. Made in 1940, this employed a 125bhp 5-cylinder Ricardo-type oil engine mounted amidships and driving traction-engine type rear wheels 6 ft. in diameter. It could haul a load of 109 tons and consumed 1¼ gallons of fuel per mile. Operated by Pickfords during the war, it ended its days with a fairground showman. *RAW/GNG*

1916 McLAUGHLIN D-4 army ambulance, HD

McLAUGHLIN (CDN) 1911-1916

McLaughlin Motor Car Co., Oshawa, Ont.

McLaughlin trucks were apparently all light delivery models similar to their Buick counterparts in the United States. One unique model was a military ambulance used by Canadian forces during World War I. *HD*

M.C.W. (GB) 1938 to date

(1) Metropolitan-Cammell-Weymann Motor Bodies Ltd., London, SW1 1938-1952

(2) Metropolitan-Cammell-Weymann Ltd., London, SW1 1952-1965

(3) Metropolitan-Cammell-Weymann Ltd., Marston Green, Birmingham 1965-1969

(4) Metropolitan-Cammell-Weymann Ltd., Washwood Heath, Birmingham 1969 to date

The M.C.W. organization was formed in July 1932 as a marketing body for the bus, coach and trolleybus bodies built by the Metropolitan Cammell Carriage Wagon & Finance Co. Ltd. (later Metropolitan Cammell Carriage & Wagon Co. Ltd.) at Birmingham, and Weymann's Motor Bodies (1925) Ltd. (later Weymann's Ltd.) at Addlestone, Surrey. Metro Cammell had been producing passenger bodies since 1930 and Weymann since 1919. The two manufacturers were early large scale producers of "all metal" bodies based on designs patented by Metro Cammell, and in 1938 this construction was embodied in a chassisless trolleybus built for London Transport incorporating AEC running units. This was followed by an order for 175 such vehicles which were built in 1939/40 and marked the first large scale attempt at chassisless vehicle construction in Great Britain. In 1948 M.C.W. introduced Birmingham-built prototypes for its robust underfloor-engined Olympic chassisless single-decker which was built in conjunction with Leyland and went into production in 1950 as the Leyland/M.C.W. Olympic. It was notably successful in overseas markets and was built at both the

1939 MCW 70 seater chassisless trolleybus, London Trolleybus Preservation Society

Birmingham and Addlestone plants. A 1953 lightweight version, employing aluminum alloy construction in place of steel and known as the Olympian, was not widely purchased. The Olympic was built throughout the 'fifties and 'sixties, and included a rear-engine Mark X version for Montreal in 1966. A batch of 300 was delivered to the Istanbul municipality in 1968 under the title of Leyland/M.C.W. Levend.

In 1963 Weymann was purchased by Metro Cammell (which became Metropolitan-Cammell Ltd. on the last day of 1964), and the Addlestone works were closed in 1966. On 1st January 1966 Metropolitan-Cammell-Weymann Ltd., which had previously been purely a sales organization, became responsible also for bus manufacture. In 1969 M.C.W. negotiated with Scania Bussar AB of Sweden to jointly manufacture an integral single-decker using Scania Vabis running units including the D11 engine mounted transversely at the rear of a mild steel body frame built by M.C.W. This was marketed as the Metro-Scania. (See Metropolitan) *OM*

M & D (GB) 1925-1927

Rhode Motor Co. Ltd., Birmingham

The M & D (Mead and Deakin) was a 30-cwt truck built by Rhode. Its 2413cc splash-lubricated ohc 4-cylinder engine was an enlarged edition of the Rhode unit; advanced features included aluminum pistons, dural rods, electric lighting and starting, pneumatic tires, and 4-wheel brakes. Final drive was by overhead worm, but the car's quarter elliptic springs were retained. Only about six were made. *MCS*

M & E (US) 1913-1915

Merchant & Evans Co., Philadelphia, Pa.

The first model of this make was a 4-tonner on a wheelbase of 9 feet, 6 inches. With a stake body and solid rubber tires, the price was $3000. For 1915, 3½- and 5-tonners were built, but details of these latter models are unavailable. *GMN*

MEILI (CH) 1958 to date

(1) Meili Traktorenfabrik, Schaffhausen 1958-1964

(2) Meili Fahrzeugbau AG, Schubelbach 1964 to date

The Meili family business had made agricultural tractors from 1934, and in 1958 they introduced a highly

1970 MEILI Agromobil 4×4 truck, Meili

unconventional cross-country vehicle called the Flex-Trac. This was a 3-axle 6x6 which could travel in water or swamp up to 30 inches deep, and on firm ground had a top speed of 60 mph. Various prototypes were powered by Ford V-8 or Willys 4-cylinder gasoline engine, or MWM 4-cylinder or Ford 6-cylinder diesel engines. Payloads varied from 1½- ton to 3-tons. However in spite of license agreements with manufacturers in Germany, England and the USA, this interesting vehicle was not made in series.

In 1959 Meili launched the Agromobil multi-purpose light truck powered originally by a BMW flat-twin engine and with rear-wheel drive. Soon 4-cylinder Volkswagen or MWM air-cooled diesel engines were adopted, and drive was to all four wheels. Payload was up to 2 tons. An industrial version was the Multimobil with 2- and later 4-wheel drive and MWM 4- or 6-cylinder diesel engines of 60 or 90 hp, the latter having a payload of 3½ tons. The lightest MA-1500 was powered by a 48 hp Perkins diesel engine. Current models are MA-2000, MA-3000 and MA-4000 with payloads of 2, 3 and 4 tons and MWM or Perkins diesel engines of 47 to 75 hp. On the MA-4000 the brakes are servo-assisted, and power-assisted steering is an option. The Multimobil is made under license in Italy as the Sirmac SAB 2500A, where it is fitted with a 160 hp Fiat V-6 engine. *FH*

MEISELBACH (US) 1904-1909

A.D. Meiselbach Motor Wagon Co., North Milwaukee, Wis.

The first Meiselbach truck was a 1-tonner powered by a horizontally-opposed twin water-cooled engine, with friction transmission and chain drive. In 1906 double disc friction drive was introduced, with discs at each end of the transverse crankshaft. In 1908 models came in three sizes, 1, 2 and 3 tons capacity on wheelbases of 84, 96 and 108 in respectively. The same engine was used as in earlier models, but there was only one forward speed as the engine was said to be sufficiently flexible. Maximum speed was 10 mph. All Meiselbachs were of the highwheeler pattern, suitable for rough country roads. *GNG*

MELEN EXPRESS CARRIER (GB) 1912-1915

F.H. Melen Ltd., Sparkbrook, Birmingham.

Although fitted with a special deep box body for laundry delivery work built by Melens in their own body shops, this three-wheeled tiller-steered tri-van was similar in virtually all other details to the Wall. This is hardly surprising, since the chassis was supplied by the latter firm. Melen also produced a number of 2-cylinder Alpha engined light cars from 1913. *MJWW*

MENARD (CDN) 1910-1919

Menard Motor Truck Co., Windsor, Ont.

Originally makers of a passenger high wheeler, this company was reorganized and began production of 1 to 3½-ton trucks including a 1½-ton model with worm drive and a 6-cylinder Beaver engine. The lineup expanded to include a ¾-ton delivery truck and at least one fire engine before the assets were sold to the Mapleleaf Manufacturing Company of Montreal. *HD*

1913 MENDIP 2-ton van, NMM

MENDIP (GB) 1908-1922

(1) C.W. Harris, Chewton Mendip, Somerset. 1908
(2) Mendip Engineering Co., Chewton Mendip, Somerset. 1914
(3) Mendip Motor and Engineering Co. Ltd., Southmead, Bristol 1914-1921
(4) New Mendip Engineering Co. Ltd., Atworth, Melksham, Wilts. 1922

Cutler's Green Ironworks was an old-established company dating from the time of the Napoleonic wars, during which swords were forged. Possessing a good foundry and smithy, the works were well equipped, despite their small size, for vehicle production and the proprietor, C.W. Harris designed a number of steam trucks in the period 1907/8. These 2/3 tonners, employed vertical water tube boilers arranged for top firing and a compound horizontal engine utilizing Stephenson's link motion. Their design was similar to that of the Straker being built in Bristol at the same time and an example was exhibited at the Bath & West Show in June 1908. In 1912, the range was supplemented by a 30 cwt van with 16/ hp 4-cylinder Aster gasoline engine. Mendip-built four speed gearbox and final drive by chain and live axle in an oil bath. A light car followed in 1913, in which year Harris sold out to W.H. Bateman Hope M.P., J.P., No vehicles were built during the war and postwar commercial vehicle production is doubtful although some cars were made until 1922. *MJWW*

MENOMINEE (US) 1911-1937

(1) Menominee Motor Truck Co., Clintonville, Wis. 1911-1928
(2) Utility Supply Co., Clintonville, Wis. 1928-1937

Named after an Indian tribe, the Menominee was a long-lived but obscure make from Wisconsin. Originally made in 1500 and 2000lb models, the range had extended up to 3½ tons by 1917, and in 1923 ran from 1 to 6 tons plus two bus chassis, for 16/20 passengers and 25 passengers. Engines were always Wisconsin, and other components came from familiar suppliers such as Cotta and Detlaff for transmissions and Columbia, Shuler and Timken for axles. Despite small scale production Menominees were sold as far afield as Michigan and New York; a New York bus operator claimed in 1923 that his Menominee single-decker was the largest unit of its type in the state. The smallest model was a 1-tonner known as the Hurryton.

In 1928 Menominee's neighbor, the Four Wheel Drive Auto Company, acquired the firm as a subsidiary, renaming the operation the Utility Supply Company. While a few Menominees were built from then on, F.W.D.'s main purpose was to acquire a source for the supply of utility bodies, pole trailers and similar equipment needed for the production of its own vehicles. Nevertheless Menominees continued to be listed, the 1932 range running from 1½ to 8 tons in company with three bus chassis, the largest a 35-passenger unit. A new line was introduced in 1933, now with Waukesha engines and the usual other components. These remained in 'production' until 1937, but by then the plant was largely occupied on the production of bodies for F.W.D. *RJ*

MEPWARD (GB) 1922

Mepstead & Hayward Ltd., London N.1

The Mepward was a short-lived assembled taxicab powered by a 4-cylinder 2,178 cc engine. Not more than 12 were made. *GNG*

1934 MERAY light truck, Haris Auto Museum

MERAY (H) 1928-1935

Meray Motorkerekpargyar R.T., Budapest

A motorcycle firm that constructed a series of light 3-wheeled cars, built also a delivery van version in the same chassis. Power came from a rear-mounted 1 cylinder JAP engine of 500cc capacity, that drove the rear single wheel through a chain. A four wheeler was also made. *GA*

MERCEDES-BENZ (D) 1926 to date

Daimler-Benz Aktiengesellschaft, Stuttgart-Unterturkheim; Berlin-Marienfelde; Mannheim; Gaggenau; Dusseldorf; Worth; Hamburg

After the amalgamation of Benz and Daimler the most significant result in the commercial vehicle field was the decision to carry on the Benz diesel engines following the pre-combustion chamber principle. An improved version was available in 1927. It was a 6-cylinder unit with 8.5 litre capacity developing 75 hp and with a payload of 5 tons. This version was awarded the Dewar Trophy in 1928. In 1932 the sale of diesel-engined vehicles from the start reach 2,000 units. Diesel engines were also used for buses, fire service vehicles and municipal vehicles. A further development was that also smaller diesel engines became available for trucks; in 1933 a 2-tonner with 3.8 litre capacity was presented. Mercedes-Benz at that time offered the widest range of diesel-engined commercials and had available the most advanced system.

1929 MERCEDES-BENZ 6×2 refuse truck, FLP

The range of gasoline engined commercials which were available in the late twenties consisted of a 10/30 PS van (based on the private car), a 1-tonner truck L 1 (or N 1 as a bus) with 3.7 litre engine, a 2-tonner L 2 with 5.7 litre engine (or as a bus N 2 with 6.4 litre engine), and a 5-

1928 MERCEDES-BENZ 6×2 tanker, OMM

tonner L 5 with 8.1 litre engine. The latter version also was available as a single or double deck bus.

In 1931 Mercedes-Benz introduced new type designations. These showed the letter L for "Lastwagen" (truck) or LO for "Omnibus" together with the payload capacity in kilograms. Available were the L 1000, L 2000, L and LO 2500, 3000, 4000, 5000 and the 3-axle LO 8500. Also in 1931 the first trolley-bus was introduced. Since 1935 only diesel engines have been installed in all commercial vehicles. In the same year the 10,000th diesel-engined commercial vehicle left the factory.

The type range which was started in 1935/36 was partially carried on until WW II. These types were the L 1500 (4 cyl., 2.6 litre), LO 2600 and L 3000 (4 cyl., 4.8 litre), L 3750 and L 4500 (6 cyl., 7.3 litre), L 5000 (6 cyl., 10.3 litre), L 6500 (6 cyl., 10.3 or 12.5 litre), L 10000 and LO 10000 (6 cyl., 11.2 or 12.5 litre, for double deck buses 14.3 litre). Various forward-control buses with front-mounted engines were developed in co-operation with coachbuilding firms. In addition there were van versions based on the passenger cars using the 1.7 litre and 2.6 litre engines. The L 3000 A and L 4500 A were 4 × 4 trucks. In 1937 the "Zwitter" (Hybrid), a half-truck version was introduced. It was not initiated for the army but was used with truck and bus bodies for mountain regions. Also not purely

1935 MERCEDES-BENZ streamlined coach, HON

1936 MERCEDES-BENZ 6×2 coach, FLP

military was the G 5, a 4 × 4 vehicle with 4-wheel steering. A special development for the army was the LG 3000 with 6 × 4 drive. During the war the Opel Blitz 3 ton truck was built under license and differed from the Opel version in its cab. This had the type designation L 701.

After WW II the L 701 3-tonner and the L 4500 were carried on, which later were replaced by the types L 3000, 4000 and 5000. The L 3250 appeared in 1949, equipped with a 6-cylinder 4.6 litre engine, which developed into the L/O 3500. New was the L 6600 of 1950 which as a bus was designated O 6600 H, it had a forward control and the engine was transversely mounted in the rear, the first Mercedes bus following this layout. This version was also available as a trolley bus (O 6600 T). Very popular for bus bodies was the type 3500 with normal control. As before all Mercedes chassis' were used with a wide variety of bodies, including municipal and fire fighting vehicles.

A new system of type designations was introduced in the early fifties. L stood for all conventional vehicles, LP for forward control versions. An additional A meant all-wheel-drive, an S indicated an articulated tractor. These letters were used together with 3 ciphers which characterized the engine used. A new forward control bus was the O 321 H (H = Heck — rear mounted engine). This was the first type where an integral construction of

1951 MERCEDES-BENZ Typ L325 3½-ton truck, Daimler-Benz

1952 MERCEDES-BENZ Typ 0319 18-seater bus, Daimler-Benz

1958 MERCEDES-BENZ Typ LP333 twin-steer truck, OMM

welded base and skeleton body frame was used. The L 319 which appeared in 1956 was a 1¾ tonner available as a van or truck and using a 4-cylinder 1.8 litre engine (gasoline or diesel). As O 319 it was also available as bus with 10-18 seats.

In 1961 the appearance of a new range of forward control trucks also brought a new system of type designations. L now stood for the short-hood versions, LP for the forward-control versions. The LP 333 for the first time was a 6-wheeler with tandem front axles. This had a 6-cylinder 10.8 litre engine and a payload capacity of 8-10 tons. In this period the range covered payload capacities from 1¾ to 10 tons. Most types were available as short-hood and forward control versions with various wheelbases and as lorries, tippers and articulated tractors. Production of the heavier types was in the Gaggenau plant, the lighter ones were produced in Mannheim. The former Auto Union plant at Dusseldorf manufactured the 1¾ tonner. In 1963 a new plant at Worth took up production and the former Mannheim and Gaggenau production was concentrated here.

A new system of type designations was introduced in 1963, even more complicated. The 2220 was a 3-axle version which was not in the program before. One year later the type 1620 with 9½ ton payload capacity appeared as the first type with a designed cab. More important was the underfloor installation of the 6-cylinder 10.8 litre engine.

1965 MERCEDES-BENZ Typ 334 articulated tanker, GNG

1968 MERCEDES-BENZ Typ 1113 sweeper/sprinkler, GNG

It was also in the early sixties that Mercedes-Benz changed from the pre-combustion chamber principle to injection type diesel engines. A cubic shaped forward control cab for some types was introduced in 1965, allowing the underfloor installation of the engine. In 1968 a new series of light-trucks, the L 406, L 408, L 508 and L 606 appeared for payload capacities of 1½ to 2¾ tons. A new V-10-cylinder engine (16 litre, 320 hp) appeared in 1969 and was installed in various new types which were characterized by tilt cabs.

In 1970 Mercedes-Benz took over the make of Hanomag-Henschel, which previously had taken over Tempo. Mercedes engines were installed in some Hanomag-Henschel trucks and in the ex-Tempo light truck. After 1973 Mercedes concentrated on forward control versions with only a few short-hood types remaining in the program. Today the program covers a complete range from the 207/307 1-ton models with 2.3-litre gasoline or 2.4-litre diesel engines, to the 2632 series with 320 hp V-10 engines, available as a 26-ton GVW rigid 6, 38-ton GTW artic or 100-ton drawbar tractor. All kinds of chassis up to 6 × 6 drive are available.

The development of buses during the sixties was the continuation of the O 321 which was series produced. The O 322 for the first time used air suspension. This and the O 317 were mainly built for city services. In 1965 the very successful O 321 was dropped after production of about 20,000 units, a record in Europe. The successor was the O 302, available in several line service and touring versions.

1971 MERCEDES-BENZ L206D 1¼-ton van, Daimler-Benz

1975 MERCEDES-BENZ 1626S 32-ton GCW truck, Daimler-Benz

New was the O 309 which succeeded the O 319 as a small bus with 10-17 seats. A new type was presented in 1968, the type O 305 following the standard bus design for city services. In 1975 the type O 303 appeared as a new touring bus version and the O 307 for long distance

1978 MERCEDES-BENZ 207 van, Daimler-Benz

services. The type O 317 is an articulated bus with underfloor engine placed amidships. The chassis is built by Steyr of Austria, bodies are made by Vetter of Stuttgart who also builds a high-decker. Both Vetter versions are part of the official Mercedes-Benz range. Ludewig of Essen uses the O 317 for a 1½-decker bus. 6-, 8- and 10-cylinder engines with up to 320 hp are used for Mercedes-Benz buses.

The "Hybrid-Bus" follows the gas-electric principle, the "Duo-Bus" is a combined battery/trolley bus. The electric motors are either fed by batteries or by the overhead wires, which also re-charge the batteries.

Today the production of trucks is concentrated at the Worth plant, Mannheim produces buses, and light vehicles are built at Dusseldorf and Hamburg. The old Benz plant at Gaggenau with a long history in production of commercial vehicles specializes in production of the Unimog (see under this heading).

Mercedes-Benz trucks and buses are made in a wide variety of foreign countries including Argentina (since 1951), Brazil (since 1953) and Saudi Arabia (since 1978.) In India they were known as Tata-Mercedes-Benz from 1954 to 1971, and since then as Tata. In 1979 it was announced that a U.S. plant would be established at Hampton, Virginia in 1980, parts for assembly coming from the Brazilian plant. In 1977 Mercedes-Benz acquired Euclid Inc. from White, giving them an entry into the heavy-duty dump truck market. *HON*

MERCEDES-ELECTRIQUE (A/D) 1906-1910

Societe Mercedes Electrique S.A., Paris

Electric driven cars appeared under this name and were built to order of Emil Jellinek-Mercedes after he had given up his interests in the Daimler company of Stuttgart. He founded the "Societe Mercedes Electrique" in Paris for distribution of these cars, which were based on the designs of Lohner-Porsche. Production was taken up in 1906 in the Austro-Daimler works, and they only differed from these by having the electric hub cap motors in the rear wheels instead of the front wheels which was favored by Lohner. Vans, trucks and buses were built. The German Daimler company took over a license and started production in 1908 in the Marienfelde plant. It is interesting to notice that these were the first commercials which appeared under the name of Mercedes, while gasoline driven commercials retained the name Daimler until 1926 when they merged with Benz. Production of "Mercedes Electrique" commercials in Marienfelde was not very important. *HON*

1916 MERCURY (i) Bulley 3-wheel tractor, Goodyear

MERCURY (i) (US) 1910-1917

Mercury Manufacturing Company, Chicago, Illinois

This make offered light open high-wheelers through 1916, with capacity of ½ ton. These initially used 2-cylinder, 2-stroke air-cooled engines with forward control, planetary transmission on wheelbase of 7 feet, 1 inch. In 1912, a progressive gearbox was used. In 1915, the Bulley tractor, named after the company's president became the major vehicle for this manufacturer. The Bulley Tractor was a 3-wheeler with the lone rear wheel driven by a chain, though there was also a model with single front wheel. *GMN*

MERCURY (ii) 1914-1915

Mercury Cyclecar Company, Detroit, Michigan

The delivery van offered on this cyclecar chassis was priced at $400. For this, a buyer got a chassis with 8-foot, 4-inch wheelbase with track of only 3-feet. The 10 hp 2-cylinder engne was air-cooled and drove the 700-pound vehicle through a friction transmission and long double belts to the rear wheels. *GMN*

MERCURY (iii) (GB) 1914

Medina Engineering Co. Ltd., Twickenham, Middx.

This light car maker offered briefly a delivery van on its 10 hp 4-cylinder chassis. The price complete was £195. *GNG*

1966 MERCURY (iv) T3 3-ton truck, OMM

MERCURY (iv) (GB) 1920 to date

(1) Mercury Truck & Tractor Co. Ltd., Gloucester 1920-1964
(2) Mercury Truck & Tractor Co. Ltd., Guildford, Surrey 1964-1972
(3) Reliance-Mercury Ltd., Halifax, Yorks 1972 to date

The bulk of this company's output has been in the field of industrial trucks not designed to run on public roads, and more recently aircraft towing tractors have been made. During their period at Guildford, when they were actually making vehicles in the Dennis factory, a number of 3-ton trucks with Perkins 4.99 or Ford 122 E engines were made; these T3 models were quite suitable for road work as well as in-plant use. In 1972 Mercury left Dennis and merged with another maker of industrial trucks, Reliance, and since then road-going vehicles have not been made. *OM*

MERIT (US) 1911

Waterville Tractor Company, Waterville, Ohio

The Model B was a ½-tonner and appears to have been the only effort by this manufacturer to produce commercial vehicles. This small chassis had a wheelbase of only 7 feet, 4 inches and was powered by a 2-cylinder, air-cooled engine mounted under the body. Drive was through a friction transmission and double chains. With open delivery body the price was $1,000. *GMN*

1970 MERK Pullax P40 tipper truck, FH

MERK (CH) 1958-1971

Merk AG., Maschinenfabrik, Dietikon ZH

Merk launched the light, handy and most verstile Merk-Pullax 4 × 4 multi-purpose vehicle in two different sizes. the P20 had a V-twin 4-stroke diesel engine of 1145 cc and 20 hp purchased from Warchalowski of Vienna. The single-tube backbone chassis offered high ground clearance and wheelbase was adjustable from 190 to 270 cm. The gearbox contained 6 forward and 2 reverse speeds and both axles had differential locks. Payload was about 2 tons. The more powerful P40 had a V-4 diesel of 2290 cc and 40 hp of the same make. Some of the early models had 4-cylinder gasoline engines. The sturdy P40 was fitted with a 4 × 2 speed gearbox with 4 reverse speeds. wheelbase was 6'10" to 9' 2" and payload up to 3 tons. Both models could be equipped with an automatic winch which could be synchronized with the wheel-traction and allowed the Merk-Pullax to climb a fantastic 100% (45°) with 1, 2 ton loads. After 1971 Merk concentrated on manufacturing of motor-tractors. *FH*

MERKUR (D) 1929-1931

Fahrzeugfabrik Quickborn, Quickborn

This was a tri-van with one driven rear wheel and back seat, platform or box being in front. Payload capacity was from 300 to 850 kg and 200, 300 and 440 cc engines were used. *HON*

MERRYWEATHER (GB) 1899 to date

Merryweather & Sons Ltd., Greenwich, London, S.E. 10

Originally builders of hand and horse-drawn manual fire engines, their first steam pump apeared in 1861 and the first steam propelled fire pump was produced in 1899. Over 30 of the "Motor Fire King", as it was called, were produced up to about 1910. It was powered by a vertical water tube boiler producing steam at 120 psi. for the duplex vertical engine with cylinder of 4 ins. and 7 ins. There were six models on offer varying with the output of the 2-cylinder "Greenwich Gem" fire pump, and they could be supplied as coal or oil fired and mounted on either steel or wooden wheels. During the frst decade a few steam trucks and cesspool emptiers were built on a chassis of similar desgn to that of the fire engines save that the boiler was mounted right at the front instead of at the rear on the "Fire King".

1903 saw the first gasoline driven chemical type fire appliance produced by the Greenwich works and in the following year the first gasoline engined motor pump was built. About the same time a few gasoline trucks were built and a design of battery electric chemical fire engine with two motors was advertised.

1904 MERRYWEATHER fire engine, GNG

1914 MERRYWEATHER fire engine, NMM

In 1906 the first centrifugal pump was installed in a motor appliance and then in 1908 a turntable ladder having the propelling engine to power the ladder movements was perfected. A motor cycle fire engine was built in 1910 and during the 1914/18 war fire pumps of up to 1,000 gallons per minute capacity were built. 1922 saw the first Merryweather fire appliance on pneumatic tires and in 1924 the first engine to deal with oil fires was built.

Early designs of vehicle were produced in their own workshops because Merryweathers also produced steam tramcars and steam equipment for brewing and other trades. As the motor industry was better equipped to supply specialist parts Merryweather went outside for the frame, engines, axles, etc., merely building such specialized items as the pumps, tanks, bodywork, hosereels, ladders, etc. Early gasoline machines were based on Aster, while during the 1920's and 1930's varying types of Albion chassis formed the basis for most Merryweather appliances. As with other fire engine builders their equipment could be mounted on chassis to suit the customer and a few other proprietary chassis were thus endowed.

During WW II many Merryweather turntable ladders were mounted on Leyland and Austin chassis and one notable experiment was to mount 100 ft. ladders on a few amphibious vehicles in order for troops to mount cliffs on the other side of the English Channel during the Normandy landings! Postwar productions have been mounted on a variety of chassis including Maudslay, AEC, Bedford, Ford and Land-Rover. *OM*

MERZ (US) 1913-1915
Merz Cyclecar Company, Indianapolis, Indiana

The Merz was a true cyclecar with a tread of but 3 feet, 4 inches and wheelbase of seven feet. As a light delivery van it used cycle fenders and a single headlamp. Its 10 hp, 2-cylinder engine was air-cooled and the drive was through a friction transmission and belts to the rear wheels. Somewhat incongrously, it had full elliptic springs all around. *GMN*

MESERVE (US) 1901-1903
(1) W.F. Meserve, Canobie Lake, New Hampshire
(2) Meserve Auto Truck Co., Methuen, Mass.

The first Meserves were steam trucks with boiler and vertical 2-cylinder engine made by Edward Clark of Dorchester, Mass. They had wooden frames, double chain drive and a capacity of 2 tons. Two were made for the Pemberton Mills of Laurence, Mass. Later Meserve made a few gasoline trucks. *GNG*

MESSENGER (US) 1913-1914
Messenger Mfg. Co., Tatamy, Pa.

The Messenger firm was primarily a manufacturer of railroad cars. The firm experimented with a 30 hp 4-cylinder 2-ton truck, but few were built. It cost $2,400. *DJS*

MESSERER (US) 1898
S. Messerer, Newark, N.J.

Messerer's delivery wagon had a 1,000 pound 4-cylinder gasoline engine with a 4-inch bore and 6-inch stroke, which developed 6 hp @ 350 rpm. The drive was by 6 inch pulley. *RW*

MESSIER (F) 1928-1931
Georges Messier, Montrouge, Seine

Messier was one of the pioneers of hydraulically retractable undercarriages for aircraft, but prior to this he built a small number of cars incorporating an ingenious all-independent pneumatic suspension. Later ones were powered by Lycoming sixes and straight-eights, the largest Messier having a 4.8-litre power unit. Though production was vey modest (only about 50 8-cylinder models were delivered), a fair number of these were fitted with ambulance body work. *MCS*

METEOR (US) 1913-1932: 1941
Meteor Motor Car Co., Piqua, Ohio

Maurice Wolfe's Meteor company was responsible for a very ordinary assembled 6-cylinder private car, with engines by Model or Continental. His other products included a special professional car chassis which he supplied to such bodybuilders as Miller of Bellefontaine, and also phonographs, hence the company's incredible 1920s slogan: 'Kills 'em with Music, and Hauls 'em Away'. By 1915 Meteor had progressed to a line of complete ambulances and hearses using the inevitable Continental Six. Prices were competitive, only $1,750 being asked for a combination car capable of fulfilling both functions. A year later an extra $300 would buy a similar vehicle powered by America's only proprietary V12, the 6.4-litre ohv Weidely. This engine was dropped at the end of the 1917 season, whereupon Meteor settled down to the familiar formula of 6-cylinder Continental engines, Warner gearboxes, and Columbia axles, progressing to the new limousine style of body in 1922. 1923 saw a cheaper companion line, the Mort, and 1924 Meteors had hydraulic fwb and balloon tires. A straight-8 engine, also by Continental, was optional in 1927, and standard in 1928 models, which had radiators not unlike those of Model-A Fords. Like S and S, Meteor switched to Buick mechanical elements in 1932, eventually followed the Cincinnati firm by concentrating their efforts on Cadillac chassis. A short-lived venture of 1941 was a 29-passenger transit bus, Model-101, but only a single prototype was built, and a more significant PSV venture was the production of bodies for Reo's 96-HT between 1945 and 1947. Meteor merged with (iii) Miller in 1957, the twin names being perpetuated in a range of professional vehicles mounted on Cadillac, Chevrolet and Dodge chassis. *MCS/MBS*

METROCAB (GB) 1970-1971
Metropolitan-Cammell-Weymann Ltd., Birmingham

An attempt to break into the London taxicab market by the well-known passenger vehicle body-builders, Metro-Cammell, the Metrocab was powered by a 1760cc Perkins diesel engine, and used a number of Ford components including gearbox and transmission from the Transit van, and radiator grille from the Cortina car. The lightweight fibreglass body had a greater window area than any other London cab. Two prototypes were operated by the London General Cab Company for some time, but the Metrocab was not put into production. *GNG*

METROPOLITAN (iii) (GB/S) 1970 to date
Metro-Cammell-Weymann Ltd., Washwood Heath, Birmingham

Originally known as the Metro-Scania, the Metropolitan is an integral-construction bus with transverse rear-mounted Scania 11.1-litre 6-cylinder diesel engine and

1975 METROPOLITAN 74-seater bus, MCW

1978 METROBUS 80-seater bus, MCW

fully automatic electro-hydraulic transmission. Both single and double deck models were made, the former for 63 passengers (44 seated). The double decker was made in two versions, a single door 75 seater and a double door 74 seater. By December 1977 more than 660 Metropolitans were in service in Britain, leading users being London Transport who had 164 double deckers, Tyne & Wear PTE (140), West Yorkshire, Leicester and Merseyside. Two Metropolitans were exported to the China Motor Bus Company in Hong Kong.

Although the higher-priced Metropolitan remains theoretically available, MCW announced in 1977 the Metrobus with Rolls-Royce or Gardner transverse rear-mounted diesels, Rockwell-Thompson semi-loadbearing frame, GKN axles, Voith, SCG or GKN-SRM automatic transmissions and Dunlop or Firestone non-independent air suspension. MCW plan to build 600 Metrobuses per year, with first deliveries in early 1978, and could expand to 1,500 with bodies by themselves or outside firms. *GNG/OM*

METROVICK (GB) 1934-1942

Metropolitan-Vickers Electrical Co. Ltd., Trafford Park, Manchester

As one would expect from such a large organisation the Metrovick range of electrics were based on a well thought out design with the controller located under the driver's seat, the single motor being immediately behind this driving the rear axle by means of a short propellor shaft. The chassis was of box section suitably braced with the wheels well covered with robust fenders. The range consisted of four models employing either worm or spiral bevel axles. The smallest was the 7/9cwt which was of 5ft 6½in wheelbase and had a 193AH battery. The 10/14cwt had a battery rated at 258AH and the chassis was of 5ft 2½in wheelbase, while the 18/22cwt was on a 6ft 7½in

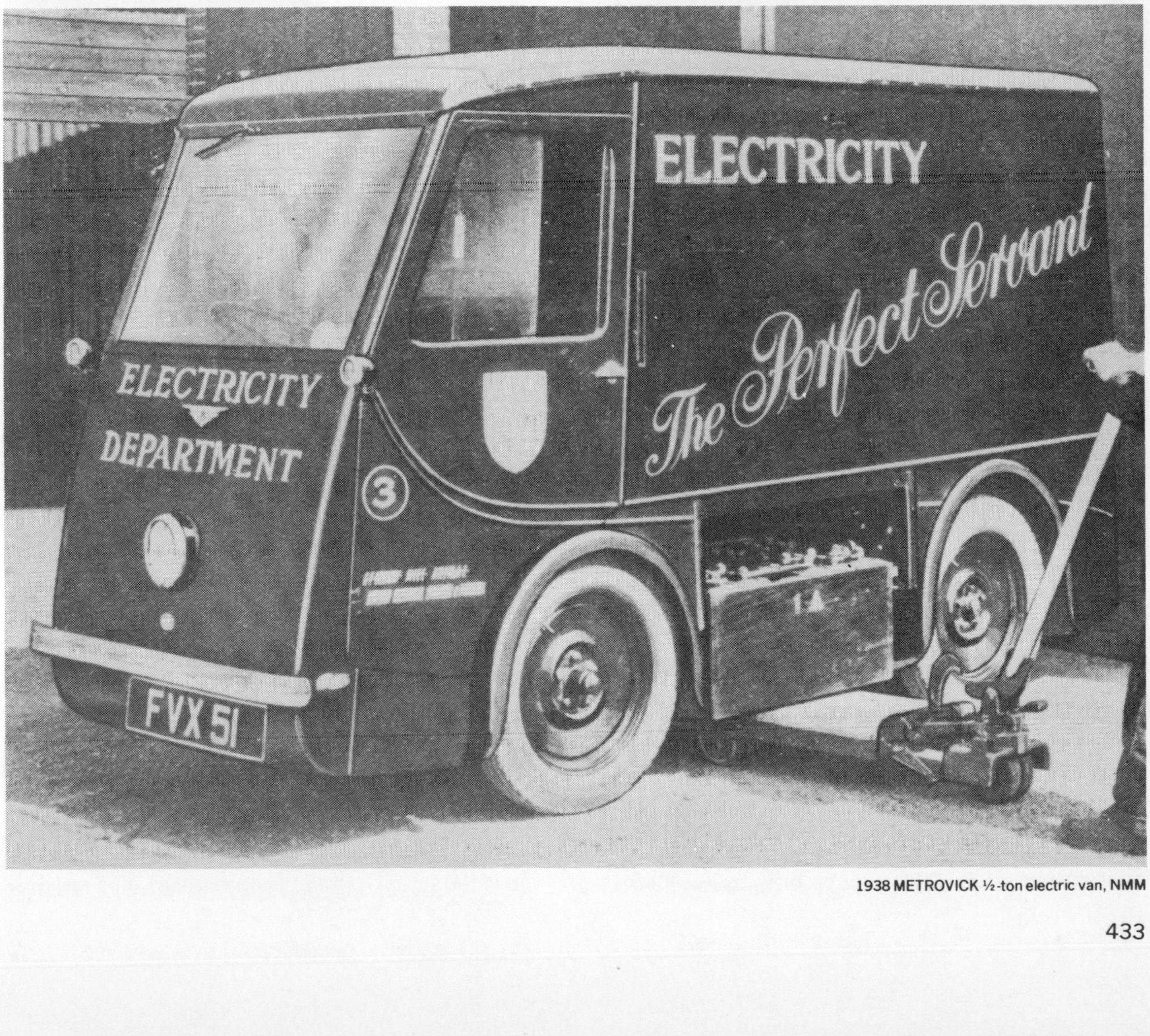

1938 METROVICK ½-ton electric van, NMM

wheelbase chassis. Largest was the 3 tonner with 11ft wheelbase and 336AH battery.

The largest model was discontinued in 1938 but the remaining models continued to be offered up to the early days of the war when the manufacture of electrical equipment was of greater importance and vehicle production was discontinued. OM

METZ (US) 1916-1917

Metz Co., Waltham, Mass.

The Metz 1-tonner was priced at $695 and had wheelbase of 10 feet, 10 inches, a 4-cylinder engine under a hood, shaft-drive and pneumatic tires. Metz was a well-known name in passenger cars. *GMN*

MEVEA (GR) 1970 to date

Mevea SA, Athens

This company began by building the British Reliant TW9 3-wheeler under license, and followed this in the same year with an ultra-light 3-wheeler powered by a 50cc single-cylinder engine developing 5.6hp. This Mevea ST150 has a 2-seater fibreglass cab and car type controls. It is also made in the form of a rickshaw taxicab with open body and tiller steering. This model is exported to many countries in the Middle East and Asia. *GA*

1950 MFO-GYROBUS bus, ES

MFO (CH) 1950-c.1960

Maschinenfabrik Oerlikon, Zurich-Oerlikon

This old company producing tool-machines, dynamos and various electric appliances launced in 1950 a highly unorthodox and unique bus for urban passenger transportation, the Gyrobus. The principle of having electricity produced by a heavy gyroscope turning at high speed was of course long known but technical problems kept it from practical application. MFO after extensive research and tests had completed a bus for 70 passengers which made use of the gyroscope principle. In the middle of the chassis, close to the center of gravity a large electro-gyro was mounted. The horizontal gyro-wheel of high quality steel measured 5'3" diameter and weighed 3300lbs. Launched at 3000rpm it stored about 9 Kw/h which was enough energy for up to 4 miles in flat country or correspondingly less if gradients of up to 20% had to be climbed. For starting the bus and putting the gyro to the required speed, electric current of the available network was drawn from a pole by means of three power collectors. The gyro was linked to a motor-generator which served to launch the gyro and afterwards produced the required electric power. This was then transmitted through a selector with 6 speeds to the electric traction-motor of 100hp linked with the rear axle. At the important bus-stops the time was utilized to draw again electric current from the net and increase the turning speed of the gyroscope.

In 1953 a small Swiss town, Yverdon, put the MFO Gyrobus in daily service on a 3 mile stretch. Total daily mileage was over 125 miles and the experiment proved quite successful. About a dozen MFO Gyrobuses were then exported to Leopoldville in the then Belgian Congo. Shortly afterwards MFO abandoned production. *FH*

MGT (F) 1950-1954

Million-Guiet-Tubauto S.A., Argenteuil

Million-Guiet-Tubauto, well-known bodybuilders constructing among others for the RATP of Paris, tried in 1950 their luck with an integral bus around a French Ford V-8 gas engine, mounted in the rear part of a very smooth, rounded body. A fleet of these buses was bought in 1952 by the French city of Rennes. Also available was a trolley-bus version, both versions being sold as well under the name Tubauto. *JFJK*

MI-VAL (I) 1950-c.1960

Metalmeccanica Italiana Valtrompia SpA, Brescia

Like many Italian motorcycle factories, Mi-Val offered a 350 kg delivery 3-wheeler of open-saddle type with two driven rear wheels. The engine was a 172cc 2-stroke single, other features being chain primary drive, backbone frame, and hydraulic brakes. *MCS*

MIAG (D) 1936-1955

(1) Muhlenbau und Industrie A.G., Braunschweig 1936-1945

(2) Miag-Fahrzeugbau GmbH., Ober-Ramstadt 1949-1955

A tractor was presented by this firm in 1936. The 10 or 20bhp diesel engines were placed in the rear.

After WW II Miag took up production in 1949 with an electric municipal vehicle and a forward control transporter using a VW engine. Also a new road tractor was presented, at first with 2-cylinder, later with 3-cylinder MWM diesel engine. *HON*

MICHAUX (F) 1870-1884

Ernest Michaux, Paris

Michaux used a conventional locomotive boiler but was unique amongst steam tractor builders in using 4 double acting cylinders placed in pairs, as separate engines, on either side of the outer firebox in a Corless frame bracketed to the boiler and carrying the crankshaft which carried, in the centre, a chain sprocket from which the drive was by pitch chain to a large sprocket on each rear wheel, the whole arrangement being duplicated on the other side of the tractor. Having no flywheel the tractor was clearly intended for haulage. *RAW*

MICHIGAN (US) 1915-1921

Michigan Hearse & Carriage Co., Grand Rapids, Mich.

The Michigan was a straightforward hearse on an assembled chassis with 6-cylinder Continental engine and worm drive. The 1921 range included an ornate 'Gothic' model with stained glass windows. *MCS*

M.I.C.M. (R) 1964-1966

MICM Usina Mecanica, Muscel, Cimpalung

MICM was a Rumanian factory that built the Soviet GAZ/UAZ 4x4 utility vehicle in simplified form. The body was identical to its Soviet counterpart but was offered only as a 2-seater utility truck with canvas top. The 70hp 4-cylinder engine was the same as in the GAZ, but unlike the Soviet model there was no auxiliary gearbox. After two years of production, MICM was re-named Aro, and under this name the factory is still active today. *GA*

MIDLAND (i) (US) 1918-1919

Midland Motor Car & Truck Co., Oklahoma City, Okla.

The single model under this tradename was a 2½-tonner with solid rubber tires on cast steel spoke wheels. *GMN*

1947 MIDLAND (ii) ¾-ton electric milk float. MJWW

MIDLAND (ii) (GB) 1935-1958

Midland Vehicles Ltd., Leamington Spa, Warwicks

Midland vehicles followed the normal layout of the period battery van by having forward control, motor placed just behind the driver and shaft drive to the rear axle. Batteries were placed either side of the chassis frame, pannier fashion. The two original models of 10 and 12cwt were later expanded into a range of five models in the 10/12, 12/15, 18/22, 25/28 and 30/35-cwt payload classes. These were designated B12, BA12, B20. B25 amd B30 respectively. Chassis or complete van or truck types were produced with body lengths from 7feet to 9ft 6in.

During WW II the range shrank to two models, the 15- and 25-cwt, but soon after the war the range was extended to 5 models in the 12 to 30-cwt range. The two smaller models — 12cwt and 15cwt — were based on a 7ft 77/8in wheelbase chassis while the 20, 25 and 30-cwt models were a foot longer. In 1951 the Vandot 10-cwt model was introduced on a 5ft 6in wheelbase chassis and in 1953 the 12-cwt model was discontinued. The remaining range continued along similar lines until production ceased entirely in 1958. *OM*

MIESSE (B) 1898-1972

(1) Jules Miesse et Cie, Brussels 1900-1939

(2) Auto-Miesse S.A., Brussels 1939-1972

Between 1898 and 1907 Miesse built steam cars, and it seems probable that some of the early chassis had light goods delivery bodies. About 1904, however, production of a somewhat heavier chassis for loads of 30cwt, designed for paraffin fuel, was started. The vertical boiler, of semi-flash type, was placed in front of the driver, and consisted of a central pot surrounded by water tubes arranged as coils with the ends set radially into the walls of the pot, and the whole enclosed in an insulated outer jacket.The engine favoured internal combustion practice, having three cylinders, single acting, with mushroom inlet and exhaust valves pushrod operated from two camshafts. The piston rods were pivoted in a hollow skirted piston and drove the crankshaft direct. In addition to goods vehicles, some buses were made, but all steam vehicle production ceased in 1907. Turner of Wolverhampton, however, continued to offer their license-built Turner-Miesse steamers as late as 1913.

Miesse were experimenting with gas engines in 1900, and four years later they had built their first 4-cylinder taxi for use in Brussels. Private cars were to engage their principal attention up to World War I, and the only goods models produced were some car-based light vans, notably a convertible tourer in the idiom much favoured by French makers of the 1920s. After the Armistice they introduced an ohc 4-cylinder engine which they applied to cars and trucks alike. By 1925 a wide range of conventional models was available, with payloads in the 1/5-ton bracket. Bus versions had fwb and could carry up to 40 passengers. Alongside their fours, Miesse also developed a straight-8 unit. It was seldom encountered in private cars (which were discontinued after 1926), but was successfully applied to a bus in that year, possibly the first commercial 8-in-line to see series production. Capacity of the 5-bearing unit was 5.2 litres with an advertised output of 100bhp, other features being magneto ignition, an engine-driven tire pump, full electrics, pneumatic tires, and double-reduction drive. Three forward speeds sufficed. A rigid 6-wheeler development followed in 1927, with 4-speed gearbox, X-braced frame, servo brakes on all wheels, and worm drive, this model seeing service not only in Brussels, but as far afield as Argentina and Syria. Forward control editions of the chassis were used as refuse collectors and furniture vans. Like most Belgian makers, Miesse developed a line of gazogenes for use in the Congo, a special 6.8-litre engine being offered for a 2½-tonner with Mateco plant sponsored by a firm in Elizabethville. The 1929 goods range included a straight-8 5-tonner, though lighter versions retained 4-cylinder units. Fwb were standard on all but the smallest Miesses, and all wore pneumatic tires. An unusual feature of forward control trucks and buses was the frontmounted spare wheel, which doubled as a bumper.

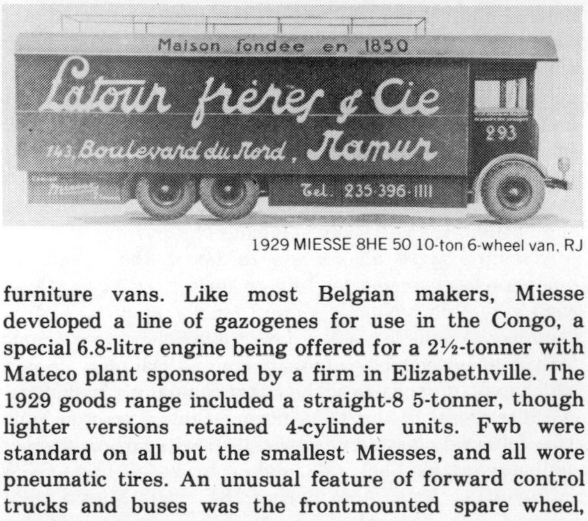

1929 MIESSE 8HE 50 10-ton 6-wheel van. RJ

1930 MIESSE 8HE 46 36-seater bus, FLP

A curious departure of 1930 was the Double Bus, a 6x4 full fronted machine for up to 100 passengers. This was designed to take either gas or electric motors, the latter fed by batteries or overhead wires. All power units were laterally mounted, with a separate worm drive to each pair of rear wheels. The footbrake was hydraulically actuated with a disc transmission brake, and plans were laid to use a pair of 4- or 6-cylinder engines in the internal combustion versions, though only the former installation, with a total capacity of 5.2 litres, seems to have been tried. Options for the 1931 season included a Bellay gas producer on the 2-tonner and Junkers 2-stroke opposed-piston diesels in the 3- and 5-ton types, but these latter were shortlived; a year later Miesse, like Bernard in France and Kromhout in the Netherlands, acquired a manufacturing license for the British Gardner unit. This had been standardised throughout the range by 1934, and came in 4-, 5-, and 6-cylinder forms. The 1939 range was extensive, covering payloads from 4 tons upward. The biggest Miesse was an 8x4 forward control 16-tonner with the unusual feature of a radiator mounted on the cab roof. Smaller forward control Miesses bore a marked external resemblance to contemporary F.Ns, while there were also full-front single-decker buses and coaches for up to 60 passengers. Buses were exported to Belgrade in 1940. During the German occupation the company made Bellay gas producer conversions.

After World War II truck activities centered round the heavy-duty class, a range of types from 5 to 18 tons using the three basic types of Gardner engine, though the straight-8 was now available in 16-tonners. Gearboxes had five or six forward speeds, air brakes were standard, and normal control models had their engines mounted well over the front axle. A new forward control bus chassis with the Gardner 6 engine and air-operated preselective gearbox appeared in 1949, followed two years later by an underfloor-engined type with six forward speeds, noted for a cranked chassis frame of immense complexity. By 1955 Miesse had had second thoughts, and were trying a simpler model with conventional ZF gearbox and the engine mounted vertically alongside the driver.

Attempts were also made to boost the company's business by agencies for foreign makes. In 1948 Miesse were assembling Nash cars and trucks, as well as Mack commercial vehicles; a few years later they were agents for the heavy vehicles of Atkinson and Daimler, a policy which explains the use of the latter company's 10.6-litre 6-cylinder diesel in the T635 normal-control tractive unit. This followed classic lines, with 6-speed gearbox, 2-speed double-reduction back axle, and air brakes; it had a GCW rating of 31 tons. Also during the 1950s Miesse collaborated with Brossel and F. N on a range of specialist vehicles for the Belgian Army.

By 1960, however, the firm had reverted to the faithful 6-cylinder Gardner (the more powerful 10.4-litre 6LX was now available), and their offerings embraced a range of 10/13-ton 4x2 trucks, as well as a 6x2 twin-steer model for heavier loads. Four years later the 8-cylinder Gardner was once again available in tractive units, and the heaviest truck was the C618, a straightforward 17-ton 6x4 with twelve forward speeds, power steering, and a new make of engine in the shape of an 11.4-litre, 210bhp Bussing — Miesse now held the agency for the Brunswick firm. Buses were Gardner-powered, and consisted of the orthodox full-front VG, and the HLC with horizontal underfloor engine. Both had air brakes, but the VG shared its 6-speed ZF box with the trucks, whereas a Daimler fluid transmission was offered on the more modern type.

1968 MIESSE T196 38-ton GCW truck, OMM

Miesse's days were, however, numbered. By 1968 annual production was down to some 50 buses and 20 trucks, and little came of a new range with the Detroit Diesel 2-stroke engine, a design which the company had exhibited at the 1948 Brussels Salon. Their rear-engined ARL6M bus bore a marked resemblance to Daimler's Roadliner, its 5.2-litre V6 engine driving forward to a 6-speed Allison automatic gearbox. The trucks and tractors, now rated for GVWs of 18 tons and GCWs of 38 tons, were of forward control type, and could be had with the 9,3-litre 322bhp engine and automatic transmission, but by late 1971 a mere forty hands were at work in the Miesse factory, and the last vehicles were trickling through. The main activities were the reconditioning of existing machines and pre-delivery checks on new Berliets destined for the Belgian market. *MCS/RAW*

MIKASA (J) 1958-1961

Okamura Manufacturing Co. Ltd., Tokyo

Named after Prince Mikasa, the Emperor's youngest brother, the Mikasa was an ingenious fwd light car with 585cc ohv flat-twin engine. Features included all-independent springing and a 2-speed (later 3-speed) torque converter transmission. Light delivery vans were listed as well as the standard sports roadster. *MCS*

MIKROMOBIL (D) 1922-1924

(1) Automobil-Gesellschaft Thomsen KG., Hamburg-Wandsbek 1922-1924

(2) Mikromobil A.G., Hamburg-Wandsbek 1924

This small car with 6/18 PS 4-cylinder two-stroke engine had an interchangeable body and could be used as private car or van. *HON*

MILBURN (US) 1914-1915

Milburn Wagon Co., Toledo, Ohio

The electric Milburn had an underslung chassis with a wheelbase of 7 feet, 6 inches. It was equipped with Philadelphia storage batteries, a General Electric motor and worm drive. With solid rubber tires, the chassis alone was priced at $985. The Milburn was more successful as an electric passenger car. *GMN*

1899 MILDE electric van, Autocar

MILDE (F) 1896-1909

Milde et Cie, Levallois-Perret, Seine

Charles Milde claimed to have built an electric fire-engine in 1888, but serious manufacture began in 1896 with a 6 hp 1-ton van; usually, this was a conversion of a Panhard gasoline-car chassis. A 25/30 cwt development, built this time from scratch, took part in the 1898 Electric Vehicle Trials; there were six forward speeds, the Postel-Vinay motors and their batteries were mounted under the driver's seat, and top speed was 9 mph with a range of 36 miles. In 1900 Milde introduced a forecarriage conversion for horse-drawn cabs and vans, while a wide range of rear wheel drive types, including a 10-seater omnibus was offered, these latter having rack and pinion steering. The avant-trains had been dropped by 1902, and a year later gasoline-electrics were added to the repertoire, these, like the battery-electrics, being of forward control type. Light models used 6 hp de Dion engines, but the 1-tonner had a 10 hp unit said to be of Milde's own make. Some chain-driven postal vans were put into service in Paris in 1904, but subsequent Mildes featured motors mounted under short frontal hoods, and shaft drive. There is no evidence of active manufacture after 1909; reports of subsequent revivals were no doubt inspired by the brief electric-truck boom of 1925-26, when Panhard, Peugeot and de Dion-Bouton toyed with such designs, Peugeot even reviving the Krieger name. The Milde-Krieger label was, however, attached to some electric conversions of light cars and vans in the 1940s. *MCS*

MILDE-KRIEGER (F) 1946-1947

Le Conducteur Electrique Blinde Incombustible SA, Courbevoie, Seine

These two historic names first appeared together on electric conversions of private cars and light vans offered during the German Occupation. At the 1946 Paris Salon the company offered a 20/25-cwt forward control electric van. It had fwd in the best Krieger tradition, being based on the small Chenard-Walcker later made by Peugeot as the D3A, but like most of the wartime electric hangovers, it lasted only a short while. *MCS*

MILITOR (US) 1917-1918

Like the much better-know Liberty, the Militor was a standardized US army design intended to replace the F.W.D. and Nash Quad which were adaptations of civilian designs. Like them it had 4-wheel drive, and was intended

1918 MILITOR 3-ton 4×4 army truck, BHV

as a load carrier and as a tractor. Powered by a 36 hp 4-cylinder Wisconsin engine, it had a radiator behind the power unit in the manner of the Walter. There were 4 speeds, and final drive was by internal gears. A total of 150 Militors were made, by the Militor Corporation of Jersey City, and the Sinclair Motor Corporation of New York City. The ending of hostilities prevented further development. *GNG*

MILLER (i) (US) 1906
Miller Garage Co. Inc., Bridgeport, Conn.

This company made goods and passenger vehicles, including sightseeing buses, powered by a 40/45 hp 4-cylinder Continental Type O engine. They had 3 speeds, chain drive and maximum speed of 20 mph. *GNG*

MILLER (ii) (US) 1913-1914
Miller Car Co., Detroit, Mich.

The Miller Model A, a ½-tonner appears to have been the only product under this name. It used a 4-cylinder side-valve engine under the hood, with a 3-speed gearbox and shaft drive. Wheelbase was 9 feet, 4 inches, pneumatic tires were standard with delivery van body, the price was $800. It was succeeded by the Kosmath. *GMN*

MILLER (iii) (US) 1917-1924
A. J. Miller Co., Bellefontaine, Ohio

Founded in 1870, this firm of coachbuilders had progressed to ambulance and hearse bodies by 1912. Initially they bought chassis from Meteor, furnishing bodies in return. In 1917, however, they started to build on their own chassis, a straightforward affair using various types of 6-cylinder Continental engine. These were produced until 1924, though Miller continued to produce bodies for other chassis during this period. They were always prepared to work on any make of car, and during the 1930s their work appeared on Chevrolets, Chryslers, Fords, Hudsons and Nashes as well as the more familiar Cadillacs and Packards. The company merged with Meteor in 1957. *MCS*

MILLER-BALSAMO (I) c.1935-1939
Ernesto Balsamo, Milan

Miller-Balsamo motorcycles used single-cylinder Rudge engines, or their own license-made variant of this type. Their light truck followed accepted lines, apart from its swing-axle rear suspension. *MCS*

MILLER-QUINCY (US) 1921-1924
E.M. Miller Co., Quincy, Ill.

This firm built ambulance and hearse bodies, some of which they mounted on their own chassis. These, like most American hearse-makes of the period, used the 6-cylinder sv Continental engine. *MCS*

MILLOT (CH) 1904-06
Eugen Kaufman, Zurich

Kaufman designed and built a few surprisingly advanced omnibuses which were in service in the German Black Forest area. Whereas most of the contemporary competitors had open cockpits for instance, the Millot bus offered full weather protection to the driver as it had not only a fixed roof but also a large windshield. The engine was placed under a proper hood above the front-axle, the radiator was of the honeycomb type and final drive by

1904 MILLOT bus, ES

chains. After having built a small number of modern and powerful touring cars — a 40/50 hp 4-cylinder-chassis was shown at the Paris Salon in 1906 — the marque disappeared. *FH*

MILNES-DAIMLER (D/GB) 1901-1914
(1) G.F. Milnes & Co. Ltd., Hadley, Wellington, Salop 1901-1902
(2) Milnes-Daimler Ltd., London W 1902-1912
(3) Milnes-Daimler-Mercedes Ltd., London W. 1912-1914

The Milnes-Daimler was a German Daimler, made either in Cannstatt or Marienfelde, with British bodywork. Up to 1904 these bodies were built by the tramcar makers G.F. Milnes but after the closure of this company, Milnes-Daimler supplied chassis only which were fitted with the

1901 MILNES-DAIMLER War Department Trials truck, Autocar

customer's own choice of coachwork. The first Milnes-Daimler truck appeared in 1901; it had an 8 hp V-twin engine which drove via a 4-speed gearbox and propeller shaft to the rear axle. The final drive was unusual in that at the end of each half-shaft was a small gearwheel which engaged with teeth cut internally on drums bolted to the rear wheels. This system was very noisy and was soon abandoned. Two of these early Milnes-Daimlers took part in the 1901 Liverpool Heavy Vehicle Trials and Aldershot War Department Trials, being the only gasoline engined vehicles to do so. By 1902 a 4-cylinder 16 hp model appeared with a capacity of 2½ tons. Smaller 2-cylinder chassis for 30 and 35 cwt loads were also made, these running on solid rubber tires whereas the 2½ tonner was shod with iron tires. The first bus also appeared in 1902, a 16-passenger on the 2-cylinder chassis.

In 1904 the appearance of Milnes-Daimlers was modernized by a new full-height honeycomb radiator which replaced the coal-scuttle hood of earlier models. In the Spring of 1904 the first Milnes-Daimler buses appeared on the streets of London, and within three years they had become the most popular make in the capital, which they remained until displaced by the B-type after 1910. The leading operators of Milnes-Daimlers were the London

1903 MILNES-DAIMLER Army charabanc, Autocar

1909 MILNES-DAIMLER 34-seater London bus, NMM

Motor Omnibus Company (Vanguard) who had 300 in 1907, and the London General Omnibus Company. Most were 34-passenger double deckers, but some were single deckers and many of the latter were used on rural routes by the Great Western Railway. The smaller chassis of 1908 had shaft drive; the range of goods vehicles ran from 2 to 5 tons, and by 1913 had been extended at both ends to include a 20 hp 1 tonner and 45 hp 6 tonner. However imports dwindled in the five years prior to World War 1, and of course ceased immediately after the outbreak of war. *GNG*

1902 MILWAUKEE steam delivery wagon, GNG

MILWAUKEE (US) 1901-1902

Milwaukee Automobile Co., Milwaukee, Wis.

This maker of steam passenger cars marketed two distinct models of goods vehicle. One was a light delivery truck based on their 5 hp 2-cylinder car, with a load capacity of 800 lbs., and the other was a heavy steam truck with paraffin-fueled fire-tube boiler and 3-cylinder single-acting engine. This had a seasoned oak frame, two speeds (4 and 10 mph) and single chain drive. It was designed by W.L. Bodman, formerly with the British Simpson & Bodman company, and had a capacity of 4,000 lbs. The light truck was marketed in Britain by Shippey Brothers under their own name. *GNG*

MINERVA (B) 1913-1957

(1) Minerva Motors SA, Antwerp 1913-1934
(2) Societe Nouvelle Minerva, Antwerp 1934-1957

Sylvain de Jong's Minerva company made its name with bicycles, proprietary motorcycle engines, and (from 1900) complete motorcycles. Serious car production dates from 1904, though in the 1899-1901 period de Jong had experimented with a voiturette and a primitive light truck. By 1913 cars had ousted the two-wheelers, and Minerva were offering a 2½-ton truck of driver-over-engine type. It had a 4-cylinder sleeve-valve engine, a 4-speed constant-mesh gearbox, all brakes on the rear wheels, and overhead worm drive, though the gasoline tank's location between the driver and his mate was somewhat alarming.

This model did not reappear after the War. Minerva sleeve-valve engines were, however, used in the Auto-Traction road tractor, and also in some Scottish Lothian buses. The first modern Minerva trucks, in the 2/4-ton class, made their appearance in 1923, and with the acquisition of Auto-Traction in 1925, Minerva acquired the services of Robert Engels. Auto-Traction models were integrated into the Minerva range, and truck development was accelerated, the new models using various types of sleeve-valve car engine, and heavy sectional radiators of more angular shape than those of the cars. Pneumatic tires were standard, and the bigger 1927 trucks featured double-reduction drive and Dewandre servo brakes on all four wheels. Gazogene versions were developed for export

1926 MINERVA 4-ton producer-gas truck, FLP

to the Congo. 1926 saw Minerva's first PSV chassis, this Type-CR being a close relative of the trucks with the same 5.3-litre 4-cylinder engine. Conventional and half-cab 32-seater HTMs followed in 1927, and the 1929 range included some smaller 20/24-seaters and a related 2½-ton truck, both using 3.6-litre power units. By this time the bigger PSVs were receiving the 6-litre 32CV 6-cylinder car engine. In 1932 Minerva, like Panhard, tried some direct-injection sleeve-valve diesels, a 5.8-litre four and an 8.7-litre six. These, however, were soon dropped in favor of more conventional Ganz-Jendrassik designs of similar cylinder capacity, rated at 60 bhp and 95 bhp respectively.

A slump in car sales led to a fusion with Imperia in 1936, but though Minerva cars faded quietly from the scene, the trucks survived. The range included normal control gasoline models from 35 cwt to 4½ tons, a bigger normal control 6½-tonner for which the old Knight engine was

1927 MINERVA 10-ton articulated truck, OMM

retained, and forward control diesel trucks and tractive units in the 5/16-ton bracket. 1938 saw a 10-cwt forward control van on which the car-type radiator looked most incongruous, this and other lighter Minervas using 2.6-litre 4-cylinder and 3.9-litre 6-cylinder sv engines by Continental.

Surprisingly, the old HTM coach chassis made a brief reappearance after World War II, but the staple Minerva truck was now the C15, a 30-cwt forward control machine with 4-cylinder Continental engine; it was still quoted as late as 1953, but not made in series after 1948. Latterly the Minerva works became a REME workshop, assembling and repairing Landrovers. None of the company's projects prospered, though Minerva tried importing Italian motorcycles and Armstrong Siddeley cars, and planned to return to car manufacture with their own edition of the abortive Italian Cemsa-Caproni. They did have a last fling in 1956 with their own light 4 x 4, the C20, a unitary construction affair with 4-speed synchromesh gearbox and hydraulic brakes. Its 2.3-litre 4-cylinder sv engine, still a Continental, was quick-detachable, but the type made no impression. *MCS*

MINI see Austin

1966 MINIBUS MB-711 small bus, MBS

MINIBUS (US) 1963 to date

(1) Passenger Truck Equipment Co., Huntington Park, Calif. 1963-1967
(2) Minibus, Inc., Pico Rivera, Calif. 1967 to date

The current wave of interest in small buses for shuttle lines and special services in major U.S. cities dates from the early 1960's, and the first builder to take advantage of it was Passenger Truck Equipment Co., which previously built various types of sightseeing vehicles for zoos and parks. The first well-known fleet of Minibuses was placed in service on a shoppers' shuttle route in downtown Washington. Dodge or Chrysler V-8 engines are used, and both propane and natural gas fuel option have been made available in recent years. Although most Minibuses look like scaled-down versions of regular buses, some have been built with bizarre body styling for special purposes. *MBS*

MINICAR (GR) 1971-1972

Zamba S.A., Athens

Minicar was an ultra light tricycle with a unitary fiberglass body and cab of angular lines, a 50cc engine, 2 seat cab and full car type controls. Payload was just 150 kilos. *GA*

MINIR see Huainan

MINNEAPOLIS (i) (US) 1910

Minneapolis Motor & Truck Co., Minneapolis, Minn.

This company announced plans to build trucks of 1, 3, and 6 tons capacity, but only one prototype was shown at the Minneapolis Auto Show of 1910. This had a 3-cylinder 2-stroke engine. *GNG*

MINNEAPOLIS (ii) (US) 1912-1913

Minneapolis Motor Cycle Company, Minneapolis, Minn.

This was a 3-wheeler equipped with a delivery box mounted over the front axle, and was rated at 300 pounds capacity. Wheelbase was 6 feet, 10 inches. Power was on the rear wheel and this was chain-driven. *GMN*

MINO (US) 1914

Mino Cyclecar Company, New Orleans, Louisiana

This vehicle was another modified cyclecar weighing 450 pounds with a wheelbase of 8 feet, 4 inches and track of 3 feet, and was furnished with a small closed delivery body. It was driven by a 4-cylinder air-cooled engine, a 2-speed gearbox and shaft drive. *GMN*

MINSEI: NISSAN MINSEI (J) 1935 to date

(1) Nippon Diesel Engineering Co. Ltd., Kawaguchi 1935-1942
(2) Kanegafuchi Diesel Industries Ltd., Kawaguchi 1942-1946
(3) Ninsei Sangyo Ltd., Kawaguchi 1946-1950
(4) Minsei Diesel Industries Ltd., Kawaguchi 1950-1960
(5) Nissan Diesel Motor Co. Ltd., Ageo-shi 1960 to date

While most Japanese truck makers developed their own oil-engine designs in the 1930s Nippon Diesel took out a license for the Krupp-Junkers opposed-piston 2-stroke installed in 90 bhp 4-cylinder form in a 7-tonner offered in 1938. this was of normal control type and had envolved by the 1950s into a vehicle closely resembling the contemporary German Bussing in outward appearance; features were four forward speeds, air hydraulic or full air servo brakes, and spiral bevel back axles. From 1955 Minsei fitted their own type of engine, still a 4-cylinder 2-stroke, but giving 155 bhp from 4.9 litres. Also in 1955 the company entered into an association with Nissan: a joint sales organization was set up, but the two firms remained independent, the only technical connection being the installation of 3-cylinder Minsei engines in diesel editions of Nissan's 680-series 6-tonner. Alongside the early post-war trucks there was also an advanced range of Minsei Condor buses and coaches; though normal-control models were marketed, the rear-engined unitary-construction Condor was on the road as early as 1946. During the 1950s there were variants for up to 68/70 passengers, available options including 5-speed overdrive gearboxes, turbocharged engines (the 1958 7.4 litre six developed 230

1974 MINSEI NISSAN TW 50P 13-ton 6×4 truck, Nissan

bhp) and air suspension, first used by Minsei in 1957. It was standardized on the 6RFL101A series of 1959, recommended for coach tours with daily stages of up to 700 miles. The company was still making air-suspended, monocoque PSVs in 1978.

The first forward-control Minsei trucks appeared in 1960, these developing into the TCK tilt-cab 8-tonners. Also new that year was a 15-ton normal control 6 × 4 with the 230 bhp 6-cylinder engine, and a conventional 7-ton 4 × 4 was added to the range. 1962 saw the beginning of a development program of 4-stroke diesels, though the big 2-stroke six was still available in 1970, and the company's latest air-spung high-speed coaches used a turbocharged 9.9-litre V8 of like type. 4 × 2 trucks in the over 14-ton GVW class however, were fitted with 10.3-litre 4-stroke sixes. Normal control Minseis were restyled with wide angled screens and alligator hoods of glassfiber, power steering and exhaust brakes were regular options, and Minsei supplied over 2,000 heavy-duty 30-ton 6 × 6 logging tractors to the Soviet Government for use in Siberia. By 1972 4-stroke engines had been standardized, while new departure was a 'lightweight' model, the 6-ton CK10 with 6.8-litre 135bhp 6-cylinder unit, 4-speed gearbox, air-hydraulic brakes and tilt cab.

1974 MINSEI NISSAN RA 50 52-seater bus, Nissan

This tendency towards smaller models was continued in 1976, with the advent of the CM90 for GVWs of 8½ tons. Intended as a replacement for Nissan's C80 and 780 series, this forward control type featured a 5.7-litre 6-cylinder direct injection diesel rated at 145bhp, a 5-speed synchromesh box, hypoid final drive, and hydrovac brakes.

The 1978 Minsei range covered normal- and forward-control 4 × 2 and 6 × 4 models, with parallel tractor and dumper types: air-servo clutches and dual-range 10- and 12-speed transmissions were regular equipment on the largest variants. The CKs and CMs apart, all Nissan Minseis had capacities of over 10 litres and outputs in excess of 160 bhp: turbocharged editions of their 10.3-litre six gave 245 bhp. The 4-stroke 8-cylinder, now developing 280 bhp from 14.3 litres, had been joined by an immense 17.9-litre V10 reserved for the heaviest tractive units, while the specialist chassis range embraced crane carriers (including a 60-tonner 10 × 4), and fire engines in 4 × 2, 4 × 4, and 6 × 6 configurations. A wide selection of buses extended from front-engined 36-seaters up to rear-engined types, both monocoque and with separate chassis. The big monocoque RAs and UAs featured 5-speed gearboxes, power steering and air suspension, and came in wheelbases of up to 21 ft. 6 in. Nissan Minsei vehicles are marketed in Australia under the U.D. name. *MCS*

1908 MITCHELL 1½-ton truck, NAHC

MITCHELL (i) (US) 1905-1908

Mitchell Motor Car Co., Racine, Wis.

Mitchell was a respected passenger car maker with quite a long life (1902-1923) who had a brief period of commercial vehicle manufacture. This concentrated on a 2,000 lb. truck with horizontally-opposed twin engine under the driver's seat, 3-speed gearbox and shaft drive to a spiral bevel rear axle. Mitchell also made a few electric hotel buses. *GNG*

MITCHELL(ii) (US) 1906

J. Henry Mitchell Manufacturing Company
Philadelphia, Pennsylvania

The only recorded vehicle by this company was a one-tonner on a wheelbase of 8 feet, 4 inches. It was powered by a 12-14 hp two-cylinder engine mounted under a front hood. This had a three-speed gearbox and solid tires. *GMN*

MITSUBISHI (i) MITSUBISHI FUSO (J) 1920: 1930 to date

(1) Mitsubishi Shipbuilding & Engineering Co. Ltd., Kobe 1920: 1930-1941
(2) Mitsubishi Shipbuilding & Engineering Co. Ltd., Tokyo: Kawasaki 1941-1950
(3) Mitsubishi Nippon Heavy Industries Ltd., Tokyo: Kawasaki 1960-1964
(4) Mitsubishi Heavy Industries Ltd., Tokyo: Nagoya: Mizushima 1964-1970
(5) Mitsubishi Motors Corporation, Tokyo: Nagoya: Mizushima 1970 to date

The famous Mitsubishi engineering combine built a handful of 4-cylinder trucks on Fiat lines in 1920, but no serious vehicle production was undertaken until 1930, when normal control buses of American type (they resembled contemporary G.M.C.s or Reos) were marketed under the Fuso name. A program of diesel engine development was put in hand in 1935; this gave the country its first diesel-engined bus as well as a range of 2½/3-ton trucks powered by 45 hp 4-cylinder and 50 hp 6-cylinder units. These were said to run happily on soya oil, and had reached the market by 1936. Vehicle manufacture was moved to Kawasaki in 1941, but Mitsubishi's main war effort was centered on other branches of engineering.

Civilian production was resumed in 1946, this taking the form of normal control 6/7-ton trucks and buses with 6-cylinder oil engines: their styling was not unlike that of contemporary Diamond Ts. Light 3-wheeler vans were also offered.

In 1950, however, the American occupation authorities dismembered the Mitsubishi empire. The vehicle interests were split between two companies, Mitsubishi Nippon and Mitsubishi Reorganized, the latter undertaking the manufacture of the 3-wheelers while the former continued development of the Fuso diesel range. This consisted by 1958 of 7/8-ton versions of the 1946 truck with 8.6-litre 6-cylinder engines giving 155 bhp, 4-speed gearboxes, and air brakes, as well as 40-seater buses. On the PSV side, however, something more sophisticated was available in the shape of a 45-seater with longitudinal rear engine: options included automatic transmission, power steering, and power operated doors, and the basic design survived into the 1970s. Nothing came of the more advanced AR470, a 1959 prototype featuring half-deck body, a 186 bhp turbocharged engine, a 5-speed overdrive gearbox, and air suspension. Mitsubishi also specialized in construction equipment such as snowplows and bulldozers; among road-going special vehicles were a

1966 MITSUBISHI FUSO 6W200R 6×6 tractor with low-loader trailer, Mitsubishi

halfcab dumper, a 6 × 6 normal control 10-tonner of military type, and a similar 20-ton tractor for low-bed semi-trailers, with 5 × 2-speed gearbox and 13.7-litre, 200 bhp diesel engine. In 1961 the normal control Fusos, now available with five speeds and power steering, were given a face-lift, emerging with streamline cabs and 165 bhp, while a new range of tilt-cab forward-control models included the T390, a trailing-axle 6-wheeler for 11-ton payloads.

1974 MITSUBISHI Rosa B210 light bus, Mitsubishi

In 1964 the two Mitsubishi companies quietly reunited themselves, though the Fuso name was still used for the heavier trucks and PSVs. Types inherited from Mitsubishi Reorganized were the Jeeps, the light vans, and a wide range of normal-control Jupiter and forward control Canter models covering the 2/3½-ton category. There was also a full-fronted bus for 25 passengers, the Rosa, based on the Jupiter, and using the model's all-synchromesh gearbox in conjunction with a 6-cylinder diesel engine. The bigger buses were all of rear-engined type with air brakes; conventional suspension predominated, though the company was still using air springing on the MAR750L, a motorway-type coach which did 78 mph on a new 210 bhp V-8 diesel of 11.4-litres' capacity. The only gap in the load-carrying range had been bridged by 1966 with the T620, a forward-control 4-tonner with 4.7-litre 6-cylinder diesel engine, 5-speed synchromesh gearbox and hydrovac brakes. By 1971 the Mitsubishi group covered every sector of the commercial-vehicle market. Car-type models were the 1,100cc 4-cylinder Colts in normal and forward control guises, both with coil ifs, as well as the

1974 MITSUBISHI Canter 2-ton truck, Mitsubishi

little forward control Minicab, now sharing its 359cc air-cooled 2-cylinder engine and mechanical elements with the Minica range. The forward control Jupiters and Canters covered GVWs of up to 6½ tons, with 5-speed boxes on the heavier types, and a range of gas and diesel power units of up to 4-litres and 105 bhp. The smallest Fuso was the T650, an uprated edition of 1966's T620, and the true heavies embraced GVWs from 14 to 21 tons, with normal control 4 × 2s, 6 × 4s and 6 × 6s as well as forward control 4 × 2 and 6 × 2 versions. All these latter had tilt cabs, and the heaviest 6 × 2s were available with a built-in hydraulic self-loading device. Alongside the established inline six and V-8 were a turbocharged 8-cylinder giving 310 bhp, and a new 10-litre 190 bhp V-6. Air servo brakes were standard, as was power steering on some models. There was also a full range of gas and diesel engined Jeeps. 4 × 2, 6 × 4 and 8 × 4 crane carrier chassis of conventional and low-bridge types, and specialist tractive units, mixers and fire engines, as well as a full line of buses, with rear engines on the bigger ones. New for the season were some outsize off-the-road dumpers with

1974 MITSUBISHI FUSO T911/912 twin steer truck, Mitsubishi

Allison automatic transmissions and GVW ratings of over 100 tons. The big Fusos were redesigned in 1972, now including 6 × 4 normal and forward control types with GVWs approaching the 30-ton mark: these used 285 bhp V-8s, 10- and 12-speed transmissions, power steering, and a combination of air, exhaust and maxi brakes. A very similar range was offered in 1978, though the Jupiter name was no longer used. Forward control was standardized on all mediums and heavies with the exception of the traditional T330s, the heavy 6 × 4 NV, and the W82 dumper with 4-wheel drive. 5-speed main transmissions were regular equipment, exceptions being the 4-speed all-synchromesh boxes of gas-engined Canters, and the 6- and 10-speed units of the biggest FUs, FVs, and NVs. 6-cylinder diesels were now all of inline type, though the smaller 5.4-litre, unusually, was built on antechamber principles whereas other units of the range featured direct injection. The biggest dumpers had 18.4-litre 8-cylinder engines rated at 430 bhp. The Jeep range was continued, but unusually among Japanese carmakers (and especially in view of their association with Chrysler) Mitsubishi no longer marketed a car-type pickup; both Minicab and Colt were listed only with forward control. The only complete front-engined bus offered by the company was the Rosa, though conventionally-engineered diesel PSV chassis were available. At the top of the PSV range was the MS, a luxury rear-engined 50-seater with air suspension and V-8 engine, capable of 75 mph. In Australia the Canter range was sold with Dodge badges, and in Switzerland by FBW as the MMC-FBW Canter. *MCS*

MITSUBISHI (ii) (J) 1950-1964

Mitsubishi Heavy Industries Reorganized Ltd., Nagoya: Mizushima

After the forcible dismemberment of the Mitsubishi combine in 1950, this company took over the light vehicle interests, which embraced scooters and light 3-wheeler vans of classic Japanese type with single front wheel. These latter were made until 1961, the Pet Leo being a 6-cwt lightweight with 310cc 4-stroke engine, and, incidentally, the first machine in this class to be made with a 3-speed synchromesh gearbox. Later ones were wheel-steered, as were the heavier 30-cwt/2-ton TMs, which had oleo-sprung front forks, transverse rear suspension, and 2-cylinder air-cooled engines. From 1953 Mitsubishi Reorganized made Jeeps under Willys license. In 1959 the Jupiter was introduced: this was a 2/3-ton conventional truck on European lines, with 4-speed all-synchromesh gearbox, column shift, hydrovac brakes, and hypoid rear axle. Standard engines were 2.2-litre ohv fours, giving 75 bhp in gas form and 62 bhp as diesels, though 3-tonners could be had with a 3.3-litre diesel 6. Another 1959 innovation was Mitsubishi's first private car, the little rear-engined 360 sedan. This led logically to the LT20 6/7-cwt van, though this, unlike the car, used a front-mounted 359cc 2-stroke 2-cylinder engine. The transverse ifs and 4-speed all-synchromesh gearbox were common to both cars and commercials. 1962 saw a bigger car, the first of the conventional 4-cylinder Colt family, and this was also produced as a car-type van. The reunion of the two Mitsubishi companies gave the new group comprehensive coverage of the truck market, other inheritances being a new Jupiter Junior with torsion bar ifs for 2-ton payloads, and the modern 2/3-ton forward control Canter with four headlamps and a choice of 2-litre 4-cylinder gas or diesel engines. *MCS*

M. & J. (GB) 1908

Martin & Jellicoe Ltd., Thames Ditton, Surrey

This company made 1- and 2-ton vans powered by 4-cylinder engines, with 4-speed gearboxes and chain drive. *GNG*

MK (NL) 1953

N.V. Motorkracht, Hoogeveen

Motorkracht, nowadays owned by Magirus and acting as their distributor for the Netherlands, manufactured in 1953 a small batch of six trucks of their own design, though using a Deutz 4-cylinder diesel engine.

The MK trade-name can still be spotted, for example in Spain, but now only on Magirus trucks which for political reasons have been exported from Holland instead of being shipped from Germany. *JFJK*

M.L.T. (F) 1900

Molas, Lamielle et Tessier, Paris

The M.L.T. was unusual in using compressed air as motive power. This was stored in eleven cylinders with a total capacity of 18½ cu. ft., at a pressure of 4,290 lbs./sq. in.; the air was heated by gas burners, then admitted to the four cylinders at varying pressures to give power ranging from 1 to 35 hp. The engine drove a countershaft, from which there was double chain drive to the rear wheels. Maximum speed was 6¼ mph. The prototype M.L.T. had a 12-seater waggonette body, and is not certain that any other vehicles were made. *GNG*

M.M.B. (D) 1899-1902

Motorfahrzeug- und Motorenfabrik Berlin A.G., Marienfelde, Berlin

This firm was founded by directors of the Daimler company and production was taken up following Daimler patents. The company concentrated on commercials and various designs of trucks and buses were carried out. Also electric vans were produced (including some for the German mail). In 1902 the firm was integrated in the Daimler company which afterwards concentrated production of commercials in Marienfelde. *HON*

MOAZ (MOAZ) SU c.1964 to date

Mogilev Lift and Hoist Plant, Mogilev

As a builder of special purpose vehicles, the MOAZ plant presently turns out a model #6401 20-ton, 200 hp tractor-truck and a #529E heavy earth-mover. *BE*

MOBILE (US) 1899-1903

Mobile Co. of America, Tarrytown on the Hudson, N.Y.

The Mobile was one of the more important makes of early American steam car, being founded by J.B. Walker who had acquired the original Stanley patents and the Stanley factory. Almost indistinguishable from the Locomobile which was also a Stanley design, the Mobile had a 10 hp 2-cylinder engine and single chain drive. Various goods models were made on the passenger car chassis, and in 1903 there was also a heavy steam truck with double chain drive and a load capacity of 3 tons. *GNG*

MOBILETTE (US) 1913-1914

Woods Mobilette Co., Chicago, Ill.

This very light delivery van was a converted passenger cyclecar and the trade name was commonly known as Woods. This vehicle used a water-cooled four-cylinder engine, a friction transmission and shaft drive. Track was only 2 feet, 6 inches and the frame was so sufficiently narrow to allow the driver to straddle it with the front fenders used as foot rests. *GMN*

MOC (GB) 1906-1908
Motor Omnibus Construction Ltd., Walthamstow, London, NE

The London Motor Omnibus Company ran a bus fleet under the name Vanguard. Buses of the time gave a lot of trouble and the LMOC decided to form a subsidiary to produce vehicles for their particular requirements. The first MOC appeared in 1906 and used a number of Armstrong-Whitworth components; Sir W.G. Armstrong being a director of MOC, as well as producer of commercial vehicles in his own right. Engines were made by Richard Hornsby and Sons. In 1907 the operating and manufacturing companies came together as the Vanguard Motor Omnibus Company and in 1908 they merged with the London General Omnibus Company. Manufacturing facilities at Walthamstow were then put to work on the X-type and eventually B-type buses. *OM*

MOCHET (F) 1951-c.1954
Charles Mochet, Puteaux, Seine

Among Charles Mochet's earlier products had been the C.M cyclecar and the pedal-powered Velocar taxis used in Paris during the German Occupation. The post-war Mochet was a rudimentary affair with bicycle-type wheels, a tubular frame, all-independent suspension, and no front wheel brakes. Power was provided by a 125cc air-cooled 2-stroke engine, which meant not only 80 mpg, but exemption from the need to hold a driving license. Early catalogues show a 3-cwt van in the range, though by 1955 this is no longer mentioned. *MCS*

MODAG (D) 1925-1926
Motorenfabrik Darmstadt A.G., Darmstadt

Among the various firms producing diesel tractors in the mid-twenties MODAG was one. A compressor-less Colo diesel engine was used. *HON*

MODERN (i) (US) 1911-1912
Modern Motor Truck Company, St. Louis, Missouri

This manufacturer launched a single model which was a two-tonner with a stake body. This used a four-cylinder engine with a three-speed gearbox and double chain-drive. Speed was governed to a maximum of 15 mph. With wheelbase of 9 feet, 10 inches, this model cost $2850. *GMN*

MODERN (ii) (US) 1911-1919
Bowling Green Motor Car Co., Bowling Green, O.

The Modern was launched with a ¾- and a ½-tonner. Both were powered by 4-cylinder engines, 3-speed gearboxes and had solid rubber tires. The ½-tonner had double chain-drive while the ¾-tonner had optional shaft or chain drive and was available with forward control. Both were available with a variety of closed or open bodies. For 1914, the models were replaced by a 1-tonner with worm drive and a 1½-tonner with double chain final drive. The same models were carried over to 1915. In 1916, a 2-tonner and a 3½-tonner were added, but by 1917, only the 1½-tonner had survived. At least from 1914, all engines were 4-cylinder types built by Continental. *GMN*

MODERN WHEEL DRIVE see S.L.M.

MOELLER (US) 1910-1914
(1) H.L. Moeller & Co., New Haven, Conn. 1910-1912
(2) New Haven Truck & Auto Works, New Haven, Conn. 1912-1914

Models A and B, introduced in 1910, were 5-tonners with four-cylinder engines. Model B had its engine under a hood while Model A used forward control. Both were limited to a speed of 9 or 10 mph. A 3-tonner was introduced in 1912 followed by a 1½-tonner in 1913. The Model B was designed especially for the hauling of block ice. This make is also referred to as New Haven. *GMN*

MOETETE see Harimau

MOGUL (US) 1911-1916
(1) Mogul Motor Truck Company, Chicago, Illinois, 1911-1913
(2) Mogul Motor Truck Company, St. Louis, Missouri, 1914-1916

The Mogul was built in capacities of 2, 4 and 6 tons and all models had forward control. Each also used a 4-cylinder engine, three-speed gearbox along with double roller-chain drive. The Model U of 1913, built for lumber hauling, had a chassis weighing 11,000 pounds with an equal-

1916 MOGUL Model M 6-ton truck, RNE

ly-large wheelbase of 15 feet, 8 inches. At least one listing carries this make into 1920, but this is unsubstantiated. *GMN*

MOHAWK (GB) 1948-1950

Erskine Motors Ltd., Gosport, Hants.

This was a forward-control 10/12 cwt van powered by a 10 hp flat-twin Coventry-Victor engine mounted between the seats. It had a 4-speed Moss gearbox and shaft drive. The frame was dropped at the front to allow a low entrance to the cab. *GNG*

1977 MOL Type HFT 1066 6×6 truck, Mol

MOL (B) 1966 to date

Gebroeders Mol P,v.b.a., Hooglede.

Mol started in 1966 to produce commercial vehicles, introducing a municipal chassis with low-line cab fitted with Kirkstall axles, Allison automatic gearbox, Deutz air-cooled diesel engine, and two additional models, normal and forward control trucks, using the same components except for the Allison box, replaced by a manual ZF transmission. Currently Mol is specializing in heavy 4 × 4, 6 × 4 and 6 × 6 vehicles, using mainly Deutz engines, Timken axles and Spicer or ZF gearboxes. They have also taken over assembly of Silver Eagle buses from Bus and Car. *JFJK*

MOLINE (US) 1920-1923

Moline Plow Co., Moline, Ill.

The Moline Model 10 was a 1½-tonner, the only type under this name. It used a four-cylinder engine with a three-speed gearbox on a wheelbase of 10 feet, 10 inches. The price of the chassis was $1695. *GMN*

MOLLER (US) 1927-1931

M.P. Moller Motor Car Co. Hagerstown, Md.

The Moller company made a variety of taxicabs sold under at least nine names. The 4-cylinder Astor and Luxor are covered under their own names, but there were also the Moller, Blue Light and Twentieth Century short wheelbase 4-cylinder cabs, and a range of larger 6-cylinder models sold under the names Paramount, Super Paramount, Aristocrat and Five Boro. These names were either chosen for the operating company, as with Five Boro, or simply because the promoters thought a stylish new name would increase sales. Production of Moller-designed cabs ceased in 1931, but a few small Diamond T truck chassis were fitted with Moller bodies in 1933, and sold under the name Town Taxi. Moller also made cab bodies for Ford V-8s in the period 1932 to 1936. At its peak in the late 1920s, the Moller factory was turning out 125 cabs per week. *GNG*

MONET-GOYON (F) 1920-1931

Ets. Monet et Goyen, Macon, Saone et Loire

This well-known motorcycle manufacturer built a number of light 3-wheeled load carriers, all of them commercial versions of passenger machines. The first was the V-2 powered by a front-mounted engine which drove the single front wheel. This was either a 500cc single-cylinder Anzani or 750cc V-twin M.A.G. The engine and transmission as well as the front wheel turned with the steering, which was by long tiller. Production of this model ran from 1920 to 1923, and alongside it was made the VT2, a 3-wheeler with single rear wheel which closely resembled the tricars of the 1904-1907 era. Steering was by wheel, and the engine was a 270cc single-cylinder Villiers. There was only one forward speed. There were apparently no goods versions of Monet-Goyon's 4-wheeled cars, but in 1929 the company returned to the 3-wheeler with the Tri-Monet. This consisted of a 500cc M.A.G.-engined motorcycle whose front forks and wheel were replaced by a tubular chassis and two wheels which carried either a passenger sidecar or a box for goods. This was made until 1931, and there was also a less powerful version with 350cc Villiers 2-stroke engine. *GNG*

MONITOR (US) 1910-1916

Monitor Automobile Works, Janesville, Wis

Between 1910 and 1916, Monitor built ½-and 1-tonners with a variety of standard body types including a wicker panel van. These trucks used both 2-and 4-cylinder engines with selective gearboxes and double chain drive. Most of the larger types had forward control and later, shaft drive. Monitor also built passenger cars. *GMN*

MONOS (D) 1928-1930

Monos Fahrzeuggesellschaft mbH., Berlin-Lichtenberg

Based on the private car versions, a van was also available with side mounted 350cc or 500cc engine. Two other van versions followed. At first a layout of two front wheels and one single driven rear wheel was used, available with 198cc Ilo or 348cc J.A.P. engine. The 1929 version featured one tiller-steered front wheel; a 200cc engine drove the rear wheels. *HON*

MOON (US) 1912-1917

Joseph W. Moon Buggy Co., St. Louis, Mo

The Moon Model A was a ½-tonner with a four-cylinder engine, capable of 35 mph. This used a three-speed gearbox, shaft drive and had wheelbase of 8 feet, 6 inches. The Model B was a 1½-tonner with chain drive, however. With an enclosed van body, the Model B was priced at $1900 and four other body types were available. For 1915 and 1916, only the Model B was built and among others, this was available with a bus body. These models of trucks did not use passenger car chassis built under this same name. *GMN*

MOORE (i) (US) 1911-1916

(1) F.L. Moore Motor Truck Company, Los Angeles, California 1911-1913

(2) Pacific Metal Products Company, Torrance, California 1913-1916

Sizeable trucks were built by these companies with ratings of 2, 3, 5 and 6½ tons capacity. The 5-tonner for 1913 used a four-cylinder engine of 605 ci displacement, with a four-speed gearbox along with jackshaft and double chain-drive. Later models included a 1½-tonner and all models had engines under frontal hoods. *GMN*

MOORE (ii) (US) 1912-1914

Moore Motor Truck Co., Philadelphia, Pa.

The initial Moore was called Model C, a ¾-tonner. For 1914, the line of trucks expanded to include 1½, 2-, 3-, 4- and 5-tonners. These all used four-cylinder engines under frontal hoods and all but the largest had three-speed gearboxes, the 5-tonner having four speeds. All used double chain final drive from jackshafts. The 5-tonner was on a wheelbase of 16 feet, 1 inch and the chassis cost $4500. *GMN*

MOORE (iii) or PALMER-MOORE (US) 1913-1914

Palmer Moore Company, Syracuse, New York

Model C is the only type listed for this make. It had a capacity of 1500 pounds with a 3-cylinder, air-cooled engine under a French-type of hood. Transmission was a planetary type and final drive was by double chains to the rear wheels. With panel body, the price was $1300. The tradename has been found in both above versions. *GMN*

MORA (US) 1911-1914

Mora Power Wagon Company, Cleveland, Ohio

This make was represented by a single model of 1500-pound capacity which used a 2-cylinder engine mounted beneath the hood. The only body style was an open express type with wheelbase of 7 feet, 10 inches. This make had no direct connection with the passenger car of the same name other than that both were formed by S.H. Mora. The truck manufacturing operation was begun after the passenger car business foundered. *GMN*

MORELAND (US) 1911-1941

Moreland Motor Truck Co, Burbank, Calif.

Moreland trucks were pacesetters technically (6-wheelers, lightweight construction and diesel power), and during its lifetime the company was one of the more important West Coast truck firms, helping to create the image of the 'Western truck' together with Kenworth, Kleiber and Fageol. Watt Moreland often served as spokesman for the truck industry, arguing for better legislation and more liberal weight allowances which recognized the 6-wheeler.

1917 MORELAND 4-ton truck, BHV

The first Morelands were made in 1½, 3, 3½ and 5 ton sizes, the larger models with chain drive, and driver-over-engine. Stock engines such as Hercules and Continental were used, together with Brown-Lipe transmissions. By 1924 the largest model was a 6-tonner, and in this year Moreland launched out into the 6-wheeler field with a bus chassis for double-decker bodywork. This massive vehicle had a 6-cylinder Continental engine, drive to both axles of the rear bogie and both Westinghouse air brakes and Lockheed hydraulics. A 60-passenger body was fitted, but

1924 MORELAND 6-wheel bus, MBS

Moreland did not proceed with the vehicle, probably because it was too expensive for bus operators. They did not, however, drop the 6-wheeler concept, and in 1925 launched the big TX6 truck. This had a novel Moreland-designed bogie whose axles were located by equalizing rockers, in turn pivoting from the centres of semi-elliptic springs attached to the chassis. Moreland claimed it was the first 6-wheeler truck though Fageol had one at about the same time. The TX6 was powered by a Continental 14H engine, was rated at 10 tons and sold for $7,000 odd. A 6-ton version was introduced the same year. The 6-wheeler led to greatly increased orders for Moreland, not only from the US but from export markets too. These included Central and South America, the Philipines and Australia where the excellent traction afforded by twin driving axles was appreciated as well as the increased payload. In fact the Moreland 6-wheelers gave long-haul road transport its start, at first in California and then in other areas.

At its peak the Moreland plant occupied a 25-acre site, and was remarkably self-contained. Although they never made their own engines, many other components were home-made, in particular the rugged axles. In time trailers, and commercial bodywork including refrigeration units became part of Moreland's output. Smaller trucks were also made including the 3,800lb Ace and 7-ton Californian, both 4-wheelers. The latter had an unladen weight of 4 tons, helped by the use of light alloys in its construction. Engines were Continental in the Ace, and Hercules in the Californian.

Moreland's best year for production was 1929, with nearly 1,000 trucks, buses and trailers delivered, but after that the figures slipped, with fewer than 30-40 per year being sold in the mid-30s. Moreland's last years were full of interest, though, with Hercules or Cummins diesel engines being offered, and attractive streamlined cabs being employed on the later models. In 1931 Moreland and Fageol entered talks for a merger, but nothing came of them. Trailers and specialist bodywork became more important parts of the business, and the later Moreland trucks were all custom-built units. Typical of the 1937/38 range was the TA-420CD, powered by a 125hp Cummins diesel engine. This was rated at 42,000lbs GVW as a straight truck, or 68,000lbs as a tractor with trailers. This and other models for loads from 4 to 10 tons were listed until 1941, but very few were made in the last two years. Moreland then became a parts/service operation which was acquired by Cook Brothers in 1949 for $35,000. *RJ*

MORETTI (I) 1952-1961

Fabbrica Automobili Moretti SpA, Turin

Early Morettis were small, specialist handbuilt sports cars; the company made practically everything in their own works, prices were high, and production on a very small scale. Thus it is surprising to find a 15-cwt truck in the 1952 range; it used the standard Moretti tubular backbone chassis and 600cc single ohc 4-cylinder engine. By 1954 a forward control 1-tonner was available, with eight forward speeds, not to mention a 1,204cc dohc power unit rated at 62bhp. As late as 1961 there was a 4-door taxi with a choice of 750cc or 980cc engines, both with ohc, but a change of policy led to a new line of sporting cars based on Fiat mechanical elements. Since then the nearest approaches to commercial vehicles have been Jeep-like open models derived from the 2-cylinder rear-engined 500 and 4-cylinder fwd 127. *MCS*

MORGAN (i) (US) 1902-1903; 1908-1913

(1) Morgan Motor Co., Worcester, Mass. 1902-1903
(2) R.L. Morgan Co., Worcester, Mass. 1908-1912
(3) Morgan Motor Truck Co., Worcester, Mass. 1912-1913

The original Morgan was a heavy steam truck powered by a 2-cylinder compound engine fed by a vertical water-tube boiler working at 600psi. The fuel was crude oil. Few were made, and Morgan's next venture in truck building came in 1908 with a forward-control gasoline truck powered by a 40hp 4-cylinder engine. This had planetary transmission, double chain drive and steel artillery wheels. For 1910 disc wheels were featured. By 1912 2- and 3-tonners were also made, and the wheelbase of the 5-tonner increased from 10 to 12ft. All three models were continued into 1913, and the make was continued for six more years as the Steele. *GNG/GMN*

1910 MORGAN (i) Model A 5-ton truck, NAHC

MORGAN (ii) (GB) 1913-1914: 1928-1935

Morgan Motor Co. Ltd., Malvern Link, Worcs.

As was the case with many light car manufacturers, Morgan's sallies into vans were spasmodic. First of these was a 1-cwt parcelcar on their standard 2-speed 3-wheeler chassis in 1913, using JAP or Precision engines: the box at the rear was interchangeable with a standard 2-seater body. A similar 3-cwt body was available on the 1928

1902 MORGAN (i) steam wagon, NMM

sv Family chassis, but this was shortlived, and the only real van to be found in Morgan catalog was the 1933 4-cwt type, also based on the Family. These last commercial Morgans had 3-speed and reverse gearboxes: sv v-twin engines were used, initially a 1,096 cc JAP and latterly a 990cc Matchless. *MCS*

MORRIS (i) (GB) 1914-1917: 1924 to date

(1) W.R.M. Motors Ltd., Cowley, Oxford 1914-1917
(2) Morris Motors Ltd., Cowley, Oxford 1924-1970
(3) Austin-Morris Division, British Leyland Motor Corporation Ltd., Cowley, Oxford 1970-1977
(4) British Leyland UK Ltd., (Leyland Cars) Cowley, Oxford 1977 to date

The first Morris delivery vans were based on the Oxford with 1-litre White & Poppe engine and the Continental-engined 1½-litre Cowley of 1915. Serious commercial vehicle manufacture did not begin until 1924, and then the Cowley factory's role was limited to the production of car-type vehicles for payloads up to 10cwt: heavier vehicles were the responsibility of a separate firm in Birmingham.

1928 MORRIS 8/10cwt postal van, NMM

Initially the staple light van was an 8-cwt version of the 11.9hp Cowley, but with a peculiar squashed-bullnose radiator that was to persist until 1930. Alongside these Morris offered a variety of commercial travellers' cars, which evolved into 5-door sedans still cataloged in 1934. For 1930 there was a new 5-cwt van on the 847cc ohc Minor car chassis, also available as a miniature fire tender: the sv engine was adopted a year later, while a

1937 MORRIS Minor GPO linesman's van, NMM

shortlived venture was the production of fast newspaper delivery vans on the 2½-litre ohc Isis 6 chassis. 1931-34 10-cwt vans used the same 1.8-litre 4-cylinder Oxford engine as the small Morris-Commercials, but there was a reversion to the 1½-litre unit in 1935, in which year the 5-cwt model became a member of the 918cc 8hp family with 3-speed synchromesh gearbox and hydraulic brakes. 1936 and subsequent 10-cwt models, though retaining the mechanics of the sv 12hp, adopted a semi-forward control layout which permitted the use of a compact 7ft 6in wheelbase. Morris light vans were much favored by the

1939 MORRIS 10cwt van, OMM

Post Office, who used not only standard types but a curious hybrid, the GPO Minor produced from 1934 to 1940: the front end sheet metal was that of the 1934 Minor private car, but mechanical elements had become pure 8hp by the end of the model's run. 1940 saw improved 5-cwt (Z-type) and 10-cwt (Y-type) vans which went back into production after the War. There were no further changes until 1950 when a new Cowley van with 1½-litre sv Oxford engine and torsion-bar ifs replaced the Y. The Z soldiered on into 1953 before giving way to a 6-cwt van version of the Issigonis-designed Minor, now of course with 803cc ohv Austin engine. Progressively updated, it survived into 1971, but a new Series III 10-cwt of 1956, based on

1961 MORRIS Minor ¼-ton pick-up, NMM

1974 MORRIS Marina ½-ton pick-up, British Leyland

later ohv Oxfords, was destined to be the last truly Morris light van, albeit Minis (from 1960) and Austin's A55-based 10-cwt model were sold with Morris badges. 1972, however, saw this latter replaced by 7-cwt and 10-cwt derivatives of the conventional Morris Marina, using 1,100cc or 1.3-litre engines. These were still marketed under a joint Austin-Morris label in 1978. *MCS*

MORRIS-COMMERCIAL: MORRIS (ii) 1924-1970

(1) Morris Commerical Cars Ltd., Soho, Birmingham 1924-1933

(2) Morris Commercial Cars Ltd., Adderley Park, Birmingham 1930-1970

(3) British Motor Corporation Ltd., Bathgate, East Lothian 1961-1967

W.R. Morris's answer to American domination of the British 1-tonner market was to produce a straightforward vehicle using mechanical elements from his private cars, among them the 1.8-litre 4-cylinder sv Oxford engine, its wetplate clutch, and 3-speed gearbox. Pneumatic tires and electric lighting were standard (starters were extra), final drive was by worm, and a complete truck sold for £225. These Morris-Commercials were made in a separate factory at Soho, Birmingham, formerly occupied by

1925 MORRIS COMMERCIAL 1-ton van GNG

Wrigley, Morris's source of transmissions which he had recently acquired. Though deliveries did not begin until May, 1924, 2,489 trucks were sold that year, 7,561 in 1926, and over 10,000 for the first time in 1928. A wide range of standardized bodywork was offered, including (by 1925) a 14-seater bus at only £310; in that year the company introduced a light 12-cwt van with the 1½-litre Cowley engine. A year later came a 1-ton halftrack, and the basic tonner was to retain its original Oxford power unit to the end in 1943. Even chassis changes were limited: the vehicles acquired enclosed cabs at the end of the 1920s, four speeds and 4-wheel brakes in 1933, and hydraulic actuation for these last in 1939. These lightweight Morrises were used in vast numbers by the Post Office.

A bigger 2½-litre Morris-Commercial-designed engine appeared in 1926, this also going into the unsuccessful Empire Oxford car. A happier application was, however, its intended one: the 25/30-cwt Z-type with dry plate clutch, four speeds, and a servo brake option. It also powered a new Morris speciality, the light 30-cwt D-type 6x4. This was predominantly a military vehicle, though

1929 MORRIS COMMERCIAL 6-wheeler, NMM

one became the first truck to cross the Kalahari Desert, and the Great Western Railway used a D-type for sightseeing trips to the summit of Plynlimon. Yet another customer was the Japanese Navy, who specified solid tires for use on coral strands, while a few 6-wheelers with 6-cylinder engines were made as private cars in 1930-31. By 1929 the Morris-Commercial range included the G-type taxicab, also Oxford-engined; this never rivalled the Austin's popularity, though sv 6-cylinder engines were standardized from 1934, and a 1.8-litre ohv six in 1938. The success of the middleweight Morris-Commercials persuaded Stoewer of Stettin to explore a manufacturing license (they exhibited Morrises at the 1931 Berlin Show), but the appointment of C.K. Edwards from AEC as Chief Engineer led to a brief sally into heavy duty types, these being made in the old Wolseley factory at Adderley Park. The Soho plant was slowly run down between 1930 and 1933.

1931 MORRIS COMMERCIAL J Courier 4-ton tanker, NMM

The 1930-32 period saw too many models. There were two 2½-tonners, a trailing-axle 6-wheeler RD with a development of the Empire Oxford engine, and the P-type Leader with a 3.7-litre sv 4-cylinder unit. Edwards's promised heavy emerged as the 4/5-ton Courier with 85bhp 5.1-litre ohv high-camshaft engine, vacuum servo brakes on all four wheels, and a wheel-out power pack for easy servicing. This last feature was common also to a brace of half-cab PSV types, the 28-seater single-decker Dictator and the double-decker Imperial, both using 6-cylinder versions of the Courier's engine: in the Imperial's case capacity was 7.7 litres for an output of 120bhp, and lhd was an option. Sales were poor, even if Birmingham patriotically ordered 51 Imperials. Curiously, Morris's smaller coach chassis, the 20-seater Viceroy, used an entirely different engine, a 5.3-litre sv six. Edwards also planned 8- and 12-ton trucks, the latter a 6-wheeler, but these did not progress beyond the prototype stage. Sales were down to just over 7,000 in 1932 (as against nearly 13,000 for the recently introduced Bedford), and Morris's answer was a new C-type range for payloads from 30-cwt to 3 tons. There were normal and semi-forward control

1934 MORRIS COMMERCIAL Imperial 51-seater bus, MAS

variants, all with spiral bevel drive and 4-wheel hydraulic brakes. Buyers had a choice of two 3½-litre sv engines developing 55bhp, a four and the six also used in Morris's most expensive private car, the 25. Civilian Cs were made until 1937, pushing annual sales back above the 10,000 mark: latterly the top of the range was a new 4/5-ton Leader coming within the 50-cwt unladen weight limit, and available also as a swb tipper or tractive unit. The company did even better with military C-derivatives, delivering some 80,000 between 1934 and 1945. The best-known WD model was the short-hood 15-cwt infantry truck, but variants included a similar 8-cwt model, and 6x4s with normal or forward control. During the War Morris developed a successful 4x4 artillery tractor with 5x2-speed box and 72bhp 4-cylinder engine, and by 1944 this had evolved into a new 15-cwt truck with all-wheel drive.

1938 MORRIS COMMERCIAL 2-ton truck, BR

The 1937 range covered the 15-cwt — 5-ton bracket, but only the traditional lightweights continued unchanged into 1938. The bigger Morris-Commercials were modernized to meet the ever-present Bedford and Fordson challenge, with normal control, forward-mounted engines, and the fashionable all-steel cabs with vee windshields. These new Equiloads retained the 3½-litre engines, but a new 2.1-litre ohv four was produced for the smallest 25-cwt model. 1939 saw two logical extensions to the range, a forward-control 5-tonner and a 20/26-seater 6-cylinder coach chassis, Morris's first purpose-built PSV since the demise of Edwards's heavyweights in 1933. Introduced on the eve of war was the PV, a full-fronted forward control 1-ton parcels van with sliding doors, using the new small ohv engine and a spiral bevel drive in place of the worm drive of the old-school tonners.

This and a slightly pruned Equiload range went back into production in 1945, 4-cylinder engines being standardized, but in 1948 Morris-Commercial stole a march on the opposition with a promising full-forward control 5-tonner powered by their own direct-injection diesel, a 4¼-litre 6 made under Saurer license. Unfortunately in Morris-modified form it was never really satisfactory, and soon afterwards the faithful old 4-cylinder gasoline engine was enlarged to 3.8 litres as a more viable alternative: 6-cylinder Oerlikon diesels were also tried in export models. Other novelties of 1948 were a companion diesel coach chassis with vacuum servo brakes, and (curiously, in view of the rival Cowley program) a 10-cwt forward control light van with hypoid back axle and the group's latest 1½-litre engine, the short-stroke sv MO-type Oxford. The Morris diesel was still available in 1951, but there was a new regular option in

1949 MORRIS-COMMERCIAL 5-ton furniture van, NMM

the shape of a 4.2-litre ohv gasoline 6, which went into modernized 2/3-ton and 5-ton Equiload models as well as into the forward control types. Hydrovac brakes, by now an option on heavy-duty Morris-Commercials, were soon standardized.

1952 MORRIS COMMERCIAL 3-ton truck, BR

1956 MORRIS (ii) 3-ton truck, BR

The Austin-Morris merger of 1951 put a stop to the latter company's engine development program. By early 1953 both the latest 30-cwt Equiload truck (Series-LC) and a PV replacement, the walkthrough-type LD, were using 2.2-litre Austin 16 engines in place of the smaller ohv Morris, and 1954 saw a complete rationalization of the two truck ranges, accentuated by the dropping of the 'Commercial' half from the Morris name at the end of 1956. Some of the old Morris types, however, were destined for long runs, being made with Austin badges as well. The LC was still available in 1959, the 10-cwt J van survived another year, and the LD did not disappear until 1968. The last innovation specifically credited to Morris was the angle-vision cab of the 1960 FG forward control truck. The end came in 1970 with British Leyland's renaming and regrouping of their commercial vehicle interests. *MCS*

MORRISON (GB) 1933
MORRISON-ELECTRIC (GB) 1934-1941
MORRISON-ELECTRICAR (GB) 1941-to date

(1) A.E. Morrison & Sons, Leicester 1933-1935 South Wigston, Leicester 1935-1941

(2) A.E.Morrison & Sons in association with Crompton Parkinson Ltd., South Wigston, Leicester 1941-1948

(3) Austin Crompton Parkinson Electric Vehicles Ltd., South Wigston, Leicester & Hall Green, Birmingham 1948-1966

(4) Austin Crompton Parkinson Electric Vehicles Ltd., Tredegar, Monmouth 1966-1968

(5) Crompton Leyland Electricars Ltd., Tredegar, Monmouth 1968-1972

(6) Crompton Electricars Ltd., Tredegar, Monmouth 1972 to date

Originally builders of cycles, motor cycles, tri-cars and electrical equipment A.E. Morrison & Sons Ltd., produced their first battery electric vehicle in 1933 using a pressed steel chassis, Bendix brakes and wire wheels of the motor car type. This was in strong contrast to the accepted style of heavy electric vehicles up to that time which had changed little in 20 years.

The first model was rated for 10cwt payload with an operating mileage of approximately 50 miles from its 48volt, 154AH capacity battery. Designs for vehicles of 12cwt, 25cwt, 30cwt and 2 tons were produced and prices were quoted at between £149 and £275 according to type. The following year saw the addition of a 3 wheeler to the range, the Trilec. This had Ackermann steering to the pair of front wheels while the single rear wheel was driven by the motor. Batteries were carried in twin side panniers above the chassis frame. The unusual feature of this model was that the driver sat at the rear of the vehicle and looked forward over the 8cwt load box. Needless to say this was not conducive to road safety and the model did not sell well.

1935 MORRISON-ELECTRIC Airflow ¼-ton electric van, OMM

After the move to South Wigston a new range was offered, the 600 series. This embraced 5/8cwt, 10/12cwt, 18/22cwt, 25/30cwt and a 2/3ton model. A departure from the usual coachbuilt bodies was announced at this time in the shape of the streamlined Airline, Airstream and Airflow models with all-steel bodies. The Airstream followed the more orthodox style in electric vehicle bodywork with van, milk truck and open body variations. The Airline looked like an early "fastback" with swept-down body at the rear with an overhead sliding cover for loading by crane, although not of all-steel construction. The Airflow was certainly eyecatching, being of normal control layout with long streamlined hood.

In 1936 the company joined Electricars Ltd., Young Accumulators and Hants Electric Chassis to form Associated Electric Vehicle Manufacturers, this arrangement continuing until 1941 when Crompton Parkinson took control of the Morrison type with Electricar design being retained for the heavier models in the 2/3ton bracket. As an aid to wartime standardization the range was subse-

1947 MORRISON-ELECTRICAR 2-ton electric van, MJWW

quently cut to just one model, a 20cwt. At the end of the war the Electricar range was discontinued and shortly afterwards, in 1948 Austin took a 50% interest in the organization and it became Austin Crompton Parkinson Electric Vehicles Ltd. The postwar range consisted of four models of 10, 20, 40 and 60-cwt capacity. In 1951 the range was extended to 7 models based on three basic chassis types of 5ft 6¾in, 7ft 5/8in and 9ft 0in wheelbase. Shortly afterwards a 1-ton pedestrian model and the GT 4-wheel articulated tractor were added. During the 1950's the range was updated by the introduction of the SD and MD dairy range and by 1958 there were 21 different

1970 MORRISON-ELECTRICAR A1 ¼-ton electric van British Leyland

models listed being based on 5 differing chassis lengths with the longest at 8ft 6in for mobile shops. 1963 saw the addition of the Electruk to the range when T.H. Lewis discontinued vehicle manufacture, and in 1966 a move was made to Tredegar. The title was changed to Crompton Leyland Electricars following the absorption of the BMC conglomerate into British Leyland, and in 1970 the new urban style of small electric vehicle, the A1 model, made its appearance. This 500lb payload van or pickup with

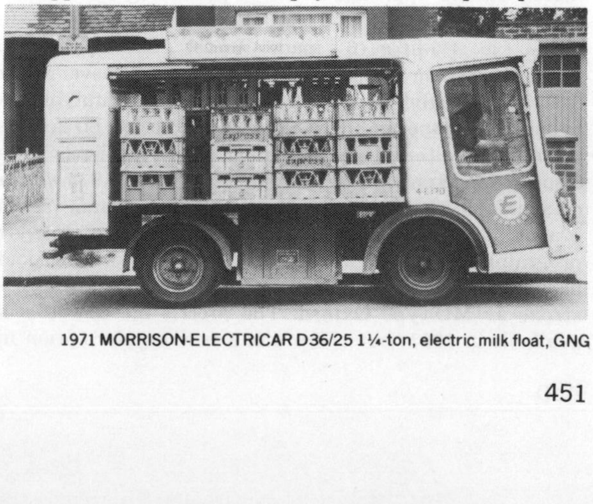

1971 MORRISON-ELECTRICAR D36/25 1¼-ton, electric milk float, GNG

fiber glass body, two motor drive to the front wheels and tilting body for battery maintenance was not the great sales leader that was hoped. Since then production has been concentrated on a conventional rear-drive chassis in several sizes from 1¼ to 2 tons. In 1976 Crompton took over production of the Oxcart which had been developed by an outside company, Oxford Electrics, using a Crompton Electricars 2-ton chassis. It had a one-man cab and was designed for the milk roundsman who also had bread and potatoes to deliver, a growing trend in the dairy business. In addition to a normal load of milk crates the Oxcart can carry 400 loaves and about 400lb of potatoes. *OMM*

MORRIS-LEON BOLLEE see Leon Bollee

1897 MORRIS & SALOM Electrobat cabs, Roger Whitehouse Collection

MORRIS & SALOM (US) 1896-1898

(1) Electric Carriage & Wagon Co., Philadelphia, Pa. 1896-1897

(2) Electric Vehicle Co., Elizabethport, N.J. 1897-1898

Henry Morris and Pedro Salom built one of America's first electric cars in 1894, and two years later began production of electric cabs for use in New York City. Known as Electrobats, two types were made, both with front wheel drive and rear wheel steering. One had the driver behind the passengers in the traditional hansom cab position, and the other seated the driver on a box ahead of the passengers. In 1897 the Morris & Salom interests were bought by Isaac L. Rice who formed the Electric Vehicle Company at Elizabethport, N.J. Electrobat cabs were made there in 1898 but the following year production was transferred to Col. Pope's recently-formed Columbia Automobile Co. of Hartford, Connecticut. *GNG*

MORRISS see Sandringham

MORS (F) 1900-1915

(1) Societe d'Electricite et d'Automobiles Mors, Paris 1900-1907

(2) Societe Nouvelle des Automobiles Mors, Paris 1908-1915

Early production of Mors commercial vehicles was on a spasmodic basis, though in 1900 the firm built an 8hp telegraph van with 4-speed gearbox, chain drive and solid tires for the French Army. The 1902 catalog depicted a conventional truck on the 12 hp 4-cylinder aiv chassis with armored wood frame, but a more serious proposition was the 1905 2-tonner, with 5½-litre 4-cylinder T-head engine, dual ignition, three forward speeds, and pressed steel chassis. A double-decker bus development had four speeds and the unusual option of a compressed air starter. A year later there were three models for payloads from 30-cwt to 5 tons, the smallest Mors truck having a driver over engine layout. The heavy ones, however, were normal control low-loaders with 6.2-litre power units, transverse rear suspension, auxiliary coil springs for the bodywork, and an unusually long wheelbase of 15ft 1in which made them suitable for char-a- banc or pantechnicon work. 1908 saw the inevitable cab chassis, distinguished by a short-stroke (80x90mm) L-head monobloc 4-cylinder engine, pressure lubrication, and the usual Mors band clutch. All these models continued without change into 1909, but the previous year's reorganization had led to the appointment of Andre Citroen as manager, and the ensuing prosperity

1906 MORS 3-4 ton van, OMM

meant less interest in trucks. Four models, including a 20/30 hp 6-cylinder, were still listed in 1914, when chain-driven Mors bullion vans were in service in Paris. *MCS*

MORT (US) 1923-1926

Meteor Motor Car Co., Piqua, Ohio

Like many private car manufacturers in the 1920s, Meteor added a junior line of hearses and ambulances to their catalog in 1923.The first Morts used the small 40hp Continental 6, though more powerful engines of the same make were available, and hydraulic fwb were standardized in 1924. There were also Mort bodies mounted on 4-cylinder Dodge chassis. *MCS*

MORTON (i) (GB) c.1900-1907

Robert Morton & Sons, Wishaw, Lanarkshire

Between 1900 and 1907 Mortons, who were general engineers, made a few light steam wagons on the Lifu principal as licensees. In 1907 when the trade appeared promising a new firm, Belhaven Engineering & Motors Ltd., was formed to take over the work. *RAW*

MORTON (ii) (US) 1912-1916

Morton Truck and Tractor Co., Harrisburg, Pa.

In 1913 Morton listed five models from 1½ to 5-tons capacity, priced from $2,500 to $4,500. A four-wheel-drive tractor was also listed. All models had 30 hp 4-cylinder engine, 4-speed transmission, and chain drive. By 1915 Morton offered 3 and 6-ton models with four-wheel-drive-and-steering, along with a standard 3-ton model. Large numbers of Morton trucks and tractors were shipped to Russia from 1914 on. The Morton was built in the factory of the Harrisburg Mfg. and Boiler Company, which later took over manufacture of the Hurlburt truck. *DJS*

MORTON (iii) (F) 1929-1930

Moteurs Morton, Suresnes, Seine.

Specialists in stationary diesel engines, this company had showed a 2-cylinder 2-stroke unit suitable for vehicle use in 1927. Their 6-ton truck, however, featured a 2.6-litre long-stroke 40 bhp engine on similar lines with aluminum block and cylinders, double reduction drive, and air brakes on the rear wheels only. There was also a compressed-air starter. The Morton did not go into production. *MCS*

MOSKVITCH (MOCKBNY) SU 1947 to date

(1) (MZMA) Moskovskii Zavod Malolitrajnikh Automobilei-Moscow 1947-1968

(2) (AZLK) Automobilnii Zavod Lovinskogo Komsomola-Moscow 1968 to date

(3) (IZH) Izhevsk Automobile Factory — Izhevsk 1969 to date

Light delivery vehicles have been built on the Moskvitch car chassis since the inception of the line in 1947.

The first series 400, based on the pre-war German Opel Kadett, contained a wooden-bodied 422 "furgon" or light van. It seated two, carried 250 kg of goods and was powered by a 4- cylinder 23 hp engine, later increased to 26 hp. This was built until 1956.

The 407 series of 1958 to 1964 had a model 430 van and series 403 of 1963 to 1965 had van 432.

About 1965 the Russians greatly revised the Moskvitch as model 408. Van 433 in this series is powered by a 4-cylinder, 55 hp ohv engine and is equipped to carry 250-

1974 MOSKVITCH 1500 van, Autoexport

400 kg of freight.

The newest 412 series includes van 434 with a 4-cylinder ohv engine of 80 hp.

A branch factory in Izhevsk opened in 1969 and also produces series 412 including a 350 kg Moskvitch-Izh 1500 GR freight carrier. *BE*

MOTALA (S) 1933-1938

Motala Verkstads A.B. Lindholmen, Motala

Motala was a manufacturer of integral buses, using Chrysler and Reo gasoline engines, and diesels by Hercules, Deutz, and Daimler-Benz. These engines were generally mounted vertically at the right side of the vehicle, as on the AEC Q-type.

In 1935 a fleet of buses was built for the Stockholm Tramways Corporation, using 6-cylinder Hall-Scott horizontal gasoline engines.

Most remarkable part of the Motala exterior was the front, with the spare wheel housed in a cavity in the front panel.

During the 'thirties nearly all Swedish metropolitan transport boards had one or some Motalas in their fleet. *JFJK*

MOTOCART see Opperman

MOTOCOR (I) 1921-1924

Armino Mezzo, Turin

The Motocor was a 3-wheeler powered by an amidships-mounted aircooled flat-twin engine of 575cc or 745cc, the bigger unit having ohv. Other features were a tilting body, a 3-speed-and-reverse gearbox, and chain drive to the single rear wheel. On commercial versions (a 4½-cwt truck or 2-seater taxi) the driver sat at the rear: private cars and taxis also had a dummy radiator in the bows. Only about 50 Motocors of all types were made. *MCS*

MOTOEMIL (GR) 1967 to date

K & A Antoniadis, Stauroupolis, Thessaloniki

Another of the successful 3 wheeled light truck producers in Greece, Motoemil uses new or reconditioned I.2 lt and I.5 lt VW engines, a glassfibre or metal cab and has a payload of 350 kilos. *GA*

MOTO GUZZI (I) 1928 to date

(1) Moto Guzzi SpA, Mandello del Lario, Como 1928-1967

(2) Societa Esercizio Industrie Moto Meccaniche SpA, Mandello del Lario, Como 1967 to date

Moto Guzzi have been the most consistent producer of *motocarri*, or light commercial 3-wheelers of motorcycle type with two driven rear wheels. As on the company's motorcycles, the single-cylinder 500cc engines were mounted horizontally. Initially these units were of the exhaust-over-inlet configuration, but ohv were standard practice from 1938, later models also having four forward speeds and shaft drive. Pre-War Guzzis could cope with payloads of up to 1 ton, and large numbers of the Trialce variant were supplied to the Italian Army. Civilian production was resumed in 1945 with the 1,500 kg Ercole, featuring a 5-speed and reverse gearbox and disc rear wheels. It acquired hydraulic rear brakes in 1955, and coil ignition (plus an electric starter) in 1957. Though a 65cc rickshaw was announced in 1948, the first lightweight to see series production was the Ercolino of 1956, with 192cc ohv scooter engine and a carrying capacity of 350 kg, later uprated to 590 kg. Even smaller trucks followed: 1962's 250 kg Aiace had a 110cc 2-stroke engine, and Guzzi's first 50cc commercial was the Dinotre of 1965 with chain drive and three forward speeds. This evolved three years later into the Furghina, a more sophisticated effort featuring a covered cab, shaft drive, a differential back axle and a

1974 MOTO GUZZI Ercole 1½-ton 3-wheel truck, Moto-Guzzi

reverse option. On the military side the company made 220 examples of a 3x3 power cart between 1959 and 1963: this one used a 750cc transverse vee-twin engine. Furghina production ceased in 1976, leaving the Ercole as the solitary truck model. The cab was now enclosed, but retained were the 500cc horizontal engine, handlebar steering, and uncoupled 3-wheel brakes. *MCS*

MOTOKART (US) 1913-1914

Tarrytown Motor Car Co., Tarrytown, N.Y.

A small delivery van with a cargo box in front of the driver was the layout of the MotoKart. This used a wheelbase of 5 feet, 9 inches with track of 3 feet, 8 inches. It was driven by a four stroke, two-cylinder water-cooled engine. This was connected with a friction transmission and single chain to the rear axle. The engine was under the driver's seat. Pneumatic tires were on wire spoke wheels. With rated capacity of 400 pounds, the price was $400. *GMN*

MOTOM (I) 1952-1966

Motom SpA, Milan

This motorcycle factory offered an ultra-light commercial 3-wheeler with two driven rear wheels. Payload was a 3-cwt, and final drive was by chain, but unusually the 48 cc engine was of 4-stroke type. Early models were sometimes known as Gavonis. *MCS*

MOTO MORINI (I) 1937-1943

Fabbrica Italiana Motocicli Moto-Morini, Bologna

This company's range included a motorcycle-based light commercial 3-wheeler with 600cc cc engine and two driven rear wheels. Air raid damage closed the factory in 1943, and the type did not reappear when motorcycle production began again in 1945. *MCS*

MOTOPORTER (D) 1973

Motoporter CmbH., Hanau

This was a 4-wheeled mini-transporter using a single cylinder four-stroke engine of 480 cc which was front mounted and drove the rear wheels. Production was limited. *HON*

MOTORCAR (GR) 1967-1970

Motorcar, Ag. Ioannis Rentis, Athens

Motorcar built a series of 3 wheeled light trucksters following the usual pattern as pioneered in Greece, new or reconditioned VW and German Ford engines, glassfibre cabs and 350 kilos payload. *GA*

MOTORETTE (US) 1911-1912

C.W. Kelsey Manufacturing Co., Hartford, Conn.

The three-wheeled Motorette was made in two delivery van versions. The single rear wheel was driven by a chain from a two-stroke, two-cylinder engine presumed to have been built by Lycoming. the parcel box was placed over the front axle while the driver's seat was in front of the rear wheel in the case of the 200lb L 1 and above the wheel in the 500lb N 1. Both models used tiller steering. *GMN*

MOTOR TRANSIT see El Dorado

1912 MOTOR WAGON Model A 800lb open express, NAHC

MOTOR WAGON (US) 1912-1913

Motor Wagon Co. of Detroit, Detroit, Mich.

Several models of light vans were offered under this name, of 800 and 1000 pound capacity. The chassis with wheelbase of 8 feet, 4 inches was priced from $610 to $900. Power was from a four-cylinder engine under the hood, in turn connected with a planetary transmission and chain drive. This was also called Detroit Motor Wagon. *GMN*

MOTOSACOCHE (CH) L

Motosacoche S.A., Geneva

This well-known motorcycle maker, like many others, launched a 3-wheeled parcel van using its own single-cylinder 350cc ohv engine, with chain drive to the rear wheel. *GNG*

MOTO SCOOTER (E) 1951-1959

Moto Scooter S.A., Madrid

This scooter manufacturer made a delivery 3-wheeler called the Titano, with single-cylinder 2-stroke engine, based on their Ronline scooter. Their factory was later occupied by the makers of the better-known Trimak, and it is possible that the last vehicles made by Moto Scooter were sold as Trimaks. *JCG*

1951 MOWAG 2-ton 4×4 truck, Mowag

MOWAG (CH) 1948 to date

Mowag Motorwagenfabrik AG, Kreuzlingen

This company was formed from the coach builders Seitz u Ruf AG, and its first motor vehicles were light vans supplied to the Swiss Post Office. From 1951 onwards Mowag produced a light 4x4 truck for the Swiss Army which was made for many years. Powered by a 6-cylinder Chrysler engine it was used as a troop carrier, command car with radio equipment, or 2-ton truck, and also as a basis for fire engines. In the early 1950s Mowag's owner W. Ruf launched into a new field with a range of cab-forward trucks with SLM horizontal diesel engines mounted under the floor. Payloads were up to 9 tons, and they were made in small numbers at first, only 34 being made in 1955. At the end of the 1950s Mowag offered a wide range including a 4-tonner with 6-cylinder Chrysler engine, a 5-tonner with SLM diesel engine and a 9-tonner

1953 MOWAG 8-ton underfloor engine truck, Mowag

with double reduction, giving 12 forward speeds. Other special models included a narrow-cab front-entrance truck for carrying long iron bars powered by a flat-8 SLM engine, and a 4x4 tipper with 5-cylinder Bussing engine. There were also three different bus chassis for touring, postal service or city work with SLM 6- or 8-cylinder engines and capacities for up to 80 passengers.

1967 MOWAG 8-ton underfloor engine steel carrier, Mowag

1967 MOWAG postal bus, Mowag

By 1965 new models with front-mounted Chrysler 6 or V-8 engines appeared for payloads of 4 and 5 tons, while the underfloor-engined models were continued, with Perkins or Bussing engines in several sizes up to 11.4 litres and 192hp. Payload of the latter was 8.6 tons. In addition there was the model M5-16 powered by an in-line 5-cylinder 2-stroke diesel engine for 9 ton payloads. A similar design of 4-cylinder engine was fitted to the M4-13F bus chassis. Gasoline engines were dropped on trucks by 1967 but a range of fire engines with V-8 Chrysler engines and 4-wheel drive was developed. These became of increasing importance in Mowag's activities as the trucks were gradually phased out, and from 1969 both

1977 MOWAG 8×4 truck, Mowag

conventional and COE fire engines were offered. In recent years Mowag have concentrated on the development of armored vehicles, but in 1975 they were working on an 8-cylinder truck engine should there be an opening in the market for commercial vehicles, and in 1977 they built an 8x4 truck powered by this engine. *FH*

M & P (US) 1911-1913

M & P Electric Vehicle Company, Detroit, Michigan

These were light battery-powered electrics of 1000- and 1500- pound ratings. They all used a wheelbase of 8 feet, 4 inches and carried 40 cells of Gould storage batteries weighing 900 pounds. Motors were by Westinghouse. Both delivery and express bodies were built. The name of this truck was changed to Victor in 1913. *GMN*

M.T. (E) 1940-1962

Maquinaria y Elementos de Transporte SA, Barcelona

This large metallurgical company began vehicle construction by making a number of trolleybuses using Seddon chassis. From 1950 onwards they made a light 3-

wheels powered by 175 cc 2-stroke engine with 3-speed gearbox and independent suspension on the front wheels. It was one of the best finished vans of its era. *JCG*

MTN see Rutland

MUCHOW (D) 1926-1931

Muchow & Co. Fahrzeug- und Geratefabrik GmbH., Berlin W 62

This company acquired the Berlin plant of Elitewagen and carried on production of electric vehicles. On the program was an *avant train* which was attachable to other vehicles or trailers. This principle was also used for various vehicles intended for all kinds of municipal purposes. Moreover a 5 ton truck and a tractor with 10 ton towing capacity were available. *HON*

MULAG (D) 1909-1913

Motoren- und Lastwagen A.G., Aachen

Mulag followed the make of Scheibler and various types of trucks were offered which were well-known for their high quality. After 1913 all products were marketed under the name Mannesmann-Mulag. *HON*

MULLER (D) 1908-1911

W.A. Th. Muller Strassenzuggesellschaft mbH., Steglitz.

This design of a road tractor was based on the electric train of Siemens-Schuckert. Gas-electric drive was used and up to six trailers could be towed. The gasoline engine and generator were placed on the tractor, the trailers were equipped with the electric motors. *HON*

1967 MULTICAR 22 light truck, OMM

MULTICAR (DDR) 1964 to date

VEB Fahrzeugwerk Waltershausen, Waltershausen

This is a city transporter, originally equipped with a 2-cylinder diesel engine of 13 PS and 2 ton payload. In 1974 an improved version with 4-cylinder diesel engine of 45 PS appeared. A single seater cabin is mounted and various bodies are available. *HON*

MULTIWHEELERS see Beardmore Multiwheelers

MURPHY see Auto Electric

MURTY (US) 1949 to date

Murty Bros., Portland, Oregon.

Murty Brothers are a small firm specializing in off-highway equipment for the logging industry, and on-highway crane carriers. They pioneered the 8-wheeled crane carrier, now featured in the ranges of many larger and better-known manufacturers.

In 1952 they announced their only on-highway load-carrying truck, the Murty Flat-top for carrying long or bulky freight such as steel pipes and girders. Made in 2- and 3-axle form, the Flat-Tops had one-man cabs and were powered by a 150bhp 486 cu. in. 6-cylinder White engine. They both had a Clark 270V 5-speed main transmission, the 4-wheeled model have an Eaton 2-speed rear axle, and the 6-wheeler a Brown-Lipe auxiliary transmission giving a total of 15 forward speeds. Payload of the 4-wheeler was 10 tons and of the 6-wheeler, 15 tons. Deck lengths were 25 and 30 ft. respectively. Fewer than 30 of these trucks were made, between 1952 and 1956, and all were sold on the West Coast. *GNG*

MUSASHI (J) 1956-1960

Mitaka Fuji Co. Ltd., Tokyo

The Musashi was a conventional 3-wheeled light truck with 359cc vertical-twin 4-stroke engine and 4-speed gearbox. The company also made a light 4-wheeler pickup, the Paddle, with similar mechanics. *MCS*

MUSKEGON (US) 1917-1920

Muskegon Engine Company, Muskegon, Michigan.

The Muskegon truck was made in only one model called 20 which was rated at two tons carrying capacity. This had a four-cylinder engine by Continental, a three-speed gearbox and shaft drive. Its wheelbase was 12 feet and chassis price was $2325. *GMN*

1901 MUSKER oil-fired steam truck, RAW

MUSKER (GB) 1900-1905

C & A. Musker Ltd., Liverpool

Early Musker wagons were built with an entirely under-mounted arrangement using a flash type boiler, oil or coke fired, with the coil laid horizontally, the engine being a 4 cylinder single acting type, using poppet valves driven by push-rods activated by a separate eccentric shaft geared to the crankshaft. A second type had a vertical flash boiler. Neither seems to have succeeded, probably because of combining too many advanced ideas in a pioneer design.

In 1903 a revised design appeared combining the vertical boiler with a conventional cross compound engine with Stephenson's link motion, all enclosed in an oil bath. The final drive was by pinions meshing on an open ring of gears fixed to the rear wheels.

The last design replaced this arrangement by a conventional double roller chain drive and incorporated a double drum marine type water tube boiler. Early in 1905 Muskers sold their wagon business to Savage Brothers Ltd. of Kings Lynn, Norfolk. *RAW*

MUTEL (F) 1905-c.1906
Mutel et Cie, Parie 15e

Mutel were mainly makers of proprietary engines which were supplied to a number of early French vehicle builders, but a few cars and commercial vehicles were sold under the Mutel name. The latter included a 12 hp 2-cylinder van, a 14 hp 4-cylinder 2-ton van and a 30 hp 4-cylinder chain-drive bus chassis. *GNG*

MUTUAL (US) 1919-1921
Mutual Truck Co., Sullivan, Ind.

The original lineup of Mutual trucks were 2½-, 3½- and 5-tonners. These all used 4-cylinder Wisconsin engines, 4-speed gearboxes and Sheldon worm-drive rear axles. For 1921, only the 2-tonner and the 2½-ton tonner were made. *GMN*

M.V (I) 1948-1973
SpA Meccanica Verghera, Gallarate

M.V-Agusta was another motorcycle maker who offered orthodox 3-wheeled *motocarri* with two driven rear wheels. In 1957, however, they branched out into 4-wheelers with a 1-ton forward control model with transverse ifs, hydraulic brakes, and eight forward speeds. Power was provided by a 1.097cc 26bhp 2-cylinder diesel. This was a short-lived venture, but in 1965 M.V announced the Diana, a cross-country type with Lypsoid tires inspired by the German Kraka. *MCS*

M.W. (D) 1925-1926
Waggonfabrik Wegmann & Co. Kassel

A ¾ ton truck was manufactured by this firm of carriage builders. Two two-stroke engines were available, either an air-cooled 412cc or a water-cooled 389cc, both by D.K.W. *HON*

M.W.D. (D) 1911-1912
Motor-Werke mbH., Dessau

A van version was available of the private cars of this make, especially based on the 8/22 PS model. Payload capacity varied from ½ to 1½ tons. *HON*

M.W.F. (D) 1924-1928
Magdeburger Werkzeug-Maschinin-Fabrik A.G., Magdeburg

This firm produced trucks and buses with 4-cylinder engines for 2½ ton payload and 6-cylinder engine for 3½ and 5 ton payload. Also buses were offered with both engine versions. *HON*

M.W.M. (D) 1924-1931
Motorenwerke Mannheim AG vorm. Benz Abt. stat. Motorenbau, Mannheim

This firm was established in 1922 when Benz sold its branch factory for stationary engines. Prosper L'Orange became their director. He was the inventor of the compressor-less pre-combustion-chamber diesel engine which Benz also used for their diesel engine experiments.

The very economical and reliable MWM diesel engines were to be used for vehicles. A 2-cylinder engine developing 18 bhp at 800 rpm was chosen and a road tractor was developed. MWM did not want to start production of vehicles themselves, so the tractors were built to their order at the Maschinenfabrik Karlsruhe. They were called "Motorpferd" (motor horse) and were produced until 1931 when MWM decided to concentrate on production of diesel proprietary engines. *HON*

MYERS (US) 1918-1919
E.A. Myers Co., Pittsburgh, Pa.

The Myers was built as 1- and 1½-tonners but further information has not been uncovered. *GMN*

1956 MYMSA Rana 3RD 200kgs 3-wheel van, GNG

MYMSA (E) 1955-1961
Motores y Motos SA, Barcelona

This company made motorcycles, sidecars, and two models of light van, the 3-wheeled 125cc Rana 3-R for 200kg loads, and the 4-wheeled 500cc diesel engined Rana 4-R for 500kg loads. *JCG*

1925 NACKE 5-ton truck, HON

NACKE (D) 1901-1929

Automobilfabrik E. Nacke, Coswig

Nacke sold his first cars under the name of "Coswiga". Small trucks and buses were available, but no specific details are known. Early models had chain drive but quite early Nacke adopted shaft drive and worm gear. Best known was the 5-ton subsidy truck. After WWI Nacke started with a 3-ton model, later concentrated on two types, a 2½-tonner with 4-cylinder engine and a 5-tonner with 6-cylinder engine. All models were characterized by worm drive which Nacke pioneered on heavier vehicles. *HON*

N.A.G. (D) 1903-1931

(1) Neue Automobil Gesellschaft mbH., Berlin 1903-1912
(2) Neue Automobil AG, Berlin 1912-1915
(3) Nationale Automobil AG, Berlin; Leipzig 1915-1931

With the acquisition of Kuhlstein N.A.G. also had taken over a design of a road tractor by Joseph Vollmer. This was the first road train in the world, it had a 50 hp spirit engine and was capable of towing two trailers. Total payload was 20 tons. This vehicle was intended for the African colonies and so was equipped with big and wide wheels. In 1904 N.A.G. presented their first omnibus for 16 passengers. The first sight-seeing bus which operated for Thos. Cook in Berlin was an N.A.G. This was in 1906.

One year later the first double-deck bus by N.A.G. was put into service in Berlin. Trucks with 2- and 4-cylinder engines and payload capacities of 2, 3½ and 6-ton were in the program and vans were available on private car chassis. N.A.G. also built the state subsidized standard truck and for several years they had the largest input of all manufacturers. In 1909 N.A.G. built the first bus with cardan drive and many double deckers were put into service in Berlin. For many years N.A.G. became the sole supplier for the Berlin bus company ABOAG. Electric vans and light trucks were another specialty chassis by N.A.G. were used for various special purposes, e.g. fire engines and municipal vehicles.

After WWI N.A.G. concentrated on a few types. There were 3½-ton and 5-ton trucks and buses based on these versions. A 45 hp engine was used. A special low-frame bus chassis appeared in 1924 using a 75 hp engine which also was installed in the heavier trucks and articulated tractors. The first three-axle chassis was presented in 1924. Vans and 1-ton trucks were based on the private car chassis with a 4-cylinder 10/45 PS or 6-cylinder 12/65 PS engine. The trucks were available with 4-cylinder 7.6-litre or 9.7-litre engines.

1926 N.A.G. 15-ton articulated low-loader, FLP

In 1927 the make of Presto of Leipzig was taken over and a well-proved design of a light truck (formerly built by Dux) was carried on. It had a 4-cylinder 3.1-litre engine. Apart from this type the program of 1930 consisted of 2¼-ton (3.6-litre), 2½-ton (4.0-litre), and 5-ton (10.8-litre) trucks, a 2½-ton six-wheel truck and buses for various body styles, including double-deck versions.

At the beginning of 1931 N.A.G. gave up production of commercial vehicles, which was taken over by Bussing. Further products were marketed as "Bussing-N.A.G." *HON*

NAIRN (GB) 1870-1871

Andrew Nairn, Leith, Midlothian

Nairn built an 8 hp vertical boilered Thomson type road steamer using his own design of resilient tread on the driving wheels consisting of three layers of rope separated by sheet rubber and protected by pivoted wrought iron shoes.

In the same year he built a 50 seater double decker steam omnibus with a Field tube boiler capable of a top speed of 16 mph. For a time, fitted with willow treads to the wheels to deaden noise, this was operated in Edinburgh.

A further omnibus made in 1871 ran, during the summer of that year, eleven or twelve trips a day over the three miles between Edinburgh and Portobello but was withdrawn after legal action. *RAW*

N.A.M. (D) 1949-1950

Niedersachsisches Auto- und Motoren-Instandsetzungswerk

This firm produced forward control buses on 2- and 3-axle GMC chassis from army surplus material. Available were the original engines or diesels by Henschel or Deutz. *HON*

NAMI (HAMN) SU

Nautshno-issledovatelskii Automobilnoi i Automotornoi Institut - Moscow

The well known Soviet design bureau, Scientific Automobile-Motor Research Institute, has lent its name to a number of Russian vehicles through the years but is engaged in design and testing only and does not do series production.

It has the only test track in the USSR. *BE*

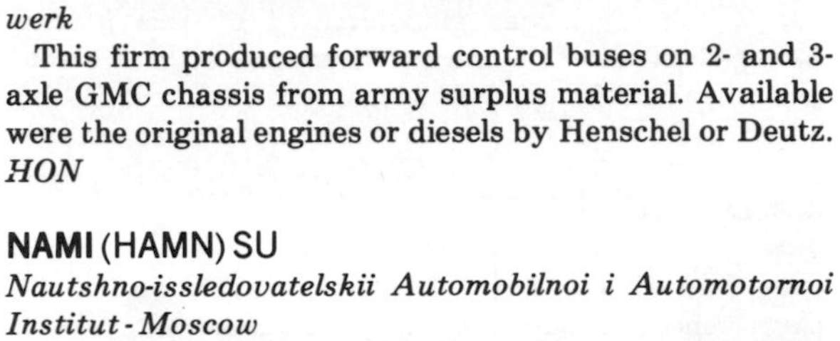

1902 NANCEIENNE 3-ton truck, Autocar

NANCEIENNE (F) 1900-1903

Societe Nanceienne d'Automobiles, Nancy

This company built vehicles to the Gobron-Brillie patents, most of them trucks. Features common to both makes were a vertical 2-cylinder aiv opposed-piston engine, an ingenious metering device in place of a carburetor, and a willingness to run on alcohol fuel; a Nanceienne won a gold medal in the 1901 Alcohol Trials. The engine was mounted vertically under the driver's seat, there were three forward speeds, and final drive was by side chains. Iron tires were fitted, though rubber damping was used for the semi-elliptic springs. Normal payload was 2 tons; a 4½-ton tipper was announced in 1902. *MCS*

NAN-FANG (p) (wg) (Southern) (CHI) 1970 to date

Kuangehou Motor Vehicle Plant, Kuangchou (Canton), Kwangtung

A large rear-engined bus. Technical details are unavailable. *BE*

NANYANG #351 (CHI) to date

Nanyang Motor Vehicle Plant, Honan Province

The Nanyang is a 7-ton dump truck using a chassis, cab, vehicle body and dumper mechanism very similar to those on the Tsingtao-built Huang-He QD-351.

A 6-cylinder diesel engine of 160 hp delivers a top speed of 63 km/h. *BE*

1902 NAPIER 5-ton truck, Autocar

1914 NAPIER 27-seater touring coach, NMM

NAPIER (GB) 1901-1920

(1) D. Napier & Son Ltd., Lambeth, London, S.E. 1901-1903
(2) D. Napier & Son Ltd., Acton, London, W. 1903-1920

Napier's early attempts at commercial vehicle manufacture were rather spasmodic, probably because S.F. Edge, their redoubtable selling agent, also sponsored de Dion-Bouton's cars (and trucks) in England. A few vans and chars-a-banc were, however, built in 1901 using modified 12 hp car chassis with vertical-twin aiv engines, side-chain drive, and solid tires; by 1905, one of these had covered 70,000 miles with only £10 spent on repairs. Nothing came of a 5-ton truck announced in 1902: it had a 4.9-litre 4-cylinder engine, twin watercooled transmission brakes, and a vertical steering column. Another short-lived venture was a 35 hp bus chassis of 1906; it was powered by a T-head 6.4-litre 4-cylinder dual-ignition engine and retained chain drive. From 1908 to 1911 the firm's main commercial-vehicle interest was a line of taxicabs, which sold well (556 delivered in 1909 as against only 366 pleasure cars). These featured L-head engines (a 1.3-litre twin or a 2.7-litre 15 hp four), three forward speeds and shaft drive: the 2-cylinder model had a unit gearbox, and Colonial models of the four operated as far afield as Canada and South Africa. Both were also available as light vans, a fleet of 15 hp luggage carriers participating in the 1909 Guards to Hastings Demonstration. A few 6-cylinder car chassis were also adapted to truck use, two such 1909 instances being a Maxim gun carrier for the Army and a police patrol van for Vancouver. It was not, however, until 1912 that a truck department was set up under the direction of A. Norris, and a year later the range embraced trucks of 30-cwt, 2 tons and 3 tons as well as a 12-cwt van on the 15 hp car chassis. The new models had paircast 4-cylinder engines, magneto ignition, unit gearboxes, worm drive, and solid tires with twin rears: the bigger ones had 4-speed boxes, found also on the 1914 30-cwt. A new 45-cwt announced for 1915 was used by the Army; it featured an American splitdorf magneto and detachable wheels, while the 6.2-litre 3½-tonner was now rated at 85-cwt. Only this latter design, now sold as a 2-tonner, reappeared after the Armistice, and the trucks were phased out towards the end of 1920 when the company elected to concentrate on aero engines. There was a final brief exploration of the market in 1931 with prototypes of a 3-wheeler mechanical horse, but the failure of Napier's bid for Bentley Motors in that year led to further rethinking, and the rights of the design were sold to Scammell. *MCS*

1904 NAPIER-PARSONS delivery van, GNG

NAPIER-PARSONS (GB) 1904-1906

G. Napier & Sons Ltd., Southampton

This light van was designed by Henry Parsons of non-skid chain fame, and built by G. Napier & Sons, no connection with the better-known D. Napier & Sons of Acton. It had a 6/7 hp single-cylinder engine with concentric valves, the exhaust valve being inside the inlet one. There was a 2-speed planetary gearbox giving speeds of 5 and 12 mph, and shaft drive. It was said that 'it is able to run on heavier fuels than gas, including ordinary lamp oil, provided that a little smell is not objected to'. In 1907 Parsons' patents were acquired by Sturmey Motors of Coventry who made it under their own name for one year, before launching the Lotis cars and commercial vehicles. *GNG*

NAPOLEON (US) 1919-1922

(1) Napoleon Motors Co., Traverse City, Mich. 1919-1920
(2) Napoleon Motor Cars & Trucks, Traverse City, Mich. 1921-1922

There were two models of this brand, a 1-tonner and a 1½-tonner. Both used 4-cylinder, ohv Gray engines, 3-speed gearboxes and bevel-gear rear axles. Only minor changes were made in the three years of manufacture. *GMN*

NARCLA (E) 1954-1966

Industrias Narcla, S.A., Barcelona

This motorcycle manufacturer also made delivery tricycles powered by single-cylinder 2-stroke engines of 6 hp. They had 4-speed gearboxes. *JCG*

1948 NASH Model 3248 3-ton truck, GNG

NASH (US) 1917-1931: 1947-1955

(1) Nash Motor Co., Kenosha, Wisc. 1917-1954
(2) American Motors Corporation, Kenosha, Wisc. 1954-1955

Charles W. Nash acquired the Jeffery concern in 1916, and with it the 2-ton Quad truck with 4-cylinder Buda engine and 4-wheel drive and steering. Both cars and trucks were sold under the Nash name from the 1918 model year, the demand for Quads being such that Nash were able to claim the title of the world's largest truck maker on their first full season's sales of 11,490 units. Nash also built conventional 1½- and 2-ton models with big 4-cylinder sv monobloc engines, coil ignition, 3-speed gearboxes, electric lighting, and shaft drive: by 1921 these had acquired starters and an extra forward ratio. Thereafter sales dropped sharply, with only 203 Nash trucks delivered in 1924, and commercial vehicles were quietly phased out, the official end coming in 1930, though up to 1931 the firm produced a few sedan deliveries based on their cheaper 6-cylinder private car chassis.

Nash re-entered the truck market in 1947 with an orthodox 2/3-tonner using the 3.8-litre 6-cylinder ohv Ambassador car engine. It was listed in chassis/cab form as an export-only item, though some were sold to American Nash dealers as wreckers. The last of 5,000 odd was built in 1955. In 1951 and 1952 Nash also offered a delivery van edition of their 2.8-litre sv Rambler compact car. *MCS*

NASR (ET) 1958 to date

El Nasr Automotive Manufacturing Co., S.A.A., Wadi Hof, Helwan

Egypt's national vehicle producer builds truck and bus chassis under Magirus-Deutz license. Medium class truck chassis with 4x2 and 4x4 drive, powered by 112 hp air-cooled diesels and fitted with the old style Magirus-Deutz cabs bearing the NASR name written in Arabic are the main products of the factory. Bus models also based on Magirus-Deutz designs, are powered by rear mounted 125 hp air-cooled diesels and are fitted with locally built bodies. Buses are named Baghdad, Kuwait, etc., and are largely exported to almost all North African and Middle East countries. The Nasr factory is supported in components, engines and technical assistance by both the German Magirus-Deutz concern and in the Yugoslavian TAM licensee. The same factory also builds Nasr passenger cars, under Fiat license. *GA*

NATCO (US) 1912-1916

National Motor Truck Company, Bay City, Michigan

Only a two-tonner was built by this company and it used a four-cylinder engine with driver's controls to the left of the hood. Wheelbase was 8 feet, 8 inches and four open and closed body types were available on the single chassis. *GMN*

NATIONAL (CDN) 1915-1925

National Steel Car Co., Hamilton, Ont.

The National truck was a sideline produced by one of Canada's major suppliers of railway rolling stock, but it was a major factor in the Canadian truck market, and the company had offices in London, Paris and Petrograd (now Leningrad). National trucks were made in several sizes from 1 to 5 tons, most with shaft drive. *HD*

NATIONALE (F) 1899-1900

La Compagnie Nationale des Courriers Automobiles, Paris

This company built their steam bus to carry 15 passengers and 12 cwt of luggage. Steam was provided by a flash boiler. A 2-cylinder compound engine with divided crankshaft was used, each cylinder driving one rear wheel by roller chain. *RAW*

1903 NAYLER 5-ton steam wagon, NMM

1906 NAYLER 5-ton steam tractor, RAW

NAYLER (GB) 1903-1909

Nayler & Co. Ltd., Hereford

Naylers' first wagons were vertical fire tube-boilered compound undertypes but their experience with these convinced them that the locomotive overtype was a much more practical proposition and they commenced to build overtype wagons and tractors, generally resembling the contemporary Foden, a proceeding which involved the makers in legal action by Fodens over patent rights. So far as is known less than a dozen vehicles in all were built, the overtypes being, reputedly, satisfactory performers, albeit somewhat prone to differential trouble, cast iron having been employed when cast steel would have been preferable. *RAW*

NAZAR (E) 1957-1967

Factoria Napoles SA, Zaragoza

This company was a fairly sizeable producer of trucks and buses during its ten years' existence. The range ran from 1500 kgs to 9 tons, all forward-control trucks with conventional chassis. Engines were the 3-cylinder Perkins diesel for the smaller models, Matacas 4-cylinder diesel and Spanish-built Henschel diesels for the largest trucks. The Perkins 6.305 6-cylinder was used in the 7-ton Nazar

1962 NAZAR 6000kgs truck, GNG

1963 NAZAR 2500kgs truck, GNG

Super 7. City and touring buses were made in sizes from 14 to 50 seats, and one was the first Spanish bus to have air-conditioning. For a while Nazars were built in Valencia as well as at their main factory at Zaragoza which was acquired by Barreiros after production ceased. Their peak year was 1963 when 1,000 units were delivered. *JCG*

NAZZARO (I) 1914-1916

Nazzaro & C Fabbrica Automobili, Turin

The famous racing driver Felice Nazzaro had built a successful 4-cylinder private car before World War I. Truck production was, however, limited to an isolated batch of 50 vehicles using 4-cylinder Anzani engines. It was not resumed after the Armistice. *MCS*

N.B. (I) 1913-1914

John Newton Fabbrica Automobili, Turin

This English-designed Italian car was also offered with delivery van bodywork. It had a 2.2-litre long-stroke sv 4-cylinder engine, 4-speed gearbox, and bevel drive. *MCS*

N.C.B. (GB) 1945-1956
SMITH'S ELECTRIC (GB) 1956 to date

(1) Northern Coachbuilders Ltd., Newcastle-on-Tyne
(2) Smith's Electric Vehicles Ltd., Gateshead-on-Tyne
(3) Smith's Delivery Vehicles Ltd., Gateshead-on-Tyne

1951 NCB 1-ton refuse truck, OMM

After gaining valuable experience in composite bodybuilding before the war with 'bus bodies and during the war aircraft Northern Coachbuilders were quick to market their range of electrics. Three models were offered at first, rated at 14-cwt, 20-cwt and 30-cwt with wheelbases of 6 ft. 3 in., 6 ft. 10 in. and 9 ft. 6 in. respectively. In 1949 a 2-tonner and a three-wheeler, the Percheron 20/25-cwt were added and then a noteworthy departure from normal practice was announced — the combination of NCB electrical gear in a large refuse vehicle by Walker Brothers (Wigan) Ltd. This was the battery electric version of the Pagefield Paragon refuse collector which was first produced for the Team Valley Estate where the new NCB factory was situated. This model was rated at 10 tons gross and used a 12 ft. wheelbase chassis. The 210AH capacity batteries were mounted pannier style either side of the chassis frame and the two BTH motors were mounted just behind the cab with drive by means of open propellor shaft to a spiral bevel rear axle.

1954 NCB Percheron 3-wheel electric milk float, OMM

1953 saw the introduction of the new style "Commuter" 1 ton and 30-cwt models which featured controls for stand-drive as well as seat-drive. As from the early 1950's the vehicles became known as Smith's NCB or Smith's Electric and considerable headway was made with exports. Later, in 1962 an agreement was made with Battronic in America to market Smith's chassis with locally built bodies.

Soon after the "Suburbanite" 20/25-cwt was announced, this also having controls for standing or sitting as in the "Commuter".

In 1959 another link was made with a normally gas engined refuse vehicle in the shape of the Karrier Bantam tractor unit with Smith's electrical gear for the Royal Borough of Kensington. During the 1960's the range was enlarged so that by 1965 there were 13 basic models from 15-cwt to 2-ton payload. The large 4/5-ton Walker-NCB had been dropped from the range much earlier.

1975 SMITHS ELECTRIC Cabac 2-ton electric refuse truck, Smiths

The most recent change of style has been the introduction of the Cabac in 1969 which offered a major departure from the accepted electric vehicle layout in that the driver could not step directly from his cab into the road or onto the sidewalk. He must first go into the body through an opening at the back of the cab and there select his delivery. The roomy cab is used for storage of certain goods. The Cabac is an 8 ft. 6 in. wheelbase chassis with 264AH battery. *OM*

NECKAR (D) 1963-1964

Neckar Automobilwerke AG., Heilbronn

This brand name was used by the German Fiat company and they presented the "Pully', a 3-wheeled small van with a single front wheel a small 2 seater forward control cabin, available as a pick up or van. A 2-cylinder 500 cc. Fiat engine developing 25 hp was installed underfloor and drove the rear wheels. *HON*

N.E.F.A.G. (CH) 1937 to date

Neue Elektrische Fahrzeuge AG., Zurich-Oerlikon

In 1937 Hans Weiss, who had been with the E.F.A.G. company since 1929 and was its managing director, took over the majority of shares and formed the N.E.F.A.G. A variety of mainly small electric vehicles was built. During the 2nd World War, when the gasoline shortage set in, a number of heavy trucks were converted for electric power and business in general was very good.

Later the company concentrated on manufacturing small, quiet and handy 3- and 4-wheel electric vehicles and tractors for the Swiss railroad and postal services, as well as modern delivery vans often favored by milkmen, butchers etc. for distributing their goods in the towns. These vehicles have 3 to 6 hp electro-motors, a payload of up to 2 tons and a range of about 20 to 35 miles. *FH*

NEGRINI *(I) 1954 to date*

Fabbrica Ciclomotori e Motocicli Negrini, Savignano sul Panaro, Modena.

This motorcycle factory also built a light delivery 3-wheeler for 200 kg payloads. Steering was by handlebar, and 48 cc Morini engines were fitted. A driver's cab was optional. *MCS*

NELSON LE MOON see Le Moon

NEMO (NL) 1948-1950

Nemo Nederlandsche Motorrijturigfabriek, Jutphaas

This was a 3-wheeled van powered by a 749 cc flat-twin Coventry Victor engine which drove the single front wheel via chains. The load capacity was 15½cwt. *GNG*

NEOPLAN (D) 1953 to date

Gottlob Auwarter KG., Stuttgart; Pilsting

Auwarter started as a coachbuilding firm specializing in buses. In 1953 they presented their first own bus under the name Neoplan, a chassis-less construction with 110 PS Kamper diesel engine. Air suspension was adopted in 1957, and 1961 saw the debut of the type "Hamburg" which became a pace-maker. In addition to the cantilever unit body, air suspension was used. Independent front suspension and the rear axle layout as a longitudinal wishbone with bellows-type pneumatic springing were further features. For extra interior comfort panorama windows and jet-air-stream ventilation were introduced. Unitized contruction became significant for all future Neoplan developments. The first double-decker touring bus, the Skyliner, was introduced in 1967 and with an air-cooled V-12 Deutz diesel engine of 340 PS it was the most powerful bus on the European market. Following the same conception the Cityliner, a high-decker, appeared in 1971.

1950 NEFAG 1-ton electric milk float, NEFAG

1970 NEOPLAN Skyliner touring coach, NMM

The logical next step in this line was the Jetliner which replaced the single-decker "Hamburg" in 1973. In the same year a new factory in Pilsting took up production. Another remarkable development was the Tropic version for overseas countries (at first developed for Ghana), featuring anticorrosive body treatment, termite-proof interior etc. This development and the increasing demands of a new market led to the opening of a new factory at Kumasi, Ghana, in 1974 where various versions following the original concept are built, but also a special type with front engine. All Ghana-built buses feature Deutz diesel engines.

Apart from the rear engine concept for all Neoplan buses, a mid-engined city bus has been available since 1974. One year later the first articulated bus under the type designated Longliner was presented, likewise mid-engine concept. The Frankfurt Show of 1975 was the debut for the biggest bus ever built, the Jumbocruiser, a double-deck articulated bus which primarily is intended for long-distance touring. A 440 PS Daimler-Benz engine is installed. For all other versions engines by Daimler-Benz, Deutz or D.A.F. are available.

The Neoplan range features a long line from the small 25-seater Jetliner to the 144-seater Jumbocruiser. Nearly all versions are available as touring or line-service buses and moreover also for combined purposes. In addition Neoplan delivers their chassis-body units to coachbuilders all over Europe. In 1975 there were plans to set up an American factory in New Mexico, but US production did not commence until 1977 when Gillig of Hayward, California started to build Neoplans with Ford engines. *HON*

NESSELSDORF see N.W.

NESTORIA (D) 1931

Bischoff & Pedall, Nuremberg

A tri-van with single rear driven wheel and rear seat and box or platform in front. It was available with 200 or 500 cc engine. *HON*

NETAM-L-CAR (NL) 1941-1942

Nederlandse Tank-Apparaten- en Maschinenfabriek Netam, Rotterdam

The Netam works had made tipper bodies, trailer and municipal machinery before the war, but their first complete vehicle was a 750 kg battery electric van made to combat the shortage of gasoline in wartime Holland. It had a Smit-Slikkerveer motor powered by 12 6-volt batteries. Top speed was 22 mph and range about 40 miles. The driver's entrance was by a door in the front of the cab. Twelve were laid down, but only five were completed, plus one passenger car. *MW*

NETCO (US) 1914-1938

New England Truck Co., Fitchburg, Mass.

The Netco was a small-production assembled truck which began life with a single model, a 1½ tonner with 4-cylinder Continental engine and worm drive. A 2 tonner was added in 1916, and in the early 1920s 2 and 2½-tonners were made, still with Continental engines, Brown-Lipe transmissions and Timken axles. A larger 4 ton model with Hercules engine was added in 1927, and by 1934 a wide range for 2/4 tons to 7/10-tons was listed, engines being Waukesha or Lycoming, the latter including straight-8s. Considering the small size of Netco's operations, it is unlikely that all these were actually built. The plant was little more than a large garage, just across the street from another small truck builder, the Wachusett. Netco's output was very small and inconsistent, probably because the firm's main business was in the supply of equipment such as snowplows and hoists rather than complete trucks. They were still active in the municipal equipment field in the 1950s. *RJ*

NEUSTADT (US) 1911-1914

Neustadt Motor Car Co., St. Louis, Mo

Neustadt is mentioned as early as 1905 as building motorized fire apparatus, and this company was an early manufacturer of passenger and commercial cars in kit form. However, their venture into complete trucks seems not to have begun before 1911 when the Model A 1-tonner and the Model B 2-tonner were made. These were both powered by 4-cylinder engines under frontal hoods, with either solid rubber or pneumatic tires. For 1912, this make was listed with E L Epperson Commercial Truck Co. as manufacturer. The latter may have been merely a temporary marketing organization. *GMN*

NEVADA (US) 1913-1916

Nevada Manufacturing Company, Nevada, Iowa

These were four-wheel-drive trucks based upon purchased design rights originated by Four Traction Auto Company of Mankato, Minnesota. The Nevada was available only as a 3-tonner with forward control and shaft drive to both front and rear axles. *GMN*

NEW CLEVELAND see Cleveland

NEW EASYLOADER see Easyloader

NEW ERA (i) (US) 1911-1912

New Era Auto Cycle Company, Dayton, Ohio

The Tricar model was the lone effort of this manufacturer and was a three-wheeler driven by a 1-cylinder, air-cooled engine which drove the single rear wheel. A parcel box of 400-pound capacity was above the two front wheels. Steering was by handlebars and possibly for this reason it might be classed as a motorcycle. *GMN*

NEW ERA (ii) (J) 1928-1937

Nippon Jidosha Co. Ltd., Ohmori, Tokyo

This typical Japanese 3-wheeler consisted of a motorcycle front end with a car-type back axle carrying a truck bed. No driver protection was furnished. Early New Eras had single-cylinder engines, though vee-twin units were fitted by 1936. A year later the name of the product was changed to Kurogane. *MCS*

NEW HAVEN see Moeller

NEW LEADER (GB) 1907-1909

New Leader Cars Ltd., Apsley, Nottingham

This passenger car maker built a forward-control chassis for light van or taxicab work, powered by a 10/12 hp 4-cylinder engine. In 1908 a normal-control 4-cylinder hansom cab type taxi was offered. All had shaft drive. *GNG*

NEW STUTZ see Stutz

NEW YORK (i) (US) 1900-1901

New York Motor Vehicle Co., New York, N.Y.

The first commercial vehicle to carry the name New York was a 20 passenger steam bus powered by a 2-cylinder horizontal compound engine fed by a vertical Morrin Climax boiler as used with stationary engines. Paraffin-fueled, it used wood alcohol as a primer to start the heating. The chassis was built by F.R. Wood & Son, and one was driven from New York to Buffalo for the Pan American exposition of 1900. This was possibly the only New York bus made. *GNG*

NEW YORK (ii) (US) 1912

New York Motor Works, Nutley, New Jersey

The short-lived New York truck was in four sizes with capacities of 1500-, 3000-, 6000- and 10000-pounds. The smaller chassis used 4-cylinder engines while the two larger ones had 6-cylinders. Possibly these were the earliest use of sixes in commercial vehicles in the U.S. Drive for all models was by double chains and all had solid tires. The motto of the New York was: Made in the East for the East. *GMN*

NEW YORK (iii) (US) 1913-1921

Tegetmeier & Riepe Co., New York, NY

The initial Model L was a 1½-tonner with a 4-cylinder, side valve engine under a frontal hood. This used a three-speed gearbox and double chain drive on a wheelbase of 10 feet, 9 inches. In 1915, an option of worm drive was available. In 1917, a 2-tonner was added to the line, with worm drive as standard. This also had a 4-cylinder engine and a wheelbase of 12 feet. Both models were continued to the end of production. *GMN*

NEWARK (US) 1911-1912

Newark Automobile Manufacturing Company, Newark, New Jersey.

This represented a series of light, open delivery vans with capacities of 1000 and 1500 pounds. They were powered by 4-cylinder, water-cooled engines with three-speed gearboxes and shaft drive. Available wheelbases were 9 feet and 9 feet, 10 inches. The 1000-pound Commercial Car weighed 1700 pounds and cost $1250. *GMN*

NEWBURY (GB) 1910

Plenty & Sons Ltd., Newbury, Berks.

This company was a well-known maker of small marine steam engines, one of their main customers being the Admiralty. Their only venture into motor vehicle manufacture was with a forward-control 15/20 cwt van powered by a vertical-twin engine. It had a 2-speed planetary transmission and chain drive, and was priced at £225. The company said that they would send a van with driver for one week to anyone wishing to test the merits of a motor van, the only charge being for gasoline and the driver's wages. *GNG*

NEWEY-ASTER (GB) 1907

Gordon Newey Ltd., Birmingham

This was an assembled vehicle, powered by a 12 hp 4-cylinder Aster engine, with 3-speed gearbox and shaft drive. Most were made as passenger cars, but a 10 cwt van was advertised. *GNG*

NEWMOBILE (GB) 1906-1907

Newmobile Ltd., Acton, London W.

This company offered a light van powered by a 9 hp de Dion-Bouton engine. *GNG*

NEWTON DERBY (GB) 1920-1926

Newton Brothers (Derby) Ltd., Derby.

Toward the end of the 1920 the Newton Derby was introduced by Newton Bros. who had been making dynamos and other electric machinery for the previous 25 years. Defined as a "refined product" this 2½/3-tonner boasted two motors — one geared to each rear wheel, two brake systems (hand and foot) both acting on the rear wheels, a timber front bumper and an unusual open fronted cab having a door actually in the front of the vehicle.

During its brief life span the vehicle was offered as the T1 (20/30 cwt), T2 (2½/3 ton) and T3 (5½ ton), each model being of similar layout. Specification was a 44 cell lead acid or 60 cell nickel iron battery, a hand controller giving four forward speeds with the final drive consisting of rear wheel pinions acting on internal ring gear. The range changed very little over the years and in common with other vehicles of the period the prices gradually fell until the marque disappeared. *OM*

NIIGATA (J) 1934-1937

Niigata Engineering Co. Ltd.

These were diesel trucks on orthodox lines with 4- and 6-cylinder engines. The 2½-tonner used a 3.9-litre, 40bhp four. *MCS*

NILES (US) 1917-1920

Niles Car & Manufacturing Co., Niles, Ohio

Initially both 1- and 2-tonners were made by this manufacturer, but the smaller model was dropped in 1918. Detailed specifications have not been found. *GMN*

NINON (F) 1928-1935

G. Vincent, Nantes

This was a light 3-wheeled parcel van using the front portion of a motorcycle powered by a 500cc Chaise ohv engine. The 3-speed gearbox was in unit with the engine, and final drive was by chain to the rear axle. *GNG*

NIPPER (GB) 1947-1948

Northern Dairy Engineers Ltd., Hull

The Nipper was a very light 3-wheeler designed for milk delivery, powered by a rear-mounted air cooled J.A.P. engine which drove via a 2-speed gearbox with centrifugal clutch. It was steered by a long tiller which extended over almost the whole length of the vehicle, as the drive stood on a platform at the rear. Two models were offered, of 8 and 10 cwt capacity, with speeds of 16 and 12 mph respectively. *GNG*

NIPPY CARRIER see Auto Mower

1937 NISSAN Type 80 22-seater bus, Nissan

NISSAN (J) 1934 to date

Nissan Motor Co. Ltd., Yokohama.

The Nissan company was formed in 1934 to take over Datsun production from Jidosha Seizo. At the same time they introduced a range of cars and trucks sold under their own name. All followed conventional American lines, the trucks bearing a marked resemblance to Federals. The same 3.7-litre 6-cylinder sv engine was used both in this and in the Graham-based private cars, other features of early types being 4-speed gearboxes and hydraulic brakes. The first 30-cwt 80 models used a semi-forward control layout, but these were followed by the normal control 180 series, continued until the early 1950s. Output rose from 69 bhp in 1936 to 85 bhp in 1952, latter models being 4-tonners also available in long-chassis form for bus or coach duties.

From 1951 Nissan's commercial vehicle activities closely parallelled those of Toyota. In 1951 they introduced a light Jeep-type 4 x 4, the Patrol, with the standard 6-cylinder engine, though unlike Toyota they used a 4-speed main gearbox. Nearly 6,000 trucks and buses were turned out in 1953, a new variation being a truck with 5.3-litre 4-cylinder diesel engine. In 1955 the company entered into an association with Minsei Diesel Industries; though both firms retained their independence, the standard truck, now a 6-tonner, was offered with the option of a 3-cylinder 2-stroke Minsei oil engine developing 100 bhp. At the same time the regular gasoline unit was enlarged to 4 litres' capacity, with pushrod-operated ohv; 1959 models had 5-speed gearboxes and hydrovac brakes as well.

Meanwhile in 1956 the company had introduced a light 35-cwt truck, the Junior, powered by the Austin-designed 1½-litre ohv engine also fitted to their license produced version of the British maker's A50 sedan. This one featured semi-elliptic front springing and hypoid final drive, and was available by 1959 as a forward control 2-tonner as well. Further extensions of the 6-cylinder range included a 30-cwt military-type 4 x 4 and a compact fire engine evolved by mounting the big 4-litre unit in a normal control Junior chassis. A rear-engined bus, the NUR690 with 3-cylinder Minsei diesel and 5-speed gearbox, was introduced in 1960 and offered for several years; normal control Juniors acquired ifs and the forward control version was developed into the popular Caball.

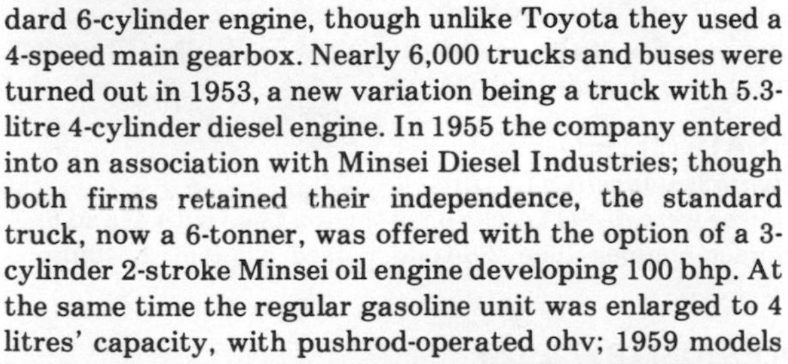

1974 NISSAN ULG780 5-ton truck, Nissan

1974 NISSAN C80 3½-ton truck, Nissan

New for 1966 was a 3½-ton semi forward control truck, the 80, with hydrovac brakes, a 4-speed all-synchromesh gearbox, and a 120 bhp 3-litre gasoline engine. With the purchase that year of the Prince interests, that concern's Homer and Clipper lightweights were integrated into the Nissan range, leading to immense complication in the 2½/3¾-ton GVW category. In 1975 five different types were listed. All save the Junior had forward control, and the lighter ones (the new E20, the Junior and the Homer) featured torsion-bar ifs. The bigger Clipper and Caball had semi-elliptics all round and vacuum servo brakes, the E20 and Caball were offered as minibuses, and all used 4-cylinder ohv gasoline engines, a 2.2-litre diesel option being limited to the Junior. The remaining Nissan commercial models were the Patrol (now with 3-speed main transmission), the 3½-tonner, and the traditional medium-heavy 780, still with the old 4-litre gasoline engine as standard, but with a new diesel option in the shape of a 6.8-litre 4-stroke six.

1978 NISSAN E20 1-ton panel van, Nissan

By 1978 the range had been somewhat simplified, with the disappearance of the Clipper and the big conventionals, though the 2.2-litre diesel four was now available in Homers and Caballs. *MCS*

NOBLE (US) 1917-1931

Noble Motor Truck Co., Kendallville, Ind.

The Noble was a conventional assembled truck made in various models from 1- to 5-tons capacity. All used Buda engines, 6-cylinder units from 1929 onwards. *GNG*

NOHAB (S) 1930-c.1935

Nydquist & Holm A.B., Trolhattan

Nohab, well-known manufacturers of anvils and diesel engines, started in 1928 in the automotive field with the license-production of the Italian Pavesi artillery tractor, for the Swedish Army, after having already produced agricultural tractors.

Two years later the product of bus chassis was taken up, offering 30- and 42-passenger chassis of driver-beside-engine lay-out, both featuring six-cylinder gasoline engine.

For a short while a four-wheeled over-the-road normal control tractor for drawbar trailers was also in production. Its towing capacity was five tons. *JFJK*

NORDE (GB) 1960-1962

North Derbyshire Engineering Co. Ltd., Darley Dale, Derbyshire.

Following the opening of the MI motorway in 1959, North Derbyshire Engineering produced a special articulated tractor to take full advantage of its lack of speed restrictions. It had a 262 bhp Cummins turbocharged diesel, 8 speed semi-automatic gearbox, Boalloy cab, and could achieve 70 mph. It was followed in 1962 by a lightweight six-wheeler with Bedford TK cab and Perkins 6.354 engine. Both models had special rubber suspension, and, though no more vehicles were produced this feature was developed by Norde Suspensions Ltd. and is now used on many vehicles, particularly tankers. *OM*

NORMAG (D) 1938-1952

Normag Zorge GmbH., Hattingen; Zorge

Normag agricultural tractors were supplemented in 1938 by a road tractor. This was of chassis-less construction and a 22 bhp diesel engine was installed. In 1948 a new model was developed but Normag again concentrated on agricultural tractors. *HON*

NORTHCOTE (GB) 1907-1908

Northcote Mfg. Co., Battersea, London S.W.

This was a motorcycle-based trivan powered by V-twin J.A.P. engines of 6 or 9 hp. It had a 3-speed gearbox and chain drive to the single rear wheel. The frame was a modified Chater-Lea. The load capacity of the 19 cu. ft. box was 3 cwt. *GNG*

NORTHERN (US) 1906-1908

Northern Motor Car Co., Detroit, Mich.

The Model C was a 1200-pound capacity delivery van which used a two-cylinder, 20 hp engine with a planetary transmission and shaft drive. Its wheelbase was 8 feet, 10 inches and it was priced at $1600. This company was better-known for its passenger cars. *GMN*

NORTHERN GENERAL (GB) 1933-1939; 1951-1953; 1972

Northern General Transport Co. Ltd., Gateshead, Co. Durham

Northern General are a progressive company with a long history of modifying and building buses to suit their own needs.Their first essays in this direction (1932/33) were lengthened Leyland and B.M.M.O. buses, and also in 1933 the first of Northern's side-engined buses was built. With the aim of providing maximum passenger accommodation within the regulation dimensions (30 ft. length for a 3-axle bus), the designer Major G.W. Hayter chose a low-height Hercules 6.3-litre engine placed beneath the floor mid-way between the front and leading rear axle. Seating capacity was 45, a record for a British single decker at this time. The first SE6, as they were called, had the entrance behind the front axle, but subsequent models had the entrance in the modern position, ahead of the axle and directly opposite the driver. Five more SE6s were assembled at Northern General's works in 1934, followed in 1935 by 31 buses and 6 coaches built for Northern General by A.E.C. at Southall. These used A.E.C. engines in place of the Hercules unit. From 1936 to 1939 5 more SE6s and 13 2-axle SE4s were built at Gateshead, the latter with A.E.C. diesel engines and 40-seater English Electric bodies. Coachwork for the SE6s was by Short or Beadle. After World War II all the SE6 buses (but not the coaches) were converted to diesel, and remained in service until 1954.

From 1951 to 1953 Northern built a series of buses and coaches to the new 30 ft. x 8 ft. dimensions powered by front-mounted A.E.C. engines. The buses, of which 4 were made, had 43-seater bodies built by Northern themselves, while the 23 28-seater coaches were bodied by Picktree. Northern then contented themselves with buses from other manufacturers until 1972 when a Leyland Titan and a Routemaster were rebuilt for one-man operation with normal control and entrance opposite the driver. These were known as Tynesider and Wearsider respectively. *GNG*

NORTHFIELD (GB) 1961-c.1965

Northfield Industrial Fabrications Ltd., Ossett, Yorks.

The Northfield was a 4-wheeled articulated dump truck with drive to the front wheels, power steering and a one-man cab. Four models were made, the 124in wheelbase F7 and the 136in wheelbase F9, with choice of Ford or Perkins diesel engines in each wheelbase. Load capacities varied from 11 to 14 tons. *GNG*

NORTHLAND see Wilcox

1922 NORTHWAY 3½-ton truck, Everitt Northway

1923 NORTHWAY 2-ton truck, Everitt Northway

NORTHWAY (US) 1918-1923

Northway Motors Corp., Natick, Mass.

Northway trucks came in 2 and 3½-tonner sizes, and were powered by 4-cylinder ohv engines of the company's own manufacture. An unusual feature for the time was a fully-enclosed and heated cab. Ralph Northway left the company in 1922 to join the Maxim fire engine company, and production of Northway trucks ceased shortly afterwards. A few passenger cars were made in 1921, and in 1925 a light assembled truck was made and sold under the name Rocket. *GNG*

NORTHWESTERN (US) 1913-c.1923

Star Carriage Co., Seattle, Wash.

Advertised as "Built in Seattle for Seattle's Hills", Northwestern trucks were conventional assembled vehicles using Continental engines and Sheldon axles. For the first four years or so only one model was made, a 3000lb truck selling at $2150, but in 1919 larger trucks of 1½ to 2 tons capacity were listed, with a final 2½-tonner coming in 1923. *GNG*

NORWALK (US) 1918-1919

Norwalk Motor Car Company, Martinsburg, West Virginia

The two commercial models by this manufacturer of passenger autos were a one-tonner and a 1½-tonner. Both were powered by Lycoming Model K four-cylinder engines, as were the passenger cars. These were connected to three-speed gearboxes and final drive was the worm-type. No electric lighting was provided. Wheelbase of both models was 10 feet, 10 inches. *GMN*

NOTT (US) 1911-c.1914

Nott Fire Engine Co., Minneapolis, Minn.

An important builder of steam fire engines, Nott made 4- and 6-cylinder gasoline pumpers as well as motorised attachments for steam pumpers. In 1912 they launched a very modern-looking worm-drive fire engine with Mercedes-like V-radiator, known as the Nott Universal. This was made at least until 1914. *GNG*

1924 NSU 3-ton truck, HON

N.S.U. (D) 1904-1931

(1) Neckarsulmer Fahrradwerke A.G., Neckarsulm 1904-1910

(2) Neckarsulmer Fahrzeugwerke A.G., Neckarsulm; Heilbronn 1910-1931

As a producer of motorcycles N.S.U. produced a tri-van on motorcycle lines with two front wheels but featuring a steering wheel. In 1906 a van version with 2-cylinder 10 PS engine was presented and during the following years various private chassis' were used for van bodies. In 1913 the production of trucks was taken up and this lasted until about 1925. After this N.S.U. again only produced vans based on private car chassis, especially the 8/24 PS and 5/25 PS types. Also some interesting versions of combination cars were available. In 1931 N.S.U. gave up production of cars and when they resumed production in 1958 no commercials were listed.*HON*

NW (Nesselsdorfer) (A;CS) 1898-1919

Nesselsdorfer Wagenbau-Fabriks-Gesellschaft, Nesselsdorf (now Koprivnice)

The President car of 1897 was the first motor vehicle to be made in Central Europe, and a year later its builders brought out a goods version with rear-mounted 4-cylinder Benz engine (actually two twins coupled together), 3-speed transmission and 2½ ton load capacity. In 1900 it was re-

1900 NW rear-engined truck, Tatra

1915 NW Type TL2 truck, Tatra

built with a 2-cylinder engine and steering column in place of the tiller. A de Dion Bouton steam bus was built under license in 1900, but then commercial vehicle production lapsed until 1906 when a bus with 25/30hp 4-cylinder engine was made. followed by two fire engines in 1911. Series production began in 1915 with 2-ton trucks featuring 35hp ohc engines and shaft drive, made until 1923. Tires were solid rubber or metal. In 1916 came the TL 4 4-tonner with the same engine which was made until 1926, though after 1919 all products went under the name Tatra. The TL 4 was made with drawbar trailer, including a side tipping trailer, and as a 22 passenger bus. When the new state of Czechoslovakia was formed in October 1918 the town of Nesselsdorf changed its name to Koprivnice, and the vehicles were re-named Tatra after the Tatra mountains nearby. *MSH*

N.W.F. (D) 1952-1955

Nordwestdeutsche Fahrzeugbau GmbH., Wilhelmshaven

This firm built forward control buses using a chassis-less construction. Ford gas and diesel engines were mounted in the rear. Also road-rail buses were built by this manufacturer. *HON*

NYBERG (US) 1912-1914

Nyberg Automobile Works, Anderson, Indiana

The Model 1½ was, of course, a 1½-tonner with a stake body. This used a four-cylinder engine with three-speed gearbox and double chain drive from a jackshaft. Engines were under frontal hoods and the wheelbase of this single model was 10 feet, 4 inches. Nyberg was better-known as a passenger car. *GMN*

NYE (US) 1920-1921

Hood Manufacturing Co., Seattle, Wash.

Listed under this tradename were 5- and 7-tonners which were tractors for the logging industry. *GMN*

1967 NYSA F501 panel van, AAR

NYSA (PL) 1958 to date

(1) Zaklady Budowy Nadwozi Samochodowych Nysa, Nysa 1958-1969

(2) Fabryka Samochodow Dostawczych, Nysa 1969 to date

Building special vehicle bodies up to 1958, the Nysa factory introduced the same year a range of light commercials in van, minibus and ambulance versions. As usual with many Eastern Block countries, Nysa vehicles shared engines and running gear with other Polish vehicles. A gas engine of 2.1 litrecapacity with 57 HP, that originated in the Soviet Gaz factory and later powered the Warszawa cars, was used in Nysa vehicles, together with Warszawa gearbox and rear axle. A batch of 200 units were exported one year later, while a special deluxe minibus version was added to the range in 1962. Built at Nysa and converted by the SAN bus factory it featured reclining seats, new grille and other refinements. The range was built practically unchanged until 1969, when the 52I series was announced to herald Nysa's second decade of life. Much modernized in appearance and including now a dual purpose Kombi van the range was powered by the old faithful engine brought up to 70 HP. This same year the name of the factory was changed to "delivery van factory" as a dedication to its current production. *GA*

O.A.F. (AUSTRO-FIAT) (A) 1911 to date

(1) Austro-Fiat AG, Vienna, 1911-1925
(2) Oesterreichische Automobilfabrik AG, Vienna, 1925 to date
(3) Oesterreichische Automobilfabrik O.A.F. & Graf & Stift, Vienna

This company was formed in 1907 to assemble and distribute Fiat products in the Austro-Hungarian Empire. There were branches in Budapest, Prague and Trieste, but actual production did not get under way until 1911, and even then the cars and smaller trucks were of Fiat design, the latter including the ubiquitous straight-frame 1-ton Tipo 2. The larger chain-drive Austro-Fiats built to Army Subsidy specifications were, however, not Fiats, though behind the more rounded radiator shells lived such Fiat features as big long-stroke sv 4-cylinder engines, 4-speed gearboxes, and solid tires. The trucks came in 2-, 3- and 4-ton sizes, the big ones running to over 6 litres with a rated output of 40-45 hp. The 4-tonner was still available as late as 1925.

The company's first post-war cars were of independent design, though it continued to distribute the Italian product until Fiat made other arrangements in 1925, and the ensuing divorce led to an association with Austro-Daimler and a change of name. After 1928 car manufacture was gradually phased out, while the main commercial-vehicle product was a modern pneumatic-tired 1½-tonner with the car's 2.8-litre 36 bhp 4-cylinder sv engine, 4-speed unit gearbox, and spiral bevel back axle. Up to World War II the smaller Austro-Fiats (the name was retained on the vehicles) continued to use gasoline engines, later 1½-tonners closely resembling 618 Fiats in appearance (even down to 1936's modern American-style cab), though they used bigger 5-bearing 2.2-litre power units. Brakes, like the Fiat's, were hydraulic. Bigger Austro-Fiats in the 2½-to-4-ton class could be had either with O.A.F.'s own 3.8-litre 4-cylinder gasoline engine or a German M.A.N. diesel, a 4.5-litre four in the smaller SRM, and an 80 bhp 6.8-litre in the big ones, which also had five

c.1938 OAF 1½-ton postal van, OMM

forward speeds. The Anschluss of 1938 led to closer affiliations with M.A.N., and during the war O.A.F. built that company's 4-ton conventional 4 × 4 truck to Wehrmacht account.

In 1945 the factory was taken over by the Russians, and there was no production for several years. Electric vans in several sizes were made for the Austrian Post Office during the 1950s, and in 1963 a new range of conventional and forward-control heavy trucks was launched under the name Tornado. Designed by Herr Kumpf, these were in the 16-ton GVW class, and were powered by a choice of Leyland, Cummins, M.A.N. or O.A.F.'s own 9½-litre diesel engine. ZF 12-speed gearboxes were offered, and the cabs of the forward-control trucks were shared with Graf & Stift. In 1966 came the Hurricane, a semi-forward-control 13-ton GVW truck with 130 hp O.A.F. engine, and

c.1960 OAF 980 12-ton truck, OMM

1966 OAF Hurricane L7-130 7½-ton truck, OMM

a military version of this had 4-wheel drive and a 90 hp M.A.N. spark ignition multi-fuel engine. During the early 1970s O.A.F.s came more closely to resemble M.A.N. trucks, sharing the same cab for the forward-control models, although the old conventional hood and cab was still used up to 1975. A 6 × 6 military truck of M.A.N. appearance was built for the Austrian Army in 1974. From 1976 onwards O.A.F.s were externally identical to M.A.N.s, though they used the older D21 engine range, and they were also selling the smaller Saviems on the Austrian market. A more individual model of 1978, though using a lowered M.A.N. cab, was an 8 × 4 crane carrier chassis. *MCS/OM*

1922 OB 3½-ton electric truck, FLP

O.B. (US) c.1921-1931

(1) O.B. Electric Vehicles Inc., Long Island City, N.Y.
(2) O.B. Electric Truck Inc., New York City, N.Y.

The O.B. electric truck was made in 1-, 2-, 3½- and 5-ton sizes, with a variety of body styles and double chain final drive. From 1925 a 10 tonner was listed as well. *GNG*

OCMA-DEVIL (I) 1953-1957

Devil Moto, Milan

This firm's shaft-driven delivery 3-wheeler differed from others in the use of a relatively powerful 245cc single-cylinder 2-stroke engine, together with a dry-plate clutch in place of the familiar wet-plate type. The gearbox had three forward speeds. *MCS*

O'CONNELL see Super Truck

1938 OD 1-ton van. HON

O.D. (D) 1932-1956

(1) OD-Werke Willy Ostner, Dresden 1932-1939
(2) Ostner-Fahrzeugwerke, Sulzbach-Rosenberg 1949-1956

O.D. produced a tri-van with one driven front wheel and 200 cc D.K.W. engine. In 1933 this version was also offered as an articulated tractor with a small two-wheeled trailer. In 1935 a 4-wheel van with 600 cc. engine was presented. In 1937 a change was made to a 1.1-litre Ford engine.

In 1949 production restarted in a new factory under the name Ostner offering the "Rex 4" a 1¼ ton van or pick-up, again with a Ford engine. It was supplemented by the "Rex-Diesel" using a 3-cylinder 1.780 cc or 4-cylinder 2.1 litre engine. In 1956 the factory was taken over by Faun. *HON*

1974 OEHLER 4-ton electric van, Oehler

OEHLER (CH) 1928 to date

(1) Eisen- & Stahlwerke Oehler Co. AG., Aarau (1928-1971)
(2) Oehler Aarau AG., Aarau (1971 to date)

In 1928 Oehler delivered the first of their electric commercial vehicles. Early models were mainly internal factory trucks; the shortage of gasoline during the 2nd World War led to a considerable expansion of the manufacturing program. There were electric trucks with payload from 1 to over 5 tons. The majority were in the 1 to 1½ ton payload class. In 1949 Oehler offered three types of delivery vans in this category. Battery weight was 600 to 900 kg and the range amounted to 25 to 40 miles. All models had forward control driver's cabs, central-tube-chassis and independent wheel suspension. In 1952 a total of 337 Oehler vehicles were registered.

Today Oehler offers two basic models with payloads of 2 and 4 tons respectively. Again both are forward controlled and are mainly used for short-distance delivery. Top speed is about 20 mph. The 4 ton truck has twin wheels at the rear. *FH*

OERLIKON see M.F.O.

OETIKER (CH) 1928-1936

E. Oetiker & Co., Motorwagenfabrik, Albisrieden-Zurich

In 1922 when the old-Arbenz truck factory collapsed, Edwin Oetiker together with a financial group took over and continued on a small scale to manufacture commercial vehicles which were still offered under the name of Arbenz. There was a 4-ton model with a 4 cylinder monobloc SV gasoline engine with Ricardo head of 6.4 litres and 60 hp and a 5-ton model with a similar engine of 6.9 liters and 65 hp. In 1928 he launched a new up to date 3-ton truck of his own design which he rightly put on the Swiss market under his own name. He used a 6-cylinder Maybach engine. The sturdy 3- (later 4- and 5-ton) chassis were rather conventional with semi-elliptic springs and twin wheels at the rear. A 3-speed gearbox, with Maybach overdrive, shaft drive and double reduction in the differential-housing and mechanical 4-wheel brakes were fitted. One year later Oetiker pioneered forward control by putting the driver's compartment on a bus on the right-hand side of the engine and on top of the front wheel-arch. Truck and bus chassis were made in small numbers only as the factory never employed more than 100 workers. By 1934 it was eminently clear that heavy commercial vehicles of the future would have to be fitted with diesel engines. The rather limited resources of the small company did however not allow for such costly developments. For a brief period Mercedes-Benz diesel engines (4-cylinder 4.9 liters 55 hp and 6-cylinder 7.4 liters 95 hp) were fitted into the 4 and 5 ton chassis. Oetiker vehicles however competed with his own customers for his patent exhaust operated brake. He therefore decided to drop truck manufacture and concentrated on exploiting his motorbrake patents. Numerous companies took out licenses from him. Edwin Oetiker died in 1952 but the company under the leadership of his wife is still active. *FH*

1929 OETIKER bus, FH

OFELDT (US) 1901

F.W. Ofeldt & Sons, Nyack-on-the-Hudson, N.Y.

The Ofeldt company was well-known as a manufacturer of steam launches, and their vehicle building was very much of a sideline. They built a few steam passenger cars and at least one 2-ton steam truck. This had a water-tube boiler, compound engine and double chain drive. They also made a 4-cylinder engine which was fitted experimentally into a delivery wagon. *GNG*

OGDEN (US) 1919-c.1929

(1) Ogden Motor & Supply Co., Chicago, Ill.
(2) Ogden Truck Co., Chicago, Ill.

Ogden trucks were made in various sizes from 1½- to 5-tons capacity, all using Continental engines. *GNG*

OHIO (US) 1912

Ohio Motor Car Company, Cincinnati, Ohio

Only two light delivery van models were offered in the single year this make was on the market. These were rated at 1000 and 1500 pounds capacity, respectively. The ½-tonner, Model 40-P had a full panel body for $2150 with a four-cylinder engine, three-speed gearbox and shaft drive. The chassis of this model was identical with that used in the 1911 passenger cars of the same name. *GMN*

OHIO (US) 1911-1913

Ohio Electric Car Co., Toledo, Ohio

The lone model of this make was a battery-powered electric with power supplied by 40 Exide cells. Its wheelbase was 6 feet, 8 inches and the price of the closed delivery van was $2000. *GMN*

OHTA (J) 1934-1957

(1) Ohta Jidosha Seizosho Co. Ltd., Tokyo 1934-1935
(2) Kohsoko Kikan Kogyo Co. Ltd., Tokyo 1935-1945
(3) Ohta Jidosha Kogyo Co. Ltd., Tokyo 1946-1957

The Ohta was a conventional small car also marketed in light van or truck form. Features included a 4-cylinder sv engine, a 3-speed gearbox and a cruciform-braced frame. Capacity of pre-War power units was 736cc, enlarged after 1945 to 903cc for an output of 23 bhp. Other improvements included the adoption of hydraulic brakes, and the introduction of a crew cab pickup. By 1954 26 bhp were claimed, and a 1-ton model was catalogued. Ohta manufacture ceased when the company was taken over by Kurogane. *MCS*

O.K. (i) (US) 1913-1916

(1) O.K. Motor Truck Co., Detroit, Mich. 1913-1914
(2) O.K. Light Delivery Car Co., Flint, Mich. 1914
(3) Star-Tribune Motor Sales Co., Detroit, Mich. 1914-1916

The earliest O.K. models had rated capacities of 1200- and 2000-pounds, respectively. The smaller was an open delivery van while the larger had a stake body. Both used four-cylinder, side valve engines. For 1914-1916, only a 1¼-tonner was made. One early reference claims the original manufacturer's name was Star-Tribune Truck Co. *GMN*

O.K. (ii) (US) 1917-1929

(1) Oklahoma Auto Manufacturing Co., Muskogee, Okla. 1917-1921
(2) Nolan Truck Co., Okay, Okla. 1921-1929

The O.K. began as 1½- and 3-tonners with wheelbases of 12 feet 6 inches or more. The larger had a 4-speed gearbox and both had worm-drive rear axles. For 1921, the line was 1½-, 2½-, and 3½-tonners and these were joined by a 1-tonner in 1923. For 1926-1927, a 2½-tonner Oil Field Special was built during the final two years of production, only a 3-tonner was offered. 4-cylinder Buda engines were used exclusively until 1928 when a range of 6-cylinder trucks named Mogul was introduced. *GMN*

O & K (D) 1938 to date

(1) Orenstein-Koppel und Lubecker Maschinenbau Ag., Berlin; Dortmund 1938-1954
(2) O & K Orenstein & Koppel AG., Berlin; Dortmund 1954-to date

O & K presented their first road tractor with their own 30 bhp diesel engine. In 1950 a combination tractor appeared which was also usable as compressor, welding engine and generator. A new road tractor was presented in 1953 which had their own 100 bhp diesel engine.

In 1951 O & K developed the first chassis-less double-deck bus for the Berlin bus company BVG. This had two axles and used the newly developed Bussing underfloor engine and other components by Bussing. This version was built in greater numbers during the following years.

As a new production line O & K took up truck cranes in 1971. They built their own chassis and used Deutz diesel engines. *HON*

OKONOM (D) 1921-1928

(1) Rudolf Ernst, Dresden 1921-1924
(2) Okonom-Grossflachen-Wagen A.G., Pirna 1924-1925
(3) Waggon- und Maschinenbau A.G., Gorlitz 1925-1928

This was an articulated truck of which two versions of tractors were available. At first a 10 ton version with 8.1 litre B.M.W. engine appeared which later was supplemented by a 3 ton version. This had a 2.6 litre Siemens & Halske engine. *HON*

OLD HICKORY (US) 1915-1923

(1) Kentucky Wagon Works, Louisville, Ky. 1914-1915
(2) Kentucky Wagon Manufacturing Co., Louisville, Ky. 1915-1923

The original Old Hickory model was a 1½-tonner with worm-drive. In 1916, only, a ¾-tonner was made with a 4-cylinder engine under a frontal hood with bevel-gear drive and pneumatic tires on a wheelbase of 9 feet, 4 inches. This model was continued to the end of 1919 and at least in 1918 it had a Lycoming engine. In 1919, a 1-tonner also was made with a 4-cylinder Continental engine. This company also built the Urban electric commercial vehicle. *GMN*

OLD RELIABLE (US) 1911-1927

(1) Henry Lee Power Co., Chicago, Ill. 1911-1912
(2) Old Reliable Motor Truck Co., Chicago, Ill. 1912-1927

The initial type was a 3½-tonner with forward control, a 4-cylinder engine with twin sparking plugs, double chain drive and a wheelbase of 10 feet, 6 inches. In 1913 there were available 2-, 4- and 5-tonners, all with forward control and double chain drive, wood spoke wheels and solid rubber tires. By 1915, the listing of models had expanded to eight kinds from 1½- to 7-tonners with worm-drive for the smaller types. There were nine models in 1917 and all but the smallest retained forward control. By 1919, the line of trucks included a 1½-tonner which would be dropped by 1924, but the balance, 2½-, 3½-, 5- and 7½-tonners, were kept to the end. The 7½-tonner still had double chain drive at least as late as 1924. *GMN*

1920 OLDSMOBILE 1-ton truck, General Motors

OLDSMOBILE (US) 1904-1908; 1918-1924; 1936-1939

Olds Motor Works, Lansing, Mich.

Oldsmobile had a delivery van edition of their best-selling Curved Dash Runabout on sale in 1904, this being virtually identical to the cars, with slow-turning 1.6-litre single-cylinder horizontal underfloor engine, 2-speed planetary gear, central chain drive, and buggy-type frame. It also wore pneumatic tires, but had switched to solids a year later, when wheel steering and a dummy hood were adopted. Also available between 1905 and 1907 were some bigger 1½-ton or 18-seater models; these followed the same general lines, but their 2-cylinder engines were vertically mounted, and final drive was by side chains. By 1908 the company had discarded gas buggy themes, though they still offered a van on their 35 hp 4-cylinder shaft-drive chassis.

Thereafter Oldsmobile concentrated on private cars until 1918, when they introduced a successful 1-tonner on orthodox lines, with 3-speed gearbox, cone clutch and full electrics, which was quite popular with smaller operators as a 14/16-seater bus. It used the same ohv 4-cylinder Northway engine as Chevrolet's bigger cars and commercials of the period, but was not offered after 1924. The last Oldsmobile trucks were export-only items, being marketed in the Low Countries, Australia and (briefly) in Britain. Essentially they were identical in appearance and specification to contemporary Chevrolets and GMCs, though the 3½-litre 6-cylinder sv engine (enlarged to 3.8-litres for 1937) was similar to that used in Oldsmobile cars. Forward control models joined the range in 1937, the biggest 5/6-tonners having hydrovac brakes and 2-speed back axles, but the name disappeared from the truck market at the outbreak of World War II. Since then the only commercial Oldsmobiles have been specially lengthened ambulance and hearse chassis, Cotner-Bevington making a speciality of the make in the 1970s. From 1968 to 1970 the American Quality Coach Company listed a 8-door 15-seater airport bus with twin rear axles, using the engine and front-wheel-drive of the Toronado. Called the AQC Jetway 707 Limousine, it had a wheelbase of 18 feet, 3 inches in its longest version. *MCS*

OLIVER (US) 1910-1913

(1) Oliver Motor Car Company, 1910-1912
(2) Oliver Motor Truck Company, Detroit, Michigan, 1913

The Oliver trucks were made only as light delivery vans with capacities of 1500 lbs on 1½ tons. These were high-wheelers with solid rubber tires, driven by opposed 2-cylinder engines. The smaller and shaft-drive, its longer, chain, and the transmission was a planetary type. Price of the "panel top express" was $1400. *GMN*

OLYMPIC (i) (US) 1922-1923

Olympic Motor Truck Co., Tacoma, Wash.

The single model of Olympic was a 2½-tonner powered by a Buda HTU engine. *GNG*

OLYMPIC (ii) (GB) 1950

Commercial Motors (Harrow) Ltd., South Harrow, Middx.

This company made a vehicle specially intended as a fish-and-chip shop or ice cream parlor, powered by a rear-mounted 804cc Coventry-Victor flat-twin engine. The prototype had chain drive, but spur gear drive was employed on the few production models made. The Olympic had forward control and the general appearance of a battery electric vehicle. *GNG*

O.M. (L) 1925 to date

(1) Officine Meccaniche SpA, Brescia, 1925-1928
(2) O.M. Fabbrica Bresciana di Automobili, Brescia 1928-1937
(3) O.M. SpA, Brescia, 1937-1968
(4) Fiat SpA (Sezione O.M.), Brescia, 1968 to date

O.M. took over the Zust concern, developing a line of 4- and 6-cylinder sv touring and sports cars to the design of the Austrian Barratouche. From 1925 both the 1½-litre 469 and the 2-litre 665 were available as light vans, the smaller car being also sold as a taxi. These outlived the cars, being quoted as late as 1935, but in 1928 O.M. had acquired a Saurer license. Saurer trucks were sold with O.M. badges until 1931. Thereafter the factory was reorganized for commercial vehicle production, which continued after O.M. was acquired by Fiat in 1933. Pre-War O.Ms. were hard to distinguish from their Swiss prototypes, even the radiator shape being very similar. Engines, too, were Saurer-type diesels, 1931 models using 5.7-litre fours and 8-litre, 90 bhp sixes; gearboxes were of 4-speed overdrive type with air brakes on the 6-tonners. The range covered payloads from 3 to 7-½-tons, all being of normal control configuration; gasoline engines were used only in military variants. The heaviest Titano series had 11½-litre, 137 bhp power units, gearboxes had five or eight speeds, and brakes were hydraulic or hydrovac on light models, with full air on the largest O.Ms. An interesting departure of 1932 was the Cappa-designed Autocarretta, a light military forward control 4 x 4 inherited from Ansaldo; early ones had the curious combination of all-independent springing, 4-wheel steering, hand starting and solid tires, pneumatics not being adopted till 1936, and power was provided by a 21 bhp aircooled four of 1.6-litres. Developments of this theme were produced by another Fiat subsidiary, S.P.A.

1932 OM Autocaretta 32 4×4 truck, BHV

1935 OM Tipo BUD 6½-ton truck, OM

1939 OM Taurus 3½-ton truck, OM

Forward control arrived in 1946 on the Super Taurus, a 5-tonner with 5.8-litre 4-cylinder engine, eight forward speeds, and air/hydraulic brakes, but from 1950 greater emphasis was laid on lighter machinery such as the 2½-ton Leoncino. Also of forward control type, this used a 58 bhp 4-cylinder diesel, a 5-speed synchromesh gearbox with column change, and hydraulic brakes. A coach version was listed, and Leoncinos were assembled in France by Unic and in Switzerland by Saurer/Berna. Developments of the family included gasoline-engined 4x4s for the army with normal or forward control, and a fwd low loader. Engine capacity went up from 3.8 to 4.2-litres in 1954, by which time there were also the aircooled Lupetto, and the 3½-ton Tigrotto with hydrovac brakes. By 1965 the range covered payloads from 30 cwt to 4½ tons. For heavier loads there were the Tigre and Super Orione; the former's 6.9-litre 4-cylinder engine gave 150 bhp in supercharged form, and the latter was a 14-tonner of 1952 with 11.6-litre V-8 unit. Air brakes and eight forward speeds featured in the specification, and it was available in 6x2 twin-steer layout. In 1960 it was replaced by a new 6-cylinder Titano with ratings of up to 230 bhp (287 bhp by 1967) with turbocharger. An unusual option for an Italian maker was an 8x4 truck.

Bus and coach production centered largely round conventional derivatives of the Leoncino family, but as early as 1948 there was a big PSV with transverse rear 6-cylinder engine and 5-speed synchromesh gearbox, this layout being applied in the late 1950s and early 1960s to Tigre and Titano variants, some with air suspension. Both unitary and separate-chassis types were listed. The Titano POS of 1954 had a horizontal engine, and O.M. supplied engines to such specialist builders as Viberti, not to mention Bianchi (for trucks). Their other products included agricultural tractors (since 1929), forklift trucks, electric and diesel-electric locomotives, and railway rolling stock. They also made van conversions of the 633cc Fiat Multipla of 1956, and by the mid-60s they were turning out 6x6 normal control army trucks of Fiat design. A new 1967 model, the 8½-ton 150, followed classic O.M. lines with air brakes and 5x2-speed gearbox, but used an 8.1-litre 6-cylinder engine made by Unic, Fiat's French subsidiary.

1968 OM Titano articulated tanker, OM

In 1968 O.M. were integrated into Fiat, and though no major alterations were apparent beyond the provision of air brakes on the Tigrotto, rationalization soon took over, in the shape of Fiat diesel engines and new angular cabs in the Fiat idiom. By 1973 only the 4x4 version of the Tigrotto retained the traditional styling: the range was still comprehensive, covering payloads from 30 cwt up to 19/22 tons, but O.M.'s own 4.9-litre engine was confined to mediums, and the heaviest models had the 306 bhp Unic V-8. Bus production was limited to modest full-front types on truck chassis.

1970 OM Leoncino E 2½-ton van, GNG

1974 OM-SAURER 90 5½-ton GVW truck, Saurer

By 1975 rationalization was complete, O.M. now concentrating on the manufacture of models in the 3-to-10-ton GVW category, sold with Fiat or O.M. badges, and made as integral vans as well as trucks. Use of the name was principally limited to Italy, though parallel Fiat and O.M. ranges were still catalogued in Switzerland in 1978, while in addition Saurer offered O.M. variations fitted with their own engine. With the advent of the Iveco consortium, the O.M. factory also produced their light-mediums for the German market, in which guise they wore Magirus-Deutz badges and used that company's aircooled engines. *MCS*

OMER (I) to date

Fabbrica Italiana Motocarri Omer, Reggio Emilia

The Omer is an ultra-light delivery 3-wheeler for 200 kg payloads. The two rear wheels are shaft driven, brakes are hydro-mechanical, and power is provided by a 48 cc single-cylinder 2-stroke engine. *MCS*

OMNIUM (GB) 1911-1914

Omnium Motor Co. Ltd., London. W.

Built for Omnium Motor Co. by the Birmingham-based Premier Motor Co. Ltd., the Omnium was one of many three-wheeled box carrier-type delivery vehicles which achieved popularity during the cyclecar craze. With a 6/7hp watercooled engine amidships under the driver's seat and chain drive to a two speed epicyclic gear on the rear hub the Omnium carried 6cwt and was favored by Gamages, Oliver Typewriters, and the London & North Western Railway. Although tiller steered, some models boasted the refinement of a canopy over the driver. *MJWW*

OMNOBIL (D) 1922

Deutsche Elektromobil-und Motorenwerke A.G., Wasseralfingen

Based on the electric-driven private car of this make, also a single-seater van version was available. *HON*

OMORT (US) 1923-1934

Omort Truck Divn., American Aggregates Corp., Greenville, Ohio

c.1925 OMORT dump truck, American Aggregates Corp

The Omort (One Man Operated Road Truck) was specially designed for road construction work, being made by American Aggregates who were, and are, major suppliers of gravel crushing equipment and construction plants. Early Omorts were based on the Model T Ford, but with chain drive and bottom dump bodies. Later models, from 1929, used Hercules engines and double reduction axles, which had been an option earlier. In the early 1930s, 2, 3, 4 and 5-ton models were listed. *RJ*

1963 OMT MF Series 8×2 truck, OMT

O.M.T. (I) 1963-1967

Officine Meccaniche Tortonesi, Tortona

The O.M.T. was unusual among European heavy trucks in being a twin-steer rigid 8-wheeler, though in other respects it followed conventional lines with forward control, 8-speed transmission, air brakes, and power steering. In addition to 11/13-ton load carriers there was a twin-steer 6x2 tractive unit. Early O.M.Ts had 6-cylinder A.E.C. AV690 diesel engines, later replaced by 11½-litre Fiat sixes. The company now makes only trailers. *MCS*

ONEIDA (US) 1917-1930

(1) Oneida Motor Truck Co., Green Bay, Wis. 1917-1923
(2) Oneida Mfg. Co., Green Bay, Wis. 1924-1928
(3) Oneida Truck Co., Green Bay, Wis. 1928-1930

Oneida is one of several American cars and trucks whose name is derived from American Indians, in this case a tribe which migrated from New York state to Wisconsin.

The first Oneida trucks were made in four sizes from 1 to 3½-tons, all with 4-cylinder Continental engines, 3-speed Cotta transmissions and Timken worm drive. By 1919 a 5-tonner had been added to the range, and new components included Hinkley engines and Wisconsin axles. For a time Oneida produced an agricultural tractor, and also a 2-ton electric truck from 1920 to 1922. This was a cab-over design like most electrics of the time, with batteries suspended from sides of the frame. Financial difficulties caused two reorganizations of Oneida during the 1920s, but production continued on a small scale with trucks in the 1 to 5-ton classes and buses for 25, 30 and 42 passengers. Engines were Continental and Hinkley, and from 1927 onwards, Hercules. *RW*

OPEL (D) 1907-1975

Adam Opel A.G., Russelsheim am Main

In 1899 Opel built a first delivery van which was based on the Lutzmann type private car. Some more vans were built in the following years but in 1907 the first-purpose built Opel truck was introduced. It was available with 2-cylinder 8/14hp or 4-cylinder 14/20hp engine; shaft drive and pneumatic tires were standard equipment. Payload was ¾ ton. Subsequently also buses and fire engines were offered.

1910 brought heavier trucks with ton payload, using a 5.0 litre engine of 45hp. Opel was among the manufacturers of the 3 ton standard subsidy-type truck. This type was also continued after WW I but production dropped and Opel concentrated on vans based on the 4/14 PS private car. They were supplemented in 1926 by an "express truck" with 4-cylinder 10/40 PS engine with 2.6 litre capacity, payload being 1 ton It was also available as a van and with special bodies (e.g. ambulances) and as a small bus. Payload capacity was increased to 1.75 ton in

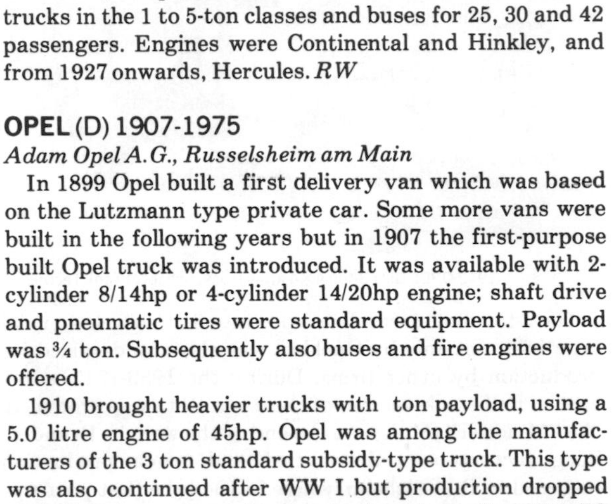

1933 OPEL ½-ton van, GNG

the following years. In 1931 Opel presented their "Blitz" (Lightning) which was to become one of the most famous of German commercial vehicles. It had a 6-cylinder engine of 3.5 litres developing 61bhp and payload capacity was 2.5 tonnes The older 1-½-ton model was continued but also received the name "Blitz". It was replaced in 1934 by a 1-tonner model using a 6-cylinder 2 litre engine of private car origin. From 1933 also van versions of the Opel 1.2 litre private model were available.

The increasing demand led to the construction of a new factory in Brandenburg featuring 100% line production and being the most modern automobile factory in Europe of that time. Truck and van versions were available but the chassis was extensively used for various purposes, e.g. fire engines, ambulances and a great variety of coaches. Most impressive was an articulated double deck bus built by Schumann for the city of Dresden.

1939 OPEL Blitz double deck articulated bus, HON

1942 OPEL Blitz 3-ton 4×4 army truck, School of Tank Technology

The 3-ton model was developed into a 3½-ton 4x4 model later built not only by Opel but was also standardized for production by other firms. During the 1939-1945 war a special half-track version of the 2-ton Blitz was produced, the "Maultier" (Mule). At the end of the war the Brandenburg factory was dismantled and truck production returned to Russelsheim, where in 1946 the first post-war Blitz left the production lines. It was the 1½-ton type with the 6-cylinder 2.5 litre engine from the Kapitan private car. A revised design appeared in 1952 with 1¾-ton payload and another facelift with semi forward control was carried out in 1959. Since 1972 apart from the 2.5 litre engine, also a 4-cylinder 1.9 litre engine and a 2.1 litre French Indenor diesel engine were available.

1971 OPEL Blitz 2-ton van, Opel

Early in 1975 production of the Blitz was given up and since then the GM Bedford models have been distributed by Opel as the Bedford Blitz. Since its first appearance in 1931 the Blitz followed the same basic design which was the reason for its lasting success. A total of about 417,000 were produced. *HON*

OPPERMAN (GB) 1947-1953

S.E. Opperman Ltd., Borehamwood, Herts.

The Opperman Motocart was an unusual vehicle designed for farm work but also usable on the road for short distances. It had an 8hp single-cylinder J.A.P. engine mounted on the front wheel, which it drove. Load capacity was 30cwt and maximum speed 12mph. In 1950 an engine modified to run on TVO (tractor vaporizing oil) was offered as an alternative to the gas engine. From 1949 to 1952 Opperman supplied Motocart chassis to Lacre for their T-type road sweeper. *GNG*

ORAVA see Praga

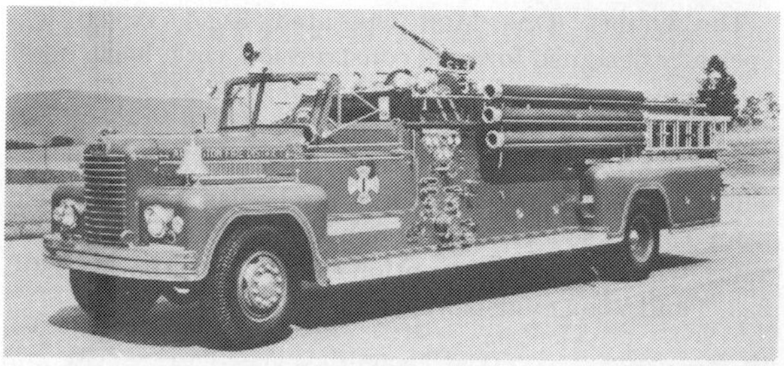

1955 OREN triple combination pumper, OMM

OREN (US) 1949-1974

Oren-Roanoke Corp., Roanoke and Vinton, Va.

Claiming to be 'the South's only fire truck manufacturer', this company built mainly equipment on commercial chassis, but in 1949 they introduced their own custom chassis using 190 and 240bhp engines. Some components were of Corbitt origin. By 1963 they were using a custom chassis made by Duplex with Cincinnati cab. In 1974 Oren-Roanoke was acquired by the Howe Fire Apparatus Co. of Anderson, Indiana. *GNG*

ORION (i) (CH) 1900-1910

(1) Zurcher & Huber, Automobilfabrik Orion, Zurich 1900-1902

(2) Zurcher, Automobilfabrik Orion AG., Zurich 1902-1910

After having built the first taxi to operate in Zurich and a few passenger cars, Orion concentrated on commercial vehicles. Zurcher was a former technical employee of Martini, Frauenfeld. The first truck was completed in 1900 and was successfully used by the army in the maneuvres. It had a horizontal single-cylinder engine placed between the frame members about midway between front and chain driven rear axle. In addition to the single cylinder models a new line with watercooled flat-twin-cylinder engines was launched in 1903. The unusual motor (160 x 180 mm, 7.2 liters) had a single camshaft to operate the inlet and exhaust valves and developed about 20hp. The wooden wheels had solid rubber tires and the final drive was by chains.

Two years later Orion was offering a broad variety of chassis with 7 and 9hp horizontal single cylinder engines

1906 ORION ⅔-ton truck, OMM

as well as three different flat-twin motors of 12/14, 16/18 and 22/24hp. Production in 1905 amounted to 72 commercial vehicles of which some were exported to Great Britain, Germany, Russia, France and South America. In the truck-competition of the Automobile Club of France the Orion entry covered 20,000km without any serious defects.

A new larger factory was founded in Zurich and an annual production of 200 vehicles was planned. The company opened a branch in Marseilles and Orion commercial vehicles were built by S.I.S. Societa Italo-Svizzera in Bologna. The Italian production comprised platform- and tipping trucks, motor-fire-engine and omnibuses, one of which was used for the regular postal service Maranello-Pavullo.

For the heavy chassis a new amidships mounted flat four engine was introduced in 1908. To improve engine cooling a front mounted radiator was used. Steel-spoke wheels fitted with solid tires were used for the heavies. Power was transmitted through 4-speed gearboxes and chains to the rear axle. The unorthodox engines and their placing in the undercarriage offered a shorter overall length and a lower center of gravity but the large companies caught up and offered stiffening competition in the field of commercial vehicles. These two reasons forced the company to stop vehicle production in 1910. At that time 133 of their commercial vehicles were on Swiss roads. Orion continued to manufacture radiators, automobile wheels, heating and later air-conditioning equipment. *FH*

ORION (ii) (D) 1952-1953

Orion-Werk GmbH., Eschwege

This firm presented a chassisless forward-control bus using a self-supporting steel body. Various diesel engines were used and were mounted in the rear. *HON*

ORION (CDN) 1977 to date

Ontario Bus & Truck Industries, Inc.
Missisauga, Ontario

A 30-foot 35-passenger city transit bus with a Detroit Diesel engine and Allison fully automatic transmission, the Orion was introduced to fill the gap that opened when Flxible announced the discontinuance of its similar model in order to change over to its "advanced design" models in 1978. Transportation Manufacturing Corp. will build the same bus under license and call it the "Citycruiser." *MBS*

ORLEANS (US) 1920-1921

New Orleans Motor Truck Manufacturing Co., New Orleans, La.

Apparently this make was offered as both 1½- and 2½-tonners but details on these are not available. *GMN*

ORWELL see Ransomes

OSGOOD-BRADLEY see Pullman

OSHKOSH (US) 1917 to date

(1) Wisconsin Duplex Auto Co., Clintonville, Wis. 1917
(2) Wisconsin Duplex Auto Co., Oshkosh, Wis. 1917-1918
(3) Oshkosh Motor Truck Mfg. Co., Oshkosh, Wis. 1918-1930
(4) Oshkosh Motor Truck, Inc., Oshkosh, Wis. 1930-1967
(5) Oshkosh Truck Corp., Oshkosh, Wis. 1967 to date

The Wisconsin Duplex Auto Company was formed in Clintonville, Wisconsin, on May 1, 1917, to develop and build four-wheel-drive trucks based on letters of patent issued to William Besserdich, the first president (who helped develop the FWD truck some years earlier), and Bernard A. Mosling, who became secretary. Late in 1917 the company moved to Oshkosh, and the first Oshkosh truck was built — actually in a Milwaukee machine shop.. This truck, informally known as "Old Betsy," is still operational and owned by the company.

This truck was of 1-ton capacity and with a stake body weighed 3280 pounds. From the first, pneumatic tires were standard, and the truck incorporated such major engineering featurs as the Dorr-Miller automatic positive locking center differential, and roller bearings on axle steering pivots. Oshkosh's first production truck was the 2-ton model A of 1918 having a 4-cylinder Herschell-Spillman engine of 72 hp with thermo-syphon cooling and a fuel system heating the gasoline at 3 different points before ignition in order to cope with the low-grade fuels of

1920 OSHKOSH Model A fire engine, Oshkosh

that time. A 3½-ton model was added in1920, and a 5-tonner in 1924. Like model A, these conventionals had set-back axles with artillery wheels, and a 5-spoke left-hand steering wheel. An accelerated road building program was launched after World War I and the major portion of Oshkosh production was used for road construction and maintenance including road scraping and snowplowing. In 1925 production started on a 6-cylinder model H with double reduction axles. A 1929 model H. long based in Van Dyne, Wis., and now in Crivitz, Wis., is very likely the oldest active snowplow in the nation. In 1932 three models were developed with gvw's of 24,000 to 44,000 pounds with 4- to 12-speed transmissions and with engines of 100 to 200 hp. These were matched by larger V-plows with side wings and rotary ploughs which were gaining in use, especially in the mountain states. The 10-ton model GD used a 6-cylinder Hercules HXD engine.

The seasonal nature of the road maintenance and snowplowing market caused an imbalance in production, so from 1933 Oshkosh started to diversify, building premium heavy duty trucks designed especially for the needs of certain specialized markets. The first of these was model TR of 1933, a 4-wheel-drive, 4-wheel steer chassis used with a bottom-dump semi-trailer or a scraper body. This made it the first rubber-tired earth-mover. Some of these tractors were mounted with a bulldozer blade, another rubber-tired first. The radiator was finned, the cab was open, and there were no fenders. The TR's were used for dam, canal, and airport construction, and some were used as prime movers in World War II. In 1935 Cummins diesel engines in the company's G-series

1935 OSHKOSH Model FB 2-ton truck, Oshkosh

were offered as an option. Also in 1935 came the J-series of 2-tons, with a V-type grille, and the cab visor removed. The more conservative FB-series had a flat front with vertical center bar and a visored cab, but later acquired the J-series cab. Improved modern styling came in 1940 with new cabs having V-windshields and gently rounded grilles. This was the beginning of the W-series, in production for twenty years. During World War II the US Government took nearly all Oshkosh truck production, notably without any militarized styling changes as found elsewhere in government-ordered trucks. Airport snow removal was the prime use, with wrecker trucks second. These were 7½-ton 4x4's having 6-cylinder 131 hp Hercules RXC engines with 5-speed transmissions and 2-speed auxilliaries. The plows were often Klauer TU-3 rotaries powered by Climax R61 6-cylinder 175 hp engines carried at the rear of the cab. Both engines were gasoline powered. In the late 1940's Oshkosh's first 6-wheel-drive trucks were produced and they were used in oil fields, sugar cane harvesting, and general hauling. They were followed in the 1950's by model W-2800, a 35-ton mining truck, a set-back conventional with planetary axles and a torque-propotioning transfer case differential. Also, in the early 1950's model WT-2206 was designed for use with a roll-over snowplough for high-speed (55 mph) airport runway clearing. These and similar trucks, many with rotaries, are still used by the US Air Force and are re-manufactured at the factory after ten to twenty years of service at two thirds of the cost of a new truck. The Air Force has 160 of these.

1955 OSHKOSH 4×4 concrete mixer, Oshkosh

In 1955 Oshkosh produced the first of the 50-50 series, a 4x4 long-nosed conventional with the front axle set far back under the cab doors. These were for the ready-mix concrete and construction industry, and the load was evenly divided between the front and rear axles. As concrete mixer barrels grew in size, so did the number of axles at the rear, resulting in 8x6, 8x8, and 10x6 drives. Eventually, concrete mixers reached the ultimate with the 12-cubic yard D-series having tandem front steering axles and four rear axles, resulting in a 12x10 drive. The last rear axle is hydraulically retractable for the return trips.

Oshkosh used International's curved-windshield cab on an additional range of conventional trucks from about 1956 to 1966.

In 1960 the first complete styling change came since 1940 with the adoption of an all steel cab with a one-piece forward-slanting windshield, rearward-slanting roof, flattop fenders, and squared-off chromium grille.

Also, in that year, Oshkosh made a 60-ton one-man off-set cab-over tractor used with a semi-trailer dumper for off-highway use. It was series 3000.

In 1962 the company came out with an all new all-wheel-drive utility tractor designed for use with earth-boring machines and other utility equipment. This was a conventional long nosed truck with a set-back front axle and two-man tandem off-set tandem cab. Formally known as U-44-L, it was also called "Big Chief" and "Pogo Stick."

1974 OSHKOSH F Series 6×6 chassis, Oshkosh

1974 OSHKOSH F Series 10×6 concrete mixer, Oshkosh

Of all the Oshkosh trucks made in recent times, the most widely used is the F-series, coming with 6x6, 8x6, and 10x6 drives, usually for construction work, or road maintenance and plowing. This is a set-back conventional with the front axle under the hood.

Conventional 6x4's otherwise generally similar to series F, are designated series R, and are generally used for highway transport, either as straight trucks or with semi-trailers.

1974 OSHKOSH E Series 6×4 tractor with low-loader trailer, Oshkosh

In the 1970's many new models have appeared in the Oshkosh range. Several more cab-overs were introduced. The first of these was the series E of April, 1971, a tilt cab-over 103 inches tall which comes in 4x2 and 6x4 variations for highway transport. These have a full-width grille, and are now made only in the South African plant.

Another is the new series H for snow plowing. It has a forward-slanting windshield, and power is furnished by two Caterpillar diesels; a 225 hp engine for the chassis and a 425 hp engine for the 2-stage spiral ribbon rotary plow which can be operated at 20 mph and has a capacity of 40 tons per minute.

1974 OSHKOSH A Series 6×4 fire engine, Oshkosh

The first of a new range of fire trucks is the 5-man cab-forward series A. This 6x4 chassis is made and then sent out of various fire equipment manufacturers for specialized fittings, and many of them are then marketed under that company's trade name. These include Pierce, Ladder Tower Inc., Snorkel Fire Apparatus and Van Pelt.

A highly specialized cab-forward CFR group (airport crash and fire rescue) is designated the M-series. The 4x4 M-1000 holds 1050 gallons of water and 135 gallons of foam concentrate and has a turret discharge and two low frontal sweep nozzles. The 6x6 M-1500's corresponding capacities are 1500 and 180 gallons with a roof turret and frontal discharge nozzle, and a separate pumping engine. The driving engine is a 510 hp diesel. Although the cab holds a crew of four, it takes only one man to operate it all, if need be. Production began in May, 1973 with the US Air Force ordering 540 of them. In 1977 Oshkosh built the largest fire engine in the world in the shape of the P-15, an 8x8 powered by two Detroit Diesels of 430 hp each.

Latest addition to the fire truck line (for 1975) is the L-series 6x4 cab-forward chassis with the very low profile of only 72 inches to the top of the cab roof. Chassis weight is 17,700 pounds, and it is powered by an 8V-71 diesel of 350 hp through an Allison automatic transmission.

For 1974 the new J-series with the Desert Prince and Desert Knight were introduced for desert use in oil field work. These 6x6 conventionals are based on series F, but fitted with 325 hp diesels, 2000 sq in. radiators, and immense doughnut tires. the J-series replaced the G-series.

In July, 1975 Oshkosh announced a completely new one-man center cab-over concrete mixer, series B, with the mixer barrel reversed for frontal discharge from over the cab roof. The diesel engine is at the rear, powering 6x4, 6x6, or 8x6 drives.

Except for series A and the International cab, flat glass has always been used all around in Oshkosh trucks. The basic styling of many series made in the early 1960's continues substantially the same today, but with some new series having their own individual shapes. In 1973 Oshkosh standardized all of its trucks with diesel engines, mostly Caterpillar, but also some Cummins and Detroit Diesels.

1978 OSHKOSH J Series descent transport truck, Oshkosh

Weights of chassis with cab vary from 10,000 pounds (series E 2-axle tractor) to 24,000 pounds (series R multi-axle tractor). All-diesel horsepowers generally range from 220 to 325 (series J), but over 500 for CFR's and Airport towers. Transmissions include Fuller 3-speed auxilliary, and others up to 13 speeds forward and 2 reverse, and the Powermatic powershifts. Oshkosh also makes a bus chassis, the V Series with 210 hp engine, mainly used for school bus work.

Although a substantial number of Oshkosh trucks are seen on the highways in the region of the factory, and in many state and county highway departments, the market is world-wide. Oshkosh trucks are manufactured in two other locations. In Paarl, near Capetown, South Africa, Oshkosh series R and E transporters are manufactured in a joint venture firm, Oshkosh Africa (Pty) Ltd. In Australia, the same series are assembled from component kits shipped from the main plant. Dealers are located not only all over the United States, but world-wide — Puerto Rico, Indonesia, Australia, New Zealand, Panama, Zambia, Kuwait,Iran and Holland, among others.

American Indian Chief Oshkosh (1795-1858) of the Menominee tribe would certainly be flattered to have his name all over the world on Oshkosh trucks. *RW*

OSSA (E) 1954-1962

Orfeo Sincronic SA, Barcelona

This well-known motorcycle maker also built delivery tricycles powered by 175cc single-cylinder ohv engines. *JCG*

OSTNER see O.D.

O.T.A.V (I) 1905-1908

Officine Turkheimer per Automobili e Velocipedi, Milan

Unlike most contemporary Italian cars, the O.T.A.V was a near-cyclecar with 863cc aircooled single-cylinder aiv engine, belt drive, no differential or reverse gear, and cycle-type wire wheels. A light truck and van formed part of the range, but though it sold well, its sponsors elected in 1908 to merge with the Junior company founded by Giovanni Ceirano the younger. This joint venture folded a year later. *MCS*

OTIS see Westcoaster

OTOSAN (TR) 1973 to date

Otosan Otomobil Sanayii A.S., Kadikoy, Istanbul

As the first Turkish producer of automobiles, Otosan has built since 1966 the Reliant FW5 prototype car powered by imported engines and components. In order to meet a local demand for a light commercial model too, they introduced in 1973 a pick-up version of their basic car. Bodywork is of glassfibre construction of nice appearance, while running gear comes from Ford of England and is the same as that powering Escorts. The 1.2 liter engine develops 63hp. *GA*

OVERLAND see Willys

1930 OVERLAND (ii) Manchester 2-ton truck, OMM

OVERLAND (ii) MANCHESTER (ii) (GB) 1926-1933

Willys Overland Crossley Ltd., Stockport, Cheshire

This offshoot of Crossley was established in 1920 to assemble Willys-Overland vehicles for the British market, but no independent truck design appeared until 1926, when a 25-cwt model was announced. Only the 2½-litre 4-cylinder sv engine, its 3-speed gearbox, and the axles were imported, but typically American were the coil ignition, spiral bevel back axle, and wood wheels with demountable rims, these last giving way to the steel detachable type by 1927. A year later the Manchester name was adopted, and a 35-cwt truck added to the range. The 5-bearing 3.6-litre engine developed 43bhp, and by the end of 1929 it could be had as a 14-seater coach or as a 6-wheeler conversion. New for 1930 was a 2½-tonner with servo fwb; all but the lightest 1931 Manchester had 4--speed gearboxes, and the 1932 range was headed by an all-British short-chassis 2½-tonner with forward control, powered by a proprietary 3.3-litre ohv 4-cylinder engine using magneto ignition. This never went into production, and the firm's steadily declining fortunes led to liquidation late in 1933. The company also assembled various types of car-based light van, as well as 6-cylinder 30-cwt American-model Willys trucks listed in the 1929-31 period. *MCS*

OWOSSO (US) 1910-1914

Owosso Motor Co., Owosso, Mich.

1911 OWOSSO 2-ton truck, NAHC

The initial Owosso commercial vehicle was a 1-tonner. This was a simple vehicle with a 20-22hp, two cylinder engine mounted under the floorboards, with a planetary transmission and double chain final drive. It had solid rubber tires and semi-elliptic springs all around. The wheelbase was 8 feet, 10 inches. While this make is listed as being manufactured into 1914, no information is available on later models. *GMN*

1911 OXFORD (i) ½-ton truck, GB

OXFORD (i) (CDN) 1911-1913

Woodstock Automobile Mfg. Co. Ltd., Woodstock, Ont.

A typical dash-mounted-radiator model of the period, the Oxford truck was built in the same factory as the Every Day highwheeler passenger car. The ½-ton vehicle, with an express body, used a 2-cylinder engine, initially air-cooled but later water-cooled. Production totalled 33 units. *HD*

1949 OXFORD (ii) taxicabs, NMM

OXFORD (ii) (GB) 1947-1953

Wolseley Motors Ltd., Ward End, Birmingham 8

The prototype of the Wolseley Oxford taxicab was built in 1940 and ran in London throughout the war years. The experience thus gained enabled Wolseley to be the first British company to get a post-war taxi into production, this being in February 1947. The Oxford had a 1,802cc 4-cylinder ohv engine as used in pre-war Morris Commercial 15cwt vans, and a 4-speed gearbox. Initially a 4-window body was used, but from 1950 onwards there was a 6-window body, which gave passengers a much better view. This body was also used on the Oxford Hirecar, a private hire version with front door on the nearside. Over 2,000 Oxfords were made, but the Austin-Nuffield merger of 1952 meant that there was no longer room for two taxicabs from the same group, and the Oxford was dropped in favor of the Austin FX3. The London distributors for the Oxford were Beardmore Motors Ltd., and a year after the demise of the Oxford they launched their own Mark VII cab. *GNG*

1942 PACIFIC (i) M26A1 6×6 heavy tractor, BHV

1944 PACIFIC (i) M26 6×6 tractor converted to civilian use in 1950, NMM

PACIFIC (i) (US) 1942-1945

Pacific Car & Foundry Co., Renton, Wash.

As part of the Armed Forces mobility program in World War II, the Pacific Car & Foundry Co., founded in 1905, designed and built a large cab-over 6x6 truck-tractor nominally rated at 12 tons. These were for towing M15 (and later M15A1) semi-trailers in tank transportation and recovery, and were possibly the most powerful production trucks of the war.

Designated as M26, these trucks were powered by a 6-cylinder Hall-Scott gasoline engine of 240 hp driving through a 4-speed transmission and a 3-speed central transfer case to a rear tandem drive and a front shaft drive. Wheels were of the divided-rim type with beadlocks. Tires were 14.00x24 20-ply non-directional military tread with duals on rear of the tractor and spread duals on the tandems of the trailer.

The Pacific was equipped with a cab-controlled front-mounted winch of 35,000 pounds capacity on the first layer, primarily for the recovery of the tractor and semi-trailer in case of becoming stuck in difficult terrain. In the rear of the cab, 2 winches were controlled in tandem or separately from a platform and had a 60,000 pound capacity on the first layer. These were used primarily for loading and unloading the semi-trailer and tank recovery.

The first version, M26, was equipped with a 7-man armored cab having ¾-inch plate in front and ¼-inch plate on the sides, rear, and top. Entrance was at the side, to the rear of the front wheels. On the roof a ring mount was provided for a .50 caliber machine gun. Windows were inclined toward the center of the cab and provided with plate openings.

Later in the war, it became fashionable to supply open cabs for military trucks. Pacific got one, too, holding a 7-man crew as before, and this model was designated M26A1. The style was entirely different and armored below the window sill, with only the windshield and window frame-rails above that level. The roof-mounted machine gun was retained. The M26A1 acquired chains to drive the rear tandem. These trucks were real heavyweights at 22 and 24 tons to pull trailers of 17½ to 22½ tons with capacities of 40 to 45 tons, for a gross combat load of some 80 to 90 tons.

Total Pacific production in WWII was 1272 trucks, many of which are still in civilian service in the United States and Europe as wreckers and very heavy specialized haulers. *RW*

c.1960 PACIFIC (ii) logging tractor, LA

PACIFIC (ii) (CDN) 1947 to date

Pacific Truck & Trailer Ltd., North Vancouver, B.C.

Started by three former executives of the Hayes Manufacturing Company, Pacific also concentrated on logging trucks, although they have since branched out into vehicles for the construction and oil industries, and have made a number of fire engines. Now a wholly-owned subsidiary of International Harvester, Pacific build four basic models including a highway truck, the P-9. Detroit Diesel and Cummins engines are used. *HD*

1918 PACKARD 4-ton truck, Goodyear

PACKARD (US) 1905-1923

Packard Motor Car Co., Detroit, Mich.

The Packard company had been making cars for six years before they turned to the truck field. Their first commercial vehicle was a 30-cwt forward control truck powered by a 15 hp horizontal twin engine under the driver's seat. It had a three-speed gearbox and double chain drive. After three years' production, this model was replaced by a larger truck with a 24 hp vertical 4-cylinder engine under a hood, 3-speed gearbox and chain drive. Load capacity was 3 tons. In 1911 one of these 3 tonners crossed the American Continent from New York to San Francisco in 46 days, being the first truck to make this journey. Although passenger car chassis were fitted with commercial bodywork, including fire engines and police patrol wagons, the 3-tonner was Packard's only truck chassis until 1912 when it was joined by a 2-tonner and a 5-tonner. The first worm-drive trucks appeared in 1914, but chains were continued on the larger models until 1920. By this date there were five truck chassis, from 1½ to 7 tons capacity. Large numbers of Packard trucks were used during World War I; in 1917/18 alone the U.S. Army took 4,856, while other armies to use them included those of Great Britain, France, the Netherlands and Russia. A few 3-ton trucks had Holt Caterpillar tracks in place of the rear wheels.

Two new developments were introduced on the 2-ton Model X chassis of 1920, 4-speed gearboxes and pneumatic tires. This model, together with 3, 5 and 7½-ton chassis were made until production ceased in 1923. Packard never made a bus chassis as such, although charabancs and other passenger bodies were mounted on truck chassis, and the first trolley buses in Toronto (1922) used Packard chassis. *GNG*

PACKERS (US) 1910-1913

(1) Packers Motor Truck Company, Pittsburgh, Pennsylvania 1910-1911
(2) Packers Motor Truck Company, Wheeling, West Virginia 1911-1913

The Packers was offered as three- and four-tonners as well as one- and two-tonners "to order". All used conventional four-cylinder engines, three-speed gearboxes and double chain drive. The largest, the 4-tonner, weighed 6700 pounds in chassis form and had wheelbase of 12 feet, 6 inches. *GMN*

PACKET see Brasie

PACO (US) 1908

Pietsch Auto & Marine Company, Chicago, Illinois

The Paco was a single model of closed delivery van priced at $500. It used a two-cylinder engine of 18-20 hp located under the hood. Steering was by wheel and final drive was by double roller chains. *GMN*

PAGEFIELD (GB) 1907-1955

Walker Brothers (Wigan) Ltd., Pagefield Ironworks, Wigan, Lancs

Walker Brothers were primarily colliery engineers who, in 1907, introduced a 2-ton truck designed by two engineers from Daimler and Beeston Humber. It had a 2-cylinder engine which in 1911 was superseded by their own 4-cylinder 28 bhp unit also used briefly in a 3-ton version. Production was about 15 before the Great War, which included a far more strongly built N model 3-tonner built to War Office Subsidy specification in 1913. This used the Dorman 4J engine and over 500 were supplied for war service. 3½-5-ton versions of the Subsidy model continued in production after the War, but sales had reached a low ebb by 1922 when Pagefield introduced the Pagefield System of refuse collection.

This development followed a chance inquiry from Southport, who, in common with other boroughs, were finding that horse-drawn refuse collectors were ideal for door-to-door work, but wasted time hauling laden carts to the increasingly distant dumping grounds. The Pagefield System overcame this by collecting special 200 cubic foot wheeled containers from the horse teams, loading them onto the back of special Pagefield trucks by winch and replacing the full container with an empty one for house-to-house collection to be uninterrupted. Southport made a cost saving of 20% with the System and in the years up to 1949 185 of these special trucks and a far greater number of containers were supplied throughout the country. As a natural development Pagefield also made more conventional municipal vehicles on maneuverable small wheeled chassis including the Prodigy from 1932.

1928 PAGEFIELD 32-seater bus, MAS

PAGEFIELD 4-ton truck and trailer, OM

The goods models and their passenger derivatives were joined in 1927 by a specifically designed PSV with drop frame, forward control layout and Dorman GJV power unit that could be withdrawn from the front for servicing. Not more than 7 or 8 buses were made. Soon afterwards they received an order from the London, Midland and Scottish Railway to supply 6-ton truck mounted cranes for container handling, for which they built special 6-wheeled, solid tired chassis used by many rail companies in the thirties. A crane chassis was also modified in 1933 to make a mobile tunnel cleaner for the Mersey tunnel and remained in service until 1964.

Walker Brothers entered into an agreement with Atkinson and Company Ltd., in 1925 in an attempt to keep their engineering department busy and Walker provided £3000 capital. However the resulting Atkinson-Walker Wagons Ltd. was wound up in 1930 with little benefit to Walkers.

1932 PAGEFIELD Plantagenet 10-ton van, NMM

1933 PAGEFIELD Pompian 4-ton van, OMM

Meanwhile Walkers became interested in the diesel engine and its promise of extra economy, particularly for the Pagefield System, and in 1930 were the first truck manufacturer to fit a Gardner diesel engine. This Gardner-Pagefield 5/6-tonner revived their flagging goods vehicle sales and in 1931 was joined by a Pegasus 4-tonner and Plantagenet 12-ton 6-wheeler. Other successive models were the Pompian, Pathfinder, Pegasix and Paladin, all Gardner powered, while the Prodigy was offered with the new Perkins diesel, or with Meadows gas engine.

Vehicle production was limited to truck-mounted cranes during the War and afterwards only municipal vehicles were produced. Then in 1947 Walker Brothers were acquired by another engineering firm who produced a small number of Perkins P6 powered 6-ton chassis for export. These and many of the municipal vehicles were now known as Walkers; vehicle production ended in 1955, many of Walkers' municipal body ideas remaining in production with a new company, Walkers and County Cars Ltd. *OM*

PAIGE (US) 1918-1923

Paige-Detroit Motor Car Co., Detroit, Mich.

The first model of the Paige commercial car was a 2-tonner on a wheelbase of 12 feet, 6 inches driven by a 4-cylinder Continental engine. This model used a 3-speed gearbox with shaft drive and a worm-gear rear axle, wood spoke wheels and solid rubber tires. In 1919, this was upgraded and classed as a 2½-tonner and was joined by a 3½-tonner. For 1921, in addition to these larger models, a 1½-tonner also was built and three sizes of Hinkley engine replaced the Continentals. After 1923 only passenger cars were made, but in 1931, by which time Paige had been acquired by the Graham brothers, a small screen-side express pick-up was made on the Graham-Paige 612 Series chassis, and marketed as a Paige. *GMN*

1927 PAK-AGE-KAR multi-stop van, NAHC

PAK-AGE-CAR (US) 1926-1941

(1) Package Car Corp., Chicago, Ill. 1926-1932

(2) Stutz Motor Car Co. of America Inc., Indianapolis, Ind. 1932-1938

(3) Pak-Age-Car Corp., Subsidiary of Auburn Central Co., Connersville, Ind. 1938-1941

(4) Diamond T Motor Car Co., Chicago, Ill. (Sales & Service) 1939-1941

The Pac-Kar, as it was originally called, was an attempt to provide a compact vehicle for metropolitan delivery work which had previously been carried out by horse-drawn trucks. The first vans were box-like in shape, with a wheel at each corner, and had a low floor sill which allowed the driver to walk straight through between the doors. The body was of unitized wood and steel construction, and the power unit was a 7 hp horizontally-opposed twin mounted at the rear. This, together with gearbox, springs and wheels, could be removed and replaced by another unit in about 15 minutes. Suspension consisted of double transverse springs attached above and below the worm-driven differential, the springs serving in place of the axle housing. The same principle was used at the front, with a long center spacer between the springs, thus giving independent suspension all round. The driver drove from a standing position with only a single hand lever control.

Lack of financial backing prevented many of the original Pak-Age-Cars from being made, and in 1932 the project was acquired by Stutz who modernized the design by adopting a larger 4-cylinder engine, a longer wheelbase and smoother appearance. Further improvements in 1936

1939 PAK-AGE-KAR multi-stop vans, HHB

included sliding doors and a V-windshield. However Stutz themselves were in financial difficulties and in 1938 they sold the design to the Auburn Central Co. who had recently discontinued their Auburn, Cord and Duesenberg cars. The Auburn-built Pak-Age-Car used a 4-cylinder Lycoming engine and was made until early 1941, by which time overall production of the make had reached about 3,500. As Auburn lacked the necessary sales and service organization, these were handled by Diamond T from 1939 onwards, and the vans carried the Diamond T trademark. *RW*

PALLADIUM (GB) 1914-1925

(1) Palladium Autocars Ltd., West Kensington, London, W. 1914-1915

(2) Palladium Autocars Ltd., Putney, London, SW 15 1915-1925

Palladium, who had built cars since 1912, broadened their activities to include commercial vehicle manufacture in 1914, commencing with a 3-4 ton shaft-driven model designed on conventional lines and assembled from proprietary units including the subsidy-type Dorman engines. 15-cwt vans were also occasionally produced, based on the Palladium private car chassis, but output of these small commercials was insignificant and ceased with the onset of war which brough a much increased demand for the 3-4 tonner, both for goods and passenger use. In 1920 Palladium announced a revised 4-tonner powered by the Continental engine and featuring a four-speed gearbox. An interesting and much publicized optional extra was the provision of double cantilever rear suspension. This consisted of a pair of eight leaf springs mounted one above the other on either side of the chassis, oscillating at their center on a stiff trunnion pin in a bracket bolted to the frame side member. At the forward end they were shackled together and to the frame, and at the rear end they were anchored to pins secured to the axle. The cantilever rear suspension was intended primarily for passenger vehicles for which Palladium received a number of orders including a few for double-deckers. The same post-war model (designated the YEE 4) continued in production, in two basic chassis lengths, until 1925 when financial troubles caused the company to be wound up. *OM*

PALMER (PALMER-MEYER) (US) 1912-1918

Palmer-Meyer Motor Truck Co., St. Louis, Mo.

This truck is listed under both of the above names. The first truck, Model B, was a ¾-tonner with a stake body. It has a four-cylinder engine under a frontal hood and was priced at $1550. For 1914, both 1- and 1½-tonners were built, also with four-cylinder, side-valve engines, three-speed gearboxes and double chain final drive, and using solid rubber tires. Shaft drive was adopted for 1915. Only 1- and 2-tonners were listed for the final two years of manufacture. *GMN*

PALTEN (A) 1954

Made at Rottenmann, Styria, the Palten was a 1-ton forward-control van generally similar to the Volkswagen in appearance, but powered by a 991cc V-twin 2-stroke air-cooled oil engine. This was designed by Professor List who also designed engines for Turner at this time; it was made by Warchalowski of Vienna. The Palten had a pressed-steel frame, all-aluminum body and independent suspension all round. *GNG*

PAN KAR (GR) 1968 to date

P. Karavisopoulos, Peristeri, Athens

Pan Kar is one of the pioneer builders of light 3-wheeled trucksters in Greece, following the usual pattern; new or reconditioned rear mounted VW engine, glassfiber cab for two, full car type controls and 350 kilos payload. *GA*

PANHARD (i) (F) 1893-1964

(1) Panhard & Levassor, Paris 1893-1898

(2) Societe des Anciens Etablissements Panhard & Levassor, Paris 1899-1964

Panhard were the pioneers of the traditional automobile layout — engine in front, gearbox amidships, and driven rear wheels. As early as 1893 their productions included a light omnibus and a waggonnette, and a price list issued in 1895 shows that they were prepared to supply a truck for 5,500 fr. A 12 hp omnibus with 3.3-litre 4-cylinder engine took part in the 1897 French Heavy Vehicle Trials, and most of the early improvements effected to their cars were

1898 PANHARD (i) 8hp 1-ton van, Panhard

passed on to the commercial vehicles. A wheel-steered 1-ton van with 8 hp 4-cylinder engine was made in 1898, and 10-cwt van of 1899 featured pneumatic tires. A 30-cwt truck took part in the French Army maneuvers of 1900. Early models were of two basic types, both with front vertical 2- or 4-cylinder aiv engines, armoured wood frames, and side-chain drive. Normal control and 3-speed gearboxes featured on lighter models, but heavier Panhards, which included chars-a-banc, heavy diligences for up to 14 passengers (these were operating in Tunisia as early as 1899) and single-decker buses as well as trucks, had four forward speeds and underseat engines. Colonial models were distinguished by their vast tubular radiators of Loyal type, though a car-based 24 hp omnibus was used by Dr. Emil Lehwess in his abortive attempt at a round the world drive in 1902. Understandably, he got no further from London than Nijni Novgorod (Gorki).

A very similar range of vehicles was offered in 1906/07, but in 1905 the company had introduced a pneumatic-tired light van on the 8/11 hp chassis with 1.8-litre 3-cylinder engine. This, like contemporary offerings by de Dion, Delahaye and Peugeot represented an attempt to unload an obsolete non-seller on the truck market. By contrast, a 20 hp bus chassis exhibited at that year's Paris Salon featured not only a 5.4-litre moiv engine, but also shaft drive, something not found on any private car offered for sale before 1908; there was also a 2-ton truck version, and this layout also featured on the company's first cab, a conventional L-head monobloc twin with ht magneto ignition and pressed-steel frame, put into service in Paris in 1908. This had evolved a year later into a 12 hp four, taken up in England by W and G (who fitted a Napier-style radiator) and also used in quantity in St. Petersburg (Leningrad). The regular truck line, however, had settled down by 1910 to a simple range of chain-driven machines with T-head 4-cylinder power units, both conventional and cab-over-engine types being available. These were still listed in 1914.

1912 PANHARD (i) 4 x 4 army truck, NMM

In 1906 tests were conducted with a 24/30 hp car chassis as a machine gun tender, but the first purpose-built military model, the Chatillon-Panhard artillery tractor with four-wheel drive and steering, did not appear until 1911. Early ones used a 6.6-litre 7-bearing 6-cylinder engine rated at 45 bhp, though later a 4-cylinder engine of slightly larger capacity was substituted, and 1914 saw a lighter model with unit 4x2-speed gearbox, which was also the first Panhard commercial vehicle to feature the 4-cylinder Knight double-sleeve-valve engine adopted by the company in 1910.

Post-1918 production centered initially around a pair of normal-control types on modern lines with monobloc 4-cylinder engines, plate clutches, 3-speed gearboxes, bevel drive, all brakes on the rear wheels, full electrics and pneumatic tires. The 30-cwt retained a poppet-valve unit until 1922, but a 3.2-litre Knight engine was fitted to the 3-tonner, Knights only being used thereafter until the late 1930s. Six basic models were offered in 1924, with payloads from 10-cwt to 4 tons. The 3½-tonner had fwb, which were available throughout the range in 1925.

The later sleeve-valve Panhards were brisk performers, the long wheelbase coaches being handsome as well. Engines were shared with the private cars, the 4.8-litre 4-cylinder 20CV unit being standard on heavier types, while the company was nothing if not versatile. From 1925 onwards they made armoured cars, as well as Kegresse-

1927 PANHARD (i) 14-seater bus with producer-gas generator, FLP

type halftracks: the soft-skin editions of these latter combined Citroen front end sheet metal with Panhard-Knight engines. A prototype gazogene truck was shown in 1925, and the 1927 catalogue featured three such models, of 30-cwt, 2½ tons and 4½ tons. A Panhard gazogene successfully underwent a 4,000-mile proving tour of the French Cameroons and the Ivory Coast in 1930. Between 1927 and 1929 there was also a brief flirtation with battery electric 2-tonners, which had short conventional hoods, rear-axle mounted motors of Oerlikon make, coil front suspension, and fwb. Engines were supplied to Chenard-Walcker for installation in their tractors, these including a twin-engined type of 1931. By 1930 the smallest Panhard was a 25-cwt machine, though an 8-tonner was listed; engines included fours of 1.7, 2.2, 2.3, 3.2 and 4.8 litres, as well as a car-type 16CV six available in the 4-ton range. 6-cylinder engines were also fitted to a fleet of 6-wheeler sleeper coaches for operation in Morocco, where Panhards were said to be very popular.

1931 improvements included servo brakes on heavy duty models, and the introduction of the silent 3rd gearbox first seen on the cars in 1929. More important, Panhard had applied the sleeve-valve principle to a pair of new diesels, a 4.4-litre 60 bhp four and a 6.8-litre six rated at 90 bhp. Comparative tests made on gas- and oil-engined 5-tonners showed that fuel consumption had been improved from 9 to 17 mpg. Silent 2nd boxes made their appearance in 1933, when the diesel 6 was enlarged to 8.9-litres, and more powerful gas engines included a 6.3-litre, 105 hp four and a 9.5-litre 6-cylinder, the latter being fitted in a high-speed coach with a wheelbase of close on 20 ft. (6 meters).

1937 PANHARD (i) Zakav 6-ton truck, BHV

Though a 30-cwt truck with 2.6-litre 4-cylinder gas engine was still listed in 1937, the last inter-War years showed an increasing concentration on the 4/8-ton category, with forward control much in evidence by 1939. Gas and gazogene Panhards were now available only with 4-cylinder engines, and the diesel range saw a new option in the shape of a poppet-valve 5.6-litre four of Gardner type, made by Bernard.

Panhard's post-War staple was a 5-ton forward-control truck with 5-speed silent 3rd overdrive gearbox, air-hydraulic brakes, and double reduction back axle. The power plant was readily removable for servicing, and at long last the old Knight engine had gone for good, buyers having the choice of three Panhard-built fours: a 5.2-litre ohv gas version giving 80/90 bhp, and Lanova-type diesels of 5.7 or 6.8 litres capacity. Included in the range were a full-front 40-seater diesel coach chassis, a tractor, a tipper, and a 6x4 conversion with 20 forward speeds and four reverses. The standard truck was uprated to a 7-tonner in 1951, and a year later 4x4 and 6x6 derivatives became available. Panhard mechanical elements were also fitted to some Tubauto and Floirat coaches, surviving in the latter make after its absorption into the new Saviem group in 1957.

1950 PANHARD (i) Dyna ¼-ton van, Panhard

The old Knight-engined sixes had also vanished from the private-car program, to be replaced by an advanced and more realistic design from the drawing board of J.A. Gregoire. This, the 610cc flat-twin Dyna, featured fwd, all-independent springing, light alloy construction, and a 4-speed overdrive gearbox. A 500 kg delivery van edition was available by 1948, and Dyna-Panhard engines were also used in the 3-wheeled commercials of F.A.R. and Sherpa. The later 6-seater Dyna 54 sedan with 850cc engine had a brief vogue in Paris as a taxicab, with 2,000 in service in the 1958/9 period.

Like many French firms in the uneasy 1940s, Panhard sought refuge in consortia, being associated with Willeme and Somua in the Union Francaise Automobile. This, however, achieved little beyond a joint Panhard-Somua bus for Paris in 1949, and in 1954 Panhard entered into an association with Citroen, as a result of which their works were used for the manufacture of 2CV light commercials. Though the classic forward-control 7-tonners lingered on into 1959, they had a badge-engineered companion in their latter days, a medium-duty normal control truck evolved by fitting a 6.8-litre Panhard diesel to a Type 55 Citroen.

1962 PANHARD (i) Dyna 850 ½-ton pick-up, NMM

With the demise of the mediums and heavies, the only remaining commercial model was the 850cc Dyna in 10/13-cwt truck and van forms. By 1964 its engine was giving 50 hp, but a year later France's *marque doyenne* was finally integrated into the Citroen company, and the Dyna range limited to a brace of sports coupes. The vans disappeared along with the sedans, though the Panhard name has been perpetuated on some specialist military vehicles produced by the group. *MCS*

1919 PANHARD (ii) 1½-ton truck, OMM

PANHARD (ii) (US) 1918-1919

Panhard Motors, Grand Haven, Michigan

Models A and B were 1- and 1½-tonners, respectively and were assembled trucks on common chassis of wheelbase of 10 feet, 10 inches. These both used Gray 4-cylinder engines, Fuller gearboxes with Torbensen rear axles and other standard parts. The name Panhard implies some connection with the famous French manufacturer but no such connection is evident. *GMN*

PANTZ (F) 1899-1907

Charles Pantz, Pont-a-Mousson, Meurthe et Moselle

The Pantz 30-cwt truck was powered by an 8 hp horizontal 2-cylinder engine, with fast-and-loose pulley transmission giving three forward speeds. A feature of the design was that the engine and transmission could be slid out of the frame and used in another vehicle of the same make. *GNG*

PARILLA (I) c.1951-1963

Moto G. Parilla, Milan

This producer of motorcycles and scooters also listed a shaft-driven 300 kg *motocarro* in the 1950s. Powered by a 153cc single-cylinder 2-stroke engine, it had four forward speeds and a backbone frame. *MCS*

PARKER (i) (GB) 1898-1899

Parker Bros. Ltd., Wolverhampton

The Parker bus was designed by Thomas Parker to accommodate some 8 to 10 passengers and used his patent system of four wheel steering. A vertical oil-fired boiler supplied steam for use in twin 2-cylinder compound engines. It is doubtful if the bus, as designed and built, was capable of useful commercial service. *RAW*

PARKER (ii) (US) 1918-c.1933

(1) Parker Motor Truck Co., Milwaukee, Wis. 1918-1924
(2) Parker Truck Co. Inc., Milwaukee, Wis. 1924-c.1933

The Parker was an assembled truck made in a variety of sizes from 1 to 5 tons capacity, and using engines by Continental, Wisconsin, and Waukesha. The 1924 1 tonner used a Buda WTU power unit, but this seems to have been the only Buda-powered model. The 5 tonners were discontinued after 1924 when the company registered a change of name and ownership. 1 to 3½ tonners were continued for a few years, but although the make was listed until 1933, little is known the last years of production. *GNG*

1959 PARK ROYAL ROUTEMASTER 72-seater bus, LTE

PARK ROYAL ROUTEMASTER (GB) 1959-1967

Park Royal Vehicles Ltd., London, N.W.10

The "Park Royal Routemaster" was the title used in 1962 when the chassisless Routemaster double-decker designed by, and hitherto built solely for London Transport, was offered for general sale. The Routemaster chassisless design incorporated alumium alloy construction with mechanical units mounted on quickly removable subframes, coil suspension (although air suspension was sometimes fitted to the rear axle), a fresh air heating and ventilation system, and AEC running units powered by engines of AEC and Leyland manufacture.

Four prototypes of 1954-7 were built by London Transport, Park Royal, Weymann and Eastern Coach Works respectively, but large scale production was entrusted entirely to Park Royal, a coachbuilding firm normally associated with the manufacture of conventional bus and trolley bus bodies. Manufacture took place between 1959 and 1967, Routemasters being produced in two lengths (27'6" and 30'0") and with entrance positions alternatively at the front or rear. Total production, excluding the four prototypes, reached 2871 of which only 115 went to purchasers other than London Transport (65 to British European Airways and 50 to Northern General). *OM*

1920 PARKER (ii) 3½-ton truck, FLP

PARR (US) 1909-1910
Parr Wagon Co., Huff Station, Pa.

This was a 3-ton forward-control truck powered by a 4-cylinder 36 hp Waukesha engine, with friction transmission and double chain drive. *GNG*

PARSONS see Napier-Parsons

PARVILLE (F) 1928-c.1930
Edouard Parville, Paris

In addition to an electric passenger car, Parville made two electric commercial vehicles, a 30 cwt van with Renault-style hood, and a 3-ton forward-control truck with pneumatic tires at front and solids at rear. One model was a refuse truck which could be controlled by the driver walking along beside it. All Parvilles employed front-wheel drive. *GNG*

PASHLEY (G.B.) 1950-1962
W.R. Pashley Ltd., Birmingham 6.

Up until 1954, Pashley offered only one model of their tri-van — a single cylinder 197cc Villiers-engined type of 4-cwt (initially 3-cwt) capacity. This was subsequently supplemented by 600cc 10-cwt version which was also, theoretically, available as a four passenger 'motor rickshaw'. A private car version, similar to the Bond Minicar, and introduced in 1953, was unsuccessful. *MJWW*

PASSE PARTOUT see Reyrol

PATHFINDER (US) 1912-1914
Motor Car Manufacturing Co., Indianapolis, Ind.

This name was much better known on passenger automobiles though light vans were also built, albeit on a small scale. The first model was a ¾-tonner with closed panel body. The chassis had a wheelbase of 10 feet, and was similar to the Model XIII passenger cars of 1913. The engine had four cylinders which drove through a three-speed gearbox and drive shaft. Later models were 1-tonners on the same chassis. Price for the 1-tonner closed van was $2000. *GMN*

PATRIOT (US) 1918-1926
(1) Hebb Motors Co., Lincoln, Neb. 1918-1920
(2) Patriot Motors Co., Lincoln, Neb. 1920-1922
(3) Patriot Mfg. Co., Havelock, Neb. 1922-1926

Patriot truck production started on October 1st, 1917 (1918 models) with the 1½-ton Lincoln and 2½-ton Washington models, both with 4-cylinder Buda engines and 4-speed transmissions; final drive was internal gear on the Lincoln and worm on the larger Washington. In mid-1918 a change was made to Continental engines. The makers built their own frames and radiators, and also bodies which they supplied to a number of other truck makers including Douglas from nearby Omaha. For 1921 a new model called the Revere was added; this was a ¾-ton 'speed model' with pneumatic tires and electric lighting and starting, features still only optional on the larger Patriots. The Revere had a Continental engine, but for the larger trucks Patriot turned to Hinkley. Patriots were widely used by farmers for whom several types of bodies were supplied, and were also seen with bus and fire engine bodies.

Poor management led to the sale of the company in 1922 to the Woods brothers who continued production of trucks in 1, 2, and 3-ton sizes with Buda or Hinkley engines, Covert transmissions and Empire or Wisconsin worm drives. In 1926 they changed the name to Woods, and continued production for a further five years. *RW*

PATTON (US) 1899
Patton Motor Vehicle Co., Chicago, Ill.

This vehicle was designed by Patton and built by the Fischer Equipment Company of Chicago. It had a vertical 3-cylinder engine made by the American Petroleum Motor Company, which drove an 8kw Crocker-Wheeler dynamo. This provided electric power for two 7½hp motors, one driving each rear wheel. The 8-ton truck had a maximum speed of 8mph. *GNG*

PAULDING (US) 1913-1916
St. Louis Motor Truck Company, St. Louis, Missouri

Trucks under this name were of varying capacities ranging from 800 pounds to 6000 pounds. The early versions used double chain-drive but for 1916, shaft-drive was adopted and engines were housed under frontal hoods. *GMN*

PAX (F) 1907-1909
Automobiles Pax, Suresnes, Seine

Like the Sorex the Pax chassis was used exclusively for taxicab work, and was made in fairly large numbers, for 200 were in service in Paris in the summer of 1908. It had an 18hp 4-cylinder monobloc engine and 3-speed gearbox. The engine castings were by Piat et Cie who had made a cumbersome steam wagon at the turn of the century. *GNG*

PAYMASTER see Ryder

c. 1966 PAZ-672 46-seater bus, FH

PAZ SU 1950 to date
Pavlov Autobus Works Pavlov

Early PAZ buses were built on GAZ truck chassis but later models show more original and sophisticated designs.

Among the various units produced by the plant is the #652 city and suburban, which is a 23-32 passenger bus of 4.2 tons unladen powered by a 6-cylinder 84 hp engine.

The PAZ 672 is a 46 passenger bus using a 130hp V-8 and four speed transmission. The roof has transparent colored glass and a fresh-air vent system. *BE*

PECARD (F) 1900-1929
L & A Pecard freres, Nevers

Pecard were noted French builders of agricultural engines and steam road rollers and also made a double high pressure 2-speed overtype wagon with long chain drive and rear axle differential, believed to have been the only overtype wagon made on the continent of Europe. Examples were noted in use in North Africa as late as 1942, still on steel tires. *RAW*

1914 PEERLESS (i) 5-ton truck, LIAM

PEERLESS (i) (US) 1911-1918

Peerless Motor Car Company, Cleveland, Ohio

The conservatively designed and rugged trucks by this manufacturer of prestigous motorcars ranged in capacity from three to six tons for the first five model years. These trucks were quite conventional types with four-speed gearboxes and double chain final drive. They all had water-cooled four-cylinder engines of up to 412 ci displacement. Peerless built their own engines. From 1916 on, this line of trucks was joined by a smaller two-tonner with worm drive. Standard color for all these vehicles was termed "Lead". Peerless also built two types of truck tractors with ratings of three and six tons. *GMN*

PEERLESS (ii) (GB) 1925-1933

Peerless Trading Co. Ltd., Slough, Bucks.

In 1925 this company took over from Slough Lorries & Components Ltd. the reconditioning of 4- and 5-ton (i) Peerless trucks from the neighbouring war-surplus dump. As this raw material ran out, the British content increased, though the basic specification did not change: by 1930 options included pneumatic tires, a special reinforced chassis for 8-ton payloads, and even a 4-cylinder Gardner diesel engine. That year also saw the introduction of the 8-ton Trader Six, which retained the traditional chain drive, but wore pneumatics at the front and was powered by an 8-litre 6-cylinder ohv Meadows engine of 115bhp. These first Traders had orthodox normal control, but the 90 series of 1931 wore their power units well over the front axles in the style of contemporary heavy duty Dennises. They were also made with worm drive, while in 1932 there was a trailing-axle 12½-ton 6-wheeler with Dewandre servo brakes on all wheels. Traders could be had with 4- and 6-cylinder Dorman or Meadows gas engines, or with 4- and 6-cylinder diesels by Gardner, though the Meadows was almost invariably specified, being standardised on 1933 models. In 1933 there was a bid for the 4/5-ton market with normal and forward control trucks using Gardner 4LW oil engines, Meadows gearboxes, and Kirkstall worm-drive back axles. The forward-control LD6 resembled a contemporary Albion or Halley in general style, and its Marelli vacuum servo brakes worked on the rear wheels only. A clock was standard, but not an electric starter. These small Peerlesses did not, however, go into production, for late in 1933 the company was split into two concerns. One of these, Peerless Motors, carried on the truck connection by acquiring a Studebaker agency, but no more vehicles were built, even if the firm served as the genesis of a very different machine, the Triumph-engined Peerless GT coupe of 1957. During their currency, British Peerless trucks enjoyed considerable popularity in the local gravel haulage business; they were,however, doomed when vehicles with unladen weights of less than 50 cwt were permitted speeds of 30mph, since this opened the market to the more economical Bedfords and Fordsons. *MCS*

1932 PEERLESS (ii) LAG 6 x 2 12-ton chassis, NMM

1949 PEGASO 8-ton truck, GNG

1950 PEGASO urban bus, GNG

PEGASO (E) 1949 to date

Empresa Nacional de Autocamiones SA, Barcelona and Madrid

The E.N.A.S.A. organisation acquired Hispano-Suiza in 1946, and three years later launched their first product under the name Pegaso. It was a forward-control 8 tonner with a 6-cylinder diesel engine, 8-speed transmission and air brakes. In 1950 it was joined by bus chassis with 125hp diesel or 145hp gas engines, and also the Monocasco integral construction one-and-a half-decker long distance coach. These were followed by more powerful trucks with 140hp for tractor/trailer work up to 16 tons capacity, 6x4 military trucks and trolleybuses. In 1955 a new factory at Barajas, Madrid was completed

1950 PEGASO Monocasco 37-seater integral coach, GNG

where production began of smaller 5- and 6-ton trucks, and the following year E.N.A.S.A. gave up its government contracts for aircraft engines to concentrate entirely on road vehicles. In 1960 Leyland became a major shareholder, and Leyland engines were used in the Pegaso Comet range of medium-sized trucks which were made in larger numbers than any previous Pegaso models. A new fiberglass cab was introduced in 1962, and remained in production until 1972 when it was replaced by a more angular all steel design which is still used today.

1963 PEGASO 2010 18000kgs articulated tanker, GNG

1968 PEGASO 1066A/1 32000kgs GVW tanker, GNG

Many new models were introduced in the 1960s including the 1063 6x2 twin steer chassis for 26,000kgs GVW and the 1066 8x2 chassis for 32,000hgs GVW. Although 8-wheelers have become more common on the Continent in recent years, the Pegaso 1066 was one of the first when it came out in 1965. Rear-engined chassis for bus and coach bodywork were made in several sizes, and Pegaso also built the Italian Monotral-Viberti integral-construction articulated bus. Other special models included a dump truck for 26-ton loads and 4x4 military trucks. In 1970 a new 5-ton 4x4 military truck was produced in conjunction with DAF, being largely of DAF design but made in Madrid. This is still in production today, together with the 3050 6x6 army truck of Pegaso design.

1972 PEGASO 1083 26000kgs GVW truck, GNG

In 1972 the new cab was introduced, and a wide variety of trucks from 6 to 38 tons GVW, in two, three- and four-axle forms, as well as artics are made. Engines range from 90 to 350bhp. In addition Pegaso makes the smaller SAVA derived range from 850kgs to 6 tons, and 30 models of passenger vehicle with 90 to 260hp engines mounted vertically or horizontally. Production capacity at the company's eight factories is about 70 vehicles per day. *JCG*

PEKING BJ-212 K(CHI) 1966 to date

Peking East Is Red Automobile Factory, Peking
(Plant Vehicle Code-BJ)

One of the important producers of light 4x4 vehicles in the People's Republic, this factory is the home of the Peking BJ-212 jeep, a unit now quite familiar throughout China.

Power is by a 4-cylinder, 4-stroke watercooled engine of 75hp @ 3,500 — 4,000rpm (similar to that used in the old Russian Volga M-21 sedan). The clutch is hydraulic with a three speed gearbox and two-gear transfer case. Seating capacity is five including driver, suspension is by semi-elliptic springs and maximum speed is 98 km/h.

The standard unit is 4-door and is fitted with a convertible canvas top. A 2-door version with less seating and a rear storage area is also produced. An odd feature is a war-type blackout light fitted as regular equipment.

The BJ-212 may now be purchased from agents in Hong Kong. *BE*

PEKING BJ-130(CHI) 1968 to date

Peking Erh Li Kou Motor Vehicle Plant (also referred to as the Peking Municipal Motor Vehicle Repair Company Plant No. 2), Peking
(Plant Vehicle Code-BJ)

A 2-ton cab-over-engine truck featuring a 4-cylinder, 75hp engine very similar to that used in the BJ-212 jeep.

The clutch is hydraulic with 4 speeds forward and maximum speed is 85km/h. *BE*

PEKOL (D) 1938-1951

Oldenburger Vorortbahnen GmbH., Oldenburg

This bus company built the first forward control buses with rear-mounted engine in Germany using Mercedes-Benz chassis' and engines. A new version was built in 1947 with Mercedes-Benz or Henschel diesel engines. In 1951 the design was taken over by Graaff. *HON*

1972 PENA 32-ton GCW articulated truck, Pena

PENA (MEX) 1956 to date

Trailers del Norte SA, Monterrey, Nueva Leon

The company was founded by the Pena family in November 1956. The company is still managed by them, and all vehicles carry the family name.

Virtually all Pena trucks are large heavy-duty models powered by Cummins diesel engines. The original models were assembled from imported parts, but current models have a high content of Mexican-made parts.

Trailers del Norte have their own engineering department where future designs are carried out. This department also designs the various semi-trailers that are manufactured by Pena.

Plant capacity is rather limited and fewer than 500 trucks are built each year. *RLH*

PENINSULA (CDN) 1961-1962

Peninsula Truck Divn., Switson Industries Ltd., Welland, Ont.

The Peninsula was an attempt by a Canadian vacuum cleaner manufacturer (Regina and others) to get in the truck business. Only 10 or 11 Peninsula trucks were built, all assembled jobs powered by Cummins, General Motors or Rolls-Royce diesel engines. Heavy-duty cab-over-engine trucks, they were intended for on- and off-road use in GVWs from 36,000lbs upwards. Despite talk of a large Cuban order, production ended after a year or so; the last Peninsula was a 55-60 ton off-road quarry truck similar to a Dart. Named after the Niagara peninsula, the company also held distributorships for Diamond T and Berliet trucks, though none of the latter sold, and the demonstrators were shipped back to France. *RJ*

PENN (US) 1911-1913

Penn Motor Car Co., Pittsburgh, Pa.

In addition to the Penn Thirty roadster, this firm built a 1500-pound delivery truck which had a 22hp 4-cylinder engine and shaft drive. It cost $1,250 in 1912. *DJS*

PENN-UNIT (US) 1910-1912

(1) Penn-Unit Car Co., Allentown, Pa. 1910-1912
(2) Penn-Unit Mfg. Co., Allentown, Pa. 1912

The Penn-Unit 1500-pound truck was powered by a 20hp 2-cylinder water-cooled engine. The engine and clutch formed an easily removed unit, as did the transmission, differential, and jackshaft. The chassis price was $1,800 in 1911. Production after the reorganization in 1912 is doubtful. *DJS*

PENTON (US) 1928

Penton Motor Co. Cleveland, Ohio

The Penton Cantilever was an early example of a 'walk-thru' delivery van with a 4-cylinder engine and front wheel drive. *GNG*

PERFEX (US) 1913-1914

Perfex Co., Los Angeles, Cal.

The Model 19 truck was a ½-tonner on a wheelbase of 9 feet 8 inches. It used a T-head 4-cylinder engine, three-speed gearbox and shaft drive. Pneumatic tires were standard and the price of this model was $875. This company also built the little known Perfex passenger car. *GMN*

PERKINS (GB) 1871-1902

Perkins & Sons, Regent Square, London

Perkins' three wheeled avant-train steam tractor was compound (1¾" and 3¼" x 4½" stroke) and ran at 450 psi on steam from a water tube boiler. The front wheel was driven and was mounted in a circular sub-frame, bearing also the engine and boiler which was enclosed in the main frame, the whole sub-frame rotating in the main frame for steering purposes. The front wheel, at least, was rubber tired. The prototype was used for some while by the Yorkshire Engine Company at Meadow Hall Works, Sheffield but though Perkins canvassed the use of his engine vigorously for many years it is doubtful if it had an extended commercial use. *RAW*

PERLINI (I) 1961 to date

Officine Mecchaniche Costruzioni Roberto Perlini, San Bonifacio, Verona

Perlini's products include trailers, semi-trailers and 3rd axle conversions, as well as dump trucks. Most of these are of off-the-road type, though the T15 of 1975, with Fiat, Scania or Detroit diesel engine, 6-speed gearbox, power steering, and air-hydraulic brakes was roadgoing. Heavier models can cope with payloads of up to 75 tons, the biggest Perlinis using V16 Detroit diesels and Allison automatic transmissions. In 1971 the firm introduced an airfield crash tender powered by twin V8 gas engines (either 8-litre B.P.Ms or 8.7-litre US Fords) mounted horizontally at the rear. Automatic transmission, air conditioning and power steering were features of the model, which could travel on one engine while the other drove the pumps. *MCS*

1975 PERLINI T-15 dump truck, Perlini

PERRY (GB) 1914-1915

Perry Motor Co. Ltd., Tyseley, Birmingham

This well-known light car maker offered a 7-cwt van on its 2-cylinder chassis. This had a vertical-twin engine of 875cc, 3-speed gearbox and shaft drive. Perry also made a 4-cylinder car, but did not make a van version of this. *GNG*

PETER PIRSCH (US) 1926 to date

Peter Pirsch & Sons Co., Kenosha, Wis.

Peter Pirsch was the son of a pioneer Wisconsin wagon builder who patented a compound trussed extension ladder in 1899 and went on to make hand- and horse-drawn ladder trucks. His first motorized ladder truck was on a Rambler chassis, and this was followed by others based on Couple Gear, White, Duplex, Nash and Dodge. In 1926 came the first complete Peter Pirsch fire engines; these were 150 to 750gpm pumpers, chemical and hose trucks powered by 6-cylinder Waukesha engines. In 1928 came a pumper with fully-enclosed cab, the first of its kind from a major US manufacturer, and in 1931 a one man operation hydromechanical aerial ladder hoist used on an 85ft articulated ladder truck. By this time Pirsch were building mostly on their own chassis, although others occasionally used were Sterling (1933), International (1936) and Diamond T (1937). Cabs were bought from General Motors for many years. In 1938 came the first 100ft aluminum alloy closed lattice aerial ladder which became a Peter Pirsch specialty and is still used today.

1936 PETER PIRSCH aerial ladder truck, Peter Pirsch

Throughout the 1930s and 1940s a wide range of fire engines, including articulated ladder trucks were made, with power coming mostly from Hercules or Waukesha engines. All these had their engines under hoods, and the first cab forward model came in 1961 with a flat-fronted cab which is still used today. Conventionals and cab-forwards were made through the 1960s with little change,

1940 PETER PIRSCH Model 38 pumper, Peter Pirsch

1956 PETER PIRSCH Model 64-KZ-6 aerial ladder truck, Peter Pirsch

1977 PETER PIRSCH Senior aerial ladder truck, Peter Pirsch

and Pirsch were also offering their specialties on other chassis such as Ford and Mack CF. Very few conventionals were made after 1970, and current production centers on rigid and articulated cab-forward units, mostly with diesel engines. Pirsch still builds on commercial chassis in addition to their custom fire apparatus. *GNG*

1939 PETERBILT 6 × 4 chassis, RNE

PETERBILT (US) 1939 to date

(1) Peterbilt Motors Co., Oakland, Cal. 1939-1960
(2) Peterbilt Motors Co., Newark, Cal. 1960 to date

T.A. Peterman purchased the Fageol Truck & Coach Co. in 1939 and continued truck manufacture there on similar lines at first, retaining Fageol's cab although abandoning the finned ventilators on the hood top. Fageols had been informally described as 'Bill-Bilt', after W H. Bill the president, so Peterman chose the name Peterbilt for his company. After his death in 1944 a group of employees bought the company which in 1958 passed into the hands of Pacific Car & Foundry who have operated it as a subsidiary ever since.

Early Peterbilts were mostly 6x4 load carriers or tractors particularly catering to the logging industry, although they were also used in sugar-cane hauling, mining, quarrying and oil field work. For highway haulers Peterbilt used extruded aluminium frames and high strength aluminium extensively in cabs, bumpers, wheels and other components to reduce weight by some 1500lbs

1941 PETERBILT fire engine, RNE

1942 PETERBILT chain drive dump truck, RNE

1949 PETERBILT off road truck, RNE

compared with steel construction which still was an option for those who wanted it. Engines were Waukesha gasoline, Hall-Scott gasoline or butane, and Cummins diesels. All early Peterbilts were conventionals, the first prototype cab-over appearing in 1950 and going into production as the Model 350 in 1952. This had a tilt cab and a very short hood, and was made until 1956. In 1955 came a new, flush-fronted cab-over, the Model 351, and this has been made up to the present day with only slight changes. The same cab is used by Kenworth, another Pacific Car & Foundry subsidiary. Some Peterbilts of the mid-1950s had a roof-mounted sleeper to save space for longer semi-trailers.

An interesting Peterbilt development was the "Dromedary", a long wheelbase tractor with a short cargo van between the cab and the fifth wheel which offers increased space and improves the versatility of the tractor when the trailer is parked. Developed in conjunction with Pacific Intermountain Express, the first Dromedary was a 2-axle tractor, later extended to 3 axles and then to a 4-axle tractor with twin steerers. During the 1950s Peterbilt made the largest fleet of 4-axle Dromedaries of any truck maker. The engines were horizontal diesels mounted behind the cab.

In 1960 Peterbilt moved from the old 12-acre Fageol plant to a new 33-acre location in Newark, and in 1969 opened a branch plant at Nashville, Tennessee. At that time Peterbilt's basic models all used Cummins NH220 diesels, Spicer 12-speed transmissions and Timken full-floating hypoid or double-reduction rear axles. GVWs ranged from 34,000 to 84,000lbs, and GCWs from 76,000 to 250,000lbs. In 1962 there was a general change to Rockwell-Standard rear axles and a new line of 6x6 conventionals for off-highway work. Generally about 12 different models were offered in 4x2 and 6x4 layouts, with additional 4x4s and 6x6s in the off-highway category. Engines were normally Cummins but Caterpillar or Detroit Diesels were standardized in some models, and the customer could order whatever engine and other components he desired, including sleeper cabs, and a set-back front axle on conventionals. A wide variety of rear suspensions was becoming available, including air. Spicer transmissions expanded to 16 speeds. In 1968 the conventional highway tractors acquired tilt hoods of fibreglass or aluminium, as well as a wide grille on some, features which continued to the present day.

1970 PETERBILT Model 359 articulated truck, GNG

1975 PETERBILT Model 352 COE tractor, EK

The 1970s saw several changes including the standardization of Fuller 15-speed transmissions, and the introduction in 1971 of a new cab-forward 200 series for city work. This shared a cab with Kenworth's Hustler model, although with a Peterbilt grille. From 1973 Peterbilt used Kenworth cabs on all conventionals with the exception of the Model 383 off-highway truck with angular fenders. Also in 1973 came the Model 346 with set-back front axle intended for the construction industry. The 1978 range consists of 10 models, mostly conventionals except for the 200 series and the 282/352 highway tractors. GVWs run from 34,000 to 62,000lbs, and GCWs from 55,000 to 125,000lbs for on highway models, and from 83,000lbs upwards for off-highway models. Engines are Cummins, Detroit Diesel or Caterpillar, in sizes from 210 to 450hp.

1977 PETERBILT Model 353 6x4 tipper, Peterbilt

In its early days when markets were confined to the Western States, Peterbilt had a modest production of two trucks per day, but with nationwide expansion the annual figure passed 2,000 in 1965, 3,000 in 1968, and climbed rapidly to the current 8,000-9,000. *RW*

PETIT BOURG see Decauville

PETROL PONY (GB) 1935-1936

The Petrol Pony was a 3-wheeled mechanical horse with a central tubular frame and the engine mounted behind the rear wheels. It had a motorcycle kick-change gearbox operated by a lever. On the prototype of 1935 a single-cylinder engine was used, but the 1936 model was Austin Seven-powered. With a semi-trailer it was said to have a load capacity of 20-30 cwt, and in 1936 'a company was being formed to manufacture it'. No more was heard of it, though. *GNG*

PEUGEOT (F) 1894 to date.

(1) Les Fils de Peugeot Freres, Beaulieu-Valentigney 1894-1897
(2) SA des Automobiles Peugeot, Audincourt 1897-1910
(3) SA des Automobiles et Cycles Peugeot, Lille 1908-1909: Audincourt 1928:Sochaux 1913-1928
(4) SA des Automobiles Peugeot, Sochaux 1928 to date

From earliest days Peugeot offered light commercial bodies on their rear-engined chain-drive chassis with handlebar steering, initially with 1.6-litre vee-twin (i) Daimler engines, and later with their own Rigoulot-designed horizontal twins; on these latter the cooling water circulated through the frame tubes. Waggonnettes, omnibuses and brakes were available, a 1-ton truck with 8hp engine making its appearance in 1898. A delivery van with vertical single-cylinder engine and 4-speed gearbox was announced in 1900, but truck production was very modest. Of 1,298 Peugeots delivered up to the end of that year probably less than 25 fell into the commercial category. With the general adoption of front vertical engines in 1902, many of the old rear-engined vehicles were sold off with truck or van bodies, these still being quoted in 1905. In that year, however, the company launched a 30-cwt truck with front mounted 1.8-litre 2-cylinder engine, solid tires, and chain drive: it was tried by the Army, and could be bought in England for £450, but very few were made. For the next few years, in fact, the only commercial types made in appreciable quantities were cabs and 10/15-cwt light vans with 2-cylinder

1902 PEUGEOT 5hp ¼-ton van, GNG

1903 PEUGEOT 12hp 1-ton truck, Autocar

engines, available with shaft drive from 1908. Side chains persisted on heavier models, which included the Type 110 3½-tonner with 3.8-litre 4-cylinder engine, also made as a double-decker bus. Up to 1913 these vehicles were produced at either Audincourt or Lille (a few were also made in Paris), but a full range of seven new models was introduced for the 1913 season, none of these being direct derivatives of private car types. Payloads ran from 10-cwt up to 5 tons; all had 4-cylinder sv engines, and all save the smallest 501 van had side-chain drive, though pneumatic tires were standard on the 1-ton 502. The 5-tonner had a cab over engine configuration. Worm drive made its appearance in 1914 on the 3-ton 1504, used by the army in World War I. A curious digression was a 10-cwt van edition of the 1.9-litre VD-type Lion-Peugeot with V4 engine, but by 1917 the big chain driven Peugeots had given way to worm-drive 3- and 4-tonners, the latter being offered also after the War with 22-seater bus or charabanc bodywork.

Heavy-duty Peugeots were still catalogued as late as 1925, with a short-lived revival in 1927, when a few 4-ton 1545s using the old 4.7-litre 4-cylinder engine were produced; but from 1919 onwards the trend was towards lighter, car-based vans and trucks. Peugeot were, however, among the earlier experimenters with diesels, trying a 53bhp twin of Tartrais type between 1922 and 1926, and following this in 1928 by the acquisition of a manufacturing license for the 2-stroke Junkers unit. This was produced in France by a subsidiary, the Compagnie Lilloise des Moteurs. Among subsequent users of the Lilloise were Latil, Lavigne, Leon Max and Willeme — but not Peugeot.

First of the post-War light vans was the Type 163, a 10-cwt car-based affair with 1.4-litre sv engine and worm drive, followed by the first of a large family of Quadrilette derivatives, the 2/3-cwt Type 171, also announced (though not marketed) as a single-seater taxicab. Last of this generation, the 5-cwt 695cc Type 190, was still available in 1931. Models in the 10-cwt/1-ton category were generally based on 10CV types, though the 30-cwt low-loading 1543 of 1923 used a 3-litre 4-cylinder sv Latil unit, and the 25-cwt 1593 of 1929 incorporated the mechanics of the unsuccessful 12CV six, as well as its spiral bevel back axle. In 1926 Peugeot built some all-independently sprung battery-electric vans under the Krieger name, but the 1930s saw a stabilisation of commercial vehicle types, based initially on the indestructible little 6CV 201 car, with 2-bearing sv 4-cylinder engine, coil ignition, worm drive, and a combination of transverse front springing with quarter elliptics at the rear. This one was rated for payloads of up to 12/14-cwt. and benefited from the refinements incorporated into private car models: ifs in 1932, bloctube frames in 1933, and synchromesh in 1935. For 1-tonners Peugeot drew on the 1½-litre 301 and the 1.7-litre

1938 PEUGEOT MKN van, Peugeot

401, styling paralleling that of touring types. For 1937 the commercials were modernised with aerodynamic front sheet metal; headlamps concealed behind a sloping grille, and a wide range of 20/25-cwt trucks and vans (bigger ones had twin rear wheels) used the 2-litre ohv Type 402 engine. The long-chassis 402 sedan itself was offered as a taxicab (Type 402LT). Wartime conditions brought a further variation in the form of a derated 34hp engine in conjunction with a Gohin-Poulenc wood-gas producer, but Peugeot managed to launch a new 2-ton forward control model in 1941. This DMA featured not only the transverse ifs of its smaller sisters, but also the unlikely option of a Cotal 4-speed electrically-selected gearbox. At the bottom of the range, from 1938 onwards, was the 202U, a car-based light van with 1,133cc ohv engine.

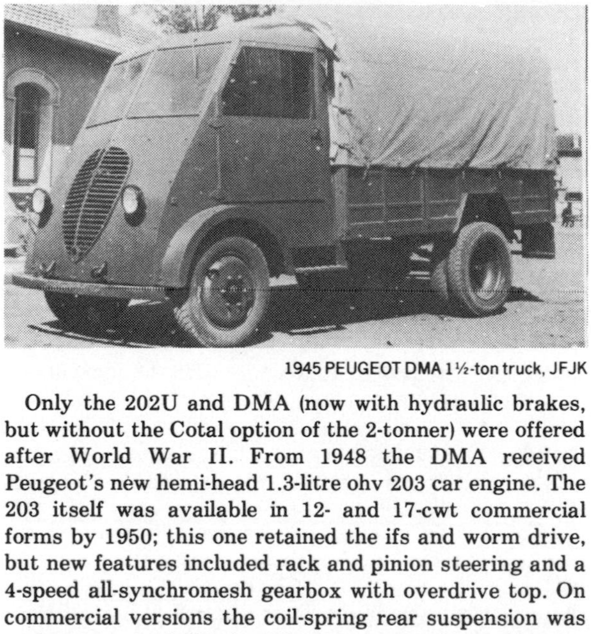

1945 PEUGEOT DMA 1½-ton truck, JFJK

Only the 202U and DMA (now with hydraulic brakes, but without the Cotal option of the 2-tonner) were offered after World War II. From 1948 the DMA received Peugeot's new hemi-head 1.3-litre ohv 203 car engine. The 203 itself was available in 12- and 17-cwt commercial forms by 1950; this one retained the ifs and worm drive, but new features included rack and pinion steering and a 4-speed all-synchromesh gearbox with overdrive top. On commercial versions the coil-spring rear suspension was replaced by semi-elliptics. The 203 remained in production until 1960, some 122,000 of the 685,828 produced being trucks and vans as opposed to the austere station wagons regarded as commercial vehicles by Peugeot. It was supplemented (and later supplanted by *camionnette*, van and ambulance editions of the similar1½-litre 403, introduced in 1956, and available from 1959 with the option of a 1.8-litre 48hp Indenor diesel. The 403 was phased out from 1962 onwards in favour of yet another car-type light truck, the 404U with gas or diesel engine.

The forward control types were also developed. In 1950 Peugeot (who already owned Chenard-Walcker) took over from that company the D3 model, already available with a 203 engine in place of Chenard's own 2-stroke twin. This one carried a payload of 27-cwt, and featured hydraulic brakes, four forward speeds, and all-independent suspension by torsion bars. This van with its side-loading facili-

1974 PEUGEOT 404 ¾-ton pick-up, Peugeot

1975 PEUGEOT J7 1½-ton side-window van, Peugeot

ties had evolved by 1955 into the 403-engined D4; some were built for Peugeot by Chausson in 1958. The D4's replacement announced late in 1965, was the J7, still all independently sprung, but now with fwd. A wide range of gas and diesel options (1.55 to 2.1 litres) enabled the heavier models to cope with payloads of up to 1¾ tons. Peugeot's 1978 commercial vehicles consisted of a delivery van edition of the 1.3-litre fwd 304 sedan (replacing a similar model based on the discontinued 204), the faithful 404U light truck, a vast diversity of J7s (including mobile homes, cattle transporters, minibuses, and a 38-passenger school bus), and ambulances derived from the 504 station wagon. All-synchromesh gearboxes were general practice and all save the 404U had front disc brakes. Every Peugeot model could be supplied with a diesel engine: in addition, their 2-litre diesel was standard equipment in the light, Jeep-type Cournil. *MCS*

PEYKAN (IR) 1968 to date

Iran National Industrial Manufacturing Co., Tehran

Peykan was the first Iranian passenger car built under Hillman license. After a few years of production, a pick-up version powered by the same 1.7 litre, 68 HP, 4 cylinder gas engine was introduced. As usual with car-based commercials, the front end of the car was retained, while the rear was built as a pick-up of unitary construction. Peykans are built by a long established company responsible also for the local production of Mercedes Benz commercials, vehicles which are sold under the name Iran National. *GA*

c. 1970 PFANDER electric milk float, GNG

PFANDER (CH) 1946 to date

Pfander AG., Dubendorf/ZH

Just after the second World War Pfander began to produce electric vehicles for various industrial and commercial purposes. In 30 years the company grew considerably and is now one of the leading manufacturers in this field in Switzerland. The present range comprises electric tractors in five sizes, platform vehicles, tipper trucks, delivery vans and small hotel and airport buses all with battery-powered electro-motors. Typical examples: EKB 900 with 7hp 48 volts motor, twin-rear wheels and hydraulic 4-wheel brakes, payload 1 ton. EKB 1000 delivery van with two 4.5hp 48 volts motors. EKB 2000 platform truck or tipper truck with two 7 or 9hp 80-volt motors, single or twin rearwheels, range 45 miles,payload 2 tons. Some 20 specially designed Pfander electric-vehicles are used at the Swiss airports of Zurich and Geneva to clean modern jet airplanes during their short stop-overs. *FH*

P.F.S. (GB) 1922-1923

Percy Frost-Smith, London, S.W. 1

Percy Frost-Smith was a specialist in gasoline-electric drive who had designed the first Tilling-Stevens bus chassis in 1911. After the war he set up on his own as a builder and operator of gasoline-electric buses. These were powered by 4-cylinder White & Poppe engines driving 24Kw dynamos, final drive being by worm gear to the rear wheels. Only six chassis were made; fitted with 48-passenger bodies by Christopher Dodson they ran for a short while in London, one of the many 'pirate' fleets that competed with the L.G.O.C. at that time. *GNG*

1931 PHANOMEN Type 4 RL postal van, HON

PHANOMEN; PHANOMOBIL (D) 1907-1945

(1) Phanomen Fahrradwerke Gustav Hiller, Zittau 1907-1910

(2) Phanomen-Werke Gustav Hiller, Zittau 1910-1945

The famous threewheeler "Phanomobil" with the engine mounted above the single front wheel which it drove by chain was also available with a van box. The first version had a V-twin air-cooled engine of 880cc which was succeeded by a 4-cylinder engine of 1,536cc in 1912. This version was also used as a taxi-cab. When production of the Phanomobil ceased in 1927 a new concept was released, a chassis with 1.55 litre 4-cylinder compressed-air cooling and 0.75 to 1.5 ton payload. It was available as van or lorry and especially the German Postal Authorities ordered large numbers for their combined mail and passenger overland services. Since 1931 a larger version with 40 hp 2.5 litre engine was offered and this one was supplemented by a 3 litre version with 2 ton payload. This latter version was also used for coach bodies. Apart from the German Mail many municipal authorities ordered this successful type e.g. as ambulances.

1937 PHANOMEN Granit 30 highway maintenance truck, FLP

After the war the production was carried on under the name Robur (q.v.).

PHILADELPHIA (US) 1911-1912

Philadelphia Truck Company, Philadelphia, Pennsylvania

This brand was built only as a 1,500-pound capacity delivery van. The engine in this truck was of four cylinders and this used forward control, with a distinctively-shaped brass-shell radiator out front. The weight of this vehicle was given as 2,065 pounds and had a wheelbase of 8 feet, 6 inches and was priced at $2,200. *GMN*

PHIPPS-GRINNELL (US) 1910-1911

Phipps-Grinnell Auto Co., Detroit, Mich.

This battery-powered electric was available only as an 800-pound delivery van with double chain drive and solid rubber tires. It was disguised as a conventional petrol van with a bonnet which housed the batteries. *GMN*

PHOENIX (US) 1908-1910

Phoenix Auto Workks, Phoenixville, Pa.

The Phoenix was a high-wheeler powered by a 12hp 2-cylinder DeTamble air-cooled engine located under a hood. Friction transmission and chain drive were used. The 1,000-pound delivery truck cost $800 in 1908 and $900 thereafter. Several 8-passenger buses were built in 1908. *DJS*

PHOENIX CENTIPED (US) c.1909-1918

Phoenix Mfg. Co., Eau Claire, Wis.

The first Centiped was a steam tractor on the lines of the Lombard, with locomotive boiler, 100hp 4-cylinder vertical engine which drove Lombard Patent tracks via bevel and spur gear open transmission, and steerable sled-type tracks at the front. It was intended for hauling logs over frozen roads in winter. In 1914 an internal-combustion-engined tractor was announced, also called the Centiped, powered by a 4-cylinder engine developing 50bhp at 700rpm, which was able to run on either petrol or paraffin. It had tracks at the rear which drove, and steel-shod wheels at the front. A sliding gear transmission gave three forward speeds, 1½, 3, and 5½mph. *GNG*

PHONIX (H) 1905-1915

(1) Phonix Automobile Works, Budapest 1905-1910

(2) Machinery, Mill and Automobile Works, Budapest 1911-1915

The Phonix factory was building passenger cars based on the German Cudell Phonix model, but a series of buses was also produced using the same chassis. A 4-cylinder petrol engine with 5 bearing crankshaft and overhead valves was fitted and drive was transmitted to the rear wheels through chains. The Phonix factory was ultimately sold to the MAG concern. *GA*

P.H.P. (US) 1911-1912

P.H.P. Motor Truck Co., Westfield, Mass.

Two truck types, designated Models 25 and 28 were 3/4- and 1-tonners, respectively. These both used 4-cylinder, 30 hp engines, three-speed gearboxes and shaft drive. Wheelbase was 8 feet, 6 inches for the smaller and 9 feet, 7 inches for the larger version. Prices were $1,050 and $1,500, respectively. *GMN*

PIAGGIO see Ape

1900 PIAT 6-ton steam wagon, GNG

PIAT (F) 1899-1900

A. Piat et Fils, Paris

The Piat 5/6 tonner had a vertical water tube boiler mounted at the rear, with double cylinders, Gooch single eccentric valve gear and an al gear drive incorporating the maker's version of the Oldham coupling. Weight in working order was about 8 tons. No specific date can be put on cessation of manufacture but nothing was seen of the design in the new century. The vehicle was 28 feet long with the steersman at the leading end and the driver at the rear. *RAW*

PICCOLO (D) 1904-1910

1. A.Ruppe & Sohn, Apolda 1904-1908

2. A.Ruppe & Sohn A.G., Apolda 1908-1910

The firm of Ruppe & Sohn were pioneers in air-cooled engines. Their first private car had an air-cooled V-twin 704cc engine which was placed unenclosed in the front. Later it was bonneted. Also a V-4 cylinder engine was available. Both versions were also offered as vans. *HON*

1910 PIC-PIC 18/24hp police bus, FH

PIC-PIC (CH) 1906-1924

(1) SAG Ste d'Automobiles Geneve 1906-1910

(2) S.A. Piccard, Pictet & Cie, Geneve 1910-1920

Piccard-Pictet took over the production of passenger cars for which SAG had obtain license manufacturing rights from Marc Birkigt of Hispano-Suiza, Barcelona. In

1910 a light Pic—Pic 18/24hp bus was delivered for the police of Rio de Janeiro. Car chassis were modified and sometimes received twin-wheel rear axles for light lorries, delivery vans and ambulances. Conventional poppet-valve as well as Argyll-type sleeve-valve engines were used. Motor Car production ceased in 1920 mainly due to the lack of exports and the cheap imports not hampered by any protective duties. *FH*

PICKERING (GB) 1905-1906

F.G. Pickering & Co. Ltd., Tweedmouth, Berwick-on-Tweed

The Pickering 2/3-ton lorry was powered by a 20-24hp 4-cylinder Simms engine. It had a 3-speed constant-mesh gearbox giving road speeds of 4, 8 and 12mph, and double chain final drive. *GNG*

PICKWICK (US) 1927-1933

Pickwick Motor Coach Works, Los Angeles and Inglewood, California

Pickwick Stages was an interurban and long distance carrier based in Los Angeles whose origins can be traced to 1912 and which was an important element in a diversified holding company known as the Pickwick Corp. In the early days Pickwick operated Pierce-Arrow passenger car chassis, stretched and extensively reworked and equipped with locally-built open bodies. The rebuilding work and construction of bodies was undertaken at the company's own shops after 1924, when Pierce's model Z bus chassis came into use. Packard, White, Fageol and other makes were used too. Featured introduced as early as the mid 1920's included reclining seats, kitchens and lavatories.

The first attempts to build up complete buses from purchased parts were apparently made in 1927, and the most spectacular example of this operation was the Nite Coach, first shown to the public in the fall of 1928. The Nite Coach was of all-metal chassisless construction, based on longitudinal beams on which the body was mounted and from which the axles were hung. There were two levels and intermediate aisle from which passengers could enter 13 interlocking compartments, each accommodating two people. Each compartment had its own running water, dressing room, storage space, and folding berths, two lavatories and a kitchen being provided elsewhere in the bus (which operated with a crew of three). The purpose of the Nite Coach was to shorten travel times on long western routes by eliminating overnight hotel stops, and the concept was that the buses would be built and owned by Pickwick but leased to local operating companies, as with U.S. Pullman cars on the railroads.

When Pierce-Arrow stopped making the model Z, Pickwick built a factory near Los Angeles and prepared to begin quantity production of Nite Coaches. The depression naturally affected the prognosis for the expensive vehicle, and only four more Nite Coaches were built of the original type. In 1930, designer Dwight Austin introduced a day coach version of the design known as the Duplex, about 40 of which were built and sold by the end of 1931. At that time the holding company entered receivership. A substantial interest in the bus operating business had already been sold to Greyhound, which now acquired the balance, and the factory was sold to Dwight Austin. During 1932 he produced a revised Nite Coach design (18 were built) with a newly patented angle drive mechanism and a transverse rear-mounted Waukesha engine. The earlier Nite Coaches and Duplexes had front mounted Sterling engines. But the economic circumstances were not right for the sale or operation of such large costly buses, and Austin soon turned his efforts to another idea (see Utility Coach). *MBS*

1929 PICKWICK Nite Coach 'Alsacia' sleeper coach, MBS

PICKWICK SLEEPER (US) 1936

Columbia Coach Works (location unknown)

In spite of its name and purpose, this experimental sleeper coach is not known to have had any connection with the earlier Pickwick bus (q.v.). It was shown in the fall of 1936 and was equipped with two Ford V-8 engines mounted in the rear and driving through a complicated system of shafts to a single rear axle. Perhaps its most distinguishing feature was a mechanical air-conditioning system, one of the first ever used in a bus. There was a plan to organize an operating company with a fleet of these buses, but nothing ever came of that, and the sample bus was sold in 1937 to All American Bus Lines, which also operated two sleeper coaches built by Crown. *MBS*

1916 PIERCE-ARROW 4-ton truck, OMM

PIERCE-ARROW (US) 1910-1932

Pierce-Arrow Motor Car Co., Buffalo, N.Y.

The first truck design from Pierce-Arrow, who were already established as one of America's leading makers of high-quality cars, was a forward-control chain-drive 5-tonner which was quickly rejected in favour of a normal-control worm-drive truck. Known as the Model R, this owed a number of features to British Dennis and Hallford designs, as the engineers in charge of Pierce-Arrow's truck division,John Younger and H. Kerr Thomas, had previously been with Dennis and Hallford respectively. In particular the worm drive was a Dennis feature, and rare on heavy trucks as early as 1911. The 5-ton Model R was joined in 1914 by the 2-ton Model X, and both types were widely used during World War I by the armies of the United States, Britain and France. In addition to their own designs, Pierce-Arrow built about 1,000 of the standardized Class B Liberty trucks for the U.S. Army.

During the 1920s the Pierce-Arrow truck range was extended to six models, from 2½ to 7½ tons, all using 4-cylinder engines and 4-speed gearboxes. In 1924 they introduced a purpose-built bus chassis, the Model Z powered by the 6-cylinder T-head engine used in Pierce-Arrow passenger cars. Two wheelbases were offered, 16ft 4in and 18ft 4in. Although intended for passenger work, the Model Z chassis was also fitted with goods bodies. In 1927 a smaller line of trucks was introduced, the Fleet Arrow series which used engines and other components

1928 PIERCE-ARROW Model Z coach, NMM

1931 PIERCE-ARROW 5-ton tipper, NAHC

from the Series 80 passenger car. The following year came the merger with Studebaker, but truck production continued, and in 1929 there were three models in the Fleet Arrow range, and six in the larger truck range. Some of the latter were little changed in appearance from the World War I era, with solid tires and open sided cabs. The 1931 range ran from 2- to 8-tons, with dual ignition on the larger models and dual rear axles on the 8 tonner. The last new model was the 1932 2-tonner which had a dual ignition straight-8 engine and was capable of 55mph. Production at Buffalo ended in November 1932 when the truck side of the business was transferred to White at Cleveland. *GNG*

PIERCY (US) 1915-1916

Hub Motor Truck Company, Columbus, Ohio

This was a gas-electric type of 2½-ton capacity. It had a four-cylinder engine under a hood and power to the rear wheels was from a generator coupled to the engine and finally by individual electric motors in each rear wheel. *GMN*

PIERREVILLE (CDN) 1969 to date

Pierreville Fire Engines Ltd., Pierreville, Que.

Founded by the sons of Pierre Thibault, builder of the Thibault fire engines, after his death, this company builds considerable numbers of fire engines, mostly on existing truck chassis. *HD*

PIGGINS (US) 1912-1913

Piggins Motor Car Co., Racine, Wis.

The Piggins was built as 1-, 2- and 3-tonners. The smallest had a 4-cylinder engine with normal control, a 3-speed gearbox and shaft-drive. While the larger models had forward control. *GMN*

PILGRIM (GB) 1911-1914

Pilgrim's Way Motor Co. Ltd., Farnham,Surrey

Makers of passenger cars since 1906, this company launched a front-wheel-drive light car in 1911, and also made a delivery van version. This was powered by a 10/12hp flat-twin engine mounted near the center of the frame, and driving forward via a 3-speed gearbox to the front axle. An unusual feature for a light van at this date was the use of solid tires. *GNG*

PINOI see Francisco

PIONEER (i) (GB) 1902

Pioneer Power Company Ltd., London

The Pioneer, assembled from American components, had a boiler stated to be "of horizontal fire tube type" with a firebox holding "sufficient fuel to last for many hours without attention". It would seem, however, that this must have referred to a fuel hopper, as the wagon was

1902 PIONEER (i) steam wagon, NMM

intended for one man control.

Each front wheel was driven independently by a 4 cylinder swash plate engine, one engine taking superheated steam from the boiler and the other the exhaust steam from the high pressure side. Steering was Ackermann on the rear axle. Load capacity was 10 tons. It is doubtful if one saw commercial use. *RAW*

PIONEER (ii) (US) 1920-1924

Pioneer Truck Co., Chicago, Ill.

The Pioneer was available only as a 2-tonner in 1920-1921 and used a 4-cylinder Continental engine. In 1921, a 1-tonner also was built but did not reappear again until 1924 with a Golden, *Belnap & Swartz* 4-cylinder engine. *GMN*

1929 PIONEER STAGE parlour coach, MBS

PIONEER STAGE (US) 1923-1930

(1) California Body Building Co., San Francisco, Cal. 1923-1927

(2) California Body Building Co., Oakland, Cal. 1927-1929

(3) Pioneer Motor Coach Mfg. Co., Oakland, Cal. 1929-1930

A taxicab garage and body-building plant was started in 1914 by W.W. Travis, operator of a San Francisco taxi fleet using heavy-duty White chassis. When these proved too costly for the duty, Travis stretched their chassis, built new bodies and sold them as "stages" (buses) to associations of California stage operators. By degrees Travis drifted away from the taxi business and into the bus business, forming California Transit Co. to succeed certain of the auto stage associations in 1921. The first all-metal bus body was completed in 1919, and the first completely assembled bus (earlier ones had been based on White chassis) was put in service during 1923. A six-wheel bus was built during 1923 and 1924, and about 50 were completed, but there were traction problems that led to a change to dual rear wheels. The "Pioneer" or "Pioneer Stage" trade name was adopted in 1924, when sales to other operators began to be significant. "Pioneer Stages" also became the operating name for California Transit Co., which had grown through the years and was by 1925 the largest over-the-road bus system in northern California, comparable to Pickwick Stages in the South.

California Transit was one of the enterprises merged in 1929 to form Pacific Greyhound Lines, and in that transition the manufacturing business became known as Pioneer Motor Coach Manufacturing Co. Only one more batch of buses was started subsequent to the merger,and late in 1929 ownership of the factory was transferred to another Greyhound subsidiary, C.H. Will Motors Co. (see Will). Production of buses at Oakland ended in 1930. Probably about 400 buses were built altogether from 1923 to 1930. *MBS*

PIPE (B) c.1905-1931

Usines Pipe,Brussels

Among the first Belgian automobile manufacturers was Pipe, starting in 1898. Around 1905 the first commercial vehicles were manufactured. In 1907 two models were available: a 16hp chassis for truck or bus use, and a 25hp chassis particularly meant to take bus bodies. The most interesting features of nearly all Pipe vehicles were the rather modern engines, with large, inclined valves in the cylinder heads, operating by pushrods from a camshaft mounted in the carter. After World War I — which took a heavy toll from Pipe: the factory had to be rebuilt completely — production was resumed in 1921, with a range of trucks and some cars. The trucks turned out to be the most lucrative so Pipe concentrated on them. Starting with a two-tonner, soon a wide range of vehicles was built, all four cylinder types with the payload reaching a peak of five tons for the heaviest models. These heavy Pipes were also available with gas-producer engine for colonial use. Additionally a range of tractors up to 20 tons GTW was built, using Minerva sleeve-valve engines. In 1932 Pipe was acquired by Brossel, who joined the marque with Bovy, the manufacturer they had acquired one year earlier, to their 'Light Vehicles Division', trading till about 1935 under the Bovy-Pipe sign. *JFJK*

PIRET (B) 1936

Ets. Piret, Brussels

Piret was one of the many truck assemblers existing in Belgium during the 'thirties. Like their competitors they used mainly American and British parts. The Piret was available with two engine sizes, 4.6 and 5.2 litre, but only very few chassis were built. *JFJK*

PITTSBURG (i) (US) 1908

Pittsburg Machine Tool Co., Allegheny, Pa.

This was a heavy steam truck powered by a 3-cylinder single-acting engine with firetube boiler. It had two speeds and double chain drive. There were two brakes, a hand brake on the rear wheels and a foot-operated air brake on the differential. The Pittsburg came equipped with a winding drum for hoisting loads which was operated from the engine, and had a payload of 8-10 tons. *GNG*

PITTSBURG (ii) (US) 1908-1911

Pittsburg Motor Vehicle Co., Pittsburg, Pa.

This company began by making relatively light electric trucks with 2hp motors, single chain drive and tiller steering. Wheelbases of Types L and 2 were 6ft 3in and 8ft 4in. In 1910 there was a wider range of six models, with capacities of 1,000 to 6,000lbs. The three largest had two motors, the others one. All had double chain drive. The

additional 'h' in the modern spelling of the city occured sometime during the first twenty years of this century. *GMN/GNG*

PITTSBURGER (US) 1919-1923

Pittsburgh Truck Mfg. Co., Pittsburgh, Pa.

This truck began as a 2½-tonner powered by a Continental C4 engine, and in 1921 the range was extended to include a Midwest-powered 5-tonner. Other models made up to the end of production in 1923 included a 1½- and 3-tonner, both using Midwest engines. All Pittsburgers had 4-speed transmissions and worm final drive. *GNG*

PLUTO (D) 1924-1927

(1) Automobilfabrik Zella-Mehlis GmbH., Zella-St. Blasii 1924-1927

(2) Pluto Automobilfabrik GmbH., Zella-St. Blasii

Although this was a license production of the sporty French Amilcar the chassis was also used for van bodies. 4/20 PS and 5/30 PS engines were used. *HON*

PLYMOUTH (i) (US) 1906-1914

(1) Commercial Motor Truck Co., Toledo, Ohio 1906

(2) Commercial Motor Truck Co., Plymouth, Ohio 1906-1908

(3) Plymouth Motor Truck Co., Plymouth, Ohio 1909-1914

Plymouth commercial vehicles were noted for the used of friction transmission in conjunction with larger engines than were normally seen with this system. Conventional and cab-over layouts were used, 1906/07 models running from ½- to 3-tons, with 4-cylinder Continental engines and double chain drive. For 1908 the largest engine was a 50hp, and sightseeing buses for 12 to 20 passengers were offered as well as trucks. There was also a combination truck and bus. By 1912 only two chassis were listed, with engines of 25.6hp for the 1-tonner and 40-hp for the 2-tonner. A cyclops headlight was centered on top of the dash, flanked by two smaller ones at the side. *RW*

1940 PLYMOUTH (ii) PT105 panel delivery van, Chrysler

1941 PLYMOUTH (ii) ½-ton pick-up, Chrysler

PLYMOUTH (ii) (US) 1935-1942

Chrysler Corporation, Detroit, Mich.

From 1935 to 1942 commercial versions of Chrysler's low-price Plymouth were offered alongside the light-duty Dodges, to give holders of the joint Chrysler-Plymouth franchise some extra sales. Initially only a 2-door commercial sedan was listed, but a panel delivery was added in 1936, and in 1937 a separate commercial range was announced, with chassis longer than those of the cars. 1939 saw not only a sedan ambulance model, but also an additional line using the smallest Dodge truck chassis; all commercial Plymouths, however, used the standard 6-cylinder sv Plymouth car engine of 3.3 litres' capacity, increased to 3.6 litres for 1942. In 1938 and 1939 Plymouth vans were marketed in Britain under the Chrysler name. *MCS*

PODEUS (D) 1905-1918

Paul Heinrich Podeus, Wismar

This firm started production of trucks in 1905 and these were known for their solid construction, which was based on designs by Joseph Vollmer. Not many details are known as these vehicles were exported to a very great extent to Eastern Europe and not widely known in their country of origin. The backbone of production were a 3- and a 5-tonner with 4-cylinder 45 and 55hp engines respectively. After WW I production was given up. *HON*

POHL (D) 1924-1930

Pohl-Werke, Gossnitz

Pohl started production of tractors during WW I for military purposes. In 1924 the first road tractor appeared, based on an agricultural type. A newly developed 4- cylinder Deutz diesel engine with 30 bhp was used from 1926. *HON*

POLSKI FIAT PL) 1934-1939; 1973 to date

(1) Panstwowe Zaklady Inzynieri, Warszawa, 1934-1939

(2) Fabryka Samochodow Osobowych, Warszawa — Zeran, 1973 to date

The best known Fiat license production of the pre-war years, Polski Fiat built light commercials, vans, pickups and ambulances based on their car model, which was the Polish version of Fiat's Balilla 508. Powered by a 36 hp, 4-cylinder gasoline engines and having nice looking lines, the range included even a Kegresse half-track version destined to military uses. Hostilities of WWII halted production of Polski Fiat but the name was revived in 1968 in the form of the FSO built Fiat 125. Produced by the same factory that built Warszawa vehicles, Polski Fiat 125 P powered by a 4-cylinder, 1½-litre gasoline engine developing 70 hp was, at first, built as a car, but a pickup and van version were added in 1973. *GA*

PONTIAC (i) (US) 1906

Pontiac Motor Car Co., Pontiac, Mich.

Pontiac 1, 1½, 2, and 3-ton deliveries and trucks were planned, all models to be equipped with patented Halfpenny auxilliary springs, a development of Mr. Martin Halfpenny, the designer and promoter. At least one prototype appears to have been built, taking nearly a year. *RW*

PONTIAC (ii) (US) 1926-1927: 1949-1953

(1) Oakland Motor Car Co., Pontiac, Mich. 1926-1927

(2) Pontiac Division, General Motors Corporation, Pontiac, Michigan 1949-1953

Pontiac's only commercial vehicles were car-based light vans. The original 1,000-pound model of 1926 used the 3-litre 6-cylinder sv chassis, but had van rather than sedan delivery bodywork, this latter style featuring on 1949 and subsequent Pontiacs. These came with sv 6 or straight-8 engines. In 1953 8-cylinder form output was 111 bhp from 4.3-litres; the smaller 6 gave only 4 bhp less. *MCS*

PONY (US) 1919-1920

Minnesota Machine & Foundry Company, Minneapolis, Minnesota

The Pony ¼-tonner with delivery van body was one of the rare vehicles which attempted a late revival of the cyclecar concept originally fostered in 1914-1915. The Pony used a small-displacement 4-cylinder, water-cooled engine which the company claimed was built on the premises. This was connected to a friction transmission and chain drive to the rear wheels. Wheelbase was 7 feet, 6 inches and the vehicle was priced at $350. *GMN*

1941 PONY CRUISER 19-seater bus, MBS

PONY CRUISER (US) 1938-1951

(1) People's Rapid Transit Co., Kalamazoo, Michigan 1938-1940

(2) Kalamazoo Coaches, Inc., Kalamazoo, Michigan, 1940-1951

People's Rapid Transit Co. operated buses over 200 miles of route in the vicinity of Kalamazoo. In 1938 the company constructed a lightweight 16-passenger intercity bus based on a Ford front-engine commercial chassis, the same chassis originally used by Beaver and also found in large numbers in the Detroit bus fleet. Restyling in 1940 made the Pony Cruiser greatly resemble small FitzJohn buses of the period; also in that year a larger Ford engine was made available, as was a 19-passenger version, and the manufacturing business was separated from the operating company under another name.

The Pony Cruiser had the same kind of appeal as the Ford Transit in being cheap to buy, economical to run, and easy to repair, with so many parts available through Ford auto dealers. A notable use of these buses was by the British Yukon Navigation Co. along the Alcan Highway in the years after World War II. Chevrolet and International K-7 chassis were listed in addition to Ford in 1947, and in 1948 there was a larger model with 25 or 29 seats known as the Kalamazoo Cruiser. Probably about 625 Pony and Kalamazoo Cruisers were built, almost all of them operated by small companies. *MBS*

POPE-HARTFORD (US) 1906-1914

Pope Manufacturing Company, Hartford, Connecticut

This well-known builder of passenger automobiles also built commercial types as well as some public service vehicles including ambulances and motorized fire apparatus. The first Pope truck had an opposed 2-cylinder, water-cooled engine of 20 hp, a 4-speed gearbox and double chain drive. Later models grew much larger with 3- and 5-tonners being included during the final two model years. These large trucks were on chassis with wheelbases as large as 14 feet, 2 inches, but to the last, adhered to the double chain drive. The 3- and 5-tonners were furnished with standard stake bodies only. The Pope Manufacturing Company was the parent organization for the Pope-Waverley of Indianapolis. *GMN*

POPE-WAVERLEY (US) 1904-1908

Pope Motor Car Co., Indianapolis, Ind.

The name of this make began as Waverley and reverted back to the single word in 1908. Pope Manufacturing Co. of Hartford, Conn. was the parent company for the above period of time. The commercial vehicles under this name were exclusively electric, battery-powered. Models ranged from light delivery vans to chassis rated as 5-tonners. All chassis tended toward rather "square" dimensions with the 1-tonner of 1906 having a wheelbase of 8 feet with track of 6 feet, 10 inches. In 1906 there were six models: one open delivery van, two closed delivery vans, plus 1-, 3- and 5-tonners. *GMN*

PORTARO see Aro

1911 POSS Model A 1000lb truck, NAHC

POSS (US) 1912-1914

Poss Motor Company, Detroit, Michigan

A half-tonner was the only type made by Poss and this was available only with open delivery body. Though small, with a wheelbase of 8 feet, 2 inches with total weight of only 1,350 pounds, it did have a 4-cylinder, water-cooled engine. With either solid or pneumatic tires, its price was $850. *GMN*

POWELL (US) 1954-1956

Powell Mfg. Co., Compton, Calif.

The Powell Sport Wagon was a pick-up based on used Plymouth chassis with reconditioned 6-cylinder Plymouth engines dating back as far as 1940. *GNG*

POWER (US) 1917-1923

(1) Power Truck & Tractor Co., Detroit, Mich.

(2) Power Truck & Tractor Co., St. Louis, Mo.

Beginning in 1917, the first model was a 2-tonner but within a year this had grown to include 1-, 3½- and 5-tonners of conventional design, all using 4-cylinder Continental engines, worm-drive and wheelbases up to 15 feet. By 1922, the range had shrunk to a 2-tonner and a 3½-tonner, both with 4-speed gearboxes, 4-cylinder Hinkley engines and worm-drive rear axles. *GMN*

PRAGA (A:CS) 1910 to date

(1) Automobilni oddeleni Prvni Ceskomoravske tovarny na stroje, Prague-Lieben, 1910-1927

(2) Auto Praga, Ceskomoravska Kolben-Danek, Prague-Vysocany, 1927-1945

1912 PRAGA Typ V 16-seater bus, VP

(3) AZKG n.p., Prague-Vysocany and AVIA n.p., Prague-Letnany, 1945 to date

The third oldest Czechoslovakian automobile factory, this concern was founded in 1907 and the name Praga used for the first time one year later. At first, foreign designs were assembled, including Benz, Charron, Renault and IsottaFraschini cars, and the first Praga trucks were made in 1910. These ran from 1½/2-tonners to 5/6 tonners, all with shaft drive. In 1911 came the Type V designed by Frantisek Kec which really established Praga as an important manufacturer. It was a 4/5 tonner with 6.85-litre 4-cylinder sv engine and chain drive. Buyers were given a subsidy and annual allowance if they kept their vehicle in good condition and ready for army mobilization, in the same manner as Thornycroft and Dennis buyers were given a War Office subsidy in Britain. The Type V was made in large numbers until 1923.

From 1912 to 1925 the Type L 2½ tonner with 3.8-litre engine from the Praga Grand passenger car was made, also as a fire engine and 25-passenger bus. Other models included the 4/5 ton Type T (1913-1924), 5 ton Type N (1916-1937) which from 1930 was available with a Deutz diesel engine of 7 litres capacity. This was developed into the Types TN and TND with 7.8-litre gasoline or 8.85-litre diesel engines and, from 1937, air brakes. In 1933 came the 3-axle bus chassis Type TO with 6-cylinder 11½-litre engine, produced from 1938 with longer chassis as the TOT 7-ton truck or TOV bus for up to 100 passengers as a city bus and also as a luxurious touring coach.

1934 PRAGA RN 2½-ton truck, VP

1937 PRAGA TN 10-ton truck, VP

Smaller chassis were made throughout the inter-war period, such as the Type MN 2-tonner with 1.85-litre 4-cylinder engine from the Mignon passenger car and Type L 3-tonner which was popular as a fire engine. The L was replaced by the 2½-tonner RN with 3.47-litre 6-cylinder engine which was made, with modifications, until 1952. Variants included the RND with 4½-litre diesel engine, SND with 6.75-litre diesel engine, and the RNG with producer gas engine. In Slovakia these trucks were made under the name Orava from 1939 to 1942, and they were also assembled in Yugoslavia where they were the prototypes for the post-war TAM trucks.

After World War 2 both RN and RND models were fitted with hydraulic brakes and all-steel cabs. Several models, including buses, had the Praga-Wilson 5-speed preselector gearbox. The RND bus had a steel body for 40 passengers. Various prototypes were tested in the years 1946 to 1950, including the forward-control 5-tonner Type

1946 PRAGA RN 2½-ton truck, VP

1965 PRAGA S5T street sweeper/collector, MSH

N5T and N4T 4-tonner, but these did not go into production because Praga was given the task of developing a new truck with capacity of 3 tons cross country and 5 tons on the road. This became the famous V3S launched in 1952, with Tatra air-cooled 6-cylinder engine, 8-speed gearbox and drive on all six wheels. It has been produced up to the present day, with a variety of bodies including tippers, mobile workshops, cesspool emptiers and road sweepers. In 1957 it was joined by a 4x2 version, the S5T for 5 ton loads on good roads only. This was made in swb form as a tractor and lasted until 1973. The original Praga factory now makes components only, and the V3S trucks are made in the former Avia factory at Letnany. *MSH*

PRATCHITT see Cumberland

PREMIER (i) (GB) 1912-1914

Premier Motor Co. Ltd., Birmingham

This was a 3-wheeled parcelcar based on the company's P.M.C. Motorette cyclecar. It had a 7hp single-cylinder J.A.P. engine, 2 speeds and chain drive to the single rear wheel. Load capacity was 5cwt, and the vehicle had a similar appearance to the better-known Autocarrier and Warrick parcelcars. It was sold in London under the name Omnium. *GNG*

PREMIER (ii) (IND) 1972 to date

The Premier Automobile Ltd., Kurla, Bombay

As a continuation of the Indian Dodge and Fargo ranges, Premier builds a full range of medium and heavy truck chassis. Powered by a Premier-built Chrysler 55hp gasoline or Perkins 110hp diesel engine, these trucks are built in 4x2 and 4x4 models and use either an American style Dodge cab or the old Kew-Dodge semi-forward control cab. The heaviest models, rigids and tractors, have an Indian-styled angular cab. Medium and large capacity bus chassis are also included in the range, these with various locally-built bodies. *GA*

PRESTO (D) 1913-1927

Presto-Werke A.G., Chemnitz

Presto started car production in 1901 but the first vans which were based on the private models appeared in 1913, using an 8/25 PS 2,078 cc engine. After 1921 only one type with 30bhp 2,350 cc engine was available as a van.

In 1926 Presto took over Dux and carried on the very successful type 22/80 PS which was offered as truck or bus. Production stayed in the Dux works. When Presto was taken over by N.A.G. in 1927 this type was continued as N.A.G.-Presto. *HON*

1968 PREVOST Panorama Coach, DL

1977 PREVOST Prestige PTS47 Coach, MBS

PREVOST (CDN) 1947 to date

Prevost Car Inc., Sainte Calire, Que.

This company began in 1924 by building wooden bus bodies, and in 1947 turned out its first complete coach, with all-steel body. Later models included Le Normand, a silverside highway coach with diesel engine and air suspension (1959), Le Travelair,a small airport bus (1962), and Le Panoramique, a sightseeing bus (1966). By 1967 these had evolved into the Champion, a split-level 3-axle coach with air-conditioning. Champions were sold in the United States as well as Canada, and a fleet of them replaced the obsolescent trans-Newfoundland passenger trains. In 1968 the Super-luxurious Panorama, with tall, curved side windows, was designed in conjunction with a Montreal operator, and went into production three years later as the Prestige. Specially suited for sightseeing and charters, it has been sold as far away as Hawaii. All current Prevost coaches have three axles, with single tired trailing axle, and are powered by rear-mounted Detroit Diesel V-8 diesel engines. Transmissions are 4- or 6-speed manual, or automatic systems. Total production to date is over 1,500 units. *HD*

PRIAMUS (D) 1903-1908; 1921-1923

(1) Motorfahrzeugfabrik "Koln", Uren, Kotthaus & Co., Cologne 1903-08

(2) Priamus-Werke A.G. fur Fahrzeugbau, Cologne-Sulz 1921-1923

The private cars of this make with 1-, 2-, 3- or 4-cylinder engines were also offered as vans. Since 1904 the cars were marketed as Priamus. After 1908 the firm concentrated on private cars but after WW I the new models 8/24 PS and 9/30 PS also were available as vans. *HON*

PRIMUS (D) 1935-1939

(1) Primus Traktoren-Gesellschaft mbH., Berlin-Lichtenberg 1935-37

(2) Primus Traktoren-Gesellschaft Johannes Kohler & Co. KG,Berlin-Lichtenberg 1937-39

Primus was the first firm to offer a mini-tractor with diesel engine. This was a single-cylinder mounted in the rear. In 1937 they changed to 2-cylinder diesel engines. *HON*

1936 PRIMUS 10hp tractor, FLP

PRINCE (J) 1952-1967

(1) Prince Motors Co., Tachikawa 1952-1954
(2) Fuji Precision Machinery Co. Ltd., Tokyo 1954-1961
(3) Prince Motors Ltd., Tokyo 1961-1967

Like the Subaru, the Prince owed its origins to the dismembering of the old Nakajima Aircraft Co. Private cars were always the firm's principal interest, but along with these was offered a normal-control 1-tonner using the car's 45bhp 1½-litre 4-cylinder ohv engine in a beam axle chassis. This model was uprated to 35cwt in 1956 when the first forward control models made their appearance. In 1959 form the power unit was giving 70bhp, and three basic light commercials were offered; the car-based Skyway delivery van, the normal control New Miler, and the forward control Clipper, all with 4-speed synchromesh gearboxes. 19,000 commercials were delivered in 1960, and a year later the heavier Princes could be had with 1.9-litre 83bhp engines. By 1966, when the company was acquired by Nissan, the biggest forward-control model could handle 2-ton payloads, and some models featured overdrive gearboxes and torsion-bar ifs, this latter feature being found on their last new design, the forward-control Homer. The Homer continued under the Nissan name, and was still catalogued in 1978. *MCS*

PRINCESS see Century (i)

PROCTOR (GB) 1947-1952

(1) Proctor Springwood Ltd., Proctor Works, Mousehold, Norwich, Norfolk.
(2) Praill's Motors Ltd., Hereford

Designed in 1939, the Proctor was a lightweight 5 to 6 tonner conceived on very similar lines to the contemporary Seddon. The first prototype was built after the Second World War at Edmonton, London, and had a Moss gearbox and Perkins P6 engine like the Seddon, and the very similar post-war Vulcan. It was used to transfer parts and machinery to a new factory outside Norwich where lightweight bodywork as well as Proctor chassis

1947 PROCTOR 6-ton truck, OMM

were produced from the end of 1947. Mk.II 7-ton rigid and 10-ton articulated tractors also joined the range. Component supply difficulties soon put an end to the company, though their Hereford distributors, Praill's Motors Ltd., produced a small number of Proctors from spares in the early fifties. *OM*

PROGRESS (i) (US) 1911-1914

Universal Machinery Co., Milwaukee, Wis.

The Progress was available in at least three capacities: ?-, 1½- and 3-tonners. All had 4-cylinder engines and forward control, with 3-speed gearboxes and double chain-drive. As fitting for the city of manufacture, vehicles for brewery and bottle hauling formed a large portion of the six models for 1913. *GMN*

PROGRESS (ii) (GB) 1930-1934

(1) Seal Motor Ltd., Manchester 1930-1933
(2) Haynes Economy Motors Ltd., Manchester 1933-1934

The first Progress 3-wheeler was derived from the Seal, but instead of control being from the sidecar, the driver of the Progress sat alongside the load-carrying platform in a bucket seat. Three engines were available, a 343cc Villiers, 680cc J.A.P. or 980cc J.A.P. Prices ranged from £75 to £92 10/-. In 1932 a more conventional-looking van was introduced which resembled the James 3-wheeler except that the drive was to the single front wheel. The engine was a 680cc J.A.P. and there was a Sturmey-Archer 3-speed gearbox. With the exception of the footbrake, controls were of the motorcycle pattern. Load capacity was 15cwt. A new model appeared at the end of 1933 with a longer wheelbase and 750cc engine. *GNG*

PROSPECT (US) 1924-1934

Prospect Fire Engine Co., Prospect, Ohio

This company built rotary pumpers called Deluge, mainly on Ford and Reo chassis, from 1923. From 1924 to about 1932 they made the Prospect-Biederman Deluge Master Fire Fighter which was a pumper on a specially-built Biederman chassis. In 1930 they used a Mars chassis with Lycoming V-8 engine. After the Depression forced Prospect to close their doors their chief designer Keenan Hanley started his own company under his own name. *GNG*

PROTOS (D) 1912-1927

Siemens-Schuckert-Werke GmbH., Automobilwerk Nonnendamm, Berlin

After 1912 Protos vehicles were also available as vans based on the 17/35 PS private car. In 1914 a 4 ton truck was presented with forward control. After WW I Protos concentrated on one model, the type C with 2.5 litre engine wich was available as van and express truck. With various purpose built bodies it was extensively used as an ambulance and by police, postal and municipal authori ties. *HON*

P.R.P. see Willeme

PRUNEL (F) 1902-1906

Ste des Usines Prunel, Puteaux, Seine

Prunel made a wide range of passenger cars and a smaller variety of commercial vehicles. The first was a light van with 9hp de Dion Bouton or Aster engine and chain drive, of 1902/03, and in 1906 they made a larger vehicle powered by a 30/33hp 4-cylinder engine, all with chain drive. A 3 ton truck took part in the 1906 Industrial

1906 PRUNEL 5-ton truck, OMM

Vehicle Trials in Paris, and a double decker bus was also built on this chassis, one of which came to England. By the time of the 1906 Paris Salon the commercial vehicle products (though not the passenger cars) were renamed U.D.P.X. (Usines de Puteaux). A new 35 hp 4-cylinder engine designed by Paul List was introduced, and normal and forward — control chassis were listed, for both goods and passenger work. Some ran on producer gas. This venture lasted for no more than one year. *GNG*

P.T.C. (NZ) c.1935-1940

Passenger Transport Co. Ltd., Otahuhu

This bus operating company was a pioneer of the oil-engined bus in New Zealand, and built a number of vehicles of their own design. These included two gas buses with Meadows engines, a 36-seater with Gardner oil engine, two 40-seaters with Leyland Cub engines. Other components included Kirkstall axles, David Brown steering gear and Lockheed brakes. *GNG*

P.T.L. see Serpollet

P.T.V. (E) 1956-1962

Automoviles Utilitarios S.A., Barcelona

Formed by Senores Perramon, Tache and Vila, who gave their initials to the car, this company made light cars and vans powered by a 250cc single-cylinder 2-stroke Ausa engine mounted at the rear. They had independent suspension all round and hydraulic brakes. They also made a 3-wheeler with the same engine. Competition from SEAT forced the company to close down after over 1,250 vehicles had been made. *JCG*

PUCH (A) 1908-1919

(1) Johann Puch Erste Steiermarkische Fahrrad-Fabriks-Aktiengesellschaft, Graz 1908-1914
(2) Puchwerke A.G., Graz 1914-1919

The private cars of Puch were available as vans from 1908 and used a 4-cylinder 20/25 PS engine. From 1913 the range covered vans, trucks, ambulances, light buses and fire fighting vehicles. During WW I there was a great demand for trucks but when this ended production of commercial vehicles was given up.

Puch later became a part of Steyr-Daimler-Puch. Commercials are still built at the Graz plant and the all-terrain vehicles Pinzgauer are marketed as Steyr-Puch. *HON*

PULLCAR (GB) 1906-1909

Pullcar Motor Co. Ltd., Preston, Lancs.

The original Pullcar was an avant-train or two-wheeled fore-carriage for attachment to horse-drawn vehicles. It

1906 PULLCAR front-drive taxicab, NMM

had a 12/14 hp Fafnir engine under the seat, with two-speed epicyclic transmission and chain drive to the wheels. These were shod with pneumatic tires, but the rear portions of the vehicle usually carried solid tires, and this feature persisted even when Pullcar offered complete vehicles, which they did from 1907. The body styles were delivery vans or taxicabs. (It was licensed by the Metropolitan Police, though few ran in London.) One Pullcar van was used to carry mail between Preston and Blackpool. Later Pullcars had 15.9 hp White & Poppe engines in place of the Fafnir twin. They were designed by J.S. Critchley who was also responsible for some early Daimlers, and the Critchley-Norris gasoline and steam bus chassis. *GNG*

1945 PULLMAN trolleybus, MBS

PULLMAN (US) 1932-1952

Pullman-Standard, Chicago, Illinois (plant at Worcester, Mass.)

A single sample trolley-coach for Brooklyn was produced by streetcar builder Osgood-Bradley in its Worcester plant during 1930, and then the company sold out to Pullman, Inc. of Chicago (afterward Pullman-Standard). Brooklyn placed an order for six coaches in 1932, and small orders were taken for other operators during the following few years. When Westinghouse and General Electric introduced single-motor drive for trolley-coaches in 1936, interest in these vehicles increased, and Pullman won a sizable share of the business. Transit systems in Boston and Providence were particularly steady Pullman customers, and other large fleets ran in Atlanta, Milwaukee and Birmingham. A modified design for the export trade was offered after 1945, and some were sold to Valparaiso and Sao Paulo. Altogether Pullman built about 2100 trolley-coaches. *MBS*

PULL-MORE (US) 1914-1917

Pull-More Motor Truck Co., Detroit, Mich.

This was a very minor make of truck and there are indications that only three-tonners were built. Further information has not been located. *GMN*

1904 PURREY steam bus and trailer, GNG

PURREY (F) 1898-1929

(1) Valentin Purrey, Bordeaux 1898-c.1908
(2) Purrey et Exshaw, Bordeaux c.1908-1913
(3) H. Exshaw et Cie, Bordeaux 1913-1929

Although famous for his self-contained steam tramcars which ran in Paris as late as 1914 Purrey also deserves to be remembered as the most successful French steam wagon builder. His first recorded wagon was exhibited in 1898 but may have been preceded by prototypes. The last was made in 1929.

Using a vertical cross water tube boiler in conjunction with a compound undertype engine with countershaft differential and twin chain final drive, Purrey's wagons, which were fitted with a single speed only, were supplied mainly in 5 and 10 ton sizes though 4, 6 and 8 tonners were also offered, the difference probably being in springing and chain sprocket sizes. By 1906 the Say sugar refinery of Paris had eighteen 5 ton and sixteen 10 ton Purreys. Harrods, the celebrated London store bought a 5 tonner in 1911 and Purrey and Exshaw had a London sales office at 81 Shaftesbury Avenue, managed by D.M. Turner from 1911 to the outbreak of the 1914 war. The war and the vast number of government surplus gasoline engined trucks placed on the market after the Armistice led to a decline in steam wagon sales and production ceased in 1929. In that year the company introduced a light steam tractor running on pneumatic tires, based on their wagon. It had a vertical boiler behind the driver, two high-pressure double acting cylinders, and chain drive. There was also an agricultural tractor of similar layout on steel tires. From 1913 onwards these vehicles were more usually called Exshaw, after the new owner of the company. *RAW*

PUMA (BR) 1978 to date

Puma Veiculos e Motores Ltda., Sao Paulo

This Brazilian sports car maker entered the truck market with a medium-sized 4-wheel chassis powered by a choice of diesel engines, Perkins 4.236, MWM or Detroit. Glassfiber cabs are featured. *GNG*

PYRODYNE (GB) 1904-1908

Bickford Burners Co., Camborne, Cornwall

Readers of the correspondence columns of the "Engineer and "Engineering" of the opening years of this century are likely to find Mr. J.V.S. Bickford expressing his views on the generation of flash steam and upon liquid fuel burners. In 1904 these were brought together in the Pyrodyne light steam truck, designed for a 30 cwt. load, using his own design of liquid fuel burner and flash boiler. Maximum pressure was 400 psi and the steam was highly superheated which cannot have pleased the slide valves used for steam distribution in the double cylinder vertical engine. Drive was by chain to the rear axle which incorporated a traction engine type differential. Both water and fuel were designed to be controlled by automatic valves and filters were provided in fuel and water feed lines to prevent impurities interfering with the operation of these devices.

The maker listed a coal burning wagon but no more than a dozen of both sorts were made. *RAW*

PURITY (US) 1914-1915

Purity Bread Company, St. Paul, Minnesota

The Purity electric was described as having been constructed for use only as delivery vans for this company, but were later listed as being for sale. These were battery-operated and were made in two models: 1200- and 2000-pound capacities. Both used chassis with wheelbase of 8 feet, 6 inches, and were furnished with pneumatic tires. *GMN*

Q (GB) 1938-1952 *Q Vehicles Ltd., Steels Engineering Products Ltd., Sunderland, Co., Durham*

The origin of the Q Electric was the German Bleichert, manufacturing rights of which were acquired by E. Cecil Kny. Several so-called Q vehicles were shown in England in 1938/39, including a conventional 15 cwt delivery van, 2 ton low-loader, 5 ton 6x4 and a municipal tower wagon, but these were almost certainly all of German manufacture. One conventional van was made by Garner during the war, and production was later taken up by Steels Engineering, makers of Coles Cranes. The first post-war was a coventional 1 ton van, later joined by a forward control model of the same capacity and typical electric appearance. *GNG*

QIAO-TONG (p), CH'IAO-TUNG (wg) (Communication) (CHI) c.1958 to date

Shanghai Cargo Vehicle Plant, Shanghai (Plant Vehicle Code-SH)

The Communication series of trucks has been produced in China for many years and the early models were similar in appearance to Czech Skodas.

Current models include the cab-over-engine 4 ton SH-141 with a 6-cylinder 90 hp engine, 5 speeds forward and 70 km/h top speed, and the model SH-361 15 ton dump truck with a choice of 210 and 220 hp diesel engines. *BE*

QUADRAY (US) 1904-1905

Commercial Motor Vehicle Co., Detroit, Mich.

This company was formed to make large electric vehicles only. Their trucks had capacities up to 6¼ tons and their largest buses could carry 50 passengers. The largest chassis had four 3½hp motors each driving one wheel, four-wheel steering and wooden tires. Maximum speed was 8mph. In 1905 there was also a gasoline-electric bus with 25hp engine generating electricity for four 2½hp motors. This was designed for interurban work too far for storage batteries to be used. *GNG*

1905 QUADRAY 4-wheel drive and steering electric van, NMM

QUADRU (US) 1911

R. Fuller (no address)

At the 1911 Detroit Auto Show sponsored by the Autombile Dealers and Manufacturers Association, R. Fuller's gasoline-electric "Quadru" was shown. It seems to have been an experimental prototype.

A gasoline engine of 32 hp generated electricity to drive all four wheels of this immense truck of 15 tons capacity. A big crane, jack, and other devices were carried on the truck for handling heavy freight, and a trailer was also attached to it. *RW*

QUAKERTOWN (US) 1916

Quakertown Auto Mfg. Co., Quakertown, Pa.

The only model offered was a 1,000-pound truck powered by a 35hp 4-cylinder engine. It cost $500. Probably only prototypes were actually built. *DJS*

1905 QUADRAY gas-electric sightseeing bus, NMM

RABA (H) 1904-1941; 1961-1963; 1970 to date

(1)-Magyar Vagon es Gepgyar Resvenitarsasag, Raab 1904-1941
(2)-Wilhelm Pieck Vagon es Gepgyar, Gyor 1961-1963
(3)-Magyar Vagon es Gepgyar, Gyor 1970 to date

Established as early as 1896 as a general engineering firm in the Austro-Hungarian city then called Raab, Raba built its first truck chassis in 1904, and these were followed in the same year by ten light vans built following Csonka designs. Forty postal vans, designed again by Csonka were built between 1907 and 1910, while Raba acquired a Praga license and started building 5 ton trucks in 1912. The Grand 4 cylinder, 40 hp car, built under Praga license too, gave birth to a series of ambulances on the same chassis in 1913, while Raba turned again for a truck license agreement to Krupp of Germany in 1920. The year 1928 marks the introduction of the first Raba-designed 3 ton trucks called Super which served also as

1936 RABA Super 3½-ton truck, AAR

1938 RABA Botond 6x6 cross-country truck, AAR

bus chassis. Maros model trucks followed in 1936 and Botond 6 x 4 military chassis were introduced in 1938, the same year that Raba buses featured M.A.N. license built

1961 RABA 106 dump truck, AAR

1977 RABA 831.03 truck and trailer, Raba

diesel engines. The Special 4 ton chassis appeared in 1941, but hostilities and occupation stopped vehicle production the same year. Total production up to that date was 6827 truck chassis and 100 buses. Following the reorganization of the automotive industry in Hungary during the post war years, Raba was allocated to rail rolling stock production, but a brief come back to the automotive world was evident in 1961, when the renamed company built a 4 x 4 10 ton half cab dumper of heavy duty construction. This same model was taken over by Dutra in 1963 in a much modernized form and is still built under the Godollo trademark. Raba's third span in the automotive field started in mid 60s, under a license agreement with M.A.N. of Germany, for the production of truck and bus axles and heavy diesel engines. High quality axles with normal or planetary drive, built at the rate of 10,000 units per year are supplied to all Hungarian vehicle manufacturers and are also exported to many marketes including West Germany. In 1970 a two axled truck chassis was introduced, built under M.A.N. license, featuring a Raba M.A.N. diesel engine and a typical M.A.N. forward control cab. Operating a workforce of 20,000 people, Raba soon extended its truck range, announcing 3 axled and tractor chassis, all fitted with the same forward control cab, and powered by their own license-built diesels developing 215 to 304 hp. In addition, Raba continues to build rolling stock, road trailers and armored military vehicles for the Eastern Bloc countries. *GA*

RAE (GB) 1910-1911

John Rae, Mirfield, Huddersfield, Yorks.

Rae's boilers had an outer water jacket with vertical water tubes expanded each end into the firebox shell. The undertype engine was a cross compound with Stephenson link motion. Drive was by short chain to the countershaft which incorporated the differential and at each end of which gears meshed with an annullar gear on each rear wheel. Solid rubbers on artillery wheels were standard. Few Rae wagons were made. *RAW*

RAF (i) (A) 1908-1913

Reichenberger Automobile Fabrik Gmbh, Reichenberg (now Liberec)

This company was founded by the racing driver and textile magnate Theodor von Liebig in 1907 to build luxury passenger cars, and commercial vehicles were added to the range in the following year. The first was a platform truck with 4½-litre 30bhp engine under the driver's seat, made later as a closed van and 12-passenger bus. In 1910 a smaller chassis was added, with 3.7-litre 25bhp engine and pneumatic tires, for 8-9 passenger omnibus bodies. This was the Type LO.

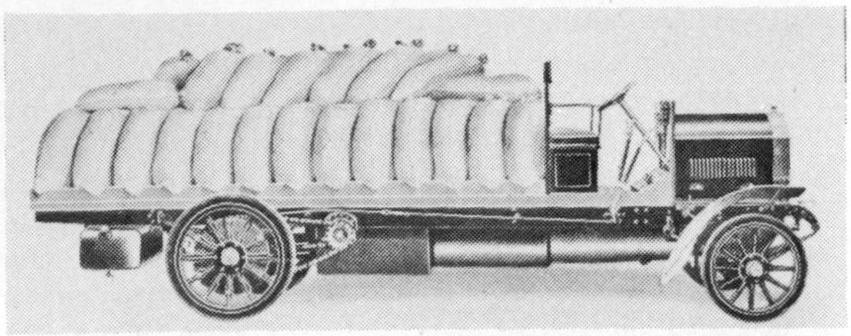

1913 RAF (i) Type HL 3-ton truck, MSH

In 1911 RAF took out a license to build the Knight sleeve-valve engine, which they sold to the Laurin & Klement and Puch factories. In 1913 RAF was bought by Laurin & Klement, and both cars and commercial vehicles of L & K design were continued under the RAF name for a year or two. In 1913 the commercial range consisted of trucks from 1½ to 6 tons capacity, and 10 to 35-passenger buses. *MSH*

1962 RAF (ii) 977D Latvia minibus, MSH

RAF (ii) (SU) c.1955 to date

Riga Autobus Works, Riga, Latvia

Based on the Volga car chassis, the RAF-977 Latvia was built as an 11 passenger microbus, an ambulance and a tourist vehicle. A choice of three 4-cylinder engines was available, driving a three speed mechanical gearbox. Suspension was coil spring in in front, leaf in rear.

A model 978 Spriditis bus has also been manufactured and a newer microbus, the 12 passenger RAF-2203 Latvia was introduced in 1975 to replace the 977. Power is by a 98 hp Volga car engine providing 120 km/h and it can be fitted for passenger, ambulance or police duties. *BE*

1936 RAGHENO bus, JFJK

RAGHENO (B) 1929-1952

Usines Ragheno, Malines.

Ragheno is a somewhat strange company, as far as their involvement in the production of commercial vehicles is concerned. They were old-established manufacturers of railway rolling stock with bus body construction as a sideline, when they produced some trolleybuses for Antwerp in 1929, using ACEC electrical equipment. They were also sub-contractors to Brossel, supplying for example in 1939 some chassis for buses to be operated by the city of Brussels. Chassis, however, were also sold under their own name, using Gardner oil engines, and probably derived from the original trolleybus chassis for Antwerp. After World War II Ragheno was for some years involved in the production of the French Isobloc buses, mainly for Sabena, the Belgian airline. *JFJK*

RAILLESS (GB) 1909-1927

(1) Railless Electric Traction Co. Ltd., London, EC 1909-1912

(2) Railless Electric Construction Co. Ltd., London, EC 1912-1918

(3) Railless Ltd., London, SW1 1918-1927

The Railless company was set up in 1908 to promulgate the use of trolleybuses and to supply and construct complete trolleybus systems. The company had no vehicle manufacturing facilities of its own, and trolleybuses supplied under the name "Railless" were built by outside manufacturers. The first trolleybus demonstrated in Great Britain, at Hendon in 1909, was a Railless with chassis built by James & Browne of Hammersmith and body by Hurst Nelson, the tramcar builders. Railless trolleybuses were used on the first British public trolleybus services at Bradford and Leeds in June 1911. These and other subsequent pre-war Railless trolleybuses had chassis by Alldays & Onions Engineering Co. Ltd. Early vehicles were small, four-wheeled single-deckers with hand-operated controllers. The first double-decker, with open top deck, was built in 1913 and ran experimentally in Brighton in the following year. In 1918 the company became a subsidiary of Short Brothers (Rochester & Bedford) Ltd. who thereafter built all the chassis — and also many of the bodies — in their Seaplane Works at Rochester. Construction of covered-top double-deckers commenced in 1922 with a batch of twelve 51-seaters for Birmingham, and it was this batch of vehicles which, more than any others, influenced the subsequent development of the trolleybus in Britain. The last Railless vehicles were supplied to Nottingham in 1927. *OM*

1922 RAILLESS 51-seater trolleybus, KCB

RAINIER (US) 1916-1927

(1) Rainier Motor Corp., New York, NY 1916
(2) Rainier Motor Corp., Flushing, NY 1917-1924
(3) Rainier Trucks Inc., Flushing, NY 1924-1927

The first Rainier was a ½-tonner with either closed or open express body. This used a Rainier-built 4-cylinder engine and worm drive. This was joined by a 1½-tonner in 1918, also with worm drive and later that year, a ¾-tonner and a 1½-tonner were added to the line. All had pneumatic tires, 3-speed Brown-Lipe gearboxes and worm drives. Each of these models was available with closed delivery bodies and all had engines under frontal hoods. The largest used a 4-cylinder Continental engine. In 1921, a larger line was offered as 2-, 2½-, 3- and 5-tonners were added to the already large number of models. By 1925, there were seven types ranging from ¾-tonners to 6-tonners, and this line was continued to the end. All these latter models had worm drive and Continental engines. John T. Rainier had previously built Rainier passenger cars in Saginaw, Michigan. *GMN*

RAITO (J) 1934-1938

Raito Automobile Co. Ltd., Tokyo

The Raito was a small car-type pickup on Datsun or Ohta lines. At peak, production ran at 60 units a month. *MCS*

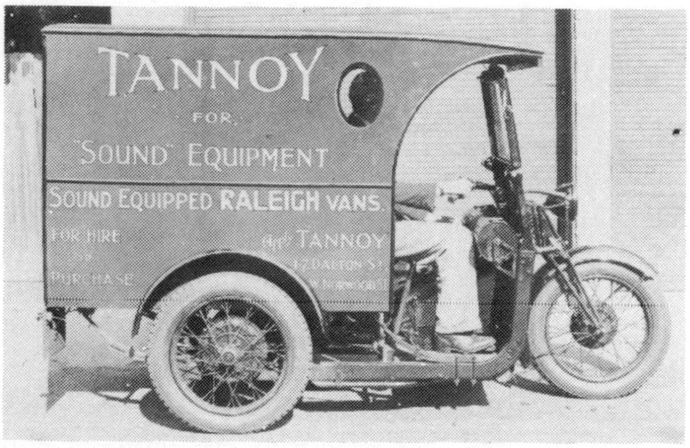

1931 RALEIGH ¼-ton 3-wheel van, OMM

RALEIGH (GB) 1929-1935

Raleigh Cycle Co. Ltd., Nottingham

Like many three-wheeled parcelcars of single front wheel type, the Raleigh started life as a direct motorcycle derivative with chain-driven rear wheels, growing more sophisticated with the years. The original 5-cwt Karryall used their own 496cc aircooled sv single-cylinder engine; the driver sat on a saddle and steered by handlebars, though all three wheels were braked and there was a differential. Capacity was up to 598cc by 1931, but the 1932 models featured car-type pressed steel frames and doorless cabs. A four-seater passenger body was available by 1933, when wheel steering and a driver's seat replaced the earlier arrangements. The 1934-5 models were even more car-like, sharing a chassis with the new Safety Seven sports tourer; this package embraced a 742cc V-twin engine, a 3-speed unit gearbox, electric pump feed, and spiral bevel final drive. The full-width cab came complete with doors; 55 mph and 46 mpg were claimed. A recession in the 3-wheeler market, however, influenced Raleigh to abandon these types, and the rights to the van design were acquired by T.L. Williams, who marketed a revised version under the Reliant name. *MCS*

RALPH (ZA) 1968-1971

(1) Rolway Enterprises (Pty.) Ltd., Ophirton, Johannesburg
(2) Rolway Enterprises (Pty.) Ltd., Alrode, Alberton, Transvaal

Ralph was a promising attempt to build vehicles specifically for the local South African market that unfortunately failed to survive. The first prototype was built by Ralph Lewis in borrowed premises with a staff force of four including himself. Rolway Enterprises was later set up with outside financial backing. Following local practice the Ralph was a heavy-duty tractor and rigid chassis using high-quality proprietary components including Cummins and GM Diesel engines, Allison, Spicer, Fuller and Clark gearboxes, and Rockwell Standard or Hendrickson axles. All-metal conventional or forward-control cabs were used. The smallest engine was a Cummins 270, and the largest, also a Cummins, was a V-12 developing 700bhp. Ralph trucks were built in sizes up to 160,000 lbs GCW. The company went into liquidation in 1971 after only 42 vehicles had been built. *GA*

RALSTON (US) 1913

Ralston Motor Company, Omaha, Nebraska

The Model ½ lasted only one year and was the lone effort of this obscure manufacturer. This was a half-tonner with an open van body driven by an air-cooled four-cylinder engine. It had a friction transmission and double chains to the rear wheels. With 36 x 2 solid tires and wood frame and wheelbase of 9 feet, 2 inches, this vehicle sold for $750. *GMN*

RAM (NL) 1968 to date

R.A. Mimiasie, Rotterdam.

Another Dutch merchant of U.S. Army surplus trucks, Mimiasie started in 1968 to sell trucks under the RAM trade-name. They used DAF engines in trucks that were otherwise left completely unchanged, except for some altering of the axle ratios since the original ratios were hardly a match for the unruly Dutch clay.

In 1970, however, RAM came with a completely new vehicle, using the semi-forward German MAN cab, and MAN engine — D2146M14, output 186 hp — Fichtel & Sachs clutch, ZF gearbox, while all further parts like axles, distribution gear, etc. came from U.S. Army surplus. The vehicle was of the 6 x 6 type and joined in 1974 by a 4 x 4 truck assembled in the same way, though with a less powerful engine of 126 hp. The 1978 Model 9000SF has a 5760cc DAF engine. *JFJK*

RAMIREZ (MEX) 1952 to date

Trailers de Monterey SA. Monterey, Nuevo Leon.

This company was founded by Sr. Gregorio Ramirez, Jr. in 1952.

Initial production began in 1953 with the introduction of the Ramirez Sultana bus. The engine used at that time was an imported General Motors. In fact, more than 80% of the vehicle consisted of imported parts. Mexican content increased rapidly and today the Ramirez is almost 100% Mexican made.

Following the Sultana bus was the Ramirez heavy-duty truck. Production of this model began in 1959. The original model came with a Dulles transmission of 12 and 15 gears. Also available were Cummins Diesel engine of 180, 220, 250, and 320 horsepower. From 1959 to 1961, less than 350 of these trucks were built by the company.

The latest model to be introduced was the Rural-

1970 RAMIREZ pick-up, RLH

Ramirez. This was a small pick-up truck with a capacity of 750 kilograms. This was one of the first pick-up trucks to be designed in Mexico. It was available with either a 4 or a 6-cylinder gasoline engine. A 4-cylinder diesel engine was also offered. At that time Trailers de Monterrey continued to expand rapidly and acquired new factories. In 1964 their affiliate, Industria Automotriz, S.A., went into the manufacture of original equipment for automotive vehicles. This plant started with 11 presses with the capacity of from 400 to 2,00 tons. By 1965 the company was supplying other Mexican manufacturers with parts.

The company has a capacity of over 5,000 vehicles a year. A few of these are exported but the majority are sold on the domestic market. Their current model lineup includes the following: Sultana buses of various sizes, including panoramic luxury models; Ramirez Reparto 1-ton microvans; Rural-Ramirez R20 and R22 diesel tractor-trucks with Cummins engines and hauling capacity of 36,000 kgs.; Ramirez semi-trailers of various sizes. Virtually all of these vehicles are designed in the engineering department of Trailers de Monterrey. *RLH*

1963 RAMSES pick-up, NMM

RAMSES (ET) 1963 to date

(1) Egyptian Automotive Co., Cairo 1963-1967
(2) Egyptian Light Transport Mfg. Co., Cairo 1967 to date

In cooperation with the N.S.U. factory in Germany, Egypt launched in 1960 its first original passenger car in the form of a N.S.U. Prinz-based light glassfibre bodied car with angular lines. This was soon followed by van and pick-up versions which due to the rear-positioned engine had a very small useful loading space. A new pick-up on Prinz lines came in 1967, while the whole range was redesigned in 1970. Power for all Ramses vehicles came from an imported N.S.U. 2-cylinder 36bhp engine driving the rear wheels. Due to the Six Day War with Israel production was sporadic between 1967 and 1970, and many times ceased altogether, but currently the Ramses is in full production again. *GA*

1910 RANDOLPH Model 14 1-ton truck, NAHC

RANDOLPH (US) 1908-1912

(1) Randolph Motor Car Company, Flint, Mich., 1908-1912
(2) Randolph Motor Truck Company, Chicago, Illinois, 1912-1913

Also known as Strenuous Randolph, this truck was made in as many as five different capacities in a given year. These ranged from light delivery vans with two-cylinder engines, to a flat-bed type with four-ton rating. All models had solid tires, three-speed gearboxes and double chain drive. *GMN*

RANGER (i) (GB) 1914

Ranger Cyclecar Co. Ltd., Coventry, Warwickshire.

Built by E.J. West who had previously made the West-Aster vehicles, the Ranger was a typical cyclecar powered a V-twin Blumfield or 4-cylinder Alpha engine. The 1914 range included a 4/5cwt light van on the cyclecar chassis. *GNG*

RANGER (ii) (US) 1920-1923

Southern Motor Manufacturing Association, Houston, Tex.

This make began as a single model, a 2-tonner with a Wisconsin 4-cylinder engine with Timken worm drive rear axle. It was derated in 1923 to a 1½-tonner , with wheelbase of 11 feet, 4 inches but still with the original components. *GMN*

RANSOMES (GB) 1842-1946

Ransomes, Sims & Jefferies Ltd., Ipswich, Suffolk.

The history of the Orwell Works dates back to 1789 when Robert Ransome, a manufacturer of plows, moved his foundry from Norwich to Ipswich. At Bristol, in 1842, Ransomes showed a self propelling engine capable of traveling at the rate of 4 or 5 miles an hour, this being probably the world's first traction engine. In 1871 four three-wheeled road steamers were built for passenger service with the Indian Government. They were actually delivered with Field tube boilers. The products of the Orwell Works, were, however, primarily for agricultural use although two 8 nhp showman's engines (no. 10608 of 1896 and no.. 20217 of 1908) were supplied, a single and compound respectively. Various other 8 nhp engines were used for road haulage but the firm did not set out to be makers of road locomotives.They did, however, supply a neat if conventional 5 ton two-speed spring mounted steam tractor (complying with the 1904 Regulations)

1908 RANSOMES road locomotive, RAW

equipped with two speeds as standard but with the option of a third. These tractors never achieved the popularity of Aveling's or Garrett's.

In 1920 Ransomes launched an overtype steam wagon incorporating a pistol boiler, built by Ruston & Hornsby of Lincoln, with circular stayless firebox so closely resembling the boiler designed by Frank Bretherton for Robeys, at the nearby Globe Works, as to suggest a license (or plagiarism!). The wagon had two speeds, Ackerman steering, long chain drive and a pressed steel chassis, but the engine performance was of no particular distinction and only 34 were made, one of them an experimental articulated 6-wheeler in 1922. Steam wagon production ceased in 1930 and the last working Ransomes wagon was scrapped in 1948.

Ransomes became interested in electric vehicle construction during the 1914-1918 war, and in 1920 a range of battery electric commercial vehicles was announced. These included trucks, municipal vehicles and tower wagons and were marketed under the name Orwell. Early models had power supplied direct to the front wheels, each of which had an electric motor mounted on it. Manufacture of trolleybuses commenced in 1924 with a single-decker for Ipswich Corporation, and the company

1920 RANSOMES Orwell 2½-ton electric van, BR

1924 RANSOMES 5-ton steam wagon, RAW

became a significant manufacturer of trolleybuses, being particularly successful as an exporter to many parts of the world. The first trolleybuses had been somewhat outdated, particularly in having a tramcar-type hand-operated controller, but later vehicles kept abreast of current design trends. A proportion of Ransomes trolleybus output consisted of three-axle machines starting with a batch built to this configuration for Maidstone Corporation in 1928, but the majority of their trolleybus production continued to consist of four-wheelers. Initially trolleybuses were also sold under the Orwell title, but this practice soon ceased.

Ransomes, range of engineering equipment was so wide that almost every item for their electric trucks and trolleybuses was capable of being constructed in their own factory, and they were by far the most self-sufficient British manufacturer of such vehicles. The only major electrical item normally purchased from other sources was the control gear which was supplied by BTH, Crompton, West and others. Ransomes also had their own coachbuilding shops where other makes of chassis were bodied as well as their own. The manufacture of electric vehicles for road use ceased with the outbreak of war except for a batch of fifty trolleybuses supplied to Singapore in 1946. The company still makes small electric trucks but purely for off the road industrial use, and it continues to make a wide range of farm and agricultrual machinery and undertakes general engineering work. *RAW/OM*

1909 RAPID (i) 1-ton truck, NAHC

RAPID (i) (US) 1904-1912

Rapid Motor Vehicle Co., Detroit, Mich 1904-1905
Rapid Motor Vehicle Co., Pontiac, Mich 1905-1912

The first of the Rapid trucks was a light delivery van with a 2-cylinder engine mounted under the driver's seat with a planetary transmission and single chain drive to the rear axle. This was on a wheelbase of 6 feet, 8 inches, weighed 1900 pounds and cost $1250. For 1906, nine different models were available including 1- and 1½-tonners and a 20-passenger bus. In 1907, there was a single 1 tonner delivery van and two types of 1½ tonners, but no less than five varieties of buses for 12 to 24 passengers. Succeeding years showed a greater variety of commercial cars. The 1909 line used 24 and 36 hp engines and the total of seventeen models included an ambulance, patrol wagon as well as a fire engine and buses of 9 to 22 passengers; the 1- and 1½-tonners were also continued. By 1910 there were only two models of 1 tonners and just one model of the 1½ tonner. For 1910, 1-, 2- and 3-tonners were made. General Motors Truck Corp. absorbed Rapid Motor Vehicle Co. in 1912 and continued the line of 1- and 2 tonners under the trade name GMC. *GMN*

(RAPID) (ii) (I) 1907-1918

Societa Torinese Automobili Rapid, Turin.

Giovanni Battista Ceirano's Rapid company, founded in 1905, was never a major producer of trucks, though a 20-seater bus was entered for the 1908 Italian Industrial Vehicle trials. By this time 25/30 hp Rapid motor water carts (which retailed in England for £900 complete) were in service in Milan and Rome. The commercial models used the 25/30 hp car engine, a 4.6-litre T-head four with separately cast cylinders. Other features were 4-speed gearboxes, shaft drive and solid tires; payload was 4 tons. Wartime Rapid trucks used leftover private-car components, and a slow rundown of the firm's activities came to an end in 1921. *MCS*

RAPID (iii) (CH) 1962 to date

Rapid Maschinen und Fahrzeuge A G., Dietikon ZH

After an abortive attempt to launch a tiny 2-seater passenger car designed by Josef Ganz after the 2nd World War — only one series of 36 cars was completed — Rapid concentrated on the manufacturing of motor scythes. In 1962 the company offered an interesting light 4x4 multi-purpose vehicle, the Alltrac 400. It was powered by an air-cooled MAG single-cylinder ohv engine type 1040 SRL of 391 cc developing 8.5 hp made by Motosacoche, Geneva. This small power plant was mounted in front of the front axle. With a wheelbase of 250 cm the versatile vehicle had a payload of 1.2 ton and was quickly adopted by many farmers in the alpine region of Switzerland. In the following years improved and slightly more powerful models were introduced. The king-size Alltrac 1500 of 1966 with a MWM 1½ litre 2-cylinder ohv diesel engine of 30 hp offering a payload of 3 tons was not as successful. In 1968 the Alltrac 550 could optionally be had with the Lombardini single-cylinder ohv diesel engine of 638 cc developing 14 hp. The heavier Alltrac 1000 received a Lombardini twin-cylinder diesel of 1144 cc and 22 hp.

1975 RAPID (iii) Alltrac 1750 tipper, Rapid

The present program includes the Alltrac 1750 which is equipped with a water-cooled Perkins 4-cylinder diesel of 40 hp. It has a constant-mesh gearbox offering 8 forward and 4 reverse speeds as well as differential locks in the rear-axle and separately engaged front wheel drive. Speed can be varied from 1 to 18 mph. Brakes are hydraulic and the rear axle can be had with single or twin wheels. Payload is 4 tons. *FH*

RASSEL (US) 1910-1912

(1) E.C. Rassel Manufacturing Company, Toledo, Ohio 1910-1911
(2) Rassel Motor Car Company, Toledo, Ohio 1912

Two truck models were made under the name Rassel. One was a 1 tonner with open delivery body and the other, also an open delivery, was a 2 tonner. Both models used 4-cylinder engines, selective gearboxes and double chain drive. Chassis prices were $1700 and $2400 respectively. For 1912, 3- and 5-tonners were added to the range. *GMN*

RASTROJERO (RA) 1952 to date

(1) IAME (Industries Aeronauticas y Mecanicas del Estado), Cordoba 1952-1967.
(2) IME (Industrias Mecanicas del Estado), Cordoba 1967 to date.

The Rastrojero Diesel is made by a Government owned factory which is part of DINFIA (Direccion Nacional de Fabricaciones e Investigaciones Aeronauticas). This is an airplane manufacturing industry which has also made farm tractors, motorcycles, cars and commercial vehicles at various times. The only road vehicles made at present are the Rastrojero Diesels.

The earlier Rastrojero Diesels had a vague exterior resemblance to Jeep pickups. The engine was a 4 cylinder 1,758 c.c. Borgward unit. They had 4 forward speeds and a half ton load carrying capacity. They were made with slight variations until 1967 when a wholly redesigned

1964 RASTROJERO NP62 1-ton pick-up, A.C. Tatlock

model was introduced. The 1967 model evolved towards the present production model with a diesel Indenor XD-4.88 engine which is a unit made by Borgward Argentina under Peugeot license. This engine has 4 cylinders and 1,948 c.c. Transmission also is made by Borgward Argentina and has 4 forward speeds. The vehicle has 0.9 tons load carrying capacity and is made as a light truck, ambulance and large and ugly four door sedan. This car version derived from the light truck is rather scarce and is sold only for taxi use. Latest additions to the line are cab-over-engine pickup, minibus and van. At present IME is experimenting with a 6 cylinder engine but this has not gone into production.

The early Rastrojero Diesel was the NP 62 model and 26,067 were made until this popular vehicle was discontinued in 1967. They are still ubiquitous in Argentina. *ACT*

RATHGEBER (D) 1909-1912; 1951-1952

Jos. Rathgeber A.G., Munich

This firm is a coachbuilder for railroad and tram cars. In 1909 production of trucks was taken up under a Bussing license.

After WW II bodies were built for buses and trolley buses and in 1951 an independent design of coach with self-supporting body was presented. Air-cooled Deutz or water-cooled Steyr engines of 90 hp were available. After suspending this own type the firm again concentrated on coachbuilding. *HON*

RATIONAL (GB) 1905-1906

Heatly-Gresham Engineering Co. Ltd., Royston, Herts.

One of the first motor cabs to run on London streets, the Rational used a 10-12 hp flat-twin engine under a centrally-mounted driver's seat, with two-speed epicyclic gearbox and single chain drive. An unusual feature was solid tires, but these were replaced by pneumatics after a year's service. A total of 13 Rational cabs ran in London, from June 1905 to October 1909. *GNG*

RAUCH & LANG; RAULANG (US) 1922-1935

Rauch & Lang Electric Car Mfg. Co., Chicopee Falls, Mass.

Rauch & Lang had been well-known makers of electric passenger cars in Cleveland, Ohio, but in 1922 they moved to the Chicopee Falls factory of the Stevens-Duryea car where they turned out a small number of electric taxicabs as well as a few with 22.5 hp gasoline engines. Both types came in limousine and landaulette form. They were made

1924 RAULANG electric taxicab, FLP

until 1927, and in 1929 a new model of gas-electric cab was announced. Known as the Raulang, this had a Willys-Knight engine and chassis with a generator and electric motor by General Electric. It was made in small numbers until 1935. *GNG*

RAYNER see Standard (i)

R.C. see Currie

REAL (US) 1914

H. Paul Prigg Company, Anderson, Indiana

This was a $375 cyclecar delivery van using an aircooled, 2-cylinder engine with a friction transmission and belt drive. Wheelbase was 8 feet, 6 inches with trend of 3 feet, and the frame was wood. The stability of the vehicle could be questioned, considering its above dimensions and its clearance, given as 15 inches. *GMN*

RECTORY (GB) 1905-1909

Rectory Engineering Co. Ltd., Sunderland

A few Rectory steam wagons were made using a vertical fire tube boiler with a smokebox superheater, feed being, unusually, by a separate steam pump.

The engine was a totally enclosed compound undertype with countershaft differential and twin roller chain final drive. The wagon was not a commercial success and in September 1909 the whole of the patterns and designs together with one complete wagon, two partially completed wagons and parts for four more were offered for sale. Nothing subsequently was heard of the wagon though the firm, who made auxiliary machinery for ships, went on for many years. *RAW*

RED BALL (US) 1924-1927

Red Ball Motor Truck Corp., Frankfurt, Ind.

The Red Ball was a captive make built by a large transport operator, the Red Ball Transit Co. of Indianapolis. Early units were straightforward assembled jobs created from stock components. Then in 1926 there appeared an ingenious and complex 6-wheeler with drop-frame chassis. This featured the firm's own bogie consisting of no fewer than eight leaf springs in a complex configuration. The tandem was single drive, the rear axle being an idler. A Wisconsin engine was used, and the chassis was intended for passenger work as well as a low-loading van. A few were sold to companies affiliated to Red Ball Transit, but the firm soon withdrew from truck making to concentrate on light-alloy van bodies which were made for some years. *RJ*

1913 REDCLIFFE bus, HD

REDCLIFF (CDN) 1913-1914

Redcliff Motors Co. Ltd., Redcliff, Alta.

Apparently a descendent of the Wallof built in Minneapolis, Minnesota, the Continental-engined Redcliff was available as a 1½-ton truck or bus. About 15 units were built. *HD*

1912 RED SHIELD HUSTLER Model A 500lb truck, NAHC

RED SHIELD HUSTLER (US) 1912

Red Shield Hustler Power Company, Detroit, Michigan

The three models under this flamboyant name were all high-wheelers and they were typical of the midwest of that time. All three were powered by 2-cylinder engines mounted under the body. Typical also was a planetary transmission and double chain drive, with solid tires. Wheelbases for the 500-pound and 1200-pound capacity trucks were 6 feet, 3 inches and 7 feet, 2 inches, respectively. *GMN*

REEVES (US) 1897-1898

Reeves Pulley Co., Columbus, Ind.

Milton O. Reeves was a pulley expert who built five vehicles which he called 'motocycles' between 1896 and 1898, and passenger cars from 1905 to 1910. Two of the 'motocycles' were buses, the 1897 "Big Seven" having three rows of seats in ascending elevation for seven passengers, while the 1898 bus seated 20 passengers with five rows of seats on a uniform level. The drive sat in the second row, and the fourth faced the rear. These vehicles were powered by 2-cylinder Sintz marine engines which drove through a Reeves variable speed geared transmission and double chain final drive. The "Big Seven" saw service in Indianapolis, while the larger bus, proving unsuitable for the roads of South Dakota for which it was intended, was fitted with flanged wheels and ran on the Big Four Railroad from Columbus to Hope, Indiana. *RW*

REGAL (US) 1911-1912

Regal Motor Car Co., Detroit, Mich.

This make, better known for passenger cars, was made in a commercial model for just one model year. The Model LB was a ½-tonner with a 30hp engine of four cylinders and wheelbase of 8 feet, 11 inches. This chassis did not correspond with any which were used for passenger cars. *GMN*

REGENT (IL) 1955-1960

Autocars Co. Ltd., Haifa

The very first Israeli vehicle was based on the *Reliant* Regent IV van, featured a glassfibre body and was powered by an imported British engine developing 36hp. Built either as a van or a station wagon, *Regent* proved the basis for future expansion of Autocars, which produced latter the *Sabra, Carmel* and *Sussita* vehicles. *GA*

1926 REHBERGER 5-ton truck, RJ

REHBERGER (US) 1923-1938

Arthur Rehberger & Son, Newark, N.J.

The Rehberger was an assembled make produced in small numbers for sale mainly in the Newark area. The range extended from 1½ to 5&7-tonners with Buda engines, Brown-Lipe or Fuller transmissions and Timken axles. The 1925 3-ton chassis was available in bus form, with the engine set back, air springs at the front, a lower frame, pneumatic tires and disc wheels. The 5-tonner had a 2-speed rear axle, giving 8 forward speeds in all. Rehberger increasingly concentrated on bus chassis from 1933 onwards, and apparently produced these in a variety of wheelbase lengths until 1937 or 1938. These found a market among smaller bus operators. During the war years they switched to heavy industrial trailers, many for the US Navy and shipbuilders. The firm had plans to re-enter the truck field in the early postwar years with a 1½ to 3½ ton range aimed at the export market. Apparently this scheme was never realized. *RJ*

1934 REHBERGER 30-seater bus, RJ

REISSIG (D) 1912-1914

Automobilwerk "Siegfried" Arno Kohl — Krugel, Reissig nr. Plauen

Based on the type 9/26 PS private car, a van version was also available. *HON*

REKORD (D) 1925-1926

Bremer Rekord Handelsgesellschaft mbH., Bremen

A light van with rear-mounted seat was built by this firm which differed from all other light vans of that period by having four wheels. A 4 or 7hp engine was used. *HON*

RELAY (US) 1927-1933

(1) Relay Motors Corp., Wabash, Ind. 1927
(2) Relay Motors Corp., Lima, Ohio 1927-1933
(3) Consolidated Motors Corp., Lima, Ohio 1933

Backed by Eastern banking interests, Relay became a truck manufacturing combine by acquiring three existing makers, Commerce of Ypsilanti, Michigan, Service of Wabash, Indiana, and Garford of Lima, Ohio. With assets of $10,000,000 the new combine claimed a capacity of 25,000 trucks per year, but never achieved a figure near that. Production was concentrated on the Wabash and Lima plants, and a closely-spaced range of eight models from 1 to 4 tons was announced. They all used Buda 6-cylinder engines and 4-speed transmissions, but while Commerce, Garford and Service trucks had worm drive, the Relay had what was mysteriously called the "Relay Surmounting Principle" which was in fact a slight variation on the internal gear drive which had been so widely used a few years earlier. Relay also used steel spoked wheels in place of the discs of the other three makes. In 1931 Relay expanded its range in both directions, with a 3/4-tonner Continental powered light model and 5 and 7-tonners, the latter a 6-wheeler. None of these was made under the other three names.

1930 RELAY 4-ton truck, NAHC

In 1931 Relay built what was claimed to be the most powerful truck in the world, the Duo-Drive. This giant was a 6x4 machine was powered by two Lycoming straight 8 engines installed side-by-side under a wide hood, each one of which drove one of the rear axles through a separate gearbox of 5 forward speeds and 2 reverse.Either engine could be used separately, driving its own axle, or both together. Output was 275hp, and top speed 60 mph. The Fuller gearboxes were air-controlled, while the Vickers steering and Jones clutch were both hydraulically operated. There was room for one sleeper berth in the cab, a rare feature in 1931. However the Duo-Drive did not have a very long career as maximum weight limits per axle were imposed in many states, besides which the tractor and semi-trailer became a more popular means of carrying heavy loads.

Relay's best production year was 1928 with 639 units, 205 of which carried the Relay name, while in 1929 the total was 679, of which Relays accounted for 511. In December 1932 Relay Motors was forced into liquidation; Commerce and Service trucks were discontinued, but a new owner, Consolidated Motors, tried to make Garfords and Relays for a further year. *RW*

RELIABLE-DAYTON (US) 1906-1909

Reliable-Dayton Motor Car Co. Chicago, Ill.

The first models of this high-wheeler had the engine under the seat which was near the center of a rather long wheelbase. A simple open box at the rear was the cargo area.

Later models were sophisticated with a choice of 15 or 20 hp 2-cylinder horizontally-opposed water-cooled engines under the Renault-style hood and having front fenders and a panel body with a roof as far forward as the dashboard. Steering was by right-hand tiller with a 2-speed forward and reverse shift on the tiller column. Among other things it had lubrication of connecting rod bearings by passages drilled in the crankshaft and an external-contracting clutch (lined with camel's hair belting!)] engaging the flywheel. The frame was ash. All models were chain-driven, the manufacturers claiming a speed of 25 mph. Price was $1100. or about $1 per pound.

Most production was for passenger cars with the trucks getting only limited production. In all, the Reliable-Dayton was one of the better high-wheelers on the market, and it came from a large factory.

The Reliable-Dayton was succeeded by the F.A.L. Motor Co., Chicago, Ill., but it is doubtful that they built any trucks. *RW*

1911 RELIANCE Model H 3½-ton truck, LIAM

RELIANCE (i) (US) 1906-1911

(1) Reliance Motor Car Company, Owosso, Michigan, 1906-1908
(2) Reliance Motor Truck Company, Detroit, Michigan, 1908-1911

The truck models offered by Reliance during its six years of existence ranged from 22-passenger buses to a five-tonner. The engines used in all these models were two-stroke types with two-, three- and four-cylinders. The earliest, the Model F maintained a fin type radiator as late as 1909. The Reliance Motor Truck Company became part of General Motors Truck Company and the brand name was changed to GMC late in 1911. The Reliance 1911 Models K and H were unchanged for 1912, other than the nameplate. *GMN*

RELIANCE (ii) (US) 1917-c 1927

(1) Racine Motor Truck Co., Appleton, Wis. 1917-1918
(2) Reliance Motor Truck Co., Appleton, Wis. 1918-1922
(3) Appleton Motor Truck Co., Appleton, Wis. 1922-c 1927

The Reliance was made in two models, 1½- and 2½-tonners, powered by Buda 4-cylinder engines, with option of 3- or 4-speed transmissions and Badger external gear final drive. Production after 1923 is uncertain, though some lists carry the make up to 1927. *GNG*

RELIANT (GB) 1935 to date

(1) Reliant Engineering Co. (Tamworth) Ltd., Tamworth, Staffs 1935-1963
(2) Reliant Motor Co. Ltd., Tamworth, Staffs 1963 to date

To-day important as makers of 3-wheelers and GT cars alike, Reliant began in a humble way in 1935 when T.L. Williams acquired the design rights of the Raleigh 3-wheeler van. A disused bus garage in Tamworth was taken over, the firm's income being augmented in early days by retail gasoline sales. The first Reliants represented something of a retro-grade step, for a 600cc single-cylinder JAP engine replaced Raleigh's V-twin, and chain drive was used. By 1936 the original 7-cwt model had been joined by a bevel-driven 10-cwt version using a more powerful 747cc JAP unit, while the rear brakes were given Girling actuation. In 1938 the company adopted the 747cc 4-cylinder Austin 7 engine; with it came a 4-speed synchromesh gearbox and all-Girling brakes, but Austin dropped their smallest model within a year. Reliant then took out a manufacturing licence, their first Austin-type unit being produced late in 1939. These were made at Tamworth until 1962; they featured chain-driven camshafts, and (from 1952) full-pressure lubrication. Limited production facilities forced a reversion to 3-speed crash gearboxes.

1951 RELIANT ¼-ton 3-wheel van, GNG

1952 RELIANT ½-ton 3-wheel van, GNG

6-cwt and 10-cwt Reliants were offered in the early post-War years, pressed-steel wheels replacing the original wire type by 1951, when production was running at 40 units a week. 1955 saw a big change: the old Raleigh layout, with the engine in the driver's cockpit, gave way to a conventional configuration inherited from the Regal tourer; at the same time glassfibre was used for the first time on Reliants bodies. Synchromesh, tubeless tires, sliding door windows, and a new coil-sprung front fork also featured in the specification. New for 1958 was the 10-cwt Regent Four, a 4-wheeler model with box-section frame, coil ifs and hydraulic brakes: engine was a 10 hp (ii) Ford. Never seriously marketed in Britain, it formed the basis of the Israeli Sabra, as well as launching Reliant on a new career as creators of simple designs for limited-volume manufacture in emergent countries.

The 1963 5-cwt 3-wheeler range used Reliant's new 600cc ohv diecast alloy engine in unit with a 4-speed synchromesh gearbox. By 1966 special 7-cwt and 10-cwt

1972 RELIANT TW9 ¾-ton 3-wheel pick-up, Reliant

1978 RELIANT Kitten ¼-ton van, Reliant

versions were being made for export, and 1967 saw a new 16-cwt pickup, the TW9. This reverted to the full-front configuration, and introduced the more powerful 700cc engine. By 1970 TW9s were being made in Athens by Mebea at the rate of 300 a year. Subsequent 3-wheeler developments were geared to the car programme, with 748cc engines and all-synchromesh gearboxes on 1974's Robin. Another 4-wheeler van based on the Rebel saloon had only a short run (1971-74); an interesting 1975 production was the Helicak, a 4-door taxi edition of the Robin built under licence in Indonesia by Italindo of Djakarta. 4-wheelers returned to the light commercial range in 1976 with a 6-cwt van based onthe 848cc Kitten, the bigger engine being fitted to the latest Robins as well. These two types represented Tamworth's 1978 commercial vehicle output, while production of the TW9 was taken up by a different company, BTB Engineering of Blackburn, who sold them under the name Ant. *MCS*

REMINGTON (US) 1911-1913

Remington Standard Motor Company, Charleston, West Virginia

The large trucks under this label were five-, seven-and-one-half- and ten-tonners. These all had forward control with 4-cylinder engines and dual sparking plugs. This make was characterized by a hydraulic transmission with progressive gear changes with "any number of speeds forward or reverse". The nature of this apparatus is unknown. The 7½-ton chassis was priced at $5500. *GMN*

RENARD (F/GB) 1903-1913

(1) Societe Francaise des Trains Renard, Paris 1903-1908
(2) Daimler Motor Co. (1904) Ltd., Coventry, Warwickshire 1908-1910
(3) Daimler Co. Ltd., Coventry, Warwickshire 1910-1913

Colonel Renard's Road Train was intended mainly for off-road haulage, his idea being to ransmit the drive to the wheels of each trailer via a worm-driven countershaft and chains. On six-wheeled trailers the front wheels were steerers and the center ones drivers, though on production trains four wheels sufficed. With two trailers a Renard outfit weighed 11 tons and required a crew of 3, but could handle 10 tons of goods or 60 passengers. Speeds of 8-10 mph were quoted.

1910 RENARD road train, Daimler-built, NMM

The first train exhibited at tge 1903 Paris Salon was made by Darracq, and powered by a 60 hp 4-cylinder Darracq engine, but later models used either a 72 hp Filtz (Turgan-Foy) unit or a steam engine, this latter method of propulsion featruing on an outfit sold to Persia in 1904. A few Renard trains were operated in France and Belgium, but sales improved after Daimler acquired a license in 1908. Early Daimler-Renards used a vast 185 × 150 mm sv 4-cylinder power unit, replaced for 1909 by a 9.4-liter 80 hp sleeve-valve six as fitted to some of Britain's Royal cars. There were four forward speeds, and weight of the prime mover was five tons. It carried 200 gallons of gasoline: export models had a supplementary 100-gallon water tank on top of the hood. Too unwieldy for use in Britain (though Daimler used on to haul components between Coventry and Birmingham), it was also expensive, at £3,300. Nevertheless Daimler-Renards found buyers in Australia, Burma, Canada, Indian, Peru and Uruguay, one of the Australian machines being used to haul copper ore from mine to railhead. The machine was not quoted after 1913, but manufacture had probably ceased several years previously. *MCS*

RENAULT (F) 1900 to date

(1) Renault Freres, Billancourt, Seine 1900-1909
(2) SA des Automobiles Renault, Billancourt, Seine 1909-1945
(3) Regie Nationale des Usines Renault, Billancourt, Seine 1945 to date

Louis Renault made his first car in 1898, branching out into commercial vehicles two years later with a forward control van edition of the C-type, using 450cc or 698cc single-cylinder de Dion engines. Pneumatic tires were always standard, though early examples featured handlebar steering. By 1905 vans and trucks for payloads of up to 1 ton were available, the biggest Renaults being based on the 10 hp twin with their own 1.9-litre engine. This year also saw the introduction of the famous 1,100cc 8 hp vertical twins offered as taxicabs or ½-tonners. Design followed the classical Renault idiom with thermosyphon circulation, dashboard radiator, 3-speed gearbox, quadrant change, and bevel drive. This would persist in principle until the end of the 1920s, though four speeds were found on heavier types, and after World War I a selective type shift was used. The little Renault was immensely popular as a cab: 950 were in service in Paris alone by 1908, while in London the General Motor Cab Co. operated a large fleet. Production continued until the War; late in 1914 large numbers of the taxis (the legendary *Taxis de la Marne*) were commandeered by General Gallieni to move his troops and so save Paris from the advancing Germans. They were the first of several generations of Renault taxis to serve the French capital, leading up to the equally indestructible 2.1-litre KZ family in the 1930s.

It was not until 1909, however, that any heavy-duty models were produced, a 4-cylinder 3-tonner being followed by a 5-ton model on similar lines with 6.1-litre engine and 4-speed gearbox; chain drive was tried, but rejected. At the same time the company made its first single-decker bus for Paris, a 21-seater with such unusual features as an exhaust-gas interior heater and pneumatic tires (dual at the front, and triple at the rear), though solids were used when the new model went into general service. Other features of these early Paris buses included a cab-over-engine layout with radiators mounted behind the driver. Also new in 1910 were a cab over engine 3.6-

1911 RENAULT 20-seater charabanc, Renault

1916 RENAULT GZ 3-ton army truck, Renault

litre 3-ton truck and a 4-cylinder cab with 2.1-litre engine. These types, plus some specialized municipal vehicles, made up the 1914 range, though just before the War Renault introduced the EG artillery tractor with four-wheel drive and steering and a huge 4-cylinder engine of 8½ times capacity. During the War years truck and tractor production ran at over 350 units a month, while Louis Renault also masterminded France's first tank program, with a successful light model which was being made at the rate of 300 a month by 1918. This tank, incidentally, was tried abortivly in demilitarized form as a sightseers' bus in Chamonix in 1919.

The immediate post-War range covered payloads from 1 to 7 tons, most of them closely resembling their 1914 counterparts, but in the inter-War years Renault assumed the role of general provider in the manner of the Italian

1920 RENAULT Type Fu 7-ton truck, NMM

Fiat and the German Mercedes. No more 2-cylinder models were made, though by 1920 there was a 10-cwt car-type van with the famous 2,120 cc monobloc 4-cylinder engine, as well as a line of pneumatic-tired coaches, and in 1922 saw a light artic on classic lines, also with the 2.1-litre unit. All engines were fours, with a 7.9-litre engine in the largest 7½-tonners, which (along with other heavy Renaults) featured double reduction drive. Pneumatic tires were standard on all models up to 2-tonners, and optional on most of the big trucks, which latter could be had in forward-control form with twin lateral radiators. Regular catalogued lines included special PSV editions of the 3- and 5-tonners, plus sweepers, refuse collectors, and fire-engines. Renault also made agricultural tractors, shunting locomotives, *autorails,* and industrial trucks. Further additions to the range included a 5-cwt van

1922 RENAULT SH 3-ton truck, NMM

1922 RENAULT J1 Paris bus, Renault

edition of the 951cc 6CV private car, and the Sahara, or MH-type, a light 6x4 with articulated bogie and brakes on all the driving wheels. Once again, power was provided by the 2.1-litre engine, and Renault made good use of the MH, not only offering a fire-engine version, but also using it to do battle with Citroen's Kegresses in the wastes of Africa. In January, 1924, Gradis and Estienne drove from Southern Algeria to the Niger, a distance of 1,600 km, in nine days; between late 1925 and July, 1926, Delingette's 6-wheelers motored from Oran to the Cape. More chequered was Courteville's 1926 expedition from Rio de Janeiro to Lima — though he made it, in spite of having to substitute a secondhand Ford engine *en route!* By 1930 the trans-Saharan transport companies had 113 Renaults on charge, including some sleeper coaches with 6-cylinder engines.

Renault, in association with Scemia, were by now the principal suppliers of Paris's buses. By 1924 single-deckers of driver-beside-engine type were in service; these had 4-speed gearboxes, servo-assisted fwb, double reduction drive, and pneumatic tires, other experiments embracing a trailing-axle 6x2 and a 65-seater 4-wheeler double-decker, which remained a one-off and was used as workers' transport by the factory. Renault also toyed with electrobuses, building a few sightseers' chars-abanc with S.A.C.M. motors in the 1925-27 period. More significant than these last were, however, the high-speed normal control coach chassis, all with servo fwb, and often with the currently-fashionable Weymann fabric body-work. Innovations on the 1927 RL-type coach were a 6-cylinder 4.8-litre engine of car type and hydraulic dampers. This one was capable of 55 mph, but even faster was the later SI, with wheelbase of 19 ft 8¼ in and the immense 9.1-litre 40 CV unit. This rapid Renault coach ran as a works entry in Paris — nice rallies of the period, as well as being energetically demonstrated in Britain by Sir Henry Segrave.

On the goods-carrying side all Renault trucks and vans

1922 RENAULT 12 hp. 5-ton articulated truck, NMM

had fwb by 1926, with servos on all but the smallest, while solid tires were now confined to the heaviest category. 1929 saw the first 6-cylinder trucks, a 7-cwt van and a taxi on the tiny 1.4-litre Monasix chassis, and a new range of 2/3-tonners powered by the 3.2-litre Vivasix unit introduced at the 1926 Salon. On these Renault introduced the novel combination of pump cooling and frontal radiator, the latter feature being universal by the end of 1930. Also new for the 1930 season were some heavy diesel trucks using 7¼ -litre 4-cylinder direct-injection engines. A still bigger 10½-litre six followed in 1931, though the old 40 CV petrol unit persisted, not only in the latest Paris buses (which featured a quick-detachable installation for servicing), but also on the larger of a pair of new 6x4 cross-country chassis with double transverse ifs and 4x2-speed gearbox. 1933 saw two new engines for the medium-duty range, a 4.3-litre 4-cylinder diesel of 45 hp, and the company's first-ever production ohv gasoline motor, with a capacity of 4 litres and coil ignition. These two were available in the YF-type 3½-tonner, while the heaviest Renaults now featured 5-speed gearboxes as standard. 1934 saw servo assistance for steering as well as brakes at the top of the range, the company's first modern forward-control trucks, and a 5.3-litre ohv gasoline engine to replace the old sv fours and sixes, in buses as well as load

1935 RENAULT ABG1 10-ton articulted truck, Renault

carriers and tractive units. Up to 1938 the range covered everything from a 10-ccwt van on the 1½-litre Celtaquatre car chassis up to 12/15-tonners with 12½-litre 6-cylinder oil engines, and normal and forward control PSV chassis for up to 45 passengers. 1936 saw the introduction of another famous engine, the 2.4-litre sv 4-cylinder 85, which developed 48 bhp and was used in conjunction with 3- or 4-speed synchromesh gearboxes in 15- and 30-cwt Renaults, the latter including a forward-control model, the AHS. Also available in 1938/9 were a light van with ifs based on the little 1-litre Juvaquatre sedan, some gazogene trucks (a method of propulsion which Renault had been testing since 1925), and a powerful full-fronted coach using a really big 6-cylinder diesel of 15.7 litres' capacity.

After the Liberation of France, the Renault factories were nationalized, and truck production was successfully resumed in 1945, with 12,000 vehicles (almost a third of the national output) delivered that year. The only normal control type retained was the Juvaquatre van; in the ½-ton class the company offered the forward control R206 with the old 85 engine, 3-speed synchromesh gearbox, and

1939 RENAULT AGKD 4½-ton truck, Renault

hydraulic brakes, their new heavy truck was a 7-tonner with 8.4-litre 4-cylinder engine, and PSV customers were catered for with the ZPD, a full-fronted diesel model closely resembling the 1939 offering. These forward control Renaults were to serve as prototypes for the State-produced Polish Stars of the 1950s. In 1949 came a new unitary-contruction bus with a horizontal underfloor 6.2-litre 6-cylinder diesel engine, 5-speed overdrive gearbox, Gregoire-type auxiliary coil rear springs, air brakes, double reduction drive and servo steering. This was followed a year later by 5- and 7-ton trucks on similar lines; unusual on so big a truck was the steering-column shift, inherited by later Saviem designs. Though a 4-cwt van edition of the rear-engined 4CV sedan made little impression, Renault did better with the Prairie, a conventional 15-cwt model, once again with the 85 power unit; it was also made in 4x4 form, as was the forward control 1-tonner. Improvements to these medium-duty types included hydrovac brakes on the 2½-ton model, and the replacement (in 1953) of the old sv engines by various versions of the 2-litre ohv Freegate car unit. Last of the sv family to depart was the Juva's 1-litre motor, replaced by the 747 cc type from the 4 CV car. These changes plus a 4x4 option in the 7-ton range helped to boost 1954's truck sales to 42,658 units.

1955 RENAULT 7-ton underfloor engine truck, Renault

1956 saw the merger of Renault with the Floirat, Latil and Somua companies to form the Societe Anonyme de Vehicules Industriels et Equipements Mecaniques (Saviem), all the group's heavy goods and passenger vehicles being marketed under the new name from October, 1957. The medium-duty trucks, however, continued as the Renault Voltigeur, Goelette and Galion, while the old Juvaquatre gave way to a new light van in the modern idiom, the Estafette, available as a 12-cwt load carrier or 9-seater minibus. Of unitary construction, it was Renault's first fwd vehicle of any type, other features

1962 RENAULT Galion 2½-ton truck, Renault

1975 RENAULT Estafette pick-up, Renault

including a 4-speed all-synchromesh gearbox and all-independent suspension. Initially the 845cc Dauphine engine (inherited from the last Juva derivatives) was fitted, but from 1962 this was replaced by the R8 of 1,108cc. A car-type van was reinstated in the range in 1962, this being a version of the 747cc fwd R4 with 3-speed gearbox, dashboard shift, permanently sealed cooling, and rack and pinion steering. 1965 saw the integration of the 1/2½-ton trucks into the Saviem program, leaving only the 4 van and the Estafettes to carry the Renault name. The former acquired a 4-speed gearbox in 1968 (open 4x4 military versions have also been produced), and both types were still listed in1978, engines for the small van being of 782cc, 845cc or 1,108cc. The Estafette now used a 1.3-litre 35 bhp unit, while there were additional car-type delivery vans based on the 956cc 5 and the 1.3-litre 12. Payload ratings were 425kg and 500kg respectively. *MCS*

RENNOC-LESLIE (US) 1918-1919

Rennoc-Leslie Motor Company, Philadelphia, Pennsylvania

A 2½-tonner chasis and a tractor were made under this name. The former had a 12-foot wheelbase while the latter had 9-foot, 8-inch. Both were powered by 4-cylinder Buda engines, a four-speed Warner gearbox along with a worm-drive rear axle. *GMN*

REO (US) 1908-1967

(1) Reo Motor Car Co., Lansing Mich. 1908-1939
(2) Reo Motors Inc., Lansing, Mich 1940-1957
(3) Reo Divn., White Motor Co., Lansing Mich 1957-1960
(4) Reo Motor Truck Divn., White Motor Co., Lansing, Mich 1961-1967

Ransom E. Olds is the only man in automotive history to have two companies named after him, both surviving into modern times, and both making passenger cars, trucks and buses. After leaving the Oldsmobile company, Olds with a group of Lansing business men formed a new company in August 1904 and produced the first car only six months later. Reo commercial car production began in 1908 with the introduction of a truck on the single-cylinder 8 hp Model H chassis, this being continued through 1914. The first all-truck Reo came in 1911, having the 4-cylinder engine under the seat, chain drive and pneumatic tires. One of these carried the baggage and equipment for the 1911 Glidden Tour from New York to Florida.

Reo entered the heavy-duty market in 1913 with the 2-ton conventional Model J which continued until 1916. In 1913 electric lighting and starting were offered as standard equipment, a first for the truck industry. The big seller for Reo was the 1-ton Speedwagon which was introduced in 1915 and continued basically the same for ten years and, with extensive modifications, into the late 1930s. The initial engine was a 30 hp 4-cylinder unit driving through a 3-speed transmission and bevel final drive. By August 1919 19,900 Speedwagons had been built, making Reo the largest producer of pneumatic tired-trucks at that time. In about 1920 Reo brought out the ¾-ton Power Wagon with twelve standard bodies all made in Reo's works. Engines and other major components were also made by Reo, which was unusual at a time when so many trucks were assembled products.

1922 REO Speed Wagon light bus, RNE

A 6-cylinder Speedwagon came in 1925, at about the time that Reo began to go after the bus market. The 6-cylinder Model W chassis was intended specifically for passenger work, following on from the popularity of the 4-cylinder Speedwagon chassis with jitney operators. Transit type (so-called "streetcar type") bodies were built by Fitzjohn and parlor car bodies by Fremont, but a great many Reo chassis had bodies by other makers too. It is estimated that about 2400 Model W chassis were sold by 1927 when it was replaced by the FB and larger GB with kick-up frames. More than 1300 FB and GB chassis, mostly for buses, were sold by 1933. Meanwhile the trucks had acquried 4-wheel internal expanding hydraulic brakes by 1928, and came in five sizes from ½ to 3-tons. For 1929 a Junior Speedwagon with 6-cylinder engine was introduced. From 1932 to 1934 Reo had one of the few straight-8 engines in a truck, a 4-tonner. The 6-cylinder Gold

1930 REO Speed Wagon 3-ton truck, Texaco Archives

1936 REO Speed Wagon 3-ton van, NMM

Crown engine made its debut in 1934, when the range ran from 1½ to 6 tons, and the smaller panel delivery vans shared the styling of Reo's passenger cars with sharp V-grille. In 1935 all trucks were re-styled with V-grilles and skirted fenders, and Reo's first cab-over appeared. During 1936 to 1938 Reo buiilt a seven-model range of trucks and buses for the Mack company to sell under the name Mack Junior. The Speedwagon name finally disappeared in 1939, when a new heavy duty range with round-nosed hood and set-back axle appeared that would be made to well into the 1950s. However, financial problems caused the company to be re-organized, and for a while lawn mowers were made to help keep the company going.

Meanwhile the buses continued to be made, the line of conventional culminating in the 3L6H of 1937 with 6-cylinder Buda engine. These were not as widely sold as earlier models, though, as operators were turning more and more to integral buses. Reo's first 'metropolitan' type of bus was the 2LM of 1937, and 3P7 pusher chassis with Fitzjohn or Bender body was introduced in the same year, though unsuccessfully. Once the decision has been made to proceed with a line of integral buses a team of engineers was hired away from Yellow Coach in order to avoid the

1937 REO 3P7 rear-engined bus, FLP

1937 REO (MACK JR.) ¾-ton van, Techniart

1942 REO 29XS 6x6 tractor with tanker trailer, OMM

problems and expense of starting from scratch, and a line of rear-engined buses known as Flying Clouds was produced from 1939 to 1942, but only 170 were sold. During the War Reo sold about 300 buses with front engines and Wayne Mate sectional bodies, mainly to the US Navy. As early as 1943 plans were laid for the 'victory' or post-war bus, to be based on a Continental 427cu in 6-cylinder gasoline engine mounted under the floor. Arrangements were made to have the body built by the Meteor Motor Car Co. of Piqua, Ohio, an ambulance and funeral car builder. Some 969 sales were recorded in three years (1945-47) a small number compared with other manufacturers or with Reo's own production of over 3000 school buses during the same period. A complete assembly line was again set up at Lansing during 1947 to produce a new monocoque series of Flying Cloud buses using underfloor Continental engines and Spicer torque converters. The expensive preparation for this line of buses never paid off as only 101 vehicles were sold, after which Reo withdrew from the bus business.

As well as the buses, Reo built military trucks during World War 2, especially the Series 29 6x6 trucks and tractors built to a common design with Federal. After the war a new engine, the Gold Comet ohv 93 hp 6-cylinder unit was introduced, and non-Reo components included Warner 4-speed transmissions and Timken axles. The new Models 30 and 31 conventionals came in 1948, with full-vision cab and flat grille. GVW was 36000 lbs, and they were powered by 170 or 200 hp Continental engines. Some long-wheelbase 6-wheelers were made for oilfield work. The name Speedwagon made a brief return for the smaller round-nosed pick up and stake trucks, and other small models included the Step-and-Serve round nosed vans, and Merchandiser forward control vans, both for multi-stop delivery. In 1953 Reo introduced liquid propane gas engines, and in 1954 a heavy-duty V-8 truck engine of its own design, and in 1956 they offered their first diesels,

1950 REO 4-ton truck with Barber-Greene asphalt paver, Vermont Dept of Highways

1916 REPUBLIC 1-tonner with bus body and trailer, LIAM

1921 REPUBLIC 2-ton tipper, RNE

1927 REPUBLIC 2-ton truck, NAHC

turbocharged Cummins units being used.

Reo's World War II experience in building military trucks was recognized when they received major contracts to make the new 2½-ton 6x6 Eager Beaver, production of which was shared mainly with GMC, though other firms such as Studebaker made some as well. Powered by Reo Gold Comet or Continental engines, the Eager Beaver remained in production for over 20 years, outlasting Reo's lifespan. In 1957 the company was acquired by White who purchased Diamond T the following year, and late in 1960 moved that operation into the Reo plant as a separate division. For 1961 a new line-haul DC series of cab-overs with hydraulic tilt cabs was introduced in the 26000 to 43000 lb GVW range with 207 and 235 hp Gold Comet engines. In 1962 came the well-known E Series conventionals with a new 200 hp 6-cylinder ohv engine which found considerable favor in the construction industry. At this time Reo had 43 basic models, seven gasoline engines of 130 to 235 hp, fourteen diesels (130 to 335 hp) by Cummins, Detroit and Perkins and the LP-gas engines. A wide range of 6x4, 6x6 and 8x6 chassis were offered as well as smaller two-axle jobs. However, as the Reo and Diamond T ranges were similar in many ways and made in the same plant, White consolidated the two divisions in 1967, and with some face lifts the trucks were continued under the name Diamond-Reo from May 1st 1967. *RW/MBS*

REPCO (AUS) 1965 to date

P.B.R. Pty Ltd., E. Bentleigh, Victoria

Repco makes the "Trademaster auto delivery van", a peculiar milk-van. An open flat-bed with a rear positioned open-top standee-driver location, the Trademaster features many interesting mechanical components, like a Ford Cortina gasoline engine, a Voith automatic transmission, a steel chassis and front disc brakes. The auto gearbox provides one-pedal driving and carrying capacity is 60 crates of milk. A vinyl-fabric tonneau cover is also provided as standard equipment in order to protect the flat-bed from weather conditions. *GA*

REPUBLIC (US) 1913-1929

(1) Alma Motor Truck Co., Alma, Mich. 1913-1914
(2) Republic Motor Truck Co., Alma, Mich. 1914-1916
(3) Republic Motor Truck Co. Inc., Alma, Mich. 1916-1929

Republic began by making conventional light trucks in the 1,500 to 2,000 lb class, and by 1917 had progressed to five models from 1,500 to 7,000 lbs. With production figures of over 10,000 units annually, they were America's largest truck makers in 1918/19, but during the 1920s they were in and out of financial trouble, with several reorganizations. Always thoroughly conventional assembled machines, they used Lycoming, Waukesha and Continental engines, with Torbensen internal gear drive on early models, replaced by Timken or Eaton worm drive axles. During the 1920s the range ran from 1 to 5 tons and included drop frame bus chassis for 16, 20, 26 and 32 passengers. 6-cylinder engines came into the range in 1927. In 1928 Republic acquired the Linn Mfg. Corp., makers of half-track vehicles, and in 1929 they merged with the commercial vehicle side of American-LaFrance to form the La-France-Republic Corp. However trucks continued to be sold under the Republic name in England until 1931. *RJ/GNG*

REX (i) (GB) 1905-1914

Rex Motor Manufacturing Co. Ltd., Coventry

Various models of the motorcycle-based Rexette tricar were adapted for parcelcar duties, some being used for newspaper delivery. Engines were watercooled singles or twins, and there were two forward speeds. The last of the series, listed in 1910, had handlebar steering and a 2-speed hub gear. In 1914 the company launched a new light car powered by an 1,100 cc 4-cylinder sv Dorman engine. Features of the design were worm drive and transverse front suspension, and a light van version was also announced but the War put a stop to any series production. *MCS*

REX (ii) (US) 1921-1923

Royal Rex Motors Co., Chicago, Ill.

This company offered six sizes of truck, all with Buda 4-cylinder engines and worm drive,, from 1 to 5 tons capacity. They were particularly intended for export, and were sold in C.K.D. form. Like the Krit car, the Rex used a swastika as trade mark. *GNG*

REX-SIMPLEX (D) 1910-1921

Automobilwerk Richard & Hering A.G., Ronneburg

Vans and some light trucks of this make were based on the private car models 9/16, 10/28 and 17/38 PS. These types in improved form were carried on until 1921. *HON*

REX VIAPLANE (US) 1932 (prototype only)

Rex Finance Corp., Chicago, Ill.

Five brothers named Fitzgerald organized intercity bus lines in Minnesota during the 1920's, later selling them to larger carriers and buying other bus lines elsewhere in the country. In 1932 the oldest brother, Roy Fitzgerald, designed an International-powered 13-passenger parlor bus, intended to be produced and sold by the brothers' financing and holding company, Rex Finance Corp., and known as the Rex Viaplane. There was also to have been a city transit version, but no buyers were attracted, and only a prototype was ever built. *MBS*

REYA (US) 1917-1919

Reya Company, Napoleon, Ohio

This was a very obscure make of truck made only in a one-tonner version for the above years. Other details are unavailable at present. *GMN*

REYNOLDS (US) 1920-1923

Reynolds Motor Truck Co., Mount Clemens, Mich.

Reynolds trucks were originally made in four sizes from 1½ to 5 tons, with a choice of solid or giant pneumatic tires on all but the 5-tonner which came only with solids. Engines were 4-cylinder Hinkleys, and the 4-speed transmission was mounted independently amidships where it had facilities for power take-offs on either side. Final drive was via a Sheldon worm axle. An unusual feature, also used by Ward LaFrance, was an engine-driven tire pump on the pneumatic models. From 1922 to 1923 only 1½ and 2-tonners were made, still using Hinkley engines. *RW*

REYNOLDS BOUGHTON see Boughton and Chubb

REYROL (F) 1905-1909

(1) Societe des Automobiles Reyrol, Neuilly, Seine 1905-1906

(2) Societe des Automobiles Reyrol, Levallois-Perret, Seine 1907-1909

Early Reyrol light cars were also offered with delivery van bodywork. All had shaft drive; engines used were 6hp singles by Buchet or de Dion, and some small sv monobloc fours of 1½ litres. *MCS*

R.F.W. (AUS) 1969 to date

The R.F.W. Truck Mfg. Corp., Chester Hill, NSW

The R.F.W. was the first Australian-designed and built heavy truck to be made for many years. The initial model was a 4-axle tipper with Scania engine and Bedford cab, but more recent productions have used purpose-built cabs and a variety of engines by Cummins, Detroit, Roll-Royce, Caterpillar or Nissan. R.F.W.s are built to order, and a wide variety of vehicles has been made including road-going 8×4s with single steered front axle, twinsteer 8×4s, a 6×4 bus chassis and cross-country 4×4 and 6×6 for fire crash tender work. The latter has a top speed of 65mph even over rough ground. *GNG*

1976 RFW 6x6 airport fire crash tender, RFW

1914 R.G. ½-ton van, NMM

R.G. (GB) 1913-1914

R.G. Motor Co. Ltd., Islington, London, N.

The R.G. 10cwt delivery van had a 10/12hp 4-cylinder engine mounted transversely behind the driver's seat, driving via a 3-speed epicyclic gear and single chain to the rear axle. The driver sat in a forward control position. The price was £195. *GNG*

RHODE (GB) 1923-1925

Rhode Motor Co. Ltd., Birmingham

Rhode produced a few light vans on private-car chassis, using their own design of 4-cylinder ohc engine. The 5 cwt version used the 1100cc 9.5hp chassis, the 7 cwt being based on the 1232cc 10.8hp. At least one 10.8 chassis was fitted with taxicab bodywork for use in Birmingham. *MCS*

RICHELIEU see Thibault

RICKETT (GB) 1864-1965

Thomas Rickett, Buckingham

Rickett is mainly remembered for his light private steam carriages built from about 1858 to 1864 but in the latter year he constructed for intended use in Spain a pair of road locomotives intended for hauling a 30-seater combined omnibus and parcel van. In appearance these were not unlike some of the smaller railway locomotives of the 1840's and 50's, having plate frames, outside cylinders, a locomotive style boiler lagged in hardwood and a front driving position. Recent researches by Mr. Anthony Heal suggest that the locomotives were not successful. They were unusual, in road practice, in having cylinders of 22 inches stroke. Though the external appearance of the boiler was not unusual, internally it was a double drum water tube type with a flue gas path equivalent to a return flue. Means were provided of clutching each wheel in or out of drive. *RAW*

RIDDLE (US) 1916-1926

Riddle Manufacturing Co., Ravenna, Ohio

This carriage building firm was established in 1831, specializing in hearses; one of these was used for President McKinley's funeral in 1901. In 1916 they started to mount ambulance and hearse bodies (the latter renowned for the high quality of carving) on their own assembled chassis, powered by a 6-cylinder Continental engine. Various types were used, from 50 to 70bhp, the 9-N being standardized in 1923, in which year Riddle adopted steel disc wheels. One of these late models featured in another Presidential funeral, that of Warren G. Harding, but three years later the company went out of business. *MCS*

1917 RIDEALGH steam wagon, R.G. Pratt Collection

RIDEALGH (GB) 1917

J.T. Ridealgh & Co., Bradford, Yorks

This shortlived vehicle was a steam wagon by the designer, J.T. Ridealgh, based on the Summerscales 3-wheeled steam tractor, but it was on 4 wheels and the relative positions of the boiler and engine were amended. It is believed to have been a total commercial failure. Actual manufacture was by Summerscales Ltd. of Keighley. *RAW*

RIEJU (E) 1954-1956

Riera & Juanola S.A., Figueras, Gerona

This motorcycle maker built an experimental delivery tricycle powered by a single-cylinder 4-stroke Fita engine, also made in Figueras. *JCG*

RIKER (i) (US) 1898-1903

(1) Riker Electric Motor Co., Brooklyn, N.Y. 1898-1899
(2) Riker Electric Vehicle Co., Elizabethport, N.J. 1899-1900
(3) Electric Vehicle Co., Hartford, Conn. 1900-1903

A.L. Riker built electric cars from 1896, and in 1898 he began manufacture of electric delivery vans, hansom cabs on similar lines to the Morris & Salom Electrobat, and

1900 RIKER (i) electric delivery wagon, LIAM

heavy trucks. In 1899 he sold his company and the rights to his name to the Electric Vehicle Company who made Rikers at Elizabethport and then at Hartford. The range included cabs, vans, hotel buses and trucks of up to 2½ tons capacity. In 1903 the Riker name was dropped, as the vehicles were similar to Columbias, made by the same company. *GNG*

1916 RIKER (ii) 4-ton coal truck, LIAM

RIKER (ii) (US) 1916-1921

(1) Locomobile Co., Bridgeport, Conn. 1916-1920
(2) Hares Motors Co. Ltd., Bridgeport, Conn. 1920-1921

Trucks with this tradename were previously named Locomobile. The change was to honor the name of the founder, Andrew Riker. Rikers were built only as 3-and 4-tonners on a single wheelbase of 12 feet, 6 inches. Both used the same T-head engine which was Locomobile-built as were the 4-speed gearbox and worm-drive rear axle. Wooden-spoke wheels were retained from the previous named line. Indicative of the outstanding quality maintained in this line of trucks, and always associated with the passenger cars were the bronze castings used for the gearbox and the lower engine parts. *GMN*

RIKUO (J) 1953-c.1956

Rikuo Motorcycle Co., Tokyo

Rikuos (like the pre-War and wartime Sawkyos) were copies of the 750cc V-twin Harley-Davidson motorcycle. The company also built a light, motorcycle type delivery truck. *MCS*

RILEY (GB) 1923

Riley (Coventry) Ltd., Coventry, Warwickshire

The only commercial vehicle offered by this well-known car firm was a 10-cwt van on their 10.8 hp 4-cylinder chassis. Few were made, and it was only listed for one year. *GNG*

RIMPULL (US) 1975 to date

Rimpull Corporation, Olathe, Kansas

One of America's newer makes of off-highway dump trucks, Rimpull began by making replacement components for mining trucks such as axles and power train installations, branching out after three years into complete trucks. These regular proprietary engines but incorporate an exclusive development known as the Quad-Reduction axle which consists of a double reduction differential and double reduction planetary transmission. End dump trucks and bottom dump coal haulers are made, as well as a water truck for road dust control with optional fire fighting equipment. This has a 600hp engine, and the dump trucks run from 600 to 1200 hp with capacities from a 65 ton two-axle to a 170 ton three-axle articulated bottom dump coal hauler. A 200-ton version of the latter is planned for the future. *GNG*

1971 RITEWAY 8x6 concrete mixer, EK

RITE-WAY (US) c.1961 to date

(1) American Rite-Way Corp., Dallas, Texas
(2) Riteway of Indiana, Fort Wayne, Ind.
(3) Arlan Mfg. Co., Arlington, Texas

The Rite-Way is a purpose-built concrete mixer, made originally in 8 to 10 cu. yard models powered by Detroit or Cummins engines and with three or four axles, one or two being tag axles. More recent models have come in 9, 10 and 11 cu. yard models with a variety of engines and transmissions, mostly Detroit and Cummins, and three, four or five axles, all with a single front axle. Six wheel drive, including front axle, was usual though not mandatory. Engines were rear-mounted and concrete discharge at front over the cab. In 1976 the Arlington-built Rite-Way was marketed by the Rexnord Company of Milwaukee, Wisconsin, some of them under the name Rex which was also used for concrete mixer and other trucks on Hendrickson, Diamond-Reo and Hahn chassis marketed by Rexnord. In 1978 Rexnord bought out Arlan and continued it as a division of the parent firm, the trucks still apparently being called Rite-Way. *GNG*

R.O.A. (E) 1952-1970

Industrias Motorizadas Onieva, SA, Madrid

This motorcycle and sidecar manufacturer also made a considerable number of light 3-wheeled vans powered by 197cc single-cylinder Hispano-Villiers engines. Models included the 250 kg Raymar and the 600 kg RC 600L. *JCG*

ROBERTS (GB) 1862

Brown, Lenox & Co., Millwall, London

William Roberts designed a massive coal-fired vertical boilered self-propelled steam fire engine using a vertical engine, for C.J. Mare, the Millwall shipbuilders. The engine was 3-wheeled and weighed over 7½ tons. Drive was by pitch chain and as no differential was fitted tight corners were negotiated by removing the driving pin from one wheel.

The Roberts was the first self-propelled fire engine in London and probably in Britain, but found no other purchasers and the prototype was not duplicated. In its time, however, it was a remarkable machine, capable of delivering 450 gallons per minute and running at 12 to 14 mph on the road. *RAW*

ROBERTS MOBILE TRUCK see Lowloader

ROBERTSON (GB) 1903-c.1912

James Robertson & Son Ltd., Fleetwood, Lancs.

The firm were general engineers and noted makers of steam winches who were drawn into the wagon mania of the mid 1900's. Their vertical boiler used a central firebox jacketed with a water space through which 9 horizontal rows of short radial fire tubes passed to an external flue annulus and thence to the chimney. The compound undertype engine was totally enclosed, 2 speeds were provided and the differential was on the countershaft with twin chain final drive. An interesting feature of the tipping version was the provision of a hydraulic tipping gear operated by an independent steam pump. Dating of building is difficult as the wagons were an incident in the career of the firm. Sales were actively canvassed in 1906/07, languished thereafter and are considered to have been dead by 1912. The Robertson was one of the first steam wagons to have internal expanding brakes on the rear wheels. *RAW*

ROBEY (GB) 1862-1934

(1) Robey & Co., Lincoln
(2) Robey & Co., Ltd., Lincoln

Robeys showed a "Patent Highway Locomotive" at the Great Exhibition of 1862 in which a domed locomotive boiler with overtype engine, having cylinders in the smokebox, drove a large pair of rear wheels by an internally toothed annullar gear. At the same period they were also building chain driven engines, probably mainly aimed at the agricultural market. Some years later the firm briefly took up the box patent design, mainly manufactured by Fowell (q.v.)

The 1896 Act revived interest in steam haulage and, like many other makers, Robeys developed a series of engines, both singles and compounds, of 6, 7, 8 and 10 nhp aimed at the road hauler. These engines incorporated road springs, belly tanks, solid flywheels, enclosed motion and larger journal areas but were not intended for heavy haulage in the same sense as Burrells, Fowlers and Fosters. Subsequently the firm developed (to comply with the 1904 Heavy Motor Car Regulations) a handsome compound steam tractor of exceptionally compact appearance. A single cylinder version (working at 150 psi compared to 200 psi in the compound) was rather underpowered for road-work and not much seen.

About 1905 the firm built a compound undertype wagon with all gear drive, using a vertical fire tubed boiler, having fully submerged tubes. Subsequently they built a very similar wagon using a Belvedere boiler, in which appear-

1924 ROBEY Express steam tractor, RAW

ance was somewhat like a Yorkshire boiler but internally very different. The centrally placed firebox was connected by a single large flue to a smokebox with water jacketed door on the offside, the products of combustion returning by horizontal fire tubes to a true smokebox on the nearside and thence to the chimney. Neither design was a great success and in 1914 the firm built the first of a series of conventional overtype wagons, of the same general design as the Foden or Garrett. In 1919, however, in recognition of the fact that such a design was by then obsolete they launched an entirely new design of overtype, largely designed by Frank Bretherton, using a pistol boiler with stayless firebox and working at 250 psi. The slide valves of the earlier wagon were superseded by piston valves and the crankshaft ran in ball bearings. Three speeds were standard but two speeders were also supplied. By the use of a nickel steel pressed chassis appreciable weight reduction was achieved. Road wheels were of cast steel with solid rubber tires. The 4-wheeler was, at first, rated as a 5-tonner but in 1923 was up-rated to 6 tons capacity. A few rigid 6-wheelers, to carry 10 tons, were made, together with a limited number of articulated 6-wheelers. At the time of writing at least two Robey articulated 6-wheelers survive as working vehicles in dock work at Colombo, Ceylon.

In addition to 266 wagons the overtype design formed the basis of the Robey tandem steam roller, the "Lion" three point roller and the Robey steam tractor. Two tractors and a wagon survive in Great Britain. The last wagon made was sent to Ceylon in 1934. *RAW*

ROBINSON (i) (US) 1909-1920

(1) Thomas F. Robinson, Minneapolis, Minn. 1909-1910
(2) Robinson-Loomis Truck Co., Minneapolis, Minn. 1910-

1913 ROBINSON (i) Model D 2-ton truck, MHS

(3) Robinson Motor Truck Co., Minneapolis, Minn. 1912-1920

Thomas Robinson's first truck was a forward-control 1-tonner known as the Gopher, priced at $1,800. A total of 57 of these were made during his partnership with Freeman L. Loomis, and when he went into business on his own again in October 1912 he offered a wider range, including 1½ and 2-ton trucks. At least one 5-tonner was made in 1913, powered by a 50 hp engine. Little is known of Robinson's subsequent production, but in 1920 he was advertising a utility truck attachment which could convert a used passenger car into a dependable truck. *GNG*

ROBINSON (ii) (US) 1915-1920

Golden West Motors Company, Sacramento, California

This was a continuation of the Golden West tractor and was rated at two tons. It used four-wheel drive and was driven by enclosed silent chains from the gearbox to the driveshafts. It had underslung springs and engine was under a hood. *GMN*

ROBUR (DDR) 1956 to date

VEB Robur-Werke, Zittau, Saxony

The first vehicles to bear this name were normal-control 1½-tonners derived from the pre-war Phanomen and sold under the name IFA-Phanomen Granit from 1949 to 1955. The name was changed to Robur Garant in 1956. In 1960 a new type with forward control known as the L02500 was introduced; it had the same well-known engine with compressed air cooling available as a 3.4-litre gasoline or 4-

1925 ROBEY 5-ton steam tar spreader, RAW

1957 ROBUR Garant 2-ton truck, MSH

1966 ROBUR LO2500 mobile shop, OMM

as special applications such as mobile shops, and current models are known as the L03000. *HON*

ROCHET-SCHNEIDER (F) 1906-1951

Ets. Rochet-Schneider, Lyon

For a long time the name Rochet-Schneider was synonimous with very sturdy, hardworking commercial vehicles. The company was founded in 1894 as a car manufacturer, and included in 1906 the first commercial vehicles in its catalogue. There was a lot of similarity between the cars and the trucks and buses, all using the same four cylinder engines and many other components. This first line of commercial vehicles was produced up to the outbreak of World War I, and their production was resumed again afterwards in 1919. The most widely known model in this range was the CIT 2, a big van with a four-in-line 80 x 130mm engine and chain drive to the rear wheels. In 1922 the first new postwar models were launched, both cars and commercial vehicles, the latter range consisting of two models, a 30-cwt chassis designated CIT and being in fact a new version of the old CIT 2, and a 50-cwt chassis with an 18 hp four-in-line engine. In 1925 a smaller model was added, a 15-cwt vehicle fitted with the 15.9 hp engine of the CIT. Because of their excellent riding comfort Rochet-Schneider chassis gained some popularity as a base for buses for all kinds of purposes. Many were in use as coaches, but the Compagnie Francaise de Tramways on the other had operated a fleet of Rochet-Schneider buses on their municipal routes in the City of Marseilles.

During the early 'thirties Rochet-Schneider started experiments with diesel engines that were built under Austrian Oberhaensli license; they were pre-combustion chamber engines, a bit like the Ricardo and Lanova engines. Rochet-Schneider finally marketed a four-in-line and a six-in-line engine, both with a bore and stroke of 110 x 150mm, of which the larger one was used in a new range

1934 ROCHET-SCHNEIDER 34-seater bus, JFJK

of heavy chassis designated Ajax. This range was produced as an addition to the gas-engined 410 chassis range, though on request the four-in-line diesel could be installed in these chassis that were then designated 375VL or 375MC.

1937 ROCHET-SCHNEIDER Model 420 3-ton truck, NMM

In 1937 a new oil-engined chassis was shown during the Paris Motor Show, the Model 425, again with an engine under Oberhaensli license, to which a ZF gearbox with overdrive was coupled.

The 115 hp Ajax chassis were also still available, as was the tandem-axle version called Centaure, and the 420. Rochet-Schneider, a keen experimenter with alternative fuels, had available gas-producer equipment for its gas-engined chassis, while on certain vehicles even compressed gas was used as engine fuel, carrying the gas in twelve large cylinders at the sides of the chassis.

In 1938, finally, four new diesel-powered bus chassis were launched, particularly for municipal and intercity transport, and named 'Marathon, Phebus, Mercure and Phenix.' In these days, Rochet-Schneider was fully concentrating on the production of buses and trucks, having discontinued all car manufacture in 1932.

After World War II Rochet-Schneider tried to regain their successful prewar position with these same models, however, without luck: in 1951 the company was taken over by Berliet and their production came to an end. The last model year had offered the following types of vehicles: 475 range, Ajax range, Centaure range, Phenix range, and 485 tractor. Payloads ranged from 3.5 to 15 tons, and the engines used were four- and six-cylinder diesels. *JFJK*

ROCKET see Northway

ROCK FALLS (US) 1912-1925

Rock Falls Manufacturing Co., Sterling, Ill.

Rock Falls ambulances and hearses were built from standardized components. Early models used 4-cylinder engines, but latterly various types of Continental Six were fitted, the last models using the big 5.3-litre 6T. Their coachwork was also mounted on other makes of chassis, such as Velie, while between 1912 and 1914 they made a small number of forward-control battery-electric ambulances. From 1920 to 1923 a 1½-ton truck was made. *MCS/GMN*

ROCKFORD (US) 1914
Rockford Motor Truck Co., Rockford, Ill.
The Rockford wau listed in 1914 as building ¾- and 1-tonners as chassis only with custom bodies to suit customers. It is possible this name may have extended to 1916 but this has not been substantiated. *GMN*

ROCKNE (US) 1932-1933
Rockne Motors Corporation, South Bend, Ind.
Studebaker's second compact car make was offered in delivery van form on the cheaper of the two models. This 65 series had a 3.1-litre 6-cylinder engine, and its 3-speed synchromesh gearbox incorporated a free wheel. The name commemorated Knute Rockne, a celebrated football coach who at the time of his death was in charge of Studebaker sales promotion. *MCS*

ROEBUCK (GB) 1930-1934
Roebuck Engineering Co. Ltd., Smethwick, Birmingham
After making a few normal-control 4-cylinder truck chassis in 1930, Roebuck announced a forward-control rigid-6 chassis powered by a 6-cylinder 8-litre Meadows 6EX engine in April 1931. It had a 4-speed gearbox and load capacity of 12 tons. Normal control was available to order. This was a very competitive field for a new company to enter, and few Roebucks were sold, although the make was listed until 1934. *GNG*

ROGERS (US) 1912-1914
Rogers Motor Car Co., Omaha, Neb.
This make was available only as a ½-tonner with an 18 hp engine. The chassis wheelbase was 8 feet, 4 inches and the price was $800. *GMN*

ROGERS UNA-DRIVE (US) 1919-c.1922
Rogers Una-Drive Motor Truck Corp., Sunnyvale, Cal.
This was a 4-wheel-drive truck for 3-ton loads in which power was transmitted to a central transfer box from which shafts led to front and rear axles. The engine was a 4-cylinder Buda. *GNG*

1932 ROKKO 1½-ton truck, BHV

ROKKO (J) 1932-1942
Kawasaki Rolling Stock Co. Ltd., Kawasaki
A branch of the Kawasaki Dockyard Co. (ships, aircraft) this firm built trucks for ten years from 1932. Early Rokkos were straight-forward normal control 30-cwt machines on American lines; diesel-powered models were introduced in 1941. Total production of Rokkos amounted to 4,200 units. *MCS*

ROLAND (US) 1914-1915
Roland Gas-Electric Vehicle Company, New York, New York
This make superseded the similarly-powered Hexter truck. As the name implies, the Roland was electrically-powered with an electrical generator driven by a gas engine. This was made in capacities of three and three-and-one-half tons. The chassis for the latter was priced at $3750. Passenger buses were also offered by this manufacturer. *GMN*

ROLLFIX (D) 1926-1936
(1) Rollfix Eilwagen GmbH., Wandsbeck 1926-1935
(2) Rollfix-Werk Frederic Schroder, Wandsbeck 1935-1936
The layout of one driven rear wheel was chosen for the first tri-van version of this firm. At first it had a very close relation to motorcycle design, but by 1928 it had improved. Engines of 200, 350 and 400cc were used. In 1933 an additional model was offered with one driven front wheel. Here the engine was placed under the driver's seat and the rear axle was driven. Following this layout also an articulated tractor with one-axle trailer was available. *HON*

ROLLS see C.I.E.M.

1977 ROMAN R-10-215 32-ton GCW articulated truck, Roman

ROMAN (R) 1971 to date
(1) Uzina de Autocamioane Brasov, Brasov
(2) Intreprinderea de Autocamioane Brasov, Brasov
The truck factory of Brasov, responsible for SR trucks since the mid-50s, took a license agreement with the French Saviem company and started building a variety of truck chassis to cover the needs of the heavy vehicle class. Built around MAN/Saviem lines and featuring the MAN-developed forward control cab, Roman's range includes two and three axled trucks, tippers, tractors, 4x4 and 6x6 units. Power comes from license-built MAN/Saviem diesels of 135 and 216 hp , while imported Raba MAN diesel were used on earlier models and the fitment of two 135 hp units in tandem was originally planned for the heaviest models. Roman is currently planning to extend its line with the production of an up-to-date city bus, designed again with MAN assistance and featuring a rear mounted diesel engine and air suspension. *GA*

ROMEO (E) 1959-1972
Fabricacion de Automoviles Diesel S.A. (F.A.D.I.S.A.), Avila
This company built forward-control Alfa-Romeo light vans, initially with a choice of Alfa-Romeo Giulietta gas engines or Alfa-Romeo-List diesels, but from 1962 onwards the latter was replaced by a Spanish-built Per-

1960 ROMEO 2 1-ton truck, GNG

kins diesel engine. The Romeo was made in a variety of forms, including delivery van, pickup, ambulance and 9-passenger minibus, the latter in utility and luxury forms. From 1967 Romeos were distributed by Motor Iberica S.A. of Barcelona, and in 1972 this company launched a new model, the F.108, under the name Romeo-Ebro. *JCG*

RONDINE (E) 1955-1963

Compania Iberica de Transported S.A., Madrid

This company made delivery tricycles with single-cylinder 2-stroke engines of 200cc. *JCG*

1898 ROOTS & VENABLES 1-ton truck, NMM

ROOTS & VENABLES (GB) 1898-1905

Roots Oil Motor and Motor Car Co. Ltd., London S.E.

This company was a pioneer of the oil-engined vehicle in Britain, building their first passenger cars for sale in 1897. Their heavy oil van of 1898 used a 6 hp 2-cylinder engine, and had tiller steering and double chain drive. Later various small goods vehicles were made on passenger car chassis with single- and 2-cylinder engines. These included at least one Royal Mail van. Many parts for Roots vehicles were made by the Birmingham Small Arms Company, and from 1902 they were built for Roots by Armstrong-Whitworth. *GNG*

ROSENGART (F) 1928-1955

(1) Automobiles L. Rosengart, Neuilly, Seine 1928-1937
(2) Societe Industrielle de l'Ouest Parisienne, Paris 1937-1955

The Rosengart was a French edition of the Austin 7, the main differences being stylistic. A light van was always offered, and by 1931 this had been joined by commercial tourers and sedans, all on the longer of two chassis options, with semi-elliptic rear springs. Developments of this family remained in production until 1941. An unusual departure of 1933 was a 4-door taxicab evolved by marrying the 747cc engine to the longer chassis used for the diminutive 1,100cc 6-cylinder. Rosengart themselves operated a fleet of these cabs, claiming that their fares were less than half those of rival companies, and this hybrid model was also used as a basis for some lengthy 5-door *commerciales.* Early post-War experiments with large fwd V8 sports sedans were followed in 1951 by a return to the Austin theme on the Ariette, a modernized 5CV with ifs, hydraulic brakes, and rack and pinion steering. Both this and its successor, the similar Sagaie with an aircooled 748cc flat-twin engine, could be had in 10-cwt van form. *MCS*

1908 ROSLER & JAUERNIG 1500kg truck, MSH

ROSLER & JAUERNIG (A) c.1908

Rosler & Jauernig, Aussig (now Usti n. Labem)

Founded in 1896 this company imported French and German cars and assembled cars and motorcycles in the early years of the 20th Century. In 1908 they issued an ambitious truck catalog listing 750kg, 1, and 1½-ton delivery vans, and heavier trucks as follows: 6hp 2 tons, 10hp 3½ tons, 14hp 6 tons and 40hp 20 tons. The latter seems improbable as its stated capacity is about twice that of any contemporary vehicle anywhere in the world. Specially modified 6 tonners were made for breweries. 'Made to order' were buses for 4 to 20 passengers, powered by gasoline, paraffin or electric motors. *MSH*

ROSS AUTO (GB) 1950 - to date

Ross Auto & Engineering Ltd., Southport, Lancs.

Ross introduced two models initially, a 10cwt with 6ft 6in wheelbase and a 25cwt with 7ft 8in, both with a 200AH battery giving a range of 40/50 miles per charge. The "Minor" soon followed, being a diminutive 5/6cwt model with 3ft wheelbase and 100AH battery.

Within a few years these early models had given way to improved types rated at 25cwt capacity and being offered with wheelbases of 5ft 6in or 6ft 6in. During the 1960's the two models were varied slightly and the shorter chassis was marketed as the Beaver at 1 ton capacity while the longer chassis model was rated as a 30cwt and called Major. This model latterly became the Stal-

1960 ROSS AUTO 25 1¼-ton electric milk float, NMM

lion around 1970 and three new models of platform truck introduced being the T1500 for 15cwt loads, the T3000 a 30 capacity model and the T6000 which was rated at 3 tons. All these were carried on 4ft 6in wheelbase chassis. *OM*

ROSSEL (F) c.1899-1900

M.E. Rossel, Lille

Rossel, steam tractors were made for haulage on canals. They had a rear mounted water tube boiler intended for coke firing and a double cylinder horizontal reversing engine placed above the frame amidships. The main axle was above the frame. The differential was on the countershaft, which was geared to the crankshaft and final drive was by pinions. Either end of the countershaft engaging with an internal gear ring on each rear wheel. Two speeds were provided. *RAW*

c.1913 ROTHWELL ambulance, OMM

ROTHWELL (GB) 1905-1916

Eclipse Machine Co. Ltd., Oldham, Lancs.

Tom and Fred Rothwell founded the Eclipse Machine Co. in 1872, manufacturing sewing machines, bicycles and ticket punches for the tramways. The Viscount premises were purchased in 1896, at which time the brothers became involved with E.J. Pennington in the manufacture of cars. Predictably, the cars were a failure but the firm survived and later cars were designed by an engineer from Royce Ltd. The first Rothwell commercial was shown at the Agricultural Hall Show in March 1905 and consisted of an 8-10 cwt delivery van with steel reinforced ash frame and 10-12 hp twin cylindered water-cooled engine. This was followed by 20 and 25 hp 30/35cwt F-head Rothwell-engined models, also available as private cars, although the commercials utilized Renold side chains for final drive. Taxicabs were built on the smaller 10 hp chassis, and in 1910 a cheaper Aster-engined 15 hp delivery van was introduced with live rear axle and 15cwt payload. This was discontinued in 1914, but the 25hp model continued in production until war contracts took precedence in 1916. When Fred Rothwell died, the business was closed in 1918 after about 600 Rothwells of all types had been built. *MJWW*

ROTINOFF (GB) 1952-1960

Rotinoff Motors Ltd., Colnbrook, Bucks.

Rotinoff specialized in heavy road tractors for abnormal loads, and not unnaturally a large number of these found favour with the military as tank transporters, "Queen Mary" aircraft transporters, etc.

Powered by 6 or 8 cylinder Rolls-Royce dieselengines and marketed as the Atlantic GR 7 and Super Atlantic GR7 respectively, these behemoths boasted a chassis weight of up to 15½ tons and no prices were quoted.Also offered was a range of 6 or 8 cylinder engined Viscount models with payloads ranging from 17 to 30 tons. After 1960 the maker's name was changed to Lomount Vehicles and Engineering Ltd and vehicles were known as Atlantics. These were made until 1962. *MJWW*

ROUSTABOUT see Trivan

ROUTEMASTER see Park Royal Routemaster

1909 ROVAL Type A delivery van, NMM

ROVAL (F) 1907-1911

Societe de Constructions de Vehicules Automobile, Levallois-Perret, Seine.

The 12-cwt Roval was a curious little vehicle on which the driver and mechanical elements were concentrated at the rear of a pressed steel frame with integral dash, leaving the entire forward part clear for the load. The 698cc single-cylinder de Dion engine was housed under the driver's feet and transmitted power to the rear wheels via a 3-speed gearbox, a transverse countershaft, and side chains. Rovals enjoyed a brief vogue in Paris as well as bring tried both in that city and in Berlin with hansomtype taxicab bodywork. Pneumatic tires were standard, but there was also a conventional 15-cwt van, the C-type, available on solids. It used a bigger single-cylinder engine of 1,039cc. *MCS*

ROVAN (US) 1911-1914

(1) Kinnear Mfg. Co., Columbus, Ohio
(2) James Boyd & Bros., Philadelphia, Pa

The Rovan was unusual among light commercial vehicles in having front wheel drive. The flat-twin engine was mounted under a short hood, and drove via a 3-speed gearbox which was bolted to the front axle. Final drive was by worm gear. The Rovan came in two wheelbases, 8ft 8in and 10ft 4in, and had a carrying capacity of 1,500lbs. Solid tires were used, and the top speed was 22mph. The price of the standard model was $1,600. *GNG*

ROVENA (E) 1960-1963

Talleres Sanglas S.A., Barcelona

This company made delivery tricycles powered by 12hp vertical-twin 2-stroke engines, under the names Rovena and Sanglas. Load capacity of both types was 500kgs. *JCG*

ROVER (GB) 1906-1915: 1923-1925: 1931-1932: 1948 to date.

(1) The Rover Co. Ltd., Coventry 1906-1932
(2) The Rover Co. Ltd., Birmingham 1923-1925
(3) The Rover Co. Ltd., Solihull, Warwickshire 1948-1976

(4) Leyland Cars-Rover, Solihull, Warwickshire 1978
(5) Land Rover Ltd., Solihull, Warwickshire 1978 to date

Before 1914 there was spasmodic production of Rover light vans, beginning with a 2-cwt type on the 6hp single-cylinder car chassis at £140, and including a commercial version of the 1911 12 hp sleeve-valve twin. In 1907 the company listed a 12hp 2-cylinder shaft-driven cab, but any chances it had were scotched by an unfortuante company promotion, the Rover Motor Cab Syndicate, whose ambitious plans never got off the ground. Between 1923 and 1925 there was a commercial variant of the popular 8hp aircooled twin with worm drive, made in Birmingham. Another brief sally into vans took place in 1931, when the principal offering was a 10-cwt machine based on the ohv 10/25hp saloon: the companion 5-cwt model using the mechanics of the sub-utility 2-cylinder rear-engined Scarab progressed no further than the Rover stand at Olympia. 1948, however, saw Britain's answer to the Jeep, the 4x4 Landrover with a short 6ft 6in

1959 LAND ROVER 88 pick-up, Rover

wheelbase and a 1.6-litre F-head 4-cylinder engine. The half millionth was sold in 1966, and production reached the million mark in June, 1976. In the course of its career it served with the military or paramilitary forces of over a hundred countries, as well as being applied to such duties

1963 LAND ROVER 1½-ton truck, Rover

as wrecker, ambulance, refuse collector, fire engine, police patrol car, armored car, and snowplow. In addition there have been tracked and air-cushion prototypes, and in 1978 the model was being assembled under licenses in 19 countries, from Australia to Zambia. Some of these licenses have evolved their own sub-variants, notably Minerva of Belgium in the early 1950's, and Santana in Spain.

Long wheelbase models were added to the range in 1954, and a forward control type in 1962. Engine capacity and power have increased: to 2 litres in 1954 and 2.3 litres, with full ohb, in 1962, while Roverbuilt diesels have been a regular option since 1957. Overdrive became available in 1975, and at long last in 1977 the vehicle was given an all-syncromesh gearbox. In 1978 guise the standard wheelbases were 7ft 4in and 9ft 1in. and standard power units the 2.3-litre gasoline four, a 62bhp diesel of like capacity, and a 2.6-litre F-head gasoline six. In the military range were an air-transportable short chassis gasoline type weighing only 2,600 lb stripped, and a forward control model using Rover's 3½-litre V8 engine. 1970 saw the introduction of the V8 Range Rover with permanently engaged four wheel drive, but though this is essentially a private car, commercial adaptations have followed, notably the 6x4 trailing-axle fire engine evolved by Carmichael of Worcester in 1971. *MCS*

1976 RANGE ROVER Carmichael Commando 6×4 fire engine, GNG

1920 ROWE V-8 3-ton speed truck, Mrs. Cameron Mateer

ROWE

(1) Rowe Motor Co., Coatesville, Pa. 1911-1912
(2) Rowe Motor Mfg. Co., Coatesville, Pa. 1912-1913
(3) Rowe Motor Mfg. Co., Downington, Pa. 1914-1918
(4) Rowe Motor Mfg. Co., Lancaster, Pa. 1918-1925

After unsuccessful attempts to manufacture 5-cylinder air-cooled automobiles in 1908 and 1910, Rowe turned to trucks in 1911. The first model, of 1500-pound capacity, had a 25 hp 5-cylinder water-cooled engine. When Rowe turned to the Wisconsin 4-cylinder engine in mid-1911, the price of the chassis was cut by $700. A complete line of trucks from 1500-pound to 5-ton capacity was offered from 1912, with chain drive on the heavier models until worm drive became standard in 1915. All models had 4-speed transmissions.

Unusual models included a 6-cylinder 5-ton c.o.e. truck offered in 1912, show models with a primitive form of "air-bag" suspension in 1913, and a chassis fitted with Farrell hydraulic transmission in 1921. Rowe's most interesting post-war model was the Model GW 3-ton truck fitted with pneumatic tires and powered by the Herschell-Spillman V-8 engine.

Rowe fitted bus bodies to several models including the Model GW V-8 and the 2-ton chassis fitted with pneumatic tires. Some Hercules and Continental engines were fitted after the war. Production peaked in 1922 with some 900 trucks built. After a fire destroyed the main assembly shops in 1923 the firm declined rapidly. *DJS*

1958 ROWE HILLMASTER 8-ton truck. OMM

ROWE HILLMASTER (GB) 1953-1962

(1) Rowe's Garage Ltd., Dobwalls, Liskeard, Cornwall 1953-1955
(2) M. G. Rowe (Motors) Ltd., Doublebois, Cornwall 1955-1962

Rowe's were coach operators who built their own design of chassis in 1953. This had a Meadows 4DC 330 5.43-litre diesel engine, 5-speed Meadows gearbox and Moss rear axle. In the first prototype this engine was mounted vertically at the front of the chassis, but by September 1954 it had been relocated horizontally under the floor amidships. At the same time a goods chassis was announced with a vertical engine mounted below the driver's seat in a position further back than in a conventional front-engined vehicle. The 7-tonner had a Meadows engine similar to the coach, and in 1956 a 9-tonner with Meadows 6DC 500 135bhp 6-cylinder engine was added. Although Rowe's had been coach operators, the passenger side of the business was gradually dropped (only five psv chassis were built), but goods vehicles proliferated in variety during the next five years. In 1958 the range covered 6 to 10-ton 2-axle chassis and 15-ton articulated 3-axle models, with Meadows, Gardner, Leyland and A.E.C. engines offered. In all, with varying wheelbases, there were 76 models in the 1958 range, far too many for a small manufacturer, though probably not all were made. A 14½-ton 6 x 4 chassis with A.E.C. or Meadows engines, Eaton axles and Hendrickson suspension was offered for 1959, and this was continued to the end of the company's life, along with 6 to 10 ton 4-wheelers. Rowe's sales were limited mainly to local Cornwall firms, especially those in agricultural business, pig food manufacturers and horse transporters. *GNG*

ROYAL (i) (US) 1914-1919

Royal Motor Truck Company, New York, N. Y.

This line of large trucks began with two types, of 3½ and 5 ton capacities. In 1916, these two models were offered with worm drive as an option to the double chain drive which previously had been standard. For the last model year on record, an incredible line of eight different capacities were offered: 1, 1½, 2, 2½, 3½, 5, 6, and 7 tons. All these types used four-cylinder Wisconsin engines with Timken worm-drive rear axle units. *GMN*

1925 ROYAL (ii) Model A bus, MBS

ROYAL (ii) (US) 1923-1927

Royal Coach Co., Rahway, N.J.

This company was organized by three prominent New Jersey bus operators to build a bus to New Jersey specifications, which were at that time unusually rigorous. As a basis they used the Ace bus chassis manufactured by the American Motor Truck Company of Newark, Ohio, and in fact hired two American Motor Truck executives as general manager and chief engineer. Chassis were assembled and bodies constructed at Rahway. Waukesha engines were used. Model A was a 29-passenger bus and Model D was slightly smaller; the letters B and C were apparently skipped because Ace was building buses with those designations. Late in 1927 Royal announced the Model E, an improved A, but it does not appear that any were built. Total production was about 50 buses. *MBS*

ROYAL ENFIELD (GB) 1935-1939

Enfield Cycle Co. Ltd., Redditch, Worcs.

Like a number of motorcycle makers, Enfield made a 3 cwt 3-wheeled parcel carrier using the rear portion of their smallest cycle, the 225 cc single-cylinder air-cooled 2-

stroke. The top speed ws 25-30 mph, and the price complete a very modest £149 15/-. *GNG*

ROYAL REX see Rex (ii)

ROYAL SCOT (GB) 1923
Knightswood Motors Ltd., Anniesland, Glasgow
The Royal Scot was a light 3-wheeled trade carrier with a payload of 2½-cwt. It was powered by a 350 cc Barr & Stroud single-cylinder sleeve valve engine, and had a Burman gearbox and channel steel frame. The driver sat on a saddle behind the box carrier, and steered by a vertical wheel and horizontal steering column. *GNG*

1908 ROYAL WINDSOR 1-ton van. NMM

ROYAL WINDSOR (GB) 1906-1908
Windsor Motor & Engineering Co. Ltd., Windsor, Berks.
This company made a 1-ton van powered by a 12 hp 2-cylinder engine, with 3 speeds, chain drive and solid tires. For 1907 a 10 cwt model powered by a 9 hp 2-cylinder engine was added; this van had pneumatic tires. *GNG*

R.R.C. see Rubber Railway

R-S (US) 1915-1916
Reading-Standard Company, Reading, Pennsylvania
This make was typical of several brands of three-wheel parcel vans of the period. The R-S used a Reading-Standard motorcycle engine mounted under the driver's seat, along with a three-speed gearbox and single chain-drive to the one rear wheel. Its parcel box, located over the front axle had capacity of one-third ton. *GMN*

1972 RUBBER RAILWAY 8×6 truck, GB

RUBBER RAILWAY (CDN) 1970 to date
Rubber Railway Co., Cambridge, Ont.
This truck was as curious in design as it was in name, for it was a 4-axle machine articulated in the center of the frame. There was no conventional steering gear, and a turn of the steering wheel directed the flow of hydraulic fluid to one of two cylinders connecting the front and rear frames. The frame hinged about a pivot pin and the action of the cylinders enabled the vehicle to steer. There were dual wheels on all four axles, three of which were powered. The engine was a Cummins VTO-903 320 hp diesel. Most RRCs, as the truck is sometimes called, have been supplied for concrete mixer work, but a dump truck has also been made. Up the the end of 1975 production had reached about 100 units. *GNG*

RUGBY see Star (ii)

RUGGERI (I) 1967-1968
Officine Enea Ruggeri, Brescia
The Ruggeri was a 4½-ton low loader forward control truck using an O.M engine and gearbox. Initially an O.M cab was used as well, though it was intended to replace this with one of Ruggeri's own design. The make did not see series production. *MCS*

RUGGLES (US) 1921-1928
Ruggles Motor Truck Co., Saginaw, Mich.
The Ruggles truck was made in various sizes from ¾-ton to 3-tons, and was unusual for a small firm in that at least some engines were of the company's own manufacture, up to 1924. Thereafter proprietary units by Hercules and Lycoming were used. Ruggles also made a number of bus chassis in sizes from 16 to 29 passengers, the latter being made from 1926 to 1927 and using a Wisconsin engine. From 1921 to 1926 Ruggles had a Canadian assembly plant at London, Ontario. *GNG*

RUMELY (US) 1919-1928
Advance Rumely Thresher Co., LaPorte, Ind.
From 1919 to 1923, the Rumely was a 1½-tonner assembled with standard parts including a Buda 4-cylinder engine, Fuller 3-speed gearbox and Sheldon worm-drive rear axle, on a wheelbase of 12 feet. For the period 1924-1927, a change in engine size was the only improvement. This company was better-known for the manufacture of agricultural tractors. *GMN*

RUMI (I) 1952-c.1958
Fonderie Officine Rumi, Bergamo
Better known for their Formichino scooter, Rumi also made light 3-wheeled *motocarri* with two driven rear wheels. The engine was a 125cc flat-twin 2-stroke in a fully enclosed mounting under the driver's seat, payload was 300kg, and other features were a 4-speed gearbox and uncoupled hyromech brakes. *MCS*

RUMPLER (D) 1926-1931
Rumpler Vorntriebs-GmbH., Berlin
After his revolutionary although not successful tear-drop shaped private cars with rear-mounted engine Rumpler turned to front-drive and used this principle mainly for commercials. A prototype appeared in 1926. Independently sprung axles were used. Production during all the years was not very significant. *HON*

RUSH (US) 1915-1918
(1) Rush Delivery Car Co., Philadelphia, Pa. 1915-1916
(2) Rush Motor Truck Co., Philadelphia, Pa. 1916-1918
The Rush was an assembled truck fitted with a 17hp Lycoming 4-cylinder engine, cone clutch, and bevel drive. A progressive rise in chassis price from $625 in December 1915 to $895 in November 1917 put the firm out of business shortly thereafter. *DJS*

RUSHTON (GB) 1929-1935

(1) Rushton Tractor Co.(1929) Ltd., Walthamstow, London, E.17

(2) Agricultural & Industrial Tractors Ltd., St. Ives, Hunts.

The Rushton tractor was originally assembled in part of the old A.E.C. works at Walthamstow. It was powered by a 4.4-litre 4-cylinder engine designed to run on gasoline, oil or paraffin. On the latter fuel it developed 29bhp, and gave a top speed of 12mph when towing a 8-10 ton load. The road tractor ran on pneumatic tires and could be fitted with a cab, while other versions were a wheeled agricultural tractor with steel wheels, and a crawler tractor.*GNG*

RUSSELL (i) (GB) 1833-c.1835

Grove House Engine Works, Edinburgh

Scott Russell (1808-82) designed six carriages for the Steam Carriage Company of Scotland to run an hourly service between Glasgow and Paisley, carrying 26 passengers. The service began in April 1834 and ran for four months until the turnpike authorities began to obstruct them with loose road metal. A fatal accident caused their running to be stopped by court order and it was not resumed, the coaches ultimately being sold.

Russell used a very light multitubular copper boiler with flat sides heavily stayed. The twin cylinders (12" diameter × 12" stroke) were vertical, the piston rod passing out through the top cover to a cross head, the latter being linked by twin connecting rods to separate crankshafts beneath the cylinders with gear drive to the axle. A separate tender for coke and water was hauled and these tenders were exchanged at fueling points.

In 1835 Russell became manager of Caird's shipyard at Greenwich and thereafter devoted his talents to shipbuilding. *RAW*

c.1909 RUSSELL (ii) ½-ton screen express truck, GB

RUSSELL (ii) (CDN) 1905-1914

(1) Canada Cycle & Motor Co. Ltd., Toronto, Ont. 1905-1911

(2) Russell Motor Car Co. Ltd., Toronto, Ont. 1911-1914

The first Russell trucks were light 2-cylinder delivery vehicles, and in 1906 a ½-ton 4-cylinder truck was introduced. A year later the range also included sightseeing buses, police patrol cars, ambulances and fire engines. Beginning in 1910 truck production concentrated on a ¾-ton delivery vehicle. During World War 1 Russell built 40 armoured cars on the 4-wheel drive Jeffery Quad chassis. *HD*

RUSSOBALT SU 1908-1915

Russko-Baltyskij Waggonyj Zavod-Riga (Latvia)

Though little is known of the commercial product of this

1909 RUSSO BALTIC Model M 2-ton truck, MHK

plant, at least three types of trucks were offered including the Model T, in 1913, with 60 hp, chain-drive, fabric top and 20 km/h. *BE*

RUSTON PROCTOR (RUSTON & HORNSBY) (GB) 1897-1930

(1) Ruston Proctor & Co. Ltd., Lincoln 1897-1918

(2) Ruston Hornsby & Co. Ltd., Lincoln 1918-1930

Rustons designed a 3 ton single cylinder steam tractor to comply with the 1896 Act but like most of its genus it had little commercial impact. Their compound 4 ton four-shaft tractor, known as the "Lincoln Imp" enjoyed somewhat better success, however and it continued nominally in production until the mid-twenties when all steam vehicle production was dropped in order to concentrate upon oil engine manufacture, the manufacture of their steam rollers being sub-contracted to their associate Ransomes of Ipswich.

Rustons, however, made the boilers for Ransomes' steam wagon up to 1930 and one of these wagons ran under Ruston maker's plates. They used one of the Ransomes/Ruston wagons for works transport until 1948. *RAW*

1952 RUTLAND Condor 7/8-ton chassis, OMM

RUTLAND: MANTON; MTN (GB 1947-1957

(1) Manton Motors Ltd., Croydon, Surrey 1947-51

(2) Motor Traction Ltd. and Waggon Rutland Ltd., New Addington, Surrey 1952-1957

Manton Motors were Commer agents in Croydon before the Second World War, after which the son of the owner started in business on his own as a commercial vehicle repairer. With strong Government incentives to the commercial vehicle industry to make export chassis Frank Manton produced a rugged and simple truck with Perkins, Meadows or Gardner engines which sold well in Spain. Around sixty were produced with a few going to home customers.

To avoid confusion with the Commer agency that had put up much of the working capital, the name of the vehicle was changed to Rutland in 1952 though most of the 75% of chassis sold for export went under the name of MTN, an abbreviation of Manton. Rutland vehicles were normally one-off designs to operators, requirements and included the 7/8-ton Albatross 4-wheeler, the conventional Troubador 4-wheeler with Perkins R6 engine and based on a chassis frame usually supplied with Gardner engine, and the twin steer Condor and Perkins engined Stuka. The latter was a 65 mph 8-ton chassis originally designed in 1952 for high-speed fish transport in Spain.

Passenger chassis were also built including 20 for Karachi and 2 advanced rear engined Clipper chassis in 1954 and 1955 with Perkins and Meadows engines. Other special products included 4 x 4 and 6 x 6 transport and crane-carrier chassis, a Leyland-powered 6-wheeler exhibited at the 1956 London Commercial Motor Show and 6-ton low-loaders for milk transport. *OM*

RYDE (GB) 1904

Ryde Motors Ltd., West Ealing, Middx

This company made two models of passenger cars, powered by 10hp flat twin or 14/16hp vertical 3-cylinder engines. They had 3-speed gearboxes and shaft drive, and both were available with light van bodies. *GNG*

RYDER (US) 1973 to date

Ryder System, Miami, Fla.

Designed by Dean Hobgenseifken, the Ryder is an unconventional line-haul tractor with aerodynamic cab with air foil spoiler to reduce front turbulence on the semi-trailer. Engines are a choice of Detroit Diesel 6-71, 6-71T, 8V-71T or Cummins VT 903, and transmission is a Fuller

1975 RYDER tractor, Ryder

RT910. The engine is mounted under the fifth wheel, and the whole power train including twin radiators, engine, transmission and rear end, is mounted on a separate tubular frame between the main aluminum frame members. This makes removal for maintenance exceptionally easy.

The prototype was called the Paymaster, but the name was changed when the Ryder system acquired the patent rights and ordered ten tractors to be built for them by the Hendrickson Mfg. Company. These are leased to Ryder System Truck Rental customers for evaluation. *RW*

RYKNIELD (GB) 1903-1911

(1) Ryknield Engine Co. Ltd., Burton-on-Trent, Staffs 1903-1906

(2) Ryknield Motor Co. Ltd., Burton-on-Trent, Staffs 1906-1911

The Ryknield had the backing of local brewery interests, and several such companies, notably Bass and Truman, Hanbury, Buxton, were among the firm's customers. Though private cars were listed up to 1906, trucks were always the primary interest. The initial 1-tonner was a simple affair using a 10hp 2-cylinder engine, lt magneto ignition, shaft drive, and solid tires; there were only two forward speeds, and the model remained in production until 1905, when a 35hp omnibus chassis was announced, examples of this being sold to Leeds and Tomorden as well as to the Great Central Railway. The 8.1-litre F-head 4-cylinder engine featured dual ignition and twin carburettors (the second one was for running on paraffin); it was also easily removable for servicing. The shaft drive

1910 RYKNIELD 5-ton truck, WB

was unusual, and special features included a screw-down hold for the clutch, and an auxiliary brake controlled by the conductor from the rear of the bus. Some Ryknields had special smokers' seats on their rear platforms. A cab-over-engine bus was a later addition to the range, while from 1906 the 4-cylinder chassis was used for 2-, 3- and 5-ton trucks. New sv Ryknields were announced in 1909, the 30 cwt model using a 20bhp 3-litre 2-cylinder engine, while the 3-tonner was a 6.1-litre four, and the 5-tonner had a 4-speed gearbox and an even bigger 9.8-litre engine. It cost £635. That year 40 Ryknield buses were sold to Brussels, but the company, which had already weathered a financial storm in 1905, went down for good in 1911. Baguley Cars Ltd. acquired not only the factory, but also the services of P. Salmon, their Chief Engineer. *MCS*

RYTECRAFT see Scootacar

1930 S & S Signed Sculpture funeral coach, CP

S and S (US) 1907-1935

Sayers and Scovill Co, Cincinnati, Ohio

This firm of carriage builders, established in 1876, had made a speciality of horse drawn hearses before turning to the internal combustion engine. Curiously, however, their first motor vehicle, sold under the Sayers and Scovill name, was a 2-ton chain-driven forward control truck with under-seat engine. Vertical 4-cylinder power units (initially of aircooled type) were used, and the model was still offered in 1912, by which time ambulance and hearse prototypes had been built. These vehicles, always known as S and S, utilized the company's own chassis, and series production got under way in 1913 with a range of Lycoming-and Continental-powered types. The latter make was standardized in 1915, and fitted also to their private cars, which carried the Sayers name and were offered from 1917 to 1923. By 1926 S and S professional cars had 5.4-litre 6-cylinder engines, but fwb were not fitted; they were, however, standardized by 1928, when the firm adopted Continental's 5.3-litre 85bhp straight-8. A sensation was created by the Signed Sculpture hearse of 1929, which cost $8,500; it followed the town car style, with sculptured bronze side panels depicting an Angel of Mercy. In 1930 ambulances of town car type were available, and late S and S machines had a truly Classic appearance, with louvered hoods, twin trumpet horns, and dual sidemounts in cellulosed covers. Synchromesh gearboxes and ride control dampers made their appearance in 1931, when engine output was up to 118bhp. From 1933 the Continental 8 gave way to an ohv Buick unit, and 1935 saw a cheaper line of lengthened Oldsmobiles alongside the regular models. A year later the vehicles were virtually pure Buick, albeit camouflaged by S and S hubcaps and the characteristic datemarks on the radiator grille. In 1938 the company forsook Buicks in favor of Cadillac chassis. S and S were reorganized as Hess and Eisenhardt in 1942, but the name survives on a comprehensive range of Cadillac-based ambulances and hearses. *MCS*

SABELLA (GB) 1914

Sabella Motor Car Co Ltd, Camden Town, London N.

The Sabella was a typical cyclecar with 10hp V-twin J.A.P. engine and belt drive, which was also offered in light van form. *GNG*

1968 SABRA Dragoon 4x4 light truck OMM

SABRA (IL) 1960-1970

Autocars Ltd., Haifa

The first Israeli factory that marketed Regent vehicles, was revived in 1960 under the Sabra trademark, named after Israel's typical cactus tree. A redesigned range included vans, pick ups and station wagons, always with fiber glass bodies and imported British engines of 41 hp and later 53hp horsepower. Production was assistedby the Reliant company of England, but during the de-cade Autocars started their cooperation with Triumph, taking from them technical assistance, engines and other components. The best result of this cooperation, though, was the introduction of the Dragoon 4 × 4 vehicle, which was based on an early Triumph experimental model known as Pony. Dragoon proved a versatile utility, agricultural and even military vehicle with its 56 hp gasoline engine, permanent front wheel drive and optional all-wheel-drive, high ground clearance, largeloading deck and fiber glass open top cab. The Sabra name was dropped ten years later in favor of Carmel, under which trademark Autocars continued their life. *GA*

SACHSENBERG (D) 1943-1944

Gebr. Sachsenberg A.G.; Dessau-Rosslau

This firm built a few steam tractors during WW II. The design principles and shape of this type to some extent resembled the LOWA tractors (see IFA). *HON*

1959 SADRIAN Articulado 1000kg 5-wheel articulated truck, GNG

SADRIAN (E) 1956-1962

Adrian Viudese Hijos, SRC, Murcia

This company made small motorcycles during the Civil War period, later supplementing these with delivery tricycles powered by Hispano-Villiers engines of 125cc and 197cc capacity. An unusual model was an articulated 5-wheeler, using the motor tricycle as the tractive unit. Payload of this model was 1 ton. *JCG*

S.A.F. (D) 1905-1911

(1) Suddeutsche Automobilfabrik GmbH., Gaggenau 1905-1910

(2) Benz-Werke GmbH. vorm Suddeutsche Automobilfabrik, Gaggenau 1910-1911

To designate this firm is a bit difficult as several forms appear. It developed out of Bergmann's Industriewerke which was known for its friction-driven Liliput cars and vans. From 1905 it became known as S.A.F. but very often the word Gaggenau appeared on the radiators. Also used were S.A.G. and Safe.

The firm specialized in commercials. When in 1906 the German Imperial Mail started to motorize their stagecoach lines they chose S.A.F. buses which were put into service all over Germany. Also available were line and excursion buses and also in 1906 some double-deck buses were ordered for the Berlin bus company. On most models the driver's seat was above the engine which gave additional capacity for passengers or freight. A speciality were tractors (e.g. for timber transport) and fire service vehicles. Special developments were trucks and trailers for a total payload of 25 tons which were delivered to Austria for transporting material for fortress-building in the Alps. In 1907 Benz bought the firm but the old name was retained until 1910 and vehicles were marketed as S.A.F. or Gaggenaus until 1911. Benz concentrated all commercial vehicle activities in Gaggenau and the plant is today owned by Mercedes-Benz. It is now entirely with production of the Unimog. *HON*

SAFEWAY see Six Wheel

1907 SAFIR 3-ton truck, FH

SAFIR (CH) 1907-1908

Safir AG, Zurich

This company built two truck chassis under Saurer license, a 30hp shaft drive and 50hp chain drive. Most models used the Saurer exhaust-operated brake and compressed air starter. Few were made, and Safir's main claim to fame was the development of the world's first small diesel engine suitable for road vehicle use, though they did not in fact mount this in a truck because of the company's closure in 1908. *FH*

SAF-T-CAB see Checker

1908 S.A.F. 6-ton truck, BHV

S.A.G.E. (F) 1908

Societe Anonyme des Generateurs Economiques, Paris

The S.A.G.E. was built under license under the German Stoltz patents. A steam bus built by this maker attended the Paris Commercial Show in 1908 and a 5 ton truck was on exhibition. The 4-cylinder compound V-engine had cam operated poppet valves. *RAW*

1903 SAGE 1-ton truck, Autocar

SAGE (F) 1902-1906
Ateliers P. Sage, Paris

The first Sage cars were made in 1900. Two years later their Abeille-engined 4-cylinder model could be had with convertible tonneau/truck bodywork, but more serious commercials followed in 1903. These were of driver-over-engine type with 4-speed gearboxes and chain drive, and came with a variety of 4-cylinder engines by Abeille, Aster, Brouhot or Mutel. Later Sages catered for payloads of up to 2½ tons, and among options were aiv or moiv power units, as well as a further choice of proprietary engine, the Filtz. From 1905 a range of gas-electric cars was also offered, though it is not known if any trucks were fitted with this transmission. *MCS*

S.A.I.M. (I) 1967-1968
S.A.I.M. SA Ind. Meccanica, Rome

Made by a commercial coachbuilder and specialist in tipping bodies, the S.A.I.M was a short-lived 8-ton forward control low loader with 15 in rear wheels and air/leaf suspension. A 6-cylinder Fiat diesel engine was used, though the company made their own 5-speed gearbox. *MCS*

ST. CLOUD (US) 1920
St. Cloud Truck Co., St. Cloud, Minn.

This company was founded by L.R. Brown who had previously been works manager of the Pan Automobile Company. A small number of 2½-ton trucks, several of which were used in local granite quarries, were assembled from proprietary components. In November 1920 a 1-ton model was announced, but the company failed shortly afterwards. *GNG*

ST. LOUIS (i) (US) 1900-1901
St. Louis Motor Carriage Co., St. Louis, Mo.

This company made light delivery wagons and covered vans powered by a 6hp horizontal 2-cylinder engine in the center of the frame. They had 2 forward speeds and bevel gear drive. *GNG*

ST. LOUIS (ii) (US) 1921-1922; 1930-1951
St. Louis Car Co., St. Louis, Missouri

An established maker of streetcars and railroad passenger cars, St. Louis was building double-deck bus bodies by 1914, when a sizable fleet of open-top double-deckers with St. Louis bodies on Mack or Kelly-Springfield chassis was placed in operation in San Francisco to convey visitors to the Panama-Pacific Exposition. St. Louis Car also built the bodies for the original fleet of Chicago double-deckers in 1917 (see American Motor Bus). Two experimental trolley-coaches and a fleet of four for Windsor were constructed in the early 1920's. The company never got deeply involved in buses, though small orders for bodies were accepted during the 1920's. With the revival of U.S. interest in trolley-coaches after 1928, St. Louis entered that market, doing moderately well before the war and quite well after 1945. Atlanta, New Orleans and Cleveland had large fleets of St. Louis trolley-coaches, over 1,100 of which were ultimately produced. St. Louis Car built a sample six-wheel gas-electric bus in 1929 and a few other prototypes of different kinds later, but never brought any complete buses to market. *MBS*

1906 ST. PANCRAS 5½-ton steam wagon, NMM

ST. PANCRAS (GB) c.1903-c.1914

(1) Saint Pancras Ironworks Co. Ltd., Holloway, London c.1903-1911
(2) The Steam Car Syndicate Ltd., Willesden, London 1911-c.1914

The St. Pancras was a vertical-boilered undertype wagon. From about 1903-07 a vertical fire tube arrangement was used which, like most of its type, was far from satisfactory. In 1907 this was superseded by a boiler using short horizontal radial fire tubes, which owed much to the Robertson design. In addition an unknown number of St. Pancras wagons carried Toward patent high pressure water tube boilers.

The totally enclosed engine was compound using a piston valve to the high and a slide valve to the low pressure cylinder respectively, driven by Stephenson link motion. Two countershafts were used, the second embodying the differential. Final drive was by double roller action and the wagons had 2 speeds.

A patent forecarriage was used incorporating both longitudinal and transverse springs. Cast steel wheels seem to have been standard.

The later wagons performed with reasonable success in town cartage work but on cross country work were outclassed by the Foden and other better overtypes. By 1911 they were of obsolete design and it is doubtful if any Willesden-made wagons found buyers. The bulk of the St. Pancras output was of the 1907 5-ton design. *RAW*

ST. VINCENT (GB) 1903-1910

(1) William McLean & Co., Glasgow.
(2) St. Vincent Cycle & Motor Works, Glasgow

Very few St. Vincent cars or commercials were built, all of them using 2 and 4-cylinder Aster engines. A 12-seater charabanc with the 14/16hp 2-cylinder engine was exhibited at the Edinburgh Show in 1908, some passenger brakes were made, and a few taxicabs followed the cessation of private car porduction in 1910. These vehicles were also known as Scottish Aster. *MJWW*

SALMSON (F) 1921-1927

Societe des Moteurs Salmson, Billancourt, Seine.

This well-known maker of cars offered the almost mandatory 100kg van and truck on their 4-cylinder cyclecar chassis with unusual 1,100cc 4-pushrod engine, but the D-Lourd of 1924 was specifically designed as a light truck. It used the 4-pushrod engine in the more substantial D touring car chassis with differential back axle. Only 70 were made, some of them in private car form. *MCS*

SALVADOR (US) 1915-1916

Mansur Motor Truck Co., Haverhill, Mass.

Previous to 1915, this had been made under the name Mansur. For 1915, the two seats straddled the hood and engine. It had worm drive and this two-tonner was available on three different lengths of wheelbase. *GMN*

SAME (I) 1963

S.A.M.E. Treviglio

This manufacturer of diesel engines and agricultural tractors exhibited an interesting range of all-wheel drive trucks and tractive units at the 1963 Turin Show. These were constructed on tractor lines, with rear engines in unit with their gearboxes and back axles. Engines were S.A.M.E.'s own aircooled diesels, a 2½-litre 45bhp twin in the 2½-ton Toro and a 7½-litre V6 in the bigger types. The 6 × 6 Elefante had a futuristic cab in the Bernard idiom, 8 forward and 4 reverse speeds, and a GCW rating of 32 tons. It was, however, decided not to proceed with these models. *MCS*

SAMPSON (US) 1905-1912

(1) Alden Sampson Mfg. Co., Pittsfield, Mass. 1905-1910
(2) Alden Sampson Mfg. Co., Detroit, Mich. 1910-1912

Alden Sampson introduced their truck range in the same year that they discontinued passenger cars. Their main product was a forward-control 5-tonner with a 40hp 4-cylinder engine and chain drive, although by 1909 the range had been widened to include smaller trucks of 1, 2, 3 and 4 tons capacity. There was also a shaft-driven ½-ton chassis powered by an 18hp flat-twin engine. Production ran at about 50 trucks per year.

1910 SAMPSON road train, CP

An unusual product of the Alden Sampson factory was the road train; this consisted of a tractor with 40hp engine and generator which provided electric power to motors in each of two six-wheeled trailers. Maximum speed was 8mph. A very limited number of these road trains was made from 1908 to 1910. In that year Sampson production was moved to Detroit, and a new, low-priced

1912 SAMPSON 1500lb van, NAHC

($1,775) truck was introduced. Known as the Hercules, this had a 30hp 4-cylinder Continental engine whereas other Sampsons used their own make of engine. By now part of the U.S. Motor Company, Sampson ceased production in 1912. *GNG*

1920 SAMSON Model 15¾-ton truck, EEH

SAMSON (US) 1920-1923

Samson Tractor Co., Janesville, Wis.

The Samson Tractor Company was W.C. Durant's attempt to make General Motors a rival to Ford in farm mechanization. In addition to the successful Model M tractor, Samson built a line of trucks in two sizes, ¾ and 1¼-tons, with Chevrolet 490 and FB car engines respectively. Samson trucks were conceived particularly for farm use, and could be had with extension bases (or rims), plain for front wheels and shallow cleated for rear, which would permit driving over plowed fields. Their cab-over-engine layout was rare for small trucks at this time. Although the trucks were successful, the tractors could not compete with the Fordson, and in 1923 the division was liquidated, the factory being re-equipped for Chevrolet assembly which is still carried on there today. *EEH*

1964 SAN H-27 40-seater bus, FLP

SAN (PL) 1952 to date

Sanocka Fabryka Autobusow, Sanok

Named after the city where it is made, San is the biggest producer of buses in Poland. Conventional in appearance, they used Star chassis with 105hp gasoline on 100hp diesel engines. Currently-built integral coaches are sold under the name Autosan. Another variant was the Sanok range of front-engined bus chassis or rear-engined integral coaches; these were powered either by a 105hp Star gasoline engine or a 125hp Wola-Leyland diesel. They were made from 1968 to 1972 only. *GA*

SANBERT see Sanford

SANDOW (US) 1915-1928

Sandow Motor Truck Co., Chicago, Ill.

The first Sandow models were 1½-, 2- and 3-tonners. The two larger ones used double chaindrive while the smallest had worm-drive rear axle. Electric lighting and starting was optional on all three in 1916. For 1921, 1- and 5-tonners were offered in addition to the three previous types. This range was continued up to 1928, with Continental or Buda 4-cylinder engines. *GMN*

SANDRINGHAM (GB) 1903

Frank Morriss, King's Lynn, Norfolk

Frank Morriss was the car repairer to King Edward VII, and from 1899 onwards made a speciality of modernizing Daimlers, in particular enlarging engines and converting them from tiller to wheel steering. In 1899 he operated a bus service in King's Lynn with a 10-passenger wagonette powered by a 5½hp Daimler engine. Although he called it a Morriss it was probably entirely Daimler apart from the body. Other similar vehicles were sold under the name Morriss, and in 1903 he built a hotel bus for the Castle Hotel at nearby Downham Market which he sold under the name Sandringham. This had a 10hp 2-cylinder engine, probably Daimler, chain drive, and two bodies, an open wagonette for the summer and an enclosed bus with seats on top in the manner of a stage coach. This version could seat 13 passengers. *GNG*

SANDUSKY (US) 1911-1914

Sandusky Auto Parts & Truck Co., Sandusky, Ohio

For its initial year, this truck was only a 1-tonner with an enclosed express body. This was revised for 1912 and re-rated as a 1½-tonner. The second portion of the manufacturer's name is given variously as "Truck", "Motor" and "Motor Truck." *GMN*

SANFORD (US) 1911-1937; 1969 to date

(1) Sanford-Herbert Co., Syracuse, N.Y. 1911-1913
(2) Sanford Motor Truck Co., Syracuse, N.Y. 1913-1937
(3) Sanford Fire Apparatus Corp., East Syracuse, N.Y. 1969 to date

The first trucks produced by this company were called Sanbert, an abbreviation of the two names of the original company. In 1911/12 there was only one model, a 1-ton engine-under-seat open truck called the Model J. It had a 3-cylinder 2-cycle air-cooled engine driving through a 2-speed transmission and double chain final drive. In 1913 this was replaced by a 4-cylinder 1 and 1½-ton truck with three speeds, and by 1916 there were five models from 1,500lbs to 2 tons. The driver-over engine layout had been replaced by a conventional hood, and worm final drive was adopted. Continental engines were used throughout the 1920s, when four or five models per year were usually

1920 SANFORD Model W-50 5-ton tipper, FLP

listed, in the range 1 to 6-tons. The 1923 models included the 1½-ton Greyhound which was a 'speed truck', one of several fast, pneumatic-tired models that were coming onto the market at this time. Also in 1923 a bus chassis was listed, but it was discontinued. 6-cylinder engines came in with the 1924 models, and a change to spiral bevel drive was made in 1926. During the 1920s fire engines began to assume increasing imporatance in the Sanford range, and in 1929 there were four models of pumper, from 350 to 750gpm, as well as other fire engine types.

After dwindling sales, production ceased in 1937, but the name was revived in 1969, again for fire engines which were now the only product. Custom chassis were made, with Cincinnati cab and choice of diesel engines, and Sanford have also built equipment on other chassis such as Duplex. *GNG*

SANGLAS see Rovena

SANOS see F.A.P.

SANSON (E) 1954-1960

Talleres Arau, Barcelona

This company built a small number of delivery tricycles powered by single-cylinder engines. Their load capacity was 600kgs. *JCG*

SARACAKIS (GR) 1970-1973

Saracakis Bros., S.A., Athens

The representatives of Volvo vehicles in Greece and bodybuilders for a long time, introduced in the early seventies a series of medium capacity city buses based on a ladder-type chassis powered by a front-mounted 6-cylinder Volvo diesel engine. Modelled SB55, these buses were delivered complete with Saracakis built bodies and were very conservative in design and construction. *GA*

SARAO (PI) 1948 to date

Sarao Motors Inc., Manila

Sarao is responsible for a typical product of Philippines, the Jeepney, which started life as a civilian version of WWII jeep. Based on surplus military jeeps with extremely customized appearance and an elongated rear body accomodating as many as 12 passengers, Jeepneys are used as taxi-cabs or minibuses. According to current availability, the original Jeep engine or an alternative gasoline or diesel unit, usually of Mercedes Benz origin, is fitted. Jeepneys are also built by a handful of other artisan workshops. The best known builder, though, is Sarao. *GA*

SAURER (i) (CH) 1903 to date

(1) Adolph Saurer, Arbon 1903-1920

(2) Adolph Saurer AG., Arbon 1920 to date

Saurer built his first stationary petroleum-motor, a single-cylinder of 1½ hp, in 1888, and exported improved versions two years later. By 1896 the first automobile engine, a horizontal single-cylinder with two opposed pistons and hot-tube ignition of 5 hp made its appearance. It was delivered in some quantities to the Parisian coachbuilder Koch who built phaetons, light omnibus and delivery vans around this Saurer powerplant. Many of them were sold to French colonies.

In 1903 the first proper Saurer commercial vehicle took the road. It was a heavy 5-ton truck with a 25/30 hp 4-cylinder T-head engine. Power was transmitted through a leather-cone-clutch, a separately mounted 4-speed gearbox, and shaft final drive. All wheels had iron tires and the handbrake acted directly on the rim at the rear. Apparently the shaft/pinion drive was not yet up to the task as Saurer reverted to chain final drive one year later with their first omnibus. Also in 1904 Saurer patented a motor-brake which changed the engine into a two-stroke air-compressor by a simple flip of a lever, thus inverting the action of the exhaust valves. This new third brake for continuous application without wear and tear was especially efficient in the mountainous roads of Switzerland. A year later the patent for a compressed air starting device was applied. Lighter trucks with 1½, 2½ and 3 tons payload were soon introduced. In 1906 the

1926 SAURER (i) A-type half-track postal bus, Saurer

Swiss postal authorities and the English Motor Car Emporium purchased Saurer omnibuses for regular services. One year later a new model was launched. The heavy truck with up to 5 tons payload received a new water-cooled 4-cylinder in line engine which delivered 30 hp at 1000 rpm. The chassis was also modernized though still retaining the final chain drive. Solid rubber tires and drum-brakes on the twin rear wheels were used. The chassis was considerably lower. Saurer entered their vehicles in numerous international competitions in Europe. Sound design, economy, excellent material and workmanship secured them many successes. 43 first places were won between 1907 and 1909.

At the same time the newly founded Safir company of Zurich took out license rights for passenger and commercial vehicles from Saurer. In 1908 the first high-speed vehicle diesel-engine was completed under Diesel's and Saurer's supervision in the Safir factory using a Saurer 4-cylinder gasoline engine as a basis.

By 1910 branch factories in Suresnes (Paris) and Lindau (Germany) began to produce Saurer vehicles for their respective markets. The Oesterreichische Saurerwerke GmbH in Vienna and the International Motor Co. in Plainfield, N.J. (USA) were also producing under license, and Saurer set up a world-wide distribution network from Russia to Uruguay, from Japan to Belgium and from Canada to Australia. In 1911 the first Transcontinental truck crossing from the American east to west coast was effected with a Saurer. Production comprised four types of commercial chassis with payloads of 1½, 2, 3 and 3½ tons. The two smaller categories had a new 16 hp 4-cylinder engine of 3 liters giving about 15 mph and shaft-drive, whereas the heavy models were equipped with the larger 30 hp engine and retained chain drive. Platform-trucks, tippers, fire-engines and omnibuses as well as special muncipal vehicles were offered. Gradients of 22%did not present any problems. Four speed gearboxes were used throughout

1922 SAURER (i) 5AD 5-ton truck and trailer, Saurer

To satisfy the specific requirements in less civilized areas Saurer created the *Kolonial-Wagen.* The emphasis lay on rugged construction and good cross-country performance. The chassis were reinforced and offered improved ground clearance by means of extra large diameter wide wheels. Normally solid-rubber tires were fitted but iron-shod wheels could also be obtained. Payload was 3 to 4 tons and the 4-cylinder engines delivered 30, 36 or 45 hp at 1,000 rpm. For tropical countries an extra radiator was mounted and governors kept the engines from overrevving. The transmission foot-brake and rear-wheel handbrake were supplemented by the Saurer motor-brake and a sprag. The rear-wheels were often equipped with a specially wide hub serving as an auxilliary rope-winch. These *Kolonial-Wagen* were used very successfully in South-America, Russia, India, etc.

In 1912 Saurer took the lead on the domestic market where 130 of their commercial vehicles were registered plus 56 passenger cars. The marque would never lose this enviable position of being the most successful Swiss manufacturer.

1930 SAURER (i) 3 BLD 4-ton truck, Saurer

1943/45 SAURER (i) M8 3½-ton 8×8 army truck, FH

In August the first World War began and interrupted sales activities abroad. The Suresnes factory was busily producing trucks and later aeroplane engines for the French Army. The British, Russian and even American military forces were using Saurer trucks as well. For the Swiss Army the company supplied trucks and developed a heavy artillery tractor employing a modified truck chassis with huge rear wheels.

Soon the new generation A-type trucks with shaft-drive and twin rear wheels made their entry into Swiss Army camps and remained in service for many years to come. They were nicknamed "The indestructible Saurers". The standard army version with a payload of 3 tons had a canvas top, a platform with hinged sides and a tarpaulin tilt. It is little known that the German MAN company worked closely together with Saurer regarding diesel engines. This co-operation led to a license agreement for the Saurer A-type truck in 1915 which was then produced by MAN for the Great War. When hostilities came to an end a considerable number of the army trucks, among them some new Saurers, were sold to the Swiss postal services and other public departments. The Saurer A-type chassis and complete commercial vehicles were offered on the civilian market from 1918 onward. In 1921 four basic models were available.

The A-chassis were made for 2 to 5 tons payload (2A, 3A, 4A and 5A). Semi-elliptic springs were used all around. The wheels — twins at the rear — were still wooden artillery types in the beginning with solid rubber tires, later replaced by the famous steel-spoke Simplex wheels made by Georg Fischer, and pneumatic tires. 4-speed gearboxes were flanged to the engine and permitted top-speeds of 15 to 20 mph in direct drive.

The two standard versions of 4-cylinder in line L-head monobloc engines were freely interchangeable. The small C-type motor (100 x 170mm 5.3 liters) delivered 32 hp and the D-type engine (110 x 180mm 6.8 liter) developed 40 hp. On special order a more powerful E-type engine (120 x 180mm 8.1 liters) with 48 hp was available for fire-engines, heavy trucks and military vehicles. General design was identical for all three powerplants with all valves on the lefthand side, pressure lubrication with automatic topping up with additional oil, multi-jet carburetor of Saurer's own design — famous for excellent economy, automatic governor, and high-tension magneto ignition with manual adjustment. The Saurer motor-brake was of course standard equipment. There was an interesting safety device automatically putting the ignition on late if the starting handle was put in place. An electric starter was usually fitted. Depending on the engine fitted the trucks would be designated as: 2AC, 4AD, 3AD, 5AE etc. With the A-type Saurers, medals and first prizes were won in competition for commercial vehicles in Spain, Sweden, Brazil and France.

By 1927 the power-output of the three engines with unchanged dimensions increased to 42, 52 and 62 hp respectively. Apart from load-carriers of many types, special vehicles for fire brigades and urban duties as well as buses and motor-coaches were built. One of the most extraordinary vehicles built on the Saurer A-chassis was an omnibus for the Swiss postal service equipped at the rear with the Nyberg rubber tracks and with the front-wheels put on skis to operate regularly on the deeply snow-covered alpine roads.

Adolph Saurer had died in 1920 and his able son Hippolyt took over the management of the newly formed public company. He restarted the further development of diesel engines broken off in 1908, but it took more time than originally expected. The new B-line of commercial vehicles was initially equipped with 4- and 6-cylinder gasoline engines. In 1926 the first 2B Saurer was shown to the public. It was a small and handy truck of 1½ to 2 tons payload with most of the general characteristics of the successful A-models but with new 42 and 55 hp 4-cylinder OHV engines of 90 or100mm bore and 150mm stroke (3.8 and 4.7 liters respectively). Gear and handbrake levers had been moved into a central position and pneumatic tires were fitted.

In 1928 the customers were offered for the first time the choice of 4- and 6-cylinder gasoline or diesel engines. Saurer thus was among the pioneers of this new engine. The first models RD 4-cylinder and LD 6-cylinder engines were built according to the Acro system. Two years later the B-line had grown considerably and various truck chassis for 2 to 6 tons payload and new lower bus chassis for 10 to 50 passengers were offered. The most famous was certainly the heavy 5BLD which for many years to come remained the typicial Saurer. The LD 6-cylinder diesel OHV engine of 7.8 liters developed 80 hp. Power was transmitted through a dry multiplate clutch, 4-speed gearbox, and open cardan-driveshaft to the spiral-geared rear axle. On respect four-wheel brakes and servo-assistance could be fitted. Saurer motor brakes were standard on all models.

Hippolyt Saurer, not satisfied with the first diesel engines, introduced an improved crossflaw version system in 1932. Two years later the great leap ahead became a reality with his invention of the direct-injection doulbe-whirl-piston system. The many advantages of the Saurer system were soon realized and license-rights were sold to many important factories abroad. Rapidly all Saurer diesel ingines were redesigned to incorporate this important improvement!!!

The heavier models (3C, 4C and 5C) were offered with the CTD and CT1D 6-cylinder OHV diesel engines of 8 litres and 100 hp at 1900 rpm.

In 1929 Saurer took over Berna, the second-biggest Swiss make of commercial vehicles. Whereas both companies continued to produce their own models for some time, Berna more and more acquired the characteristics of Saurer engines and vehicles.

In 1932 the Swiss motor vehicle law came into effect prescribing maximum total weight and payload. The advanced and interesting 6 × 4 Saurer truck with both rear axles driven could therefore not be sold in Switzerland. It was however produced in the Paris factory for the French market. The new law led to the C-line of Saurer vehicles which were introduced from 1934 onward. This range covered the wide variety of trucks for 1 to 6 tons payload. The smallest models LC 1 and LC 1.5 were still available either with the "CA" 6-cylinder-SV-gasoline engine of 2.9 litres and 52 hp or the "CDB" 4-cylinder OHV diesel engine of 2.8 liters and 50 hp. The gas engine had a detachable light-alloy cylinder-head and the crankshaft in 7 plain bearings. The diesel monobloc engine was of light alloy and the wet cylinder-liners were interchangeable. 5 plain bearings were fitted to the carefully machined crankshaft. Both engines possessed aluminum pistons and pressure lubrication. They were 3-point rubber-block mounted and water-cooled. Power was transmitted via a dry single plate clutch to the 5-speed gearbox (5th speed was overdrive, 3rd and 4th gears were synchronized). On request a 4-speed gearbox with 3 silent ratios could be supplied. The hydraulic 4-wheel brakes could be supplemented with the Saurer exhaust brake and the mechanical handbrake acted on the rear wheels only. Steering was right-hand as always and by worm and sector. Electrical equipment was 12 volts for the gas and 24 volts for the diesel version. GF Steel spoke wheels were fitted.

The heavier models (3C, 4C and 5C) were offered with the CTD and CT1D 6-cylinder OHV diesel engines of 8 liters and 100 hp at 1,900 rpm. Especially for heavy tipper-trucks a dual-ratio rear-axle was fitted offering 8 forward and 2 reverse speeds. The hydraulic 4-wheel brakes were air servo-assisted. For the medium range 1C and 2C models the new CRD and CR1D 4-cylinder diesel engines of 4½ and 5.3 liters respectively and developing 55 and 65 hp were used. As before low-slung omnibus chassis were also made. Depending on the rear-axle ratio a speed of 35 to 50 mph was attained by the 5 ton truck 3C.

With the outbreak of the Second World War all models

could be had with wood-gas generators. Again many special-purpose vehicles were built based on the C-line, for example an extra-short wheelbase road-tractor for trailers etc., fire-fighting-vehicles, urban and excursion buses in many sizes, etc. Whereas the Swiss Army relied on fairly standard trucks of the Swiss marques and on a large number of requisitioned commercial vehicles for road transportation, special cross-country vehicles were required for more specific tasks for the artillery and other units. In the thirties Saurer had developed various all-wheel-drive military vehicles of which three were introduced. They were all forward-control and equipped with diesel engines similar to the civilian types. Along the backbone chassis 2, 3 or 4 axles with single wheels were independently suspended on coil springs and offered excellent cross-country performance. According to the number of wheels designations were M4, M6 and M8 of which the M6 was produced in the largest quantity. These versatile and handy vehicles remained in service until very recently. In 1946 a new artillery tractor and ammunition transporter, the Saurer M4H with 4-wheel-drive, forward-control, 1½ ton payload and 70 hp rear-mounted 4-cylinder diesel engine was introduced.

In the forties the C-range was extended to comprise forward-control models, which were designated L2C, N2C, L4C, N4C & S4C. The very first forward-control Saurer was shown in 1935. General specification and the diesel engines were the same as on the conventional types. Later a new powerful V8 engine CH1D of 10.6 litres and140 hp at 2,000 rpm was fitted into the heaviest truck chassis. Official payload increased to 7 tons but often much heavaier loads were hauled. One of the highly successful motor-coaches on the L4C chassis was pruchased in large numbers by the Swiss postal services and some are still in daily use after having covered tremendous mileages.

1956 SAURER (i) 6C 10-ton truck, Saurer

1955 SAURER (i) 42P 22-35 seater (100 passenger) bus, GNG

In 1950 not less than 11 different diesel engines for motor vehicles were produced by Saurer. 4-cylinders: CDB 85 × 125mm 45 hp, CR1D 110 × 140mm 68 hp, CR2D 115 × 140mm 80 hp. 6-cylinders: CDD 85 × 125mm 60 hp, CTD 105 × 130mm 95 hp, CT1D 110 × 140mm 110 hp, CT2D 115 × 140mm 150 hp, 8-cylinders CH2D 115 × 140mm 160 hp, 12-cylinders VD1D 115 × 140mm 250 hp and CV1DL turbo-supercharged 115 × 140mm 300 hp.

Two new chassis with rear-engines were launched at this time for buses 3H and 4H for 30 and up to 70 passengers respectively. The 6 or 8-cylinder diesels CT2D and CH2D were mounted in the lefthand rear corner driving the twin-wheel rear axle via an 8-speed gearbox, the intermediary ratios were changed by compressed air. On the modern city buses the motor was mounted transversely at the rear (type 4HP) or just in the fornt of the left rear wheel (4ZP).

For army and civilian tasks a new line of forward control all-wheel-drive trucks was introduced in the early fifties. Whereas the 2CM for 3½ to 4 tons was equipped with the CR2D 4 cylinder diesel engine, the CT2D 6 cylinder engine was fitted in the 4CM and 5CM with 5½ and 6½ tons payloads respectively. Wheelbase for all models was 11'2" and the Tracta-type front-axle-drive could be separately engaged. 5-speed gearboxes had twin-ratio auxiliary tramsmissions to offer 5 speeds each for road and cross-country use. Climbing potential was up to 66% fully loaded.

In 1953 two prototypes of a 6 x 6 lorry were built for the Swiss Army. This 6CM was similar to the 5CM but with an additional driven twin-wheeled rear axle.

By 1958 at the top of the C-line, the S4C for 7 to 10 tons payload and the 6C for 10 to 11 tons were offered. The last C-type Saurer disappeared from the catalogs in 1963. To compete successfully with the foreign imports in the light class Saurer from 1952 onward offered the forward control LC1 which was built under Saurer license by OM. It was equipped with a 4-cylinder diesel engine of 65 hp and offered 2.9 tons payload.

A brief look at the various license agreements between Saurer and companies abroad will show that some of these co-operations are very old and have endured difficult times. One of the earliest, with the Austrian Saurer Werke AG., Vienna dates back to 1906. In 1959 Steyr-Daimler-Puch took over the majority of shares. This company has manufactured in series the Saurer light tank 4K (1960) which was developed in Arbon but not adopted by the Swiss Army. There is a very close collaboration with the Fiat-owned OM in Brescia and Milan. Saurer-designed diesel engines for vehicles, ships, railroad locomotives and stationary purposes were produced by OM which on the other hand sells its lorries exclusively through Saurer/Berna in Switzerland.

Development continued through the years and already in 1955 the first D-type trucks were shown. The management realized that concentration and rationalization of the manufacturing program was a necessity. The range of the preceding C-line had grown into a too wide spread with individual solutions for almost any transportation problem. In 1965 two basic D-chassis namely type 2D and 5D in various wheelbase lengths and equipped with 6-cylinder diesel engines of 120 to 240 hp were offered as normal control, forward-control and under-floor vehicles depending on the task. The impressive range of 15 truck, 10 bus, 6 all-wheel-drive and 5 trailer-tractor types was possible due to a clever combination of standardized components. These models were designed for the home-market and covered all needs of medium and heavy commercial vehicle requirements. Whereas normal leaf-springs, sometimes supplemented by rubber-cushion springs were used for the trucks, the more comfortable air-suspension was fitted to bus chassis. Compressed air brakes and motor-brakes were generally used and the handbrake acting on the rear wheels only was equipped with a compressed-air servo. The 4-speed synchro gearbox in conjunction with a separate reduction gear offered 8 forward speeds. For the town-buses pre-selector gearboxes were chosen. Payload ranged from 6.8 to slightly over 10 tons and the buses had a passenger capacity of 22 to 180 persons. The diesel engines fitted were partly developments of the C-engines and partly of the new D-type powerplants. The smallest, type CT4D of 6.8 liters developed 120 hp at 220 rpm. The CT3D with 8.1 liters supplied 140 hp. Next in line, the CT2D Lm of 8.7 liters was equiped with the patented Saurer supercharger and offered 192 hp. The new under-floor horizontal engine, the DCU of 10.3 liters and 160 hp, could also be had in a boosted vesion type CDUL of 210 hp. Especially designed for the four-wheel-drive models, the DC-128 engine of 10.8 liters developed 180 hp. The supercharged models DCL of 10.3 liters and 210 hp and the most powerful of the line, the type DCL-128 of 240 hp were also mounted. Similar engines were also fitted under-floor and in the rear of the bus chassis. All engines were 6-cylinder OHV diesels with 7 crankshaft bearings, direct injection and compression ratio of 15 to 17.5:1. The only surviving 4-cylinder engine was the CR2D Lm of 5.8 liters developing 100 hp.

1962 SAURER (i) C Series 3½-4½ ton truck, GNG

In 1971 the successful 2D line was replaced by the new 4D models which received a new 6-cylinder diesel engine type CKT of 8.8 liters and 200 hp at 2500 rpm. Unlike the earlier C-type engine, which had an aluminium block, the new powerplant, also with direct injection, received a cast-iron block and head. The 4DM was a four-wheel-drive chassis mainly for tipper-trucks and army requirements with a wheelbase of 14'9" and 8½ tons payload. It had a 6-speed ZF synchro-gearbox and an additional cross-country reduction box, thus offering 12 forward speeds. Front axle drive could be engaged separately and power-distribution is ⅓ : ⅔. Both front and rear differential were equipped with a positive lock. Supplemented by the motor-brake and the hand-brake. Semi-elliptic springs with added rubber-cushion springs were used all around. The 4DF was a forward-control chassis of similar general specification with the following exceptions: only the rear axle was driven, the 6-speed ZF gearbox was combined on request with an additional overdrive unit offering 12 forward speeds and 60 mph top speed. For urban special-purpose vehicles a version with an automatic Allison 4-speed gearbox was offered.

1973 SAURER (i) 5DM 4×4 truck, Saurer

The heavier 5D line was equipped alternatively with the 6-cylinder in line diesel engines D2K of 12½ liters and 250 hp or the turbo-supercharged D2KT of 12 liters and 330. The normal control truck 5D had a wheelbase of 14'9" or 16'5", a 9-speed ZF gearbox including a crawler. Gear-change between 4th and 5th speeds was electro-pneumatically controlled. All gears with the exception of the rear speed and crawler are synchronized. The other specifications were similar to the 4DM and payload is about 8½ tons. The 5DF was a forward-control chassis with wheelbase of 10'8", 12'2", 13'6", 14'9" and 16'5". The 5DM was an all-wheel-drive heavy truck. Here an additional reduction-gear offered a total of 18 forward speeds, ranging from 2 to 48 mph at peak-rpm. Only the turbo-supercharged D2KT engine was fitted into this chassis. In the heaviest class, Saurer offered the 5DF 6 × 4 with two driven rear axles each with twin wheels. The D2KT 300 hp engine is fitted. Top speed is 60 mph. Payload of the tipper-truck was about 14 tons. In 1974 the 5DF 8 x 4 with two steered front axles and two driven rear-axles was launched; payload was 18 tons. On request this model could be had with an automatic Allison gearbox instead of the normal 9-speed ZF gearbox.

In the medium and light class Saurer offers three different OM models under their combined names. The Saurer-OM Type 35 forward-control truck tractor with a payload of about 2½ tons, the Saurer-OM Type 90 with a Saurer designed 103 hp diesel and 5½ tons payload and the Saurer-OM Type 130R with a 145 hp-diesel engine and about 8 tons payload.

1974 SAURER-LEYLAND bus, Saurer

In the bus department a co-operation with the Danish-Leyland (DAB) became effective early in 1974. Contrary to earlier practice where the motor was placed up front, midship or in the rear — all models of the standardized range especially designed for urban traffic received the horizontal under-floor-mounted 6-cylinder diesel engine D2KUT with 240 hp the two-axle models and 270 hp for the 3-axle models for up to 150 passengers and a total length of 17.5m.

1974 SAURER (i) 5DF 8×4 chassis, Saurer

1978 SAURER (i) D330 8×4 truck, Saurer

In 1975 an interesting short wheelbase tractor 6 × 2 with two steered front axles and the 330 hp engine was launched. From 1976 onward the old designations were dropped and replaced by the D-series. The present line comprises the medium D 180 4 × 2 with the C2K 6 cylinder of 8,820cm 3 and 180 hp. The D 230 4 × 2 has the C2KT of the same size but with turbocharging and 230 hp output. The D 290 and D 330 are offered in various 4 × 2, 6 × 2, 6 × 4 and 8 × 4 versions. Both have a 12 litre turbo 6-cylinder diesel engine. The earlier D2KT developed 330 hp whereas the D3KT is slightly de-tuned and output is 290 hp. In the all-wheel-drive sector Saurer offers the normal control D 230 N 4 × 4 and the D 330 NK 4 × 4 and 6 × 6 as well as the Saurer-OM 75 and 90 4 × 4 with 122 hp engine. The co-operation in the bus field came to an end and Saurer again offers various models of their own design with rear and underfloor mounted engines D3KTU. In the light and medium class of 4 × 2 vehicles Saurer traditionally offers the OM 65, 80, 90, 100, 110 and 130. Saurer designed and developed the new Fiat V8 diesel engine of 352 hp and in 1978 launched their new D4KT, a 6-cylinder turbo-diesel engine of 315 hp as well as a gas-engine, the D2K-G for their G 230 F. *FH*

SAURER (ii) (A) 1906 to date

Oesterreichische Saurer Werke AG, Vienna

This company was founded when the production capacity of the Swiss Saurer company could not cope with the demand and to evade import duties. As no special Austrian types are mentioned in the Saurer history it is to be supposed that a selection of the standard truck and bus chassis as produced in Arbon were manufactured over the years for the Austrian market. In 1937 the mother company sold all their shares of the Oesterreichische Saurer Werke AG, but the company continued to make use of the Saurer designs under license agreement. Interestingly enough the regulations for the standardization of automobile manufacturing in Nazi Germany as set up by Fieldmarshal Goering in 1939 included one basic type of 4½ ton truck by Austrian Saurer, Austro-Fiat, Magirus and MAN. All four works would use the same uniform design but Saurer was permitted to fit their own diesel engine.

In 1959 Steyr-Daimler-Puch took over the controlling interest. There is still a loose technical co-operation between Saurer Arbon and Austrian company. *FH*

1927 SAURER (iii) Type BH 12-seater bus, FH

SAURER (iii) (F) 1910-1956

1) Adolph Saurer, Suresnes (Seine) 1910-1917
2) Societe des Automobiles Industrials Saurer, Suresnes (1917-1956)

During 1910 Saurer, purchased the old Darracq-Serpollet omnibus factory in Suresnes near Paris in order to further expand their activities in one of the most promising markets for commercial vehicles.

At the Paris Show 1910 Saurer exhibited 3½ and 5 ton trucks with chain-drive as well as an omnibus seating 20 passengers. Sales in France were very satisfactory. Toward the end of 1917 the firm was reformed into Societe des Automobiles Industriels Saurer. Swiss and French bankers put up to 20% of the share capital. One year later Saurer was exclusively producing trucks and aircraft engines for the French Army. Shortly after the armistice the heavy depression set in and in the early twenties Saurer Suresnes was in serious financial troubles. Slowly things improved again. Principally the designs and models of the mother-company were taken over.

In 1927 a new fully equipped Saurer omnibus type 2BH with a 4.7 liter 4-cylinder OHV engine of 55 hp made headlines in France and Europe. Driven by the famous sportsman Lamberjack it won the Criterium de Tourisme Paris-Nice and was the only entry finishing this rally without any penalty. The light Weymann-bodied omnibus with 12 passengers aboard reached a measured 57.1 mph in the speed contest. One year later Lamberjack repeated this fine performance with the famous Saurer bus "Popol" using the new 6-cylinder engine.

In view of the modern transport regulations in France allowing heavy gross weight, Saurer, Suresnes built trailer-vehicles using the basic chassis types B, BH and BL for the tractors. These heavy-load vehicles were not available in Switzerland. The standard truck and bus models were of course also manufactured in Suresnes. At the Geneva Motor Show of 1932 Saurer, Arbon exhibited a very up-to-date heavy 6x4 truck with the LD engine which was subsequently made in Suresnes for the French market. The same model was also built in England.

Prior to the 2nd World War some of the latest C-type Saurer vehicles were produced. In 1937 the Swiss mother company increased their share in the capital. In 1948 Saurer Suresnes made 689 trucks and buses and about 1,000 workers were employed. Apart from Saurer, Arbon the following companies had financial interests: Hotchkiss, Latil and Peugeot. There were 6 sales companies and 12 agents in France. The factory was acquired in 1956 by Unic of the Simca group. *FH*

1914 SAURER (iv) articulated tipper, LA

SAURER (iv) (US) 1911-1918

Saurer Motor Co., Plainfield, N.J.

Saurer trucks were first imported into the United States in 1908, followed by assembly by the Quincy, Manchester & Sergent Company in 1909. These were 2½ and 4-tonners, but when actual manufacture began only the larger model was made, followed in 1912 by a 5 and a 6½-tonner. In October 1911 the International Motor Company was formed, a holding company for the sale of both Saurer and Mack trucks, joined in 1912 by Hewitt. For several years all three makes were advertised together, Saurer representing the heavier side of the combined range, though exceeded by the enormous 10-ton Hewitt. In 1916 production of the Mack AC engine began at Plainfield, and demand for this led to the discontinuance of the American Saurer two years later. *GNG*

SAUTTER-HARLE (F) 1908-1913

Harle et Cie, Paris

This firm of government contractors built steam engines, searchlights for the French Navy and (from 1907) cars. Their commercial vehicles were little known apart from the mobile searchlight chassis. The bigger ones were chain-driven machines with 18 hp 4-cylinder engines, but the smaller type, announced in 1913, was in the private car idiom with 2.3-litre engine, shaft drive, pneumatic tires and a sporting style of bodywork. 40 mph were claimed. Harle et Cie also built municipal vehicles. Their sweeper was powered by a 1.8-litre vertical-twin engine, but their driver-over-engine refuse collector had a 5.2-litre 4-cylinder power unit, with loading and discharging mechanisms driven off the 4-speed gearbox. Machines of this type were used in Rouen. *MCS*

1958 SAVA P. 54 2000kgs 3-wheel truck, GNG

SAVA (E) 1957 to date

Sociedad Anonima de Vehicules Automoviles, Valladolid

This company began by making a 3-wheeler with 673cc single-cylinder engine and shaft drive to the rear axle, but soon afterwards they launched a range of trucks based on Austins, though for some time these were made with Sava's own design cab. These had gas and diesel engines, and were made in sizes up to 6 tons. In 1963 they added the Sava-BMC model S-76 with the FG-type BMC cab incorporating sliding doors, and this was followed by the J-4 10/12-cwt van and pickup and other models in the Austin range including the normal-control WF 3-tonner, and forward-control FF 5-tonner and FG 7-tonner. All these were identical to Austins in appearance. In 1966 Sava passed under the control of E.N.A.S.A., makers of Pegaso heavy vehicles, thus giving the latter an entry into the

1960 SAVA P. 58 4R 2500kg van, GNG

1975 SAVA S-511 aircraft servicing truck, Sava

light truck and bus market. The current range of Sava vehicles extends from 850 kgs to 6 tons capacity. From 1957 to 1965 various models of Berliet were made by Sava, of which the best-known was the type GPS of 38 tons G.C.W. *JCG*

SAVAGE (GB) 1895-1913

(1)Frederick Savage & Co. Ltd., Kings Lynn, Norfolk 1895-1898
(2) Savage Bros. Ltd., Kings Lynn, Norfolk 1898-1911
(3) Savages Ltd., Kings Lynn, Norfolk 1911-1913

Savages were noted for their fairground machines, had a good business as founders and general engineers, and made agricultural traction engines, but they also supplied

1908 SAVAGE 3½-ton steam wagon, OMM

five road haulage engines to showmen, the first (No. 647) in 1895 and the last (No. 847) in 1909, the total being made up of two 7 nhp compounds, two 8 nhp compounds and a single. They also made between 1910 and 1913 six 4 nhp compound steam tractors and one single cylinder tractor of 4½ nhp, the class being known by the trade name of "Little Samson," probably in imitation of Taskers "Little Giant."

1910 SAVAGE Little Samson compound steam tractor, RAW

Parallel with these activities they made a series of steam wagons (probably no more than 35 in all) in very diverse types. The undertype compound engine was used in all, some having piston valves to both cylinders but others having a piston valve to the high pressure and a slide valve to the low pressure, a wise modification giving protection against the effect of condensate trapped in the low pressure cylinder. As to boilers they used, variously, the Musker water tube type (the patent rights of which they bought in 1903), their own amendment of the Musker design, a top-fired short locomotive type and a vertical cross water tube type. Savages were the patentees of a cast steel wheel with end grain wood-block treads used in some of their wagons.

Savages abandoned road vehicle manufacture in 1913 to concentrate upon their specialist work for showmen and their general engineering. *RAW*

1960 SAVIEM MTPV 6×4 dump truck, NMM

SAVIEM (F) 1957 to date

(1) Societe Anonyme de Vehicules Industriels et Equipements Mecaniques,Suresnes, Seine: Blainville, Normandy 1957-1977
(2) Renault Vehicules Industriels, Suresnes, Seine: Blainville, Normandy 1977 to date

This company came into existence in 1955 as the result

of a fusion between Renault's heavy goods vehicle interests and the Floirat, Latil and Somua concerns: Chausson, renowned for its buses, joined in 1959. The Saviem name was not, however, seen on any vehicle before the 1957 Paris Salon, and up to 1960 the range was a curious conglomeration of types inherited from the group's component elements. The trucks were all forward-control diesels in the 12/19-ton GVW class, Renaults having horizontally-mounted 6-cylinder engines, while Latils and Somuas were fours or sixes with conventional vertical installations. The dumpers were of Somua type, Latil contributed their famous 4-wheel-drive-and-steer timber tractor, and a variety of Renault and Floirat coaches could carry up to 50 passengers. Some had rear engines, though the addition of the Chausson strain from 1959 onwards led to an increasing concentration on unitary structures and horizontal, amidships-mounted power units. Interesting features of the 1961 PSV range included automatic (Renault Transfluide) and semi-automatic (Wilson) gearboxes, air brakes, power steering, and air-leaf suspensions. Also in 1961 came the first of Saviem's international involvements, a technical agreement signed with Henschel of Germany.

During the early 1960s a degree of rationalization became apparent, with Saviem's own 4.6-litre 4-cylinder and 6.8-litre 6-cylinder Fulgur diesel engines replacing older types, and the acquisition (in 1964) of the Limoges Arsenal where previously the French Government had built power units for AFVs. Here Saviem diesels were developed alongside a line of multi-fuel types for military purposes. A widening of the range began the same year with the introduction of new 5- and 7-ton forward control trucks with 4-cylinder Renault and 6-cylinder Perkins oil engines, while at the end of 1965 Saviem entered the 1/2-ton category by taking over Renault's old-established Galion-Goelette family. These were evolved by 1969 into improved models with new 3.3-litre 85 bhp diesels (there was still a gas option), hydrovac brakes, and coil-spring ifs. At the top of the range both the heavy trucks and Paris's new buses with horizontal underfloor engines were powered by 6-cylinder M.A.N units of German make.

In 1968 Saviem and M.A.N agreed to pool their technical development and marketing. The German factory would furnish 6- and 8-cylinder engines of up to 285 bhp for the heavy range, Saviem's principal contributions being gearboxes and their new tilt cab. The same year saw an association with Alfa Romeo of Italy, who developed a new fwd 2-ton forward control van, the FC20, and also marketed the lighter Saviems in their own country. In 1971 Saviem became a partner (with D.A.F, Magirus-Deutz and Volvo) in the Club of Four, a European consortium to produce standardized commercial vehicles. Saviem's entry in the 9/13-ton GVW class, the J model, appeared in 1975: it was a forward-control tilt cab machine using a Limoges-built 5½-litre 6-cylinder engine of M.A.N design, a 5-speed ZF gearbox, and air/hydraulic brakes. Among the variations available were turbocharged power units giving 170 bhp and power steering.

Between 1960 and 1973 the company strengthened its position, with production climbing from 5,000 to 36,971 units in a thirteen-year period, at the end of which Saviem were responsible for 32 per cent of France's medium duty trucks and 61 per cent of her buses. With Berliet passing from Citroen to Renault control in 1974, some integration was inevitable, but in 1978 it had as yet been confined to the grouping of the truck interests into a single company, Renault Vehicules Industriels.

1971 SAVIEM E7N 45-seater coach, GNG

Saviem's 1978 line-up covered everything save the smallest car-based types, still a Renault preserve. In the under 5-ton GVW category were the forward control S-types as made since 1969. 4 × 4 versions were available and the lightest SG2s had irs as well as ifs. The Js had been extended downwards to embrace the 6-ton bracket on the JK60 model using a 3.6-litre 4-cylinder engine rated at 100 bhp, while the heavier tilt-cab family covered GVWs of up to 20 tons and GCWs of close on 40. The most powerful SM340 tractor featured a 335 bhp 15½-litre V8, 9- or 10-speed transmissions, air/exhaust braking and power steering, these two latter features being standard on most of the large Saviems. The only normal control types were the TP dumpers, thinly disguised 4 × 2, 4 × 4, 6 × 4 and 6 × 6 M.A.Ns rated up to 48 tons, while also offered were fire engines, municipal types, and the EPG range of crane carriers with M.A.N. engines and transmissions, which came in 3, 4-, 5- and even 6-axle forms. PSV design now centered on unitary single-deckers with 7.3-litre 6-cylinder horizontal underfloor engines capable of carrying up to 72 passengers. Features of these were power steering, 6-speed synchromesh gearboxes, and Saviem's air-leaf suspension. *MCS*

1974 SAVIEM SM32 240 articulated tanker, Saviem

SAXON (US) 1914-1916

Saxon Motor Co., Detroit, Mich.

The basic Saxon was a popular light passenger automobile and this company offered an open express van on the smaller of two passenger car chassis. Rating on this was only 400 pounds. It was powered by a 4-cylinder, side-valve Continental engine. *GMN*

SAYERS & SCOVILL see S & S

SCAMMELL (i) (GB) 1919 to date

(1) G. Scammell & Nephew Ltd., Spitalfields, London 1919-21

(2) Scammell Lorries Ltd., Watford, Herts 1922 to date

Scammell & Nephew had been cart and bodywork makers since the 19th century and had subsequently sold, serviced and bodied commercial vehicles, particularly Foden and Mann steamers.

In 1919 they started to experiment with a heavy four wheel tractor with articulated trailer, which was found to be able to haul seven tons at similar running costs to a rigid 3-tonner. In 1921 a factory was opened in Watford to produce the vehicle, which was the first complete articulated vehicle to be made in quantity in Britain, though its inspiration came to a great extent from the American Knox.

The basic vehicle changed very little for over fifteen years apart from growing into a 10, then 12, then 15-tonner by 1926, or a 20-ton machinery carrier. Drive was via 3-speed gearbox and chains to the back axle, and the engine was an overhead valve 7094cc, four cylinder unit. Though offered with shaft drive and pneumatic tires in the Thirties both solid tires and chain drive could still be specified on some models as late as the Forties.

80% of the early production was of tankers, mainly for gas companies, the earliest for Mex having slab sides. Scammell were pioneers of frameless tank semi-trailers which, with pumps driven off the front of the crankshaft, were in service by 1925 and could carry 3300 gallons. By 1930 some 200 frameless Scammell tankers were in use.

The first sign of diversification took place in 1925 when Scammell started work on a local-delivery vehicle for 2½ ton loads called the Auto-Van. It had front wheel drive and a three cylinder radial engine with vertical crankshaft. Though too novel to be a commercial success it sowed the seeds for Scammell's famous mechanical horse in 1933, which was based on a design by Napier.

1926 SCAMMELL 8-ton articulated truck, NMM

In 1927 Scammell produced their first rigid 6-wheeler, the 6x4 Pioneer 6-tonner, primarily for heavy-duty overseas use. It had an unusual system of wheel drive in which each was driven through a train of gears housed in beams pivoted from a central axle.

It was soon adopted by the British and other Armies as the basis of articulated tank transporters and experimental armoured cars, and by 1929 could be equipped with all-wheel-drive.

Also in 1929, a six ton rigid four wheeler was introduced with a shaft driven rear axle for the first time, and work started on the first truck specifically designed to carry 100 tons. Initially this used the usual 80 hp gas engine, though it was converted to Gardner diesel in 1931. The articulated tractor was unusual in having a divided rear axle, each portion of which carried two sets of double wheels.

1931 saw the first chain drive 6x2 road-going Scammell rigid six wheelers, whilst developments in time for the 1933 London Commercial Motor Show were rubber suspension on the trailer of the articulated wheeler, the option of the Gardner 6LW diesel in the 15 tonner, and the 3 ton Mechanical Horse. Over 20,000 of these were ultimately built, some as rigids, some with electric drive and some as oil engined 6 tonners, and Scammell's patent

1935 SCAMMELL MH6 6-ton mechanical horse, NMM

automatic coupling and trailer have also been used on many other articulated tractors, whilst the horse has been built under license in France as the F.A.R. In 1948 the familiar round nose Scarab replaced the original Mechanical Horse and in 1964 this was replaced by the Townsman, with restyled fibreglass cab and Leyland diesel engine, which was eventually killed by legislation favoring four wheel tractors. Scammell also built a few four-wheelers of similar design, the original ones with air-cooled, 2 cylinder engines for rigid use in 1937 and the later ones as artics based on Standard Atlas components from 1962.

1946 SCAMMELL R8 15-ton truck, OMM

In the Thirties, Scammell built numerous one-off vehicles for special purposes at home and overseas, including all-wheel drive military and oilfield machines and fire engines, whilst in 1937 they introduced an eight-wheel forward control rigid which changed very little over the next twenty years. The original articulated concept with conventional tractors continued right through to 1970, having been given the name Highwayman in 1955 and given the option of Leyland 11-litre engine at the same time.

To the end it had an open gate gear change, though the original 3 and later 4 speed gearboxes were replaced in the mid-Thirties by six speeds and an epicyclic rear axle.

1949 SCAMMELL Scarab 6-ton mechanical horse, Scammell

1960 SCAMMELL Highwayman 3600 gallon articulated frameless tanker, Scammell

During the Second World War over 2000 Pioneers were built for a variety of military purposes. Afterwards these were replaced by the 6x6 Explorer, whilst special Meadows engined oilfields 4x2 trucks were joined by the Mountaineer 4x4 in 1949. This was used as the basis of dump trucks and other off-road vehicles.

In 1952 the Constructor 6x6 appeared as a tractor for heavy road haulage or a variety of off-road uses. It had a 6 cylinder Gardner engine, now also used in the Mountaineer, and was joined by the 6x4 Junior Constructor in 1956 and the Super Constructor, with choice of engines up to 250 hp for gross train weights of over 150 tons, in 1958.

In 1955 Scammell were acquired by Leyland Motors, after which a number of Leyland components were included in Scammell models, although to this day a wide choice of other makers' engines and transmissions are available.

The forward control Handyman joined the Highwayman in 1960 when the Routeman eight-wheeler appeared and a new 6x4 articulated Trunker was developed with Leyland cab. This gave way to a Trunker II in 1965, with second steering axle in front of the back axle, which had a Michelotti-styled fibreglass cab also used on the Routeman II eight wheeler announced in 1962, and Handyman III in 1964.

To compliment the Mountaineer dump truck, the Sherpa 4x2 and Himalayan 6x4 half-cab forward control dump trucks had joined the range in 1959 and 1961. Another special product at the time was an 8x8 snowplow/gritter, of which seven were built in 1960.

New for 1964 was the normal control 6x4 Contractor range which could either be a heavy haulage tractor or a high speed intercontinental rigid or articulated vehicle depending on engine (usually Cumins, A.E.C. or RollsRoyce of up to 375 hp) and transmission. Some were even used as

1959 SCAMMELL Constructor 6×4 heavy road tractor, Scammell

1963 SCAMMELL Routeman II 8×2 truck, Scammell

1965 SCAMMELL Trunker II 32-ton GCW tanker, Scammell

conventional 8x4's in Australia.

1968 saw the Routeman available as an 8x4 for the first time, whilst the start of a new generation of articulated tractors was the Crusader with steel Motor Panels' cab. This was initially a 6x4 for 42 tons gtw with a General Motors 290 hp engine, though for British use it evolved as a Rolls-Royce 220 or 280 hp engined 4x2 32 tonner. It was also the basis of the Samson 8x4 heavy haulage tractor in 1970.

1974 SCAMMELL Crusader 32-ton GCW truck, Scammell

In 1976 a new version of the Contractor heavy haulage tractor adopted a six cylinder 450 hp Cummins engine and in the following year Scammell's old trailer division was sold to York trailers.

With the end of Thornycroft production at Basingstoke, Scammell produced their Bushtractor and Nubian Crash Tender chassis. In November 1976 the tipper version of the Bushtractor was renamed the Scammell LD55, which in 1977 was uprated to 24 tons gvw and given the Leyland L12 engine in place of its former AEC unit. The Nubian is still produced and in 1978 was revised with a rear engine. *OM*

SCAMMELL (ii) (GB) 1933

G. Scammell & Nephew Ltd., Spitalfields, London E.1

After production of Scammell trucks was transferred to Watford in 1922, the parent firm of G. Scammell & Nephew reverted to their original business of body building and repairing. In 1933, however, they announced a low-loading 5-tonner powered by a 4-cylinder Meadows 4EL engine. It had forward control, a 4-speed gearbox, and a claimed top speed of 40 mph when loaded. At least one was sold, to the Steel Barrel Company of Uxbridge, but production never got under way. *GNG*

1903 SCANIA 1-ton truck, Scania

SCANIA (S) 1903-1911

Maskinfabriks AB Scania, Malmo

This bicycle and motorcycle making company built a passenger car in 1901 and their first commercial vehicle two years later. it had a 2-cylinder 10 hp engine made by Kamper in Germany which was mounted under the driver's seat, and chain drive. Capacity was 1½ tons. From the end of 1903 Scania built their own engines, and by 1906 they were making a conventional 2-tonner with driver behind the engine. This chassis was used for tower wagons and buses as well as ordinary trucks, and Scania

1911 SCANIA 2 ton truck

enjoyed a good export market. Small postal vans based on passenger cars were also made, these and the 2 tonners being made up to the merger in 1911 which led to the foundation of Scania-Vabis AB. *GNG*

SCANIA-VABIS: (ii) SCANIA (S)

(1) Scania-Vabis AB, Malmo 1911-1923
(2) Scania-Vabis AB, Sodertalje 1924-1969
(3) Saab-Scania (Scania Division), Sodertalje 1969 to date
(4) Scania Bussar AB, Katrineholm 1969 to date

Scania-Vabis AB was the result of a merger between Scania of Malmo and Vabis of Sodertalje. Initially the former factory handled commercial vehicle production, with the private cars (and all the group's engine requirements) being made at Sodertalje. This state of affairs continued until 1923, when cars were dropped from regular production. (The last one, a special order, was delivered as late as 1929). There was no immediate rationalization, though by 1914, when the N.A.G-style horseshoe radiator made its appearance, Scania-Vabis had settled down to a diet of 4-cylinder sv engines with magneto ignition. Capacities ranged from under 2½-litres for car-based delivery vans up to over 9-litres for the real heavies. Foot transmission brakes and 4-speed gearboxes were general practice, with a low 'underdrive' range available for snow work.

1915 SCANIA-VABIS 1-ton truck, Scania

Light-duty models rode on pneumatic tires, bevel drive featured on the up-to-2-ton family, and bigger trucks, such as the 5-ton ELa, favored side chains. 1916 saw a military 8-tonner with four-wheel drive and steering, not to mention a second steersman's post at the rear. This was not developed, though at least one 4×4 fire engine was built in 1917, by which time the company's mediums used 4.7-litre and 5-litre power units. From 1913 to 1922 there was also a branch factory at Fredericksburg in Denmark, where some peculiarly Danish types (including an electric truck in 1917) were produced alongside the standard offerings.

1925 SCANIA-VABIS Type 3752 20-seater bus, Scania

Chain drive did not finally disappear until 1927, but in 1924 there was a switch to ohv. Bigger vehicles — which included 6×4s for 3- and 6-ton payloads — featured double reduction back axles, while there were also some special mail buses equipped for winter work, with skis to the front wheels and creeper tracks at the rear. New angular radiators and dry plate clutches made their appearance in 1926, when the range included buses for up to 30 passengers. Also offered was an American-looking 1½-ton truck on pneumatic tires and demountable rims, but thereafter the trend was towards heavier machinery from 2½ tons upward. By 1927 there were larger buses with 4-wheel brakes and 6.4-litre 6-cylinder ohv engines rated at 100 bhp. These included half-cab single-deckers of very British appearance, though a full-front 37-seater was introduced in 1932, alongside a parallel range of forward-control

1930 SCANIA-VABIS articulated logging truck, Scania

trucks. In 1930 Scania-Vabis, like Volvo, espoused the Hesselman semi-diesel engine, made both in 4- and 6-cylinder forms: it had ousted the gas type effectively by 1935. Both engines were progressively enlarged, the six giving 120 bhp from 7.8 litres in 1935, while the final pre-War fours ran to 5.7 litres and were also offered with charcoal gas generators, even before the shortages of

1936 SCANIA-VABIS Type 35111/10-ton truck, Scania

1939-40. The standard truck range covered the 4/8-ton bracket, and Scania-Vabis were early in the field with large rear-engined buses, a model with a wheelbase of over 6 meters making its appearance in 1936. Early examples used the big six, later replaced by an 11.3-litre Hesselman-type straight-8. Trolley buses were first offered in 1939: these used running gear made by Asea of Vasteras, and were still listed in the 1950s. In 1942 Scania-Vabis built a 4½-ton 4×4 with the 4-cylinder engine, which featured the classic normal control styling destined to persist for some sixteen years.

1944 SCANIA-VABIS L11 6-ton truck, Scania

1946 SCANIA-VABIS B20 42-seater bus, Scania

1963 SCANIA-VABIS LB5-7642 articulated van, Scania

Though some buses had been exported to Estonia, the company's pre-War production (about 300 units a year) had been aimed almost exclusively at the home market. Scania-Vabis's first serious bid for export sales came in 1949, when they already accounted for 90 per cent of Stockholm's buses and had scrapped their old Hesselman units in favor of direct injection diesels — a 5.2-litre four, an 8½-litre six, and an updated edition of the straight-8, this last fitted to a unitary construction bus, the Metropol, capable of carrying 130 passengers. In 1953 guise this rear-engined giant had a wheelbase of 22 ft. 8 in., and featured a Spicer automatic gearbox, air brakes, power doors, and power steering. Its structure owed much to American Mack ideas: Scania-Vabis repaid the compliment in 1953 by selling their engine design rights to the Pennsylvania firm and later (from 1963) supplying them with complete power units for their urban delivery trucks. Smaller Scania-Vabis buses could be had in separate-chassis form: these were conventional in layout (apart from the option of engines mounted well forward of the front axle), and used 5-speed synchromesh gearboxes.

The post-War trucks were orthodox normal control machines for payloads of upwards of 5 tons, with diesel engines, 5-speed synchromesh gearboxes, and single-reduction spiral bevel back axles. The lighter L50 used the 4-cylinder unit and hydrovac brakes but on the big Scanias (which also came in 6×2 form) were 150 bhp sixes, full air brakes, and the option of an auxiliary gearbox giving 10 forward speeds. Turbochargers were first seen in 1955 on the straight-8, but this seldom went into trucks: an exception was the 6×6 8-ton Anteater (so called because of its sloping nose) evolved in 1957 for the Swedish Army. Forward control also made a tentative reappearance that year, though on the L70 tractive unit reserved for the Dutch market, and fitted with a Dutch-built cab.

1958 heavy trucks had 10.3-litre engines, exhaust brakes, and power steering, some dumper versions being used underground in the Kiruna mines, where by 1963 miners were being transported to work in specially modified Scania-Vabis buses, complete with exhaust brakes and Telma retarders to cope with the sharp gradients. Air suspensions were tested on the biggest buses, though the largest standard type, the CF75, while using the Metropol's structure, now wore its engine over the front axle. By 1961 annual production had built up to 7,000 units, and all standard trucks featured 6-cylinder engines and air brakes. Smallest of the range was the 7.2-litre L55 for 7/8-ton payloads: at the other end was the 6×4 LT75, which could cope with 14/15 tons. In 1963 the big six was enlarged to 11-litres, and output went up to 225 bhp with the optional turbocharger: at the same time dual-circuit air brakes were standardized, while forward control came back in earnest on the LB76, a power-steered 11-tonner available with such options as a 6×2 configuration, double reduction drive, and sleeper cabs. Output rose steadily from 255 bhp with turbocharger in 1965, to 275 bhp by 1967. This permitted tractor versions to achieve GCW ratings as high as 40 tons. 1965 saw the company's idea of a light truck, the normal control L36: it could carry 7½ tons, and was a hefty affair with the 5.2-litre 4-cylinder engine, wheelbases of 12 ft. 2 in. or 15 ft. 8 in., and a choice of five or ten forward speeds. It was really too heavy for its class, and was not quoted after 1968.

More and more impact was being made in export markets. Trucks had been assembled in Brazil as early as 1953, with local engine manufacture starting six years later: thereafter only gearboxes would be imported from Sweden. Dutch assembly began at Zwolle in 1964: subsequent developments included a state-controlled plant in Iraq (1972), and an Argentinian branch (1976) capable of turning out 1,500 vehicles a year. The make, introduced to the British market in 1966, formed the basis for Metropolitan Cammell-Weymann's MetroScania bus, which went into production in 1970. From February, 1968, the Vabis half of the name vanished from radiator badges, though the company itself did not assume its new style until the 1969 merger with Saab. This put Scania back into the car business, though it had kept a useful foothold there since 1948, when the Swedish Volkswagen concession was acquired.

1975 SCANIA LBS-140 6×4 truck and trailer, Scania

Modern tilt cabs had arrived on 1968's LB110 forward control range. These used 285 bhp 11-litre turbocharged engines in conjunction with 5- or 10-speed gearboxes, air-servo clutches, and power steering. Truck versions had GVWs of 16 tons, but the 110 would not long remain at the head of the family. In September, 1969, Scania announced a 14.2-litre V8 (350 bhp in turbocharged form)

1975 SCANIA LS-140 6×4 truck and trailer, Scania

which went into the LB140 with a 19-ton GVW. Normal control 140s had made their appearance in 1972, along with stiffer frames and new rangechange gearboxes, though there was still a light-weight (12-ton GVW) in the shape of the normal-control 4-cylinder L50. Bus development centered round integral rear-engined types. The urban CR111 used the 202 bhp six, a Scania-built automatic gearbox, power steering, and air suspension. The CR145 coach followed similar lines, but had its engine (a normally-aspirated, 275 bhp V8) set longitudinally over the back axle. On this one, too, a synchromesh gearbox was regular wear.

The Brazilian factory makes a number of models specially adapted for the local market. These include the LK140 with set forward front axle (to meet regulations limiting single tire axles to a loading of 5 tons), and the BR116 rear-engined bus chassis with longitudinal engine as opposed to the transverse engine of all Swedish-made Scania buses.

Automatics were also invading the load-carriers. A dual range 6-speed type was seen in 1971 on the LBAT/SBAT series of tilt-cab, forward-control 4×4s and 6×6s built for the Army. These vehicles could attain 55 mph on the road, wade through 3 feet of water, and climb a 60 per cent gradient; they were on commercial sale by 1977. While these military Scanias favored the Lysholm-Smith torque converter, an Allison box was favored for roadgoing types: it was first listed on 81s in 1975. A year later it could be had on the 86 as well.

1978 SCANIA CR111M 81-passenger city bus, Scania

In 1977, Scania made 20,700 trucks and buses, the latter in a separate factory at Katrineholm. Heavies were the order of the day: even the lightest 81s were rated at 16 tons GVW, and engines were 8-litres sixes of 163 and 205 bhp. These came in forward control form only, whereas both the 110s (11 litres, 280/305 bhp) and the V8-engined 140s for GVWs in the 26/30-ton bracket came with normal control as well. The CR111 and CR145 made up the basic PSV range. Both could be had in chassis form for specialist coachbuilders and the Katrineholm works also offered conventional full-front machines, though they did not build bodies for these. Engines were 8-litre or 11-litre sixes, and could be mounted either over or ahead of the front axle. *JFJK/MCS*

1978 SCANIA SBAT-111S 6-ton 6×6 truck, Scania

S.C.A.T. (I) 1913-1918

Societa Ceirano Automobili Torino, Turin

Giovanni Ceirano the younger established this company in 1906. Only private cars were produced before World War I, though the 3-litre 4-cylinder 15/20 could be had in cab form by 1913. During the War years a series of 2- and 4-ton trucks with 4-cylinder engines were produced to the designs of Giuseppe Coda, most of these going to the Italian Air Service. After Ceirano reacquired the company in 1925, truck manufacture was resumed under the Ceirano name. *MCS*

SCEMIA see Somua

1924 SCHACHT Super Safety bus, OMM

SCHACHT (US) 1910-1938

(1) Schacht Mfg. Co., Cincinnati, Ohio 1910
(2) Schacht Motor Car Co., Cincinnati, Ohio 1911-1913
(3) G.A. Schacht Motor Truck Co., Cincinnati, Ohio 1913-1927
(4) LeBlond-Schacht Truck Co., Cincinnati, Ohio 1927-1938

Schact began as a manufacturer of highwheel buggies and conventional passenger cars, abandoning these lines in 1910 although a few cars with combination truck/tourer bodies were sold up to 1913. Early trucks were conventional machines with load capacities from 1,000 lbs. to 4 tons, and by 1922 the range ran from 2 to 7 tons. Schachts of this period used Continental or Wisconsin engines but many other components were of the firm's own manufacture, making them less of assemblers than many of their rivals. By the late 1920s this was less true, with axles coming from Wisconsin, transmissions from Fuller etc. In 1926 the trucks were supplemented by the Super Safety Coach, a low-chassis vehicle with 48.6 hp 6-cylinder engine and 8-speed transmission. This chassis cost $5,900, reduced to $4,900 the following year.

1925 SCHACHT 4-ton truck, NAHC

In 1927 the company name was changed to LeBlond-Schacht with the intervention of LeBlond interests which included finance, machine tools and aircraft engines. The new capital thus obtained enabled Schacht to expand and to acquire the Armleder Truck Company in 1928, the two ranges being gradually integrated over the next eight years. By 1930 Schacht had ten dealerships in the Northeastern United States, but sales were hardly in proportion; 280 vehicles in 1929 and 359 in 1930, although the latter was an encouraging increase in what was a bad year for the industry. There was a wide range offered in the early 1930s, from 1½ to 10 tons, including tractors from 1932. Engines were Continental in the smaller models, Hercules and Wisconsin in the larger, and all were sixes from 1929 onwards. They were stylish vehicles, with big headlights, broad radiators and rakish fenders. 1935 models resembled Whites, and in 1937 they were redesigned with more original cabs, grilles and fenders. There were two series, the A series conventionals from 1½ to 3½ tons, and the CU cab-overs from 2½ to 5 tons. CU cabs slid forward on outriggers and rollers for easy engine maintenance. Apparently LeBlond-Schacht withdrew from the truck field in 1938, perhaps 1939 at the latest, to specialize in fire apparatus (they had acquired Ahrens-Fox in 1936). Fire engines of Ahrens-Fox design and Schacht models based on the A Series were offered into the early 1940s. *RJ*

1930 SCHACHT 3-ton truck, NAHC

1937 SCHACHT 3-ton truck, Old Cars

1901 SCHEELE electric van, GNG

SCHEELE (D) 1899-1925
(1) Heinrich Scheele, Cologne-Lindenthal 1899-1906
(2) Kolner Elektromobil-Gesellschaft Heinrich Scheele, Cologne-Lindenthal 1906-1925

This is one of the pioneer firms of electric cars and the only one originating in the last century and lasting into the twenties of this century. Only electric driven vans and trucks were built. *HON*

SCHEIBLER (D) 1899-1909
(1) Scheibler Motoren Industrie, Aachen 1899-1903
(2) Scheibler Automobil-Industrie GmbH., Aachen 1903-1909

Scheibler was one of the pioneers in production of commercials. At the beginning vans and hotel buses were offered; light trucks followed. Later Scheibler specialized in the heavier type of vehicles, and payload capacity went up to 3 tons. After 1909 the company was renamed and further models were offered as Mulags. *HON*

SCHIEMANN (D) 1901-1911
Gesellschaft fur gleislose Bahnen Max Schiemann & Co., Wurzen

Max Schiemann was the German pioneer of trolley buses. In 1901 he built the first line at Konigstein (Saxony) with the rolling stock built by Siemens & Halske according to his design. These first cars were equipped with front drive and bogie steering. Later developments had rear drive and steering-knuckle type of steering. Later also goods vehicles were built and traction engines for pulling horsedrawn vehicles up steep gradients. These also used the trolley system. *HON*

SCHILTER (CH) 1958 to date
Schilter AG., Maschinenfabrik, Stans NW

Schilter was one of the first Swiss factories to produce a multi-purpose vehicle for agricultural transportation tasks. In 1958 a rear-wheel drive vehicle equipped with an air-cooled Universal proprietary flat twin cylinder gas engine was launched. One year later a four-wheel drive version appeared. MAG 9 hp or 12 hp engines in unit with the gearbox and the differential rear axle were fitted. Payload was 1.8 tons. In the next years improved versions were offered.

1974 SCHILTER 1600 multi purpose truck, Schilter

The range in 1978 includes four models. The Schilter 1,000 1-ton model is equipped with air-cooled MAG single cylinder, 10 hp or twin-cylinder 16 hp gas engines or with Lombardini single cylinder diesel engines of 14 hp fitted conventionally over the front-axle. The gearbox has 6 forward and 2 reverse speeds. Front-wheel drive can be disengaged. Model 1600 with a 1.9 ton payload has a front-mounted water-cooled Perkins 4-cylinder diesel engine of 36 hp and a 8 speed gearbox. Model 1800 has the same engine, tuned to 40 hp, but instead of the central tube chassis, an interesting solution with two frames, allowing considerable torque is used. Payload is 2.7 tons. The shorter wheelbase Schilter 2500K is a 4-ton tipper truck also used as a snowplow. *FH*

SCHLEICHER (US) 1911-1919
Schleicher Motor Vehicle Company, Ossining, New York

The trucks under this label were essentially built-to-order trucks of large capacity. The three- and five-tonners used 4-cylinder, 45 hp Continental engines. Also offered were 6-, 8- and 10-tonners with prices up to $10,000 for the largest chassis. These all had four-speed gearboxes and double chain drive. Available wheelbases for the various chassis were up to 13 feet. *GMN*

SCHNABEL (US) 1914-1916
G.A. Schnabel and Son, Pittsburgh, Pa.

This specialist in hearse bodies also assembled a few of his own chassis. These were produced either with conventional radiators or with the Renault-style dashboard type. *MCS*

SCHNEIDER (F) 1908-1914
Ets. Schneider, Le Havre

After the bankruptcy of Brillie, Schneider decided to continue commercial vehicle production on their own, manufacturing them mainly in their Le Havre plant, though some also came from Le Creusot and Paris. The main part of the production was again done for the city of Paris, constituting of buses of the PB2 types. These PB2's were single deckers with a four-in-line 125x140mm engine of 35 hp. The radiator was again the well-known round Goudard & Menesson type. The PB2 was in production until 1920, first as Schneider, later as CGO-Schneider produced by Somua.

Most of the PB2's went to the French Army in 1914 where they were used particularly as carriers for the RVF-

1914 SCHNEIDER PB 2 Paris bus, OMM

section (Ravitaillement Viande Fraiche), troop carriers and ambulances. Apart from buses Schneider also manufactured trucks, which were of similar layout, and some specialized vehicles like an Army tractor constructed in 1914 and particularly notable for the position of the engine, the round radiator and the driver, which were placed all behind the front axle and very high in the vehicle.

After the take-over of Schneider's automotive division by Somua, the original brand-name was still used for various years for the buses as late as 1929. Produced in these years was one of the most interesting Schneiders, the H16 with a steerable third axle at rear. *JFJK*

SCHUCKERT (D) 1899-1903

Elektrizitats-Aktiengesellschaft vorm. Schuckert & Co., Nuremberg

A few electric vehicles were built by this company and used as vans. In 1900 two versions of electric-driven three-wheeled vans appeared either with single front or rear wheel. These were used by the mail for letter collecting. After 1903 vehicles were manufactured by the Siemens-Schuckert company. *HON*

1909 SCHURMEIER Model D 2-ton truck, AACA

SCHURMEIER (US) 1910-1911

Schurmeier Wagon Co., St. Paul, Minn.

The Schurmeier was the product of a buggy and wagon company who made a few trucks at their wagon factory before opening a new plant specially built for motor vehicles. Their trucks had 2-stroke engines, vertical twins in the 1-ton model and vertical 3-cylinder units in the 2- and 3-ton models. They had forward control and chain drive. About 100 Schurmeiers were made in all. *GNG*

SCHUTZE (D) 1900-1902

Giesserei und Maschinenfabrik Paul Schutze, Oggersheim

Electric trucks for 10 ton payload were produced by this firm. The design featured a front-driven bogie. *HON*

1921 SCHWARTZ 2-ton truck, FLP

SCHWARTZ (US) 1918-1923

Schwartz Motor Truck Corp., Reading, Pa.

H.B. Schwartz was an automobile dealer prior to introducing a line of 4-cylinder worm-drive trucks in mid-1918. In 1920 the firm listed 1½-ton and 2 ½-ton trucks with Continental engines and a 5-ton model with Buda engine. In 1922 a Lycoming-engined 1½-ton "speed truck" with bevel drive was added to the Schwartz line. In late 1923 the firm was taken over by Clinton Motors. *DJS*

SCOOTACAR; RYTECRAFT SCOOTACAR., (GB) 1934-1940

(1) British Motor Boat Mfg. Co., London, W.C.1.
(2) B.M.B. Engineering Co., London

Jim Shillan commenced in business in 1920 selling Evinrude outboard engines in London's Cannon Street, graduated to building and racing speedboats on the Welsh Harp at Hendon in the late twenties and thirties, and evolved the Scootacar, initially as a fairground 'dodgem' car and logical extension of his leisure-oriented business. Butlins operated a fleet of these at Clacton. It was as a light delivery vehicle that the Scootacar became best known, however, its diminutive size ensuring ideal publicity for its operators. Three main types were evolved; a light 5-cwt truck with dropsides and closed cab, a forward control box van and the dodgem type with a small box compartment fitted at the rear. Customers included Castrol, Englands Glory Matches, Chrysler, Vauxhall, and Piccadilly Cigarettes among others.

Initially fitted with a 98cc Villiers industrial engine (and occasionally with the B.S.A. C.10 unit) mounted in a sub frame which supported the rear axle, later models developed 8-10hp and became progressively more sophisticated. Tubular chassis were employed throughout, however. The company built powered life rafts for Coastal Command during the war and were taken over by Brockhouse Engineering Ltd., of Southport, when hostilities ceased. *MJWW*

1974 SCOT C1H 6×4 tanker, HD

SCOT (CDN) 1972 to date

Atlantic Truck Mfg. Co. Ltd., Debert, Nova Scotia

The first Scot truck was a conventional 6 × 4 tractor powered by a Cummins NTC335 diesel, with Ford Louisville cab. Later a 6 × 4 cab-over chassis for dump truck and garbage body work was added, and in 1976 the original highway tractor was replaced by the A2HD with the company's own cab and hood. Other recent models include fire engine chassis, aircraft refuellers and special vehicles for off-highway logging and mining work, the latter up to 400,000 lbs capacity. Engines run from 180 to 600 hp, mostly Cummins or Detroit diesels. *GNG*

1903 SCOTT (i) 2-ton steam wagon, NMM

SCOTT (i) (GB) 1903-1904

G.D. Scott, Castle Works, Derby

Scott's boiler was described as "a plain cylinder with concentric rings of Field tubes with a common petroleum burner in the middle". The rear wheels and crankshaft were concentric and his own design of "equalizing" gear was fitted. 3- and 5-ton sizes were contemplated but possibly no more than the prototypes were constructed. *RAW*

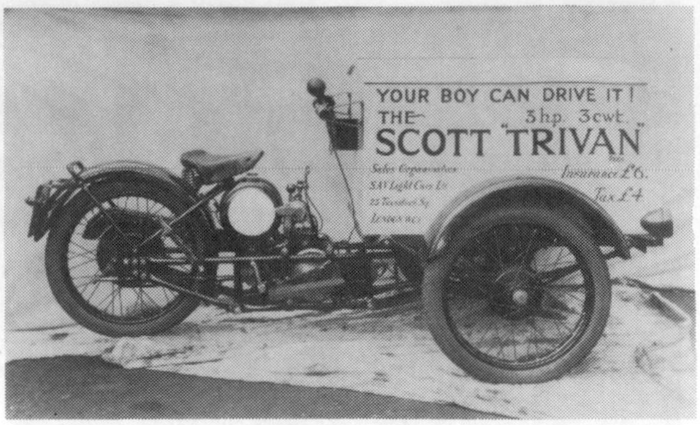

1929 SCOTT (ii) 340lb tri-van, Scott Owners Club

SCOTT (ii) (GB) 1929-1931

Scott Motor Cycle Co. Ltd., Shipley, Yorks.

Scott were pioneers and well-known builders of 2-stroke motorcycles, and their commercial vehicle venture was a light motorcycle-based 3-wheeler powered by a single-cylinder horizontal 3hp engine. The 2½ cwt load was carried in a box ahead of the rider, between the front wheels. Maximum speed was 45mph, and the price £80. *GNG*

SCOTT (iii) (GB) 1952

Scott Electric Vehicles Ltd., Kidderminster, Worcs.

Most Scott electrics were works and railroad platform trucks, but in 1952 they listed two road-going vehicles for milk flat or general delivery work. They were 3-wheelers with a similar appearance to the Brush Pony, and came in 10 cwt and 1-ton forms. The former had a 1½hp motor, the latter a 2hp. Drive was to the single front wheel. *GNG*

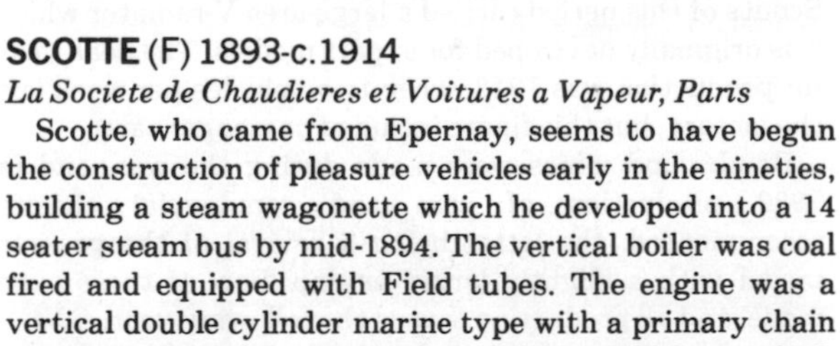

1904 SCOTTE steam tractor and road train, Autocar

SCOTTE (F) 1893-c.1914

La Societe de Chaudieres et Voitures a Vapeur, Paris

Scotte, who came from Epernay, seems to have begun the construction of pleasure vehicles early in the nineties, building a steam wagonette which he developed into a 14 seater steam bus by mid-1894. The vertical boiler was coal fired and equipped with Field tubes. The engine was a vertical double cylinder marine type with a primary chain to a countershaft embodying the differential from which the rear wheels were driven by twin roller chains.

By 1897 he had produced the "train Scotte"-a postal bus coupled to a trailer omnibus, aimed at rural services of the type catered for by the roadside steam trams. Later he made a heavy haulage tractor and as late as 1905 this was tested by the French Army but not adopted. An ambulance train was supplied to the Societe Francaise de Secours aux Blesses Militaires in 1909 but thereafter little was heard of the make which seems to have perished in the early days of the 1914-18 war.

Scotte returned to Epernay when he set up in business as a hatter. *RAW*

1914 SCOUT 3-ton truck, OMM

SCOTT-STIRLING see Stirling

SCOTTISH ASTER see St. Vincent

SCOUT (GB) 1909-1921

Scout Motors Ltd., Salisbury, Wilts.

The first commercial vehicle chassis from this regional car maker were 2- and 4-cylinder shaft-drive units for 10, 15 and 20 cwt loads. Larger chassis for 2- and 3-ton loads with 32 and 38 hp 4-cylinder engines and chain drive were introduced in 1910, and a number of these were fitted with bus and charabanc bodies. Most were sold locally, operating services through the New Forest to Southampton and Bournemouth, but at least one was in service in Suffolk. Worm drive was introduced in 1914, and some Scouts of this period carried a large-area V-radiator which was originally developed for export models. The peak year for production was 1912, when two vehicles per week left the factory, but this figure included passenger cars.

Bombs and mines were made during the war, and in 1920 production of cars and commercial chassis recommenced, the latter being a revival of the pre-war model with a slightly larger engine. Few of these were made, and all production ceased the following year. *GNG*

SCRIPPS-BOOTH (US) 1914-1915

Scripps-Booth Cyclecar, Detroit, Mich.

The cyclecar version of this fairly well-known marque was available with a delivery van body which weighed 750 pounds and was priced at $395. It was powered by an air-cooled, 2-cylinder engine of 10 hp. Final drive was through a planetary transmission and belts to the rear wheels. Wheelbase was 8 feet, 4 inches with tread of three feet. Like the other cyclecars, this was not a success and the manufacturer went to manufacturing the more popular "light car" for passenger use, but did not offer a commercial version. *GMN*

1932 S.D. Freighter 2-ton truck, NMM

S.D. (GB) 1923 to date

Shelvoke & Drewry Ltd., Letchworth, Herts.

Launched in the summer of 1923, the S.D. Freighter was a new conception of small-wheeled vehicle for short-distance transport. It was powered by a 2.2-litre 35/bhp 4-cylinder E.T. White monobloc engine mounted transversely at the driver's right, driving a 3-speed epicyclic gearbox to his left, and thence by bevel gear to a propeller shaft and to a worm rear axle. Control was by two tram-type handles, the right hand one for steering and the left for gear-changing and rear wheel braking. There was a pedal-operated front wheel brake. As introduced the Freighter had a 6 ft., 6 in. wheelbase and a body length of 10 ft., but almost any wheelbase could be had; in 1928 there was a 2-ton van on a 12 ft. wheelbase with a 20 ft. body. Turning circle of the original model was 21 ft., 4 ft. less than the regulations for a London taxicab. Maximum speed was 14 mph which could be obtained in reverse, although top gear in reverse was usually blanked off for safety reasons.

Among the first orders for the Freighter was one from Deptford Corporation for two refuse trucks; as time went by the company came to be identified increasingly with municipal vehicles though the earlier Freighter was used for a wide variety of work including cable carriers for the General Post Office, furniture vans, glass carriers, mobile canteens and torpedo carriers for the Royal Air Force. There were also a number of buses; the 10th chassis to be built, late in 1923, had an 18-seater bus body and was used as a demonstrator. The first orders came from Gates of Worthing who started their Tramocar service along the seafront in April 1924. Eventually they had a dozen Freighters as well as two rear-engined E-type buses delivered in 1938. Other operators to use S.D. buses included the Corporations of Plymouth, Bournemouth, Blackpool and Belfast, and private operators in Rhyl, Barmouth, Aberystwyth and Jersey. Wheel steering was introduced on the buses in 1933, though not on other vehicles until the E-type of 1938.

By 1928 over 100 municipalities were using S.D.s, and export customers included Rangoon who had 30 and Poznan, Poland who had 10. The 1929 models featured a new 2.4-litre 38 bhp engine made by S.D., supplemented in 1932 by a 3-litre 44 bhp unit. Other makes of engine were said to be available if specified by the customer, but most, if not all, S.D.s were powered by these two units which continued to be offered until World War II. The basic design changed little, though pneumatic tires, and fully-enclosed cabs were available from 1929, and a self-starter from 1936. A works truck with 5 ft. 3 in. wheelbase was added to the range in 1928, and a completely different line for the company was the building of the Latil Traulier 4-wheel drive tractor from 1932 to 1939. In 1933 the patents

1939 S.D. E-type gulley emptier, OMM

of the Principality moving-floor refuse collector were acquired by Shelvoke & Drewry for their sole use. In 1938 came the completely new E-type which had its engine ahead of the driver, though still transversely-mounted, and broke with tradition in having wheel steering from a conventional right-hand postion. It was the first S.D. to have a frontal radiator.

In 1946 a new model known as the W-type appeared. It marked a further step towards conventional design, and also an increase in size, with longitudinally-mounted 3.9-litre 55 bhp S.D. engine. By now S.D.s were almost exclusively municipal vehicles, the W-type being made as a Chelsea-type side-loading, or moving-floor rear-loading refuse collector, and as a gully emptier. It could be had with a single or double cab, the latter with accommodation for a crew of six. The old transverse-engined model was made in small numbers after the war, as the N-type, but production ceased in about 1950. A few of these were supplied as ordinary goods vehicles to a fruit-packing firm in Jersey. Fork-lift trucks were a new activity for

1950 S.D. W-type 3-ton truck, OMM

Shelvoke & Drewry from 1952 onwards, and from 1954 a Perkins P4 diesel engine was optional in the W-type. In 1960 came a new range which marked a further increase in size; the TW models had S.D. gasoline or Perkins P6 diesel engines and were rated for 10-11 ton GVW, while the TY had a Leyland 0350 engine and 14 tons GVW. Features of the new models included new composite fiber glass and coachbuilt cabs, 5-speed gearboxes and air-pressure hydraulic brakes. Wheelbases were 8 ft. 6 in. to 11 ft. 6in., and capacities 12 to 25 cu. yds. with four-and-aft tipping bodies.

An important new development of 1961 was the Pakamatic compressing body with double acting packer plate and shredding tongues to break up refuse. Originally available on the larger models, it was introduced on the 8 ft. 0 in. wheelbase TN in 1963; this had a 4-cylinder Perkins 236 engine and at 8½ tons GVW was the baby of a range extending up to the 14-ton GVW Leyland-engined TY-type. Gully and cesspool emptiers continued to be offered, and in 1967 there was a 6-wheeled street washer supplied to Westminster Council. By 1970 gasoline engines were no longer offered, and there was a new body type, the ejector discharge Revopak which discharged without tipping, in addition to fore-and-aft tippers in 18 and 35 cu. yd. sizes, and Pakamatics from 35 to 60 cu. yds.

1974 S.D. NX Revopak refuse truck, S.D.

A new Motor Panels cab came in 1973 and was used on all but the smallest NN series by 1975. The range is now the widest S.D. has ever offered, with tankers of 11½ to 16 tons GVW, fore-and-aft tippers and Pakamatics from 8¾ tons GVW and Revopaks from 11½ to 22 tons. The largest of the latter is the 6 × 4 NT model with Leyland 410 turbocharged engine and 6-speed gearbox.
410 turbocharged engine and 6-speed gearbox. In 1979 S.D. returned to making their own cabs.

A completely new field for Shelvoke & Drewry was entered in the summer of 1975 when they built, in col-

1977 S.D. WX and WY series fire engine, S.D.

laboration with the fire engine specialists Carmichaels of Worcester, the CSD fire engine with 210 hp Cummins V-8 engine as standard, and options of Perkins V-8 or Rolls-Royce straight-8 engines. This was available as a road-going 4 × 2 water tender or a 4 × 4 airfield crash tender. 1978 models of the latter could be had with Detroit Diesel or Rolls-Royce engines from 235 to over 700 hp and there were also the WX and WY series of road-going fire engines. In 1976 S & D again broke fresh ground with the NY series of 4×4 on/off-highway truck chassis in the 16-ton class. These had a Leyland 144 hp diesel engine, 6-speed transmission and Motor Panels tilt cab. *GNG*

1938 S.D.S. 4-ton truck, JFJK

SDS (B) 1938-1940

This was a Belgian make of heavy duty trucks, patterned on the contemporary American trends, and assembled from parts bought from outside suppliers. Parts used were Hercules gasoline engines, Gardner oil engines, Timken axles, Clark gearbox and Lockheed hydraulic brake with Dewandre servo-assistance. Only truck chassis were manufactured. *JFJK*

1914 SEAGRAVE ladder truck, LA

SEAGRAVE (US) 1907 to date

(1) The Seagrave Co., Columbus, Ohio, 1907-19
(2) The Seagrave Corp., Columbus, Ohio, 1919-1963
(3) Seagrave Fire Apparatus Divn., FWD Corp., Clintonville, Wis. 1963 to date

One of America's best-known manufacturers of fire apparatus, Seagrave's first motorized vehicles were powered by a 4-cylinder air-cooled engines; the first three were delivered to Vancouver, B.C. late in 1907. Two years later came the AC90 tractor, also with 4-cylinder air-cooled engine, for articulated ladder trucks, while in 1911 came the first fire engines with water cooling. These centrifugal pumpers carried their 6-cylinder engines under a long hood, though the air-cooled driver-over-engine 'buckboards' were made up to 1914. All Seagraves had chain drive up to 1922.

1915 saw a fwd conversion for 65, 75 and 85 ft. ladder trucks, the Model K with 4- or 6-cylinder engine. Seagrave also used Couple Gear electric chassis for their ladder trucks. In 1917 came the first motor water tower, and in 1922 a shaft-drive pumper with rounded hood, artillery or disc wheels which supplemented the older chain-drive models with Mercedes-type gabled hood, though the latter continued for six years longer. In 1923 a smaller pumper, the 350 gpm Suburbanite with 6-cylinder Continental engine appeared, and there were also larger pumpers of 750 to 1,300 gpm. A wide variety of fire apparatus including articulated ladder trucks were made in the 1920s.

1930 SEAGRAVE aerial ladder truck, NMM

In 1932 appeared Seagrave's 240 hp V-12 engine, designed to counter American La France's V-12 which had come in 1931. A smaller V-12, based on Pierce-Arrow's passenger car unit, was added in 1935, and the still smaller Seagraves such as the Continental-powered Suburbanite were still made. Very few Seagraves used commercial truck chassis, but some were built on Ford and Reo chassis in the1930s because of the Depression. In 1935 new styling with a V-radiator grille was adopted, and this lasted until 1951. The first limousine "Safety Sedan Pumper" came in 1936, also smaller pumper series called

Sentry, of 500 to 600 gpm capacity. Articulated ladder trucks with both open and closed cabs were still made during the 1930s and 1940s.

1950 SEAGRAVE quad combination pumper, EK

In 1951 came the 70th Anniversary Series, completely restyled with the siren built into the center of the radiator grille; this lasted until 1970 and was used in a wide variety of apparatus, pumpers, rigid and articulated ladder trucks, with open and closed cabs. The big V-12 engine was retained and a new model with 300 hp came in 1955. Segrave equipment was offered on a number of commercial chassis in the 1950s including Ford and

1958 SEAGRAVE 70th Anniversary Series pumper, OMM

International. In 1959 came the first cab-forward models, though conventionals continued until 1970. Seagrave was the first major fire engine builder to offer an aerial platform (snorkel) in 65 and 85 ft. sizes, in 1961. The following year Waukesha and Hall-Scott engines were available; production of the V-12 dwindled during the 1960s. The company was sold to FWD in 1963; the Columbus plant was gradually run down and production transferred to Clintonville. Seagrave had introduced the Rear Admiral, a rear-mounted turntable designed for the new cab-forward chassis, but because of the move to Clintonville none were delivered for several years. Seagrave fire engines were made at Clintonville alongside FWD's own Tractioneer cab-forward pumpers. In 1969 a new company was formed

1970 SEAGRAVE aerial ladder truck, OMM

in Columbus to make fire equipment on commercial chassis, sold under the name Seagrave Commercial-by-Timpco.

The last conventional pumper of the 70th Anniversary Series was delivered to Jackson, Mich. in 1970. In 1972 Seagrave introduced a new custom cab-forward range with Detroit Diesel engines, made in combination pumper and articulated ladder truck form. They also built chassis for the Pierce Mfg. Co. of Appleton, Wisconsin.

Seagrave fire engines were assembled in Walkerville (now Windsor) Ontario from 1910 to 1918, and in St. Catherines, Ontario from 1930 to 1936. (See also Bickle.) *GNG*

SEAL (GB) 1922-1930

Seal Motors Ltd., Manchester

The Seal (Sociable, Economical and Light) was a most unusual vehicle resembling a motorcycle and sidecar, but steered from the sidecar. Passenger versions were made from 1912, and a goods model was introduced in 1922. This used the 980 cc V-twin J.A.P. engine of the passenger model, and came in van, pick-up and 'convertible' forms, the latter suitable for business or pleasure. Transmission was by a Burman gearbox and chain final drive. Production of the commercial version continued until 1930 when a new model was introduced under the name Progress. *GNG*

SEARS (US) 1909-1911

Sears & Roebuck Co., Chicago, Ill.

The Sears was a high-wheeled light farm wagon with chain-drive, left-hand tiller steering, full elliptic springs, and fenders front and rear. The 2-cylinder-horizontally-opposed air-cooled motor was under the seat and the general layout was a cab-over with the front axle under the dashboard. Most of Sears' production was of high-wheeled cars.

Afterwards the Sears became the Lincoln (i) *RW*

S.E.A.T. (E) 1953 to date

Sociedad Espanola de Automoviles de Turismo, SA, Barcelona

This company was formed to manufacture Fiat cars and commercial vehicles under licence in Spain. The first products were taxicabs and light vans on the 1400 chassis, followed by the 1500 in van and pick-up form with gasoline or diesel engines. When Fiat introduced the 600 and forward-control Multipla SEAT soon built commercial versions of these, the 600D having an additional door on the right hand side to make for easier loading. In 1974, after SEAT had built over 300,000 of the 127 cars, they launched the 127 Comercial which could carry up to 300kgs of cargo. This is still made today. *JCG*

SEATON-PETTER (GB) 1926-1927

British Dominions Car Co Ltd, Yeovil, Somerset

The Seaton-Petter was a short-lived attempt at a £100 utility car, using a 1,319cc vertical-twin water- cooled 2-stroke engine in a simple chassis. The rear seats of the standard tourer were detachable for occasional commercial use, but the chassis was also availble with van bodywork in two sizes, for 7-cwt and 10-cwt payloads. These were advertised for immediate delivery in January, 1927, but little was heard thereafter. *MCS*

SEDAN (GB) 1909-1910

Sedan Auto-Car Syndicate Ltd, Wolverhampton, Staffs.

The Sedan was a front-wheel-drive fore-carriage design powered by a 22hp flat-twin engine. The brakes were on the front wheels, but there were also rear wheel brakes 'for emergency use'. Vans and trucks with a capacity of 2 tons were listed, but very few went into service. At least one was delivered to Coalite Ltd in early 1910. *GNG*

1940 SEDDON 5L 6-ton truck, Seddon

SEDDON (GB) 1938-1975

(1) Foster & Seddon, Salford, Lancs., 1938-45.
(2) Seddon Motors Ltd., Oldham, Lancs., 1947-50
(3) Seddon Diesel Vehicles Ltd., Oldham, Lancs 1951-1973
(4) Seddon Atkinson Vehicles Ltd., Oldham, Lancs, 1974-1975

Foster and Seddon were hauliers and commercial vehicle distributors who in 1938 decided to market a Perkins P6 diesel engined truck to take maximum advantage of the 2½-tons unladen weight tax and speed concessions. They succeeded in making a full size vehicle within the limit which qualified for 30 miles per hour operation and could carry 6 tons. Approximately 20 were built before 1940, with a further 60 early in the war, until the Ministry of Supply requested Seddon to concentrate on trailer manufacture.

After the war production at Salford built up to six chassis per week, but space was cramped so a move was made to a new factory in Oldham where the Mk. 4 and 5 were built as goods vehicles, tippers, and, mainly for export, as bus and coach chassis. In 1950 a new 3-tonner with Perkins 4-cylinder engine appeared, and in 1952 a Seddon specifically designed for passenger work was introduced with a mid-mounted 6-cylinder Perkins engine for 32 seat bodywork. Seddon moved into an even lighter sector in 1954 with the Twenty-Five, a Perkins 3-cylinder-engined light delivery vehicle.

By using proprietary components for all except parts that they could make more cheaply themselves, Seddon were able to offer vehicles priced below the other small producers, but at the same time to incorporate individual features to customers' requirements that would have been out of the question for the mass producers. They were able to offer a payload advantage because of the use of lightweight components, and from 1954 were the first manufacturers to experiment with fiber glass cab panels.

The combination of low cost and custom building thus enabled Seddon to find gaps in the British market that would have been uneconomic for other manufacturers, and they had a similar success in certain export markets, notably the Far East, Central and South America, Spain and Portugal, and Holland, where they were assembled by, and as, Van Twist.

From the mid fifties Seddon began to move away from the highly competitive light-weight field towards the maximum capacity 4-wheeler market. In 1956 the traditional

1954 SEDDON 6-ton truck, OMM

1954 SEDDON 1¼-ton van, OMM

pattern of Seddon cab acquired a wrap-around windshield on the 6/7-tonner and its articulated derivative, whilst for 1957 two new lightweight cabs were adopted for the medium and heavy models. Amongst these was the Mark 15 for 11 tons gross operation, and the Mark 12 with set back front axle.

1958 SEDDON DD8 15-ton truck, OMM

1958 was an important year for the company when they moved into the heavyweight market with the DD8 24-tons gross 8-wheeler, which used a similar plastics cab to the Mark 15, and a choice of Gardner or Cummins diesel engines. Also announced was the Sirdar 40-ton g.t.w. 6 × 4 conventional export tractor with Cummins I68 hp engine, a version of the Mark 15 with Leyland 116 hp engine for 14 tons gross operation, and the Pennine Mark 19 bus for up to 43 seats. This had an AEC horizontal mid-mounted 98 hp engine and gearbox.

Leyland engines were also offered in the larger 1959 goods models, which now had new rounded plastics cabs and could be supplied as trailing axle 6-wheelers. The Sirdar was now available with a 200 hp Cummins engine for 30 tons rigid operation, while in 1961 a conventional 6 × 4 articulated tractor was available for up to 45 tons g.t.w. In 1962 the range was simplified to reduce the variety of major components offered, and all the 6- and 8-wheelers were fitted with a Maxartic bogie which helped to save over a ton of laden weight on the DD8.

Having moved into the heavy market, Seddon replaced most of their medium range in 1964 with the 13: Four which had a new steel cab and used the Perkins 6.354 engine. This, and the uprated 16: Four announced in 1965 with Perkins V-8 170 hp engine was extremely cheap, the smaller model initially costing only £1,710 in chassis/cab form, and enabled Seddon greatly to increase production to 2,500 vehicles per year by 1970.

By 1967 the V-8 engined tractor had grown to a 28-tonner, whilst a Gardner 180 hp or a Rolls Royce 220 hp engined version could handle 32 tons, or 38 tons on the continent with the larger engine. These and most of the lighter models incorporated axles produced by Seddon as part of a new policy to be less dependent on outside suppliers.

Meanwhile the Pennine bus chassis in Mark IV form had been available with a Perkins 6.354 engine from 1967, with the option of the V-8 in 1968.

Developments in 1970 included the option of a turbocharged Rolls Royce engine in the 38-ton tractor, whilst a rear mounted Gardner engine was available in the

1971 SEDDON 32/4 32-ton GCW truck, GNG

1977 SEDDON-ATKINSON 400 32-ton GCW truck, Seddon-Atkinson

Pennine RU bus, now made by a Seddon subsidiary, Pennine Coachcraft Ltd.

Seddon were also experimenting with air cooled Deutz engines in some of their existing models, while a joint company with Magirus-Deutz was marketing the latter's products in Britain until the German company set up its own British organization.

By now Seddon claimed to be Britain's largest independent commercial vehicle producer, and in December 1970 strengthened their position by acquiring Atkinson Vehicles Ltd.

More recently Seddon found a new niche in the bus market with their small Midi-Bus, and also make a large Gardner 180 hp mid-engined model.

In 1974 Seddon were acquired by the International Harvester Corporation, and in 1975 the Atkinson and Seddon heavy models were rationalized in the 400 series with new steel cabs and a wide choice of engine and transmission options. *OM*

SEDDON-ATKINSON (GB) 1975 to date

Seddon-Atkinson Vehicles Ltd., Oldham, Lancs

The first product of the newly formed combine was the 400 Series comprising 4-, 6- and 8-wheeled rigid chassis and an articulated tractor for 32 tons GVW. Power plants included Cummins, Gardner or Rolls-Royce diesels from 204 to 271 hp. In 1976 came the 200 Series 4-wheeler in the 17-tons GVW class, powered by a 134 hp 6-cylinder International diesel engine. Survivors from the former Seddon range included municipal vehicles which retained the old cab, and the Pennine 7 underfloor-engined coach chassis. All these models were continued into 1978 when they were joined by the 300 Series, a 6-wheeler in the 24-tons GVW class powered by a 200 hp International DT-466 engine, with 6-speed ZF gearbox, and available in three wheelbase lengths. *GNG*

1936 SEFA fire engine, JCG

SEFA (E) 1931-1936

Sociedad Espanola de Fabricacion de Automoviles, Madrid

This company was formed to make cars and commercial vehicles, but in fact concentrated entirely on the latter. They were conventional medium-sized trucks in the 3- to 5-ton range, with 4-cylinder engines, and bore a great similarity with the contemporary de Dion Bouton chassis. A number of fire engines were made, and delivered to the municipality of Valencia. Not more than 35 Sefas were made in all, and production ended with the Civil War. *JCG*

1911 SEITZ (i) 3-ton truck, NAHC

SEITZ (i) (US) 1908-1913

Seitz Automobile & Transmission Company, Detroit, Mich.

All trucks with this name used forward control and were furnished with the "Seitz double friction transmission", even up to the five-tonner. Other models included two- and three-tonners as well as a delivery van rated at 1,500-pound capacity. The three-tonner had a 4-cylinder engine of 40-45 hp with wheelbase of 10 feet, 4 inches, double chain drive and solid tires. It was claimed that the friction transmission was designed to be used as an emergency brake by putting it into reverse.*GMN*

SEITZ (ii) c.1940-c.1949

Fahreugfabrik Seitz & Co. AG., Kreuzlingen

The old coach-building company Seitz offered electric delivery vans and light trucks during and immediately after the 2nd World War. In 1949 two models were made: the forward-control Type A with 4.5 kW motor and 1½-ton payload and the normal control Type E with 8 kW motor and 2-tons payload. Range was 50 miles. The company was reformed and became Mowag. *FH*

1915 SELDEN 2-ton truck, GNG

SELDEN (US) 1913-1932

(1) Selden Motor Vehicle Co., Rochester, N.Y. 1913-1919
(2) Selden Truck Corporation, Rochester, N.Y. 1919-1928
(3) Selden-Hahn Motor Truck Corp., Allentown, Pa. 1929-1932

George B. Selden achieved fame in 1906 when he ran his car claimed to be of 1877 manufacture, and thereby gained a patent on which most U.S. car makers paid royalties until 1911, when Seldon was defeated by Henry Ford. After this he turned to vehicle manufacture, introducing passenger cars in 1906 and trucks in 1913. The latter were conventional shaft-driven vehicles powered by 4-cylinder Continental engines of 20 and 40hp. Brown-Lipe 3- or 4-speed gearboxes were used, and rear axles were by Timken and Russel. 1, 2, and 3½-ton models were made, and Seldens were exported in large numbers to Great Britain, France, Scandinavia and Japan. They were also one of the most important firms connected with the standardized Class B Liberty truck made for the U.S. Army in World War I, of which they built 3,700.

Post-war models still had Continental engines, and were made in several sizes from 30cwt to 3½ tons. By 1924 the largest model was a 5/7-tonner, and there was also a purpose-built bus chassis in the range. In 1928 came a new series powered by 6-cylinder LeRoi engines, the 1½ and 2½-ton Pacemakers and 3/4-ton Roadmaster. Top of the range was a 5/7-tonner known as the Model 77. In 1929 Selden merged with the Hahn Motor Truck Corporation of Allentown where limited production continued for a further three years. *GNG*

SELVE (D) 1920-1929

Selve Automobilwerke A.G., Hameln

Selve started with production of vans and later turned to private cars too. Both versions used the same chassis' and engines, which were available with 1.5 and 2.0 litre capacity. Selve chassis' were also used for light fire engines. In 1928 a 6 × 6 all-terrain vehicle with 6-cylinder 50 PS engine was presented, but production was not taken up. *HON*

SENECA (US) 1916-1921

Seneca Motor Truck Company, Fostoria, Ohio

A half-tonner was the only model by this manufacturer. It used a 4-cylinder LeRoi engine, had a three-speed gearbox and a wheelbase of 9 feet. Price of the chassis alone was $1,020. It is likely this company was connected with the manufacturer of passenger autos by the same name, also located in Fostoria. *GMN*

1912 SENTINEL Standard 6-ton steam wagon NMM

SENTINEL (GB) 1906-1956

(1) Alley & McLellan Ltd., Polmadie, Glasgow 1906-1917
(2) Sentinel Waggon Works Ltd., Shrewsbury 1917-1920
(3) Sentinel Waggon Works (1920) Ltd., Shrewsbury 1920-1936
(4) Sentinel Waggon Works (1936) Ltd., Shrewsbury 1936-1950
(5) Sentinel (Shrewsbury) Ltd., Shrewsbury 1950-1956

Stephen Alley was the force behind the Sentinel wagon and patentee of many of the essentials. His firm had a high reputation as marine engineers and builders of small vessels though, curiously, they never built their own boilers, using instead specialists such as Abbott & Co. of Newark. The essentials of the 1906 5-ton design were a vertical boiler with cross water tubes and a really effective superheater capable of imparting 150° F of superheat to the steam, an undertype engine with twin high pressure cylinders and poppet valves operated by camshaft. Other features were Ackermann steering, single speed and single chain drive to rear axle differential. After the spate of poor undertypes put on the market under the 1904 regulations the Sentinel was like waking from a bad dream — a wagon soundly engineered, strong and simple in the mechanical parts, fitted with a boiler providing ample supplies of dry, hot steam. This design, the Standard, continued without major changes until the new Super appeared in 1923, the latter examples of having solid rubber tires on cast steel wheels.

Whilst the Standard was in production the firm had a brief dalliance in 1911 with overtypes of which 16 were sold. The only really distinctive feature was its use of cylindrical firebox in a locomotive boiler, followed later by Robeys and Rustons, the countershaft running in a tunnel

1924 SENTINEL Super 6-ton steam wagon, OMM

through the steam space. Otherwise the design was not dissimilar to the Foden 5-tonner.

The appearance of the Super in 1923 brought with it several important changes. In the boiler, still at 230 psi, the cross water tubes gave way to inclined water tubes expanded into recesses pressed into the inner firebox but in the engine the stroke of the pistons was increased from 5" to 9", the diameter remaining 6 3/4", thus, speed for speed on the piston, increasing power output and making the road speed potentially faster. Other changes were the transfer of the differential to the crankshaft, permitting double chain drive and redesign of the valves and camshafts but the wagon was still a single speed which, though fine for simplicity and weight saving, handicapped it on longer hauls.

1930 SENTINEL DG8 15-ton steam wagon, OMM

This led to the introduction of the DG series, in two, three and four axle models in which the boiler reverted to cross water tubes, and pressure was raised to 275 psi, permitting the cylinders to be reduced to 6" × 8". The 2 speed gears were interposed between the crankshaft and a countershaft, with twin chains thence to the rear axle. For the first time, therefore, the engine of a Sentinel undertype could be run whilst the vehicle was standing, without disconnecting the chain. Pneumatic tires were introduced about 1930 but the tare to laden weight ratio placed the wagon at a disadvantage under the revised taxation rules of 1933, based on unladen weight.

After the brief intermediate dalliance with the SD series, using shaft drive in a wagon that otherwise had a strong resemblance to the DG's, the company embarked, in 1934, upon the production of the S type wagons in which a very serious attempt was made to reduce tare weight and to bring steam wagon practice into line with contemporary good class internal combustion truck design. Aluminum alloys were used extensively in the

1934 SENTINEL S4 7/8-ton steam wagon, OMM

engine and gearbox and the engine itself was a 4-cylinder single acting horizontal inline with longitudinal crankshaft. Poppet valves operated by camshaft were used and the well tried cross water tube boiler and superheater were retained but placed a little further back. Pneumatic tires and electric lights were standard. For the cab, sheet steel was used for the roof and front apron with armored ply side panels and boarded back. Full windshields were fitted and wind-up windows were provided in the doors. The 'S' type was available in 4, 6 and 8 wheeled versions. Despite every effort, however, the need for the boiler and its attendant water made the wagon heavier than its i/c rivals and its principal users were the gas companies, who were interested in promoting coke sales, and a limited band of traditional steam wagon users — mainly millers, oil cake makers, brewers, grain merchants and cement manufacturers. Production virtually ceased with the outbreak of war in 1939 and, despite postwar efforts to interest the Coal Board and other Government agencies was not resumed for some time. In 1950, however, one hundred 6 wheeled wagons, mostly new but including some rebuilds, were supplied to the Argentine Government, one of which survives.

In addition to wagons Sentinel produced a limited number of heavy steam tractors for haulage, mainly directed at the round timber trade but these never achieved as much popularity as the Foden timber tractors as they were somewhat heavier on their feet than the Foden.

In 1936/7, in conjunction with Abner Doble, Sentinel produced a very advanced fully condensing truck with mono-tube boiler (delivering steam at 1,500 psi) and compound engine but high production cost meant that, though very successful in engineering terms, the prototype was not repeated.

A fleet of 'S' type wagons remained in use by the North Thames Gas Board in London until the early fifties and a small fleet of tar sprayers on the same type of chassis were used by M.R. Woolley of Bucknell, Salop until the sixties. The most remarkable Sentinel survival, however, was the fleet of Standards used by Brown Bayley's steelworks, Sheffield for internal transport until the sixties. Apart from these, however, the last working Sentinels, notably in the Liverpool area, were the Super and DG models which survived because of their exceptionally rugged construction. The very last working steam Sentinel, owned, at the time of writing, by Lloyd Jones Bros. of Llanfair, Denbigh, North Wales is a DG tar-sprayer.

Probably the most celebrated of the tractors was the "Elephant" employed to shunt railway wagons on Teignmouth Quay until the 1960's. This tractor was not only interesting in the technical sense but also because it superseded an i/c tractor unsuccessfully tried on the same work. This tractor is preserved.

It is difficult to overestimate the importance of the Sentinel in the steam wagon scene, representing, as it does, the most sustained attempt to market a steam vehicle able to hold its own with the diesel. In terms of loads carried and road speed there would be little to choose between an up-dated Sentinel design and a diesel but as to cab comfort, ready availability from cold, hours of manning and time spent on fuelling (both coal and water) it would lag seriously behind. Probably only the loss of oil supplies could revive interest in steam and in this event the Sentinel S type would, equally probably, have the best claim to revival.

Apart from their steamers Sentinel had several interesting ventures into the internal combustion field. From 1934 to 1935 Garner trucks were made at Shrewsbury under the name Sentinel-Garner, with Meadows and Austin gasoline engines and Perkins Leopard diesels. Then production was transferred to London, and the next non-steam venture was with the H.S.G. (High Speed Gas) system. Introduced in November 1938, there were two models of the Sentinel-H.S.G., a 5-ton truck with 4-cylinder horizontal underfloor 5,778cc engine and gas producer beside the driver, and a 32/35-seater passenger chassis with 6-cylinder 8.7-litre vertical engine at the front in conventional position. In this the gas producer was at the rear. Neither of these vehicles went into production.

1955 SENTINEL 12-ton 6-wheel truck, OMM

During the war Sentinel built and tested an underfloor gasoline-engined truck, and production was announced early in 1945. It had a horizontal 4-cylinder engine of 5.7 litres developing 85hp, 4-speed gearbox and overhead worm final drive. Although listed for a year or two very few of the gasoline model were made, but in 1946 an oil-engined 7/8-tonner went into production. This also had a horizontal underfloor engine, of 6.08 litres and 90bhp. The engine had Ricardo Comet cylinder heads, and there was a 5-speed Meadows gearbox and hydraulic servo brakes. In 1948 a 9.12-litre 6-cylinder engine was added to the range, and this was used in a 10-ton rigid 6-wheeler launched at the end of 1949, and also in an integral-construction bus for 39 or 42 passengers originally introduced in 1948. Home models of this had 4-speed gearboxes with 5 speeds on export models. The earlier Sentinel buses were built in conjunction with Beadle the coachbuilders from Rochester, Kent, though other firms such as Burlingham also contributed bodies. In 1952 came direct-injection engines and vacuum servo in place of hydraulic brakes, and there were two 6-wheelers, a lightweight 6 × 2 with 4-cylinder engine and a heavy 6 × 4 with 6-cylinders. Vehicle production dwindled in the mid-1950s when Sentinel went into automation equipment, and ceased in 1956 when the factory was acquired by Rolls-Royce for the manufacture of diesel engines. Many Sentinel components were acquired by Transport Vehicles (Warrington) Ltd who used them in the earlier models of their T.V.W. trucks. *RAW/GNG*

SERGEANT (F) 1903

Charles Sergeant, Calais

For his tractor Sergeant used a rear mounted Serpollet steam generator. The engine was centrally mounted above the chassis and drove the rear axle through a gear drive. Rope tires were used. The tractor was intended for barge towage. *RAW*

SERPOLLET (F) 1894-1907

(1) Leon Serpollet, Paris 1894-1899
(2) Gardner Serpollet, Paris 1899-1907

Although Serpollet's earlier efforts were all directed at private vehicles, he essayed a steam wagonette for the

Paris-Rouen Trial of 1894, and built sundry small omnibuses and other light commercials using his well-known flash boiler. By 1898 he was using paraffin as the standard fuel, with a Longuemare burner.

After forming his partnership with the American, Frank Gardner, in 1899 Serpollet designed a number of rather heavier vehicles including several steam buses, but as operators were reluctant to purchase them he and

1905 SERPOLLET steam bus, RAW

Gardner helped to form the Darracq-Serpollet company to build and operate steam buses. Serpollet died in 1907 and his firm did not survive him, although Darracq-Serpollet lingered on until 1912.

How the engine was arranged in his earlier commercial vehicles is not entirely clear. The final drive was by roller chain from a sprocket behind the rear axle and he may have used a separate engine to each wheel, similar to the layout of Le Blant vehicles. Certainly the whole of the boiler and machinery was beneath the vehicle. Latterly he used a compound undertype engine of conventional design.

From 1901 to 1904 a small number of Gardner-Serpollets were made in England by the British Power Traction & Lighting Co. Ltd. of York. They were sold under the name P.T.L. *RAW*

SERTUM(I) 1938-1940

Officine Meccaniche Fausto Alberti SA, Milan

Sertum motorcycles included a successful 500cc ohv vertical-twin. They also made delivery 3-wheelers on motorcycle lines with two driven rear wheels. *MCS*

SERVICE (US) 1911-1932

(1) Service Motor Car Co., Wabash, Ind. 1911-1914
(2) Service Motor Truck Co., Wabash, Ind. 1914-1923
(3) Service Motors Inc., Wabash, Ind. 1923-1926
(4) Relay Motors Corp., Lima, Ohio 1927-1932

The first Service trucks, Model A, were delivery models with 22½hp 4-cylinder engines, friction transmissions and chain final drive. They were of the highwheeler pattern with 2-inch solid tires and semi-elliptic springs all round. Like other truck makers Service soon expanded their range, and by 1917 they had conventional trucks in five sizes from 1 to 5 tons, with 4-cylinder Buda engines, 3- or 4-speed transmission and Timken worm drive. These models were made with little change until 1927 when the company was acquired by Relay Motors. During World War I Service built a number of Liberty trucks alongside regular truck production, after considerable plant expansion. In 1920 Service added a lighter truck to their range; a ¾-tonner with spiral-bevel drive and pneumatic tires, it was typical of the 'speed models' which many truck makers were introducing at this time.

Early in 1927 Service was bought by Relay Motors who transferred production to Lima, Ohio and introduced a new range of Service trucks which were identical to Relays except that they used worm drives and steel disc wheels in place of Relay's internal gear drive and artillery wheels. In this they were similar to Commerce and Garford trucks, and the only difference between the three makes lay in the nameplates. They did not sell well, with about 80 units delivered in 1928 and 40 in 1929, the record prosperity year. So when Relay went into liquidation in December 1932 it was inevitable that Service production should be suspended, although a further brief attempt was made to continue Relay and Garford. *RW*

SETRA (D) 1951 to date

Karl Kassbohrer Fahrzeugwerke GmbH., Ulm

Kassbohrer was a well-known coachbuilding firm for many years when in 1951 the first Setra bus was presented. Setra stand for SElbstTRAgend which means self-supporting. This new design principle was used for their first own construction of a bus. A 95bhp Henschel engine was mounted in the rear. The first versions were touring coaches but public service buses followed.

In 1955 a special high-decker version was developed which was delivered to Continental Trailways in the USA. This was the first Golden Eagle which, with the smaller Silver Eagle, was made by Kassbohrer until 1961 when production began at Trailways' subsidiary plant in Belgium. It had a 240bhp MAN turbocharged engine. It was the first time that a German built bus was used in the USA for transcontinental service. In 1958 a 4-axle articulated version following the same principle was ordered by the same company. This was equipped with a Rolls-Royce engine.

The current program offers several version of touring coaches including one 3-axle high-decker. A city bus follows the standard principle of the VOV and is also available as an articulated version. Daimler-Benz and M.A.N. engines are installed. *HON*

SHAKESPEARE see Kalamazoo

SHAKTIMAN (IND) 1958-1963

Ministry of Defence, Indian Ordnance Factories Jabalpur

A product of the Jabalpur ordnance factory, responsible for the production of military vehicles and tanks, Shaktiman trucks were built under West German MAN license. Built mainly of imported parts, powered by a 130hp multifuel engine, having a payload of 5 tons and 4 × 4 driving configuration, Shaktimans were built in a grand total of 5,000 units. *GA*

SHANGHAI (i) (CHI) 1957 to date

Shanghai Motor Vehicle Plant, Shanghai (Plant Vehicle Code — SH)

A rather common sight in the cities of China is the little 3-wheeled Shanghai 58-1 truck. Powered by a V-twin, 27hp aircoooled engine, it carries a one ton load and does 20 mpg.

From 1957 to 1958 a 4-cylinder, 50hp Shanghai #58 jeep was assembled in a lot of 500 units. This vehicle was very similar to the Willys CJ3A.

There is evidence that another Shanghai jeep is now in

production, powered by a 75hp engine.

A cab-over-engine 2-ton truck, the Shanghai SH-130, is in current production using a 4-cylinder, 75hp engine with four forward gears.

The Shanghai (formerly Phoenix) passenger car is also built in this plant. *BE*

SHANGHAI (ii) (CHI) to date

Shanghai Bus Factory — Shanghai (Plant Vehicle Code — SK)

The series of buses built on Jay Fong truck chassis at this plant includes the SK-644 23 passenger city bus, the 36 passenger SK-644A and the SK-660 articulated 48 passenger 6 × 4.

A Hsiangp'ai (Elephant) light bus was exhibited in 1975 and may also be in current production. *BE*

SHANGHAI SH-380 (CHI) to date

Shanghai Cargo Vehicle Plant, Shanghai (Plant Vehicle Code — SH)

Built in the same plant that produces Qiao-Tong (Communication) brand trucks, the Shanghai SH-380 is a 32-ton dump truck.

The cab is installed on the truck's left and seats one in front and two behind. A Shanghai V-12 diesel engine of 400 hp & 2,000 rpm drives with a 3-speed gearbox. *BE*

SHARPS MINITRUCK see Bond

SHAW (US) 1918-1920

Walden W. Shaw Livery Co., Chicago, Ill.

As early as 1913, this company manufactured a taxicab, but its first venture into trucks appears to have been in 1918 when a 2-tonner was introduced. No information on this is available. In 1920, the company also built passenger cars. *GMN*

SHEFFIELD (GB) 1899

Sheffield Motor Dray & Engineering Co., Hillsborough, Sheffield.

The Sheffield steam wagon was front steered, with a vertical Field tube boiler at the rear fired by coke, working at 150 psi. The engine was a vertical 3-cylinder single acting with Wilkinson's patent valve gear. Wagons were offered in 1, 2 and 4/5 ton sizes but seem to have failed commercially. *RAW*

SHEFFLEX (GB) 1921-1935

(1) Sheffield-Simplex Motor Works Ltd, Tinsley, Sheffield, Yorks. 1921-1924
(2) Shefflex Motors Ltd, Tinsley, Sheffield, Yorks. 1926-1935

During World War I luxury car maker Sheffield-Simplex had built Commer 2-tonners while the Commer works was fully occupied with the heavier RC military truck. By 1922 Commer had over-capacity, and the contract with Sheffield-Simplex ended. However for a time they sold their surplus Commers under the name Shefflex, and even sold some to Scottish Commercial Cars for resale under the name Caledon. Probably no more than 50 found homes, and in 1923 Sheffield-Simplex sold the remnants to motor dealers R.A. Johnstone Ltd who soon found customers for them and decided to take up manufacture. Those were 1½ and 2 tonners initially, increased to 2½ tons or 24 passenger models, and low-loading dust carts. All had Commer-designed 24. 8hp 4-cylinder engines with ball-bearing crankshafts and, surprisingly for such a late date, non-detachable cylinder heads. In 1930 22.4hp Dorman engines were adopted, and the range extended to include trailing axle 6-wheelers for 4- and 5-ton loads, plus a 6-ton articulated unit in 1932 when forward

1928 SHEFFLEX 2-ton truck, OMM

1933 SHEFFLEX DL6 5-ton 6-wheel van, OMM

control was also offered. Meadows engines and gearboxes were sometimes used, and in 1932 Shefflex adopted the unusual Petter 3-cylinder 2-stroke diesel; Dorman and Gardner diesels were also available.

After about 150 of the Johnstone-built Shefflexes had been sold, production ended in 1935, though in 1937 a final Meadows-engined refuse truck was made under the name Ideal, a name used on the last Shefflex of 1935. Thereafter a few A.E.C. Monarchs were converted to electric traction for municipal work, and the company still exists today making refuse disposal bodywork. *OM*

SHEPPEE (GB) 1905-1914

Sheppee Motor & Engineering Co., York

Colonel F.H. Sheppee was a retired officer of the Indian Army with a consuming interest in and great knowledge of steam vehicles using high pressure flash steam. In pursuance of this interest he had acquired a stake in the British Power Traction & Lighting Co. in York, from which he withdrew in 1904, setting up his own works the following year with John Gibbs as works manager and a number of promising workmen from B P T L as staff.

During the next nine years he built (or perhaps rebuilt) 14 trade vehicles including his celebrated steam charabanc, of which probably three were purely experimental and no two exactly alike as Sheppee was, in fact, conducting a quest for the ideal steam wagon, a path trodden for a lifetime by Doble without a final conclusion being reached.

Sheppee used a liquid boiler with continuous generating coils, arranged within a rectangle and one above the other producing steam at 900 psi and 1000°F. The engine was fabricated, totally enclosed and had double high pressure single acting cylinders, with pushrod operated poppet

1908 SHEPPEE steam wagon chassis, WB

valves. A gilled tube condenser was fixed in the conventional radiator position and the finished vehicle resembled a gasoline truck. Sheppee aimed at total automation and had achieved his purpose but not at an economic price. The experiment was terminated by the 1914 war and his death. His steam goods vehicles probably came as near to technical perfection as any save the Sentinel-Doble and the Henschel Dobles. *RAW*

SHERPA (F) 1954-c. 1960

Cie Generale Automobile Parisienne, Noisy-le-Sec

The Sherpa was a front-wheel-drive 3-wheeled van powered by an 850cc Dyna-Panhard 2-cylinder engine mounted above the single front wheel. It had a central tubular frame and could be supplied with either van on camionette bodies. An unusual feature was the gearbox which gave two series of three speeds according to whether the vehicle was empty or loaded. *GNG*

SHUTTLECRAFT see American Carrier Equipment

1955 SHERPA 3-wheel van, NMM

1972 (EBRO)-SIATA Combi-1 van, GNG

SIATA (E) 1960-1971

(1) Siata Espanola SA, Tarragona 1960-1970
(2) Motor Iberica SA, Barcelona 1971

Although the Italian Siata company did not offer commercial vehicles, the Spanish branch made quite a number of vans and pick-ups derived from the SEAT 600 and 1400 models. The last model was the Siata S.4, made as a van or light bus on the SEAT 850 chassis. This was in fact manufactured by Motor Iberica who also make the larger Ebro trucks. In 1971 the name was changed to Ebro-Siata. *JCG*

SIBAT (PI) 1975 to date

Renault Philippines Ic., Makati, Rizal

Assembling Renault cars since 1959, the Filipino factory introduced, a light utility multipurpose vehicle under the name of Sibat. Sibat has a Rodeo-like doorless open-top body with angular lines, a very low silhouette and a folding rear bench seat. Mechanically it follows the usual Renault practice of a front-wheel-drive unit powered by a 11+ gasoline engine. *GA*

SIBRAVA (CS) 1921-1924

Jaroslav Sibrava, Prague

After Walter 3-wheelers were discontinued, a small factory began to make modified Walter designs under the name Sibrava Trimobil. These had 1¼-litre 9hp V-twin engines, shaft drive and tiller steering. Both passenger car and delivery van models were made. *MSH*

SICARD (CDN) 1938-1968

Sicard Inc, Sainte Therese, Que.

Sicard was best known as a successful builder of snow-blowers, the first of which, mounted on a F.W.D. chassis, was made in 1927. In 1938 the first Sicard-built chassis

1948 SICARD street sprinkler, LA

appeared, a semi-forward control truck with an unusual body which was a tipper in style but which shifted its load of snow by means of a cable-drane scraper which traveled from the front of the body to the rear pushing the load ahead of it. Later this chassis was used with conventional tipper bodies, and with various designs of refuse collectors. A branch plant was opened in Watertown, N.Y., and in 1958 Sicard brought out its first highway trucks. Kenworth and KW-Dart trucks were also built by Sicard, some being sold under the Sicard name. In 1967 Sicard was taken over by Pacific Car & Foundry of Seattle, Washington, and the following year production of Sicard vehicles ceased. (Production of own trucks ended by 1969 with total output of about 2,500 units). *HD*

SIEBERT (US) 1911-1916

The Shop of Siebert, Toledo, Ohio

A 1-tonner and one of 1,200-pound capacity were the first trucks under this name. The smaller managed with a two-cylinder engine while the larger had four cylinders. The 1-tonner was on a wheelbase of 10 feet. Later, a ¾-tonner was made with a four-cylinder engine under the hood with a three-speed gearbox and double chain drive. A 1-tonner was added for the last two years of manufacture, of the same general configuration as the ¾ tonner. *GMN*

SIEGEL (D) 1907-1910

Feodor Siegel Maschinenfabrik, Schonebeck

The ¾ ton van by this firm was marketed as "W.M.W." (Waren-Motor-Wagen). It had a light chassis and a 2-cylinder 9 hp engine. This engine and a 4-cylinder 12 hp were available for the 1 ton truck or van of 1909. *HON*

SIEMENS & HALSKE (D) 1899-1900

Siemens & Halske A.G., Berlin

This firm constructed an experimental trolleybus system in 1882, but this was not commercially used and the system itself was not further developed.

In 1899 a "Strassenbahn-Omnibus" (tram bus) was presented. This vehicle ran like a tram on a certain part of the route with two smaller front guide wheels running in the rails only; electric power was taken from the overhead wire. So also the battery was fed and this provided power when the vehicle operated free from rails and wire elevated guide wheels. Siemens & Halske did not continue their own developments, but supplied electric equipment for Schiemann (q.v.) trolley buses and also built the first vehicles for that company according to their design. *HON*

SIEMENS-SCHUCKERT (D) 1903-1913; 1935-1939

Siemens-Schuckert AG, Berlin

After the takeover of Schuckert (q.v.) manufacture of their three-wheeled electric vans was carried on. In 1906 a new factory in Berlin-Nonnendamm was opened and production of electric vehicles was taken up on a large scale. Available were vans, trucks and buses. Also some versions of gasoline-electric road tractors were built. The gas engine fed a generator which on the other hand supplied the electric motors of the tractor itself and of the trailers. Electric or gas-electric commercials were marketed under the name of Siemens-Schuckert, while gasoline driven vehicles were available under Protos (q.v.)

In 1934 an electric driven 2-ton model was introduced. This was available until 1939. *HON*

1941 SIG 4-ton electric tipper truck, FH

1943 SIG EL300 300kg electric van, GNG

SIG (CH) c.1940-1950

Schweizerische Industrie Gesellschaft, Neuhausen a/Rhf.

Founded in 1853 and producing rolling-stock for Swiss and foreign railroads as well as infantry weapons, SIG expanded its activities in the early thirties by manufacturing electric vehicles. When the Second World War broke out a severe shortage of gasoline and diesel oil set in quickly and SIG launched various electric-vehicles for road use. They ranged from the light delivery van EL 300 with 670 lbs payload to the heavy 4 ton type EL 4000. Several hundred were produced. After 1945 supplies of gasoline were back to normal soon again. SIG electrics were used for specific tasks only and the company turned its main manufacturing effort to electro-locomotives for mines, fork-lifts etc. In 1964 there were still 537 SIG commercial vehicles, mainly of the 1- to 2-ton class, registered in Switzerland. *FH*

SIGNAL (US) 1913-1923

Signal Motor Truck Co. Detroit, Mich.

The initial Signal was a 1½-tonner with a side-valve

four-cylinder engine, a three-speed gearbox and double chain drive. This was continued through 1914 with both open and closed bodies available. For 1915, a 2-tonner with double chain drive was added as well as 1- and 3-tonners. In 1916 the drive system was changed in all models to worm gear drive, and capacities of the models were 1, 1½, 2 and 3 tons. Left-hand drive was standard with optional right-hand drive for the then large Allied demand for trucks in Europe. In 1917, a 5-tonner also was built. In the last years of this make, the line of truck types shrunk rapidly and in the last year of record, only the Model F, a 1¾-tonner, was built. *GMN*

1967 SILVER EAGLE 6×2 coach, MBS

SILVER EAGLE ADDRESSES

(1) Bus & Car SA, St. Mihiel, Belgium 1961-1974
(2) Eagle International Inc., Brownsville, Texas 1975 to date
(3) Mol, NV, Hooglede, Belgium 1976 to date

The largest component of the association of intercity bus companies known as the National Trailways Bus System has, since the late 1940's, been a group of operating companies based in Dallas, originally known as Transcontinental Bus System and now Continental Trailways, Inc. In 1956, in an effort to compete with the 40-foot bilevel Scenicruiser bus built by GM for Greyhound, this company contracted with Karl Kassbohrer, A.G. for a prototype "Golden Eagle," delivered in 1956 and followed by 50 more in 1957 and 45 (including four articulated buses) in 1958. These had MAN diesel engines. Late in 1960 an additional 85 buses were acquired from Kassbohrer, incorporating numerous modifications. These, as well as the 1958 batch, had more seats and fewer interior frills, and were designated Silver Eagles.

Transcontinental Bus System organized a subsidiary in 1961 to build its own buses, basically using the Kassbohrer design but incorporating a Detroit Diesel 8V-71 engine. The plant was set up in Belgium under the name of Bus & Car, S.A., and it was later included in a group of overseas affiliates spun off to Transcontinental stockholders in the form of a new corporation, Western Sales, Ltd. Bus & Car also built a small number of buses of other types for European tour operators, under the "Eagle" name. With minor modifications, approximately 3,500 Silver and Golden Eagles were built from 1961 to 1974, the majority for National Trailways Bus System operators, but others sold as well to independent regular- route and charter carriers. A few have also been marketed in South Africa and Australia.

A second manufacturing plant at Brownsville, Texas, was set up in 1975 and now supplies the U.S. market. The St. Mihiel factory also built transit buses, the initial purchase comprising 140 for Israel, and the U.S. plant is also beginning to make an effort to sell these buses, which are now built by another Belgian plant.

With the steady decline in the value of the dollar against many other currencies, importing buses became an expensive undertaking for the Continental Trailways system, especially when its traffic levels declined, and late in 1976 the purchases were discontinued; approximately 3,630 Eagles were imported in 16 years. Production of identical buses has been continued by Eagle International of Brownsville, Texas, lately at fewer than 100 vehicles per year. *MBS*

S.I.M. (i) 1953-1955

Societa Italiana Motorscooters, Reggio Emilia

This short-lived concern produced commercial 3-wheeler editions of both their 125cc scooter and their 150cc shaft-driven motorcycle. Engines were single-cylinder 2-strokes, with three speeds and chain drive on the smaller, 250kg edition. The 150cc S.I.M. had four forward speeds. *MCS*

SIMA-STANDARD (F) 1929-1932

Societe Industrielle de Material Automobile, Courbevoie, Seine.

SIMA had formerly built 500cc cyclecars to Violet designs, replacing these in 1929 with a conventional 4-cylinder 5CV. This was in effect an updated edition of Citroen's 856cc model of 1921-26, with fwb added. It used some Amilcar as well as Citroen parts, and, unlike the Citroen, was available as a light van for 300kg payloads. *MCS*

1956 SIMCA Aronde 1300 Pick-up, Simica

SIMCA (F) 1935-1964: 1968 to date

1) Societe Industrielle de Mecanique et de Carrosserie Automobile, Nanterre, Seine 1935-1961: Poissy, Seine-et-Oise 1954-1970
2) Chrysler France SA, Poissy, Seine-et-Oise 1970 to date

H.T. Pigozzi took over the old Donnet factory, where he built Fiats under license. Most of these were private cars, but light vans were offered on the 6CV (508), Simca-5 (500) and Simca-8 (1100) chassis, the two latter being reinstated after the war, and giving way in due course to commercial editions of the improved Simca-6 and the 1.2litre 8CV. 1951 saw the first all-French Simca car, the unitary construction Aronde with 1.2-litre engine, coil ifs and hypoid rear axle, this being offered in detuned 37hp form as a van or pickup. Development followed that of the basic car line, with capacity increased to 1.3 litres in 1956, and 5-bearing crankshafts on 1961 and later versions. When Chrysler acquired an interest in the company, they started to assemble private and commercial Arondes in their Australian factory at Keswick. Simca's purchase of the French Ford company in 1954 gave them a ready-made 5-tonner, this model being continued without major change as the Cargo. Some of these were supplied to the army,

1978 SIMCA 1100 pick-up, Simca

both in soft cab 4 × 2 form and as 4 × 4s for 30-cwt and 3-ton payloads; the heavier 4-wheel drive types were commercially available. Also inherited from Ford was the genesis of a successful taxicab, for by marrying the redesigned small V8 car to the Aronde engine they produced the roomy Ariane 4 widely used in French cities in the later 1950s. Since 1951 the company had also been allied with Unic, and their normal control 5-ton V8 of 1957, the Caboteur, used Unic front-end sheet metal. A year later came a 25-seater full-front coach, the Iseran, on which a 2-speed back axle was standard. That year, however, the car and truck interests of the group were separated, and production of the bigger trucks and buses transferred to the Unic works at Puteaux. The V8 range was not quoted after 1962; Chrysler acquired a controlling interest in Simca during 1963. With the demise of the Aronde at the end of the 1964 season, there was a four-year hiatus on the commercial vehicle side, broken when the new 1100 range came out complete with a 7½-cwt van option. This had a transversely-mounted 4-cylinder ohv engine driving the front wheels, a 4-speed all-synchromesh gearbox, all-independent suspension, and front disc brakes.

It was still available in 1978, while Chrysler-France's specialist associate, Matra, offered the Rancho, a 4 × 4 station wagon. This was based on the 1100, but used the 1.4-litre engine from the 1307 sedan. *MCS*

SIMCA-MARMON see Marmon-Boquet

SIMMS (GB) 1904-1907

Simms Mfg. Co. Ltd., Kilburn, London N.W.

This well-known maker of electrical equipment built a number of cars and commercial vehicles. The latter included light vans with single- and 2-cylinder Simms engines of 8, 10 and 12hp and capacities ranging from 8 to 20cwt. These were made from 1904 to 1906, and were supplemented by a larger 4-cylinder chassis in 1905. This could be had with 20/25 or 28/35hp engines, for loads of 2 and 5 tons respectively. It had a 3-speed gearbox and chain drive. Simms engines were also used in the 1905 Simms-Coulthard 4-ton truck made by Coulthard the steam wagon builders of Preston, Lancashire. *GNG*

1956 SIMO 400kg 3-wheel truck, JCG

SIMO (E) 1924-1936; 1952-1959

Miguel Simo, Barcelona

This motorcycle maker built a few delivery tricycles in the first period, and from 1952 to 1959 a 3-wheeled truck powered by a 197cc single-cylinder Hispano-Villiers engine. This had 3 speeds chain drive to the rear wheel, and tiller steering. *JCG*

SIMPLO (US) 1908-1909

Cook Motor Vehicle Co. St. Louis, Mo.

For $700 the Simplo conventional delivery wagon offered a 16 hp 2-cylinder gas engine, air or water-cooled, driving through a friction clutch to a double chain final drive. Brakes were double internal expanding, Wheelbase was 86 inches, capacity was 1,000 pounds, and the truck was the standard 56 inches, with 61 inches optional. Tires were 28 x 3 pneumatic or 36 x 1½ solid, a size used on high-wheelers. *RW*

SIMSON (D) 1913-1917

Simson & Co., Suhl

This armaments factory took up car production in 1911. In 1913 also a light truck was available which was based on private car components and used the 10/30 PS engine. This production was carried on during WWI but it was not very important and ceased in 1917, while private cars were carried on also after the war. *HON*

1901 SIMPSON-BIBBY steam wagon, Autocar

SIMPSON & BIBBY (GB) 1896-1902

Simpson & Bibby, Cornbrook, Manchester

Despite the publicity given to Simpson & Bibby wagons they must be considered almost entirely experimental and manufacture was practically 100% sub-contracted.

Their vehicle of 1896/7 was a steam van with compound cylinders driving direct onto the cranked rear axle. Experiments followed with a divided axle and then with separate engines to each wheel. Their wagon in the 1901 Liverpool trials had a 3-cylinder radial engine to each rear wheel with spring loaded mushroom inlet valves, cam operated from the crankshaft, and central exhaust valves on the uniflow system. The boiler was their own semi-flash design. Each engine drove a rear wheel via a short countershaft and roller chain.

In 1902 a Colonial wagon was introduced with rear-mounted boiler, engine and driving position, carried on a heavy chassis with traction engine wheels. A single acting V4 engine was used and hydraulic steering was incorporated, the necessary water pressure coming from the feed pump. *RAW*

1932 SINGER 1¼-ton truck, NMM

SINGER (GB) 1905-1916: 1928-1940

1) Singer & Co. Ltd., Coventry, Warwickshire 1905-1936
2) Singer Motors Ltd., Coventry, Warwickshire 1936-1940

Before 1914 Singer's commercial vehicle offerings were intermittent, though between 1905 and 1907 the 12/14 with horizontal underfloor 2-cylinder engine and chain drive (made under Lea-Francis licence) was available as a forward control delivery van, the conventional 12/14 hp four of 1909 was used as a cab in at least one provincial city, and the bigger 2.8-litre 16/20 also appeared in van form. More serious was a 7-cwt edition of the 1914 Ten with 1.1-litre paircast sv 4-cylinder engine and 3-speed transaxle, some of which were supplied to the War Office. No more Singer commercials were listed until 1928, when 5-cwt and 10-cwt vans were introduced. The former was the 848cc ohc Junior with 3-speed gearbox and fwb, but the latter typified the thinking of many firms with peripheral truck interests, in that it used up obsolete parts, in this case those of the recently discontinued 1.3-litre ohv 10/26 private car. The radiator was, however, peculiar to the van range. By late 1929 the stock of 10/26 components had been exhausted, and Singer was supplementing the Junior with a bigger 14-cwt model powered by a 1.8-litre ohv 6-cylinder engine, which retained righthand shift and magneto ignition. At the 1929 Commercial Vehicle Show, however, they launched an all-out attack on Ford and Morris-Commercial with their new Singer Industrial Motors. These had nothing in common with existing car types, using 3.1-litre 4-cylinder pushrod engines developing 60hp. Unusual features were the 5-bearing crankshafts, one-shot chassis lubrication, coil ignition, and servo-operated fwb; final drive was by overhead worm, and twin rear wheels were standard. The Industrial was available as 2-ton truck or 20-seater coach; by mid-1930 a swb edition had been developed for newspaper delivery work. 1932 saw a shortlived 35-cwt Prosperity model powered by a 3.4-litre ohv 6-cylinder engine, but neither the Industrials nor an intermediate 25-cwt truck

1934 SINGER Nine van, GNG

using 1929 car-type sheet metal and the 2,050cc sv 6-cylinder unit also used in the 18hp sedan came toanything. After 1932 only light vans were offered. Even then the variety was disconcerting. There were three delivery types in 1931, the 5-cwt and 14-cwt being joined by a 10-cwt model based on the 1,261cc sv. Ten (with 1930-style 6-cylinder private car radiator), while a new 15-cwt with the 18/6 engine, servo brakes, and a built-in illuminated sign over the cab made its appearance during 1932, only to give way to a similarly-styled 12-cwt based on the 1,440cc sv 12/4. New for 1933 were an improved 5-cwt with the 972cc 9 hp engine (but still with 1932 Junior sheet metal), as well as seldom-seen 5-door traveler's sedans on the 12/4 and 14/6 car chassis. 1935 saw the Nine — now with 1935 styling and hydraulic brakes — as the sole commercial model, though Singer engines were being fitted to Staussler's lighter specialist vehicles. An associated company, Motor Units Ltd, were marketing light gasoline rollers, and the RAF placed an order for 100 9's with light tender bodies. Last of Singer's vans was the Bantam 9 of 1936, still with three forward speeds. Unusual features were detachable rear doors and fixed starting handles, but few were sold, and the van was not revived after the War. Singer's last 'commerical' venture was the Ota light agricultural tractor made by a subsidiary company from 1946 onward: it used a (ii) Ford engine. *MCS*

SIRECOME (I) 1946 to date

(1) Sirecome s.n.c., La Spezia 1946-1973
(2) Sirecome S.p.A., La Spezia 1974-to date

Sirecome started life in the first post WW II years trading surplus military vehicles, but soon faced the need to reconstruct and customize the vehicles sold. The first model to leave the Sirecome works was the GMC 2.5 ton 6x6 truck fitted with a Perkins diesel of 89 hp and right hand drive, as common with heavy Italian vehicles. The 3-4 ton 37 followed soon together with the Borgward NATO class 0.75 ton model, both powered by a Fiat 70 hp diesel, closed cabs and the Sirecome trademark on their hood. Sirecome elaborated also the M series of 2.5 ton and 5 ton 6 x 6 trucks, and the whole of its production found its way to various Italian construction companies. The M35/M52 series trucks were fitted with hard-top cabs, right hand drive and Perkins 6 cylinder diesels of 120 hp, but were soon replaced by a series of forward control chassis of 4 x 4 and 6 x 6 configuration which were of Sirecome design, though based on the M series military trucks. Power for these heavy duty off highway vehicles comes from either a Fiat or a Perkins diesel of 88 up to 230 hp, while the cabs fitted are tall metal cabs of angular lines. Current production consists of series of all-wheel-drive chassis of original appearance, while Sirecome is also building special vehicles to order. *GA*

SIRMAC (I) to date

Sirmac SpA, Calcara, Bologna

The Sirmac is a 4 x 4 forward-control truck for on or off-highway work, with a payload of 2500 kgs. based on the Swiss Meili. The standard engine is a 165 hp Fiat V-6 gasoline unit, but alternatives include Ford V-8 gasoline or Fiat 6-cylinder in-line diesel. The transmission has 10 forward and 2 reverse speeds, and suspension is independent all round by air-filled rubber cylinders. *GNG*

1976 SIRMAC SAB2500A 4×4 truck, Sirmac

SISU (SF) 1931 to date

OY Suomen Autoteollisuus, Helsinki

Pioneer of the Finnish automobile industry and the nation's best known commercial vehicle make, Sisu was the creation of Tor Nessling. Operations were initially on a very modest scale, with only 12 trucks delivered in the first year; the company supported itself by building streetcars. The staple model was the SH, an American-looking 3-tonner with 85hp 6-cylinder sv engine, and 4-speed gearbox. The same chassis sufficed for trucks and buses. In 1943 Sisu and Vanaja were nationalized into the Yhteissisu concern to build vehicles for the army, but though this consortium had a 5-year life, development of the SH family continued. In immediate post-war from the Sisu was a 5-tonner with 5 litres of engine and 90hp, a 5-speed overdrive gearbox, and hydrovac brakes. Styling was early 1940's American, and most, if not all Sisus of the 1945-48 period ran on wood-gas. A more powerful 110hp gasoline engine was available by 1949, along with 80hp and 100hp diesel options. There was also a forward-control bus chassis. In 1953 Sisu's production amounted to 350 vehicles, GVW ratings of up to 13 tons were listed, and the heaviest models used 8.7-litre, 140hp diesel engines.

By the late 1950's Leyland diesel engines were standard equipment, and Sisu were building some real heavies, notably a 335hp 6 × 6 normal control tractor for use in Lapland, which could haul 180 tons. There was also a heavy normal control dumper with 185hp Rolls-Royce engine, power steering, ten forward speeds, and air-leaf suspension. The regular line covered GVWs in the 13/ 20-ton bracket, with 5-or 6-speed gearboxes, hypoid rear axles, and hydrovac or full air brakes. Various 6-cylinder Leyland units of up to 11.1 litres and 165hp were installed; the K34 6 × 2 type (and subsequent Sisus of this configuration) had the unusual feature of a trailing third axle with electro-hydraulic lift to raise it off the ground when the vehicle was running light. This type of axle was also applied to heavy 4 × 4s. The buses continued to be conventional forward-control models sharing the mechanical specification of the trucks, though by 1965 these had been supplemented by a new range with horizontal underfloor engines and wheelbases of up to 6m (19ft 8in). Sisu PSVs could also be had with British M.C.W. bodywork.

1931 SISU SH 3½-ton truck (right), JFJK
1965 SISU K141 10-ton (left), JFJK

By 1964 Sisu were ready to explore serious export sales, their campaign being spearheaded by a modern tilt-cab forward control design, the KB117 for 9/10-ton payloads. A 6 × 4 edition was available, other features including power steering and a 6-speed gearbox of XF make. By 1966 there was a 7-tonner with Cummins V6 engine, normal control types were restyled with fiber glass hoods, and the catalog covered almost every category save the lightest. At one end of the range was the 3-ton KB124 using a 70/80hp engine; at the other there were 6 × 2s and 6 × 4s with a 16-ton capacity and power options as high as 330hp. 4 × 4 types included the 3½-ton KB45 for military use, with 160hp 6½-litre turbocharged Leyland engine mounted behind the cab; it had evolved into a tilt-cab 6 × 6 by 1968. 1970 saw a wide range of Leyland-engined buses with front, amidships or rear engines, as well as some terminal tractors for dockside use on which Allison automatic transmissions were standard. The 3-tonners apart, the truck range now centered around two basic types, the forward control Bulldog inherited from Vanaja (whom Sisu had ultimately absorbed in 1967), and the normal control Bear. The former came in 4 × 2 and 6 × 2 configurations, with 13-speed Fuller rangechange gearbox and power steering; tilt cabs were standard, and engines were turbocharged 6-cylinder Leyland or Rolls-Royce, and A.E.C.'s V8, with outputs of up to 295hp. The Bear had a 16-ton GVW, double-reduction hypoid final drive, and six forward speeds: it came with the smaller 165hp Leyland unit. By 1976 both Saab-Scania and Leyland had 12 per cent stakes in the company, but this Swedish involvement led to no immediate change in the choice of engines. The range covered the terminal tractors, the buses (rear-engined versions were the principal export item), and the usual line-up of heavy-duty normal-and forward-control trucks and tractive units. Leyland and Rolls-Royce power units were standard, and at the top of the load-carrier range were machines for 33-tonner GVWs, using 12.2-

1975 SISU LE-137 8-ton, Sisu

1975 SISU M-162 14-ton 6×2 truck, Sisu

litre, 312hp Rolls-Royce sixes, servo-assisted twin-plate clutches, Fuller rangechange transmissions, and dual-circuit air brakes. *MCS*

S.I.V.E. (I) 1899-1903

Societa Italiana Vetture Elettriche Turrinelli & C. Milan.

These six-seater electric cabs were designed by Gino Turrinelli, who was later to make the Ausonia electric car. *MCS*

SIX-WHEEL (US) 1924-1928

Six-Wheel Co., Philadelphia, Pa.

American Motor Body Corp. was formed in 1923 by Charles M. Schwab of Bethlehem Steel and other investors as a reorganization of American Motor Body Co., formed in 1920 to succeed Wadsworth Manufacturing Co. The automobile body plant in Detroit that Wadsworth had operated was sold to Chrysler in 1925. Meanwhile in 1923, American Motor Body acquired the Philadelphia factory of Hall & Kilburn Co., an old established manufacturer of railroad car and streetcar seats, and expanded its line to include tandem-rear-axle buses and trucks marketed under the Six-Wheel name but also sometimes known as "Safeway" buses. There were a few 4/5-ton trucks, which were sold in Turkey, South Africa, India and the Sudan as well as in the United States, and the heavy-duty bus design with its Continental engine was favorably received in several large cities, particularly New York, Cleveland, Detroit and Kansas City. Most of the bodies were built by Wolfington in Philadelphia, but some were supplied by Auto Body Co. (Lansing), American Car Co., St. Louis Car Co., Fitzgibbon & Crisp, Kuhlman, Lang and Hoover. Approximately 400 Six-Wheel buses were sold. The company also had interests in several small operating companies in New Jersey during the 1920's. *MBS*

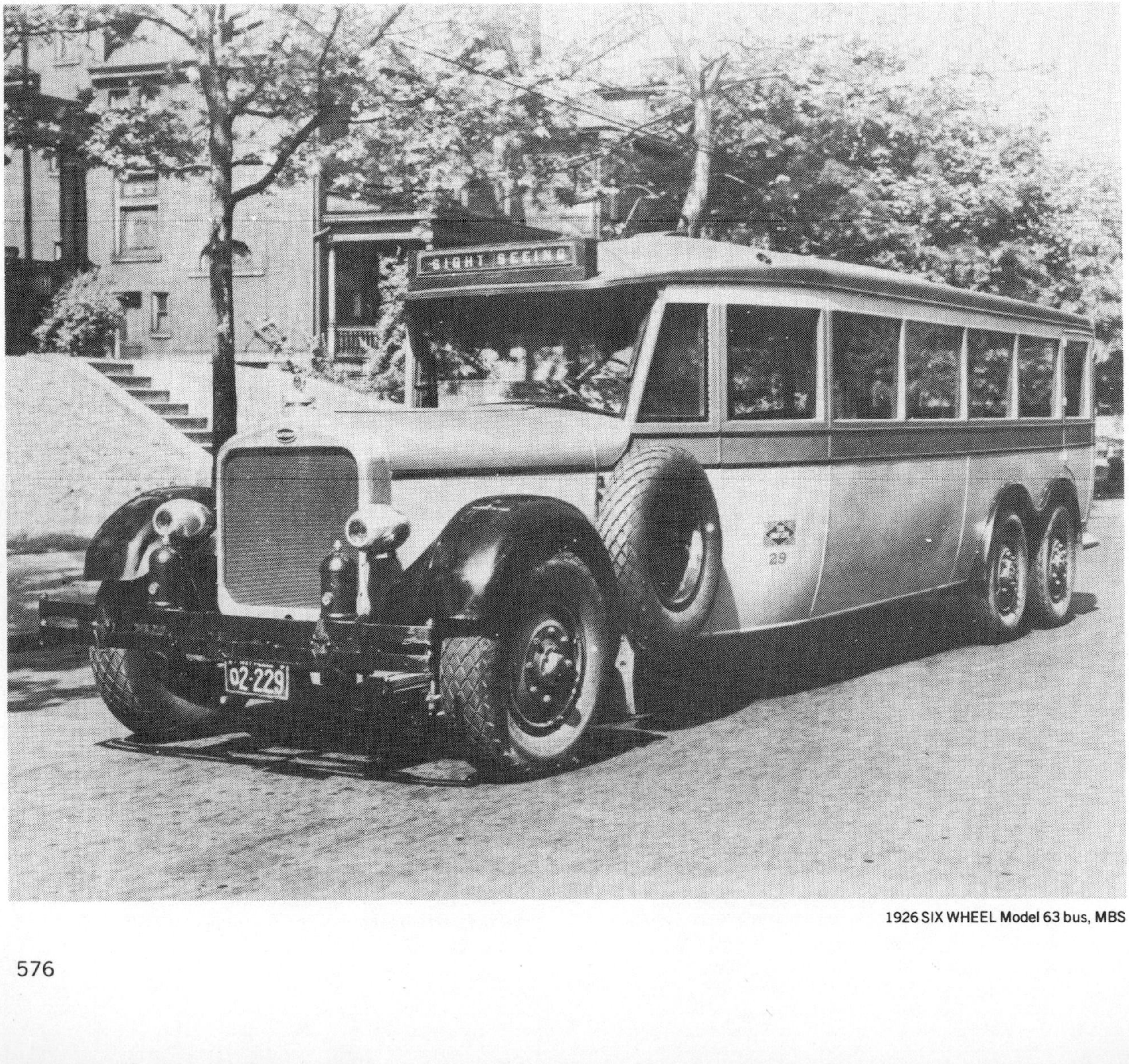

1926 SIX WHEEL Model 63 bus, MBS

1925 SKODA-SENTINEL 6-ton steam wagon, VP

1930 SKODA Typ 304 3-ton truck, VP

1936 SKODA Typ 6-ST-6 4-ton 6×6 army truck, VP

SKODA (CS) 1925 to date

(1) Skoda zavody AS, Plzen; Mlada Boleslav 1925-1930
(2) A.S.A.P., Mlada Boleslav 1935-1945
(3) Automobilove zavody n.p., Mlada Boleslav 1946 to date
(4) Zavody V.I. Lenina, Plzen; Ostrov nad Ohri 1948 to date

In 1924 the Skoda armaments syndicate took out licenses to build the British Sentinel steam wagon which was made in 4- 5- and 6-ton sizes for several years. Some of these steamers survived in service until the 1950s. In 1925 the old established vehicle maker, Laurin & Klement was acquired, and the 1½ and 4-5 tonners made by this company were continued under the Skoda name until 1927. The range of Skoda vehicles grew in the late 1920s and early 1930s, running from 1½ to 5 tons load capacity or buses for 12 to 35 passengers. The first diesel-engined model, the 606D truck or 606DN bus, appeared in 1932, as did the first 3-axle truck, the 8 tonner 706N. A 3 axle bus with two driven axles and 7.8-litre engine appeared in 1932. By 1936 the largest trucks were 6 × 4s for 8 to 10 ton loads with diesel or producer gas engines, while diesels were found among the smaller trucks down to 3 tons capacity, and air brakes were featured.

1937 SKODA Typ 404 4-ton truck, VP

From 1936 onwards trolleybuses were made, first with two axles and then with three, and these were continued in a wide range after World War II. In 1937 two prototypes were built of a streamlined 3-axle bus with integral construction and rear-mounted 6-cylinder engine, but with the approach of the war these never went into production. By 1940 four main types were being made, from 1 to 7 tons, with gasoline, diesel or producer-gas engines. Special military vehicles including 6 × 4 and 6 × 6 trucks and armoured vehicles were made at Plzen.

1938 SKODA Typ 606 DN touring coach, MSH

1947 SKODA Typ 706 RO bus, MSH

In 1946 the factory was nationalized, and production of heavy vehicles transferred from Mlada Boleslav which from then on made only passenger cars and the light commercials derived from them. However the lighter Tatra Type 805 trucks were made there from 1951 to 1953. The 8-ton Skoda 706 was made in the AVIA factory from 1946 to 1951, and was then re-named LIAZ (which see). Delivery vans, pick-ups and ambulances were made on the Skoda 1200 and 1201 car chassis, and from 1965 the

1975 SKODA 1203 pick-up, MSH

forward-control 1203 has been the staple model, made as van, pick-up, minibus, ambulance and hearse.

Skoda components were used in the New Zealand Trekka and Pakistani Skopak light pick-ups. Trolleybuses are still made under the Skoda name in the Ostrov nad Ohri factory; the latest is the T11 using the chassis and body of the Karosa SM11 bus. *MSH*

SKOPAK (PAK) 1969 to date

1) Haroon Industries Ltd., Karachi
2) Republic Motors Ltd., Karachi

Built by local Skoda representatives, the Skopak is a light utility fiber glass bodied vehicle. Using Skoda mechanics with a doorless canvas top body resembling Renaults Rodeo, Skopak features a 1.2 litre gasoline engine developing 47hp and independent swinging rear axle, familiar with all front-engined Skoda vehicles. *GA*

SLEEPER COACH (US) 1937

Sleeper Coaches, Inc., Detroit, Mich.

A number of experimental sleeper coaches were constructed in the 1930's, after the depression had largely ended, in an effort to capitalize on interest created by the Pickwick Nite-Coach several years earlier. One such attempt was made by Paul W. Seiler, former president of General Motors Truck Co. The prototype had berths for 16 passengers and was constructed on a rear-engine Reo chassis. no further examples were built. *MBS*

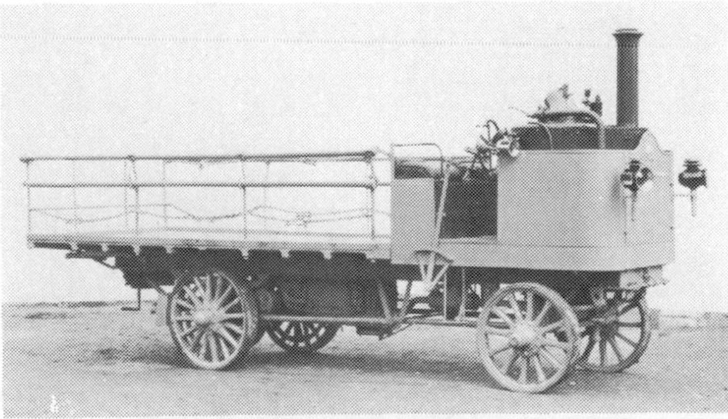

1906 SLM 5-ton steam wagon, SLM

S.L.M. (CH) 1906-1907; 1924-1932

Schweizerische Locomotiven & Maschinenfabrik, Winterthur

This well-known maker of locomotives had two separate phases of commercial vehicle production. The first was in 1906 when they launched two models of steam wagons, in

1925 SLM 3-ton front-drive truck, SLM

3½-and 5-ton sizes. One had a front-mounted engine and chain drive, while on the other the engine was just ahead of the rear axle which was gear driven. Few were made.

In 1924 S.L.M. brought out an unconventional front-wheel-drive truck powered by a 35hp 4-cylinder engine mounted ahead of the front axle Power. was transmitted through a remarkable hydraulically-operated 3-speed gearbox which included the differential and was mounted just behind the front axle. There were two sizes, a 2-tonner on pneumatic tires and a 3-tonner on solids. It was advertised as being highly suitable for municipal work, and was offered on the British market under the name Modern Wheel Drive. However only about 15 trucks were made. *FH*

SM (GB) 1910

SM Car Syndicate Ltd., Willesden Junction, London N.W.

Apart from its interest in the latter days of the St. Pancras wagon the SM company also built a shaft drive steam truck of its own design using a paraffin-fired semi-flash boiler beneath the driver's seat and a 2-cylinder vertical engine placed in the i/c position under a hood. Chassis and running gear components were bought-in-the front axle from Butler and worm drive rear axle from Dennis Bros. Superficially it resembled the Sheppee and shared the same fate, namely, to be almost totally ignored by commercial users. *RAW*

SMIT (NL) 1970 to date

Carrosseriefabriek Smit B.V., Joure

Using the engine and transmission of the Citroen ID, and Ford D-400 Smit builds mobile shops according to the example introduced some years before by Spijkstaal, another Dutch manufacturer of this type of vehicle. *JFJK*

SMITH (GB) 1906-1907

Frank Smith, Manchester

The Smith was a conventional 3-ton truck powered by a 42hp 4-cylinder engine, with chain drive. At least one was supplied to Baxendale & Company, a Manchester firm. In July, 1906 it was stated that a bus chassis is to be produced shortly, but it is not known if this ever materialized. *GNG*

SMITH — MILWAUKEE (US) 1912-1915

A.O. Smith Co., Milwaukee, Wis.

The initial Model A was a 3-tonner with a twin-ignition 4-cylinder engine under a hood, a 3-speed gearbox and worm-drive. Wheelbase was 14 feet. This was upgraded to a 3½-tonner for 1913 and was joined by the Model B, a 6-tonner. The Model B with a platform body, was priced at $4,750. These two types were continued essentially unchanged into 1915. *GMN*

1912 SMITH-MILWAUKEE Model A 3½-ton truck, A.O. Smith Co.

SMITHS ELECTRIC see N.C.B.

1908 S.N.A. 2-ton truck, ES

S.N.A. (CH) 1903-1913

Ste Neuchatelois d'Automobiles, Boudry (NE)

After having built motorcars together with his younger brother in Biel, Fritz Henriod founded this small company. Around 1903 a few trucks were built by S.N.A. and they were possibly the first in the world with an air-cooled four cylinder engine which was placed under the driver's seat. Probably the 25/30 hp OHV car engine of 4,941cc (110x130mm) with four separate and finned cylinders and two big lateral fans was used. A special device mounted on the steering-wheel allowed an automatic gear-change. The heavy-duty wood-wheels had iron tires and final drive was by chains. Financial difficulties led to the company's liquidation. *FH*

SNYDER (US) 1914

Snyder Motor & Manufacturing Company, Cleveland, Ohio

This was yet another obscure cyclecar which was available as a delivery van with a wheelbase of 8 feet, 4 inches. It was driven by a water-cooled, four-cylinder engine and had a three-speed gearbox and shaft drive. Its tread was 4 feet, 2 inches. Price for this delivery van was $425. *GMN*

SOAMES (GB) 1903-1904

Langdon-Davies Motor Car Co. Ltd., Southwark, London S.E.

The Soames, or Langdon-Davies, was made in car and van form, being powered by an 11 hp vertical twin engine driving through a constant-mesh gearbox and double chain drive. The latter were mounted close together near the center of the rear axle instead of near the wheels. Both engine and gearbox were mounted on a sub-frame separate from the chassis. *GNG*

SOEST (D) 1909-1911

Soest & Co., Dusseldorf

This firm built one type of truck only following the regulations of subsidized vehicles with 5-ton payload capacity. *HON*

SOLLER (CH) 1904-1913

Eugen Soller AG., Lastwagenfabrik, Basel

Soller specialized in heavy vehicles. The very massive 6-ton-truck of 1905 was equipped with a vertical single-cylinder engine of 12 hp, a huge gearbox with eight speeds (gears in constant mesh!) final drive by chains and very fat iron-tired wooden wheels. Steering this monster with a top speed of 7½ mph must have been quite a chore, especially as the steering wheel was of very small diameter. Smaller trucks for 1 to 5 tons payload were also offered.

In 1912 a new model was launched with a very unorthodox single-cylinder opposed piston engine which

1905 SOLLER 6-ton truck, ES

was horizontally mounted above the front axle. Chain drive and iron tires were retained but six speeds in either direction were now considered enough. Production after having reached several dozen vehicles ceased just prior to the first World War. The company remained in business however for repairs and service on commercial vehicles.*FHL*

1950 SOMUA 14-ton articulated truck, GNG

SOMUA (F) 1914-1955

Societe d'Outillege Mecanique et d'Usinage Artillerie, Saint-Ouen

Somua was founded in 1914 to take over the activities of three companies, the Usines Bouhey and the Ets. Farcot, both well-known general engineers and constructors of heavy military equipment, and the automobile construction division of the Societe Schneider. The main activity of the new group would remain the production of commercial vehicles, making good use of the fame the Schneider trucks and buses had already established for themselves. In fact, the Schneider name was still used up to the mid-twenties, particularly on bus chassis. For example, all buses supplied to the CGO and its successor, the SCRTP, were known as Schneider, having bodies by Scemia. One of the most interesting vehicles delivered was a tandem-axle bus, of which not only the front axle steered, but also the third axle.

Somua truck chassis, till about 1920 also partly known as Schneider, were very popular among manufacturers of municipal equipment like street-sweepers, refuse collectors, sprinklers, etc. as for example Laffly and Scemia. They bought the bare chassis, fitted them with their body, and then sold them as Laffly-Schneider vehicles, or Scemia-Schneider, or Laffly-Somua, Scemia-Somua. Somua itself also was a well-known supplier of municipal equipment, manufacturing refuse collectors on chassis which still had the lay-out of the original Schneider bus with the driver seated above the engine. The familiar round Solex radiator was retained on these vehicles up to the mid-twenties, when they were completely revised, receiving a closed cab and a more conventional radiator. On these chassis Somua produced during the twenties, under license the German Faun refuse collectors, among others for the city of Paris. On normal control chassis a range of fire engines was produced.

Somua was a typical manufacturer of heavy duty chassis, very sturdy equipment that could stand the roughest job. The Ateliers et Chantiers de la Loire used for example Somua chassis as carriers for their cranes, and Drouville constructed some of their finest fire engines on Somua chassis.

During the early thirties up to World War II various Somua normal control chassis were converted to half-tracks, using metal tracks at the rear. There were the four-cylinder MCG and MCL, produced from about 1933 onwards, and the six-cylinder MCSL that came a few years later. Some of them were fitted with armor-plating.

In 1933 Somua announced a completely new range of heavy-duty in vehicles, available among others with a diesel engine constructed after the German Lanova principle of a pre-combustion chamber. A range of four- and six-cylinder engines was built, for mounting in heavy chassis with a payload of 10 to 13 tons and single or tandem rear axles. Still the original Schneider lay-out, with the driver above the engine, was retained, creating thus a kind of semi-forward truck. Besides these heavy oil chassis, a gasoline engined range with payloads from 5 to 8 tons was available. Buses still were very important in the Somua range, with models like the JZSA chassis for coaches, and the BZSCA for municipal vehicles. From 1936 onwards the latter chassis would also be available in a trolleybus version, with the internal combustion engine replaced by a SW electric motor.

Full forward control trucks were the GLF and the GULSF, the former a two-axle vehicle, the latter a tandem-axle chassis. The GLF was available in three versions: with a 75 HP gas-producer engine, with a 90 HP oil engine or with a 105 HP gasoline unit. The GULSF could be had with either a 165 HP gasoline engine or a 125 HP oil engine.

During the war years, many Somua truck models were converted to gas-producer use, until 1944, when the whole production came to a halt. In 1946 production was resumed with the gas-producer version of the GLF. But soon the Lanova range of diesels were also in production again and with them the normal range of Somua vehicles became available.

The first new announcement after the war was the JL 15, an 11-tonner with a six-in-line 120 HP diesel engine.

In 1949 Somua scored a big success when the RATP, the Paris transport board, decided to buy a large batch of the new Somua OP5 bus chassis, with 120 HP oil engine and Wilson pre-selector gearbox. They were fitted with a body by Milion-Guiet-Tubauto, whose most interesting detail was that it could be easily lifted off the chassis in its entirety. A trolleybus verison of the OP 5 was also available, with SW electrical equipment. Immediately before the merger with Latil and Renault, Somua introduced a new range of truck chassis, the JL 19, with a 9,300 cc 150 HP oil engine, available in various wheelbase lengths, as a tractor and as single- or tandem-axle truck.

The heaviest Somuas produced in these years were the MTP and the MTPV, available as single and tandem-axle tipper trucks, heavy duty tractors and crane carrier chassis. *JFJK*

SOREX (F) 1906-1909

Automobiles Sorex, Levallois-Perret, Seine

So far as is known the Sorex was made only as a taxicab, with 12hp vertical twin engine. A few ran in London as well as in Paris and other French cities. *GNG*

S.O.S. see B.M.M.O.

SOULES (US) 1905-1908

Soules Motor Car Co., Grand Rapids, Mich.

This was a 1-ton shaft-driven truck powered by a 22hp horizontally-opposed twin engine. *GNG*

SOUTH BEND (US) 1913-1916

South Bend Motor Car Works, South Bend, Ind.

Initial trucks, from the same city as Studebaker, were 2- and 4-tonners. For the last year of manufacture, the entire line was revised from chain drive to worm gear drive or optional internal-gear drive. Made in the last year were ¾-, 1½-, 2- and 3½-tonners. *GMN*

SOUTHERN (i) (US) 1919-1921

Southern Truck & Car Corp., Greensboro, NC

Apparently 1- and 1½-tonners were made under this name but details of design are not available. This company was one of the very few truck manufacturers in North Carolina. *GMN*

1954 SOUTHERN (ii) F-35 bus, MBS

SOUTHERN (ii) (US) 1945-1961

Southern Coach Manufacturing Co., Evergreen, Alabama

Stanley Green formed Southern Coach Manufacturing Co. in 1941 to rebuilt a group of Southeastern Greyhound Lines front-engine Whites to cab-over-engine styling with Wayne bodies, and during World War II the plant was also used to perform heavy overhaul work for operating companies. Production began on a line of underfloor-engine transit buses in 1945, starting with a 32-passenger version and working up gradually to 35, 41, 45 and 50-passenger buses. Waukesha engines and Spicer transmissions were used at first, with most later buses having Fageol Twin Coach engines or else Leyland or Cummins diesels, with hydraulic transmission. About 1,400 buses were built in all, but very few after 1956; most customers were in the southern states, and a few Southerns were exported. There were also some large government orders. After the plant had closed it was sold in part to Flxible, which used it to build buses and a few truck bodies until it burned down in 1968. Flxettes are now built in a smaller plant in another part of Evergreen. *MBS*

1963 SOVAM 400kg van, Sovam

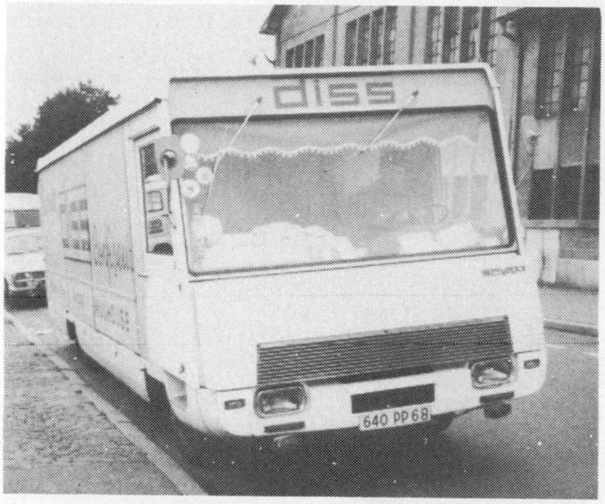

1975 SOVAM mobile shop, OMM

SOVAM (F) c.1963 to date

S.A.Morin Automobiles Sovam, Parthenay

Like Spykstaal in Holland, Sovam is a company that has specialized in mobile shops, using a low floor and front drive. Their first vehicle was a small van based on the Renault 4 car, but gradually sizes grew, and in 1968 came Sovam's first six-wheeler, designed for 9 tonner GVW and powered by a Perkins 6.354 diesel engine. In 1971 there were three models, for 3½-, 5.9- and 7-tons GVW, all with Peugeot engines, both gasoline and diesel, Peugeot gearboxes and Sovam axles. Bodies were by Etalmobil, an associated company. Most Sovams are used as mobile shops attending the weekly markets so familiar in French towns, though other uses have included mobile libraries, demonstration vans and airfield ground support vehicles. In 1973 a prototype ambulance with Reeves bodywork was built for the London ambulance service, but it was not followed up with production models. Recently a change has been made to Renault engines, but otherwise Sovam design remains as it has been for several years. *GNG*

1936 SOVEL 5-ton electric truck, JFJK

SOVEL (F) 1925 to date

Societe Sovel, Villeurbanne

Sovel was founded in 1925 to manufacture battery-electric vehicles for municipal use and delivery purposes, using the, — in those days, — newly introduced American Ironclad battery, manufactured under license in France by Tudor. An interesting feature of these first Sovel electric vehicles was the use of two electric motors, in such a way that a differential became superfluous: one engine drove the left rear wheel, the other the right, both by chains. These engines were produced by the Ets. Jacquet Freres of Vernon and constructed for a rating of 45 amps, 85 volt current. The engines were initially mounted in front of the rear axle, but later moved to a place behind the axle.

1960 SOVEL electric refuse truck, OMM

Besides manufacturing chassis, Sovel also produced bodies from 1935 onwards, particularly municipal ones, for example for refuse collection.

Up to the mid-thirties most Sovel vehicles were still fitted with cushion tires. During the late thirties a new range of electric vehicles was introduced, from small delivery vans to really heavy vehicles. They were fitted with a closed van body, or a very modern, forward control cab combined with a flatbed or truck body.

After World War II the range of Sovel vehicles was broadened. Small vehicles for internal transport were added, as well as electric dumper trucks for use in mines, or the type P, a predecessor of the current commercial vehicle breed with interchangeable body, and a special electric roadrail tractor pulling on the tracks 80 tons at a speed of 15 km/h. But most popular were the Transwatt vehicles, in use with the French railways SNCF,

1975 SOVEL electric refuse truck, JFJK

warehouses, department stores, etc. Like so many small manufacturers Sovel sought a somewhat safer basis for further existence by diversifying its production: the municipal bodies were also mounted on internal combustion engined chassis, like Latil, Berliet, Renault, Saviem, etc. Ant the production of airport passenger vehicles was taken up. But the electrics also remained, in fact Sovel is one of the last to exist from quite a number of French electric vehicle manufacturers. Currently in production at Villeurbanne are the AR10, AR15 and AR19, the last one with a payload of nearly twelve tons. Additionally, an electric city bus is produced, the C20, in co-operation with Currus, a French body manufacturer. *JFJK*

SOWERS (US) 1913-1914

Sowers Motor Truck Co., Boston, Mass.

The Sowers was a 1½-tonner built for only two years. Further information has not been located. *GMN*

1941 SPA Dovunque 5/6-ton 6×6 army truck, BHV

S.P.A. (I) 1908-1947

Societa Ligure Piemontese Automobili, Turin

Like many Italian factories, S.P.A. owed its origins to the Ceirano family. In this case the guiding spirit was Matteo, partnered by Michele Ansaldi, recently responsible for the Fiat-Ansaldi cars. Though serious truck production did not begin until 1909, S.P.A. fielded several vehicles — 30-cwt and 2/3-ton trucks, as well as a couple of buses — for the previous year's Industrial Vehicle trials, and would defeat the Fiat entry in the army's 1910 light truck competition. That year a 2-tonner was cataloged; it featured a 3.4-litre 4-cylinder T-head engine, pump cooling, 4-speed gearbox, twin transmission brakes, and, unusually, shaft drive; most early S.P.A.s outside the car-based class favored chains. By 1914 trucks had become the company's principal interest, and S.P.A.s came in all sizes from 10/12-cwt car-type delivery vans with 1.8-litre sv monobloc engines and pneumatic tires up to a chain-driven 3½-tonner with the remarkable cylinder dimensions of 95 × 200mm. 30-cwt, 2½-ton and 3½-ton types were produced in considerable numbers during the war; the firm also built a prototype forward control 10-tonner.

After the armistice the two bigger chain-driven models were continued, as well as a smaller 35-cwt truck with 2.7-litre monobloc engine, bevel drive, and pneumatics, available with an electric starter by 1923. It could also be had as a 20-seater coach with double reduction back axle, a larger PSV model having the 2½-tonner's 4.4-litre power unit. A Torinese bank failure in 1925 led to a liquidation and a Fiat takeover, which in its turn killed off the private car line. The trucks were, however, continued, all but the smallest using 4.4-litre pressure lubricated engines, 4-speed unit gearboxes, fwb, pneumatic tires, and full electrics; the 5-tonner had its engine mounted well forward of the front axle. By 1927 the 35-cwt S.P.A., now uprated to 2 tons, had brakes on the front wheels as well. In the meantime S.P.A. had taken over production of the Pavesi articulated tractor, and the range continued with little alteration until 1931, when the company added Ceirano trucks to its repertoire. From 1929 S.P.A.s were made under license in Poland under the Ursus name.

Thereafter S.P.A. concentrated on specialist types for the Army, though some of these, like the long lived Tipo 38 2½-tonner, were of essentially civilian type; it had a 4.1-litre 4-cylinder sv engine, magneto ignition, and mechanical fwb, subsequently replaced by hydraulics. There were also the Dovunque (go anywhere) family of forward control 6-wheelers, initially 3-ton 6 × 4s with 4-cylinder S.P.A. or 6-cylinder Fiat gasoline engines. Later Dovunques were modern, Fiat-like 6 × 6s with 9.4-litre, 108 bhp 6-cylinder diesels. 1937 saw the first of the 4×4 artillery tractors, the 1-ton AS37, which had 4-wheel steering and rode on 24 in. wheels. A development of this, the TM40, featured the big 6-cylinder Fiat diesel and air brakes. Some of these specialist types survived the war, but in 1947 S.P.A. was finally integrated into Fiat, and the name officially dropped. To this day, however, the Fiat truck plant at Stura is always referred to as 'the S.P.A.', while the radiator badges of the heavier Fiat goods vehicles carry the words Costruzione S.P.A. *MCS*

1948 SPANGLER Dual 8×4 twin-engined truck, NAHC

SPANGLER (US) 1947-1949

D.H. Spangler Eng. & Sales Co., Hamburg, Pa.

The Spangler "Dual" was a heavy duty four axle truck. The front two axles steered. Each of the rear axles was driven by a separate 100 hp Ford V-8 engine. The engines were mounted side-by-side and had separate drive trains. The Spangler was made of "Genuine Ford Parts," and could be serviced at any Ford dealer. Models built included a large flatbed truck and a fire engine. There was also a Spangler "Dual" with three axles, and in the early 1950s Spangler dual front conversions, giving twin steering axles, were made for various trucks such as G.M.C., Ford and White. Production took place in the Hahn Motors plant, for D.H. Spangler was president of Hahn from 1937 to 1954. *DJS*

SPARTAN (i) (US) 1946-1949

Spartan Coach & Manufacturing Co., Sturgis, Mich.

In the years following World War II, as automobiles became plentiful, bus riding declined, and the smaller companies in the U.S. intercity bus industry wanted new vehicles that would cost less to buy and operate. One of the answers was provided by the Spartan coach, designed by Howard Munshaw (formerly with Pony Cruiser). A 21-passenger bus on a 170-inch wheelbase and equipped with an International engine and 5-speed Fuller transmission, the original type of Spartan had a framework of welded steel tubing similar to that of the Aerocoach. A few Spartans were also sold to major operators, which used them for feeder routes and other lightly traveled lines, and five went to Nairn Transport of Syria. Two larger models seating 25 and 29 passengers were introduced in 1949, but by that time the trend in the industry was to the introduction of new features such as air-conditioning to attract more business rather than to cut costs, and only about 20 buses were sold in 1949. The company was shut down, and Howard Munshaw went on to form Cub Industries and build small transit buses instead. *MBS*

SPARTAN (ii) (US) 1975 to date

Spartan Motors Inc., Charlotte, Mich.

Following the demise of Diamond-Reo a group of former employees started the Spartan company in September 1975. They built the 2000 series chassis which could be used for either fire engines or trucks, and the HH-1000 6 × 4 off-road coal hauler with a load capacity of 40 tons. Various engines such as Detroit Diesel and Cummins can be specified. For 1978 Spartan plans to build over-the-road trucks similar in appearance to Diamond-Reo, with finance and factory space provided by a supplier to the original firm. *OM*

SPAULDING (US) 1913

Spaulding Manufacturing Co., Grinnell, Iowa

The Spaulding Model T was a 1-tonner with a wheelbase of 9 feet, 7 inches whose chassis weighed 2300 pounds. Its 4-cylinder engine was the same as used in the 1912 Model E passenger cars under the same trade name, although the commercial vehicle used double chain drive. It also used a 3-speed gearbox and had an express body. With either solid rubber or pneumatic tires, the price was $1100. *GMN*

SPEEDWELL (i) (GB) 1900

Speedwell Motor & Cycle Co., Aberdeen

The Speedwell 3-ton wagon used a Toward patent boiler working at 200 psi and a compound undertype engine with two road speeds of 3 and 5½mph. Artillery wheels were used. The only known example was supplied to Persley Quarries. *RAW*

SPEEDWELL (ii) (US) 1908-1915

Speedwell Motor Car Company, Dayton, Ohio

The initial trucks by this manufacturer were light

delivery vans but these were soon dropped in favor of much larger types and by 1912, only 2- and 3-tonners were being made. The larger types all had forward control and 4-cylinder engines with double chain-drive and solid tires. An option in 1912 was a power winch mounted behind the cab, for an additional $200. In 1913 and 1914, a 6-tonner was also made with chassis weight of 7200 pounds and fitted with a stake body which sold for $4400. The name Speedwell was much better known for high quality passenger cars. *GMN*

SPERBER (D) 1911-1919
Norddeutsche Automobilwerke, Hameln

The private cars of this firm were the basis for van versions. 4-cylinder 15 hp engines were used. The factory was taken over by Selve. *HON*

SPHINX (US) 1915
Sphinx Motor Car Co., York, Pa.

This firm briefly offered a ½-ton truck with 17 hp Lycoming 4-cylinder engine. Cone clutch and bevel gear drive were used. It cost $675 with panel body. *DJS*

1956 SPIJKSTAAL 3-wheel van, A. de Boer

SPIJKSTAAL (NL) 1955 to date
Spijkstaal B. V., Spijkenisse

Spijkstaal began their existence during the 1930s as manufacturers of agricultural trailers. A range of electric trucks for municipal purposes and internal works transport was added in 1955. More than ten years later, in about 1966, they added a range of mobile shops, manufacturing their own chassis and axle casings, but using foreign components such as Opel or Ford engines, Ford or ZF gearboxes, ZF steering and Salisbury or Dana differentials. In 1975 a range of front-drive vehicles with very low loading height was launched, using British Ford 115 or 152 hp diesel engines and Allison automatic gearboxes. The 1978 range covered 3- and 4-wheeled electric vehicles including works trucks and aircraft tugs, and 4- and 6-wheeled diesel-engined mobile shops. *JFJK*

SPOERER (US) 1912-1914
Carl Spoerer's Sons, Baltimore, Maryland

The Spoerer was built only as light closed delivery vans which used the same chassis as used for Spoerer passenger autos. The two commercial types differed only in the size of the four-cylinder, water-cooled engines. The larger Model 40C had displacement of 8.5 liters while the smaller Model 25A had displacement of 4.6 liters. The Model 40C, with wheelbase of 10 feet, had shaft drive and a capacity of 1,500 pounds, and its price was $3,000, while the Model 25A sold for $2,000. Both models were quite attractive for the time. *GMN*

SPRINGFIELD (US) 1901
Springfield Motor Vehicle Co., Springfield, Mass.

This was a steam van with two compound engines, one on each side, connected directly to a rear wheel. It had a range of 50 miles on one supply of fuel and water, and a load capacity of about 1,000 lbs. *GNG*

SPYKER (NL) 1921-c.1923
Nederlandsche Automobiel- en Vliegtuigenfabriek, Trompenburg, Amsterdam

Spyker was the best-known Dutch make of passenger car until the advent of the DAF, but although a number of commercial bodies were built on passenger car chassis in the pre-war period, the first purpose-built truck chassis did not appear until 1921. It was a 2-tonner powered by a 4-cylinder sv monobloc engine in unit with the 4-speed gearbox, and had worm final drive. Wheelbase was 11 ft. Few were made, and in 1925 Spyker abandoned vehicle manufacture altogether. *GNG*

1954 S.R. 101 3-ton truck, AAR

S.R. (R) 1954 to date
(1) Uzina Steagul Rosu, Brasov
(2) Uzina de Autocamioane Brasov, Brasov
(3) Intreprinderea de Autocamioane Brasov, Brasov

The former ASTRA factory of Brasov, responsible for the repair of vehicles and locomotives and the building of vehicle bodies, was engaged in the post-war years in the production of tools and machinery, under the SR (Red Star) name. It was thus fully equipped to produce the first Rumanian post war vehicles as early as 1954. Choosing as model the Soviet ZIL 150 4 ton truck, the first SR truck chassis was named model 101 and was powered by a 5.5-litre gasoline engine developing a modest 95 hp and appeared in May of the same year. Model 101 was built until 1962 when the Carpati range, named after the neighboring Carpathian moutains, was introduced. Modeled, once again, after the contemporary ZIL range and fitted with a nice looking cab with mid-50s American style panoramic windshield, it had a V8 gasoline engine developing 140 HP and a payload of 3.5 to 5 tons. SR trucks were built since their introduction, practically unchanged. Later additions included long and short wheelbases, tractor and 4x4 variants, while a diesel engine option has been offered since 1968. Diesels used were 126 hp Mercedes Benz, 112 hp Perkins or Yugoslavian Torpedos of 95 hp. Unusual was the fact that the foreign customer specifying a Mercedes Benz or Perkins diesel, had to supply the engine himself, in order that local currency was not spent. A forward-control range including truck, tractor and tipper versions and based on existing models was the only important innovation in

1975 S.R. Bucegi 5-ton truck, BHV

more recent years. Powered by the same V8 gasoline engine it featured a cab derived from the Carpati range and was also later supplemented with a 6x4 model. SR is largely exporting to many countries in the Eastern Bloc, in Africa and Asia while the V8 engine and other components are regularly supplied to the TV bus factory. The Brasov factory is also responsible for the Roman vehicles built under Saviem license. Total capacity in 1973 was reported to be 36,000 units per year.

The SR 114 4x4 chassis is also used as the basis of AT202 fire engine which is the main fire fighter used in Rumania. A purpose-built cab, and front end with 4 headlights and body are constructed on the chassis giving to the vehicle a customized appearance. *GA*

STANDARD (i) (GB) 1906-

(1) Standard Steam Lorry & Omnibus Co., Rayleigh, Essex 1906-1907
(2) J.T. Rayner & Sons, Rayleigh, Essex 1907-

The Standard was a 5-ton top-fired locomotive-boilered compound undertype with countershaft differential and double chain final drive, the principal novelty being the use in some wagons of Rayner patent resilient wheels, the essence of which was a circle of radial cylinders arranged round the hub, each cylinder containing a piston attached to a rod carrying a hardwood shoe. The shoes formed the wheel periphery in contact with the road and the entrapped air in the cylinders was supposed to give the wheels resilience. Leakage and other infirmities made the wheels a failure.

1907 STANDARD (i) 5-ton steam wagon, RAW

Rayner later made a few gasoline engined lorries and omnibuses but the total production of steam types was commercially negligible.

1911 STANDARD (iii) ¾-ton van, NMM

Some later vehicles seem to have been sold as Rayners. *RAW*

STANDARD (ii) (US) 1907-1908

Standard Gas-Electric Power Co., Pa.

This unusual truck was powered by a horizontally-opposed twin engine under the seat which drove a shunt-wound generator. Unlike most gasoline-electric trucks this was not intended to drive, but when the engine speed dropped below 1,000 rpm it became a motor, taking current from the battery and restoring the engine to its normal speed. If the engine were out of action the truck could run on the batteries alone for a few miles. It had 3 speeds and final drive by double chains. *GNG*

1935 STANDARD (iii) Atlas ½-ton van, John Davy

1959 STANDARD (iii) Atlas ½-ton, OMM

STANDARD (iii) (GB) 1911-1915; 1931-1936; 1939-1965

Standard Motor Co. Ltd., Coventry, Warwickshire

Standard did not become seriously involved in commercial vehicles before World War II, though there were earlier ventures beginning with a fast delivery van for 10/15-cwt payloads offered on the 15hp 4-cylinder monobloc chassis in 1911. Some of the 20hp 6-cylinder cars sent to India for the Delhi Durbar also carried light truck bodies. In 1913 the new worm-drive 9.5hp with 1,097cc 4-cylinder engine was available as a 3-cwt van. In 1931 Standard introduced a 7-cwt van based on their 1.3-litre Big 9 with coil ignition and 3-speed gearbox, payload going up to 10-cwt in 1932 when a 6-cwt type based on the 1-litre Little 9 was added to the range. These used the same sheet metal as the cars, but lacked bumpers, chromium plating, or running boards. In 1934 they gave way to new 4-speed Atlas models with 1.3-litre 10hp or 1.6-litre 12hp engines, but neither was a big seller, and they disappeared once their private-car counterparts were superseded by the streamlined Flying Standard range. World War II saw substantial production of light commercials based on the Flying 12 and 14, the former for the Army and the latter for the RAF; the Beaverette light armored car also used the 14hp chassis, and experiments with ultra-light 4 × 2 and 4 × 4 vehicles of jeep type led to the announcement in 1945 of an interesting Farmer's Utility intended to sell at £140. A 4 × 4 less than 8ft long, it used the 1-litre 8hp sv engine, and featured a tubular frame, independent suspension, and six forward speeds. It never went into production, though a civilian version of the 12hp WD Utility was exported in small numbers, and there was also a van edition of the post-war 12hp car, made for Standard dealers, as well as for those handling the Ferguson tractors made in Standard's factories until Ferguson contracted an alliance with Massey-Harris in 1954.

1948, however, saw a one-model policy based on the 2.1-litre 4-cylinder ohv Vanguard, with full-width styling, 3-speed gearbox, coil ifs, and hypoid axle, available also as a 12-cwt van or pickup. These light commercials continued with little change until 1955, though from 1954 they could be had with Standard's own 40bhp 2.2-litre diesel engine, also offered as a proprietary unit: some were used in London taxis. Price of the 1955 diesel van was £816, over £200 more than was asked for the gasoline model. The reintroduction of a range of small cars led to a 6-cwt van variant in 1954, this being basically the 948cc 4-speed Ten: Standrive 2-pedal control was a 1956 option on commercials as well as cars. In 1956-57 the 6-cwt was Standard's staple truck offering, since only in Australia was a Phase III Vanguard utility offered, though in 1958 and 1959 the factory catalogued a chassis/cab version also available with the 1.7-litre Ensign engine.

In the autumn of 1959 Standard made their bid in the new forward control walkthrough light van class with the 10/12-cwt Atlas on a 7ft wheelbase. The mechanics were essentially those of the Ten, but the engine was slightly inclined in the frame, and transverse ifs replaced the car's coils. A wide range of variants was catalogued, including personnel carriers, ambulances, and mobile homes, but in original form it was underpowered, and a year later it was supplemented by a new Atlas Major using the Ensign engine. 1962 models of the 6-cwt were uprated to 7-cwt with 1,147cc Triumph Herald engines, and a year later the forward control types were further improved, emerging as the 15-cwt Ensign-powered 15, and the 1-ton 20 with either the 2.1-litre Vanguard unit or a 2.3-litre Leyland diesel. In September 1963 Leyland (who had acquired Standard in 1961) integrated these two models into their own range, though production continued at Coventry. This left the 7-cwt van and pickup as the only vehicles still carrying the Standard name; car production had been halted during the summer. This state of affairs persisted into 1965, but vans of Standard design continued to be made as Leylands until 1968.*MCS*

STANDARD (iv) FISHER — STANDARD (US) 1912-1933

Standard Motor Truck Co., Detroit, Mich.

The Standard was a conventional truck using Continental engines throughout its lifetime, with Brown-Lipe transmissions and Timken worm-drive rear axles on many models. Chain drive was used on the larger models up to about 1920, these running up to 5 tons capacity. In 1925 Standards were made in sizes from 1¼ to 7 tons, the 2½ to 7-tonners having a choice of 4 or 9-speed trans-

1920 (iv) 3½-ton truck, FLP

1929 FISHER-STANDARD moving van, NAHC

missions. There was also a speed model, popular with many truck makers at this time, which was called the Fisher Fast Freight. By 1928 all the smaller trucks were called Fishers, bearing such names as Fisher Junior Express (1 ton), Fisher Fast Freight (1½ tons), Fisher Mercantile Express (2 tons) and Fisher Heavy Duty Six (2½-3½ tons). There were also Standard trucks in the 2½ to 7½ ton range, and a 28 — passenger bus, the Standard AK. They sold well in the Detroit area, particularly to the municipality for refuse collection, snow removal etc., and also to some extent in Canada. From 1930 the name Fisher-Standard was used for al models. *RJ/GNG*

STANDARD (v) (US) 1913-1914

Standard Motor Truck Co., Cleveland, Ohio

This is another Standard about which little is known. Under this name were a 1-and a 1½-tonner with no technical details available. *GMN*

STANDARD (vi) (US) 1913-1915

Standard Motor, Truck Co., Warren, Ohio

The Standard consisted of a line of 3/4-, 1-, 1½-, 2- and 3½-tonners. Despite this impressively complete line of vehicles, no other details have been found. In 1916 the name was changed to Warr°n Motor Truck Co. *GMN*

STANDARD (vii) or, STANDARD TRACTOR (US) 1915-1916

Standard Tractor Company, Brooklyn, New York

The Standard Tractor was designed for the pulling of independent trailers, and had forward control. Its rear drive was unusual inas-much as the worm-driven jackshaft was to the rear of the back axle and was connected by roller chains to the rear wheels. This presumably allowed for a shorter unit. The overall gearing allowed an 18:1 axle wheel ratio. The tractor was equipped with air brakes and with attachments for air connections to a drawn trailer. *GMN*

1934 STANDARD (viii) ½-ton van, NMM

STANDARD (viii) (D) 1933-1939

Standard Fahrzeugfabrik GmbH., Ludwigsburg; Stuttgart-Feuerbach

When Standard started to build tri-vans they followed the layout of one driven front wheel and rear mounted box or platform. 400cc and 500cc engines were available. In 1936 the tri-van was supplemented by a 4-wheel version of ½-ton payload capacity. This had a 500cc engine which was placed under the platform driving the rear axle. *HON*

STANDARD (ix) (IND) 1965 to date

Standard Motor Products of India Ltd., Madras

The only factory to still bear the Standard name, builds a light commercial model based on the Triumph Herald car. Using the Herald front-end and built as a chassis/cowl only, it forms the basis of van, pick-up or similar bodies of 250 kilos payload. The outdated Standard Atlas, alias Leyland 20, 1 ton forward control model is also built in chassis front-end form and the same bodies are fitted. 1 litre and 2 litre 68hp gasoline engines power the two models respectively. *GA*

STANLEY (US) 1909-1916

Stanley Motor Carriage Co., Newton, Mass.

The best-known commercial vehicle made by the celebrated steam car builders was the Mountain Wagon, a 12-passenger open-sided hotel bus originally developed to serve the Stanley Hotel at Estes Park, Colorado, built by the Stanley brothers. Later, many other hotels and organizations used Mountain Wagons, and one is still in regular service today, at the Magic Age of Steam Museum at Yorklyn, Delaware. They were powered by a 30 hp 2-cylinder engine which was in fact a detuned and lower geared version of that used in the larger of the 'Gentleman's Speedy Roadsters'. The Mountain Wagon was made from 1909 to 1916, and was supplemented by delivery vans and trucks for 1,500 lbs., 1 ton and 1¼ ton capacity.

Commercial vehicles were not listed after 1916, but two attempts to revive the firm both involved trucks and buses. The first was in 1924 when an organization called the Steam Vehicle Corp. of America was formed to make cars at Newton and commercial vehicles in the former Watson truck plant at Canastota, N.Y. Nothing came of this, nor of announcements in 1935 and 1936 that Stanley steam buses would be made by the Stanley Steam Motors Corp. of Chicago. *GNG*

1929 STAR (i) 1¼-ton newspaper van, OMM

STAR (i) (GB) 1904-1931

(1) Star Engineering Co., Wolverhampton, Staffs 1904-1909
(2) Star Cycle Co., Wolverhampton, Staffs 1905-1906
(3) Star Engineering Co. Ltd., Wolverhampton, Staffs 1909-1928
(4) Star Motor Co. Ltd., Wolverhampton, Staffs 1928-1931

Early Star commercial vehicles were based on their lighter private car chassis with 3-speed gearboxes, chain drive, and pneumatic tires on the front wheels only. Smallest offering was a 3-cwt van based on the 1905 6 hp transverse-single made by the associated Star Cycle Co. (later Briton); at the other end of the scale was a 25-cwt machine based on the 14/16 hp 4-cylinder chassis, listed in 1907. In that year shaft drive made its appearance on cabs and 15-cwt vans with 1.9-litre 2-cylinder or 2.4-litre 4-cylinder engines. 1909 saw a full range of commercial vehicles from 1 to 4 tons, all with 4-cylinder engines and chain drive: the big ones had 4-speed gearboxes, twin rear wheels, and capacities of up to 6.2 litres. A charabanc chassis with a 12 ft. 6 in. wheelbase was also available. There was continuing coverage of the market up to 1914, when the smallest Star was a 5-cwt van on the 10 hp 4-cylinder car chassis, and the heaviest the 4-tonner. This last was the only model that could not be bought with shaft drive; the 2-ton and 50-cwt trucks featured double reduction back axles, also found on the wartime 50/60-cwt and 4/5-ton types.

The immediate post-1918 range comprised a worm-drive 30-cwt model with 3.8-litre 4-cylinder engine, twin rear wheels and the option of pneumatic tires, a similar 2½-tonner available with solids only, and a 4.1-litre 3-tonner retaining double reduction drive, though worm drive was standardized with the advent of new types in 1924. Other features were 3.1-litre monobloc engines, 4-speed unit gearboxes, and all brakes on the rear wheels. They were available with pneumatic tires and (from 1926) with fwb as well, payloads ranging from 15-cwt up to 3 tons. This series forged the long-standing connection between Star and the Selfridge department store chain (who specified spiral bevel back axles on their early orders); a less likely customer was the King of Saudi Arabia, who bought a fleet of Star harem wagons in 1927. New for 1927 was a low-loader 20-passenger coach chassis with 3.4-litre engine, twin-plate clutch, full electrics and pneumatic tires. This evolved into the Star Flyer with 3.2-litre 7-bearing ohv 6-cylinder engine and fwb, an impressive performer capable of 50 mph, and much favored as a horsebox as well as for passenger work; the Prince of Wales ordered such a vehicle with Vincent body. Later Flyers had 3.6-litre engines, vacuum servo brakes, and a somewhat American looking radiator in place of the traditional Star style. 4-cylinder trucks and buses were discontinued after

1927 STAR (i) 30 cwt. van

1928, but the success of earlier newspaper vans led to an interesting design created for *The Evening Standard* in 1929. Payload was 25-cwt, it used a specially reinforced frame with twin rear wheels, and the 6-cylinder Flyer engine was fitted. In the late 1920s Star also offered a line of ambulances based on the 18/50, 20/50 and 20/60 car chassis.

The Lisle family sold out to Sydney Guy in 1928, and truck production, never on a large scale, dwindled steadily from 284 in that year to a low 84 in 1931, the last year in which Flyers were available. Car production ceased in May, 1932. *MCS*

STAR (ii) (US) 1913-1914

Star Motor Car Co., Ann Arbor, Mich.

Two models of trucks were made during the short life of this make. A 1-tonner used a four-cylinder, side-valve engine mounted under the hood. It had solid rubber tires, a three-speed gearbox and double chain drive. The 1½-tonner, at a price of $1,800 had a wheelbase of 10 feet, 10 inches and a similar drive system. *GMN*

1931 STAR (iii) RUGBY 1½-ton van, NAHC

STAR: (iii) RUGBY (US) 1922-1932

Durant Motors Inc., Lansing, Mich.

William C. Durant's Star Four with 2.2-litre sv Continental engine represented a challenge to Ford and Chevrolet at a list price of under $400. Logically, the range included a delivery van; more surprisingly, there was also a depot wagon, a station wagon ancestor with roll-up side curtains. Durant's challenger in the 1-ton class was the Mason, made by another of his companies, but in some export markets the gap was bridged by a 15-cwt van on the ohv Durant Four chassis. A 2.8-litre six, also by Continental, was added to the Star lineup in 1926, this forming the basis for a new 1/1½-ton truck called the Star Six Compound Fleettruck, sold under the Rugby name from the end of 1927. Previously, however, all Stars had been sold as Rugbys in British Commonwealth countries, to avoid confusion with the well-established (i) Star from Wolverhampton. The new name called for few basic changes; the ½-ton van was now based on the 36 bhp Durant Four, and boasted fwb, a refinement missing from the similarly-powered 1-ton truck. There was, however, a more sophisticated tonner, offered with either the small six or a bigger four; on this one there were four forward speeds and the handbrake worked on all four wheels. By mid-1929 it had acquired a 3 × 2-speed transmission, but this departure was short-lived, and the bigger 1931-32 Rugbys reverted to a conventional 4-speed box. The same 58 bhp Continental 6 was used both in this model and in the ½-tonner based on the Durant 6-14 car. *MCS*

1975 STAR (iv) 200 6-ton truck, MSH

1967 STAR (iv) 25 5-ton articulated truck, OMM

STAR (iv) (PL) 1948 to date

Fabryka Samochodow Ciezarowych, Starahovice

Starahovice is a major industrial city in central Poland where an old established machinery engineering factory was chosen, immediately after the war, to become the first producer of Polish-built vehicles under the name of Star, derived from the first half of the city name. Polish engineers designed the first Star trucks in 1948 and a batch of 10 units were produced using the Ursus factory facilities in Warsaw. After being approved for production, Model 20, as it was known, powered by a gas engine of 85 hp and having a payload of 3.5 tons was built in 20 units during the first year, but in increasing numbers subsequently. Star vehicles, later built in tractor and tipper versions also, and mechanically improved, powered by 87.5 and 105 hp gas engines, retained the old style cab for many years and have been exported since 1954, mainly to Eastern Bloc countries. A 100 hp diesel engine option was introduced in 1961, while a 6 × 6 military or civilian model with canvas top cab and front winch was in regular production as early as 1958. Series 28/29 was introduced in the late 60s and had an uprated payload of 5 tons, a 100 hp diesel or 105 hp gas engine option of Star manufacture and a modern style cab designed by Chausson of France. This same cab was later fitted to the 6 × 6 chassis which was largely redesigned, as well as to a 150 hp diesel engined 4 × 4 chassis used mainly as the basis of a fire-fighting vehicle with Jelcz body and equipment. Star also supplies chassis, engines and other components to the San bus factory. *GA*

STAR-TRIBUNE see O.K.

STARBUCK (US) 1912-1913

Starbuck Automobile Co., Philadelphia, Pa.

The single model of this make was a 1½-tonner with an open express body. It used a four-cylinder engine with forward control, a three-speed gearbox and double chain drive. Platform springs were used at the rear. This sold for $1,700. *GMN*

START (CS) 1928-1929

"Start" Kralovohradecka Tovarna na Automobily, Petrasek a Spol., Hradek Kralove

Founded in 1921, this company made small cars and delivery vans in 1928/29, powered by 1.45-litre 4-cylinder sv engines developing 20 bhp. *MSH*

STEAMLINE see Baker (ii)

STEAM-O-TRUCK (US) 1918-1920

Steam Automotive Works, Denver, Colorado

An early letter by this manufacturer gives the tradename as Stokesbary, but later truck journals refer to this as Steam-O-Truck. This was built only as a five-tonner with the boiler under the hood and steam led to the two-cylinder engine directly-geared to the rear axle with a 3:1 reduction. (Prior to 1919, this had been a four-cylinder, single-expansion engine.) Boiler operating pressure was initially 700 psi, later reduced to 600 psi. The chassis had a wheelbase of 13 feet, 1 inch and cost $5000. Its water reservoir held 40 gallons. *GMN*

STEAMOBILE (US) 1919

Winslow Boiler & Engineering Co., Chicago, Ill.

Probably the last American steam truck to be announced, the Steamobile had an advanced Uniflow V-4 engine and Winslow high-pressure boiler. Final drive was by shaft and load capacity about 5 tons. *GNG*

STEAMOTOR (US) 18 1917-1920

(1) Steamotor Truck Company 1917-1918

(2) Amalgamated Machinery Corporation 1919-1920

As implied in the tradename, this was a steamer which used a 600 psi, 45 hp boiler to feed a two-cylinder Doble-built engine. The boiler was under the hood with the engine under the driver's seat. The final drive was by shaft and worm gear. This two-tonner had a wheelbase of 12 feet and the chassis alone was priced at $3,000. No standard bodies were available. *GMN*

STEARNS (US) 1911-1914; 1915-1916

F.B. Stearns Co., Cleveland, Ohio

Stearns was an early builder of passenger automobiles with an enviable reputation for high quality. Their first commercial vehicle was a 3-tonner with a 44 hp, four-cylinder engine, double chain drive and solid rubber tires. From

1912 STEARNS 5-ton truck, NAHC

1912 on, only 5-tonners were made and in that year, offered only a platform body on chassis of any wheelbase from 15 feet, to 19 feet, 8 inches. This had a three-speed gearbox and double chain drive. An unusual feature was a lock for the jackshaft differential to limit wheel slippage. After dropping the manufacture of commercial vehicles for nearly two years, a re-designed 5-tonner was offered in the middle of 1915. This used a four-cylinder engine with Knight sleeve valves. This engine was spring-mounted on a subframe using inverted semi-elliptical springs. However, the double chain drive was retained. Only platform bodies were offered on wheelbases as great as 22 feet, 6 inches. *GMN*

STEEL SWALLOW (US) 1908

Steel Swallow Auto Co., Jackson, Mich.

Steel Swallows were built as enclosed delivery vans and mail vans on very light chassis with a 7-foot wheelbase. The engine was an 8 hp, two-cylinder type and was connected with a friction transmission. This car was differential-less and slippage was provided by friction drive between driving pulleys and the rear wheels. *GMN*

STEELE (US) 1914-1919

W.M. Steele, Worcester, Massachusetts

W.M. Steele had built the defunct Morgan trucks, previously of Worcester. Steele trucks were 2-, 3-, 4- and 5-tonners which were powered by engines built by Steele. These were equipped with Cotta three-speed gearboxes and final drive by double chains from a Steele-built jackshaft. In all cases, the two seats straddled the hood. *GMN*

STEGEMAN (US) 1911-1917

Stegeman Motor Car Co., Milwaukee, Wis.

The Stegeman was a conventional truck made in six sizes from 1,500 lbs. to 5 tons capacity. The smallest model ran on pneumatic tires, while the larger ones used solids. Chain drive was featured on all models from 1 ton upwards, and this could be had with a fully-enclosed oil bath for an extra $150. Most Stegemans used 4-cylinder engines, but in 1917 they used a six with an electric starter, both unusual features for trucks at this date. Their 1917 7-tonner had a fully-floating worm-drive rear axle of their own manufacture, and in that year they announced plans to double their production capacity. However 1917 proved to be their last year. *RW*

STEIGBOY (D) 1927-1930

Steigboy Apparatebau GmbH., Leipzig W 31

The layout of two front and one driven rear wheels was featured in this design. Engines by DKW (200cc), Villiers (350cc) and Sturmey-Archer (500cc) were installed. *HON*

STEINKONIG see World

STEINMETZ (US) 1922-1926

Steinmetz Electric Motor Car Corp., Baltimore, Md.

The Steinmetz electric trucks adopted the name of the Schenectady, N.Y. electrical genius, Charles P. Steinmetz. There were two models, a ½-tonner and a ¾-tonner, both using Diehl DC motors and Russel bevel-gear rear axles. The smaller had a wheelbase of 9 feet while the larger was 6 inches longer. Both models remained unchanged through 1924 but only the ¾-tonner was still built for 1926. *GMN*

STELLITE (GB) 1915

Electric and Ordnance Accessories Co. Ltd., Birmingham

The Stellite light car was built by a subsidiary of Wolseley. It used an 1100cc 4-cylinder F-head engine with detachable head, a 2-speed transaxle, and an armored wood frame. A 5-cwt van was briefly available in 1915. *MCS*

STEPHENSON (US) 1910-1913

Stephenson Motor Truck Co., Milwaukee, Wis.

The Stephenson models were 1- and 3-tonners with forward control. These were powered by 4-cylinder, water-cooled engines which drove through friction transmissions and double chain drives. Solid rubber tires were used. Wheelbases were 9 feet, 4 inches and 11 feet, respectively, with a price of $2000 for the 1-tonner and $3500 for the 3-tonner. *GMN*

STERLING (i) (US) 1909-1910

Sterling Vehicle Co., Harvey, Ill.

Apparently the only type of truck under this name was the Model C. This had a water-cooled 2-cylinder engine with a 3-speed gearbox and shaft drive. The chassis weighed 2700 lbs. and the wheelbase was 7 feet, 4 inches. *GMN*

1927 STERLING (ii)DW8 2-ton truck, OMM

STERLING (ii); STERLING WHITE (US) 1916-1953

(1) Sterling Motor Truck Co., Milwaukee, Wis. 1916-1933
(2) Sterling Motors Corp., Milwaukee, Wis. 1934-51
(3) Sterling Division, White Motor Co., Milwaukee, Wis. 1951-1952
(4) Sterling Division, White Motor Co., Cleveland, Ohio 1952-1953

After the name change from Sternberg, Sterling trucks became conventionals in a 1½- to 7-ton range. In 1918 Sterling made 479 USA "Liberty" model B trucks, being one of the 15 manufacturers selected by the US Army to make them to the original Gramm-Bernstein design. The civilian range was also continued, much of which was worm-driven, although still chain-driven on the 7-ton and some 5-ton models.

From the mid-teens until the sale of the company, the name "Sterling" was with rare exceptions cast into the smooth metallic triangular shell crown as a prominent identification feature.

The exclusive wood inlay of the frame developed during the Sternberg days was patented on Feb. 7, 1922 and continued to be used in Sterling trucks. Sterling made its own 4-cylinder engines cast in pairs, 4-speed sliding gear transmissions on models up to 2½-tons, 3-speed constant mesh transmissions on the 3½- and 5-ton models, and 6-speed constant mesh transmissions on the 5- and 7-ton chain drives. Pneumatic tires were used with duals on some models up to 3½-tons, and solids, including duals, on larger size models for 1922. Most Sterlings had cycle-type fenders from the mid-teens to the early 1930's, and some were still used far later. Solid tires continued to be used until about 1927, being phased out completely by late 1931.

1932 STERLING (ii) 1½-ton van, OMM

In the mid-1920s Sterling added a 1½-ton worm drive to the range at $3,345. Several other straight-truck sizes with worm or chain drives ranged from 2- to 7½-tons priced from $3,545 to $6,500. These were heavyweights, with the 5-ton chain drive chassis weighing 10,000 pounds. This one had a transmission of 6 speeds forward and 2 reverse. At the top of the Sterling range were tractors of 12-, and 20-ton capacity priced from $5,850 to $6,600. Buses were also offered for 21 and 25 passengers at $6,800 to $7,575. The general styling was virtually unchanged from the mid-teens to the late 1920s.

In 1928 Sterling adopted the new high-speed 6-cylinder engines on the market and offered a 1-ton model. In 1928 Sterling used an early multiple transmission, an idea developed by the Schacht Motor Truck Co. about 1920. Although most truck manufacturers had abandoned chain drive, Sterling continued to offer them for many years afterwards on the large models. Some tandems came into use. For 1930 Sterling's new 6-cylinder gasoline engine of 779.3 cu. in. developed 185hp, a new record for truck engines. Sterling reached its record production with 1,000-1,600 trucks in these last three years. 1931 saw Sterling's handsome new F-series of the mid-range trucks which resembled Brockway and Indiana, among others. Some even had rear fenders.

In 1932 Sterling bought the La France-Republic Corp. of Alma, Mich., which helped foreign sales substantially, as La France-Republic had extensive overseas dealer outlets. Sterling continued La France-Republic production until 1942.

Cummins diesels were now available, and Sterling was one of the first to offer them as an option.

By 1935 truck manufacturers had started the cab-over revival, and Sterling developed an unusual rear-tilting cab. The windshield, front-quarter windows, seats, and fenders were stationary while the doors and the remainder of the cab, with its rear-quarter side windows, tilted backwards on hinges at the rear base of the cab.

Later, for 1937, Sterling's completely new and handsomely styled G-series cab-over tilted in orthodox

1936 STERLING (ii) FB70-ML 6×4 tanker, OMM

fashion, i.e., to the front. The engine was a 125hp Cummins diesel, some of them driving tandem rear axles.

These tilt-cabs were among the first of the new era although the tilt feature was little copied until the early 1950's. In both Sterling cab-overs, the doors opened from the front, windshields were V-type, and the familiar radiator grille graced the front of the cab.

Sterling's conventional styling was, on the other hand, very conservative. Front brakes were hydraulic with the rear mechanical, actuated by a vacuum booster. Air brakes were also available.

1939 STERLING (ii) Series J 6-wheel truck NMM

On Jan. 1, 1939 the Fageol Truck and Coach Co. of Oakland, Cal. ceased their production and Sterling bought their sales outlets. Since more Sterlings were delivered to California than anywhere else, this purchase made good sense.

About the same time, Sterling conventionals got new streamlined cabs with large rectangular V-windshields. The chain drives were included in the H-series, while other series had shaft drives. One of the latter was the rare J-series with a very different front-end styling. The theme of the grille was a cross between iron grille-work and a waterfall, while the fenders were full-blown pontoons, making it the most beautiful truck in Sterling history. The J-series 6-wheeler weighed 12,775 pounds with a capacity of 8 to 12 tons and was priced at $8,165.

Typical weights of the other conventional 10- to 13-ton 6-wheeler chassis and cabs were in the 13,000 to 17,000 pound range. Sterlings could be light or heavy in the overall range of 7- to 20-tons capacity with weights of 10,375 to 20,000 pounds priced at $4,840 to $15,200.

Developing the chain-drive idea further, Sterling engineers applied it to a tandem bogie. Power was supplied through three differentials and concentric jackshafts to drive the chains, all amazingly co-ordinated with the springs and radius rods.

During World War II Sterling made many heavy trucks of 7½- and 15-tons in the HCS and DDS series to special army order using the standard cabs and fitted with heavy wrecker and airport fire equipment.

Special projects included 12-ton 8 × 8 T-26 8-man cab-forward tractors and cargo trucks using a swan-neck frame and powererd by American-La France 275hp engines driving through tandem bogies, front and rear, and equipped with 14.00 × 24 dual tires all around. The weight was 50,000 pounds.

A special experimental project (this one after WWII) was the T-26 El, another 12-ton cargo truck, a set-back, conventional with tandem bogies front and rear which were all chain driven. Dual tires all around were 14.00 × 24 20-ply, and steering was of the hydraulic platform type.

1940 STERLING (ii) articulated low-bed truck, RNE

Power was furnished by a Ford GAA 425hp V-8 engine normally used in certain Sherman tanks, which gave a top speed of 41mph to this 55,900 pound behemoth. These were some of the largest trucks built anywhere in the 1940's.

In the civilian field annual sales hit a post-war peak near 600 followed by a decline. In 1951 Sterling was sold to the White Motor Co. of Cleveland, Ohio, and the following year the Wisconsin operations were shut down and removed to Cleveland.

The trucks themselves had the new Sterling White nameplate, and the front axle was set back a little more, but otherwise they were, little changed from late pre-war models in appearance. Also in 1951, White had contracted to be the sales and service organization for the Freightliner truck, and in 1953 bought the Autocar Company of Ardmore, Pennsylvania. The sum total of all these operations seemed rather too much especially as Sterling and Autocar trucks were pretty much in the same class, so the Sterling truck was discontinued at this time.

Sterling's lifetime production is likely around 12,000 trucks, with the biggest years in the late 1920's. *RW*

STERLING (iii) (US) 1973 to date

Sterling Custom Built Trucks Inc., Kansas City, Kansas

The name of Sterling has been revived by this small company who even use the same trade mark as the famous Milwaukee concern. Their products include trucks and prime movers as well as small mobile cranes, trailers and railroad service trucks. *LA*

STERNBERG (US) 1907-1915

(1) Sternberg Motor Truck Co., Milwaukee, Wis. 1907-1913
(2) Sternberg Mfg. Co., Milwaukee, Wis. 1913-1914
(3) Sternberg Motor Truck Co., Milwaukee, Wis. 1914-1915

Most of Sternberg trucks were cab-overs with right-hand steering in 1, 1½, 3½, and 5-ton sizes driven by 29 to 44hp 4-cylinder T-head engines cast in pairs and powering through a multiple disc clutch and 3-speed selective sliding transmission mounted amidships to a double chain drive. However, the 1-ton model had a friction drive. Springs were semi-elliptic all around except, strangely, the 1½-ton model which had platform springs at the rear. Solid tires were mounted on artillery wheels. Radiators were in the front, and bow-shaped on the top.

An unusual salient feature of Sternberg frames was that they were lined with solid oak planks pressed into the main steel channels and then further secured by many bolts throughout the length of the planks. Road shocks were said to be substantially reduced to the chassis and load with this type of construction. The remainder of the frame was also of bolted construction, in contrast to the usual riveting used in that era.

A more conventional truck series was introduced for 1914, and this had a worm drive. A 7½-ton cab-over model was also in the range.

Anti-German reaction stirred up by the war in Europe was felt all over the nation, even in small cities. Accordingly, Mr. William Sternberg, the company's founder, changed the truck's name to Sterling, and production continued under that name. *RW*

1935 STEVENS (i) ¼-ton 3-wheel van, GNG

STEVENS (i) (GB) 1932-1936

(1) Stevens Bros. (Wolverhampton) Ltd., Wolverhampton, Staffs.
(2) Stevens & Bowden Ltd., Wolverhampton, Staffs; Willesden, London NW10

This was a light 3-wheeled van on the lines of the James or Reliant, made by the Stevens family who had made A.J.S. motorcycles, buses and cars. It was powered by a 588cc single-cylinder engine, with chain drive to the rear axle. In October 1932 it was announced that the design would be made by Bowden (Engineers) Ltd. of Willesden as well as at Wolverhampton. Load capacity of the Stevens was 5cwt, and the price was £79 in 1932/33, later increased to £82. The 1935/36 models had shaft drive in place of chain. *GNG*

1975 STEVENS (ii) Model B van, Stevens

STEVENS (ii) (GB) 1972 to date

Anthony Stevens Automobiles Ltd., Warwick

The Stevens Light Delivery Van is built in the style of an Edwardian vehicle, yet has entirely up to date running gear and equipment. The vans are made in five sizes, from 6 to 22cwt capacity, and are powered by 4-cylinder Ford engines of 1.1 to 2.0 litres. Automatic transmissions are optional extras. 12-seater estate buses are also made. A total of 40 Stevens vehicles have been made, and the vans are still available to special order. *GNG*

STEWART (GB) c.1902-1910 (STEWART THORNYCROFT)

Stewart & Co. (1902) Ltd., Glasgow

The firm were builders of fixed and marine steam engines and are said to have experimented with a vertical fire tubed boiler and compound undertype engine in 1902, but evidence both as to details and whether or not it came onto the market are scanty.

The bulk of production, however, was under license from Thornycroft and consisted of locomotive-boilered undertypes using radial valve gear and the Thornycroft helical gear transmission. The licensors ceased to build steam wagons in 1907, but Stewart went on to develop a massive Colonial design of wagon in which the engine and transmission were much as before, though enclosed in a sheet iron casing, but reverting to the Thornycroft water tube boiler in place of the locomotive type. Other features were cast steel wheels all round, traction engine steering by chain and bobbin and the incorporation of a winding drum into the rear axle. These wagons were said to have been still available in 1910 but production had probably ceased before this. *RAW*

STEWART (i) (US) 1912-1916

Stewart Iron Works, Covington, Ky.

This particular Stewart Commercial vehicle was a 1-tonner which remained as Model 1 during the five model years. It had a four-stroke, two-cylinder engine with forward control and double chain drive with wheelbase of 8 feet. The frame side members were of steel but cross members were of hickory. The manufacturer was engaged principally in the making of cast iron fences. *GMN*

1931 STEWART (ii) straight-8 articulated truck, RNE

STEWART (ii) (US) 1912-1941

Stewart Motor Corp., Buffalo, N.Y.

Thomas R. Lippard and R.G. Stewart of the Lippard-Stewart company severed their connection with that firm and organized the Stewart Motor Corporation in July 1912. The first Stewart trucks resembled the still contemporary Lippard-Stewarts in having a Renault-styled hood and dashboard radiator. They featured a 4-cylinder Continental engine and Timken bevel drive. Capacity was 1,500lbs. This model was made up to 1916, and was joined by the totally different Model K 1-tonner powered by a 2-cylinder engine under the seat, with 2-speed transmission and double chain drive. Unlike other Stewarts, the Model K had solid tires.

The 1916 Stewart trucks were completely redesigned, with conventional frontal radiators, and were available in a range of ½, ¾ and ; ½-tonners, joined by a 2-tonner in 1917. This had a Buda OU 4-cylinder engine, but the others, like most of Stewart's production, were Continental-powered. Milwaukee and LeRoi engines were available in the 1918 models which included a 3½-tonner. The largest models had internal gear drive and solid tires until

1935 STEWART (ii)-ton van, NAHC

the early 1920s, by which time Stewart trucks had wide distribution, working in 800 American cities and 39 foreign countries. In 1921 a 'speed model' was added to the range, and in 1925 a 6-cylinder 18-25 passenger bus chassis. Electric lighting and starting became standard at this time, and 6-cylinder engines were standardized from 1926, although a four was optional in the 1 and 1½-ton sizes. A new model in the 1926 range was the Buddy, a ¾-ton speed model aimed at the light delivery market and usually available with an open express body with side curtains. Made until 1930, the Buddy was reintroduced in 1935 as a ½-tonner with 35bhp 4-cylinder Waukesha engine.

Unlike many truck makers, Stewart built their own bodies, although of course custom bodies were also available. Their aluminum panel of 1929 was the first aluminum body to be made by a chassis maker. For 1930 Stewart's range consisted of six models from 1½ to 6/7 tons, now with Lycoming engines in all but the largest, which was Waukesha-powered. In 1931 there were two new models with 6-cylinder 100hp and 8-cylinder 130hp engines, both Lycomings. The latter was installed in a 3½-tonner which had an excellent power /weight ratio, and although expensive at some $4,000 (comparable with Mack and White), it was appreciated by long-distance operators who needed its power to overcome the wind resistance of high van bodies. The Stewart eight was made until 1937, some with a Truxmore third axle which allowed a payload of 8 tons.

In 1935 the smaller Stewarts blossomed out with streamlined cabs and V-windshields and grilles, although the larger models remained more conservative as was generally the case in truck design. Hydraulic brakes were standard by this time, and the largest sizes was now 7/8 tons. Further restyling took place with the 1937 a series which had pontoon fenders resembling those of the Diamond T, and teardrop headlamps. Engines were now all Waukeshas, with Waukesha-Hesselman semi diesels available in the heavier trucks. 1937 was the last year of the 4-cylinder Buddy Stewart. Cab-overs in four sizes from 1½ to 3 tons were listed in 1938 and 1939, but few were made.

Stewart's best year for sales was 1930 with 2,315 units delivered, but during the 1930s the figure dropped, with only 390 in 1938 and 90 in 1939. President T.R. Lippard left that year to go to Federal, and a new company backed by Indianapolis capital took over Stewart. They concentrated on the heavy end of the range, with trucks from 3 to 7 tons in 1940/41, but few of these were made. During the 1930s Stewart had a Canadian assembly plant at Fort Erie, Ontario they enjoyed export sales to Europe and other parts of the world as well. A few early-1930s Stewart trucks were still at work in Seville, Spain in 1965.
RW

1950 STEYR 5-ton truck, OMM

STEYR (A) 1922 to date

(1) Oesterreichische Waffenfabriks-Gesellschaft A.G., Steyr 1922-1926
(2) Steyr-Werke A.G., Steyr 1926-1935
(3) Steyr-Daimler-Puch A.G., Steyr; Graz; Wiener-Neustadt;
Vienna 1935 to date

Steyr took up production of cars after WW I when this arms factory had to look for new employment. The first truck appeared in 1922, it was the type III with a 6-cylinder 12/34 PS engine and 2½ ton payload capacity. It was succeded by the type 40 with 6-cylinder 8/40 PS engine. Several types with 4- and 6-cylinder engines followed, available as vans, trucks or light buses. Some special vehicles, especially 6 × 4 all terrain types were built from about 1935 to 1942. These retained the type designations AD with a suffix and were widely known as Austro-Daimler. But they were produced in the Steyr plant and marketed as Steyr. The Steyr type 640 was derived from them; it was a 6 × 4 all-terrain vehicle also, appearing in 1937 and featuring a 6-cylinder 2,260cc engine. 4 × 4 trucks, types 1500 A and 2000 A were developed for the army and appeared in 1941. A V-8 engine of 3,517cc was used. These military versions were the basis for the post-war type 370 truck with the same engine and 3 ton payload capacity. From 1948 also a diesel engined version was available, at first a 4-cylinder, later a 6-cylinder. Also a bus was developed.

1963 STEYR-PUCH Haflinger 4×4 van, GNG

These types were succeeded by the 4-ton type 380, the 5-tonner type 480 (also available as a 6-tonner as type 480z), the 7-tonner type 586z and 680 and the 8-tonner type 780. These remained in production until 1968. Another development was the 4 × 4 all-terrain vehicle Haflinger (also known as Steyr-Puch) which appeared in 1959 and was produced in the Puch plant at Graz. It had an air-cooled opposed twin engine of 643cc developing 27hp.

In 1968 the old range of trucks was succeeded by the so-called "Plus" range, very modern forward control vehicles. This range covers payload capacities from 5 to 16 tons and engine outputs from 110 to 320hp. They are available as trucks, tippers, dumpers and articulated tractors and with 4 × 2, 4 × 4, 6 × 2, 6 × 4, or 6 × 6 drive. In 1975 a new 8 × 4 version and a 6 × 6 tractor or articulated tractor were added, both using the 320hp engine.

1970 STEYR 880Z refuse truck, GNG

The small Haflinger was succeeded by the Pinzgauer, available with 4 × 4 or 6 × 6 drive and equipped with an air-cooled 4-cylinder 2.5 litre engine developing 87hp. The central tube chassis layout allows a very good ground clearance and maneverability in rough terrain. Also the Pinzgauer bears the marque name Steyr-Puch. A new bus program was presented in 1970. This was based on the former Saurer (Austria) buses after this firm had given up production under their own name and was totally integrated in the Steyr concern. The new types were available as line and touring versions and covered a wide range of seating capacities. Own diesel engines with outputs from 132 to 230hp are used. In touring coach design there is a close co-operation with the Hungarian Ikarus works. Also an articulated bus with underfloor engine is available.

1977 STEYR 1490 6×6 dump truck, Steyr

A unique development is the City Bus. The first version was the type L which was introduced in 1973. It used certain chassis components of the Haflinger and also the opposed twin 643cc engine which drove the front wheels. A propane-butane mixture was used. For the unitary body plastic material was used to a great extent. There was a rear entrance for the passengers, the capacity being 10 seats and 10 standees. This bus was intended mainly for city centers and precincts. The type L was succeeded by the type S in 1975. The original purpose was extended to that of a feeder bus. For the type S a Mercedes-Benz 2-litre diesel engine of 55hp is used and again the front wheels are driven. The unique body styling of the type L is also to be found on this new version, but the entrance is now at the right side. Passenger capacity was increased to 14 seats and 14 standees.

Steyr trucks and tractors have been made in Greece since 1974. *HON*

STIGLER (I) 1921-1925

Officine Meccaniche Stigler SA, Turin

The Stigler was a light battery electric car of conventional appearance, with dummy hood and radiator. It was also offered as a delivery van and even a hearse. *MCS*

STILL (i) see C.M.S.

1952 STILL (ii) 2-ton electric truck, BHV

STILL(ii) (D) 1950-1955

Hans Still A.G., Hamburg 48

Two versions of electric vans were produced by this firm. They had 1½ ton payload capacity. *HON*

1930 STILLE 8-wheel bus with gas producer, HON

STILLE (D) 1930

Maschinen-und Fahrzeugfabrik Stille, Munster

The only type of this firm was a 4-wheeled bus with two front axles, which were steered. It was a chassis — less steel construction following a design of Dr. Deiters. A 6-cylinder 7-litre Maybach engine was used. Production was only on a small scale. *HON*

STIRLING; SCOTT-STIRLING (GB) 1897-1908

(1) Stirling Motor Carriages Ltd., Hamilton, N.B. 1897-1905

(2) Scott, Stirling & Co. Ltd., Edinburgh; Twickenham, Middx. 1905-1907

(3) Scott-Stirling Motor Co. Ltd., Twickenham,

1903 STIRLING 14-seater bus, NMM

Middx. 1907-1908

Stirlings were one of the first motor vehicle makers in Britain, and were also the first to start a passenger service operated by motorcars. This was at their home town of Hamilton, and was carried out by wagonettes on their Daimler-engined car chassis. Larger, purpose-built buses with 12hp 2-cylinder engines under the driver's seat were made in 1902; these had 16-passenger wagonette bodies, 3-speed gearboxes and internal gear final drive. One of these ran for 12,500 miles in Edinburgh, and in 1903 a fleet of similar vehicles with 12 seater closed bodies was put into service in London by the London Motor Omnibus Syndicate Ltd., operating the Oxford Circus-Cricklewood route. Buses were also supplied to the North Eastern Railway, and export orders came from South Africa, Australia and New Zealand. In the Argentine town of Bahia Blanca seven Stirling buses were fitted with flanged wheels and operated on tramways. 2-ton trucks were also made, for the War Office and civilian users.

In 1905, after the move to Twickenham and change of name to Scott-Stirling, a 24hp 4-cylinder chassis was introduced, which could be fitted with 36 seater double-deck bodies. A fleet of 100 of these was ordered by the London Power Omnibus Co. Ltd., successors to the London Motor Omnibus Syndicate, and operated over the same route. However, competition proved too great, and the company collapsed in 1907; this loss of their best customer was probably the main reason for Scott-Stirling's closing their doors in the summer of 1908. In 1906 it was announced that Argyll would make large numbers of buses and trucks of SS design in their new factory at Alexandria but nothing came of this. *GNG*

1911 STODDARD 30 2½-ton truck, CP

STODDARD-DAYTON (US) 1911-1912

Dayton Motor Car Co., Dayton, Ohio

This well-known quality car manufacturer entered the truck field at the end of its life with 1- and 2½-ton forward-control trucks with chain drive and solid tires. These were only offered during the 1911 season, but a light delivery van and truck on the 28hp car chassis were continued into 1912. *GNG*

1908 STOEWER 3-ton truck, HON

STOEWER (D) 1900-1927

(1) Gebruder Stoewer, Fabrik fur Motorfahrzeuge, Stettin 1900-1916

(2) Stoewer-Werke A.G. vorm. Gebr. Stoewer, Stettin 1916-1927

Stoewer started production of commercials in 1900, the first being a 3-ton truck and a bus for about 15 passengers using the same chassis and a 2-cylinder engine of 10/20hp.

Subsequently electric driven commercials were built for a few years, trucks and buses as well as fire service vehicles. In 1905 a 4-cylinder 4.6 litre engine of 24hp was introduced, supplemented one year later by a 5.9 litre engine of 30hp. Buses became a speciality; in 1906 the London and District Motor Bus Company ordered 200 double-deckers.

A new range was introduced in 1912, 4-cylinder 4.9 litre 38hp and 7.3 litre 42hp engines were used. Trucks were built according to the subsidy construction principles, so these types were built in large quantities for the army. After WW I trucks and buses were built only on a small scale until a new 1½ trucks appeared in 1924 using a 2.6 litre 28hp engine. This was supplemented a year later by a 3-ton type with 5.7 litre 40hp engine. But production was only on a small scale, ceasing in about 1927.

Vans were based on the private car types D9 (2.1 litre 32bhp), D 12 (6 cyl., 3.4 litre 45hp) and F 6 (1.6 litre 30hp). A new 2 ton truck, built under Morris-Commercial license, was presented at the Berlin Motor Show in 1931, but production was not taken up. *HON*

1979 STONEFIELD P3000 6×4 TV van, Stonefield

STONEFIELD (GB) 1974 to date

Stonefield Vehicles Ltd., Paisley, Scotland

With prototypes running since 1974 and production models from 1977, the Stonefield is a light off-road vehicle available with 4 × 4, 6 × 4 or 6 × 6 drive. It has Ferguson positive traction, automatic transmission and a choice of engines including Ford's 3-litre V-6. Original cab design and prototype work was by Jensen Motors Ltd., and the vehicle is jig-built from a box-section girder frame to ease overseas assembly. *OM*

STONELEIGH (GB) 1913-1914; 1922-1924

Stoneleigh Motors Ltd., Coventry

Though the original Stoneleigh car, an offshoot of the Siddeley-Deasy, was a thinly disguised 13.9hp BSA, the 30-cwt truck used the same 3,308cc 4-cylinder Knight sleeve-valve engine as was fitted to some Siddeley-Deasy models. The frontal radiator was more substantial than the car's, and the worm final drive was common to both types, but the truck's 3-speed gearbox was centrally controlled. 14-seater bus and ambulance versions were available, the latter being sold under the Siddeley-Deasy name. In 1922 Armstrong Siddeley revived the Stoneleigh name for a cyclecar with 1-litre air-cooled V-twin engine, differentials back axle, and central driving position. Th' was also offered with 4-cwt van bodywork. *MCS*

STORMS (US) 1915

Storms Electric Car Co., Detroit, Mich.

The Storms was the only US-built battery electric cyclecar, and offered a ¼-tonner delivery van on its passenger car chassis. *GMN*

STOUGHTON (US) 1920-1928

Stoughton Wagon Co., Stoughton, Wis.

This make began as a series of 1-, 1½- and 2-tonners. These were assembled from stock parts which included Waukesha engines for the two smaller and Hercules engine for the largest. All used Brown-Lipe 3-speed gearboxes and worm-drive. A 3-tonner with wheelbase of 13 feet, 2 inches was a 1922 addition. Later years saw various changes in capacities from 1¼-tonners to a last effort in 1928 with a 3½ to 4-tonner. During the last five years, a variety of Waukesha, Midwest and Continental engines was used. In 1926 and 1927, three sizes of fire apparatus were offered with 250, 350 and 500 gallon rated capacities. *GMN*

STRAKER (GB) 1899-c.1912

(1) Bayley-Straker Ltd., Newington (London) and Bristol 1899-1901

(2) Brazil, Holborow & Straker Ltd., Bristol 1899-1901 (both involved in making early vehicles)

(3) Straker Steam Vehicle Co. Ltd., Bristol 1901-1906

(4) Sidney Straker & Squire Ltd., Bristol 1906-1912

Sidney Straker, a London consulting engineer with manufacturing interests in Bristol, joined with his friend Edward Bayley, a London vehicle builder to produce a wagon for the 1899 Liverpool Trials, giving it a de Dion boiler, vertical compound in line engine, shaft drive and Ackermann steering. Production models, however, though retaining the de Dion boiler, had a transverse horizontal engine under the chassis, with 2-speed gearing and single chain drive to a rear axle differential. The wagons were offered in a bewildering range of sizes ranging from 2 to 12 tons, many steps in the range doubtless existing only in Sidney Straker's fertile imagination. The wagons, however, were practical workers, though, like all wagons using de Dion boilers, very heavy on water tube replacements and over 200 were stated to have been built by 1906, when, probably in deference to the changed Construction and Use regulations, coupled with the success of the Foden, Straker went over to a compound overtype, first made in 1905, dropping the Ackermann steering in favor of chain and bobbin type — a retrograde step.

Straker was quick to realize the growing importance of the gasoline engined vehicle and after tentative experiments in Bristol set up factories in London and Twickenham specifically for making i/c chassis, with an eye particularly on the psv market. These, however, were sold under the Straker-Squire name (see below), which was applied to some of the later overtypes, the last of which, launched in 1908, had a side-fired boiler and a more compact wheelbase. Production seems effectively to have ceased about 1912.

During the period 1901/03 Straker made a number of steam buses on his standard 3-ton steam wagon chassis with no commercial success and his name was linked with Lawson's London bus fiasco in 1899-1900. *RAW*

STRAKER-MCCONNELL see Arbenz

1909 STRAKER-SQUIRE ¾-ton truck, BR

STRAKER-SQUIRE (GB) 1905-1926

(1) Sidner Straker & Squire Ltd., Bristol 1906-1913
(2) Straker-Squire (1913) Ltd., Bristol; Twickenham, Middx. 1913-1917
(3) Straker-Squire Ltd., Twickenham, Middx; Edmonton, London N. 1918-1926

The first gasoline-engined vehicles sold under the Straker-Squire name were German-built Bussing chassis with 28/30hp 4-cylinder engines, intended for 3-ton loads or double-decker bus bodywork. They later became very popular in London, being operated by the London Road Car Co. and the London General Omnibus Co.; when the two amalgamated in 1908 there were more Straker-Squires running in the city than any other make. By 1907 the range had been diversified to include a worm-driven 1-ton chassis and a short-lived gasoline-electric chassis as well as the Bussing-type. A 25 cwt 2-cylinder van was made in 1908, but from 1909 onwards the company standardized on 4-cylinder vehicles of their own design, having no further connection with Bussing. In 1910 there was a 5-ton colonial truck with steel rear wheels and chain drive which was made in small numbers for at least three years, and gasoline-engined tramcars were also made at this time. In 1913 came a new 3/4-ton worm-drive chassis for goods or passenger work, completing a range which

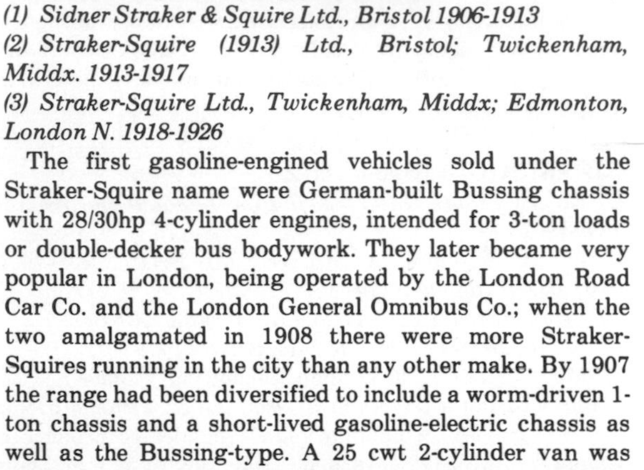

1923 STRAKER-SQUIRE 34-seater bus, LTE

included 25 and 35 cwt worm drive and a 5-ton chain drive chassis. Several hundred 3-tonners were used by the War Department and the Admiralty during World War I.

In 1919 Straker-Squire took over a shell factory at Edmonton and began production of a new design, the 5-tonner A-type powered by a 55bhp 4-cylinder monobloc engine, with 4-speed gearbox and worm drive. Of semi-forward control layout, it was made with 14 ft. 6 in. wheelbase for trucks and buses, and 12 ft. 6 in. for tipper work. The bus became popular with the independent or 'pirate' operators in London who appreciated its speed (useful when racing rival buses to a bustop) and were prepared to overlook its unreliability. In 1922 the A-type was joined by the smaller BW-type, a 22.4hp normal-control chassis for 2½ tons or 18 passengers, and these two models were made up to the end of production in 1926. In 1921 Straker-Squire entered the trolley-bus field with a single-decker based on the A-type chassis with electric motors and other equipment by Clough, Smith & Co. Ltd. Known as Straker-Cloughs they were probably the British trolleybuses to have foot-operated controllers as opposed to tram-type hand controls. They had shaft drive from a single front-mounted motor. Among cities which used Straker-Cloughs were Keighley, Rotherham, Wigan and Teesside, while they were exported to Penang and Bloemfontein. Production of all Straker-Squires, including passenger cars, came to an end in 1926, and the Edmonton factory was sold to Rego Clothiers Ltd. The Twickenham factory had been disposed of at the time of the move to Edmonton, and the Bristol works were vacated in 1918. *GNG*

1938 STRAUSSLER Hefty 4×4 tractor, BHV

STRAUSSLER (GB) 1935-1940

Straussler Mechanization Ltd., Brentford, Middx.

Nicholas Straussler was a Hungarian-born consulting engineer who designed a number of advanced and individualistic vehicles both for civilian and military use. In 1935 several of the former were announced, including a 4-wheeled mechanical horse powered by an under-seat mounted Ford Ten engine, with differential-less narrow track rear axle, known as the Nippy. A larger vehicle was the Zulu, a 7-ton chassis with rear-mounted Ford V-8 engine, 4-wheel drive and tubular backbone frame. These were both built in Straussler's small factory at Brentford, but the most radical civilian design was made for Straussler by the Manfred Weiss company in Hungary. This was a rigid 8-wheeler powered by a 150hp 7.2-litre twin-ohc V-8 engine which drove the front pair of axles. The engine was virtually a combination of two of the 4-cylinder units used in Straussler-designed armored cars. All eight wheels were independently sprung. The lone example of this 8-wheeler was fitted with a 3,700 gallon tanker body and used by the Anglo-Iranian Oil Company to transport gasoline from the oilfield to Teheran.

Among Straussler's military vehicles were two tractors, the Singer Ten-powered Sturdy and the Ford V-8-powered Hefty. Both had 4-wheel drive and tubular backbone frames which were split so that the rear axle could pivot independently of the front. Series production of the Hefty took place in the Alvis factory, and these vehicles were sometimes called Alvis-Strausslers. Yet another Straussler design was the 3-ton truck with two Ford V-8 engines mounted side-by-side, known as the G3. Fifty of these were made by Garner in 1939. *GNG*

STRICK (US) 1978 to date

Strick Corporation, Fairless Hills, Pa.

The Strick Cab Under is a most unusual design consisting of a chassis and cab which can be slotted under a large trailer to give the maximum amount of payload space within a given length. The chassis is a twin-steer 6-wheeler powered by a Cummins 903 V-8 turbocharged engine which is located behind the 4 foot high cab. Transmission is a 13-speed Roadranger. The general appearance of the Cab Under is similar to that of the 1965 Bussing Decklaster which was also a twin-steer chassis. *GNG*

STUDEBAKER (US) 1902-1964

(1) Studebaker Automobile Co., South Bend, Ind. 1902-1912

(2) Studebaker Corporation, South Bend, Ind. 1913-1964

The Studebaker brothers had been making horse-drawn wagons since 1852, and continued this activity until 1919. In 1902, they branched out into electric cars, producing over 1,800 units in ten years. These featured twin Westinghouse motors and chain drive, a brake body being featuring in the original catalog. By 1906 the commercial models covered payloads from ½ to 5 tons; the smallest vans had tiller steering and a single chain, though bigger Studebakers were wheel-steered. The first gasoline commercial vehicles sold by Studebakers were light vans based on the Flanders car, but from 1913 onwards similar bodies were mounted on their own 4-cylinder chassis with 3-speed transaxle. In the same year Studebaker also exhibited, but did not market, a 3-ton truck designed by Albert Mais, of Fremont-Mais; it had a 4-cylinder T-head engine, a 4-speed all-indirect gearbox, and spur gear drive.

1909 STUDEBAKER 2½-ton electric van, NAHC

1913 STUDEBAKER Four ½-ton van, Goodyear

1917 saw a pneumatic-tired 1-tonner, once again car-based, but the demise of the 4-cylinder line at the end of 1919 led to a virtual abandonment of trucks until 1925. In that year the company marketed a line of ambulances and hearses with bodies by Superior, using a lengthened edition of their 5.9-litre Big 6 private car. The Studebaker-Superior connection would continue up to 1937, when Studebaker switched to Bender of Cleveland for their professional carriages. The last such models appeared in 1940.

In 1926 there were some further Big Six derivatives, 14/18 seated-passenger coaches with twin rear wheels and (initially) hydraulic fwb, dropped a year in favor of mechanical actuation. By 1929 the aged six had given way to the 5½-litre, 118 hp President straight-8 for PSV work, brakes were servo-assisted, and a complete coach could be purchased for a little over $6,000.

At the top of the range was a 'parlor' type on an 18ft. 4in. wheelbase. Truck-based PSV chassis would be listed until 1942.

Already in 1927 there was once again a car-based panel delivery with 4-litre 6-cylinder sv engine, followed soon afterwards by a lighter type using Studebaker's compact Erskine chassis. In 1932-33 there would also be a van edition of the firm's second compact, the Rockne 6. Serious truck manufacture began in 1928 with a 4-litre 1-tonner, and a 3-ton type with the Big Six unit. These two were said to have boosted commercial vehicle sales by 93 per cent between 1928 and 1929, but on the home market, at any rate, Studebaker trucks never bulked large. Only 2,100 units found buyers in 1935, when Ford sold over

1929 STUDEBAKER straight-8 coach, MBS

180,000. In 1929, the 3.6-litre, 68hp engine was standardized in all models of up to 2 tons; that year's Studebaker-Pierce-Arrow merger (with which White would briefly be associated in 1932) led to a Studebaker-Pierce-Arrow label on some trucks. (In England however, such machines were plain Studebaker). Early 1930s models used the company's own 6-cylinder engines (the regular unit gave 75hp from 3.8 litres), with 4-speed gearboxes on the bigger ones; servo brakes and 2-speed back axles featured on the 3-tonner by 1932. Car and truck styling did not always coincide; the 1931s shared the same front-end sheet metal but thereafter the two lines diverged, the 1935 trucks closely resembling the cars of the previous year. No similarities were to be observed between 1936 and 1940. The 1936 range included normal and forward control types for payloads of up to 3 tons. The biggest ones had 385ci (6.3-litre) F-head Waukesha engines and five forward speeds. A ½-ton pickup based on the Dictator 6 car chassis made its appearance in 1937, and a year later there was a switch to Hercules engines on the heavy-duty models, the largest of these having the same capacity as the superseded Waukesha, with an

1932 STUDEBAKER 1½-ton truck, OMM

output of 106hp. Also new for 1938 was a 2/3-tonner with 68hp Hercules diesel engine, this range-structure persisting until 1940; by now, of course, hydraulic brakes were standard. 1941 saw a rationalized range of M-types, all with Studebaker's own engines; the modest 2.8.-litre Champion 6 went into the ½-ton and 1½-ton types, and the 3.7-litre, 94bhp Commander into the heavier versions. Styling once again paralleled that of the cars, with hydrovac brakes and 2-speed rear axles available on the big ones. Interestingly, the company reverted to Hercules power for the normal-control 6 × 4 and 6 × 6 2½-tonners they built, mainly for Lend-Lease, during World War II. 197,000 such vehicles were produced, as well as many land-going and amphibious light Weasel fulltracks which were Champion-powered.

Until 1948, only the M-types were offered, but a redesigned 2R line made its appearance in 1949, still with the old sv 6-cylinder engines. Light-duty types were available from 1950 with overdrive or automatic. Four years later, even the ½-tonners ran to four forward speeds, while a modern 3.8-litre ohv short-stroke V8 was

1957 STUDEBAKER Transtar 2-ton truck, NAHC

available in the 1½- and 2-tonners. V8s gained in both capacity and power; to 4.3 litres in 1955, and to a formidable 182hp by 1958. Hydrovac brakes were now standard on the heaviest trucks, options including 5-speed gearboxes. At the lower end of the range there was a ½-ton 4 × 4 and a pair of cheap lightweights, the car-based Panel with ifs, and the Scotsman pickup using the latest 3-litre development of the faithful Champion unit. It sold for a low $1,595. 1959 Scotsmen could be had with V8 and automatic options; the type was replaced in 1961 by the ½-ton Champ. This combined the styling of the compact Lark sedan with a beam front axle, and Studebaker's long-overdue small ohv 6. 1962 saw the return of diesel power on a tractive unit for 18-ton GCWs, though this time the company opted for GM's Detroit unit, a 3½-litre 4-cylinder 2-stroke rated at 130hp. A 5-speed gearbox was standard, and full air brakes optional.

The 1963s, last of the regular truck line, covered nominal payloads from ½ to 3 tons, all but the lightest using V8 gas engines as standard. Detroit Diesels were, however, available even in 1-tonners. By 1964 the rundown of Studebakers automotive activities was beginning, with the transfer of car production to Canada. The commercial vehicles faded away, though there was a final fling with the Zipvan built for the Post Office. Features were forward control, rhd, an automatic gearbox, and a quick-detachable power pack. Appositely, the engine was the Champion's ohv descendant. *MCS*

STURGIS (US) 1900-c.1901

S.D. Sturgis & Bros., Los Angeles, Calif.

The Sturgis was probably the heaviest truck of its day, with a load capacity of 5 tons on the truck and a further 5 tons on the full trailer with which it was intended to operate. It was powered by a 40hp 4-cylinder horzontally-opposed engine driving through friction clutches and a train of gears to the rear axle. The engine was located amidships, below the load-carrying platform, while the driver sat over the front axle and steered from the right-hand side with a huge horizontal steering wheel. The speed range of the Sturgis was 1½ to 6mph. The truck was ordered by W.H. Manchester who used it for several years on a freight route between Los Angeles and Pomona, California. It was said to have cost $4,000, and the makers stated that they would build other trucks in different sizes, but it is not known if they did so. *RW*

STURMEY see Lotis and Napier-Parsons

1924 STUTZ Pumper/ladder truck, RNE

STUTZ: NEW STUTZ (US) 1919-1940

(1) Stutz Fire Engine Co., Indianapolis, Ind. 1919-1928
(2) New Stutz Fire Engine Co., Hartford City, Ind. 1931-1940

Built by a separate company from Stutz passenger cars, the Stutz fire engine was made in pumper, ladder truck and combination form, with 4- and 6-cylinder Wisconsin engines. Their peak period was the mid-1920s when deliveries were made to fire departments all over the country, and also to Tokyo, Japan. In 1926 they turned to their own 175hp 6-cylinder ohc engine. A new company was formed in 1931 which was no longer under Harry Stutz' control. In 1939 they built the first American fire engine to be powered by a diesel engine (Cummins), which was delivered to Columbus, Ind. Despite this pioneering development, New Stutz was too small to compete successfully, and they delivered their last appliance, a triple combination pumper, in 1940. *GNG*

STYLKAR (GR) 1965-1970

(1) St. Karakatsanis, Thessaloniki 1965-1967
(2) St. Karakatsanis, Rouf, Athens 1967-1970

The very first producer of 3-wheeled light trucks in Greece that set the basis for a handful of other builders of similar vehicles. Fiber glass cabs, new or reconditioned engines of VW or BMW origin, and FK (Taunus) rear axles were soon the basic specifications for hundreds of vehicles built up to today. *GA*

SUBURBAN (US) 1912-1913

Suburban Truck Co., Philadelphia, Pa.

A 1½-ton worm-drive truck with 29 hp 4-cylinder engine was the only model offered in 1912. The chassis price was $2,500. A 2-ton truck priced at $3,000 was listed in 1913. The smaller model had a disc clutch while the larger had a cone clutch; they were otherwise similar. *DJS*

1963 SUBARU Sambar 800 lb. pickup FLP

SUBARU (J) 1963 to date

Fuji Heavy Industris Ltd., Isesaki

Formed, like Prince Motors, from the disbanded Nakajima aircraft empire, Fuji introduced their Subaru minicar in 1958, following it up five years later with a 7-cwt forward control van on similar lines. Features were a rear-mounted 2-cylinder 2-stroke aircooled engine, a 3-speed synchromesh gearbox, and all-independent springing by torsion bars. By 1975 the original Sambar had given way to the ½-ton Minijumbo on similar lines, now with water cooling (assisted by an electric fan) and

1978 SUBARU 1600 pick-up, Subaru

four forward speeds, though the 4-stroke 490 cc ohc engine already used in the cars was not standardized until 1977. Fuji, associated since 1966 with Isuzu, also make agricultural tractors and specialized truck and bus bodies. A light conventional 4 × 4 pickup, the Brat, was introduced in 1978. *MCS*

SULLIVAN (US) 1910-1923

(1) Sullivan Motor Car Co., Rochester, N.Y.
(2) Sullivan Motor Truck Co., Rochester, N.Y.

This company began by making a light delivery wagon powered by a 16 hp horizontally-opposed twin engine, with 2-speed planetary transmission and double chain drive. Payload was 800 lbs and the wagon had solid tires. By 1912 they had 2-1 cylinder engines and two models of 1,000 and 1,500 lbs, and two years later the largest model was of 2,000 lbs payload. In 1916 there were larger models still, from 1 to 2 tons, with 4-cylinder Buda engines, Brown-Lipe 3-speed transmissions and Timken worm drive. These were continued with little change until 1923. *GNG*

SULTANA see Ramirez

SUMIDA see Ishikawajima

SUMMERSCALES (GB) 1917
Summerscales Ltd., Keighley, Yorks.

J.T. Ridealgh resigned as a designer at Manns in 1917 and designed the Summerscales spring mounted, three wheeled vertical boilered steam tractor built in 1918. The engine was a 4-cylinder high pressure poppet valved uniflow type with roller chain final drive. Intended for road or agricultural use it was described by its only known commercial user (S. Rollinson, East Ardsley, Barnsley) as "useless". The design formed the basis of the Ridealgh steam wagon. The tractor was also referred to as the "R & T". Total production was, reputedly, two. *RAW*

SUN (D) 1906-1908
Kraftwagen-Gesellschaft Roland mbH., Berlin

Various types of trucks and buses were produced by this firm. 4- and 6-cylinder engines by Argus were used, ranging up to 70 hp. *HON*

1938 SUNBEAM ¾-ton electric van, NMM

SUNBEAM (GB) 1929-1963
(1) The Sunbeam Motor Car Co. Ltd., Wolverhampton 1929-1933
(2) Sunbeam Commercial Vehicles Ltd., Wolverhampton 1934-1948
(3) Sunbeam Trolleybus Co. Wolverhampton 1948-1963

Like the products of many other car manufacturers a number of early Sunbeam chassis were fitted with commercial bodywork, including a considerable number of 12/16's for ambulance service in the Great War. Many of these were built under license by the Rover Co. Ltd., whilst Sunbeam concentrated on aero engines.

The slump in car sales in the late twenties encouraged Sunbeam to develop high grade bus and coach chassis which appeared in 1929 as the Pathan 4-wheeler and Sikh 6-wheeler. They had 6-cylinder, dry-sump-lubricated, 7 bearing engines producing 142 hp from almost 8 litres (initially a slightly smaller engine was fitted to the Pathan). The 6-wheeler only attracted 2 customers, but a few dozen four-wheelers were sold before Sunbeam decided that the field was too competitive. However an unsold 6-wheeler was made the basis of a trolleybus in 1931 and thereafter these became a Sunbeam speciality, surviving takeovers by Rootes in 1935, (during which time a solitary Gardner-engined double decker was produced), by Brockhouse in 1946, and by Guy in 1949. The Company remained in being through the acquisition of Guy by Jaguar followed by British Motor Holdings followed by British Leyland and still exists, at any rate theoretically, today, at the Guy factory, though no orders have been completed for some fifteen years. Approximately 2,000 Sunbeam trolleybuses were produced, some bearing the name Karrier in the late thirties and forties after Rootes merged their trolleybus department with Sunbeam.

In October 1937 Sunbeam entered the battery-electric field with a 12/15 cwt chassis with equipment by British Thomson-Houston, which was made until 1940. *OM*

SUNGRI-58 (Victory) (NORTH KOREA) to date
Sungri Automobile Combine, on the Taedong-Gang River

The Sungri-58 truck, based on the 2.5-ton Russian GAZ-51, contains a 4-stroke, 6-cylinder engine of 70 hp at 2,800 rpm, providing 70 km/h. *BE*

SUNNYSIDE (CDN) c.1940-1945
Sunnyside Auto Body Works, Calgary, Alta.

The Sunnyside was a highway coach produced briefly by a firm which had previously built bus bodies and today builds truck bodies. *HD*

SUPER-TRACTION see Wisconsin

SUPER TRUCK (US) 1919-1936
(1) O'Connell Motor Truck Co., Waukegan, Ill.
(2) O'Connell Motor Truck Co., Chicago, Ill.

The most familiar Super Truck was a construction service vehicle similar to the Hug, but with an important difference. It featured a driver's seat which pivoted around the steering column, allowing for vehicle travel in two directions. The chassis of the Super Two-Way Drive, which came in sizes from 2½ to 7½ tons was otherwise conventional, with Wisconsin engines, O'Connell's own transmission and a cast-iron Packard-type radiator. The driver's seat was located behind and to the side of the short hood which was in fact the only sheetmetal on the vehicle.

Other and more conventional Super Trucks were also made, featuring Wisconsin engines (mainly 4s, but 6s from 1928 as well), Fuller transmissions, Timken and Sheldon axles. These were made in sizes from 2½ to 7 tons. Production was small and mainly for local distribution. *RJ*

1939 SUPERIOR (iii) Model 411-25 Avenue Coach, MBS

SUPERIOR (i) (US) 1911-1912

Superior Motor Car Co., Detroit, Mich.

The enclosed delivery van built under this name was rated at 1,200-pound capacity. It was powered by a 4-cylinder, water-cooled engine of 25 hp. Drive was through a planetary transmission and shaft drive. Wheelbase was 10 feet, 4 inches and it cost $1,500. *GMN*

SUPERIOR (ii) (US) 1912-1914

F. G. Clark Co., Lansing, Mich.

The Superior Model A was a 1-tonner with an express body powered by a 4-cylinder engine. The chassis weighed 2,500 pounds and had a wheelbase of 9 feet, 2 inches. The drive train included a three-speed gearbox and double chain drive. With solid rubber tires, the price was $1,700. *GMN*

SUPERIOR (iii) (US) 1938-1948

Superior Coach Corp., Lima, Ohio

The Superior Motor Coach Body Co. was organized to build bodies for Garford bus chassis in 1923 and after 1930 (as Superior Coach Corp.) built principally school bus bodies, introducing what was said to be the first all-steel school bus with safety glass throughout in 1931. Its first complete bus was an integral type known as the Avenue, with a Ford V-8 rear-mounted engine, put on the market in 1938 and joined in the next year by an over-the-road version called the Rocket. There was a wartime hiatus, and a redesigned transit bus was again offered briefly after 1946. Probably fewer than 100 Avenue buses were actually sold for transit service, the largest fleet comprising 14 vehicles used to motorize the streetcar lines in Lima (Superior's home town) in 1939. *MBS*

SUSSITA (IL) 1973 to date

Autocars Ltd., Tirat Carmel

This is the latest metamorphosis of the Israeli national automotive industry, after Regent, Sabra and Carmel names were used. Following tradition, fiber glass bodied vans, pick-ups, station wagons and the 4x4 Dragoon utility vehicle are built, all fitted with the Triumph 1.3 litre 55 hp and 1.5 litre 59.5 hp engine and running gear of same origin. *GA*

1974 SUTPHEN aerial tower fire engine, EK

SUTPHEN (US) 1967 to date

Sutphen Fire Equipment Co., Amlin, Ohio

Sutphen were well-known builders of fire equipment on other chassis before they began making their own chassis in 1967. Their aerial tower with telescopic lattice-type aluminum boom appeared in 1963, and hundreds have been made since then. Their custom chassis was a 3-axle job with Cincinnati cab and a choice of diesel engines, mainly Detroits, from 265 to 525 hp, and carried the Sutphen Aerial Tower. These have also been built on commercial chassis, as have pumpers. In 1972 Sutphen built an experimental turbine-powered 2,000 gpm pumper using a Ford 3600 gas turbine. Production of custom chassis and equipment on commercial chassis continues today. *GNG*

1978 SUZUKI ST20K ½-ton pick-up, Suzuki

SUZUKI (J) 1959 to date

(1) Suzuki Motor Co. Ltd., Kamimura 1959-1967
(2) Suzuki Motor Co. Ltd., Iwata 1967 to date

Best known for the 2-stroke motorcycles they have built since 1952, Suzuki branched out in 1959 with a dual-purpose light vehicle. All four wheels were independently sprung, and the 359cc air-cooled twin 2-stroke engine drove the front wheels. The need for more payload space soon dictated a switch to underfloor engines and rear wheel drive on the 360 commercial range, and a similar layout was found on 1978's ST20 trucks and vans, though from 1974 power units were watercooled, and 1977 saw the original twin replaced by a vertical-three of 539cc developing 33 hp. Since 1971 Suzuki has also offered the Jimny, a diminutive 4 × 4 with jeep-type or pickup bodies. This shares its power unit with the vans. *MCS*

SWIFT (GB) 1904-1916; 1924

(1) Swift Motor Co. Ltd., Coventry, Warwickshire 1904-1916
(2) Swift of Coventry Ltd., Coventry, Warwickshire 1924

Swift of Coventry progressed from sewing machines and bicycles to motor tricycles in 1899, and to cars in 1900. Light vans were, however, produced on a spasmodic basis. At least one 10 hp chassis with 1.7-litre moiv 2-cylinder Aster engine is known to have been so bodied in 1904, and vans were also made on the 1906 8/10 hp with White & Poppe motor. A biggish shaft-driven truck of their own make was in use at the factory in 1908, but it was not until 1909 that a van was actively promoted. This was a 15-cwt type on the 10/12 hp 2-cylinder chassis with cone clutch, 3-speed gearbox, and pneumatic tires. 4-cylinder engines had been adopted by 1912, and in 1914 the company announced a 3-cwt edition of the 972cc 2-cylinder cyclecar. A similar body for 5-cwt payloads was also offered on the model's successor, a straightforward 1.2-litre 10hp four which was new in 1915. The last Swift van was another 10 hp model, the 1924 version with coil ignition. *MCS*

SWP (CH) 1958-1965

Schindler Waggon AG., Pratteln (BL)

In the late fifties Schindler, a company specialized in building railroad coaches, took up the manufacturing of an advanced forward-control bus with unitary construction. A watercooled V8-ohv-diesel engine of 8,7 litres on the indirect injection principle was purchased from Kamper. It had a centrally located camshaft, a compression ratio of 18:1 and a Bosch injection pump.

Maximum power was 145 hp at 2,500 rpm. This engine was placed upright in the rear of the chassis. Power was transmitted via a pneumatically-hydraulically operated single plate dry clutch and the mechanical ZF 5-speed gearbox, with additional second ratio gearbox with pneumatical control, to the twin-wheel rear-axle. Independent wheel suspension with wishbones and optional air-cushion springing offered excellent riding comfort to the 30 passengers. Wheelbase was 13 ft. 2 in. and the hydraulic brakes with air-pressure servo (Westinghouse/Perrot) were supplemented with an exhaust-motor-brake. The ZF-Gemmer steering had hydraulic servo-assistance. This model was offered till 1965, later buses being equipped with a Henschel diesel engine.

In addition SWP offered an omnibus with unitary construction where the mechanical, engine and drive-train parts were supplied by FBW. This offered 26 seats and additional space for 60 standing pasengers. Both models were made in small quantities only and were sold exclusively in Switzerland. *FH*

1914 SYMES 1-ton truck, GB

SYMES (CDN) 1912-1914

Symes Motor Truck Co., Chatham, Ont.

This company built handsome ½-ton and 1-ton trucks for farmers and merchants, while 3- to 5-ton models could be built to order. *HD*

SYNNESTVEDT (US) 1904-1907

Synnestvedt Machine Co., Pittsburg, Pa.

The Synnestvedt was a battery-powered electric, built also as a passenger car. The commercial vehicles began as relatively small delivery vans with wheel steering and double chain drive on a wheelbase of 8 feet, 3 inches. Passenger buses were also built on this chassis. During the last year of manufacture, the Type F 3-tonner and Type D 5-tonner were made. Type D had a chassis weight of 5 tons, a wheelbase of 10 feet, 4 inches and track of 5 feet, 8½ inches. In chassis form it cost $4,500. The Type F had a wheelbase of 7 feet, 3 inches with track of 4 feet, 8½ inches. Both used double chain drive. *GMN*

SYNRI 1010 (NORTH KOREA) to date

The Synri 1010 is reported to be a 6-ton, 6 wheel truck. Further details are not known. *BE*

SYRENA (PL) 1975 to date

Fabryka Samochodow Malolitrazowych, Bielsko-Biala

Based on the Syrena passenger car, the R20 pickup is a light 300 kilo payload commercial vehicle powered by a 3-cylinder, two stroke, 842cc gasoline engine developing 40 hp with front-end and front-wheel-drive same as found on the Syrena car. Another commercial model, powered by the same engine was shown in 1973 and 1974 Poznan Fair in the form of a van called Bosto, but it has not reached production stage so far. *GA*

T.A.F. (R) 1972 to date

Gircuil, Bucharest

TAF model 65D is a forestry tractor powered by a 65hp diesel engine with articulated steering and all-wheel-drive. It is built by a factory responsible for the production of non-automotive engineering products. *GA*

1923 TALBOT (i) 25/50hp ambulance, NMM

1935 TALBOT (i) 75 ambulance, NMM

TALBOT (i) GB 1914-1938

Clement Talbot Ltd., London, W.10.

Talbot built 15-cwt truck versions of their 4½-litre 4-cylinder 25/50 private car to military account during World War I, these being marketed after the Armistice in two forms, a 20-seater coach chassis on a 12ft. 9 in. wheelbase, and an ambulance. By 1923 70 per cent of London's ambulances were said to be Talbots, and both variants were still current in 1926. New in 1923 was a 30-cwt WD Subsidy-type vehicle designed by Georges Roesch; it had a 54bhp 4-cylinder ohv engine, a 4-speed gearbox incorporating a power tire pump, and pneumatic tires, but never saw serious production. Another 30-cwt Talbot was announced in 1928, this time with 3-litre sv engine, coil ignition, 3-speed unit gearbox, and worm drive. This was later offered by the associated W and G firm with four-wheel brakes added. In 1930 Talbot introduced a new ambulance based on Roesch's 6-cylinder ohv 75 car chassis, from which it differed in having a double-reduction back axle and artillery wheels. Initially capacity was 2.3 litres, but later models had preselective gearboxes in place of the original 4-speed silent third type, and the option of more powerful 3-litre and 3.4-litre 7-bearing engines. By 1937 216 such chassis had been made, most of them serving in London. An attempt to market an ambulance version of the Humber-based 3-litre sv Talbot of 1938 came to nothing. *MCS*

1938 TALBOT (ii) ¾-ton electric van, OMM

TALBOT (ii) (D) 1937-1939

Waggonfabrik Talbot GmbH., Aachen

This firm built electric vans of ¾- and 2½-ton payload capacity using normal car chassis of various manufacturers. *HON*

1949 TAM Pionir 3-ton truck, OMM

T.A.M. (YU) 1947 to date

(1) Tovarna Automobilov Maribor, Maribor, 1947-1960
(2) Tovarna Automobilov in Motorjev, Maribor, 1960 to date

Originally built in 1942 by occupation forces to produce aircraft components, the TAM factory was destroyed during hostilities and was rebuilt in 1946 by the local Communist Party members with the intention to start producing vehicles. Eventually TAM, standing for "Maribor Automobile Works", turned to the East for cooperation and thus the first Pionir model trucks of 3.5 ton capacity rolled off the lines in 1947, in which year only 27 units were built. Pionir was nothing more than the contemporary Czechoslovakian Praga truck built in Maribor. This same model and its bus variant were built for 15 years, though TAM signed in 1957 a license agreement with Klockner Humboldt Deutz concern, calling for the construction of certain Magirus Deutz engines and vehicles in Yugoslavia. The first product of this cooperation was introduced the same year as TAM 4500 with 4.5 tons payload and a 4-cylinder 85hp Deutz air cooled diesel engine imported from Germany. In-line air cooled diesel engines under Deutz license were built in Maribor from 1960, permitting thus the factory to change its name to "Maribor Automobile and Engine Works". The great demand for commercial vehicles in post-war years and the immense backing of the KHD organization, gave TAM a unique growth. V4 and V6 air cooled diesels, 4 × 4 chassis, bus chassis and integrally built coaches were soon in production, while a number of specialist firms were added to the TAM group of companies; Automontaja as a bus body builder, Vozila Gorica as a municipal vehicle producer and Karoseriest as a specialized body builder are the most important. Truck capacities were increased to 6.5 tons payload, and buses and coaches were close in following Magirus Deutz models in appearance and construction. The year 1960 saw the first original TAM vehicle which was, at the time, the first vehicle designed

1975 TAM 2001 2-ton truck, AAR

1975 TAM 5000 5-ton truck, AAR

entirely in Yugoslavia. Called 2000 from its 2-ton payload, it was powered by an IM, the Yugoslav version of the Perkins, 4-cylinder diesel developing 55hp and featured a two seat forward control cab on conservative lines, but was generally well-built. A forward control version of the 6500 model, fitted with a TAM-designed angular line cab was also marketed in the late 60s as a tractor or municipal chassis. V8 diesels are also currently built in Maribor, while all in-line air cooled diesels, used by KHD group worldwide are of TAM construction. Current production includes a much modified 2-ton model, named 2001, built as truck, van or minibus, 5- to 6.5 ton trucks still fitted with the old style Magirus Deutz cab, 10 ton tractors, and 4 × 4 chassis buses and coaches of all capacities. The assembly of certain selected heavy duty Magirus Deutz 6 × 4 chassis is also programmed, while the extension of cooperation with Zastava, Fiat's associate in Yugoslavia, is also a reality after the Iveco group formation in Europe. TAM is exporting to many countries, one of its best markets being South Africa, while following a recent reorganization, it envisages a production target of 14,000 units, almost double its 1971 production. *GA*

TAPLIN (GB) 1861-1862

B.D. Taplin & Co., Lincoln

Taplin's road haulage engines used a reversed locomotive boiler with the cylinder above the firebox and the driven axle under the boiler barrel, the drive being by gear throughout. The driving and steering platform was at the firebox end and some, at least, of the engines incorporated a screw jack arrangement in the front suspension to level the boiler when ascending hills. The engines were offered in 12 and 16 hp sizes. *RAW*

TARPAN (PL) 1974 to date

Fabryka Samochodow Rolniczych, Poznan

Originally introduced at the 1973 Poznan Fair in the form of an angular-lined 4-door van based on Syrena mechanics, Tarpan 233 entered production a year later as a large dual purpose vehicle. Redesigned with more pleasant lines, it features a double cab pick up body of unitary construction offering accomodation for 6 persons and carrying 750 kilos of payload. One wide door each side permits access to the interior, and mechanics are shared with other Polish vehicles, as usual. The old faithful 4-cylinder, 2.1 litre gasoline engine developing 70hp, as used on the Warszawa range, powers the Tarpan, while gearbox, axles, etc., are similar to those used by Nysa and Zuk light commercials. *GA*

c.1905 TASKER Little Giant steam tractor, RAW

TASKER (GB) 1902-1925

(1) W. Tasker & Sons Ltd., Andover Hants 1902-1903
(2) W. Tasker & Sons, Andover, Hants 1903-1907
(3) W. Tasker & Sons Ltd., Andover, Hants 1907-1925

Though Taskers began engine building in 1869 their limited output was for use in agriculture and they did not begin building steam tractors until 1902, when they produced their first 3-ton tractor, followed in 1904 by the 4-ton "Little Giant", a compound, gear drive type, conventional in layout but very capable in performance. This was followed in 1920 by the chain drive tractor in which very much improved springing was obtained by long leaf springs bearing upon steel channel frames bolted to the hornplates, radius rods being fitted, after wagon practice, for tensioning the chain.

1910 TASKER 5-ton steam wagon, RAW

The chain drive tractor was a most workmanlike machine and had a devoted following, though, as with all Tasker products, production was on a limited scale by very dated workshop practices.

In addition to these popular tractors the firm made overtype compound steam wagons. After an initial venture in 1909, in which four crankshaft discs took the place of a flywheel and provision was made for locking the differential from the footplate, a conventional design was adopted in 3- and 5-ton sizes incorporating single chain drive with the differential in the rear axle. By the time production ceased in 1925, 122 wagons had been made but they never matched the tractors as performers. One experimental 10-ton artic was made in 1922 but never sold.

During the twilight years of road steam the firm went through very difficult times. In 1925 a medium-weight gasoline-engined truck was attempted using a Dorman engine but, apart from the body it was an assembled job and did not sell. The firm remained in the doldrums until the thirties when it was revived as a specialist builder of trailers and semi-trailers. In 1968, following liquidity problems, the company became a wholly owned subsidiary of Craven Industries Ltd. *RAW*

TATA (IND) 1954 to date

Tata Engineering & Locomotive Co., Jamshedpur

The Tata engineering company assemble Mercedes-Benz trucks and buses in India, products being known as Tata-Mercedes-Benz up to 1971, and plain Tata since then, when the M-B 3-pointed star was replaced by a large 'T' on the grilles. The old semi-forward control cab is still used on some models, though the forward-control models bear a close resemblance to the M-B LP810 series. *GA*

TATE (CDN) 1912-1914

Tate Electric Ltd., Walkerville, Ont.

Four models of electric truck, from a light, shaft-driven panel delivery to a 2-ton chain-driven stake truck, were built by this firm, which also made electric passenger cars. *HD*

TATRA (CS) 1919 to date

(1) Tatra akc. spol. pro. stavbu automobilu a zeleznicnich vozu, Koprivnice 1919-1945

(2) Tatra, n.p., Koprivnice 1945 to date

Formerly Nesselsdorfer, Tatra is the oldest Czechoslovakian make. After the change of name in 1919 the former Nesselsdorfer TL 2 and TL 4 trucks were continued for some years, but in 1923 the brilliant engineer Hans Ledwinka designed his famous Type 11 car, with flat twin engine, central tubular frame and swinging half axles giving independent suspension to front and rear wheels. The commercial version, known as the Type 13, was introduced in 1925 and made until 1933 in many forms including vans, buses and ambulances. It led to a whole range of larger vehicles, all employing the basic tubular backbone frame, such as the Type 26 with 1.05-litre flat twin engine, and later 1.68-litre flat-four engine, and six wheels, surely one of the smallest three-axled commercial vehicles ever made. As well as a load carrier, the Type 26 was made as a fire engine and light bus. Production ran from 1926 to 1933 when it was succeeded by the Type 72 with 1.9-litre engine, also a 6-wheeler. 328 of these were made, up to 1937, after which the line of really small Tatra 6-wheelers was discontinued. Meanwhile the 2-cylinder 4-wheeled Type 13 had grown up

1925 TATRA T.13 1-ton truck, Tatra

into the 4-cylinder 1.68-litre Type 43 for 1½-ton loads, replaced by the 1.9-litre Type 43/52 made up to 1937. There were also a number of light vans built on the 1,155cc Type 57 and 57a passenger car chassis between 1932 and 1938. The coal-scuttle hood of the original small Tatras was continued until 1935 on these models, then replaced by a conventional frontal grille, though the engines were still air-cooled. About 200 8cwt delivery 3-wheelers were made in 1929/30 on the type 49 frame with 528cc 7hp single-cylinder engine.

At the other end of the scale, Tatra introduced in 1923 a 3 tonner with 7.48-litre 4-cylinder water-cooled engine and tubular backbone frame. This was the Type 23 made up to 1931, and supplemented by the 3-axle Type 24 with 11-, 12- and eventually 16.6-litre 6-cylinder engines. Load capacity of the Type 24 was 10 tons, and they were made with a wide variety of goods, bodies, tankers, furniture vans, fire engines and open and closed buses. From 1935 to 1938 the 24 was available with a 140bhp diesel engine. Other 2- and 3- axle models were made during the 1930s, many of them with high cross-country mobility which made them very suitable for military use. These included the Type 85 6-wheeler with 8.2-litre 4-cylinder gasoline or 6-cylinder diesel engine for 5-ton loads and also widely used as a bus chassis. In 1939 came the Type 81 10-ton 6-wheeler with 12.46-litre 160bhp V-8 diesel engine, or 14.73-litre 120bhp V-8 producer-gas engine. More significant was the introduction in 1942 of a new range of air-cooled diesel engines made in 4, 6, 8, and 12-cylinder versions, all with the same cylinder dimensions of 110 × 130mm. The 4-cylinder unit was used in the Types 114 and 115 3-tonners, but the best-known truck of the series was the Type 111, a 10-ton rigid 6 with 14.82-litre 180hp V-12 engine, made from 1942 to 1962, by which time 33,690 had been delivered, a remarkable figure for such a large and

1931 TATRA T.24/58 6-ton truck, Tatra

1933 TATRA T.43 1½-ton truck, Tatra

1938 TATRA T.92 2-ton 6×4 truck, Tatra

1938 TATRA T.85/91 30-seater bus, Tatra

expensive machine. In 1957 it was joined by the Type 138 with 11.76-litre V-8 engine, and this replaced the V-12 in 1962, being still in production today, alongside the heavier Type 148 introduced in 1968.

1950 TATRA 111 10-ton 6×6 truck, Tatra

Other models of the 1950s included the 1.7-ton off-road 4 × 4 Type 805, powered by a de-tuned version of the 2½-litre V-8 used in Tatra's luxury Type 603 passenger car. Passenger vehicles did not form a large part of Tatra's post-war activities, except for the Type 500HB 6-wheeled

1967 TATRA 138 8-ton 6×6 truck, Tatra

'mountain bus' of 1955, with rear-mounted 9.85-litre engine and 60-passenger integral body/chassis, and a range of 3-axle trolleybuses made between 1947 and 1960.

1977 TATRA 813 8×8 heavy tractor, Tatra

In 1967 came the new Type 813 range of forward-control heavy vehicles in 4 × 4, 6 × 6 conventional and twin-steer, and 8 × 8 form, mainly as tractors for drawbar trailers, though the conventional 6 × 6 was also used with tipper bodies. These are powered by an 18.98-litre 270bhp air-cooled V-12 diesel engine and can be used for the heaviest of indivisible loads of up to 300 tons, when two or more tractors may be used, and also as aircraft tugs. These and the conventional Type 138 and 148 make up the current Tatra range. They are exported all over the world, and the absence of water cooling makes them suitable for work in extremes of hot and cold climates. *MSH*

TAYLOR (i) (GB) 1859-1864

James Taylor, Birkenhead

Chiefly noted for cranes and dockside machines Taylor also produced a 5 nhp haulage engine for dockside work. Using a modified short locomotive boiler he incorporated it into a chassis of plate and angles. Vertical duplex cylinders were employed in conjunction with all gear drive and a differential. The driving and steering position was at the front, the forecarriage being in a turntable, giving a very tight steering lock. Railroad type buffers and couplings were fitted and the machine was clearly intended, inter alia, for shunting rail wagons. At least one example was used at Keyham Dockyard.

In addition Taylor built Bray engines under license.*RAW*

TAYLOR (ii) (US) 1917-1918

Taylor Motor Truck Co., Fremont, O

This company bought the former H.G. Burford Co. of Fremont and continued the business of truck assembly from standard parts. The line of Taylor trucks were 1-, 1½-, 2½-, 3½- and 5-tonners, all with 4-cylinder Continental engines, Covert gearboxes and Timken worm-drive rear axles. Wheelbases ranged from 10 feet, 10 inches for the smallest to 13 feet, 4 inches for the 5-tonner. *GMN*

T.B. (GB) 1922-1924

Thompson Brothers (Bilston) Ltd., Bilston, Staffs.

The T.B. was one of the better-looking 3-wheelers of its day, and was made in van form with a capacity of 7½-cwt in addition to the more familiar passenger car. It was powered by a 961cc V-twin J.A.P. engine, and had a 3-speed gearbox and shaft drive to the single rear wheel. *GNG*

TCAVDAR (BG) 19 - to date

Uzina Tcavdar, Botevgrad

A national Bulgarian producer of buses and coaches, Tcavdar uses Skoda chassis, engines and components, building medium and large capacity buses and coaches.

Outdated in appearance and heavy looking, Tcavdar buses were retained for local use only until 1975, when a cooperation agreement with the West German Kassbohrer body building firm resulted in a modern coach called 11M3. A unique combination of Western and Eastern world products, the 11M3 is built according to Setra methods and is very modern in appearance and finish, but is still based on a Skoda chassis of the 706 family, powered by a Skoda front placed diesel engine developing 160hp. *GA*

1962 TECHNO container truck, Techno

TECHNO (US) 1962

Techno Truck Co., Cleveland, Ohio

The Techno was a most unusual attempt to introduce a new concept of loading and unloading cargo. Its basis was an International B 170 short conventional truck which Techno converted to front wheel drive, a necessity as there was no conventional body to the rear of the cab. Instead there was a framework to hold a container which could be lowered to ground level by hydraulic actuation, and had an adjustable height to meet any dock level between ground and 66 inches, for loading or unloading. The container could also be deposited on the ground or on a portable docking stand. Two half-size, or four quarter-size containers could be accommodated, and open-type lumber or pipe carriers were also usable in the Techno system.

This truck was planned for production in capacities of 4, 5, 6, and 8-tons, but only the one 6-ton prototype was actually built. *RW*

T.E.C.O. (US) 1948

Tibbetts Engineering Co., Highland, Ill.

Keith Tibbetts was the son-in-law of C.J. Hug and had been vice-president and general manager of the Hug company. In 1948 he and his two sons built three trucks for a local quarry, using many parts left over from Hug production, including Buda diesel engines. Two of these trucks are still in daily use, after nearly 30 years, as well as four 1937 Hugs now used as drilling rigs and water tankers. *RW*

TEC-TRUCK (US) 1920-1921

Terminal Engineering Co., New York, NY

This was a battery-powered electric tractor for trailers, rated as a 2½-tonner. *GMN*

TEMPO (D) 1928-1968

Vidal & Sohn Tempo-Werk GmbH., Wandsbek; Hamburg-Harburg

The first Tempo design followed a very popular van layout of that time: two front wheels with front mounted box or platform and one driven rear wheel with the driver's saddle seat. Two-stroke Rinne engines of 195cc and 350cc were used during the following years. In 1933 Tempo changed to a layout the other way round, with one driven front wheel and two rear wheels. Now there was also a two-seater cabin. The first 4-wheeled 1 ton van was presented in 1936 and used a 2-cylinder 600cc Ilo engine. Tempo was very successful in the field of vans and had a share of about 40%of the German market in 1937. After WW II Temp resumed production in 1945 and a new start was made with a ¼ tonner which was followed by a ½ ton version a few year later. A new four-wheeled forward control transporter appeared in 1949. This carried a 1 ton

c. 1952 TEMPO ¼-ton 3-wheel truck, GNG

1954 TEMPO Matador 1000 1-ton van, GNG

1965 TEMPO Matador 2-ton 6X2 truck, GNG

payload and was equipped with a Volkswagen engine which was placed under the driver's seat and drove the front wheels. It had the type designation Matador. In 1952 — when Volkswagen enlarged their own transporter program — the VW engine was no more available. Tempo presented two new versions, the Matador 1000 with their own 3-cylinder 672cc two-stroke engine and the Matador 1400 with a 4-cylinder 1,092cc Heinkel engine. A new ½-ton van was the Wiking with a 2-cylinder 452cc two-stroke Heinkel engine. In 1958 the Matador changed to Austin engines. All versions retained the original front drive. This enabled Tempo not only to offer only a big variety of vans, pick-ups and micro buses but to offer it for various special purpose vehicles. From 1955 Hanomag had an interest in Tempo which led to a total takeover in 1963, but until 1966 vehicles were sold under the name of Tempo, after which they were known as Hanomag (q.v.). When Hanomag-Henschel were taken over by Mercedes-Benz the old Matador transporter became a part of the Mercedes program.

Foreign license production of Tempo vehicles included a Spanish factory which made 3 wheelers, followed by 4 wheelers in the Barreiros factory, and an Indian factory at Chinchwad, Poona (Bajaj Tempo Ltd.) which began production of Matador and Viking models in 1966 and was still making them in 1975. *HON*

TEN CATE (NL) 1935-1947

Fa. J. & I. Ten Cate, Automobiel-en Trailerfabriek, Almelo

This company began by building special trailers for Chenard-Walcker tractors which were imported into Holland by Beers of the Hague. They were also major manufacturers of tipper and tanker bodies, and built the chassis for the Beers Trambus of 1934. A year later they started to make tractors of their own, so that they could offer complete tractor/trailer units. These had Deutz diesel engines, central tubular chassis and came in four- or

1936 TEN CATE articulated truck MW

six-wheeled form. Finance was always a problem, and the war spelled the end of Ten Cate as vehicle manufacturers. From 1945 to 1947 they repaired and modified dump trucks and the last ones, with White engines, were sold under the Ten Cate name. *MW*

1870 TENNANT 3-wheel steam tractor, RAW

TENNANT (GB) 1867-1872

Tennant & Co., Leith

Tennants were general engine makers mainly concerned with ship work. After R.W. Thomson ceased to build engines himself he selected them to build his three wheeled road steamers in which he used his vertical "pot" boiler and horizontal duplex engine with gear drive to the rear wheels which were shod with the inventor's patent solid rubber tires protected with wrought iron linked shoes. They continued to build his engines for some years, most subsequent examples having vertical engines. They were partly responsible for the design of later engines and produced at least one engine, with a locomotive boiler, which was very largely of their own design. The firm was, however, in low financial water and the standard of workmanship was poor. They finally became insolvent. *RAW*

TENTING (F) 1898

Societe Nationale de Construction de Moteurs H. Tenting, Boulogne-sur-Seine

Though Tenting cars with friction-and-chain transmission had been made as early as 1891, the company's only attempt at a commercial vehicle was a 22-seater omnibus produced in 1898. Power was provided by a 16hp 4-cylinder engine with the gargantuan dimensions of 140 × 220mm, electric or tube ignitions were optional, friction drive was retained, and the exhaust pipe was mounted across the cab roof. The vehicle was credited with 18mph. *MCS*

1972 TERBERG SF 1400-437 14-ton 6×4 dump truck, OMM

TERBERG (NL) 1965 to date

Automobielfabriek W.G. Terberg & ZN. B.V., Benschop.

After World War II Terberg of Benschop was one of the various Dutch truck dealers selling and reconditioning U.S. GMC trucks. The GMC's were replaced by Diamond and Reos, and Terberg gradually became a real truck manufacturer, initially using parts of Diamond and Reos in new tipper trucks, but currently manufacturing some of its own parts, like driven front axles. The first Terberg truck model, N 800, still closely resembled the U.S. Army Reo, though it was fitted with a DAF oil engine. The accompanying model, SF 1200, was fitted with a Mercedes-Benz oil engine, and also used the semi-forward Mercedes-Benz cab. Both models are still built, but have meanwhile been joined by further types. Some of these, introduced in 1974, use the cab and engine of the new Volvo N-line of semi-forwards, and are sold in some countries outside Holland through the Volvo dealer network. *JFJK*

TEREX (GB/US) 1969 to date

(1) General Motors Scotland Ltd., Motherwell, Lanarkshire 1969 to date

(2) Terex Divn, General Motors Corp., Hudson, Ohio 1972 to date

In 1968 General Motors was forced to sell its American-based Euclid division to White (see Euclid), but the Scottish plant which had been set up in 1950 continued under GM ownership, using the new name Terex (Latin 'Earth-King') for its products. In 1973 the Terex name was used for new GM-built dump trucks made in United States. By 1974 the range covered Detroit and Cummins-engined models from 17 to 150 tons capacity, and in that year they were joined by the 350-ton 3-axle Titan model with GM locomotive diesel engine of 3,300bhp and electric drive. By 1977 the largest model had grown to 550 tons capacity.

1975 TEREX R-17 17-ton dump truck, Terex

As well as the Scottish plant, Terex has overseas factories in Canada, Luxemburg, Brazil, Australia, India, and South Africa. *OM*

TERRAPLANE see Hudson (i)

T.G.E. (J) 1917-1939

Tokyo Gasu Denki KK, Tokyo

Tokyo Gasu Denki (Tokyo Gas & Electricity) was a large industrial group whose activities also included aircraft and aero engines. The first serious producers of trucks in Japan, they built vehicles on American lines,

1975 TEREX Titan 350-ton dump truck, Terex

1932 TGE-CHIYODA Q-type 2½-ton 6×4 truck, BHV

starting with an orthodox 1-tonner in 1917; this was subsequently uprated to 3-cwt, though production was described as intermittent, with only 80 vehicles delivered in 1930. A year later came the Chiyoda range of American-type trucks and buses, named after an Imperial residence in Tokyo where a T.G.E. truck had been taken into service. Like the private cars of the same name, Chiyodas were mainly destined for army service, and included some 6 × 4 2½-tonners. Along with those of Ishikawajima (Sumida), T.G.E.'s automobile activities were merged into the Isuzu concern. *MCS*

T.H. see Ideal

1911 THAMES charabanc, NMM

THAMES (GB) 1905-1913

The Thames Ironworks, Shipbuilding & Engineering Co. Ltd., Greenwich, London S.E.

Thames Ironworks was established in 1857 and was a major shipbuilding company among whose landmarks was the construction, in 1860, of H.M.S. Warrior, the first seagoing ironclad ever built. Vehicles were a sideline, and were begun as a diversification to counterbalance the steadily declining economics of shipbuilding on the Thames. The company purchased ship's engines from, among others, William Penn of Greenwich, and took over their works when it came on the market in 1898. Road vehicles were made there.

The Thames 5-ton steam wagon launched in 1905 had features that, if it had been allowed the time for development, might have been an excellent wagon, having an ample sized locomotive boiler, transverse compound enclosed engine, two road speeds and shaft drive to a rear axle differential. The two missing ingredients were an effective superheater and a double high pressure (as opposed to compound) engine, and the Thames was overwhelmed by the change in customer feeling in favor of the overtype in about 1908

The first Thames gasoline-engined vehicles, introduced in 1905 were a 1-ton van powered by a 2-cylinder 10/12hp Aster engine, and a bus chassis with 24/30hp 4-cylinder engine and chain drive. These were joined in 1906 by a 25/40hp 6-cylinder chassis, one of the first examples of a 6-cylinder commmercial vehicle, and in 1908 by a 10/12hp 2-cylinder worm drive chassis for either van or taxicab bodies. The latter had sloping, Renault-type hoods. These were replaced by a 15hp 4-cylinder chassis in 1910, though single- and 2-cylinder passenger car chassis continued to be made, as well as larger models. Charabancs formed an important part of Thames' output, and in addition to large normal-control models, an unusual semi-forward control double-decker of stage coach layout was introduced in 1911. This was developed for Motor Coaches Ltd. of London who were to operate them over a zone of up to 100 miles from London. Later in 1911 it was anounced that Motor Coaches Ltd. were to take over the marketing of all Thames commercial vehicles, but by this time production was practically at an end. Only one Thames commercial vehicle is known to survive, a 1913 stage coach belonging to the National Motor Museum at Beaulieu. *RAW/GNG*

THAMES (ii) see Ford (ii)

1959 THIBAULT pumper, Thibault

THIBAULT (CDN) 1938 to date

Pierre Thibalut (Canada) Ltd., Pierceville, Que.

Thibault had built hand-drawn fire apparatus as early as 1908, then horse-drawn units, and in 1918 its first motorized 5 engine which used a Ford chassis. By 1938 the firm was producing complete fire eninges of sophisticated design which were sold under the name Richelieu. During World War 2 the company developed an airport crash truck, and after the war a completely new chassis and chab were developed, and the product name changed to Thibault. Current models use Detroit Diesel engines as standard equipment. They include the Tibocar pumper with custom enclosed cab, four-wheel and tractor-drawn aeriol ladder units, salvage and foam trucks, and quick delivery stock units on Ford, G.M.C. or Interanational chassis. *HD*

THIRION (F) 1902-1904

A. Thirion et fils, Paris

The Thirion was a fire engine powered by a horizontal 2-cylinder engine mounted under the seat, with a 3-speed gearbox and shaft drive. There were two pumps, fore and aft, driven by chain from the propeller shaft. It had seats for five firemen. *GNG*

THOMAS (i) (US) 1905-1911

E. R. Thomas Motor Co., Buffalo, NY

The manufacturer of the motorcar which won the New York to Paris race also built taxicabs. The chassis for this taxi differed from those used for passenger autos. Originally, the taxi used a 4-cylinder engine rated at 14-16hp and used a wheelbase of 8 feet, 4 inches. In 1910, the Model R taxi for 6 passengers also used a 4-cylinder engine, had a wheelbase of 10 feet, 3 inches and cost $4000. *GMN*

THOMAS (ii) (US) 1906-1908

(1) Thomas Wagon Co., Vernon, N.Y. 1906-1907

(2) Thomas Wagon Co., Lititz, Pa. 1908

This firm built farm wagons with a patented steering-knuckle front axle from 1904-1910. The truck was simply the wagon fitted with a 2-cylinder air-cooled engine and wheel steering. Friction transmission and dual chain drive were used. The 3-ton model cost $1,500 in 1907. *DJS*

THOMAS (iii) (US) 1916-1917

(1) Thomas Auto Truck Co., New York City, N.Y.

(2) Consolidated Motors Corp., New York City, N.Y.

This company was formed by Charles K. Thomas, former vice-president of Federal. The product was a 2-ton assembled truck powered by a 4-cylinder Buda engine, with Covert-Brown-Lipe 3-speed transmission and Timken-David Brown overhead worm rear axle. *GNG*

THOMPSON (US) 1905-1906

Thompson Auto Co., Providence, R.I.

This steamer was made in two models. Model A was a delivery van with a price of $1,800 which had a Stanley burner and a 10hp Fitzhenry engine. Unlike most steamers, drive was not direct but through a single roller chain. It had a reach frame with solid rubber tires, a wheelbase of 8 feet and track of 5 feet. The model B was on a wheelbase of 8 feet, 8 inches and was a 10-passenger "Wagonette" for $2,200. *GMN*

THOMSON (GB) 1867-1873

R.W. Thomson, Leith

Thomson is remembered for his 3-wheeled road steamers in which he employed his own design of vertical boiler combining vertical fire-tubes with a copper "pot" protuding downward in to the firebox. These engines were fitted with his resilient wheels. In early examples the engine was horizontal but subsequently he used the

1868 THOMSON 3-wheel steam tractor, RAW

vertical engine. After building five or six in his own works he sublet actual production together with some detailed design work, to Tennant & Co. of Leith (of which firm he was a director) as well as to Robey, Ransomes, Burrell and other noted traction engine builders. He died in 1873.

The resilient wheels were shod with a solid rubber tire which was fitted over the center but not vulcanized to it. Protection from road stone was afforded by an armor of interlocking pivoted iron shoes. The longest lived of his engines were a pair built by Tennant which were used by Road Engines Limited of Glasgow, until the early 1930s. *RAW*

THOR (GB) 1905

Thor Motor Car Co., London S.W.

The Thor was a 10cwt van powered by a 6/8hp 2-cylinder Simms engine, with 3-speed gearbox, chain drive and solid tires. It was also made in passenger car form, and a 12/14hp version of the latter was also listed. Whether this had van bodywork as well is not certain. *GNG*

THORNE (US) 1929-c.1938

(1) Thorne Motor Corp., Chicago, Ill.

2) Thorne Gas Electric Corp., Chicago, Ill.

The Thorne was one of a group of multi-stop delivery vans that appeared in America in the late 1920s, better-known examples being Divco and Pak-Age-Car. Powered by an 18hp 4-cylinder Continental engine mounted at the front, it drove via a 90volt electric motor just ahead of the rear axle. Locked hydraulic four wheel brakes were featured, and the driver stood, as in some other vehicles of this type. Larger Continental engines of 19.6 and 24.02hp were used in 1929 and 1932 respectively, but the gas-electric drive was not entirely satisfactory, and Thornes did not enjoy the sales of better-known makes. *GNG*

THORNYCROFT (GB) 1896-1977

(1) John I. Thornycroft & Co. Ltd., Chiswick, London W. 1896-1898

(2) John I Thornycroft & Co. Ltd., Basingstoke, Hants. 1898-1947

(3) Transport Equipment (Thornycroft) Ltd., Basingstoke, Hants. 1948-1969

(4) Scammell Motors Divn., British Leyland Motor Corporation, Watford, Herts 1969-1977

John I. Thornycroft built steam launches beside the river Thames at Chiswick. In 1896 one of his lightweight vertical marine engines was adapted for use in a van. This had rear wheel steering and front wheel drive by chain and was the only true industrial vehicle to be exhibited at the 1896 Crystal Palace Motor Show.

In 1897 production versions with compound engines were sold to a number of local users including Chiswick Urban District Council, who had the first of many mechanically tipped Chiswick models.

In 1898 Thornycroft opened a new factory at Basingstoke to keep pace with the demand for wagons and produced the first articulated platform lorry by attaching a two wheel trailer to their 4-ton chassis, an idea that was not to gain acceptance for another twenty years.

1901 THORNYCROFT (American) steam wagon, OMM

1901 THORNYCROFT steam van and trailer, OMM

1901 THORNYCROFT colonial steam wagon, RAW

In 1899 Thornycroft started a long connection with military vehicles when they supplied a fleet of steam wagons for service in the Boer War. In 1902 they also produced a double deck bus for service in London and others were supplied overseas as early as 1900. Steam wagon production finally came to an end in 1907, by which time they were being produced under license by Duncan Stewart & Co. Ltd., in Glasgow and had been made by the Berlin railway engineering company of Schwartzkopff, and by the Cooke Loco works of Patterson, New Jersey, U.S.A. The reason for the early eclipse of Thornycroft steam vehicles was the adoption of paraffin and gasoline-driven lorries from 1902. The paraffin engines were particularly suited to the low octane fuels obtainable in the British Colonies at the time, and they built up an important export trade. They were also used by the War Office who had experimented with Thornycroft paraffin vehicles since the turn of the century and in 1904 ordered a number of heavy paraffin tractors. One of these, 50hp 15-tonner, won the premier award in the 1909 Adlershot Trails.

The gasoline vehicles were initially 4-tonners followed by 24hp 30cwt, 2- and 2½-ton models, of which virtually all the parts were made by Thornycroft themselves. From 1904 the 2- and 2½-tonners were also available with passenger bodywork. By 1905 the original exposed horizontal tube radiators gave way to a design with conventional header tank and shell.

Thornycrofts continued to do well in the trials of military and motoring organizations and for £25 all could be equipped with special carburetors to permit the use of paraffin fuel.

In 1908 a new range appeared with choice of 2-cylinder 16hp or 4-cylinder 30hp engines for goods or up to 34 passengers. 1913 saw a 3-ton model built to War Office Subsidy specification join the Pickfords fleet, the first Subsidy vehicle to enter civilian service. Approximately 5,000 of this J model were produced by Thornycroft during the First World War. Afterwards, like most of their contemporaries, they continued to produce as many chassis as the sale of ex-WD vehicles to the saturated civilian market would permit. Initially these were 2- to 6-tonners, the smallest of which won the Dewar trophy in 1921, and Thornycroft were less hard hit than many of their contemporaries on account of the export business that they had built up before the war.

1922 THORNYCROFT J-type 4-ton van, OMM

Reconditioned J models proved to be popular as charabanc chassis and from 1922 Thornycroft began to produce new chassis intended to replace them. These included the 34 seat Patrician based on the 30hp long chassis, the 24 seat BZ and the 30 seat Boadicea, which all had L-heads from 1924 when the old T-head engine from the J model was discontinued. In 1923 the largest 6-ton capacity W model became available with forward control, also available on its London bus chassis derivative. Thornycroft also revived their interest in articulated vehicles, offering three models from 4 to 12 tons capacity. Also in 1923 Thornycroft experimented with producer gas vehicles as a continuation of their crude fuel colonial models. In 1924 the successful Subsidy model 30 cwt A1-Type was introduced. It had unit engine and gearbox for the first time on a Thornycroft and in common with the other light Subsidy models, it had pneumatic tires with gearbox driven tire pump, though solids could still be specified. It was also obtainable as the Dragon coach or as a 20 seat bus, and 1,000 A-types were in service by the end of 1925.

1924 had also seen the introduction of the 4 × 4 Hathi gun tractor. This followed War Office experiments with four wheel drive vehicles made from captured German components and was one of the first British vehicles so equipped. It had a 100hp 6-cylinder engine, six forward speeds, and a winch. It exerted a 9,000lb. drawbar pull, was capable of up to 12 miles per hour, and a total of around 25 were built, most finding their way to India and Australia, for heavy haulage work. At least one was converted to 6 × 6 layout by the War Office.

In 1926 the A1 and its 2-ton sister, the A2, were joined by a rigid 6-wheel A3 for 3-ton loads and later by the XB for 5-ton loads. The A3 was also eligible for the War Department Subsidy and over 100 were supplied in the first year, primarily for overseas off-road operation. Also in 1926 the old BX 2½-tonner was modernized as the KB with unit engine and gearbox and pneumatic tires, and for 1928 the J received similar treatment, becoming the JJ 5/6-tonner.

On the passenger vehicle side the Lightning coach of 1927 was one of the first in Britain to receive a 6-cylinder engine and was also fitted with 4-wheel servo brakes for the first time on a Thornycroft.

In addition to passenger variants of the A type, including export 6-cylinder 6-wheelers in 1929, there were the larger 32 seaters as well as LC and BC double deckers

1930 THORNYCROFT PB 10-ton 6-wheel truck, BR

with 48 seats and, new in 1929, the HC 6-wheel double decker for up to 68 seats. This later was also the basis of some Brush-equipped trolleybuses. Also new in 1929 was a forward control JC 10-ton 6-wheeler with 6-cylinder engine, followed by a QC 12-tonner three years later. By the end of 1931 Thornycroft were offering around 40 different passenger and goods models and were amongst the top half dozen British commercial vehicle manufacturers. At the time of the 1931 London Commercial Motor Show the passenger range was revised with the 32 seat model now known as the Cygnet, and the 4-wheel double decker as the Daring. The latter had fabricated box section axles and only semi-floating half shafts.

The 2- and 2½-ton versions of the A series were now the Bulldog and Speedy, whilst the heaviest 4-wheeler became the Jupiter, which had a feature to remain popular with Thornycroft, though less so with operators, throughout the thirties, a normal-control layout with the front axle behind the engine. The first Thornycroft road-going diesel engine was announced at the time, though after indecision as to whether it should have direct or indirect injection, it

1932 THORNYCROFT Jupiter 5-ton truck, OMM

did not seriously enter production for another 2 years. For 1932 all the rest of the range had acquired model names, many of which were derived from the parent Thornycroft company's battleship building interests at Southampton.

A name to become synonymous with the lighter goods models for over 20 years was the 4-ton Sturdy. There was also the trailing axle 6-wheel Wolfhound for 4 tons, the Tartar 3-ton 6-wheeler based on the old 6-wheel Subsidy model, the cross-country 6-ton 6 × 4 Amazon, the 5-ton Strenuous, the Taurus which replaced the Jupiter, the Mastiff 7-ton 6-wheeler, the Iron Duke 6½-ton tipper and the 11-ton 6-wheeler now called the Dreadnought, but briefly announced as the Colossus in 1931. In 1933 came the Handy and Dandy, small manuevrable 4-wheelers,

1933 THORNYCROFT Cygnet 32/35-seater bus, OMM

which became popular with the railroad for 2- and 3-ton loads. These marked the end of the old A models, though they survived for passenger transport until 1935.

Following an order for 40 lightweight 6-wheelers from the Metropolitan Supply Co. Thornycroft produced the Stag. This was a forward control 6-wheeler with choice of 6-cylinder diesel or gasoline engine, and 8 speed Thornycroft or Maybach gearbox. It was designed to weigh under 7 tons complete with Thornycroft-built insulated van body, and was intended as a high speed transporter on the new arterial roads.

In 1934 came the Trusty, a 7½/8-tonner embodying everything that Thornycroft had learned about lightweight construction. It had a new 4-cylinder diesel engine, which, like the Handy's made extensive use of Elektron metal, and deep light gauge chassis members with cruciform bracing. Total weight was only 4 tons as a platform truck and it had a forward-control layout with set-back front axle.

At the same time a diesel-engined 3-tonner, the Bullfinch, was announced, which was the first to use a proprietary engine, the Dorman-Ricardo. Meanwhile the

1934 THORNYCROFT Speedy 4-ton tanker, OMM

passenger range had been joined by the 34-seat Charger and the lightweight Ardent 20-seater. The larger models had never become particularly popular, though after the Gardner 6LW became an option in the Daring, a few were supplied to the Stalybridge, Hyde, Mossley and Dukinfield Joint Board bringing their total of Thornycroft vehicles to over 80. In fact only about 65 Thornycroft double deckers were built for operation in Britain.

The original Sturdy, and ultimately its 5-ton stablemate, the Beauty, were replaced by a new Sturdy in 1935, which had a 4-cylinder 62hp gasoline engine and very light build to qualify for tax and speed concessions for vehicles weighing under 2½ tons.

In 1936 the lightest passenger model became known as the Dainty and in 1937 it was joined by the 26-seat Beautyride based on the Sturdy. With one exception of export buses, notably Gardner-engined Amazon buses to

1937 THORNYCROFT Trusty 6½/8-ton truck, BR

Iraq in 1937, these were Thornycroft's last serious attempt at the passenger market, and by 1939 only the Beautyride was offered.

With increased concentration on goods models including the Nippy 3-tonner in 1938 to replace the Dandy, Thornycroft were soon busy with military models once again. They supplied 122 normal-control Sturdy searchlight generator trucks and in 1938 were granted a

1938 THORNYCROFT Stag 10/12-ton truck, OMM

repeat order for 400 more. In addition the Amazon was supplied for military purposes, notably as the basis of over 2,000 Coles Mk. 7 truck mounted cranes, following its successful overseas off-road use as a heavy goods model during the thirties. 2,000 Nippy and Sturdy models were made during the war for essential civilian transport and were joined by a new military model, the 4 × 4 Nubian. This had a choice of 61hp diesel or 85op gasoline 4-cylinder engine and was nominally rated as a 3-tonner. It was able to climb a 1 in 2 gradient and work in difficult off-road conditions, yet have a top speed of 40mph. Total wartime vehicle production amounted to 13,000 plus 8,230 tracked Bren Gun carriers. These figures included a number of 8 × 8 amphibious Terrapins with twin Ford V-8 engines, over 5,000 Nubians and a further 1576 generator trucks, plus several thousand Tartar 6 × 4 trucks.

In the last year of the war a diesel-engined Sturdy was introduced. This had a 6-cylinder unit which reverted to indirect injection and had been intended for 1939. The Nippy continued in production and both it and the Sturdy were the basis of a few small buses, whilst the Trusty reappeared in various guises, including an 8-wheel 14/15-tonner from 1946. This had the 7.88-litre 100bhp diesel engine used in many of Thornycroft's wartime products, but from 1947 was also available with direct injection. This unique feature was primarily to make the chassis suitable for overseas use in countries where its extra speed, refinement and 6.5 mpg fuel consumption could be used to advantage. The Trusty was also available as a 6-wheeler whilst a specifically export 12-ton gross chassis usually with normal control called the Trident was announced in 1948, but not produced in any quantity until 1950 because of material shortages. During the first three years of peace approximately 40% of Thornycroft products were exported.

1949 THORNYCROFT Amazon 14-ton articulated tanker, OMM

1949 THORNYCROFT Nippy 20-seater bus, AJHB

New in 1948 was an updated version of the Sturdy called the Sturdy Star, featuring a direct injection 4.18 litre 6-cylinder diesel. This chassis was similar to the Trident though the latter had a 5.51 litre engine. In the same year the vehicle side of the Thornycroft business was renamed Transport Equipment (Thornycroft) Ltd. as a wholly owned subsidiary of J.I. Thornycroft & Co. Ltd.

1947 THORNYCROFT Sturdy 5/6-ton truck, OMM

This was primarily because both this and the shipbuilding side were still under Government supervision after the war but answerable to different Ministries.

The Nubian and Amazon remained in production for special purposes, mainly overseas, and were joined in 1950 by the massive Mighty Antar 85-ton tractor. This initially was powered by an 18-litre Rover Meteorite diesel tank engine producing 250hp. It had a 4-speed gearbox and 3-speed auxiliary box giving 12 forward ratios. It carried 200 gallons of fuel, did four miles per gallon and had twin radiators. Initially supplied to the Iraq Petroleum Company, it was soon used extensively for oil field, heavy haulage and military purposes and over 750, mainly with Rolls-Royce diesel and gasoline engines, were in service by 1964.

Also in 1950 the Nippy was offered with a diesel engine for the first time, this being a direct injection version of the original post-war Sturdy unit. By the end of 1952 the Nippy had become the Nippy Star 4-tonner and had the distinction of being the only vehicle in that weight category produced in Britain which had all its components apart from tires and electrics built under the same roof. Also in 1952 the Sturdy acquired a proprietary steel cab, and the Mighty Antar could be bought as a 4 × 2 tractor with rigid chassis to rear axle attachment and giant earthmover tires on the driving axle. This was followed by a 6 × 4 Big Ben heavy export chassis which started life as a variation of the Nubian, by now available in 3-axle form, but grew to become a cross between this and the Antar. It had an 11.3 litre 6-cylinder diesel.

1959 THORNYCROFT Trusty 15-ton 8-wheel van, OMM

By 1957 the Swift and Swiftsure had replaced the Nippy and Sturdy and in 1958 the plastics-cabbed Mastiff for 14 tons gross vehicle weight filled the niche left by the old 4-wheel Trusty. A lighter MA Antar was introduced with a 216hp turbocharged version of the Big Ben's 11.3 litre engine and by now Nubians in both 4 × 4 and 6 × 6 form were being supplied as airfield crash tenders. The Trusty in heavy duty 6 × 4 conventional layout was used for various overseas purposes including oil exploration and both the Big Ben and Antars were available in Sandmaster form with special tires and cooling systems for desert operation.

In 1960 a 4 × 4 dumptruck chassis for 20 tons gross weight joined the range and by now the normal control Trusty had similar frontal treatment to the Antar. Vehicles for the home market were mainly limited to the 8-wheel Trusty and the articulated tractor version of the Mastiff, now with a new fiber glass cab, though Swifts and Swiftsures were still listed. With increased specialization in ultra heavy-duty overseas vehicles, Thornycroft were finding it difficult to keep their large works at Basingstoke fully occupied and in 1961 their vehicle building interests were taken over by AEC who needed extra capacity. Thornycroft's conventional road models which clashed with AEC were soon discontinued, though their specialized products were encouraged. The smallest Nubian model acquired an AEC AV410 engine whilst the 6 × 6 version normally used the 8-cylinder Rolls-Royce gasoline engine, though Thornycroft continued to make their own unit for the Big Ben. The Mighty Antar was now using a supercharged 16.2 litre Rolls-Royce 8-cylinder diesel engine developing 333hp, increased to 363hp by 1964, when the Nubian Major was introduced. This was designed specifically as a high speed airfield crash tender and used the 300hp Cummins V-8 diesel. Considerable rationalization was by now taking place between AEC and Thornycroft with common axles and gearboxes on the Militant and Nubian.

Following the Leyland merger with AEC the two special vehicle producers, Scammell and Thornycroft were linked. Thornycroft then concentrated on making gearboxes for the Group as well as Scammell Trailers, though its special vehicles continued to be produced at Basingstoke until the factory was sold in 1969. Vehicle production then

c. 1970 THORNYCROFT Nubian Major Mark 101 airport engine, GNG

moved to Scammell's factory at Watford, and in 1970 the last new Thornycroft model appeared, an overseas 6 × 4 Bush Tractor based on the AEC 690 Dumptruck, then being marketed by Aveling-Barford.

Scammell continued to build Thornycroft models to special order and the Nubian chassis was produced to carry a number of other manufacturers' fire fighting equipment. However the new rear-engined Nubian chassis introduced in 1977 bears the Scammell name, and this marked the end of Thornycroft even as a brand name within the Leyland group. *OM*

THREE POINT (US) 1919-1924

Three Point Truck Corp.-New York Air Brake Co., Watertown, NY

The Three Point was an odd vehicle with a pivot-type front axle to eliminate frame distortion and torsional "weave". The unit was marketed by Three Point but produced in New York Air Brake's Watertown plant. Other features included a curious radius rod setup for front and rear axles (veed in the manner of the Model T, again in the interests of 3-point suspension) and crudely copied radiator more or less after Rolls-Royce. Flat "pit" or "military type" fenders were other details. The job was assembled, essentially of Buda engines and other stock components. Only one model was offered from 1922 on, the A13 with a rating of 6 tons. Production may have continued as late as 1926. *RJ*

c. 1970 TIAO-JIN NJ-230 1½-ton 4×4 truck, BE

TIAO-JIN (p) T'IAO-CHIN (wg) (Leap Forward) (CHI) 1958 to date

Nanking Motor Vehicle Plant — Nanking, Kisngsu
(Plant Vehicle Code-NJ)

With 1,500 employees, the Nanking plant was one of the first major producers of Chinese trucks and buses.

The Tiao-Jin NJ-130 is a 2.5 ton truck with a 79 hp, 6-cylinder engine providing 82 km/h and is similar in design to the Soviet GAZ-51.

Other models include the 4 × 4 NJ-230 all-terrain 1.5 ton truck with an 88 hp, 6-cylinder engine similar to the GAZ-63, and large buses known as Wei-Xing (Satellite). *BE*

1910 TIDAHOLM charabanc, OMM

TIDAHOLM (S) 1903-1932

Tidaholm Bruk A.B., Tidaholm

Tidaholm started constructing vehicles in 1903, calling their number one the 'Tor I'. It had a 4-cylinder watercooled engine of 26 hp at 800 revs, and could easily carry 5 tons in an unladen weight of 2.7 tons. In 1905 a second vehicle was finished, the 'Tor II'. Being faced with the increasing success of the automobile and the surprising results of their own experiments, the board decided on small scale production. Initially the engines were imported, first 12- and 16 hp Fafnirs from Germany, later, from the same country, Argus units. After a short while, however, the Argus engine was copied, thus making Tidaholm independent from outside suppliers. Particularly keen users of Tidaholm vehicles were the Swedish Army, the postal authorities and various state enterprises. Right from the beginning Tidaholm was very advanced with regard to new designs. For example, gazogene trucks were made as early as 1924; engines burning crude petroleum were manufactured in 1929; and in 1930 the company started production of large truck and bus chassis with double-drive rear bogie. In 1932, the year in which the company finally ceased production, an impressive tandem-axle bus was manufactured, advertised as the largest omnibus in Scandinavia with a length of 10.5 metres and a capacity of 72 passengers. During their 29 years of existence Tidaholm constantly produced all parts, including bus and truck bodies, in their own premises. In the period 1906-1913 some private cars were also manufactured. A number of Tidaholm fire engines were still in service in Sweden in the late sixties, the last remnants of a total vehicle production of some 5,000 units. Near the end of its life Tidaholm had produced some oil engined vehicles fitted with their own power units of Hesselman type. All assets of the company were finally acquired by Scania-Vabis. *JFJK*

1932 TIDAHOLM T6 10-ton truck, OMM

c. 1970 TIENSIN TJ-G20 bus, BE

TIENTSIN (CHI) to date

Tientsin Bus Factory — Tientsin, Hopei
(Plant Vehicle Code—TJ)

This plant, a former repair shop, turns out a series of buses including the 10 passenger TJ-620 with 67 hp, the TJ-644C 23 passenger model using 95 hp, and the TJ-660 41 passenger articulated design with a 110 hp engine and five speeds forward. They also made 4 × 4 jeep type vehicles. *BE*

TIFFIN (US) 1913-1923

Tiffin Wagon Works, Tiffin, Ohio

Early models of the Tiffin were of light to medium capacities (1,200 to 4,000 pounds) and were of a design typical of the period: 4-cylinder side-valve engines, 3-speed gearbox, and double chain drive from a jackshaft. For 1916, this line was supplemented by 1½-, 5- and 6-tonners. These latter models had an option of double chain drive or internal reduction gears running in drums on the rear wheels. Electric starting and lighting were standard features on all but the two largest models. These six models were continued through 1920, but the post-WWI slump reduced the line of trucks to the two largest capacities for the final year of production. *GMN*

TIGER (US) 1914-1915

Automobile Cyclecar Co., Detroit, Mich.

This was a cyclecar fitted with small delivery body. It had a water-cooled, four-cylinder engine of 12 hp, with wheelbase of 7 feet, 2 inches and tread of 3 feet, 8 inches. The price of the delivery van was $300. *GMN*

1914 TILLING-STEVENS bus, NMM

TILLING-STEVENS (GB) 1911-1952

(1) W.A. Stevens Ltd., Maidstone, Kent 1911
(2) Tilling-Stevens Ltd., Maidstone, Kent 1911-1919
(3) Tilling-Stevens Motors Ltd., Maidstone, Kent 1919-1930
(4) T.S. Motors Ltd., Maidstone, Kent 1930-1937
(5) Tilling-Stevens Ltd., Maidstone, Kent 1937-1952

The name of Tilling-Stevens was long synonymous with the manufacture of gas-electric vehicles. The first model, the TTA1, appeared in June 1911 and, like much of the early production, was purchased by Thomas Tilling Ltd. who had participated in the design and had a substantial financial stake in the manufacturing company. The TTA1 was intended basically as a passenger chassis for double-deck bodies and was distinguished by its Renault-style hood with radiator behind the engine. It was joined in 1912 by the more powerful TS4 with conventional radiator, and both models continued in production up to the war. In 1917 manufacture commenced of the TS3, a similar vehicle to the TS4 but with smaller radiator, and this was joined by the forward-control TS7 in 1923. Various other less important gas-electric models included the TS3AX long-wheelbase charabanc of 1921-5 and the small 20-25-seater TS5A of 1925. The TS6 of 1925-8 was a heavier and stronger vehicle than hitherto, and came in both normal and forward-control configuration suitable for single and double-deck bodies. Although, as with most Tilling-Stevens gas-electrics, the majority were built as buses, many later found a renewed life as mobile generating sets with fairground showmen.

Manufacture of vehicles with ordinary clutch and gearbox transmission began in 1919 with two models, the 4-ton TSB3 and 2½-ton TSB4. Sales initially were low compared with those of gas-electrics, but as interest in the latter waned the gear-driven Tilling-Stevens came more into prominence, culminating in the excellent "Express" model (B9A forward-control and B9B normal-control) of 1926. A drop-frame version of the Express, the B10A and B10B of 1927, proved highly popular and sold in large numbers. The demand for gas-electrics dropped significantly in the late twenties, and two new designs of 1929, the TS15A six-wheeler and TS17A four-wheeler, failed to revive it. Surprisingly, Tilling-Stevens showed comparatively little interest in trolleybuses which it marketed only from 1921 to 1926. An interesting hybrid was produced in 1924 for the Tees-side Railless Traction Board, this being a normal TS3A gas-electric bus fitted with trolley booms and a changeover switch to allow it to be used as a trolleybus where overhead wires existed. A similar vehicle, but this time on a converted B10B chassis, was built experimentally in 1931 for export to Turin.

Following disposal by Thomas Tilling Ltd. of its shareholding, the business was reconstituted in 1930 as T.S. Motors Ltd. A significant drop in trade was experienced as Tilling's associated bus companies began to order new vehicles elsewhere. Trade remained at a low ebb throughout the thirties although the acquisition of Vulcan in November 1937 helped to employ factory capacity and gave the company a renewed foothold in the goods vehicle market. An entirely new range of passenger chassis was introduced in 1932 including diesel-engined options employing Gardner 5- and 6-cylinder units. Up to six models were available throughout much of the decade, the ones most usually found being the HA39 with 4-cylinder gasoline engine, the D5L with 5-cylinder Gardner and the very similar J5L which differed only in having a 5-speed gearbox. The whole range was marketed as T.S.M.,

c. 1922 TILLING-STEVENS TS4-PE 30-seater bus, GNG

1931 TILLING-STEVENS TSM 52-seater bus, OMM

and these letters were carried on the radiator in place of the old "Tilling-Stevens" inscription. A remarkably advanced six-wheeler with independent suspension, designed to accommodate an 8-cylinder horizontally-opposed underfloor diesel engine and Maybach-type 7-speed preselector gearbox, was announced in 1937 as the Successor, but it came to nothing.

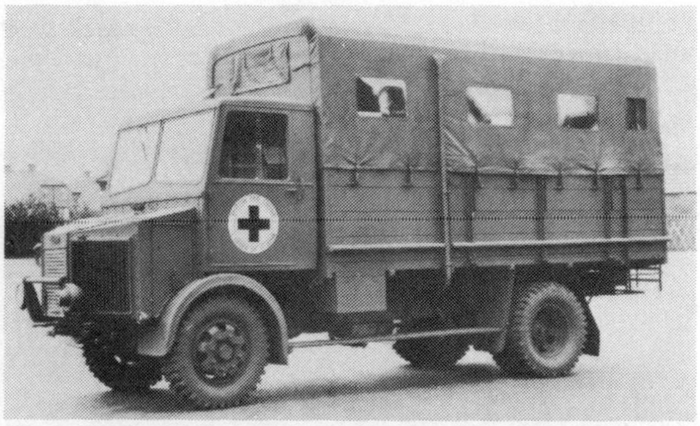

1938 TILLING-STEVENS 3-ton mobile workshop, BHV

The war years saw a revival of gas-electric transmission for military vehicles required as mobile searchlights, and many examples of models TS19 and TS20 with 78 hp gasoline engines of Vulcan origin were built up to 1944. An early post-war battery-powered 5-ton goods model failed to go into production, but the Tilling-Stevens name was revived in a new 1947 range of coach chassis. The K5L and K6L were Gardner-powered models of 5 and 6 cylinders respectively, but much more common was the K6M, a Meadows-engined coach with outstanding road performance. There was also a high-framed Perkins-engined model which sold in small numbers, the L6P, but this gave way in 1950 to the Express Mk. II (designated L4M), an unimpressive lightweight 4-cylinder Meadows-engined coach. This also replaced the heavier range and was Tilling-Steven's last production model. The company was purchased in September 1949 by the Rootes group who discontinued production in 1952. *KCB*

TITAN (i) (DK) 1905

Titan Maskinfabrik, Copenhagen

This was a 3-wheeled electric van whose driver sat above the rear wheel with the 250 kg load ahead of him. It was powered by a 1½ hp motor which drove the rear wheel by chain. *GNG*

TITAN (ii) (US) 1911

Central Motor Co., Detroit, Mich.

The Central Motor Co. was a division of US Motor Co., and the Titan taxi was built on the Brush chassis, including its unusual wood frame and coil springs at all four corners. This diminutive vehicle used a single-cylinder, water-cooled engine with a planetary transmission and double chain drive and its wheelbase was only 6 feet, 8 inches. *GMN*

TITAN (iii) (US) 1916-1917

American Machine Company, Newark, Delaware

The Titan was another unsuccessful steam-powered truck and was made as a 2½-tonner. This Model A chassis used a wheelbase of 12 feet and weighed 4,650 pounds. The two-cylinder engine with 4-inch bore and 5-inch stroke was directly-geared to the Torbensen rear axle. The cost of this chassis was $3,000. One contemporary journal lists this make as late as 1920. *GMN*

TITAN (iv) (US) 1917-c. 1932

(1) Titan Truck & Tractor Co., Milwaukee, Wis.
(2) Titan Truck Co., Milwaukee, Wis.
(3) Titan Truck Service Co., Milwaukee, Wis.

Living up to their name, Titans entered the market as 5 tonners with 4-cylinder engines, Titan's own 4-speed constant-mesh transmissions and internal gear final drive. They had solid cast-steel disc wheels and solid tires. In the early 1920s the Titan range was extended to include lighter models of 2, 2½, 3½ tons, with prices from $3,400 to $5,400, rather above the average. Engines were 4-cylinder Budas. The smallest Titan was the -tonner of 1925. The end of Titan production is uncertain; lists do not carry it beyond 1927, but a Wisconsin parts dealer remembers scrapping several Titans of 1931-32 vintage. *RW*

TITAN (v)(D) 1974 to date

Titan Stahl-und Geratebau GmbH., Berghaupten-Gengenbach

This firm builds special vehicles. On the program are heavy chassis for truck cranes and other purposes. They are available as 6 × 4, 6 × 6, 8 × 4, 8 × 6, 10 × 4, 10 × 6 and 10 × 8 layout. For prime movers, dump trucks and some other special purposes chassis with 4 × 4, 6 × 6 and 8 × 8 layout are on the program. Daimler-Benz engines are used. *HON*

TMC (US) 1975 to date

Transportation Manufacturing Corp.
Roswell, New Mexico

TMC is subsidiary of Greyhound that builds almost all

of the buses required by its parent's U.S. operations, roughly 350 per year. The buses are identical to the current MCI model except for nameplates. TMC has announced that it will build the Canadian Orion bus under license for U.S. customers as well. *MBS*

TODD (GB) 1869-1872

Leonard J. Todd, Leith.

Todd's first road locomotive was a small spring-mounted tractor with 2½" x 4" duplex cylinders reported to have covered 100 miles in 10 hours, but in 1872 he made a large locomotive. Using a locomotive boiler at 150 psi he paired it with double 10" x 10" cylinders. Drive was by gear to a countershaft and from discs on the extremities of the countershaft by side coupling rods to the main driving axle. Solid wooden disc wheels and iron tires were fitted and both axles were sprung. For a while in 1872 Todd ran a steam omnibus between Leith and Edinburgh but was discouraged by legal obstacles. *RAW*

TOLEDO (i) (US) 1901

American Bicycle Co., Toldeo, Ohio

This company made light steam cars and at least one paraffin-fuelled steam wagon with water-tube boiler, horizontal cross-compound engine with piston valves and Stephenson link motion. Final drive was by internal gears, a familiar system on later gas-engined trucks, but rare on steamers. It had a capacity of about 2 tons, and was said to be in daily operation at the company's factory. *GNG*

TOLEDO (ii) (US) 1912-1913

Toledo Motor Truck Co., Toledo, Ohio

This company bought the Rassel Motor Car Co. in 1912, although the subsequent Toledo trucks did not copy the earlier Rassels. The Toledo Model A was a 1-tonner with forward control which had a four-cylinder water-cooled engine along with a three-speed gear-box and double chain drive. It was offered only with a stake body for a price of $1,850. The Model B was a 2-tonner also with a stake body and wheelbase of 10 feet, 10 inches, at $2,600. *GMN*

TOMLINSON (GB) 1947-1961

Tomlinson (Electric Vehicles) Ltd., Minster Lovell, Witney, Oxon

The Tomlinson was aimed at equipping the dairy or bakery roundsman with a powered pram or truck to replace his old manual barrow or pram. Vehicles (pedestrian controlled) were supplied as either chassis or complete with bread van or milk float bodies. Payloads varied in the 10, 15 or 20 cwt bracket with wheelbases from 3ft 9in to 4ft 5in. Some models were also available fitted as internal works trucks.

The conventional roadgoing chassis was the "Goliath" a 10/15cwt, 4ft 4¾in wheelbase machine introduced in 1949 with either milk float or bread van bodywork but this did not appear for very long and the company concentrated on pedestrian controlled types. The general style of vehicles remained unchanged right through to the end of production. *OM*

TORBENSEN (US) 1906-1910

Torbensen Motor Car Co., Bloomfield, NJ

This was a small delivery van which at first used a 3-cylinder, 2-stroke, air-cooled engine, with forward control. It was a ¾-tonner. Later versions used 2-cylinder engines with planetary transmissions and double chaindrive, and

1907 TORBENSEN 1500lb delivery wagon, LIAM

in 1910, wheelbase was 7 feet, 8 inches. Torbensen Motor Car Co. was a subsidiary of the Torbensen Gear Co. of the same city which was a major supplier of axles to the auto industry. *GMN*

TORPEDO (YU) 1972 to date

Tvornica Motora i Motornih Vozila, Rijeka

A general engineering firm established since 1853 and the first producer of diesel engines in Yugoslavia, Torpedo was building a variety of diesel engines, generating sets, agricultural tractors and wheeled loaders, when they entered the automotive field building the Rumanian SR truck and tipper, appropriately powered by a Torpedo air cooled 11O HP diesel engine. A 3-axled half-cab dumper was introduced also in 1973 and is built since then in collaboration with the RZD factory, along with the 5-ton payload truck and tipper chassis. Power for the dumper comes from a Torpedo 210 HP Din diesel engine. *GA*

TOURIST (D) 1907-1920

(1) Tourist Automobil-Werk GmbH., Berlin-Tempelhof 1907-1911

(2) Berliner Automobilfabrik "Torpedo" Georg Beck & Co., Berlin-Tempelhof 1911-1920

The first design featured an open three-wheeled private car. Later it was available with a rear van box. The V-twin air-cooled 7 hp engine was placed in the front, transmission was to the rear wheels by shaft and chains. *HON*

TOWARD (GB) 1897-c.1900

Toward & Co., Newcastle-upon-Tyne

Toward's first steam vehicle was a steam wagonette or small charabanc built in collaboration with Atkinson & Philipson, the Newcastle coach builders in 1897, Meek, one of the partners in Towards, having long had an interest in steam cars. The same year they built a steam van, to carry about a ton, for a Newcastle wholesale chemist in 1897, in which they used their own design of inclined vertical boiler incorporating water tubes across the firebox in conjunction with a duplex cylindered engine having Stephenson link motion. The crankshaft and countershaft, which incorporated the differential, were geared together and final drive was by chain to each rear wheel. In 1899 they built a 3½-ton steam wagon for a Yorkshire iron ore mine.

They also built a compound steam tractor of about 3½ N.H.P. but otherwise seem not to have pursued wagon or

1898 TOWARD PHILIPSON steam van, VCC/GB

tractor building after 1900, although their other business continued and they manufactured boilers, engines and wheels for other makers. *RAW*

TOWER (US) 1915-1923

Tower Motor Truck Company, Greenville, Michigan

Tower trucks were limited to two-tonners with a worm drive through the 1920 model-year. For the last two years of its existence, the line was changed to 2½- and 3½-tonners. These used four-cylinder Continental engines, Fuller gearboxes and Timken worm-drive axles. Wheelbase on the 3½-tonner was 13 feet, 9 inches, and this cost $4,100. *GMN*

1936 TOYOTA G1 1½-ton truck, BHV

1939 TOYOTA 6-wheel bus, FLP

TOYOTA (J) 1935 to date

(1) Toyoda Automatic Loom Works Ltd., Kariya City 1935-1936

(2) Toyota Motor Co. Ltd., Toyota City 1937 to date

Toyota's first commercial vehicle effort was the Kiso Coach, an advanced full-fronted machine powered by an underfloor-mounted Hercules engine; only 12 were made. By contrast, their 30-cwt G.1 truck owed much to contemporary Chevrolet designs, though cab styling suggested a Diamond T; its 3.4-litre 6-cylinder engine developed 65hp, and there were four forward speeds. Its successors, the GB (1938) and KB (1942) were scarcely distinguishable from Chevrolets: over 40,000 were made up to 1944, as well as some half-tonners with 2¼-litre 4-cylinder engines. As early as 1937 a 6-cylinder Toyota diesel was announced, but did not apparently reach series production.

Production of the KB was resumed almost immediately after World War II, but in 1951 this type was superseded by a more substantial truck, the 4-ton BX. At the same time the company made a bid for the light 4 × 4 Jeep market with the BJ, also with the traditional ohv six; this was later given the Land Cruiser designation and was still cataloged in 1975. Both models acquired 3.9-litre, 105hp engines in 1952, while variations on the BX theme included conventional and forward control buses, as well as a fire engine. Also in the range was a car-type light pickup with 995cc 4-cylinder sv engine, which accounted for 3,709 of the 9,600-odd Toyota commercials sold in 1953. In 1958 form it featured a 1½-litre ohv power unit and coil spring ifs, while a wide range of light trucks with 3- or 4-speed synchromesh gearboxes catered for the 10-30-cwt category; the heavier-duty variants, which included the forward control Dyna, had beam front axles.

The BX evolved into the 5-ton FA and DA, the latter with 5.9-litre diesel engine, and Toyota, like Nissan, were supplying local SEATO military requirements with 4 × 4 and 6 × 6 tactical trucks modelled on the American Dodge and GMC. Both versions used the regular 3.9-litre gasoline six. Truck production rose from 71,000 in 1959 to 110,000 in 1960.

This basic range was progressively developed over the ensuing decade, with pickup editions of such private car models as the 790cc flat-twin Publica, the 1½-litre 4-

1975 TOYOTA Dyna 1½-ton truck, Toyota

1975 TOYOTA Landcruiser 1-ton pick-up, Toyota

cylinder Corona, and the 2-litre 6-cylinder Crown, this last being available with Toyoglide automatic transmission. Dynas were offered with hydrovac brakes, and the big trucks were uprated to the 6-ton class, with hypoid final drive, and a choice of 4- or 5-speed synchromesh gearboxes: 2-speed axle options also featured. The big diesel now ran to 6½ litres and 130hp. 1970 saw a new line of light trucks and vans, the forward-control Hi-Ace series with 1.6-litre 4-cylinder gasoline engine, 4-speed all-synchromesh gearbox, and coil ifs; in 1971 it became the first Japanese commercial vehicle to be regularly marketed in Britain. 1975 models were given servo brakes, and in 1977 this type was joined by the smaller Lite Ace on similar lines, with an 80¼-in. wheelbase and the 1.2-litre unit. Also new was a more powerful (4.2 litres, 128hp) gasoline engine for the FA and the Landcruiser, the latter now coming with a choice of two diesels, a 3-litre four and a 3½-litre six. During 1977 Toyota announced their answer to GM's and Ford's Basic Transport Vehicles for emergent countries: this BUV was of semi-forward control type, used the Lite Ace's engine, and could carry an 850kg payload; initially production ws confined to the Philippines. Landcruisers (and in some export markets), the Dyna as well were offered with power front disc brakes.

1978 TOYOTA Hi-Ace 1-ton van, Toyota

In 1978 Toyota offered a comprehensive range of everything save true heavies, the preserve of Hino, an associate company since 1966: Daihatsu joined the group in 1967. At the top were the FA and DA 6-tonners. In the 2-ton bracket were the Dynas with beam front axles; on similar lines, though somewhat lighter, were the Toyo-Ace (forward control) and Stout (normal control). Smaller Toyotas, all with coil ifs and 4-speed all-synchromesh gearboxes, were the Hi-Ace, Lite Ace, Hi-Lux (a car-type pickup) and a delivery van based on the 1.2-litre Corolla sedan. The Landcruiser was continued, but the sole PSV (minibuses apart) was the Coaster, a forward-control 25-seater based on the Dyna and available with air conditioning. A 2-litre ohc gasoline engine was now an option in the Hi-Ace, while all the larger Toyotas could be had with diesel as well as gasoline power. Toyota made 836,438 commercial vehicles in 1977, exporting over 440,000. Manufacture or assembly was being undertaken in fourteen foreign countries: Toyota do Brasil produced their own version of the Landcruiser with a 4-cylinder Mercedes-Benz diesel engine. *MCS*

1923 TRABOLD 2½-ton truck, Victor A. Trabold Sr.

TRABOLD (US) 1911-1932

(1) Trabold Truck Mfg. Co., Johnstown, Pa. 1911-1922
(2) Trabold Motors Co., Johnstown, Pa. 1922-1924
(3) Trabold Motors Co., Ferndale, Pa. 1924-1929
(4) The Trabold Co., Johnstown, Pa. 1929-1932

Adam G. Trabold buit experimental automobiles in 1898 and in 1905 and ran an automobile agency for ten years prior to introducing the Trabold 4-cylinder c.o.e. truck in 1911. Chain drive was used. A range of trucks with the Buda 4-cylinder engine under the hood was introduced in 1913. Bevel gear drive was used in some models from 1915 and worm drive was adopted in 1923. Throughout manufacture Trabold relied on Buda engines. Production exceded 100 trucks per year in the mid-1920s, when 1½-ton and 2½-ton models were offered. After 1929 production was on a custom basis. Some of the last trucks were fitted with the Lycoming 8-cylinder engine and hydraulic four-wheel-brakes. The Trabold Company built truck bodies until 1960. *DJS*

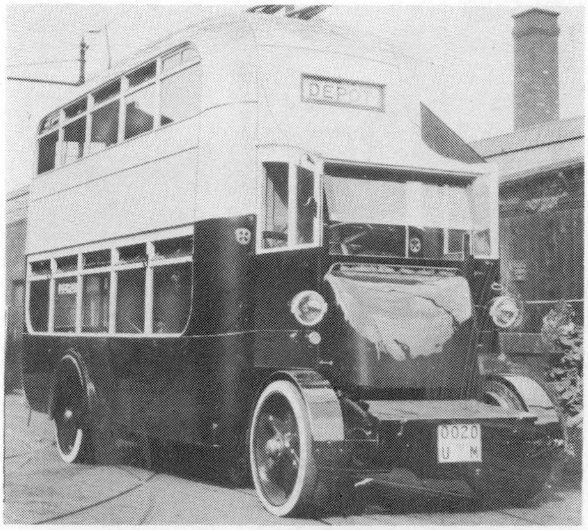

1921 TRACKLESS 64-seater trolleybus, KCB

TRACKLESS (GB) 1921-1924

Trackless Cars Ltd., Leeds, Yorks

This small company produced four trolleybuses in as many years using, it is believed, frames and axles, etc. provided by the Kirstall Forge, the final erection of the chassis being sub-contracted to the Blackburn Aeroplane & Motor Co. Ltd. of Leeds. All four were double-deckers for Leeds Corporation and were built to the unconventional designs of G.A. Bishop for the Electric Traction Company of Leeds. To achieve a very low saloon floor height the vehicles were front wheel driven by two electric motors, each driving a front wheel direct from a motor shaft pinion on the vehicle forecarriage. The whole forecarriage gave the appearance of being added on as an afterthought, and its bizarre appearance was heightened by the front axle which swivelled as the vehicle cornered. None lasted in service after 1925. *OM*

TRADER see Peerless (ii)

TRAFFIC (US) 1918-1929

(1) Traffic Motor Truck Corp., St. Louis, Mo.
(2) Traffic Motors, St. Louis, Mo.

The Traffic was a generally conventional assembled truck with 4-cylinder Continental Red Seal engine, Covert 3-speed gearbox and Russel internal gear final drive. On pre-1925 models an unusual feature was that the frame side members were joined together at front and rear by semi-circular members of the same section channel steel.

The front cross member served as a bumper. Pneumatic tires were extra on earlier models. In 1925 a new Traffic was introduced on which the curved chassis members were abandoned; this had a larger Continental engine of 4,151cc in place of the 3,610cc unit previously used, and a heavier Clark internal gear rear axle. Load capacity was up to 2½ tons, and this was further increased to 3 tons for 1927 because of a stronger frame, although the engine remained unchanged. In its last year, Traffic offered a 2/2½ ton truck with a 6-cylinder engine. *GNG*

1974 TRANSCOACH, MBS

TRANSCOACH (US) 1974 to date

Transcoach Division, Sportscoach Corp., Chatsworth, Calif.

Previously a producer of truck bodies and motor homes, Sportscoach set up a new division and purchased an existing product line, rather than modifying one of its own designs, when the decision was made to enter the small bus market. Gillig Brothers had previously offered its Microcoach on Ford or Dodge chassis of 137, 158½ or 178-inch wheelbase, with a variety of optional seating arrangements accommodating 17 to 27 passengers. It had been produced since 1970. Transcoach made no changes in the design except to offer a built-in wheelchair lift as an extra-cost option and to add an electric brake operated by the battery on the eddy current principle and acting on the driveshaft. This device lengthens the life of the hydraulic brakes, which are needed only below 5mph. In 1975 Transcoach announced an experimental diesel-powered bus with a Detroit Diesel 4-53 engine and placed a prototype in trial service in Oakland. The sample bus had a chassis assembled by Transcoach and equipped with air suspension. On the production-model gasoline-powered buses, the current chassis models used are the Dodge RM-400 or Ford M-500. *MBS*

1948 TRANSICOACH, MBS

TRANSICOACH (US) 1948-1950

Richmond, Indiana

The last revival of C.J. Hug's sectional bus body idea was in 1948. Crown Coach Corp., Los Angeles, had become the western distributor for Wayne, and both Crown and Wayne offered the Hug-designed Transicoach as a low-cost underfloor-engine school bus. Most Transicoaches had Hercules engines and five-speed Fuller transmissions. About 200 were sold. *MBS*

TRANSIT (i) (US) 1902

Steamobile Co., Keene, N.H.

This company made light steam passenger cars under the name Steamobile or Keene Steamobile, and a truck under the name Transit. This had a 6 hp vertical double-acting 2-cylinder engine and single chain drive. The driver sat at the rear, with a container for the load ahead of him. *GNG*

TRANSIT (ii) (US) 1912-1916

(1) Transit Motor Car Co., Louisville, Ky. 1912-1913
(2) Transit Motor Truck Co., Louisville, Ky. 1913-1916

The Transit began as a 3-tonner with a 32 hp engine on a chassis of 12-foot wheelbase, a 3-speed gearbox and double chain drive. The next year (1913), 1-, 2-, 3½- and 5-tonners were built, all with forward control and double chain drive. The 1914 line included a 5-tonner with a dump body as well as 2- and 3½-tonners. For the final two years of production, a 1-tonner also was built. The latter had its engine mounted beneath the floorboards while the others had engines under hoods, with seats both sides of the hoods. Double chain drive was used on all models. *GMN*

1948 TRANSIT (iii) Model 81 bus, MBS

TRANSIT (iii) (US) 1948-1949

Transit Buses, Inc., Dearborn, Mich.

Transit Buses were formed in 1941 as a selling organization for the rear-engine Ford Transit bus (see Ford), but went off on its own at the end of 1947 after disagreements with Ford over the proper sort of change to make in order to meet post-war demands. The company owned Union City Body Co., and that plant was used, starting in the fall of 1947, to produce a new design of 31-passenger bus body. Chassis were built by Checker Cab Manufacturing Co., and Continental engines mounted crosswise at the rear were standard equipment. In the changed economics of the post-war years, many former operators of lightweight buses were unable to afford new vehicles, and the few cities (particularly Detroit) that had earlier pursued small-bus policies were finding that increased labor costs forced a revision of their thinking. Detroit did buy 300 Transits in 1949, but fewer than 200 were sold to other operators in two years, and in January 1950 Transit Buses were sold to Checker Cab (See Checker). *MBS*

TRANSPORETTE (D) 1925-1926

Maschinenfabrik Schwabenthau & Gomann, Berlin

This was a light tri-van with a single driven front wheel. The engine was mounted above the front wheel. *HON*

TRANSPORT (i) (US) 1919-1925

Transport Truck Co., Mt. Pleasant, Mich.

The models built by this manufacturer were typical of the period, beginning with 1-, 1½- and 2-tonners built from off-the-shelf components. Continental and Buda engines. Fuller gearboxes were types of sub-assemblies used. The number of models expanded to six for 1925, the last year of production. *GMN*

TRANSPORT (ii) (GB) 1946-1948

Glover, Webb & Liversidge, London Transport Engineering Ltd.

This design of front wheel drive low loading refuse collector was produced by a company specializing in the construction of refuse collection bodies, and being old

1948 TRANSPORT (ii) moving floor refuse truck, OMM

established bodybuilders of all types.

Of monocoque construction the vehicles had a set back front axle which was both steered and driven. Power was supplied by a Meadows 4-cyl. gasoline engine driving through a David Brown gearbox to a Moss front axle, Rzeppa constant velocity joints being used for the drive line and outer ends of the driving axle. Bodywork consisted of a bulk refuse body with a Transport moving floor for discharge without tipping. *OM*

TRANSPORT TRACTOR (US) 1915-1917

Transport Tractor Co. Inc., Long Island City, N.Y.

This make was somewhat unusual in that their only product was a tractor to haul trailers of 5-ton payloads. The driver sat over the 25 hp 4-cylinder engine, and the tractor had a 3-speed transmission and worm final drive. It had an exceptionally low bottom gear ratio of 45.8:1. *GNG*

TRAYLOR (US) 1920-1928

Traylor Engineering & Manufacturing Co., Allentown, Pa.

The Traylor line of trucks began with 1¼-, 2-, 3- and 4-tonners typically assembled from standardized parts, including 4-cylinder Buda engines, Brown-Lipe 3- and 4-speed gearboxes and Sheldon worm-drive rear axles. Beginning in 1925, the models were trimmed to just 1-, 1½-, 3- and 5-tonners, which models were maintained until the end in 1928. *GMN*

TREKKA (NZ) 1966-1973

Motor Lines (Bodies) Ltd., Otahuhu, Auckland

A product of a body building company, the Trekka was a very successful vehicle in combining the utilitarian body of a jeep-type vehicle with rear wheel drive only and a small capacity engine, for use in everyday city and light off-road work. The all-metal body was much like a Land Rover;s in general appearance, having eight variants, canvas top, fiber glass hard top, truck cab, station wagon, etc., while mechanical components were of Skoda origin. A 1.2 litre, 4-cylinder gasoline engine developing 47 hp and independent half axles of swinging design, a Skoda charactistics, were of particular interest. Trekka was

1967 TREKKA ½-ton utility vehicle, OMM

exported to many Asian countries, while an assembly line was also developed in Surabaja, Indonesia in 1971, but the whole project collapsed a couple of years later. *GA*

TRIANGLE (US) 1917-1924

Triangle Motor Truck Co., St. Johns, Mich.

The first Triangle was a 1½-tonner on a wheelbase of 12 feet, had a Waukesha 4-cylinder engine and a 3-speed gearbox. This model was continued through 1924 with the addition of a 2½-tonner in 1920 which had a Rutenber engine and 4-speed gearbox by Fuller. A 1-tonner was added in 1922 which used a Herschell-Spillman engine, along with a 2½-tonner. This line of four models was continued into 1924. *GMN*

1936 TRIANGEL fire engine, OMM

TRIANGEL (DK) 1918-1950

Die Forenede Automobilfabriker A/S, Odense

This company was the result of the merger of three of the most renowned Danish car manufacturers: Thrige, Anglo-Dane and Jan. The inspiring mind behind this merger was Thomas B. Thrige, who had founded his own car works in 1909. After the merger the new company decided to concentrate on the production of commercial vehicles, which were to be sold under the name Triangel, thus being a permanent memory of the three founders. Initially a large part of the components used were machined in the Odense factory, such as the very

1930 TRIANGEL 4-ton truck, JFJK

interesting four-in-line monobloc 50 hp engine with alloy pistons. But gradually Triangel became more and more an assembled make, concentrating particularly on the use of American truck parts. White & Poppe, Continental, Hercules engines were used, though some models had French Ballot engines.

Triangel never manufactured really heavy vehicles: payloads ranged between two and five tons. The Triangel Mignon, for example, manufactured in the mid-twenties, could carry 2½ tons. The T62 of 1938, the heaviest Triangel vehicle produced during the prewar years, had a capacity of five tons. Based on the T35 3-tonner of 1936 was a fleet of military vehicles for the Danish Army, about the only vehicles Triangel ever delivered to them.

Already as early as 1930 Triangel had produced its first forward-control vehicle, the 'Special'. Some six years later they came with their first diesel-engined models, using initially American Hercules diesels, but later the Danish-built Bur-Wain engine. In 1941 one of the last new Triangel models was launched, the T50X, payload 4½ tons, fitted with a really neat cab. After World War II for some years forward control trucks were produced, but not for long: soon truck production was discontinued and the Forenede Automobilfabriker concentrated on the import of Austin cars and trucks. *JFJK*

1907 TRIBELHORN electric hotel bus, FH

TRIBELHORN (CH) 1902-1919
(1) A. Tribelhorn & Co., Feldbach (1902-1916)
(2) A. Tribelhorn & Co., AG., Feldbach (1917-1918)
(3) A. Tribelhorn AG., Zurich-Altstetten (1918-1919)

Soon after having founded the company, Tribelhorn announced a 5-ton truck. In 1907 the company displayed, apart from light passenger cars with electric-motors a similarly powered small omnibus. The batteries had to be recharged after about 30 miles. The motor of 10/30 hp allowed a top speed of 12 mph. Amazingly this bus was still in daily use a few years ago in Lucerne for one of the traditional hotels.

c. 1917 TRIBELHORN 5-ton electric truck, FH

Electric-trucks of various sizes with engines of 6 to 40 hp and payload of 2 cwt to 5 tons were built. This type of commercial vehicle was much favored by the Swiss postal services and town administrations. During the first World War there was a definite need for a small and handy delivery van in the Swiss postal services and Tribelhorn

1919 TRIBELHORN 500kg electric van, FH

neatly filled this requirement with a new battery-powered electric three-wheeler.

In order to increase range and climbing performance Tribelhorn developed a combined powerplant with a gasoline engine coupled to a generator which was patented in many countries.

In 1918 six models of commercial vehicles were offered. The lightest was the three-wheeler called "Tank electrique". Model 4 was a delivery van with payload of about 10 cwt, pneumatic tires and a conventional hood. Then followed four models with forward control, payloads of 1 to 5 tons and final drive by chains. One year later the company was reformed and continued its activity under the name E.F.A.G. *FH*

TRI-KON (GB) 1936

Grandex Motor Tri-Kons Ltd., St. Albans, Herts.

This was a motorcycle-based 3-wheeler powered by a 247 cc 2-stroke Villiers engine, with a 3-speed Burman gearbox and chain drive to the single rear wheel. The front wheels, which were smaller than the rear one, were mounted in cycle-type forks, and the load-carrying portion had an Accles & Pollock tubular frame. Steering was by handlebar, and the price of the Tri-Kon was a very modest £52 complete. *GNG*

TRIMAK (E) 1959-1972

(1) Trimak SAE, Madrid 1959-1968
(2) Trimacar SAE, Sabadell, Barcelona 1968-1972

The Trimak was the best-known and longest-lived of the many makes of Spanish 3-wheeler, sales exceeding 2,500 during the mid-1960s which was the company's best period. It was more car-like than many of its contemporaries, having wheel steering and shaft drive to a differential, and also it was the only Spanish 3-wheeler to have a heater in the cabin. The Trimak was powered by a 250cc Lew engine built under Polish license, though a few of the last models had small diesel engines. Load capacity was 700 kgs, and Trimaks were made as van, pickups and light refuse vehicles. *JCG*

1965 TRIMAK Lew 700kg refuse truck, GNG

TRIRO (D) 1950-1953

Triro-Werke, Mockmuhl

A tri-van was manufactured by this firm. It had one driven front wheel and used a 250cc Triumph two-stroke engine. Payload capacity was ½ ton. *HON*

TRITOMOBIL (D) 1926-1930

Bruno V. Festenberg-Pakisch, Hamburg

This was a very unconventional tri-van. There was one single rear wheel and a rear driver's seat. The engine was mounted under the box driving the left front wheel. Further details are not available. *HON*

TRITRACTOR (GB) 1925

Tritractor Ltd., London E.C. 2

This was a most unusual short-wheelbase tipper of 3-wheel configuration, although in fact there were two small wheels at the front. The prototype, powered by a Continental engine, was driven from the rear, with the load ahead of the driver, but the production model was revised to locate the driver in a one-man cab at the front over the engine. This was now an A.E.C. unit, and other components by this firm including gearbox and radiator were also incorporated. Drive was by shaft to the rear wheels. The Tritractor could carry a 6½-ton load, and had a turning circle of only 23 feet. *GNG*

TRIUMPH (i) (US) 1909-1912

Triumph Motor Car Co., Chicago, Ill.

This passenger car maker launched a light delivery van powered by a 16/18 hp horizontally-opposed twin Monarch engine located under the seat, with planetary transmission and double chain drive. Air- or water-cooling was available to choice, and prices ran from $650 to $850 according to body style and engine. *GNG*

1963 TRIUMPH (ii) Courier ½-ton van, NMM

TRIUMPH (ii) (GB) 1932-1935: 1962-1965

Triumph Motor Co. Ltd., Coventry, Warwickshire

Between 1932 and 1935 Triumph made a few car-based light vans with hydraulic brakes and worm drive. The 5-cwt was based on the 832cc Super 7 (with 1931 front-end sheet metal), while the 8-cwt derived from the Ten with 1,122cc ioe Coventry-Climax engine. A slightly better seller was the 1962 5-cwt Courier, a commercial edition of the 1,147cc Herald 1200 with all independent springing. A price nearly £150 higher than Ford's corresponding model can hardly, however, have helped. *MCS*

1963 TRIVAN 1-ton 3-wheel truck, DJS

TRIVAN (US) 1962-1964

Roustabout Co., Frackville, Pa.

The Trivan, successor to the Roustabout, was a 3-wheeler of ½-ton capacity. It was powered by a Kohler 32 hp 2-cylinder air-cooled engine which drove through a 3-speed transmission to the single rear wheel. A steel tube frame was used, with air-bag suspension. Production totaled 150 trucks. *DJS*

TRIVER (E) 1952-1960

Construcciones Acorazadas S.A., Bilbao

This company made delivery tricycles powered by 125 and 175cc engines, and also light vans based on their Cervato cars. These were 4-wheelers with close-mounted rear wheels. *JCG*

TROJAN (i) (US) 1914-1920

(1) Toledo Carriage Woodwork Co., Toledo, Ohio 1914-1915
(2) Commercial Truck Co., Cleveland, Ohio 1916-1920

This company began with a light truck for 1,500 lb. loads, and added in 1916 a 2,000 lb. model. Both had 4-cylinder engines and cost between $1,400 and $1,600. *GNG*

TROJAN(ii) (GB) 1923-1965

(1) Leyland Motors Ltd., Kingston upon Thames, Surrey 1923-1928
(2) Trojan Ltd., Croydon, Surrey 1928-1965

Leslie Hounsfield's Trojan Utility Car went into production in 1922 at Leyland's Kingston works, a 7-cwt van following a year later. The Trojan featured a underfloor-mounted 1½-litre horizontal square-4 2-stroke water-cooled engine with paired combustion chambers. This drove via a 2-speed epicyclic gearbox and roller chain to a differentialless back axle. Other features were the punt-type frame, cockpit-mounted mechanical starter, cantilever springs, and solid tires: pneumatics remained an extra on commercial models at least until 1932. The hood housed only the fuel tank and carburetor. For all the modest output of 10 hp, the engine's flat power curve made it ideal for commercial work, and major customers were Brooke Bond Tea (who took some 5,000 assorted Trojans over a quarter of a century), the R.A.F., and the G.P.O. Though

1924 TROJAN (ii) ¼-ton van, NMM

the basic van persisted without change into 1933, there were numerous sub-variants, including a taxicab for Japan, a 12/15-cwt military 6 × 4 with six forward speeds (1926) and a bigger-capacity model with semi-elliptic rear suspension (1927). In 1928 production was transferred to Trojan's own works near Croydon Airport, where it was to remain until the end.

Friction differentials made their appearance on the 10-cwt Victory and 12-cwt Atlas of 1931; the latter also had an electric starter, three forward speeds, and an automatic clutch. The 1933 7/10-cwt Lightweight featured preselection and a worm-drive back axle, this latter featuring persisting on some Trojan models until 1938, though it was seldom encountered. Forward control vans were 1935's principal novelty, new for 1936 being the Lowdall, a 25-cwt type based on the 15 hp Mastra car and sharing that machine's rear-mounted 2.2-litre 6-cylinder engine and synchromesh gearbox. It did not progress beyond the mockup stage, and that October Trojan dropped their private car program in order to concentrate on light commercials.

1949 TROJAN (ii) ¾-ton van, OMM

The post-war 15-cwt Trojan had little in common with earlier types, its 2-stroke 4-cylinder engine apart, and even this had its cylinders set in a 90-degree V and lived under a frontal hood. The drive line was conventional, with single-plate clutch, 3-speed synchromesh gearbox, and hypoid rear axle. On all but the earliest ones, brakes were hydraulic, and by 1950 Trojans were being exported to nine countries. There was even a short-lived Electrojan with 6 hp series-wound motor and car-type controls, but this met with no demand and only about a dozen were sold, between 1951 and 1953. As early as 1952 there was a bigger 20/25-cwt Trojan powered by the 2.4-litre Perkins P3 diesel, and by 1957 this had supplanted the gas-engined types. The range now embraced pickups, 13/20-seater light buses, and personnel carriers, and light artics.

1957 TROJAN (ii) 1-ton van OMM

1960 TROJAN (ii) 13-seater coach, NMM

Also new that year was another forward-control model, which evolved into the staple 1959 type with trailing-arm ifs, wrapround windshield, and composite steel and fiberglass bodies. It used the 42 hp Perkins 4/99 engine. In 1959 Trojan merged with Lambretta Concessionaires Ltd., and scooters became the group's dominant interest, though the truck line survived into the summer of 1964. Since 1962 Trojan had been building the German Heinkel cabin scooter with 198cc ohv engine, and this could be had as a miniature parcel car; it outlived the true Trojans by only a year. The company's subsequent activities involved sports and racing cars, an astonishing volte face for a factory whose original objective had been utilitarian transport. *MCS*

TROJAN (iii) (US) 1937-1940
Trojan Truck Mfg. Co., Los Angeles, Calif.

Like their rivals Maxi and Knuckey, Trojan made outsize dump trucks for strip mining and similar purposes. They were powered by a 190 hp Caterpillar V-8 engine normally intended as a stationary unit, driving through a conventional sliding gear transmission plus an auxiliary offering a 40% overdrive and 50% underdrive ratio. Both boxes provided 9 forward speeds and 3 reverse. Final drive to the dual bogie was by central shaft to sprockets on the wheels of both axles. Payload of the 55cu yd. body was over 70 tons. The frame consisted of no fewer than four channel sections nested inside each other for a laminated side rail 12 in. deep. *RJ*

TRUMBULL (US) 1914-1916
Trumbull Motor Car Co., Bridgeport, Conn.

The Trumbull was one of the more popular and better-designed light cars of the period and also offered a ¼-tonner on the passenger car chassis. This used a 4-cylinder engine, a 3-speed gearbox and shaft-drive on wheelbase of 6 feet, 8 inches. Its price was $395. *GMN*

TSINGHUA (CHI) to date
Tsinghua University Machine Shop, Tsinghua, nr. Peking

Cab-over-engine trucks of about 2 tons, built by student workers in a plant associated with the University. *BE*

T.S.M. see Tilling-Stevens

TSUBASA see Daihatsu

TSUKUBA (J) 1934-1943
Tokyo Automobile Manufacturing Co. Ltd., Tokyo

More advanced than the contemporary Datsun or Ohta, the Tsukuba light car had a 736cc V-4 engine and worm drive to the front wheels. The hood and Renault-like radiator grille were of alligator type. Most of the 470 vehicles built carried light commercial bodywork. *MCS*

TUBAUTO see M G T

TUBUS (E) 1940-1952
La Hispano de Fuente En Segures SA, Castellon de la Plana

This company which had operated buses for many years went into manufacture because of the shortage of vehicles owing to the Civil War. Their first product used a Bedford chassis, but later they made chassis and bodies, only buying out engines which came from well-known firms such as A.E.C., Cummins and Perkins. *JCG*

TUGGER (GB) 1930
Arthur Stewart Auto Services Ltd., London S.W. 1

The Tugger was a front-wheel-drive 5-cwt van using a reversed Austin Seven engine and gearbox, with a Tracta front axle. The designer was J. Budge who had formerly been with Standard. Planned selling price was £110, but it never progressed beyond the prototype stage. *GNG*

TULSA (US) 1913-1916
Tulsa Automobile & Manufacturing Co., Tulsa, Okla.

The Tulsa was made as ¾-, 1- and 1½-tonners. One reference claims this company was formed from Harmon Motor Truck Co. of Chicago and Pioneer Automobile Co. of Oklahoma City, Okla., in 1912. Complete information has not been found. *GMN*

TURBINE (US) 1904
Turbine Electric Truck Co., New York, N.Y.

The electrical power for this sturdy and possibly unique truck was supplied from a generator driven by a steam engine. A 24 hp Roberts water tube boiler supplied the steam. Electrical power was applied to General Electric motors geared to the rear axle. Axles were pivoted at the center with steel guide plates to maintain wheel alignment under spring deflection. This monster weighed 6 tons and was on a wheelbase of 9 feet, 5 inches with track of 6 feet. With steel tires and enclosed cab with condensor above, it had an appearance similar to a railway locomotive. It was claimed that coal consumption was 40 lbs./hr. *GMN*

TURGAN (F) 1900-c.1907
Turgan, Foy et Cie, Levallois-Perret, Seine

Turgan began making cars in 1899, and soon afterwards turned to commercials. A steam bus was entered in the Paris Commercial Vehicle Trials in October 1900. By 1905 two models of steam truck were made, with load capacities of 3 and 6 tons. They used a double drum water tube boiler placed in front of the driver and fired with coal. Separate compound engines were used for each rear wheel.

1906 TURGAN 34-seater Paris bus, NMM

The engines were mounted above the chassis under the driver's seat from which each wheel was driven by a long roller chain. The wagons were single speed.

In 1905 a 24 hp 4-cylinder gas chassis was also made, for goods or passenger work. One Turgan double-decker bus ran briefly in London at this period. In 1907 there was a forward-control 4-ton truck with round Solex radiator and double chain drive. *RAW/GNG*

TURNER (GB) 1954-1956
Turner Manufacturing Co. Ltd., Wolverhampton

During Turner's long period of car manufacture (1902-1930), their only commercial vehicles had been Turner-

1907 TURNER-MIESSE 1½-tone steam truck, NMM

1956 TURNER 1½-ton 4×4 pick-up, BHV

Miesse steamers. After World War II, however, they made two forays into this field. The first of these was the ultra-light L.D.V. produced by an associate company, but more interesting was the fwd prototype exhibited at the 1954 London Show, with Whitson minibus body. Its Turner-built 1.4-litre Roots-blown 2-stroke twin-cylinder List diesel engine, 4-speed David Brown gearbox, and hypoid axle were mounted as a quick-detachable unit. 10/12-cwt load carrying versions were planned, but never materialized. Turner, however, continued to experiment, and in 1956 they showed two further types: a milk delivery van with Divco-like bodywork, irs, and 4-speed Manumatic gearbox, and a 4 × 4 pickup with the 3-cylinder version of the List diesel. *MCS*

TURNER-MIESSE (GB) 1906-1913

Turners Motor Manufacturing Co. Ltd., Wolverhampton, Staffs

Turner were licensees of the Miesse (B) patents, making steam cars and light steam wagons (for loads about 30-cwt) following the practice of the patentees. The Turner boiler was a paraffin fired vertical, with a central pot, into the shell of which coiled water tubes were set, the horizontal coils surrounding the pot within an external insulated casing. The engine was a horizontal three-cylinder single acting with mushroom inlet and exhaust valves, operated by twin camshafts and pushrods, the whole engine closely following motor practice and dispensing with connecting rods and crossheads. The arrangement included two speeds, counter-shaft differential and twin chain drive. rubber tires were standard.

Relatively few Turners were made and 1909 is believed to mark the end of this particular manufacture though other vehicle activities of the company continued and steam wagons were nominally available until 1913. It is believed that some car chassis made at Wolverhampton may have been used as the basis for tradesmen's delivery vans.

Exports included a batch of steam charabancs for Arabia in 1909 and 30-cwt flat goods vehicles for Japan. *RAW*

TUTTLE (US) 1913-1914

Tuttle Motor Co., Caneastota, N.Y.

This commercial was made only as a 1½-tonner. It used a 4-cylinder Hazard engine mounted under a hood. It was an assembled affair with Sheldon axles, Sheldon cast spoke wheels and solid rubber tires. Final drive was worm gear and the wheelbase of the lone model was 10 feet, 10 inches. *GMN*

T.V. (R) 1960 to date

Uzina Autobuzul Tudon Vladiminescu, Bucharest

Originally a producer of medium class buses and trolleybuses using SR built components, TV soon started building light commercials in van, pick-up and minibus versions. Built along the Soviet UAZ vehicle lines, which they resembled in general, TV models are heavy looking and are powered by the same 70hp 4-cylinder gasoline engine that powers the ARO utility vehicle and which originated in the Soviet GAZ factory. TV shares with ARO the rest of its components also, as gearbox, axles,

1975 TV 11-R 1-ton van, MSH

etc. A facelift of the range took place in 1969 along with the introduction of 4 × 4 variants of all models produced, while the 1971 range was redesigned and modernized with a lower and wider Western-style appearance. In the meantime buses were regularly built along with the light commercials. Though the first models built since the early 60s were simple and conservative in construction and appearance, current models are built in 3 capacities and have a forward entrance body with power derived from the SR built V8 gasoline engine develops 140hp and placed at the rear of the body. TV trolley-bus production ceased at the end of 1975. *GA*

T.V.W. (GB) 1958-1962

Transport Vehicles (Warrington) Ltd., Warrington, Lancs.

A varied range of haulage and tipping vehicles produced by a company set up to carry on the production of trucks when the Sentinel diesel vehicle range came to an end. Much of the Sentinel parts stock was obtained and early designs bore a close resemblance to their parentage but the Sentinel power unit and underslung position were not continued with. Proprietary engines such as Rootes TS3

1958 TVW 15-ton 6-wheel truck, OMM

two-stroke, Leyland and Meadows were used in the normal front of chassis position. Models included 4-, 6- and 8-wheelers, also twin steering 6-wheelers. As the old Sentinel cabs were used up so a new design of cab appeared and two models were advertised, a 4-wheeler with the TS3 but using a Meadows gearbox, and an 8-wheeler employing the Gardner 6LW and DB main and auxiliary gearboxes. Many of the vehicles produced were tippers with light alloy bodywork for coal transport. *OM*

TWIN CITY (i) (US) 1917-1922

(1) Twin City Four Wheel Drive Co., St. Paul, Minn.
(2) Four Wheel Drive Mfg. Co., Minneapolis, Minn.

The Twin City truck was made in two factories simultaneously, in the twin cities of Minneapolis and St. Paul which are separated only by the Mississippi river. The 4 × 4 design was the work of J.L. Ware who had made a truck of his own name in St. Paul from 1912 to 1915. Two models were made, a 2-tonner and a 5-tonner, both with 4-cylinder engines and 3-speed gearboxes. The 1917 model had four wheel brakes. These trucks should not be confused with the Twin City (ii) listed below, or with the Twin City made by F.R. Brasie. *GNG*

1925 TWIN CITY (ii) Model DW 25-seater coach, MHS

TWIN CITY (ii) (US) 1918-1929

Minneapolis Steel & Machinery Co., Minneapolis, Minn.

This company was best-known for its agricultural tractors, and was succeeded by the Minneapolis-Moline tractor company. In 1918 a line of conventional shaft-drive trucks of 2- and 3-½-ton capacity were introduced, and these were joined in the 1920s by buses. The best known was the Model DW introduced in 1925. This was a typical low-built parlor coach of the period, with 60hp engine, seats for 25 passengers and air springs at the front. *GNG*

TWIN COACH (US) 1927-1953

Twin Coach Co., Kent, Ohio

William B. and Frank R. Fageol formed the Twin Coach Co. in 1927 to produce and market a 40-passenger dual-engine bus principally intended for heavy-duty city transit service, but also made in deluxe and parlor versions. Prior to that time they had been employed by

1927 TWIN COACH Model 40 40-seater bus, MBS

ACF, which was not interested in their dual engine idea. The Twin Coach plant at Kent was acquired from the Thomart Motor Co. by the Fageols in 1925. Construction of Fageol buses at this location lasted until the sale to ACF in 1926; the plant was again acquired by the Fageol brothers in 1927 (see ACF; Fageol).

The original Twin Coach, one-third larger than the biggest single-deckers then on the market, was a great success and resulted in all other large builders of U.S. buses enclosing their engines within the bodywork by 1933. Originally equipped with 4-cylinder Waukesha motors, the Twin Coach changed quite early to Hercules engines when Waukesha would not make requested modifications. Hercules engines were used in all Twins from 1928 to 1943.

Although the Twin Coach name was retained, smaller buses added to the line beginning in 1929 had a single motor conventionally placed at the front (with forward control of course). Four experimental streetcars were built, and small railbuses and railroad maintenance-of-way vehicles were produced in limited numbers. Delivery trucks, both battery and gasoline-powered, with front as well as rear wheel drive, were constructed from 1929 to 1936, when this operation was sold to Continental-Divco (see Divco).

1931 TWIN COACH 1-ton delivery van, MBS

The dual-motor buses, by then known as model 40, and the front-engine styles with seating capacities between 17 and 20, were superseded in 1934-36 by a line of rear-engine buses. With modifications these sold well through the late 1930's and up until 1943, when bus production was suspended because of the war. The smaller types were interesting because the engine was over the rear axle, instead of behind it, and the drive shaft therefore pointed downward instead of forward. Torsion bars replaced leaf spring suspension in 1939.

In 1935 Twin Coach built and delivered the first diesel bus ever built as such in the U.S., and about 300 large diesel-electrics (plus a smaller number of gas-electrics) were constructed thereafter. Most of these were used in New York City. The heavy and costly electric drive was never superseded in Twin diesels by anything better. In 1938 the Super Twin made its debut; in its original form this was a four-axle 56-passenger diesel-electric bus, hinged vertically in the center but not truly articulated. Four samples were built and tested, the last two being three-axle versions, but the Super Twin failed to catch on. A trolley-coach version of the original model 40 had been produced from 1928 to 1934, and new trolley-coaches in the style of the rear-engine buses were made in 40- and 44-passenger styles from 1936 to 1942.

1938 TWIN COACH Model 27-R 27/29-seater bus, MBS

During the wartime hiatus Twin Coach made control cabins for U.S. Navy blimps and tail assemblies for Curtiss-Wright airplanes at Kent, and also operated a government owned aircraft modification plant at Buffalo, New York. This factory was purchased in 1946 and converted into a second bus assembly plant. Canadian customers were served from a third plant at Fort Erie, Ontario, from 1948 to 1951.

The postwar Twin Coach bus was completely new, with styling by Dwight Austin. Its most distinctive feature was a six-piece windshield entirely of flat glass, versions of which are used today by all three major U.S. makers of transit buses. A new engine plant in Kent was used to produce a 6-cylinder gasoline motor of high compression and light weight. In the postwar Twin, this engine was turned on its side beneath the floor to gain the benefits of good weight distribution and minimal loss of power in transmission. It was coupled to a Spicer torque converter, wartime production of these transmissions for military vehicles having greatly speeded their development into

1947 TWIN COACH Model 41-S 41-seater bus, MBS

reliable and useful devices. The larger models of postwar Twins, the 41- and 44-passenger versions, were originally intended to have dual engines, but only the first few 44-passenger buses were actually built in this way.

In turning away from heavy and expensive diesel motors, but considering the sale of dual-engine buses, Twin Coach banked on a postwar return to prewar transit

1938 TWIN COACH Model 58-GDE 58-seater diesel-electric bus, MBS

operating conditions. Instead, labor and material costs skyrocketed; simple and cheap maintenance became the industry's demand as the great postwar growth of private automobile travel caused sharpe declines in transit use. Ambitious plans to reintroduce the Super Twin, trolley-coaches, and over-the-road coaches were shelved. Only two orders for Super Twins and two for trlley-coaches were filled in the postwar years. 1948 was Twin's last good year, for by that time many older buses retained for service during the war years had largely been replaced, and customers were buying fewer buses as well as being more selective in their purchases. Diesel power was on the rise, and Twin's gamble had failed.

In 1950, attempting to boost sagging sales, Twin Coach introduced an engine modification that permitted use of liquefied petroleum gas, commonly called "propane" though actually a mixture. At the time, propane was cheap and plentiful; several transit operators in the midwestern states adopted the system and bought numerous Twins while converting others to propane (most notably Chicago). The phenomenon was short-lived. In 1953, Twin sold its bus manufacturing business to Flxible and also sold part of the original Kent plant. The engine factory stayed in business supplying motors for buses and trucks of other manufacturers, while the Buffalo factory had been turned back into an airplane component plant. Highway Products Co. (qv) later acquired the engine plant at Kent, and in 1968 introduced a small bus using the Twin Coach name but having no other link with the former firm. Total Twin Coach bus production was approximately 14,700 vehicles (plus trucks of an unknown quantity in the 1930's), divided as follows: dual-motor and front-engine designs of 1927 to 1936, about 2,700; rear-engine buses of 1934 to 1943, about 6,200; and postwar buses, about 5,800. *MBS*

TWISTER DRAGON WAGON (US) 1972 to date

Lockheed Missiles and Space Co. Inc., Sunnyvale, Calif.

This is one of a group of extraordinary all-wheel-drive vehicles developed for on/off highway use by a subsidiary of the Lockheed Aircraft Corp. It is a forward-control 8 × 8 truck which is articulated between the front and rear pairs of axles, the rear part being able to roll as well as yaw. It is powered by a Caterpillar 1160 225hp diesel engine driving through an Allis 6-speed transmission with a 2-speed transfer case to a manually-selected choice of drive on the rear four, or all eight wheels. Rockwell-Standard tandem bogies and high-traction differentials are used, and the 6-rod independent walking beam type suspension is also by Rockwell-Standard. Air brakes are used on all four axles, with a disc parking brake on the drive train.

1971 TWISTER DRAGON WAGON 8×8 truck, Lockheed

The Dragon Wagon has a top speed of 55mph on the highway and can climb a 60% gradient and traverse a side slope of 40%. Load capacity is 8 to 15 tons according to the difficulty of the terrain. Development began in 1972 and commercial production in March 1974. *RW*

TWYFORD (US) 1905-1906

Twyford Motorcar Co., Brookville, Pa.

In addition to its four-wheel-drive automobiles, Twyford listed an 8hp delivery truck in 1905 and a 16hp truck in 1906. In addition, Twyford listed 6-, 10-, and 15-passenger buses in 1906. All Twyford vehicles had 2-cylinder vertical engines. The trucks may have existed as prototypes but no buses were built. *DJS*

1969 UAZ-452 800kg 4×4 van, OMM

1975 UAZ-469 4×4 utility vehicle, MSH

UAZ SU 1957 to date

Ulyanovsk Automobile Plant, Ulyanovsk

As the large Molotov Works at Gorky began to show signs of age, the UAZ plant was constructed to take over some of its production.

The GAZ/UAZ-69 4 × 4 field car ultimately gave way to the more modern UAZ-469 in the new factory. It, too, has been improved since introduction and is currently powered by a 4-cylinder, in-line engine of 79 hp providing over 100 km/h. It will seat up to seven, or two plus cargo.

Cab-over-engine light trucks were added including the 0.8-ton UAZ-450D, a 4 × 4 with a 65 hp 4-cylinder engine. Ambulance, van and bus models were also built on this chassis. These were joined by a 4 × 2 series 451 of similar styling.

The current 4 × 4 series is now built as the 452 with power increased to 80 hp. *BE*

U.D. see Minsei

U D P X see Prunel

UERDINGEN (D) 1930-1958

Waggonfabrik Uerdingen A.G., Krefeld-Uerdingen; Dusseldorf

This specialist firm in railroad coachbuilding was engaged in construction of the first modern trolley-bus in Germany, which was put into operation in 1930 in Mettmann (Rhineland). Krupp components were used. In 1932 the first chassis-less trolley-bus was produced for Idar-Tiefenstein. The firm carried on development of chassis-less trolley-buses and in 1949 a new range was presented using Henschel components and a VW auxiliary engine driving a generator to permit driving without wire for short distances. Also chassis-less buses and articulated buses were built during the fifties, mainly with Bussing engines and components. When the demand for trolley-buses diminished production was given up. *HON*

ULTIMATE (US) 1919-1925

Vreeland Motor Co., Inc., Hillside. N.J.

The Ultimate was a conventional assembled truck powered by two sizes of Buda 4-cylinder engine, a 25.8 hp in the 2-ton Model A and a 28.9 hp in the 3-ton Model B. There were also two models of bus chassis, the 25-seater AJL and the 30-seater BU. Both had Westinghouse electric lighting and starting sets, unlike the trucks which relied on hand starting. The larger bus chassis was the only Ultimate made for the last two years of production. *GNG*

UNIC (F) 1905 to date

(1) Societe des Anciens Etablissements Georges Richard, Puteaux, Seine 1905-1914
(2) SA des Automobiles Unic, Puteaux, Seine 1914-1958
(3) SA Unic (Simca Industries), Puteaux, Seine 1958-1966
(4) Fiat France SA, Division Vehicules Industriels, Suresnes and Trappes 1966-1974
(5) Unic-Fiat SA, Trappes 1975 to date

After the divorce from Brasier, Georges Richard continued the manufacture of cars under the Unic name, adopted in view of his initial one-model policy. This first Unic was a 10/12 hp T-head twin with lt magneto ignition, cone clutch, 3-speed gearbox and shaft drive, which became very popular as a taxi in many European countries; 2,500 were in service in London alone by 1911. By 1908 the 10/12 had acquired a ht magneto; it had also been joined by an even more popular 1.9-litre L-head monobloc four, though a heavier cab with 3-litre 23 hp engine never caught on, any more than did the curious 2-cylinder G1 of 1911, which had a dashboard radiator and masqueraded as a Renault. Unic taxis had a long career, reappearing in the 1920s with smaller, 1.8-litre 4-cylinder power units, four forward speeds, and spiral bevel drive. As late as 1934 the company offered the L11F2, a more car-like 2-litre affair with fwb, disc wheels, and the magneto ignition to which the company remained loyal until 1936. Unlike its 1920s counterparts, it had a flat radiator, and some of these Unics were still working in London in the early 1950s.

By 1907 the 10/12 was also offered as a 10/15-cwt van, in which guise it won a Gold Medal in the British Commercial Vehicle Trials. The introduction of a 24/30 hp 4-cylinder private car added a line of ambulances to the range, and by 1909 the 2- and 4-cylinder lightweights had been joined by bigger Unics for payloads from 25 cwt to 2½ tons. A 2.3-litre 4-cylinder power unit was available,

1912 UNIC ¾-ton newspaper vans, OMM

1922 UNIC M1AZ charabanc, NMM

with the option of chain drive in the over-2-ton class. 4-speed gearboxes were first listed in 1910, and a year later came the O-type, a forward-control machine available as a 2-tonner or a 15-seater coach. By 1913 it had a 3.3-litre L-head monobloc engine, the twins had gone, and the smallest van used a new 1½-litre 4-cylinder unit.

The continuation of the taxi line in 1919 furnished the company with a light van chassis, but the trucks (the 30-cwt M1A2 and the 2-ton M2-O) were modernized with rounded-vee radiators, electric lighting, 4-speed gearboxes and pneumatic tires with twin rear wheels. Bigger ones had double reduction drive, also applied to Unic's first 3-tonner, the 3-litre M5C of 1925. Also new that year were fwb of uncoupled type, with or without servo assistance, and coach chassis for up to 24 passengers were available, with a 3.2-litre drop-frame version in the 1929 catalog. Unic's first true heavies came in 1931, in the shape of the

1932 UNIC 11CV ambulance, Unic

normal control CD2 and CD3, continued up to the outbreak of war. These were powered by 8.6-litre diesel sixes made under Mercedes-Benz license, other features being vacuum servo brakes on all wheels and double reduction drive. The CD3 was a 6-wheeler for 11-ton payloads, and a year later a smaller 4.6-litre engine enabled the company to offer a diesel in the ¾-ton bracket. The 1934 range covered payloads from 18 cwt up to 11 tons, a 6-tonner using a 5-litre 4-cylinder oil engine and 5-speed gearbox. The lighter Unics were restyled to bring them into line with contemporary private car types, with silent 3rd gearboxes from 1935, and (at long last) ohv and coil ignition on the 1937 models. In the intermediate bracket

1933 UNIC CD2 7-ton truck, Unic

were 4- and 5-tonners with 4-cylinder gasoline, diesel or gazogene engines, servo brakes, and the choice of four or five forward speeds; a long wheelbase coach edition was offered. The CD used a bigger 10.3-litre engine, and the Unic commercial range was completed by a halftrack of Kegresse type for the Army, using the 2.2-litre gasoline engine common to the 1-ton S25/27 trucks and the U4 car.

During the war Unic joined the G.F.A. consortium along with Bernard, Delahaye, Laffly and Simca, but this association was short-lived, and from 1951 Unic threw in their lot with the last-mentioned company, becoming the heavy-vehicle division of Simca Industries in 1958, and ultimately taking over production of Simca's 5-ton forward control truck with Ford V-8 gasoline engine. A 30-cwt military 4 × 4 development of this theme was still being produced for the NATO powers in 1964. The private cars were, however, discontinued, leaving Unic free to concentrate exclusively on heavy goods vehicles for payloads of over four tons. The new ZUs of 1946 were normal control trucks (only a few bus chassis were made) with American-style grilles and cabs, dry-plate clutches

1948 UNIC ZU51 12-ton articulated van, Unic

and 4- or 8-speed transmissions according to payload rating. The 7-tonners used 110 hp, 9.8-litre 6-cylinder diesels, with 6.8-litre fours in lighter types; other features were air brakes, disc-type transmission handbrakes, and pneumatic selection of the auxiliary ratios. ZU engines were also fitted to Labourier trucks, and the Unic range

1955 UNIC ZU100 8-ton tipper, Unic

continued without major alteration until 1955, by which time 4 × 4 versions had made their appearance, and the marque dominated the 10/15-ton class in France. The heaviest Unics had 180 hp turbocharged engines, power steering, and an air-assisted gearchange. The company kept a foothold in the smallest category by acquiring an O.M. license; in 1956 they acquired Saurer-France, subsequent French Saurers having Unic-type cabs. 1957 saw an extensive restyling, and comprehensive coverage of the 4/13-ton bracket, with 6.6-litre fours on the smaller Unics, and the big six in the heavy Lautarets and Izoards. Forward control, already available, arrived in earnest in 1960, an unusual departure being the adaptation of Fiat front-end sheet metal (from the unsuccessful C40/C50 series) for normal control editions of the 5-ton Vosges. This had a 5-litre 4-cylinder engine rated at 90/100 hp, a 5-speed synchromesh gear box, and air-hydraulic brakes, by contrast with the 8-speed rangechange boxes, full air brakes, and power steering at the top of the range. By 1964 the largest six developed 210 hp with the aid of a turbocharger, and more power still would soon be available in the shape of a 10.8-litre 255/270 hp V-8 fitted to the top-line Izoard. Along with the conventional trucks, there were tractors for GCWs of up to 65 tons, normal control 6 × 4s, and forward control 6 × 2s; all-synchromesh boxes were standard by 1966. The smallest power units were fours of 4.5 and 5.4-litres with ratings of up to 135 hp; 5- and 6-cylinder derivatives were used in intermediate Unic types.

In the meantime there had been a managerial reshuffle, with Simca changing hands. The car side went to Chrysler, but Fiat bought into Simca Industries, the truck division, emerging in full control of Unic by 1966, when the firm was renamed to indicate its latest status. In 1968

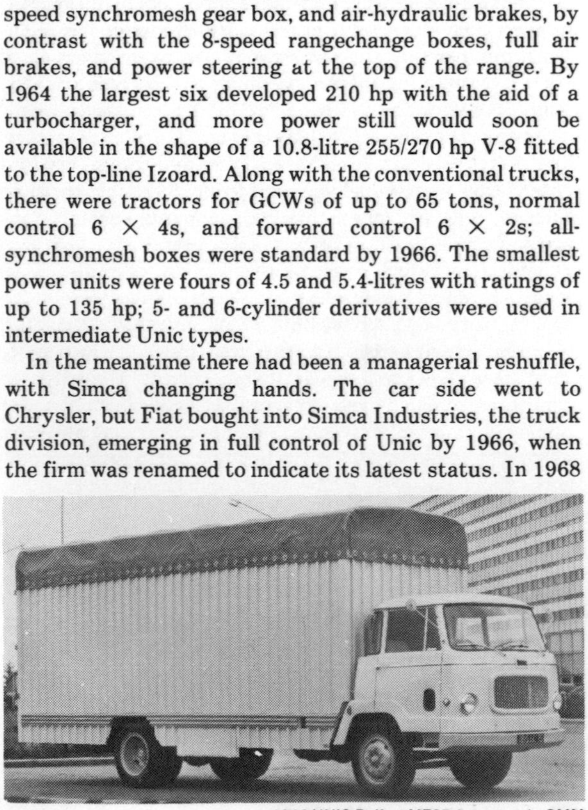

1962 UNIC Belfort MZ37 6-ton truck, OMM

some Unic models featured tilt cabs and 7.4-litre O.M. diesel engines, and 1970 Unics were extremely hard to distinguish from Fiats, thanks to their Fiat-style cabs and the abandonment of the distinctive, long-snouted normal control family. Engine development, however, continued, other members of the Fiat group utilizing the French concern's latest V-8, a 14.9-litre 340 hp affair mated to an 8-speed splitter box with synchromesh.

By 1973 production had been transferred to a new plant at Trappes capable of turning out 30,000 units a year, and under a new program of rationalization Unic became responsible for Fiat products in the 10/16-ton GVW bracket. The Unic name was used only at home and in Belgium. During 1976 and 1977 Unic badges appeared on some heavy 4 × 4 and 6 × 4 normal control construction trucks of Magirus type for the French market, while the company's own product was supplied to Germany with Deutz diesel engines. *MCS*

c. 1955 UNIMOG 4×4 tractor/truck, GNG

UNIMOG (D) 1948 to date

(1) Gebr. Bohringer GmbH., Goppingen 1948-1951
(2) Daimler-Benz Aktiengesellschaft, Gagenau 1951 to date

In 1948 the UNIMOG (UNIversal-MOtorGerat = Universal Motor Unit) appeared following a totally new concept. It was mainly developed for agricultural use as a tractor for a wide variety of accessories but also as a light truck for about 1½ tons payload. A 4-cylnder 1.7 litre Mercedes-Benz diesel engine was used, the vehicle had 4 × 4 drive, maximum road speed was about 35 mph. It was not only used in agriculture but became a popular road tractor and basis for municipal purposes.

In 1951 production was taken over by Mercedes-Benz and transferred to the Gaggenau works. In 1954 a new version appeared with the UNIMOG S, a cross-country 4 × 4 truck with 6-cylinder 2.2 litre gasoline engine and 1½ ton payload capacity. During its production the UNIMOG has become a really universal vehicle and today is used with a wide scale of applications for agricultural purposes, as a road tractor, articulated tractor or just as a truck, as road-rail vehicle, for underground mining work, and with fire fighting equipment, while the front axle plus cab allows a wide variety of lift trucks. It is available with diesel engines ranging from 34 to 150 bhp and the S version retains the 2.2 litre gasoline engine.

A tracked version is available as the Unitrac, produced by Tractortechnic of Gevelsberg and a 6 × 6 chassis for a wide variety of bodies is offered by LESA of Stolberg. *HON*

UNION (i) (US) 1901-1904

Union Motor Truck Co., Philadelphia, Pa.

The Union was a tall, awkward vehicle with 380 ci 2-cylinder engine slung under the frame. Rear wheels were larger than those in front. Transmission was by "reversible roller ratchet and movable crank pin." Two Unions were entered in the 1903 commercial vehicle contest in New York City; one broke down and the other lost a solid tire and overturned. A Union finished first in class in the 1904 contest. *DJS*

UNION (ii) (US) 1905

Union Automobile Manufacturing Company, St. Louis, Mo.

This obscure brand of truck appeared only as a closed light delivery van. Its power was provided by a 2-cylinder, 16 hp engine. A friction transmission was used with shaft drive. Either solid or pneumatic tires were available. Wheelbase was 7 feet, 8 inches and the weight was given as 1,800 pounds and the price as $1,275. *GMN*

UNION (iii) (US) 1912-1914

Union Motor Truck Co, San Francisco, Calif.

This make offered just a 1½-tonner in its first year, designated Model U-1. For 1913 and 1914, only a 2-tonner is listed. This is the whole of the information available on this obscure make. *GMN*

UNION (iv)(D) 1914-1917

Union-Werke A.G., Mannheim

During WW I this firm built trucks but no details are known. *HON*

UNION (v) (US) 1917-1925

Union Motor Truck Co, Bay City, Mich.

Beginning with a 2½-tonner assembled from stock parts, the Union added 4- and 6-tonners in 1921. In 1925, the line of models included 1½-, 2½- and 4-tonners, plus a bus. Wisconsin engines and Fuller gearboxes were used exclusively in these trucks. Rear axles were all bevel gear types. *GMN*

1939 UNION CARTAGE tractor, OMM

UNION (vi) (GB) 1935-1939

Union Cartage Co. Ltd., London E3.

Union Cartage specialized in transport in and around London's dockland. They required heavy road tractors to tow drawbar trailers and as the only suitable machines available were gasoline engined they decided to build their own tractors around the more economical Gardner 5LW diesel engine. In all some 42 Union tractors were made and many of these remained a familiar sight in London until the 1960's. One has subsequently been preserved by the company. *OM*

UNIPOWER (GB) 1937 to date

(1) Universal Power Drives Ltd., Perivale, Middlesex 1937-1973.

(2) Unipower Vehicles Ltd., Chiswick, London W4 1974-to date.

Unipower were well-known for their conversions of popular 4-wheel trucks into rigid 6-wheelers when in 1937 they produced their first 4 × 4 tractor on similar lines to the contemporary Latil. This had the Gardner 4LW engine and was intended as either a heavy haulage road tractor or for off-road use in forestry or oilfields.

1938 UNIPOWER Forester 4×4 tractor, GNG

As the Forester tractor it continued in production throughout the war as the result of a Government effort to increase home-grown timber production. It was joined in the late forties by a similar vehicle called the Hannibal with more powerful 5LW engine, able to haul gross train weights of 25 tons or give a 70,000 lb. winch pull with land anchor in place. A rigid low-loading machine with 4 × 2 drive was also offered and in 1950 the Junior 4 × 4 tractor for 12.5tons gtw with Perkins P6 was announced, following an order for a lighter tractor from Southern Rhodesia. Primarily for timber extraction, Unipower conventional 4 × 4 tractors remained in production with little

1971 UNIPOWER 6×4 28-ton GCW articulated truck, OMM

change apart from the addition of the 4-wheel steering Centipede in 1956, until 1968, by which time they were out-dated by cheaper and more versatile 4 × 4 conversions of agricultural tractors by such firms as County Commercial Cars.

In 1968 Unipower's former tractors were superseded by the forward-control Invader 4 × 4 truck with Perkins V-8 170 bhp engine. It was intended to replace aging ex-WD 4 × 4 vehicles for various off-road and recovery purposes in the 13- to 20-ton category, and found its greatest success as the basis of fire-crash tenders. It was renamed the Unipower P44 in 1972 and since then has gained Rolls-Royce and Cummins engines of up to 365 bhp to give it rapid acceleration for emergency duties. Six-wheel conversions to proprietary vehicles were discontinued in 1973.

In 1977 the firm was acquired by AC Cars Ltd. and production transferred to Thames Ditton. *OM*

UNIQUE (GB) 1914

Motor Carrier & Cycle Co, Wimbledon, London S. W.

This company made a forward-control 7cwt van powered by an 8/10hp 2-cylinder engine, with shaft drive. The engine and gearbox were mounted on a sub-frame below the driver's seat. The price was £145, and the company's 'registered foot starter' was £3 3/-extra. *GNG*

UNITAS (GB) 1919-1924

Scottish Co-operative Wholesale Society Ltd., Glasgow

The Unitas was built for the SCWS by Belhaven and was based on their own commercial chassis. It differed only in having a radiator bearing the Unitas name, and a body supplied by the SCWS' own body building units at Glasgow and Leith. Finished vehicles were used only by the SCWS and the United Co-operative Baking Society, and production ceased when Belhaven stopped making vehicles in 1924. *MJWW*

UNITED (i) (US) 1914-1915

National United Service Company, Detroit, Michigan

This was an obscure cyclecar built in passenger car and delivery van versions. It had a wheelbase of 8 feet with tread of 3 feet, 4 inches. For $425, it sported a four-cylinder water-cooled engine, friction transmission and double chain-drive. The load rating is not available. *GMN*

UNITED (ii) (US) 1915-1930

(1) United Motor Truck Co., Grand Rapids, Mich. 1915-1916
(2) United Motors Co., Grand Rapids, Mich. 1916-1922
(3) United Motors Products Co., Grand Rapids, Mich. 1922-1926
(4) Acme Motor Truck Co., Cadillac, Mich. 1927-1930

The United was a conventional truck made initially in 1½-, 3- and 5-ton sizes, all powered by 4-cylinder Continental engines. The 1½- and one 3-ton model had worm drive; the other 3-tonner and the 5-tonner were chain driven. Production in the 1920s ran from 1- to 5-tonners powered by a variety of engines including Buda up to 1923, and thereafter Herschell-Spilman, Waukesha and Wisconsin. One model, the 1-1½-tonner of 1926 was listed with a United engine, though later trucks of the same size had Hercules units. In 1927 the company was taken over by Acme and the range merged with that of the new owners. *GNG*

UNITED (iii) (US) 1917-1920

United Four-Wheel Drive Co., Chicago, Ill.

For the first four years of production, only a 1½-tonner was built, and apparently drive was by all four wheels. This is another make about which few data are available. *GMN*

1911 UNIVERSAL Model A 3-ton truck, NAHC

UNIVERSAL (US) 1910-1920

Universal Motor Truck Co., Detroit, Mich. 1910-1916
Universal Service Co., Detroit, Mich. 1916-1920

This make began by offering 3-tonners with forward control on a wheelbase of 11 feet. Typically, it used a four-cylinder, 30 hp engine with double chain final drive. In 1913, this was joined by 1- and 2-tonners and only the smallest used shaft drive and an U engine under a hood. In 1915, the smallest truck was upgraded to a 1½-tonner and the 2- and 3-tonners were unchanged. This line of three sizes was maintained to the end in 1920. *GMN*

UNIVERSELLE (D) 1926-1929

Universelle Cigarettenmaschinen-Fabrik J.C. Muller & Co., Dresden A 24

The tri-van of this manufacturer followed very closely motorcycle lines with a rear-mounted box. *HON*

UPPERCU (US) 1924-1927

Aeromarine Plane & Motor Corp., Keport, N.J.

Inglis M. Uppercu built training planes and seaplanes, and after acquiring the old-established coachbuilding firm of Healy & Co. in 1921 he turned to ambulances, hearses and special passenger cars on Cadillac chassis. In 1924 he developed a line of single and double-decker buses with front wheel drive, powered by Continental engines, which, with the transmission, were detachable in the manner of the Chicago tractor buses of 1917. Probably not more than two double deckers were made, and about 30 single deckers, of which most were sold to Tompkins Bus Corp. of Staten Island who later resold them to Chicago. 1926 and 1927 models were listed with Waukesha Six engines. *GNG*

UPTON (US) 1902-1903

Upton Machine Co., Beverly, Mass.

This firm was primarily a manufacturer of planetary transmissions. A few touring cars and delivery wagons were built. Trucks offered were a 20 hp 4-cylinder 3-ton truck and a 10 hp 2-cylinder 2-ton truck, both with wheel steering, planetary transmission, and double chain drive. Ten trucks were said to be under construction in May 1903. *DJS*

URAL-ZIS, URAL (SU) c.1942 to date
Ural Automobile Plant, Miass

With advancing German armies threatening Moscow in World War II, a portion of the Zis factory was moved to the Ural Mountains to insure continued truck production.

Vehicles manufactured there bore the Ural-Zis nomenclature and were somewhat different from their Moscow counterparts.

The Ural-Zis-5 was a 3-tonner with a 6-cylinder, 76 hp engine of greater compression-ratio than the Zis-5.

A 2.5-ton gas-generator truck, the Ural-Zis-352 was similar to the Moscow-built Zis-21.

Various wartime modifications were carried out on these vehicles including a flattened fender design.

The plant remained intact after the war ended and production continued for awhile with the war models, eventually giving way to the 3-ton Ural-Zis-355 in 1956 and in 1958 a more modern 355M. This was a 3.5-ton cargo with a 6-cylinder, 95 hp engine, four speeds forward, 75 km/h.

Now referred to simply as Ural, the product has evolved into more rugged vehicles of indigenous design commencing with the Ural-375D, originally introduced about 1961. This is a 5-ton, 6 × 6 cross country truck with collapsible and detachable seats. Tire pressure may be controlled on the move. The engine is a V-8 of 200 hp at 3,000 rpm driving a 5-speed mechanical gearbox. A winch is optional equipment.

The Ural-377 6 × 4 series, based on the Ural-375, comprises semi-tractors, cargos and dumpers and were introduced about 1965. These are powered by 180 hp V-8s. *BE*

URBAN (US) 1911-1918
Kentucky Wagon Manufacturing Co, Louisville, Ky

The Urban was a battery-operated electric. The initial model was a modest ½-tonner but in later years a number of chassis were offered, up to 2-tonners. Edison alkaline batteries were used in all models, and final drive was by double chains. Open and enclosed models of delivery vans were offered on chassis with wheelbases to 10 feet, 10 inches. *GMN*

URSUS (PL) 1924-1939
Zakladow Mechanicznych Ursus S.A., Czechowice, Warszawa

Ursus was a mechanical engineering concern that built a series of light tonnage truck and bus chassis, powered by either imported Citroen or locally-built Fiat gas engines. Main model was "Type A" of 1.5 and 2 ton payload, built under Italian SPA license. A batch of armored cars was also built on the same chassis, while Ursus facilities were also used in the post war years for the trial building of the first prototype Star truck chassis. Production was stopped during WWII and restarted in post war years, but only agricultural tractors have been built since then. *GA*

U.S. (US) 1909-1930
United States Motor Truck Co., Cincinnati, Ohio

The first product of this company was a light truck powered by a 20 hp flat-twin engine under the seat, with double chain drive, for loads of 1500/2000 or 2000/3000 lbs. By 1912 two 4-cylinder models had been added though the twin was still made; there was a driver-over-engine 1½-tonner and a conventional 3-tonner. The range was widened to include 3½-, 4- and 5-tonners by 1916, with worm and chain drive. During the 1920s conventional trucks were made from 1½- to 7-tons capacity, the latter a higher figure than was usual for small assembled makes at this time. They were Buda-powered as were most other models, though Continental and Hinkley engines were used in the early 1920s. *GNG*

U.S.A. see Liberty

UTIC (P) 1967 to date
Uniao de Transportadores para Importacao e Comercia Ltda., Lisbon

Representing the Leyland group and running successfully, for many years, assembly and body building facilities, Utic pioneered the construction of integrally-built

1915 U.S. 3-ton truck, RNE

1968 UTIC Integral coach, AAR

buses and coaches in Portugal, using Leyland or A.E.C. underfloor diesel engines and running gear. Utic buses and coaches have pleasant lines and are exported to many European and South American countries. Two factories situated in Lisbon and Porto, have a current capacity (1978) of 450 units per year. *GA*

UTILITY (US) 1910-1912

Stephenson Motor Car Company, South Milwaukee, Wisconsin

The Utility was available as one- and three-tonners. Both used four-cylinder engines with forward control. Drive system in both consisted of friction transmissions and double-chains. The larger Model C was available with a stake body on a wheelbase of 11 feet, 4 inches at a price of $3500. *GMN*

UTILITY COACH see Austin Utility Coach

1903 VABIS 1500kg truck, Scania

VABIS (S) 1902-1911

Vagnfabriks Aktiebolaget i Sodertalje, Sodertalje

This company, whose name means Wagon Factory Ltd. in Sodertalje, built wagons from 1891 and an experimental passenger car in 1897. The first truck came in 1902. It had a 15p V-twin engine mounted at the front under a short hood, shaft drive and iron tires. It was shown to the public at the same 1903 Stockholm Motor Show which saw the first Scania truck, and the two companies remained close rivals until the merger in 1911. Vabis employed shaft drive up to 1906 when they launched the Type 5 chain drive 3-tonner which was the staple model until the end of the company's independent existence. Like Scania they also made small delivery vans based on their passenger cars. *GNG*

VALIANT (ZA) 1973 to date

Chrysler South Africa (Pty) Ltd., Elsier River, Cape Province

A pick-up version of the Valiant passenger car, specially designed to fill local needs, is the main commercial vehicle product of the South African Chrysler plant. Called The Rustler, it follows the American style of large car-based pick-ups, sharing the front end of the South African designed and built car and powered by the well known Slant 6 Chrysler gasoline engine developing 145hp. *GA*

VALLEY see Huffman

VALMET (SF) 1945 to date

Valmet Oy, Helsinki

A very important engineering concern, better known for its diesel engines, agricultural tractors and diesel locomotives, Valmet makes also regular appearances in the automotive field. A trolleybus model was built early after the war, while all-wheel-drive forest tractors have been the main product for many years. Powered by Valmet's own 82hp diesel engine and exported throughout the world, these 4 × 4 tractors were used as the basis of the most interesting Valmet product, the articulated 4 × 4 vehicle intended for military use. Built from two independent open-top hulls, with drive to all 4 large diameter wheels and steering by articulation, this vehicle is used either as a gun tractor or as a troop-carrier. Power in this case too comes from an up-rated Valmet diesel developing 90hp and a front-mounted winch is standard equipment. Driver and engine assembly are positioned in the front hull, while the rear one is used as a load. Recently a 6 × 6 timber tractor powered by a 135hp Scania engine has been made. *GA*

c. 1948 VALMET trolleybus, AAR

VAN (US) 1909

H.F. Van Wambeke & Sons, Elgin, Ill.

Trucks under this name were archaic-looking high-wheelers of 1,600- and 2,000-pound capacity. These were driven by 2-cylinder, air-cooled engines through friction transmissions and double chains to the rear wheels. The smaller was a light delivery van while the larger was called an express delivery. Their only concession to engineering advances was the use of wheel steering, rather than tiller. *GMN*

1960 VANAJA TB-type 32-ton GCW articulated truck, GNG

VANAJA (SF) 1948-1967

Vanajan Autotehdas OY, Helsinki

Originally commercial bodybuilders, Vanaja were nationalized in 1943 and fused with Sisu under the Yhteissisu name. The combined operation built trucks for the Finnish armed forces, but Vanaja became independent again in 1948. Their trucks bore a close resemblance to Sisu's, early ones having 5-litre 6-cylinder gasoline

c. 1963 VANAJA 6×4 van, OMM

engines, though by 1954 a 5.7-litre diesel was standard equipment. Later models were medium and heavy types with 5-, 6- and 10-speed gearboxes and hypoid final drive. On these, engines and axles were of British A.E.C. origin (though some Vanajas used Leyland's 0680), regular variants having diesel sixes of 7.7, 9.6, and 11.1 litres. The range covered normal and forward control trucks in 4 × 2, 4 × 4, 6 × 2,and 6 × 4 configurations, a peculiarity of Vanaja's 6 × 4s being the drive, taken to the front axle and one of the rear pair. Early Vanaja buses were of conventional normal or forward control type, but in 1958 the company introduced the VLK500, with horizontal-underfloor mounted 7.7-litre A.E.C. unit. The firm was taken over by Sisu in 1967, and the name disappeared: Sisu's forward control Bulldog was, however, a continuation of a Vanaja design. *MCS*

1913 VAN AUKEN 1-ton electric van, HHB

VAN AUKEN (US) 1913-1914

Van Auken Electric Car Co., Connersville, Ind.

This was a small battery-powered electric truck with a wheelbase of 6 feet, 8 inches. Carrying capacity was either 750 or 1,000 pounds. It used a General Electric motor, had four forward speeds and drive gear was a worm. The front axle was tubular and chassis weight was given as 1,240 pounds. *GMN*

VANDEN PLAS see Austin

VAN DYKE (US) 1910-1912

Van Dyke Motor Car Co., Detroit, Mich.

Van Dykes were built on a single chassis during the short life of this make. This used a wheelbase of 7 feet, 2 inches, with a 2-cylinder engine, friction transmission and shaft-drive. It had a 12hp engine and delivery van capacity was ½-ton. Either solid or pneumatic tires were available; the weight of this vehicle was given as 1,900 pounds and the price as $950. *GMN*

VANETTE (GB) 1923-1930

The Stepney Carrier Co. Ltd., High Holborn, London W.C.1

This was a 3-wheeled parcelcar powered by a 247cc single-cylinder 2-stroke engine, with 2-speed gearbox and chain drive to the single rear wheel. Payload was 150lbs. In 1929 a 3-speed gearbox was introduced, and in 1930 the name was changed to Karivan. *GNG*

1962 VAN HOOL Type 340 coach, JFJK

VAN HOOL (B) 1955 to date

Van Hool P.v.b.A., Koningshooikt

After having acquired experience as a manufacturer of bus bodies, Van Hool started in 1955 with the construction of integral buses around Fiat mechanical components. These buses were an instant success in Belgium and soon obtained a foothold abroad, particularly in Holland and France, the reason for this success being not least their excellent appearance.

In the early sixties a new range of buses were introduced, showing already the beginning of the shape Van Hool is currently so renowned for and sales companies were founded in France and Holland. Van Hool expanded further and set up a manufacturing plant in Spain (Saratoga), bought the bus plant of the Irish CIE to found Van Hool McArdle, and designed a special bus chassis for production by Cummins Nordeste of Salvador, Brazil. In Belgium a full range of integral city, intercity and luxury buses is built, still using Fiat running units. *JFJK*

VAN-L (US) 1911-1912

Van-L Commercial Car Co., Grand Rapids, Mich.

Three chassis were made by this manufacturer; a 1-, 1½- and 2-tonners. All used 4-cylinder engines and had forward control. These also used three-speed gearboxes and double chain-drive. The two-tonner had a 32hp engine, chassis weight was 4,000 pounds and with solid tires the price was $1,900. The manufacturer was succeeded by Commercial Service Company. *GMN*

VAN TWIST (NL) 1955-1967

Kemper & Van Twist Diesel N.V., Dordrecht

After World War II Kemper & Van Twist Diesel was the Dutch distributor of Seddon diesel vehicles, assembling these for some time in their own premises and offering them as Seddon Van Twist.

During the early fifties the company, which also distributed the Perkins diesel engines in Holland, started thinking about their own vehicles using Perkins engines, Kirkstall axles, Moss gearboxes, etc., thus clearly patterning their vehicles on the Seddon. In 1955 production started with a range of five models, including a normal control truck. On the civil market the Van Twists were not so successful, but as chassis for municipal vehicles they were built up to 1967. Some Van Twist vehicles can still be seen working in The Hague. *JFJK*

VAUXHALL see Bedford

V-C (US) 1912-1913

V-C Motor Truck Co., Lynn, Mass.

The only model of this make which has been discovered was a 1½-tonner known as Model B which had a selling price of $2,350. *GMN*

1975 V-CON Model 3006 270-ton 8×6 diesel-electric dump truck, Marion Power Shovel Inc

V-CON (US) 1971 to date

Marion Power Shovel Co. Inc., Vehicle Constructors Division, Dallas, Texas

V-Con diesel-electric end-dump trucks are among the largest in the world. There are four models, from 250 to 270 tons capacity, powered by Alco diesels of 8 or 12 cylinders, or Detroit Diesels of 12 or 16 cylinders, with horsepower ranging from 1,340 to 3,000. Engines are turbocharged, and mounted amidships, generating electric power through a GTH 11 alternator to drive General Electric 772 motorized wheels. The wheel arrangement differs from other dump trucks in that the eight wheels are arranged four abreast. Usually six wheels are powered, but other power arrangements are optional. The front wheels steer in pairs, by hydraulic actuation, with a 51-foot turning radius. Brakes are electronically actuated, hydraulic; blended with discs on the powered wheels and internal expanding drums on the unpowered.

Because of their 28ft. width, the V-Cons cannot be delivered under their own power on the highway, so they are transported in sections and assembled on the site. The price of the largest model, the 3006, is about $1,200,000, and plant capacity is one or two units per month. The makers plan other sizes from 200 to 400 tons. *RW*

V.E.C. (US) 1901-1906

(1) Vehicle Equipment Co., Brooklyn, N.Y. 1901-1905
(2) Vehicle Equipment Co., Long Island City, N.Y. 1905-1906

This was one of the most important early builders of electric vehicles in America, making many of the sightseeing 'rubberneck' buses which plied in New York, Washington and other cities. Other products included ambulances, brewery trucks, tipping coal trucks and special vehicles for lifting safes to the upper stories of office buildings, handling machinery and withdrawing telephone cables from underground conduits. In 1906 the name was changed to General Vehicle Company, and the products to G.V. *GNG*

1905 V.E.C. electric sightseeing bus, LIAM

1912 VEERAC 1500lb truck, AACA

VEERAC (US) 1910-1914

(1) Veerac Motor Company, Minneapolis, Minn. 1910-1914
(2) Veerac Motor Company, Anoka, Minn. 1914

The odd name Veerac was an acronym for "Valveless, Explosion Every Revolution, Air-Cooled". In other words, the engines were two-stroke types and air-cooled. The commercial versions were light, open vans with planetary transmissions and double chain-drive to the rear wheels. A

¾-tonner and a one-tonner were the only sizes offered. The one-tonner used a two-cylinder, 20hp engine and had a wheelbase of 7 feet, 2 inches and was governed to a maximum speed of 15mph by a cylinder "cut-out". *GMN*

1912 VELIE Model Z 3-ton moving van, NAHC

VELIE (US) 1911-1929

(1) Velie Motor Vehicle Co., Moline, Ill. 1911-1915
(2) Velie Motors Corporation, Moline, Ill. 1915-1929

This car maker added a 2-ton truck to his range in 1911. It used a 5.7-litre 4-cylinder paircast engine with dual ignition in a straight forward chassis with 3-speed gearbox and side-chain drive; pneumatic tires were an option. By 1915 there were models for payloads from 1½ to 3 tons, and worm drive had been adopted, Monobloc engines of Continental make were standardized in 1916, and the 1½-tonner, at any rate, survived into 1925 with little change. From 1915 to the end in 1929 the company also offered a specialized ambulance or hearse chassis with the 6-cylinder sv Continental unit. Some such Velies were supplied to Rock Falls. *MCS*

VELOX (i) (A) 1906-1910

Prazska tovarna automobilu Velox, Prague-Karlin

The Velox was a taxicab powered by a vertical single-cylinder water-cooled engine under the driver's seat. Capacity was 1,020cc and output 10bhp at 2,000rpm. There was a 3-speed constant-mesh gearbox and single chain final drive. These Velox cabs were known as the 'Russian type' as many of them were delivered to Moscow. *MSH*

VELOX (ii) (D) 1929-1930

Maschinen- und Motorenfabrik Scharrer & Gross, Nuremberg

The principle of one front wheel, which was tiller steered, was featured by this tri-van built on motorcycle lines. The rear axle was driven by chain. A single-cylinder two-stroke Velox engine of 350cc, 5000 or 600cc was used. *HON*

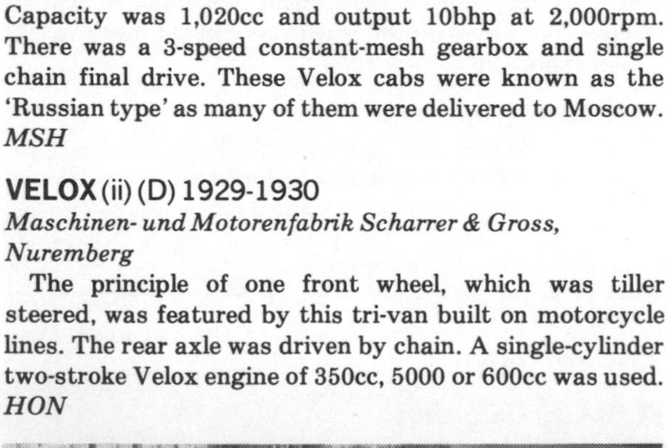

1959 VERHEUL 6-wheel cab over truck, TBG bus and 4-wheel tractor, OMM

VERHEUL (NL) 1948-1971

NV Auto-Industrie Verheul, Waddinxveen

Verheul was one of the oldest Dutch bodybuilders, with a history going back to the turn of the century, when they started after World War II to make an integral bus using Leyland running gear. Sales of these, in export as well as the domestic market, were successful throughout the 1950s, and in 1958 Verheul turned to goods vehicles when they acquired the truck manufacturers, Kromhout of Amsterdam. These were continued at Verheul's own factory with little change apart from a new cab; Kromhout and Rolls-Royce engines were used, but truck production was not a success, and was phased out in about 1965. In 1960 Verheul had been acquired by AEC and subsequently most of its buses were fitted with AEC engines unless anything else was specified by the customer. After the AEC/Leyland merger in Britain Verheul was renamed Leyland Verheul Nederland NV, and later British Leyland Nederland BV. Buses were sold under the name Leyland-Verheul and were once again fitted with Leyland running units. The last range was the LVB, still the most widespread bus model in Holland. Verheul production came to an end after a factory fire in December 1971. A prototype Leyland-Verheul of 1973 did not go into production. *JFJK*

1899 VERITY steam wagon, Autocar

VERITY (GB) 1899

Verity Motor Co., Bradford, Yorks

E.A. Verity produced his first, and possibly only, steam wagon the the spring of 1899 and it worked for a while in Leeds. Coke fuel was used in the maker's own design of flash boiler working at 250 psi. The engine (or engines for it is not clear whether or not a separate engine was used for each rear wheel) was mounted under the chassis and final drive was by roller chain to a sprocket bolted to each rear wheel. Wheels were wooden throughout and were fitted with steel tires. In this and other respects it was far too lightly built to survive and did not, in fact, do so. *RAW*

VERMOREL (F) 1908-1932

Etablissements V. Vermorel, Villefranche, Rhone

Most Vermorel cars were of medium capacity, and most of their commercial vehicles were car-based machines in the 10-cwt/1-ton category, though a normal control 2½-tonner was entered for the 1912 French Army subvention trials. Pre-war Vermorels used T-head (later L-head) 2.2-litre 4-cylinder engines in conventional shaft-driven chassis, this capacity being standard until 1923/4, when 1.7-litre units were fitted even to 1-ton trucks. By 1927 light-duty models had the ohv and fwb of their private-car counterparts, and there was also a small van on the 1,100cc AG chassis. Cars and vans alike survived into 1932, when vehicle production was abandoned. During the German Occupation Vermorel produced gazogene conversions of their own design for Chevrolets and similar trucks. *MCS*

VERNEY (F) 1937-1975

Autocars Verney SAMV, Le Mans

In 1937 the Societe Centrale de Chemins de Fer,

1963 VERNEY 44-seater bus, JFJK

founded ten years before by Charles Francois Baert and Louis Verney to operate and construct small local railroad, started to build road vehicles too in one of its Le Mans plants. They manufactured for some years a one-ton battery-electric forward-control van, and also started producing integral buses of their own design.

After the war bus manufacture was resumed, producing in small numbers — about 70 buses per year — buses and luxury coaches, using various engines, mainly Latil gearboxes and Chenard & Walcker axles. About 1958 the R1 and the T were introduced, viz. offering 35 and 50 seats and using AEC, DAF or Perkins diesel engines, and Dunlop Pneuride springs in combination with fully independent suspension to all four wheels. In 1962 a fleet of R1 buses was delivered to the RATP. The last novelty by Verney was a bus with fully independently sprung six wheels, before the company was reorganized in 1975 as the CBM, Car & Bus Le Mans. *JFJK*

VERSARE (US) 1925-1931

(1) Versare Corp., Albany, N.Y. 1925-1928
(2) Cincinnati Car Co., Cincinnati, Ohio 1928-1931

The first type of Versare bus, introduced with great fanfare in 1925, was built on the principle of a double-truck streetcar and represented an attempt to produce an extremely large bus capable of doing streetcar duty. There were two bogies, each driven by an electric motor, with the current supplied by a generator driven by a Buda gasoline engine located under a conventional front hood. The power plant was said to be readily removable for repairs, as were the bogies. Body construction was also unique for the period, consisting of fabricated aluminum alloy framing built up in sections, welded together, and covered with an aluminum alloy skin. Four buses and a prototype truck are known to have been built; there could have been more.

1925 VERSARE 8-wheel bus, MBS

In 1927 Versare announced a second type of gas-electric bus with its engine inside the body at the rear, the earliest U.S. example of so-called "streetcar-type" bus construction with the front entrance door ahead of the front axle. There were again two electric motors and two driving axles. This concept proved somewhat more palatable to potential customers, and with interest being shown in the design, the Cincinnati Car Co., an old established streetcar builder, acquired Versare in 1928. A trolley-coach version was marketed as well, initially having the same three-axle layout as the motor bus, but later revised with a single rear axle, and after sale of the company the trolley-coaches were sold under the Cincinnati name. The buses continued to use the name Versare and may have still been built at the original plant in Watervliet, N.Y., near Albany. Approximately 100 buses and 40 trolley-coaches were produced, and buyers included transit companies in New York, Albany, Montreal, Cleveland, Boston and Salt Lake City. *MBS*

VESPA see Ape

1962 VESPACAR 450kg 3-wheel van, GNG

VESPACAR (E) 1951-1973

(1) Motomecanica S.A., Madrid
(2) Motovespa S.A., Madrid

The Vespacar was a delivery tricycle derived from the famous Vespa scooter made in Italy by Piaggio of Genoa. Five different models were made, for loads of 250 to 550kgs. They were available with or without doors to the 2-seater cab. *JCG*

VETERAN (CDN) 1920

Built in Sherbrooke, Quebec, the Veteran gained its name from the fact that it was designed by ex-servicemen and as far as possible the company's policy was to employ only returned soldiers. The truck itself was a 3½-tonner powered by a 4-cylinder Buda engine, with Cotta 3-speed gearbox, overhead worm drive and all-steel fully-enclosed cab. Some were reportedly sold to the Canadian Post Office. *HD/GNG*

VETRA (F) 1925-1966

Societe de Vehicules et Travaux Electriques, Paris

When the trolleybus was introduced in Europe for the second time, and this time with more success than before, Vetra was founded in France to install trolleybus systems. The main founder was Alsthom, the French electrical engineering company. Besides installing overhead wiring Vetra also constructed the trolleybuses, initially using Renault chassis like the popular PY. In 1939 a trolleybus with integral body/chassis construction was produced for Paris, using the running gear of the Renault TN4H. After the war a co-operation with Berliet was arranged resulting in the joint manufacture of a range of single- and tandem-axle trolleybuses, which were sold by both companies under their own names and with their own model designations. In 1966, after most trolleybus systems had disappeared in France, the Vetra company was wound up. *JFJK*

VIBERTI (I) 1953-1966
Officine Viberti SpA, Turin

Viberti were primarily commercial-vehicle coachbuilders, in which field they were still active in 1976. They built ambulance, tipper, tanker, and workshop van bodies, as well as semi-trailers. By contrast, their Monotral unitary-construction buses qualified the Viberti as a make in its own right. These came in 4 × 2 and 6 × 4 forms, and featured horizontal rear engines, with air and air-leaf suspensions making their appearance from 1957 onward. A speciality was the articulated autotreno for up to 130 passengers, and the CV60 of 1960 was designed to pull a 4-wheel passenger-carrying trailer of their own construction. Most Vibertis used Fiat diesel mechanical elements, though they were also made with Lancia, O.M., and Pegaso engines and gearboxes. At the 1956 Turin Show they exhibited a futuristic gas-turbine powered coach, the Golden Dolphin with refrigeration, cloakrooms and all-independent springing. If this never took the road, their 1960 double-deckers went into service in Turin. These were 6 × 4s with accommodations for more than 140 passengers. Features were a 200bhp Fiat engine mounted vertically at the left front of the structure, a 4-speed automatic transmission, and air suspension. Specialist trucks were also built; the BVF203 6 × 6 fire engine of 1955 had two side-by-side 140hp Fiat units, each with its individual air-assisted clutch and 4-speed gearbox, not to mention a backbone chassis. Other such Vibertis were an articulated 6 × 6 10,000-gallon tanker and a 4 × 4 forward control dumper, both with O.M.-built V8 diesel engines. *MCS*

VICKERS (GB) 1928-1971
(1) Vickers-Armstrongs Ltd., Crayford, Kent
(2) Vickers All Wheel Drive, Swindon, Wilts

This well-known engineering and armaments company has made a number of widely differing vehicles during its history. From 1901 to 1927 they owned the Wolseley company and in the 1920s made a number of Wolseley-based tracked vehicles which could run on retractable wheels when on the road. From 1928 they built the Carden-Loyd which was one of the very few full-tracked vehicles offered for sale on the civilian market. It had a 50hp 6-cylinder engine, 5-speed transmission and load capacity of 1½-tons.

A larger vehicle for carrying 6½-ton loads, powered by an Armstrong Siddeley engine, was produced in the early 1930s with half tracks at both front and rear.

Military vehicles and heavy tractors were made from the 1930s to 1960, and in 1962 Vickers bought a 60% interest in All Wheel Drive of Camberley who made 4 × 4 and 6 × 6 conversions of truck chassis. At their Swindon factory Vickers continued with the conversion business but also made crane carrier chassis under the name Vickers-AWD. Their last product was the Jetranger, a 6 × 6 cross-country fire engine chassis powered by the rear-mounted 28-litre Cummins V-12 engine, with body and equipment by Carmichael of Worcester. This was announced in 1971. *OM*

1931 VICKERS-CARDEN-LOYD 1½-ton tractor/truck, NMM

VICTOR (i) (US) 1910-1914
Victor Motor Truck Co., Buffalo, N.Y.

This was an overly-ambitious manufacturer who, for 1911 offered delivery vans in five different six sizes as well as an ambulance, police patrol wagon, and fire apparatus as well as sight-seeing buses. The line of trucks for 1912 listed no less than seven sizes from a 1-tonner to a 10-tonner. For the last two model-years, only 3- and 5-tonners were offered. The 5-tonner used dual 40 × 6 solid tires at the rear. *GMN*

VICTOR (ii) (US) 1913-1914
Victor Automobile Manufacturing Co., St. Louis, Mo.

This make was a battery-powered electric built only as a ½-tonner. It used 32 cells made by Gould, with four forward speeds and motor by Westinghouse. Final drive was by bevel gear. Elliptical springs were used all around. Wheelbase was 7 feet, 8 inches, the chassis weight was 1,800 pounds and the price was $1,500. *GMN*

1923 VICTOR (v) 2½-ton truck, LIAM

VICTOR (iii) (GB) 1914-1915
(1) Victor Motors Ltd., Eynsford, Kent 1914-1915
(2) Victor Cars Ltd., Ealing, London W. 1915

The Victor cyclecar, powered by a 965cc V-twin Precision engine, was made in 5cwt van form with open driver's cab. The only modification to the chassis was that of additional rear springs. *GNG*

VICTOR (iv) (US) 1918-1920
Victor Motor Truck & Trailer Co., Chicago, Ill.

This brand was built as 1½- and 2-tonners apparently on a common chassis with a wheelbase of 11 feet, 8 inches. These were furnished with 4-cylinder Continental engines, Fuller 3-speed progressive gearboxes and Clark internal-gear rear axles. *GMN*

VICTOR (v) (US) 1923-c.1928
Victor Motors Inc. St. Louis, Mo.

The Victor was a conventional truck made in several sizes from 1¼ to 6 tons, though the latter was a short-lived model only made in 1925/6. It and the 3½-5-ton model used Continental engines, but the smaller trucks were all Hercules-powered. One Continental-powered bus chassis for 35 passengers was listed in 1926/27. *GNG*

1927 VICTOR (vi) 1-ton electric van, OMM

VICTOR (vi) (GB) 1927-1961

Victor Electrics Ltd., Burscough Bridge, Ormskirk, Lancs.

The Victor was the result of experiments by a Southport baker who, in 1923 connected lengthened Model T Ford to electric power. Production models of 1927 onward still used many Ford components. The model A was a 1-ton capacity van based on a 10ft wheelbase chassis, the model B was a 23cwt model, and the C type was listed as a 30cwt, all being of a similar layout. Early in the 1930's the LL was introduced, being similar to the C type except that it offered a rather lower loading line through being carried on smaller steel disc wheels than the higher model. Redesign of the standard models then went ahead to give the appearance of lower, more compact vans than the old truck style of early models. The old conventional type was dropped in favor of the accepted design of electric with side batteries, forward control and small disc or car-type wire wheels. The range offered included vans and trucks in the 10- to 30-cwt range with wheelbases between 6ft and

1937 VICTOR (vi) ½-ton electric van, NMM

7ft 6in and driven by either bevel or worm axles. Minor changes in 1937 resulted in four basic models being listed with capacities of 8cwt, 10cwt, 20cwt, and 30cwt, these being of the single motor type with batteries of 124, 155, 186 and 217AH size. Steel disc wheels were fitted and wheelbases varied between 5ft 3in and 7ft 6in. In 1938 an additional model of 15cwt capacity was added to the range.

A somewhat similar range was offered during the postwar years although only four models were listed, these being between 15cwt and 50cwt, with wheelbases varying between 6ft 3in and 9ft 3in and employing overhead worm rear axles. During the 1950's the range was updated with a variation in the wheelbase of some models and the choice of larger capacity batteries. The 10cwt model was reintroduced to the range and a drawbar tractor (model K) was offered with a towing capacity of between 3 and 6 tons according to battery size. *OM*

1934 VICTORIA 200cc 3-wheeled truck, HON

VICTORIA (D) 1905-1909; 1934-1935

(1) Victoria Fahrradwerke vorm. Frankenberger & Ottensteiner A.G., Nuremberg 1905-1909
(2) Victoria Werke A.G., Nuremberg 1934-1935

From 1905 the Victoria private cars are available as vans, especially the 2-cylinder models of 800 and 1,250cc.

In 1934 a tri-van was introduced with one front wheel. A 200cc. engine was side-mounted driving one rear wheel by chain. This version was not produced in great numbers. *HON*

VICTORIA COMBINATION (F) 1900-1903

Ste Parisienne E. Couturier et Cie, Paris

The Victoria Combination was one of the more unusual light cars of the turn of the century with its engine (2 ¾hp de Dion Bouton or 3½hp Aster) mounted over the front axle which it drove. Both axle and engine turned with the steering, which was by tiller. Chiefly seen as a two seater car, the Victoria Combination could also be had as a light box van with capacity of 150kg. *GNG*

VILLARD (F) 1925-1935

Cyclecars Villard, Colombes, Seine.

Though private cars were offered, the principal Villard product was a 3-wheeler van for 3-cwt payloads. A 350cc single-cylinder 2-stroke engine drove the single front wheel via a 6-speed friction-and-chain transmission. Oil lamps were standard at the price of £60-odd, but the make was quite popular, a large fleet being operated by the Felix Potin grocery chain in Paris. 1930 and subsequent Villards were more sophisticated affairs with 500cc 4-stroke ohv Chaise engines and conventional 3-speed gearboxes, in which form payloads of 11/12cwt were advertised. *MCS*

1958 VILLOF Mira 500kg 3-wheel van, JCG

VILLOF (E) 1949-1962

Construcciones Mecanicas Villof, Valencia

These delivery tricycles were made by Vicento Llorena

Ferrer, from whose name the word Villof was derived. The original models had single-cylinder engines and tiller steering, but in 1957 a new model known as the Mira appeared. This had an enclosed cab with wheel steering and car-type controls. The engine, 3-speed gearbox and tubular frame were similar to those of the earlier model. *JCG*

1920 VIM ¾-ton van, OMM

VIM (US) 1913-1923

(1) Touraine Co., Philadelphia, Pa. 1913-1915
(2) Vim Motor Truck Co., Philadelphia, Pa. 1915-1923

The Vim ½-ton truck was the product of a firm which had found its 6-cylinder touring cars difficult to sell. The truck had a 14hp 4-cylinder Northway engine, cone clutch, and bevel drive. It was made entirely of purchased parts. The chassis cost $620 in 1915, when four body types were offered. Sales were in excess of 13,000 trucks per year from 1915 to 1917 but declined sharply thereafter.

The firm announced 1½-ton and 3-ton models for 1918 and operated its own engine shop for a time. Post-war models had Continental or Hercules engines. A takeover by Standard Steel Car, makers of the Standard V-8, in 1921, and subsequent sale of Vim assets to Baltimore interests in 1922 hastened the end of production. *DJS*

VINOT (F) 1902-1925

Vinot et Deguingand, Puteaux, Seine: Nanterre, Seine

The Vinot (or, more correctly, Vinot-Deguingand) was available as a 1-ton truck within a year of its introduction. This was of driver-over-engine type, and had the 10hp vertical-twin aiv engines, coil ignition, and armored wood frame also found on the cars: pneumatic tires were fitted. Their next serious attempt at a truck was in 1908, when they entered a chain-drive normal control vehicle for the French Truck Trials; it had a gilled tube radiator at each end of its 4-cylinder engine. Production 2/3-tonners were, however, conventionally-cooled affairs with 4-speed gearboxes and 3.7- or 4.8-litre power units. Alongside these were some straightforward 2.2-litre shaft-driven fours offered either as 15cwt vans or taxicabs, the latter version being used in London. The acquisition of the Gladiator company led to some badge-engineered editions of the lighter Vinot commercials as well as of the private cars. In 1912 the catalogue listed models from 10cwt to 2½-tons, including some cab-over-engine types, and a 30-cwt 2.2-litre with Vinot's vertical gate gearshift, transverse rear suspension, and a double reduction back axle. After the Armistice the firm's main efforts centered around a 10-cwt car-type light van and a modernized 30-cwt truck with 2.6-litre engine, twin rear wheels, and pneumatic tires. A 15.9hp (10CV) cab was also briefly listed in 1922, but commercials were not offered after 1925, and a year later the private car line expired as well. *MCS*

V.I.T.E. (F) 1919-1920

Voiturettes Industrielles de Transport Economique, St. Cloud, Seine-et-Oise

This was a light van powered by a flat-twin motorcycle engine which drove the front wheels via a 3-speed gearbox and vertical shaft to the center of the axle. The wheels were mounted close together, which gave the V.I.T.E. the superficial appearance of a 3-wheeler. *GNG*

VOLGA see GAZ

VOLKSWAGEN (D) 1949 to date

(1) Volkswagenwerk GmbH., Wolfsburg; Hannover 1949-1960
(2) Volkswagenwerk A.G., Wolfsburg; Hannover 1960 to date

The Transporter was first presented in 1949 and followed a concept which was not practiced before. It was no longer a van body on a private car chassis, but was an independent design of a chassis-less all-steel forward control van body, air-cooled 1.131 cc. flat four engine mounted in the rear and rear-wheel drive. Payload was 850 kg. Later versions included a pick-up and a micro-bus. Engine capacity was raised to 1.192 and 1.493 cc. and the total payload increased to 1 ton.

1966 VOLKSWAGEN 1-ton pick-up, Volkswagen

In 1965 a van version appeared on a beetle chassis and with rear-mounted beetle-engine. It is built by the "Westfalia" works but is part of Volkswagen's official program. The German Postal Authorities are one of the most prominent customers for this version. They also built a taxi version of the Transporter but this was not accepted by the public.

In 1968 the 2 millionth Transporter left the Hannover works. 1971 and 1973 saw further increases in engine capacity of 1.6, 1.7 and 1.8 litre (55 and 66 PS).

In 1974 Volkswagen built 200 of their transporters with electric motors for experimental purposes. More were ordered by various customers, e.g. the Deutsches Bundesbahn.

Since 1975 a new transporter version has been offered under the designation LT. It features the orthodox layout of front engine and rear drive, a 2-litre water-cooled engine (following Audi 100 principles) being used. Forward control pick-up and van versions are available in sizes up to 4½ tonners. Also a diesel engine is offered, this being a Perkins produced under license.

1975 VOLKSWAGEN 1-ton van, Volkswagen

1976 VOLKSWAGEN LT35 2-ton van, Volkswagen

In 1973 a transporter in kit form was produced for assembly and completion in developing countries. The kit contains gearbox, front-drive component steering assembly, and the 1.600 cc flat four engine.

Planned for introduction in 1979 was a range of larger trucks, developed in cooperation with M.A.N. *HON*

VOLPI (I) 1901
Societa Volpi, Milan

Volpis were special chassis made in very small numbers for Milan's fire brigade. French engines (probably de Dion or Aster) were used. *MCS*

VOLTACAR (US) 1914-1916
Cyco-Lectric Car Company, New York, New York

This electrically-powered parcel van was a crude affair with a 500-pound capacity box in front of the driver's seat. Its wheelbase was but 5 feet, 8 inches with tread of 3 feet, 4 inches. Surprisingly the drive to the rear axle was by worm gear. It was equipped with solid 28 x 2 tires and was priced at $585. *GMN*

VOLTZ (US) 1915-1918
Voltz Bros., Chicago, Ill.

The Voltz was available as 3- and 5-tonners with engine under hood. In both models, final drive was by jackshaft and double chains to the rear wheels. Electric headlamps and tail lights were standard equipment. *GMN*

VOLVO (S) 1928 to date
AB Volvo, Gothenburg

Assar Gabrielsson and Gustav Larson set out to give Sweden a national car. Though the truck version did not follow until a year later, in 1928, it dominated the company's thinking in pre-war days. Like the car, it was based on American ideas, both using 1.9-litre 4-cylinder sv engines of a modest 28hp in a conventional chassis with 3-speed gearbox and fixed wood wheels. The first commercial Volvos were light pickups for the Gothenburg

1929 VOLVO LV40 2-ton tipper truck, Volvo

postal authorities, but these soon evolved into 1-tonners on longer wheelbases which included some small buses. 1929 saw the company's first six, a side-valve 7-bearing 3-litre not unlike the U.S. Continental. It gave 55bhp in original form, and went into the 2-ton LV60 family with 4-speed boxes. At the same time, long-chassis editions of the private car were adapted for taxi use, thus starting a long line which continued until 1957. The last of the family was the PV830 with 3.7 litres and 90bhp, which differed only from private-car versions in retaining a beam front axle to the end.

Though a 4½-litre straight 8 truck engine was planned, this never materialized, and development continued along American lines: the heavier duty LV66s of 1931 used 4.1-litre sixes differing from the private-car line in their use of overhead valves. Included in the new range was the company's first trailing-axle 6-wheeler, the LV64LF, this configuration being preferred in early days to tandem drive. In 1932 came a preliminary essay into forward control with the LV75 Bulldog, also used for PSV bodies, though only 250 were made before the model was dropped in 1935. 1933's main changes were the adoption of hydraulic brakes and an alternative power unit for heavier Volvos, a Hesselman-type semi-diesel, also of 4.1 litres, offered as an alternative to the conventional gasoline type until the mid-40s. A purpose-built bus chassis came in 1932, but this LV70B was essentially a modified long wheelbase truck. New 1½-tonners (LV76/78) came in 1934, these resembling contemporary Opels in appearance and using the sv car engine, already enlarged to 3.3 litres: the 3.7-litre version came out during 1936. There were some smaller pickups on the car chassis, and 1934 saw a forward-control, purpose built bus capable of seating up to 34 passengers, this configuration superseding all the conventional PSV models by 1942. Engines were of 4.1-litre gasoline or Hesselman type, and these buses formed the basis of a modest export business, with sales (by 1940) to several South American states as well as to South Africa and to Belgium, where Volvo commercials were being supplied at the rate of some 150 units a year. In 1936 the truck range was extended upwards to embrace

1937 VOLVO PV51 ½-ton pick-up, OMM

the 4-ton LV93s with engines mounted over the front axle. A year later came even bigger models, the LV290s using 6.7-litre units rated at 120hp, coping with 5-ton payloads in four-wheel form, and up to 6½ tons as a six-wheeler. The same engine went into the B40 forward control bus. While in 1938 came a large city model, the B50. This featured a wheelbase of 17ft 5in, a 7.6-litre Hesselman engine, and a Lysholm-Smith torque converter transmission, but was made only in small numbers. The 1939 range covered payloads from 1½ to 6 tons, and styling was much on Ford lines, the grille being shared with contemporary private cars. Wartime shortages led to wood-gas versions (the Swedes usually mounted their producers on the front bumper, giving a very odd appearance) and also to a line of electric trucks including a 3-tonner. Volvo had also gone empire-building: the Skofde Gjuteri & Mekaniska Verkstad at Skovde, acquired in 1931, became their engine division, and further facilities were obtained in 1935 with the purchase of the Penta marine-engine firm. In 1941 the company secured a majority holding in Svenska Flygmotor (aero-engines, printing presses), followed in 1942 by KMVA of Koping (machine tools). Bolinder-Munktells would join the group in 1950, their tractors and earthmoving machinery being subsequently marketed under the Volvo-B.M. name.

No further new models appeared until 1944, when the range was augmented with the LV140, a 5-tonner with a 5.7-litre ohv gasoline engine, and a full-front 40-seater bus, the B512, which was similarly powered and featured

1947 VOLVO LV150 3-ton truck, OMM

hydrovac brakes. By 1946 it was available with five forward speeds and Volvo's first true diesel, the 95hp VDA, a six of 6.1 litres' capacity: this also went into their heaviest truck, the LV150, though the rest of the immediate post-war time up followed classical themes, with sv and ohv gasoline engines and hydraulic brakes, double-reduction back axles featuring on 5- and 6-tonners. Even bigger 6.7-litre diesels made their appearance in 1947, when the company commanded 35 per cent of national truck sales and an impressive 47 per cent of PSVs, soon increased to over 50 per cent. In 1950 Volvo commercial models were available in seven European countries, four in South America, and in several parts of Africa as well.

Volvo were ready to move up-market. While light mediums remained American in concept and appearance, 5-speed gearboxes had reached the 5-ton sector by 1951, and a new departure was the L395 for 8/12-ton payloads. It used Volvo's own 9.6-litre, 130bhp direct injection diesel six, came in 6 × 2 as well as 4 × 2 form, and featured a 5-speed gearbox with synchromesh and overdrive, a hypoid rear axle, and a choice of hydrovac or full air brakes. It was made without change for several seasons, though as early as 1954 there were not only a 6 × 6 military derivative, but also the option of a turbocharger which boosted output to 195hp. There were also some more sophisticated PSV designs: the B658 of 1952 had its big diesel mounted horizontally under the floor, a semi-automatic preselector gearbox, and full air brakes: wheelbases of up to 19ft 8in were catalogued. A year later their were rear-engined derivatives (the B635 and B727) as well, while diesel power was bulking larger in the truck range, with a 90bhp 4.7-litre unit in the 4/5-ton L375 and a similar 6.7-litre type in the L385, a 6/7-tonner. At the other end of the scale there was a car-type delivery van, the PV445, essentially a commercial edition of the successful PV444 with the latest 1.6-litre ohv power unit. Such vehicles were still being marketed in a modest way as late as 1970, when the range included the PV154, based on the current 142 family. Advanced thinking was reflected by the early use of Kienzle tachographs in the bigger trucks, and even in 1957 some gasoline-engined models for export could be had with LPG conversion. 1958's heavy-duty L495 line came with ZF power steering as standard, but the lighter models were not forgotten, two novelties being the L2304 Laplander and the L420/L430 for 3/5-ton payloads. The former was a cross-country forward control 4 × 4 on a 6ft 10½in wheelbase using the 4-cylinder car engine, while the latter represented Volvo's first serious essay into forward control trucks for many years, and used a 3.6-litre ohv V8 gasoline engine originally intended for a big American-type sedan, the Philip, which never progressed beyond the prototype stage. The vehicle was on conventional lines, with 4-speed synchromesh gearbox, 2-speed rear axle, and hydrovac brakes. It continued without change until 1964, when a 3.6-litre 4-cylinder diesel, already an option, was standardized. Annual production of commercial vehicles had built up to close on 13,000 units by 1961.

c. 1960 VOLVO 495 11-ton 6×4 truck, GNG

Volvo's first international challenge in the heavy goods market came in 1963, with the 7½-ton forward control L4751. This featured Europe's second tilt cab (Foden had beaten them to it by a few months): it also used the familiar 5-speed synchromesh gearbox and hypoid final drive with a 2-speed axle option, other extras included turbocharging (which boosted output of the 4.7-litre engine from 97 to 123hp), air, and exhaust brakes. A year later the same formula had been applied to the top of the range, the normal control L495 being supplemented by a big tractor, the L4951, which had power steering as standard and use of the 9.6-litre engine in 240hp turbocharged form. It could cope with GCWs of 35 tons, and headed a range of smaller normal and forward control types in the 3/8-ton class. Standard buses used 6-cylinder diesel engines (the biggest one had a horizontal underfloor installation) and could seat from 34 to 51 passengers, though for lighter work it was possible to mount PSV coachwork on the L430 chassis.

The famous F85, F86 and F88 families made their appearance during 1965, with a 6 × 4 version of the biggest model, in base form a 10-tonner with 9.6-litre engine, power steering, and 8-speed dual range gearbox. 16-speed splitter boxes and torque converter transmissions had arrived by 1969, when Volvo were

1975 VOLVO F86 8½-ton truck Volvo

exporting a good 50 per cent of their output. New for 1971 was a semi-integral city bus, the B59, with horizontal 9.6-litre engine over the back axle, semi- or full-automatic transmission, power steering, and self-levelling rear suspension, the underfloor-engine theme being perpetuated on the B58, a coach chassis on which a manual box was standard. Outputs rose steadily; by 1972 the 86's 6.7-litre diesel was giving 207hp with the aid of a turbocharger, the 80's bigger unit was good for 260hp, and the 12-litre TD120A fitted to the biggest Volvo of all, the F89 with a GVW rating of 26 tons, disposed of a formidable 330hp. Volvo were also producing special export versions: for Britain, where Ailsa began serious assembly (as well as the manufacture of Volvo-engined PSVs to their own designs) in 1974, there was an eight-wheeler 86 and the FB88, an uprated 88 with wheels and brakes from the 89 and a 312hp turbocharged engine, and 1975 saw a 'Middle East Special' F88 with cooking and washing facilities in the sleeper cab. There were also low-emission F86s aimed at the municipal market.

1975 VOLVO-BM 6×6 logging truck and trailer, Volvo

Volvo's acquisition of D.A.F. in 1975 concerned only the car side of the Dutch company, but 1975 saw the two firms (along with Saviem of France and Magirus-Deutz of Germany) collaborate in the Club of Four scheme for a rationalized truck in the 6/13-ton GVW class. Volvo's contributions had tilt cabs and 5-speed synchromesh gearboxes: engines were either Perkins fours or their own 6-litre sixes, the latter giving 180hp in turbocharged form. During 1973 the big normal control trucks had been updated to bring them into line: cabs were shorter, power steering was standard, and the heaviest N12 (available as a 4 × 2, 6 × 2, or 6 × 4) was rated at 26½ tons GVW. The Laplander family was redesigned in 1975 as the C30, with 6-cylinder ohv car engine, eight forward speeds, and a payload of 2½ tons in optional 6 × 6 guise. This one was made under license by Csepel of Hungary.

A proposal for a merger with the rival Saab-Scania group in 1977 came to nothing, but there was more important news from Volvo in the shape of modern replacements for the well-tried F88 and F89. These F10s

1978 VOLVO F611 7.3-tonne GVW truck, Volvo

and F12s had independently sprung cabs, a power window on the passenger side, low emission levels, adjustable steering columns, and an air conditioning option. The biggest 12-litre turbocharged units now gave 350hp, and the specification, embraced air, exhaust and trailer brakes, with a choice of 16-speed splitter or 8-speed automatic gearboxes. The Club of Four range had been extended to embrace the heavier F614 with turbocharged 6-cylinder engine: GVW and GCW ratings were 13.5 and 25 tons respectively. The F85 and F86 were continued, but there was a new F4 for urban delivery work. GVW rating was 6½/7 tons, and other features were a walkthrough tilt cab, a 5-speed all-synchromesh gearbox, and power steering. Most interesting of all was the engine, a small diesel six with indirect injection and a turbocharger. It gave 120hp at a high 3,600rpm. Bus types embraced the front-engined B57 and B58 with front-mounted diesel and sixes, the latter model available with semi-automatic and automatic gearboxes, and in articulated form as well. Air-leaf suspension was optional. Air bellows springing and automatic transmission were standard on the B59, which had its 9.6-litre power unit set horizontally at the rear, and could be had as a luxury conference coach complete with television monitors, video tape recorder, and internal telephones: the body was by Johckheere of Belgium. A smaller conventional 30/40-seater, the B609, was also catalogued, using the mechanical elements of the Club of Four truck range. *JFJK/MCS*

1978 VOLVO F12 45-tonne GCW truck, Volvo

VOLVO BM (S) 1963 to date

(1) Bolinder Munktell, Eskilstuna 1963-1973

(2) Volvo BM AB Eskilstuna 1973 to date

Munktells was an old-established manufacturer of steam traction engines and rollers dating back to the 19th century, who made agricultural tractors with Bolinder engines from 1913, and in 1950 became part of Volvo. Production of dump trucks began in 1963, and four years later came the 860 series of articulated 6-wheel dump trucks which have been the division's staple product ever since. The frame pivots both horizontally and vertically behind the front axle, giving excellent traction on rough ground and a much smaller turning circle than in a rigid 6-wheeler. Drive from the 150 hp Volvo 6-cylinder engine is to the front and leading rear axle. The dump truck model is known as the DR860, and there is also an all-purpose chassis of similar design known as the TC860. With a load capacity of more than 18 tons, this has been used for log and pipe hauling, cable laying, cement mixing and even, with a 4,000 gallon tank, for fire fighting. *GNG*

1928 VOMAG Type 5CZ 6-ton truck, HON

VOMAG (D) 1915-1944

(1) Vogtlandische Maschinenfabrik AG. vorm. J.C. & H. Dietrich, Plauen 1915-1932

(2) Vomag Betriebs-AG, Plauen 1932-1938

(3) Vomag Maschinenfabrik GmbH., Plauen 1938-1944

This firm originally built textile and printing machines but during WW I took up production of trucks. Two types were available after the war, a 3- and a 4-tonner, both with chain- or cardan drive; a cardan driven bus and a 1½ ton van followed. In 1924 three-axle versions were presented. On buses the third axle, which was not driven, was steerable. Available were 3, 4, 5, 6 and 7 ton versions with own 4-cylinder engines of 45, 50 and 65 hp output. A Maybach 120 hp engine was used for the buses. In 1928 Vomag presented a bus with front-drive. This type was later built in considerable numbers although the principle was not to have a lasting break-through. Vomag specialized in the heavier types of trucks and buses, but production was not too significant compared with other manufacturers. Buses were used to a large extent by the KVG, a state owned company operating in the province of Saxony.

1930 VOMAG Type 60V57 bus, HON

1938 VOMAG streamlined bus and trailer, body and trailer by Gaubschat, Ingo Kasten

1939 VOMAG 4½-ton truck, FLP

In 1930 the first diesel engine was produced following the Oberhansli principle. In the mid-thirties trucks ranging from 3½ to 9 tons payload capacity were available with diesel engines fro 80 to 140 hp. 2- and 3-axle chassis' were used for trucks as well as buses. An express road tractor with 100 bhp diesel engine was added in 1937. A last new development suffered from the outbreak of war. It was a unitary construction which was developed in co-operation with the coachbuilding firm of Crede and Kassel. After the war production was not resumed. *HON*

VORAN (D) 1928-1929

Voran Automobilbau A.G., Berlin

After front-driven private cars this firm turned to commercials. Experiments were made with trucks and buses. In the development of buses the company co-operated with the Berlin bus company ABOAG and some front-driven double-deck buses were built. One of these was acquired by General of London. *HON*

VULCAN (i) (GB) 1907-1953

(1) Vulcan Motor & Engineering Co. Ltd., Southport, Lancashire 1907-1938

(2) Vulcan Motors Ltd., Maidstone, Kent, 1938-1953

Though better known for their commercial vehicles, Vulcan did not market these until five years after their first car. Before 1914 production was limited to light vans for payloads of 15 cwt or less, initially with sv 2-cylinder engines: by 1912 fours of 2.1 and 2.4-litres were standard. Design was conventional, with 3-speed gearboxes and worm drive. In 1914 the company introduced a 30-cwt truck, still with cone clutch and worm drive, but now with four speeds. Capacity of the 4-cylinder T-head engine was 3.3-litres: post-war editions, though basically similár, were distinguishable by their L-head monobloc layout.

The early post-war years were punctuated by unhappy financial adventures. In 1919 Vulcan joined the Harper Bean consortium, serving as the truck division, though private cars would still be made until 1928. By mid-1920 commercial vehicle production was said to be running at 100 units a week, but the group collapsed, all the same. In 1923 Vulcan forged an equally profitless link with Lea-

1923 VULCAN (i) 26-seater bus, NMM

Francis of Coventry, even offering the disastrous twin ohc 16/60 hp car model as an ambulance chassis in 1928. This was not the only attempt at a light, car-type commercial; others included a 2.6-litre taxicab with T-head engine in 1922, and a 7-cwt van on the 12 hp touring chassis in 1925. In the main, however, Vulcan concentrated on medium-duty trucks in the 1¼-cwt to 4-ton class, all with 4-cylinder sv engines (Dormans were used on some of the bigger ones), magneto ignition, cone clutches, transmission footbrakes, and worm drive. Pneumatic tires and electric lighting were available on light duty models as early as 1920, and a 4-ton light artic came in 1922. From 1925 onwards there were some WD subsidy types — a 30-cwt 6 × 4, a 2-ton halftrack, and even an extraordinary 4 × 4 cross-country machine made under Holverter patents, with 4-wheel steering and all-independent springing. 1930 models of the 30-cwt and 2½-ton standard Vulcans were available with forward control, while the firm was making a speciality of low-loading municipal models on small-diameter wheels shod with solid tires, on which the driver sat beside his engine. Even more complex was a chain-drive sweeper-collector of 1926, with 4.1-litre engine and 7 ft. wheelbase, complete with a 100-gallon water tank on the cab roof, but refuse collectors continued to be a regular Vulcan line until 1939. Later models featured conventional forward control and pneumatic tires.

1925 VULCAN (i) 1½-ton Subsidy-type truck, OMM

1930 VULCAN (i) RSW 1½-ton 6×4 army truck, BHV

PSVs also engaged Vulcan's interest for several years, starting in 1922 with 20-26-seaters on the 2-ton chassis, but progressing by 1926 to purpose-built models of half-cab type, these being made with worm or double reduction bevel drive, pneumatic tires, twin rear wheels, and full electrics. Big 4-cylinder engines were general practice, though sixes made their appearance in 1927 on the small normal control 20-seater Brighton, which used a 2.7-litre twin-carburetor ohv Meadows unit. A year later came Vulcan's own 6.6-litre sv engine in the 32-seater Brisbane, and the 1930 bus and coach range ran to six models, from the modest 20-seater Duke with 49 hp 4.1-litre 4-cylinder engine up to the Emperor, a classic double-decker with Dewandre servo fwb. Its 6-cylinder engine developed 130 bhp, but the only major operator to show serious interest was Vulcan's home town of Southport, and the smaller PSVs were never best sellers either, though a number of 26-seater half-cab Duchesses found their way to Guernsey. By early 1931 Vulcan had followed Lea-Francis into receivership, even if production continued, the

1935 VULCAN (i) Retriever 2-ton truck, OMM

popular refuse collectors acquired a new-style ribbon radiator shell which persisted on Vulcans up to 1939.

The PSV range was still listed as late as 1933, but that year's main effort centered round a range of normal and forward control trucks on classic lines, from a 3-litre 30/35-cwt to a 4-tonner with 5.3-litre 78 hp engine. All but the smallest had vacuum servo fwb, plate clutches replaced the old cones, and fully enclosed cabs of new design made their appearance; on forward control Vulcans a section of the front wing swung up to give access to the engine. a 5/6-tonner with forward control was introduced in 1934, in which year there were also 4-cylinder diesel options, a Dorman in smaller types, and a Gardner in the heavy duty range. Hydraulic brakes and spiral bevel back axles featured on normal and forward control 2-tonners announced in 1935/6, though the older arrangements persisted on the 5-tonners, which now had new 4-cylinder engines of Vulcan's own make.

A takeover by Tilling-Stevens led to the transfer of operations to Maidstone in 1938, but design changed little, apart from the standardization of forward control and the replacement of Gardners by Perkins P6s as the recognized diesel option. An interesting side-issue of 1939 was a range of 2-ton battery electrics marketed under both Tilling-Stevens and Vulcan names. In 1941 authority

1946 VULCAN (i) 6VF 6-ton truck, OMM

was given for the production of improved 6-ton 6VF and 6PF models for essential civilian users. These had either the Perkins or an improved 4.6-litre 78 hp Vulcan 4-cylinder engine with coil ignition; brakes were hydraulic, the gearbox was of 4-speed constant-mesh type, and like all previous Vulcans the 6-tonners retained worm drive. With the return of peace tractor and tipper models were added to the range, followed in 1950 by a full-front coach chassis.

Meanwhile losses incurred by the parent Tilling-Stevens company had led to a takeover by the Rootes Group in 1950. At that year's Show Vulcan exhibited a new 7-tonner with Gardner 4LW engine, servo brakes, 5-speed gearbox, and hypoid final drive, but this was nearly the end, and production of both makes at Maidstone was quietly run down. *MCS*

VULCAN (ii) (US) 1913-1916

Driggs-Seabury Ordnance Co., Sharon, Pa.

The Vulcan succeeded the American-built Commer. Five models from 3-ton to 7-ton capacity were listed in 1913. Driggs-Seabury made all parts for the Vulcan, which had a 4-cylinder engine, cone clutch, chain drive, and pressed steel frame. When Driggs-Seabury became involved in war work the Vulcan range was cut to three models from 2-ton to 5-ton capacity in mid-1915 and was discontinued in late 1916. Driggs-Seabury was also responsible for building the Twombly, Sharon, Driggs-Seabury, and Ritz motor cars. *DJS*

VULKAN (D) 1899-1905

Vulkan Automobil GmbH., Berlin SW13

This company offered a variety of electric driven vans. Only one motor was used for the front driven wheels. *HON*

1977 WABCO Model 3200B 235-ton diesel-electric dump truck, Wabco

WABCO (US) 1957 to date

(1) Le Tourneau-Westinghouse Co., Peoria, Ill. 1957-1968
(2) Westinghouse Air Brake Co., Construction Equipment Divn., Peoria, Ill. 1968-1972
(3) Wabco Construction & Mining Equipment Group, Peoria, Ill. 1972 to date

Wabco's roots go back to two old-established companies, the Westinghouse Air Brake Co. of railroad fame, established in 1869, and the R.G. Le Tourneau Co., makers of road-building machinery since 1919. In 1953 Westinghouse purchased the earth-moving equipment part of Le Tourneau, and four years later launched a line of giant rear dump trucks under the trade name Haulpak. The first models were 27 and 30 tonners, but as the demand for larger trucks grew Wabco extended their range to include a 65-tonner in the mid-1960s, a 100-tonner by 1970 and in 1971 a 200-tonner diesel-electric semi-trailer. This has since been replaced by a rigid 6 × 4, the M3200B with a capacity of 235 tons.

1974 WABCO Model 50 50-dump truck, Wabco

The current range consists of diesel-powered trucks of 35, 50, 75 and 85 tons, and diesel-electrics of 120 and 170 tons, in addition to the M3200B. The 35- to 85-ton group is powered by Cummins 6 or V-12 engines of 420 to 700 hp, or Detroit Diesel V-12 or V-16 engines of 475 to 700 hp. These drive through 6-speed Allison powershift transmissions with electric shift control to Wabco's own double reduction rear axle. Service brakes are air over hydraulic, and there is full-time power steering. For the diesel-electrics, engines are V-12 Cummins, Caterpillar or Detroit Diesel for the 120-tonner, V-12 or V16 Detroits for the 150- and 170-tonners, and a General Motors EMD V-12 of 2,000 to 2,475 hp for the M3200B. This unit is normally used in railroad locomotives. Drive is through two EMD drive motors (General Electric on the smaller diesel-electrics) and Wabco spur and planetary gear reductions. Wabco also makes bottom-dump articulated coal haulers of 120 to 150 tons powered by Cummins V-12 or Detroit Diesel V-16 engines, both of 700 hp.

Wabcos are distributed worldwide, and there are factories at Gembloux, Belgium, Campinas, Brazil, and Rydalmere, N.S.W., Australia. The latter makes a specifically Australian model, the W22, which with a 230 hp 6-cylinder Detroit Diesel engine is smaller than any of the U.S. models. *RW*

WACHUSETT (US) 1922-1930

Wachusett Motors Inc., Fitchburg, Mass.

The Wachusett company was started by a former partner in the New England Truck Company who made the Netco. Fred Suthergreen erected a new building just across the street from the Netco factory and began to make a line of conventional assembled trucks using Continental engines, Brown-Lipe transmissions and Timken rear axles. Load capacities were in the 1 to 2½-ton range. *GNG*

WADE (US) 1913-1914

Wade Commercial Car Co., Holly, Mich.

The Wade was a crude looking vehicle, even for a high-wheeler, with rated capacity of 800 lbs. and an open express body. It used a single-cylinder, air-cooled engine mounted under the body, with friction transmission and double chain-drive. Its wheelbase was only 6 feet, and its price only $400. *GMN*

1914 WAGENHALS 800lb 3-wheel mail van, US Postmaster General

WAGENHALS (US) 1910-1914

(1) Wagenhals Manufacturing Co., St. Louis, Mo. 1910-1911

(2) Wagenhals Motor Car Co., Detroit, Mich. 1912-1914

The single model of this make was a 3-wheeler, a type which had a short vogue at that time. This was claimed to be a 750 lb. and used a 14 hp 2-cylinder engine through 1913, with a 4-cylinder engine for the last year. The transmission was a planetary type and final drive was by a single chain to the lone rear wheel. Steering was by wheel to the front axle. The driver sat behind the delivery box. In 1912, the chassis was underslung apparently in an attempt to obtain better stability. Wheelbase was 6 feet, 8 inches. *GMN*

WALKER (i) (US) 1906-1942

(1) Automobile Maintenance & Mfg. Co., Chicago, Ill. 1906-1911

(2) Walker Vehicle Co., Chicago, Ill. 1911-1942

The Walker was America's best-known and longest-lived make of electric truck. The first models were sold under the name Walker Balance Gear and had separate electric motors for each rear wheel. This system was replaced in 1909 by a single 3½ hp motor mounted integrally in the hollow rear axle. There was also a gas-electric powered by a 3-cylinder 2-cycle engine, but this did not last long. By 1912 there were five models in the range, from 750 lbs. to 3½ tons capacity, all with rear axle motors. These were continued through the 1920s and 1930s with relatively little change except for updating in such matters as pneumatic tires which came in with the lighter models in the mid-1920s. At this time the lighter delivery trucks had small dummy hoods though the heavier models were all forward control. The 1929 Model 10 Special ¾-ton panel delivery had a full-length hood and was as stylish as the

1915 WALKER (i) ½-ton electric pick-up, NAHC

1932 WALKER (i) 4-ton electric truck, NAHC

best gasoline panel deliveries. Capacities ran from ¾-ton to 7 tons in 1929.

In 1938 came another gas-electric, the Walker Dynamotive. This was a multi-stop delivery powered by either a 4-cylinder Waukesha or 6-cylinder Chrysler engine, with capacities of 1 and 1½ tons respectively. It had a 15KW DC generator on the flywheel bellhousing, and the standard Walker axle-mounted motor. The Dynamotive, together with electric trucks of 1½ to 5 tons capacity, was made up to 1942, but production was not resumed after the war.

Walkers were exported to Britain in some numbers, and were widely used by London stores such as Selfridges and Harrods. When the latter began to make their own delivery vans in 1936 they used a number of Walker components. *GNG*

1949 WALKER (ii) 5-ton truck, OMM

WALKER (ii) (GB) 1947-1955

Walker Bros. (Wigan) Ltd., Pagefield Ironworks, Wigan. Lancs.

After Walkers were bought by the engineering firm of Walmsleys in 1947 most of the former Pagefield municipal vehicle models like Paragons and Paladins were renamed Walker. They were joined by some Walker-NCB battery electric chassis converted by Northern Coachbuilders, and in 1948 by a 5-ton export chassis. This was made from bought-in components, as Walkers' machining facilities were fully occupied by Walmsleys, and was powered by the Perkins P6 engine. Production ended in 1955. *OM*

WALKER-JOHNSON (US) 1919-1924

(1) Walker-Johnson Truck Co., East Woburn, Mass. 1919-1920
(2) Walker-Johnson Truck Co., Boston, Mass. 1920-1923

From 1919 to 1922, this was a 2½-tonner only with a Buda 4-cylinder engine, a 4-speed Brown-Lipe gearbox and Timken worm-drive rear axle. Wheelbase was 12 feet, 6 inches. In 1922, this was replaced by a shorter 1-tonner with a 4-cylinder Midwest engine. *GMN*

WALL (GB) 1911-1915

A. W. Wall Ltd., Roc Motor Works, Tyseley, Birmingham

Better known as builders of three-wheeled cyclecars, Walls also offered a small delivery van on the same V-shaped tubular frame. Initially powered by a forward mounted 4-5 hp single cylinder inclined air-cooled engine (enlarged in 1914 to an 8 hp V-twin) transmission was by Roc 2-speed epicyclic gear and cardan shaft to the live rear axle. Capacity was 5-cwt (increased to 6-cwt with the larger engine) and despite tiller steering, the Wall found favor with Boots the chemists and was even exported to Brazil. *MJWW*

1922 WALLACE coach, NMM

WALLACE (US/GB) 1919-1922

Richmond Motor Lorries Ltd., Shepherd's Bush, London W.12

Wallace vehicles were assembled in London from American-made components, under the direction of S.A. Wallace who had formerly been chief engineer of A.E.C. They used a 4-cylinder Continental Red Seal engine, 3-speed gearbox and bevel drive rear axle. The capacity of the trucks was 30-cwt, and a char-a-banc model was also made. The company said that they hoped to build the whole vehicle in Britain before long, but there is no evidence that they did so. *GNG*

1910 WALLIS & STEEVENS steam wagon NMM

WALLIS & STEEVENS (GB) 1895-1930

Wallis & Steevens Ltd., Basingstoke, Hants

Wallis & Steevens were at their best in their uncomplicated free steaming agricultural engines and their Advance rollers but they supplied a number of road haulage engines in 5, 6, 7 and 8 nhp sizes from about 1895 to 1915, 13 of which went to showmen. A few, in the last century, were singles but most were compounds.

Under the freedom of the 1896 Act they produced a 3-ton single cylinder tractor, a dizzily temperamental design which could, with careful handling, do useful work. This was followed in 1905 by a 4-ton compound tractor, incorporating the Wallis patent oil-bath enclosure to the engine also used in their wagons. Though a good idea, the oil-bath was not so good in use, it being difficult to keep the oil in and the water out. The firm did not believe in high boiler pressures, generally favoring 140 psi for singles and 170 psi for the compound tractors (180 psi in later road locos). The agricultural engines worked well at modest pressures by having (generally) 2½" diameter fire-tubes but in the tractors the makers yielded to theory using more and smaller tubes, which made the steaming qualities unpredictable, a characteristic that carried over into the first overtype compound 5-ton wagon in 1906. A 3-tonner working at 200 psi followed in 1911 and a few 2-ton wagons were made together with an experimental vertical engined steam van. Early wagon boilers had 3 tubes (out of a total of 44) of 2¾" diameter and the rest 1¾", the idea being that the large tubes would assist steam production when it was needed but could be closed by dampers when steam was being produced to excess. Early 5-ton wagons worked at only 150 psi but in latter examples this was stepped up to 150 psi and (after 1920) to 200 psi with much improved performance, early Wallis wagons being notable sluggards. All 5-tonners were fitted with the oil-bath but 3-tonners had an open engine. Total wagon production was 127.

The steam tractors continued to be listed until the mid-thirties but by this time self-propelled vehicle production was concentrated upon the firm's conspicuously successful Advance steam or diesel road-rollers. The last design of steam tractor was a 5 nhp engine with two speeds and road springs, mounted on solid rubber tires, which was launched in 1927 but, in a contracting market, it failed to make headway against the Foden tractor and only 5 were made. Roller production has continued to date. *RAW*

WALTER (i) (US) 1909 to date

(1) Walter Auto Truck Mfg. Co., New York, N.Y. 1909-1911
(2) Walter Motor Truck Co., New York, N.Y. 1911-1923
(3) Walter Motor Truck Co., Long Island City, N.Y. 1923-1935
(4) Walter Motor Truck Co., Ridgewood, L.I., N.Y. 1935-1957
(5) Walter Motor Truck Co., Voorheesville, N.Y. 1957 to date

William Walter, a Swiss immigrant, came to the U.S.A. in 1883 and established himself as a manufacturer of candy and confectionery machinery. He built himself a passenger car in 1898 and from 1904 to 1909 made high-quality cars, at first in New York City and later at Trenton, N.J. Truck production began in 1909 at the New York factory on West 66th Street, and in 1911 the first 4-wheel-drive trucks appeared, which were to become the staple

1914 WALTER (i) 4×4 truck, Walter

1934 WALTER (i) 75ft ladder truck, OMM

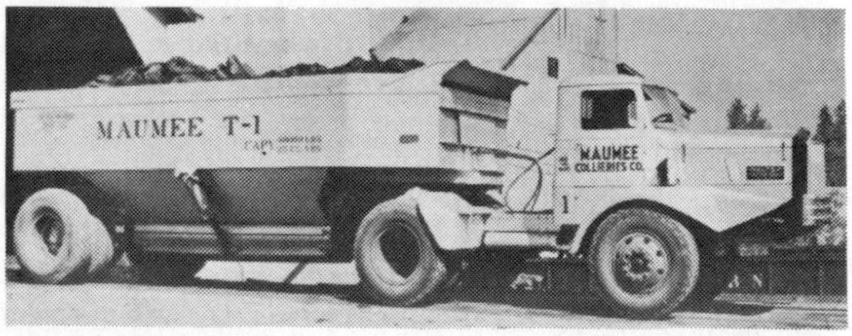

1937 WALTER (i) 20-ton coal truck, RW

product of the company. Based on the French Latil and of similar appearance with radiator behind engine, they were made in sizes from 1½ to 7 tons. Conventional rear wheel drive and also front wheel drive trucks were also made, all with internal gear drive to the wheels. Engines were Walter's own make up to 1920, then mainly Waukesha during the 1920s. Gradually the rear-wheel-drive models were phased out, although a 15/25-ton rwd tractor with 5-speed gearbox was made as late as 1924. By the mid-1920s Walters had assumed their characteristic appearance with engine projecting ahead of the front axle; in 1929 the first Walter Snow Fighter appeared, and this was a field in which the company later became well-known, as well as for highway maintenance work and carrying cement mixers. During the 1930's Walter supplied a number of fire engines to New York City. Articulated dump trucks were used in open-cast coal mining, and Walters were also seen

1949 WALTER (i) 4×4 heavy wrecker truck, LA

1975 WALTER (i) 4×4 Model CBK airport fire crash truck, Walter

in the logging industry. By 1940 there were six models, all with 4-wheel-drive, of 3 to 12 tons capacity. Engines were 6-cylinder units by Waukesha, Hercules and Cummins, the latter a diesel.

During World War II Walter supplied 4 × 4 artillery tractors with 672ci 6-cylinder Hercules engines to the U.S. Army, and also snow removal trucks with Waukesha engines to both U.S. and Canadian forces. After the war the 4-wheel-drive trucks were continued, and Walter entered a new field with the building of airfield crash tenders. These were developed in conjunction with the Federal Government, the Port of New York Authority and the National Fire Protection Association. Current production includes crash tenders with single and twin engines, refuse collection trucks and the familiar 4-wheel-drive trucks and snowplows. *LA*

WALTER (ii) (CS) 1922-1946

(1) Akciova Tovarna Automobilu Joseph Walter, a spol., Prague-Jinonice 1922-1932
(2) Akciova Spol. Walter, Tovarna na Automobily a Letecke Motory, Prague-Jinonice 1932-1946

Joseph Walter built 3-wheeled cars from 1910, but his first commercial vehicle was a 30-cwt delivery van powered by the 6/18 hp 1.54-litre 4-cylinder single ohc engine, introduced in 1922. This was increased to 20 hp in 1924, in which year the larger W1Z1 van and truck was introduced, using a 2.1-litre sv engine. Other models of this era included the Commercial with the 4-cylinder 1.9-litre ohc engine from the firm's 4B passenger car, and the Universal powered by a 6-cylinder 2.86-litre ohv engine, again a passenger car unit. This 6B engine had an aluminum crankcase. These two models were made from 1926 to 1932, and a few additional ones in 1935. Also in 1926 came the PN 2-tonner, powered by a 4-cylinder 2.37-litre ohc engine. This was also made in bus form, and in 1927 a regular service from Prague to Berlin was started with these vehicles. In 1928 the PN was replaced by a larger 3-axle

1928 WALTER (ii) PN 16-seater bus, MSH

1936 WALTER (ii) D-3-V street sprinkler, Techniart

model with 2.84-litre engine. Larger still was the FN with 5.2-litre 4-cylinder engine made as a 3½/4-ton truck or 37-passenger bus. In 1932 a 30-passenger bus was built using an enlarged version of the V-12 engine of the Walter Royal pasenger car; its capacity was 7.3-litres. From 1932 onwards the larger Walters used 4- and 6-cylinder double-piston Junkers Diesel engines; the 4-cylinder was a 2.72-litre 55 bhp unit, and the 6-cylinder a 4.08-litre 80 bhp unit.

The last series of PN trucks was made in 1946, after which the factory began to make engines for Praga RN trucks. Walter also made stationary diesel and gas engines, carburetors, starters, fuel pumps and aero engines and propellors. Production of the latter continues today. *MSH*

WALTHAM or WALTHAM-ORIENT (US) 1906-1908

Waltham Manufacturing Company, Waltham, Mass.

Commercial vehicles under these names were very light vans ranging in capacity from 600 pounds to 800 pounds. As many as eight types were offered in a single year, all powered by one and two cylinder engines of 4 and 8 hp. All used friction transmissions and had wheelbases of 8 feet, 2 inches or 8 feet, 3 inches. The largest model was called a Democrat Wagon and was a bus for 4 to 6 passengers with a price of $1,850. *GMN*

WANDERER (D) 1928-1939

Wanderer-Werke A.G., Siegmar

Private cars of this make were the basis for van versions which were offered from about 1928. These were available with 4-cylinder engines at first and during the thirties had 6-cylinder units of 1,692 cc and 1,963 cc. *HON*

WANTAGE (GB) 1901-1913

Wantage Engineering Co. Ltd., Wantage, Berks.

The building of traction engines began at Wantage in 1887 and although some engines were turned out with plated flywheels and covers to the motion, with an eye on road haulage, the firm cannot, with the definition adopted for this book, be considered builders of road locomotives.

1901 WANTAGE steam wagon and trailer, RAW

In 1901 the firm made a vertical boiler undertype wagon of primitive appearance to compete in the War Department Trials but it failed to appear, and this was followed in 1902 by a wagon of more developed appearance, being a compound undertype with a countershaft differential and chain drive, steamed by a vertical boiler. On their own showing the firm seem to have tried both water tube and fire tube types before satisfying themselves that the locomotive boiler was the best for use in wagons; a decision they put into practice in 1904 when they launched the wagon onto the market using a top fired locomotive boiler. Whether this was a rebuild of the vertical boilered wagon is not known but apart from the boiler the resemblance was close. The wagon was rated as a 4-tonner. The makers also offered to build a 2-tonner on "pneumatic puncture-proof tires" but there is no evidence that this was done.

A steam tractor was built following generally the arrangement of the wagon but rather larger in the cylinders. A Wantage wagon was the chassis of the elaborate "Tarmaciser" machine exhibited at the Staines Road Tar Trials in 1907, which swept, tarred and gritted the surface in one operation but perished from over complication before more had been built than this prototype. Though the company continued to list wagons for some years 1907/8 marked the effective end of manufacture notwithstanding the fact that, dissatisfied with the compound engine for undertypes, the company went to the lengths of commissioning the design of a four cylinder single acting engine, which was never put into production. *RAW*

1930 WARD 4-ton electric van, NAHC

1929 WARD ½-ton electric van, NAHC

WARD (US) 1910-1934

(1) Ward Motor Vehicle Co., Bronx, N.Y. 1910-1914
(2) Ward Motor Vehicle Co., Mt. Vernon, N.Y. 1915-1934

Ward was long one of the principal manufacturers of battery operated electric commercial vehicles. This make began with five delivery van types all with chain drive and with rated capacities from one of 800 lbs. to a 2-tonner. By 1912, a 3½-tonner was added with a speed of 7 mph and a 4-tonner was made for 1914. Yet another, a 5-tonner, was added for 1915. Essentially no changes were made to these models until 1922 when the smallest was a ½-tonner. In 1925, a 10-tonner was offered. There were some minor changes in the ratings of the several models during the last years but from 1925 through 1932 there were more than ten different models which were cataloged, from ½-tonners to 7½-tonners. Westinghouse supplied the DC motors used in Ward electrics until 1920, and after that year, motors were from General Electric. Production of complete vehicles ceased in 1934, but Ward continued to make truck bodies until 1965. *GMN*

WARD LAFRANCE (US) 1918 to date

Ward LaFrance Truck Corporation, Elmira, N.Y.

Founded by A. Ward LaFrance, a member of the same family who mae American LaFrance fire engines, although there was never any business connection between the two concerns, Ward LaFrance was an

1937 WARD LA FRANCE pumper, Ward La France

assembled truck which made an important contribution to the war effort and today specializes in fire engines.

Early Ward LaFrance trucks were offered in a range from 2½ to 5/7 tons, and featured Waukesha engines, Brown-Lipe transmissions and Timken axles. They were generally conventional, although employing a self-lubricating system which was complex and bulky. The 1920 2½-tonner was specially designed for pneumatic tires, and an engine-driven 2-cylinder Kellogg pump for the tires was standard equipment. The range was widened in 1926 with 6-cylinder engines in some models and more heavy-duty models in the 5- to 7-ton area. Two bus chassis were added in 1929, followed in 1930 by the 'Bustruk'. This was a high-speed chassis adaptable for bus or van-type bodies, powered by a straight-8 Lycoming engine.

Ward LaFrance sales, which rarely exceeded 100 units annually, were confined for the most part to New York

1945 WARD LA FRANCE Model D articulated truck, FLP

State, the City being a major market. The 1930s saw an increasing emphasis on purely custom-built units such as the 4 × 4 crane truck for hauling away illegally parked cars, delivered to New York City in 1934. As a small assembler Ward LaFrance adopted diesel power early, with a Cummins-engined 6-wheeler catalogued in 1934. From this date onwards diesels became an increasingly important part of the Ward LaFrance range. Big and handsome tractors for gross loads of up to 20 tons were made in the 1930s, together with a heavy-duty cab-over-engine 6-wheeler from 1935. One of the more unusual options at this time was a fabricated chassis frame in steel or Duralumin to customer's choice. This was a deep 14 inches just behind the cab. Costly to make, it was dropped on later models for a more conventional heat-treated channel frame.

During World War II Ward LaFrance made large numbers of heavy-duty wreckers. Designated M1, and later M1A1, these 6 × 6 10-ton trucks with Continental 6-cylinder engines were also made by Kenworth. In addition to the wreckers, Ward LaFrance made a number of 6 × 4 and 6 × 6 load-carrying army trucks. Wartime production necessitated substantial additions to the small Elmira plant, and to capitalize on this Ward LaFrance introduced a new range of trucks in 1945, the D Series. These were offered in sizes from 40,000 to 60,000lbs GCW, and used Continental Gasoline or Cummins Diesel Engines. Styling was functional with military overtones, the fenders having flat tops in the style of quarry trucks. Attempts were made at large-scale marketing, including in Canada,

1975 WARD LA FRANCE 8×8 HET tractor, Ward La France

and for a time sales were well up on pre-war (509 in 1947 and 271 in 1948), but production fell off severely once the postwar boom was over. By the mid-1950s ordinary load-carrying trucks had been given up in favor of fire engines, bodies, shipping containers and trailers. In 1945 Ward LaFrance attempted to market buses in knocked-down form for export and used the sectional body construction pioneered by C.J. Hug and used during the war by Wayne Works. If the post-war plans had succeeded, Buda diesel engines would have been used and Hug is said to have been engaged as the chassis engineer. Westinghouse became interested and proposed a trolleybus version called the Westram, some of which were actually produced and sold in Argentina and Mexico. There is no record of any Ward LaFrance bus being sold in the U.S.

Ward LaFrance built their first fire engine in 1931, and these vehicles became of increasing importance in the firm's activities. Conventional open-cab ladder trucks were made until 1960, joined in 1959 by the modern type of forward-cab appliance which has been made in 4- and 6-wheeler models with a great variety of pumper and aerial platform bodies. Engines used include Waukesha, Roiline, Hall-Scott, International and Ford and the fire engines have 5- or 6-speed transmissions and air brakes. Fire equipment is also built on other chassis such as Ford, International and Chevrolet, while the most powerful

1975 WARD LA FRANCE Ambassador custom pumper, Ward La France

Ward LaFrance is a twin-V8-engined 4 × 4 airfield crash tender with a total power of 532hp and a maximum speed of 60mph. In 1971 Ward LaFrance pioneered a move away from red as the traditional fire engine color; experiments by an optometrist indicated that lime yellow was more clearly visible by both day and night, and by 1975 the company had received orders for lime yellow engines from more than 140 fire departments all over the United States and in El Salvador, Saudi Arabia, Colombia and Venezuela. Ward LaFrance also supplies the US Army with the HET tractor, an 8 × 8 heavy duty transporter powered by a 600hp diesel engine. *RJ/GNG*

WARE (US) 1912-1915

Ware Motor Vehicle Co., Saint Paul, Minn.

Designed by J.L. Ware, this was an early example of a 4-wheel drive truck in which the power, unusually, was taken from the 4-cylinder engine by propeller shaft to the rear axle where there were power dividers each side of the differential. From there power was transferred by two long shafts back to the front axle. Three sizes were made, from ¾ to 3-tons. The Ware company was succeeded by the Twin City Four Wheel Drive Company who continued the design. *RW*

WARREN (i) or WARREN—DETROIT (US)1911-1913

warren Motor Car Company, Detroit, Michigan

The Warren light delivery vans were half-tonners and were based on the Warren Model 11 passenger car chassis. Though this was a 1911 design, it remained unchanged for threee production years of the commercial types. Both open and enclosed bodies were offered which used a 30hp, 4-cylinder engine with a 3-speed transmission and shaft drive. Wheelbase was 9 feet, 2 inches. The "Winged Express" model cost $1300. *GMN*

WARREN (ii) (US) 1912-1913

Warren Motor Truck Co., Warren, Ohio

The Model 30 was the only truck made by this manufacturer. It was a ½-tonner with an open express body on a wheelbase of 9 feet, 2 inches. It was powered by a 4-cylinder, 30hp engine. Possibly this make was continued into 1916, but the evidence is questionable. *GMN*

WARREN-LAMBERT (GB) 1914-1915

Warren-Lambert Engineering Co. Ltd., Shepherd's Bush, London W.

The Warren-Lambert light car was powered either by a 2-cylinder Blumfield or 4-cylinder Dorman engine, and a 4/5-cwt light van was offered on the 2-cylinder chassis. *GNG*

WARRICK (GB) 1911-1931

John Warrick & Co. Ltd., Reading, Berks.

The Warrick parcelcar was a 3-wheeler similar to the Autocarrier, made by a firm who had begun in business with pedal-driven parcelcars. It was powered by a 723cc single-cylinder air-cooled engine of Warrick's own manufacture, which drove via a 2-speed epicyclic transmission and chain to the single rear wheel. As in the Autocarrier, the driver sat over the engine, with the load ahead of him. In 1912 a prototype was tested of a front-seated version with double chain drive, but this did not go into production. About 2,000 Warricks were made between 1911 and 1925, and design hardly changed over the years. A few were assembled from existing parts up to 1931. *GNG*

WARSZAWA (PL) 1958-1972

Fabryka Samochodow Osobowych, Warsaw-Zeran

The FSO factory undertook the production of Soviet Pobeda cars, early in 1951, using at first imported engines and components and building locally only the body. Warszawas were for many years the only cars built in Poland and soon a ½-ton payload pick-up version was introduced. Sharing the car's front end and mechanical components, now almost completely Polish built, Warszawa pickup were built unchanged for many years, apart from a grille facelift in 1968. Power came from the old Pobeda designed 4 cylinder, 77 hp gasoline engine, the same as used in Warszawa cars and Nysa or Zuk light commercials. A station wagon and an ambulance were also introduced after the 1968 facelift. The introduction of Polski Fiat cars in 1968, saw the end of the old style Warszawa generation, production of which was dropped in 1972. *GA*

WARTBURG (D) 1901-1904

Fahrzeugfabrik Eisenach, Eisenach

This firm started to produce cars under the name of Eisenach. In 1900 the name Wartburg was chosen for a private car, but one year later also commercials were presented. A truck and a bus were available. 2-cylinder engines and 4-cylinder engines were used. The cars featured an underfloor engine. After 1904 vehicles were offered as Dixi. *HON*

WASHINGTON (i) (US) 1909-1912

Washington Motor Vehicle Co., Washington, D.C.

Four models of battery-powered electrics were made under this name. These ranged from a 750-pound delivery van to a two-tonner. They were equipped with Edison alkaline batteries and were claimed to give 50 miles per charge. Final drive for all types was by double chains. The four-tonner used a wheelbase of 9 feet, 4 inches and the chassis cost $2,800. One reference claims this name was changed to Capitol car in 1911.*GMN*

WASHINGTON (ii) (US) 1914-1916

Washington Motor Car Co., Hyattsville, MD.

Little information is known about this make other than the three models which were listed: 5-, 6- and 7-tonners. Possibly this could have been a continuation of the earlier make of the same name from the District of Columbia. *GMN*

WATEROUS (US) 1906-c.1923

Waterous Engine Works, St. Paul, Minn.

An old-established maker of horse-drawn steam fire engines, Waterous is credited with delivering the first gasoline-powered fire engine in the United States. Sold to Radnor, Pa. Fire Department, it had two engines, one for propelling and one for driving the pump. It was of forward-control layout, but in 1907 Waterous introduced a 4-cylinder fire engine with engine under a large hood, and this was made in small numbers at least until 1923. The company still makes pumps today. *GNG*

1920 WATSON (ii) 5-ton articulated truck, FLP

WATSON (i) (CDN) 1912

The Watson Carriage Co. Ltd., Ottawa, Ont.

Watson built light delivery trucks and at least six taxicabs, all using Hupmobile engines and friction drive. *HD*

WATSON (ii) (US) 1917-1925

(1) Watson Wagon Co., Canastota, N.Y. 1917-1919
(2) Watson Products Corp., Canastota, N.Y. 1919-1922
(3) Watson Truck Corp., Canastota, N.Y. 1923-1925

Watson "Trucktractors" were assembled cab-overs along Roman chariot lines with a crescent cab and a shallow flat parbolic radiator in front. A bumper was attached to the forward protruding frame.

Specifications included a capacity of 5 tons with a Continental 4-cylinder engine, Brown-Lipe clutch and 4-speed gearbox (4 forward, 1 reverse), Timken Worm drive, centrifugal water pump, solid-tires — duals on the rear, artillery wheels, and right-hand drive. The price was $4,050, but this did not include lights.

The semi-trailers with dump bodies were heavily built with huge artillery wheel shaving steel tires. Those for ordinary road transport were lighter with solid rubber tires.

Starting with their 1920 models Watson broadened their range by assembling conventional trucks with crescent cabs in 1 and 3½ ton capacities. The engines were now 4-cylinder Buda, lights were now standard, and so was the left-hand drive for these new models. One unusual feature seems to be a spring-loaded front bumper so as to give on impact. *RW*

WATSON (iii) (GB) 1918-1929

Henry Watson & Sons Ltd., Newcastle-on-Tyne

This company was a manufacturer of metal castings of all kinds who had previously made the British Berna and officially announced their range in 1920. It was a conventional machine rated at 3½/4½ tons capacity and powered by a 4-cylinder 5.3-litre engine. It had a 4-speed gearbox and final drive was by internal gears in the rear wheels, this American practice being comparatively rare on British vehicles. There were two wheelbases, 13 ft. and 14 ft. 6 ins. In 1922 a larger model rated at 6 tons was added to the range. This had a 6.3-litre engine mounted ahead of the front axle in the manner of some Continental trucks. Watsons were listed until 1929, but received little notice in the press after 1924, and may not have been made for the full period of their listed life. *GNG*

WAVERLEY (US) 1899-1903; 1908-1916

(1) Indiana Bicycle Co., Indianapolis, Ind. 1899

(2) American Bicycle Co., Indianapolis, Ind. 1899-1901

(3) International Motor Car Co., Indianapolis, Ind. 1901-1903

(4) Waverley Co., Indianapols, Ind. 1908-1916

This well-known electric vehicle maker listed commercial types throughout its life, and by 1900 there were 18 different models, including open and closed deliveries and a station bus. Tiller steering was used. In 1903 the company was acquired by Colonel A.A. Pope and for the next five years vehicles were made under the name Pope-Waverley. With the collapse of the Pope empire Waverley became independent again, and continued to make a wide range of passenger and goods vehicles. The latter came in several sizes from 1 600 lb. delivery van to a 5-ton brewery truck. *RW/GMN*

WAYNE (i) (US) 1914

Wayne Light Commercial Car Company, New York, N.Y.

This tricycle type had an 800-pound capacity box in front of the driver and was driven by an air-cooled, two-cylinder engine, with belt drive to the single rear wheel. It had a two-speed gearbox and was steered by handlebars. Price was $475. This could be classed as a three-wheeled motorcycle. *GMN*

1946 WAYNE-GMC bus MBS

WAYNE (ii) (US) c.1931 to date

(1) The Wayne Works, Richmond, Ind. c.1931-1959

(2) Wayne Works Divn., Divco-Wayne Corp., Richmond, Ind.

(3) Wayne Corp., Richmond, Ind.

Starting as a wagon builder in the 1840s, Wayne became a major supplier of composite school bus bodies and small transit bus bodies for conventional Ford, Chevrolet, Dodge and other light truck chassis, at least by 1931. Wayne also built school bus bodies forforward-control front- and rear-engined chassis in later years, and still does so today. A particularly notable use of Wayne bodies for other than school use was by Ford in the 1930s, and again in 1949-50. From 1941 to 1946 Wayne built about 300 sectional bodies, essentially the same as those designed and built earlier by C.J. Hug, on rear-engined Reo chassis, but sold under the Wayne name. Purchase of Wayne by Divco in 1959 resulted in a small forward-control transit bus based on a Divco chassis and known as the Bantam, but it was not successful. Since then Wayne has continued to build school buses, and some transit buses, on a variety of chassis. *MBS*

W. & E. (GB) 1945 to date.

(1) Wales & Edwards Ltd., Wyle Cop, Shrewsbury, Salop 1945-1957.

(2) W & E Vehicles Ltd., Harlescott, Shrewsbury 1957 to date

The first two models offered were of 20cwt and 25cwt capacity and were of three wheel layout. Both had a wheelbase of 7 ft. 2 in., overall length of 11 ft. 5 in. with 259AH batteries carried in the center of the chassis frame and employed bevel rear drive. During the 1950's a longer-7 ft. 10 in. wheelbase was offered as an alternative, and in 1960 the 1-ton model became the Rangemaster and

1952 W & E 1¼-ton 3-wheel electric milk float, GNG

featured a more powerful motor giving a running speed of 13 mph as against the 8-10 mph of the previous models. A diesel-engined 25 cwt 3-wheeler was also made from 1957 for a few years.

1968 W & E 4/40 2-ton electric milk float, GNG

In 1962 the Rangemaster was uprated to 25 cwt and larger capacity batteries offered. 1963 saw the introduction of the I-range or Intermediate 25 cwt and the 2-ton Loadmaster which was a 5-wheeled, 3-axle articulated outfit with a combined wheelbase of 12 ft. 6 in. and overall length of 19 ft. Lightweight models were also on offer, these being variations of Standard models but with different battery capacities.

In the 1970's the range continued on similar lines with Standard, Lightweight, Intermediate and Rangemaster types in capacities from 25- to 30-cwt and in two wheelbase lengths. A new four wheeler made its appearance — the Four-Forty. This was a 40cwt model while a slightly heavier model for 50cwt loads was named the Freightleader. Current range is of 3-wheelers rated at 28½ and 30cwt while the 4-wheeled models are the 4/40 at 40-cwt and the 4/96 for a 34/36-cwt payload. *OM*

WEEKS (US) 1907-1908.

Weeks Commercial Vehicle Co., Chicago, Ill.

This was a ½-tonner with a closed delivery body. Its engine, mounted under the floorboards, had two cylinders, was "vapor-cooled" and developed 20 hp. This engine was built by Advance Engine & Manufacturing Co. The transmission was a friction disc type and final drive was by double chains to the rear wheels. Gross weight of this van was 1,500 lbs. *GMN*

WEGMANN (D) 1951.

Wegmann & Co., Kassel.

This firm built a forward control bus with electric drive. The batteries were carried in a one-axle trailer. This system was not accepted at that time and so only a few experimental vehicles were produced. The same system was taken up by M.A.N. in 1975. *HON*

WEIDKNECHT (F) 1896-1898.

F. Weidknecht, Paris.

The Weidknecht vertical boilered tractor was one of several designed in the mid-nineties to convert horse drawn buses and lorries to steam power by making them into the semi-trailer of an articulated unit. It was demonstrated in Paris in 1897 but there is no clear evidence of successful commercial use.

In 1897 also he made the Weidknecht & Bourdon steam bus using double cylinders with Soims valve gear, a

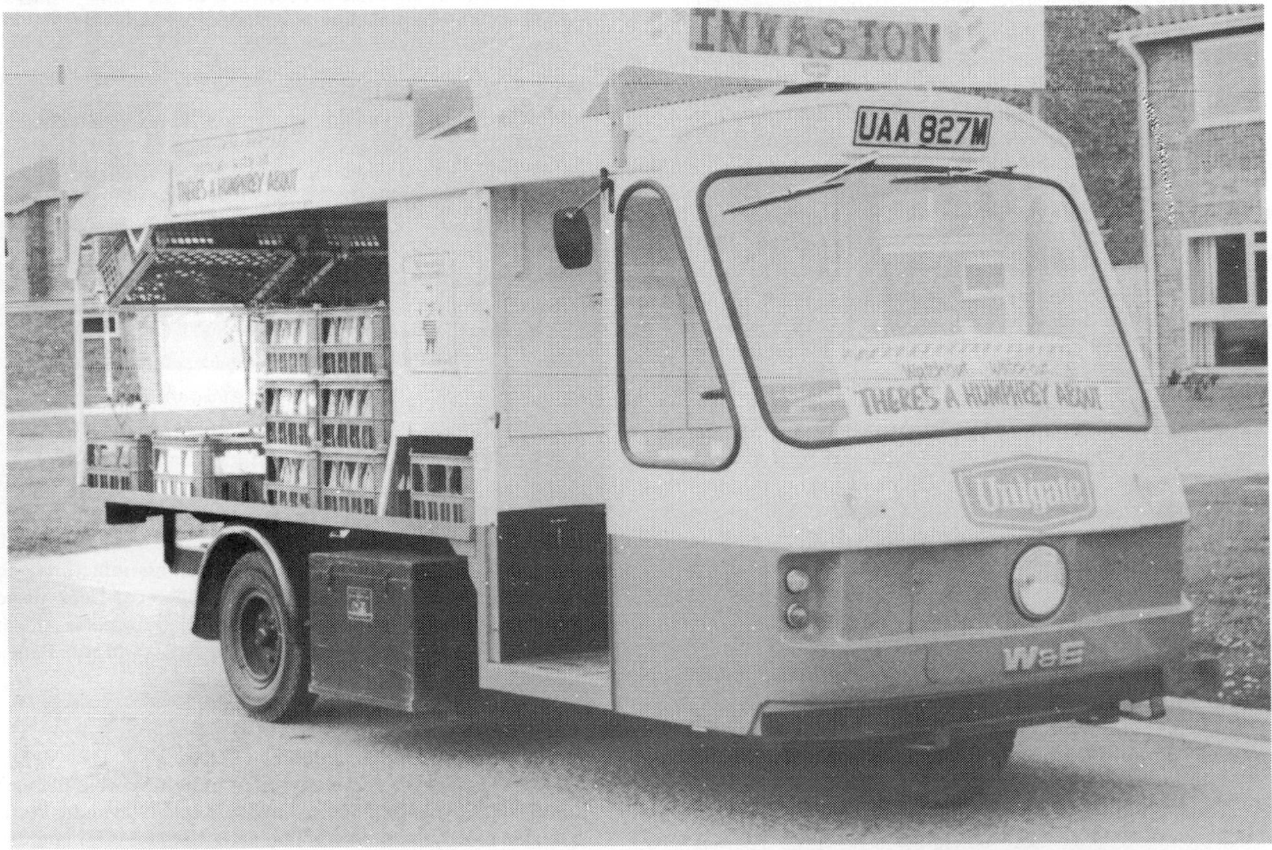

1974 W & E 1½-ton 3-wheel electric milk float, GNG

countershaft differential and chain drive.

The Weidknecht vertical boiler used cross water tubes in the firebox and vertical smoke tubes between the top of the firebox and the smokebox. *RAW*

WEIER-SMITH, or W-S (US) 1915-1918.

Weier-Smith Truck Co., Birmingham, Mich.

The W-S for 1916 was a 1½-tonner and the single model for the succeeding year was a 2½-tonner. The one model built in 1918-1919 was a 3½-tonner driven by a 4-cylinder Continental engine. The last model had an 8-speed gearbox and worm-drive rear axle. Wheelbase was 13 feet, 2 inches. *GMN*

WEISE (D) 1929-1939

Weise & Co. GmbH., Berlin No. 55

In 1929 Weise presented a tri- van with one driven front wheel, the 200cc. Rinne engine mounted above it. Steering was by tiller. Later a modernized version was available with enclosed engine and normal steering. 1939 saw the debut of a 1-ton van with diesel engine. *HON*

WEISS (i)(D) 1902-1905

(1) Maschinenfabrik Otto Weiss & Co., Berlin NO 55 1902-1904

(2) Automobil- und Motorenfabrik vorm. Otto Weiss, Berlin NO 55 1904-1905

Based on the private car designs of this firm, van versions were available. 2- and 4-cylinder French Herald engines were used and so cars were also known as Weiss-Herald. Also a small bus with 10hp engine was offered. The friction drive transmission was almost an exact copy of the Maurer system. *HON*

WEISS (ii) (D) 1931

Konrad Weiss, Munchen 2

This was a light tri-van with two front wheels which was more a motorized bicycle using a 96cc Sachs engine. *HON*

1927 WEISS MANFRED 1½-ton truck, Haris Muzeum

WEISS MANFRED (H) 1925-1929; 1935-1939

(1) Weiss Manfred Loszer, Acel es Femarugyar R.T., Csepel, Budapest

(2) Dunai Repulogepgyar, Csepel, Budapest, 1935-1939

Weiss Manfred was a large engineering firm that introduced their own design of a light car powered by a 4-cylinder, 2 stroke engine. The same chassis was also used as the basis of a few light commercials, but production of both versions was dropped in 1929, after some 300 assorted units had been built. The firm reorganized in 1935, participating in a schedule calling for the production of various military products and soon built military vehicles, including 4 × 4 trucks, armored cars, personnel carriers and light tanks, some 3,000 all total, as well as airplanes and aircraft engines. The famous Hungarian engineer Nikolas Straussler started his career with Weiss Manfred. Best known of his early efforts, the twin-engined G3 4 × 4 military truck, later series produced by Garner in England, was built and tested by Weiss Manfred, but hostilities in Hungary led to the transfer of one prototype to England under somewhat adventurous conditions. Following post-war reorganization, no more vehicles were built by Weiss Manfred, but its premises on Csepel island were later taken over by the Csepel truck factory. *GA*

WEI-XING see Tiao-Jin

WELLS (GB) 1915

Wells Motors Ltd., King's Cross, London N.

The Wells was a conventional 3-ton truck built to War Office Subsidy specifications, powered by a 4-cylinder Dorman JJ engine, with the choice of 3- or 4-speed gearbox and worm drive. *GNG*

WENDAX (D) 1935-1951

Wendax Fahrzeugbau GmbH., Hamburg

In 1935 Wendax presented their first tri-van following the layout of one driven rear wheel. A 200cc Ilo engine was used. Also after the war this layout was continued, although it was outdated. In 1949 Wendax presented a four-wheel forward-control transporter for which a 1.1 litre Volkswagen engine was used. It was front-mounted and drove the front wheels. *HON*

1974 WERKLUST 6×2 front-drive container truck, JFJK

WERKLUST (NL) 1974 to date

B.V. Machinefabriek Werklust, Apeldoorn.

Werklust started in 1974 with the production of a special container tipper truck, having no longer rear axle drive but only a driven front axle, manufactured by Terberg. Power is supplied by a Mercedes-Benz diesel engine, and the transmission is a fully automatic Allison box. Werklust's own version of the British Motor Panels cab is supplied. *JFJK*

WEST-ASTER (GB) 1907-1908

E.J. West & Co. Ltd., Coventry

This passenger car maker also built taxicabs, delivery vans and travellers' broughams, all with 2-cylinder Aster engines and shaft drive. The cabs had 10/12hp engines, the other models 12/14hp. *GNG*

WESTCAR (GB) 1922-1926

(1) Strode Electric Light Co. Herne, Kent. 1922
(2) Strode Engineering Works, Herne, Kent 1922-1926

Built in the stable block of the Prescott-Westcar mansion at Strode Park, Westcars were rarely seen outside their native area — apart from their stand at the British Empire Exhibition at Wembley.

A number of light delivery vans were built on the private car chassis, and sold in the local area only. Bodied by the works, using wood cut on the Strode estate, or by Cheesemans of Maidstone, these were straightforward 10cwt types with Dorman 1.4 litre engines and other bought-out components. *MJWW*

1975 WESTCOASTER electric mail van, Westcoaster

WESTCOASTER (US) 1927-1975

(1) West Coast Machinery Co., Stockton, Calif. 1927-1970
(2) Westcoaster Co., subsidiary Otis Elevator Co., Stockton, Calif. 1970-1975

The West Coast Machinery Co. was formed to make farm equipment, and soon added a line of light 3-wheeled gasoline and electric vehicles for personnel and cargo carrying, similar in conception to the Cushman. These were made up to 1975 when the range consisted of thirteen 3-wheelers powered by either a 17.6hp 50cu. in. 2-cylinder air-cooled engine or 36 volt electric motor. Drive was automotive hypoid type to the rear axle, and most Westcoasters had wheel steering, though some personnel carriers for hotel or resort use were tiller-steered. Typical uses for Westcoaster 3-wheelers were for police patrol work, mail service, refuse haulers, in-plant ambulances etc. There were also two 4-wheelers, both electric, a 1-ton flatbed truck and a delivery van with 750lb. load capacity and top speed of 43mph. The latter was called an Otis, as were some of the 3-wheelers, after the Otis Elevator Co. which had owned Westcoaster since 1970. Another Otis project was the 20-passenger Electrobus (q.v.), but all vehicles were discontinued in September 1975 because of low-volume sales. *RW*

WESTERN (US) 1917-1923

Western Truck Manufacturing Co., Chicago, Ill.

A 7-tonner was the first model under this tradename. This used a 4-cylinder Wisconsin engine, a 4-speed gearbox with double chain drive, on a wheelbase of 12 feet, 2 inches. This model was listed into 1919 but was replaced in 1920 by a series consisting of 1½-, 2½- and 3½-tonners. The 1½-tonner had a 3-speed gearbox while the two larger ones used four speeds. All three models had Timken worm-drive rear axles. *GMN*

WESTERN STAR see White

WESTERN FLYER see Flyer

WESTFALIA (D) 1910-1914

Rahmesohl & Schmidt A.G., Oelde; Bielefeld

This firm produced vans which were based on their private car models. Especially the type 12/30 PS was available. *HON*

WESTLAND (GB) 1906

F.W. Baker Ltd., Stourbridge, Worcs.

This was a 30cwt van powered by a 15hp 4-cylinder White & Poppe engine, and having shaft drive. It had a handsome circular radiator and bonnet in the Delaunay-Belleville style. *GNG*

WESTMAN (US) 1912-1914

Westman Motor Truck Company, Cleveland, Ohio

A 1½-tonner was the only size commercial vehicle built by the manufacturer and this had forward control with a 3-speed gearbox and shaft drive. The 4-cylinder engine had a dual ignition system. The Model E, a covered express, had a wheelbase of 8 feet, 9 inches, the chassis weighed 3,800 pounds and other body types were available to order. *GMN*

WESTRAM see Ward La France

WEYHER (US) 1910

Weyher Manufacturing Co., Whitewater, Wis.

The single model which carried this name was a ½-tonner and used a 16hp, 2-cylinder water-cooled engine under a hood. The drive was through a friction transmission and then by double chains to the rear wheels. Wheelbase was 7 feet, 10 inches and solid rubber tires were standard. *GMN*

WEYHER ET RICHEMOND (F) 1903-1912

Stedes Ans. Etablissments Weyher et Richemond
Pantin, Seine

The firm was mainly concerned with the manufacture of steam fire engines some of which were self-propellors similar to the Merryweather Fire-King, the engine being just forward of the boiler with countershaft differential and double chain drive.

A limited number of steam goods vehicles are said to have been made with the boiler moved to the front of the chassis but were abandoned by 1905. *RAW*

W. & G. (GB) 1920-1936

W. & G. du Cros Ltd., Acton, London W. 3

This company were well-known operators of taxicabs before World War I, and their first vehicle was a conventional 4-cylinder chassis for 2- and 2½-ton loads and charabanc bodies. The 'new W & G taxi chassis' of 1922 was in fact a Talbot-Darracq with W & G were going to equip with a British-built body, but it never materialized. A later taxicab venture was the operation of a fleet of about 100 Yellow Cabs which bore the name W & G on their radiators, causing people to think of them as being made by W & G in the same way as the pre-war Napiers and Panhards had done. In 1925 came a new 30cwt truck and 26-seater charabanc chassis, and in 1926 a low-frame bus chassis with 5.4-litre 70hp 6-cylinder engine and underslung worm drive. With a 30-passenger body this was capable of 55mph. Passenger vehicles made

1921 W & G 1½-ton truck, OMM

up a large part of W & G's output from now on, including a forward-control bus chassis with 6.6-litre 6-cylinder engine in 1928, but two other lines were developed. One was the ambulance developed by the Metropolitan Asylums Board in December 1926; this had offset drive to the nearside rear axle and Lockheed hydraulic four wheel

1927 W & G MAB-type ambulance, NMM

1928 W & G 24-seater coach, NMM

brakes. The prototype had a Continental 6-cylinder engine, but production models were Meadows-powered. A total of 200 were made before they were superseded by the Talbots in 1930. Talbot and W & G were both part of the Sunbeam-Talbot-Darracq combine. The other line of vehicle was the low-loader truck, mainly for municipal work, made in normal and forward control form from 1930. These were usually called duCros to distinguish them from the more classy buses and coaches. W & G vehicles were listed up to 1936, but production probably ceased several years earlier, and is most unlikely to have survived the collapse of the S-T-D group in 1935. *GNG*

WHIPPET see Willys

WHITCOMB (US) 1928-1930

Whitcomb Wheel Co., Kenosha, Wis.

The Whitcomb was an unusual 6-wheeled bus with integral construction and coil ifs. It was powered by a 66.15hp 6-cylinder Wisconsin Z engine developing 105hp, and had a claimed maximum speed of 60mph. As a regular coach it seated 24 passengers, but for deluxe work this was reduced to 18. Prices ranged from $13,000 to $15,000. In 1930 a 3-ton truck was also listed by Whitcomb. *GNG*

WHITE (i) (US) 1900-1903

(1) White Engineering Works, Indianapolis, Ind. 1900-1901
(2) White Steam Wagon Co., Indianapolis, Ind. 1901-1903

No connection with the well-known White from Cleveland, this was a 2-ton steam wagon with a marine-type water-tube boiler and double compound engine with four horizontal cylinders. Final drive was by double chains, and maximum speed 5 mph. *GNG*

WHITE (ii) (US) 1901 to date

(1) White Sewing Machine Co., Cleveland, Ohio 1901-1906
(2) The White Co., Cleveland, Ohio 1906-1915
(3) White Motor Co., Cleveland, Ohio 1916-1965
(4) White Trucks, Cleveland, Ohio 1966 to date

Rollin H. White of the Cleveland sewing-machine concern (unconnected with (i) White) started to build steam cars in 1900. Early ones had 2-cylinder simple engines mounted under the floor, underslung frontal condensers, tiller steering, and chain drive: front-mounted compound engines, radiator-type condensers, wheel steering, and shaft drive made their appearance on the 1903 line. White boilers were of semi-flash type with a steaming capacity of 100 miles between refills.

The firm's first van was delivered to the Denver Dry Cleaning Co. in 1901. Thereafter car-based light commercials on pneumatic tires became a regular part of the catalog range, the 1904 10hp version carrying a 10-cwt payload. By 1906, a wide diversity of bodies was available: these included buses (one was exported to Japan in 1907), police patrol wagons (the 30hp type found favor in Rio de Janeiro), fire appliances, and mail trucks. White Steamers were the US Army's first standard motor ambulances. Some larger 2½-, 3-tonners with double compound engines, vertical boilers, and side-chain drive were tried but not made in quantity.

Though steamers were still available in 1911, 1910 had seen a line of gasoline cars based on the French Delahaye. Along with these came a range of trucks using the same type of 4-cylinder L-head monobloc engine. 4-speed

1914 WHITE 5-ton truck with tractor wheels, White

overdrive gearboxes were standard, with conventional bevel drive, pneumatics, and twin rear wheels on the ¾-ton GBE, double reduction shaft drive on the 1½-tonner, and chain drive (plus solids) on the 3-ton type. By 1912 there was also a chain-driven 5-tonner, the TC, this having a 5.3-litre engine. These basic variants were continued without major change until 1918, though later 5-tonners ran to 5.9 litres, power dump trucks made their appearance in 1914, and in 1913 the company built an unusual steel-tired logger using the new 60hp 6-cylinder car engine. A year later Rollin White left the company to found the Cleveland Tractor Co. (Cletrac). 1- to 3-ton Whites were standardized by the American Army in World War I, some 18,000 being delivered.

White became more seriously involved in the bus business during 1917, when they built the first of a large fleet of open-sided sightseeing vehicles for the Yellowstone National Park. Commonly known as the YP-type, these were based on the 20-45 TDB truck chassis, subsequently used for other types of PSV. The municipally-owned transit system of San Francisco was running a small fleet of Whites as early as 1918, and examples are known to have operated in interurban service in Ohio by 1919. Rebuilt White taxicabs aided in the rapid expansion of the Star Auto Stage Association in central California in 1916, and Whites also helped build up the extensive system of Motor Transit Co., based on Los Angeles and initiated by a White truck dealer.

1920 WHITE Model 45 5-ton truck, White

1923 WHITE Model 45 5-ton 6×2 tanker and trailer, White

1918 saw the abandonment of private cars (apart from a few 'specials' on light commercial chassis which persisted in penny numbers until the late 1930s). Also dropped was chain drive, which gave way to double reduction bevels, while the 4-cylinder engines were given detachable heads. The range structure continued as before. Widespread interest in the company's buses led to the introduction of the first White chassis specifically intended for PSV use, the Model-50 of late 1921. Essentially a modification of the 20-45, it continued with the well-tried 4-cylinder GN engine (subsequently evolved into the GR and then into the GRB), but was both longer and wider than earlier

1923 WHITE Model 50 bus, RNE

designs. When air brakes were added to create the 50-B in 1925, the White bus was fully competitive with the currently popular AB Mack and Type-Y Yellow, and sold well for both local city transit and over-the-road duties. Production estimates are difficult to work out, but probably not more than 10 per cent of White's annual output in the later 1920s (the years of the greatest expansion in the US bus industry) consisted of bus chassis.

White made no precedent-setting strides in bus design, their vehicles selling on durability and consistent performance. The company's first series-production 6-cylinder commercial vehicle was the Model-54 bus of 1926: a 4-cylinder type with similar styling carried the Model-53 designation. The 54 had a 519ci 7-bearing ohv engine, dual coil ignition, a 4-speed gearbox, and Westinghouse air brakes on all four wheels. The 54-A of late 1928 was an important improvement: the dash was pushed forward over the two rear cylinders, and the engine set over the front axle, increasing passenger capacity from 29 to 38 on city transit version, in return for a modest wheelbase increase from 20ft to 20ft 10in. There was also a 15ft variant, the 65, later joined by the intermediate 65-A. In 1928 the company built an experimental gasoline-electric bus, which combined the big 6-cylinder engine with two rear-mounted G.E.C. electric motors.

The trucks continued on established lines, though pneumatic tires and electric lighting were now regular equipment, even if oil lamps were still cited in the 1929 catalog. Among 1927's new models were the 1¼-ton 57, which dispensed with a transmission brake, and the 3½-ton 58, available with an air-brake option, 6,260 commercial vehicles found buyers in 1928, when models were available for payloads from 15-cwt to 7½ tons. In 1929 the ohv 6-cylinder Model-54 engine was applied to the Model-59 heavy tractor, while a modern lightweight was the 1-ton 60 with 4.3-litre, 54bhp 6-cylinder sv unit, spiral bevel drive, and hydraulic fwb; orthodox mechanicals would not be quoted after 1933. The new small White was not cheap ($1,850 for a chassis), but it found favor for high-class delivery work, being often seen with town-car style bodywork and dual sidemounts. The old sv fours survived in the up to 2½-ton class (they would linger on into 1934), but hydrovac brakes on all wheels were now general practice, and were found on a new heavy-duty family, the 620/640 series for GVWs of up to 16 tons. Engines were ohv 6s of 75 or 100 hp, pneumatic tires were standard, and features of the heavier variants included auxiliary transmissions, electric pump feed,

1932 WHITE Model 64T 12-ton articulated truck, White

double reduction drive, all full air brakes. Sub variations were the K-series with engines projecting back into the cab, and White's first catalog 6 × 4s for 10-ton payloads. These featured Timken worm-drive back axles and were supplied in small numbers to the US Army. 1932 was a poor year, with only 2,138 vehicles sold, but during the season White absorbed Indiana, transferring that concern's operations to Cleveland. They also entered into a brief association with the Studebaker-Pierce-Arrow consortium, during which period a few Pierce-Arrow trucks were assembled in the White factory.

A more important development of 1932 was a 505ci, 143 hp sv flat-12 engine with which White hoped to take the lead with heavy-duty city buses. Subsequently made also in 811ci, 225 hp form, this unit featured dry-sump lubrication and twin downdraught carburetors, and was located amidships and underfloor in a range of PSVs for up to 100 passengers introduced in 1933-4. Other

1933 WHITE Model 642 8-ton tanker, Texaco Archives

characteristics of the design were twin starter motors, air-assisted wet-plate clutches, and 5-speed constant-mesh gearboxes, but these so-called Pancakes soon gained a reputation for thirst and poor performance. Both the engine and the composite wood and steel body construction were dropped at the end of 1937, but the basic underfloor-engine concept was retained in a new series of city buses, also available in parlor-car layout, so that the ageing 54-A and 65-A could be dropped. The new 24 engine was much more modern, and in bus form the new White was successful, though the over-the-road version failed to attract much attention. The smaller flat-12 engine also found its way into some heavy forward-control trucks, but these made little impression and disappeared during 1938.

A restyled 700 truck series, distinguishable by its vee radiator, appeared in 1934, helping to boost annual sales from a low 1,384 to close on 4,000. These followed classic lines with flexibly-mounted 6-cylinder coil-ignition engines, ohv being retained for the heavy-duty models, some of which ran to 9½-litres. 5-speed gearboxes were standard in the over 3-ton class. Even more elegant were the 1936s, with streamlined cabs designed by Alexis de Sakhnoffski; thereafter the shape of normal control Whites changed little until the later 1950s. Light-duty

1935 WHITE Model 731 12-cylinder truck, White

models included a 1½-tonner, the 703, with 80 hp sv engine, available with factory-built streamlined van bodywork; chassis prices were as low as $1,185. Though White's subsidiary, Indiana, had pioneered the use of the Cummins diesel, White themselves stayed with gasoline power, apart from a few special-order heavies with Cummins units made for export from 1937 onwards. The 1937 range covered everything from lightweights up to 16½-tonners, these including some 6 × 4s as before. All had 6-cylinder engines, mainly sv, with ratings of up to 130 hp. Air brakes and 5-speed gearboxes characterized the heavier Whites, while there were now parallel forward control models in the 1½-, 10-ton bracket with streamlined cabs. In the bus field, White had some more successful offerings in the shape of modified normal control truck chassis; the 2-ton 704 (for school bus use) and the larger 706 (for transit and intercity work) sold better in the mid-1930s than the well-liked but outmoded regular PSV line. These were later superseded by forward-control versions designated 706-M, 800-M, 805-M, and 810-M. Early White bus types had been supplied either in chassis form or with bodies by Avery or Lang, but by the late 1920s a close association had developed between White and the Bender Body Co. of Cleveland, who built most of their PSV coachwork. The change to a new type of construction in 1938 involved a new White bus manufacturing plant on the east side of Cleveland, where bodies as well as chassis were built. Bender tried to keep alive by making bodies on other makes of chassis, but expired around 1942.

1938 WHITE Model 788 bus, MBS

White was building normal control 6 × 6 trucks for the Army in 1939, but in the meantime they had explored the multi-stop delivery van market with two unusual models. The first of these was the underfloor-engined Merchandor of 1938 followed a year later by the more radical White Horse 2-tonner, a Franklin design. It featured forward control, full unitary construction, a 3-speed gearbox, coil rear springing, and a rear-mounted, quick-detachable 2.4-litre aircooled flat-4 engine giving 40 hp. Of stand-and-drive type, it sold 2,000 units in two years and was the last true lightweight White for twenty years.

During World War II White produced some 20,000 Hercules-powered M3A1 scout cars of Indiana design, as well as more than 4,000 similar M3 halftrucks powered by their own 147 hp sv 6. Heavier military models were 4 × 4 tractors and 6 × 4 and 6 × 6 trucks, some of which used proprietary engines, either Hercules gasoline or Cummins diesel. The full normal control line was resumed in 1946, with hydraulic torque converters and air conditioned cabs as regular options a year later.

1942 WHITE Model WA-122 articulated moving van, White

By the 1938-42 period White had annexed some 10 per cent of the available heavy duty transit bus business, major buyers being transit systems in Cleveland, Washington and Boston, as well as the Pacific Electric Railway of Los Angeles. Like the trucks, the buses went back into production unchanged after the war, some very large orders being fulfilled between 1945 and 1947. Once the backlog had been cleared, however, sales fell off in favor of more modern rival machinery with diesel engines mounted transversely at the rear.

Buses continued to play second fiddle to the trucks. There was a stylistic facelift in 1949, and Cummins diesels became a regular option after 1951, but both sales and the company's share of the market stayed low. White's last bus, a 50-passenger Cummins-powered transit type for Washington, was completed in October, 1953. Total bus production had amounted to some 15,000 units. A school bus chassis based on the normal control truck with 6-cylinder gasoline engine, was however, listed as late as 1968.

Along with the expansion of their truck business, White went empire-building in the 1950s. First to fall to them were Sterling in 1951, followed by the Freightliner custom truck (1951), Autocar (1953), Reo (1957) and Diamond T (1960). Of these concerns, Autocar survives to the present, and the Diamond T and Reo companies were merged into a single unit, which White eventually sold off in 1968.

Forward control was revived on the Super Power 3000 range of 1949. These featured power tilt cabs, with the usual options of 5-speed gearboxes, 2 speed rear axles, air brakes, and disc-type handbrakes. Up to 1955, some of the lighter models were fitted with Packard's obsolete 6-cylinder sv gasoline engine. Also in 1949, Cummins diesel engines were regularly available in 12.2-litre 6-cylinder form, while the traditional sv gasoline units ran up to 8.1 litres and 184 hp. The heaviest tractive units catered for GCWs in the 100,000 pound class, and by 1955 more power was forthcoming all round, with turbocharged editions of the Cummins engine, and the uprating of White's Mustang gasoline engines to as much as 215 hp. Weight-paring techniques were applied in 1959 on the 5000 forward control and TDL normal control tractors. These featured glassfibre cabs and front wing assemblies,

1949 WHITE Model WC-22 articulated van, White

1958 WHITE Model 3400TD articulated van, White

1959 WHITE Model 5464TD articulated van, White

as well as liberal application of aluminum which lopped a ton off the basic TDL. Engines were Cummins diesels from 180 to 262 hp (335 hp on the 6 × 4 forward control Turnpike Cruiser of 1960); other features included multi-speed transmissions by Clark, Fuller or Spicer, and (on the cab 5000) power-assistance for gearshift driver's seat and cab windows. In the range were further specialist types, notably 4 × 2 and 6 × 2 twin-steer developments of the 3000 family with automatic transmission for airfield-tanker work, and the heavy duty 6 × 4 Construktor, an off-highway or mixer chassis with 5 × 3-speed transmission, normal control, and a choice of gasoline or diesel engines in the 145/220 hp bracket. At the other end of the scale White made another attack on the urban delivery van market with two types. Of these the Highway Compact van had a GVW of 26,000 pounds and was made for them until 1965 by Highway Products; thereafter Highway handled their own marketing. Engines were gasoline units by Ford or Chrysler, diesel options being by Perkins or GM-Detroit. The smaller PDQ revived the White Horse theme, though its quick-detachable power unit was conventionally located. As White no longer made any small engines, an astonishing variety of types found their way into this one; the F-head 4-cylinder Willys, the Continental 6, the Plymouth Valiant's ohv Slant 6, a Chrysler marine V8, and the British 4-cylinder Perkins diesel. A fire at White's branch plant at Montpelier, Ohio, brought PDQ production to a halt in 1965, and thereafter the company was content to stay with heavies.

By the late 1950s there were ohv gasoline Mustang engines as well as the traditional sv types, and by 1961 the 3000 had evolved further into the Utilideck, a half-cab type for the carriage of steel girders. Alongside these were some more compact forward control models, the 1500s for city work, with low tilt cabs mounted over the front axles and a heavy bumper protecting both grille and lamps. Wheelbase of the 1500 tractor was only 6 ft. 2 in. and 4-

1965 WHITE 2000 Series 5-ton truck, GNG

1966 WHITE 7000 Series articulated tanker, EK

speed gearboxes, gasoline engines, and hydrovac brakes were standard, though a wide range of options included air brakes and power steering. By 1964 the British Perkins diesel in 6-cylinder form was also available. Half-cabs had been applied to mixer chassis, not to mention the White-Freightliner range. A so-called Mustang V8 gasoline engine was announced in 1966 as an option in the 4000 and 9000 normal control trucks and tractors; this 250 hp unit was, however, nothing more than a modified Cummins diesel, and never saw series production. Thereafter gasoline engines were quietly phased out, the last sv Mustangs making their appearance in 1971-2. Some models were even quoted with Chevrolet-built gasoline V8s in 1971.

The 1967 line-up embraced the 1500 Compact (now available in a 6 × 4 configuration, as well as a wide selection of normal control trucks and tractors in 4 × 2, 6 × 2, 6 × 4 and 6 × 6 guises, 8x6s being added in 1968. As the White-built engines became obsolescent, proprietary units took over with diesels by Caterpillar, Cummins,

1974 WHITE Construcktor 8×4 dump truck, White

1978 WHITE Road Boss articulated van, White

Detroit, Diamond Reo and Perkins featuring in the later 1960s, albeit only the first two makes were still regularly quoted in 1978. For 1968 White made a bid for the specialized Western-state haulage business with the Western Star line, made in branch plants at Ogden, Utah and Kelowna, British Columbia. These were available only with normal control and diesel power.

Essentially the same heavy-duty themes persisted into 1978. Descended from the Compact was the Road Xpeditor 2, a low-tilt cab type for urban work with a choice of 10.4-litre Caterpillar or 14-litre Cummins engines, both sixes. For GVWs of up to 68,000lb. or GCWs as high as 125,000lb. there was the forward control Road Commander, made as a 4 × 2 or 6 × 4 with a wide choice of transmissions and engines of up to 450bhp. Its normal control counterpart with tilting glassfibre hood was the Road Boss. A comprehensive range of Western Stars included a 6 × 6, though the Construcktor was now made only with Autocar badges. Power steering and Allison automatic gearboxes were generally available, air brakes were standardized throughout the range, and the 1978 color chart embraced 306 different shades. An interesting feature of tandem-axle models was the use of White's four-spring rear suspension, and on Road Commanders and Road Bosses there were centralized servicing points for electrics and air lines. Despite a trading loss of $50 million in 1975, the group's production averaged 30,000 units a year, one-third of these marketed with White badges. *MCS/MBS*

WHITE FREIGHTLINER see Freightliner

WHITE HICKORY (US) 1917-1921.

White Hickory Wagon Manufacturing Co., Atlanta, Ga.

The Model H, a 1½-tonner was built from 1917 to 1920. It used a 4-cylinder engine from Continental, a 3-speed gearbox with progressive change and a Timken worm-drive rear axle. In 1921, 2½- and 3½-tonners also were offered. *GMN*

WHITESIDES (US) 1911-1912

Whitesides Commercial Car Company, Franklin, Indiana, 1911-1912. Newcastle, Indiana, 1912.

This commercial was available only as a -tonner with a four-cylinder, 30 hp, water-cooled engine. Both open and enclosed vans were offered as well as "flat dray" and stake types. Prices were $1,265 and $1,285. *GMN*

WHITE STAR (US) 1912-1914.

White Star Motor & Engineering Co., Brooklyn, NY.

A 2-tonner and a 3-tonner were listed under this name for 1913. The 2-tonner was a closed van with a 4-cylinder engine, a 3-speed gearbox and double chain drive. The 3-tonner had a stake body with a 4-cylinder engine under a hood with a 4-speed gearbox on a wheelbase of 14 feet. For 1914, these two models were joined by a 5-tonner. *GMN*

WHITING (US) 1904-1905.

(1) Whiting Foundry Equipment Company, Harvey, Ill., 1904-1905.

(2) Chicago Commercial Auto Manufacturing Company, Chicago, Ill., 1905.

The Whiting was a massive truck for this early period with a gross weight of 10,000 pounds, powered by a 4-cylinder of 680 ci displacement. Drive was through a 3-speed gearbox with roller chains to each rear wheel. This had forward control, structural steel frame and was limited to a maximum of 10 mph. The only body available was a flat bed. *GMN*

WHITLOCK (i) (GB) 1903-1906.

Whitlock Automobile Co., London, W.

This obscure firm was responsible for Britain's first gasoline-driven taxicab design. Bodywork was in hansom style, but the mechanics were conventional, with 12 hp 2-cylinder front-mounted Aster engine, 3-speed gearbox, and shaft drive. It did not go into service. In 1906 Whitlock announced a 15-cwt van version of the 12/14 hp 2-cylinder Aster-engined car, with pneumatic tires at the front, and solids at the rear. *MCS*

WHITLOCK (ii) (GB) 1963.

Whitlock Brothers Ltd., Great Yeldham, Essex.

Whitlock made a wide variety of construction equipment including special modifications of Fordson tractors. Their DD105 dump truck was an unconventional vehicle powered by a choice of Perkins or Ford diesel engines. It was an articulated 4 × 4 with Dowty hydrostatic drive which powered the rear wheels only for road use and all four for off-road work. Other features of the DD105 were air brakes and power-assisted steering. Load capacity was 12cu. yds. Only a few were made. *GNG*

1914 WICHITA Model B 1-ton truck, RNE

WICHITA (US) 1911-1932.

Wichita Falls Motor Co., Wichita Falls, Texas.

This company specialized in trucks for southwest and oilfields use, and a number were also exported to Mexico and Central America. Over the years the range ran from 1½ to 5-tonners, all with Waukesha engines, the Timken or "own" axles. The company was said to have weathered the Depression thanks to big orders from Mexico, but did not survive beyond 1932. *RJ*

WIKOV (CS) 1925-1940.

Wichterle & Kovarik akc. spol., Prostejov.

The Wikov company was founded in 1918 by the merger of two agricultural machinery makers, Frantisek Wichterle and Frantisek Kovarik. Their first car was made in 1925, and had a 1,480cc 4-cylinder engine with single ohc. This was used as the basis for a number of fire engines made up to 1933, with special equipment by such firms as Sigma pumpy of Lutin, Hrcek & Neubauer of Brno-Kralovo, and Pole, Hasickse zavody of Cechy pod Kosirem. From 1936 to 1938 a 30cwt truck was made using the Wikov 40 1,980cc 40bhp engine, also with single ohc. These were built mainly for the Czechoslovak army, but a number of fire engines, ambulances, funeral cars and 18-seater buses were also made on this chassis. The final order was for 28 trucks for the German army of occupation in 1940, this bringing the total number of 1½-tonners made to 450.

After the war the company name was changed to Agrostoj, and as such makes agricultural machinery to the present day. *MSH*

WILCOX (US) 1910-1927

(1) H.E. Wilcox Motor Truck Co., Minneapolis, Minn.
(2) H.E. Wilcox Motor Co., Minneapolis, Minn.
(3) Wilcox Trux Inc., Minneapolis, Minn., 1921-1927

This company began its career in vehicle construction with the Wolfe passenger car of 1907. Some car-based delivery trucks were also called Wolfe, but the name of all products was changed to Wilcox in 1910 when two trucks were listed, a 1-tonner with driver either behind engine or over it, and a 3-tonner. Also that year Wilcox shipped a bus to South Dakota, described as a combination mail wagon and stagecoach. Truck production grew over the

1912 WILCOX Model K 1½-ton truck, NAHC

next few years so that Wilcox became the most important vehicle maker in Minneapolis. By 1918 the range consisted of six models, from 3/4-ton to 5-tons, the larger being cab-over-engine models which Wilcox was particularly noted for. Buda or Continental engines were used, although Wilcox also made some of their own engines, and were something more than mere assemblers of trucks. A number of Wilcoxes carried bus bodies, used to transport iron and copper miners in areas where there were no railroads, and in 1922 Wilcox made their first purpose-built bus chassis. This was a sophisticated low-loading vehicle with drop frame (with fabricated arches rather than one-piece side rails), a cast-aluminum radiator and Huck-type live axle with differential-mounted planetary gear train for final reduction. Bodies were mainly by Eckland, a Minneapolis firm who were to be

1922 WILCOX bus, MBS

associated with Wilcox and subsequently Will until the end of their history. Wilcox buses used either Continental or Waukesha 6-cylinder engines, and later models had a top speed of 62 mph with 29-passenger bodies. In 1925/26 the Northland Transportation Company ordered 39 of these buses for which the trade name of Northland was used, possibly to distinguish them from the Wilcox truck. The latter were now made in 1- to 5-ton models, with Buda or their own make of engine. However buses came to dominate the company's output, and in March 1927 H.E. Wilcox sold the enterprise to principals of the Motor Transit Corp., formed in 1926 as a holding company for bus lines operated under the Greyhound name. (see WILL(. *RJ/MBS*

WILL (US) 1927-1930

C.H. Will Motors Corp., Minneapolis, Minn.

The Greyhound system of bus companies purchased the former H.E. Wilcox Motor Co. in 1927 and turned its production over entirely to buses, most of which were delivered to midwestern Greyhound companies. The operation was named for its general manager, Carl H. Will, and the buses were known at first as "W.M.C." and later as "Will" buses. In response to Greyhound's requirements, Will introduced a redesigned parlor car on 239 or 249-inch wheelbases later in 1927, and with minor modifications these constituted the front line of Greyhound's fleet until 1930. Waukesha 6-cylinder engines were used, together with Timken axles, robust drop frames (now one-piece side rails) and air springs at the front.

1927 WILL Greyhound bus, MBS

As part of the formation of Pacific Greyhound Lines in 1929, the California Body Building Co. of Oakland (see PIONEER STAGE) was acquired, and its buses, slightly modified, became known as "Pioneer-Will" and later as Will. With an order for 60 of these for Pacific Greyhound completed in the summer of 1930, the Oakland plant was closed. In the meantime Yellow Coach and Greyhound agreed on a manufacturing contract, according to which

Greyhound would underwrite part of the development expenses of new Yellow models built to Greyhound specifications, and the first purchase contract pursuant to this agreement was signed in November 1929. Greyhound wound down Will production at Minneapolis, the last buses being delivered to Northland Greyhound Lines in January 1931. Virtually all Will buses had Eckland bodies, and very few were ever sold to companies other than Greyhound. Probably about 500 were built.

The corporation continued in existence as Greyhound Motors & Supply Co., directed by Carl Will and located in Chicago, where it operated a bus overhaul and rebuilding plant for the parent company. *RJ/MBS*

WILLEME (F) 1919 to date

(1) Etablissements Willeme, Neuilly, Seine 1919-1936
(2) Etablissemtns Willeme, Nanterre, Seine 1937-1963
(3) Camions Willeme, Nanterre, Seine 1963-1970
(4) Perez et Raimond, Villeneuve-la-Garenne 1971 to date

Like (ii) Peerless in England, Willeme began by reconditioning war-surplus American trucks, in this case 3/5-ton Libertys. These were offered up to 1929 (and later) in unmodified form, down to the solid tires and radiator brush guard. Gradually improvements were incorporated; such options as pneumatics, a more powerful 7.7-litre engine, and the almost mandatory gazogene. By 1930 the Willeme-Liberty range included artics, a 7½-ton dumper, and a 12-ton trailing-axle 6-wheeler; this last retained the traditional Liberty overhead worm drive, but had eight forward speeds, and brakes on the four front wheels only. A year later the company adopted the Junkers opposed-piston 2-stroke diesel engine; initially C.L.M.-built units were fitted, but later Willeme built their own. Heavy-duty models, now with Westinghouse air brakes, used the 80 bhp 3-cylinder version, but further down the range there were twins, as well as a modest 1-tonner, the LH, with single-cylinder engine, 3-speed unit gearbox, and no front wheel brakes. 1934 saw the introduction of Deutz-type 4-stroke 4- and 6-cylinder oil engines, and though the old gasoline engined Liberty model was still available in 1939, the firm was now turning towards true heavy trucks, including really large tractive units for indivisible loads. There was still a 3-tonner with Junkers-type engine, but most Willemes were in the 8/15-ton class, with 8-speed transmissions, and air brakes. The biggest 6-cylinder engine had a capacity of 11½-litres, and the range included both 6-wheelers and forward control versions.

After World War II, nothing smaller than a 10-tonner was marketed, while some of the specialized Willemes reached herculean proportions, notably a 50-ton soft-cab tank transporter, and an 8 × 4 twin-steer 150-tonner tractor made in 1948 for the Portuguese State electricity authorities. There were also on- and off-the-road dumpers, 6 × 6 and 8 × 4 crane chassis, and the huge W8SAT 6 × 6 250 hp tractor built for Saharan use in 1957. The 1946 truck range used Willeme-built diesel engines — a 9-litre four, a 13½-litre six, and an 18-litre straight-8 giving 225 hp. Common to all were conventional control with forward-mounted engines, eight forward speeds, air brakes, and worm drive. Initially only 4 × 2 and 6 × 2 configurations were offered, but a 6 × 4 was added in 1947. 1954 saw more powerful engines, 6-speed constant-mesh gearboxes, and new streamlined cabs not unlike those of the latest Citroen trucks. Full forward control was an option by 1959, and two years later the 4-cylinder Willemes had been dropped, while modern wide-vision cabs in the Unic or Bernard idiom now featured. In 1962 Willeme allied themselves financially and technically with A.E.C. of Great Britain, offering 7.7-litre and 11.3-litre 6-cylinder A.E.C. engines as alternatives to their own six, now giving 255 hp with the aid of a turbocharger. At the same time a bid was made for the medium-duty market

1928 WILLEME-LIBERTY 6-ton truck, FLP

1957 WILLEME S.411 articulated tanker, OMM

1962 WILLEME RD .201 6×4 dump truck, OMM

with license-assembly of B.M.C.'s Austin/Morris FG and FH models. Other Willeme changes included double reduction bevel drive and ZF 6-speed gearboxes; on models with GVWs of over 19 tons power steering and 12 speeds were either optional or standard. 1967 saw the introduction of tilt cabs applied in 1968 to a 38-ton GCW 6 × 4 forward-control tractive unit using a 12½-litre A.E.C. engine and a 12-speed splitter box. Financial troubles supervened during the year, and production was halted. The last Willeme to be seen was a version of their big 6 × 4 tipper/dumper powered by a 275 hp Volvo engine, and featuring a 13-speed Fuller transmission, but rumors of an association with the Swedish maker proved unfounded, and the Willeme disappeared.

1978 WILLEME TG2000 heavy tractor, Perez et Raimond

A manufacturing license was, however, acquired by Perez et Raimond, makers of the P.R.P., who have resumed production at the rate of about 40 vehicles a year. The new owners' speciality is large forward control tractors for indivisible loads of up to 1,000 tons, built in 6 × 4, 8 × 4 and 8 × 8 configurations. Detroit Diesel engines are standard, the heaviest Willeme TG300 using the 516 hp V-16 in conjunction with a Clark torque converter. Caterpillar, Cummins and Mercedes-Benz units may also be specified. *MCS*

WILLEMS (B) 1934-1940

S.A. des Ets. Willems, Antwerp

Willems manufactured a range of trucks and bus chassis, using the American system of assembly. Nearly all parts used were also of American origin, like Hercules gasoline engines, Clark gearboxes, Timken axles. The brakes were by Lockheed, with Dewandre servo-assistance. Production never reached high numbers. *JFJK*

WILLET (US) 1911-1915

(1) Willet Engine & Carburetor Company, 1911-1913
(2) Willet Engine & Truck Company, 1913-1915

Prior to 1913, the Willet was made only as low-capacity delivery vans using 2- and 3-cylinder engines. For 1914, the Model L was introduced which had a 4-cylinder engine, was a 2-tonner with friction transmission and chain-drive. This model had a French-type hood and was very similar in appearance to the Mack Bulldogs. The 4-cylinder engine was a two-stroke type and the chassis had a 12-foot wheelbase and used solid tires. For 1915 only a 3/4-tonner was made which had shaft drive, 11-foot, 1-inch wheelbase with pneumatic tires and whole chassis price was $2,100. *GMN*

WILLYS (i) (US) 1903-1963

(Including (i) OVERLAND 1903-1926:
WILLYS-KNIGHT 1924-1931)

(1) Standard Wheel Co., Terre Haute, Ind. 1903-1905
(2) Overland Co., Indianapolis, Ind. 1905-1907
(3) Willys-Overland Co., Toledo, Ohio 1908-1963
(4) Gramm Motor Truck Co., Lima, Ohio 1913-1915; 1927-1930

The story of these interlinked makes is, if anything, even more complicated on the commercial vehicle side than it is in the realm of private cars. Thus the generic Willys label is the most logical, albeit John N. Willys did not enter the picture until 1907. There were affiliations with Federal and Gramm, not to mention a Stearns truck (admittedly made before this company came under Willys-Overland control).

The original Overland runabout of 1903, with solid tires and tiller steering, was nominally available as a delivery van. There is, however, no evidence of active commercial vehicle manufacture until 1908, when some postal vans were built on the contemporary private-car chassis with four separately cast cylinders and 2-speed, pedal-controlled planetary transmission. An 800-pound commercial car, the Overland 37, was listed in 1910, and a year later came a driver-over-engine 1-tonner on solid tires, powered by a 40 hp 4-cylinder engine. This was almost certainly a Federal product (though advertised as an Overland), and until 1913 the only Toledo-built commercials were the vans,

1922 WILLYS Overland 4 van, RNE

now with 3-speed sliding-type gearboxes. The Willys name first appeared on the 1½-ton Utility of 1913-15, made by Gramm at Lima; the 240 ci (3.9-litre) 4-cylinder engine followed classic Overland lines, but final drive was by side chains, and only the front tires were pneumatic. Light van development continued, with full electrics and lhd in 1915 (when the list price was $850), and a L-head monobloc engine on the 1916 models. This had evolved by 1919 into the classic Light Four; descendants of this engine were still being produced in 1963. The vans were to be the staple commercial Willys products once more until 1927, though from 1924 both 4- and 6-cylinder Willys-Knight sleeve-valve cars were offered in taxicab form, and in 1923 the firm's British branch at Stockport marketed a curious 1-tonner based on the Overland Four car chassis. Though this was never offered in the USA, it had little or no affinity with the later, British-made (ii) Overlands and Manchesters.

In 1926 the Overland Four gave way to the 2.2-litre Overland Whippet with fwb (known, confusingly, as plain Whippet in 1927 and 1928, and thereafter as the Willys Whippet!). This was offered throughout its career as a panel van, later with the option of a 2.4-litre 6-cylinder unit. From 1927 to 1931 there was also a line of Willys-Knight 6-cylinder sleeve-valve trucks for payloads from 1 to 2½ tons, with 2.7-litre and 4.2-litre engines, joined briefly in 1928 by an export-model coach on a 15 ft. 10 in. wheelbase; this last featured four forward speeds and vacuum servo brakes. By the end of 1929, however, the company was concentrating on a pair of 1½-tonners, the C101 and the T103; they had four forward speeds and Whippet front-end sheet metal, engines being respectively a 7-bearing 3.2-litre sv six and the small Knight six. From

1930 WILLYS C-101 1½-ton truck, GNG

1927-1930 Willys trucks and buses were built by Gramm. In 1932 only the C101 and a car-type screen express were offered, both with the sv unit, while the entire car and truck line was jettisoned for 1933 in favor of the sub-utility 2.2-litre 4-cylinder 77, offered in panel delivery form. This one and its redesigned successor of 1937 tided the company through a receivership, and in final 1941-2 form the commercial range consisted of a conventional ½-tonner and a forward-control variant for urban delivery work. Both featured 2-speed synchromesh gearboxes with column change, hypoid rear axles, and hydraulic brakes. A 4-speed 1½-tonner with similar engine had made a brief appearance as an export-only item in 1938.

Thereafter the name of Willys was indelibly associated

1937 WILLYS ½-ton pick-up, GNG

with the wartime ¼-ton 4 × 4 Jeep, the production of which they shared with Ford, though its concept was that of Bantam's 1940 prototype. In its definitive Willys form it used the familiar sv 134 ci, 2.2-litre engine, a 3 × 2-speed Warner synchromesh gearbox, hypoid drive to all four wheels, and hydraulic brakes. Nominal payload was 800 pounds, and the vehicle was to serve as the inspiration for a whole generation of similar vehicles, notably the British Landrover, the Russian Gaz, and the Japanese Toyota. Among makers who took out Willys licenses after the War were Mitsubishi in Japan, Hotchkiss in France, and Viasa in Spain.

1951 WILLYS Jeep van, GNG

More important, Willys, unlike Ford, continued the development of the Jeep after VJ-Day, having a civilian edition on the market at $1,090 late in 1945. Jeep business would delay their re-entry into the passenger-car field proper until 1952, though from 1947 the range included a station wagon that was more car than truck. By 1949, however, panels and pickups had joined the basic Universal model, and a 75 hp ioe development of the 134 unit made its appearance in 1952, though its companion six was not fitted to Willys commercial vehicles. The restyled short (CJ5) and long (CJ6) wheelbase Willys Jeeps were announced in 1955, along with an austerity lightweight model (the Despatcher) with sv engine and 2-wheel drive only.

For the Army the company produced a new generation of Mechanical Mules with air-cooled flat-4 engines rated at 17 hp; there was also a 100 hp ¾-tonner, but neither type became commercially available. There were, however, new 1- and 1½-ton forward control Jeeps in 1957, the 1½-tonner using the 3.7-litre, Continental-based sv six inherited from Kaiser, with whom Willys had merged in 1954. By 1961 a wide range of Jeep types extended from the Despatcher up to normal and forward control 1/1½-ton models. The Universal Jeep was now available with a 4-cylinder Perkins diesel engine, and there was even a multi-

1961 WILLYS Jeep FC-170 van, GNG

stop forward control delivery model, the Fleetvan, only 12 ft. 10 in. long. An element of styling crept in on the 1962 Panel Van and Gladiator pickup; these used Willys' new 3.8-litre phc 6-cylinder engine and could be had with automatic transmission. A year later, the company assumed the name of Kaiser Jeep Corporation, and with this change of name the vehicles themselves, though continued without alteration, became plain Jeeps. Willys Overland do Brasil, who had been building Jeeps under license since 1954, perpetuated the old name for another four seasons before a merger with the local Ford interests once again put a Ford label on a Jeep for the first time since 1945. *MCS*

WILLYS (ii) (IL) 1965-1967

E. Ilin Industries Ltd., Haifa

Ilin Industries were assembling various car and commercial vehicles in Haifa, including Studebaker, Hino and Willys. In order to fill the need for a light pickup, not included in the Willys range, Ilin introduced a model that used the same chassis and front-end as used in the Willys station wagon, but the rear part was designed as a high sided pickup body. Power came from a 4-cylinder "Hurricaine" gas engine. The introduction of the "Gladiator" series, ended production of Willys pickup, but Jeep vehicles are still built in Haifa by Mat-mar Ltd., that took over in 1969. *GA*

WILLYS-VIASA (E) 1956 to date

Vehiculos Industriales y Agricolas S.A., Zaragoza

Jeep vehicles of American type were made under license from the Kaiser-Jeep Corporation in Zaragoza from 1956, and in 1963 Viasa introduced a range of forward-control vehicles of their own design in addition. These used Spanish-built Perkins Diesel engines of 63 hp, had 5-speed gearboxes and 4-wheel drive. Various body styles are made, including the Duplex with double cabin seating six passengers and cargo space for 800 kgs load, and the Toledo 9-seater minibus with cargo space for 300 kgs. In 1968 there appeared the Jeepster Commando, similar to the American model but with 53 hp Perkins diesel engine. From 1974 Willys-Viasa vehicles have been distributed by Motor Iberica S.A., makers of Ebro vehicles. *JCG*

WILSON (i) (US) 1914-1925

J.C. Wilson Co., Detroit, Mich.

This company had long been manufacturing horse-drawn wagons. The first motorized truck was a 2-tonner with double-chain drive which was changed to worm-drive for 1916. In 1917, 1- and 3-tonners were added, and for 1918, 3½- and 5-tonners were listed also. The 5-tonner had a 4-speed gearbox. In 1920, this brand included models which were 1½-, 2½-, 3½- and 5-tonners, all with 4-speed Brown-Lipe gearboxes and Timken worm-drive rear axles. Continental engines were used in all four types. *GMN*

WILSON (ii) (GB) 1934-1954

Partridge, Wilson & Co. Ltd., Leicester

First Wilson models were the 5-cwt LW and 15-cwt MW introduced in 1934. By 1936 there were four models listed including the LW and MW which had both been uprated to 8-cwt and 25-cwt respectively. The two additional models were a pair of 6-cwt payload types designated the SLW with a 198AH battery, and the "Speedy" when the chassis was equipped with a smaller 129AH battery. All these vehicles were of the single motor type and were fitted with either worm or spiral bevel rear axles.

For 1937 there were 11 different models on offer, although the variations concerned battery size on three basic chassis designs. These were the XW, a 4-cwt 5 ft. wheelbase bevel driven machine, the MW, a 6 ft. 6 in. wheelbase worm axle chassis varying in capacity from 10-cwt to 25-cwt, and the LW which covered the 5-cwt to 8-cwt payload bracket and was of 6 ft. 1 in. wheelbase with bevel rear axle. There was also an electric conversion of the Scammell Mechanical Horse.

1949 WILSON (ii) ¾-ton electric van, OMM

The early postwar range centered around four models — Senior, Major, Junior and Minor with payload capacities of 30-cwt, 25-cwt, 18-cwt and 15-cwt respectively. The models were soon renamed the Beavermajor range with the name Beaver as a prefix to these previous title. Of similar layout, these chassis had the batteries positioned at the rear and center within the chassis frame, with the motor placed just behind the controller which was under the driver's seat, and the propellor shaft ran between the side batteries to the rear axle. Post-war production was in fact subcontracted to Hindle Smart of Manchester, as the Leicester works were entirely devoted to transformers and battery charging equipment. *OM*

WINCHESTER (GB) 1963-1972

Winchester Automobiles (West End) Ltd., London, S.W. 10

The Winchester was a taxicab designed by a group of owners and drivers, led by K.E. Drummond. It was the first London cab to have a Fiberglass body, and was powered initially by a Perkins 4-99 diesel engine, later replaced by a slightly smaller Ford Cortina gas engine. The chassis were made by Rubery Owen, the bodies by James Whitson of West Drayton up to 1965 and then by Wincanton

1962 WINCHESTER Mark 1 taxicab, GNG

Transport & Engineering of Wincanton, Somerset. A major change in body styling came in 1968 when the highly distinctive lines of the original Winchester were replaced by a more conventional appearance. At the same time chassis production was transferred to Keewest Developments Ltd. of Botley, Hants. *GNG*

WINDHOFF (D) 1910-1914

Gebr. Windhoff Motoren und Fahrzeugfabrik GmbH., Rheine

The private cars of this firm were the basis for their vans. The types 6/18 PS and 10/30 PS were available. In some cases also the 15/40 PS was used, especially for the army. *HON*

WINKLER (US) 1911-1912

Winkler Brothers Manufacturing Company, South Bend, Indiana

The two models of the Winkler used 4-cylinder engines with forward control and had open cabs. These were one- and three-tonners whose engines were rated at 25 and 45 hp, respectively. The three-tonner used a three-speed progressive gearbox, had wheelbase of 10 feet and with stake body cost $4000. *GMN*

1975 WINNEBAGO shuttle bus, EK

WINNEBAGO (U.S.) 1973 to date

Winnebago Industries, Inc., Forest City, Iowa

Winnebago was one of the earliest house trailer manufacturers to turn to so-called "motor homes", the self-propelled version of the house trailer that enjoyed a phenomenal success in the U.S. during the 1960s. With the drop in demand for these vehicles, Winnebago and others modified their motor home design into a small bus, in this case based on a 159-inch-wheelbase Dodge chassis (RM-350 with a 318-cubic-inch six or RM-400 with a 440-cubic-inch V-8). The total number of vehicles of this type, of all makes, sold in the U.S. to the end of 1975 has been small, and most of them are used for specialized transportation rather than common-carrier service. *MBS*

WINTHER (US) 1917-1926
WINTHER-MARWIN (US) 1918-1921
WINTHER-KENOSHA (US) 1927

(1) Winther Motor Truck Co., Winthrop Harbour, Ill. 1917-1918
(2) Winthrop Motor Truck Co., Kenosha, Wis. 1918-1921
(3) Winther Motors Inc., Kenosha, Wis. 1921-1926
(4) Kenosha Fire Engine & Truck Co., Kenosha, Wis. 1927

Martin P. Winther, a former Jeffery engineer, formed his own company in 1917. The rear-drive Winther truck was closely followed by the 4-wheel-drive Winther-Marwin truck, and, in 1920, by the Winther passenger car

Except for the drives, both trucks were similar in layout, being powreed by 4-cylinder Wisconsin engines of various sizes driving through Borg & Beck clutches, Cotta 3- or 4-speed transmissions and Celfer internal gear axles. Cabs were open, but fitted with low doors. Initial capacities were 2, 3, 4 and 6 tons, priced from $2,750 to $4,600. Later additions extended the range from 1 to 7 tons, the latter model having a 4-cylinder Herschell-Spillman engine. Transmissions were Warner, Brown-Lipe or Fuller, and internal gear axles Torbensen, Medway or Clark. The 4-wheel-drive Winther-Marwin was made in the same sizes, with a shaft driving from the engine to a central transfer case, and from there to a shaft to each axle.

1918 WINTHER-MARWIN Model 430 1½-ton truck, FLP

As early as 1919 the company claimed that Winthers were the dominating truck in the U.S. Navy. The 1½-tonners were aimed at the farmers' market, while the heavier models were made for logging (in Orgeon), fire-fighting and as snowplows. The latter made early use of rotary plows, and one of the largest used two engines, the rear one over the rear axle to drive the truck, and the front one for the plow, with the fully-enclosed cab between.
Throughout the 1920s Winthers continued much the same mechanically, but with electric starters added. The 1926 range included five models from 1½ to 5/7 tons, all with Wisconsin engines. In its last year the products were renamed Winther-Kenosha, and in the summer of 1927 the plant was sold to H.P. Olsen and truck manufacture was discontinued. *RW*

WISCONSIN (US) 1912-1926

(1) Wisconsin Motor Truck Works, Baraboo, Wis. 1912-1915
(2) Myers Machine Co., Sheboygan, Wis. 1915-1918
(3) Wisconsin Truck Co., Loganville, Wis. 1919-1925

This company began by making light trucks in the 1500 lb. to 1-ton category increasing to a 2-tonner in 1916 and a 5-tonner in 1921, with a variety of models from 1½- to 5-tonners being made thereafter. Engines were mostly Waukeshas, though Continental and Herschell-Spillman units were also listed. In 1923 Wisconsin took over the Six Wheel Truck Company of Fox Lake, Wisconsin who had made a 6-wheeler under the name Super-Traction. This led to the introduction of a 6-wheel bus chassis in 1924. Intended for 28 passengers, it had a 6-cylinder Continental 6B engine and two underslung worm axles. A 4-wheel bus chassis with the same engine was also listed in 1924. *GNG*

WITTENBERG (US) 1966 to date

Wittenberg Motor Co., Midway, Wash.

For more than 30 years Wittenberg has dealt in used military vehicles, and from 1966 onwards they offered rebuilt military trucks with new cabs, hoods and fenders and their own nameplate. They are mostly based on 6 × 4 and 6 × 6 trucks of the U.S. ARMY M-series made by Reo and GMC, but they also offer a smaller 4 × 4 based on the ¾-ton Dodge, and a 5-ton 6 × 6 cab-over with one-man offset cab. A wide variety of custom bodies can be made by Wittenberg as well as equipment such as front-mounted winch, transfer case with power take-off etc. *RW*

WITT-WILL (US) 1911-1931

Witt-Will Co. Inc., Washington, D.C.

The Witt-Will was a conventional assembled truck using Continental engines, Brown-Lipe transmissions and Timken worm or bevel axles. It was made in sizes from 1½ to 5½ tons, with 6-cylinder engines coming into the range from the mid-1920s. The plant was little more than a large garage, but a point of distinction was that it was virtually in the shadow of the White House, and in fact Witt-Wills found many customers among Federal agencies. Few were sold outside the Washington area, and production tapered off in the 1930s with a shift of interest to truck bodies and auxillary truck equipment on other chassis. *RJ*

W.M.C. see Will

WOLF (GB) 1905-c.1908

Wearwell Motor Carriage Co. Ltd., Wolverhampton, Staffs.

This long-lived (1901-1939) motorcycle maker built a few tricar-based trade carriers during the period when passenger tricars were popular. They had 7 hp 2-cylinder engines of the company's own make, 3 speeds and chain drive to the single rear wheel. *GNG*

WOLFE see Wilcox

1961 WOLFWAGON 6×4 chassis, LA

WOLFWAGON (US) 1956-c.1964

(1) Wolf Engineering Corp., Dallas, Texas 1956-1960
(2) St. Louis Car Co., St. Louis, Mo. 1960-c.1964

The Wolf Wagon was an unusual concept which involved a series of trucks which could be hooked together with one operator. Each unit had a conventional A-type drawbar which could be stored vertically in front of the cab when the truck was traveling solo. The controls for throttle, gearchange and brakes for the 'trailer vehicles' was transmitted by cables. Two- and three-axle models were made, and a pair of three-axle trucks could operate at 40 tons GVW. Most applications were doubles, though the system was advertised as usable with up to six units. The power plant and transmission were mounted either above the front axle or below the floor between front and rear axles. It was designed by L.J. Wolf of the St. Louis Car Company, who undertook manufacture of the production models. *GNG*

WOLSELEY: WOLSELEY-SIDDELEY (GB) 1901-1921

(1) Wolseley Tool and Motor Car Co. Ltd., Birmingham 1901-1914
(2) Wolseley Motors Ltd., Birmingham 1914-1921

In early days this pioneer maker explored every possible application of the internal-combustion principle — trucks, buses, marine and railcar power units and light locomotives, all designed by Herbert Austin, who was the company's general manager until 1905. In 1901 they offered a 10-cwt delivery van on their 5 hp single-cylinder horizontal-engined chain drive chassis, and a year later the range had been extended to embrace 15- and 30-cwt models with the 2.6-litre 2-cylinder unit. Next came fire-engine and light bus developments of the 24 hp four, the latter featuring a front vertical radiator in place of the wrap-around

1905 WOLSELEY ½-ton van, BR

tubes of the private car. By 1905 a full range was being offered, from a 2-cwt parcelcar on the little 6 hp chassis to forward-control 2-tonners using 2- or 4-cylinder engines and 4-speed gearboxes, also available with single- or double-decker bus bodywork. There was also an immense 4-ton army lorry with an unladen weight of 6 tons; this had a 4-cylinder horizontal engine or nearly 13 litres' capacity, lt magneto ignition, a paraffin carburetor, a 100-gallon fuel tank, a vertical exhaust, iron tires, and a transversely-sprung front axle aimed at clearing obstacles up to a foot high. With Austin's resignation, J.D. Siddeley took over the management of Wolseley. The new line of vertical-engined Wolseley-Siddeleys included commercials as well as cars; by the end of 1905 there was a 30-cwt model with 3.7-litre ioe 4-cylinder engine, 3-speed gearbox, and shaft drive, offered with forward or conventional control. The War Office ordered some conventional ambulances in 1908. The bigger 30 hp X-type was chain-driven, being usually seen as a 35-seater omnibus, though a 3½-ton truck version was also available. Over 100 of the former type were sold, some of them going to the London General Omnibus Co. A gas-electric model with 40 hp engine and twin BTH electric motors was tested in 1907, but did not go into production. Serious truck production petered out during 1908, but in the meantime Wolseley had plunged into taxicabs, the principal types being 8/10 hp and 10/12 hp twins with ht magneto ignition, 3-speed gearboxes, and shaft drive, though a bigger 18 hp 4-cylinder model was also offered. Among those who used Wolseley-Siddeley cabs was W.R. Morris, then an Oxford garage proprietor, who would acquire the Wolseley interests in 1926. In 1910 Wolseley built some motor sledges for the ill-fated Scott Antarctic Expedition, and in 1912, after Siddeley's departure, there was a revival of truck production under the direction of A.A. Remington. Initially only a car-based 12-cwt light van and a 25-cwt truck were offered, but by 1914 there were six commercial models, the largest of them the 6.6-litre HR-type for 5-ton payloads. All used sv 4-cylinder engines with magneto ignition and thermosyphon cooling, and solid tires were standard on all but the smallest versions (and charabancs on the 1-ton chassis). The 12-cwt and 1-ton had worm drive, with double-reduction back axles on bigger Wolseleys. The 30-cwt and 4-ton were approved War Office Subsidy types, continuing in limited production during the War years. Thereafter Wolseley abandoned commercial vehicles, apart from a short-lived 7-cwt delivery van of 1921, mounted on the 1.3-litre 10.5 hp ohc light-car chassis. The company was, however, responsible for the production of the Oxford taxicab between 1947 and 1953. *MCS*

WOLVERINE (US) 1918-1922

American Commercial Car Co., Detroit, Mich.

This minor make began as a ¾-tonner along with a 1½ tonner. The smaller was a delivery van with pneumatic tires, but this type was not continued after 1918. The 1½-tonner remained unchanged for the duration of this make. It had a 4-cylinder Continental engine under a hood with a wheelbase of 11 feet, 8 inches, a Fuller 3-speed gearbox and rear axle by Russel. *GMN*

WOLVERINE-DETROIT (US) 1912-1913

Pratt, Carter, Sigsbee Company, Detroit, Mich.

Only one model of commercial vehicle was offered in each of these two years. In 1912, an open express type was made which had a one-cylinder, water-cooled engine with a

1905 WOLSELEY 20hp bus, NMM

friction transmission and double chain drive. Either solid or pneumatic tires were available and the wheelbase was 7 feet, 5 inches. Chassis price was $775. In the final year of manufacture the Model C half-tonner was made. This also was a one-cylinder type but had worm drive and a wheelbase of 8 feet. The only body type ws a flare board express, with the engine mounted under the body. *GMN*

WOOD (US) 1902-1905

(1) Wood Vapor Vehicle Co., Brooklyn, N.Y.
(2) J.C. Wood, Brooklyn, N.Y.

Mr. Wood experimented in motor propulsion for several years. The truck described here was designed to transport asphalt and was completed in 1905. It was very large and powerful for its time, being a 7-ton coal-fired low cab-forward steam motor truck with a rather different method of producing motive power.

The steam was used in two single-acting engines hung below the frame, which drove the rear wheels directly through driving chains. The truck could be started from a standstill without clutches or other special devices. The maximum hp developed was 100 for this truck weighing 4½ tons. Heavy artillery wheels were steel-tired, with the rear ones being much larger.

In front, steering was by wheel, and the steering column rose out of a low platform between the wheels, which the driver ascended from the front with the help of an auxiliary step. Once on the low platform he turned, slid under the steering wheel, and sat on the main elevation in front of the large body which was of the rear-dumping type. *RW*

WOODALL NICHOLSON (GB) 1905

Woodall, Nicholson & Co. Ltd., Halifax, Yorks

This coachbuilding firm made a least one delivery van with 12/14 hp 2-cylinder Aster engine, 3-speed gearbox and shaft drive. It was supplied to the Halifax Economic Stores. The company is still in business as a manufacturer of hearse bodies on Ford and other chassis. *GNG*

WOODROW (GB) 1914-1915

Woodrow & Co. Ltd., Stockport, Cheshire

Powered by a V-twin Precision engine, the shaft-driven Woodrow cyclecar was made in light van and truck versions, with a load capacity of 5-cwt. Even the commercial versions were more rakish than most cyclecars, with sharply-pointed V-radiators. *GNG*

WOODS (US) 1927-1931

(1) Patriot Mfg. Co., Havelock, Neb. 1927-1929
(2) Patriot Mfg. Co., Divn. of Arrow Aircraft & Motors Corp., Lincoln, Neb. 1929-1931

The Woods was a continuation of the former Patriot truck, the same assembled trucks in 1 to 3 ton sizes being continued under the new name. In 1929 Patriot merged into the Arrow Aircraft interests, and production was transferred to Arrow's main plant at Lincoln. They also enlarged the dealership network for Woods trucks which were sold to telephone companies, state highway departments and Arrow's airport holding as fuel and servicing vehicles. Semi-trailers and truck bodies were added to the line. The 1930 range was typical of Woods production; trucks from 1½ - to 4-tons, including a 6-wheeler, powered by Hercules engines and using Timken and Shuler axles. The later Woods resembled the Diamond T, an important rival. *RJ*

WOODS MOBILETTE see Mobilette

WOOLSTON (US) 1913

C.T. Woolston, Riverton, N.J.

Four models of commercial vehicles were listed for this single year of manufacture. These were 1-, 2-, 3- and 5-tonners. Despite the large capacities, these were made only as express types. These used 4-cylinder engines and the smaller two had forward control while the two larger types had engines under hoods. Model A, the one-tonner had a three-speed gearbox, solid tires and was govered to a maximum speed of 15 mph. *GMN*

WORLD (US) 1927-1931

World Motors Co., Cincinnati, Ohio

The World truck was the outcome of a reorganization of Steinkoenig Motors Company, makers of a handsome range of Waukesha-powered assembled trucks which largely appeared to buyers in the Cincinnati area; the firm was smaller than its local rivals such as Armleder, Schacht and Biederman. World's main claim to fame is that it used straight-8 engines for many of its trucks from 1928 to 1930. Continental engines were used in most models, though there were a few Lycomings too. World trucks were in the 1½ to 5-ton range, but they were expensive, and failed to survive the Depression. *RJ*

WORTH (US) 1907-1910

Worth Motor Car Manufacturing Company, Evansville, Ind.

This make offered a preponderance of buses with ratings of 5, 9 and 16 passengers. The smallest was a high-wheeler with a 2-cylinder engine. The largest model had a wheelbase of 11 feet, 8 inches and had a 60 hp, 4-cylinder engine. This manufacturer also offered Model D delivery van on a wheelbase of 8 feet, 4 inches. *GMN*

W.S. see Weier-Smith

W.S.C. (GB) 1907; 1912-1914

Wholesale Supply Co. Aberdeen.

The Wholesale Supply Co. were a branch of the Aberdeen Co-op and their vehicle building activities appear to fall into two separate phases. The first, in 1907, saw the introduction of a small three wheeled cyclecar cum parcels carrier, but this was unsuccessful. A larger JAP-engined cyclecar followed in 1912, and concurrent with this was a larger range of cars, pick-up trucks, vans and taxis. Little is known of the technical specifications of these, but a large number of Albion components were used in their construction, and they were operated by the Aberdeen Co-operative Society. *MJWW*

WUHAN WH-130 (CHI) 1970 to date

Wuham Motor Vehicle Plant, Wuhan, Hupeh
(Plant Vehicle Code-WH)

The general construction of the engine and chassis of the Wuhan WH-130 is much the same as the Nanking Tiao-Jim (Leap Forward) NJ-130.

This 2.5-ton truck is of conventional layout with a Nanking 6-cylinder motor and a maximum vehicle speed of 70 km/h. (BE)

WUHAN 211 (CHI) to date

Wuhan Number Two Motor Vehicle Plant, Wuhan, Hupeh

The Wuhan 211 is a 4 × 4 jeep seating five or carrying a load of ½ ton. There are four half-doors and a convertible canvas top.

A 4-cylinder, 80 hp engine powers it and there are three speeds forward with a two-gear transfer case.*BE*

WUHAN #250K (CHI) 1970 to date

Wuhan Pedicab Factory, Wuhan, Hupeh

The model #250K 3-wheeler serves as both taxi and delivery. It is fitted with a removable canvas top and can be had in blue or buff.

Power is by a 1-cylinder, aircooled engine of 12 hp @ 4,600 rpm and as a taxi it seats three plus driver.

There are four forward speeds and the transmission is chain driven. *BE*

XENIA (US) 1914

Hawkins Cyclecar Co., Xenia, Ohio

With a delivery body, this cyclecar was priced at $395. It was powered by a 2-cylinder, air-cooled engine rated at 10 hp and drive was through a planetary transmission and belts to the rear wheels. Its track was 3 feet with wheelbase of 8 feet, 4 inches, and it sported a single headlamp. *GMN*

YA SU 1925-c.1945
YAAZ or YAZ c.1945-1959

Yarolavl Automobile Factory, Yaroslavl

Along with the AMO factory, the Yaroslavl plant commenced truck manufacture in 1925 in accordance with Lenin's plans.

A 3-ton YA-3 was built from 1925 to 1928, using an AMO 35 hp, 4-cylinder engine providing 30 km/h.

A 3.5-ton YA-4, with a German Daimler-Benz 6-cylinder, 70 hp engine was built from 1928 to 1929.

From 1929 to 1934, a 4.5-ton, 93 hp YA-5 was produced, and variations were made into World War II including dumpers and a 6×4 8-ton YAG-10 with an American Hercules 6-cylinder engine.

An unusual truck appeared about 1932 in the form of the YAG-12. This was an 8×8 cargo truck with four wheels steering in front. It was rated at 12 tons and was originally powered by a Continental 6-cylinder of 93 hp. Russian sources report that some versions were also powered by 105 hp engines, increasing the maximum speed to 45 km/h. Length of production is uncertain but it was possibly made until 1941.

Buses manufactured at the plant included the YA-2 city 6×6 and the 70 passenger YA-1, both running experimentally in Leningrad before the war.

A confusing amount of prefixes accompanied the many models built at this plant. The G in YAG stands for "gruzovik" or truck, the S in YAS means "samosval" or dumper. The model prefix was revised to YAAZ after the end of World War II.

Among the postwar vehicles were the YAAZ-200, a 7-ton truck of 110 hp similar to the Minsk-built MAZ-200, the YAAZ-210 series of cargos, dumpers, semi-tractors and prime movers, the YAAZ-214 7-ton 6x6, the YAAZ-219 12-ton general purpose truck and the YAAZ-222 10-ton dumper. All were powered by various 6-cylinder diesels.

In 1959 truck production was transferred to the new Kraz plant at Kremenchug. Further information will be found under that entry.

The former YAAZ plant is now known as Yaroslavskii Motornoi Zavod (YAMZ) and constructs diesel engines for other truck plants including Kraz, MAZ and Belaz. *BE*

YALE (US) 1920-1922

Yale Motor Truck Co., New Haven, Conn.

Obviously named after the famous university at New Haven, the Yale was a conventional truck made in only one model, a 1½-tonner powered by a 4-cylinder Herschell-Spillman engine. *GNG*

YELLOW CAB (US) 1915-1929

(1) Yellow Cab Mfg. Co., Chicago, Ill. 1915-1925
(2) Yellow Truck & Coach Mfg. Co., Chicago, Ill. 1925-1928
(3) Yellow Truck & Coach Mfg. Co., Pontiac, Mich. 1928-1929

The Yellow Cab business was started in Chicago in 1910 by John Hertz, using various makes of cab, and actual production began in 1915 with a conventional machine powered by a 4-cylinder Continental engine, and with a Racine body. Sales of these cabs soon took place to other companies than Yellow, and in other cities. In 1924 a batch of 120 were turned out for assembly in London with English landaulette bodies, and were operated by W & G du Cros of Acton.

In 1924/5 a 1-ton truck was marketed under the name Yellocab Truck. In 1923 production of buses and coaches began (see Yellow Coach) and two years later Yellow's operations were taken over by General Motors, Hertz remaining as president. In 1924 he had started a self-drive hire company using his own make of Ambassador sedan,

1923 YELLOW CAB 4-cylinder taxicab, TCV

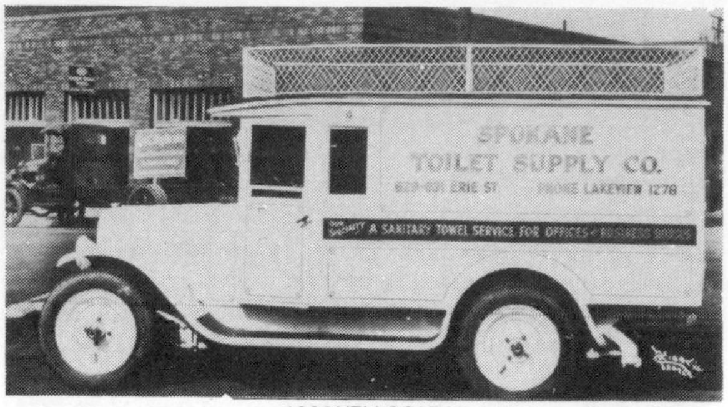

1926 YELLOCAB Model T-2 van, General Motors

1928 YELLOW CAB Model O÷ taxicab, TCV

renamed Hertz in the latter part of 1925.

Meanwhile the Yellow Cab line was expanded with the introduction of the Yellow-Knight powered by a Knight sleeve-valve engine which was offered alongside the Continental-engined cabs. A few Lycoming and Northway engines were also used in the cabs and Hertz sedans. In 1927 came a new cab with front-wheel brakes, similar to the Hertz car, followed in 1928 by the 6-cylinder Model D6 with Buick Standard Six engine. The Yellocab Truck had been joined by a Yellow-Knight truck, and these together covered a capacity range of 1500 lbs. to 4 tons, the smaller trucks being Continental-powered, and the larger using Knight or Buick engines. The trucks were dropped at the end of 1927, and in 1929 all Yellow Cabs had Buick engines. In 1930 the name was changed to General Cab. *GNG*

YELLOW and GM COACH (US) 1923 to date

(1) Yellow Coach Manufacturing Co., Chicago, Ill. 1923-1925

(2) Yellow Truck & Coach Manufacturing Co., Chicago, Ill. 1925-1928

(3) Yellow Truck & Coach Manufacturing Co., Pontiac, Mich. 1928-1943

(4) GMC Truck & Coach Division, General Motors Corp., Pontiac, Mich. 1943 to date

John D. Hertz was a Chicago automobile salesman who had the idea of making and selling a line of autos built as taxicabs, together with advice on how to run taxi operating companies. Between 1915 and 1922, his Yellow cabs were sold by the thousands, often on credit or in return for shares in the operating companies. When the struggling Chicago Motor Bus Co. appeared to be making a successful stand against a competitive franchise bid by agents for the powerful Fifth Avenue Coach Co. of New York, Hertz's eye turned toward organizing a similar chain of motor bus operating companies. He obtained control of Chicago Motor Bus Co. and its manufacturing affiliate American Motor Bus Co. and then joined it with Fifth Avenue Coach in a new holding company called The Omnibus Corp.

The cab manufacturing company was joined by a new bus plant headed by Col. George A. Green of Fifth Avenue Coach. Born in Australia and trained in the early days of the London bus business, Green had designed the dependable Fifth Avenue Coach double-decker. In the summer of 1923 he worked out a plan to modify the larger Chicago double-decker according to his New York experience to produce a third type combining the best features of each. Since earlier Fifth Avenue buses had been designated Type A and later ones Type L, Green moved to the end of the alphabet and called the first Yellow Coach "Type Z."

1926 YELLOW COACH Type X bus, MBS

He accurately forecast a demand for a heavy-duty single-deck version seating 29, which was introduced by modifying the double-deck chassis, and for a deluxe 25-passenger bus with low headroom for fast express and suburban lines (the "Type Y" of 1924), and finally for an economical 17 to 21-passenger feeder bus (the "Type X" of 1925).

A key feature common to the Chicago and New York double-deckers of the 1917-1922 period was the four-cylinder Silent Knight sleeve-valve engine, manufactured under license from Daimler of Coventry by the R&V Engineering Co. of East Moline, Illinois. Hertz added this company to his group in 1923 and renamed it the Yellow Sleeve-Valve Engine Works. Originally hostile to the sleeve-valve concept, Green later endorsed it and became reluctant to turn away from it for the Type Z. The fact

1924 YELLOW COACH Type Z 67-seater bus, MBS

that this engine had been tried and proved it buses over a period of several years, whereas competitors were still in the stage of experiments and tests, greatly aided Yellow's early sales efforts. The Type Z gained renown as a durable and reliable city transit bus, which was more expensive than others, but attracted many repeat orders.

In 1925, at the request of the street railroad system of

Philadelphia, Yellow stretched the Type Z chassis from a wheelbase of 200 inches to 230 inches and cooperated with General Electric in the design and construction of a fleet of gas-electric buses, the first ones seen in the U.S. since the unsuccessful trial of 10 DeDions by Fifth Avenue Coach in 1912. The so-called Z-230 or Z-33 was then offered (both gas-electric and gas-mechanical) along with Z-200 or Z-29. In fact, every order for Yellows that specified any kind of substantial change in equipment or dimensions was distinguished for record-keeping purposes by its own model number, but there were basically only a few general types.

General Motors bought control of Yellow Coach from Hertz and his associates in 1925 for $16 million and merged its own GM Truck manufacturing operation into Yellow. The Yellow Sleeve-Valve Engine Works was closed; engine production was transferred to Pontiac and incorporated into GM Truck manufacturing operations. Bus manufacture followed in 1927, and the Chicago plant was sold.

The small Type X was the least successful of the original Yellows, its engine in particular being not too well regarded. Many operators rebuilt their X's with Ford or Buick engines in later years. In 1928 Yellow suspended production of the Type X and replaced it with the Type W with new styling and a Cadillac V-8 engine. Many X's and an even larger proportion of W's were sold as intercity parlor coaches to smaller operators, a usage which Green with his city transit orientation had not perceived. Consequently the Type W was offered with a smart-looking parlor car body built by either Lang or Yellow.

In response to the success of the original 40-passenger Twin Coach, Yellow added another 10 inches to the wheelbase of its Type Z single-decker in 1929 to produce the Z-240 or Z-39. The increase in seating capacity came about in part because the dashboard was pushed forward over the back part of the engine. By that time the double-decker was virtually a thing of the past, though 100 were sold to Fifth Avenue Coach and 12 to Baltimore in 1930. The market for the Z-200 had also dried up, and both it and the Z-230 were superseded by the Z-225, which had seats for either 29 or 33 passengers and was styled like the Z-240.

Improvements in technology had rendered the sleeve-valve engine obsolescent, and in 1930, reversing its historic stand and contradicting its previous advertising and promotion, Yellow introduced a line of poppet-valve engines of substantially greater horsepower. Although the last few Type Y deluxe buses were built with these motors, the Y was soon discontinued and replaced by the Type V, available in transit and intercity versions; it was quite similar in dimensions and appearance to the Z-225, but had a smaller engine. Also in 1930 the Type W was joined by the similar Type U, which had a Buick six-cylinder in-line engine, for economy-minded operators of smaller buses.

1929 YELLOW COACH Type W, Lang-bodied bus, MBS

Greyhound, the dominant U.S. intercity bus operator, arranged to sell its wholly owned bus manufacturing subsidiary C.H. Will Motors Corp. (see Will) to Yellow Coach during 1929, and Yellow subsequently designed and built a 250-inch-wheelbase Type Z parlor coach chassis to Greyhound specifications. This type of bus was the last conventional Yellow chassis to be introduced, as work was already under way on new designs that enclosed the engine within the body. The big Z-250 used a 707-cubic-inch six-cylinder engine, while smaller Yellows were equipped with either 616 or 568-cubic-inch motors. After 1930, GM Truck engines were used in the smallest models in place of the earlier Cadillac or Buick automobile engines.

1934 YELLOW COACH 715 small bus, MBS

Between 1931 and 1934, Yellow built and sold a small number of city transit buses with rear-mounted engines that drove forward. These were not particularly successful, the largest types encountering significant clutch trouble because the largest engine that could be accomodated within the bus was too small for the size of the vehicle. In the meantime the small types U and W were superseded by front-engine forward-control buses. The use of letter designations was given up, and buses (and a few trolley-coaches) of the new designs were labeled with model numbers in the 700 series. Production of types V and Z, especially the parlor versions, continued until 1936.

At least as important as the continuing technical innovations during the 1930's was the powerful marketing effort that Yellow put behind its products. Sales manager Herbert J. Listman involved Yellow in holding companies that bought interests in operating companies or tried to obtain competing franchises, in order to boost sales. The dominant carriers in the U.S. industry, especially Omnibus Corp., Greyhound, Public Service Coordinated Transport, and later National City Lines, were kept in Yellow's camp by careful cultivation of their special needs. With these large companies serving as Yellow's proving ground and also paying the bills for improvements and changes that they wanted made, Yellow strengthened its existing position as the U.S. bus industry's dominant manufacturer.

In 1934 Yellow Coach hired a talented designer and engineer named Dwight Austin, who had been vice-president for design of the old Pickwick manufacturing operation and who had later acquired the former Pickwick factory to build Nite Coaches and small Utility Coaches on his own. Austin's principal contribution to Yellow was an invention patented by him, whereby a bus engine could be placed transversely across the back of the vehicle. It consisted of a set of gears so arranged as to turn the output shaft by more than 90 degrees and was known as "angle drive." The final shaft then ran forward at an angle to an offset differential. Angle drive permitted greater utilization of the available space within the bus body as well as easier access to the engine for maintenance than could be had with longitudinal placement of the motor. These advantages were achieved with somewhat greater expense, not only in terms of the initial cost of the mechanism itself, but also because fuel economy was not as good with the loss in efficiency created by the extra set of gears.

1935 YELLOW COACH 718 41-seater bus, MBS

1936 YELLOW COACH 720 71-seater bus, MBS

After a struggle lasting several years, The Omnibus Corp., still closely tied to Yellow Coach, received approval in 1934 to substitute buses for streetcars on most of the major routes in the borough of Manhattan, New York City. A 40-passenger bus was designed utilizing the angle drive idea and the same 616-cubic-inch motor that had replaced the sleeve-valve engine four years before, but with an air-assisted clutch mechanism for easier handling in heavy traffic. Eventually close to 400 of these buses, designated as Model 718, were placed in service by Omnibus Corp. companies, and a small number were sold as well to other operators. By 1937, production of heavy-duty front-engine buses had ceased at Yellow in favor of transverse rear engines, and the other major U.S. bus builders followed suit unless they had already committed themselves to underfloor engines. Yellow built 300 rear-engined double-decker buses, Models 720 and 735, between 1936 and 1938. New York's Fifth Avenue Coach Company took 160, while 140 went to Chicago. All were one-man-operated, and some were later converted to diesel engines.

The diesel engine was slow to catch on in the U.S., where in the early years there were no particular advantages to its use, and it was seen as a costly and troublesome alternative to gasoline power. Yellow Coach did not begin work on diesel power until 1936, when Public Service Coordinated Transport, a very large company, specified diesel engines in a fleet of 27 new Yellows for experimental purposes. At that time the only tried and tested engine in the U.S. was Hercules, six-cylinder four-cycle motor, which had been installed in a small number of Twin Coaches with good results, and these engines were used in the Public Service Yellows. General Motors Research undertook to develop a new diesel engine specifically for bus use after expressions of interest were obtained from several large customers. The results was a two-cycle engine announced in 1938 and offered in two, three, four and six-cylinder versions; the smallest two were soon dropped, at least as far as the bus business was concerned. The range was known as the "71" series after the displacement of each cylinder in cubic inches. Modifications for heavy truck and marine uses were soon developed.

Providing an adequate bus transmission to handle the increased torque of the diesel engine was a problem initially, the first solution tried by Yellow and others being to revert to electric drive, but by 1939 a torque converter was on the market and was being tried by many operators. Troubles with the new components were numerous and frequent, but Yellow persevered to the extent of shipping replacement transmissions and diesel engines at no charge to customers when original units failed.

In 1939 Yellow adopted a system of bus model numbers that continues in use today. As an example of the nomenclature the first type to use the new system was model TD-4501, in which "T" means transit as opposed to parlor (intercity), "D" stands for diesel, 45 is the nominal seating capacity and the final digits refer to the particular model of that general type. A third prefix letter was used for many years to denote the transmission (hydraulic, mechanical or electric).

1940 YELLOW COACH TD-4502 bus, MBS

The outbreak of World War II was in some respects fortunate for this developmental effort. Military demands required that bus production be stopped, while diesel engines and torque converters proved ideal for armoured vehicles and were, so to speak, proven under fire. By war's end both components were as reliable as they could be made, and the GM diesel-hydraulic bus rose rapidly to prominence on U.S. transit properties. General Motors Corp. had bought out the minority interests in Yellow Truck & Coach during 1943, and when bus production was resumed in 1944 the nameplates read "GM Coach" instead of "Yellow Coach."

Dwight Austin was also directly involved in the development of new over-the-road Yellows in the mid 1930's. Financed by Greyhound, the Model 719 "Super Coach" with transverse rear engine and underfloor luggage space brought a new standard of passenger comfort to the intercity bus industry. Through a number of modifications the 719 developed into the diesel-powered, air-conditioned "Silversides," of which almost 2500 were placed into Greyhound service between 1940 and 1948, and then into 41-passenger postwar versions that introduced the 6-71 diesel to many over-the-road carriers. Torque converter drive was not used, because it offered poor fuel economy at highway speeds.

As the use of private cars for both local and intercity travel soared after 1950, GM stepped up its promotional

1954 GM COACH TDH4801 bus, NMM

activities and its service to its customers in order to continue capturing a dominant share of the shrinking market for new buses. Air suspension, in which rubber bags hold compressed air under varying pressure depending upon load and road conditions, replaced conventional leaf springs on both transit and intercity buses in 1953, and for a period of several years after that, GM had only one competitor for the heavy-duty transit bus market (namely Mack).

Again using Greyhound as its financial partner, GM developed the split-level 43-passenger "Scenicruiser" in

1959 GM COACH TDH-5301 bus, MBS

1953 and built 1000 of them for Greyhound between 1954 and 1956. At this time the old concept of bi-level seating with increased underfloor baggage space, as well as provision of lavatory facilities on board, both known in the 1920's, took hold of the U.S. intercity bus industry. By the mid 1960's all seats were on an upper level, further increasing luggage carrying capacity and allowing development of an extensive "package express" business to replace railway parcel service.

The Scenicruisers were built with two 4-71 diesels because Greyhound did not believe that a single 6-71 could provide sufficient power for fast acceleration and for climbing hills. A fluid coupling was used to merge the output of the two engines into a single final driveshaft. Right from the start there were reliability problems which led to considerable bad feeling between GM and Greyhound. In 1958, development work was started on a line o1 V-form "71" series diesels; the 6V-71 made its debut in a new series of transit buses in 1959, and the 8V-71 began to be used in intercity coaches in 1961 (later also in transit buses for better performance with engine-driven air-conditioning). The Scenicruisers were then rebuilt with 8V-71's. Since 1961 this engine has been used in virtually every intercity bus in the U.S. and Canada, no matter who the builder is. It should be noted that engines and transmissions are not sold by GM Truck & Coach but by a separate GM corporate division, Detroit Diesel-Allison of Indianapolis, which sells them as well to GM Truck & Coach.

1968 GM COACH PD-4903 coach, MBS

From 1959 to 1977 GM offered many different specific models of buses but essentially only a few types: 35-foot and 40-foot split-level intercity buses with 8V-71 engines and Spicer mechanical transmission; 35-foot city transit buses with 6V-71 engines and Allison torque converter transmission; and 40-foot city buses either 96 or 102 inches wide with 6V-71 or 8V-71 engines and Allison transmission. Production of this series of transit buses ceased in 1977 with 33,500 built since 1959.

Introduction of the new "Rapid Transit Series" or RTS type, with stainless steel understructure and fiberglass exterior panels, hand been planned for the early 1970's. The RTS was delayed by a U.S. government program to devise a low-floor city bus more accessible to elderly and handicapped travelers, ultimately to be built to a common

1975 GMC COACH RTS 47-seater bus, GMC

specification by all interested manufacturers. This "Transbus" has been mandated as the only federally funded 40-foot transit bus that can be built after 1981, although at the end of 1978 there were as yet no prototypes operating successfully. Meanwhile GM introduced the RTS in 1977 as an interim design incorporating many Transbus styling features but not the revised axles, tires and brakes that the 22-inch floor height of Transbus will require. A Canadian subsidiary which has built GM transit buses since 1962 continues to offer the old desgin and has sold some to U.S. customers.

As units of a highly profitconscious corporation, Yellow Coach and GM Coach have dominated bus production in the U.S. since 1926. Intelligent marketing efforts in the early years, together with a shrewd willingness to undertake risky experiments as long as the customers paid some of the bills, resulted in Yellow becoming the largest bus maker.This position is maintained today in spite of standardization on Detroit Diesel engines by all manufacturers and also in spite of government subsidization of city transit bus purchases with awards made to the lowest bidder. Approximately 112,000 Yellow and GM buses have been built since 1923. *MBS*

YORKSHIRE (GB) 1903-1928

(1) Yorkshire Patent Steam Wagon Co., Hunslet, Leeds, Yorks
(2) Yorkshire Commercial Motor Co., Hunslet, Leeds, Yorks

The core of the Yorkshire wagon was the celebrated double-ended locomotive boiler patented jointly by G.W. Mann and J. Clayton in 1901. These boilers, placed transversely across the front of the chassis, consisted of a circular firebox with two short horizontal barrels, the top of the inner firebox extending upwards to a point a little below the horizontal center line of the two barrels. Firetubes ran from the inner firebox out to the two smokebox tube plates, the flue gases being carried back to a central smokeheader, placed above but separate from the firebox, through return tubes and discharging up a central chimney. In earlier boilers the exhaust steam entered hollow smoke box doors and was directed through the return flues by an arrangement of multiple jets, but experience showed this to be an unnecessary complication and the later wagons had an exhaust nozzle below the chimney. This boiler remained the essence of the Yorkshire wagon until the last one made (in 1937). The only noteworthy amendment was the later adoption of a flat sided tapered firebox. The boiler was compact and free-steaming but rather expensive to build, and, as to the smoke header under the chimney, somewhat tedious to keep clean.

Early Yorkshires had a compound undertype engine geared to a countershaft differential and with gear final

1904 YORKSHIRE 4-ton steam wagon, RAW

1913 YORKSHIRE 5-ton steam wagon, RAW

drive. The cylinders were placed respectively on the outside of the chassis members, eliminating a crankshaft at the expense of a long pipe between high and low pressure cylinders. In 1908 an entirely redesigned arrangement was adopted, using a transversely placed vertical compound engine with modified Hackworth valve gear and final drive by long roller chain. In the 1920's two series of wagons were made with shaft drive. In the first of these the engine was arranged longitudinally on the center line with gearbox and cardan shaft in line behind it, but in the second the engine, still with the crankshaft longitudinal, was offset to the near side and the gearbox placed alongside it on the center line. A Yorkshire of this latter type, pneumatic tires and enclosed cab, was a very presentable vehicle and probably the only Yorkshire steamer aimed seriously at the long and medium distance market, most of Yorkshire's sales having been for municipal or local delivery work in which they had a faithful following and in which there were notable examples of longevity. Chain drive was never dropped from production and the last steamer made (in 1937) was so equipped. The smallest Yorkshire was a 2 tonner and the largest the 10 ton 6 wheeler, offered from 1927-33. The preponderance of production was, however, the 5 tonner. Limited numbers of tractors were made.

In 1911/12 the company had a brief dalliance with a 25/30 cwt.gasoline engined chassis using a 15.9hp White & Poppe engine, it being obvious that for 3 tons capacity and under customer preference was for internal combustion, but the venture was not pursued and it was not until 1933/4 that the company made a serious attempt to market a motor truck. The vehicle then offered was a 6 tonner with Dorman-Ricardo 4-cylinder oil engine, fully forward cab and the option of a Wilson pre-selector or a conventional 4-speed and reverse box. The two options, known as the WK(PS) and WK(C) were offered at £ 1225

1927 YORKSHIRE WG-type gulley emptier, NMM

(chassis) and were among the first to abolish the vestigal radiator shell, substituting a central series of perforations in the cab front. In 1935 a 13-ton 6 wheeler was added, followed by a 15-ton 8 wheeler in 1936, both powered by Gardner 6LW engines. Though the vehicles were very satisfactory, the economics of their manufacture in which all major components were brought-in, made them unable to compete in price with the mass producers and although the company succeeded in interesting a number of major fleet owners (notable the Cement Marketing Company) production was discontinued after 1938 in favor of concentration upon more specialized work. Post-war Yorkshire vehicle production has been principally motor road sweepers based upon complete chassis by other makers. Total diesel production was very limited but almost 2,000 steam wagons were made.

The firm was a branch of Deighton's Flue & Tube Co. Ltd. and was not separately incorporated during its period of vehicle production. Both styles seem to have been used interchangeably. *RAW*

YOUNG (i) (US) 1920-1923

Young Motor Truck Co., Geneva, Ohio

This was a conventional assembled truck made in 1½ to 2½-ton sizes, powered by Continental engines. *GNG*

YOUNG (ii) (US) 1970 to date

Young Fire Equipment Corp., Lancaster, N.Y.

This company introduced two lines of custom fire engine, the two-axle Bison and the three-axle Crusader, the latter with an unusually low-profile cab. It carries a snorkel with an 85 foot boom. Engines are Detroit or Caterpillar diesels. *GNG*

YUE LOONG (RC) 1958 to date

Yue Loong Motor Co., Ltd., Taipei, Taiwan

Yue Loong is the most successful experiment of cooperation between many firms. Having the license agreements with Nissan Motor Co. of Japan, and Kaiser Jeep of USA, Yue Loong is steadily building and marketing under its own name a variety of vehicles including light trucks, vans, pickups, station wagons, medium and heavy truck chassis, bus chassis and 4 × 4 jeep vehicles. This form of cooperation permits the frequent changing of models and the inclusion of a variety of types in each year's range. Basic models are identical, mechanically and in appearance to Datsun, Nissan and Jeep vehicles, but many models are of local design, containing a Chinese percentage of components and parts of various origins. Yue Loong builds passenger cars on the same pattern, while scooters and light gasoline engines are also included in the product range. *GA*

Z (CS) 1927-1932; 1945-1946

Ceskoslavenska zbrojovka a.s., Brno

This well-known armaments works manufactured cars from 1924 and their first commercial vehicle appeared in 1927. It used the engine of the Z-18 car, a 2-cylinder 2-stroke 3-port unit of 990cc developing 20 hp. It had a larger chassis than the car, and with truck or van body had a load capacity of 700-1,000kgs. From 1930 to 1932 the Z-9 delivery van with 2-cylinder 2-stroke 1-litre engine was built, but it was underpowered.

In 1936 some military four-wheel drive vehicles were made, powered by 4-cylinder 2-stroke air-cooled engines of 2 litres capacity. They were made as cross-country scout cars and as light armoured vehicles, but in 1938 all vehicle production by Z came to an end, only armaments being made thereafter.

After World War II a number of Canadian Dodge and Ford trucks and Farmall tractors were assembled in the Brno factory, but this came to an end in the autumn of 1946. *MSH*

1958 ZABO bus, JFJK

ZABO (NL) 1957 to date

N.V. Carrosseriefabriek Zabo, Ridderkerk

In 1957 Zabo constructed an integral bus called the Junior, meant for municipal use with a capacity of 60 passengers. It was fitted with a 83hp Perkins diesel engine, Bedford clutch and gearbox and Clark axles, but nevertheless was not very successful. After a period making only bodies Zabo became again a manufacturer of complete vehicles in 1973, with the introduction of a semi-integral bus around DAF running units. *JFJK*

ZAPPA & SCHARS (F) 1905-1906

E. Zappa & Schars, La Souis-Floirac, Gironde

At the 1905 Paris show Zappa & Schars exhibited a compound steam tractor with a water tube boiler and single chain drive to the rear axle, but it is doubtful if many were made. *RAW*

ZASTAVA (YU) 1958 to date

(1) Crvena Zastava Metalna Industrija, Kragujevac 1958-1968

(2) Zavodi Crvena Zastava, Kragujevac 1968 to date

The metal industrial firm of Crvena Zastava (Red Flag) manufactures various models of Fiat under license, forming the light vehicle end of the Yugoslav industry, while FAP and TAM supply the heavier models. The first to be built were the old-style Fiat 1100 van and the 1½-2-ton Tipo 615 with 48 hp diesel engine, made in van, pick-up, minibus and ambulance versions. The Fiat Campagnola 4 × 4 utility vehicle was soon added to the range, and was made in civilian and military versions. The light 750T van/minibus is also built, together with a van version of the old-style Fiat 600 car. The 2-ton range was modernized in 1973/74 with the latest Fiat cabs and engines, while the cooperation between Fiat and Magirus-Deutz in the Iveco groupe is likely to lead to closer ties between Zastava and TAM as the latter firm use Magirus-Deutz components. *GA*

1965 ZAPOROZHETS ZAZ-969 560lb 4×4 utility vehicle, OMM

ZAZ (SU) 1965 to date

Kommunar Automobile Plant, Zaporezhe

Derived from the Zaporozhets passenger car, this is a small 4 × 4 utility vehicle of Jeep type, powered by a 887cc air-cooled V-4 engine. The original ZAZ-968/9 was intended for air transportation, and was replaced in 1970 by the slightly heavier 969 with wider hood. This could carry four passengers or a 1,000 lb. load, and was also available with 4 × 2 drive and as a low-profile field ambulance. A 4-door forward-control model was known as the ZAZ-971. *GNG*

ZEITLER & LAMSON (US) 1914-1916

Zeitler & Lamson Motor Truck Co., Chicago, Ill.

This truck was made in five sizes from 1 to 5 tons, priced at $1,550 to $4,150. Engines were by Continental. Production ceased in 1916 or 1917, but the design was revived under the name King-Zeitler in 1919. *GNG*

1970 ZELIGSON 12-ton 6×6 oilfield truck, LA

ZELIGSON (US) 1946 to date

Zeligson Co., Tulsa, Okla.

Zeligson was launched by three ex-servicemen who later

founded the Crane Carrier Company (C.C.C.). The Zeligson name continued as a company mainly concerned with remanufacturing military trucks for sale to civilian operators, and the conversion of conventional trucks to all-wheel-drive. Custom-built chassis for the oil industry and other specialized work are also made, using military and civilian proprietary components. These include Detroit Diesel engines, and special bodies, cabs and winches are mounted at the plant. *LA*

ZETTELMEYER (D) 1910-1915; 1936-1939

Maschinenfabrik Hubert Zettelmeyer, Konz nr. Trier

Steam driven traction engines were the first vehicle produced of this firm. They were produced from 1910-1915. In 1936 Zettelmeyer followed the trend of developing light road tractors. It was unique as it had unitary construction. A 20 bhp diesel engine was installed. *HON*

1957 ZIL-151 2½-ton 6×6 army shop van, BHV

ZIL (SU) 1957 to date

Zavod Imieni Likhacheva, Moscow

During the period of de-Stalinization in the Soviet Union, the ZIS automobile factory was renamed ZIL in honor of designer and former plant manager I.A. Likhachev.

ZIS models continued in production with only the name changed, but gradually new units replaced the earlier designs.

The ZIS/ZIL-150 4 × 2 truck was modified and became the ZIL-164 in 1957, and the 6 × 6 ZIS/ZIL-151 gave way to the ZIL-157 in 1958.

1970 ZIL-135L4 10-ton 8×8 truck, Motor Jahr

This was a 4.5 ton cargo truck with a 6-cylinder engine of 104 hp, built for civilian and military use.

About 1964, the ZIL-164 was phased out and a ZIL-130 introduced. This truck is currently produced and is rated at 6.6 tons. Power is by a 170 hp gasoline V-8 through a 5-speed mechanical gearbox. The ZIL-130G is an extended wheelbase version and the 130V-1 is a semi-tractor.

The Mitishi Factory assembles dumpers on the 130 chassis as the ZIL-MMZ-555. This chassis is also used for a variety of special purposes including refrigeration van, cement truck, water tanker and refuelling vehicle.

1974 ZIL-131 6×6 fire engine, NMM

ZIL also produces heavy duty cross-country trucks in the form of models 131 and 131A. These 6 × 6 vehicles replaced ZIL-157 and make use of many Model 130 parts. They have power steering and centralized tire pressure control. A 6-ton ZIL-137 semi is also based on the 131.

Model 130 forms the basis for the ATs-30-130 fire engine, and model 131 is used for fire engines ATs-40-131 and AA-40-131, the latter built for airfield use. From 1964 the ZIL factory has made the 135 series of 8 × 8 trucks

1975 ZIL-133G 8-ton 6×4 truck, MSH

and tractors, mainly for military use, with twin 180 hp V8 engines.

Buses built by ZIL include model 118 "Yunost" (Youth) carrying 15-17 passengers. This was introduced in Moscow in 1963.

The ZIL-158 B, based on an earlier ZIS/ZIL-155, is capable of carrying up to 62 passengers, weighs 6.5 tons unladen and is powered by a 109 hp engine providing 65 km/h. It functions as an urban or tourist bus.

In addition to trucks and buses, ZIL luxury limousines are produced at this plant as well as various household goods and bicycles. *BE*

ZIM see GAZ

ZIMMERMAN (US) 1912-1916

Zimmerman Manufacturing Co., Auburn, Ind.

This was a ½-tonner based on a high-wheeler chassis. Components were typical of this type with a 2-cylinder engine, planetary transmission and double-chain drive. Springs were ¾-elliptic-front with full-elliptics at the rear. This model was re-rated as a 1½-tonner in 1915 and 1916. *GMN*

ZIS (SU) 1933-1957

Zavod Imieni Stalina, Moscow.

As an outgrowth of the old AMO factory, the revamped and newly renamed Stalin plant finished manufacture of the AMO/ZIS-3 truck and introduced, in 1934, the 3-ton ZIS-5. This was a 4 × 2 cargo featuring a 6-cylinder engine of 73 hp giving 60 km/h and was influenced by Inter national Harvester designs of the late 20s.

A 6 × 4 ZIS-6, was also constructed using the same basic chassis and engine.

1934 ZIS-5 2½-ton truck, MHK

The Spanish Civil War (1936-1939) saw the use of these ZIS models by the Soviet-backed Republican forces and it is possible some units may actually have been constructed in Spain during that period.

These designs, and their subsequent variations, con tinued in production in Russia through World War II and served an important role in military transportation. Some had a single headlight, flattened fenders and strengthened parts.

A portion of the plant was moved to the Ural mountains during the war and trucks built there were known as URAL-ZIS.

Other models appearing during the years of ZIS manufacture included the 2.5-ton producer-gas ZIS-21, a ZIS-30 using gas cylinders and half-track trucks built mainly for military use.

1935 ZIS-6 4-ton 2½-ton 6×4 truck, MHK

A ZIS-8 bus was built on the ZIS-5 chassis and was eventually replaced, about 1938, by the modern 26-passenger ZIS-16. An ambulance version, the ZIS-16C was also constructed. A ZIS-11 fire engine was introduced in 1935.

When the war ended, new trucks were brought forth including the ZIS-150 4-ton, 4 × 4 and the ZIS-151, 6 × 4.

The 150 cargo was powered by a 90 hp engine and was based on the IHC K-series. A similar vehicle is still produced in the People's Republic of China as the Jay Fong (Liberation) CA-10 thanks to Soviet technical aid in the 50's.

Semi-tractors and dumpers (MMZ series) were also introduced after the war and continued on through the plant name-change in 1957.

1939 ZIS-16 26-seated bus, MHK

ZIS buses included the model 154 city bus and the smaller 155. A ZIS-127 bus of 1955 was a 32-passenger vehicle powered by a 180 hp diesel six.

The prestigious ZIS limousines, as well as bicycles, refrigerators and related household goods, were also manufactured at this plant.

In 1957 the plant was renamed Zavod Imieni Likhacheva in honor of a former manager. Vehicles then became ZIL, with some models continuing on under the new prefix.

Further information will be found under the ZIL entry. *BE*

ZMAJ (YU) 1969-1971.

Zmaj Industrija Poljoprivrednih Masina, Zemun.

Builders of airplanes since 1927 and agricultural machinery since the early post war years, Zmaj launched in late 60s a medium class truck of very conventional design. A ladder-type chassis, powered by the IM, alias Yugoslavian Perkins, diesel, developing 62 or 64 hp for the 4-cylinder unit and 84 hp for the 6-cylinder unit and fitted with a high standing forward control metal cab for two, the Zmaj was built in 3-, 3.2-, and 3.5-ton capacities in truck and tipper. Unfortunately Zmaj could not compete with better established firms, and truck production was dropped a couple of years later, but production of agricultural machines and wheels for vehicles continues today. *GA*

ZUBR (PL) 1960-1968.

Jelczanskie Zaklady Samochodow, Jelcz k/Olawy.

Built by the same factory that later produced the Jelcz vehicles, the Zubr was once Poland's heaviest truck with its 8-ton payload. An old style forward control cab, reminicent of early post-war Fiat cabs and a Wola 155 hp diesel engine were the main features of the Zubr A80 truck, which was very conservative in other details. A

c. 1965 ZUBR A-80 8-ton truck, BHV

slight cab restyling was evident in mid 60s, together with the introduction of a 4 × 4 variant, while the factory reorganized its activities in 1968 and had a new lease of life under the Jelcz name. *GA*

1975 ZUK 900kg pick-up, MSH

ZUK (PL) 1959 to date.

Fabryka Samochodow Ciezarowych, Lublin.

Giving up production of Lublin trucks in late 50s, the FSC factory undertook the building of 900 kg payload pick ups. General lines and mechnical components were the same as Nysa, but the body was modernized. Originally a 57 hp gasoline 4-cylinder engine was used, but output was raised to 70 hp since 1973, when a grille face-lift was announced, together with minibus, kombi and double cab pick up variants. A van version had already been added to the range in 1966 and currently the whole range is produced, though vehicles are in the same class as the Nysa range and compete with each other. *GA*

1934 ZUNDAPP ¼-ton pick-up, HON

ZUNDAPP (D) 1928-1935.

Zundapp Ges. mbH., Nuremberg.

As a manufacturer of motorcycles Zundapp built a tri-van following motorcycle lines in 1928. In 1933 a tri-van with one front wheel and driven rear wheels was announced. It was replaced by a four-wheel van in the same year which had a 400 cc motorcycle engine; later also the 500 cc engine was used. The rear wheels were driven by cardan shaft. *HON*

1912 ZUST Tipo 4 4-ton truck, NMM

ZUST (I) 1908-1917.

(1) Brixia-Zust SA, Brescia.
(2) Ing. Roberto Zust Fabbrica Italiana di Automobili SA, Milan 1908-1911.
(3) Fabbrica Automobili Zust, Brescia 1912-1917.

Though the parent Zust concern had started to make cars in 1905, it was, curiously, the Brescia-based offshoot that offered the first commercial model, a cab edition of the 10hp 3-cylinder car chassis with T-head 1.4-litre power unit and shaft drive. 150 of these were in service in London by 1910. In this year the first Zust truck appeared; it was a chain driven 2½-tonner on orthodox lines with solid tires and 4-cylinder L-head engine. A 4-tonner followed, and Zusts remained in production until the company was absorbed by O.M. The 1916 catalog listed models from 2 to 5 tons, all with 4-cylinder sv monobloc engines; the bigger ones had chain drive. *MCS*

ZYPHEN & CHARLIER (D) 1925-1926.

Eisenbahn- und Maschinenfabrik van der Zyphen & Charlier GmbH., Cologne-Deutz.

A chassis was presented by this firm in 1925 using a 4-cylinder B.M.W 45/60 PS engine. It was available as a 4 ton truck or with a bus body. *HON*

ALPHABETICAL INDEX

A

B

C

D

E

F

G

H

I

J

K

L

M

N

O

P

Q

R

S

T

U

V

W

X

Y

Z